HISTORY OF
PRINCE EDWARD
COUNTY, VIRGINIA

Portrait by Richard Wilson. Used by Permission, National Portrait Gallery, London.
Courtesy Metropolitan Museum of Art, New York.

PRINCE EDWARD AUGUSTUS (left) and PRINCE GEORGE FREDERICK

HISTORY OF
PRINCE EDWARD
COUNTY, VIRGINIA

*From its Earliest Settlements
through its Establishment in 1754
To its Bicentennial Year*

BY

HERBERT CLARENCE BRADSHAW

THE DIETZ PRESS, INCORPORATED
Richmond, Virginia

Printed in the United States of America

© 1955, BY
HERBERT CLARENCE BRADSHAW

From the Presses of the Dietz Printing Company

Dedication

Those on whom the writing of a book falls heaviest are the members of the writer's family. To the author, the work is pleasure. To his wife, it means neglect or postponement of his household duties and the disarrangement of household routine. To the children it means adjustment to a different order, so exacting that even questions about school work must have a set time. For all the inconveniences to the household the preparation of this history has entailed, the writer's family has maintained its interest and has given continuing help. It is fitting, therefore, that he dedicate this book

TO HIS WIFE

MILDRED CUNNINGHAM BRADSHAW

AND TO THEIR CHILDREN

KATE WEAVER BRADSHAW

HERBERT CUNNINGHAM BRADSHAW

ELIZABETH SCOTT BRADSHAW

Acknowledgments

NO one can accomplish alone the writing of a book such as this. Along the way there are many to whom he must turn for help. This writer acknowledges with the deepest gratitude the assistance which has been given him so freely and so generously.

J. Barrye Wall has been the source of great help and wise counsel. He has generously made available the columns of the Farmville *Herald* for inquiries by the writer and for publicity about his work. He has made available materials which he had, notably the list of soldiers of World War II, and has generously given permission to the writer to use freely materials from the Farmville *Herald* files and *Today and Yesterday in the Heart of Virginia* and has furnished some of the illustrations. He facilitated research by permitting the writer to bring to his home bound volumes of the Farmville *Herald* files and has given him microfilm reproductions of these files. For all this help, for assistance and counsel in planning the publication of this book, and for warm encouragement, the writer expresses his sincere thanks.

Mrs. W. S. Morton has for many years carried on a painstaking research in Prince Edward records. She has also accumulated manuscript materials relating to Prince Edward history. She has generously made available to the writer extensive notes made and materials found during her research. In addition, she did some special research for the writer, which greatly helped. The numerous references to Mrs. Morton's notes and mss. material in the reference notes in this work show how extensive has been her help and how greatly indebted to her the writer is.

Horace Adams, clerk of the county, and his assistants, Mrs. Richard Tunstall and Mrs. C. I. Noble, Jr., were gracious in making available to the writer the county records for research and in providing a place in which he could work comfortably while using the county records.

The writer would bear testimony to the unfailing courtesy and the cordial assistance extended him by the staffs of the libraries in which he carried on his research.

In the reference room, in the manuscript and rare book room, in the newspaper and film department of the Duke University Library, and in the libraries of the Law and Divinity Schools and the

Woman's College of that university, his research was facilitated by understanding and cordial assistance. The writer was given access to the stacks of these libraries and a carrel placed at his disposal; this courtesy enabled him to carry on research with the freedom of a graduate student or a member of the university staff; it is especially appreciated.

Special mention should be made of the help given by Miss Mattie Russell, curator of manuscripts, and Edwin J. Hix and Miss Mary Wescott of the newspaper and film department of the Duke Library.

The staff of the Southern Historical Collection in the library of the University of North Carolina helped greatly with the research in the manuscript collections there. A courtesy of the U. N. C. Library which was also much appreciated was in making available microfilm of the Journals of the Virginia House of Delegates for special periods.

The staff of the manuscript room of the Alderman Library of the University of Virginia helped in research there. Before the writer visited that library, his research there was greatly aided by having had furnished him, at his request, a list of the mss. materials relating to Prince Edward.

As he had found in previous research experiences, the staff of the Virginia State Library was most helpful. The facilities of both the general reference department and the Archives Division were used. The interest of staff members, especially in the Archives Division, revealed materials which might not otherwise have been found.

Paul L. Grier, librarian at Hampden-Sydney, made a thorough search for some mss. materials which the writer had examined in the library before the fire of 1941 but had failed to make notes from at that time.

Catesby ap C. Jones of the Virginia Historical Society furnished a list of materials in its library relating to Prince Edward. William M. E. Rachal, editor of the society's publication, *The Virginia Magazine of History and Biography*, graciously published the first chapter of this work in the October, 1954, issue of the magazine.

Miss Mildred Harvey, Prospect, generously lent a copy of Woodrow W. Wilkerson's history of Olive Branch Methodist Church.

Mrs. Ruby Redd, Farmville R. F. D., generously made available the class books of Mt. Pleasant Methodist Church and a biography of the Rev. John Wesley Childs.

The Rev. John B. Cunningham, D.D., Lynchburg, lent a mss. history of Buffalo Presbyterian Church.

Mrs. B. T. Taylor, Farmville, kindly furnished a mss. copy of a history of the Prospect Methodist Church delivered at the 1953 homecoming.

The late R. B. Wilson, Green Bay, generously sent a mss. history of Liberty Christian Church and negatives of photographs of old homes in Leigh District which are among the illustrations of this book.

Col. D. W. Paulett kindly provided details of the history of Company G of the Virginia National Guard.

Charles A. Garden and Nelson Hix gave directions to old homes in the Prospect area; Frank Schultz guided members of the writer's family to Brooklyn and lent a copy of a newspaper article containing a historical account of the old home.

Stephen L. Farrar, clerk of Amelia County, and his staff made available the Amelia County records for research.

The writer would acknowledge his appreciation to Steed Rollins, editor of the Durham *Morning Herald* and vice-president of the Durham Herald Company, for arranging periods during which the writer could make special trips for research which could not conveniently be done on Saturdays, his "day off" from newspaper work.

Mrs. J. Keith Marshall, Marshall, Va., generously lent the writer the Walton family papers which had been preserved by her father, John F. Walton, and her grandfather, William M. Walton.

Members of the Weaver family permitted him to copy mss. papers which were found in the effects of James R. Weaver.

Mrs. Branch Clements permitted him to copy the letter notifying Alexander Marshall of the death of his son in a Confederate hospital.

When the writer was preparing a history of the Baptists of Prince Edward in 1935 for *Today and Yesterday in the Heart of Virginia,* G. R. Nunnally, clerk of Bagby Memorial Church, O. L. Vassar, clerk of Mt. Nebo Church, and Mrs. B. L. Wilkerson, clerk of Glenn Memorial Church, furnished mss. historical sketches of their churches, and Miss Margaret Payne (Mrs. J. L. Green) prepared a history of Spring Creek Church for the writer.

John H. Bruce, clerk, has always been gracious in making available to the writer the records of Sharon Baptist Church.

Thomas J. McIlwaine kindly checked records in his office of Superintendent of Schools to provide lists of School Board members and Electoral Board members and other data pertaining to the schools.

Miss Elizabeth Royer, librarian of the theology library, Emory

University, located the source of information and kindly sent the writer the information and reference concerning the establishment of the Prince Edward Circuit of Methodist churches. Mrs. Grace N. Teague, librarian of the religious section of the Joint University Libraries (Peabody and Scaritt Colleges and Vanderbilt University) of Nashville sought the same information for the writer, but did not find it; her efforts are sincerely appreciated. (The determination of the date at which the Prince Edward Circuit was established proved one of the most difficult facts to ascertain in the preparation of the book. In the Duke library, there are no annuals of the Virginia Methodist Conference prior to 1868. The writer was told that both Emory and Vanderbilt University libraries had good collections of Methodist history. He directed inquiries to both libraries; Vanderbilt's materials on the subject were similar to Duke's.)

Dr. Garnett Ryland made available the facilities of the Virginia Baptist Historical Society's library at the University of Richmond for research.

Walter H. Evert, Jr., assistant to the secretary of Princeton University was quite painstaking in searching the Princeton records for Prince Edward students prior to 1800. This entailed considerable time, and the writer is deeply appreciative of this cooperation.

Theodore Louis Trost, curator of the Samuel Colgate Baptist Historical Collection, examined minutes of the Middle District and Appomattox Associations not available to the writer in the libraries which he used to determine facts about the history of Mountain Creek Baptist Church.

D. C. Morris consulted the records of Spring Creek Baptist Church, of which he is clerk, to provide certain information.

W. W. Fitzpatrick, Rougemont, N. C., provided information about the Quail Roost Guernsey stock purchased in Prince Edward.

W. C. Fitzpatrick, mayor of Farmville, kindly provided a list of the officials of the town of Farmville since 1948, when the writer's research in the records of the town for its sesquicentennial history ended.

Mrs. Anne Atkinson Chamberlayne painstakingly traced the ownership of the "old stone house" near Overly.

Mrs. J. Woodfin Hughes made available papers of Col. John Foster, her great-grandfather.

Mrs. S. H. Bondurant lent a copy of the sermon the Rev. Daniel Witt preached at the funeral of Elisha Woodfin, Jr.

Dr. J. H. Cocks sent a photograph of Dr. W. W. H. Thackston and a copy of the *Bulletin of the Virginia Dental Association* containing articles about Dr. Thackston.

Miss Lucy Brittle of Emporia gave the writer a copy of the recipe for cucumber cold cream used by her aunt, the late Miss Jimmie Prince.

W. A. Garner of Roanoke lent mss. letters and other papers concerning the McGehee and related families.

W. D. Mason provided information concerning the operation of the "block system" on the Norfolk and Western Railroad.

W. S. Weaver, Mrs. Weaver, and Edward T. Bondurant provided information concerning the dissolution of Beulah Christian Church.

The writer has drawn heavily upon the sesquicentennial history of Farmville which was published in the Farmville *Herald* of Oct. 22, 1948. He made acknowledgments of assistance in the preparation of that work in the publication; special reference is due here to the help of the late Major D. Burton Blanton, Mrs. J. L. Bugg, Mrs. W. G. Dunnington, and Mrs. J. M. Grainger in giving information used in both that work and this.

The late Morton Carter, who died in February, 1955, at the advanced age of 102, provided the writer with valuable information which has been indicated in the notes. His mind remained remarkably clear throughout his long life, and his memory was clear and accurate when the writer last visited him, at Christmas, 1954.

Mrs. Gertrude G. Vilaska of the Metropolitan Museum of Art in New York located the portrait of Prince Edward Augustus for the writer.

The National Portrait Gallery of London granted permission to use the portrait of Prince Edward Augustus in this book.

Mrs. G. P. Tschebotarioff of the Princeton Art and Archaeology Department sent a copy of the portraits of Samuel Stanhope Smith.

Union College, Schenectady, N. Y., sent the print of the portrait of John Blair Smith reproduced in this work.

The Richmond *Times-Dispatch* lent the print of the Patrick Henry miniature.

Mrs. Graves H. Thompson, of the Hampden-Sydney *Alumni Record,* lent several photographs.

Mrs. Meade L. Shackelford of Longwood College lent photographs.

Miss Mary Dupuy, Worsham, lent a rare copy of a photograph of the old Courthouse, used 1832-72.

Charles H. Cooper, chief photographer for the *Herald-Sun* papers, made the print of the old courthouse, 1832-72, from the original photograph.

Mrs. Louisa Venable Kyle, London Bridge, Va., lent a print of a portrait of Richard N. Venable.

The writer acknowledges a debt of gratitude to several people who are no longer living but whose assistance and encouragement in historical research have contributed materially to the writing of this book:

Dr. C. E. Burrell, who years ago gave permission to use materials in his *History of Prince Edward County, Virginia* and gave the writer copies of some manuscript materials which he had; Dr. Joseph D. Eggleston; Dr. W. H. Whiting, Jr.; Miss Emma Cabell Venable; Miss Addie Carrington Venable; Miss Sally Bruce Dickinson; Mr. J. M. Mottley; Mrs. Mamie O. Garnett; the writer's grandparents James R. Weaver and J. S. Bradshaw and Ann Mildred Jenkins Bradshaw; and his father, Herbert L. Bradshaw.

All the photographs used in this book, for which no credit is given, were, with one exception, taken by the writer's oldest child, Kate Weaver Bradshaw; the exception, Jamestown Church, was taken in 1937 by the writer's wife. The writer's mother, Mrs. Herbert L. Bradshaw, has made available papers and other materials in her possession. The writer's son, Herbert Cunningham Bradshaw, has helped with the preparation of copy. And the writer's wife, Mildred Cunningham Bradshaw, has made possible the writing of this work by seeing that the writer was able to devote a great amount of his time at home to the work. She also helped copy some manuscript materials. Members of the writer's family have also helped prepare the index.

Contents

List of Illustrations

Prince Edward Augustus and Prince George Frederick—*Frontispiece*

Introduction

WHEN he completed writing the sesquicentennial history of Farmville, for the Farmville *Herald*, the writer suggested to J. Barrye Wall the preparation of a bicentennial history of Prince Edward County. Plans were accordingly made. Shortly thereafter the writer moved to Durham, North Carolina, to join the editorial staff of the Durham *Morning Herald*. In 1952 I began intensive research, looking to the writing of this work. When I mentioned to Mr. Wall that the research was under way, he replied that he thought the undertaking had been abandoned because of removal from Virginia. Fortunately, residence in Durham facilitated the research.

Duke University has an excellent collection of Virginia newspapers and pamphlets, manuscript materials relating to Prince Edward, and nearly all the published books of which the writer knows which deal with Prince Edward County. Nearby, at Chapel Hill, the University of North Carolina Library has the Southern Historical Collection with important manuscript materials, some of which contain Prince Edward materials, microfilm of the Journals of the Virginia House of Delegates, and some secondary sources which were not available at Duke. Because of the opportunities for research during the evenings, Durham is an ideal place for a person engaged in historical research on Southern topics to live. I could not have written this book living anywhere else, with the possible exception of Charlottesville, without losing a great deal of time from regular work.

It had been my hope to complete the manuscript in time for publication by the final bicentennial celebration, October 15, 1954. The work proved more time-consuming than anticipated, and this aim was not realized.

In writing this book, I have undertaken to link Prince Edward history with the history of Virginia and the United States, to show the part that the locality has in contributing to the main stream of events in state and nation. I have also tried to bring into this history the participation of as many people as possible. Consequently there are lists which may seem to some readers unnecessary. They are given to show the extent of participation in affairs by Prince Edward people and to inform the descendants of these people of the interests and, to some extent, the attitudes of their forbears.

As the research in Prince Edward history continued, I was amazed to find the wealth of material, especially source material, about the county. In putting the fruit of the research into this history, I have had to be selective, because the scope of the work as planned could not include all the material found. Throughout, however, I have endeavored to omit nothing which might interfere with giving as full and clear a picture as possible of life in Prince Edward in its various aspects. The sources of information are given in the reference notes, and the acknowledgments of assistance form a special section of this work.

H. C. B.

Durham, North Carolina
December, 1954

CHAPTER I

The Settlement of Prince Edward

THE first century of Virginia's history saw the settlement of Tidewater. As the colony entered its second century, immigrants and the descendants of earlier settlers were beginning to push into the forests beyond the fall line to open the rolling hills and narrow valleys to settlement and cultivation. Once the migration into the wilderness which became Middle Virginia began, there continued a steady influx of settlers. Organized local government followed the settlers, with new counties set up as rapidly as the population justified.

In the division of the settled portion of Virginia into eight shires in 1634, Charles City, named in honor of Charles I then ruling in England, included territory on both sides the James River.[1] On the south side of the James, the area designated Charles City lay south of the Appomattox River and extended westward; to the east was the portion of James City County which in 1652 became Surry County.[2] For the convenience of the inhabitants of Charles City, county courts were held alternately on the south and north banks of the James, beginning in 1658.[3] In 1702 the area south of the James was erected into a new county, named Prince George in honor of the husband of Queen Anne.[4]

The migration beyond the fall line began while the region south of the Appomattox was Prince George County. The area south of the Nottoway River was organized as Brunswick County as a buffer against the Indians and the French in 1720, but the territory remained under the jurisdiction of the Prince George Court until the new county could support a local government in 1732.[5] During this period the first land grants were made in the region which was to become Prince Edward County. From an early period in Virginia's history, land grants had been made on the basis of fifty acres for each person who came into or was brought into the colony. After 1705 grants were also made for cash payments, at the rate of five shillings for fifty acres. The new method of granting land was especially advantageous to persons already settled in Virginia who were looking for fresh lands or more land than they could expect to acquire in the older settled regions. Under the new system a person

1

who wished to receive a grant of land paid to the Receiver-General
of the colony the stipulated fee for the acreage he wished to patent.
Then he took the certificate of payment from the Receiver-General
to a surveyor, whose survey was returned to the office of the Secretary of the colony, and a patent was issued,[6] in the name of the King,
signed by the Governor. The patents were written on parchment,
and some of them are still preserved.

Interestingly enough, the first land grants made in the Prince
Edward area were located in what was then Brunswick County. The
first of these grants was made September 28, 1728, to Richard Jones,
Jr., of Prince George County, for 337 acres on Bush River.[7] Although
the first patentee in Prince Edward never lived on his Bush River
holding, he is numbered among the pioneers of Southside Virginia.
He was one of the pioneer settlers of Amelia County, moving to his
plantation on Deep Creek probably about the time he patented land
on Bush River. Jones was one of the first justices of the peace of
Amelia, was one of its first representatives in the House of Burgesses,
serving 1734-40, a militia officer, and a vestryman of Raleigh Parish.[8]
The second grant in the Prince Edward area was to Charles Williamson, also of Prince George County, also on Bush River, and was
made for 252 acres; the date of the grant was September 8, 1729,
and the boundaries indicate that it lay along the Prince George-
Brunswick line.[9]

In 1734 Prince George was divided, the western section being
made a new county named in honor of the Princess Amelia Sophia,
daughter of King George II. To the area taken from Prince George
was added a portion of Brunswick County to include the ridge between the watersheds of the Roanoke and Appomattox Rivers, the
area drained by the Appomattox becoming a part of Amelia.[10] The
first court of Amelia met May 9, 1735. In addition to administering
the oaths of office to the justices, to John Burton as sheriff and
Samuel Cobbs as clerk, the court appointed John Bentley constable
for the section of the county above Deep Creek and directed John
Dawson, one of the magistrates, to take the list of tithables above
Flat Creek.[11] A commission of the peace dated October 29, 1736, was
directed to Edward Booker, Charles Irby, Richard Jones, Richard
Booker, Henry Anderson, John Burton, Abraham Green, Robert
Tucker, Thomas Jones, John Dawson, James Clarke, James Branch,
Francis Anderson, Thomas Tabb, William Watson, and Joseph
Scott, justices.[12]

The list of tithables, who included all males sixteen years of age and over and all Negro, mulatto, and Indian women sixteen and over who were not free,[13] was the nearest approach to a census during the colonial period. The lists were taken annually, since the county and parish levies were poll taxes on the tithables. The returns for Amelia, reported when the first county levy was set November 19, 1735, showed 588 tithables in the new county.[14] How many of these were in the section which became Prince Edward is not known, but they were few. Prior to 1735 only six land grants had been made in the Prince Edward area;[15] of the five persons to whom these grants were made, certainly four never lived on their holdings in the area, although they may have settled overseers and slaves on the land to work it. The one grantee who may have settled on his Prince Edward land was Charles Williamson, but it is not known whether he did. The next three grants in succession to the Williamson grant were made in 1733, one for 3,800 acres on the Appomattox River to William Randolph, and two on Sailor's Creek, for 503 and 238 acres respectively, to Edward Booker, then of Henrico,[16] later presiding justice of the Amelia Court. In 1734 Peter Jefferson of Goochland County, father of Thomas Jefferson, received a grant of 400 acres on Sailor's Creek.[17]

As many grants to Prince Edward land were made in 1735 as had been made in the preceding seven years; patentees in 1735 were Joseph Ligon, with two grants totaling 781 acres on Sandy River; William Ligon, 492 acres on Sandy River; Richard Randolph, 1,782 acres on Bush River; Matthew Talbott, 1,258 acres on Bush River; and William Townes, 118 acres on Sailor's Creek.[18]

The first tax levied in Amelia County amounted to sixteen pounds of tobacco per tithable; the total income of the county in 1735 was 9,408 pounds of tobacco. The sheriff and the clerk each received a salary of 1,040 pounds of tobacco, and the constables each received 280 pounds of tobacco.[19]

The population of Amelia County increased rapidly. In six years the number of tithables doubled, 1,185 being listed in 1741. The cost of operating the county government almost doubled, too, 17,775 pounds of tobacco being required, but the increase in tithables made it necessary to levy only fifteen pounds of tobacco per poll to meet the expense.[20] In 1753, the last year Amelia included Prince Edward, there were 3,462 tithables listed; each was taxed six pounds of tobacco to raise the 20,772 pounds of tobacco needed to operate the county government that year.[21] In eighteen years the number of tithables had increased almost sixfold.

Between 1736 and the end of 1753, 258 land grants were made in the area which became Prince Edward.[22] This gives no indication of the growth in population, for several grants were made to the same person. Substantial grants, too, were made to persons speculating in frontier land, who sold their grants in smaller tracts to settlers. Some who patented land settled overseers and slaves and indentured servants on their holdings on the frontier.

As the number of settlers in the western portion of Amelia increased, the county court was concerned with the building of roads in the section. John Dawson was appointed surveyor of a road to be cleared from Flat Creek to or near the fork of Sailor's Creek in 1736 and to call upon the people who lived near the route, who were not employed on other roads, to assist in clearing it.[23] Work on the roads was required of male laboring tithables. Another road into Prince Edward was authorized to be cleared during the next year, this one from Craddock's on Flat Creek to Bush River, with Samuel Hudson as surveyor.[24] These early roads took the place of the hunting path, mentioned in the grant to Charles Williamson in 1729.

At the December, 1738, Court, Joseph Morton asked that a road be cleared from George Walker's plantation (on Bush River) to Buffalo River. The Court granted the request, and, in an action which will be apreciated today by people who make motions, named Morton surveyor. The same Court ordered a road cleared by the Walker tithables from Walker's plantation into the road from Colonel Randolph's quarters.[25] In 1739 Joseph Morton, Jr., was directed to mark and clear a road from Colonel Richard Randolph's quarters to the ridge which divided Amelia from Brunswick.[26] Two subsequent orders of the Amelia Court apparently refer to this road: in 1740 Joseph Morton, Sr., was named surveyor of a road to be cleared from Colonel Richard Randolph's quarters by "the nearest and best way" to meet a road cleared by order of the Brunswick Court and directed that Colonel Randolph's hands, three of John Nash's hands at Camp Creek, Hudson Akin, and Akin's tenant clear the road;[27] in 1741 John Hardin was named surveyor of this road to succeed Morton.[28] Morton in the same year had been named surveyor of another road to the Brunswick line, this one beginning at John Hudson's.[29]

While the Prince Edward area was a part of Amelia, a network of roads was cleared from north to south and from east to west. The names of the surveyors, who directed the clearing and upkeep of the roads, and of those assigned to help them provide a partial list of the earliest settlers in Prince Edward:

George Walker, road to be cleared from the mouth of Bush River below the mouth of Sandy River into Walker's road by Rutledge and Walker's and Nash's hands, 1740.[30]

William Barns, road from Stocks Creek to Sailor's Creek, 1740.[31]

Jacob McGehee, road from Craford's to John Hudson's, to be worked by male tithables of Joseph Morton, John Hudson, Robert Bowman, Thomas Morton, David Brown, and Colonel Randolph at Mountain Creek, 1741;[32] later, Bush River road "to where Covington stops."[33]

Henry Walthall, road to be cleared from Nash's quarter on Bush River into Osborne's road by male tithables of John Mullins, Charles Cottrell, Edward Haskins, and John Nash, 1741.[34]

Batho. Austin, road to be cleared from the Appomattox River near Colonel Richard Randolph's quarter to Hill's fork on Vaughan's Creek by all who lived near the route and were not employed on other roads, 1742.[35]

John Childrey, road from Sailor's Creek to Sandy Creek, 1742.[36]

Henry Ligon, successor to George Walker, 1742.[37]

John Nash, road from Bush River bridge across Sailor's Creek into Walker's road, with his male tithables and those of James Rutledge, Richard Rutledge, John Mullins, Edmund Groat (Gross ?), Charles Cothril, Douglas Puckett, Mrs. Cobb, and Edward Haskins, 1743.[38]

Richard Rowland, directed to clear a bridle way from Anthony Griffin's road to "Sandy River Chappell," 1744.[39]

Anthony Griffin, road to be cleared from Mallory's Creek along the ridge to Randolph's road at the heads of Bush and the Meherrin Rivers by his hands and those of Stephen Collins, Peter Davis, John Mayes, Colonel Richard Randolph at the quarter of which Harding is overseer, and at Captain John Nash's quarter, 1745.[40]

Charles Anderson, road to be cleared from the head of Little Roanoke along to ridge between Briery and Buffalo Rivers to Rutledge's Ford over the Appomattox River by Charles Kirkey, Hugh Kirkey, Alexander Kirkey, Francis Rice, Richard Woodson, Ralph Elkin, John Hudson, John Bibb, Joseph Morton, John Martin, Hugh Nixon, John Mullins, Anderson, and their tithes and "all other persons convenient" who were not employed on other roads, 1745.[41]

John Davis, road to be cleared from Bush River road near John Bragg's to the church by Stephen Collins, Richard Womack, George Stewart, John Braggs, John Hudson, James Ball and their tithables and the tithables of Colonel Richard Randolph at Mountain Creek, 1745. The same order directed Jacob McGehee to make a division in the road of which he was surveyor and to apportion the hands to each section as he thought best.[42]

Daniel Brown, road to be cleared from the new road near Mallory's Creek into the Sandy River road and thence to the church by Charles Burks, Joseph Ligon, Thomas Morton, William Soirrey, James Gravely, Matthew Womack and their tithables, 1745.

Stephen Collins, the upper part of the road of which Anthony Griffin was surveyor, 1745.[43]

Robert Baker, road to be cleared from the Sandy Ford on the Appomattox to the main branch of Spring Creek, with Colonel Richard Randolph, Colonel William Randolph, James Cunningham, John Cunningham, Samuel Evan, James Alexander, James Ewen (Ewing), Samuel Baker, John Thompson, James Parks, Joseph Little-John, Robert Martin, and others convenient, 1746.[44]

William Brown, road to be cleared from Bush River road below the pole bridge along the ridge into Mallory's Creek road by Lester, Saresay, Potter, Thomas Morton, Ambros, and Berstrey's hands, 1747.

George Foster, road to be cleared from Bush River road at Busby's Path crossing the creek below Watson's mill into Watson's road near Tunstall's quarter, 1747.

James Atwood, permission to clear a bridal way from little Briery River into the chapel road, 1747.[45]

George Moore, authorized to clear a road from Snail's Creek to his house and on to Colonel Richard Randolph's upper quarter, Anthony Griffin, George Jones, John Owens, and John Carroll to help him, 1747.[46]

Joseph Rice, road to be cleared from the place Captain Walker's old road crossed Sandy River by the nearest and best way to Bush River, the Parson, Thomas Turpin, John Holloway, Richard Witt, Michael Rice, John Waddell, and their tithables to do the work, 1747.[47]

William Womack, road from Great Sailor's Creek into the road a little below Crawford's house, with Thomas Certain, Abraham Vaughan, John Gentry, Jonathan Howell, William Brooks, Charles Spradling and their tithables and those at John Nash's and Benjamin Ruffin's quarters to do the work, 1747.[48]

Joseph Morton, Jr., bridle way to be cleared from the road near Charles Anderson's to *Bush River Church*, with Anderson, Richard Woodson, Alexander Cunningham, Theodorick Carter, Joseph Shelton, John Chessright, and their tithables to do the work, 1748.

Richard Woodson, road from the road near Nash's to the bridge over the Appomattox, 1748.[49]

John Nash, road to be cleared from the race paths at Abraham Womack's and Sandy River bridge to Bush River Bridge and into the Buffalo road by George Walker, Henry Ligon, Abraham Womack, Thomas Haskins, Jonathan Cheatham, William Lewis, and Douglas Puckett, 1750.[50]

Robert Atkins, road from George Moore's to Sandy River, 1750.[51]

Samuel Goode, road from Sailor's to Sandy Creek, 1751.

Peter Davis, road from George Moore's to the fork of Randolph road, 1751.

David Flournoy, road from head of the pole bridge to the fork, 1751.

Anthony Griffin, road from Snail's Creek to George Moore's, 1751.

Daniel Dejarnet, road from Mallory's Creek to Snail's Sreek, 1751.[52]

James Nicks, road from the ridge at the head of the Appomattox River joining Callaway's road the best route to the point it crosses the river, 1751.

James Walker, road from Vaughan's Creek to Randolph's road, 1751.[53]

William Womack, road from Crawford's house to Great Sailor's Creek bridge, 1751. The hands under Womack were also directed to help Thomas Haskins repair the bridge.[54]

Henry Ligon, road from the fork above Sandy River bridge to the fork above George Walker's, 1751.

Douglas Puckett, road from Bush River bridge to the church, 1751.

Benjamin Woodson, road from the fork to Rutledge's Ford, above the mouth of Bush River, 1751.[55]

For the convenience of travelers, the Amelia Court in 1739 ordered the road surveyors to place at each crossroads inscriptions in large letters directing to the most noted place to which each road leads."[56]

A 1742 order suggests that road clearing involved merely the cutting of trees along the route selected for the roadway, for it directed the surveyors to grub and cut down the stumps.[57]

As roads were cleared, bridges were built over the streams in some places. There was a bridge over Bush River in 1744, when John Nash complained that it was in such a state of disrepair that no wheeled carriage could pass over it safely. The builder, Edward Robertson, was summoned to the next court to hear the complaint.[58] It was the custom then for the builder of a bridge to agree to keep it in repair for a period of years, usually seven, after it was built and to give bond for keeping it in repair.

Charles Anderson presented to the April, 1748, Court a petition for a bridge over the Appomattox, above the mouth of Bush River and opposite the land of Colonel Peter Randolph. Clement Read was named to ask the Goochland Court to consider the bridge, and Anderson and John Nash were appointed to represent Amelia in drawing up specifications.[59] An agreement with the "undertaker" (persons who contracted to do construction work were then called undertakers instead of contractors) was reported to the August Court, and Nash and George Walker were authorized to receive the bridge when it had been completed.[60]

Anderson, Nash, Richard Woodson, and Joseph Morton were directed to select a site for a bridge over Buffalo by the May, 1748, Court, in response to a petition from the "upper part" of the county.[61] In August Nash and Anderson were authorized to let the building of the bridge over Buffalo at the place where the road crossed.[62]

Bush River bridge continued to give trouble, and it was decided to change the location to a site upstream. Nash and Walker were authorized to arrange for its construction and also for the construction of a bridge over Sandy River at or near Hawkins' plantation in 1749.[63] In October of the next year Joseph Morton and Charles Anderson were commissioned to arrange for the building of bridges over Bush and Briery Rivers;[64] later in 1750, in March, the same men were directed to have Buffalo River bridge repaired and to have a bridge built over Mountain Creek.[65]

Three bridges were built and one was repaired in the Prince Edward area in 1752: Charles Anderson received £7:5 for building Briery River bridge; Thomas Morton was paid £4:10 for building a bridge over Mountain Creek and £2:15 for repairing Buffalo bridge; and Richard Morton was paid £70 for building the bridge over the Appomattox River.[66] The Appomattox bridge, on a site long abandoned a few miles downstream from the present site of Farmville and not far above the mouth of Bush River, was an undertaking of considerable size; its completion by a resident of the area indicates a high degree of competence as a contractor and the presence of workmen of considerable skill among the pioneers of Prince Edward.

Two streams of settlers converged upon the territory which became Prince Edward and met here. The first settlers came from Eastern Virginia, and their move into the upper part of Amelia was the natural migration westward of a people seeking more and fresh

Courtesy Richmond Times-Dispatch

PATRICK HENRY

Courtesy Mrs. Louisa Venable Kyle

RICHARD N. VENABLE

Courtesy Department of Art and Archaeology, Princeton University

SAMUEL STANHOPE SMITH

Courtesy Public Relations Office, Union College

JOHN BLAIR SMITH

PLATE 1

BRANCH J. WORSHAM   DR. JOHN PETER METTAUER

Photograph by C. R. Rees and Co., Richmond, 1871

JOHN HOLT RICE   DANIEL WITT

PLATE II

HENRY E. WATKINS

DR. W. W. H. THACKSTON

PHILIP W. McKINNEY

ASA DICKINSON WATKINS

PLATE III

Prince Edward Court House

Copy by Charles H. Cooper of photograph lent by Miss Mary Dupuy

THE COURTHOUSE, 1832-1872

Courtesy Hampden-Sydney Alumni Record

VENABLE HALL, HAMPDEN-SYDNEY COLLEGE

Plate IV

THE COURTHOUSE, 1939-

THE COURTHOUSE, 1872-1939

Courtesy The Farmville Herald

PLATE V

THE CLERK'S OFFICE, 1855-1872

Courtesy The Farmville Herald

THE CLERK'S OFFICE, 1896-1939

PLATE VI

COLLEGE PRESBYTERIAN CHURCH

THE ROTUNDA, LONGWOOD COLLEGE

PLATE VII

Courtesy Longwood College

LONGWOOD HOUSE

THE LOCKETT HOUSE

Plate VIII

SHARON BAPTIST CHURCH (Sandy River Church)

SHARON BAPTIST CHURCH (Side View)

PLATE IX

KINDERTON

FOREST GREEN

PLATE X

BUFFALOE

GOLGOTHA

Plate XI

BUFFALO PRESBYTERIAN CHURCH

THE BUFFALO COMMUNION SILVER

PLATE XII

GENERAL TARLTON WOODSON'S HOME

JAMESTOWN'S MAIN STREET, 1953

PLATE XIII

WOMACK'S MILL

JAMESTOWN CHURCH, 1937

PLATE XIV

ROTHERWOOD

OAKLAND

PLATE XV

CORK

BURKE'S TAVERN

PLATE XVI

STAIRCASE AND PANELING, CHATHAM

PARLOR CEILING CENTERPIECE, CHATHAM

PLATE XVII

LOCUST GROVE (Redd)

LOCUST GROVE (Crute-Mottley)

PLATE XVIII

PROSPECT METHODIST CHURCH

BRIERY PRESBYTERIAN CHURCH

PLATE XIX

THE JACKSON-WHITE HOUSE

PANOLA

PLATE XX

LINDEN (Watson-Stokes-Cox)

Courtesy R. B. Wilson, Jr.

LINDEN (Dupuy)

PLATE XXI

THE McKINNEY HOUSE

ASPEN HILL

PLATE XXII

INGLESIDE

THE RUDD-OWEN HOUSE

Courtesy R. B. Wilson, Jr.

PLATE XXIII

TRAVIS

OAK GROVE

Plate XXIV

WALNUT HILL

THE PAULETT HOUSE

PLATE XXV

PLATE XXVI

STONE KNOLL

SUNNYSIDE

Plate XXVII

Courtesy Hampden-Sydney Alumni Record

SLATE HILL IN THE 1890's

SLATE HILL

PLATE XXVIII

CLOVER HILL

Courtesy R. B. Wilson, Jr.

OAKLAND

PLATE XXIX

MIDDLECOURT

PENSHURST

PLATE XXX

FARMVILLE HIGH SCHOOL

R. R. MOTON HIGH SCHOOL

PLATE XXXI

THE DEBTORS' PRISON

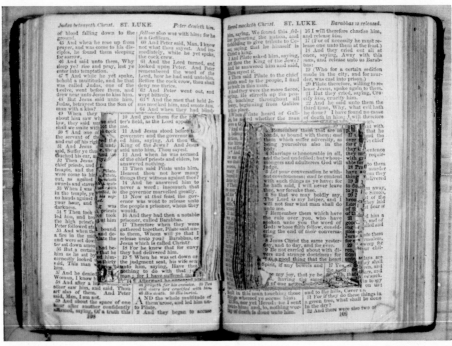

A MEMENTO OF WAR

PLATE XXXII

land. They came from various sections of the eastern part of the colony, from south of the James to the Northern Neck. Some of the immigrants belonged to the movement into Southern Virginia and Northern North Carolina known as the Hanover migration. The number of people who went out from Hanover and its neighboring counties during the four decades before the Revolution was almost phenomenal. These settlers from Eastern Virginia were largely of English stock. There were some exceptions. Jacob McGehee, who came from King William and whose first land purchase is recorded in 1741 and who in the same year was named a road surveyor (indicative of residence there), was of Scotch descent.[67] John Nash, who moved from Henrico County to the Prince Edward area about 1743, was a native of Wales, where his father, Abner Nash, was living in 1732.[68]

Neither record nor tradition has preserved the identity of the first person to make his home in the region now Prince Edward. Joseph Morton came very early to the upper part of Amelia—it may have been Prince George and Brunswick when he came—as a marksman for the Randolphs. As marksman, he sought out desirable lands in the wilderness for his employers and recommended these lands to them for patenting.[69] There was much interest among wealthy Virginians of that day in acquiring extensive acreages in the sections being opened to settlement, both for speculation (to sell to settlers) and for cultivation (following the location of "quarters" on them with overseers and slaves settled there). It is not known how many of the Randolphs Morton represented in his land hunting. William Randolph patented 3,800 acres on the Appomattox in 1733; Isham Randolph patented 6,000 acres on Buffalo River in 1737; and between 1735 and 1745, Richard Randolph took out six patents for a total of 18,946 acres on Bush River, the Appomattox, Mountain Creek, Falling Creek, and Buffalo. Morton also selected lands for himself and acquired considerable holdings: Joseph Morton, Jr., patented 1,200 acres on Briery River in 1739, and Joseph Morton, in 1745 and 1747, patented 5,553 acres in four grants on Briery, Sandy, and Buffalo Rivers.[70]

The second major stream of migration consisted of Scotch-Irish settlers from Pennsylvania. These people, who were Scotch in nationality, had the Irish hyphenated as a result of a sojourn of approximately a century in Northern Ireland. They had been settled there by James I to repopulate a land desolated by the armies of Queen Elizabeth I. There they had prospered until economic discrimination by the English government cut off the market for their goods, and severe depression followed. Many migrated to Pennsylvania, where they settled on the frontier. Indian troubles made life precarious there, so many took again to the weary road and sought a haven in the "back parts" of Virginia.

About 1735 two Scotch-Irish settlements, both under the leadership of John Caldwell, were made in Southside Virginia, one on Cub Creek in Brunswick, now Charlotte, the other on Buffalo River in Amelia, now Prince Edward. The Scotch-Irish for the most part moved in companies and made their homes in a settlement, for the threefold purpose of mutual protection against the rigors of the wilderness, of maintaining social contacts, and of convenience for religious worship.[71]

The first Scotch-Irish name to appear in the Amelia Court orders is that of Michael McDearmon (spelled McDearmond there), who appeared as a witness at the April, 1737, Court.[72] Two months later he made oath that he had not received any allowance provided by law for bringing persons into the colony, and the court ordered the testimony certified,[73] evidently to the Council of State.

By 1743 there were several Scotch-Irish settlers in the Prince Edward area. The suit of Samuel Wallace vs. Caleb Baker brought a number of neighbors from the Buffaloe Settlement as witnesses for the litigants: for the plaintiff, Francis Baldwin, Douglas Baker, Samuel Baker, James Stewart, and the one non-Scot among them, Joseph Morton, Jr.; for the defendant, John Caldwell, who traveled fifty miles to attend court, William Dudgins, William Caldwell, Thomas Caldwell, James Cunningham, and Andrew Wallace.[74]

The Scotch-Irish settlers designated to clear a road from Sandy Ford to Spring Creek in 1746 have already been named.

To the English, Scotch-Irish, Scotch, and Welsh racial strains in the upper end of Amelia was added the French Huguenot. At Manakin, in Goochland, was the principal settlement in Virginia of the Protestant refugees from France, who left their homeland to escape persecution under Louis XIV. They first went to England and Holland, some going from Holland to England with William of Orange when he and his wife Mary came to the English throne in 1689. William made a grant of land in Virginia to the Huguenots, and it was on this grant, at Manakin, that many settled. They spread from Manakin into the adjacent countryside. From the Manakin area to Prince Edward came three sons of Jean Jacques Flournoy— David, Mathew, and Thomas—and a daughter, Mary, with her husband, William Booker.[75] Peter and Alexander LeGrand, sons of the second Peter LeGrand and his wife, Jane Michaux, also came. Two sisters of the mother of the LeGrand brothers, who were daughters of the Huguenot immigrant, Abraham Michaux and his wife, Suzanne Rochet, with their husbands were among the early settlers; they were Ann Madelin Michaux, who married Richard Woodson, whose first land grant in the county was dated 1743, and Easter Mary Michaux, who married Alexander Cunningham, who received a grant on Little Mountain Creek in 1746. Still another of the pioneer wives of Michaux stock was Elizabeth, daughter of Jacob Michaux, niece of Mesdames Woodson and Cunningham, and wife of Abraham Venable, who settled on the Appomattox River. Woodson and Venable were of English stock. Cunningham was Scotch-Irish and came into Prince Edward from Goochland. Peter LeGrand married as his second wife Lucy Nash, daughter of the Welsh John Nash, and his brother Alexander married Lucy Walker, daughter of William Walker, a pioneer settler of Cumberland County.[76] Elias and Daniel DeJarnett, of a Huguenot family which had settled in Gloucester County, moved to the Snail's Creek area. They had probably been attracted to the section because their sister Eleanor had moved to it with her husband, Jacob McGehee.[77]

Thus early began that racial blending which was to produce in Prince Edward a race of British and Gallic heritages.

The pioneers in Prince Edward had no trouble with Indians. There is nothing to indicate that there were any Indians living in the area when the white settlers came. Jefferson mentions no Indian tribe as resident in Prince Edward in his *Notes on Virginia*. Relics of Indian culture have been found in the county, and there has been handed down the tradition of Indian sites: settlements on Fort Creek and at Slippery Rock, both in the central part of the county, Indian Rock near Buffalo Church, and an Indian burial ground near the fork of Sandy River.

The most extensive search in Prince Edward for Indian relics has been carried on along Little Buffalo Creek, on the farm Buffaloe. Here have been found in abundance flint and white quartz arrowheads and flint and slate spearheads. Here, too, have been found numerous relics of Indian domestic life. "Potsherds give us an idea of Indian skill and appreciation of beauty: bricklike legs of pots, pieces of pottery with lines and designs, a pot-ear with a place for two fingers. Some of the pottery seems to have been molded in baskets, and the markings come from the weave. Across the rim of the vessel the potter seems to have made marks to correspond with those on the side. There are also tools: an awl, almost needle-sharp; a saw with three teeth remaining; scrapers of igneous rock for cleaning poles for houses; a stone hatchet; a stone for shaping the inside of pots; an axe, one end rounded, the other shaped for cutting; finger stones used for grinding, shaping stones, and stones for scraping animal skins; a whetstone; hand-stones, large and small—as useful and essential to the squaw as the can-opener to the modern housewife. Several breadstones remain; on these corn was ground into meal, and the dough was kneaded; the stone was then heated, and the bread baked on the hot stone. Pottery beads or marbles, which may have been used in games; tiny bricks—the Indian dominoes; white pipe-stems tell something of Indian amusements. One pipestem has an enlargement at one end—a bowl not used for smoking, but apparently a burial pipe.

"Among bits of jewelry are a piece of copper lacework with egg-shaped bevelled holes and two hair lines and a broken brass bangle."[78]

The broken brass bangle has on it the design of a snake, suggesting a Mayan origin. When found, it had attached a piece of cloth of sinew. There were contacts between the Indians of Eastern Virginia and those of Mexico prior to the English settlement at Jamestown. A Virginia Indian, known to history by his Spanish name, Don Luis de Velasco, spent some time in both Mexico and Spain, returning to Virginia with the Jesuits whose efforts to establish a settlement he thwarted by assassinating them. Dare one speculate upon the possibilities that this piece of jewelry found its way from Mexico to Virginia, to turn up in a Prince Edward field? The egg-shaped bevelled holes of the copper piece are said to be similar to Costa Rican gold lacework.[79]

Prince Edward was probably the hunting ground of the Appomattox and possibly other tribes of Indians. The Nottoways may have come upstream to the springs from which flowed the river to which they gave their name and hunted in southeastern Prince Edward. So may the Meherrins. In 1670 the Men Heyricks (Meherrins) with 50 bowmen, the Nottoways with 90 bowmen, and the Appomattox with 50 bowmen, were listed among the tributary Indians living in Charles City County. The figure for the Appomattox Indians showed a decline of ten since Captain John Smith's time. At the command of Powhatan, the Queen of the Appomattox once gave Smith bread, water, and a "turkie cocke."[80]

The Appomattox Indians may have had a settlement on Little

Buffalo, where so many relics have been found, where they lived when hunting in the vicinity. Game abounded in the wilderness which became Prince Edward, and the streams were teeming with fish. The numerous pottery relics suggest that the tribe may have had an atelier at some clay bank overlooking Little Buffalo.

The first resident of the Prince Edward area to become a justice of the Amelia Court was George Walker, who was recommended to be added to the commission in July, 1739.[81] He attended the May, 1740, Court as a magistrate[82] and continued to figure prominently in county affairs. In 1741 and 1742 he was a church warden of Raleigh Parish,[83] the only Prince Edward resident who is known to have been warden and vestryman of Raleigh Parish which then embraced the entire county of Amelia. In February, 1742, Walker took the oath of an officer of the Amelia militia,[84] and in August, 1747, he became sheriff of Amelia.[85] Walker took the list of tithables above Sailor's Creek in 1744.[86]

The only other Prince Edward resident to serve as an Amelia magistrate was John Nash, who in March, 1743, was recommended to the Governor to be placed in the commission of the peace with the same rank he had had in Henrico County.[87] Four months later (July, 1744) Nash appears fifth in the list of Amelia justices.[88] (The rank in the commission was quite important to the justices; it determined when he would become sheriff in the rotating system in which magistrates shared that important office.) In 1746 and again in 1749 Nash took the list of tithables in the "upper part" of Amelia.[89] Nash had served twice as sheriff of Henrico,[90] but he did not serve as sheriff of Amelia, apparently because his place in the commission had been passed when he became a justice and Prince Edward had been cut off from Amelia before the rotation reached again the justice holding fifth rank.

Charles Anderson was recommended three times to the Governor for appointment to the magistracy in Amelia (February, 1746; August, 1749; and November, 1750), but his name was never added to the commission. No other resident of the section which became Prince Edward (other than Walker and Nash, of course) was recommended for appointment to the Amelia Court.[91]

In colonial Virginia the ecclesiastical organization was as important as the political. The Church of England was the Established Church. Just as the county was the local unit of of political government, the parish was the local unit of ecclesiastical government. The act which created Amelia County created Raleigh Parish and made it coterminous with the new county. Just as Amelia was formed of parts of Prince George and Brunswick Counties, Raleigh Parish was formed from part of Bristol Parish (the portion of Prince George included in the new county) and part of St. Andrew's Parish (the portion of Brunswick included in Amelia).[92]

Raleigh Parish was divided in 1748; the portion of Amelia which is now included in the counties of Nottoway and Prince Edward became Nottoway Parish. Two petitions asking for a division of Raleigh Parish, one presented by James Anderson, the other by the Parish vestry, were read at the June, 1748, Court and ordered to be certified,[93] evidently to the House of Burgesses. The bill for dividing the parish passed the House of Burgesses November 28, 1748; two days later it was reported that the Council had agreed to the bill without amendment, and the Governor signed the bill December 17.[94]

Election of vestrymen for both Raleigh and Nottoway Parishes followed the division of Raleigh, freeholders in the respective parishes voting in the elections. In Nottoway Parish Charles Anderson, Charles Irby, John Nash, Joseph Morton, William Watson, James Attwood, George Walker, Richard Jones, Jr., Abraham Cocke, Henry Ward, Daniel Dejarnet, and William Baldwin were elected; they took the oath of vestrymen May 19, 1749, in Amelia Court.[95] Of the vestrymen, Anderson, Nash, Morton, Attwood, Walker, Dejarnet, and probably Baldwin were residents of the western portion of the parish which became Prince Edward.

Apparently dissatisfaction with the Nottoway vestry developed not too long after the election. Acting upon a petition of the inhabitants of the parish, the Assembly of 1752 dissolved the vestry, pronounced all its subsequent acts void (but its previous acts and levies "good, valid and effectual"), and directed the freeholders of the parish to elect prior to June 10, 1753, a new vestry, whose members should take the prescribed oaths in Amelia Court.[96]

The vestry of Raleigh Parish established a place of worship in the "upper part" of Amelia prior to April 20, 1744, when the first reference to "Sandy River Chappell" was made in the Amelia records.[97] As far as can be determined, the chapel was on the site of the present Sandy River meeting-house, now house of worship of Sharon Baptist Church. When the chapel in the wilderness, built for the convenience of the pioneers on the frontier, became a church is not known, but two entries in the court orders in 1745 refer to it as "the church."[98] A 1749 entry mentions Sandy River Chapel,[99] but in the same year a grand jury presented five men for selling liquor at Sandy River *Church* and in the church.[100]

The Scotch-Irish settlers brought with them to their new home in Buffaloe Settlement their Presbyterian faith. They are described as having "great unanimity" in interpreting the Westminster Confession and in adhering to the Scotch or Geneva model in church government and forms of worship. In Virginia they were Dissenters. John Caldwell, with the approval of Donegal Presbytery, asked the 1738 session of the Synod of Philadelphia to petition Governor Gooch of Virginia "on behalf of himself and many members of our persuasion about to settle in the back parts of Virginia" for recognition of their right to worship "in a way agreeable to the principles of their education." The synod appointed a committee to present the request to Governor Gooch, who assured the committee that there would be no interference with any ministers who conformed to the Act of Toleration.[101]

The status of church organization among the Scotch-Irish settlers is not clear. They were ministered to by visiting evangelists from presbyteries in the Middle Colonies. There is nothing to indicate that they had in the earlier years of their settlement in Virginia either church organizations in their new home or regular pastors. The Rev. John Thomson, pastor of the Chestnut Level Church in Donegal Presbytery, preached at Buffalo and Walker's (places of worship for the Scotch-Irish settlers in Amelia) in 1739. In that year Thomson asked to be released from the Chestnut Level pastorate, quite likely in order to enable him to move to Virginia, but the request was refused. He apparently spent much of his time during the next few years in Virginia, and in September, 1743, Donegal Presbytery directed him to supply "the back parts of Virginia" until November. The next year the presbytery released Thomson from his pastorate, and he moved to the Buffaloe Settlement where he bought a farm of 386 acres in 1745. Thomson retained his ties with the church organizations in the North, attending the Philadelphia Synod of 1745. At the request of the synod, he answered a complaint of Governor Gooch over some "religious disburbances"; Thomson evidently satisfied the Governor by pointing out the distinction between the "New Lights," who were apparently responsible for the disturbances, and the Presbyterians. In 1747 Donegal Presbytery named Thomson to a commission of three ministers and authorized it to act with full power in Presbyterian affairs in Virginia.[102]

Meanwhile New Brunswick Presbytery had sent the Rev. William Robinson to preach to Presbyterian settlers in Virginia and Carolina

in the winter of 1742-43. On his return northward in the spring of
1743 he preached with great effectiveness in the Cub Creek and
Buffaloe settlements.[103]

The Prince Edward tradition of interest in education and literary
matters had its origin in the work of John Thomson during his
residence in the Buffaloe Settlement. These years, in the opinion of
his most exhaustive biographer, were the happiest and perhaps the
most useful of his life. Here he conducted a school which was well
attended. Some of the students built cabins in which they lived
while studying with this minister. It was a fortunate frontier community to have as its schoolmaster a Master of Arts of the University
of Glasgow.

While Thomson was living in the Buffaloe community, he wrote
a book, the first to be written in the confines of Prince Edward. It
was the *Explication of the Shorter Catechism,* and the title-page
described the author as John Thomson, M.A., V. D. M. (Verbi Dei
Minister), of the County of Amelia. It was published at Williamsburg in 1749. As the title indicates, the work is a study and an
explanation of the Shorter Catechism; it is praised by one of Thomson's biographers as "probably the keenest analysis of the Shorter
Catechism yet written." An appendix compares the doctrines of the
Church of England and the Presbyterian Church; in this comparison,
Thomson showed that Presbyterians conformed to all the Thirty-nine
Articles of the Church of England except four which relate to arch-
bishops and bishops and the ordination of priests and deacons. Did
Thomson add this appendix to show the doctrinal unity of the two
Churches in an effort to keep down controversy among the settlers
of the two communions who were meeting and mingling on the
frontier which became Prince Edward?

Thomson was the author of another work, *The Poor Orphan's
Legacy,* but where he was living when he wrote it is not known.
Both books are listed in the inventory of the estate of his daughter,
Martha Baker, in Prince Edward in 1759. Thomson's grandson,
Andrew Baker of Prince Edward (Martha Baker's nephew), had the
Legacy reprinted in 1792, and the Presbyterian Board of Publication
republished it again in 1860.[104]

It is a pleasant picture, and it helps to complete the frontier
scene: while most of the settlers were opening land for cultivation,
building homes, and clearing roads in the 1740's, John Thomson was
preaching (although there is no indication that he was pastor of a
church) to pioneer congregations, was instructing classes of pioneer

youth, and was writing his book on the Shorter Catechism. Work and study, agriculture, theology, and learning had an early emphasis and blending in the upper part of Amelia.

The clearing of roads through the western section of Amelia indicated an increasing travel through that part of the country. As travel increased, inn-keeping offered opportunities for profit and at the same time became a requirement for the accommodation of the traveling public. Lands to the west and southwest were being opened, and settlers were moving to the new country. The Hanover migration, for example, was in full swing by the later 1740's; the north-south roads through Prince Edward provided access to the watersheds of the Staunton and the Dan, and to North Carolina as well.

George Moore received a license from the Amelia Court on August 17, 1748, to keep an ordinary at his house.[105] Moore's home was located on the road which crossed what became the southeastern corner of Prince Edward. His opening of a tavern there marked the beginning of Moore's Ordinary, which continued as the name of the community for more than a century; it is the present Meherrin. Moore's license was renewed by the Amelia Court in 1749 and again in 1751.[106]

Charles Anderson received a license to keep an ordinary at his house on June 16, 1749.[107] He, like Moore, had an advantageous location for a tavern, for his home was situated convenient to the intersection of an important east-west road and an important north-south road. The former led by Sandy River Church past Anderson's and through the Buffaloe Settlement to the west; the latter linked Rutledge's Ford on the Appomattox (the present Farmville) with a road through Lunenburg near the head of Little Roanoke River. Anderson's inn became the site of the courthouse of Prince Edward when the county was established,[108] and the opening of his inn may be regarded in a sense as the founding of Worsham, just as the opening of Moore's Ordinary may be regarded as the founding of Meherrin. Anderson's ordinary license was renewed in 1750 and in 1751.[109]

Richard Burk received a license to keep an ordinary at Crawford's in January, 1750.[110] This may have been located in Prince Edward.

There were occasional requests to the court for a valuation to be put upon the improvements which had been made for land holdings. Two such petitions were filed with the Amelia Court for Prince Edward land. In 1751 George Forrest asked for an evaluation of the improvements he had made on his 400-acre farm on Sandy River,[111] and the next year Edward McGehee asked that the improvements he had made on 5,000 acres which he owned between Bush and Briery Rivers be valued.[112]

In 1748 the people of the upper part of Amelia were excited by reports of two cases of horse stealing, then a capital offense. One of the cases heard by the Amelia Court proved a false alarm; the accused, a Negro slave belonging to Richard Woodson, was acquitted in May, 1748.[113]

The second case proved more spectacular. Circumstances suggest that Charles Anderson and Joseph Morton, Jr., engaged in some rather clever detective work and made a rather thrilling capture of the suspect, who was subsequently tried, convicted, and executed. They petitioned the June, 1748, Court for a reward for taking up a horse thief, and the petition was certified. The neighbors thought Anderson and Morton deserved more, so they petitioned the General Assembly "to allow such reward . . . for trouble, expense and loss of time in pursuing and apprehending . . . as will encourage others to detect such offenses and pursue and take those who commit them." The Committee on Propositions and Grievances of the House of Burgesses was unimpressed by the argument. Anderson and Morton had received the reward allowed by law (twenty shillings), and that, thought the committee, was enough.[114]

The roads which had been cleared through the forests did not provide the best access to the markets on the Appomattox River at and below the falls. Early settlers in the upper end of Amelia (and Goochland) had found the river "useful for carrying tobacco in boats near seventy miles above the falls." By 1745 this use of the river had been impeded by obstructions both natural, such as falling trees and accumulating sand bars, and artificial, such as milldams and stone stops and hedges for catching fish.[115]

The Amelia Court in June, 1745, directed that all male laboring tithables living within two miles of the Appomattox who would assist in clearing the river be relieved of their obligation to work on the roads. The same order directed owners of dams to keep open passages adequate for the safe passage of boats and other vessels. Surveyors were named to supervise the cleaning of the Appomattox channel from the mouth of Buffalo downstream: Edmund Gross was supervisor for the stretch of river from the mouth of Buffalo to the mouth of Bush; Douglas Puckett, from the mouth of Bush to Townes Quarter; Henry Dawson, Townes Quarter to Lovells Mill; and John Echols, Lovells Mill to Clements Mill.[116]

County court action was apparently inadequate to bring the relief desired by those who wanted to use the river as an avenue of commerce. A petition from Amelia was presented to the Virginia Assembly in March, 1745/6, asking that a law be passed requiring the owners of dams to build "convenient passages" in the dams and that the dams, if the owners did not construct such passages, be demolished; the petition further asked that the law "for the more effectual clearing of rivers and creeks" be amended. The Committee on Propositions and Grievances of the House of Burgesses regarded the petition as reasonable and agreed that the law in question needed explanation and amendment.

The mill owners did not permit this petition to go unchallenged. John Smith and other mill owners of Amelia presented a counter petition that they have the permission of the House of Burgesses to keep their milldams across the Appomattox. This petition did not get beyond the Committee on Propositions and Grievances.[117]

This controversy over the Appomattox was the first clash, insofar as has been found, between public and private interests in Prince Edward. The former wanted the river open for boats to the falls above Petersburg to facilitate the transportation of their produce to market. The mill owners claimed the right to keep the dams across the river.

The Assembly of 1745/6 decided in the public interest. It empowered the county courts of Henrico, Prince George, Amelia, Goochland, and Albemarle to order the clearing of the James and Appomattox Rivers of trees and stumps and to levy the costs upon the tithables of the county or counties. A fine of ten shillings was set as the penalty for the first offense of permitting a tree to fall in the river and failure to clear it out immediately, with a penalty of fifteen shillings fixed for subsequent offenses. Stone stops, hedges, and milldams were ordered demolished, but owners of milldams were given until October 1 to construct locks or some other form of passage through the dams. When a dam had to be destroyed, the county court was to designate four justices to appraise the value of the dam, report to the next court for the proof of public claims, and certify the valuation to the Assembly which in turn would compensate the owner for the loss. The courts were further authorized to appoint two or more surveyors for the river to clear it of obstructions, to view locks, and to report the sufficiency or the insufficiency of the locks.

The act of 1745 was in effect only four years.[118] Navigation of the Appomattox was again impeded by obstructions. An act of February, 1752, directed that the river be cleared and named eight trustees, three of whom were from the section of Amelia which became Prince Edward, to clear the river and remove the stops they thought necessary. John Nash, George Walker, and Joseph Morton were from the Prince Edward section;. the other trustees were Peter Randolph, William Randolph, George Carrington, Clement Read, and Benjamin Harris. Owners of dams were given six months in which to install gates or locks or other passages "sufficient and convenient for the passing of any boat or other vessel," with the destruction of the dam the penalty for non-compliance, "any law, usage or custom to the contrary notwithstanding." Persons whose land lay on the river where stone-stops and fish hedges had been placed were assessed the charge of removal after July 10, 1752. The trustees and their employees were authorized to go on private land without being liable for trespass and were permitted to cut from adjacent land the timber needed for their work, which was to be valued and paid for.[119]

Distance was a compelling reason for residents of sections remote from the courthouse to want a county divided and a courthouse located more convenient to them. The first petition for dividing Amelia was presented to the June, 1748, Court by John Nash; after it had been read, it was ordered certified,[120] evidently to the Assembly. This proposal probably involved Lunenburg as well, for on March 17, 1748, the Committee on Propositions and Grievances of the House of Burgesses rejected propositions from Amelia and Lunenburg "to erect part of those counties to be divided from them by a line running from the head of the westernmost fork of Sandy River in Amelia County through Lunenburg County such a course as will strike the Staunton River below the mouth of Little Roanoke River, opposite a place called the Sandy Bar, into one distinct county."[121]

The next move to divide Amelia was made in 1752. The Assembly deferred action on the petition until the 1753 session. On November 6, 1753, a petition from "sundry inhabitants" of Amelia was presented to the House, reminding it of its postponement of action on the petition of the year before. The petition was referred to the Committee on Propositions and Grievances that day.[122] This was probably the petition presented to the Amelia Court October 20, 1753, by Edward Thweatt on behalf of himself and others for a division of the county, which was certified to the Assembly.[123]

The bill to divide Amelia was reported favorably by Charles

Carter, chairman of the Committee on Propositions and Grievances, on November 14, 1753.[124] It was read the third time the next day and passed the House. One of the burgesses from Amelia, Thomas Tabb, carried the bill to the Council,[125] and two days later the Council reported its agreement to the bill.[126] For over a month the bill which had passed both houses of the Virginia Assembly awaited the Governor's signature. Then, in the phrase of the day when the Governor of Virginia was viceroy of the King of England, Governor Robert Dinwiddie "commanded" the House of Burgesses to attend him in the Council-Chamber and to bring to him the bills ready for his signature on December 19. The fifteenth bill presented him that day, "to which he was pleased to give his assent," was the act "for dividing the County of Amelia."[127]

The act took effect January 1, 1754. It divided Amelia by a line from Ward's Ford on the Appomattox to the mouth of Snail's Creek on Nottoway River. The area on the "upper" or western side of the line was designated Prince Edward County. Courts were ordered held on the second Tuesday in each month. The sheriff of Amelia was authorized to collect any taxes or fees remaining unpaid by residents of the new county, and the Amelia Court was authorized to retain jurisdiction in all actions and suits pending before it.[128]

The name of the new county honored a young prince, Edward Augustus, Duke of York and Albany, second son of Frederick, Prince of Wales, deceased son of the reigning sovereign, His Majesty, George II.[129]

CHAPTER II

Establishing A County

LESS than a month after Governor Dinwiddie had signed the bill which established Prince Edward County, the justices of the peace were meeting to set up the government for the new county. The law directed the county court to be held on the second Tuesday of each month; and on the second Tuesday in January, 1754, six of the justices appointed for Prince Edward met to hold the first court.[1] The place where the first court was held is not preserved in the records. Circumstances indicate that the first courts met in the public room of Charles Anderson's tavern,[2] near the intersection of the road from Amelia Courthouse and other points east by Sandy River Church and through the Buffaloe Settlement westward and the Roanoke road from Rutledge's Ford on the Appomattox into Lunenburg.

At the first meeting of the court the Commissions of the Peace and of Dedimus Potestatem which designated the justices of the peace who made up the county court and conferred upon them the authority to act as magistrates were read. Two of the group, David Flournoy and John Nash, Jr., administered the oaths of government, of a Justice of the Peace, and of a Justice of the Peace in Chancery to John Nash, Sr., who for a decade had held fifth rank in the commission for Amelia and who was listed first in the commission for Prince Edward; George Walker, who had also been a magistrate in Amelia, Joseph Morton, and James Wimbish. The elder Nash then administered the oaths to Flournoy and the younger Nash.[3]

When the county court had been constituted by the subscription to the test by the magistrates, John LeNeve, who since 1749 had been deputy clerk of Amelia under his father-in-law, Samuel Cobbs,[4] presented a commission from Secretary Thomas Nelson of the Colony to be clerk of the new county; he took the required oaths, subscribed the test, and was sworn clerk.

The Governor had not appointed a sheriff for the new county, so in accordance with the practice of the times, the court recommended three of its number, John Nash, Jr., David Flournoy, and James Wimbish, from which list the Governor would make the appointment. John Nash, Sr., was first in the commission and was accordingly first in line for appointment as sheriff; it is likely that he yielded his place to his son, probably in order to become a candidate for the House of Burgesses. The younger Nash was appointed sheriff; at the February court he took the oath of office and gave bond in the sum of 1,000 pounds current money for the faithful discharge of his duties; Samuel Cobbs and Matthew Flournoy were his securities.[5] Other magistrates took the oath at subsequent courts: Abraham Venable in May[6] and Joel Watkins in June.[7] The commission read at the November, 1754, Court contains the first list of justices which has been preserved: it was directed to John Nash, George Walker, Charles Anderson, Joseph Morton, James Wimbish, Abraham Venable, Joel Watkins, David Flournoy, John Nash, Jr., Thomas Scott, Samuel Ewing, and Thomas Haskins.[8] Although this is the first list to be preserved in its entirety, the first commission was probably directed to all those named except the last three. Scott, Ewing, and Haskins were recommended to the Governor by the October Court to be added to the commission.[9]

The office of justice of the peace was one of considerable dignity and importance. The justices made up the county court, which combined legislative, administrative, and judicial functions. The court managed the county's business, drew up the budget, set the levy, provided for the clearing and maintenance of roads and the construction and upkeep of bridges, granted licenses to ordinaries or taverns, set the prices which could be charged at those places of entertainment for food, refreshments (especially alcoholic), and lodging; issued permits for the building of milldams. The Court heard civil and criminal cases, admitted wills to probate and deeds to record, granted letters of administration for estates. It could impose the most severe penalties, even death, upon slaves convicted of crime, but it acted as a court of hearing for freemen accused of crime; when it found cause in cases of accused freemen, these were sent to the General Court in Williamsburg for trial. Appointments to the county courts were made by the Governor. Since vacancies were filled by the Governor on recommendation of the Court, it was in effect a self-perpetuating body. The office of magistrate carried no salary, but the dignity of office and the respect in which a magistrate was held attracted the services of the ablest and most successful men of the county. The responsibilities of a justice required both intelligence and integrity, and the method of appointment combined with the indefinite term to insure the selection of men who possessed these qualities. It also required knowledge of the law which today is not

expected to be found in a layman. But when the county court composed of magistrates directed the affairs of the county, it provided
each of its members with a copy of the laws of the colony and with
copies of the acts of each session of the Assembly as soon as they
were compiled and printed after the close of the session.[10] One item
of county expense was the payment of some person for "bringing
up" the acts of Assembly from Williamsburg. These volumes were
considered the property of the county, and upon the resignation or
death of a magistrate, the return of these books was expected and
sometimes asked.[11] It is no surprise that the county court of colonial
Virginia was a training ground for statesmanship and leadership.

One of the first concerns of the Prince Edward Court was to
provide the buildings necessary for the conduct of county government. The great room of an inn was at best only a makeshift courthouse, and a jail where prisoners could be made secure was a
necessity. Charles Anderson offered to the Court at its second meeting the use of his kitchen (kitchens were then outbuildings) as a
jail. The court accepted the offer, and when Sheriff Nash advised
that the kitchen of Anderson's tavern was not sufficient as a jail, the
Court authorized him to summon a guard whenever he needed one.
At this second court (February, 1754), a committee consisting of
George Walker, James Wimbish, and David Flournoy was authorized to review proposals for building a courthouse and to report to
the next court.[12]

Charles Anderson's proposals for building the county buildings
were the most acceptable to the March Court. The place where he
proposed to build them was satisfactory, described as "scituated
centrically and convenient &c, and well watered," and at or near
Anderson's house. The courthouse, stocks, pillory, and whipping-
post (the latter three essential to the administration of colonial
justice) were to be built after the plan of the courthouse, stocks,
pillory, and whipping-post in Cumberland County. The Court had
certain specifications for the jail: it was to be constructed of logs,
twelve feet by sixteen in the clear, the inside walls to be ceiled with
four-inch plank, two floors of hewn timber, brick underpinning, and
a brick chimney.[13] This prison, for which Charles Anderson was
paid £52:15,[14] did not serve the county long. In 1755 it burned;[15]
the October, 1755, Court directed the sheriff to enter into an agreement with workmen to build a prison twelve feet square of "Hughed
logs."[16] In December a runaway indentured servant was acquitted
of the charge of burning down the jail, but he received thirty-nine

lashes on his back well laid on for appearing in women's clothes and often changing his name before being returned, by being conveyed from constable to constable, to his master, William Eaton, on the Roanoke River in North Carolina.[17]

Before the courthouse was completed, the Court changed its idea about some features of the plan. In October, 1754, it appointed George Walker to treat with Anderson or some other person to paint the building on both the inside and the outside and to tar the roof; instead of "dorment windows" there was to be a large window at each end of the building (evidently in the gable ends), with two windows on each side below; the building was to be underpinned three feet clear of the ground, and a pair of brick steps was to be built at each door.[18] The next year James Wimbish was appointed to get someone to build a table with a drawer which could be locked for use in the courthouse.[19] Glass windows were put in the courthouse in 1757.[20]

The site proposed by Anderson and approved by the Court for the location of the courthouse and its appendages was on a tract of 3,000 acres belonging to Anderson. Here was a tavern, described in the year of the establishment of Prince Edward as a "well accustomed ordinary." Here, too, was located a store at the time the place was selected as the site for the courthouse.[12] When the courthouse and the jail had been built, Prince Edward Courthouse took on the appearance of a frontier village. The Anderson land was described as being convenient to church and mill; the nearest church was Sandy River.

Repairs to courthouse and jail were made frequently during the colonial period. Each sheriff in turn upon taking office protested the insufficiency of the prison. A new jail was ordered built in 1759 with the same dimensions as the Cumberland jail, John Morton letting the contract.[22] When John Martin and James Thackston reported to the February, 1762, Court that the prison had been well built, Joel Watkins, who was then sheriff, protested its insufficiency.[23] A new jail was under construction in 1764, when a committee consisting of Peter LeGrand, John Morton, Henry Watkins, James Scott, and Nathaniel Venable was appointed to view and receive it if satisfactorily completed.[24]

In 1767 the Court levied 4,000 pounds of tobacco to build a new clerk's office and 3,000 pounds of tobacco to repair the courthouse.[25] Peter LeGrand and Nathaniel Venable were appointed to let to the lowest bidder extensive repairs to the courthouse, to be completed by September 1, 1767: turning the end of the building to the east; putting in five large windows with shutters; repairing the old windows and putting shutters and iron bolts on them; underpinning the courthouse with well burnt bricks.[26] Nathaniel Venable built the clerk's office; Venable was also directed to build brick steps at the courthouse.[27] In the same year Peter LeGrand repaired the jail, for which he received £2:6.[28] Whether the courthouse was repaired within the time limit set is not apparent. In 1769 an order noted that the Court received the courthouse from Daniel Dejarnett as done by Peter LeGrand, agreeable to the contract of Dejarnett, the undertaker (contractor).[29]

In 1765 Alexander Kain was paid twenty-five shillings for a courthouse table;[30] in 1768 John Popham was paid fifteen shillings for six chairs for the Court;[31] and in 1769 Peter LeGrand was directed to have the lawyer's bar repaired.[32]

The Court planned to build a new courthouse in 1772. The building was to be forty-six feet long, twenty-four feet wide, with a pitch of twelve feet; the roof was to be hipped from the joists. The courthouse was to have two jury rooms, each twelve feet square and each equipped with a fireplace. The contractor was allowed two years in which to complete the structure. Peter LeGrand and John Morton were named the building committee, charged with drawing a draft of the proposed building, with advertising the time bids would be let, with letting the work to the lowest undertaker; and with taking the undertaker's bond with security.[33] In July, 1775, the Court named Peter LeGrand, John Morton, Richard Morton, and Archer Allen to receive the new building when it had been completed by Christopher Ford.[34] Apparently some time was yet to elapse before the building was completed, for in March, 1776, James Thackston, Reuben Coleman, and Benjamin Allen were appointed to view the new courthouse and report whether it had been completed according to specifications.[35]

During the more than twenty years of the county's existence, the Court had never gotten title to the land on which the courthouse and the other county buildings stood. The July, 1775, Court noted the opinion "that Joseph Smith, under his right to lands purchased of Henry Benskin Lightfoot, formerly Charles Anderson's, will when this court adjourns to the new courthouse be the only proprietor of the old and present courthouse and he has leave then to remove it from this place."[36] In December the Court paid Charles Venable ten shillings for his survey and plat of one acre of land on which the courthouse was built.[37] Title to the land was not forthcoming, despite an agreement by Smith to sell the land and the Court's confirmation of Smith as the owner of the old courthouse. In May, 1777, the Court tendered to Smith two pounds, the consideration stipulated in the deed for the acre of land on which the courthouse was built and demanded his wife's relinquishment of dower in the land, apparently the technicality which stood in the way of getting title after Smith had agreed to sell; he refused both to give up his wife's relinquishment and to take the money.[38] Perhaps the inflated value of the Continental currency of the time was Smith's reason for holding up conveyance of title.

The March, 1754, Court directed the sheriff to summon twenty-four "of the most capable freeholders" of Prince Edward to serve as a grand jury at the May Court.[39] The first grand jury consisted of James Atwood, Peter Davis, Samuel Southerland, Richard Childress, William Cambell, Henry Baker, Robert Elliot, James Thaxton, Philemon Holcomb, George Davis, Charles Ritchie, Michael McDearmon, Robert Galispie, James McMackin, and John Owing. Their one indictment was discharged.[40]

The second grand jury in Prince Edward history functioned at the November, 1754, Court. It began the practice, long maintained, of presenting road surveyors for not keeping roads under their supervision in repair. Grand jurors at this session of Court were Elias Dejarnet, Henry Childs, James Donald, Robert Black, James Reed, Joseph Littlejohn, James Parks, James Callicoat, Henry Baker, Samuel Baker, William Hill, Jacob McGehee, James Thaxton, John Morrow, William Baldwin, and John Fulton.[41]

The earliest orders concerning the summoning of grand jurors directed the sheriff to summon twenty-four of "the most capable freeholders." After September, 1767, certain occupational groups were excluded from grand jury service: owners and operators of mills, keepers of ordinaries, constables, and surveyors of highways.[42]

When persons summoned for jury duty failed to appear, they were cited to appear and fined. If the person gave an excuse satisfactory to the Court, he was excused and his fine was remitted.[43]

The first will probated in Prince Edward was that of Caleb Baker; his will was presented in April, 1754, by Martha Baker and Henry Baker, executrix and executor.

The first civil case was heard at the April Court; Charles Anderson brought suit against John Coldwell for £1:7:5. The defendant confessed judgment.[44]

The first criminal case was heard at the May Court under the style, Our Lord the King plaintif vs. John Coldwell, Thomas Coldwell, and John Galispie, deft. The defendants were discharged, but the court ordered that James Ewin, Sr., John Coldwell, Jr., and Samuel Wallace be fined "if they do not appear at the next Court and show cause." The offense is not listed.[45] The first charge listed by the Prince Edward Court and the first fine levied was against Robert Bird, who at the June, 1754, Court was fined five shillings for not going to church.[46] It is probable that the charges against the six whose cases were considered by the May Court were the same, since all those named were Scotch-Irish and therefore Presbyterians and dissenters; those discharged could have explained their right to worship as dissenters which was confirmed by Governor Gooch and thereby have been excused for failure to attend worship of the Church of England. Bird, who was fined, failed to appear.[47]

The Scotch-Irish, and the Coldwells (John LeNeve's spelling of Caldwell), chalked up another first in Prince Edward. John Coldwell was the first person to be imprisoned in the county; he was fined five shillings sterling by the July, 1754, Court for "assaulting Samuel Wallace during the setting of this Court." He was then committed to jail until he could give security on a bond of five pounds under which he was put, conditioned on his good behavior, for a year and a day.[48]

In November, 1754, the Court drew up the first county levy. It amounted in all to 33,040 pounds of tobacco, which meant an assessment of 40 pounds of tobacco on each of the 926 tithables in the new county. The items of the levy show what a county in the colonial period spent money for:

		(Pounds of Tobacco)	
To the Clerk for his ex officio....................	1240		
To the Sheriff for his ex officio...................	1240		
To Mr. Clement Read, the King's Attorney..........	936		
To John LePeve for laying off Ten acres Land the Prison Bounds..........	350		
To the Honourable the Secretary for Commission of the Peace and Dedimus and Writ of Election of Burgesses	357	4139	
To John LeNeve for two record books at 43 shillings each			
To do for one do at 26 shillings £5:12:0			
To the Honourable the Secretary for the Second Commission of the Peace and Dedimus.............	112	112	

(Pounds of Tobacco)

To John LeNeve for sending for a Commission of the
   Peace and c £1:10:0
To Richard Washborn for one old Wolf's head, certified
               by George Walker   100
To Abraham Baker for one old Wolf's head, certified
               by James Wimbish   100
To William Searcey for one young wolf's head Certi-
            fied by George Walker   50   250
To the Sherif for sundry service gross......300......   240
To the Clerk do........................90......   63
To Captain Anderson for Guarding Abraham Womack
            25 days   750
To do   for Guarding Timothy Sullivant 19 days   570   1220   1523
To William King 57 Days Guard over Womack)   690
To do   6 Days Guard over Chapman)
To Joel Stubblefield 29 Days a Guard.............   870
To Alexander LeGrand 6 Days a Guard...........   180
To John Philips 6 Days a Guard.................   180   1920
To Capt Anderson for the use of his Kitchen as a Prison
         49 Days   £4:0:0
To do   for cleaning the Court House...........   300
To Mr. Nash for Paid John Bentley sending
   for books........................ £2:10:0
To Richard Perryman for Prison chimney.. £1: 6:0
To Capt Anderson for Labouring, Diet & time £1:15:0 ————
                        £16:13:0

To Tobacco to be sold to discharge money Debts...... 22593
To Sherif's Commission at 6 per cent on 33040...... 1902

               33040

The County credit By 926 tiths at 40 lbs. Pole....... 33040[49]

    The levies show that most of the bills were paid in tobacco. Skilled workmen and some others who rendered services charged in sterling or current money. Since cash money was scarce, the levy was fixed in tobacco, and a sufficient amount of tobacco, calculated at prevailing prices, was levied to be sold for cash to discharge the cash obligations of the county.

    Residents of the new county found taxes higher than they had in

Amelia, when in 1753 the tax on each tithable had been six pounds of tobacco.[50]

In the 1755 levy appeared such items as To Thomas Scott, Coroner, for inquiring on Dejarnett's and Hudson's Negroes, 133 pounds of tobacco each; To Peter LeGrand for Buffalo Bridge, 500 pounds tobacco; to John Bigger for building a bridge over Spring Creek, £6:7:6; To Charles Anderson "for his Burgesses wages as per acct" £25:4:0; To John Martin for the prison, £10:17:6; To Hugh Challis for cleaning the Courthouse, 300 pounds of tobacco. The number of tithables had declined this year to 893; each was assessed twenty-two pounds of tobacco.[51]

The tax rate remained the same in 1756, when there were 900 tithables, and the county expenses amounted to 19,800 pounds of tobacco.[52]

The following table shows the number of tithables, the amount of tobacco levied per poll, and the total amount of the county expenses:

Year	Tithables	Levy per Poll (Pounds of Tobacco)	Total Levy (Pounds of Tobacco)
1757	902	20	19640[53]
1758	910	8	7344[54]
1759	1011	23	23252[55]
1760	1090	15	16350[59]
1761	1194	14	16716[57]
1763 (January, for 1762)	1134	9	10206[58]
1763	1187	8	9496[56]
1765 (January, for 1764)	1276	61	77836[60]
1765 (December)	1367	8	10936[61]
1767 (May, for 1766)	1381	12	16572[62]
1767 (December)	1402	12	16824[63]
1768	1576	9	14184[64]
1770 (January, for 1769)	1620	16	25920[65]
1770 (December)	1782	7	12474[69]
1771	1863	6	11178[67]
1772	1980	9	17820[68]
1774 (January, for 1773)	2048	28	57344[69]
1774 (October)	1964	7	13748[70]
1775	1948	7	13636[71]

The fluctuation in the levy shows the simplicity of the approach of the county Court to the problem of finances. The bills for the year were added up at the end of the year, the number of tithables ascertained, the total expense divided by the number of tithables and the individual assessment made accordingly. Sometimes additional expenses would be discovered after the levy had been set, and it would then be increased.[72]

Members of the Court were appointed to take the lists of tithables. In 1754 John Nash took the list of those between Bush River and the Amelia line, Joseph Morton those between Bush and Buffalo Rivers, and Abraham Venable those above Buffalo River.[73] A part of the list of tithables taken in 1755 has been preserved, the list taken by Thomas Scott of those between Bush and Buffalo and the list taken by Samuel Ewing above Buffalo.[74] This division was followed for several years in taking the list of tithables. In 1767, when in addition to the list of tithables land and wheel carriages were ordered to be listed, the number of magistrates taking the list had increased to five; in that year Charles Venable, William Booker, Joel Watkins, Peter Johnston, and Philemon Holcombe took the lists, no specific district being indicated.[75] In 1773 six magistrates were directed to take the list of tithables, land, and wheeled carriages: Abraham Venable, Thomas Haskins, Henry Watkins, Charles Venable, Peter LeGrand, and Peter Johnston.[76]

The colony imposed a tax of six pounds of tobacco on each tithable in 1761 to pay expenses incurred between February 22, 1759 and March 6, 1761. At this time 1,775 pounds of tobacco was due the public (colonial) treasury from Prince Edward, and the sheriff was directed to sell the tobacco collected to meet the charge at the July, 1761, Court to the highest bidder and pay the proceeds to the treasurer of the colony before October 20.[77] For the period March 6, 1761, to November 2, 1762, a tax of seven pounds of tobacco was levied on each tithable, and the balance due from Prince Edward was 2,657 pounds.[78] For the next period, November 2, 1762, to November 30, 1764, the rate was multiplied, the levy being 46 pounds of tobacco per tithable.[79] This rate was continued by the October, 1765, session of the Assembly, to pay the expense of the militia in the defense of the frontier. For Prince Edward this levy was adjusted to forty-one pounds of tobacco per poll. Virginians who wished to pay in cash could discharge their obligation by paying at the rate of twelve shillings sixpence per hundred pounds of tobacco.[80]

In 1769 "sundry inhabitants" of Prince Edward joined with others of similar feeling in Charlotte and Amherst Counties in petitioning the Assembly for relief from "the oppressive exactions of collectors of public (colonial), county, and parish levies." The Committee of Propositions and Grievances of the House of Burgesses reported the petition as reasonable; with this finding the House agreed, and the committee was directed to draw up bills to implement the resolution. The bill was reported November 22, 1769, read the first time, and ordered to be read a second time.[81] This is the last reference to it.

A major concern of the county court was the maintenance of law and order. Grand juries were alert to indict those who offended. Some of the offenses which provoked indictments two centuries ago are lightly regarded now. In general penalties were heavier then. The Grand Jury in May, 1755, indicted one man for getting drunk and swearing, another for swearing two oaths, still another for swearing, another "for living in the Bed of Adultery," and four men "for not going to any Place of Worship in one month."[82]

Court action on indictments presented by the Grand Jury in May, 1757 give the penalties for some of these offenses. Five men, indicted for profane swearing and drunkenness in May, were fined ten shillings each in July; another was fined five shillings for getting drunk and swearing; another five shillings for getting drunk; two, indicted for swearing, were not prosecuted. Nine men were indicted for not going to their parish church; two of them were fined five shillings each for the offense.[83] Several in the group who were dismissed on this charge were Scotch-Irish, who evidently pleaded the Act of Toleration. The Court was not partial to its members in imposing fines, nor did grand jurors fear the magistrates when it came to making presentments. In 1760 a magistrate was indicted for swearing one oath,[84] in 1762 another was indicted for the same offense,[85] and in 1763 still another was fined twenty shillings for swearing four oaths.[86] An inn-keeper found himself indicted in 1761 "for suffering unlawful gaming in his house."[87] This inn-keeper was among three men presented by the grand jury in 1773 for retailing liquor without a license. The 1773 jury indicted two men "for absenting themselves for divine service" and a man and a woman for living together in adultery.[88] The grand jury in 1763 presented one man for keeping a tippling house, two for unlawful gaming, and eight for not going to the parish church.[89]

The county court acted as a court of inquiry in criminal cases; it could mete out severe punishments to slaves, but freemen accused of serious offenses were sent to the General Court at Williamsburg for trial if there appeared satisfactory evidence. This distinction, however, did not lead to careless consideration of cases in which slaves were involved. And a slave brought into court had a chance to be acquitted. A Negro woman slave belonging to George Brown was tried for murder in 1755 and was acquitted.[90] On the other hand a man who reported that he had accidentally killed one of his slaves was put under bond of one thousand pounds sterling, as was his brother, who was "present at the said Correction of said Slave." The owner was acquitted at the hearing in December, 1755.[91] A slave of John Ford of Amelia was convicted of felony in 1765; when it was ascertained that he enjoyed benefit of clergy, the sheriff was directed to burn the man in his right hand, give him thirty-nine lashes on his bare back and discharge him.[92] In 1759 a Negro formerly belonging to Colonel Clement Read of Lunenburg was found guilty of murder and sentenced to death; execution of the sentence was delayed, for more than a year and a half later, in December, 1760, the man claimed that he was not the same person who had been convicted in April, 1759. The Court held that he was, and set an early date for execution.[93] In September, 1759, a slave girl belonging to John Nash was acquitted of a charge of murder when evidence indicated that the death was accidental.[94] In 1769 a slave belonging to William Booker was convicted of rape and sentenced to be hanged; the Court valued him at ninety pounds.[95]

In 1770 there was an epidemic of charges brought against Negro slaves in Prince Edward County for "feloniously administering poisonous medicines." In April of that year a slave of William Hudson was sentenced to be hanged, since he did not come under benefit of clergy; his value was fixed at 110 pounds.[96] The next month a slave belonging to the estate of Colonel William Randolph received a similar sentence on a similar charge, since he, too, lacked benefit of clergy.[97] Two other Negroes, one belonging to Robert Walton and the other to Peter LeGrand, were acquitted of the charge of administering poisonous medicines; LeGrand's slave was found guilty of stealing, but not to the extent that he should be hanged; accordingly the sheriff was ordered to nail the slave's ears to the pillory, then cut them off, give him thirty-nine lashes on the bare back at the whipping-post, and discharge him.[98] Three years later a slave belonging to John Crenshaw was acquitted of the charge of administering poisonous medicines, but was convicted of administering medicines contrary to law, for which he received twenty-one lashes.[99]

An extremely dangerous situation developed in the case of a slave of William Womack in 1756. After having been outlawed, the slave took refuge in the quarters of John Stanton, where he defended himself with a broad ax and sharp-pointed darts which could kill a man at a considerable distance. With these he had attempted often, so the record puts it, to kill his master and the neighbors who undertook to capture him alive. A group consisting of Abraham Womack, Isham Womack, William Barry, James Moor, and William Masters tried to frighten him by firing guns through the quarters. The slave continued to defend himself by attempting to kill the men trying to capture him. When they heard the slave groan, they broke into his refuge and found him dying of wounds received in the shooting. William Womack applied to the court for a valuation of the slave, which was made and certified to the Assembly.[100]

Offenses were not limited to slaves in colonial Prince Edward. One of the most surprising discoveries in reading the court order books of the period is the number of times Scotch-Irish settlers were involved in such charges. Some of them seem to have been contentious and hot-headed, quick to anger and prompt to strike.

One man, convicted of stealing a saddle, asked to be whipped instead of being sent to the General Court for further trial; he received twenty-five lashes, the man from whom he stole the saddle laying them on. That was in 1763;[101] four years later another man, accused of stealing green tobacco, consented to be whipped instead of being remanded for further trial.[102] One man, who was under suspicion of having cut open the jail and removing a slave from it, asked to be examined on the charge; he was found not guilty at the hearing in April, 1763.[103] The Court in 1764 dismissed a man who admitted shooting another, when it was apparent that the victim was in no danger of losing his life, but was expected to recover.[104]

The influence of a magistrate did not outweigh the rules of evidence in colonial Prince Edward. One of the justices in 1766 accused two men of burning a tobacco house belonging to him, but both men were acquitted of the charge.[105]

The county found biting off part of a man's ear an expensive crime. The man who committed the assault was sent to General Court, but until he could be moved to the Publick Gaol in Williamsburg he was kept in custody in Prince Edward. In laying the county levy for 1771, the justices included 700 pounds of tobacco payable to eight men at the rate of twenty pounds for a day's service for guarding the accused.[106] In another biting case, this one in 1774, the Court acquitted the accused of the charge of biting a man's nose.[107]

In the records are cases of persons brought to trial for one offense of which they were acquitted, but in ascertaining the facts in the case the Court found them guilty of another offense. Two men in 1765, for example, were suspected of horse stealing. They were acquitted of that charge, only to be found guilty of being imposters. They admitted to being convict servants of Colonel John Chiswell. Their penalty was ten lashes each, and they were delivered to a constable who in turn was directed to deliver them to Colonel Chiswell at his mines in Augusta.[108]

One Prince Edward man was sent to General Court in 1773 on the charge of robbing a Williamsburg man of six pair of gold sleeve buttons valued at £7:10.[109] The accused escaped, and the Governor advertised for his apprehension.[110] In the same year two men were sent to General Court for pushing a man who died as a result of the fall from the pushing. Five witnesses were put under bond for £1000 pounds each, current money, to attend the General Court as witnesses against the accused.[111]

People in those days had their differences as well as they do now. In a suit for slander, a young woman was awarded damages of £100 current money, after a jury found the man she accused guilty.[112] Sometimes the Court put a person under bond for good behavior for a period of twelve months.[113]

The witness in a case in colonial times was allowed twenty-five pounds of tobacco for each day he attended court for the purpose. In the suit of Adam Jones vs. Joshua Davidson in 1757, Jones was ordered to pay Elias Dejarnett 100 pounds of tobacco for four days' attendance as a witness for him and William Young 175 pounds of tobacco for seven days' attendance. The defendant Davidson had a much heavier witness bill: John Morton, 175 pounds tobacco for seven days' attendance; William Brown, 200 pounds tobacco for eight days; John Popham, 175 pounds tobacco for seven days; Charles Right, 100 pounds tobaco for four days; and Parsons Anderson, seventy-five pounds tobacco for three days.[114]

Sometimes the witness was also allowed expenses for traveling. Charles Hudson, who appeared as a witness for Abraham Venable, Jr., in his suit against Alexander Kain in 1757, was allowed seventy-seven pounds of tobacco for one day's attendance and for coming and returning fourteen miles.[115] In 1764 Charles Anderson received 843 pounds of tobacco for attendance fifteen days and traveling thirteen miles twelve times as a witness for Alexander Spiers and Company; at the same time that firm paid William Tyree 296 pounds of tobacco for attendance eight days and traveling eight miles four times as a witness for the company.[116]

Throughout the period when slavery was the prevailing type of labor, patroling played a part in keeping slaves under control. Patrolers, deputized for the service, went through sections of the county, inspecting passes of slaves found away from home and bringing to jail Negroes found without satisfactory passes, visiting slave quarters to see that all was in order and that there were no clandestine meetings or plotting of insurrections. The pay for this work in colonial times was twenty pounds of tobacco per day. The levy for 1766 provided payment for several patrolers: William Womack, William Frazier, Ike Rice, William Rice, Dudley McDermonroe, Royal Bowman, John S. Bowman, and Ambrose Crawford, three days each; John Baulding, Thomas Caldwell, Williamson Bird, Charles Hudson, four days each; Alexander Legrand and William Walker, two days each.[117]

The first petition for a road presented to the Prince Edward Court asked for one from William Watson's across Buffalo to intersect the Roanoke road near the Courthouse. Watson, Alexander Hambleton, Robert Elliott, and Edward Brathwaite were directed by the February, 1754, Court to view a route for this road and make recommendations.[118]

The road through Thomas Haskins' plantation was a source of controversy in 1761. The road crossed Haskins' lowgrounds and lay between his house and a branch in such a way as to deprive him of the use of the branch as a source of water for his pasture. Although the road had been used twelve years, the Court closed it. A petition for its re-opening was presented to the Court, which in July, 1761, appointed John Morton, Theodorick Carter, and Jacob McGehee to see if a road could be run around Haskins' property. They reported to the August Court that there was "no good passable way around," and the Court ordered the road to be cleared and re-opened along the former route. Phileman Holcomb testified in behalf of Haskins that he would not have the road go in the way directed if it were through his property for fifty pounds. Samuel Goode set a more conservative figure for the damages, twenty pounds, while Matthew Rice, one of the petitioners for re-opening the road, thought twenty-five pounds a fair estimate of the damages.[119]

Thomas Haskins was not the only person who sought to have the road through his property changed. In 1766 Richard Randolph petitioned to have a road changed at Sandy Ford when he built a mill on the Appomattox there, and he was given permission to make the change; his own hands were ordered to do the necessary work, and the route followed should be that recommended by viewers appointed for the purpose.[120] This new road was completed by the spring of 1767, when John Nash, Jr., John Morton, Philemon Holcomb, and Peter Johnston were appointed to view it.[121] Another new road in the Sandy Ford area, this one leading to James Ewing's, was cleared about the same time. Peter LeGrand, Abraham Venable, Williamson Bird, and Samuel Southerland were named to view it, but the road was ordered to be dropped.[122] The April, 1767, Court, which named the two sets of viewers for the two new roads mentioned, ordered a road to be opened from James French's to Buffalo River. The order followed the recommendation of Nathaniel Venable, who had been named to view the route.[123] John Nash, Jr., also wanted the road run around his plantation, and in May, 1767, Philemon Holcomb, Benjamin Haskins, and John Watkins were appointed to recommend a way from the road from Bush River bridge around the Nash plantation to Sandy River bridge. The change was approved and Nash was ordered to open the new road.[124]

Routes for three new roads were ordered to be viewed in 1768: from Hoggatt's road to Venable's Mill, William Simmons, Abraham Venable, James Scenter, and John Peck, viewers;[125] from Sandy River Church to Miller Woodson's store, John Clarke, Thomas Clarke, Thomas Owen, and Stephen Neal, viewers;[126] and a road from the branch below the Widow Thaxton's to her house on the road from the Courthouse, Henry Walker, Manness McFeiley, John Martin, and John Crockett, viewers.[127] Paschal Greenhill received permission in 1769 to clear a road from his house into the road to Sandy River Church.[128]

The Prince Edward records abound in references to the building and repair of bridges. The first bridge the Prince Edward Court had built was over Buffalo River in 1754.[129] Following a report from James Wimbish, David Flournoy, and Thomas Scott in May, 1755, that a way they had viewed over Spring Creek was impassible for wheeled carriages, a bridge was ordered built; the work was reported "well done" to the September Court.[130] In 1759 Richard and John Morton acknowledged bond for building Appomattox bridge, and Thomas Haskins was ordered to let the contract for building a bridge over Sandy River below Ligon's Mill.[131]

In compliance with a petition for a bridge over the Appomattox at or near Rutledge's Ford, the June, 1761, Court appointed Abner

Nash, John Morton, and Richard Morton to view a site and report to the Court.[132] The building of the bridge was approved in July, and John Nash, Jr., and John Morton were appointed to inform the Cumberland Court and represent Prince Edward in letting the contract for the bridge and its upkeep for seven years.[133] Charles Anderson and Maurice Langhorne represented Cumberland County in letting the contract.[134] Abner Nash acknowledged bond for an unrecorded amount for the building of the bridge, with Peter LeGrand and John Nash, Jr., his securities, in September.[135] Philemon Holcomb reported to the Court of February 9, 1762, that the Appomattox bridge was passable ever since last Friday.[136] Seven years later, another bridge was built over the Appomattox at Rutledge's by Peter LeGrand.[137]

A petition for a bridge over the Appomattox at Sandy Ford, where the new road crossed the river, was presented to the September, 1769, Court. Peter Johnston and William Watts were appointed to notify the Cumberland Court of the decision of the Prince Edward Court approving the construction of a bridge at Sandy Ford, and Johnston and John Morton were named to represent Prince Edward in letting the contract for the bridge and its upkeep for seven years.[138]

It was customary to pay for the building of bridges in cash, rather than in tobacco. Richard Morton was paid six pounds for building a bridge over Briery River in 1757.[139] William Hudson received fourteen pounds for building Buffalo bridge, and Joseph Rice seven pounds for repairing Bush River bridge in 1758.[140] Thomas Haskins was paid ten pounds for Sandy River bridge in 1760,[141] and Charles Anderson received £1:15 for repairing Bush River bridge in 1761.[142] Even the minister worked on the bridges. The Rev. James Garden was paid £1:15 for "mending" Briery River bridge in 1766.[143]

Peter LeGrand was the county's principal bridge builder in the colonial period. In addition to Rutledge's bridge in 1769, LeGrand built a bridge over Bush River in 1762, for which he was paid £19:5,[144] a bridge over Buffalo in 1766,[145] a bridge over Briery in 1773.[146] He also repaired a number of bridges: Buffalo bridge, 1771[147]; several unidentified bridges in 1773, for which he received £10:10[148]; later in the same year he was directed to repair the upper bridge over Bush River and the bridges over Briery and Buffalo[149] and in 1774 the lower bridge over Bush River.[150]

Philemon Holcomb was frequently entrusted with letting contracts for bridges. He had Bush River bridge repaired in 1756.[151] In 1761 he was directed to salvage and sell the plank and timber which could be found at Nash's bridge and account for the sale at the laying of the next levy.[152] In 1767 Holcomb let contracts for repairs to the lower bridge over Buffalo and the two bridges over Bush.[153] The next year he was authorized to let contracts for rebuilding the Bush River bridges and the bridge over Buffalo.[154]

Usually, though not always, the Court entrusted the letting of contracts for bridge construction and repair to magistrates. Among the justices, in addition to Holcomb, given this responsibility were Thomas Haskins,[155] John Leigh,[156] John Nash, Jr.,[157] John Morton,[158] Nathaniel Venable,[159] and Robert Goode.[160] Among the men who were not on the bench who were directed to attend to letting contracts were Thomas Watkins,[161] Richard Burks,[162] Hugh Challis,[163] John LeNeve (the county clerk),[164] Theodorick Carter,[165] and Thomas Carter.[166] Douglas Puckett[167] and Robert Atkins[168] were other colonial bridge builders.

The early settlers paid more attention to road signs than their descendants prior to the building of the present highway system. Two road surveyors were presented by the grand jury in 1759 for not keeping up the signboards at crossroads on their highways.[169] In the same year Daniel Ayres was paid eighty-three pounds of tobacco for two signs with 166 letters.[170]

At least two taverns were in operation when Prince Edward County was established, Charles Anderson's and George Moore's. Anderson's license was renewed successively until 1763.[171] George Moore last received an ordinary license in 1757.[172] Hugh Challis was granted an ordinary license in May, 1754;[173] there was only one renewal, in 1755.[174] William Simmons' first license was granted in 1760; there were successive renewals until 1773.[175]

Prior to the beginning of the Revolution other ordinary licenses were granted to Samuel Ewing, 1758;[176] David Bond, 1759;[177] John Robbins, 1760;[178] Grimes Holcomb, 1760 (this is mentioned as a renewal);[179] Thomas Wilmuth, 1762;[180] Thomas Wild, 1765;[181] Philemon Holcomb, 1767 (where Douglas Puckett dwelt);[182] James Cole, 1767[183] John Moore, 1768[184] William Wiley, 1768 (at Burks');[185] Samuel Wright, 1768 (listed as a renewal);[186] Benedict Alderson, 1769 (where Samuel Wimbush "lately dwelt");[187] Charles Cooper, 1770 (at the store lately kept by Richard Burks);[188] Lewelling Williamson, 1771, mentioned as a renewal;[189] Daniel Stone, 1771, at James Cole's;[190] Charles Williamson, 1773;[191] Joseph Smith, 1773, at the Courthouse;[192] George Moore, 1773, where Daniel Stone "lately lived";[193] Joseph Moore, 1774, at Lightfoot's store.[194] There are references to Wimbush's Ordinary[195] and to Chappell's Ordinary, near Sandy Ford,[196] but there is no record of license issued to either.

In addition to licensing the operation of the tavern, the County Court also set the rates which could be charged for entertainment, both food and lodging for man and horse and for a variety of liquors. These rates were usually set at the March Court.[197] Among prices fixed in colonial times for ordinaries were rum, ten shillings per gallon, 1755;[198] corn, twelve shillings, sixpence per barrel, 1757;[199] whiskey, five shillings per gallon, 1758;[200] rum, twelve shillings, sixpence per gallon, 1759;[201] brandy, ten shillings per gallon, 1760[202] corn, seventeen shillings, sixpence per barrel, and rum, twelve shillings, sixpence per gallon, 1762;[203] corn, sixteen shillings per barrel, 1764.[204]

The name of the tavern-keeper at the Courthouse between Charles Anderson and Joseph Smith is not shown among the ordinary licenses granted by the Court. Henry Benskin Lightfoot owned the property on which the Courthouse and other county buildings stood between the Anderson and Smith ownerships,[205] and very likely the tavern property also, since Anderson and Smith both owned it. He may have leased the tavern. It was advertised in 1767 for rent or lease for a term of years. Then it had "a large garden in good order, a valuable apple orchard of fine fruit, and land sufficient for working five hands." Prospective lessees were referred to Peter Johnston for terms.[206]

One of the responsibilities of colonial county government was to see that accurate weights and measures were used. In June, 1754, John Nash was directed by the Court to send for standard weights and measures to be used in Prince Edward.[207] In the levy of 1757 the Court put in the item of 3,000 pounds of tobacco for the weights and standards.[208] These standards were kept at Colonel Nash's.[209] An item in the 1759 levy listed the sum of six shillings, threepence to be paid James Stuart for three stamps for the standard.[210]

An important phase of the colonial county government was the militia. Made up of able-bodied men in the county, the militia was the nucleus of colonial defense against enemies real and potential. The militia of a county was organized on a regimental basis. At the head was the county lieutenant, a rather deceptive title from the current use of the term. Then, as the governor was the King's lieutenant in the colony, the county lieutenant was His Majesty's lieutenant in military affairs in the county; he held the rank and carried the title of colonel. Residents of prescribed areas in the county made up companies of militia.

John Nash, Sr., presented his commission as county lieutenant in September, 1755, and took the required oaths.[211] Others who held a colonel's commission in the colonial militia were George Walker (1755),[212] John Nash, Jr., and Thomas Scott (1756).[213] There is a reference to the burgess, Charles Anderson, as Colonel Anderson;[214] majors in the Prince Edward militia included John Nash, Jr. (1755),[215] Thomas Haskins (1756), David Flournoy (1756),[216] Robert Hastie (1759),[217] and John LeNeve (1763).[218] Captains' commissions are recorded for David Flournoy (1755),[219] Charles Venable (1755), John LeNeve (1755),[220] Philemon Holcomb (1756),[221] Peter LeGrand (1758),[222] Joel Watkins (1761),[223] John Morton (1762),[224] Abraham Venable (1762),[225] Henry Watkins (1763),[226] George Walker (1768),[227] Archibald Buchanan (1768),[228] Obadiah Woodson (1769),[229] William Bibb (1773), and John Holcombe (1773).[230]

Peter LeGrand became quartermaster general of the Prince Edward militia in 1762.[231]

The French and Indian War created much concern on the Virginia frontier. In a letter to Philip Ludwell dated February 10, 1756, the Rev. James Maury of Louisa proposed a chain of forts some thirty miles apart on the frontier, each to be garrisoned by a company of approximately fifty men, some of whom would be whites, some Indians, but all expert woodsmen. He further proposed that the courts of the "upper counties"—and he included Prince Edward along with Frederick, Hampshire, Halifax, Lunenburg, Bedford, Albemarle, Louisa, Orange, Culpeper, Prince William, and Fairfax—recommend expert woodsmen to be given commissions in the garrisons.[232]

Prior to April, 1757, the Prince Edward militia, along with the militia of other "upper counties" had been called to actual service. Its nature is not known, but because the accounts for pay of the men and for provisions could not be determined by the Governor, the General Assembly appointed a special commission, consisting of William Randolph, Richard Bland, and Archibald Cary to settle the accounts of the militia of Prince Edward, Bedford, Halifax, and Lunenburg.[233] In June, 1757, Landon Carter, of the Committee to Examine Accounts of Officers of Militia, reported that the account of Colonel John Nash for the pay of a Prince Edward militia company in the amount of £207:18 was just. The report added that £350 had been paid Colonel Nash and that the balance of £92:2 was in the hands of John Nash, Jr., for settling the provisions account.[234]

When Prince Edward was called upon to draft eight men from its militia for service in the war, a special court consisting of five magistrates and four militia captains (Captain Samuel Ewing was also a justice and was listed among the magistrates) met June 20, 1757, to select the men. John Nash as county lieutenant presented the muster rolls to the court, showing 316 men in the five companies: 74 in Captain LeNeve's company, 64 in Captain James Scott's, 56 in Captain Philemon Holcomb's, 55 in Captain Samuel Ewing's, and 62 in Captain Charles Venable's. The Court listed eighteen men, whom it "deemed . . . idle, vagrant, dissolute persons" and directed the sheriff, Lieutenant Elias Dejarnet, Lieutenant Henry Watkins, Lieutenant William Baldwin, Ensign John Morton, Ensign Samuel Goode, Ensign George Moor, and Ensign George Ewing to bring those listed to a second session of the court called for June 28. From this list the eight draftees were to be selected.[235]

There must have been considerable consternation produced by this action, which was in compliance with an Act of Assembly, more because of the Court's estimate of the eighteen than because of the prospect of being drafted into military service. Five of the eighteen secured bondsmen in their behalf, one who was in prison enlisted, six were classified as runaways, one appeared and "proved himself an industrious man," two were shown to be residents of adjoining counties, one was not found, and still another escaped. One of the men summoned had already gone to a fort as a soldier. In addition to the volunteer, two others were "deemed a soldier," delivered to the county lieutenant, who in turn delivered them to Captain Holcomb to take to Fredericksburg, one of the places of rendezvous. Eight who did not appear were designated deserters "for His Majesty's service." Of those who secured bondsmen, one proved himself industrious, another was excused, still another "made it appear" that he was over fifty years of age and he was excused, one was found to be under age. One of the non-residents "made it appear" that he was an overseer in charge of five hands and he was excused.[236]

The county's account of expenses for militia in service presented in 1758 included an item for carrying the draftees to Fredericksburg. The account was approved:

	£	s	d
To Henry Watkins, ensign, for pay for self, two sergeants, and sixteen men, militia of the county as by muster roll	80	13	
To Henry Watkins, ensign, for horse hire for expresses	1	17	
To Henry Watkins, ensign, for salt	1	15	
To Charles Gilliam, for horse hire		13	9
To John Cloyd, for provisions		7	
To Samuel Ewing, for provisions for Indians		16	4
To James Wimbish, for provisions for Indians	1	5	4
To Capt. Philemon Holcomb, pay for himself and guards for carrying drafted soldiers to Fredericksburg	6	9	4
To Mr. John Nash for provisions	20	7	8
To Capt. John Nash, Jr., for pay of his company, June 8, 1757-July 8, 1757	82	8	
	£196	14	5[237]

In 1770 Nicholas Alley presented a bill for provisions furnished the Prince Edward militia in 1757, explaining that his earlier request for payment in 1764 had been rejected by the House of Burgesses because he did not explain why he did not present the account earlier. Alley explained that he had been wounded in an engagement with the Indians soon after he had furnished the provisions and had later moved to South Carolina where he lived until 1764. The House approved payment of £3:9:9½ for 372 pounds of pork and two barrels of corn which he furnished the militia.[238]

If one thinks Alley slow in presenting claims, let him consider a number of soldiers in the French and Indian War who did not file until 1780 claims for land to which they were entitled under a proclamation of the King of England in October, 1763. Between January and May, 1780, the following Prince Edward residents who had been soldiers in the French and Indian War filed claims for land: John Morton, first lieutenant in Major Andrew Lewis' detachment from the 1st Virginia Regiment of Regulars; Thomas Morton, second lieutenant in the same command; Alexander LeGrand, sergeant in the same command;[239] Richard Foster, private in Captain Samuel Overton's company; Henry Pigg, private in the 2nd Virginia Regiment; Joseph Truman, private in Captain Obadiah Woodson's company of volunteers under Major Lewis;[240] Freeman Llewelling, John Gaulding, Charles Howell, James Foster, and Edward Penix, privates under the late Colonel William Byrd;[241] Jonathan Smith, first lieutenant, John Pettry, Bryant McDearmonroe, privates under

Colonel Byrd; Samuel Burton, private under Colonel Washington; William Carter, Ezekiel Hendrick, Hezekiah Coleman, Daniel Murray, John Smith, and John Tibbs, privates under Colonel Byrd;[242] Philemon Hawkins, soldier under Colonel Byrd;[243] and Charles Hervey, under Major Lewis in 1755.[244]

Charles Anderson furnished a wagon, driver, team, and provisions for hauling arms, ammunition, and goods to Fort Frederick in 1756. The driver, team, and wagon, which had been impressed for the service, were employed twenty-eight days. He was allowed £24:10 for the work.[245]

When Captain Obadiah Woodson went on the expedition against the Shawnee Indians, he impressed wagons and horses of Abraham Venable, Jr., to haul supplies. Venable's petition for compensation was referred to a committee consisting of Archibald Cary and Peter LeGrand.[246]

The expedition against the Shawnees was a most unsatisfactory experience for Captain Woodson, who lived in Prince Edward. Not only was the expedition unsuccessful, but responsibility for the failure was charged to Woodson and some other officers by a Council of War held by Major Lewis. The officers involved were declared mutinous. In 1757 Woodson petitioned the House of Burgesses for a hearing, and the request was deferred until the next session of the Assembly. Another officer, John Smith, also asked for a hearing on the charges. The House investigation found that Smith did not misbehave himself on the expedition as had been charged and he was allowed pay. The special committee, of which Archibald Cary was chairman, gave Woodson only partial satisfaction. It found that "want of success" in the Shawnee expedition was due to lack of supplies but it added that Woodson did not behave as an officer should have. The House of Burgesses, on October 4, 1758, approved the findings of the Committee.[247]

The decision concerning Captain Woodson involved his command in loss of pay. John Morton and Thomas Morton petitioned the House in March, 1759, for pay for themselves and the private soldiers in Woodson's company. The Committee on Claims approved the request for pay for the two Mortons, but rejected the portion of the petition relating to the non-commissioned officer and private soldiers. The House ordered that allowances be made to pay the Mortons.[248]

Peter LeGrand, Thomas Tabb, and John Nash were named commissioners for Amelia and Prince Edward in 1758 to examine and settle accounts for pay and provisions for the militia in the two counties and for provisions furnished the Indians who had come to the assistance of the colony, for damages done by those Indians to the inhabitants of the counties, and for the pay of officers and guards who took drafted soldiers to Fredericksburg or Winchester.[249]

In 1758 Samuel Ewing presented to the Prince Edward Court a bill for seven shillings for goods furnished six Cherokee Indians; the bill was certified to the General Assembly.[250]

By modern standards, the training of the militia was scant. Some companies seem to have been drilled more frequently, but the county regiment drilled only once a year, on muster day. The militiamen, however, had much more practice in the use of guns than the infrequent drills imply. In their hunting, they gained experience which served them better than drilling when they were fighting the French and Indians on the frontier.

In the years toward the close of the colonial period, the days of the annual musters are known. Colin Campbell of Surry, adjutant of the Southern District, advertised the dates for the general musters in each of the counties of the district. He attended the musters, having worked out a schedule by which he could attend all the musters in his district. The dates on which musters were requested in Prince Edward by Campbell were: Friday, March 22, 1771;[251] Friday, March 27, 1772;[252] Monday, March 29, 1773;[253] Thursday, March 24, 1774;[254] Monday, March 27, 1775;[255] Saturday, September 9, 1775.[256] The trend of the colonies to resist by force the attempt to force compliance to objectionable requirements of the mother country may explain the two musters held in 1775.

Administratively the processioning of land belongs with the activities of the parish vestry. It may properly be included in the history of the activities of the civil government, because it was designed to fix the land boundaries. The act of 1748 governing processioning was in force when Prince Edward became a county; this law provided that "the bounds of every persons land shall be processioned or gone round every four years and the landmarks renewed." County courts were required to direct the parish vestries, between June 1 and September 1, 1751, and every fourth year thereafter to have the land processioned. The vestry divided the parish into precincts and appointed for each precinct two or more "intelligent, honest freeholders" to procession the land between the last of September and the last of the following March, to report each person's land which was processioned, the persons present at the processioning, the lands which were not processioned, and the reasons for not processioning them. The church wardens were required to give notice at church, at least three Sundays in advance, of the precincts in which the lands were to be processioned and the names of the processioners. Disputed boundaries, not settled at the processioning, could be settled by a surveyor and jury appointed by the court. Three processionings fixed permanently the boundaries of land.[257]

The first processioning in Prince Edward was ordered September 12, 1759 and was directed to be done between October 10, 1759, and March 31, 1760. A partial list of the processioners assignments by precincts and a partial list of their returns has been preserved. Robert Atkins was the last of three or more processioners for the precinct between Mountain Creek and Bush River as far out as the old road to George Moore's and the Lunenburg line. Other processioners and their precincts were:

James Yargain and Joseph Ward: below Sailor's Creek as low as the county line and between the old road from Hawkins' by Major Haskins and the Appomattox River.

Peter Duryea and John Childress: between the old road called Roanoke road and Sailor's Creek as far up as Ligon's rolling road, down Sailor's Creek to the old Sailor's Creek road and along the road to the county line.

Matthew Rice and James Moore: between Ligon's rolling road and Sailor's Creek old road, Sailor's Creek and Sandy River.

Thomas Turpin, Abraham Brown, Thomas Chandler, Jacob McGehee: Ligon's rolling road up Sandy River to Griffin's road, down that road to the county line.

Michael McDearmon, Thomas Clark, John Clark, John Owen: in the fork of Sandy River from the Church road to Griffin's road.

Elias Dejarnett, James Callicoat, Anthony Griffin, Nicholas Hudson: between Griffin's road and the county line as high as George Moore's Ordinary.

Henry Ligon, Jr., and Godfrey Piles: Griffin's road and the old road to Moore's Ordinary and Sandy River.

Returns reported of this processioning have been recorded and preserved as follows: Godfrey Piles and Henry Ligon; Henry Ligon and Thomas Crafford; Joseph Ward and James Yeargain; John Watkins, Benjamin Haskins, William Sadler, and Joseph Rice (between Bush and Sandy Rivers); Thomas Graham, Edward Shilladay (dated January 31, 1760); John Caldwell, Richard Walden, Pugh Price, Jr.; Matthew Rice and James Moore; John Owen, John Clark, and Thomas Clark; William Davidson and Alexander Cunningham; Elias Dejarnett, James Callicoat, Anthony Griffin (their processioning was begun February 11, 1760); Joseph Cunningham and William Baldwin; William Boyd and Thomas Caldwell (their processioning began February 2, 1760); Charles Venable and John Simmons (dated June 4, 1760); William Watson and Robert Baker (between the north and south forks of Buffalo); Samuel Arbuckle and John McElroy (between the church road and Buffalo); William Price, John Biggars, John Martin, Richard Childress (between Griffin's road, Randolph's old road, George Moore's Ordinary, and Sandy River, dated April 7, 1760); William Simmons and Alexander Hambleton; John Popham and John Morton (between Bush and Briery Rivers and Scott's road); John Watson, John Gaulling, Josiah Chambers, Richard Morton; William Hudson and Charles Hudson; Samuel Sutherland, Robert Bird, James Ewing, William Hall (from Abraham Venable's upper wagon road which leads to Randolph's mill between Falling Creek, Buffalo, and the Appromattox); Robert Williamson, Elkanah Jenings, Robert Thirman; and William Brown and Theodorick Carter.[258]

Nathaniel Venable as clerk of the vestry was paid 250 pounds of tobacco for making out the orders for the first processioning.[259]

The complete record of the processioning which was ordered at the vestry meeting August 15, 1763, to be made between October 10, 1763, and March 31, 1764, has been preserved. The processioners and their precincts for that processioning were:

John Wright, William Thirman, Richard Bennett, Marvel Stone, Richard Wooldridge: all lands from the upper end of the county to Sawney's Creek.

John Chiles, George Oliver, Peter Ford: between Sawney's and Vaughan's Creeks, Walker's road and the Appomattox River.

Peter Coffee, John Parks, John Hill: between Sawney's Creek and Vaughan's Creek from Walker's Road to the county line.

John Caldwell, Jr., James McMahan, Thomas Caldwell: from Vaughan's Creek as low as Abraham Venable's upper wagon road between the Appomattox and Randolph's road.

David Tyree, Robert Peak, William Penix, Jeremiah Penix: from Abraham Venable's upper wagon road leading to Randolph's mill, between Falling Creek, Buffalo, and the Appomattox.

Thomas Caldwell, Samuel Baker, Samuel Wallace: from the road which leads from Randolph's mill by Buffalo Church to Spring Creek bridge, between Falling Creek, Spring Creek, and Buffalo.

Joseph Parks and Henry Caldwell: above the road from Woodson's mill to Spring Creek, between Spring Creek and Walker's road, as far up as the head of Vaughan's Creek.

Robert Baker, Andrew Baker, Samuel Smith, Robert Johnson: between Buffalo and Spring Creek which runs by Douglas Baker's to the county line.

Thomas Graham and John Hill: between the creek that runs by Douglas Baker's and the creek that runs by Robert Baker's as far as the county line.

Archibald McCroy and John McCroy: above Wimbish's road leading from Buffalo by Wimbish's to the Roanoke road between the county line and Buffalo.

Edmond Archdeacon, James Wimbish, James Thackston: below Wimbish's Church road, as far as the county line between Briery and Buffalo as low as Caleb Baker's path which leads to Nathaniel Venable's and from then to Briery River as the road runs to John McGehee's.

Caleb Baker and John Bauldwin: between Caleb Baker's path to Nathaniel Venable's between Buffalo and Briery as low as the path from Richard Woodson's to John Morton's.

Alexander LeGrand, Pugh Price, Sr., John Watson, Josiah Chambers, John Gaulding: below the path from Richard Woodson's to John Morton's between Briery, Bush, Buffalo, and the Appomattox.

John McGehee, John Brown, Samuel Burton: in the fork of Briery and Bush Rivers as far out as Brown's mill path.

Thomas Green, John Popham, Jr., William Purnell, William Atwood: between Briery and Bush from Brown's mill path to the county line.

John Watkins, Samuel Goode: below Bush River from the mouth to Nash's mill, from the old road from the mill to Sailor's Creek, by the creek and the Appomattox River.

William Ligon, John Sutton Bowman, Thomas Crafford: between Bush and Sandy Rivers from the road by Nash's mill to the road that leads from upper Bush River bridge to lower Sandy River.

Abraham West, Robert Atkins, Thomas Hill: the area bounded by Mountain Creek, Bush River, the old road to Moore's Ordinary, and the county line.

James Yargain, Samuel Poe, Edward Patterson: Sailor's Creek to the county line between the old road from Haskins' to Hawkins' and the Appomattox.

Joseph Nun, Matthew Rice, John Chapman: the area bounded by

the old road called Roanoke road, Sailor's Creek, Ligon's rolling road, old Sailor's Creek road, and the county line.

Noel Waddell, Charles Rice, Icay Rice: the area bounded by Ligon's rolling road, Sailor's Creek old road, Sailor's Creek, and Sandy River.

Edmund Harper, John Bradshaw, Jacob McGehee: the area bounded by Ligon's rolling road, Sandy River, Griffin's road, and the county line.

Mumford Dejarnett, Brackett Owen, John Atkins, James Atkins: the area bounded by the old road from Bush River bridge to Sandy River Church, Sandy River, Mountain Creek, and Bush River up to Moore's Ordinary.

George Morton, James Hamblet, Alexander Womack, William Davidson: in the fork of Sandy River from the church road to Griffin's road.

John Thomas Dejarnett, Steven Neal, Thomas Hudson: between Griffin's road and the county line as high as Moore's Ordinary.

Rice Scott, Henry Ligon, William Young, Benjamin Parrott: between Griffin's road, the old road to Moore's Ordinary, and Sandy River.

Processioners' returns were listed in order: Edmund Harper, John Bradshaw, Jacob McGehee; Robert Baker, Robert Johnson, Andrew Baker, Samuel Smith; Jeremiah Peniks and David Tyree; Thomas Hudson, Steven Neal (dated March 15, 1764); Noel Waddell, Charles Rice, Icay Rice (dated March 5, 1764); Thomas Caldwell, Jr., Samuel Baker, Jr., Samuel Wallace (dated January 17, 1764); Thomas Caldwell, John Caldwell; Robert Peak, William Penick; Caleb Baker; Thomas Crafford; Peter Coffee, John Hill (dated March 16, 1764); James Yargain, Edward Patterson; Thomas Green, William Purnell, William Attwood (dated March 23, 1764); John Watkins, Samuel Goode (dated January 30, 1764); a report dated March 20, 1764, with the names of the processioners torn off; John Watson, John Gaulding, Josiah Chambers, Alexander LeGrand; John Hill, Thomas Graham; Henry Caldwell, Joseph Parks (dated March 12, 1764); Thomas Hill, Robert Atkins.[260]

A third processioning was ordered at the vestry meeting on October 19, 1767, to be made between October 10 and March 31. In many instances the same processioners viewed the land boundaries who had noted them four years earlier. Marvel Stone was not on the list in the westernmost precinct. Lawrence and Charles Smith had the precinct from Vaughan's Creek to Abraham Venable's upper

wagon road between the Appomattox and Randolph's road. John
Porter replaced John Parks in his precinct. David Tyree and Robert
Peak were not listed in 1767, and Alexander LeGrand was named
processioner in their stead. Rice Scott, Thomas Scott, Mumford Dejarnett, and Brackett Owen had a precinct with new bounds: Mountain Creek, Bush River, the old road to Moore's Ordinary, and the
county line; so did John Brown, James Atkins, William West, and
John Atkins: between the road from Bush River bridge to Sandy
River and the old road to Moore's Ordinary and between Sandy River
and Mountain Creek. Mac [kerness] Goode and Thomas Osborne
joined James Yargain and Edward Patterson; they replaced Samuel
Poe. Thomas Turpin, Miles Turpin, and David Rice were associated
with Matthew Rice in that precinct, in place of Joseph Nun and
John Chapman. Benjamin Lewis was processioner in place of Charles
and Icay Rice. Jacob McGehee was not among the processioners in
1767-68, leaving his colleagues of 1763-64 to procession that precinct.
A new group processioned the area in the fork of Sandy River be-
tween the church road and Griffin's road: John Hamblin, John
Penick, Thomas Morton, Thomas Clark, Jr. William Griffin, James
Callicoat and George Burks replaced John Thomas Dejarnett and
Steven Neal. Richard Thomason and Jesse Owen replaced Rice Scott,
William Young, and Benjamin Parrott, leaving Henry Ligon the only
processioner to serve that precinct in both 1763-64 and 1767-68.[261]

At its second session the Prince Edward Court decided to have
the line dividing Amelia and Prince Edward surveyed. John Nash
and George Walker were appointed to ask the Amelia Court to
appoint four members to meet them for the survey. The committee
was instructed to provide chains, carriers, markers, and the other
necessities for running the line.[262] A year later, in February, 1755,
Nash was appointed to settle the expense of surveying the line and
report the cost.[263] At the August Court that year Prince Edward's
proportion of the cost of the survey was reported as £7:5, and Nash
was directed to sell enough of the county's tobacco to raise the money.
These expenses did not include the surveyor's fee. John LeNeve
received 214 pounds of tobacco for surveying the line from Ward's
Ford on the Appomattox to the mouth of Snail's Creek in Nottoway
River.[264]

When Prince Edward County was formed, the adjacent counties
were Amelia on the east, Lunenburg on the south, Bedford on the
southwest, Albemarle and Cumberland on the north.[265]

A petition requesting an addition to Prince Edward was presented to the September, 1758, Court; it was certified to the General Assembly, but was rejected by the House of Burgesses March 3, 1759.[266]

After Charlotte County had been cut off from Lunenburg, the Prince Edward Court in September, 1765, appointed Peter LeGrand and Nathaniel Venable commissioners to meet with commissioners from Charlotte to settle the boundary between the counties.[267]

In colonial days young men who wished to become lawyers took examinations under examiners appointed for the purpose by the General Court. County courts frequently recommended young men to the examiners for the examination. In February, 1754, Charles Cupples applied for recommendation to the examiners and received it from the Prince Edward Court.[268] The first attorney to present his commission to practice law to the Prince Edward Court and take the oath required of lawyers upon their admission to practice was Paul Carrington, who qualified at the Prince Edward Court of June, 1755.[269] Abner Nash qualified as an attorney in January, 1757,[270] and Clement Read, Jr., the following July.[271] Other lawyers who qualified to practice in Prince Edward Court before the Revolution were Robert Saunders (1759),[272] Thomas Carr (1760),[273] Benjamin Bryan (1761),[274] George Walker (1762),[275] Thomas Griffin Peachy (1762),[276] William Watts (1765),[277] John Williams (1765),[278] James Milner (1765),[279] Isaac Read (1770),[280] David Stokes (1771),[281] Edward Carrington (1773),[282] Benjamin Lawson (1773),[283] and William Cowan (1773).[284]

Benjamin Lawson was the second prospective lawyer to be recommended "for honesty, probity, and good demeanor to the gentlemen appointed by the General Court as examiners into the capacity, fitness, and ability of persons applying for license to practice as an attorney." The recommendation was given at the May, 1773, Court. Lawson lost no time in taking the examination; at the next Court he presented his commission and took the oath of an attorney.[285]

Robert Lawson was practicing law in Prince Edward in 1773 and had apparently become established in his profession in the county by that year.[286] There is no record in the Prince Edward Order Books of his qualifying as an attorney before the County Court.

Clement Read was King's Attorney for the new county. He resigned in September, 1755, and Thomas Nash was recommended by the Court to the Governor to succeed him.[287] The appointment came through, and Nash took the oath of King's Attorney in January, 1756.[288] Clement Read, Jr., qualified as King's Attorney in September, 1757.[289] Read served until 1770, when he was succeeded by

George Walker, Jr., who took the oath of King's Attorney at the November, 1770, Court.[290]

There was some feeling among the early settlers of the county that lawyers' fees were too high. In this feeling the Prince Edward pioneers were not unlike others on the frontier in both Virginia and North Carolina. One of the grievances which provoked the Regulator movement in the latter state was the high fees charged by lawyers and public officials; the Regulator movement broke into open rebellion against the colonial authority and was put down at the battle of Alamance in 1771. In Prince Edward the protest took the form of a petition, which was presented to the September, 1758, Court and by it certified to the General Assembly, asking that fees charged by lawyers and county officers and the prices of wheat and corn be fixed by law.[291]

The petition, drawn up because a severe drought had cut the yield of tobacco and grain heavily, asked for a law stating the price of public (colonial) taxes payable in tobacco at twelve shillings sixpence the hundred pounds as well as a price ceiling of two shillings per bushel for wheat and eight shillings per barrel of Indian corn. The petition was presented on the second day of the session beginning September 14, 1758, and after it had been read it was tabled.[292]

The portion of the petition asking for regulation of fees charged by county officers was answered by extending for one year the act passed in 1746 which set up a detailed schedule of fees to be charged for services rendered by colonial and county officials. The effective period of the law had been extended twice before, the second extension expiring April 12, 1759.[293] It may have been in anticipation of this expiration that the people in Prince Edward asked that the fees be fixed. Before the expiration date, the Assembly modified its third act extending the law by making the period of extension two years instead of one. In March, 1761, the act fixing the officials' fees was extended two years, and in May, 1763, for still another two years.[294]

It was more than two years after the petition was presented that the relief it requested in setting attorneys' fees was granted. In the Assembly of March, 1761, lawyers who practiced in the General Court were permitted to charge £1:1:6 for giving advice when no suit was brought, fifty shillings (£2:10) for any suit at common law, and five pounds for a chancery suit or a suit in which a land title or boundary was involved. A lawyer whose practice was limited to the county courts could charge ten shillings for giving advice when no suit was brought, fifteen shillings for a suit at common law, thirty shillings for chancery suits or those involving land titles and boundaries, seven shillings sixpence for petitions for small debts, and £1:1:6 per day for attending a land survey in the country. The penalty for overcharging was set at fifty pounds.[295]

An idea of the lawyers' fee may be had from the account of Francis Eyre, attorney for the plaintiff in the suit of Thomas Howlett, executor of Thomas Howlett, vs. Thomas Osborne. (William Watts was attorney for the defendant.) Eyre's bill for his fee and expenses came to £166:8:4. He wrote to his client: "I have been very frugal in your cause which has been attended with great success." Howlett recovered £437:11:11½ damages from the defendant after a jury trial in June, 1768.[296]

Even in those days, of which the impression prevails that manners were uniformly suave and gentlemen uniformly unruffled, there were cases of tension and probably temper in court. In May, 1771, the greatly respected Paul Carrington went too far for the Prince Edward magistrates. The justices showed no leniency; the eminent attorney from Charlotte, who was later to serve with distinction as a judge of the highest court of Virginia, was fined five pounds sterling and costs for contempt of court.[297]

The court day designated when the county was formed was the second Tuesday in the month. This was changed in February, 1762, to the third Monday in the month, to avoid conflicts with other court days.[298] The third Monday was destined to remain Prince Edward Court day for many years.

A succession of commissions from the Governor to magistrates provides a list of the justices of the peace of the Prince Edward Court. In January, 1757, Robert Hastie, James Scott, Peter LeGrand, and John Leigh were recommended to the Governor by the Court to be added to the commission, and they were included in the commission dated August 9, 1757; others in that commission were John Nash, James Wimbish, Joel Watkins, David Flournoy, John Nash, Jr., Thomas Scott, Samuel Ewing, and Thomas Haskins.[299]

A new commission in 1758 was directed to John Nash, James Wimbish, Joel Watkins, John Nash, Jr., Thomas Scott, Samuel Ewing, Thomas Haskins, Robert Hastie, James Scott, Peter LeGrand, John Leigh, Henry Watkins, and John Morton. The last two, along with Hugh Challis, had been previously recommended.[300] The same justices, except Samuel Ewing who had since died, were named in the commission presented at the March, 1761, Court.[301] A commission from Governor Fauquier dated October 29, 1761, added Abraham

Venable, Abner Nash, Charles Venable, Nathaniel Venable, and
Benjamin Haskins.[302] Abraham Venable's high rank in this commission, the first to which he had been named since 1754, gave
offense to James Scott.[303] (The list and rank of this commission has
not been preserved, but Abraham Venable signed as presiding justice
in January and July, 1762, and in the next commission, dated May
26, 1763, he ranked second.)[304] In January, 1762, Scott refused to
take the oath of a justice under the new commission, giving as his
reason that "he disliked Abraham Venable's being placed so forward
in this commission." It was not until March, 1763, over a year later,
that James Scott is listed among the magistrates present at Court.[305]
Whether time assuaged his feeling, or whether there was some agreement no one can say now. Justices were meticulous about their rank,
one reason being that the rank determined their place in the rotation
for sheriff. It may be noted here that Abraham Venable never held
the office of sheriff in Prince Edward. There may have been an agreement on his part to yield his place when his time came to be sheriff
as a concession to Scott and possibly some others who may also have
resented his "being placed so forward," but of this, too, no one
now can say.

Wimbish, who was dead, Joel Watkins, who was sheriff, Hastie,
who had left the county, and Abner Nash were not listed in the
commission of 1763. Watkins returned to the court in 1764.[306]

A new commission was issued by Governor Fauquier under date
of November 6, 1766, to John Nash, Abraham Venable, Joel Watkins,
John Nash, Jr., Thomas Scott, Thomas Haskins, James Scott, Peter
LeGrand, John Leigh, Henry Watkins, Peter Johnston, John Morton,
Abner Nash, Charles Venable, Nathaniel Venable, Benjamin Has-
kins, William Booker, and Philemon Holcomb.[307]

It was of members of this Court that Samuel Wallace was charged
with saying "many scandilous and defamatory" things at the April,
1767, session. Wallace plead guilty and was fined five pounds sterling "for the use of our Sovereign Lord the King." He was also put
under a good behavior bond of £500 for twelve months. Andrew
French and George Ewing were his securities.[308]

Three vacancies in the commission occurred in 1772. Joel Watkins expressed a desire to be left out of the commission; Abraham
Venable refused "to do the business of a magistrate for this county";
and Abner Nash had removed to North Carolina, where he was later
to serve as Governor of the State. The clerk was directed to certify
these vacancies to the Governor with the Court's recommendation of

Thomas Flournoy and Obadiah Woodson for appointment as magistrates.[309] There is reference to a new commission in July, 1772;[310] the list of justices is not preserved, but neither Flournoy nor Woodson was included. Both were again recommended for appointment in December, 1774.[311] There is no record of their appointment by the colonial Governor.

It was the practice in Virginia counties as long as the magistrates and sheriffs were appointed by the Governor (until the Constitution of 1850-51 went into effect) for the justices to serve as sheriff of the county in rotation, the order being determined by their rank in the commission of the peace. Usually the sheriff served two years. The Court would recommend three persons, the magistrate whose turn it was to serve being named first and the next two in the rotation order the others. The Governor would appoint and commission the magistrate who was listed first among the three.

John Nash, Jr., was the first sheriff of Prince Edward.[312] David Flournoy was the successor, taking the oath of office at the August 1756, Court, although it seems that his term did not begin until the first of the following year. Flournoy served during 1757 and had as "undersheriffs" his brother, Thomas Flournoy, and Richard Burks.[313] James Wimbish was sheriff during 1758 and 1759; Hugh Challis and Samuel Wimbish were his deputies.[314] Succeeding colonial sheriffs were John Nash, Sr. (1760-61);[315] Joel Watkins (1762-63);[316] Thomas Scott (1764-65);[317] Thomas Haskins (1766-67);[318] James Scott (1768-69);[319] Peter LeGrand (1770-71);[320] John Leigh (1772-73);[321] Henry Watkins (1774-75);[322] John Morton (January, 1776);[323] Charles Venable (after Morton's resignation at February Court, 1776).[324]

Morton's resignation may have been prompted by Peter Johnston's challenge of his recommendation for appointment. After Morton had been recommended (Charles Venable and Nathaniel Venable were the other two recommendations), Peter Johnston asked the Court why Morton should have been recommended when he (Johnston) outranked him in the commission. The Court reminded Johnston that he had promised John Nash, Sr. and John Nash, Jr., who in turn had informed the Court which recommended him for the magistracy, that he would not interpose for the office of sheriff if he would be given a preferred place in the commission.[325] The wording of the explanation is not altogether clear, but it appears that Johnston meant that he would yield his claim to the sheriff's office when it came to him the first time if he were given a higher rank than some of the justices who had been named in the commission prior to his appointment. In the commission of 1766 Johnston was placed ahead of Morton, Abner Nash, Charles Venable, Nathaniel Venable, and Benjamin Haskins, all of whom, except Nash, had been listed in the commission of 1763, and Nash had been in the commission of 1761.[326]

Aiding the sheriff in the performance of his duties were his deputies and the constables. Philemon Holcomb was deputy to John Nash, Sr. and Joel Watkins.[327] Philemon Bird was also deputy to Watkins.[328] Thomas Carter was "undersheriff" to Thomas Scott.[329] George Davidson, Francis Watkins, and David Woodson served as deputies to Thomas Haskins. [330] Jonah Cole and Joseph Moore were deputies to Peter LeGrand,[331] and during LeGrand's term John Holcomb was sworn "undersheriff" for the specific purpose of collecting his father's arrears,[332] that is, the taxes which his father, Philemon Holcomb, had failed to collect when he was deputy and which were charged against him. Joseph Moore also served as deputy to Henry Watkins and John Morton.[333] John Leigh's deputies were William Lawson, George Davidson, and John Dejarnett.[334] John Venable and Thomas Moore were deputies under Henry Watkins.[335] Charles Venable recommended John Watson as his deputy.[336]

Arthur Neal is listed as the first constable appointed by the Prince Edward Court; his appointment was made in June, 1754.[337] Later appointments included George Stubblefield (1755) in place of Isham Womack;[338] Simcock Cannon (1756) in place of Daniel Davidson;[339] Abraham Brown (1756) replacing Stubblefield;[340] Samuel Wallace (1756), in place of William Crockett;[341] Pugh Price, Jr. (1757), succeeding Thomas O'Bryant;[342] William Simmons (1757);[343] James Dyer (1757), succeeding Abraham Brown;[344] William Young (1758), in place of Dyer;[345] George Davidson (1759), replacing Ambrose Davidson;[346] John May (1760), in place of William Crockett;[347] Thomas Bryant;[348] Elkanah Jennings (1761), succeeding Arthur Neal;[349] John Popham (1762), in place of James Atkins;[350] Dudley McDearmon (1762);[351] Manness McFeiley (1767);[325] John Holloway (1767), replacing Powell Stamper;[353] Daniel Fowlkes (1768), succeeding Popham;[354] John McClard (1768), succeeding Daniel Rice;[355] Edmund Harper (1769), in place of John Holloway;[356] David Tyree (1770), in place of Zachariah Robertson;[357] Alexander Gaulding (1771);[358] Alexander Guille (1771);[359] Alexander Kain (1773), in place of John Popham;[360] William Brown (1773), succeeding Alexander Kain, deceased.[361]

Throughout the colonial period, John LeNeve served as both clerk and surveyor of Prince Edward County.[362] On April 20, 1767, Francis Watkins, who in 1766 had been deputy sheriff, qualified as deputy clerk.[363] He continued as LeNeve's deputy as long as LeNeve was clerk. Thomas Scott, Peter LeGrand and Peter Johnston served as coroners of the county, the second qualifying in June, 1758.[364] William Watkins was escheator for the county, taking the oath of office in April, 1767.[365]

The only public officials who were elected by the people in colonial times were members of the House of Burgesses. Vestrymen of the parish were elected when the parish was established and occasionally thereafter when an election was ordered by the General Assembly. Magistrates and sheriffs were appointed by the Governor, upon recommendation of the Court. Clerks were commissioned by the Secretary of the Colony, and surveyors by the president and faculty of the College of William and Mary. The election of the burgesses was the democratic leavening in the prevailingly aristocratic loaf of government. Yet it was effective, for it required the man ambitious to serve as burgess to maintain friendly contact with the electorate.[366]

To be a voter a man had to be a freeholder; each person who had an estate or freehold for his own life or for the life of another or a greater interest in at least fifty acres of land if there were no settlement on it or twenty-five acres if there were a settlement on it could vote. He could vote in the county in which he held the property. Women, infants under the age of twenty-one, persons who refused to attend the services of the Church of England, convicts, free Negroes, mulattoes, and Indians were denied the vote, regardless of the property they might hold. Joint tenants or tenants in common on a piece of property were allowed one vote, if all the parties could agree.

Each county had two representatives in the House of Burgesses, which was the lower house of the Virginia General Assembly. The burgess had to be a freeholder in the county which he represented. The Governor issued writs for the election of the burgesses. These were sent by the Secretary of the Colony to the county sheriffs, who in turn delivered them to each minister and lay reader in the county, endorsed with the time and place (always the Courthouse) of the election. After each Sunday worship service, after receiving the writ and before the day of the election, the minister or reader read the notice of election to the congregation. The freeholder was required to vote in the election; if he failed to vote, he was subject to a fine of 200 pounds of tobacco.

The sheriff conducted the election. If he could not determine who was elected "upon the view," he was required to take a poll, in which each freeholder voting was listed under the names of the candidates for whom he voted (he could vote for two candidates for burgess). If more freeholders appeared on the day set for the election than could be polled on that day, the sheriff could continue the election to the next day. The two candidates getting the most votes were declared elected, but if there were a tie, the sheriff (or undersheriff, if he happened to be conducting the election) "shall and may return which of them he thinks fit."

The burgess was exempt from arrests, attachments, executions, and any other process except treason, felony, or breach of the peace while attending the Assembly and for ten days before and after. After 1762 he was allowed fifteen shillings per day for travel to and from the Assembly and for attendance upon its session. The Prince Edward burgesses were allowed four days each way for travel to and from Williamsburg for the sessions.[367] Prior to 1762, under act of 1755, the burgess was allowed 130 pounds of tobacco a day for travel and attendance, and before that the burgess was paid ten shillings a day.[368]

The first election for burgesses in Prince Edward was held March 22, 1754. There were four candidates: Charles Anderson, John Nash, Joseph Morton, and George Walker. Anderson and Nash were elected. Anderson's poll has not been preserved, but the polls for the other three have been. Nash received 161 votes, Walker eighteen, and Morton fifteen. Anderson's and Walker's polls, taken in the election held December 8, 1755, have been preserved; Anderson received 117 votes, and Walker 48.[369]

Anderson and Nash are reported as having attended the House of Burgesses for the first time during the third session of the Assembly of 1752-55.[370] Nash was appointed to the Committee on Public Claims, and Anderson to the Committee on Courts of Justice at the session which began May 1, 1755.[371]

Nash and Anderson represented Prince Edward in the House of Burgesses through the session of March 30, 1758.[372] From the session beginning September 14, 1758, through the session of 1761, Peter LeGrand and Anderson were burgesses from Prince Edward.[373] LeGrand and Abner Nash represented the county from the session beginning November 3, 1761, through the session beginning May 1,

1764.[374] LeGrand and Nathaniel Venable were burgesses from the session beginning October 30, 1765, through the session beginning March 31, 1768.[375] Both were placed on the Committee on Courts of Justice in 1766[376] Thomas Scott and Peter Johnston represented Prince Edward at the session of May, 1769.[377] Scott and Paschal Greenhill were burgesses from the session beginning November 7, 1769, through the session which began July 11, 1771.[378] Greenhill and Peter LeGrand represented Prince Edward at the sessions beginning February 10, 1772 and May 5, 1774.[379] The last burgesses from Prince Edward were LeGrand and William Bibb. LeGrand does not appear to have attended the last session, but Bibb was present for it, which began June 1, 1775.[380]

Prince Edward sent representatives to the Virginia Conventions, which for all practical purposes took the place of the House of Burgesses in the immediate pre-Revolutionary period and the early days of the Revolution, prior to the formation of the Commonwealth. Robert Lawson and John Nash attended the convention which met at St. John's Church, Richmond, on March 20, 1775,[381] and heard Patrick Henry's most famous speech, which ended with the classic alternative, "Give me liberty, or give me death." Lawson and William Bibb attended the conventions of July 17 and December 1, 1775.[382] William Watts and William Booker attended the convention of May 6, 1776,[383] which framed the Constitution of Virginia under which the Commonwealth was established. With this convention, Virginia's colonial history came to its formal end.

CHAPTER III

The Established Church and the Dissenters

St. Patrick's Parish

WHEN Prince Edward County was established, it was within the bounds of Nottoway Parish. There was a disposition to want a separate parish for the new county, and a petition was presented to the County Court in February, 1754, asking that Prince Edward be made a parish. Charles Cupples, representing the petitioners, presented the petition, which was certified to the General Assembly.[1] The petition reached the House of Burgesses on May 3, 1755, and was referred to the Committee on Propositions and Grievances.[2] In addition to asking that a new parish be created for Prince Edward by a division of Nottoway Parish along the county line, the petition also asked that Nottoway Parish be required to pay to the new parish a proportionate part of the money which had been raised by levy for building two large churches and buildings on the glebe land. The petition was reported by the committee as reasonable on May 6, and the House directed the committee to prepare a bill in line with the request.[3]

The bill dividing Nottoway Parish was read the first time May 16, 1774,[4] and after the second reading on May 21, it was referred for amendment to a special committee consisting of Richard Bland of Prince George, William Randolph of Henrico, Matthew Marable and William Embry of Lunenburg, Samuel Harris and George Currie of Halifax, William Callaway and John Phelps of Bedford, and John Nash and Charles Anderson of Prince Edward.[5] The bill with amendment was reported June 27[6] and was read the third time and passed on the next day.[7] The concurrence of the Council was reported June 30.[8]

The act made Prince Edward County a separate parish, to be called St. Patrick's, effective September 1, 1755. An election of twelve vestrymen by the freeholders of the parish was directed to be held before September 1 after having been advertised for twenty days. The vestrymen were directed to take in Prince Edward Court the oath appointed to be taken in the first year of George I by "an act for the further security of his Majesty's person and government, and the succession of the crown in the heirs of the late Princess Sophia, being Protestants, and for extinguishing the hopes of the pretended Prince of Wales, and his open and secret abettors"; the oath of abjuration; the test; and the oath to be conformable to the doctrine and discipline of the Church of England. The vestrymen were authorized to fill vacancies among them.

Nottoway Parish was directed to pay to the vestry of St. Patrick's £197:14:6 and 16,947 pounds of tobacco, the proportion due the part of the parish which became St. Patrick's of the sum raised for building two churches and buying a glebe and erecting buildings on it.[9]

Ten vestrymen of the twelve chosen in the first election took the prescribed oaths at the September, 1755, Court: John Nash, John Nash, Jr., George Walker, Thomas Scott, Charles Venable, Peter LeGrand, Thomas Haskins, David Flournoy, James Wimbish, and John LeNeve. They met on the same day, September 9, and appointed Hugh Challis clerk at an annual salary of 500 pounds of tobacco and chose John Nash and James Wimbish church wardens.[10] The eleventh vestryman was Charles Anderson and the twelfth was probably Samuel Goode.[11] Walker moved away, and Anderson resigned; to succeed them the vestry, at its meeting November 26, 1755, chose John Martin and James Scott. Thomas Haskins and David Flournoy were chosen wardens at that meeting.[12] Robert Hastie was elected a vestryman October 28, 1757, to succeed David Flournoy, deceased. James Wimbish and Thomas Scott were elected church wardens for 1758.[13]

The people of St. Patrick's were not satisfied with their vestry. They presented a petition to the House of Burgesses on March 2, 1759, charging the vestry with illegal, arbitrary, and oppressive proceedings and asking that it be dissolved.[14] The Committee on Propositions and Grievances reported the petition reasonable, apparently being influenced to this decision more by a fact which the petition did not mention, that one vestryman was a dissenter, than by the content of the petition.[15] The vestry was dissolved, and an election of a new vestry was directed to be held before August 1, 1759, after a month's notice. The Assembly took cognizance of an increasing tendency on the part of vestrymen to leave the Church of England to join a dissenting congregation and in this act prohibited a dissenter from serving as a vestryman. When a vestryman became a dissenter, the vestry was directed to elect another person in his place. A vestryman who had become a dissenter could be re-elected to the vestry if he returned to the Established Church.[16]

The election was held July 31, 1759; eight of those elected took the oaths of office at the August Court: Robert Hastie, Peter Le-Grand, Richard Woodson, John Nash, Jr., Richard Burks, Philemon Holcomb, John Graham, and John Nash.[17] Three other vestrymen qualified at the September Court: Obadiah Woodson, Zachariah Leigh, and John LeNeve.[18] The new vestry met on the day the first eight members took the oaths (August 14) and chose Nathaniel Venable clerk and John Nash and Peter LeGrand church wardens for 1760.[19]

In February, 1762, John Leigh qualified as vestryman.[20] Since only eleven of the twelve elected in 1759 had taken the oaths of office previously, and the records mention no subsequent election, it is probable that Leigh was elected in 1759, but did not qualify until 1762. In December, 1762, Zachariah Leigh resigned as a vestryman and Thomas Scott was elected to succeed him; at the same time Robert Hastie resigned because he intended to leave the country, and Thomas Haskins was chosen to succeed him.[21] Peter Johnston was unanimously elected vestryman in 1766 to succeed the late Obadiah Woodson.[22] Upon the resignation of John Graham in 1771, Paschal Greenhill was elected his successor.[23] Paschal Greenhill moved out of the parish, and Obadiah Woodson was chosen his successor in 1774.[24]

The vestry elected the following church wardens: Richard Burks and John LeNeve, for 1761;[25] Philemon Holcomb and Obadiah Woodson, for 1762;[26] Holcomb and John Graham, for 1763;[27] Thomas Scott and Richard Woodson, for 1764;[28] Scott and John Nash, Jr., for 1765;[29] Peter LeGrand and Thomas Haskins, for 1766;[30] Haskins and Peter Johnston, for 1767;[31] Johnston and Philemon Holcomb, for 1768,[32] and again for 1769;[33] Peter LeGrand and Johnston, for 1770,[34] and again for 1771;[35] John Leigh and LeGrand, for 1772;[36] Thomas Scott and Leigh, for 1773;[37] LeGrand and Holcomb, for 1774.[38]

At the second meeting of the vestry, which was held at Sandy River Church December 3, 1755, the Rev. James Garden was unanimously received as minister of the parish. Garden was recommended by the Hon. Thomas Dawson, commissary of Virginia, and he was also favorably known to the vestry. His salary was set at 17,280 pounds of tobacco annually; and he was paid 2,160 pounds of tobacco at the rate of twopence per pound (this would yield in cash £18) for his services from September 1 until October 15.[39] Garden served as minister of the parish until his death, February 19, 1773.[40]

Three ministers applied for the parish after Garden's death: the Rev. Messrs. Oglesby (or Ogilvie), Sanders, and McCartney. James McCartney brought good recommendations from Granville Parish in North Carolina, where he was minister, and was chosen minister on August 10, 1773. He preached and administered the sacrament of Holy Communion at Sandy River Church on the second Sunday in October, 1773; at the Upper Church on the next Sunday; and at the Chapel on the fourth Sunday in October. He agreed to move his family to the parish and take possession of the glebe on December 1, 1773.[41]

MacCartney, a native of Ireland, settled in North Carolina, where he enjoyed the favor of Governor Tryon. He taught school before entering the ministry. Writing from Granville to the secretary of the Society for the Propagation of the Gospel on October 28, 1769, MacCartney mentioned the numerous dissenters there: "Many Presbyterians," who had a minister settled there, and "likewise many Baptists who are great bigots." But MacCartney assured the society's secretary that he would "take every prudent method I am capable of to abolish Dissention and make converts to the Church." In 1771 MacCartney was chaplain to Governor Tryon's army which defeated the Regulators at Alamance. MacCartney was not entirely satisfied in Granville, and his influential friends in New Bern, where he had taught, tried unsuccessfully to help him become located in New York. Among these friends was Abner Nash, who had gone to New Bern from Prince Edward.[42] This friendship suggests that Nash was influential in helping MacCartney get the appointment to St. Patrick's Parish.

MacCartney's ministry in Prince Edward was of short duration. Within two years after coming to the parish he had died. His will was probated at the August, 1775, Court.[43]

One of the applicants for the parish ministry when MacCartney was chosen put in a bill for his services in the parish, which probably consisted of preaching what today might be termed a "trial sermon." The vestry rejected this request of the Rev. Mr. Ogilvie;[44] evidently his services were neither great nor numerous, or the vestry would have compensated him.

When St. Patrick's Parish was created, there were two churches in its territory, Sandy River and Buffalo. At the vestry meeting which called Garden as minister, Richard Rutledge was elected sexton at Sandy River and Francis Rice at Buffalo, and Alexander Fraser was chosen clerk or lay reader at Sandy River and Samuel Wimbish at Buffalo. The sexton's salary was set at 300 pounds of tobacco a year, and the clerk's salary at 1,200 pounds of tobacco a year.[45] The next year, 1756, James Thackston was elected clerk at the upper church (Buffalo), and Thomas Day at Sandy River. Day served only a short time; in March, 1757, John Turner was elected clerk at Sandy River.[46] Turner served until his death, and in August, 1759, Alexander Fraser was again chosen clerk for Sandy River.[47] For a few months in late 1766 and early 1767, Fraser served as clerk at both churches, Sandy River and the upper church (this upper church was at French's).[48] In May, 1773, David Rice was named clerk for Sandy River Church.[49] John Crockett became clerk for the chapel in 1765.[50] Philemon Bird was named clerk for the upper church in July, 1767.[51]

Judith Rutledge succeeded her husband as sexton at Sandy River in 1757.[52] The parish levy for 1758 includes an item allowing her twelve shillings sixpence for washing and keeping the surplice; the same allowance was made to Elizabeth Rice for the same service.[53] John Crockett became sexton at Buffalo in 1760;[54] in 1763 he became sexton at the upper chapel.[55] Thomas Hastie was named sexton of the new church at French's in 1764.[56] Mrs. Mary Barnwell succeeded Hastie in the late summer of 1771.[57]

The clerk read the service in the absence of the minister. Since the minister in St. Patrick's had two churches and a part of the time a chapel in addition to the churches at which to preach, the clerk had to conduct services frequently. The sexton kept the church clean, opened it for services and closed it afterwards, and in St. Patrick's Parish kept the surplice which the minister used at the church the sexton served.[58]

The vestry of the parish had many duties, some of them secular to the modern mind. Some of the more important were: to call the parish minister; to have land processioned; to look after orphans and see that they were bound out to suitable persons; to make provision for the care of the poor; to investigate cases of suspected moral delinquency and to present them, if the evidence justified, to the county court, and also to collect fines imposed for offenses of this nature; to lay and collect the parish levy (which provided the financial support of the parish); to provide for the erection, maintenance, equipment, and worship of churches and chapels; to purchase and maintain a glebe and to build and keep in repair thereon the necessary buildings.

It was five years after the parish was established before the vestry gave attention to the building of churches. Sandy River and Buffalo, which was also called the upper church, had been built before the parish was formed. It is not known whether the structure at Sandy River was the chapel which was standing in 1744 or whether the chapel had been replaced. And it is not known when Buffalo Church was built or whether it was built by the vestry of Raleigh Parish or later by the vestry of Nottoway Parish.[59] It appears that a new church was built at Buffalo in 1760, for the vestry on December 12 of that year directed the persons who let the contract for the upper church to have it floored and to provide doors, window shutters, and a pulpit.[60]

On November 10, 1761, the vestry decided to close Buffalo Church and to end the services of the Church of England there because it was situated among dissenters. The minister, the clerk, and the sexton were notified of this decision.[61] The dissenters who evidently had become so numerous in the neighborhood that there were not enough Anglicans left to justify the continuation of worship were the Scotch-Irish Presbyterians. Lately they had been augmented by a considerable migration from Pennsylvania under the leadership of the Rev. Richard Sankey.[62]

At its meeting in December, 1761, the vestry decided to build two new churches, one at or near Sandy River Church, the other on the land of Buchanan and Co. near Robin's Spring. Peter LeGrand was asked to draw plans for the churches, which were to be forty-eight feet by twenty-four with a pitch of sixteen feet and a compass ceiling.[63]

In March, 1762, the vestry decided to change the location of the church planned for Robin's Spring to Price's Path on Thomas Hamblett's land.[64] The site was again changed in January, 1763, and the location originally designated was chosen. John Nash agreed to build the church with some alterations in the plans: a square ceiling was substituted for the compass ceiling and a "mindallion" cornice was substituted for the cornice in the plan. The alterations applied to both church buildings.[65]

The vestry at this time seemed determined to meet the building needs of the parish. On March 10, 1762, it decided to build a chapel, thirty-two feet by twenty, in the upper end of the county at or near the schoolhouse on Obadiah Woodson's land. The chapel was to have doors, a floor, window shutters, seats, and a pulpit.[66]

The letting of the contract to build Sandy River Church was ordered to be advertised in the *Virginia Gazette*; March 25, 1763, was the date set for letting the contract, and the undertaker was given two years to complete the building.[67]

Colonel John Nash was given permission to build a pew in Sandy River Church on condition that he add to the east end of the church as much in proportion as his pew was to the church; Peter LeGrand was granted the same privilege, on the same condition, at the upper church (at Robin's Spring). John Nash, Jr., was given permission to build a gallery in the upper church, and John Leigh was given permission to build one in Sandy River Church.[68]

The new Sandy River Church burned just before it was completed. The Virginia Assembly of November, 1762, authorized the vestry to add to the levy to provide compensation to Thomas Wood, who was undertaker of the church which burned, for his expense, trouble, materials, and workmanship.[69] In February, 1763, the vestry asked John and Richard Morton to value the church which was burned. An additional levy of two pounds of tobacco per tithable was set to provide compensation for Wood.[70]

The Mortons were paid five shillings each for appraising the value of "Wood's church," and fifteen shillings each for valuing "LeGrand's church" and riding to the place. Since they were directed in November, 1763, to value the upper chapel, report their valuation to the vestry, and receive the chapel if well done, it seems that Peter LeGrand built the chapel near Obadiah Woodson's.[71] An order in January, 1765, to pay LeGrand £17:9, the balance due on the "upper church,"[72] seems to refer to the chapel, instead of the church at French's, which was known as the upper church. In November, 1765, the vestry directed that the church built by LeGrand and Christopher Ford be received if done according to specifications and that the "undertakers" be paid the balance due them of £113, with an additional £33:3:9 paid to LeGrand for alterations.[73] Over a year earlier, in September, 1764, "so much of the church" as had been completed was ordered received from John Nash, and several payments were directed made to Thomas Nash for special work, such as building brick steps to the church and putting up a balustrade in front of the stairs, and for the balance of £44:1:9 due him for building the church.[74]

In May, 1764, the vestry directed that the grounds at the new church at French's be grubbed and cleaned.[75] Sundials were ordered placed at the two churches and the chapel.[76] In 1772 a gallery was ordered built in the upper chapel, with Peter LeGrand doing the work, and Obadiah Woodson was given permission to build a gallery there at his own expense.[77]

When the vestry decided to build a church at Robin's Spring (French's), it added to the parish levy 12,000 pounds of tobacco for the purpose. This raised the levy to 41,790 pounds of tobacco, or thirty-five pounds of tobacco per poll for the 1,194 tithables in the county in 1761.[78] In 1763 the vestry ordered a special levy of 14,000 pounds of tobacco to pay for building Sandy River Church; this levy brought the total levy set that year to 57,408 pounds of tobacco or forty-eight pounds of tobacco per tithable.[79]

While the church at French's was being built, worship services were held at the Courthouse on alternate Sundays. William Purnall was lay reader at the Courthouse during 1762.[80] The first service held in the church at French's was set for the fourth Sunday in June, 1764.[81]

The first parish levy, set in September, 1755, amounted to £157:17:6, which the vestry ordered paid from the sum of £197:14:6 due from Nottoway Parish.[82] John Nash bought 16,947 pounds of tobacco due St. Patrick's Parish from Nottoway and gave the vestry, under the agreement £151 for the tobacco and for £38:16 cash received from the Nottoway vestry. Later Colonel Nash sold the tobacco and money to Robert Hastie for £171. Reluctant to make twenty pounds in a deal involving church tobacco and money, Nash offered "the benefit of the bargain" to the vestry. The transaction had been fairly handled, thought the vestry, and it declined to accept the profit Nash made.[83]

Parish levies tended to run higher than the county levies. The 1756 levy came to 40,500 pounds, or forty-five pounds per tithable.[84] Subsequent parish levies were:

Year	Total Levy (pounds of tobacco)	Levy per Tithable (pounds of tobacco)
1757	40,262	41[85]
1758	39,474	43[86]
1759	53,689	53[87]
1760	37,060	34[88]
1761	41,790	35[89]
1762	44,236	39[90]

Year	Total Levy (pounds of tobacco)	Levy per Tithable (pounds of tobacco)
1764	52,401	41[91]
1765	38,276	28[92]
1766	33,144	24[93]
1767	38,025	27[94]
1768	37,824	24[95]
1769	29,160	18[96]
1770	35,640	20[97]
1771	33,534	18[98]
1773	36,884	18[99]
1774	39,600	20[100]

These were the taxes paid by Prince Edward people for the support of the Established Church. They were levied in addition to the county and public taxes (public taxes were those levied by the colony).

Although the St. Patrick's vestry was prompt enough in laying plans for the purchase of a glebe, it was five years before the dwelling house on it was ready for the minister to move into.[101] At the first meeting (September 9, 1755 at the courthouse), the wardens were authorized to receive proposals for a glebe and to report to the vestry.[102] Three tracts, each of 300 acres, were offered to the vestry at its meeting at Sandy River Church December 3, 1755. George Walker offered a tract near Leigh's for £100, Theodorick Carter a part of his tract for £90, and Philemon Holcomb a part of his tract for £105. A committee consisting of Thomas Scott, David Flournoy, Thomas Haskins, and John Nash, Jr., was appointed to view the lands offered and report.[103] Apparently none of the tracts offered pleased the committee, for in March, 1757, another committee, Scott, Haskins, James Wimbish, and Samuel Goode, was appointed to view lands offered for the glebe and report.[104] At its October, 1757, meeting, the vestry decided to buy 300 acres for £200 from Charles Anderson, George Walton, Abraham Martin, and Henry Ligon.[105]

Detailed plans for buildings on the glebe were made at the vestry meeting in January, 1758. These plans give a good description of a typical Prince Edward home of the period. The dimensions of the dwelling on the glebe were fifty-four feet by eighteen feet with a pitch of twelve feet. There were two rooms, one eighteen feet square, the other sixteen by eighteen, with a passage between twelve feet wide running the full width of the house. The person approaching the story-and-a-half house from the front would see five windows and a door with a glass transom over it and a bonnet over the door. Each of the two rooms had two windows on the front and one on the back. There were front and back doors in the passage, each with its "light" and bonnet. There was also a large window in the passage on the front. The staircase was in the passage or hall, and there was a window just above the "half-space" or landing on the stairway. There were two windows in each gable end upstairs. Brick chimneys were built on the inside the framing of the house, and in the two downstairs rooms there were two closets each, one on each side of the chimney. Wash boards and chair boards were built in the passage. Each gable end was wainscoted with paneling and quarter round.

The roof was sheeted with three-quarter inch plank and covered with heart-pine shingles. The underpinning of the dwelling was two and one-half feet above the ground, and there was a cellar, sixteen feet by twelve, seven feet deep. The floors were of pine quarter plank one and one-fourth inches thick and six inches wide. The house was weatherboarded with plain and beaded pine plank and was primed and painted. Brick steps were built at each door. Sawed timber shutters, which were painted, were put in the side windows, and the eaves were to be "neatly cornished."

A kitchen, twenty-four by eighteen, with a pitch of eight feet, was also planned. This building also had a brick inside chimney, was underpinned with brick one foot above the ground, was weatherboarded with beaded plank, shingled, and boxed, and had one glass window on the front. The kitchen had an earth floor. The practice of having the kitchen separate from the dwelling prevailed until after the War Between the States. Various reasons for the separate building have been advanced: to reduce danger of destruction by fire and to keep the odors of cooking foods out of the living quarters are two likely ones.

The vestry included plans for a dairy at the glebe. This building was twelve feet square with a pitch of eight feet. It was plastered, had a brick floor, was weatherboarded and shingled, but like the typical old dairy was latticed under the eaves of each side. A smokehouse the same size of the dairy was built.

A garden one hundred feet square was laid off and fenced with oak posts and three square rails, which were "tenanted" into the posts their full thickness of half an inch.

The vestry directed the wardens to advertise for bids in the

Virginia Gazette, the contract to be let the second Tuesday in April
(court day) at the courthouse.

When the vestry met in April, it made some changes in the plans;
the width of the dwelling was increased from eighteen to twenty feet,
windows were directed to be put in each closet, and a lock worth five
shillings sterling was to be put on each outer door.[106]

The contract for the buildings with Peter LeGrand, who did so
much building in colonial Prince Edward, gives additional details.
Since it was prepared after the changes in the plans had been made,
it gives the inside dimensions of the chamber as seventeen by nineteen feet. The staircase in the hall was to be open, with rails and
banisters (in many of the older houses the staircase was enclosed).
The upstairs passage was fourteen feet wide. The upstairs floors
were tongued and grooved, and the boards were not to exceed twelve
inches in width (downstairs the flooring was not to exceed six inches
in width). The dwelling was weatherboarded with good featheredge
plank, plain and beaded, to show no more than six inches and to
have a lap of at least two inches. The contract does not mention the
hall window on the front, calling for seven windows on the first
floor, four in front and three in the back. The staircase window
opening on the back had eight panes and the other windows had
eighteen panes, and there were six panes in the "light" over each
door leading to the outside. The panes were eight by ten inches in
size and were of crown glass. Neat casing of all windows and doors
was called for, the doors having quarter-round and raised panel
work. The walls were to be plastered and whitewashed. The closet
windows had four panes and the windows in the gable ends eight
panes each, all panes of the same size as those used in the other
windows. The contract called for two fireplaces upstairs as well as
the two downstairs. Shutters of quarter round and raised panel were
to be at each window, and each room, as well as the passage, had a
wash and chair board or rail, as it would be called today. The exterior of the dwelling was to be primed and painted, and the roof
was to be tarred twice.

LeGrand undertook the work for 595 pounds current money.[107]
The 1759 levy included an item for £90:8:4, the balance due him for
the glebe buildings.[108] The original plans called for an initial payment of 10,000 pounds of tobacco to the builder in September, 1758,
with the balance in two equal installments in September, 1759, and
1760.[109] In December, 1760, the glebe buildings were deemed ready
for occupancy, and LeGrand was directed to deliver the keys to the

wardens and the wardens in turn to deliver them to the Reverend Mr. Garden.[110]

Since the parish had not provided a glebe for the minister the first year Garden served, he was given twenty pounds for his board.[111]

Through the rest of Garden's ministry after he moved into the glebe, the vestry seems to have assumed that all was well with the buildings and that no repairs were needed. How characteristic that is even today of church boards in their management of the minister's home. But the coming of a new minister opens eyes to the need of repairs and refurbishing. Perhaps it is the new minister's wife. At any rate, in June, 1774, following MacCartney's occupancy of the glebe in the preceding December, the vestry authorized extensive repairs and renovation of the glebe buildings. Broken window panes, twenty-four in all, ten inches by eight in size, were replaced. New chair boards were put in the hall, a little lower than they had been; the new boards had moulding on them. New shingles and new weatherboarding were added where needed. The cellar passage got new underpinning, and all the underpinning was pointed and repaired where needed. New steps were built at the doors. The plastering was patched and whitewashed, and the inside (evidently the woodwork) was painted blue. The outside was painted a stone color. A brick oven, evidently for keeping food warm, and new hearths were built in the "mansion house" and four new locks were bought.

The kitchen was ceiled and had a new window.

Door racks, a manger, and stalls were built at the stable. The dairy and smokehouse had new underpinning, and the weatherboarding was repaired.

A larger garden, this one forty-five yards square, was laid off and enclosed. A plank fence was built around this garden, with plank six inches broad at the bottom of the palings, which were five feet high. A necessary house, ten feet by eight feet, was built in the garden.[112]

In 1767 the vestry established an order of worship services which had the minister preach at the Chapel each fifth Sunday and administer the sacrament of the Lord's Supper there as he saw fit. The sacrament was to be administered at Sandy River and French's at Christmas, Easter, and Whitsuntide. The hour of service was 11 o'clock from April 1 to October 31 and noon November through March.[113] The levy for 1763 provided payment of six shillings for wine at Sandy River Church at Easter and of twelve shillings for three bottles of claret used at Sandy River.[114]

An important duty of the vestry was the care of the needy. The first levy provided for payment of £2:2:6 to John Holloway for care, trouble and burying a needy man; for the relief of a needy woman; and for the payment of five pounds to Dr. Foster for salivating an indigent person.[115] The 1759 levy provided payment of eight pounds to William Crockett for caring for a poor woman three months and burying her, of 125 pounds of tobacco to Daniel Newman for caring for another needy woman at the time of her death, and of 1,000 pounds of tobacco to Alexander Womack for caring for a needy woman one year.[116] In 1761 William Campbell was paid fourteen shillings for linen for burying a poor man.[117]

Items in the 1760 levy show the expense of a case of smallpox. For one case the vestry paid Charles Cobrall five pounds and Michael McDearmon £2:3 for caring for the ill man, paid Theodorick Carter £1:2 and Philemon Holcomb five shillings for blankets for him, and paid George Walker £1:15 for a rug for the man.[118] In 1770 two needy families were victims of smallpox; the vestry provided new clothing for them and directed that their old clothing be burned.[119]

In 1770 the vestry paid Robert Jennings £4:3:4 for caring for a crippled child.[120]

Peter Johnston acted as the vestry's agent in buying a new communion service in 1770. The service included a flagon, a pint can, and a salver of silver. A special levy of two pounds of tobacco per tithable was laid to buy the church plate (3,025 pounds) and pay the collector's commission (215 pounds).[121] The service had come by July, 1772, when it was delivered to the minister. It did not prove as expensive as anticipated, and the parish had a credit balance of £15:2:5 with Hyndman and Company in London. Johnston was directed to spend the balance for superfine crimson broadcloth to be made up with silk lace and tassels fringed for use in the churches as directed by the wardens, with proper cushions.[122]

For all its sense of obligation to care for the needy, the St. Patrick's vestry did not welcome prospective relief cases. One man was sent back to Cornwall Parish (Charlotte County) promptly upon his removal to Prince Edward; the vestry "adjudged" that he had "not gained a legal settlement in this parish and is likely to become very chargeable."[123] Public Welfare departments are sometimes confronted with a similar problem today.

Fines imposed for offenses against good morals were paid to the parish vestry. In 1763 the vestry received fines amounting to thirty shillings from four persons for swearing (one paid a fine of fifteen shillings, the others five shillings each), a fine of five shillings from one man for getting drunk, and two fines of five shillings each from two men for not going to church.[124]

Responsibility for "binding out" orphans rested with the church wardens, but they performed this duty at the direction of the county court. The court orders abound in authorizations to the wardens to bind out orphans.[125] Older children could choose their own guardians,[126] but the wardens selected guardians for younger children. Guardians gave bond for faithful care of their wards. The conscientious guardian looked out for the child's best interests. Peter Davis, for example, after having given a ward, John Wotton Nelson, "book learning," asked that the indentures binding the boy to him be cancelled and that the boy be bound to Matthews Flournoy to learn a trade.[127] An inconsiderate guardian might have kept the boy as his ward in order to have the advantage of the labor of a growing lad. Just before George Ewing, Sr., left the colony, the indentures which bound Elizabeth Morrain, whose father was dead, to him were cancelled, and he was directed to return the child to her mother.[128]

The Presbyterians

Presbyterianism in Prince Edward stems from two sources. The first Presbyterians in the county were the Scotch-Irish settlers from Pennsylvania who planted the Buffaloe Settlement. To them John Thomson preached in 1739 and William Robinson in 1743. One wonders at the reception Robinson may have received, for he belonged to the "New Side" New Castle Presbytery in the Presbyterian controversy of that era. The Scotch-Irish generally belonged to the "Old Side," and John Thomson was one of the "Old Side" leaders. Probably the scarcity of preaching made the pioneers welcome any minister who preached the Gospel according to the interpretation of Calvin.

The principal points at issue between the two "sides" were evangelism and the education of the ministry. The "Old Side" did not like the evangelistic methods used by ministers like the Tennents and Samuel Blair; they also insisted that the ministers be educated in a Scotch university. The "New Side" felt that the Presbyterian Church should be evangelistic; their methods were moderate enough, in comparison with those of the New Lights and those later used by the Separate Baptists and still later by the Methodists. The "New Side" was willing to ordain ministers educated in the "Log Colleges,"

which some of their ministers conducted for the training of young
men who wanted to preach but lacked other opportunities to get
an education.[129]

The other source of Presbyterianism in Prince Edward was provided by the "New Side." Samuel Davies came to Virginia in 1747
as evangelist to the Presbyterian congregations worshipping in meeting-houses on the lands of Samuel Morris, David Rice, Stephen
Leacy in Hanover County and Thomas Watkins in Henrico County.[130]
These congregations had their origin in Samuel Morris' dissatisfaction with the spiritual ministry of the Established Church and his
effort to find a more satisfying one. He built a "reading house," in
which he read sermons to people who came to hear him. William
Robinson preached to them on his visit, with the result that Morris
and his neighbors who had similar religious ideas found a spiritual
haven in Presbyterianism.[131]

Davies "found time, strength, and disposition" to travel far afield
from these four meeting-houses at which the General Court of Virginia had licensed him to preach. In 1752 he wrote to the Bishop of
London about Presbyterian settlers in frontier counties "about one
hundred miles west and southwest from Hanover lately settled by
people who came chiefly from Ireland originally, and immediately
from the Northern colonies, who were educated Presbyterians . . . ."
These he visited in "frequent missionary excursions" to what are
now Cumberland, Powhatan, Prince Edward, Charlotte, Campbell,
Nottoway, and Amelia Counties.[132]

It was Davies' practice to make some appointments on his missionary tours in advance and others as he went along. He would
send someone ahead to make arrangements for lodging and entertainment for the night, and it was his custom to preach to the family
and slaves and neighbors, if they could be gotten together, at the
places he stayed. Preliminary arrangements were necessary, for
many people did not care to receive a dissenting minister, especially
a "New Light," as evangelists and their converts were often called in
that period, into their homes. John Morton of Prince Edward frequently performed this service for Davies, and on one occasion
arranged for him to stay at the home of Joseph Morton, who was
then living either at Slate Hill in Prince Edward or Little Roanoke
Bridge in Lunenburg (Charlotte). Both Morton and his wife, *née*
Agnes Woodson, were profoundly impressed by Davies. When he
left, they went with him to Cumberland, where he was to administer
the Lord's Supper. Mrs. Morton wished to participate and asked her

husband; "he told her to do as she thought proper," to quote Alexander. Then Morton himself, in an intermission between the sermon and the sacrament, told Davies he wished to take part in the service. The minister and Morton discussed the matter briefly, and Davies gave Morton a token admitting him to the Lord's Table. Husband and wife together partook of their first communion under Presbyterian auspices at this time and thereby publicly identified themselves with this faith. Their conversion laid the foundation of Briery Church, which was built shortly afterward by Morton and others who had became Presbyterians under the preaching of Davies.[133]

The membership of Briery in its earlier years was entirely non-Scotch-Irish. Morton, Walton, Wimbish, Craghead, Pettus, Watkins, Dabbs, Venable, Vernon, Booker, Jackson, Clark, Tanner, Breedlove, Billups, Rowlet, Flournoy, and Blanton were the family names of the forty-nine members received during the pastorate of the Rev. Robert Henry, 1755-67. The first Scotch-Irish name in the roll of members is that of Adam Calhoun, which is seventy-sixth on the list; he became a member between 1776 and 1780.[134]

The Rev. Robert Henry was installed as pastor of Briery and Cub Creek (in Charlotte) churches June 4, 1755. Prior to his coming, which could not have been long after the organization of the church, Joseph Morton, who had been chosen one of the ruling elders, would read a sermon each Sunday to the assembled congregation and question the children from the Shorter Catechism. The worship services conducted by Morton each Sunday began before the church was organized and these services, together with Morton's conversations with his neighbors on matters of religion, were important factors in making possible the founding of Briery Church.[135]

Through Davies and Henry, the latter a graduate of the College of New Jersey (Princeton) in the class of 1751,[136] Briery was identified with the "New Side" Presbyterians.

Another Presbyterian church, also the fruit of Davies' labors, was Cumberland; this church, though located north of the Appomattox, drew members from Prince Edward as far south as the Courthouse community. The Rev. John Wright was installed as pastor of Cumberland on the last Sunday in July, 1755. Wright was a graduate of Princeton in the class of 1752.[137]

Davies, Henry, and Wright were three of the six ministers appointed by the Synod of New York to constitute Hanover Presbytery. The first meeting of the new presbytery was held at Hanover December 3, 1755. Davies was chosen moderator; he and Henry were two of the four ministers present for the organization of the presbytery.[138]

The Buffaloe Settlement received a large infusion of Scotch-Irish settlers about 1759. In that year the Rev. Richard Sankey, a son-in-law of John Thomson, moved to the settlement with a large part of his congregation. Indian depredations forced their removal from Pennsylvania; as of August 19, 1759, fourteen members of Sankey's congregation had been killed by Indians. Sankey purchased a farm in Prince Edward in October, 1759. Eight years earlier, his father-in-law had moved to North Carolina.[139]

Sankey became pastor of Buffalo Church after coming to Virginia.[140] He seems to have been the first settled pastor of this church. While there are references to worship services in the Buffaloe Settlement from 1739 on, there is no reference to Buffalo Church or to a place of meeting prior to Sankey's arrival. Land for a church for "the Presbyterian Congregation in Buffaloe Settlement . . . . under the Immediate Care and Inspection of the Rever'd Mr. Richard Sankey . . . ." was bought in 1761.[141] There is a reference to the road to Mr. Sankey's meeting-house in a court order dated September 11, 1759.[142]

Although the breach between "Old Side" and "New Side" had been healed officially by a reunion at the joint meeting of the Synods of Philadelphia (Old Side) and New York (New Side) the year before Sankey came to Prince Edward,[143] Buffalo Church through him was identified with the "Old Side." He joined Hanover Presbytery as its thirteenth member.[144]

The Presbyterians in the Buffaloe Settlement evidently relied upon Governor Gooch's arrangement with John Caldwell to provide the religious toleration necessary for their undisturbed worship as dissenters. The Briery congregation lacked that protection, since Davies had no place of worship licensed in Prince Edward. (Under the law, congregations which did not belong to the Church of England were required to be licensed, and their ministers were required to take certain oaths of loyalty to the Sovereign and to the Protestant succession to the throne and of belief in the Triune God and in the inspiration of the Scriptures.)[145] George Walton applied to the Prince Edward Court in September, 1759, "on behalf of Presbyterians performing divine service at the head of Bryery River in the Presbyterian way." His application, evidently that the Briery meeting-house be licensed, was received and ordered to be recorded.[146]

After Henry left the pastorate of Briery in 1767, Joseph Morton resumed again his early practice of conducting service in the absence of a minister. At this time, George Walton shared the responsibility. Morton, George Walton, and Sherwood Walton were the first elders of the church.

In 1766 Briery established what was called "a permanent fund for the support of the Gospel." It was an endowment fund, subscribed by the members, the income from which was used to support the church. There were seventy-two subscribers, a number of whom were not members of the church; in subscriptions ranging from ten shillings to fifty pounds, they pledged £308. George Walton with fifty pounds, Joseph Morton with twenty-five, John Pettus with fifteen, and Henry Watkins with twelve were the largest subscribers. The money was spent in the purchase of slaves; these were hired out and the money derived from their hire was used for the support of the church.[147]

The colonial Presbyterian churches exercised a strict discipline. Reference has already been made to the use of tokens for admission to Davies' communion service in Cumberland. Church members attended services prior to the Lord's Supper and prepared themselves for it. Those who did received tokens, and only those with tokens could receive the bread and wine. A certificate given members removing from the Buffaloe Settlement shows the emphases of these early churches:

"Certificate

"That Mary Hanna, widow, her son Robert and her daughter Jane, were for some years orderly members of this congregation, have behaved honestly, soberly, Christianly, are free from any scandal or church censure. They have been admitted to sealing ordinances with us, and are now recommended to Christian communion wherever Providence may order their lot. Is certified at Buffaloes, Prince Edward County, Virginia, August 30, 1765. By Mr. Richard Sankey, R. D. M."[148]

The Baptists

The earliest Baptist influence in Prince Edward originated in the portion of Amelia County which is now Nottoway. In a way strikingly reminiscent of the origin of Presbyterianism in Hanover County, the Baptist beginnings in this section are to be found in the spiritual experience of Samuel Thomson who had moved from Hanover to Amelia. About 1768 Thomson became a "pious and devout Christian without ordinary means, in the midst of wicked neighbors." He invited to his home his neighbors to whom he would read the Bible and other books and with whom he would pray and converse about their spiritual obligations. He invited Samuel Harriss and Jeremiah Walker, two Separate Baptist ministers who had been converted in the revival which had begun under the preaching of Shubael Stearns at Sandy Creek Church in Guilford County, North Carolina, to preach in his community.[149] It is not clear whether a petition to license George Walton's home as a place for Baptist worship was presented to the Amelia Court before or after the visit of Harriss and Walker. But a petition dated October 27, 1768, to that effect was presented to the Amelia Court and was rejected on November 24. Two residents of Prince Edward, John Thomas Dejarnett and his wife Millisant (*née* Hall), signed the petition.[150]

Although the petition was rejected, the revival was held with powerful effect, and sixty-six persons were baptized, of whom the names of forty-six are known. Among those were Millisant Dejarnett and Elizabeth Dejarnett, although John Thomas Dejarnett who signed the petition is not in the list of forty-six. Also among those baptized were David Ellington and his wife and Robert Foster and his wife of Prince Edward. As a result of the revival, those who were baptized constituted Nottoway Baptist Church on December 10, 1769. They built a meeting-house forty by twenty feet in size on land given by John Fowlkes near Little Nottoway River on the road leading from the present Burkeville to the present Victoria. In many respects the Baptists at Nottoway were more like the Regular Baptists than the Separate Baptists. The Regular Baptists usually had their meeting-houses licensed as places of worship, and their ministers took the prescribed oaths for dissenting ministers. Not so the Separate Baptists who took the view that God was the Christian's sole authority and that the minister should preach and the believers should worship whenever and wherever the opportunity presented itself. The first pastor at Nottoway, Jeremiah Walker, "renounced the tones, actions, and violence" characteristic of Separate Baptist preachers and "discouraged the outcries, ecstacies, and epilepsies so much thought of by them." Ellington is listed among the assistants to Walker in 1772.[151]

Samuel Harriss, on one of his many missionary tours of Virginia, preached in the western part of Prince Edward in 1771, where among his converts was Robert Jennings. As a result of this revival Rocks Baptist Church was constituted about 1772 with fifteen members. William Johnson became the first pastor of the church, of which Jennings is described as for many years "an ornament."[152]

The year following the organization of Rocks Church, Appomattox Baptist Church was constituted in Prince Edward with twelve members. Its organization was the result of a revival conducted by the vigorous minister, Samuel Harriss, who on this occasion had associated with him James Read. John McLeroy, a native of Ireland, became first pastor of this church. He is described as "a wretched traitor to the cause," and his ministry proved an obstacle to progress in the church. The meeting-house, which was known as Peak's, from Richard Peak on whose land it was built, was about four miles north of the present Prospect.[153]

About 1775 William Rice built a meeting-house for dissenters "on the main road" a short distance west of the present Rice. The four acres on which the meetinghouse stood were deeded by Rice to Jacob Waddill, Thomas Tinsley, Robert Goode, James Wade, Icay Rice, and William Rice as trustees in an indenture dated August 1, 1775.[154] The deed does not identify the meeting-house as connected with any denomination, but the organization there in 1781 of Sailor Creek Baptist Church, with Robert Foster as pastor,[155] suggests that it was a preaching station of Nottoway Church built for the convenience of members living in that vicinity.

One Prince Edward meeting-house escapes identification by denomination. Upon the petition of Joseph Rice, the Court in December, 1759, gave him permission to build a meeting-house on his land.[156] Who used it, or whether it was built after Rice received permission to build it is not known.

CHAPTER IV

Life in Colonial Prince Edward

THE staple of colonial Virginia was tobacco. It was the principal agricultural product and warehouse inspectors' notes for tobacco were used as a medium of exchange. The practice has given rise to the current concept that tobacco was used as money in colonial times. Taxes, as readers have seen, were levied in tobacco; salaries and fees of county officers were paid in tobacco, as well as the salary of the parish minister. One should not think, though, that when the sheriff or his deputy came to collect the tax due, the farmer took the collector to his tobacco packing house and weighed out the pounds of tobacco due; or that when he went to the store to get tea and sugar and salt or silk for a Sunday dress for his wife, he carried with him a wagon load of tobacco and passed across the counter enough tobacco to pay for his purchases. The use of tobacco as money was not barter.

In the public warehouses, to which the farmers delivered their tobacco, were two inspectors of tobacco who were appointed by the Governor upon recommendation of the court of the county in which the warehouse was located. The inspectors were bonded and under oath to conform to regulations governing the sale of tobacco. All tobacco offered for sale in Virginia was required to pass inspection. It was a violation of the law to load uninspected tobacco on boats for shipment abroad or to carry uninspected tobacco into Maryland or North Carolina for sale. After examining and weighing the tobacco, the inspectors gave to the seller promissory notes for the full quantity of the tobacco received. These notes stated whether the tobacco was sweet-scented or Oronoko, whether it was stemmed or leaf, and gave the date it had passed inspection. The inspectors were required to give the seller as many notes as he asked. A person who delivered a hogshead of tobacco of the minimum weight, 950 pounds, could receive, for example, five notes for one hundred pounds, six notes for fifty pounds, four notes for twenty-five pounds, and five notes for ten pounds. He was thus able to get notes for his tobacco in denominations most convenient for his own use, just as a person now may get when cashing checks in money denominations convenient for his uses. These notes, covering tobacco delivered to the warehouse for sale and shipment to England, were used as money to pay obligations and were received in settlement of accounts. The Virginia Assembly stipulated which warehouse notes would be legal in each county. The notes of a warehouse were legal in the county in which the warehouse was located, but the upper counties did not have warehouses. An act of 1748 made notes of all warehouses on the south side of the James above Jordan's Point legal for the payment of public, county, or parish levies, for quit-rents, and of fees of public and county officials in Amelia and Lunenburg Counties. A rebate was allowed in Amelia and other upper counties of thirty pounds of tobacco for every hundred pounds due. That is, if a person's taxes amounted to one hundred pounds of tobacco, he was required to pay only seventy. Warehouses were built by individuals and then rented for public use at rental fees fixed by the Assembly. A rental fee of eight pence per hogshead was allowed in most warehouses, though a stated fee for the year was set for some. The inspector charged a fee of three shillings per hogshead for his services. Out of these fees his fixed annual salary was paid. Income in excess of the inspectors' salaries was paid into a general fund, which was used to pay the salaries of inspectors when the fees were insufficient to provide them.

There were several warehouses, notes of which were payable in Amelia: Bolling's Point, Maycock's, and Jordan's in Prince George County, Warwick and Col. John Bolling's in Henrico; and after November 9, 1748, John Osborne and Rocky Ridge.[1]

After the creation of Prince Edward County had been authorized by the Assembly, an act was passed listing the warehouses, the notes of which should pass in the new county in payment of levies, fees, and quit-rents: Bolling's-point, Blandford, John Bolling's, Byrd's, Warwick, Osborne's, Shoccoe's, and Rockyridge. Prince Edward people were also given an "abatement" on quit-rents and fees paid to officials; for every hundred pounds of tobacco due for such payment, the person paying was permitted to retain thirty pounds.[2] This abatement was discontinued in 1765.[3]

The act of 1765 made notes of the following warehouses legal for the payment of public obligations in Prince Edward: Blandford, Bollings Point, Bollingbroke, John Bolling's, Warwick, Osborne, Rocky Ridge, Shockoe's, and Byrd's.[4] Blandford was adjacent to Petersburg; Shockoe's was in Richmond; Warwick was a town in Chesterfield County on the lower Appomattox, an important trading

place in colonial times; Osborne's and Rocky Ridge were also in
Chesterfield. The warehouses were on waters navigable by ocean-
going vessels; from the warehouses tobacco could be shipped directly
to England.

A transaction between Robert Cowan and Richard Burks of Prince
Edward shows how the tobacco notes were used in selling tobacco.
Cowan bought twenty-one tobacco notes from Burks. They were
listed thus:

Number of Note	Pounds of Tobacco	Warehouse	Inspector
1446	1135	Bolling Brook	John Watkins
1447	1138	" "	" "
173	983	Blandford	Thomas Austin
255	960	"	" "
775	1210	"	" "
776	1100	"	" "
1127	1174	"	" "
1128	1162	"	" "
1863 (stemmed)	1170	"	" "
	10032	at 22 s ---- £110.7.0	
1397	1171	Bolling Brook	Richard Beasely
1126	1049	" "	" "
1127	1061	" "	" "
2202	1130	Col. Bolling	Thomas Edwards
2203	1225	" "	" "
1891	1101	" "	Miner Wilks
2008	1158	Osborne's	John Lea
33	1182	Warwick	Carter Braxton
34	1161	"	" "
35	1196	"	" "
	11434	at 21/6 ----£122. 18. 3	
1713	1112	Osborne's	James Mitchell
1967	1137	"	" "
	2249	@ 21 shillings ---- £23. 12. 3	

Total   £256. 17. 6

To Douglas Hamilton: 23. 12. 3
To R. Cowan: 46. 18. 10½   70. 11. 1½
                                        ———————
                          Balance   £186.   6.   4½[5]

Burks apparently received only one note for each hogshead of tobacco which he delivered to the warehouses. On the basis of the inspection, Cowan bought his tobacco notes, paying him twenty-two shillings per hundred for one lot, twenty-one shillings sixpence for another, and twenty-one shillings for the third. Burks then discharged his obligations to Hamilton and Cowan and received the balance left from the sale.

Prince Edward people shared in at least three petitions for additional inspections of tobacco. One was presented to the House of Burgesses in May, 1770, from freeholders from Prince George, Dinwiddie, Amelia, Brunswick, Lunenburg, Mecklenburg, Charlotte, Prince Edward, and Sussex; it asked for an additional inspection at Colonel Robert Bolling's in Blandford, because the large quantity of tobacco brought to the warehouses on the Appomattox made it impossible for the inspectors to inspect tobacco promptly. The petition was reported as reasonable, but it was not until 1772 that a bill establishing an inspection of tobacco on the land of Robert Bolling at Cedar Point was passed.[6]

In March, 1773, a petition from Chesterfield, Cumberland, Amelia, Buckingham, Bedford, and Prince Edward asked for an additional inspection in Manchester, because so much tobacco was being brought to Rocky Ridge in Manchester that the inspectors could not "execute their offices with proper dispatch." Within a week after the petition had been presented, the inspection was established.[7]

In the third petition inhabitants of Bedford, Pittsylvania, Lunenburg, and Amelia joined with those of Prince Edward in asking for an inspection on the land of Archibald Walthall or on some other lot in the town of Gatesville, "where there is a good landing," because the inspectors at Osbornes had more tobacco brought to them than they could inspect promptly. This petition was referred to the Committee on Propositions and Grievances, but on the same day (May 26, 1774) the Governor dissolved the Assembly, because a paper published by the House of Burgesses reflected "highly upon his Majesty and the Parliament of Great Britain."[8]

While some tobacco from Prince Edward was hauled to the warehouses on wagons, some went to the warehouses on the Appomattox by canoe. The river may not have been used as much in the two decades between the founding of the county and the outbreak of the Revolution as it had been earlier. But navigation of the Appomattox was talked, and during the Revolution the hope was expressed that the legislature would take steps to clear the river and make it suitable for navigation. Even then some people were carrying tobacco from some distance above the mouth of Buffalo to Banister's mill near Petersburg, "and the canoe men say it is a much better river to carry tobacco down than James River."[9] William Simmons paid into the Prince Edward treasury seventy pounds of tobacco which was the reward allowed Thomas Caldwell for taking up Simmons' Negro boatswain.[10]

While the advertisements of land for sale in Prince Edward stress the suitability of the land for tobacco, some mention the peach and apple orchards and one advertised a "remarkable fine orchard from which 1300 gallons of Brandy may be made in a season."[11] A typical advertisement was that of Matthews Flournoy, who in 1766 advertised his farm of 789 acres at the head of "Briar" River in Prince Edward: exceeding good soil for tobacco, fresh land cleared sufficient to work ten hands, dwelling house with brick chimneys, all convenient outhouses, plenty of good tobacco houses on the land, good apple and peach orchards, a new overshot grist mill.[12]

Grain, both wheat and corn, was produced in substantial quantity in colonial Prince Edward. It provided food for man and stock, and the comparatively numerous mills show the importance of the grain production.

The construction of grist mills was licensed by the county court. Prior to authorizing the construction, the court would authorize the sheriff to summon a jury and view the site and assess damages to any property owner other than the petitioner which a mill-pond would involve. Permission was granted by the Prince Edward Court to the following persons to build mills: Robert Baker, orphan of Robert Baker, Jr., to build at or near where Robert Baker's mill stood, 1763;[13] Zachariah Leigh, 1765;[14] Nathaniel and Abraham Venable, on the Appomattox River, 1766;[15] William Ligon, on Sandy River, 1766;[16] Francis Watkins, on Briery River, 1769;[17] John Leigh, on Mountain Creek, 1770;[18] Thomas Redd, on Vaughan's Creek, 1771;[19] John Crenshaw, 1771;[20] Richard Thomason, on Mountain Creek, 1772;[21] William Gooch, on Snail's Creek, 1774;[22] William Watts, Mountain Creek, 1774.[23]

Many more petitions for mills were presented. Inquisitions were ordered for many, but it does not appear whether or not the license to build was granted. Samuel Wallace's petition for a mill on Falling Creek in 1766 was rejected after the jury found it would damage six acres of land and timber above the mill site.[24] Caleb Baulding had a mill, which William Harrison petitioned to rebuild in 1769.[25] Martain's Mill was in the county in 1769.[26]

An effort was made to grow hemp in Prince Edward. Its cultivation was encouraged by the payment of a bounty on its production and manufacture. Joel Watkins presented two certificates "for hemp he has manufactured and made" to the April, 1767, Court.[27] A month later he produced a certificate for 1,305 pounds of hemp of his manufacture.[28] Obadiah Woodson presented a certificate for 582 pounds of hemp in September,[29] and Manness McFeiley a certificate for 731 pounds in November, 1767.[30] Watkins manufactured 1,344 pounds in 1769,[31] and in 1771 Henry Walker manufactured 1,214 pounds.[32]

The farm in colonial times was usually as nearly self-supporting as a Virginia farm could be made. Some farms had stills, the usual product of which was brandy. The inventory of Thomas Caldwell's estate (1774) includes a still worm and head valued at £25. Other items in this inventory show the equipment early Prince Edward farmers used: one wagon and hind gears, one plow, two sets of irons, one three-horse tree and three olivets, one hand saw, four augurs, one hammer and chisel, two small rings and two wedges, one trowel, four old casks and a runlet (a small barrel, sometimes spelled rundlet), bells, bridles, and wagon harness, three axes, three hoes, and one drawknife, two smoothing irons, two pot racks, one gun, powder horn, and shot bag, one grubbing hoe and old irons, hogsheads, three harrows, two saddles, a cutting knife, old iron tools.

His livestock included three hogs (a smaller number than one usually finds on farms in those days), fifteen sheep, four cows, two yearlings, and two heifers, a bay mare valued at £8, two bay horses, and a black horse, geese and ducks, and, this appears the most likely classification, a beehive.

Also on hand was a supply of products: ten and one-half gallons of brandy, a piece of woolen cloth, eight barrels of corn, hay, oats, flax, and Indian fodder. The crop of tobacco had evidently been sold.

In the house the appraisers found two spinning-wheels and spools, six pots, a pair of tongs, a tub, pewter dishes and basins, tea cups, candlesticks, a looking-glass, thre beds and furniture, a chest, a table, chairs, a flax haskel, a loom, jugs, bottles, a case of knives and forks, and a parcel of old books valued at seventeen shillings.[33]

The inventory of Douglas Baker's personal property, made in 1765, shows some additional items: among household furnishings, books, valued at £3:11:6, tables, chests, chests of drawers, chair, looking-glass, tea "acquepage," pewter, brass, copper, beds and furniture, guns, pot racks, table linen, flax and cotton wheels and cheke reels, earthenware and copper vessels. Supplies on hand included wool and flax to the value of £1:6:9. Farm equipment included plow irons, traces, smith's tools, bells, men's and women's saddles, and the inevitable "old irons," as well as "other plantation utenshals." Horses, mares, and colts were valued at £31, cows at £13:10, and sheep and hogs at £5:11. The Negroes were valued at £135, and there was the substantial, for the times, amount of £74:5:11 due on bonds and open accounts.[34]

The farm and household equipment indicates that there was plenty to do both indoors and out. Spinning-wheels and looms show that thread was spun and cloth woven at home for the clothing the household. Some materials were bought, but much of the clothing, as well as food, was grown and processed at home.

Slaves, indentured servants, the individuals themselves and members of their families provided the labor which operated the early farms. Early lists of tithables show a considerable number of people without slaves. Two of the three lists of tithables (those for the areas between Bush and Buffalo and west of Buffalo) for 1755 remain; in the two lists Colonel Randolph is charged with more tithables than any other person; of the twenty-nine, twenty-seven appear to be slaves; the property on which these slaves and apparently two overseers were located was west of Buffalo River. Abraham Venable with twelve tithes had the next largest number, of whom eight were slaves. John Martin was third with ten tithables, of whom eight appear to be slaves. Richard Woodson had listed nine tithables, as did Colonel Charles Anderson. Pugh Price, Sr., also had nine tithables, seven of whom were slaves. Of James Walker's eight tithes, five were slaves. Listed with seven tithables were Thomas Scott, Jr., six of whom seem to have been slaves; James Wimbish with five slaves; John Watson, who had six slaves; and Robert Bird, with four slaves. Listed with six tithables each were Jacob Williamson, with five slaves; David Flournoy, with five slaves; Peter Davis, with five slaves; Thomas Baldwin, with three; John LeNeve, with five; Thomas Stone, with four; Charles Venable, with four; Captain Innes, with five, the sixth being apparently his overseer. There were several listed with five tithables: Matthews Flournoy, with two slaves; Guy Smith, with three; Peter LeGrand, all five of those tithables listed at the place between Bush and Buffalo were slaves; Theodorick Carter, with three slaves; Colonel Richard Randolph, an overseer and four slaves; Douglas Baker, three slaves; Obadiah Woodson, an overseer and four slaves;. Martha Baker, four slaves; Robert Baker, three slaves.[35] The section of the county for which the 1755 list is missing lay east of Bush River; subsequent lists show that similar conditions obtained there at this time. These lists show a steadily increasing number of slaves in the county, an increase explained by natural causes and by purchase of additional slaves.

Slaves were sold at public auction in Prince Edward along with other forms on property on court days and at special sales. "A parcel of choice slaves, house carpenters, sawyers, house wenches, and ground negroes" was offered at auction at the November, 1768, Court.[36] In disposing of the estate of the Hon. Philip Grymes, his executors brought 140 slaves, "including several good tradesmen and some valuable house servants" to Prince Edward Courthouse and offered them for sale on Thursday, December 20, 1770. "Proper allowance made for ready money" was offered those who paid in cash, although credit until June Court was allowed, and "notes of merchants" and "their bills of exchanges" would be received in payment.[37]

In Prince Edward were to be found some slaves who had come directly from Africa. From the emphasis given "Virginia-born slaves" in the advertisements, it seems that these were regarded as more desirable purchases, no doubt because they had been trained for farm work or some trade. Their understanding of the English language also was a factor. Two of four runaway slaves from Robert Donald's Prince Edward plantation in 1775 were African-born slaves; one was described as speaking badly, the other as speaking "very broken English." A third of these runaways was a native of Jamaica.[38] It appears from this that some Prince Edward Negroes were brought from the West Indies. Thomas Tabb of Amelia, a merchant whose business extended into Prince Edward, with John Wayles imported Negroes from Africa; they advertised in the *Virginia Gazette* of May 25, 1769: "Just arrived in James River from Africa, the ship *Amelia*, Thomas Duncomb, master, with about 230 fine healthy slaves, men, women, and children, sale of which will begin at Bermuda Hundred, Tuesday, 6th of June next."[39]

Slaves in colonial times ran away far more frequently than one might suppose. Provision was made to allow persons who took up runaways seventy pounds of tobacco and expenses of caring for them, which was paid by the county, but which the owner of the slave reimbursed the county on claiming his slave. Three claims for taking up runaways were allowed by the August, 1754, Court. One of these runaways was from Brunswick County; the home of the others is not listed, although the names of the masters are.⁴⁰ In 1758 claims for taking up a slave from Goochland and another from Brunswick were allowed.⁴¹ In 1767 Richard Woodson took up runaway slaves from Caroline, Gloucester, and Essex Counties, and in the same year Reese Osborne took up one from Chesterfield; Noel Waddell one from Bedford and one of James Smith's of Prince Edward; Matthews Flournoy one from Bedford and one from Charlotte; John Thomas Dejarnett a slave of Thomas Haskins of Prince Edward and Haskins took up one from Amelia; and Joseph Ward took up a runaway from Amelia.⁴²

Among the runaways from Prince Edward was a slave of John Nash, Sr., who was taken up in Amelia in 1758.⁴³ William Simmons' runaway boatswain has already been mentioned. Richard Woodson advertised for a runaway in 1766, offering in addition to the legally prescribed allowance two pistoles for his Virginia-born slave.⁴⁴ Benjamin Wimbish advertised for "a white mulatto man slave named Toby, and about 23, of middle stature, spare made, grey eyes, light curled hair, little or no beard, stoops in shoulders of brisk motion, difference in thumbs, small scar on face, brought up to planter's business," who ran away June 19, 1771, whom he expected to pass as a free man and possibly as a white man. He offered an additional reward of ten pounds if the slave were taken up in North Carolina and five pounds if taken up in Virginia.⁴⁵ The most persistently sought slave from Prince Edward, at least in the public print, was Windsor, a fourteen-year-old slave of William Watts. Windsor had been Watts' body servant and had evidently traveled rather widely with his master, who was a lawyer. The boy was a "sensible and artful fellow, about five feet high, handsome lively look, speaks quick." He was taken up in York County, jailed in spite of his protest that he was free, but broke out of jail. Watts suspected that he was hidden by his father in New Kent or by someone near Williamsburg, where he was reported as having been seen. Watts also suspected that the boy would try to board ship to escape from

Virginia and warned masters of vessels against taking him. He advertised for the boy at intervals from August, 1770, to November, 1771.[46]

As the advertisements described the dress of runaways, they tell how slaves dressed in that period. Woodson's slave wore an old German serge coat, a fine linen shirt, and oznaburg breeches.[47] Watts' boy wore a blue broadcloth sleeveless jacket, an Irish linen shirt, and oznaburg breeches. He had evidently carefully planned his escape, for he took with him a brown Holland coat, a blue broadcloth waistcoat, two white linen shirts, two pair of oznaburg breeches, and good shoes and stockings.[48] A runaway slave of Robert Lawson in 1774 wore or carried with him an upper jacket made of blanket, an underjacket of negro (black) cotton, an oznaburg shirt, a pair of blue velvet breeches, but had neither shoes nor stockings.[49]

Sometimes the runaway got into trouble, as did the slave of Edward Wood of Prince Edward, who was taken up in Chesterfield, charged with, convicted of, and executed for a capital crime, of all of which his master was ignorant. The Chesterfield Court valued him at seventy-five pounds, not knowing that he was a skilled carpenter; upon Wood's petition for additional allowance, the House of Burgesses raised it to 100 pounds.[50]

In addition to living in the prospect of economic loss through failure to apprehend a runaway slave, the owners, their families, and neighbors lived in continuing apprehension of an insurrection. The part of the patroller in keeping on the lookout has already been mentioned. Insurrections came only rarely, however, only two in Virginia, Gabriel's in Goochland County in 1800, and Nat Turner's in Southampton in 1832, having been of consequence. In 1775 a slave of John Baulding of Prince Edward was accused of conspiring to murder his mistress and to raise an insurrection. He was acquitted on these charges, but found guilty of another which was not specified and was given for it fifteen lashes.[51]

These runaways and the offenses charged to slaves in the criminal records were, however, the exception. Prince Edward slaves were generally faithful, and some were conspicuously industrious. There were skilled persons among them in the various crafts useful in that day: blacksmithing, carpentry, bricklaying, operating mills and brandy stills, to mention a few. The bulk of them worked in the fields, cultivating tobacco and corn and the other crops. In most instances, because the master owned only a few, the slave did all kinds of work about the farm, working in the crop, doing chores around the house and stable. While some were dissatisfied with their lot, most of them accepted it philosophically and remained faithful in return for the care provided and in many instances the friendship which masters and their families gave. The slave who had a good master, who fed him well, clothed him warmly, and provided him decent lodging, undoubtedly regarded his lot as better than it had been in Africa, where his own kind had captured him and sold him to the slave trader. In some, of course, the desire for freedom burned strongly, outweighing whatever advantages of economic security they might have enjoyed.

In addition to slaves, there were both indentured and convict servants in Prince Edward. The indentured servant sold his services to a master in return for some favor or service which he could not provide for himself. Many people sold their services for a term of years to some person who paid the cost of their transportation to the New World. The convict servant was one who had been convicted of some crime, but who was released to the custody of the person whom he served.

Indentures binding a person could be transferred from one master to another. Dorcas Jackson complained to the Prince Edward Court in 1758 of the ill usage she received from her master, Samuel Wallace. It was found that Wallace was the third person to hold the indentures binding her; she had been bound by the church wardens of St. Paul's Parish, Hanover, to Edward Wade. She next was in servitude to Rice Hughes, who endorsed the indenture to Wallace. Wade, however, had not endorsed the indenture to Hughes, so the Court held the endorsement not sufficient to keep Dorcas Jackson in servitude, freed her, and decreed that she recover the costs of her suit; she was directed to pay John Caldwell, Letitia Caldwell, and William Crockett, her witnesses, fifty pounds of tobacco each for two days' attendance at the court.[52]

If the indented (the term is used interchangeably with indentured) servant ran away and was found, he was required to serve additional time for that lost. In 1764 an indented man servant was required to serve 119 days above the time stipulated in the indenture binding him to John Hill for absenting himself from service.[53] In 1772 an indented woman servant of Henry Caldwell was required to serve 270 days extra for "abscond[ing] from his service."[54] An Irish servant man, indented to John Thompson, Jr., ran away, wearing a brown linen shirt and jacket, duffil breeches, a felt hat, but was barefoot.[55]

John Leitch of Warwick advertised for a convict servant who was a weaver by trade and who had run away from Prince Edward in October or November, 1772. A reward of thirty shillings was offered if the man, one of whose identifications was his strong Welsh accent, was returned to Leitch or to Henry Benskin Lightfoot in Prince Edward.[56] A convict servant of Christopher Curtis ran away in 1774; a native of Bristol, the servant spoke good English and was a shoemaker by trade. His speech was better than his chirography, however, for his master, supposing that the servant would forge a pass, added that he could "write a blotched hand." The servant wore an old blue coat, a striped waistcoat, and spotted stockings.[57]

The status of the apprentice belongs somewhere between servitude and education. Children, both boys and girls, were bound as apprentices to learn some useful trade. The master received the service of the apprentice, but in return had to take care of him and teach him a trade. Poor children were bound by the church wardens, and the indentures were under the supervision of the court. The periods for which children were bound apprentices were sometimes quite long. One boy, son of an indented woman servant, in 1773 was bound twenty-one years to his mother's master, John Caldwell;[58] he may have been an infant at the time. A girl was bound fourteen years, with her father's consent, as apprentice to Alexander Frazier in 1772.[59] One indenture presented in court showed that a woman had been indented to Miller Woodson until she was thirty-one years of age.[60] The apprentice could have his day in court. Upon the complaint of his mother, a boy indented as apprentice to Charles Rice had this indenture cancelled with an order to the church wardens to bind him out to someone else.[61] On two occasions, once in 1767 and again in 1769, apprentices of George Walker complained about him, and he was summoned to court to answer; no disposition is recorded in either case,[62] as was none in the case of the complaint of an apprentice against John Thomas Dejarnett, who also was summoned to explain.[63] Apprentices were bound to learn various trades; the cooper's trade was designated in one case.[64] Apprentices, too, sometimes ran away; when John Thompson, Jr., advertised for his runaway indented servant, he also advertised for a runaway apprentice boy, who like the servant left barefoot; his clothing consisted of an oznaburg shirt, Russian drill breeches, and a negro cotton coat.[65]

Today's youngsters thoroughly familiar with the practice of branding cattle on the Western ranges may be surprised to learn that their ancestors in colonial Prince Edward also branded their livestock—horses, as well as cattle. Branding was necessary for identification of animals which strayed, as they frequently did. The *Virginia Gazette* abounds in advertisements of strayed horses which were found; more advertisements of this nature appeared than any other type of advertisement from Prince Edward. The brand was given as a part of the identification, though occasionally the animal had not been branded. Many Prince Edward residents had their brands or marks, as they called them then, recorded. The first on record was that of John Martin, and his brand, recorded in October, 1754, was a cross and two slits in each ear.[66]

The horse served a dual purpose: he was a work animal and he was also a riding animal. The only transportation many people had was to ride horseback. Some of the more well-to-do Prince Edward people had carriages. A popular type of vehicle in colonial times was the chaise, which was called then a chair. These were taxed, and from the failure of five people to list their "chairs" for taxes in 1771 we know five owners of such: Peter LeGrand, George Walton, James Scott, Jesse Hughes Walton, and Andrew French. All paid the prescribed fine for failing to list this item of property for taxation.[67] Much of the heavier work on the plantation was done by oxen. They were used for the heavier plowing, for the rougher hauling. Strong and steady, though slow, a yoke of oxen was invaluable to the colonial farmer.

By the beginning of the Revolution, the people of Prince Edward had become interested in blooded horses. William and Edward Watts brought the first blooded horse to the county for breeding purposes of which there is record. *Junius,* a beautiful bay stallion, belonged to Edward Watts, but was kept by his brother William. *Junius'* first season in Prince Edward was in 1776, when he was six years old. He had been bred by Nathaniel Harrison. His sire was the race-horse *Yorick* which belonged to Colonel Tayloe. The sire of *Junius'* dam was *Othello,* described as "as high a bred horse as ever came to America"; the sire of *Junius'* granddam was *Money,* an imported horse, whose dam was "an old Spanish running mare" imported by Colonel Nathaniel Harrison's father. *Junius* was advertised as having "distinguished himself by the activity and symmetry of form of his colts." The fee charged in 1776 were twenty shillings, with a season fee of forty shillings. In 1777 the season's fee was increased to three pounds and the insurance from four to five pounds. Good pasturage was provided for mares, though the Watts brothers declined to assume responsibility for those which got away or were stolen.[68]

The people of Prince Edward depended upon the fish caught in the Appomattox River and its tributaries as an important source of food. As milldams were built across the Appomattox, the fish supply was reduced to the extent that the people in 1761 petitioned the Assembly to require owners of milldams to put slopes in their milldams to permit the passage of fish upstream.[69] This petition was supplemented by petitions from Brunswick and Lunenburg making a similar complaint about milldams in the Meherrin and Nottoway Rivers. The Assembly in 1761 passed a law requiring owners of dams in those rivers to construct an opening or slope at least ten feet wide sufficient for the passage of fish.[70] This act was amended in 1762 to provide that the length of the opening be at least three times the height of the dam, that the bottom and sides of the opening be planked, the sides at least fourteen inches deep to admit a current of water at least twelve inches deep between February 10 and May 31. This act included provision for building locks for the passage of boats and canoes, and Archibald Cary, Richard Eppes, Thomas Tabb, Robert Bolling, Peter LeGrand, Ryland Randolph, Thomas Nash, William Archer, Christopher Hudson, Alexander Trent, and John Morton were named trustees for the clearing of the Appomattox.[71]

The early settlers found the abundant wild game as well as the fish a desirable supplement to the food they could raise.

The Prince Edward mercantile scene was dominated by Scotch merchants in colonial times. Early firms operating stores in the county included Robert Hastie and Company, Archibald Buchanan John Bowman and Company (1757),[72] Alexander Spiers John Bowman and Company (1762),[73] Robert and James Donald and Company (1764).[74] Andrew French operated a store for Alexander Spiers and Company at what is now Kingsville,[75] apparently succeeding his brother James French as manager about 1767.[76] French left the county about 1772 and was replaced in the management of the store of Alexander Spiers John Bowman and Company by Andrew McKenzie. Andrew French left the colony in 1774.[77] McKenzie was succeeded as manager on September 1, 1773, by James Cross.[78] Dreghorn, Murdock and Company of Glasgow had a store in Prince Edward. Henry Benskin Lightfoot was succeeded as its manager by John Graham in 1774.[79]

Miller Woodson kept a store in the eastern part of the county, apparently for Robert and James Donald, whose headquarters were at Warwick in Chesterfield County.[80] Robert Routledge and John Pleasants were partners in a store prior to Routledge's murder in

1766.[81] Nathaniel Venable and Company was a locally owned firm which was in business in 1772.[82] There is mention in 1770 of a store "lately kept" by Richard Burks;[83] the store was sold about 1768 to the Donald firm.[84] Archibald Buchanan was living in the county and operating his store in 1763.[85] Buchanan and Company, which had a store at the present Kingsville where the church at Robin's Spring was built, were described as "merchants of Glasgow."[86] Peter Johnston seems to have had connections with Hyndman and Company, London merchants.[87]

Peter Johnston in 1769 advertised for sale in the lower end of Prince Edward 150 acres of land on which were a storehouse, a counting house and lodging room with brick chimneys, a warehouse, a tailor's shop, a smith's shop, a convenient house for an ordinary, and all other necessary houses, located "on a very publick road, commodiously situated for trade and ordinary keeping."[88]

One practice of the colonial era on which this age looks with horror was the treatment of debtors. The Prince Edward court orders record imprisonment for debt. The debtor then remained in the county jail for at least twenty days; then he could come into court, take the oath of an insolvent debtor, render a schedule of his estate, and be discharged from custody. At least four persons were imprisoned for debt in Prince Edward between 1764 and 1774. One of these was a woman, who rendered to the July, 1766, Court a pathetically meager list of property: one feather bed and furniture, one iron pot, one pair of pot hooks, one woolen wheel, one pair of cards (for working with wool), one pair of shears, one small chest, one candlestick.[89]

Provision for the support of insolvents was made in the county levy. In 1770 there were forty-nine insolvents in the county.[90] Evidently not all these had been imprisoned for debt. Imprisonment usually followed a suit for judgment which the debtor was unable to pay.[91]

Mail service to colonial Prince Edward seems to have been uncertain. The nearest post offices seem to have been Petersburg and Warwick. People were expected to call for or send for their mail to these places, it would appear from the advertisements of letters being held there for them. In 1767 a letter was held for Walter Spence of Prince Edward at the Petersburg post office; four letters for Peter Johnston were held at the Warwick post office at the same time, and also at the Warwick office there were held letters addressed to Captain Theodorick Munford and John Moor of Prince Edward.[92]

Owners of land in Prince Edward who lived outside the county usually employed overseers to look after their property, manage their slaves, and cultivate the land. The lists of tithables give the names of a number of overseers. In some instances people employed overseers for the property where they lived. An agreement between John Leigh and his overseer, Thomas Owen, in 1762 indicates what an overseer received for his work. Under this contract Leigh paid Owen two shares of corn, wheat, and tobacco; eight pounds cash; and 600 pounds of pork and beef.[93] The lists of tithables indicate that a working force of approximately ten slaves was considered a fair responsibility for an overseer. The 1769 list for William Randolph shows that there were five overseers for his Prince Edward holdings: one had ten slaves, one twelve, a third eleven, a fourth eleven, and a fifth ten.[94] John Leigh's contract lists ten slaves, presumably those he was assigning to his overseer. Some of the men listed in the lists of tithables as overseers later became men of property and influence; one of the Randolph overseers in 1769 had been appointed a magistrate before the close of the Revolution. A prudent man could use the opportunity, it is evident from the Leigh contract, to save money with which to buy land and slaves for himself. Many indented servants, too, after their terms of service acquired property and became persons of respectable standing. Except for slaves, the lines dividing social classes in colonial times were rather fluid. A person who by industry and economy acquired means and who by bearing and respectable conduct showed himself of gentlemanly instincts, regardless of lowly origin, could become accepted in the highest circles of society.

The lottery was a form of legal gambling in colonial times. Worthy causes even used lotteries to finance themselves. The promoter of a lottery would determine his needs, then add to them a sum to be distributed in prizes in sufficient amount to make participation in the lottery attractive. He would divide the total into small amounts, which he would charge for a ticket. The drawing would take place at the stipulated time, and tickets drawn to the number determined would be declared winners. The first drawn tickets might win substantial prizes. Joseph Calvert of Norfolk promoted a lottery in 1767; to make certain a wide distribution of tickets, he appointed managers in various parts of the colony. Peter LeGrand was Calvert's manager in Prince Edward, selling tickets for him.[95]

Little is known of the schools of colonial Prince Edward. John Thomson who is credited with being the county's first schoolmaster had already left the Buffaloe Settlement before Prince Edward County was organized. William Capples was teaching a school in Prince Edward in the 1760's, which apparently had a good and wide reputation among the Scotch-Irish settlers. To this school in 1761, after the end of the French and Indian War, came two students from western North Carolina, Ephraim Brevard and his cousin, Adlai Osborne.[96] There was a schoolhouse on Obadiah Woodson's land, which in 1762 was selected as the site for a chapel.

The coming of Presbyterian ministers who had been educated at the College of New Jersey, better known as Princeton from its location and present name, resulted in the formation of close ties between the "back parts" of Virginia and North Carolina and the New Jersey institution. The incompleteness of the early Princeton records makes it impossible to ascertain the homes of all the students in those days, but they show that Caleb Baker Wallace of the class of 1770 came from Prince Edward. He was a son of Samuel Wallace and his mother Esther was a daughter of Caleb Baker. Father and maternal grandfather were Prince Edward pioneers.[97]

At least one young Prince Edward man attended the College of William and Mary in the colonial period. Francis Scott, son of Colonel Thomas Scott of Prince Edward, was on March 25, 1771, charged board to this date, £18:1:2, at the college.[98] The amount suggests that he was a student there during the 1770-71 session.

There was a Dr. Foster practicing in Prince Edward in 1755, when the parish levy included an item of five pounds paid to him for salivating a person, evidently an indigent. The fee suggests that he may have lived at some distance.[99]

The practice of Dr. William Cabell, who lived in the section of Albemarle (later Amherst) which is now Nelson County, extended into Prince Edward. Since his fees ranged from one to five pounds, depending on the distance he had to travel, his services must have been expensive for the Prince Edward patient.[100]

Though no physician is known to have lived in Prince Edward prior to the Revolution, one of its residents made quite a stir in the medical world. In the 1760's the word spread that Mrs. Constant Woodson of Prince Edward could cure cancer. In 1766 Thomas Dosson, address unknown, advertised in the *Virginia Gazette* that Mrs. Woodson had cured him of a cancer on his neck, which a physician had diagnosed as one of the worst of cancers and gave the patient no hope of recovery.[101]

A month after Dosson's advertisement appeared, Mrs. Woodson

petitioned the Assembly for a reward for her discovery, which she promised to reveal to the public if a reasonable reward was forthcoming. The House of Burgesses took a cautious course; it was not willing to run the risk of losing so valuable a contribution to medical science as Mrs. Woodson might be in a position to make; on the other hand, there were risks involved. The House decided to give Mrs. Woodson £100 upon her presentation of a certificate from Drs. Theodorick Bland, James Field, William Black, and Robert Brown, or any two of them, that her method was a reliable cancer cure; the four physicians were directed to experiment with Mrs. Woodson's remedy. The Governor signed the bill April 11, 1767.[102] It appears that the physicians did not endorse Mrs. Woodson's cure, for there is no indication that the reward was paid.

Mrs. Woodson advertised her cure in 1768 and invited all doctors of medicine, especially Dr. Brown of Southampton and Dr. Walker of Hanover, to advise their cancer patients of her and to certify to her their diagnosis of cancer by the patient. The advertisement noted that she was "successful in curing cancers."[103]

Meanwhile James Kirk of Augusta County had advertised in a letter written November 27, 1767, that Mrs. Woodson had made "a perfect cure" of a cancer in his wife's breast, which had first been noticed as a lump twelve years before and which had burst before she went to Mrs. Woodson. Mrs. Kirk had consulted a number of physicians, including Dr. Cabell, all of whom told her there was no cure for it.[104] By June, 1768, however, Mrs. Kirk had taken a decided turn for the worse; Mr. Kirk felt constrained to set the public aright, since Mrs. Woodson was claiming that she had cured several women, including Mrs. Kirk, of cancer. Becoming worse after the treatment, Mrs. Kirk again consulted physicians who advised her that her condition had been aggravated by "improper medicines" used by Mrs. Woodson. At the time, Mrs. Kirk had been confined to bed over three months "in a languishing condition."[105]

Kirk's warnings apparently did not make too great an impression. The obituary of Anthony Hay, master of the Raleigh Tavern in Williamsburg, who died December 4, 1770, states that he died of cancer; he underwent several operations on his lip and face and then went to Prince Edward where he spent some time under the care of Mrs. Woodson, "famous for the cures she has made." Hay sought Mrs. Woodson's treatment too late, however, according to the account.[106]

The early Prince Edward inhabitant depended a great deal upon home treatment in cases of illnesses. Through experience in caring for the sick, many people, both men and women, developed a certain degree of skill in diagnosing illnesses and in prescribing home remedies. Often mistakes were made, but in simple illnesses such attention proved helpful.

The young couple in colonial Prince Edward included a practical as well as a romantic approach to courtship and marriage. This practical approach was detailed in the suit of a young couple against the wife's father who allegedly had failed to give them the property promised. Robert Martin and Elizabeth, his wife, brought suit against her father, Peter Johnston, in 1771. Isaac Read represented the plaintiffs, Paul Carrington the defendant.

Martin explained that he had been encouraged "to make addresses" to Miss Johnston under the prospect that her father "was to make her a fortune suitable to the said Robert's expectations." When Martin found his suit received with favor, he so advised his father, John Martin, in order that the fathers might work out the details of the practical settlement. The elder Martin wrote Johnston, "inquiring what portion he designed to give with his . . . daughter Elizabeth on her intermarriage with Robert."

Johnston replied to the inquiry:

"I have considered the proposed match between your Son and my Daughter, and am willing to make up her fortune to the Value of Five hundred pounds, but as I told you before it was not in my power to do it, til such times as I could Collect my Debts due me. I now repeat it again that no mistake may arise on that head, what I can do without Detriment to my present Scheme of life shall be done, and that as fast as possible, in the meantime I intend to buy a Couple of negro Girls or young wenches and give to her and will assist in fitting them out for housekeeping. If the above is agreeable to you, I make no doubt but it will be to them and be a great means of making both easy, as they can meet with no other Interruption in the plan of Happiness proposed to themselves."

Young Martin and his wife claimed that Johnston had refused to give them the £500 promised although often requested to do so. The case was postponed to the next Court,[107] but there is no record of further hearing. The case was evidently settled by agreement.

As regrettable as a family unpleasantness is, this suit gives a vivid picture of the financial arrangements which entered into a marriage agreement when bride and groom were members of families with property. Not every bride had the handsome dowry of £500 as this one, but parents helped young couples get established to the best of their ability. If the young man's father owned an extensive acreage, he could look to him for a farm and some livestock and farming implements. The bride's father might not have the cash, but his gift was frequently one of Negroes and household equipment, and perhaps some livestock. Sometimes gifts of property were not made on the occasion of marriage, but when the father wished to make such gifts. John Leigh in 1763 gave eight Negroes to his son, Zacharias Greenhill Leigh, six to his daughter Ellena Leigh, and seven to his daughter Elizabeth Leigh.[108] Edward McGehee, who lived in Cumberland but had large land holdings in Prince Edward, gave to each of several of his sons 700 acres of land in Prince Edward.[109] Such gifts, of land, Negroes, or other property, were often confirmed in the donor's will. Jacob McGehee gave to each of his children, daughters and sons, substantial tracts of land, some Negroes, livestock, farming equipment, and household furniture and utensils.[110] The aura of romance may linger about the colonial era, but it was a practical age. It had to be.

CHAPTER V

The Talk of the County

LET no one suppose that colonial Prince Edward lacked excitement beyond that normal to frontier living. Several events took place which would arouse interest and provoke comment were they to happen today; the early Prince Edward residents were as equally interested and as disposed to discuss them as this generation would be.

The event which created the greatest excitement in the county before the Revolution did not take place in Prince Edward, but it involved a popular resident. The murder of Robert Routledge, a popular Prince Edward merchant, by Colonel John Chiswell was more than another murder case. It probed more deeply into public feeling than a murder ordinarily would, for it involved class feeling and aroused a people already becoming jealous of their personal liberties and prompt to resent any threat to them.

The clearest account of the murder was given in the *Virginia Gazette* by a correspondent from Prince Edward who signed himself "Dikephilos"—friend to justice. Dikephilos was obviously a person of education, for he wrote well; he knew the people, for his letter expresses their viewpoint; he was courageous, for he refused to back down from his account when confronted with what obviously were testimonies designed to be favorable to Colonel Chiswell; withal, Dikephilos was eminently fair, although it was obvious he saw no excuse for Colonel Chiswell's conduct and none for the effort of some of his friends to shield him from the dispensation of justice.

Routledge, "a worthy, blunt man, of strict honesty and sincerity, a man incapable of fraud or hypocrisy," as Dikephilos described him, was at Benjamin Mosby's tavern at Cumberland Courthouse on June 3, 1766. He was joined in the evening by a good friend who was to be his bedfellow that night, according to one account. Routledge had been at the inn with friends for most of the day and had been drinking. His state of intoxication, however, was not sufficiently great for him not to notice and disapprove of Chiswell's rather liberal use of oaths in his talk. Although the men were intimate and regarded as friends, Chiswell resented the correction of a man he regarded his inferior; he then proceeded to abuse Routledge roundly, calling him " a fugitive rebel, a villain who came to Virginia to cheat and defraud men of their property, and a Presbyterian fellow" (which to a staunch Church of England man was an epithet along with the rest of them). Routledge threw a glass of wine in Chiswell's face; Chiswell tried to throw the bowl of toddy at Routledge, but was restrained by the company, and in turn a candlestick and tried to hit Routledge with the fireplace tongs, each time being prevented. Then he ordered his servant to bring him his sword on pain of being killed himself, and the servant obeyed. Joseph Carrington was taking the intoxicated Routledge, who had protested that he meant Chiswell no harm, from the room when he paused to get the key to the room to which he was taking Routledge; Routledge stepped to a table, and Chiswell reached across it with his sword and stabbed Routledge through the heart. As some witnesses later told it, to the disgust of Dikephilos and the contradiction of earlier testimony and other witnesses, Routledge walked into Chiswell's extended sword. Thompson Swann was standing near the table "with the breast of his coat projecting over it"; Chiswell's sword passed through Swann's coat near the third buttonhole from the bottom as it was thrust at Routledge's heart.

Chiswell was lodged in Cumberland jail and refused bail. The Cumberland Court, acting as an examining court in the case, sent the case to the General Court at Williamsburg and Chiswell, in custody of the county sheriff, Jesse Thomas, to the Publick Gaol there.

At this point public resentment began to rise. The King's Attorney left Cumberland on the day of the examination by the Court, leaving no representative "to interrogate for the Crown." Arrived in Williamsburg, Chiswell was given bail by three judges of the General Court, which was not then in session. The judges acted, it was charged, before they had examined witnesses or seen depositions of witnesses. It was not surprising that the public wrath flamed. Was the King's Attorney permitting his friendship for Colonel Chiswell to interfere with his duty to represent the Crown in the examination of those accused of crime? Were not the judges being guided by friendship rather than by principles of law and justice in the way in which they released Chiswell on bond?

Routledge's Prince Edward friends and others throughout the section were "extremely uneasy"; if one "atrocious murderer" escaped punishment through the influence of friends, they were "apprehensive that it [would] not be the last opprobrious stain of the kind on the colony." Dikephilos found "patriots alarmed, foreigners

alarmed, the middle and lower ranks of men acquainted with the particulars, extremely alarmed."

There were threats from Prince Edward: Routledge's neighbors, many of whom had enjoyed favors from "his humanity and bounty," said bluntly that "if the law be disregarded, violated, and trampled on, to save from justice the assassin of their worthy benefactor, they can never enjoy a moment's ease until they take proper revenge for the cruel and cowardly assassination." They promised to be quiet pending the outcome of the trial, but if there be "injustice and partiality . . ." Dikephilos' standing as a person of influence is at this point revealed in his statement that he persuaded Routledge's neighbors not to take matters to an extremity, although he "applauded their honest, grateful hearts."[1]

The conduct of the affair was warmly debated in the newspaper. Depositions of witnesses were published.[2] One Richard Hartswell in a letter which subsequent knowledge of events makes almost pathetic confessed to his anxiety over two manifestations of the sad state of affairs to which the world was coming: one of his friends, Mr. Robinson, the Colony's treasurer, had been charged with breach of trust; another, Mr. Chiswell, had been accused of willful murder. Mr. Hartswell had known both men for twenty-eight years; he found it impossible to suspect either of bringing blemish upon his name. As for the reported oaths of Colonel Chiswell at the time of the murder, he had never heard him use one, although he had been with Chiswell for days at his house in Hanover. But he would leave the outcome to the trial, glad if Chiswell's innocence should be established, but should he be proved guilty, he should bear the punishment.[3]

Meanwhile Colonel Chiswell who had given no outward indication of remorse[4] went about his business while free on bail. He returned to Williamsburg September 10 from his mines.[5] But Colonel Chiswell never came to trial in the General Court; death, not his high standing or his influential friends, prevented his coming to trial. On October 15 he died at his Williamsburg house after a short illness. Public feeling was still so high that the case had to be handled with the utmost discretion. Physicians testified under oath that death was caused by nervous fits, "owing to constant uneasiness of mind."[6] The physicians' testimony did not dispel the popular belief that there was another cause; in making notes from old newspapers in an almanac John Randolph of Roanoke noted concerning the item: "notwithstanding he is believed to have committed suicide."[7]

June, 1766, brought another exciting event, this one a family's remarkable experience during a storm which occurred on Saturday, June 14. The house of James Smith, a tailor, which was near some houses belonging to James French, the merchant, was struck by lightning. It struck the end opposite the chimney, which, incidentally, was of wood, shivered two pieces of studding above the plate and one piece below, melted the tin on the stirrup iron of a saddle hanging from two nails on the upper studding and tore the saddle to pieces, drew over 100 nails from the clap boards and some from the shingled roof, melted pewter basons, spoons, and plates on a shelf, and broke a looking-glass. The bolt did not stop at this, however. Mrs. Mary Smith, James Smith's wife was knocked down, the lightning leaving a trail of blisters down her body. She was lifeless for half an hour, could not speak for more than two hours, and did not stop having spells of unconsciousness until the following Wednesday. Although feeling "pretty well" since then, she was complaining of some pain the Sunday following. The box iron with which she was ironing when the bolt hit was not damaged, but a pair of sleeve buttons was not found afterward. Smith was struck across the thighs as he was sitting at his work board and required assistance in rising for some time after the experience. A young man resting on a feather bed in the room was slightly shocked about the legs. A boy about twelve or thirteen years of age who was sifting meal in the room had his hair singed, the hair of his right eyebrow and most of his right eyelashes burned off. The bolt left a trail of blisters from his forehead down his body to his thigh and tore to pieces his left trousers' leg. More impressive, perhaps, than the almost miraculous escape was the gratitude of James Smith and his wife. On Sunday, June 22, the couple publicly returned thanks for their deliverance from death. There is no finer picture standing out in all Prince Edward history than that of this pious couple going to the church (evidently the church at French's) and before the congregation expressing their gratitude to God that their lives has been spared in their terrifying experience.[8]

One event which left its mark on much of colonial Virginia Prince Edward escaped. That was the flood of May, 1771, described as "the greatest freshet in James River ever known," and even to this day one of the greatest floods that river has experienced. High water in the Rappahannock also reached record levels, and the damage on the Roanoke River was considered even greater than that on the James. Much tobacco and livestock were lost and over fifty people were drowned along the James, and from the valley of the Roanoke came news of ruined land and loss of Negroes, stock, and horses. The Appomattox, however, was little affected, since the heavy rains fell farther west than the headwaters of the stream which drains most of Prince Edward. There was little rain in Richmond, but wagoners from Augusta and Albemarle arriving in Richmond late in May reported rain every day of their twelve-day trip.[9]

Prince Edward played a leading part in the counterfeit money disturbance of 1773. The circulation of counterfeit money became known in January, 1773. Robert Carter Nicholas, treasurer of the colony, published a warning "against dangerous and ingenious forgeries of five-pound bills emitted in November, 1769, and July, 1771," and pointed out the differences between the genuine and the counterfeit. As soon as the situation became known, the Governor, Lord Dunmore, on the advice of the Council, summoned the Assembly to meet. He felt it necessary to do this because the credit of the paper currency of the two emissions had been destroyed by the counterfeiting.

After the Assembly had been summoned, a person from "one of the most remote counties" who had been associated with the counterfeiters informed the Governor of those involved in the counterfeiting and advised that if they were not apprehended shortly they would either assemble such a force of friends that they could with difficulty be taken or that they would escape into the neighboring province of North Carolina. The Governor then called into consultation Speaker Peyton Randolph of the House of Burgesses, Attorney General John Randolph, and Treasurer Robert Carter Nicholas. On their advice, John Lightfoot was sent to Pittsylvania County to round up the counterfeiters. Lightfoot had a dangerous, though successful trip. He returned to Williamsburg with the engraver, the papermaker, the printer of the paper money, and the coiner of pistoles and dollars, with their plates, tools, and implements, and a considerable quantity of paper money ready for circulation. The accused were committed to the Publick Gaol to await trial.[10]

When the House of Burgesses met early in March, it took several actions relating to the counterfeiting. First it adopted resolutions drawn up by the committee of the whole; the resolutions thanked the Governor for his vigorous efforts; called attention to the practice that an examining court for the accused be held in the county where the arrest was made or the crime committed (evidently Lightfoot had brought the accused to Williamsburg without going through with that formality); voted Lightfoot a reward of £200 over and above his expenses because of his diligence and the risks he took; agreed that persons who assisted Lightfoot should be rewarded by the colony.[11] To the proposed rewards the Council agreed, and the Governor signed the act granting them, as well as the acts "for better securing the publick Credit of the Colony" (which provided for a new emission of money to take the place of two which had been counterfeited) and to prevent counterfeiting of paper money.[12] Among those who received payment for assisting Lightfoot in his undertaking was Daniel Stone, a tavern-keeper in Prince Edward, who was voted the sum of £5:5:8.[13]

Before Treasurer Nicholas' notice was published, the counterfeit notes had been circulating in Prince Edward. The first news that Prince Edward people had that some of the notes they had been passing for money were counterfeit came when Robert Lawson returned from a merchants' meeting held in January and returned some money which had been either paid him or entrusted to him to deliver with the news that the merchants had pronounced the notes counterfeit. One man (evidently Miller Woodson) who had given him forty pounds to pay to Andrew McKenzie, the merchant, took the money back, as did George Davison, a deputy sheriff, who had collected £49:10 for Lawson, when they were advised by Lawson that it was counterfeit. Davison testified that he had received the money when he collected it as good money.[14]

Meanwhile certain Prince Edward citizens were charged with having knowingly passed the counterfeit money by Moses Terry of Halifax County. Lawson heard that he was on the list given by Terry to the Governor, but upon investigation found that he was not. Paschal Greenhill, a member of the House of Burgesses, however, was on the list.[15] The Governor notified the House of Burgesses of this accusation against Greenhill. The House thanked the Governor for the information, "entreat[ed] his Lordship to take every legal step to secure said Greenhill and bring him to justice. . . ."[16] Greenhill was in a difficult spot; he had not gone to the meeting of the Assembly. Further, he had announced that he was leaving the colony. Gossip lost no opportunity to jump to conclusion. Greenhill did decide not to go to the Assembly after hearing that the Governor had issued a warrant for him, although he had previously intended going; he determined to wait for examination by the County Court where he was confident of establishing his innocence; then it was his intention to attend the Assembly. So he informed Lord Dunmore.

Greenhill had determined to leave Virginia on a trip to Rhode Island before he learned that he had been implicated in the counterfeit money charges. His father had recently died in that colony, leaving a substantial estate which Greenhill, as heir at law, was going to receive. Not only did Greenhill deny paying out counterfeit money knowingly, but George Davison, Lewellin Jones, Lawson, Miller Woodson, and Daniel Jones, all of whom were said by Terry to have received counterfeit money from Greenhill, denied ever having received any money of the emissions of 1769 and 1771 from Greenhill.[17]

Two people were tried in Prince Edward Court on charges of passing counterfeit money, one in March, 1773, the other in April, and both were found not guilty. The former was Lewelling Williamson. The latter, George Davison, the deputy sheriff, had been suspended as deputy five days prior to his trial until his "character" could be "acquitted respecting the late information of the King against him." Happily it was.[18]

It has never been made clear why Terry should have implicated Paschal Greenhill in the counterfeit money deal. Not only did he accuse Greenhill of having passed the counterfeit money knowingly, but he claimed that Greenhill himself had told him that he had passed the money to Lawson and Daniel Jones.[19]

At any rate, the counterfeit money was circulated in Prince Edward, to the great embarrassment of some of the people. The evidence now at hand indicates that no one in the county passed the counterfeit money knowingly, and that the counterfeiting was so well done that it was difficult to distinguish between the good and the bad money of the paper currency emissions of 1769 and 1771.

CHAPTER VI

The Break With the Old Country

THE protest against the Stamp Act in 1765 served notice that the American colonists claimed the full political rights of Englishmen and that they did not intend to yield the claim. With the passage of the Stamp Act the dominant political leaders in England, with the support of the reigning Sovereign, George III, elder brother of Prince Edward Augustus, began a series of acts designed to assert the full authority of the British Parliament over the American colonies. Through the Townsend Act taxing various commodities, including tea, the Boston port bill and the stationing of British troops in Boston, through differences between Lord Dunmore, the Governor of Virginia, and the House of Burgesses, resentment against British measures and finally British rule mounted in the thirteen colonies until it broke out into open fighting.

No resolution of the attitude of Prince Edward County toward the Stamp Act has been preserved, but a comment in Dikephilos' letter describing the Routledge murder may be regarded as showing the sentiment prevalent in the county:

"People generally say that every true American justly detested the late intolerable Stamp Act. . . ."[1]

A sense of alertness toward acts of the British government concerning the colonists continued. The people continued resentful of acts which contravened their rights as they saw them. The differences with the English government were discussed and gave concern. The attitude of the upcountry Virginia Southside has been described by Henry Blagrave, a member of the House of Burgesses from Lunenburg County. Blagrave wanted to find out exactly how his constituents felt on so important and controversial a matter, so he made inquiry among them and recorded his findings in a letter dated April 4, 1768. A digest of Blagrave's letter reveals this state of mind in Lunenburg, a state of mind undoubtedly shared in the neighboring counties:

A strict inquiry among constituents concerning the taxes the Parliament of Great Britain insists upon levying shows that the people do not think that they should be taxed there since they have

107

authority from their most gracious Sovereign to hold assemblies here
for that purpose and for others. They think themselves exceeding
happy in having the best of kings, but they perceive that his Majesty
has some mischievous subjects. They understand that they (the
American people) are represented in Great Britain to be rebellious
but they have no such intentions and intend to be faithful and loyal
subjects of King George and his successors. If his Majesty wants
money or men from America to support the Crown or to preserve
his sacred person or good subjects from an enemy, they are willing,
upon his Majesty's requisition, for their own assembly to tax them
to the utmost farthing they are able to pay and they will pay it
cheerfully. They will risk their lives and fortunes in his Majesty's
service when required with all pleasure imaginable. But for Briton
to strive against Briton is the most shocking thing they ever heard
of. They counsel his Majesty's liege people to keep the king's com-
mandment, not to be hasty, and not to stand in an evil thing.[2]

The leaders of the dominant Tory party, even King George himself, seem to have found it impossible to reconcile the loyalty to the
Crown which Americans expressed with resistance to the taxes levied
upon them by the British Parliament. The principle of "taxation
without representation" was seemingly incomprehensible to the ruling clique in England. So matters went from bad to worse, though
loyalty to the Crown continued to prevail.

In 1774 resolutions were adopted in Prince Edward County
containing "like patriotick Sentiments with the Resolutions of several
other Counties already published, and profess all due Obedience to
the Sovereign of the British Empire." They were not published for
lack of space.[3]

In Virginia Patrick Henry had proclaimed "Give me liberty or
give me death." In Massachusetts battles had been fought at Lexington and Concord. Governor Dunmore decided to remove the powder
from the public magazine at Williamsburg, and Patrick Henry
marched at the head of company to demand restitution from the
Governor. Events were moving swiftly toward crisis, and men had
to make choices. On June 19, 1775, the committee of Prince Edward
met at the Courthouse to consider the trend of the times. Present
that day were John Nash, Jr., who was chosen chairman of the
meeting, John Morton, Robert Lawson, William Booker, Francis
Watkins, Obadiah Woodson, Thomas Flournoy, James Allen, Sr.,
and Thomas Haskins. Benjamin Lawson acted as clerk of the committee. They adopted resolutions condemning Lord Dunmore's action

in removing the powder, but their first resolution avowed "unfeigned attachment and affectionate loyalty" to the King and expressed the prayer for "speedy pacification" between Great Britain and the colonies "upon permanent, constitutional, and generous principles as the only probable means of preserving to us the inherent, legal, and just rights and privileges which his Majesty's subjects have ever laid claim to." Governor Dunmore was rebuked for not being fair and impartial in his reports to the British government and his letter to Lord Dartmouth of December 24, 1774, was cited as an example of his "disingenuous, illiberal, and viciously subtle representations" calculated to keep up the "unhappy ferment." Then his action in removing the powder was condemned as "despotic, cruel, and unwarrantable" and his answer to the protest of the mayor, aldermen, and council of Williamsburg concerning his action as "unmanly, evasive, and affrontive." The last resolution thanked Captain Patrick Henry and the volunteers under him for "their firm, prudent, and spirited conduct" which resulted "in obtaining an equivalent for the powder so unjustly removed."[4]

The Virginia Assembly was no longer functioning as a legislature, so the people acted through conventions. One such convention met in Richmond July 17, 1775, to adopt measures under which the public interest would be protected while there was practically suspension of government because Governor Dunmore would not call the Assembly and the people had lost respect for him. Robert Lawson and William Bibb represented Prince Edward in the convention, and Lawson served on the committee to draw up forms for commissions for officers of the regular forces, the minute men, and the militia. The convention also adopted measures for the defense of the colony. Prince Edward, Charlotte, Halifax, Lunenburg, and Mecklenburg were created a district to furnish a battalion of 500 men between the ages of sixteen and fifty in ten companies. Officers of the battalion were to be a colonel, a lieutenant colonel, a major, ten captains, ten lieutenants, ten ensigns, twenty sergeants, a drummer and fifer for each company, a chaplain, an adjutant, a quartermaster, a surgeon, two surgeon's mates, and a sergeant-major.[5]

The Prince Edward committee, at a meeting October 26, 1775, endorsed the resolution and ordinances of the July Convention and gave to them the weight of having the full force of law, adding that they should be binding upon the people of Virginia and pledging to execute them in their true sense and spirit. After stating that the committee would consider anyone who tried to hinder their execution an enemy, it thanked the delegates to the convention for their "zeal for the American cause and the interest of their constituents . . ." John Nash, Jr., served as chairman of this meeting also.[6]

The July Convention provided for the election of committees of safety in the counties. At the November Court the freeholders of Prince Edward elected a committee of twenty-one: Robert Lawson, John Nash, Jr., William Booker, William Bibb, Nathaniel Venable, James Allen, Sr., Thomas Scott, Sr., John Morton, the Rev. Samuel Stanhope Smith, John Nash, Sr., the Rev. Richard Sankey, John Holcombe, Henry Walker, Thomas Flournoy, James Clark, Obadiah Woodson, David Walker, John Watson, Philemon Holcombe, Joseph Parks, and Andrew Baker. John Nash, Sr., the county patriarch, who since the founding of the county had been named first in the commission of the peace, was unanimously chosen chairman, and the young lawyer, Benjamin Lawson, was elected clerk.

The committee then proceeded to adopt resolutions. It realized that matters could get out of hand and that the committee iself could become a menace to the rights of the people by assuming unlimited powers. It decided to confine its course to the instructions of the Continental Congress and the colonial convention. The members had changed their minds about the prospects of reconciliation with Great Britain since June; now they saw little prospect of it. At this time Lord Dunmore was waging war against the Virginia patriots in the Eastern part of the colony which he could strike from the water; many of the patriots were forced to flee their homes because of Dunmore's depredations; the Prince Edward committee invited the refugees who felt so inclined to come to the county, where "humanity and the laws of hospitality" would provide them a share from the possessions of the county people. Finally the committee looked to order in its own house and directed its subcommittees which were set up in various sections of the county to be "vigilant and active" in finding "all inimical and disaffected persons to the American cause" and in informing the chairman of them.[7]

How many "inimical and disaffected persons" were found in Prince Edward is not known. There is the record of one, John Hamblin, who was summoned to appear before the committee on January 25, 1776, to answer the information given the committee that he was "an enemy to the American cause." Hamblin appeared and admitted that he had been "unfriendly to the measures adopted in America," but that he had since been "convinced of his error," that he was now a friend to America and would so conduct himself.

Asking the forgiveness of the committee and his countrymen, he promised to sign the Association of the Continental Congress which heretofore he had refused to sign. The committee, with John Nash, Jr., acting as chairman pro tem, adopted a resolution considering Hamblin "a friend to his country" and recommending him to the public for forgiveness.[8]

Meanwhile it was beginning to be more and more apparent that action would be required to supplement the resolutions asserting the rights of Americans. The act of the July, 1775, Convention providing for a military establishment had to be put into effect. Tarlton Woodson of Prince Edward was commissioned an ensign in the First Battalion of Virginia forces on September 16, 1775. Robert Lawson was commissioned major on February 13, 1776, and was soon promoted to lieutenant colonel.[9] On February 19, 1776, officers of the Second Company of the Fourth Regiment were commissioned: John Morton, captain; John Holcombe, first lieutenant; Obadiah Woodson, second lieutenant, and Edward Wood, ensign.[10] The payroll of this company for the month June 28-July 28, 1776, has been preserved. Captain Morton received eight pounds, the lieutenants £5:8 each, the ensign four pounds. Four sergeants, James Morton, Samuel Anderson, Charles Stagg, and Charles Anderson, each received three pounds. The four corporals, Robert Lorton, Thomas Hastie, William Wright, and William Chambers, received two pounds ten shillings each. Anderson Cocke, the fifer, and William Cary, the drummer, also received two pounds ten shillings each. The sixty-three privates received two pounds each, to make the total payroll £210.[11]

Morton's company left Prince Edward Courthouse in March, 1776, for Suffolk. There and at Portsmouth it was engaged in skirmishes with Lord Dunmore's forces. After Dunmore left Virginia waters in September, 1776, the Fourth Virginia Regiment went by water to the head of the Elk (in Maryland) and thence marched through Philadelphia and Newark to New Brunswick, New Jersey, where it joined Washington's army after its retreat from Fort Washington. The regiment was in the battles of Trenton, Princeton, Brandywine, and Germantown and was at Valley Forge in the winter of 1777-8. During this period Lawson had been promoted to colonel.[12]

The transition from allegiance to the British Crown was accomplished smoothly at the local level in Prince Edward. A convention, which assembled in Williamsburg May 6, 1776, and at which Prince Edward was represented by William Watts and William Booker, drew up a Constitution for Virginia and established the Commonwealth.[13] The allegiance of the Virginian was henceforth (at least until the Federal government was established over a decade later) to the Commonwealth of Virginia. Magistrates who had been commissioned by the royal governor who would swear allegiance and take the prescribed oath to the Commonwealth were authorized by the Convention to continue in office and sheriffs who had been commissioned were directed to remain in office until October 25. Where there were not enough magistrates to carry on the county government, the Governor (who now was to be elected by the Assembly) was authorized to appoint, with the advice of the Council, as many as would be needed in each county. Quitrents and arrears thereof, duties, aids, penalties, fines, and forfeitures heretofore payable to the King were declared payable to the Commonwealth.[14]

When the Prince Edward Court assembled July 15, 1776, it proceeded to comply with the act of the Convention. Peter LeGrand and Nathaniel Venable administered the oath prescribed, that of loyalty to the Commonwealth of Virginia, to support, maintain, and defend the Constitution of Virginia and the government as established by the Convention, to faithfully execute the office of a magistrate, and to do equal right and justice to all men to the best of judgment and according to law, to John Nash, who had prior to his father's death early in the year been designated Jr. One can only wonder how Nash felt as he took the new oath, if he thought of the January day twenty-two years before when he took the oath of a magistrate to the King of England, the oath of allegiance and supremacy, the abjuration oath and the test. Nash then administered the new oath to Thomas Scott, Thomas Haskins, Peter LeGrand, Nathaniel Venable, Benjamin Haskins, William Booker, and Philemon Holcombe. Peter Johnston had come to Court that day, too, but he did not join his fellow magistrates to take the new oath. They sent for him to come into Court and asked him to qualify under the ordinance of the Virginia Convention. Johnston asked to be excused, "alledging for reasons his deafness."

Then the officers of the Court, John LeNeve, the clerk; Francis Watkins, his deputy; Charles Venable, the sheriff; and John Watson, his deputy, took the oath of office.[15]

LeNeve and Watkins took the oaths of clerk and deputy clerk respectively at the August Court.[16] George Walker took the oath as deputy attorney general for the county at the November Court.[17]

Meanwhile two more justices had declined to serve. At the August Court John Leigh gave deafness as an excuse for not taking the new oath required of magistrates, and Henry Watkins, gave his general disability as the reason for his declining to take the oath. The Court then recommended to the Governor, now Patrick Henry, Thomas Flournoy, William Bibb, John Clarke, Jacob Woodson, John Watson, Robert Goode, and Thomas Scott, Jr., to be added to the commission.[18] All were appointed, and all, except Watson and Goode, took the oath of office at the November, 1776, Court; Watson and Goode qualified at the December Court.[19] Old members who qualified under the new commission were John Nash, Thomas Scott, Thomas Haskins, Peter LeGrand, James Scott, Benjamin Haskins (in November), William Booker, Philemon Holcombe (in March, 1777), and John Morton (in July, 1777).[20]

The old order was changing rapidly, but for some Prince Edward people the changes were not going far enough. A petition signed by Richard Sankey and 160 other inhabitants of the county, predominantly the Scotch-Irish in the Buffaloe Settlement, urged the House of Delegates to implement the last article of the Bill of Rights by granting complete religious liberty . . . "make Virginia an asylum for free inquiry, knowledge, and the virtuous of every Denomination." It urged the immediate disestablishment of the Church of England in the Commonwealth and an accurate definition "between civil and ecclesiastic authority." The petition was referred to the Committee on Religion.[21] It was nine years before the aims of this petition were completely realized, although in the intervening years gradual steps were taken in that direction.

By 1776 it was clear that the insistence of Americans upon their rights coupled with the equally strong insistence of the Tory government in Britain that Parliament had the right to tax the colonists had reached the stage of rebellion. Insistence upon rights had to be backed up by force. Prince Edward reported 550 men of military age (between sixteen and fifty) in 1776.[22] Recruiting was under way early in the year; in February, the Virginia Committee of Safety sent by Paul Carrington the sum of £288 to be equally divided among the chairmen of the committees of safety in Prince Edward, Charlotte, Halifax, and Mecklenburg for the recruiting service in their respective counties.[23] In March the Virginia committee issued to William Bibb a warrant for £20:10 to be used by John Morton for bounty money and recruiting expenses in Prince Edward. At the same meeting, March 8, two other warrants were issued to Bibb: one was for £408:10 for sixty-three rifles furnished the Prince Edward company of regulars and for twelve muskets stored for the public use; the other was for £1:13 to be paid John Watson for escorting slaves from Williamsburg to the lead mines.[24] Three days later the committee paid Major Robert Lawson £5:10 for a valuable gun furnished the public.[25] In May warrants were issued by the Virginia committee to William Booker for £61:4:5 to be used by Charles Allen to pay his company of Prince Edward minute men and to pay for hunting shirts furnished them; for £135 for one month's pay for the Virginia company ordered to North Carolina; and to William Watts for £5:7.4¼ to be paid John Nash for rugs, blankets, and other necessary items furnished Captain John Morton's company.[26]

To provide guns for some of the soldiers, the committee had to purchase some from private individuals. Not only Major Lawson sold a gun to the public, but in June warrants were issued to William Booker to pay for five guns: Thomas Hamblett, £5:10 for a rifle bought of Adam Jones for the Prince Edward minute men; Samuel Baker, £5:10 for a rifle; Joshua Baker, four pounds for a rifle; George Shellody (Shilladay), £4:10 for a rifle (these three also for Captain Allen's company of minute men); and Douglas Baker, £5:10 for a rifle for Captain Brent's company of the Fourth Virginia Regiment.[27]

Warrants were also issued in June to William Booker to be used by Captain Allen: £18:3:9 for blankets and kettles; £1:16:3 for provisions for Allen's company of minute men; and eleven pounds to Nicholas Broadway for a wagon furnished Allen's company.[28] In July—on the memorable fourth—the committee issued a warrant for £1:8:6 to Captain George Muter to be paid James Lyle for six iron pots furnished the Allen company.[29]

Accounts for the Prince Edward militia paid in 1777 included: exact date uncertain, Captain Charles Allen, £5:0:9 for expenses with his company upon its return in December, 1776;[30] July 11: Nicholas Brewer, £12:15 for wagon hire;[31] September 13: Charles Collier, £7:18 pay as commissary of the Prince Edward militia;[32] September 18: Captain John B. Smith, £146:11:1 for pay and rations for his company;[33] September 22: Nathaniel Venable, £9:18:3 for wagon hire;[34] September 23: George Walker, £21:7:4 for pay, forage, etc., as major of the Prince Edward militia;[35] September 29: Captain Thomas Flournoy, £165:17:5 for pay, etc.;[36] November 4: Richard Randolph, £8:13:4 for flour etc. furnished Prince Edward militia.[37]

Captain Charles Allen's company of minute men was recruited in the spring of 1776. Joseph Parks was lieutenant, and James Allen was ensign of the company. The company served four months at

Hampton during the year, a service which explains the expenditures for guns, blankets, kettles, and pots.[38]

Congress called for eighty-eight additional battalions in 1776, and the Virginia legislature in 1776 passed legislation to provide the fifteen extra units asked for Virginia. Since nine battalions had been provided (another additional five battalions had been stationed on the Ohio River), the Governor was authorized to recruit six more battalions on the basis of quotas assigned each county. The Assembly followed a rather unique method of setting up quotas: a certain number of men was assigned for each officer (for a captain, twenty-eight men; for a first lieutenant, twenty men; for a second lieutenant, sixteen men; for an ensign, ten men), and counties were called upon for certain officers. Prince Edward was assigned a first lieutenant and a second lieutenant, an assignment which required the enlistment of thirty-six men. Congress promised the men who enlisted at this time a bounty of $20; annually a suit of clothes consisting of two linen hunting shirts, two pair of overalls, a leather or woolen waistcoat with sleeves, two shirts, two pair of hose, and two pair of shoes, or $20 to the soldier who provided those articles for himself. Land grants were promised at the close of the war: 100 acres for each private and non-commissioned officer; 150 acres for an ensign; 200 acres for a lieutenant; 300 acres for a captain; 400 acres for a major; 450 acres for a lieutenant colonel; and 500 acres for a colonel.[39]

To carry the baggage of Captain John Morton's company to Suffolk in August, 1776, Nathaniel Venable had two wagons, with teams and drivers, impressed into service. Venable provided provisions and forage for drivers and teams for fifteen days. Dissatisfied with the allowance of twelve shillings, sixpence per day which he claimed was two shillings, sixpence less than the usual price of "wagoning" at the time, Venable petitioned the legislature for an additional payment of £7:3:3; the request was refused. In September, 1777, he had a wagon and team impressed to carry the baggage of Captain Smith's company of militia to Williamsburg. Since he had been paid only ten shillings a day for the nineteen days his team and wagon were employed, which was three shillings a day less than the figure William Bibb and Pugh Price had appraised as a fair payment for their use, he asked additional compensation for this "wagoning," a request which was endorsed as reasonable.[40] This was the company of Hampden-Sydney students, under the command of one of the teachers, John Blair Smith. Venable's oldest

son, Samuel Woodson Venable, was lieutenant of the company, and
Samuel Hackley was ensign. The company served six weeks at
Williamsburg.[41]

The legislature of October, 1777, passed a law to recruit enough
men from the militia to complete fourteen regiments of eight companies each for the Continental Army. A quota of twenty-men was
set for Prince Edward, and the county lieutenant and the field officers
of the militia were directed to meet before the second Monday in
the following February, select all single men in the militia rolls,
summon them to meet in ten days and draft "by fair and equal lot"
the number of men needed. A bounty of $15 was offered by the
Commonwealth and to encourage enlistments, volunteers were promised an extra bounty of $10. One year's service was required of
volunteers and draftees for this service.[42]

In order to raise 2,000 reinforcements for Washington, the legislature in May, 1778, promised a bounty of $30 and a complete suit
of regimentals (coat, jacket, pair of breeches, two pair of shoes, two
stockings, two shirts, and a hat) to volunteers; they were also to be
exempt from drafting for military duty, unless the State was invaded,
and from taxes for twelve months after discharge. The method of
enlistment used in 1776 was revived, and Prince Edward was called
upon to furnish a captain, with a quota of twenty-four volunteers,
and an ensign, with a quota of ten.[43]

Captain John Blair Smith's company of students saw services
again in 1778. The students spent six weeks in service at Petersburg.[44]

Throughout the war various militia companies from the county
were called to duty at different places in the State. Captain Ligon's
and Captain Charles Allen's companies were stationed at Petersburg
for a time in 1778. Captain Thomas Flournoy's company of which
John Moore was lieutenant and John Allen ensign was on guard
duty three months at the public magazine in Williamsburg in 1779,
and during the same year Captain John Holcombe's company was
on duty at Petersburg for three weeks. Either in that year or the
next Captain Clarke's company was also stationed at Petersburg.
Both Captain Charles Allen's and Captain Philip [sic] Holcomb's
companies were on duty at Petersburg in 1780; the latter used the
Masonic Hall as barracks during its stay of two to three months. In
1780 Captain Richard Holland's company of which Philip Mathews
was lieutenant was assigned to duty guarding prisoners of war at
the Albemarle barracks.[45]

Prince Edward met its draft quotas consistently until the end of

1780. The twenty-two drafted by act of October, 1777, were furnished in February, 1778; the twenty-two required by act of October, 1778, were sent in May, 1779. To meet the quota of thirty men set in May, 1780, nineteen recruits were raised, and eleven deserters were delivered to the military authorities. The thirty-four men called for in October, 1780, could not be sent. Just as the drafting got under way, General Greene retreated across the Dan River, Lord Cornwallis' army in pursuit. These movements alarmed the Southside counties to the extent that every man who could get arms joined the companies hurriedly marching to join Greene. The continuing threat through the summer of 1781 kept over half the militia on continuous duty, so the quota was never filled.[46]

Deserters, mentioned as having been delivered in 1780 to help meet the quota, were something of a problem. William Porter, lieutenant of the 12th Virginia Regiment, advertised in November, 1777, for six deserters "from my quota of Prince Edward draughts," offering a reward of $10 each upon delivery of the deserter to the Continental forces or to any jail in the State. Hezekiah Morton, also a lieutenant of the 12th Virginia, advertised at the same time for three deserters from his quota of Prince Edward draftees.[47] Earlier in the year, Robert Ward, lieutenant in the Second Georgia Battalion advertised a reward of $10 each for six deserters from his company upon delivery to him at Prince Edward Courthouse.[48]

The retreat of General Nathanael Greene, commander of the American army in the South, into Virginia early in 1781 called into service numerous militia companies. Affidavits of old soldiers over a half-century later tell of Prince Edward militia companies which joined Greene. Captain Andrew Baker's company (Joseph Parks lieutenant and Joseph Read ensign) joined Greene near Dan River. Captain Nathaniel Cunningham's company (John Dupuy lieutenant) joined Green at Irvin's Ferry and took part in the Battle of Guilford Courthouse; later the company carried prisoners to Halifax County and later carried prisoners who had been wounded at Guilford to a British ship at Jamestown. Cunningham's predecessor as captain of the company was John Bibb. Captain Ambrose Nelson's company joined Greene in North Carolina, but was not in the Battle of Guilford. Captain Richard Allen's company (Abner Watkins ensign) was stationed at Ratcliffe's Old Field in 1781. Captain Richard Holland's company guarded prisoners on the march from Prince Edward Courthouse to Albemarle Barracks. Captain Cunningham's and Captain Bird's companies were at the siege of

Yorktown, and after the surrender Captain Cunningham's company guarded prisoners on the march to Winchester. The militia was also used to guard military stores at Prince Edward Courthouse where Major Mazaret was in command and Henry Lipner commissary and to collect provisions for the army at Yorktown.[49]

In July, 1777, there were ten militia companies in Prince Edward, seven of which were commanded by Clarke, Owen, Ligon, John Biggars, Thomas Flournoy, Josiah Chambers, John Bibb; captains of the three upper companies were not listed, but it appears from subsequent appointments that these captains were Charles Venable, Henry Walker, and David Walker.[50]

During the course of the Revolution the following militia officers are recorded as having been appointed and as qualifying in Prince Edward Court:

May, 1777: Josiah Chambers, John Bibb, David Walker, captains; Charles Allen, Jacob Woodson, John Dabney, lieutenants; Benjamin Allen, James Carter, Richard Holland, ensigns.[51]

July, 1777: Robert Goode, William Wooton, second lieutenants; Jesse Watson, William Rice, ensigns.

August, 1777: Henry Young, second lieutenant (in Captain Chambers' company).[52]

September, 1777: Andrew Baker, captain; Sharpe Spencer, Nathaniel ———, John Dabney, first lieutenants.[53]

February, 1778: Ambrose Nelson, captain, succeeding John Biggars.[54]

March, 1778: Charles Allen, adjutant.[55]

June, 1778: John Bibb, captain; James Bibb, first lieutenant; John Dupuy, James Reid, second lieutenants; ——— Biggars, Jr., Yancy Bailey, Robert Black, ensigns.[56]

July, 1778: ——— Vaughan, Thomas Lorton, second lieutenants (the latter in Captain Chambers' company); Samuel Burton, ensign.[57]

August, 1778: George Carrington, captain.[58]

December, 1778: Martin Smith, adjutant (payment for six months' service).[59]

March, 1779: Richard Holland, recommended lieutenant to succeed George Booker.[60]

May, 1779: Thomas Haskins, colonel; George Walker, lieutenant colonel; Williamson Bird (succeeding Charles Venable), Sharpe Spencer, Thomas Moore, Samuel Venable, captains; Nicholas Davis, George Booker, William McGehee, first lieutenants; Robert Venable, James Parks, Jesse Watson, Ambrose Nelson, John Langhorn, second lieutenants; John Clark, Jr., Drury Watson, Thomas Watkins, ensigns.[61]

July, 1779: Thomas Flournoy, major.[62]

August, 1779: Richard Holland (succeeding Henry Walker), Jacob Woodson (succeeding David Walker), captains.[63]

June, 1780: Thomas Lorton, Dick Holland, Jacob Woodson, captains; Jesse Watson, William Price, Jr., Joseph Parks, first lieutenants; Drury Watson, James Clarke, second lieutenants; Nathaniel Allen, Stephen Pettus, John Bell, ensigns.[64]

August, 1780: James Wright, first lieutenant; William Booker, ensign.[65]

June, 1781: John Nash, county lieutenant; George Walker, colonel; John Clarke, major.[66]

July, 1781: Thomas Flournoy, lieutenant colonel.[67]

October, 1781: Stephen Neal, James Clarke, captains; John Richards, William Wooton, James Parks, first lieutenants; Nathaniel Allen, George Pullam, George Foster, John Clarke, Jr., John Bell, second lieutenants; Philip Matthews, Robert Walton, Peyton Glenn, ensigns; William Galespie, no rank stated.[68]

November, 1781: Nathaniel Bassett, captain; Robert Shelton, ensign.[69]

January, 1782: Ambrose Nelson, captain, succeeding John Bibb.[70]

August, 1782: Jesse Watson, captain, succeeding Thomas Lorton; Samuel Carter, lieutenant.[71]

When Greene needed reinforcements, Thomas Watkins raised a company of dragoons and joined the army. Philemon Holcomb was lieutenant, Samuel Venable cornet, and Thomas Munford sergeant. Captain Watkins' company charged the Queen's Guards in the Battle of Guilford Courthouse; the command surprised the British, who at that point thought that they had won the battle, by leaping a ravine and charging. Many of the enemy were killed before they realized what was happening.[72]

Richmond Smith and Samuel Venable, of Captain Watkins' Dragoons, were detached by Colonel Washington on a reconnoitering party and were captured with their horses by the enemy. Both petitioned the Assembly for compensation for their horses, Smith's being valued at 10,500 pounds of tobacco and Venable's at 18,000 pounds of tobacco. Both petitions were rejected since they had been allowed by the court of claims in Prince Edward.[73]

The war made it difficult to obtain salt. To help maintain a supply of salt, the county bought salt from time to time for sale to the people. Nathaniel Venable deposited with Francis Watkins in February, 1777, £91:8:6 which he had collected from selling 138 bushels of salt for the public.[74] The following May Venable and John Nash each deposited £13:7 which they had collected from the sale of salt; at the same time Venable loaned the county £78:16:8 to pay for salt which had been bought.[75] Venable also filed a report of the sale of county salt in September, 1777.[76]

The care of needy families of soldiers also presented a problem to the Prince Edward Court. From October, 1777, when the court directed the justices to furnish needy families in the county with provisions under an act of the Assembly "for providing for the poor whose husbands or fathers are in the Continental service" until the end of the war, there are numerous entries of accounts of such provisions supplied which were certified to the Commonwealth for payment. Not only magistrates, but others, probably on authorization of a magistrate, also furnished provisions. The first account was certified in October, 1777, at the Court which authorized the justices to furnish provisions to needy families; it was presented by John Biggars for £11:14:6 for bacon "furnished sundry women whose husbands are in the Continental service."[77] In November John Nash presented an account for £20:10:6 for sundries furnished wives of servicemen and Benjamin Haskins £1:5 for a peck of salt furnished a serviceman's wife.[78]

The list for 1778 was much longer—January: William Ligon, £4:12 for sundries; Charles Venable, £15 for pork; John Ligon's estate, £27:12:6 for provisions; James Wade, £27:12:6 for provisions; Francis Watkins, £11 for salt; Daniel Foulks, £9 for pork; Thomas Scott, eighteen shillings for bacon.[79]

March: Rice Scott, £5 for two and one-half pounds of salt (an expensive necessity then!); Manness McFeiley, £13:14 for provisions; George Cardwell, £10 for ten barrels of corn for several women.[80]

April: Repes Childress, £3:3 for provisions; at this Court William Booker was directed to provide supplies for a soldier's wife and report the cost.[81]

June: Thomas Haskins, £4 for provisions; Rice Scott, an unrecorded amount for salt.[82]

July: William Booker, £10 for provisions, provided in compliance with the directive given him in April; William Pillow, £1:18 for provisions.[83]

October: Thomas Scott, £12:15 for sundries; William Wooton, £3 for wheat.[84]

November: William Bibb, £10:10 for sundries; William Collins, an unrecorded amount for sundries; Henry Young, £1:17 for sundries; Thomas Scott, £39:15.[85]

December: John Ligon, £27 for sundries; George Caldwell, £10 for two barrels of corn; Thomas Flournoy, £20 for provisions; Thomas Scott, £40 for provisions.[86]

There were substantial allowances certified for payment in 1779:

February: Wiliam Bibb, £75 for provisions[87]

March: Thomas Haskins £24 for provisions; Thomas Scott, Jr., £64 for provisions; George Walton, £12 for six bushels of wheat.[88]

April: Maness McFeiley, £70 for sundries; Philemon Holcombe, £73:10 for sundries; Thomas Scott was authorized to supply corn to a family.[89]

May: Thomas Scott, £20 for corn provided in compliance with order issued him in April.[90]

June: Robert Goode and Jacob Woodson were authorized to furnish corn to soldiers' families.[91]

July: Thomas Scott, Jr., £86:18 for provisions; Sharpe Spencer, £30 for one barrel of corn; John Dixon, £15 for one-half barrel of corn (these prices show inflated values and a depreciated currency).[92]

August: John Holcombe, £74:16:2 for provisions; Jacob Woodson, £39 for sundries; Robert Goode, £63:14 for sundries; Thomas Morton, £30 for one barrel of corn.[93]

September: Sharpe Spencer, £41 for provisions; William Bibb, £37 for provisions; Robert Goode, £23 for provisions.[94]

October: Jacob Woodson, £39 for corn; Thomas Scott, Jr., £88 for provisions.[95]

The load become lighter in 1780, probably because of the expiration of the term of the enlistment of a number of the soldiers. Thomas Scott, Jr., filed an account of £81:11 and Philemon Holcomb an account of £54:10 for provisions furnished soldiers' families.[96] Jacob Woodson was authorized to furnish the family of a soldier fifty pounds of pork and one barrel of corn.[97] Woodson's bill of £1,050 for 350 pounds of pork furnished this family was certified in January, 1781, and in September his bill of £350 for more pork furnished this family was certified to the State Treasurer. The husband and father of the family was at this time a prisoner of war in Charles Town (S. C.).[98] The mounting inflation is seen in the rising price of corn. Manness McFeiley's account for corn furnished a soldier's family, certified in September, 1781, showed that a barrel of corn sold for £50 a barrel, an increase of £20 since the summer of 1779.[99]

As the war moved toward its end—an end, however, which did not appear imminent to the Americans—the people were called upon to furnish additional supplies. Earlier in the war they had sold guns for use by the army. They were called upon to provide food supplies, for which they were paid, throughout the war. Payment in many instances, especially for goods furnished during the latter part of the war, was not made until after the war was over. In 1780, Prince Edward was asked to furnish thirty-eight suits of clothes for soldiers, each suit to consist of two shirts of linen or cotton, a pair of overalls, two pair of stockings, a pair of shoes, one wool, fur, or felt cap, and a leather cap. The four senior magistrates and the county militia field officers were directed to meet prior to February 1, 1781, and lay out the county into districts equal in number to the suits it was asked to furnish; an equitable division on the basis of assessable property was ordered. The people in each district were to have a meeting at which the contribution of each individual to the suit was to be set, "observing as far as possible the rules of equality according to property." Each of the districts was also directed to deliver to a receiver appointed by the Governor one good beef weighing at least 300 pounds. Each county was also called upon to furnish before March 1, 1781, a good wagon and a team of four horses with complete harness and a driver, the driver to render one month's service.[100]

Prince Edward moved to comply with this legislation. In May the Court directed the Sheriff to pay Nathaniel Venable £19,680 current money for a wagon which he bought for the county for the public use.[101] Elizabeth Venable was paid £2 current money for pasturing and feeding the public cattle—those collected for the Army.[102] In October John Nash reported that the clothing from the county was ready and that the commissioners and their assistants were busy forwarding supplies; then he added, in a line which expresses the weariness of the people with the sustained struggle and its heavy demands upon them, "we wait impatiently to hear of the time when such supplies will be no longer necessary."[103] On the day that he wrote that letter an event was taking place at Yorktown which was to lessen, although not remove entirely, the demand for supplies.

Robert Walton of Prince Edward acted as purchasing agent for Georgia in buying horses. General Greene sent him a draft for

126,000 pounds of James River tobacco, which he sent to Governor Jefferson in April, 1781, with the request that the Governor send him a cash draft on the Treasury to use to buy the horses.[104]

After Morgan defeated Tarleton at Cowpens, General Greene moved his army into Virginia to the north side of the Dan River. Cornwallis was pressing hard upon Greene, and the American commander was confronted with two major problems: getting enough men to strengthen his army to enable him to strike back at Cornwallis with some hope of success and sending his heavy equipment to a place where it would be reasonably safe from capture.

Accordingly he sent his stores to Prince Edward Courthouse.[105] Major John Mazaret, commanding the artillery, brought five pieces of artillery, two howitzers, twenty wagons loaded with ammunition and all the heavy baggage to the Prince Edward county seat on February 20, 1781, after a "tedious retreat" of six weeks. In reporting his arrival, Mazaret took occasion to point out that officers and men needed clothing badly—some had not received a "single farthing" or any clothing for over a year.[106]

Meanwhile, Brigadier General Robert Lawson, having learned of Greene's retreat to the Dan, assembled the Prince Edward militia at the Courthouse February 16 in response to Greene's appeal for militia reinforcements. General Lawson's problem was arms. There were not enough to equip the militia. He sent a company of twenty-four picked riflemen to Greene that day. The evening before Captain Moore had left with his company, armed with very good guns. And Lawson collected that day enough guns to send another company the next day, about 100 men altogether from Prince Edward in three days. Lawson suggested to the Governor that he be appointed commander of the militia in that area,[107] a request which was evidently granted, for within ten days he had reported that he had ordered out the militia of Prince Edward, Cumberland, Amelia, Charlotte, Lunenburg, Mecklenburg, Brunswick, Buckingham, and Amherst to Greene's support. Approximately 1,000 militia went from these counties to reinforce Greene's army.[108]

As spring came on and planting time approached, members of the militia showed reluctance to join Greene. Some counties failed to send their full quotas; some counties sent no soldiers. Lawson regretted that they had to be called from their farms at the critical planting season, but he recognized the priority of the needs of the Army.[109] The objections of the militia went beyond mere desire to plant the crop. Lawson learned of the dissatisfaction and reported it in July to Governor Thomas Nelson, who had succeeded Jefferson, in replying to orders to send one-fourth of the Prince Edward militia to join Greene. In the first place, the militia officers could not procure arms; the continued calls for arms from the early part of the war had practically stripped the country of arms. When the militia had been called out to join the command of the Marquis de Lafayette after Lord Cornwallis had united his army with that of General Phillips, not more than one-third of the Prince Edward militia had been able to secure the necessary arms. The prospect of a period of service with Greene's army in the South considerably longer than would be required if they served in Virginia "distresses [the people] greatly." It was true that the militia was called upon to serve only two months in the Southern army; but to that period of active duty there had to be added additional time for going to the army and returning home to make the time the militiaman had to be away from home nearly five months. In contrast, a tour of duty in Virginia did not take more than three months. Nor were reports from the South calculated to make the service there appear attractive. Some magnified the "horrors" of the Southern climate; some reports stressed the fatigues of the march. Then comparisons entered the picture. The counties of Southside Virginia had on four different occasions sent militia to South Carolina, calls which had not been made upon the counties of Northern Virginia, and yet the Southern counties had done equal duty within the State.[110]

The problem continued through the summer. Strong reinforcements for Greene were called for in August; the call gave concern to Lawson, who expressed regret at the necessity.[111] In September Colonel John Nash, as county lieutenant for Prince Edward, asked for twelve blank commissions for militia officers in the county, "so no excuse can be made by them when called into the field."[112]

From February until March, 1781, Prince Edward Courthouse was designated a special post for the collection of supplies from Prince Edward, Charlotte, Lunenburg, Mecklenburg, and Bedford Counties. These had formerly been in the districts of Carter's Ferry and Boyd's Ferry. Captain Charles Russell was put in command of the stores at the Courthouse. In May the post was discontinued, the counties were returned to their former districts, and Captain Russell was sent to take charge of the stores at Albemarle Old Courthouse.[113]

Prince Edward, along with Amelia, Dinwiddie, Chesterfield, Powhatan, Cumberland, and Goochland, was the principal source of flour for LaFayette's army in the summer of 1781. Low water made the grinding of meal uncertain, and the army had to depend upon flour for its bread. As LaFayette moved eastward, the problem of supply became more difficult. His army required fifty barrels of flour daily, and at least forty wagons were needed to supply him.[114]

In addition to being a place for the collection of food supplies for the army and the rendezvous for Greene's heavy equipment and baggage trains, Prince Edward Courthouse also had a laboratory for the manufacture of gun-powder and ammunition and a magazine for storing it. About the last of May, 1781, a supply of ammunition was sent to General Greene. At this time plans were made to move the laboratory (as the manufactories of ammunition were called) and magazine from Prince Edward Courthouse, because of danger of capture by the "enemy's partisan troops"; so many men had been called into service from Prince Edward and the other Southside counties that there was no effective force remaining to protect such an important establishment.[115] It is not certain that the laboratory and the magazine were moved, however; in 1782 a report from New London stated that all the powder used at the New London laboratory before the "reduction of York" (i.e., the surrender of Cornwallis which ended the siege of Yorktown) came from Prince Edward Courthouse.[116]

Prince Edward Courthouse also served as a rendezvous for militia and troops gathered from Southside counties to join the armies. Some soldiers from Cumberland spent ninety days at Prince Edward Courthouse in 1780. Among the officers mentioned as being there at the time were three from Prince Edward: General Robert Lawson, Colonel John Holcombe, and Major John Overstreet. This Cumberland company, under Captain Benjamin Overstreet, marched from Prince Edward Courthouse through the home county to join General Stephens in Henrico County.[117]

When Lord Cornwallis' army reached Cobham, a town in Surry County on the James River, on July 8, 1781, the commander sent Lieutenant Colonel Banastre Tarleton with the legion cavalry and eighty mounted infantry on a raid to Prince Edward Courthouse and New London in Bedford County. The detachment left Cobham the next morning.[118] Tarleton was at Prince Edward Courthouse on Saturday, July 14.[119] Tarleton's raid did not prove successful in capturing and destroying stores. Evidently anticipating such a move by the British as Cornwallis' army moved on into Virginia, Thomas Smith, deputy commissary general of military stores, had all the supplies moved from Prince Edward Courthouse even before Lord

Cornwallis dispatched Tarleton on the expedition.[120] Tarleton did break up a hanging scheduled for Prince Edward Courthouse the day he reached that point.[121] When news of Tarleton's arrival at Prince Edward Courthouse reached New London, Captain Nathan Reid hid the stores there. "I ashure you I never worked more tightly in all my life, than I did for about twenty-four hours," he wrote. Some 500 men assembled and were stationed in close woods and underbrush along the route Tarleton was to travel, but he did not get to New London.[122] After spending the night at Prince Edward Courthouse, Tarleton moved southward. He crossed Briery River and then took the road to Moore's Ordinary where he spent the rest of the day. As he went, his men continued to pillage and burn and take prisoners. From Moore's Ordinary the raid continued through Lunenburg and other Southside counties.[123]

General Anthony Wayne had been sent to Virginia to join the Marquis de Lafayette, who was in command of the Continental Army in the State. Not only was Virginia menaced by Lord Cornwallis' army coming into the State from North Carolina, but also by raids from British detachments landed in the Hampton Roads area. General Phillips and the traitor Benedict Arnold led raiding parties up the James during the summer of 1781. General Lawson was notified in June that the militia from Prince Edward then serving with Lafayette would be required to serve two months from the time of "their joining camp." None would be permitted to leave until a sufficient body of the militia joined the army for their relief. Later in the summer, to strengthen Lafayette's army for resisting the enemy raiders, half the militia of a number of Southside counties was ordered to join his army and as many more as could arm themselves were directed also to join. Supplementing the order, General Lawson addressed an appeal to several Southside counties urging that the orders be complied with as quickly as possible. The aid of the King of France gave prospect of destroying the enemy in Virginia; "an instantaneous and manly exertion may end our fatigues, and troubles, and crown our just cause with glory and success—the least delay—the smallest inattention, or backwardness will greatly injure if not ruin the success of farther opposition." Not only were men urgently needed, but provisions as well; and Lawson urged in particular that the people furnish wagons, teams, and carriages to transport the provisions.[124] At this time only one-third of the Prince Edward militia could be sent because of lack of arms.[125]

As the American armies closed in on the British at Yorktown, lack of supplies posed a serious problem. The people did not realize how desperately supplies were needed by the army. Governor Nelson sent General Lawson from Williamsburg to Prince Edward late in September to speed up the flow of food to the army. Lawson, coming through Powhatan and Cumberland, found no mills grinding flour. He set them to work at once; assembled wagons, ox-carts, and other carriages to haul wheat to mills and flour to landings to be shipped to the army. Lawson proposed that all coopers in the militia of Amelia, Powhatan, Cumberland, Prince Edward, and Buckingham Counties be sent back from the army to make barrels for the flour, that most of the wagons of the Southside be put to hauling flour to the army. He reported that a large quantity of beef had been sent down, so much that he judged "the army will not suffer on this head." Some wagons with flour had already been started to Manchester and Petersburg to be loaded on vessels to be shipped to the army.[126]

The summer of 1781 was not a pleasant time for Virginians. The State was invaded by enemy armies; raiding parties went far into various sections, including Prince Edward. There were persistent and continuing demands for men and for supplies, until from counties like Prince Edward most of the able-bodied men of military age—a wide scope from sixteen to fifty—were in service. The people were called upon to furnish provisions, wheat and beef, until some must have wondered if enough would be left to carry them through the winter. Calls for firearms from the beginning of the war had left few guns in the county. Summer lengthened into fall, and the pressure, especially for supplies, mounted. To add to the worry and the perplexity, there was at this season an "exceeding and unusual unhealthiness" in Prince Edward and the neighboring areas, so debilitating that the people could not work to assemble supplies "with the vigor their readiness to help would otherwise insure."[127] Exhaustion from such sickness combined with weariness of the long struggle and fear inspired by the raids to stimulate the attitude reported by John Nash. Men like Lawson saw clearly that it was now or never; his exertions in the light of his understanding of and sympathy for the situation of the people were made in the confidence that a superlative effort would bring victory. His judgment was vindicated. On October 19, the second major British Army in this country surrendered to the Americans. The war officially was not over; but Cornwallis' surrender at Yorktown ended the fighting and the British efforts to crush the rebellion.

CHAPTER VII

The Aftermath of War

IF any American expected the surrender of Cornwallis or even the treaty of peace with Great Britain which in 1783 recognized the independence of the onetime American colonies to end his troubles, he was thoroughly disappointed. The war removed some problems, but it brought others, weighty and perplexing.

Until the treaty of peace, the American colonies had to continue to maintain an army, which meant that men had to remain in service and had to be paid and fed. A recruiting station was maintained at Prince Edward Courthouse to secure enlistments for periods of six months, but the results were disappointing. Lieutenant Nathaniel Price, who was in charge, reported that only five soldiers had enlisted as of January 2, 1782, and he recommended that the post be abandoned, because in his opinion no more enlistments could be secured. It was difficult, too, to get supplies.[1] The Cumberland commissioner to secure commodities for the army was criticized early in 1782 for neglecting his duties, although there was an abundance of pork and flour in that county. The same report noted that there was plenty of beef in Amelia, Bedford, and Prince Edward Counties, but that it could be gotten only by impressment. There was a general tendency on the part of the people to withhold supplies as soon as they thought the provisions law had been repealed.[2]

The prevailing state of mind was reflected in the apprehensions of trouble with the men going into service. Colonel Thomas Posey, with a detachment headed for General Greene's army in the South in February, 1782, had his officers prepare themselves for trouble. Their "steady and determined carriage" kept order among the men, although on the first night out of Cumberland Old Courthouse six men deserted of whom two returned before the detachment left Prince Edward Courthouse, from which Colonel Posey wrote on February 17, the day after his arrival there. He left on the 18th; later he noted that there were no desertions on the trip to Peytonsburg.[3]

In March, 1782, Nathaniel Venable took charge of the recruiting service at Prince Edward Courthouse, but no provision was made to finance its operations. John Morton, who was commissioner of taxes for Prince Edward, had run into difficulties in undertaking to provide beef for the French soldiers quartered at Charlotte Courthouse; he had sent to Henry County for forty head of cattle, but received only twenty; and of those ten were so poor he had to sell them, getting nothing for them except the price of the hide. He suggested that what was left from paying the expenses of bringing the cattle from Henry be turned over to Venable for the recruiting.[4] In May Morton reported that he had on hand about 150 barrels of flour, thirty poor cattle, and a considerable quantity of corn and oats.[5] John Nash as county lieutenant collected the taxes imposed to finance the recruiting service; in 1782 he collected £323:9 in Prince Edward. He reported 453 men in the county militia that year.[6]

One of the most critical problems war brought was inflation. The great rise in the price of corn has already been noted. Captain John Morton received £60,000 from Captain John Pierce, quartermaster general of the Continental line to pay thirty soldiers for October, 1781; this was not quite enough, since Captain Morton's payroll came to £60,200 for that month.[7] In a suit in which the decision was rendered in October, 1784, the Court found that the plaintiffs (Elizabeth Young and Edward Morecock, executors of Henry Young, deceased) had sustained damages amounting to £277:15 paper money; it directed that the plaintiff recover of the defendant (Philemon Holcomb, administrator of John LeNeve, deceased) £3:9:5 in specie or current money and costs.[8] The difference shows the depreciation of currency in those days.

In Prince Edward there was dissatisfaction with the management of public affairs. A petition presented to the House of Delegates on May 16, 1782, criticized the last session of the Assembly for leaving the country in "dangerous circumstances." Confusion and injustice were the result of the session; the legislature failed to take advantage of the opportunity "to introduce order and justice into the management of public affairs . . . ." "We are left without system and without defense," the petition noted in pointing out that property was insecure, that the public faith had been "grossly violated." The petitioners "recollected with deepest resentment" the assistance the representatives of the people gave to the "speedier distruction" of public faith. They called upon this session of the Assembly to restore the public credit as far as possible and to act for the public welfare. The objects of particular complaint were the laws dealing with taxes, paper money, and certificates issued by Virginia. The petition asked for the redemption of paper money by taxes and also of the certificates unless the latter were redeemed in cash. The tax in specie was held especially burdensome; a reduction was sought, and the petition asked that sheriffs not be permitted to distrain "until a later day," because it appeared impossible to the petitioners to be able to pay such an amount in so short a time. The petitioners then pointed out that the Southern part of the State had carried a greater burden in supporting the Revolution than other sections; because of the great amount of provisions furnished—the petitioners had "supplied the army with all the provisions we could spare and more than we could with convenience"—they considered it "extremely unjust that we should be obliged to furnish as much cash as those who have parted with nothing unless we can be paid for what the public (i.e., the State) has received." They also asked that attention be given to "the law which takes a retrospective view of contracts between individuals" and asked justice here. The chief beneficiaries of this law would be those "disaffected from the country from the commencement of the war," evidently a reference to the British merchants who could recover prewar debts due them under this law. The petition also called attention to inequality in the valuation of real estate for taxation. By implication it criticized the indifference on the part of the members of the previous Assembly by asking that heavy penalties be imposed upon members of the Assembly who do not attend its sessions.

The petition covered a lot of ground. Its significance was heightened by the signers. They were not chronic malcontents, but men of standing, reputation, and property. Heading the list were the names of John Blair Smith, John Nash, Thomas Haskins, Benjamin Haskins, Henry Watkins, James Ligon, John Richards, John Smith, and William Booker; among the other petitioners were Archibald McRobert, John Holcombe, Robert Lawson, Thomas Clark, Jr., William McGehee, Peter Johnston, William Bibb, John Morton, Richard Burks, John Hill, John Overstreet, Alexander Marshall, John Clark, George Booker, Joel Johns, Abraham Venable, Thomas Watkins, John LeNeve, Samuel W. Venable, George Walton, William Wootton, John Rowlett, James Allen, Christopher (who signed briefly Xr) Dejarnett, Samuel Carter, Henry Dickenson, William Ligon, Thomas Clark, Joseph Rice, John Dupuy, John Purnall, Caleb Baker, Francis Rice, and Rice Scott.

The petition was referred to the Committee on the State of the Commonwealth.[9]

One prayer of the petition was granted by the October, 1782, session of the Legislature. To equalize the land tax, the State was divided into four districts, Prince Edward and the middle tier of counties (running north and south) being placed in the second class or district. John Pendleton, Jr., and Samuel Jones were directed to examine the returns of all land valuations in each county, to ascertain the average price of land per acre, and to apply the difference between the average price per acre and the valuation to the account of each individual in the district, either by adding or deducting, whichever was necessary. They were to make out account books for each county and send them to the two tax commissioners who were to be appointed by the county courts for three-year terms. The standard or average tax set for the second district was seven shillings, sixpence. (In the first district it was ten shillings, threepence; in the third five shillings, sixpence; and in the fourth three shillings.)[10]

Early in 1782 John Morton, Richard Foster, and Thomas Scott had been named commissioners for Prince Edward under the "Act for ascertaining certain Tax's and Dutys, and for establishing a permanent revenue"; Peter LeGrand and William Bibb were appointed to assess the lands belonging to the commissioners.[11]

The men who bore the brunt of collecting the heavy and unpopular taxes from an economically distressed people were the county sheriffs. A petition of Benjamin Haskins, sheriff of Prince Edward in 1782, shows how that official was caught between the upper stone of general difficulty and the nether stone of an exacting government. After pointing out that he took the sheriff's office reluctantly because he knew it would be impossible to collect the taxes in time on account of the scarcity of money in circulation, Haskins recited his experience; one-half the collection amounted to £1550; in September he paid into the treasury £726; in October he was prepared to pay £618 more and on the 19th so notified the treasury. But "owing to the great throng of business and the tardiness of their doing of business," he could not get the treasury to receive the money until after the treasury had obtained a judgment against him for £797. On the day after the judgment was obtained, he paid the £618, but the solicitor refused to allow him credit for that sum in the discharge of his judgment. (And this generation thinks bureaucratic blindness and inefficient a peculiar phenomenon of its own age!) Haskins thought that this decision worked an unjust hardship upon him because it was the fault of the treasury, not his, which prevented his payment before the time limit. He advised the Assembly that he could pay the entire judgment if he were given credit for the £618. The petition was reported as reasonable; the committee thought the sheriff should not have to pay ten per cent interest on £575, a part of the sum for which the judgment was obtained.[12]

Haskins' petition is only a sample of the petitions of sheriffs for consideration and relief during the decade of the 1780's. The Prince Edward sheriff in 1787 (Thomas Flournoy), along with others, petitioned for relief because the people were uanble to pay their taxes.[13]

Philemon Holcombe in 1789 was reported in arrears £1768:13:5 on returns on his collections for 1784. Patrick Henry had interceded with Governor Edmund Randolph on Holcombe's behalf the year before. The Legislature had permitted payments to be made as late as April 1, but Henry and some others were under the impression that it was May. The Acts of Assembly did not reach Prince Edward until late in April, so the extended time limit had passed before Holcombe knew of it, although he knew the time for payment had been extended. Henry asked the Governor "such Indulgence [for Holcombe] as you think is right and proper."[14]

In response to a petition from John Holcombe, who had "farmed" the sheriff's place of Thomas Flournoy in 1786, Governor Beverley Randolph and the Council of State suspended execution of a judgment against the estate of Flournoy until November 2, 1788. An additional suspension was asked until the General Assembly, which was considering a bill on the matter, should reach a decision. Flournoy's difficulty had arisen from the failure of Robert Watkins, to whom Holcombe had let out half of Prince Edward for the collection of taxes after he had been appointed Flournoy's deputy to collect taxes, to collect all the taxes due from his district.[15]

Flournoy's petition to the General Assembly for more time in which to pay the taxes due which had not been paid for 1786 was rejected. "Not well versed in the business of the office, [he had] farmed it out to Colonel John Holcombe." As he had not settled the 1786 accounts by 1791, Flournoy's property was advertised for sale to make good the unpaid accounts; it was then that he petitioned for time in which to collect from Holcombe and his securities.[16]

Another problem involving tax collections arose in Prince Edward when William Bibb, sheriff in 1788 and 1789, moved to Georgia; his removal meant that no land could be sold to discharge payment of taxes, because he alone was authorized to sell it for the purpose. Since his deputies would be held responsible for arrears, an act of the Assembly authorized John Watson to make such sales as were necessary to collect the taxes for 1788 and convey property thus sold.[17]

The people were not leaving the responsibility for asking for relief entirely to the sheriffs. Benjamin Haskins headed the list of petitioners in 1784 asking the postponement of the collection of the current taxes until they could harvest and sell another crop. They noted that they had had only one crop since the war, that they would have gladly paid a "great proportion" of that "to answer the public demands," and that the small balance remaining after paying their taxes from this crop "private necessity and importunate and merciless creditors forced from them." To the petition some of the most substantial property owners in the county subscribed, men like George Walker, John Nash, William Wootton, Woodson Knight, Thomas Clark, James Wade, William McGehee, Jacob McGehee, John Morton, William T. Walker, James Allen, Jr., William Bibb, Giles Fuqua, and Douglas Baker. They also proposed the cession by Virginia of the State's lands northwest of the Ohio to Congress, in order to "rid the State of many claims of creditors with their enormous demands." They also proposed the sale of all State property except that necessary to be reserved for its use.[18]

In the effort to equalize the tax burden, appraisers were directed to be appointed in the counties. In January, 1788, Charles Allen, James Allen, William Wooton, Tarlton Woodson, John Fontaine, Thomas Watkins, Joseph Moore, John Holcombe, and Samuel W. Venable were appointed "valuers of property" for Prince Edward.[19]

During the Revolution the County Court ended the practice of levying taxes in tobacco and substituted money for tobacco. The impending change was foreshadowed in setting the costs of administration in both tobacco and money in the 1777 levy. The salaries of the clerk, the sheriff, and the attorney were not only set at 1,248 pounds of tobacco, but the cash equivalent, £7:16, was also stated. The total levy for 1777 came to £83:18:3¾, which meant an assessment of two pounds of tobacco per poll for each of the 2,020 tithes.[20] The 1778 levy was the last in which the assessments were made in tobacco; that year each of the 2,044 tithables was taxed six pounds of tobacco, to yield £306:12.[21] In 1779 the 2,075 tithables were taxed at the rate of three shillings, sixpence each to yield £363:2:6, the sum needed to operate the county government.[22] It was the first year in which the people were required to pay their county levies in money. The change from tobacco to money as the legal medium of exchange in part accounts for the burden of the taxes in the next decade; tobacco had been an fairly abundant commodity; money was scarce and remained so for some time.

The county tax rate was set as low as ninepence per tithable in 1788, but this had to be raised threepence to one shilling per tithable a month after it had first been set.[23] The next year the rate was doubled to two shillings per tithable. It required £272:16 to operate the county government in 1789, and there were 2,728 tithables, a decline of fifty from 1788.[24] But in 1788 the number of tithables had increased by over 400, from 2,345, to 2,778.[25]

In 1786 the office of commissioner of the revenue was established, and the Prince Edward Court was authorized to appoint two and to divide the county into the districts for their work. The commissioners were to visit each person subject to taxation in their respective districts and list all the taxable property of that person, who was to make affirmation to the list. One of the four lists which the commissioners were required to make was to be placed in the clerk's office; this list, open to public inspection, was to be used in laying the county levy and in fixing the poor rates. One copy the commissioner was to keep. A third copy, certified by the clerk, went to the high sheriff for use in collecting taxes; and the fourth, also certified by the clerk, was delivered to the solicitor, to be used as evidence in court for the amount of taxes charged the sheriff.[26] The commissioners of the revenue named in Prince Edward were John Morton and Richard Foster.[27]

Forms were prescribed for the land tax books to show the name of the owner, the number of lots owned, the annual rent of lots, the quantity of land owned (in acres), the rate of land per acre, the total vale of land exclusive of town lots, and the amount of the tax at one and one-half per cent. Forms were also fixed for listing taxable property, with columns for the date of receiving the lists from the individual, the name of the person chargeable with the tax, the names of white male tithables over twenty-one, the names of white males over sixteen and under twenty-one, the number of blacks above sixteen, the number of blacks under sixteen, the number of horses, mules, mares, and colts; the number of cattle; of carriage wheels; whether there was an ordinary license; the number of billiard tables; the number of stud horses; the rates of covering for the season; and for practicing physicians, apothecaries, and surgeons.[28]

Additional tax relief was granted in 1786 when the Legislature permitted taxes to be paid in notes for inspected tobacco, as they had been paid in the colonial period, for both 1786 and 1787. The rates fixed for 1786 were twenty-eight shillings per hundred for tobacco inspected in the Richmond, Manchester, and Warwick warehouses, twenty-six shillings for the warehouses in and around Petersburg and on the Appomattox. There were other rates lower, some as low as eighteen shillings per hundred, but practically all Prince Edward tobacco was marketed through the warehouses mentioned. For 1787 the rates were somewhat higher. Credit on tobacco notes from Richmond, Manchester, Warwick, and Osborne's warehouses was allowed at thirty shillings per hundred pounds, and from the Petersburg warehouses and those on the Appomattox at twenty-nine shillings per hundred.[29]

During the Revolution the Court had continued to give attention to roads and bridges. Despite the fighting, bridges had to be repaired and rebuilt and some had to be built new; roads had to be kept passable, and occasionally new roads had to be viewed and cleared. Surveyors were appointed to superintend the upkeep of the roads from time to time. The bridge over the Appomattox at Rutledge's was rebuilt in 1779 by Peter LeGrand and William Bibb.[30] In the same year another new bridge was built over the Appomattox at Randolph's Mill at Sandy Ford.[31] A third bridge over the Appomattox River was built, this one in 1780 near Josiah Chambers', Peter LeGrand being the contractor. The inflation of the times is to be noted in his bond of £50,000 to build the bridge and guarantee it for six years. Prince Edward's share of the cost was £1271.[32] Something had happened to Chambers' bridge by April, 1783; a petition from Cumberland was presented, asking that the road crossing the river "where the Appomattox bridge near Chambers lately stood" be discontinued and that a new road be opened to the bridge near Nash's mill. Philemon Holcombe and William Bibb were named representatives of Prince Edward to meet the Cumberland deputies, and Holcombe was authorized to view a way for the necessary changes in the road the plan would require in Prince Edward.[33]

Changes in religious matters affected the civil life of the county. Before either the close of the Revolution or the breakdown of the Establishment, the dissenters gained one objective, permission for a limited number of their ministers to perform the marriage ceremony. In June, 1781, the Rev. Archibald McRobert (who had left the Church of England to become an Independent) was licensed to perform marriages in Prince Edward;[34] in August, the Rev. Richard Sankey, now the venerable pastor of the Buffalo Presbyterian congregation, received his license to marry people;[35] and in December the

Rev. Robert Foster, "on the recommendation of the elders of the Baptist congregation in this county," was licensed to perform marriages.[36] The Baptist congregation of which Foster was minister was Sailor Creek, worshipping in William Rice's meeting-house. In 1785 each of these three ministers presented their credentials, certificates of ordination and communion in their respective denominations, took the required oaths, and received testimonials from the Court authorizing them to perform marriages.[37] In July, 1785, the Rev. John Blair Smith received a license to marry people; he was president of Hampden-Sydney College and pastor of Briery and Cumberland Presbyterian Churches; James Allen and Francis Watkins were his securities.[38] Abner Watkins, a Baptist minister who was pastor of Sailor Creek Church, received a license to perform marriages in May, 1787.[39] The first Methodist minister to produce his credentials and receive testimonials from the Prince Edward Court authorizing him to perform marriages was the Rev. John Robinson; Thomas Watkins and Richard Foster were his securities when he received his testimonials in January, 1792.[40]

The management of the public welfare program was also affected by the disestablishment of the Church of England. To carry on this portion of the responsibility of the parish vestry, the office of overseer of the poor was established in 1786. Prince Edward was divided into four districts by the March, 1786, Court for the purpose of electing overseers. District One lay east of a line from the Appomattox River by John Nash's and thence along the road leading to Joseph Moore's to the county line; the election for this district was scheduled for the second Tuesday in April, 1786, at Clark's store under the superintendency of William Wooton. District Two extended from the county line by Joseph Moore's to the Roanoke road, up this road to Buffalo bridge by Caleb Bakers, and down Buffalo to the Appomattox; the election in this district was to be held the second Wednesday in April at the Courthouse, under the direction of Charles Allen. District No. 3 was the north side of the road from Buffalo bridge by Fountain's (Fontaine's) via the fulling mill and Andrew Porter's to the county line; the election in this district was set for the second Thursday in April at Walker's Church, with John Holcombe as superintendent. The fourth district lay south of the road from Buffalo at Fontaine's to the county line. Richard Foster was authorized to conduct the election in this district at Sankey's meeting-house, also on the second Thursday in April.[41]

The results of the 1786 election have not been preserved; the second election of overseers of the poor took place Saturday, March 28, 1789. The only change in voting place was in District One, with Mackness Rowlett's the polling place, and the only change in superintendent in District Three, where John Watson was in charge. The boundary line of District Two was clarified, the western line following the Roanoke road to Hector's shop and thence up Buffalo road to Baker's bridge. Samuel Booker's is substituted for Joseph Moore's as the southern landmarks for the boundary between Districts One and Two.[42] John Morton, William Womack, James Ewing, John Miller, James Harper, Benjamin Moore, Stephen Pettus, Robert Goode, Christopher Dejarnett, William Walker, Charles Allen, and Francis Watkins took the oath of office as overseers of the poor at the April, 1789, Court.[43] Ewing, Miller, and Robert Kelso were elected from District Three, and Womack, Moore, and William T. Walker from District Four.[44]

An entry in 1788 described the first group elected as "overseers of the poor of St. Patrick's Parish"; they were directed to divide the parish into precincts for processioning the land and to appoint processioners.[45] This was the second processioning ordered after the Revolution; the first was ordered to be held in 1784, the parish vestry, which was then still in existence, having been directed to set up the precincts and appoint the processioners.[46] Overseers of the poor now bound out orphans, instead of the church wardens.[47]

For all the changes some things did not change. Old punishments still prevailed. Two Negro slaves were given thirty-nine lashes on the bare back for stealing bacon in 1783 and 1784.[48] A man accused of horse stealing was sent to the General Court for trial in 1784, after the County Court, as an examining body, thought him guilty.[49] In the same year a grand jury presented four men for retailing spiritous liquor without a license, one man for a breach of the Sabbath day and breaking the peace by assaulting another; one man for getting drunk and profanely swearing three oaths; and another for getting drunk.[50] A Negro slave, accused in 1785 of "preparing, exhibiting, and administering medicines contrary to law" was found guilty on the first two counts, but because the medicine was not administered and because it seemed harmless, the accused was let off with the "light" punishment of having his hand burned in open court and of getting thirty-nine lashes on his bare back at the whipping-post.[51] The services of a vagrant were ordered to be hired out by the sheriff at public auction in 1782; if no one hired him for the month for which he was offered, he was to receive thirty lashes.[52]

In times of war and in the years afterward, the jail as usual needed repairs.[53] A jail for debtors was authorized in 1786, Thomas Scott and Charles Allen being directed to let bids.[54] The next year it was viewed and received, and Richard Bibb was paid £52 for building it.[55] Benjamin Allen built a jail for the county in 1784.[56] A new jail, evidently for criminals, was built in 1791; Peter LeGrand was authorized to remove the old jail for criminals and in return for the iron and other materials in it he was to deduct £4 from the price he was charging to build the new jail.[57] A pillory and stocks were ordered built in 1785.[58] Some attention was given the courthouse also; Christopher Ford was notified that it needed repairs in 1783,[59] and Samuel W. Venable and John Fontaine were directed to let contracts for its painting and repair in 1788.[60]

With the end of the war, young men could turn their thoughts to entering a profession. The bar proved popular. In 1783 David Witherspoon was recommended to practice law in the county "for honesty, probity, and good demeanor" in 1783.[61] Samuel Anderson qualified to practice law in the same year.[62] Others recommended to practice law were David Walker (December, 1783)[63] and Abraham Venable (September, 1784).[64] Venable produced his license and took the oath of an attorney in October, 1784;[65] Daniel Allen in July, 1785;[66] Richard N. Venable in July, 1786.[67] Patrick Henry and Paul Carrington, Jr., took the required oaths at the February, 1788, Court.[68] For Henry, this was the resumption of the practice of law after retiring from it in 1774.[69]

During this period the Court acted as certifying agent for pensions for widows and heirs-at-law of soldiers who died in service and for veterans who were entitled to pensions. Certification was made to the Auditor of Public Accounts. Soldiers from Prince Edward who died in service and whose next of kin were certified were James Harefield,[70] James McDearmonroe,[71] Thomas Brooks,[72] Parsons Anderson,[73] William Robbins,[74] James McCormick,[75] William Harrison,[76] Josiah Foster,[77] and James Hawfield.[78] William Hines was certified as wounded in an engagement with the Indians while in service under Colonel Clarke in Kentucky County.[79] The service of William Hubbard as a sergeant in the First Virginia Regiment and the claim of Robert Redding, a wounded soldier, to a pension were also certified.[80]

There were veterans of the Revolution who lived for many years after the end of that war. The census of 1840 reported the following persons receiving pensions for Revolutionary service (either of themselves or their husbands) living in Prince Edward and their ages: Charles Brightwell, 83; John Crute, 85; John Cunningham, 82; Bartholomew Cyrus, 82; Joseph Davidson, 86; Mary Dupuy, 73; Nathan Grubbs, 81; Obediah Hendrick, 82; William Hill, 82; William Jesse, 81; James Moss, 80; Ann Pugh, 74; William F. Scott, 80; Jehu Simmons, 78; and Samuel Walker, 84.[81]

After the war the Court righted an old injury. Lieutenant Archer of Lee's Legion had impressed a horse from John Hamblin and refused to give him a certificate for it, charging that Hamblin was "an enemy of his country," although he had been cleared of the charge by the Committee of Safety. The Court in September, 1786, on petition of Hamblin's widow, certified the value of the horse to the Auditor at £30.[82]

Charles Venable was serving as sheriff when Virginia became a Commonwealth, and he was reappointed for 1777.[83] John Morton, who had resigned in 1776, possibly because of anticipated duties as captain of a company which was to go into service, possibly because of the complaint of Peter Johnston, served in 1778.[84] When Nathaniel Venable was recommended in his turn for the office in 1779, he resigned his right to the office in favor of his brother Charles, who was appointed and served through 1781.[85] Benjamin Haskins was sheriff in 1782 and 1783.[86] William Booker, who was in line for the sheriff's post for 1784, was recommended, but he died before he was appointed.[87] Philemon Holcombe was sheriff in 1784 and 1785.[88] Thomas Flournoy served in 1786 and 1787;[89] William Bibb, in 1788 and 1789.[90]

John LeNeve died in March, 1783, and his deputy, Francis Watkins, was chosen his successor as clerk by the Court in April.[91] In 1780 John Scott had been recommended to the masters of William and Mary College to be surveyor of the county[92] (LeNeve had been surveyor since 1754). David Walker was recommended as surveyor in 1783.[93] The old forms and the old way still prevailed in 1786 when John Fontaine was recommended to the president and masters of William and Mary College for appointment as surveyor of the county.[94]

John Morton and Richard Foster filled the new office of commissioner of the revenue when it was established in 1786.[95] In 1787 Morton and Thomas Watkins were the commissioners, Morton working in the district west of the road from Rutledge's bridge to the Charlotte line (the Roanoke road), Watkins in the district east of it.[96]

Charles Allen was later a colleague of Morton in this work and was succeeded by John Booker in 1792.[97]

George Walker resigned as deputy Attorney General for the county in 1784 and was succeeded by Robert Lawson.[98] He was succeeded in April, 1788, by Abraham B. Venable.[99] Abraham B. Venable resigned in May, 1789, and was succeeded by his cousin and fellow Princetonian, Joseph Venable, who took office in June, 1789.[100] Since 1785 the office had been called deputy attorney for the Commonwealth.[101]

Joseph Moore, Charles Allen, Richard Foster, Joseph Parks, William Wooton, and Richard Winn were recommended to be added to the commission of the peace in May, 1781. Allen and Wooton qualified in June, Foster in January, 1782, and Moore in June, 1782.[102] Joseph Parks refused to qualify in October, 1784,[103] and Nathaniel Venable resigned as a justice at the same time.[104] The next month Robert Goode resigned, and the clerk was directed to notify the Governor of the vacancies: Abraham Venable and William Booker had died; James Scott and Thomas Scott, Jr., had moved away; Nathaniel Venable, Robert Goode, and Joseph Parks had resigned. Richard Bibb, James Allen, Sr., Thomas Watkins, and Thomas Gibson were recommended for appointment.[105]

In May, 1785, a new commission was received, naming as magistrates John Nash, Jr., Thomas Scott, Thomas Haskins, Peter Le-Grand, John Morton, Charles Venable, Benjamin Haskins, Philemon Holcombe, Thomas Flournoy, William Bibb, John Clarke, Jacob Woodson, John Watson, Joseph Moore, Charles Allen, Richard Foster, William Wooton, Richard Winn, Richard Bibb, James Allen, Sr., Thomas Watkins, and Thomas Gibson. Scott, LeGrand, Morton, Flournoy, Moore, the two Allens, Foster, Wooton, Winn, Richard Bibb, Watkins, and Gibson were present and qualified at the May Court.[106] In November, 1786, John Holcombe, Samuel W. Venable, Tarleton Woodson, and John Fontaine were recommended to be added, and they were included in the commission presented in June, 1787.[107] In July, 1787, a warrant from Lieutenant Governor Beverly Randolph removing Charles Venable and Thomas Haskins from the magistracy was read and ordered recorded.[108]

The difficult times in Prince Edward during this period reflected the unsettled situation throughout the newly independent states. Under the Articles of Confederation, which had been approved by each of the states as the basis for union, the authority of the central Congress was hamstrung by the requirement of unanimous approval by each state, and the supreme authority of each state made for confusion. A dispute over navigation of the Potomac between Maryland and Virginia led to a conference at Mount Vernon. There it was recognized that there were commercial problems of concern to all the states, so a conference was called to meet at Annapolis to discuss them. There in turn it was recognized that the scope of the problem extended beyond commercial matters, so a convention was called to meet in Philadelphia to consider revising the Articles of Confederation.

Patrick Henry, who had moved to Prince Edward in 1786 after declining to stand for election to a sixth term as Governor, was elected a deputy to the Philadelphia Convention. Writing to Governor Edmund Randolph from Prince Edward on February 13, 1787, Henry declined to serve. He gave no reason; ill health may have been one reason, but James Madison foresaw the possibility of Henry's opposition to the work of the convention and expressed to Washington the opinion that Henry declined in order to be free to oppose that work. The Convention met during the summer of 1787 and instead of revising the Articles of Confederation drew up an entirely new Constitution which it submitted to the states for ratification or rejection. After the close of the Philadelphia Convention, Washington, who had served as its president, sent Henry a copy of the Constitution as it had been drafted there. Henry acknowledged its receipt and expressed opposition to it, but left the way open for a change of mind.

When the matter of calling a convention in Virginia to consider the Constitution was presented to the Legislature in the fall of 1787, Henry, who was a member of the House of Delegates from Prince Edward, opposed the call as proposed because it did not give to the convention the privilege of proposing amendments to the document. George Mason seconded Henry's amendment to permit such consideration. The bill which passed was a substitute offered by John Marshall, which authorized the convention to consider the proceedings of the Philadelphia Convention "with full and free investigation and discussion."

At the Prince Edward Court in February, 1788, Henry announced his candidacy for the convention to consider ratification of the Constitution by Virginia. In one of his notable speeches he opposed ratification, pointing out the defects he found in the instrument of government prepared in Philadelphia to a large crowd which had come to hear him. Support for the Constitution in Prince Edward was led by the Rev. John Blair Smith, president of Hampden-Sydney. Smith intended being present when Henry announced his candidacy and to make a speech in reply in favor of the Constitution. On the day Henry spoke, Smith was called to visit a dying woman who was a member of one of his congregations, and there was no reply to the great orator. A young man in Smith's family took down Henry's speech in shorthand. Not long thereafter, at a public speaking at the College Hall, one of the students delivered Henry's speech; another replied, giving Smith's reply to Henry and defense of the Constitution. Henry, who attended the program as did a large crowd, objected to Smith that advantage had been taken of him. Smith replied that no advantage which had been taken unless Henry's speech had been incorrectly reported and if that were the case, he would make amends. Henry thought the speech accurately reported, but "complained," as Foote relates it, "of the abrupt introduction of the subject, the tartness of the reply, and the appearance of an attempt to expose him before that large audience." Smith replied that Henry's speech had been made publicly and that it was generally known that he had intended to reply to it when made; the only ground for complaint on Henry's part, he insisted, would have been incorrect reporting. Henry was not satisfied, and he stopped going to hear Smith preach, although he had been a regular attendant upon his preaching.[110]

Henry was elected to the convention from Prince Edward at the election held at the March, 1788, Court. Robert Lawson was chosen his colleague[111] As Henry left the yard at Prince Edward Courthouse before going to Richmond to attend the convention, there took place an incident which he afterward enjoyed telling: an old fox-hunter tapped him on the shoulder and said:

"Old fellow, stick to the people; if you take the back track, we are gone."[112]

Henry stuck to the interests of the people as he saw them. He led the opposition to ratification of the Constitution in the Virginia Convention which assembled on June 2. One of his greatest speeches —and this is saying a great deal of an orator who was noted for his great speeches—was made before the Convention June 5. The defects of the Constitution as he saw them may be summarized in his objections that the consolidated government derived its power directly from the people (and not from the states) and operated directly on the people of the states; that not sufficient responsibility attached to the men who were to conduct the affairs of the government under the Constitution; and that no bill of rights was provided to protect the liberties of the people. He spoke on seventeen of the twenty-two days the Convention was in session, often as many as three times a day; on one day he made five speeches, on another eight, and one day he was on his feet for seven hours in one speech.

Henry lost one phase of his fight, to prevent ratification of the Constitution by Virginia. He won another, to secure a bill of rights. The bill of rights proposed by Henry was incorporated substantially in the eight amendments to the Constitution.[113] In the light of history one may say that both Henry's defeat and his victory in the Virginia Convention of 1788 were both fortunate and significant for the future welfare and prosperity of the United States. With the adoption of the Constitution, the foundations of the nation were securely laid.

CHAPTER VIII

The Lamp of Learning

O N the eve of the Revolution there began in Prince Edward a movement destined to have the greatest influence upon the life of the county and the surrounding country. In 1772 the ministers of Hanover Presbytery made an unsuccessful attempt to establish an institution of learning. Two years later the effort was renewed when the Presbytery, meeting at Cub Creek Church on October 13, 1774, proposed to the congregations of Cumberland and Prince Edward the raising of subscriptions to buy a library with philosophical and mathematical apparatus; since Samuel Stanhope Smith was "inclinable to take charge of such a seminary," the presbytery promised to approve the establishment of a seminary in Prince Edward or the upper end of Cumberland when the status of subscriptions to the undertaking provided the "proper encouragement." When Hanover Presbytery met at Slate Hill in Prince Edward on February 1, 1775, the retiring moderator, Samuel Leake, reported that the Prince Edward and Cumberland congregations had succeeded "beyond expectation" in raising subscriptions, which then amounted to £1300. The presbytery then proceeded to lay the foundations for an institution of learning. The trustees who were to be nominated later and Joseph Morton, James Allen, William Smith, Warren Walker, William Morton, and Robert Goode were authorized to raise or to borrow £400 to be used to purchase books and mathematical and philosophical equipment; since the Non-Importation Agreement was expected to remain in effect for some time, Samuel Stanhope Smith was directed to purchase this equipment in the Northern colonies, upon the advice and approval of the Rev. Robert Smith of Pequea, Pennsylvania; the Rev. Robert Davidson and John Bayard, merchant, of Philadelphia; and the Rev. Dr. John Rodgers and Samuel Brown, merchant, of New York.

After looking at several proposed sites for the school on February 2, the presbytery selected one hundred acres of land at the head of Hudson's branch in Prince Edward which was offered by Peter Johnston for the purpose and decided to build thereon an academy and a dwelling for the rector and other necessary buildings to the extent the subscriptions permitted. Johnston, John Nash, Jr., James Allen, Sr., John Morton, and Nathaniel Venable were named a committee to draw plans and to let the contracts for the buildings.

The next step was the appointment of trustees, and the following were chosen: the Rev. Richard Sankey, the Rev. John Todd, the Rev. Caleb Wallace, the Rev. Samuel Leake, Peter Johnston, Paul Carrington, John Nash, Jr., John Morton, Nathaniel Venable, Thomas Read, James Venable, Francis Watkins, and the rector, ex-officio. Sankey, Johnston, Nash, Morton, Venable, and Watkins were from Prince Edward. The presbytery reserved the privilege of naming the trustees, the rector, and the assistants.

On February 3 Samuel Stanhope Smith was chosen rector, and he, with his father, the Rev. Robert Smith of Pequea, and William C. Houston, a professor in the College of New Jersey, was directed to choose his assistants.

The presbytery then turned to matters of policy after setting tuition at four pounds per year (twenty shillings to be paid on entrance) to be divided among the rector and his assistants by the trustees. The strictest regard would be given the morals of the youth in attendance, and divine worship, according to the Presbyterian mode, would be conducted both morning and evening. But every effort would be made to avoid developing any bias in students toward the Presbyterian faith, and students of every denomination would be permitted to enjoy their own religious opinions and to attend public worship services of their own denomination when convenient.[1] This statement was made obviously to get the patronage of members of the Church of England. At this time, worship of that communion was conducted regularly at the Upper Church at French's, only a mile from the site chosen for the academy, at a distance considered quite convenient in those days.

Samuel Stanhope Smith planned a comprehensive course of study for the proposed institution: Greek, Latin, and the sciences usually taught in colleges and academies; geography "to greater perfection" than usually taught; arithmetic, algebra, geometry applied to surveying, natural philosophy in all its branches; eloquence; criticism; and the science of morals.[2]

Through 1775 the work of getting the school ready to open went on apace. It was hard enough work as it was to start a new institution. At least one stone was thrown, but Smith retained his calmness.

The stone was in reply to an advertisement of the academy, dated September 1, 1775, from the pen of a staunch Church of England man who used the *nom de plume* Luther. Smith's Presbyterian doctrines, he held, were repugnant to those of the Church of England (he had evidently not read Thomson's *Explication of the Shorter Catechism*) and were in his opinion "subversive of morality." He feared that if the civil war (the Revolution) continued, gentlemen of fortune from the lower part of the country would take refuge in the back counties and that they would send their sons to the Prince Edward school. The result would be, he feared, both Senate-house and pulpit filled with dissenters; it was absurd to say that a dissenter was a proper person to bring up a Church of England member. Smith's dignified reply called attention to the "catholic plan" of the academy and to the fact that the trustees were chiefly members of the Church of England.[3]

The effort to raise or borrow £400 was a failure, so Smith sent his own letter of credit for £300 and £20 cash to buy books and apparatus. Purchases made in the amount of £240 had been received by November 8, 1775. At this time it was reported that contracts had been let to build the academy house and the rector's residence for £694. The undertaker agreed to take subscriptions in payment on condition that any subscriptions found insolvent be made good with other subscriptions. At this meeting Hanover Presbytery enlarged the board of trustees by adding the Rev. David Rice, Patrick Henry, John Tabb, William Cabell, and James Madison, Jr.[4] Smith reported the engagement of two assistants, his brother, John Blair Smith, and John Springer.[5] Philemon Holcombe was elected steward at this meeting of Presbytery. The contract required him to provide "wholesome diet"; one-half the meat served was to be fresh, and one-half the bread made of fine wheat flour. He was also to furnish servants to keep the students' rooms clean, although the students were required to furnish their own beds or rent them, their own candles, and laundry, then simply called washing. The steward was to receive eight pounds per annum for each student. It was advertised that by January 1 the steward, with the assistance of "a few neighbors who live well," would be able to take care of all the students. For the time being the student could cut the wood he needed for his fires from the academy land at no charge.[6]

The school, called both Prince Edward Academy and Hampden-Sydney Academy, began classes January 1, 1776. John Springer had been detained from joining the faculty, but Samuel Stanhope Smith secured Samuel Doak in his place and in addition his brother-in-law, David Witherspoon, who was only sixteen at the time.[7] The entire faculty was made up of Princeton graduates: Samuel Stanhope Smith of the class of 1769, John Blair Smith of the class of 1773, Witherspoon of the class of 1774 (he was fourteen then), and Doak of the class of 1775. In addition, five of the trustees were also Princeton graduates: the Rev. John Todd, 1749; the Rev. Samuel Leake, 1764; the Rev. Caleb Wallace, 1770; Colonel James Madison, Jr., 1771; and the Rev. David Rice, 1761.[8]

The number of students at Hampden-Sydney was much greater than anticipated. Holcombe advertised in April that he would no longer be able to furnish beds for many more; he found it "too chargeable" to provide beds at the rate he had been furnishing them and he also found young people disposed to be less careful of others' property than of their own. Accordingly he requested gentlemen who would send their sons to the academy in the future to send beds with the boys. He added to his advertisement inquiry for a man "who understands cooking, and managing the Business of the Kitchen and Table in such a large family."[9]

Francis Smith of Hanover was contractor for the academy buildings. He died in 1776, and his son and the executor of his estate, Thomas Smith, who held a number of subscriptions which had been taken by his father for payment, urged those who had not paid the half installment due in October, 1775, to pay him or Francis Watkins in Prince Edward.[10] Work on the building did not proceed as rapidly as desired. In May, 1776, the walls were only three feet high, and students were permitted by the new undertaker, a man named Coleman, to build eight or ten little huts of shingles intended for the roof. In September Nathaniel Venable and Paul Carrington were given permission to build cabins for their sons because the number of students was taxing the facilities of the college.[11]

The students had little recreation, spending most of their time in study, but they were patriotic; sixty-five of them, over sixteen, organized a company, with John Blair Smith as captain, David Witherspoon as lieutenant, and Samuel Venable as ensign. About September 1, 1777, the Governor requisitioned a company of Prince Edward militia to come to Williamsburg to resist an expected invasion by the British. At the advice of President Smith, the Hampden-Sydney company went, but was discharged in a few days. As it was time for the academy vacation, some students went home, some joined the

Continental army, and a number never returned to Hampden-Sydney.[12]

The need for buildings was so pressing that in 1777 the trustees secured permission to hold a lottery to raise money to erect them. The goal for the effort was $4,200 or £1,260. Paul Carrington, William Cabell, James Madison, Jr., John Morton, Thomas Read, Nathaniel Venable, and Francis Watkins were named managers of the lottery. The plan was to sell 5,600 tickets at $5 each, to yield $28,000. Of the tickets, 3,117 would be blanks, and 2,483 would yield prizes. The entire amount expected from the venture, $28,000, was appropriated in prizes, but fifteen per cent of each prize would be deducted upon payment to raise the $4,200 required for the buildings. The first prize was to pay $2,000; there were two second prizes of $1,000 each; four prizes of $500 each; six of $200 each; ten of $100 each; twenty of $50 each; thirty of $25 each; one hundred of $15 each; 1,000 of $10 each; and 1,310 of $5 each.[13] The drawing was scheduled to begin July 27, 1778, at Prince Edward Courthouse, and those who were selling tickets were asked not to sell any after that date and return those unsold then to the managers. There were still tickets to be sold in early July.[14]

Naturally there was much interest in Prince Edward in the academy; the Court in 1777 decided to reroute the road by the academy and named a commission composed of Thomas Hamblet, Pugh Price, John Bauldin, and James Allen, Jr., to view a way to "turn" it by the academy and report to the court the conveniences to the public and the inconveniences to individuals.[15]

One of the greatest problems at Hampden-Sydney in its earlier years was keeping a steward. When Philemon Holcombe took the job, food was plentiful and currency values stable. The war soon completely changed that situation. Holcombe was permitted to increase the charge for board from £8 to £9, but his request in December, 1776, for an additional increase was refused; the trustees criticized his "diets" for breakfast and supper and strictly prescribed the food he was to provide. Holcombe gave notice, and the trustees let the stewardship to the lowest bidder for the job, William Bibb, who was to begin his duties July 1.[16] Bibb evidently found he had made a bad bargain because of the depreciation of money and left without notice about Christmas, 1777. In this emergency Nathaniel Venable, James Allen, Sr., and John Morton agreed to furnish provisions for a year. They engaged a Mr. Young, most likely Henry Young, who kept an inn at French's, and his family to cook at the rate of £20 per student; under this arrangement students were fed during 1778.[17] At this time breakfast was served at eight o'clock, dinner at one o'clock, and supper at eight o'clock in the evening. The three teachers were boarded free. If a student died or entered military service, the proper proportion of any fees he had paid in advance was refunded.[18]

After 1778, presumably until after the end of the Revolution, students were responsible for providing their own board.

At first grading was by grouping into one of three classes, first, second, and third, or as the students said at examination, white, yellow, and black. Those who did outstanding work received the public praise of the rector, and those who did poorly were also mentioned in public but with disapproval. Two literary societies were organized in 1776, the Cliosophic and the Tully Whitefield.[19]

In 1783 the Prince Edward institution was chartered as Hampden-Sydney College with the following trustees: the Rev. John Blair Smith, Patrick Henry, William Cabell, Sr., Paul Carrington, Robert Lawson, James Madison, John Nash, Nathaniel Venable, Everard Meade, Joel Watkins, James Venable, Francis Watkins, John Morton, William Morton, Thomas Read, William Booker, Thomas Scott, Sr., James Allen, Charles Allen, Samuel Woodson Venable, Joseph Parke, Richard Foster, Peter Johnston, the Rev. Richard Sankey, the Rev. John Todd, the Rev. David Rice, and the Rev. Archibald McRobert.[20]

The rechartering of Hampden-Sydney as a college appears a part of the postwar effort to strengthen the institution and to make it more attractive to students. The buildings were repaired; Major John H. Overstreet was engaged as steward, with board at £16 per year. Tuition was fixed at £5 per year. The curriculum emphasized the English language, geography, mathematics, philosophy, and "a very accurate acquaintance with Greek and Latin added where desired." A native of France would be engaged to teach pronunciation of the French language provided enough students would provide themselves with French textbooks to justify it.[21]

Samuel Stanhope Smith had resigned as rector in 1779 to return to Princeton to teach and to assist his father-in-law, John Witherspoon, in the direction of the college. His brother and assistant at Hampden-Sydney, John Blair Smith, succeeded him.[22] During this administration the first degrees were granted by Hampden-Sydney. Kemp Plummer, David Meade, James Watt, Ebenezer McRobert, Thomas McRobert, Nash LeGrand, and John W. Eppes received the A.B. degree on September 22, 1786; William Baker and Clement

Read of the same class received degrees in April, 1787, and at that time Hampden-Sydney conferred the honorary A.M. degree on the Rev. Henry Pattillo.[23]

The college was now flourishing after the difficulties of war. But, as so often happens, trouble entered to disturb its tranquility. The controversy between President Smith and Patrick Henry has already been mentioned. Although it had its origin in political differences over the ratification of the Constitution, it was not long in becoming personal. Henry stopped his heretofore regular practice of going to hear Smith preach. In July, 1788, a few months after the unpleasantness developed between the college president and its most prominent trustee, Smith notified the board that he intended to leave the college, though he did not plan to leave the neighborhood. He was asked to continue, and Drury Lacy was named vice-president, to live at the college and to assist Smith.[24] In July, 1789, Smith notified the board that he intended to sever his connection with the college on October 1, and a committee consisting of Smith, Archibald McRobert, Henry, and Francis Watkins was named to correspond with members of Congress and "any other literary characters" in an effort to find a successor.[25] Foote implies that Henry's disagreement with Smith contributed to the "discontent" with Smith and to charges that students were being proselyted which were investigated in 1790.[26] At its meeting on March 16, 1790, the board questioned five students from different regions as to whether they had observed any effort on the part of the president and masters to influence students in their religious principles. They unanimously reported that they had observed no such attempt.[27]

Smith had played a prominent and important part in the revival in 1787, and his encouragement made Hampden-Sydney one of the principal centers of that stirring of interest in matters spiritual. Not everyone looked with favor upon the revival. A biographer of William Henry Harrison, Hampden-Sydney's only son to occupy the White House, implies that Harrison's short stay as a student at the college was because of family disapproval of the revival to which Smith gave so much encouragement. He quotes Jefferson's comment to the effect that it would do Hampden-Sydney no good and that parents disapproved of it. Harrison transferred to an academy in Southampton County.[28]

Hampden-Sydney had a difficult time getting a president in succession to Smith. William Graham, the founder of Liberty Hall (now Washington and Lee University) declined three offers in three successive years. Drury Lacy as vice-president directed the affairs of the college, but resigned in 1796 to devote his entire time to the ministry. This was not surprising, because the board had been critical of Lacy's practice of spending so much time away from the college in preaching. This practice probably explains why he was never made president. In April, 1794, the board had decided that if Lacy would be away from the college no more than half the Sabbaths—"if he can avoid these weekly calls from the college"—and get an able assistant it would be agreeable for him to stay on.[29]

Archibald Alexander became president in 1796, and joining him as tutors were John Holt Rice and Conrad Speece.[30] This was a period of disciplinary troubles in most American colleges. Samuel Stanhope Smith was having them at Princeton. In 1799 Martin Smith complained that some students went to his peach orchard one night, shot his dog, and shot at his overseer. He was invited to present his evidence to the board, but that body felt that he did not sustain his charge. Three students were expelled in 1805 for ringing the bell, putting timbers against the teachers' doors to fall on them when the doors were opened, and throwing bricks through the windows at a tutor.[31] Some of the young men were of an independent stripe sufficiently broad to do credit to the most extreme versions of the psychology which holds that restraining a child curbs the development of his personality. One youngster in the grammar department, summoned to appear before the trustees to answer questions about shooting a pistol near the college, was not fazed by that august body; he "showed the utmost contempt of the board, left their presence in an abrupt manner, and told them they could do what they could."[32]

The board, of course, was concerned about conditions. In 1793 it named Charles Allen and Archibald McRobert to expostulate with the officers of the college on the necessity of preventing damage to the buildings by the students, whose injuries had brought the college buildings to a "ruinous condition."[33] In 1794 and again in 1801 a directive of the board prohibited the playing of "fives" against the college buildings—a game in which balls were bounced against the side of the buildings.[34] Dr. Joseph Mettauer complained in 1804 that his son Peter has been "improperly and passionately corrected" by a teacher in the grammar school; the board decided not to investigate, but to rule that no boy over fourteen should receive corporal punishment except in the presence of the president and faculty.[35] The demoralizing influences at Prince Edward Courthouse were recognized—or imagined—in a rule adopted in 1809 prohibiting students to go there unless compelled by legal authority—"going is a loss of time, generates vice, and is a corruption of morals and ought not to be tolerated." At the same time it rescinded a rule fining students fourpence for not attending public prayers.[36]

Dr. Alexander, gentle soul, resigned in 1806, to return to the ministry as pastor of Philadelphia's Pine Street Presbyterian Church. Subsequently he was to become the first professor in the theological seminary at Princeton, New Jersey, where he was to be recognized as one of the foremost trainers of young ministers.[37] William S. Reid was put in charge of the college for the session.[38] Moses Hoge was the next president of the college;[39] under his administration conditions became more stablized and the college prospered.

A perennial problem of Hampden-Sydney was lack of funds. In 1784 the General Assembly granted the college a tract of 412 acres which had belonged to Alexander Spiers John Bowman and Company and which had been confiscated during the Revolution because it belonged to a loyalist.[40] Ten years later the Assembly granted to the college four tracts of land which had belonged to Robert Routledge, whose murder in 1766 had aroused so much interest and concern. Routledge left no will and no known heirs. His administrator and former partner managed the property. Altogether the college received 1,272 acres of land from this act, except 100 acres which were reserved for the lifetime use and occupancy of Charles Gray and his wife who had long lived on a part of the Routledge property which they thought that they had purchased, being unaware that title could not be given to the property.[41]

The tract acquired in 1784 was known as French's Old Store from James and Andrew French who before the Revolution had managed the store of Alexander Spiers John Bowman and Company of Glasgow. This property, located at the present site of Kingsville, was regarded as "fairly valuable," since it yielded an annual rent.[42] In 1792 the rent was £30.[43] The college trustees and the vestry of St. Patrick's Parish in 1784 agreed upon the removal of the church at French's to the college, where it would be used as the common hall, though title would remain in the Episcopal Church. The last mention of this arrangement is reference to postponement of the removal of the church.[44]

In 1789 the college sought through the delegates from Prince Edward to the legislature to secure the surveyors' fees formerly paid to the College of William and Mary, the escheated lands of the vestry of St. Patrick's Parish, and the money formerly in the hands of the vestry. The college did not get any land or money from these sources.[45]

When it was learned in 1796 that President Washington had shares in the James River Navigation Company to give to some college in the upper part of the state, William Cowan, Richard N. Venable, and Samuel W. Venable were appointed to address him in regard to presenting it to Hampden-Sydney. This stock was given to Liberty Hall, which in appreciation changed its name to Washington Academy and later became Washington College; it is now Washington and Lee University.[46]

Another fund sought by the college was that of the Society of the Cincinnati. The trustees instructed its committee seeking these funds to advise the society that the name of the college would be changed to any name the society suggested and the board would also agree to any other reasonable condition. John B. Scott, Charles Scott, Clement Carrington, and Abraham B. Venable represented Hampden-in its effort to secure the Cincinnati money. The money had been accumulated from the gift of a month's military pay into a fund for the relief of unfortunate members, their widows, orphans. When it became evident that the money would not be needed for that purpose, the society in 1802 decided to give the money to Washington College subject to a majority vote of those attending the next annual meeting, scheduled for the second Monday in December, 1803, in the Capitol in Richmond. A determined effort was made to secure this fund for Hampden-Sydney, which in the opinion of its friends would make the Prince Edward college "one of the most respectable and useful institutions in Virginia or in the United States." One member preferred Hampden-Sydney, because "the Rockbridge Academy is already very rich"; another favored it if it would take the name Cincinnati Academy. When the deciding vote was taken December 13, 1803, the vote was eighteen to sixteen in favor of Washington College over Hampden-Sydney. The only member of the society from Prince Edward present at the meeting was Major John L. Crute;. he voted to give the fund to Hampden-Sydney as did Clement Carrington of Charlotte, John Scott of Halifax, Willis Wilson of Cumberland, George Carrington of Halifax, William Bentley of Powhatan, William Moseley and Marks Vandewalt of Richmond, Charles Scott of Kentucky, John Harris and Jordan Harris of Powhatan, Matthew Clay of Pittsylvania, William B. Wallace of Stafford, Larkin Smith of King and Queen, Samuel Clemons of Richmond, and John Trabue of Chesterfield. The funds in 1822 amounted to $16,388.82. Hampden-Sydney thus lost what was in those times a handsome endowment; but it is still Hampden-Sydney College and not Cincinnati College.[47]

Hampden-Sydney in 1820 asked for an appropriation from the Literary Fund. Consideration of the request continued sometime, for in 1823, William S. Morton, clerk of the board, sent to Henry E. Watkins (then a member of the House of Delegates) a detailed account of the college in support of the petition at the request of the president and directors of the Literary Fund. The college then had two brick buildings for the accommodation of students: one, built in 1776, was three stories high, forty-four by thirty-four feet in size, and contained twelve rooms. The other, construction of which had begun in the spring of 1822, had not yet been completed, but it had one wing four stories in height seventy-two feet long and forty feet wide with twenty-four rooms and a center section forty-three by forty-eight feet containing five large rooms for public purposes. (This was the present Cushing Hall.) On the first floor of the brick dining hall was the students' dining room, and the steward's family occupied the second floor; this building was forty-eight by forty-four feet. There were three small frame buildings, one containing the library and apparatus, another, the old steward's house now occupied by students; and the third, built for the president shortly after the college was founded, was too small and too decayed to be used for that purpose. These buildings cost about $38,000. There were 450 volumes in the college library, and the chemical and philosophical apparatus, though small in quantity, was in good condition and adequate for current needs. Textbooks were listed for the academy attached to the college and for the freshman, sophomore, junior, and senior classes, the five divisions established in 1812. The 137 students were divided thus: nineteen in the grammar school, fourteen seniors, thirteen juniors, twenty-eight sophomores, forty-five freshmen, and eighteen science students. Salaries of officers varied according to income from tuition. The college had received 1,540 acres in escheated land, of which it had sold 1,100 acres for $5,600. Individuals had contributed $40,000 in gifts of money and other property. The college at the time owned 440 acres of the land granted by the Commonwealth, but the old tenement on it was of little value; 120 acres on which the college buildings were located; forty-eight shares of stock in the Bank of Virginia, of which a considerable part had to be sold to pay the debts incurred for the new buildings. The income from the college property amounted to only $200 annually.[48]

In 1821 the college accepted in trust the gift of a house and lot from the late Dr. Hoge intended to be used as a place of worship for the part of Cumberland congregation worshipping at the college. Prior to this, worship services had been held in the college hall.[49]

Jonathan P. Cushing, a professor in the college, was chosen president in 1821. He enjoyed a successful administration.[50] During his administration, Christmas vacations were granted for the first time, as a result of a student petition.[51] Cushing has the distinction of being the first layman and the first non-Presbyterian to serve as college president. The Rev. Daniel Lynn Carroll of Brooklyn, New York, was elected president in 1835 following Dr. Cushing's death.[52] He resigned in 1838 and was succeeded by William Maxwell,[53] who resigned in 1844 and was in turn succeeded by the Rev. Patrick J. Sparrow.[54] The years had been difficult for Hampden-Sydney since the Cushing regime because of lack of funds,[55] the result of the panic of 1837. Conditions improved under the Rev. Lewis W. Green, who became president in 1849.[56] Green resigned in 1856; the Rev. A. L. Holladay was named his successor, but he died three months after his election. The Rev. J. M. P. Atkinson was elected president in May, 1857.[57]

For many years the year at Hampden-Sydney was divided into two sessions, a winter session of six months beginning in November and ending in April, and a summer session of four months beginning about June 1 and ending the latter part of September.[58] May and October were thus vacation months for the college student. Commencements were held in September, at the close of the summer session, for almost three-quarters of a century after the college was founded.[59] In 1851 commencement was held in June.[60] In earlier years students were the commencement speakers; the 1827 commencement program included a Latin oration, several English orations (two of which were given by Prince Edward graduates, William M. Tredway and James D. Ligon), a philosophical oration, a Clio-sophic oration, and a master's oration. The college that year conferred eight bachelor of arts degrees and seven master of arts degrees. The day following the commencement, the anniversary of the Literary and Philosophical Society was observed at which Jesse B. Harrison of Lynchburg spoke and Frederick Speece of Campbell County read a poem; speakers for the next year were announced as William C. Rives of Albemarle and Nelson Page of Cumberland, with Daniel Bryan of Alexandria giving the poem.[61] The Literary and Philosophical Society had been organized at Hampden-Sydney in 1824 by President Cushing with the assistance of John Holt Rice and Professor James Marsh.[62]

At the end of the winter session there was an exhibition, featured by music, orations, and debate. The exhibition held April 26, 1827, featured a Latin oration ("The Character of Germanicus"), a Greek oration ("The Character of Aristides"), several English orations, two "forensics" (one in which two freshmen took part, "Is the Advancement of Knowledge and Civilization Conducive to the Progress of Poetry?" and the second, debated by sophomores, "Ought the Catholics in Great Britain to be Entitled to Representation in Parliament?"), and three dialogues.[63] Independence Day was also celebrated at the college in those days. In 1828 the program began with the invocation by John Holt Rice, followed by a reading of the Declaration of Independence and four orations, two by representatives of the Union Literary Society, two by representatives of the Philanthropic Literary Society.[64] By 1851 speakers from outside the college were being secured for commencement programs; that year George W. Purkins of Halifax, a member of the State Constitutional Convention (designated Reform Convention in the notice), gave the literary address.[65]

In 1828 charges for the winter session amounted to $85.75, divided among tuition ($24), board ($54), room ($6), and servant's hire ($1.75). Summer session expenses amounted to $57.25, apportioned thus: tuition, $16; board, $36; room, $4; and servant's hire, $1.25. The cost of laundry was $10 per year; fuel would cost a student $6 and candles $1; any more that $20 pocket money would be "unnecessary" and "injurious."[66] Yet there were numerous items for the student to buy. In accounting for $195, Edmund W. Hubard listed his expenditures in November, 1824, and January, 1825:

Nov. 8:	cash paid J. Morton for tuition............	$34.00
"	" Am. Burwell for board...........	60.00
"	" one geography and atlas.........	7.00
"	" 3 yards baize and one inkstand....	2.50
"	" wood, together with cutting.......	5.00
"	" admittance in Society...........	3.00
"	" one algebra and Bible...........	4.00
"	" one silk cravat.................	2.00
"	" two chairs	1.50

Nov. 9:	cash paid	one silver pencil case	....	.75
	"	"	confectionery &c	2.00
Jan. 3	"	"	one almanac	.12½
4	"	"	horse feed	.50
8	"	"	two dozen apples	.25
Jan. 9	"	"	one duck	.50
	"	"	one pitcher	.25
	"	"	letters	.30
Jan. 15	"	"	dinner	.36
	"	"	kisses	.25
	"	"	wood	2.12[67]

Hampden-Sydney sponsored a medical school in Richmond from 1837 until 1854 when the school received an independent charter as the Medical College of Virginia.[68]

In 1847 Hampden-Sydney put into effect a scholarship program in which 1,200 scholarships were to be sold at $100 each. The purchaser of such a scholarship secured for himself or for his sons a full college course without the payment of tuition; if the purchaser had no sons, he was given the privilege of nominating a succession of students to receive a college education without payment of tuition for twenty years. The funds received from the sale of scholarships was to be invested in state and United States stocks and the interest was to be used to pay the faculty. A scholarship of $500 entitled the donor to keep one student in college without payment of tuition in perpetuity.[69]

In addition to the members of the original board of trustees from Prince Edward, the following men from Prince Edward served as trustees of Hampden-Sydney prior to the outbreak of the War Between the States: Richard Bibb, Joseph Moore, Abraham B. Venable, James Morton, Richard N. Venable, Joseph Venable, Archibald Alexander, Charles Scott, Dr. Robert L. Smith, the Rev. Matthew Lyle, Dr. Goodrich Wilson, the Rev. Drury Lacy, the Rev. John Holt Rice, John Booker, William L. Venable, Henry E. Watkins, William Berkeley, Thomas A. Morton, William S. Lacy, Dr. William S. Morton, James Madison (not the President but the Farmville tobacco manufacturer), Henry N. Watkins, Nathaniel E. Venable, the Rev. Benjamin Franklin Stanton, Samuel C. Anderson, Asa Dupuy, James D. Wood, Thomas Tredway, the Rev. Patrick J. Sparrow, Branch J. Worsham, Dr. Peyton Randolph Berkeley, Frank N. Watkins, Dr.

Nat A. Venable, the Rev. Samuel Lyle Graham, Robert C. Anderson, Asa Dupuy Dickinson, the Rev. Samuel Davies Stuart, Thomas E. Perkinson, John Thruston Thornton, Stephen Osborne Southall, Henry Stokes, Dr. Francis B. Watkins, and Thomas T. Tredway.[70]

Union Theological Seminary

The first step toward the founding of Union Theological Seminary was made when Hanover Presbytery in 1797 adopted a proposal made by Archibald Alexander to raise a fund to help educate "poor and pious" youth for the ministry, support missionaries, and distribute books to the poor.[71] Nearly a decade later, in 1806, the presbytery, in considering an overture presented to the General Assembly in 1805 enjoining presbyteries to look for pious and promising youth and to endeavour to educate them for the ministry, appointed a committee consisting of Archibald Alexander, Matthew Lyle, John Holt Rice, Conrad Speece, James Morton, Robert Quarles, and James Daniel to raise money and make other plans toward establishing a theological seminary at Hampden-Sydney College and to help educate "poor and pious youth" for the ministry. Rice was named agent of the committee to raise funds.[72] This committee entered into an agreement with the trustees of the college under which the trustees held the funds and library belonging to the presbytery. Moses Hoge became president of the college in 1807 and continued, with the trustees' approval, the practice of early Hampden-Sydney presidents in giving instruction in theology; the Presbytery approved Hoge as teacher under the agreement which provided that when the committee had raised enough funds to employ a teacher of theology, such a teacher would be recommended by the presbytery and approved by the Hampden-Sydney trustees.[73]

In a debate over whether the Presbyterian Church should have one central seminary; or two seminaries, one in the North and one in the South; or synodical seminaries, the Virginia presbyteries favored the third choice. The General Assembly broke the tie between the first and third choices by approving the first. In 1812 the Synod of Virginia selected Lexington as the permanent site for a seminary, but chose Hampden-Sydney as a temporary location and named Hoge as teacher of theology.[74]

An application to the Virginia legislature to incorporate the seminary was refused in 1816.[75]

In 1818 funds collected for theological education amounted to almost $4,800, and there was an additional $4,000 in pledges. Hoge had twelve students in theology that year. The theological classes were postgraduate courses for young men who planned to enter the ministry.[76]

When Hoge died, Archibald Alexander was elected president of Hampden-Sydney and the Synod named him professor of theology, but he declined the call to remain at the theological school at Princeton. At this time there was widespread support among Presbyterians in the Valley of Virginia of a plan to abandon the theological school at Hampden-Sydney and to support exclusively Princeton Theological Seminary. John Holt Rice was a leader in opposing this move, in which opposition Hanover Presbytery joined. The synod, divided between two opinions, did little to carry on its theological school and in 1822 turned over its funds to Hanover Presbytery in trust for the education of ministerial students. The sum received from the synod was $8,756.04, and the presbytery had twelve shares of Farmers Bank of Virginia stock, two shares of Bank of Virginia stock, and $1,115.68 in money. A committee of presbytery, consisting of Matthew Lyle, John B. Hoge, John D. Paxton, Nathaniel Price, and James Madison, drew up plans for a seminary and chose John Holt Rice professor at a salary of $1,200 per year. About the same time Rice was offered the presidency of Princeton College, but he declined the offer because of his health. He accepted the appointment as professor of theology in the theological school and resigned the pastorate of the First Presbyterian Church in Richmond in June, 1823.

Hanover Presbytery authorized the collection of funds to erect the seminary buildings at its April, 1823, session and named Rice special agent to raise the funds. While at Saratoga, Rice attended a meeting of Albany Presbytery, which promised to help support the new seminary. In addition to Albany, Rice received gifts for the seminary in Boston, Salem, Philadelphia, Baltimore, and Fredericksburg. In the fall of 1823 Rice began his classes in the seminary with three students, and with the beginning of instruction, the Union Theological Seminary began. At that time there were no buildings; Rice, at the invitation of President Cushing, who was then a bachelor, lived at the house provided for the college president. Through the instrumentality of Cushing, Martin Sailors gave the seminary five acres of land on which the buildings were erected. Construction of the east wing of the proposed seminary building got under way shortly after classes began; it was 1831 before the central portion and the west wing were completed. (This building is the present Venable Hall dormitory at Hampden-Sydney College.)

Efforts to raise funds for the seminary proved quite successful; the sum of $14,000 was contributed from Prince Edward and Charlotte Counties in 1825. Rice was popular in the North; in 1828 a group of ministers in Boston promised to give Union Seminary all the patronage in their power and to give "pecuniary aid" the following spring. In 1829 a professor's home was built with funds contributed by friends of Rice in Boston, and Dr. Rice and his assistant, the Rev. Hiram P. Goodrich, moved into "Boston House." This dwelling is now called Estcourt. Goodrich's salary was paid from the interest on funds contributed by friends in New York. Much of this fund was lost in the financial crash of 1837. A legacy from Andrew Baker of Prince Edward to buy books under the supervision of Hanover Presbytery was turned over to the Seminary in 1826.

In 1826 the General Assembly took the Theological Seminary of Hanover Presbytery under its care and control and placed it under the care of the Synods of Virginia and North Carolina: "The Union Seminary of the General Assembly, under the Care of the Synods of Virginia and North Carolina." The two synods accepted the responsibility, although Dr. Joseph Caldwell, president of the University of North Carolina, opposed it in his synod because he wanted the seminary in his state.

John Holt Rice died September 3, 1831, and was succeeded by Dr. George A. Baxter in the professorship. The three students with whom Rice had started eight years before had increased to forty-six; and one of his last acts was to recommend the Rev. Elisha Ballantine as assistant.[77]

Creed Taylor's Law School

Although Creed Taylor's law school was not located in Prince Edward, it deserves mention because the students there usually boarded in Farmville.[78] Taylor opened his school in 1821 at his home, Needham, not far from Farmville in Cumberland County.[79] He tried to limit his enrollment to twenty, and took four students to live in his own home; he declined to take a student for less than six months. Sessions continued from early March until late December.[80] Taylor gave no lectures. His students read law books and applied their learning in moot courts.[81] The law school was regarded by some of the more devout of the section as a center of infidelity.[82] The school was in session in 1827, but the account of the closing of that session did not mention one for 1828.[83]

The Medical School

In 1837 Dr. John Peter Mettauer opened a medical school at Prince Edward Courthouse known as the Prince Edward Medical Institute. A session began November 1, 1845, to continue until September 1, 1846. Dr. Mettauer was assisted in teaching the students by Dr. Francis Joseph Mettauer. The Doctors Mettauer offered all branches, theoretical and practical, taught "according to the discoveries and improvement of the present enlightened state of medical science." Anatomy was emphasized, and students were given the opportunity to witness Dr. Mettauer's surgical operations and to observe his treatment of medical cases in the infirmary which he conducted at Prince Edward Courthouse. Instruction was given by lectures, demonstrations, daily examinations, and dissections. In a sense the Prince Edward Medical Institute was preparatory to the Washington University of Baltimore, and students who had completed a year at the Mettauer school were admitted to the second year in the Baltimore institution. The fee at the Prince Edward Medical Institute was $100, in advance, for the course, with an additional fee of $20 for the course in dissections. Students boarded in the community.[84]

The Prince Edward Medical Institute became the Medical School of Randolph-Macon College in 1847. The change evidently made some complications for Dr. Francis Joseph Mettauer, who at the time was professor of chemistry and natural philosophy at Hampden-Sydney. Upon the application of Dr. John Peter Mettauer in September, 1847, Dr. Francis Joseph Mettauer was permitted to fill the chair of chemistry in the medical school provided he did not teach there any courses he taught at Hampden-Sydney.[85] Apparently this arrangement did not suit the Mettauers, for two years later, the board reiterated its position and Dr. Francis Joseph Mettauer resigned his professorship at Hampden-Sydney.[86]

As the institute, the Medical Department of Randolph-Macon (the college was then located at Boydton) had a ten months' session beginning in November. Dr. John Peter Mettauer was professor of the principles and practice of medicine, surgery, and clinical practice; Dr. Francis Joseph Mettauer was professor of anatomy, physiology, and chemistry; and in October, 1849, there was no occupant of the chair of therapeutics and materia medica, midwifery, and the diseases of females and infants. The fee for the course was $115, and the graduation fee was $30. Board convenient to the college was advertised as available at $100 for the session, and textbooks could be bought in Farmville.[87]

The Education of Women

One of the manifestations of the growing social consciousness of the early nineteenth century was a widespread interest in the education of girls. Little attention had been given to providing formal education for the daughters of the family previously. Some had studied with their brothers under the teachers engaged by the father, and some of the more fortunate had received instruction in such arts as music and dancing; for the most part, though, the girls' education was principally in the domestic skills at the instruction of the mother. Early in the nineteenth century this pattern was changed, and schools for the education of girls appeared in many places.

The first girls' school in Prince Edward was in the now abandoned town of Jamestown on the Appomattox River. It was in operation in 1817, when a lottery was conducted to raise money to erect a building for the school. The managers of the lottery offered 10,000 tickets at $5 each; of these, 3,362 were to yield prizes, and the rest were blanks. The first prize was $10,000; the second, $5,000; the third, $2,000; there were two prizes of $1,000 each; three of $500 each; four of $250 each; ten of $100 each; twenty of $50 each; one hundred of $20 each; and 3,000 of $5 each. In addition there were special or stationary prizes: the first five numbers drawn on the first day's drawing (the drawing was to last twenty days, 500 tickets being drawn daily) each would receive a prize of $50 each; the first five numbers on the fifth day, $100 each; the first five drawn on the tenth day, $150 each; the first four on the fifteenth day, $250 each; and the last number drawn on the twentieth and last day, $5,000. All the prizes were subject to a discount of fifteen per cent, which would provide the money needed to erect the building.

Edmund Booker of Jamestown was treasurer of the lottery and one of the managers; other managers were Tscharner Woodson, James D. Wood, Allen Wilson, Abner Nash, Blake B. Woodson, Maurice Langhorne, Peter Rison, Robert Jones, William Randolph, Edward Booker, and Thomas B. Randolph. James H. Fitzgerald was named a manager, but he declined to serve.[88]

Mrs. Mary R. Cowardin was in charge of the school at that time, at least during the 1817-18 session. A public examination of the students (which was the practice of the day) took place on June

14, 1818, and William B. Smith, Philip T. Southall, Blake B. Woodson, William Randolph, and William F. Randolph were so favorably impressed that they wrote a commendatory notice. The results of the examination gave entire satisfaction to the large audience, and the "proficiency [of the students] in grammar and geography" merited special emphasis. Mrs. Cowardin was generously praised as "ably calculated" to conduct a school, as being of mild temper and disposition, of correct judgment and pleasing manner.[89]

The school was in operation in the early 1830's when William White was in charge.[90]

The next school for young ladies in the county, of which there is record, was opened by Eleazar Root, Jr., at Prince Edward Courthouse on January 1, 1832.[91] A "next" session was announced as scheduled to begin the first Monday in July, 1832, when a "large and commodious edifice will . . . be in readiness." An additional teacher in the English department had been employed; Miss Mansfield would continue to teach music, painting, and drawing. For the ten months' session, board and tuition in all branches cost $130 and in the English branches, including washing and candles, $100. Tuition for day students in music was $25; in language, $20; in painting and drawing, $15; and in the English branches, $25. Board in "genteel families" around Prince Edward Courthouse could be had for $7 per month. In December the students had a month's vacation. President Cushing of Hampden-Sydney, Samuel C. Anderson, the well known attorney, and the Rev. B. F. Stanton were given as references.[92] During that session E. Root, Jr. and H. Root were listed as principals, Mrs. E. Todd as assistant teacher in the English department, and Miss L. Mansfield, teacher of music, painting, and drawing. Dr. William Dupuy of Nottoway was added to the references in 1833.[93]

In 1838 the Young Ladies Seminary of Prince Edward was incorporated, the petitioners being of the opinion that the institution operated by E. Root, Jr., "should be placed on a permanent footing." Samuel C. Anderson, Branch J. Worsham, William H. Venable, John P. Mettauer, Jared Todd, Henry Thweatt, Joseph Todd, and James D. Wood were named trustees.[94] Fees had increased somewhat by 1838, board being $120 for the term; tuition in the English branches $25; in French $20; in painting and drawing $30; in music $50; and use of the piano $10. There were daily lessons in the English branches and in French, two lessons weekly of one-half day each in painting and drawing, two lessons of one hour each in music and one hour daily assigned for practice.

Some of the restrictions associated with girls' schools of another day were to be noted in 1838: pupils were not allowed to attend parties; nor were they allowed to receive visits except from near relatives.[95]

In 1840 George W. Dame advertised the session of the Young Ladies' Seminary at Prince Edward Courthouse.[96]

In 1845 Robert G. Branch, who had been professor of ancient languages at Hampden-Sydney, became head of the young ladies' seminary.[97] In an advertisement in March, 1845, Branch proposed to open a school for young ladies on June 1 in the buildings erected for a female seminary. The summer session ran from the first of June to the last of September, the winter session from the first of November to the last of April. Tuition for the summer session was $12, board including bed and washing $40, music $12.[98]

H. D. Brown and his wife conducted the Brownsville Young Ladies Institute at Prince Edward Courthouse in the 1850's. Closing exercises for the 1857-58 session were held June 7-8, 1858. The school was described as "flourishing and growing in reputation." The Brown school has been identified as successor to the school conducted by Root and Branch.[99]

A school for girls was opened in Farmville in the spring of 1835. Twenty-five pupils were quickly enrolled. The principal, the Rev. A. J. Huestis, brought with him testimonials concerning his qualifications from President William Fisk of Wesleyan University in Connecticut and from John Burrage and William A. J. Bradford, school commissioners of New Bedford, Massachusetts. A. M. Huestis was preceptress. Tuition was $20 in the junior or elementary class in English, $25 in the senior class or higher departments of English science. Instruction was also offered in music, painting, drawing, French, and ancient languages. Board could be obtained in town in respectable families for $7.50 per month. The location of the school is described as being in a "commanding and romantic part of town," with good facilities for health and proficiency in science.[100] By July, 1835, thirty students were enrolled; the summer session was scheduled to end July 27, and the winter session to begin August 24.[101]

It is not certain how long Heustis remained in Farmville; he is listed as one of the principals of the Buckingham Female Collegiate Institute in 1837.[102]

In 1839 a group of men secured a charter for the Farmville

Female Seminary, which was incorporated with a capital of $30,000. The incorporators were W. C. Flournoy, Joseph E. Venable, Thomas Flournoy, William Wilson, George Daniel, Willis Blanton, and others who may become stockholders. Those listed were named trustees and were empowered to select a president and fill vacancies among them.[103] The building which was erected had on it a silver plate bearing the inscription: "Farmville Female Academy. Built by Joint Stock Company. 1839"; when it was taken down about 1897, the time of the construction of the building provoked some discussion, since the deed to the land on which it was built was not conveyed by George Whitfield Read and his wife Charlotte to the trustees until 1842. Inquiry was made of old residents, including W. W. H. Thackston, W. T. Rice, and C. H. Erambert, and the conclusion was reached that the corner-stone was laid in 1839, the construction proceeded, and that the building was completed, occupied, and paid for in 1842, when the deed was given. The land, lots 105 and 107 of the Josiah Chambers survey,[104] is the nucleus of the present site of Longwood College, the building standing where the present Rotunda building is now located. The lots then were at the corner of High and Spruce Streets, but Spruce Street has been closed for over half a century and absorbed into the college campus.[105] Solomon Lea was the first principal of the academy conducted under the auspices of the joint stock company. He was succeeded by his brother, the Rev. Lorenzo Lea. Their successors were Benjamin Tinsley, Benjamin Gould (1855-59), and George LaMonte (1859-62).[106]

A visitor from Cumberland at the public examinations on June 24, 1856, praised the showing of the students highly. Principal (then Benjamin Gould), teachers, and several gentlemen conducted the examinations. The examination of Miss Susie Dunnington in chemistry would have done credit to a college junior, thought this member of the audience; he mentioned Misses Bettie Watkins, Hattie Read, Christiana Osborne, Hattie Venable, and Louisa Fuqua as showing a knowledge of textbooks "which would elevate them to the highest grade of scholarship." Examinations were conducted for classes in Latin, French, astronomy, chemistry, botany, rhetoric, philosophy, algebra, grammar, geography, and arithmetic. A dialogue by three young ladies pointed out the deficiencies of superficial education, literary polish, and parlor accomplishments "afforded by two many female schools."[107]

In 1860 the seminary received a charter as The Farmville Female College, with W. C. Flournoy, Joseph E. Venable, Thomas Flournoy,

H. E. Warren, George W. Daniel, F. N. Watkins, and James B. Ely the incorporators.[108]

Schools for Boys

In addition to the grammar or academy department conducted at Hampden-Sydney College, there were many schools for the education of boys in ante-bellum Prince Edward. Hampden-Sydney was largely responsible, for it generated much interest in education in the county; its convenience made it possible for many Prince Edward boys to look forward to getting and to get a college education; and it also provided a supply of teachers in young men who wished to teach for a year or two before continuing professional studies or while reading law in the office of some attorney or while studying theology under the college president before Union Seminary was formally opened.

Drury Lacy began a notable teaching career in Prince Edward about 1779, when he became teacher in the family of Colonel John Nash. After four years he joined the faculty at Hampden-Sydney[109] and served as vice-president and chief executive officer of the college in the seven-year interval between the departure of John Blair Smith and the coming of Archibald Alexander. After resigning at Hampden-Sydney, Lacy conducted a grammar school at his home, Ararat, from about 1800 until his death in 1815; it was continued for several years thereafter by his son, the Rev. William Lacy, who later went to Arkansas. This was one of the most famous of Prince Edward preparatory schools; John Randolph of Roanoke, when living at Bizarre, sent his wards to Drury Lacy; he would often ride over to hear the Latin and Greek grammar lessons, which were held before breakfast! At the opening of the day's formal session, at nine o'clock, the boys read verses from the Bible until the assigned portion was finished. Randolph sometimes stayed for this exercise and took his turn. He was also accustomed to take part in the spelling bees on Friday afternoon, always starting at the foot and usually going to the head of the line. In the afternoon reading classes, when passages from the Bible, *The Spectator*, Shakespeare, and Milton were read, Randolph would sometimes take a turn and show the boys how the passage should be read. It must have been a thrilling experience to hear his fine and musical voice read, but what an exasperation his participation in classes must have been to the schoolmaster! But because he did, this picture of Drury Lacy's school has been preserved.

Hugh Blair Grigsby was prepared for Yale at Ararat; sixty-one years later, in 1876, he could still feel and distinguish (which is the test) Lacy's influence and bear testimony to his thoroughness as a Latin teacher. The school at Ararat was well attended, many pupils coming from a distance and boarding with Lacy or some of the neighbors.

John Hatchett left a record of the schools which he attended as a boy in Prince Edward. In 1780 he attended classes taught by William Booker in a room of Colonel Thomas Flournoy's home. His teacher in 1781 and 1782 was Ulitious (Ulysses ?) Rogers. He attended Joseph Price's school in 1783, John Bibb's in 1784, William Russell's in 1775, and John Bassette's in the summer of 1786, when he was in his seventeenth year. Hatchett himself taught a school at his home, beginning in 1805.

Among other schools in Prince Edward were those conducted by Franklin Gilette Smith before 1822; by David Duncan at or near Prince Edward Courthouse about 1819; by William Branch, Jr., at his home, Golgotha, about 1820; by the Rev. Hiram P. Goodrich, before 1828; by the Rev. Elisha Ballantine at Prince Edward Courthouse in the old home of Captain William Worsham, beginning about 1837, in which he was assisted for a time by the Rev. Stephen Taylor.[110] The Rev. William S. White, while studying theology, taught a school in Farmville in 1824-25.[111] Andrew W. Millspaugh taught a school at Longwood, before becoming a manufacturer of railroad spikes.[112]

It is interesting to note the number of people who were identified with education in Prince Edward during the first half of the nineteenth century who were Northerners and especially New Englanders. President Cushing was from New England and a graduate of Dartmouth; Professor James Marsh, who taught acceptably in both Hampden-Sydney and Union Seminary, became president of the University of Vermont;[113] A. J. Huestis was from New England, from his credentials presumably a graduate of Wesleyan with teaching experience in New Bedford, Massachusetts; Eleazar Root, Jr., was a native of New York and a graduate of Williams; he later became superintendent of public instruction in Wisconsin and shared in the founding of the University of Wisconsin.[114] And there was at least one young lady from New England who came to Prince Edward to teach school at one of the homes; Miss Emily Howe of Princeton, Massachusetts, taught at the home of the Rev. Matthew M. Dance; she subsequently married Colonel Asa Dupuy of Linden.[115]

William B. Featherston began teaching a school at the home of

Colonel Samuel D. Burke, Burke's Tavern, in 1840; the first session of this school began February 15 and ended July 15; the second session began August 1 and ended December 20. Burke advertised that he could accommodate eight or ten boarders and that board and tuition would cost $65 per session. Featherston was a graduate of William H. Harrison's celebrated preparatory school in Amelia, and was recommended by his old teacher as a teacher of English, Latin, and Greek. Burke's practice was not unusual in those days.[116] A man would engage a teacher for his children and admit others to the classes upon payment of tuition. Usually the other students came from neighboring farms, but Burke had accommodations for boarding students at his inn. James D. Ligon of Walnut Hill admitted children of neighbors to classes conducted at his home. In the late 1850's two of the teachers were W. W. Woodson of Goochland County and Albert Todd, a graduate of Hampden-Sydney in the class of 1857.[117]

Union Academy, in the section of Prince Edward which became Appomattox County, was chartered in 1838 by William Mathews, Philip Mathews, Edmund Conner, Samuel Watkins, Peter LeGrand, Samuel Mitchell, Jr., Rezin Porter, E. M. W. Durphy, J. McDearmon, William L. Wood, Samuel B. Hill, and Davis Hill.[118]

A school, whose prospect of great usefulness was cut short by the War Between the States, was opened in Farmville in the late 1850's. W. J. Morrissett, M.A., taught mathematics, natural sciences, and French; G. E. Booker, M.A., taught languages; L. Morrissett was assistant in languages; and S. B. Partin assistant in mathematics at the Southside Institute. The 1858-59 term began September 1, 1858 and continued until the end of June, 1859.[119] It will be noted that throughout this period a ten-month school term prevailed. Classes met in the old Baptist Church at the corner of Main and Fourth Streets, a building made vacant by the building in 1856 of a new church on the present site occupied by the Baptist Church.[120]

It is not certain that the Southside Institute was the school chartered as the Farmville Institute in 1852 with F. N. Watkins, C. C. Read, Joseph E. Venable, J. W. Dunnington, and B. M. Robertson as trustees.[121]

Public Education

Public education began in Virginia with the creation of the literary fund in 1811. Income from this fund was appropriated among the counties to be used to pay tuition for poor children.

School commissioners were appointed in each county to administer the fund made available to the county.

Prince Edward's first school commissioners, who qualified in June, 1818, were: James D. Wood, Francis Watkins, Jr., John J. Flournoy, Anderson P. Miller, Osborn Lockett, John Clark, Charles Woodson, Nathaniel Price, Jesse Michaux, Robert Kelso, William Mathews, and Rezin Porter.[122] At this time, the principal officers of the commissioners were the clerk and treasurer, who handled the money. Richard N. Venable, who in 1820 succeeded James D. Wood, qualified as treasurer in June, 1823, giving bond for $2,000.[123] Charles Woodson became treasurer in 1825; he served until 1837. James McDearmon was treasurer 1837-45, and Luther C. Jeffress 1845-46.[124]

Others named commissioners and the dates of their appointments, were: William Doswell, 1825;[125] John W. Redd, Richard Booker, Josiah Rice, 1825;[126] Robert Hill, William C. Bell, 1827;[127] John Foster, 1829;[128] James McDearmon, 1830;[129] William C. Hill, Simeon H. Wootton, 1831;[130] Robert Venable, 1832[131] William Holland, John A. Scott, 1834;[132] John W. Gilliam, James H. Wilson, 1836;[133] John Dupuy, William B. Baker, and Griffith Dickenson, 1837;[134] James T. Price, Jacob McGehee, 1839;[135] Luther C. Jeffress, 1840;[136] Thomas O. Rowlett, Joseph Phillips, 1844.[137]

In November, 1846, the county was divided into ten districts, for each of which a commissioner was appointed. The number of the district is given with the commissioner in this list: 1. (Town of Farmville) George W. Daniel; 2. James Venable; 3. James H. Wilson; 4. William B. Baker; 5. Luther C. Jeffress; 6 John W. Redd; 7. John A. Scott; 8. Thomas O. Rowlett; 9. William H. Venable; 10. Joseph Phillips.[138] Subsequent appointments as commissioners were: James D. Ligon, 1848;[139] Benjamin W. Womack, 1849;[140] William Elliott, 1850;[141] Stephen O. Rowlett, 1851;[142] Thomas H. Almond, 1853;[143] Jechonias Overby, George W. Vaughan, 1854;[144] Gabriel S. Harper, William A. Womack, William L. Womack, 1856;[145] P. H. Jackson, John H. Knight, Francis D. Redd, Samuel W. Vaughan, Joseph T. Ligon, 1857;[146] William Walton, Samuel B. Scott, 1858;[147] S. T. Clark, Alexander S. Clark, 1860;[148] William H. Cary, James M. Wootton, 1861.[149]

After 1846 the principal officer of the commissioners was called superintendent, and that title has continued to designate the administrative officer in the local school unit. Luther C. Jeffress was chosen superintendent for Prince Edward in 1846.[150] James Venable was named superintendent for Prince Edward in 1850 and served through 1857.[151] John H. Knight became superintendent January 1, 1858;[152] he was succeeded by Samuel B. Scott in 1861.[153]

The school commissioners were permitted to build school buildings and employ teachers for them beginning in 1829 if that procedure seemed more advisable to them than paying tuition for children in a particular district. Residents of the district were required to provide three-fifths of the cost of the building, and the commissioners could pay the remaining part if it did not exceed ten per cent of the annual apportionment for the county from the Literary Fund. They were empowered to appropriate up to $100 of the county quota to employ a teacher for the school so built, but the teachers for such schools had to be approved by persons designated by the directors of the Literary Fund.[154] The Prince Edward commissioners objected to many of the requirements of this act, including the new forms for reports, and petitioned for changes, but the petition was not acted on by the Schools Committee of the House of Delegates to which it was referred.[155]

The sums allotted Prince Edward by the Literary Fund were never large. In 1839 it was $204.45.[156] In 1844 it was $426.24.[157] The year before, of 500 indigent children in Prince Edward, only 159 were in school.[158] The highest amount received was $465.08 in 1845, but a portion of this had to be re-appropriated for the new county of Appomattox.[159] In 1846 Prince Edward received only $249.12, and Appomattox was allotted six cents more.[160] The allotment for Prince Edward rose to $384 in 1851.[161] For the session 1844-45, the Prince Edward school commissioners paid teachers four cents per pupil per day to teach indigent children.[162]

It was the duty of the commissioner to report to the superintendent all children between the ages of five and sixteen; to enter indigent children in the district with teachers and to have the teacher keep a record of each indigent child's attendance. The superintendent in 1846 assumed the duties which had been performed by the clerk and treasurer; he was required to prepare and keep a register of children at school, report to the annual meeting of the commissioners the condition of the school system, see that the commissioners reported the number, ages, names, and sex of children in their districts and to designate the children who were entitled to receive instruction under this act, to set the per diem compensation of teachers for teaching indigent children, subject to the approval of the commissioners.

The people could after 1846 petition for an election to establish district free schools; a favorable vote of two-thirds was required to establish them.[163]

The Libraries

Two library societies were in existence in Prince Edward early in the nineteenth century. The Library Company of Prince Edward had been organized prior to January 1, 1803, when the trustees of Hampden-Sydney, meeting at James Morton's store, named Morton, Samuel W. Venable, and Richard N. Venable to draw plans for a library building for the college and to enter into an agreement with the library company under which the company would be provided a room in the library in which to keep its books.[164] In December, 1804, the company petitioned the General Assembly for incorporation. Signing the petition were Samuel W. Venable, Archibald Alexander, Isaac Read, Archibald McRobert, W. M. Watkins, Drury Lacy, Joshua League, William L. Venable, Edward Dillon, Henry A. Watkins, C. Scott, F. Watkins, Jr., F. Watkins, Sr., Henry E. Watkins, Nathaniel Venable, Jr., Thomas Morton, and Charles Morton.[165]

A charter was promptly granted to the society which had been organized to procure a library for the benefit and improvement of its members. Samuel W. Venable, Goodridge Wilson, Archibald Alexander, Matthew Lyle, Drury Lacy, James Morton, John B. Scott, William Cowan, and John H. Rice, who had been listed as directors in the petition, were confirmed as directors in the charter of incorporation. The director's term was one year.[166]

The Library Company of Prince Edward ceased to function about 1820. On April 26, the clerk of the Hampden-Sydney Board of Trustees was directed to write to members of "the late Library Company of Prince Edward" that if the company did not meet on the next Prince Edward court day, the trustees would consider the company dissolved and would take possession of its property, "agreeably to the constitution of the company."[167] In September, 1821, the trustees directed the college librarian to take charge of the books and property of the company, but to permit the Union Literary Society to withdraw from the library the books which it had deposited as a contribution for shares.[168]

The Buffalo Circulating Library operated in the territory of the Buffalo Presbyterian Church. The first meeting was held April 13, 1803, at which William Womack was chosen clerk and John Cunningham librarian and treasurer. The following shareholders were listed: Andrew Baker, Sr., three chares; William Baldwin, Nathaniel Price, and Samuel Baldwin, two shares each; and John Cunningham, John Hamilton, Thomas W. McGlasson, Robert Hill, Andrew Baker, Jr., John Andrews, William Womack, Jr., Nancy Elliott, Thomas Clark, James McKle (the name later became Mickle), and Adam Calhoun, one share each. Shares cost $10 each, and annual dues of one dollar per shareholder were set. As soon as the money had been paid in for seventeen shares, it was to be spent in the purchase of "useful books." Each subscriber could take out at one time one book for each share he held in the library; folio books could be kept out three months, quarto books two months, octavo or less books one month. A fine of ten cents a month was levied for books kept out overtime. A book seriously damaged had to be replaced or paid for. Shares in the library could be sold if the purchaser agreed to the rules. New subscribers could be received at any time upon the purchase of a share, and whenever the sum of $20 had been accumulated, it was to be spent for new books.

The catalogue of books in the Buffalo Library was heavily weighted with volumes on religious subjects. Such poetry as Thomson's *Seasons*, Milton's *Paradise Lost*, and Goldsmith's *Deserted Village* was included. Works of history, biography, and travel were also found in the list.

In August, 1803, William Baldwin was elected chairman of the library. Thomas W. McGlasson succeeded Womack as clerk in 1811. William Berkeley was elected president in 1821.

From time to time there were changes in the ownership of shares. In 1804, after Andrew Baker, Sr.'s death, his shares were transferred, one each to Robert Hill, Elliott Baker, and the legatees of Samuel Baker, deceased. The last-mentioned share was transferred to Captain Andrew Baker in 1806, and at the same time one of Robert Hill's shares was transferred to Samuel Hill. Charles Raine's share was transferred to Allen W. Elliott in 1809. Thomas B. Clarke acquired Thomas Clarke's share in 1812, and Lillious D. Womack William Womack's share in 1817.

As early as 1816 proposals were made to dissolve the society and divide the library, but it was not until January 31, 1822, that a motion to dissolve, made by Nathaniel Price who had proposed dissolution in 1816, passed by a majority of one vote. The library was divided among the members, each shareholder receiving books and cash to the amount of $7.50. To prevent breaking up a set of books worth more than that amount, the recipient paid into the treasury the difference between that figure and the value of the books. Such was the case with Elliott Baker, who drew Marshall's *Life of Washington*, valued at $14, and with Nathaniel Price, who drew Russell's *Modern Europe*, valued at $10. Provision was also made for members who so desired to give the books received to the trustees of Buffalo congregation for the benefit of the congregation.[169]

Students at Other Institutions

After the founding of Hampden-Sydney College, most of the young men of the county who went to college chose Hampden-Sydney. Some, however, chose other institutions. From Hampden-Sydney, three sons of Nathaniel Venable went to Princeton. Samuel Woodson Venable and Abraham Bedford Venable graduated at Princeton in 1780, and Richard Nathaniel Venable graduated there two years later. A fourth son of the family, Nathaniel Venable, Jr., graduated there in 1796. Their cousin, Joseph Venable, who was later to succeed Abraham Bedford Venable as commonwealth's attorney for Prince Edward, graduated from Princeton in 1782. George M. Bibb went from Prince Edward to Princeton, graduating there in 1792.[170] Henry E. Watkins was a Princeton graduate in the class of 1801, and Abraham Watkins Venable in 1819.[171] Watkins also studied law at William and Mary.[172]

Francis J. Mettauer, a son of Dr. John Peter Mettauer, attended the College of William and Mary, where he was a junior in 1834-35 and a senior in 1836-37.[173] He apparently was not enrolled 1835-36.

Edwin Womack and R. J. Overton of Prince Edward were appointed cadets to the Virginia Military Institute in 1853 and 1855 respectively.[174]

Dr. Flournoy of Prince Edward studied at the University of Edinburgh before 1800.[175]

Two Prince Edward students, one a Watkins (not otherwise identified), the other James D. Ligon, studied law under Judge Henry St. George Tucker in Winchester; the former was there in 1827-28, the latter, 1828-29.[176]

Two law students at William and Mary, listed from Prince Edward, were A. D. Dickinson in 1841-42, and William A. Leigh, son of Paschal G. Leigh of Sandy River Church, in 1841-42 and 1842-43.[177]

Thomas Watkins Ligon, after studying at Hampden-Sydney and the University of Virginia, studied law at Yale.[178]

CHAPTER IX

A Great Age for Politics

THE ratification of the Federal Constitution increased the opportunities of freeholders in Prince Edward and elsewhere to participate in government. The transition of Virginia from colony to commonwealth had made some changes: in addition to the two members of the House of Delegates (who took the place of the two members of the House of Burgesses), freeholders voted for the members of the State Senate from the district. In 1786 the office of overseer of the poor was established and made elective. But there remained the qualification of property ownership for voting; the Governor of the state was elected by the legislature—a step toward greater democracy, it is true, from appointment by the Crown of England; the magistrates and sheriffs continued to be appointed by the Governor.

The establishment of the Federal government gave freeholders the right to vote for two officers: presidential electors and members of the lower house of Congress, the House of Representatives. Members of the upper house, the Senate, were elected by the State legislatures.

Virginia was entitled to twelve presidential electors, so the General Assembly in November, 1788, divided the State into twelve districts. Prince Edward was placed in the tenth electoral district, with Campbell, Pittsylvania, Charlotte, Halifax, Bedford, Franklin, and Henry Counties. The time of the election was set for the first Wednesday in January, 1789, and the place in each county was the courthouse. Persons eligible to vote for members of the General Assembly were eligible to vote for the electors. The election was conducted by the high sheriff, and each voter was to announce his choice of elector from the district publicly. Determination by view, that is, by the sheriff calling for the expression of choice from the assembled freeholders in a body, was forbidden in this election. The electors were called to meet in Richmond on the first Wednesday in February, 1789, to cast their votes for President and Vice-President.[1]

Patrick Henry, who was living in Prince Edward at that time, was chosen elector from the district. He, as did every other elector, cast his vote for George Washington for President. Henry's choice for Vice-President was George Clinton of New York, but John Adams of Massachusetts was elected.[2]

The same Assembly divided the State into ten districts for the election of members of the House of Representatives. Prince Edward was placed in the sixth district, with Charlotte, Campbell, Buckingham, Bedford, Franklin, Henry, Pittsylvania, and Halifax Counties. The first election of representatives took place February 2, 1789,[3] and Isaac Coles of Halifax was elected.[4] In 1791 the choice of the district was Abraham Bedford Venable,[5] second son of Nathaniel Venable of Slate Hill, graduate of Princeton, lawyer, and formerly attorney for the Commonwealth for Prince Edward.

The Constitution had allotted to Virginia ten representatives, who with the two senators, determined the number of presidential electors from the State. The census of 1790 showed that Virginia was entitled, on the basis of population, to nineteen representatives. In 1792 the Assembly redistricted the State for the election of both electors and representatives. Prince Edward, Buckingham, Cumberland, and Lunenburg were constituted one of the twenty-one electoral districts; the first Monday in November every fourth year beginning in 1792 was set as the day for electing Presidential electors.[6] Prince Edward, Charlotte, Buckingham, Cumberland, and Fluvanna were constituted one of the nineteen congressional districts; the third Monday in March, 1793, was set as the day on which to leect members of the House of Representatives, and subsequent elections were set for that day on each second year thereafter.[7] Venable was elected from the new district for the Third, Fourth, and Fifth Congresses.[8]

Tarlton Woodson of Prince Edward was elected presidential elector in 1792, and he, together with all the other electors, voted for Washington.[9]

In Virginia political party organization became effective in 1800. Friends of Jefferson, determined that their candidate should not lose this year as he had done in 1796, met in Richmond early in the year to plan the campaign in Virginia and set up an organization reaching into the counties. A committee of correspondence was set up in Prince Edward (as in the other counties) to arouse interest in Jefferson's candidacy, to get out the vote in support of Creed Taylor of Cumberland, nominee for district elector on the Jeffersonian ticket, and to inform the state committee of developments locally. The Prince Edward committee consisted of Archibald McRobert,

Tarlton Woodson, Thomas Green, Theodorick B. McRobert, and Daniel Carter. Jefferson received 345 votes in Prince Edward to four for John Adams.[10]

Commissioners were named to conduct the election of presidential electors in 1800 instead of the sheriff. The Prince Edward commissioners were Archibald McRobert, Tarlton Woodson, and John Kelso.[11] The concentrated efforts proved successful for Jefferson was elected, and for many years thereafter committees of correspondence in behalf of candidates were organized for campaigns.

Candidates for the post of presidential electors were then nominated by a caucus consisting of the members of the party in the General Assembly. The caucus was held during the session of the Assembly during the winter preceding the November election. In 1804 the caucus nominated Peter Johnston of Prince Edward on the Republican ticket (the party of Jefferson was then called Republican; later Democratic-Republican, from which it has become Democratic). The electoral districts had been changed, and Prince Edward had been put in the district with Charlotte and Halifax. Colonel Thomas Read of Charlotte, who had been elected on the Jeffersonian ticket for his district in 1800, was upset because he had been left off the electoral ticket and so advised the party committee in Charlotte. When news of Read's "excited" feelings, which were shared "by many respectable persons in the district," reached Johnston, he wrote the Rev. Archibald McRobert, chairman of the Republican committee in Prince Edward, resigning the nomination and proposing to the state General Committee of Correspondence that Read be nominated in his stead. McRobert forwarded Johnston's letter to Philip N. Nicholas, chairman of the state committee, and in a covering letter endorsed Johnston's proposal, as "justly due the early, uniform, firm and now aged patriot and manly and constant advocate of the Republican cause." The substitution was made as proposed, and Johnston gained in respect far more, perhaps, than he would have had he persisted in holding the nomination. McRobert spoke of the "prompt and polite manner" in which he declined the nomination as bringing him respect, and the state committee praised his candor and liberality.[12] Johnston's conduct may have been a factor in his election as speaker of the Virginia House of Delegates in 1805.[13]

Behind this difficulty which Johnston kept from becoming more unpleasant was Colonel Read's political animosity toward Isaac Coles, who was then state senator from the district composed of Prince Edward, Charlotte, and Halifax. Coles had been earlier a Federalist (although now he had changed parties), and Read a Republican who was a staunch enemy of Federalists. He had opposed Coles for the State Senate because of the latter's earlier political affiliation. As reported to Read, and accurately, Coles had nominated Johnston in the caucus. In doing so, Coles had informed the caucus that Colonel Read's health was poor and that he did not wish to be on the Republican ticket again. When the Republican committee, in inquiring of Read why he declined the nomination, asked if Coles had been authorized to make the statement, Read replied no. One gets the impression that Read was provoked on two counts: one, that his political opponent should presume to speak for him; the other, that his political opponent might be trying to move him out of the place of party leadership he had enjoyed in the past.

Coles, however, was speaking not so much for himself as for Creed Taylor, who was also in the caucus. Sometime before, Taylor, on a visit to Read, invited Read to come by his home, Needham, just outside Farmville, and ride to Richmond with him. Read replied that he was getting too old to go so far from home again; Taylor remonstrated that he would certainly be going to the meeting of the Electoral College as he would undoubtedly be on the ticket again. Read replied—he must have been feeling particularly unwell that day—that the election was so far off, someone else in the district would be thought of whom it would suit better to go. Taylor assumed responsibility for suggesting to Coles to propose Johnston, and so wrote Read in an effort to divert his wrath from Coles. Read recalled more specifically the invitation Taylor had given him which was for the trip to Richmond for the Electoral College meeting: Taylor had invited him to come to Needham on the Friday prior to the election on Wednesday, have dinner with him that Friday, spend the night with him, and ride with him to Richmond the next day, since Taylor was a member of the legislature which was convening on Monday; as Read remembered it, his reply was that it was earlier than he intended going, that it did not suit him to go so far from home and to leave earlier than necessary if he had to go. When Taylor then said he would probably have to go as an elector, Read replied that the time was distant and many changes might take place. He indicated that he had not abated one whit his antagonism for Coles and that he saw in Coles' action more than a "tender regard" for his health. He found himself embarrassed that his friends and political allies would think from Coles' supposed speaking for him some change in his political attitude. Taylor's reply recognized that the two did not remember the incident at Read's home alike and regretted any dissatisfaction he may have caused his friend.[14]

Archibald McRobert, Tarlton Woodson, and Thomas Green were election commissioners in Prince Edward in 1804.[15] Read was elected presidential elector.[16]

When Abraham Venable did not seek re-election to Congress in 1799, three candidates sought the seat he was vacating: John Randolph, then living at Bizarre in Cumberland just across the Appomattox from Farmville, Powhatan Bouldin of Charlotte, both of whom were Republicans, and Clement Carrington of Charlotte, Federalist.[17] Randolph, who entered politics at the proposal of Creed Taylor,[18] was elected and promptly became one of the leaders of the Republican party in Congress. He later broke with Jefferson and Madison over the Yazoo issue. Until this dissension he had no Republican opposition (and only weak Federalist). He was re-elected in 1805 without campaigning; but the break came that year and Randolph found the administration working to discredit him in his district. A near neighbor announced his candidacy in opposition in 1807, but later withdrew it.[19] This neighbor was almost certainly Peter Johnston. Johnston went to Washington where he conferred with Jefferson; he did not call on Randolph, and the latter, upon learning of Johnston's visit to the capital, implied that he thought that Johnston was seeking administration support to oppose Randolph for the House of Representatives.[20] Randolph was feeling keenly the enmity to him. Early in 1807 he wrote his friend and neighbor, Edward Dillon of Sandy Ford, Prince Edward: "In these days of mutability we hardly know who to select as *friends*, or who to set down as *enemies*."[21]

Randolph's first Republican opposition after 1799 came in 1809 when Jerman Baker, a brother-in-law of John W. Eppes, who was Jefferson's son-in-law, ran against him. Randolph defeated Baker by more than two to one, carrying Prince Edward 342 to Baker's 84. Eppes himself was Randolph's opponent in 1811, and again Randolph, who appeared to enjoy the support of his district, although it was Jeffersonian in presidential politics, won by more than two to one.[22] Randolph was among those who tried to block Madison's nomination for the Presidency on the Republican ticket in 1808. Creed Taylor, who was as staunch a supporter of Randolph in the controversy with the Jefferson administration as he had been a decade before when persuading his young neighbor to become a candidate for Congress, was active in supporting James Monroe for the nomination instead of Madison. Taylor regarded Monroe as "the man, of all others, in the United States to succeed Mr. Jefferson."[23]

The great congressional fight came in 1813, with John W. Eppes opposing Randolph a second time. This time an important factor was Randolph's opposition to the War of 1812. At first confident, Randolph soon found that Eppes had been making a thorough house-to-house canvass of the district. This sort of campaign disgusted Randolph, who after the fashion of time campaigned by addressing the people on court days in the counties of his district. The Eppes campaign strategy undertook to present Randolph in as unfavorable a light as possible; he was represented as charging the administration with being under French influence, and, as Randolph wrote Josiah Quincy, "ignorant people were made to feel the British fleet had come into the Chesakeake to aid my election." One of Randolph's great speeches, one which lasted three hours, was made at Prince Edward Courthouse. When an Eppes supporter from Buckingham, a man who served a sentence for forging bank notes and who had been convicted by a jury of which Randolph was a member, spoke impertinently to the candidate when he was on the bench, the indignation of the audience was so great that the visitor had to leave or risk a beating. Randolph once said that this was the only speech he ever made in which he felt that he was eloquent while speaking.[24] In the election Prince Edward and Charlotte remained loyal to Randolph; the Prince Edward vote was 303 for Randolph to 218 for Eppes, the administration candidate;[25] the Charlotte vote was 345-117 in favor of Randolph, but Buckingham went 509 to 141 for Eppes, and the Cumberland vote was 206 to 146 for Eppes. Eppes carried the district by 176 votes.[26] Randolph thought that had he been able to attend the election at Cumberland—he was prevented by the fire which destroyed Bizarre—he might have won.[27]

Randolph defeated Eppes in 1815.[28] Randolph did not run in 1817, and Archibald Austin of Buckingham went to Congress.[29] Austin was defeated by Randolph in 1819,[30] who continued to represent the district in the House until he resigned to enter the United States Senate in 1825. Dr. George W. Crump of Cumberland was elected to complete the term, and Randolph was returned in 1827.[31] Randolph did not seek re-election in 1829.[32] During the next two terms Judge Thomas T. Bouldin of Charlotte represented the district.[33]

Randolph served for a time as minister to Russia during this period. On his return his friends in Prince Edward received him with the unique courtesy that gave him attention during a speech which lasted six hours! But Randolph's voice had a singular charm, and he was a popular figure in Prince Edward.

The speech was political. There had been the understanding that Judge Bouldin would not run for Congress when Randolph wished to return. But Randolph announced from Russia through a friend that he would be a candidate in 1831 and did not notify Bouldin; he found that he could not get back in time so withdrew from the race, but his friend, Dr. George W. Crump, who had filled out the term when Randolph went to the Senate and had then made way for him to return to Congress in 1827 announced his condidacy in opposition to Bouldin in order to keep a place for Randolph in the event he should get back before the election. Randolph did not appreciate this unauthorized action, spoke bitterly of Dr. Crump, and behaved ungraciously toward him, for he was present. Nor was he altogether kind in his remarks toward Judge Bouldin. The speech was typical of the Randolph of later years; he dwelt upon the theme of decadence of the younger generation of that day—the sons were not what their fathers had been, and he made, in the comparison, some unkind remarks about the descendants of some men for whom he had great esteem.[34] No doubt this characteristic of the speech held the attention of the audience; everyone wondered what was coming next. No doubt many understood that Randolph, certainly because of his physical health and possibly also because of his mental health, was hardly accountable at the time for what he said. And they must have been grieved that the great man they admired had given back so much. But they joined with their fellows in sending him back to Congress. Randolph had not long to serve, for he died May 24, 1833, and Judge Bouldin was elected to fill the unexpired term.[35]

The United States had a difficult time keeping out of the wars in Europe which centered around the French First Consul and Emperor, Napoleon I. There were pressures from the principal rivals for victory, England and France. The impressment of seamen from American vessels for British naval service was a point of continuing and rising controversy. In 1807 the British ship of war, the *Leopard*, attacked an American vessel, the *Chesapeake*. The attack provoked widespread hostility toward Great Britain throughout the United States; in Virginia mass meetings were held in many counties and resolutions of protest were passed. Prince Edward was among them; a meeting was held at the Courthouse July 29, 1807, called for the purpose of expressing the sentiment of people on the attack on the *Chesapeake*. General Tarlton Woodson was chairman of the meeting, and Francis Watkins, Sr., was its secretary. The resolutions committee consisted of General Peter Johnston, Colonel John Purnall, Major Robert Kelso, Colonel Samuel W. Venable, Colonel Charles Allen, Osborne Lockett, Thomas Haskins, Robert Venable, Major Thomas Green, John Nash, Sr., Major James Morton, Major Archer Allen, Richard N. Venable, and Dr. Goodrich Wilson. The resolutions which they drew up were prefaced with a preamble noting that news of the "lawless and atrocious attack" was heard "with horror" which excited the "warmest indignation" in Americans and that if American citizens may be seized and killed with impunity, the Revolution was in vain. The resolutions pledged the lives and property of those sharing in their adoption to the United States government in support of "measures of redress or vengeance"; urged the non-importation of British goods and the "vigorous use of the rifle and the bayonet" to redress the wrongs done; thanked the citizens of Norfolk, Hampton, and vicinity for "their prompt, spirited, and decided measures" on the occasion; and directed that copies be sent to the President, the Governor, and the Richmond newspapers. To these resolutions the mass meeting gave unanimous assent.

The day before the mass meeting, the Prince Edward Volunteer Troop of Cavalry, of which Captain William L. Womack was commander, also adopted resolutions expressing "indignation and resentment for the many aggressions committed on our rights by the British government and especially the attack of the *Leopard* on the *Chesapeake*, an attack in which the blood of our countrymen has been shed and the dignity of the American flag violated." The cavalrymen could be neither silent nor indifferent nor did they wish to be idle under such circumstances. Captain Womack was authorized to tender their services to the Governor, and they resolved to hold themselves "in readiness to march at a moment's warning wherever the interest of our country and the command of government requires." Captain Womack acted as chairman of the meeting of the cavalry company (a unit of the county militia), James D. Wood as secretary, and Samuel V. Allen, William A. Allen, Abner Nash, Henry E. Watkins, and Samuel F. Lockett served as the resolutions committee.[36]

John Randolph was opposed to war with England. When the "War Hawks," as the young and dominant element in the 12th Congress was called, were on the verge of carrying the country into war, Randolph introduced a resolution declaring it inexpedient to go to war with Great Britain. The House of Representatives refused to hear him, so the amazed and aroused congressman issued an address to the freeholders of Charlotte, Prince Edward, Buckingham, and Cumberland Counties in which he expressed the viewpoint he had not been permitted to express in Congress. Randolph's address, usually styled his Manifesto, in some of its expressions of principle and basic concept has a familiar ring to those who observe closely the political trends of the 1950's. The refusal of the House to hear him marked the first time that body had refused to hear a member in his place; this was a proscription of freedom of speech, an invasion of liberties, this move by the House to reserve the right of free debate in Congress to self-styled Republicans; not even the fathers of the Sedition Act had the hardihood to go that far. Having heard that the leaders of Congress would attempt to get a declaration of war passed the Monday after he wrote this address, which was dated May 30, 1812, Randolph felt it his duty, "by the exercise of [his] constitutional function," "to arrest . . . this heaviest of all possible calamities . . ." Since he was not permitted to finish his argument in Congress, he would give it to his constituents.

Randolph contended that war with England was not in the American interest nor was it necessary to maintain American honor, describing it as "an idolatrous sacrifice of [interest and honor] on the altar of French rapacity, perfidy, and ambition." Then, in familiar terms, he pointed out that the times were not ordinary times, that war would be against the liberty and happiness of mankind. He asked pertinent questions: "Are you willing to become the virtual allies of Bonaparte?" To annex Canada to the Northern states? And if the United States did annex Canada, would any of you people in Charlotte, Prince Edward, Buckingham, or Cumberland be any better off—any richer? Any freer? Any happier? Any more secure? Are you willing to submit to an ever growing system of taxation which sends the European laborer supperless to bed and for the nominal privilege of licensed trade with France would you abandon your lucrative commerce with Great Britain, Spain, Portugal, and their Asiatic, African, and American dependencies—this commerce which gives an outlet for your tobacco, grain, flour, and cotton which are denied a market in France? Small wonder that Henry Clay, the new Speaker of the House, and his fellow "War Hawks" wanted to silence Randolph! Randolph concluded with the characteristically over-modest apology for his "poor ability"; Americans are "in the toils of French duplicity," but "if you and your posterity become hewers of wood and drawers of water, it shall not be for want of my best exertions to rescue you from cruel and abject bondage."[37]

For all Randolph's exertions the "War Hawks" had their way and declared war on England. And though Randolph was popular and influential in Prince Edward, the county went for the re-election of Madison in the November election by 107 to 28 votes for his opponent Rufus King.[38]

In 1816 another Virginian, James Monroe, was in the line of succession for nomination for the Presidency by the Republican party. Although opponents of Madison had undertaken to capitalize on his popularity, achievements, and standing in the party to block Madison's nomination in 1808, Madison subsequently named him Secretary of State. In the caucus of the Republican members of Congress, where Presidential candidates were then nominated, Monroe won, although the Virginia members of the caucus refrained from pushing his candidacy not from indifference but from good politics.[39] When the Republican caucus in the Virginia legislature named the electors, it did not indicate a choice of nominee. The veteran elector from the district, Thomas Read, was nominated elector,[40] but evidently this year he felt unable to go to Richmond, so General John Purnall of Prince Edward was named elector from the district on the Republican ticket.[41]

General Purnall had been active in politics in Prince Edward for years. In 1808 he, Peter Johnston, and Thomas Green had been commissioners to conduct the Presidential election.[42] He had also been named a commissioner for 1816, his colleagues that year being Robert Kelso and Charles Woodson.[43] Purnall, Francis Watkins, Jr., John Booker, Richard N. Venable, Robert Kelso, Charles Woodson, and Samuel Lockett composed the Republican Committee of Correspondence for Prince Edward in 1816.[44]

The political situation as Monroe's second term approached its end was confused. In the first place, the advisability of the congressional caucus as the means of nominating Presidential candidates was questioned, 181 of the 261 members of Congress publicly calling it an inexpedient method.[45] Nor was there in 1824 a single outstanding candidate for whose claims aspirants would stand back. Yet 160 Democratic (the party name at this time was in transition) members of Congress attended the caucus February 21, 1824, and their balloting showed a considerable unanimity of feeling for the year: William H. Crawford of Georgia, Monroe's Secretary of the Treasury, received 132 votes for the nomination for President, and Albert

Gallatin, who had been Jefferson's Secretary of the Treasury, received 120 votes for the Vice-Presidential nomination.[46] The party organization in Virginia appeared pleased with the caucus choices, and the legislative caucus named General Purnall elector on the Crawford-Gallatin ticket and appointed James D. Wood, Osborne Lockett, John Clarke, Jesse Michaux, Robert Kelso, James Madison, Edward Booker, and Samuel C. Anderson the Prince Edward committee for Crawford and Gallatin.[47] In the Virginia caucus the three representatives from Prince Edward, State Senator Joseph Wyatt and Delegates Asa Dupuy and Henry E. Watkins, supported Crawford, but split on the Vice-Presidential nomination, Wyatt supporting Gallatin and Dupuy and Watkins Nathaniel Macon, long a representative from North Carolina and at one time Speaker of the House.[48]

The rank and file of Virginia Democracy, however, did not feel bound by the approval which the legislative caucus gave Crawford and Gallatin. A convention of supporters of General Andrew Jackson met in Fredericksburg in July and named electors on a Jackson-John C. Calhoun ticket, Colonel Thomas Davenport of Halifax being nominated for the district of which Prince Edward was a part.[49] Henry Clay's admirers did not wait so long, but on March 8 his friends in the Virginia legislature held a caucus and nominated electors pledged to his support. Dr. Samuel Pleasants Hargrave of Halifax was nominee from the Prince Edward-Charlotte-Halifax electoral district on the Clay ticket.[50]

In the balloting 117 Prince Edward voters voted for the Crawford elector, three for the Adams elector; the Jackson and Clay electors did not receive a single vote in the county.[51] When the electors met November 30, General Purnall was not well enough to go to Richmond for the meeting. The electors, all of whom with the exception of Purnall were present, advised the General Assembly of the absence of the distinguished citizen of Prince Edward; so the Assembly, in accordance with the law, elected Joseph Wyatt as substitute elector for General Purnall; Virginia's twenty-four electoral votes were cast for Crawford for President and Nathaniel Macon for Vice-President.[52] None of the four candidates for the Presidency who received electoral votes received a majority, so the election had to be decided by the House of Representatives. Although Jackson led in the number of votes received, the House chose Adams with the support of Clay. When Adams named Clay Secretary of State, Jackson's supporters charged a political deal and proceeded to harass the Adams administration and plan for the 1828 election.

Jackson had devoted friends; he had equally determined enemies. His enemies were as determined to keep him out of the Presidency as his friends were to put him in. In 1827 there were meetings in many counties of people opposed to Jackson's candidacy, but this writer has found no record of such a meeting in Prince Edward. There was, though, a meeting of Jackson's friends at the Courthouse on December 17, 1827. Samuel Carter was chairman, and Branch J. Worsham and Jacquelin A. Berkeley were secretaries. The object of the meeting, to endorse the candidacy of Jackson, was explained by Samuel C. Anderson. According to custom a resolutions committee was appointed and retired to draw up a report. Members of the committee were Thomas Scott, James Madison, John J. Flournoy, Samuel C. Anderson, James W. Womack, William T. Wootton, James H. Dillon, William Brightwell, Richard Booker, James H. Wilson, Peyton Randolph, Littleberry Watson, and Abraham W. Venable. The resolutions proposed General Jackson as the only candidate of those opposed to the present administration and expressed the belief that a change was necessary: "We feel the blight and mildew which the pestilential influence of a northern monied aristocracy is spreading over our beloved State; the hopes of our agriculturist perishing and our commercial energies withering, whilst our hard and scanty earnings are transferred to the favored and protected manufacturers of the North." The resolutions endorsed Virginia's opposition to a broad construction of the Constitution and criticized the tariff, internal improvements, and patronage policies of the Adams administration as leading to the ultimate ruin of the South. They called upon Asa Dupuy and Stephen C. Farrar, members of the House of Delegates, and State Senator Joseph Wyatt to attend the Jackson meeting scheduled to be held in Richmond during the winter as their representatives.

At this meeting a Jackson Committee of Correspondence and Vigilance was appointed: Henry E. Watkins, Samuel D. Burke, Nathaniel E. Venable, Charles Woodson, Robert Kelso, Jesse Michaux, Jaquelin A. Berkeley, Thomas E. Haskins, Thomas Flournoy, Robert Hill, Samuel Watkins, Thomas A. LeGrand, Edward Booker, James T. Price, Thomas Haskins, Sr., and Branch J. Worsham together with the resolutions committee.[53]

The prevailing sentiment for Jackson in Prince Edward is indicated by the absence of any representative from Prince Edward at the anti-Jackson meeting which met in Richmond January 8, 1828 and named General Edward C. Carrington elector for the district; nor has this writer found the list of any anti-Jackson committee in Prince Edward for this year.[54] The anti-Jackson leadership in Prince Edward is found in the list recommended to the Governor by the Central Anti-Jackson Committee as election commissioners: Richard N. Venable, Dr. John Peter Mettauer, and Osborne Lockett. They proposed that election commissioners be equally divided between Jackson and anti-Jackson men.[55]

Wyatt, Dupuy, and Farrar attended the pro-Jackson caucus and joined in endorsing Jackson. In the vote on which Vice-Presidential candidate to endorse, Wyatt supported John C. Calhoun, and Dupuy and Farrar supported Nathaniel Macon; Calhoun received 162 votes to 20 for Macon. Richard Logan of Halifax was named elector for the district.[56]

In the election of 1828 Prince Edward went overwhelmingly for the Jackson ticket, giving it 323 votes to 8 for the Adams ticket.[57] A correspondent of the Richmond *Enquirer* from Prince Edward wrote after the polls closed that "heavy rains made much against us and in favor of the Coalition. However, we, the *rabble*, hope that we have not fallen far short of our duty. Mr. Adams' men attended like good, loyal, well-disciplined, regular troops . . . I hope Mr. Adams will now be convinced that Prince Edward is not yet prepared for his government."[58] The vote showed it.

Prince Edward voters in the second half of the decade of the 1820's demonstrated two contradictory attitudes in politics. On the one hand there was widespread support of Andrew Jackson, representative and champion of the more equalitarian democracy of the Western United States. On the other hand there was opposition to amending the Virginia Constitution of 1776.

That Constitution set up a government which was aristocratic in character; under it, the eastern and older counties were more favored than the western and newer in representation in the General Assembly. In the western part of the state there was a growing desire to amend the old Constitution. A meeting was held in Staunton on July 25, 1825, which proposed a convention "to amend defects in the State Constitution." The East got busy. Petitions, with a printed text in which opposition to such a convention was expressed, were circulated. Numerous signatures were obtained in Prince Edward on three petitions, one headed by Eaton Hudson, the second by J. McDearmon, and the third by A. C. Venable. One reason, that the petitioners were "content with ancient institutions and fearful of the spirit of innovation," sounds strikingly inconsistent with the endorsement of Andrew Jackson for the Presidency. The petitions were presented to the House of Delegates on December 21, 1825.[59] When the issue of a constitutional convention was put before the people in the election in April, 1828, Prince Edward voters were ten to one against it; only 26 in the county voted in favor of a convention; there were 260 opposed.[60] In the state, there was a majority of 6,975 in favor of the convention;[61] the next session of the Assembly called a convention; each senatorial district was represented by four delegates, who were elected, the persons qualified to vote for the House of Delegates being the electors.[62] To this convention, the senatorial district composed of Prince Edward, Charlotte, and Halifax Counties sent John Randolph of Roanoke of Charlotte, Richard N. Venable of Prince Edward, William Leigh and Richard Logan of Halifax.[63]

The changes made in the Constitution by the Convention of 1829-30 were relatively few. A more equitable representation in the General Assembly was put into effect. Under this change Prince Edward lost one delegate; instead of having two, the county was given only one. The county was put into a new senatorial district; since 1776 Prince Edward, Charlotte, and Halifax had formed a district; the new district consisted of Prince Edward, Charlotte, Lunenburg, and Nottoway.[64] But the property qualifications for voting were retained; the legislature continued to elect the Governor; and the Governor continued to appoint the sheriffs and the magistrates.[65] The aristocratic character of the government was continued.

In 1832 the political discussion within the ranks of the Virginia Democratic party centered around a Vice-Presidential nominee, since John C. Calhoun had resigned that office after his break with Jackson. At the Virginia caucus Jackson was unanimously endorsed, but some wanted Philip P. Barbour of Virginia for Vice-President, others Martin Van Buren of New York. The caucus decided it inexpedient to nominate a candidate for Vice-President at the time, Wyatt favoring, Dupuy opposing the resolution. A change had been made in the electoral district since 1828; Archibald Austin of Buckingham was elector on the Jacksonian ticket from the district of which Prince Edward was a part.[66] The Democratic National Convention, the first such meeting, assembled in Baltimore in May; Asa Dupuy was one of the delegates from Virginia. Van Buren was nominated by the convention for the Vice-Presidency; in a resolution introduced by

William S. Archer, the Virginia delegation concurred in the Van Buren nomination.[67]

The Jackson committee in Prince Edward in 1832 consisted of Jesse Michaux, Nathaniel Price, Edward Booker, Charles Woodson, Henry E. Watkins, Samuel C. Anderson, Thomas Scott, James D. Wood, John J. Flournoy, James Madison, Joseph Redd, William T. Wootton, Nathaniel E. Venable, Thomas E. Haskins, James McDearmon, Samuel D. Burke, Henry Thweatt, James H. Dillon, Thomas Flournoy, James Wilson, Branch J. Worsham, Dr. John T. Ligon, Richard Booker, and Thomas E. Perkinson.[68]

Although the Virginia delegation concurred in the Van Buren nomination, Barbour supporters put a Jackson-Barbour ticket in the field, with Samuel P. Christian of Buckingham elector for the district.[69] Austin, elector named by the party caucus, had declined to commit himself to support any particular candidate for the Vice-Presidency, stating that his choice would be the candidate "that might prevent an election by the United States Senate," that is, the candidate most likely to get a majority of the electoral votes. He pledged to support Jackson.[70] Barbour expressed regret at the division of the ticket and urged support of the regular ticket.[71] In the election of 1832 Jackson maintained his strength in Prince Edward, his elector getting 323 votes. Henry Clay did not make as good a run as Adams had made four years before; his elector, Samuel Branch of Buckingham, polled only two votes in Prince Edward. The Jackson-Barbour ticket received no votes in the county.[72]

The pattern of political thinking in the Prince Edward area is indicated in John Randolph's opposition to the United States Bank (which Jackson opposed so strongly) and the protective tariff.[73] Judge Bouldin voted against the tariff of 1832 which was supported by the Virginia delegation in the House eleven to eight and which passed the House 132 to 65.[74] Judge Thomas T. Bouldin died before the end of John Randolph's unexpired term to which he had been elected.[75] Before his death, he became strongly anti-administration and opposed the withdrawal of government deposits from the Bank of the United States and favored their redeposit.

When it became necessary to elect a third representative for the 1833-35 term, the shift in attitude toward the administration was of such strength that the anti-administration people were confident of winning. They had three candidates in the field, Daniel Wilson, Philip Bolling, and Judge Beverley Tucker, John Randolph's half-brother. One of them might have been elected had not friends of the administration in Charlotte determined to run a Jackson man. They selected James W. Bouldin, a brother of the late representative, who took the opposite side on the issues of the bank and the restoration of deposits. In an attempt to concentrate its support, the anti-administration party in Buckingham withdrew Wilson and Bolling. James W. Bouldin carried the district, an indication that among the people Jackson and his policies were still popular. The vote at Prince Edward Courthouse was 177 to 116 in favor of Bouldin over Tucker. (Walker's Church, a new precinct, had not been heard from for the report, but was credited to Bouldin.) One observer described the campaign as a battle between "pure democracy" and Federalists, Clay men, Calhoun men, and the Bank of the United States. It is interesting to note the revival of the term Federalist to describe opponents of Jackson.[76] In a classification of Virginia state senators in 1835 as administration men and the opposition, Henry E. Watkins of Prince Edward was listed among the twelve "opposition" senators, indicating that this former member of the Jackson committees in Prince Edward in both 1828 and 1832 had changed his political affiliation.[77] The election of James Madison, an administration man, to the House of Delegates from Prince Edward by a vote of 78 to 56 for the opposition (the candidate's name was not given in the report) was regarded as a Jackson victory; the line-up in the House of Delegates showed the loss of a Whig member from Prince Edward in 1834 (Asa Dupuy) and the gain of a Republican (Madison) in 1835. In the congressional election that year James W. Bouldin defeated the Whig candidate, Philip A. Bolling.[78]

Jackson's supporters realized that they had a fight on their hands in 1836 to elect a successor who would carry out Jackson's policies. On May 13, 1835, Prince Edward Democratic-Republicans met in Farmville to nominate delegates to the national convention which was to meet in Baltimore May 20. Nathaniel E. Venable and Thomas Tredway, Sr., were named delegates. The Farmville meeting, of which Robert Kelso was chairman, Abraham Z. Venable secretary, and at which James Madison stated the object of the meeting, passed resolutions praising Jackson for "most laudable exertions to put down a most unjust, unequal and oppressive system of Tariff duties; the corrupting, bribing and wasteful system of Internal Improvements by the Federal Government, and that unconstitutional, dangerous and alarming monopoly, the Bank of the United States." The resolutions urged support of the administration and continuation of these policies by the next administration.[79]

Venable attended the Baltimore convention which nominated Van Buren for the Presidency and Richard M. Johnston of Kentucky for the Vice-Presidency. The Virginia delegation opposed Johnston (its choice had been William C. Rives of Virginia). Venable attended the meeting of the Virginia delegation at Beltzhouser's Hotel in Baltimore at which it was decided to notify the convention that the delegates could not recommend Johnston for support—they were not satisfied that Johnston would "support and carry out the doctrines Virginia has ever maintained and holds dear."[80]

At home the Democrats got busy. The state corresponding committee for Van Buren, at a meeting in Richmond January 11, 1836, named a committee of seventy-three for Prince Edward: Nathaniel E. Venable, Thomas Hickson, James M. Jackson, Clement C. Read, Joel W. Womack, William H. Chappell, James B. Ely, A. Z. Venable, George Daniel, Samuel W. Venable, Thomas B. McGehee, Dr. Thomas Overton, Thomas Goode, Branch J. Walthall, Richard Marshall, J. W. Ellington, James T. Price, E. B. Miller, Thomas Clarke, William Clarke, Thomas Scott, William T. Wootton, Francis T. Wootton, John Rudd, Jr., James Scott, Branch O. Scott, Simeon Wootton, Henry N. Watkins, John Redd, Sr., Joseph Redd, John W. Redd, William Carter, James S. Allen, Samuel Watson, George W. Bell, Nathan Bell, William Scott, (B) John Scott, James H. Wilson, James Bigger, John Bigger, John Carter, James Carter, James W. Womack, Lillious D. Womack, William Elliott, William Baker, Samuel Baldwin, Ralph Merriman, Robert Kelso, Bannister S. Pryor, Thomas LeGrand, Wray Moss, Peter LeGrand, Jacob Tibbs, Rezin Porter, James McDearmon, Samuel McDearmon, William Brightwell, Joel Elam, Charles Brightwell, Robert Venable, Henry J. Venable, James Venable, Thomas Tredway, Moses Tredway, George King, Branch J. Worsham, Joseph Wilson, Benjamin H. Price, Amplius Tuggle, Thomas H. Anderson, and Nathaniel Price.[81]

Thus the organization for Van Buren reached into every community of the county. The Democrats carried the county with 273 votes for Van Buren, but the Whigs polled 216 votes.[82] This was quite a gain in four years, for in 1832 only two votes were cast for Henry Clay in Prince Edward.

In 1838 the Whigs put up a candidate for the House of Delegates, William C. Flournoy, but he was defeated by Nathaniel E. Venable.[83]

James W. Bouldin declined to run for re-election to the House of Representatives in 1839. The Democrats of the district had a meeting at Prince Edward the third Monday in October, 1838, to nominate a candidate. The Charlotte delegation was instructed to nominate and support Nathaniel E. Venable, then a member of the House of Delegates from Prince Edward, for the nomination.[84] This writer has not found a record of the results of that meeting. The Democratic candidate (there is some indication that he was Daniel A. Wilson) lost, and John Hill of Buckingham was sent to Congress in 1839,[85] the only Whig ever to represent Prince Edward in the national House of Representatives. Hill's statement shortly after his election strikes a note not infrequently heard in these times: "My most ardent wish is to lessen the powers of this government—and if it cannot be done, I believe that in twenty years it will be an absolute despotism."[86]

The Democratic and the Whig parties were now well-matched in strength, not only in Prince Edward but throughout the nation. Dissatisfaction under Jackson had increased under Van Buren; a crippling economic depression in 1837 contributed to the strengthening of the Whigs. The Whigs had elected their candidate to Congress from the district in 1839. In April, 1840, Samuel D. Burke, Whig, defeated Henry N. Watkins, Democrat, for the House of Delegates from Prince Edward by sixteen votes. Watkins had been nominated at a county States Rights Republican meeting February 17, 1840, of which Moses Tredway was chairman and John Rice secretary.[87] The Presidential campaign in 1840 promised to be hot. It lived up to its promise.

The Democrats held a state convention February 22, 1840, which named the county committee: Henry N. Watkins, James H. Wilson, James W. Womack, L. D. Womack, Joseph Redd, John W. Redd, John Redd, Jr., William T. Wootton, Littleberry Clarke, William Clarke, Thomas Clarke, William Carter, Robert Kelso, Dr. B. Pryor, William Trent, T. LeGrand, A. LeGrand, William Brightwell, Robert Venable, Abram M. Venable, Allen Watson, James T. Price, Dr. R. Dejarnett, Clement C. Read, George Daniel, John Tuggle, Drury Watson, Joseph Williams, Samuel Baldwin, Samuel W. Venable, Jr., Dr. Thomas Overton, Beverly Scott, Edwin Edmunds, Thomas McGehee, Dennis R. Fielder, and James Edwards.[88]

A dinner was given for the delegates to the convention at the Terpischore in Richmond on February 24, which though well attended did have as many out as the Whig dinner the next day.

Nathaniel E. Venable proposed one of the toasts at the Democratic dinner: "Direct Taxation: The true mode of informing the people of the expenses of the State and of providing for the payment of the principal and interest of the public debt."[89]

The Cumberland "Republicans" called for a meeting of delegates from the electoral district (at the time Buckingham, Prince Edward, Charlotte, Cumberland, and Fluvanna) at Buckingham in October to promote Van Buren's candidacy.[90] At a state Democratic convention in Charlottesville September 9-11, Samuel C. Anderson and William C. Flournoy (who had moved politically in the opposite direction to most of the people who were changing political affiliations by leaving the Whigs to become a Democrat) took active parts and served on important committees; Anderson made one of the closing speeches of the convention. Anderson, Thomas Tredway, Luther Jeffress, and Flournoy were delegates from Prince Edward.[91]

The Whigs, too, were active. The Tippecanoe Club of Prince Edward and Nottoway met at Burkeville (the present Burke's Tavern) April 28. Major H. R. Anderson of Nottoway was chairman of the meeting, which was attended by the following delegates from the two counties: Isaac Read, Richard H. Burruss, Thomas Branch, Henry M. Vaughan, Francis N. Watkins, Asa D. Dickinson, George B. Hughes, Edward B. Miller, Vincent Phillips, Sterling J. Cole, Booker Foster, John McGehee, Thomas E. Scott, Anderson E. Scott, Creed T. Harper, Thomas E. Perkinson, Nathaniel Motley, William B. Featherston, Paschal G. Leigh, James D. Ligon, John B. Cobbs, James Agnew, William E. Noble, M. F. Noble, M. W. Vaughan, John Motley, and S. D. Burke. A committee was named to distribute campaign documents; those in Prince Edward were S. D. Burke, William B. Featherston, Vincent Phillips, Paschal G. Leigh, and Booker Foster. Henry E. Watkins, Francis N. Watkins, Isaac Read, and Asa D. Dickinson were invited to attend the next meeting to discuss the merits of the two candidates for the Presidency.[92]

August Court day at Prince Edward Courthouse saw a great battle in which Henry E. Watkins for the Whigs and Samuel C. Anderson for the Democrats were the chief duellists, with others, notably Samuel D. Burke, joining in. Watkins began the speaking and spoke until he was nearly exhausted. Anderson followed him; having taken notes on Watkins' speech, he replied to it. In his speech Anderson charged that General Harrison (the Whig candidate for President) had voted for a law in Ohio by which poor white men could be sold for debt. As he did not read the entire law to which he referred, Burke challenged him to do so; as he did not, Burke quoted the portion in question from memory. Anderson told him, "If you want to talk, come up here; here's the place—talk after me." Burke answered: "You know, sir, I am not in the habit of public speaking." Then Anderson retorted: "Don't talk at all." Burke then took a copy of the law to Isaac Read who was speaking and asked him to read it. Anderson questioned whether what was read was a certified copy of the law in question. Read asked him if he denied it was a true copy; Anderson did not respond to the challenge. To one of Anderson's admirers, Anderson completely carried the day: his on this occasion was the "most powerful political effort made at our courthouse since Randolph of Roanoke was taken from amongst us."[93]

Van Buren carried Prince Edward; he received 361 votes to 268 for Harrison.[94] Among Harrison's supporters were five men who had served on the county committees for Jackson in both 1828 and 1832: John J. Flournoy, Henry E. Watkins, Samuel D. Burke, Thomas Flournoy, and Edward Booker; and two who had served on the Jackson committee in 1832: Henry Thweatt and Thomas E. Perkinson.[95]

Asa Dupuy, Samuel C. Anderson, and Nathaniel E. Venable were the election commissioners in 1840.[96]

The 1840 Presidential campaign had not gotten under way when the Democrats began the 1841 congressional campaign. Edmund W. Hubard of Buckingham announced his candidacy in May, 1840, almost a year before the election. His platform opposed a national bank, a protective tariff, and internal improvement by the Federal government; it denied the right of the Federal government to abolish slavery in the District of Columbia, endorsed the Independent Treasury scheme, and favored the re-election of Van Buren. Hubard had been nominated at a convention which met at Prince Edward Courthouse in the winter of 1839, but then declined the nomination because D. A. Wilson, who had since been elected a judge, was a candidate.[97] In Hubard's platform one sees in addition to a reiteration of the Jacksonian doctrine an emerging pattern of the Southern Democratic position. Hubard was elected and served three terms in the House.[98] The state was redistricted in 1843; Prince Edward, Campbell, Buckingham, Charlotte, Cumberland, Fluvanna, and the city of Lynchburg constituted the Fourth District, and it was from this district that Hubard was elected for his second and third terms. The population of this district was 76,139, the largest of any congressional district in the state at this redistricting.[99]

The Prince Edward Democrats were described as the States Rights Republican party in the account of their 1840 meeting.[100] The state Democratic meeting in 1842 in Richmond was described as the States Right Convention. James H. Wilson, Samuel C. Anderson, Branch J. Worsham, Thomas T. Tredway, and Joseph A. Watson were the delegates from Prince Edward. Anderson was chairman of the nominating committee of seven members and a member of the committee of seven on arrangements for furthering the objects of the meeting and of the committee of twenty-three to prepare an address to the people of Virginia; Worsham was one of seven members of the resolutions committee. The resolutions regarded a national bank as unconstitutional, "deleterious to the interests, and subversive (yes, they were using that word in 1842) of the liberties of the people"; held that the bankrupt bill passed at the last session of Congress impaired the obligations of contracts; disapproved the acts of the special session of Congress, viewed "with regret and disapproval the profligate extravagance of the party in power"; welcomed party victories in other states; pledged to get out the vote in the spring elections (for Congress and the state legislature); commended the resolutions of 1799 as the best commentary on the Constitution and urged their circulation through the state. The last item has significance for the future, for it furnishes an indication of the trend of political thinking on the relationship of state to nation. Local committees were appointed; that for Prince Edward added Luther C. Jeffress and Robert C. Anderson to the five delegates to the convention.[101]

For all the concern for states rights, however, it does not appear that John C. Calhoun, now regarded as the foremost of that political school in this period, was popular in Prince Edward, though Samuel C. Anderson did deny the charge of the New Orleans *Bee* that the redistricting act of 1843 had been designed to injure Calhoun in Virginia.[102]

The Democrats made a concerted effort in the 1843 spring elections. Prince Edward voted for representative, state senator, and delegate in that election. The Democrats won each of the offices. Edmund W. Hubard defeated the Whig Richard H. Toler for Congress, carrying both precincts in Prince Edward by a majority of forty-six; William H. Dennis of Charlotte defeated the Whig Wyatt Cardwell, also of Charlotte, for the State Senate, carrying Prince Edward (both precincts) by a majority of seventeen; and Samuel C.

Anderson was elected to the House of Delegates by a majority of nineteen over the Whig candidate, Mathews (William ?); Mathews carried Walker's Church precinct by twenty-six,[103] an unusual circumstance because Walker's Church precinct had been regarded as strongly Jacksonian; the candidate Mathews, however, was probably one of the Mathews family from that part of the county. The 1843 elections marked a comeback for the Democrats, but the majorities were small. There was widespread interest in the voting in the county, and the Richmond *Enquirer* editorially urged Anderson's election in the course of the hard campaign.[104] The Whig convention for the congressional district was held in Farmville March 22, in the public room of F. H. James' hotel.[105]

Dr. J. R. McDearmon, John A. Scott, Clement Barksdale, S. O. Southall, Wood Bouldin, and B. W. Leigh represented Prince Edward Whigs at the state convention in Richmond February 7, 1844. This convention endorsed Henry Clay for president; it named Henry E. Watkins assistant to the elector in Prince Edward to carry on the campaign.[106] The Democrats carried the county in the election, James K. Polk's elector receiving 377 votes to 264 cast for the elector on Henry Clay's ticket.[107]

As in the 1843 campaign, the Democrats organized well for the 1845 election. William C. Flournoy, Samuel W. Venable, Moses Tredway, Branch J. Worsham, Nathaniel J. Price, William Brightwell, Luther C. Jeffress, Thomas Clark, and Francis T. Wootton made up the county committee that year; they were instructed to enlarge their committee by appointing members in every section.[108] Democrats won the three races again. Hubard defeated John Hill for Congress, Prince Edward voting 381 for Hubard and 228 for Hill; Dennis defeated Samuel D. Burke for the Senate, carrying Burke's home county (Prince Edward) by 393 to 217; and S. D. McDearmon was elected to the House of Delegates over the Whig candidate, Asa D. Dickinson, by 441 to 176. McDearmon was described as "a Polk, Texas, anti-bank, anti-tariff, anti-Distribution man . . ."[109] The description gives a clew to the thinking of the majority in Prince Edward on the issues of the mid-1840's. The county Democrats showed a considerable gain in strength in their vote for a delegate over 1844, when Samuel C. Anderson, Locofoco (this term was applied to the Democrats because a member of a Democratic convention a few years before had used the newly developed "locofoco" matches when the lights went out), defeated the Whig Henry E. Watkins by 318 to 271.[110]

In at least one instance, voters in a particular section of the county organized to propose and endorse a man from their section for office. Democrats of the Southeastern section of Prince Edward met March 8, 1848, with James T. Price as chairman and Thomas O. Rowlett as secretary. Since B. W. Womack, who was at the time a member of the House of Delegates, had declined re-election, these voters proposed their neighbor, William T. Wootton, as the party's candidate to succeed him. They paid him high tribute: "from his age and experience, unimpeachable probity and unwavering political fidelity, habitual moderation and comity, good standing and general popularity," he was recommended to the party meeting at March Court which nominated candidates for the House of Delegates. The nominating committee consisted of Thomas O. Rowlett, Pettus Perkinson, Ens. Stern, William B. Rowlett, John Queensbury, and N. S. Robertson. A certain amount of community feeling entered the recommendation; as one of the chief strongholds of the Democratic party in Prince Edward, the southeastern section felt entitled to some recognition.[111] The effort bore fruit, for Wootton was elected.[112]

Edmund W. Hubard announced that he would not seek re-election in 1847. A meeting of Prince Edward Democrats was held January 18, 1847 (Court day), at which delegates were named to the district convention to meet in Farmville January 27 to nominate a candidate in his stead. James H. Wilson was chairman and John W. Redd secretary of the meeting. These officers and Branch J. Worsham, Joseph A. Watson, Thomas H. Almond, James Venable, Newton Cunningham, David F. Womack, James Cobbs, Thomas T. Tredway, William Elliott, L. D. Womack, L. C. Jeffress, B. W. Womack, J. T. Carter, R. S. Carter, N. G. McGehee, William T. Carter, William F. Scott, George W. Bell, Sr., Nathan Bell, Thomas C. Clark, George W. Bell, Jr., James A. Bell, Henry N. Watkins, Joseph Redd, B. O. Scott, Elbert F. Redd, Thomas J. Redd, James Scott, Charles A. Scott, Edwin W. Scott, Samuel B. Scott, James T. Price, William T. Wootton, F. T. Wootton, S. H. Wootton, John W. Fowlkes, Thomas O. Rowlett, John Queensbury, Thomas Clark, Jacob McGehee, William J. McGehee, William Walton, P. G. Leigh, J. Leigh, John Foster, Joseph Phillips, William Bradshaw, Benjamin F. Flippen, William Weaver, Richard Marshall, John T. Ligon, Thomas Goode, Henry Tucker, Joseph D. Chambers, Thomas Hickson, S. W. Venable, S. Woodson Venable, Thomas F. Venable, N. E. Venable, William H. Chappell, Edwin Edmunds, Beverly S. Scott, William C. Flournoy,

C. C. Read, Robert C. Anderson, Edwin J. Redd, F. D. Redd, Henry J. Venable, Samuel Watson, and Allen Watson attended as delegates from Prince Edward.[113]

The convention met in the Presbyterian Church and was opened with prayer by the Rev. Dr. James H. C. Leach. James W. Bouldin of Charlotte was temporary chairman, and Thomas H. Almond temporary secretary. John P. Wilson of Cumberland was chosen president, and Robert H. Glass of Campbell and Almond secretaries. Each county, for all its delegates, had one vote, except Campbell, which had two votes. Appomattox nominated Thomas S. Bocock of that county as the candidate, and Buckingham seconded Bocock's nomination. Campbell nominated Adolphus D. Read of Campbell, Charlotte James W. Bouldin, and Cumberland William C. Flournoy of Prince Edward, who declined "being supported." Prince Edward supported Bocock. On the first two ballots Bocock received four votes, Read two, and Flournoy two. On the third ballot Bocock received six votes and Flournoy three, Campbell giving one vote to each and Cumberland and Lunenburg supporting Flournoy. Flournoy, H. D. Flood of Appomattox, Glass, Samuel I. Booker and Colonel Joseph Fuqua of Buckingham constituted the notification committee.[114]

Henry P. Irving of Cumberland was the Whig candidate; he had been nominated at the Whig convention which met January 19, also at Farmville, from a field of candidates: Colonel Thomas H. Flood, nominated by Appomattox; Wyatt Cardwell by Charlotte, Thomas M. Bondurant by Buckingham; R. Ivanhoe Cocke by Fluvanna. On the first ballot Irving received four votes (Campbell's two and one each from Cumberland and Prince Edward) and each of the others one. On the second ballot Irving received six votes, Lunenburg and Fluvanna joining his supporters on the first ballot, and Bondurant, Flood, and Cardwell one each. Francis N. Watkins was the notification committee.[115]

In the April election Bocock defeated Irving, carrying Prince Edward by a majority of forty-seven. In the district Bocock's majority was only three. Irving contested the election, but was unsuccessful in trying to unseat the Democrat.[116]

Henry E. Watkins, Samuel C. Anderson, and Robert C. Anderson were the commissioners for the 1848 Presidential election.[117] The Democratic candidate, Lewis Cass, carried Prince Edward, receiving 253 votes to 211 cast for General Zachary Taylor, the Whig candidate[118] (who won the election in the nation).

The district Whig convention met in Farmville January 25, 1849,

and nominated Henry P. Irving for Congress. Irving had lost two
years before; Bocock was again successful.[119]

In 1851 the Whigs again held their district convention in Farmville, meeting in the Presbyterian Church March 12. F. N. Watkins
of Prince Edward was president of the convention, and C. R. Barksdale represented Prince Edward on the nominating committee. R. L.
Saunders of Prince Edward and W. G. Miller of Charlotte were the
secretaries. Delegates from Prince Edward were F. N. Watkins,
Colonel J. L. Carrington, William J. Porter, T. B. Rice, A. A. Eram-
bert, William C. Bell, Ryland J. Matthews, William A. Womack,
Colonel Joseph Dupuy, Booker Foster, Dr. A. S. Dillon, Dr. James
T. Spencer, J. J. Rice, Dr. W. H. H. Thackston, Dr. B. C. Peters,
John T. Thornton, John A. Dalby, F. P. Wood, George O. Scott,
S. O. Southall, A. D. Dickinson, J. E. Venable, J. B. Tinsley, John A.
Scott, Joseph T. Morton, D. P. Gregg, R. L. Saunders, F. Booker, and
——— Wootton. Resolutions pledged support to "any true Whig
who will abide by the acts of the last session of Congress known as
the [California] Compromise who shall receive a majority vote of the
convention. Prince Edward supported Hunter H. Marshall of Charlotte for the nomination; other candidates were P. A. Bolling of
Buckingham and the Rev. John Early of Campbell. The latter received the nomination on the second ballot, defeating Marshall five
to three.[120] Early declined, pointing out that he had written to a
member of the convention that he would not accept.[121] Subsequently
Philip A. Bolling was nominated; he was defeated by Bocock, Prince
Edward giving the Democratic candidate a majority of 139.[122]

Prince Edward, Charlotte, and Appomattox made up the Thirteenth District for representation in the Constitutional Convention
of 1850-51. Willis P. Bocock, Branch J. Worsham, and Thomas H.
Flood were delegates from the district.[123]

In 1851 the new state Constitution went into effect. It provided
for the popular election of Governor, Lieutenant-Governor, and
Attorney General, as well as of county officials. The parties adopted
the convention plan of nominating state officials. The state Democratic convention was called to meet in Staunton September 24 to
make the nominations. Prince Edward Democrats met August 25 to
nominate delegates, Moses Tredway serving as chairman and B. W.
Womack and John W. Redd as secretaries. A nominating committee,
composed of the chairman, secretaries, and Thomas Clark, Samuel
W. Venable, and Robert S. Carter named a delegation of fifty:

Thomas Clark, Samuel C. Anderson, B. W. Womack, Samuel W. Venable, William C. Flournoy, Robert S. Carter, Daniel M. Saunders, Thomas H. Almond, Colonel John T. Carter, F. T. Wootton, William T. Wootton, Thomas Hickson, James H. Wilson, H. G. Richardson, T. T. Tredway, James A. Bell, William Brightwell, Joseph Phillips, Newton Cunningham, D. F. Womack, James Venable, Dr. William T. Walker, James Cobbs, William Elliott, William T. Carter, Samuel Carter, John W. Redd, Joseph Redd, E. F. Redd, S. B. Scott, B. S. Scott, John T. Ligon, Dr. Simeon Walton, William Walton, Jacob McGehee, S. H. Wootton, William Bradshaw, James Flippen, J. B. Hilliard, P. H. Jackson, Dr. William H. Chappell, George Daniel, Joel W. Womack, John Thackston, D. W. Calhoun, James W. Womack, H. S. Guthrey, G. W. Clibourn, William S. King, Thomas H. Anderson, and C. C. Read.[124]

The Democratic nominees were Joseph Johnson of Harrison County (the present West Virginia was then a part of Virginia) for Governor; Shelton F. Leake of Madison for Lieutenant-Governor; and Willis P. Bocock of Appomattox for Attorney General. The Whigs nominated George W. Summers of Kanawha for Governor, Watts for Lieutenant-Governor, and Baxter for Attorney General.

Two elections were scheduled for the fall of 1851. On October 23, the elections for the officials who had been elected by popular vote—representatives, state senators, and delegates—were held. At the same time the referendum on the amended Constitution took place; different qualifications for voters were set up for the constitutional referendum; every white male citizen twenty-one years of age or over who had resided in the state two years and in the town or county where he offered himself to vote was eligible to vote on the Constitution; the old qualifications held for voters in the election of legislators. The new Constitution would remove the property qualifications for voting; it marked a long step forward in making the state government more democratic. If the Constitution was approved in the referendum, an election would be held December 8 for Governor, Lieutenant Governor, and Attorney General and also for the State Senate and the House of Delegates; qualifications for voters in the December election were the same as those for voters in the constitutional referendum.[125]

Virginia approved the amended Constitution by a vote of 67,562 to 9,933, and the election on December 8 was called by Governor John B. Floyd.[126] The Democrats elected the three state officials. In

Prince Edward Johnson received 279 votes to Summers' 203; Leake 275 to Watts' 191; and Bocock 290 to Baxter's 185.[127] The Constitution created new senatorial districts, and Prince Edward, Nottoway, and Lunenburg constituted the Ninth District; no Whig sought the Senate seat in the district, but two Democrats ran, Thomas H. Campbell defeating Scoggin; Prince Edward voted 369 for Campbell to 99 for Scoggin.[128] James H. Wilson, who had been nominated at the county Democratic meeting August 25 for the House of Delegates, had no Whig opposition and received a vote of 394 in the December election.[129]

The new Constitution also provided for the popular election of the members of the Board of Public Works by sections. Prince Edward was placed in the first section with Nottoway, Pittsylvania, Franklin, Campbell, Buckingham, Appomattox, Roanoke, Bedford, Giles, Grayson, Wythe, Washington, Dinwiddie, Chesterfield, Princess Anne, Prince George, Nansemond, Petersburg, and Norfolk.[130]

In the Presidential campaign of 1852, Stephen O. Southall was county Whig elector, and William C. Flournoy was one of the regular electors on the Democratic ticket.[131] The use of the term elector to designate the person chosen from the electoral district to vote in the Electoral College and the person in the county who managed the campaign for a party is confusing; it developed from the activity of the nominee for district elector in behalf of his ticket. Franklin Pierce, the Democratic nominee, led in Prince Edward with 302 votes to Winfield Scott's 227; the Whig candidate, however, carried Farmville, which was now a separate precinct, by nineteen votes.[132]

In the congressional redistricting, Prince Edward remained in the Fourth District, but Appomattox was placed in the Fifth District. This meant that Prince Edward could no longer be represented by Bocock. A Democratic meeting at the Courthouse on April 18, 1853, of which Samuel W. Venable was chairman and Dr. William T. Walker secretary, indicated its preference for a convention to select a candidate for the House from the new district. It named E. H. Bass, John T. Carter, R. H. Watkins, John P. Hughes, Newton Cunningham, J. W. Womack, George W. Daniel, J. B. Hilliard, W. T. Wootton, F. T. Wootton, D. F. Womack, T. T. Tredway, W. C. Flournoy, E. J. Redd, W. C. Arms, and any other Democrat from the county who could attend delegates to a district convention to select a nominee.[133]

W. O. Goode of Mecklenburg was chosen the Democratic nominee for Congress and Wyatt Cardwell of Charlotte the Whig nominee in 1853.[134] Goode was elected.[135] Prince Edward this year elected a Whig to the House of Delegates, Stephen O. Southall. He was the second Whig to represent the county in the lower house.[136]

In the mid-1850's the Whig party in the South tended to become absorbed into the Know-Nothing movement, which was known as the American party, and in the North to become divided between the new Republican, anti-slavery party, and Know-Nothingism. In 1855 the opposition to the Democratic party in the Virginia state election was called the American ticket; on the ticket were Thomas Stanhope Flournoy, a native of Prince Edward who was living in Halifax and a brother of the Prince Edward Democratic leader, William C. Flournoy, for Governor; James M. H. Beale of Mason County for Lieutenant Governor; and John M. Patton of Richmond City for Attorney General.[137]

Democratic nominees were chosen at a convention in Staunton November 30, 1854. Delegates from Prince Edward were chosen at a party meeting November 20, at which Joseph A. Watson presided and of which J. H. Knight was secretary. These and five persons from each of the five magisterial districts were delegates: Courthouse District: Samuel C. Anderson, William C. Flournoy, R. H. Watkins, B. J. Worsham, William T. Carter; Farmville District: Beverly Scott, Joel W. Womack, H. G. Richardson, P. H. Jackson, Thomas Hickson; Prospect District: Thomas H. Almond, James Venable, H. J. Venable, Daniel C. Glenn, Captain William Brightwell; Darlington Heights District: T. T. Tredway, D. F. Womack, John T. Carter, Newton Cunningham, Joseph Daniel; Sandy River District: Thomas Clark, John Foster, F. T. Wootton, William Walton, William T. Wootton.[138]

The Staunton convention nominated Henry A. Wise of Accomac for Governor, Elisha W. McComas of Kanawha for Lieutenant Governor, and Willis P. Bocock of Appomattox for Attorney General.[139] Wise waged an active campaign; he was one of the first candidates to travel by railroad in his campaigning. This new method of transportation made it possible for him to visit many parts of the state after his nomination. He spoke at Prince Edward Courthouse in January "in an able, eloquent and masterly speech" lasting over three hours; in it "he fully avowed his opinions upon every cardinal topic of the day, State and Federal, with a boldness, vigor, ability and independence which, we (the Farmville *Journal*, a neutral paper in the campaign) are free to say, we have never heard surpassed by any man."[140] The part William C. Flournoy played in support of Wise and the other Democratic nominees, although his brother was the American nominee for Governor, attracted attention. The *Southside Democrat* called William C. Flournoy's speech at Prince Edward Courthouse on March 19 "the most telling and eloquent effort made in Eastern Virginia in the present canvass . . ." That paper reported that "some of the most respectable Whigs" in Prince Edward would support the Democratic ticket: "they say they can swallow most anything to beat democracy, but can't go Know-nothingism."[141] In Prince Edward Wise received 427 votes, Flournoy 355; McComas 428, Beale 337; Bocock 435, Patton 334. In the congressional race, Goode received 437 votes to 330 for L. Tazewell, the Know-Nothing and Whig candidate.[142] The Democrats carried the state by approximately 12,000.[143]

Prince Edward Democrats were well organized for the 1855 campaign. A meeting was held, as usual, at the March Court. Thomas T. Tredway acted as chairman, and John H. Knight as secretary of the meeting. Samuel C. Anderson in stating the object of the meeting urged unity and energy among the Democrats and spoke of the "evil and corrupt tendencies of secret political organizations" (a reference to the Know-Nothing party). William C. Flournoy was called for and spoke. Then Thomas H. Campbell, state senator, was called for, but he asked to be excused because of the late hour. The meeting endorsed the nominees of the Staunton convention and nominated John Wesley Redd for the House of Delegates. Redd subsequently declined the nomination, and at a meeting at the April Court Thomas T. Tredway was nominated. A committee of vigilance was appointed in each district at the March meeting: Courthouse: John W. Redd, H. S. Guthrey, Colonel H. D. McCargo; Darlington Heights: William P. Baker, T. T. Tredway, John P. Hughes; Farmville: George W. Daniel, S. W. Venable, James B. Hilliard; Sandy River: Thomas Clark, F. T. Wootton, James Scott; Prespect: H. J. Venable, James R. Carter, James Venable.[144]

R. H. Allen of Lunenburg on the Know-Nothing ticket opposed Thomas H. Campbell, Democrat, for the State Senate. Campbell was elected, receiving 445 votes to Allen's 323 in Prince Edward. Stephen O. Southall, Whig, opposed Tredway for the House of Delegates, but was defeated 430 to 357. In a clever phrase which probably expressed his own bias, the newspaper correspondent reporting the returns from Prince Edward described Allen as a "Know-Nothing voted for by Whigs," Southall as a "Whig voted for by Know-Nothings."[145]

Religion was injected into the 1855 campaign in Prince Edward when a letter to the *Penny Post* dated Farmville, May 14, 1855, related that a Baptist minister with independence to speak and act for himself who united with the order (Know-Nothings) was notified by some of his most prominent members that they had no further need for his services; it further reported that the minister replied that in agreeing to preach he did not resign his conscience or political feelings to their keeping and that he expected to fulfill his part of the contract and knew of no way they could absolve themselves of theirs and not pay him. William T. Wootton, John Rudd, Samuel B. Bruce, Francis T. Wootton, and Thomas Clark in a letter dated June 11 replied. They identified themselves as the persons about whom the unidentified correspondent to the *Penny Post* was writing, since the only Baptist minister in the county who had become a Know-Nothing was the Rev. Samuel J. Atkins, whom they had employed to preach for them during 1855. They denied sending any such communication to Atkins and expressed regret that they had to defend themselves against a false charge and were "more deeply pained that one who ministers to us should be the occasion to compel us to this course."[146]

Branch J. Worsham, John Wesley Redd, and Colonel Joseph Dupuy were commissioners for the 1856 election.[147] James Buchanan, the Democratic candidate, received 429 votes in Prince Edward, and Millard Fillmore, the American party candidate, received 214.[148]

When Willis P. Bocock resigned as Attorney General in March, 1857, a state Democratic convention was called to nominate a candidate to succeed him. The Prince Edward delegation, named at a county convention held April 20, 1857, of which John W. Redd was chairman and Samuel B. Scott secretary, was instructed to confer with other delegations from the district before deciding upon a candidate to support. Branch J. Worsham, George W. Daniel, Samuel B. Scott, William T. Wootton, and Asa D. Dickinson attended the state convention and supported James Garland of Campbell for the nomination; John Randolph Tucker was the convention's choice.[149]

In 1857 William C. Flournoy opposed William O. Goode for the Democratic nomination for the House of Representatives from the

Fourth District.[150] At the convention which met at Burkeville May 20, Goode was nominated by a vote of 4,219 to 783 for Flournoy. The Prince Edward delegation gave Flournoy 299 votes and Goode 130.[151] The vote in the convention may appear unusually large for a convention; it was the practice at that time in state and district party conventions to allow each county as many votes in the convention as had been cast in that county for the party nominees at the preceding election. Prince Edward, having cast 429 votes for Buchanan, was allowed 429 votes in the convention.

In the election May 28, 1857, Prince Edward cast 321 votes for Goode and 75 for R. R. Collier, his Know-Nothing opponent, and 329 votes for John Randolph Tucker and 11 for John M. Patton, the Know-Nothing candidate.[152]

The Democratic nomination for Governor in 1859 attracted more than normal interest. The Democratic meeting at the Courthouse, of which William T. Wootton was chairman and Branch J. Worsham was secretary, named twenty delegates to the state convention which met in Petersburg December 2, 1858. They were F. T. Wootton, Thomas Clark, Samuel B. Scott, Cornelius Tucker from the First (Sandy River) District; William T. Carter, Asa D. Dickinson, William C. Flournoy, Edwin J. Redd from the Second (Courthouse) District; Branch J. Worsham, John P. Hughes, Thomas T. Tredway, David F. Womack from the Third (Darlington Heights) District; James H. Dillon, John A. Dalby, John H. Knight, James Venable from the Fourth (Prospect) District; George W. Daniel, James W. Dunnington, Francis P. Wood, James M. McNutt from the Fifth (Farmville) District.[153]

In the convention Governor Wise strongly opposed the nomination of John Letcher of Rockbridge to be his successor. Letcher's endorsement of Dr. Henry Ruffner's plan for removing the Negro population from Western Virginia rose up to plague him. William C. Flournoy of Prince Edward championed Letcher in debate with Wise and charged the Governor with being politically inconsistent; Wise replied that the party had been inconsistent, not he; he reminded the convention that he had opposed Van Buren in 1840 because Van Buren opposed the annexation of Texas. When the vote was taken, the Prince Edward delegation was divided; nine of the delegates named were in attendance, and Prince Edward's 429 votes were equally divided among them, forty-seven each. McNutt, Wood, Knight, Womack, Tredway, and Flournoy cast 282 votes for Letcher;

Daniel, Dalby, and Dickinson cast 141 votes for Henry A. Edmundson of Roanoke. Letcher received the nomination for Governor, Robert L. Montague of Middlesex the nomination for Lieutenant Governor (William C. Flournoy received 456 votes on the first and second ballots), and John Randolph Tucker of Frederick the nomination for Attorney General.[154]

The "Opposition" (to the Democratic party) ticket consisted of W. L. Goggin for Governor, W. T. Willey for Lieutenant Governor, and Walter Preston for Attorney General.[155]

Meanwhile the congressional race had been working through the intricacies of a political maze. Thomas F. Goode of Mecklenburg had twice announced and twice withdrawn; Henry L. Hopkins[156] of Petersburg, formerly of Powhatan, had announced and withdrawn.[157] William C. Flournoy announced in March.[158] William O. Goode, the incumbent, had announced in February; admitting that his health was delicate, as it had been for years, Goode reminded his constituents that his vote was usually recorded and that he was chairman of the District of Columbia Committee, a post which required ten to twelve hours' work daily.[159]

In the election on May 26, Prince Edward voters cast 316 ballots for Letcher, 271 for Goggin; 294 for Montague, 240 for Willey; 301 for Tucker, 240 for Preston; and in the congressional race 437 for Flournoy and 103 for Goode. Flournoy carried Prince Edward, Cumberland, and Charlotte Counties; Goode carried the others and was re-elected; the Letcher ticket won in the state.[160]

A little over a month after the election, William O. Goode died.[161] The convention to name his successor met in Farmville September 21 and, although Henry L. Hopkins and Thomas F. Goode were also candidates, nominated Roger A Pryor of Petersburg by acclamation. Goode opposed Pryor for the election on what he called the platform of Senator James M. Mason of Virginia, Senator Clay of Alabama, and the champions of Democracy and Southern rights.[162] In a debate with Pryor at Prince Edward Courthouse, Goode charged him with political inconsistency and with supporting Senator Stephen A. Douglas and his "squatter-sovereignty" plan. Pryor criticized Goode for not abiding by the decision of the district convention and said he would support Douglas for the Presidency if he were nominated by the Charleston convention. Goode's course in running was defended because he had not gone into the convention. Both men received their due portion of applause.[163] Pryor carried the district in the special election October 27, winning in every county except Goode's home county, Mecklenburg. His majority in Prince Edward was eighty-four.[164]

Local Government

Until the Constitution of 1851 became effective, sheriffs and magistrates continued to be appointed by the Governor. The rotation of the sheriff's office in order among the magistrates was continued.

In succession to William Bibb, whose last term was in 1789, the following Prince Edward sheriffs were appointed by the Governors: John Clarke, 1790-91;[165] Jacob Woodson, 1792-93;[166] John Watson, 1794-95;[167] Charles Allen, 1796-97;[168] Richard Foster, 1798-99;[169] Tarlton Woodson, 1800-01[170] James Morton, 1802-03;[171] John Purnall, 1804-05[172] William Price, Jr., 1806-07;[173] Robert Kelso, 1808-09;[174] Archer Allen, 1810-11;[175] Samuel Carter, 1811-13 (Carter took office in February, 1811, succeeding Archer Allen, deceased);[176] John Booker, 1814-15;[177] Samuel Baldwin, 1816-17;[178] Jacob Woodson, 1818-19;[179] Samuel Watkins, 1820-21;[180] Edmund Lockett, 1822-23;[181] Josiah Perkinson, 1824-25;[182] Robert Venable, Sr., 1826;[183] James Morton, 1827-28;[184] Osborn Lockett, 1829-30;[185] Thomas Scott, 1831-32;[186] Robert Kelso, 1833-34;[187] Nathaniel Price, 1835-36;[188] Charles Woodson, 1837;[189] John J. Flournoy, 1838-39;[190] John Clark, 1840-41;[191] Jesse Michaux, 1842-43;[192] Asa Dupuy, 1844-45;[193] Moses Tredway, 1846-47;[194] Jack Vaughan, 1848-49;[195] Lillious D. Womack, 1850-51;[196] William T. Wootton, 1852.[197]

Joseph Venable continued as deputy attorney for the Commonwealth until 1810.[198] Samuel L. Lockett was named his successor, but he held the office only a short time, and Henry E. Watkins was appointed Commonwealth's Attorney in October, 1810.[199] Watkins resigned in April, 1813, and Samuel Branch was appointed by the Court to succeed him.[200] Branch served until June, 1846; William C. Flournoy became the next Commonwealth's Attorney for Prince Edward.[201] He continued until the office became elective under the amended Constitution of 1851.[202]

John Morton continued as commissioner of the revenue until his death, and Thomas Green was appointed to succeed him in December, 1796.[203] Charles Allen was Morton's colleague until 1792, when John Booker was named his successor.[204] Additional commissioners were sometimes appointed: James Allen and John Hudson in 1796, for example.[205] Samuel V. Allen succeeded Booker as commissioner in the lower district in 1813 and was serving in 1814. Abner Nash was commissioner in this district in 1816.[206] Thomas Green and John Booker served as commissioners of the revenue in 1818, and Booker and John P. Green in 1819 and 1820.[207] After 1820 there was only one commissioner; John P. Green served until his death, James Foster succeeding him in August, 1826.[208] Watkins Dupuy was appointed in September, 1839, to succeed Foster, who had died, and continued to serve until the office became elective in 1852.[209]

Francis Watkins resigned the office of clerk in July, 1825, and Branch J. Worsham, who had been writing in the clerk's office since boyhood and had been deputy clerk since 1810 and clerk of the Superior Court since 1816, was named his successor.[210]

The last person recommended by the Court to the professors of William and Mary College to be appointed county surveyor of Prince Edward was William Hamlin, who was nominated to succeed Charles Allen in January, 1800.[211] Hamlin resigned in November, 1815, and was succeeded by James R. Allen.[212] Among other antebellum county surveyors were Thomas W. McGlasson, appointed in 1834;[213] Anderson Hill, appointed in 1835;[214] and Booker Foster, who qualified in 1846.[215]

Charles Allen succeeded Francis Watkins as escheater in 1794 and resigned the office in 1795.[216] Charles Woodson was escheater for the county in 1810; he was succeeded by Samuel V. Allen in 1814, but was serving again in 1816.[217]

Charles Allen was also coroner; he held this post in 1787, resigning in 1795 at the same time he resigned the escheater's office,[218] when he became sheriff. John Nash was coroner 1796-99; he resigned, and it was with difficulty that he was replaced.[219] John Booker declined recommendation to the Governor for appointment, and Samuel Carter and Edmund Lockett were recommended in October, 1799;[220] a year later Joel Jackson and Thomas Haskins were recommended, but Jackson, who was appointed, declined to serve. Simeon Walton was then recommended to the Governor;[221] he qualified as coroner in February, 1802, giving bond for $10,000, with Anderson Wade and Thomas Scott his securities.[222] Charles Woodson succeeded Walton upon his resignation in 1804.[223] When Woodson resigned in 1806, it was proposed to have two coroners in the county, one in the lower, the other in the upper district; Walton and Samuel Wootton were recommended for the lower district, Samuel Allen and William A. Allen for the upper district.[224] Thomas

Pettus and Robert Hill became coroners in 1811.[225] Later there was only one coroner for the county. Samuel Allen resigned in 1842 and was succeeded by John Foster.[226]

The county was divided into two constables' districts in 1837. The first district included the town of Farmville and its environs; the line began at Sandy Ford bridge, followed the road to the road which crossed Big Buffalo, then followed that road to the bridge over Little Buffalo, and from the bridge went upstream to the road from Drury Watson's, which it followed to the road from Farmville to the Courthouse. From this road the line followed the boundary between the property of Watson and Mrs. Womack and of Mrs. Womack and Thomas F. Venable to Briery River; then it went down Briery and Bush to the Appomattox and up the Appomattox to the Sandy Ford bridge. John P. Hawkins was named constable of this district, and Josiah M. Rice constable of the second district, which included the rest of the county.[227]

John Nash resigned as a magistrate in December, 1788.[228] In September, 1791, Benjamin Haskins resigned, and the clerk was directed to notify the Governor of his resignation, of the death of Joseph Moore, and of the removal from the county of William Bibb and John Holcombe. James Morton, Peter Johnston, John Purnall, John Lamkin Crute, William Price, Jr., and Robert Kelso were recommended to be added to the commission,[229] and their appointments were read at the November Court.[230] William Worsham, Thomas Haskins, Jr., George Foster, George Booker, and Martin Smith were recommended for appointment in February, 1794.[231] The vacancies on the Court apparently remained unfilled; in June, 1795, the Court certified to the Governor that John Nash, Jr., Thomas Haskins, Charles Venable, and John Clarke declined to act as magistrates; that William Bibb had moved from Virginia; that Benjamin Haskins had moved from Prince Edward; that Joseph Moore, James Allen, Sr., and John Fontaine were dead; and that Thomas Gibson and John L. Crute refused to qualify as justices; Archer Allen, Samuel Carter, Charles Scott, John Booker, Alexander Marshall, and Samuel Baldwin were recommended to be added to the commission.[232] Allen, Carter, Booker, Baldwin, and Marshall qualified in July.[233]

John Nash, Jr., John L. Crute, Thomas Haskins, Jr., Josiah Perkinson, Robert Watkins, Augustus Watson, and Richard D. Pincham were recommended as justices in October, 1797.[234] Another list of recommendations was submitted in August, 1798: John L.

Crute, Augustus Watson, Samuel Watkins, Robert Watkins, John Nash, Jr., Edmund Lockett, Josiah Perkinson, Robert Venable, and Thomas Clarke.[235] Watson, Perkinson, Watkins, Lockett, and Venable qualified in October.[236]

To fill vacancies created by the deaths of Philemon Holcombe, Robert Watkins, and Thomas Flournoy, the removal from the state of John Watson, and the resignation of Alexander Marshall, Osborn Lockett, Thomas A. Morton, Thomas Scott (son of James Scott), and Edward Dillon were recommended in November, 1804.[237] The four took the oath of office in February, 1805[238]

In 1806 Jesse Wootton, Armistead Miller, Richard K. Randolph, and James Ming were recommended. They were appointed and qualified, all except Ming in January, 1807, and he in February, 1807.[239] Among those whom they replaced were William Wootton and Samuel W. Venable, who resigned in 1806.[240]

Thomas A. Morton (who had qualified, moved away, and returned), Nathaniel Price, Samuel Wootton, Francis Watkins, Jr., Charles Woodson, William L. Venable, and John James Flournoy were recommended for appointment as magistrates in December, 1809. All of these except Venable qualified by September, 1810; Venable took the oath in May, 1816, evidently on appointment following this recommendation for in the subsequent recommendations he is not listed.[241]

Anderson P. Miller, Zachariah Rice, Rezen Porter, and John Clarke took the oath of a justice in December, 1810, having been recommended for appointment three months before.[242] John Booker qualified in November, 1811, after having been recommended the month before.[243] Francis Watkins, Jr., resigned in November, 1812.[244]

The next recommendations were made in May, 1816: Jesse Michaux, Samuel V. Allen, Asa Dupuy, John Booth, Moses Tredway, Jack Vaughan, James D. Wood, and James Madison. They were appointed, and all qualified in the following October, November, and December.[245] Thomas A. Morton resigned in February, 1817.[246]

After Jacob Woodson resigned in May, 1821, the Court recommended seven men to be added to the commission: Lillious D. Womack, William Doswell, William T. Wootton, William Mathews, Augustus Watkins, Thomas A. LeGrand, and Thomas E. Haskins.[247] These qualified in August and in October. The next year Samuel Wootton resigned the magistracy, and Samuel Watkins resigned in March, 1825.[248]

The Court nominated Henry E. Watkins, Joseph Redd, Henry Thweatt, Abraham L. Venable, Robert Venable, Jr., and Vincent Philips in May, 1825, to be added to its membership. These, and James Wilson, whose nomination was not recorded, were appointed; all, except Watkins, qualified in July, 1825, and he took the oath of office in March, 1826.[249] Edmund Booker and Samuel D. Burke were recommended in June, 1827;. they took office the following November.[250] Upon the deaths of General John Purnall and John Booker, the Court in February, 1825, decided that its members and officers would wear crepe upon the left arm for sixty days in their memory.[251]

James W. Womack, Thomas E. Perkinson, James McDearmon, and Joseph Todd were recommended as justices in March, 1830, and during subsequent months qualified.[252]

John Rice joined the Court in December, 1832.[253] Additions in 1833 were Richard Booker, Paschal L. Ligon, William Trent, Thomas Flournoy, William S. Morton, and Thomas C. Overton.[254]

In 1836 Frederick Hobson, C. C. Read, Peyton R. Berkeley, Nathaniel Jones, John W. Redd, and John A. Scott were recommended to the Governor for appointment; all, except Berkeley, took the oath of office.[255]

Nominations were sent to the Governor in 1840 for John Dupuy, Joel W. Womack, James Venable, Joel Elam, Luther C. Jeffress, Henry S. Guthrie, Francis T. Wootton, James McDearmon, and George W. Lockett. All except Lockett qualified.[256]

A slate of nominees was also presented to the Governor in 1843: Paschal L. Ligon, Thomas Clark, Isaac Read, David F. Womack, Edward F. Booker, Newton Cunningham, William M. Walton, James Cobbs, Benjamin W. Womack, and Thomas T. Tredway. Of the group, Clark, David F. Womack, Cunningham, Cobbs and Benjamin W. Womack qualified.[257]

The Court recommended in 1845 that William Brightwell, Joseph Phillips, Albert G. Green, Thomas B. McGehee, Joseph E. Venable, George W. Clibourn, Thomas H. Venable, and Clement R. Barksdale be appointed justices. Brightwell, Green, the Venables, Clibourn, and Barksdale qualified in October.[258]

The terms of all the officers of the Court expired June 30, 1852, and of the magistrates July 31, 1852, under the amended Constitution. The officers of the court who were elected on the fourth Thursday in May qualified at the June Court, 1852. The terms of the sheriff, the commissioner of the revenue, and constables (one for each district) were two years each; the term of the commonwealth's attorney and the overseers of the poor (also one for each magisterial district) was four years; and the term of the clerk and surveyor was six years. Branch J. Worsham was the first elected clerk; Hilary G. Richardson the first elected sheriff; Watkins Dupuy the first elected commissioner of the revenue; William C. Flournoy the first elected commonwealth's attorney, and Booker Foster the first elected surveyor.[259]

Justices of the peace were elected by districts for terms of four years each; their term began August 1, and they qualified at the July, 1852, Court. The county had been divided into five districts, and four magistrates were elected from each: F. T. Wootton, John A. Scott, Thomas Clark, and Giles A. Miller, from the district usually called Sandy River; Henry S. Guthrey, Thomas E. Haskins, John W. Redd, and Robert S. Carter, from the Courthouse district; Newton Cunningham, David F. Womack, John T. Carter, and Thomas T. Tredway, from the Darlington Heights district; William Brightwell, John A. Dalby, Charles A. Morton, and Robert V. Davis, from the Prospect district; Joel W. Womack, C. C. Read, H. E. Warren, and Francis P. Wood, from the Farmville district.[260] Thomas E. Haskins was elected presiding justice.[261]

The first overseers of the poor elected under the amended Constitution for the four-year term were William Weaver, first, or Sandy River, district; William T. Carter, second, or Courthouse, district; Henry C. Thackston, third, or Darlington Heights, district; Samuel F. Hunt, fourth, or Prospect, district; Benjamin C. Peters, fifth, or Farmville, district.

The first constables elected under the Constitution of 1851 were Nathaniel M. Mottley, district one; Thomas L. Hines, district two; James Mickle, district three; Edward R. Brightwell, district four; and Samuel A. Moore, district five.[262]

In 1854 Newton Cunningham was elected sheriff; he was reelected in 1856.[263] Henry B. Brightwell was elected sheriff in 1858 and again in 1860.[264] Watkins Dupuy continued to be elected commissioner of the revenue. [265]

The Court held that Flournoy was neglecting his official duties as commonwealth's attorney through his service as a member of the House of Delegates; it removed him from office and ordered a special election held March 8, 1853, for commonwealth's attorney.[266] It is not known whether the election was held; if it was Flournoy was re-elected; the levy in August, 1853, compensated Flournoy for services since June, 1852; and the levy in July, 1854, paid him for services since August, 1853.[267] He continued as commonwealth's attorney until he failed to qualify after the election in May, 1860; the Court ordered an election of commonwealth's attorney on October 17;[268] in November, 1860, John T. Thornton qualified for the office.[269]

Three vacancies occurred among the magistrates before the second election; William B. Baker replaced Thomas T. Tredway who resigned in 1853;[270] James Whitehead succeeded Newton Cunningham, who resigned when he was elected sheriff in 1854;[271] Joseph T. Morton came to the bench from the fifth district (Farmville) in 1855.[272] James S. Lockett was the only new justice elected in 1856; he was from the first district.[273] Samuel S. Baker became a justice from the third district in 1858.[274] Thomas E. Haskins, who had been re-elected presiding justice in 1856, resigned in 1859, and Edwin J. Redd was elected a magistrate.[275] In 1860 Robert V. Davis, Richard W. Price, William T. Lee, Thomas B. Rice, Joseph T. Ligon, Robert C. Anderson, John P. Hughes, James E. Flippen, Richard B. Thackston, James T. Gray, James Whitehead, James S. Lockett, Charles A. Morton, Edwin J. Redd, James B. Ely, William T. Carter, Samuel S. Baker, Samuel B. Scott, John A. Dalby, and David F. Womack were elected justices.[276]

The justices continued to set the county levy in pounds, shillings, and pence until December, 1792. That year each tithable was assessed one shilling, threepence, to yield £193:2:6 from 3,090 tithables.[277] The next levy, which was set in February, 1794, was the first in dollars and cents; the levy per tithe was thirteen cents, to yield $414.50, the amount required to operate the county government.[278] It was 1806 before it cost $1,000 to finance a year's operation; the levy set that year was designed to raise $1,041.19 at an assessment of seventeen cents per tithe.[279]

The state set the taxes on various forms of property. The rates for taxes in 1803 were fixed at forty-eight cents on the $100 valuation on land; forty-four cents per slave over twelve years of age; twice the season covering fee for each stud horse and jack ass, and twelve cents each for all other horses, mules, mares, and colts; $1.25 per wheel for four-wheeled carriages except phaetons and stage wagons, for which the tax was eighty-four cents per wheel; forty-three cents per wheel for two-wheeled riding carriages; $1.56 for each $100 rent on town houses and lots. Ordinary licenses were $12.50; wholesale merchants handling goods of foreign growth or manufacture paid tax of $40, and retail merchants paid a tax of $15.[280] The land tax for 1807 was reduced to forty-two cents on the $100 valuation. To the list of taxes was added a tax of $20 on hawkers or peddlers.[281]

Tax rates had increased considerably in 1813, and the list of taxable items was lengthened. The land tax was sixty-four cents on the $100; the tax on slaves over twelve was fifty-nine cents; the tax on stallions and jack asses was increased to three times the season covering fee; the tax on other horses, mares, colts, mules sixteen cents each; fifty cents per wheel on two-wheeled carriages valued at less than $100; $2.50 on carriages valued at $100 to $200; one per cent of the value on carriages valued at over $200; $2.08 per $100 annual rent or value on houses and lots in towns; $2.00 on the $100 valuation on mills (grist, manufacturing, merchant, and saw-mills); $1.00 on the $100 valuation on tanyards and smith's shops; $6.66 on the $100 on ordinaries (minimum, $16.50); $60 on wholesale merchants; $23 on retail merchants; $45 on hawkers or peddlers of dry goods and $20 on peddlers trading in tin and pewter; $30 on tobacco manufacturing plants and stemmeries; $60 on apothecaries; $12.50 on physicians; $5.00 on auctioneers; $5.00 on lawyers practicing in county courts, $10 on lawyers practicing in superior courts, $15 on lawyers practicing in superior courts of chancery, and $20 on lawyers practicing in the court of appeals; newspapers were charged a tax equal to the charge for four annual subscriptions; and the clerk of court was taxed one per cent of the fees he received. A poll tax of $1.50 was levied on free Negroes and mulattoes. A scale of taxes on notes and bills was also set: ten cents on $20-$100; twenty-five cents, $100-$500; fifty cents, $500-$1,000; seventy-five cents, $1,000-$2,000; $1 over $2,000; $1.25, over $3,000; $1.50, over $4,000; and for each $1,000 in excess of $5,000 an additional twenty-five cents.[282]

The Board of Principal Assessors of the State of Virginia set $8,703.09 as Prince Edward County's quota of the direct tax for 1816; to raise this sum, a levy of twenty-eight cents on each $100 property valuation was imposed.[283] Laban Hawkins' tax bill for that year amounted to $21.73, with taxes paid on these items: on ten tithes, $5; on eleven blacks, three horses, and one gig or carriage, $8.75; on 220 acres of land, $3.57; on tickets, $4.42.[284]

In 1820 the land and buildings in Prince Edward had an appraised value of $1,986,659.23, and the valuation of town property in the county was $18,575, to give a total real property valuation of $2,005,234.23.²⁸⁵ Real estate valuation for tax purposes had not gone up appreciably by 1850, when it was $2,071,121; but there was a marked increase during the next six years, when the assessed valuation was $2,613,910.²⁸⁶ In 1850 license and revenue taxes amounting to $6,511.24 were paid in Prince Edward.²⁸⁷

There were also federal taxes to be paid. Early in January, 1816, Samuel Jones of Buckingham, collector of the revenue for the Thirteenth Collection District of Virginia, announced his schedule to visit "certain places to receive the entry of carriages, with harness, agreeable to Act of Congress passed December 12, 1814." Retailers and distillers were directed to apply for licenses at these places. Jones or a deputy was scheduled to be at Prince Edward Courthouse January 15, 1816; at Sandy River Church January 16; and at Walker's Church January 17.²⁸⁸ Laban Hawkins paid a "direct tax" of $12.46 for the year 1815, according to a receipt given him April 25, 1816, by J. N. Williams, deputy to Samuel Jones, collector.²⁸⁹

In August, 1784, a new jail was reported by a commission not named in the court orders as having been completed according to contract. Benjamin Allen was the undertaker. This jail seems to have replaced the jail built on the acre of land bought from Joseph Smith for the county buildings in 1775.²⁹⁰

Another jail was built in 1791. In May of that year Peter LeGrand was directed to remove the "jail used for criminals" for which he was allowed the timbers and irons; an additional condition was the deduction of £4 from his charge for building the new jail. The new jail had a window in the front of eight panes, each pane eight by ten inches, "with new strong shutters and iron bolts" and a frame "of hart pine." Samuel W. Venable, John Morton, Thomas Scott, and Charles Allen were appointed in November, 1791, to view the new jail and receive it when it had been completed.²⁹¹

In June, 1822, William L. Venable submitted a plat of the town of Prince Edward Courthouse; the Court agreed to accept the land designated public square on the plat, through which the north-south road led, in lieu of the public lot on which the courthouse stood, except for the jail; the Court decided to retain that building and the land within ten feet around it.²⁹²

A new jail was ordered to be built in August, 1823, on land bought from William L. Venable near the site of the old jail.

Nathaniel Price, James D. Wood, Jesse Michaux, Asa Dupuy, Robert Kelso, Moses Tredway, and William S. Morton were named commissioners to let the contract for building it.[293]

In June, 1830, the Court determined to build a new courthouse. Henry E. Watkins, Samuel C. Anderson, Charles Woodson, Branch J. Worsham, and James D. Wood were named commissioners to receive plans and report them. The commissioners presented plans to the July Court, which adopted plan number one of William A. Howard; it determined that the building should be erected in the center of the public square, as near as possible to the north stiles of the enclosure, in order to preserve the trees. On the second day of the July Court, however, the action adopting plans was rescinded. In August the Court adopted plan number two instead of number one and added Joseph Todd to the commissioners. A new enclosure was ordered in November, 1830, to be built of posts and rails of good timber. A year later the sale of the old building was ordered. The Court in June, 1832, directed the commissioners to receive the new building and gave permission to John Pearson, who had bought it, to remove the old building. Pearson was subsequently appointed keeper of the courthouse and its grounds and was made responsible for supplying water and fires for the building. In August, 1832, tin gutters were ordered placed on the courthouse and benches on the lawn; and the Court received the commissioners' report. Porches were reported completed in November of that year. Hudson Wilson and Jack Thackston built the courthouse.[294]

The jail burned in 1845, and the Court in October directed that it be repaired or rebuilt. Branch J. Worsham, David F. Womack, Henry S. Guthrey, Luther C. Jeffress, Nathaniel Jones, George W. Clibourne, Joseph Redd, and John W. Redd were named commissioners to build or repair the jail after the plan of the building which burned. Guthrey received the contract for "repairing" the jail; other references refer to its "building" or "rebuilding"; thus it is not clear how the burned jail was replaced.[295] Early in 1855 this jail burned; in March of that year Branch J. Worsham, Asa D. Dickinson, William C. Flournoy, Samuel C. Anderson, and George W. Cliborne were appointed commissioners to let the contract for repairs to the jail. The commissioners' report was accepted by the November Court, and payment for the repairs was made an item of business for the next session of the court.[296]

A new clerk's office was built 1809-10, probably replacing the "office house" built on the acre of ground bought from Joseph Smith in 1775. The new office was built of brick, twenty by twenty-two feet in size with a twelve-foot pitch, on a lot forty-five yards square on the road from Farmville to the Courthouse. James Morton, Richard N. Venable, John Booker, Francis Watkins, Sr., and Henry E. Watkins were named commissioners to let the contract for the building in June, 1809; when the deed by which William L. and Frances W. Venable conveyed the lot to the magistrates was written in August, 1810, the "new brick clerk's office" had been erected.[297]

This building served until a new office was built in 1855 on the courthouse square, the center of the office being in line with the center of the north and south doors of the courthouse. Dickinson, Anderson, Worsham, and Henry S. Guthrey were named commissioners in July, 1854, to draw up plans and let the contract for the new office. It was received "as done according to contract" in December, 1855, and the sheriff, Newton Cunningham, was directed to pay Guthrey and Thackston, the contractors, $1,785 on account, which included payment for the stone window sills.[298] Since the land on which the office built in 1809-10 had been conveyed to the county for "the sole and only purpose of a clerk's office," it reverted to the original owner, and the Court in May, 1857, "surrenders the lot to the persons entitled thereto."[299]

The old practice of processioning land was kept up until 1830. The county was divided into twenty-two precincts and processioners were appointed to go over the boundaries and set the landmarks of the boundaries between farms. The precinct divisions generally followed those determined in colonial times by the parish vestry.[300] In 1792 the overseers of the poor were directed to lay off the precincts and appoint the processioners.[301] In 1827 the Court recorded its opinion that it would not be necessary to procession land oftener than every six years.[302] The practice was revived in an Act of the General Assembly of 1884 directing the Board of Supervisors of Prince Edward and some other counties to divide the counties into precincts, appoint processioners, have the lands processioned then and each five years thereafter.[303]

After 1786 the overseers of the poor directed the welfare work caried on by the county. They were elected by districts. In 1792 Thomas Scott, William Price, Jr., Samuel W. Venable, John Richards, Charles Allen, Joseph Parks, William Porter, John L. Crute, John Miller, Robert Kelso, and John Perkinson took the prescribed oath after the election.[304] George Booker succeeded Joseph Parks when he left the county in 1794.[305] After the election in 1795, James Morton, James Wade, Jr., John Richards, Jacob Woodson, John L. Crute, John Booker, Jr., Samuel Carter, William Lindsey, Jacob Venable, and Robert Venable qualified as overseers of the poor.[306] Those who qualified for the office in 1798 were Tarlton Woodson, Nicholas Davis, William Matthis (Mathews), Thomas Clark, Josiah Perkinson, James Price, Simeon Walton, John Daniel, Samuel Baldwin, James Morton, and John Booker.[307]

In 1801 bad weather prevented the election scheduled for March 28 in three districts. The Court appointed overseers for those districts: John Booker, Abner Nash, Martin Smith for the second district; Hezekiah Morton, Baker LeGrand, John Barrett for the third district; and Nathaniel Price, Dudley Barksdale, George Booker for the fourth district.[308] The election apparently was held in the first district, for three residents of that district qualified: Richard Phillips, Simeon Walton, and Thomas Clark. John Cunningham qualified instead of George Booker from the fourth district.[309]

The record of Philip Mathews' qualification as an overseer of the poor in 1810 is distinctive in noting that Mathews, instead of taking the oath, "made affirmation in solemn form as the Law directs."[310] Mathews was a Baptist minister.

In 1823 the Court determined to build a poor house or work house for the accommodation of the poor; Charles Woodson, Robert Kelso, Nathaniel Price, James D. Wood, Thomas E. Haskins, and John Booker were named a committee to draw plans and to recommend a site.[311] Land was bought for the purpose in 1826, and the next year the overseers of the poor were directed to receive the poor house from the commissioners as soon as it was finished and to place all persons on the poor list who were willing to go there in the newly completed almshouse. Woodson, Wood, Price, and John J. Flournoy were then directed to build a steward's house on the land bought for the poor.[312] Robert C. Land and James Fore built the poor house for $450.[313]

The General Assembly in 1828 made provision for voting places in counties at other places than the Courthouse. Voting at these polls was to be under the supervision of a deputy sheriff, who would attend the voting with a copy of the commissioner's land book, and commissioners.[314]

Voters in the upper end of Prince Edward presented a petition with numerous signatures (headed by James McDearmon) to the legislature in 1830 asking that a separate precinct be established at Walker's Church. They made a good case: because of the distance from the Courthouse, only three or four of the 100 qualified voters in that end of the county were accustomed to vote. That so few voted is understandable; voters had to travel from thirty to sixty miles to the Courthouse and had to incur a tavern bill in order to vote. The petition proposed as the dividing line between the two precincts a line from the mouth of Vaughan's Creek to Southey Bell's, thence a straight line to John Cunningham's mill, thence a straight line to Isham and John Harvey's store near the Charlotte line.[315] Early in 1831 a bill was passed authorizing a separate election in Prince Edward at the storehouse of Samuel and William Matthews at Walker's Church.[316]

The next separate precinct established in Prince Edward was at Mrs. Prudence Perkinson's in the lower end of the county on the east side of Bush River. The precinct was established in 1845 in response to petitions signed by William T. Wootton, James Scott, and others. In the petition Sandy River Church originally appeared as the polling place desired, but it was scratched through and Mrs. Perkinson's house substituted.[317] In 1845 and 1846 other petitions were circulated; these, signed by John Foster, James Leigh, Branch J. Worsham and many others, asked that the law establishing a separate voting place at Mrs. Perkinson's be repealed, observing that the Courthouse could be reached from all parts of the county. The law was repealed in 1847.[318]

As early as 1841 a petition to the legislature, signed by Jacob W. Morton and others, asked that a voting precinct be established at Farmville. A second petition to the same effect, with Morton again the first signer, was sent to the legislature in 1844; the second petition proposed Randolph's Warehouse or H. G. Richardson's hotel as the voting place.[319] A third petition, signed by William C. Flournoy and 276 others, asked that a separate election precinct be established in Farmville. Oddly enough, at the same time this petition was presented to the House of Delegates in 1847, another, to which William C. Flournoy's was the first signature, opposed the establishment of a precinct in Farmville. The law designating the Town Hall in Farmville the voting place for a separate precinct was passed March 31, 1848.[320]

Although the separate precinct at Mrs. Perkinson's had existed only two years and had been abandoned after petitions requesting such abandonment had been presented, there was still strong sentiment for a separate polling place in the eastern or lower part of the county. The names of Samuel C. Anderson, Branch J. Worsham, William Walton, and Thomas Rowlett head a long list of signers of a petition asking in 1850 the establishment of an election precinct at Sandy River Church.[321] A law granting the request was passed in March, 1850, and Martha Williamson's storehouse near Sandy River Church was designated the voting place.[322] Prince Edward now had three precincts: the Courthouse, Farmville, and Sandy River Church.[323] (Walker's Church was in the section which became Appomattox County in 1845.)

The Constitution of 1850-51 provided that the justices of the peace should be elected from districts. An Act of Assembly passed April 2, 1852, directed that Prince Edward be divided into five districts and appointed as commissioners to divide the county Branch J. Worsham, S. O. Southall, Benjamin W. Womack, William T. Wootton, Newton Cunningham, Thomas E. Perkinson, Joseph Philips, Joel Elam, Joseph E. Venable, Edward F. Booker, and Francis T. Wootton. The commissioners were also authorized to establish polling places, one of which was to be the Courthouse.[324]

A majority of the Prince Edward commissioners met at the Courthouse April 15, 1852, and set the boundaries of the five magisterial districts and established the polling places:

1. Sandy River District: beginning at the mouth of Bush River, up the river to Mountain Creek, up Mountain Creek by Rudd's Mill to the source of the fork at or near Aspen Grove on the Lunenburg line, and thence with the lines of Lunenburg, Nottoway, Amelia, and Cumberland to the beginning. Sandy River Church was established as the polling place.

2. Courthouse District: beginning at Aspen Grove on the Lunenburg line, thence along the Lunenburg and Charlotte lines to the Roanoke road (the present road from Farmville to Abilene, then usually described as the road from Charlotte Courthouse to Prince Edward Courthouse), down the road to the fork by Hampden-Sydney College, thence by the college to King's tavern and eastwardly to French's old church spring, thence by a straight line to Briery bridge east of the Courthouse, thence by the road to Bush River upper bridge, and thence along the line of District One. Two polling places were established in this district, one at the Courthouse, the other at Marble Hill "now owned by James H. Brame and William F. Scott."

3. Spring Creek District: beginning at Roanoke road on the Charlotte line, along District Two line to the road by Hampden-Sydney College to the fork to Martin's bridge on Buffalo, up the road by Martin's, Londonderry near Buffalo Meeting House and by Robert Hill's to the Sandy Ford road to the county line near Pamplin's, and thence with the county lines of Appomattox and Charlotte to the beginning. Polls were established at Darlington Heights, "now owned by Josiah Cunningham and William B. Beach."

4. Prospect District: beginning on the Appomattox River at the place where the bridge called Sandy Ford formerly stood, thence along the road crossing Buffalo at LeGrand's bridge to the road running west by Martin's and Londonderry (the line of District Three), thence with the county lines of Appomattox, Buckingham, and Cumberland to the beginning. The polling place was fixed at Davis' "now owned by Robert V. Davis."

5. Farmville District: beginning on the Appomattox where Sandy Ford bridge formerly stood, up the District Four line to the road from Martin's bridge, thence along the District Two line to Bush River upper bridge, thence down Bush and up the Appomattox to the beginning. The polling place was established at Farmville.[325]

The division required two days, for which the commissioners were paid at the rate of $2 per day. Worsham, William T. Wootton, Cunningham, Perkinson, Elam, Venable, and Booker were engaged in the work both days and signed the report. Womack, Phillips, and Francis T. Wootton spent one day, the first, in working out the division. Southall apparently did not participate in the division of the county into districts.[326] The number of voting places in Prince Edward had now doubled. The Courthouse, Marble Hill, Spring Creek, Prospect, Farmville, and Sandy River[327] continued the polling places until the War Between the States.[328]

A move to change the long-established court day from the third Monday to Tuesday or Wednesday began in the 1830's. On January 8, 1839, the House of Delegates rejected a petition asking for the change, although it had been signed by such influential persons as Samuel C. Anderson, John A. Smith, A. D. Dickinson, Henry N. Watkins, Francis N. Watkins, Henry E. Watkins, William Berkeley, Wiltshire M. Lewis, Francis A. Smith, John Rice, J. W. Wilson, George H. Matthews, William C. Flournoy, George D. Saunders, Charles Smith, C. C. Read, and James H. Dupuy. The reason advanced for the change reflected the growing, and for lawyers, a comparatively recent, concern for religious matters; Monday court required many to leave home on the Sabbath and otherwise make preparation for court on the Lord's Day. In 1841 J. McDearmon and others asked that court days in both Prince Edward and Buckingham be changed from Monday to Wednesday to enable those who had to attend to avoid preparations on Sunday. A petition signed by A. C. Anderson and numerous others was presented to the legislature in January, 1842, asking that Prince Edward court day be changed from the third Monday to the Tuesday after the third Monday.[329] On March 25, 1842, the General Assembly passed a law to make the change.[330]

Opposition to the change of court day developed at once. Three petitions urging repeal of the change were filed with the General Assembly in January, 1842; the names of J. D. Sayler, B. W. Womack, and F. V. Morton head the lists of petitioners.[331] These proved effective; on February 9, 1844, the legislature restored the court day to the third Monday, the day on which the County Court in Prince Edward had been held for eighty years before the change was made.[332]

The highest court of the colony of Virginia was the General Court. The Commonwealth continued the General Court. In 1788 the General Assembly established several district courts throughout the state, the law observing that "delays inseparable from the present constitution of the General Court may often be equal to the denial of justice, the expense of criminal prosecutions [is] unnecessarily burdensome, violations of law frequently pass with impunity because of the difficulty of attendance by witnesses." Prince Edward, Buckingham, Charlotte, Halifax, and Cumberland were constituted one district, for which the court was held at Prince Edward Courthouse twice yearly, the terms beginning April 1 and September 1. The General Assembly added three judges to the nine of the General Court and these judges of the General Court conducted the district courts, two being assigned to each court. If one of the judges could not attend, the other could constitute the court. The General Court appointed the clerk of the district court, and the Governor and Council appointed the jailor.[333] The General Assembly also established a Court of Appeals of five members in 1788.[334]

Francis Watkins was clerk of the District Court. John Fowlkes was district jailer, resigning in 1792.[335] Wray Moss was appointed jailer in 1795.[336] Paul Carrington, Jr., was serving as attorney for the commonwealth for the district in 1793. Richard Parker and Edmund Winston served as judges for the September, 1793, term.[337] Among the judicial assignments to the Prince Edward District Court were Edmund Winston and James Henry, 1799;[338] Edmund Winston and Paul Carrington, Jr., 1804;[339] Edmund Winston and Archibald Stuart, June, 1805;[340] Richard Parker and Creed Taylor, December, 1805;[341] Edmund Winston and Paul Carrington, Jr., June, 1806;[342] Edmund Winston and William Nelson, Jr., November, 1806;[343] Edmund Winston and Paul Carrington, Jr., June, 1807;[344] Edmund Winston and William Nelson, Jr., December, 1807.[345]

The district court did not prove altogether satisfactory in meeting the public needs; some of the same objections which had been raised to the General Court could also be raised about the District Court. To provide more convenient courts at a higher level than the county court, the legislature in 1807 established the system of circuit courts. Virginia was divided into twelve circuits, with one judge of the General Court assigned to each circuit; he was required to hold a superior court twice a year in each county in the circuit. Judges were assigned to circuits by the Governor. The superior courts were given the jurisdiction which had been given to the district courts. The terms of the Circuit Court of Prince Edward were scheduled to begin April 28 and September 28.[346] The law was amended in 1809 to set up thirteen circuits and to fix the date of the opening of the terms in Prince Edward as the fourth Monday in April and the fourth Monday in September. Clerks of county courts were designated clerks of the circuit courts in their counties; in counties where district courts were held, the clerk of the district court was to be clerk of the circuit court.[347] Branch J. Worsham became clerk of the Prince Edward Circuit Court in 1816.[348]

In 1852 Prince Edward, Buckingham, Cumberland, Appomattox, Campbell, Charlotte, Halifax Counties and the town of Lynchburg were constituted the Third Judicial Circuit. Under the Constitution as amended in 1851 circuit judges were elected by popular vote.[349]

The period between the Revolution and the War Between the States was the golden age of the Prince Edward bar. Patrick Henry had returned to the practice of law when living in the county. Abraham B. Venable, who was to have a distinguished career as member of the House of Representatives, the United States Senate, and as president of the Bank of Virginia, had been admitted to the bar in 1784; his brother, Richard N. Venable, had been admitted to practice in 1786.

Among the other lawyers who began practice in the earlier part of the period by qualifying before the Prince Edward Court were Creed Taylor and Theodorick McRobert, 1791;[350] Richard Randolph, 1795;[351] Francis Watkins, Jr., 1796;[352] Henry E. Watkins, 1803;[353] Samuel L. Lockett, 1806;[354] James W. Womack, 1808;[535] George Booker, 1809;[356] Henry N. Watkins, 1810;[357] Nathaniel E. Venable, 1813;[358] Samuel Anderson 1815;[359] Anderson Morton and William P. Booker, 1818;[360] William Branch, Jr., 1822;[361] Samuel L. Venable and Alexander B. Walthall, 1826;[362] James D. Ligon, 1829;[363] Mercer M. Booker, 1832.[364] Edward Booker was a Prince Edward lawyer in that period.[365]

Two accounts of the Prince Edward bar of the latter part of that era give vivid pictures of the leading attorneys. Henry E. Watkins had retired from active practice in 1850, but still attended court. In a case in Nottoway in which he was associated with Benjamin Watkins Leigh, the audience was unable to decide on the merits of the two, so well matched were they in abilities. Watkins' client was so well pleased with his work in this case that in addition to paying him a generous fee he gave him a fine edition of Shakespeare. He was remembered as a "warm friend and patron of education," for his fine address and courtly manners and the refined and elegant hospitality of his home.

Samuel C. Anderson was at the end of the period dean of the Prince Edward bar. He was described of being of splendid appearance, large and portly, of commanding and attractive presence. One account describes him as "the most venerable and impressive looking man I ever saw." Anderson was especially effective as a debater. A self-made man, he was not considered a finished legal scholar, but his sound common sense and good judgment made up for his lack of learning. In the legislature he was a popular and convincing speaker. He won his greatest fame in debate in the Presbyterian General Assembly in Philadelphia in 1837, where one of his hearers called him "the most powerful debater I ever heard" and said he should be in the United States Senate. In his later years he suffered greatly from palsy.

There was more fire about William C. Flournoy than about his contemporaries, if one may draw conclusions from the description of his characteristics which remained in the memory of an observer years afterward: "the gleam of his eye, the glow of his words, the force of his logic, the sting of his sarcasm."

John T. Thornton was remembered as being "of superb person, of superior mind, of great gifts as an orator, unusually accurate and thoughtful in the preparation of legal papers." Stephen O. Southall was remembered as scholarly, wise, and witty.[366] Asa D. Dickinson, F. N. Watkins, and Richard H. Watkins were practicing attorneys in Prince Edward during this period.

Both accounts mention Judge William Leigh of the Circuit Court, "a perfect master of law," as one remembered him, presiding with an "ability and [a] justice rarely if ever surpassed." Both remembered, too, the clerk, Branch J. Worsham. Distinctive in person, his white hair closely cut, his dress neat and tidy, he had the manner of the "oldentime Virginia gentleman" and he made his office a pattern of neatness and order where any record could be found in a moment. He was regarded as "a good statute lawyer."[367]

The Formation of Appomattox County

Similar pressures to those which had led the freeholders in the upper end of Amelia County to have a new county created in the late 1740's and early 1750's prompted the citizens of the upper ends of Prince Edward, Charlotte, and Buckingham and the lower part of Campbell to have their section erected into a new county. The residents of these sections of the various counties had to travel over twenty-five miles to court. The plan of forming a new county from these areas was proposed in the 1790's. There seems to have been no further agitation of the matter until 1825, when petitions from the four counties asked that the new county be created. The General Assembly declined to create a new county of the area then, because for one reason, there was considerable feeling among the western counties that the counties east of the Blue Ridge had a better share of representation in the General Assembly; to create a new county in that part of the state, when the western counties were seeking a convention to equalize, among other objects, representation, would increase the agitation. After the Convention of 1829-30 had made changes in the representation allowed the counties, this objection was removed. In 1831 another petition, bearing over 500 names, sought the establishment of a new county from the upper parts of Prince Edward, Charlotte, and Buckingham and the lower part of Campbell.[368]

This petition proposed that Prince Edward be divided by a line run from the Cutbanks on the Appomattox River to the junction of

Vaughan's Creek and the Mill Fork, thence up Vaughan's Creek to its source and thence across to Cub Creek. The portion of Prince Edward west of this line would be added to parts of the other counties to form the new county.

The proposed boundary along Vaughan's Creek provoked opposition. Some of the residents of the area between Vaughan's Creek and the Mill Fork did not wish to leave Prince Edward County. A petition signed by Robert Kelso, Edwin Gray, Samuel G. Daniel, Alexander Swan, B. L. Pryor, and James Gilliam all of whom lived between Vaughan's Creek and the Mill Fork, presented a counter petition to the General Assembly on December 21, 1831, asking that the Mill Fork be made the boundary instead of Vaughan's Creek; this would permit them to remain in Prince Edward.

Robert Kelso continued an opponent to any plan which would take him out of Prince Edward. Later he proposed that Sawney's Creek, instead of Vaughan's, be made the dividing line between the new county and Prince Edward. Petitions from Samuel Wheeler, Creed T. Mitchell, J. McDearmon and others opposed this plan, one of the petitions noting that such a change in the line "would make an ugly place in the new county." The petitions opposing Kelso's plan reached the legislature before his did; the two of Wheeler, Mitchell, and McDearmon were presented in February and March, 1839; Kelso's in January, 1840.

On April 23, 1840, there was a vote at Mathews' store at Walker's Church on forming a new county, with 45 voting for it and 13, one of whom was Robert Kelso, voting against it.

Four years later another vote on the issue was taken at Walker's Church, with the freeholders in the part of Prince Edward proposed to become part of the new county taking part. The April, 1844, vote showed 55 in favor of a new county, 14 opposed.

Notwithstanding the popular sentiment within the area involved for a new county, H. G. Richardson and others in December, 1844, presented a petition opposing the creation of a new county because "it will greatly and unnecessarily increase county taxes."[369]

The General Assembly was now ready to act; under a bill passed February 8, 1845, it created Appomattox County from parts of Prince Edward, Buckingham, Charlotte, and Campbell. The eastern boundary began at the mouth of David's Creek on the James River and proceeded in a straight line to the head of Holliday Creek and thence down Holliday to the Appomattox River; the line then followed the Appomattox downstream to the Cutbanks from which it kept a straight line to the mouth of Cabin branch on Vaughan's Creek; thence it followed the creek to its head, from which it followed a straight line to Merryman's or Land's; thence it followed the public road leading by McKinney's old store to a fork on the Lynchburg road about a mile north of Red House.

Clover Hill, the residence of Captain John Raine in what had been Prince Edward, was designated the county seat, and the Thursday after the first Monday in May, 1845, was set as the day on which the first court was to be held. Justices of the peace of the four counties from which Appomattox was formed who lived in the new county were to be appointed magistrates of the new county and commissioned in order of their seniority in the commissions of the old counties. The four sections of Appomattox were continued in the same senatorial districts to which they had belonged when a part of the older counties, but the new county was placed in the same judicial circuit, the same congressional district, the same presidential electoral district, and the same militia brigade as Buckingham County. The county surveyors of the four counties from which Appomattox was formed were directed to run the lines of the new county.[370]

Major Samuel D. McDearmon, who had been elected to the House of Delegates from Prince Edward in 1844, was elected to the House of Delegates from Appomattox County in April, 1846, without opposition.[371]

The Militia

The militia provided the basis of defense of the colony and later of the Commonwealth. The militia system was a type of universal military training with the training provided at home. The training was meager, but it acquainted the men with the rudiments of military experience; and the militia was at the call of the Governor in the event of emergency. The county was the unit in the militia organization. Through the colonial period the county lieutenant was at the head of the county militia; there were also a colonel, a lieutenant colonel, and a major; the county was divided into districts, each of which furnished a company, at whose head was a captain; the other commissioned officers of the company were the lieutenant and the ensign.

During the Revolution the Prince Edward militia was frequently called into service. The organization continued through the war. In

1783 Thomas Flournoy became county lieutenant, John Clarke colonel, Charles Allen lieutenant colonel, and Thomas Watkins major.[372] Company captains in 1784 were Jacob Woodson, Williamson Bird, Dick Holland, Nathaniel Bassett, ———— Clark, Ambrose Nelson, Jesse Watson, James Ligon, ———— Owen, William Wooton, and John Purnall.[373]

Robert Lawson, who had been a brigadier general of volunteers in the Revolution[374] and who had been made a member of the Council of State in 1782,[375] became county lieutenant in 1785. John Holcombe was commissioned lieutenant colonel, and Charles Allen and Thomas Watkins were commissioned majors.[376] Captains commissioned that year included James Morton of the first company, Joseph Scott of the second company, Philemon Holcombe, Jr., of the company of light horse (the militia cavalry), James Allen, Jr., of the seventh company, Ambrose Nelson of the ninth company, William Porter of the tenth company, Berryman Green of the sixth company, John Purnall of the eighth company, and Charles Scott of the fifth company.[377]

Thomas Flournoy was again county lieutenant in 1787. Colonel Clarke's resignation the year before opened the way for promotions to Charles Allen to be colonel, Thomas Watkins lieutenant colonel, and Tarlton Woodson major. Abner Watkins was named captain to succeed James Ligon, resigned, but he evidently did not accept the appointment as John Lamkin Crute was later appointed captain of this company. William Porter succeeded Bassett as captain, James Parks, Clarke, and James Harper, Owen. Parks served only a few months and was succeeded by John Scott (Spring Creek). Samuel W. Venable was a new captain qualifying in 1787, and Robert Kelso succeeded Dick Holland.[378]

The General Assembly reorganized the Virginia militia in 1792 to conform to an Act of Congress to establish a uniform militia. The militia of Prince Edward, Charlotte, Halifax, and Pittsylvania made up one brigade, which with three other brigades from Southside Virginia constituted a division. Divisions, brigades, and regiments were to be numbered by the Governor. Counties were to be divided into districts for regiments, battalions, and companies. There was to be a company of grenadiers, light infantry, or riflemen for each battalion. Musters were ordered each two months, except in the winter, for the companies of grenadiers, light infantry, riflemen, artillery, and cavalry, and once every three months for all other companies at or near the center of the company district. The annual battalion musters were set for May, and the annual regimental musters were set for October. Musters began with roll call and inspection at eleven o'clock. Commissioned officers were required to meet twice a year for a two-day training by the brigade inspector.

The law exempted from militia service certain state officials, clerks of courts, inspectors of tobacco, professors, tutors, and students at "public seminaries of learning," ministers, keepers of jails and the public hospital, millers, Quakers, and Mennonists.

In addition to being subject to call in case of invasion or insurrection, the militia also was used for patrol duty. The battalion commanding officer was authorized to appoint an officer and as many as four men for patrol duty, which included visiting slave quarters or other places suspected of being a meeting place of "slaves, servants, or other disorderly persons" and slaves suspected of "strolling about from one plantation to another without pass[es]." Slaves found wandering without passes and those meeting in unlawful assemblies could be taken before the nearest magistrate who could impose a penalty of up to twenty lashes on the bare back. Patrollers received fifty cents for each twelve hours they were engaged in patrolling.[379]

The Prince Edward officers appointed after the reorganization were Tarlton Woodson, lieutenant colonel and commander of the regiment, Samuel W. Venable, major of the first battalion, James Morton, major of the second battalion, and the following captains: Jacob Woodson, John L. Crute, Philemon Holcombe, Jr. (the cavalry company), William Porter, John Purnall, Jesse Watson, Robert Kelso, Samuel Carter, Robert Watkins, and William Price, Jr. Philip Mathews became a captain in 1794, but his predecessor is not indicated.[380] In 1794 there were 1,044 free white males aged sixteen and over in Prince Edward's 63rd Regiment of militia.[381]

Samuel W. Venable was commissioned lieutenant colonel and commander of the Prince Edward militia in 1796, and Philemon Holcombe, Jr., and Jesse Watson became majors. Charles Scott qualified as a captain that year.[382] Philemon Holcombe, Jr., became commander of the county militia in 1797 with the rank of lieutenant colonel.[383]

In 1798 there was talk of locating an arsenal in Prince Edward County, but there is no indication that it was ever built.[384] Charles

Scott in 1799 bought forty horsemen's swords for the Prince Edward cavalry at a cost of £74:17:6, for which he asked to be reimbursed.[385]

Within the next few years Thomas Green, Jr., (1798), Samuel Watkins (1799), John Hudson (1801), and Charles Woodson (1803) were commissioned captains.[386] Jesse Watson became colonel of the Prince Edward militia in 1803; Robert Kelso was commissioned major the same year.[387]

The Prince Edward militia constituted the 63rd Regiment of the Virginia militia; it was one of six regiments in the 11th Brigade, which was one of four brigades in the First Division. The Virginia militia consisted of four divisions in 1804.[388]

John Purnall received his commission as colonel and commander of the 63rd Regiment in 1804, and Thomas Green his commission as major. Captains commissioned that year were John Cunningham of the cavalry company (in May), Emanuel J. Leigh of the artillery company, Archer Womack of cavalry company (in October), Thomas Clark, William Carter, Jr., and Nathaniel Price.[389] William Ligon was commissioned captain in 1805.[390]

Peter Johnston was appointed brigadier general of the 11th Brigade in 1805, succeeding John B. Scott, who resigned.[391] Scott was a native of Prince Edward, but was at this time living in Halifax County.[392] At this time Tarleton Woodson was a major general of the state militia.[393] Andrew Baker was a general of the militia in 1805.[394] New captains in the Prince Edward militia in 1806 were Rezin Porter, Francis Watkins, Jr. (the cavalry company), Henry Penick, and James Ming; Samuel Baldwin and Henry Ligon received major's commissions that year.[395] William L. Womack became captain of the cavalry company in 1807, and Zachariah Rice was also commissioned captain that year.[396] Lieutenant Colonel Philemon Holcombe commanded the first regiment of cavalry in 1807.[397] In 1809 Archer Womack was commissioned major, and Paschal G. Leigh captain.[398] Two new captains were commissioned in 1810: Anthony W. Woodson of the artillery company and James Madison.[399]

In 1811 Augustus Watson became colonel of the county militia, Thomas Scott major, and Daniel Hamblin and Josiah Penick captains. Penick commanded the light infantry company.[400] Richard Marshall was commissioned captain in 1812,[401] and Samuel V. Allen succeeded William L. Womack as captain of the cavalry company in 1813. Samuel Wootton is mentioned as a militia captain in 1813.[402] In 1814 three new captains were commissioned: William C. Scott,

Thomas Redd (artillery company) succeeding Paschal G. Leigh, and Benjamin Watson succeeding William Carter.[403]

At least some companies of Prince Edward militia saw active service in the War of 1812. Captain Josiah Penick's company was stationed at Camp Bottoms Bridge.[404] The cavalry company was also called into service, and a muster roll, dated September 12, 1814, was preserved. At that time Samuel V. Allen was captain; W. L. Venable, first lieutenant; H. E. Watkins, second lieutenant; S. L. Lockett, cornet; A. Fuqua, P. Randolph, and B. Foster were sergeants; J. J. Foster, H. N. Watkins, and O. Morton, corporals; and J. D. Wood was musician.[405] Captain Richard Marshall's company was another Prince Edward militia unit which was on active duty during the War of 1812.[406]

A company from Hampden-Sydney, commanded by John Kirkpatrick, also saw service during the war.[407]

Thomas Scott became colonel of the county militia in 1815,[408] and the next year Andrew Baker and James Madison were commissioned majors, and John Stevens and Lillious D. Womack captains.[409] John Foster became a captain in 1818.[410]

In 1821 John Clark succeeded James Madison as lieutenant colonel, and James Ewing succeeded Clark as major. Hudson Wilson was promoted to the captaincy to succeed Ewing.[411]

Samuel V. Allen qualified as lieutenant colonel of the First Regiment of the First Division Cavalry in 1822.[412]

John Clark became colonel of the militia in 1827, James Ewing lieutenant colonel, Asa Dupuy major, and Joseph Dupuy and Thomas Pettus captains.[413] John Shepperson was commissioned captain in 1828.[414]

The roll of officers of the 63rd Regiment has been preserved for the year 1830. Asa Dupuy and Samuel V. Allen were colonels, John Foster, lieutenant colonel, John Rice and Jedithan Carter majors, Samuel D. Burke adjutant; the captains were Hudson Wilson, John Shepperson (artillery), George O. Bowman, Henry M. Vaughan, and Samuel Scott (cavalry). First lieutenants in the militia were Griffith Dickinson (artillery), Henry Thweatt, William A. Swann (artillery), William J. Bigger (cavalry); the second lieutenants were Samuel W. Venable (artillery), Charles Woodson (artillery) Josiah M. Rice (cavalry), Thomas Vernon, Stephen Fore (rifle), Harwood Cary (cavalry), Robert F. Mosley, and John D. Calhoon. Joseph Philips (light infantry), Samuel Baker, Tarleton Woodson (rifle),

Charles C. Hudson, and Creed T. Nunnally were ensigns. Cornets were Harwood Cary and Vincent Philips (cavalry). William S. Morton was surgeon, and John P. Mettauer was surgeon's mate. James McDearmon was quartermaster, and William Matthews quartermaster sergeant. William Hines was drum major.

Several promotions had been made in the First Battalion by October, 1830; officers of the battalion then were John Foster, lieutenant colonel, George O. Bowman, Henry M. Vaughan, Samuel D. Burke, Griffith Dickinson, and Henry Thweatt captains, with Burke also adjutant, whose duty was to attend to the training of officers. The lieutenants were Joseph Phillips of the light infantry, Samuel W. Venable and Benjamin B. Watson of the artillery, Josiah M. Rice and Vincent Phillips of the cavalry, Micajah McGehee and Robert F. Moseley of infantry of the line. Creed T. Nunnally (light infantry), Thomas E. Scott, and Thomas Worsham (both of infantry of line) were ensigns; Nathaniel Price was cornet of the cavalry.[415]

Officers of the Prince Edward militia became dissatisfied with the "languishing state" of the militia and met on September 17, 1832, to consider it. Colonel Asa Dupuy presided at the meeting, and Lieutenant Colonel John Foster served as secretary. A resolutions committee consisting of Colonels Dupuy and Foster, Major John Rice, Captains Henry Thweatt, Samuel D. Burke, Tarlton Woodson, and Lieutenant Josiah M. Rice was appointed to draw up resolutions to be presented at a meeting called for October 27. The preamble expressed the belief that a well organized and properly trained militia was "the surest and best defense of the rights and liberties of a free people." The militia system of the day was regarded as "defective and nugatory," and the system in effect fifteen to twenty years before, while not perfect, was better. Under the older system there were regimental, battalion, and four company musters yearly, and the officers "had something to do"; the current system called for only one regimental and one company muster a year, and they were usually taken up in enrolling names, electing officers, drafting for routine or duty, laying off squads for patrol duty, activities which left little time for drill and other military training. The preamble also criticized the patrol system as "oppressive" in getting the men together, as "inefficient in practice and more expensive than formerly." Under the new system patrolling would cost $2,373, while the average annual cost to the county during the preceding four years was $257.79. The resolutions proposed increasing the company musters to at least four and preferably six a year, restoring the battalion muster, and returning to the former system of patrolling. Militia fines (for failure to attend musters and to perform other duties) were recommended at from one to two dollars. One resolution proposed that all militia east of the Blue Ridge and all volunteer companies in the state be armed.

The militia accepted an invitation of the 26th Regiment (Charlotte) for the officers of the 11th Brigade to meet at Halifax Courthouse in November to consider the militia problems. Colonel Dupuy and Captain Burke were named delegates.[416]

Colonel Dupuy attended the Halifax meeting, which recommended four company musters and the restoration of the battalion muster. It also proposed that regimental commanders inspect and review the battalion muster and one company muster. The meeting also favored repeal of the patrol law passed by the last session of the Assembly and recommended fines of seventy-five cents to two dollars on privates for failure to attend musters.[417]

Militia officers in 1818 included Charles Woodson, colonel; James Madison, lieutenant colonel; John Clark, major; Peyton Fuqua and John Foster, captains.[418] Francis A. Martin became a captain in 1819.[419]

John Rice was promoted to lieutenant colonel and Samuel D. Burke to major in 1833.[420] In 1834 Henry Thweatt was commissioned major and Josiah M. Rice captain.[421]

The Mexican War apparently was little felt in Prince Edward. There was a recruiting office for Southside Virginia opened at Petersburg in 1847, with Captain E. C. Carrington, Jr., in charge. The purpose was to secure volunteers in sufficient number to bring the companies of the Virginia Regiment of Volunteers to the full standard of 100 men. A soldier's pay then was seven dollars a month.[422] Only one person from Prince Edward is now known to have served in the Mexican War; he was William Hines, popularly known as "Drummer" Hines, because he was drummer to the Prince Edward militia and played the drum at musters.[423]

In 1855 Samuel Carter was sergeant major of the county militia, James R. Whitehead trumpeter, and William Hines drummer.[424]

John T. Carter became commander of the 63rd Regiment of militia in 1858 with the rank of colonel, John F. Rice lieutenant colonel, and Joseph T. Ligon major.[425]

Muster day was one of the great events of the year. Great crowds attended to see the companies drill and even engage in maneuvers. In one muster of the 1850's the cavalry would charge toward the infantry which awaited the horsemen with bayonets; a bugle signal would order retreat just before contact.[426]

The Spirit of '76

The spirit of '76 long prevailed in Prince Edward and was demonstrated in various aspects of life. Advertisements of Hampden-Sydney College for many years did not lose the opportunity to call attention to the identification of the college with the cause of independence. In 1783 the trustees determined that no person should be chosen a professor "unless the uniform tenor of his conduct manifest to the world his sincere affection for the liberty and independence of the United States of America," in order "to preserve in the minds of the students the sacred love and attachment they should ever bear to the principles of our glorious Revolution."[427]

Devotion to the principles of the Revolution was carried into church life. A letter signed by G. C. Moore, obviously written at the instruction of some group and sent to a meeting of the Sailor Creek Baptist Church, illustrates this:

"I will inform the Baptist conference that may meet in assembly at Mr. Jacob McGehee's on the 24th Jan. 1807 lest they should not meet the information that on the 17th Instant the funeral of the illustrious Richard D. Pincham was preached and the eminent character who exhibited on the occasion was the Reverend John Pollard the text was I know that my redeemer liveth and that he shall stand upon the earth in the latter day. And as an honor which he Justly merited and which does you much honor you inserted the time of his death in your records. Therefore in order to render his name immortal on account of his noble character and worthy conduct in defense of liberty, I hope you will record the time of his funeral si si. Jan. 22, 1807."[428]

Another demonstration of this spirit was the celebration of Independence Day. On July 4, 1843, the Farmville "Blues," the local military unit, gave an "elegant collation," followed by "sentiments proposed and received with applause." At such celebrations, thirteen toasts were proposed by arrangement, evidently in honor of the original colonies; then came volunteer toasts. At the Farmville celebration, each of the thirteen toasts was followed by appropriate music. The thirteen toasts proposed and the music which accompanied each were: the Fourth of July, *Hail Columbia*; the American Revolution, *The Star-Spangled Banner*; the memory of Washington, *Pleyel's Hymn*; the heroes of the Revolution, *United States March*; liberty of conscience, *Bird of Liberty*; the Old Thirteen, *Auld Lang Syne*; the right of search—the arrogant claim of haughty nations to which no freeman could submit without degradation, *Yankee Doodle*; our Navy, *Wet Sheet and Flowing Sea*; agriculture and commerce, *Farmer's Daughter*; the Old Dominion, *Old Virginny Never Tire*; the treaty of Washington, *Hicks' March*; the tree of knowledge, *Bruce's Address*; and the American fair—the daughters of noble mothers, *Haste to the Wedding*.

One unusual feature of the Farmville celebration was that three toasts were proposed to temperance; one was sent by a lady to "the cold water celebration"; another proposed by John Erambert; and the third proposed by Edward J. Erambert to the Fourth of July, 1843, "may it long be celebrated as the first temperance celebration in Farmville." Lieutenant Dimmington (Dunnington) toasted the farmers of Virginia in a sentiment perennial in Prince Edward: "may their wheat escape the rust, their tobacco the worm, so that we may all be enabled to pay our debts." Numerous patriotic toasts were offered. Adjutant Nathaniel D. Price showed interest in foreign affairs in calling the British war in China "the darkest blot on the escutcheon of any civilized nation." A. W. Millspaugh proposed the sentiment, perhaps nostalgic, "Scotland." Political toasts vied with the patriotic in number and were frequently negative: E. M. Barksdale proposed John Tyler (then President): "he stands alone, a renegade, against the country he betrayed"; Lieutenant R. F. Lester proposed Thomas Ritchie, the leading Democratic editor (his paper was the Richmond *Enquirer*); Thomas J. Davis hoped John C. Calhoun may "soon be called to preside over the destinies of the people of the United States"; Joseph W. Watson proposed Van Buren as next president and also got off a Democratic taunt: the Whig promises, two dollars a day and roast beef—"when shall we see them?" The Whigs put in some good licks too: R. B. Cole thought a Clay foundation the best of soils; S. O. Southall toasted the enemies of Henry Clay who "vainly seek to disparage what they cannot rival"; T. Cox hoped Clay would be the next president; and J. M. Poindexter would give "a cobweb pair of pantaloons, a porcupine saddle and a hard-trotting horse to the enemies of Henry Clay." Lewis M. Carter hoped that "religion, virtue and temperance [would] always characterize the people of Farmville." M. W. Vaughan concluded the sentiments with the hope of "a speedy return to good old Virginia times when the true Anglo-Saxon spirit animated the bosom of her sons, when argument and reason were the weapons of her warfare, and the music by which she pressed to victory, when on the flag under which she fought and bled and died was written in indelible characters—Truth."[429]

In 1848 the people in the "upper end" of Prince Edward had a great Fourth of July celebration at Spring Creek Baptist Church. On a day clear and beautiful and pleasantly cool for the season, the throng assembled in the church for a program which began at 11:30 A. M. The Rev. E. W. Roach, pastor of the church, offered a prayer "for the perpetuation of the many civil and religious blessings we now enjoy." Richard H. Watkins read the Declaration of Independence. William T. Walker delivered the speech of the occasion which lasted for about an hour. The program over about two, the crowd adjourned to the grove where "they partook of a bountiful and well-prepared barbecue with a plentiful supply of lemonade and wine." When dinner was over, the table cloth was removed, and the toasts were drunk. Newton Cunningham presided over this portion of the program, assisted by Samuel Allen, Richard Woodson, and James R. Whitehead as vice-presidents.

There were the usual thirteen prepared toasts: the day we celebrate; the memory of Washington; Lafayette, DeKalb, Kosciusko, and Pulaski; the heroes of the Revolution; our country—"right or wrong we know no other principle than that of *amor patriæ*"; old Virginia; the signers of the Declaration of Independence; France, our ancient ally; Ireland and Poland, "in their noble struggle for nationality and freedom, they have the heart of every votary of liberty"; the Army and Navy of the United States; Generals Scott and Taylor; the President of the United States; and the ladies—"the fairest and sweetest part of creation: we always toast them last, because we like to finish on the best."

The volunteer toasts were predominantly political, though pleasantly interspersed with light and gay sentiments. Local people were also toasted. The "president of the day," Newton Cunningham, set the prevailing tone when he led off the volunteer toasts by proposing Generals Cass and Butler, "may they be elected President and Vice-President." Samuel Allen toasted the Polk administration; Abner Moore, Cass and Butler; Samuel B. Drinkard, General Lewis Cass; R. J. Matthews, General Cass. Allen proposed a toast to Jefferson,

Madison, and Monroe—"since their day the nation has had nothing but turmoil and strife"; James D. Mickle toasted Jefferson, and Caleb T. Baldwin, Madison. A. W. Smith urged Democrats to oppose a third triumph of old Federalists, young Whigs and no party. The Whigs, if not in the numerical majority at Spring Creek that day, were if anything more vocal than the Democrats: William Harvey proposed General Zachary Taylor; C. Hancock warned Southerners to look well to the North running a Wilmot Proviso man, so vote for Taylor and Fillmore; Thomas M. Cobbs criticized the Mexican War—"commenced in weakness, profligacy and in violation of the Constitution—may its end not be the dissolution of the union"; William A. Womack and J. R. F. Moseley proposed General Taylor in a succession of toasts; James Mickle, Jr., described General Cass as "eulogist of Louis Philippe in power," proposed that he follow him into retirement; A. Womack reminded that "Old Zac is a Taylor and will take Lewis' measurements well in November"; E. B. Beach toasted Henry Clay, and John P. Hughes Clay and Taylor; E. B. Jeffress and J. R. F. Moseley (again) proposed Taylor, and A. W. Allen, Whig principles; E. B. Jeffress questioned where were now the Southern principles of Martin Van Buren, once described as a Northern man with Southern principles (Van Buren was this year candidate of the Free Soil party for the Presidency); Captain D. F. Womack proposed Cass and Taylor—"may the people have the choice in selecting them to fill [the Presidency] and may he fill it with credit to himself and honor to the nation."

A Bailey, Jr., William B. Beach, Jr., D. F. Womack, and S. H. Crenshaw proposed toasts to the orator of the day, William T. Walker; a committee of D. F. Womack, Newton Cunningham, and R. J. Matthews asked Walker for a copy of his speech for publication, but the orator declined, saying that "your politeness and friendship call forth the request" and depreciating the value of the speech.

D. F. Womack toasted Asa D. Dickinson, who responded; John S. Mickle proposed a toast to Joseph R. Bailey of Charlotte, who also responded; Captain D. F. Womack also proposed Clement Hancock, who responded and proposed the sentiment in reply, "Old Zac and his temperance principles forever"; A. D. Dickinson toasted B. W. Leigh and Richard Booker, late of Spring Creek; William T. Walker proposed R. H. Watkins, who responded with a toast to the ladies of Spring Creek; Walker also toasted R. J. Matthews whose reply was a speech on education; Matthews proposed the Rev. E. W. Roach;

Edwin B. Jeffress and William T. Walker toasted William Scott, who responded when he was first toasted.

The ladies were several times proposed, and in reply to a toast offered by Edwin B. Jeffress specifically to the ladies of Spring Creek, A. D. Dickinson responded on behalf of the ladies with a toast "to the beaux of Prince Edward and Charlotte—they are worthy of marrying the brightest jewels—even the fair damsels of Spring Creek." J. W. Daniel hoped that "the lovers of the fair sex may never want means to support nor spirit to defend them." And a bachelor (otherwise unidentified) proposed "money, above all, matrimoney."

More serious toasts were offered, too, as Richard H. Watkins': "true religion—corner-stone of every good and enlightened government—the religion of Christ as proposed by the Protestants is the only true religion." Daniel Allen proposed the success of the common school system. Anderson Hill of Appomattox was truly expansionist: "may the Star-Spangled Banner wave from the Atlantic to the Pacific, from the Frozen Ocean to the Isthmus of Darien."[430]

It is on this note of political interest, of love of the Union, and of devotion to the principles of the Revolution that this chapter on Prince Edward's political history appropriately ends. The next period of the county's political history has a different accent; yet it is not a surprising change. The South, following John C. Calhoun, had made the right of secession of the state a basis for the preservation of the Union. In Calhoun's thinking the two were intimately connected; yet they led to different extremes, and ultimately, almost, it would seem, before the South realized what was happening, one extreme had been reached.

CHAPTER X

Faith's New Day

THE vestry of St. Patrick's Parish called an ideal selection for the special needs of the parish upon the death of the Rev. James McCartney. Their choice fell upon the Rev. Archibald McRobert, a native Scotchman, who was minister of Dale Parish in Chesterfield. Only one other clergyman of the Church of England in Southside Virginia if not in all Virginia could have been calculated to check the rising tide of dissent in Prince Edward as well as McRobert. He was McRobert's good friend, the Rev. Devereux Jarratt, minister of Bath Parish in Dinwiddie County.[1]

St. Patrick's needed a minister who could cope with the dissenters who even now appeared to be sweeping all before them. The Presbyterians had two churches in the county, Briery and Buffalo, the latter serving the large Scotch Irish settlement, with Cumberland Church including a sizable portion of the county within the bounds of its congregation. When McCartney died, they were laying the foundation of a college within the county, in which work, however, they were being assisted by Anglican laymen. Hanover Presbytery held its meeting in February, 1775, at the home of Nathaniel Venable, who until the year before had been clerk of the vestry.[2] The Baptists had organized two churches in the western part of the county, Rocks and Appomattox, while the influence of Nottoway Church in the lower part of the county continued strong, and a meeting-house which seems to have been a preaching station of Nottoway had been built at William Rice's.

The fitness of McRobert and Jarratt in meeting the dissenters was not in a vigorous opposition. Rather it was in their emphasis, in the pulpits of the Establishment, of doctrines which the dissenting ministers were preaching with such telling effect. McRobert and Jarratt were not unorthodox Anglicans; they were simply preaching doctrines of the Church of England which their fellow ministers were neglecting and had been neglecting so long that they seemed new when the Presbyterian and Baptist evangelists expounded them. In the sermons of McRobert and Jarratt hearers heard about salvation by grace and final perseverance, explained in the same way they heard them proclaimed in Presbyterian meeting-houses and under Baptist brush arbors.[3]

McRobert came to Prince Edward about 1776.[4] During the next four years his evangelical sentiments, instead of holding the fort for Anglicanism in St. Patrick's, carried him into open dissent. In 1780 he described himself as an Independent, holding that "the Church of Christ is truly and properly independent." But his inclination was toward Presbyterianism, and he expressed the opinion that he would ultimately find his theological haven there. He drew up a Constitution and Discipline of the Christian Church along with articles covering what he regarded as the essential parts of natural and revealed religion and presented them to the people. His hearers at the chapel (at or near Obadiah Woodson's schoolhouse) organized an Independent congregation, which some of the members of Buffalo Presbyterian Church joined shortly thereafter, and some individuals in the congregations at French's and Sandy River Churches accepted McRobert's articles of faith. John Blair Smith and the elders at Cumberland invited McRobert to assist in a communion service at Cumberland in 1780. The vestry does not appear to have been greatly disturbed by McRobert's dissent. It permitted McRobert to continue preaching in the churches and the chapel after he became a dissenter and while he was undertaking to form congregations of Independents at each place of worship. He was planning in the summer of 1780 to continue preaching at each of the three stated places of worship in the parish and, if Independent congregations had not been formed at the churches by the beginning of 1781, to devote his time fully to the congregation at the chapel and to any other Independent congregations which might invite him to preach to them.[5] McRobert's hopes of forming Independent congregations at French's and Sandy River were not realized.[6]

When Hanover Presbytery met at Buffalo Church in April, 1787, "a small society in the neighborhood of Walker's Church, formerly considered as an Independent Church and under the pastoral care of Mr. McRobert" sent its elder to the presbytery with the request that it be taken under the care of the presbytery and considered a part of the Presbyterian Church and asked for supplies. Drury Lacy was appointed to preach there twice a month.[7]

During the Revolution additions continued to be made to the vestry of St. Patrick's Parish. Robert Lawson became a vestryman in 1775;[8] Benjamin Haskins and William Bibb, 1777;[9] William

Watts, 1778;[10] John Watson, 1779;[11] John Holcombe and Richard Foster, 1780;[12] Joseph Moore, 1782.[13] Foster and Philemon Holcombe were named church wardens in 1785.[14]

In 1777 the vestry was given permission to sell the glebe and apply the proceeds of the sale to the purchase of a new glebe, since the lands of the old glebe were worn out, its uncleared land inconvenient, and the timber supply insufficient to keep the place in repair.[15] The glebe was sold in 1778 to the Rev. Archibald McRobert.[16]

The plight of the Established Church in Prince Edward is clearly indicated in a petition which the parish vestry sent to the General Assembly late in 1781. It requested that all vestries be dissolved, that elections of new vestries be ordered, and that members of all denominations be eligible for election to the parish vestry. The St. Patrick's vestry seems to have lost sight of the religious functions and responsibilities of vestries in regarding the "exclusion of Dissenters from vestries and other privileges they may have as freemen relics of British tyranny." The petition was signed by Thomas Scott, Robert Lawson, William Watts, William Bibb, Philemon Holcombe, John Holcombe, Richard Foster, George Walker, Archibald McRobert, John Watson, and John Nash. It was referred to the Committee on Religion of the House of Delegates on December 21, 1781, and was rejected June 9, 1782.[17] After the petition had been prepared, Joseph Moore and Richard Foster (the latter for the second time) took the ancient oath of a vestryman to be conformable to the doctrine and discipline of the Church of England as by law established.[18]

Meanwhile steps toward disestablishment were being taken. The Baptists and Presbyterians were memorializing the General Assembly to grant religious liberty. Captain John Morton was the ruling elder appointed by Hanover Presbytery to go with the Rev. John Todd to the General Assembly in 1773 to urge passage of a bill to extend the Act of Toleration to Virginia.[19] Richard Sankey and others asked for full religious liberty in the Buffalo petition presented in 1776.[20] In that year the first long step toward religious freedom and separation of church and state was taken in Virginia; dissenters of every denomination were exempted from paying parish levies and any other taxes or impositions for the support of the Established Church.[21] Dissenting ministers were given the right to perform marriages in 1780, county courts being authorized to license as many as four ministers of each denomination to perform marriages.[22]

As sentiment in favor of religious liberty increased, concern for financing the various denominations also increased. People accustomed to an established church supported by taxation could not understand that a church could be supported in any other way. A bill was proposed to impose a tax upon every person for the support of some religious teacher. When the assessment proposal was first discussed, it attracted widespread support. There was favorable sentiment toward it in Hanover Presbytery, which went so far as to set up a standard under which an assessment would be agreeable, which included provision that each citizen could choose annually the religious group he wished to support.

Even so staunch a friend of liberty as Patrick Henry supported an assessment. James Madison, Thomas Jefferson, and George Mason opposed it, and they were supported by many dissenters. Baptists uniformly opposed the General Assessment bill, and Hanover Presbytery later sent a committee, of which John Blair Smith was a member, to oppose it. Smith made an able speech before the committee considering the bill in 1784; it was defeated in the committee by three votes. The defeat of the assessment left the support of the churches to the voluntary liberality of their members and friends.[23]

Religious liberty became a reality in Virginia with the passage of Jefferson's Statute for Religious Freedom in 1785. The delegates from Prince Edward, John Clarke and Richard Bibb, voted for the bill.[24] Starting with the most superb premise of any of the great documents of human freedom—"Well aware that Almighty God hath created the mind free"—the act ended a religious establishment in Virginia and gave to every one the right to exercise freedom of conscience in belief, in propagating, defending, and supporting his belief. In the enactment of this law a new day dawned for faith.

When a law dissolving vestries under the Establishment passed, the vestry of St. Patrick's Parish ceased to exist. By 1792 there were no people left in Prince Edward who called themselves Episcopalians known to the signers of a petition asking that certain funds which had belonged to the parish be appropriated for public use. Of the £1,500 paper currency for which the glebe had been sold, there remained, after some expenditures by the vestry, 1,653 paper dollars and £211:2:3, which had been in the hands of Nathaniel Venable since 1784; another fund of about £100 realized from the sale of plate and furniture was in the keeping of Peter LeGrand and Richard Foster, church wardens at the time of the sale. Francis Smith headed the list of petitioners; among them were the Baptist minister, Robert Foster; Archibald McRobert; and Drury Lacy, Presbyterian minister and vice-president of Hampden-Sydney. Some of the signers were active in public affairs, as John Dupuy, John Morton, William Worsham, James Allen, Jr., Jacob Woodson, William Wootton, Joseph Parks, Dick Holland, Thomas Watkins, and James Wade, Sr. The Scotch-Irish community was well represented, Andrew Cunningham, Samuel Baldwin, Samuel Graham, Jr., Robert Hill, John Caldwell, John Hill, Hugh Porter, Samuel Graham, Thomas Thompson, Samuel Ewing, Samuel Cunningham, Alexander Hamilton, Adam Calhoun, and George Calhoun being among the signers.[25]

The General Assembly in 1792 named Thomas Scott, Charles Allen, John Morton, William Wootton, and James Morton trustees of these funds, which were to be held subject to appropriation by the County Court for the "most just and beneficial" use for the county. At least twelve magistrates had to be present when the appropriation was made.[26] In September, 1793, the court appropriated £250 of parish funds to the county's poor fund.[27] In October, 1786, the court ordered two accounts presented against the parish paid, the last bills presented to St. Patrick's Parish.[28]

The Revolution affected dissenters as well as Established Church. Interest in spiritual matters sank to a low level, accompanied by a deterioration in morals. A Presbyterian writer speaks of the "cold and lukewarm indifference to the ministrations of the Gospel in all that region" (referring to Prince Edward and its neighboring counties); a Baptist historian, writing of a meeting of the Middle District Association at Rice's meeting-house in 1785, states that "a general dearth in religion existed almost throughout the state" and a little later describes the religious conditions as "cold and wintry."[29]

Refreshing came in 1787. A revival, begun by John Williams, a Baptist minister of Charlotte, spread quickly to other denominations and to other counties. Many Baptist churches reported to the Middle District Association at its May, 1787, meeting that revivals had already begun or were about to begin in them. The interest which Williams' preaching created among some of the young people of Briery attracted the attention of John Blair Smith, who was pastor of that church and Cumberland as well as president of Hampden-Sydney.[30]

At that time not one of the eighty students at Hampden-Sydney was known to have serious religious convictions; on the contrary, they were "generally vicious and profane and ridiculed religion." Several students came under the influence of the revival and became concerned about their spiritual condition. William Hill, whose spiritual concern had been aroused when he was home on vacation, borrowed the family Bible of Major James Morton. At his request for a religious book, a fellow student, William Calhoun, son of a Presbyterian elder who lived near the college, brought him Allein's *Alarm to the Unconverted*, the selection of his sister. While reading it in secret, he opened the door to the persistent knocking of another student, James Blythe, and, when asked, embarrassedly admitted that he was reading the book. Blythe then admitted that he had professed religion in North Carolina but had since neglected its cultivation. He joined Hill in reading the book. Meanwhile another student, Cary Allen, had made a profession of religion while at home on vacation. Learning of Hill's and Blythe's reading, Allen introduced them to Clement Read, a graduate student, who was undergoing a religious experience. The four met the following Saturday for prayer meeting, "the doors being locked," as they had been on a prayer meeting much earlier in the history of the Christian faith. Some of the students heard what was going on behind the locked doors; they shouted, they cursed, they knocked on the door—made such a disturbance in their effort to break up the meeting that the college president and tutors came to see what the trouble was. President Smith invited the prayer group to meet in his parlor the next Saturday; the room was filled; two Saturdays later the prayer meeting was held in the college hall. Of the students at the college at that time, Read, Blythe, Allen, Hill, Nash LeGrand, and William Calhoun became ministers.[31]

Smith organized a prayer meeting among the elders of Cumberland and soon there were "praying circles" in the various parts of the congregation. Smith's father, Robert Smith of Pequea, Pennsylvania, writing of the revival in his son's congregations in 1788, stated that 225 communicants had been added to the Lord's Table in eighteen months. These were principally young people; they would usually go in companies to worship and other religious meetings and converse on spiritual matters on the way; upon arrival at the place of meeting, they would sing until the minister arrived. The father did not fail to note that his daughter-in-law, Betsy, and her father, Colonel John Nash, were growing "apace in piety" as were some of Colonel Nash's Negro slaves.[32] It was a conversation on religion with Drury Lacy, who was spending a night at Colonel Nash's, which sent Nash's nephew, Nash LeGrand, "a young man of promise and irreligion [at midnight] to prayer and lamentation in the garden until morning" and then to a prayer meeting at Nathan Womack's in Cumberland where he was converted.[33]

The revival continued to spread. After a week's visit in Prince Edward and Charlotte, Henry Pattillo returned to his home in North Carolina to start a revival in Granville and Caswell Counties. James McGready, stopping in Prince Edward on his way to North Carolina, noted its powerful effectiveness and carried it to Orange and Guilford Counties in that state.[34] It was worthy of particular note that nearly every magistrate and nearly every lawyer in Prince Edward and Charlotte became members of churches,[35] for at this period men of standing in many sections showed scant interest in religious affairs, and lawyers were notoriously lacking in spiritual concern, even to the point of infidelity in many.

Young people were especially influenced by the revival. An irreligious young person became a rarity, and in their profession they abandoned frivolities and amusements[36] to intensify the Puritan atmosphere which has been so characteristic of Prince Edward through the years.

The period between the Revolution and the War between the States was for the Presbyterians of Prince Edward an era of growth. Because the supply of ministers was inadequate to the needs of growing churches after the revival of 1787, Drury Lacy proposed a plan by which different congregations would unite and have ministers rotate in conducting services. Under this plan Cumberland, Buffalo, Briery, and Cub Creek united with the plan to call two ministers who would preach in rotation at the four churches, the college (a preaching station of Cumberland), and Charlotte Courthouse (a preaching station of Cub Creek). Archibald Alexander, who had come to Prince Edward with Benjamin Grigsby in missionary labors in-1792, was called in 1793 to be co-pastor of the four congregations with Lacy. The plan as conceived was not working out too well, so the next year Alexander, who had delayed accepting the call in 1793 and had been invited to supply the churches until he could decide, was called by Briery and Cub Creek. Briery and Buffalo united to call the Rev. Matthew Lyle, who also had come to Prince Edward as a missionary in 1792. Lacy preached at Cumberland, with Alexander as co-minister for a time. These ministers succeeded John Blair Smith, who left Prince Edward for the Pine Street Church pastorate in 1791, at Briery and Cumberland, and the Rev. Richard Sankey, who died in 1790, at Buffalo.[37]

About 1797-99 Archibald Alexander began to have doubts about the authority for infant baptism. Both he and Matthew Lyle determined to give up the practice "until," as Alexander put it, "we should receive more light." Both ministers advised their congregations of the question in their minds and the intention to refrain, at least for the time being, from baptizing infants. Their plan was agreeable to the congregations they were serving, both at Briery, and Lyle at Buffalo. In May, 1799, Conrad Speece became a tutor at Hampden-Sydney; he, too, began to study the matter of baptism and came to the conclusion that he should be baptized by immersion upon a profession of faith. On a Sunday in April, 1800, without having discussed his intention with Alexander or any other of his Presbyterian friends and associates, he was baptized by the Rev. James Saunders, pastor of Appomattox Baptist Church. He promptly began preaching among the Baptists. Speece attended the meeting of the Middle District Association at Tarwallet meeting-house in Cumberland in October, 1800. Shortly after this meeting, he announced that he was convinced of the validity of infant baptism and wrote to Saunders advising him of the change of mind. He returned to the Presbyterian Church and was licensed to preach by Hanover Presbytery in April, 1801. Speece's action, both in joining the Baptists and in rejoining the Presbyterians, was the subject of wide comment. Presbyterian historians take the view that he was influenced by Alexander, who had from intensive study concluded that infant baptism was a valid practice for the church, to return to his earlier position. Semple, the Baptist historian, thought that Speece found the manners and customs of Baptists so different from those to which he was accustomed that he became dissatisfied. He quoted the opinion of some that the Middle District Association meeting which he attended was so confused, unpleasant, and turbulent that Speece was disgusted with Baptist proceedings; he also quotes a less charitable opinion that Speece became disappointed on finding that Baptists paid their preachers little or nothing for their work. Alexander noted impulsiveness as one of Speece's characteristics and observed that it was evident that he was not happy while affiliated with the Baptists. Of Speece's ability there is no doubt; as evidence, the college paid him £100 for his first year's service, £20 more than the agreement called for. Meanwhile Alexander and Lyle, after refraining from baptizing infants for some two years, quietly resumed the practice.[38]

This generation of ministers, too, grew old. Lyle died in 1827 and was succeeded at Briery by the Rev. James W. Douglas in 1828 and at Buffalo, after a succession of supplies, by the Rev. Isaac

Cochran in 1831.[39] As the generation which had been quickened in the revival of 1787 grew old and passed away, a new revival sprang up in 1828. Much of its success at Briery was credited to the faithful seed-sowing of Lyle; and Douglas, with the assistance of the Rev. Asahel Nettleton who helped as his strength permitted, cultivated the field diligently. This revival was felt, too, at Hampden-Sydney College and Union Seminary, and the first meeting of inquiry, attended by more then one hundred, was held at the home of John Holt Rice. This revival, too, appealed to lawyers and men of education; for as at the time of the revival of forty years before, lawyers, especially, were notoriously irreligious. It made something of a stir when five of the leading lawyers of the section, including two from Prince Edward, Henry E. Watkins and Samuel C. Anderson, professed religion; and the presence at a session of Nottoway Court about this time of seven lawyers in the bar at the same time, all of whom were professing Christians, was labeled by one chronicler as "unexampled in Virginia."[40]

Briery at this time was reaching westward in its ministry. It held preaching services at the Welch Tract meeting-house, one of the church buildings open to all denominations for worship, not far from the present site of Bethlehem Presbyterian Church. A new building, to which the name Bethlehem was given, was dedicated in 1829 by the Rev. James W. Douglas. The Rev. Isaac Cochran began preaching there in 1831, although it was a branch, or arm, as such congregational groups were sometimes called, of Briery. Bethlehem was constituted a separate church in 1834, with Cochran as pastor.

From the founding of Hampden-Sydney, Cumberland Church maintained a place of worship there for the students and members of the congregation residing in the vicinity. This was until the completion of a separate church building in 1820 the College Hall. The land for the building had been given in 1819 by Dr. Moses Hoge; when the church was built, Samuel W. Venable gave the church eleven acres adjoining to provide the church with timber, fire wood, and fencing. After Farmville had become a village of some size, the Presbyterians built a place of worship there in 1828, which was a preaching station of Cumberland Church. With several preaching stations, more than one minister served the church.

When the Farmville meeting-house was built, the Rev. John Kirkpatrick was pastor of Cumberland Church, but the Rev. John D. Paxton was preaching at the college, and in 1829 the Rev. J. H. C.

Leach was engaged to preach twice a month at Farmville. Cumberland Church was divided in 1835, the members in Prince Edward joining the newly constituted Hanover Church which had as its principal place of worship the church at Hampden-Sydney with Farmville as a preaching station. The Rev. B. F. Stanton was first pastor of Hanover Church, and Clement C. Read, Samuel C. Anderson, John Rice, and Moses Tredway were the first elders. The church was officially Hampden-Sydney Presbyterian Church 1846-49; since 1849 it has been College Presbyterian Church. The Farmville Presbyterian Church became a separate organization, with its own pastor and officers, in 1844. The first pastor, the Rev. William C. Scott, did not come until two years later; in the interim supply ministers filled the pulpit.

During this period several church buildings were erected by the Presbyterians in Prince Edward. Buffalo Church moved from its old site near the present Five Forks to the lot it now occupies about 1808, when the land was purchased from George Booker by William Baldwin, Nathaniel Price, and Samuel Baldwin, trustees. The church built then is still used by the congregation. Briery erected two buildings during this period; the second meeting-house was built in 1824, and the third, designed by Dr. R. L. Dabney, was built about 1855. Briery did not acquire title to the land on which its meeting-house stood until 1789, when Thomas Flournoy sold to trustees James Venable, Jacob Morton, and Obadiah Claybrook three acres. David Flournoy gave an acre in 1822, on which the second house of worship was probably erected, and in 1855 George W. Bell gave four acres "adjoining at the east the old meeting-house tract." The meeting-house built in Farmville about 1828 became the home of the Farmville Presbyterian Church upon its organization in 1844; this is still used by the church, the original building having been remodeled and enlarged. William C. Flournoy, Jacob W. Morton, John Dupuy, William M. Womack, and William G. Venable were trustees of the church to whom it was conveyed in 1845 by N. E. and Mary E. Venable, Samuel W. Venable, Clement C. and Ann Read, and Samuel and Martha Lyle in a transaction to clear the title. Dr. Dabney drew plans for the remodeling in 1859. A brick church was erected at Hampden-Sydney in 1819-20. When this proved inadequate for both white and Negro members, a new building, the present, was erected in 1860; Dr. R. L. Dabney drew the plans.[41]

The Presbyterians of the Meherrin community planned to erect a church on the road from the Courthouse to Meherrin, about a mile

and one-half from the railroad. The land for the church was conveyed by indenture dated January 30, 1853, from Addison Brightwell and his wife, Adaline, to Thomas E. Haskins, Daniel S. Mc-
Cormick, and Joseph Dupuy, trustees of Forest Church. It was proposed to move to this lot the building known as Old Forest Church,
near the Lunenburg-Prince Edward line, for use as a Presbyterian
church.[42]

Among the changes in Presbyterian practice during this period
may be noted the abandonment of the use of tokens for admission to
the communion service at Briery in 1828,[43] the introduction of
instrumental music with the use of a melodion in the Farmville
Church in 1857, and in the same year, in the same church, the removal of the partition separating the men's side from the women's.[44]
The practice of having men sit on one side, women on the other, was
general in churches of all denominations, and it was long continued
in the rural churches; it is still observed, only a few violating it, at
Spring Creek Baptist Church.

During this period, Presbyterianism was expanding to such an
extent that it was deemed advisable to divide Hanover Presbytery in
1829. The Prince Edward churches were west of the dividing line
(which at that point was the county line separating Prince Edward
from Nottoway and Amelia) and therefore became affiliated with
West Hanover Presbytery.[45]

Presbyterian support of foreign missions, an interest which was
spreading through the major Protestant denominations at this time,
was given through cooperation with the American Board of Commissioners for Foreign Missions, an organization which was inter-
denominational in theory but in practice dominated by the Congregationalists. John Holt Rice, who reflected in his interests and concerns the broadening interests and concerns of the churches of the
era, in 1831 drew up a plan for a distinctively Presbyterian foreign
mission program under "The Committee of the Presbyterian Church
of the United States for Foreign Missions." The plan would not
exclude support of the American Board, but called for the closest
cooperation between the Presbyterian committee and the board and
permitted Presbyterian churches to support either, since many
churches were committed to the support of the board.[46]

Denominational support of foreign and home missions, which
developed from Rice's plan, was one of the sources of disagreement
which flared into the open at the historic General Assembly in
Philadelphia in 1837. Another controversial issue was that of cita-

tion, under which presbyteries could cite synods, synods presbyteries, and the General Assembly synods. There were also doctrinal differences developing, to a considerable extent the result of the Act of Union of 1801 with a Congregational group, the General Association of Connecticut. The Assembly of 1837 declared the Western Reserve, Utica, Genessee and Geneva Synods out of connection with the Presbyterian Church. The exclusion followed the failure of an elder from Western Reserve Synod to answer the question "Have you adopted a Confession of Faith?" Samuel C. Anderson, the Prince Edward lawyer, and George A. Baxter, then president of Union Seminary, spoke in favor of excluding Western Reserve Synod, and Anderson won national fame in the denomination from this speech. Archibald Alexander also favored exclusion, reminding the Assembly that the Union of 1801 was a temporary arrangement which had not worked out satisfactorily.

The Presbyterian Church split as a result of controversy over the action of the 1837 Assembly; those supporting it became the Old School, those opposing it the New School, as the church which the opponents set up, the Constitutional Presbyterian Church, was popularly known. No section was more affected by the split than Prince Edward. Hiram P. Goodrich and Stephen Taylor, professors in the seminary, and Elisha Ballantine, assistant in the seminary, opposed the exclusion of the four synods; after the Synod of North Carolina in 1837 asked that all professors in the seminary who could not concur in the decision of the Assembly resign, they resigned. Daniel Lynn Carroll, president of Hampden-Sydney, asked West Hanover Presbytery to dismiss him to join one of the presbyteries connected with one of the excluded synods; since that presbytery was not recognized by West Hanover, it merely gave him a letter to the effect that he was in good standing in West Hanover Presbytery when he applied for dismissal. The pastor of the church at Hampden-Sydney, the Rev. B. F. Staunton, supported Dr. Baxter in the controversy.[47]

When the New School controversy was at its height, Staunton preached a vigorous sermon in College Church. From the text 1 John 2:19, he attacked the New School position. So hard did he press the matter that a large minority in the congregation, both men and women and some entire families, "arose with utterances of disapproval, left the church and went home."[48]

In Briery Church, Henry N. Watkins resigned as clerk of the session in 1840 and read a paper that the differences between Old

School and New School adherents within the congregation were irreconcilable and that "peace, harmony, and prosperity" would be promoted by separation of the two factions; he then proposed a meeting of the congregation to effect "an amicable separation" and to divide the church funds equitably. The proposal was defeated by the session five to two, only Thomas C. Spencer supporting Watkins, and William Scott, Adam Calhoun, Lillious D. Womack, James W. Womack, and the moderator, the Rev. S. L. Graham, opposing. Watkins and others withdrew and organized a church of the New School, to which the name Douglas was given; this church, located in Charlotte, was built about 1841. In 1870 Briery Church received fifteen members from Douglas upon its dissolution.

Another church of the New School was organized at Prince Edward Courthouse; property for this building was bought in 1845. Henry N. Watkins was a trustee of this church as well as of Douglas Church. Other trustees of the Prince Edward Courthouse church were Jared Todd and William H. Venable. Elisha Ballantine was first pastor of both these churches of the New School, which drew members from both College and Briery Churches.[49] In 1857 the New School church at the Courthouse, with Edward H. Compton pastor, had 115 members, and the New School church called Farmville, with the Rev. J. H. C. Leach as pastor, had 106 members.[50] Although there remained a formal division until after the War Between the States, the bitter feelings engendered by the controversy seem to have soon died down. In 1856 the Rev. E. H. Compton was invited to act as moderator of a meeting of the session of College Church.[51]

A Presbyterian congregation worshipping at Walker's Church was reported to the General Assembly in 1833; it had thirty-two members, and the Rev. David C. Proctor was stated supply. In 1873 this church united with the Presbyterian Church at Appomattox Courthouse.[52] Walkers Church building was one of the free churches; in the indenture Dr. James Walker, Dick Holland, and Martha Holland conveyed the "tract on which Walkers Church now stands" in 1802 to Stephen Pettus, Phil. Matthews, and William Gray, trustees, "for the use, benefit, and emolument of Publick worships for the — societys of Christians, Presbyterians, Baptist and Methodist or any other religious society or sect who wish to use the said house for the aforesaid purposes either in common or jointly or separately as to them shall seem best for preaching the Gospel, administering the sacraments and c."[53]

Appomattox Church was organized as a Constitutional Presbyterian Church in 1840 at Grove meeting-house, about two miles nearer Farmville than the present church. The Rev. J. H. C. Leach was the first pastor. Property for the church was bought in 1843 from Amplius Tuggle by the trustees James H. Wilson, Merrit B. Allen, John Tuggle, and Nathaniel J. Venable. Appomattox Church was received into West Hanover Presbytery in 1865; it had been a church of Piedmont Presbytery. In the same year Dr. Leach was enrolled as a member of Hanover Presbytery.[54] The breach was being healed.

It was apparently the practice of Buffalo Church to have either evangelistic or summer services in an arbor. Thomas T. Tredway instructed his overseer to send two slaves to help build the arbor whenever Mr. Hunt asked for them.[55]

Like the Presbyterians, the Baptists grew greatly during this period, and they also had divisive controversies. Sailor Creek Church was organized at Rice's meeting-house in 1781 with thirty-five members. Jeremiah Walker, pastor of Nottoway Church, was the leader in the organization of Sailor Creek, apparently from members of Nottoway who lived in northeastern Prince Edward. Robert Foster was first pastor of the new church.[56] He and his wife were two of the first six people in Prince Edward to become Baptists.[57]

In 1788 Mountain Creek Baptist Church was organized with twelve members by the Rev. Thomas Crymes.[58] There had evidently been a place of worship here for several years, for Mountain Creek meeting-house is mentioned in a road order in 1785.[59]

A third Baptist church was organized in eastern Prince Edward in this period. Known as Liberty, it united with Sailor Creek Church July 22, 1797, but the place of worship continued to be used and to bear the old name. At the same time Angola Church in Cumberland united with Sailor Creek. Sailor Creek records prior to 1827 list the members of the church as worshipping at either Rice's or Liberty.[60]

The Prince Edward churches belonged to the Middle District Association, which held its organization meeting in 1784; the association's second meeting was held May 9, 1785, at Rice's meeting-house.[61] In 1791 Robert Foster and John Smith represented Sailor Creek at the meeting of the association; Henry Lester, Joel Johns, Elisha Betts, and William Fears, Mountain Creek; and William Baldwin, Liberty.

Committees were appointed to visit vacant (pastorless) churches and stir them up; Simeon Walton, Robert Foster, and Abner Watkins were sent to Liberty; Foster, Watkins, and Henry Lester to Mountain Creek; and James Saunders and John Weatherford to Rocks[62] In 1797 James Saunders and Philip Matthews represented Appomattox Church at the Middle District Association.[63]

In 1802 David Holt, Branch Walthall, Joseph Ligon, and Simeon Walton were deacons at Sailor Creek; Thomas Clark was treasurer; and Richard Marshall was elected clerk that year to succeed Richard D. Pincham. Abner Watkins had succeeded Foster as pastor.[64]

The Middle District Association at a meeting at Walker's Church in 1803 decided to divide its territory. The great interest which accompanied the revival of 1787 had led to a division in 1788, the southern part of the territory becoming the Roanoke Association. The division proposed in 1803 was made the following year, with two new associations being formed, the Appomattox and the Meherrin, from the Middle District. The last meeting of the Middle District before division was held at Rice's the second Saturday in October, 1804; Mountain Creek was represented by Armistead Miller and John Rowlett, Sailor Creek by Abner Watkins and Owen Haskins, and Appomattox by James Saunders and John Feilder. Saunders was moderator of this session.[65]

The Prince Edward churches fell into the territory of the Appomattox Association, which held its first meeting at Walker's Church in 1805. Miller and Rowlett represented Mountain Creek; Thomas Pettus and William Walker, Sailor Creek; James Saunders and Abraham McGehee, Appomattox; and William Hill and Richard Wooldridge, Rocks.[66]

From Mountain Creek the second pastor, Henry Lester, extended his ministry into Charlotte County, where in 1803 he led in the organization of Ash Camp Church. The ministry of Ash Camp in turn extended into southwestern Prince Edward, and in 1815 a Baptist church was constituted at Welch Tract meeting-house. The Welch Tract Church called as its pastor Richard Dabbs, who was also pastor at Ash Camp. John Whitehead and John Adams were the first deacons, and Whitehead and Thomas Bunting represented the church at the Appomattox Association in 1815. Abner W. Clopton succeeded Dabbs in the pastorate at Ash Camp and Welch Tract in 1823 and served until 1833. Welch Tract did not flourish, although Clopton was one of the ablest Baptist ministers in the state. Its membership, according to available records, never exceeded forty.

In 1833, when Elisha Collins had succeeded Clopton as pastor, the church moved to a new site and took a new name, Spring Creek. A meeting-house was built by Richard Woodson on land given by Wilkerson Watson, on a knoll just west of the present Spring Creek Church. Philip Adams, John Whitehead, John Harvey, Elisha Collins, Richard Woodson, Robert Morgan, and Jesse Michaux were the trustees. The change invigorated the church; there were twenty-three baptisms during the first year on the new site.[67]

In June, 1827, a letter was prepared at Sailor Creek Church petitioning the Appomattox Association to appoint a presbytery to inquire into the expediency of organizing a church at Sandy River meeting-house. It was evidently deemed expedient, for on September 21, Sailor Creek directed its clerk, Elijah McGehee, to give letters to all members who applied for dismissal to join the new church.[68] The church was constituted as Sharon Baptist Church October 27, 1827, by twenty-three men, thirty-seven women and three slaves, all female. Attending the organization session, of which Simeon Walton was moderator, were Daniel Witt, Walton, Peter Nunnally, Absalom Nunnally, Willis R. V. Crute, Thomas Clark, William Ligon, William Walton, Francis Marshall, Alexander Marshall, Jr., Francis T. Wootton, John G. Lowden, Samuel H. Pettus, and Elijah McGehee. Daniel Witt was elected pastor; Elijah McGehee clerk, and Thomas Clark treasurer, the two latter to posts they had held at Sailor Creek. Clark and William Walton were elected deacons in addition to the deacons who had transferred from Sailor Creek, Simeon Walton, Willis R. V. Crute, and Elijah McGehee. Other business at the organization meeting consisted of the adoption of rules of decorum, an order to purchase a church book, and one to buy a table and cloths for the observance of the Lord's Supper. The members subscribed to a covenant which was entered in the record book.[69]

Sharon Church was organized in the building which had been erected by the vestry of St. Patrick's about 1763-65 on a site which had been occupied by a church or chapel of the Establishment for at least twenty years previous. After worship according to the rites and discipline of the Church of England ceased in Prince Edward, Sandy River Church was used by various denominations. The people of the community evidently wanted to keep such a place of meeting, for they repaired the building by popular subscription.[70] The Presbyterian John Holt Rice and the Methodist Matthew M. Dance were preaching there when Witt visited the community. Witt's first sermon in the building in which he was to preach for forty-four years was delivered before a meeting of the Appomattox Baptist Association on the fourth Sunday in February, 1827. He became popular at once, and his personal winsomeness and his preaching ability were important factors in the move to establish a Baptist church there.[71]

A few years later a controversy developed with the Methodists over the use of the building. The Baptists in 1832 secured a deed to the property from William Clark, who inherited the property from his father Thomas Clark, who bought it from John Jackson, representative of Royall and John Sutton Bowman. The Bowmans had conveyed the property to the church wardens in 1764. The Baptists also secured a deed from Paschal G. Leigh to a part of the property. Judge Thomas T. Bouldin and Charles Smith, who were consulted in the matter, held that the title from Clark was invalid and that the only valid title rested with the churchwardens of the parish, unless there was an older and better title than that made to the wardens, which they were inclined to think; they proposed that a line be run through the church since in their opinion only a part of it was legally the property of the church wardens and afterward of the Commonwealth. The Methodists wanted to build a wall through the church along the proposed line, but it was not done.[72] The Baptists retained the property, and the congregation of Sharon Church continues to worship there. The illness of the minister's wife and contentions with the Methodists were given as reasons for a decrease in the church membership in 1834.[73]

On November 25, 1836, a Baptist Church was organized in Farmville by William Moore, Daniel Witt, and E. W. Roach with twenty-three members. Several of these had been members of Sharon Church.[74] The year before subscriptions had been taken to raise money to buy a lot and build a Baptist church in Farmville, and $950 had been pledged. Members of other denominations were among the subscribers, and members of Sharon Church were particularly generous.[75] The first church was located at the southeast corner of Main and Fourth Streets, and the dedicatory sermon was preached November 30, 1839, by Daniel Witt. It was built in 1837. The first pastor of the church was William Moore, and the first deacons B. M. Robertson, Francis H. Robertson, Granville Nunnally, and Washington Nunnally. In 1856 a new church was built on the site now occupied by the Farmville Baptist Church.[76]

Pisgah Baptist Church was organized on August 15, 1857, at Union meeting-house, which had been erected a few years before by the Union Baptists. Daniel Witt played an important role in the organization of this church and became its first pastor. There were thirty-nine charter members, eighteen of whom came from Sailor Creek Church. John Redford, Benjamin F. Flippen, James N. Marshall, and J. W. Phillips were the first deacons, and Phillips was the first clerk. Richard A. Marshall was the first messenger to the Appomattox Association, carrying with him the request of the church for admission in 1858.[77]

During this period the oldest Baptist church in the county, Rocks, was lost to Prince Edward when Appomattox County was created. John Weatherford, remembered in Baptist history as a minister imprisoned in Chesterfield jail in 1773 for preaching the Gospel without a license, became pastor about the time of his visit as a committee of the Middle District Association in 1791 and served for some years, probably until his removal to Halifax in 1813. Philip Matthews succeeded him as pastor.[78]

The other old churches had fallen on difficult times. Sailor Creek lost some of its most active members to Sharon in 1827; in that year it reported 362 members; the next year the membership was down to 154.[79] On June 4, 1834, Rice's meeting-house was destroyed by a cyclone; Sailor Creek moved its place of worship to the meeting-house at Jamestown. The church never flourished there.[80] In 1850 members of a Baptist church at Brown's in Cumberland combined with Sailor Creek, as they were too few to maintain a church of their own. Sailor Creek drew members from Cumberland as well as Prince Edward; its longtime clerk and one of its leading members, Elisha Woodfin, lived in Cumberland.[81]

Two churches were organized from Rocks Church in 1834. As a result of "difference of sentiment respecting a temperance society," a number of members of Rocks followed their pastor, Philip Matthews, in organizing Matthews Church at Walkers Church with a charter membership of twenty-two. These were the pro-temperance faction. The associational comment for 1834 observes of the new church that "if their Christian enterprise in all things can correspond with their zeal on the subject of temperance and with their kindness to us . . . they must necessarily be an honored and distinguished people." The comment then dropped a hint of advice to the new church, enjoining it to "be temperate in all things" and to move "prudently in aiming a blow at the fell destroyer." Matthews and

J. Gilliam represented this church at the association in 1834. A. A. Baldwin succeeded Matthews as pastor at Rocks after the division. The other church organized from Rocks in this year was Liberty, which was represented at the association by its pastor, T. A. LeGrand, and A. A. LeGrand.[82]

Mountain Creek Church went out of existence between 1816 and 1823.[83] Armistead Miller, who was pastor in 1809, for some years filled that office.[84]

Appomattox Church continued until the late 1850's. It was last represented at the Appomattox Association in 1856, when Richard Jenkins, who seems to have been its pastor, was its messenger; it reported in that year four baptisms and 104 members. In 1857 the church sent neither letter nor messenger, and beginning in 1858 it was no longer listed as one of the churches in the association. The Rev. James Saunders was pastor of this church during its most flourishing period.[85]

A new Baptist church was constituted in 1859 which has had through the years members resident in Prince Edward. This was Elon, at Pamplin's Depot. J. S. Mason was the first pastor, and he and Charles Gilliam were the first delegates from the church to the Appomattox Association.[86]

Baptist churches paid little attention to the title to the property on which their houses of worship were erected. Rice's meeting-house had been deeded to trustees when it was built in 1775, and there is no indication that the title was vested in any other persons or group. Mountain Creek meeting-house was standing in 1785 and the church had been organized in 1788; it was 1811 before Edward Scott and his wife Elizabeth conveyed the acre of land on which the building stood (including the spring) to trustees Alexander Marshall, Branch O. Scott, and Robert Redd for the use and benefit of the meeting-house.[87] Liberty Church had consolidated with Sailor Creek in 1797; twenty-one years later Rowlett Perkinson gave the land and building for the purpose of divine worship free for any denomination of Christians, conveying title to Thomas Penick, Jacob Waddill, Henry M. Penick, and Simeon Walton.[88] Appomattox Church did not secure title to its land and meeting-house until 1838, when Thomas Jones and his wife Elizabeth conveyed the property to Jehu Simons, Nathaniel Simmons, and Shepherd Thaxton, trustees, on condition that if the church was discontinued the land would revert to the former owner and the building to the church.[89]

The Baptist churches of Prince Edward shared in the broadening interests of the churches which followed the beginning of the modern foreign missionary movement when William Carey went as a missionary to India in 1793. Sailor Creek Church organized a mission society at a meeting at Jamestown July 19, 1817. The members of this first mission society in Prince Edward were Abner Watkins, Thomas Pettus, Simeon Walton, John Walthall, Elisha Woodfin, Branch Walthall, Sterling Smith, John Sanders, George Holman, Elijah McGehee, John T. Watkins, Henry Walthall, Samuel W. Walthall, Booker Woodson, Richard S. Marshall, Barret W. Walthall, Alexander B. Walthall, William C. Ligon, William G. Overton, Josiah Lancaster, William N. Ellett, and David B. McGehee.

This church licensed three of its members to preach: Hezekiah Ellington, David B. McGehee (1807), and Sterling Smith (1819), and ordained McGehee to the ministry (1812).[90] Sharon Church ordained William C. Ligon to the ministry in 1830.[91]

Another phase of the broadening interest of the churches was the establishment of Sunday Schools. Spring Creek Church reported a Sunday School in 1834; it was organized by Richard Booker and Jesse Michaux to teach the children of the community to read. Primers, spelling books, and readers were used. The first library cost $40. Although the school was sponsored by a Baptist church, it was at first conducted by a student from Union Seminary at Hampden-Sydney. Each week some person in the Spring Creek community sent to Hampden-Sydney for the student. In 1835 a Bible class was reported "attached to the Sunday School."[92] Sharon Church had a Sunday School in 1842; it was organized "for the present year" in April, with Francis T. Wootton, superintendent, James Nunnally, secretary, and Thomas Clark, Samuel B. Bruce, William McGehee, John McGehee, and J. M. Holt directors.[93] Sailor Creek Church organized a Sunday School in 1843; the church collected $15.25 to buy books for the school.[94]

By 1830 two movements had arisen to create dissension among Baptists. One was the preaching of Alexander Campbell; the other was the opposition to the mission program.

The controversy over Campbell's doctrines was particularly strong at Sharon Church. At the church meeting June 26, 1830, Elijah McGehee expressed his disapprobation of the action of the Appomattox Association in adopting and recommending to the churches for adoption certain articles from the Beaver Association which were said to contain the sentiments of Campbell. Efforts to explain the intent of the association in adopting the articles failed to reconcile McGehee, and the church met again the following Monday, June 28. There was a large attendance, and full and free discussion. The prevailing opinion held that Campbell's opinions were "contrary to the sacred Scriptures, destructive to the peace and harmony of churches wherever they obtain, and the fruitful source of strife and confusion." The church agreed unanimously with the article which held "that no creed is necessary for a church but the Scriptures as they stand." The records on action on the other resolutions are confusing; the confusion may result from subsequent removal of the records of that meeting from the book by order of the church; by subsequent correction and recording again. The records note approval of other articles of the resolution; then they state: "While the church feels no disposition to interfere with the private opinions of its members to bind their consciences or to condemn whatever is good in the writings of the above named author (Alexander Campbell), the articles extracted from the minutes of the Association seem to them so glaringly false and dangerous that they are unwilling they should be propagated under their authority. . . .

"As this church conscientiously believes that the sentiments expressed in the foregoing articles, & published in the minutes of the Appomattox baptist Association held at Wolf Creek Meeting House on the 15th, 16th, & 17th of May 1830 are unscriptural & pernicious, calculated to sow the seeds of discord among bretheren, & dishonor the cause of Christ. Thereupon resolved that if in future any member of this church shall—late these doctrines, he shall be called to account & dealt with as an offender."

Elijah McGehee sought unsuccessfully to have the records of the meeting removed. He resigned as clerk, and a year later with his wife requested a letter of dismissal from the church.

Nothing more appears in the records of this controversy until August 27, 1836. A minute for that day runs: "Brother William Walton having communed with the Campbellites & favoured their sentiments contrary to the rules and regulations of this church and in opposition to the views and feelings of his bretheren, on his refusal to refrain from such conduct in the future, was expelled from the church."

When that action was taken, Walton's father, Simeon Walton, presented a resolution that "if any of our members shall in the future join in communion with the sect called Campbellites, they shall by that act forfeit their membership."

For the next half-century there were dismissals in compliance with this resolution.[95]

At first Alexander Campbell's writings which urged a restoration of primitive apostolic Christianity in the churches were popular with his fellow Baptists. Some disagreed later with some of Campbell's ideas; among these was Abner W. Clopton, who successfully urged the Appomattox Association to pass a resolution recommending that the churches not only discountenance Campbell's writings, but also refuse to invite into the pulpits any minister "who holds sentiments expressed in the Beaver Anathema." The last was directed at Silas Shelburne, a Baptist minister in Lunenburg, who was strong in his endorsement of Campbell's views, and some other ministers in the neighboring Meherrin Association who supported Campbell. A Clopton supporter failed to get the Meherrin Association to take a stand similar to that of the Appomattox Association.[96]

Shelburne often preached in the Appomattox Association,[97] and his influence explains in part the interest in the reform movement in southeastern Prince Edward, which was neighboring to Lunenburg, and between which sections there were many ties. Peter Ainslie, a Baptist minister who was dismissed from his church in 1832 and became a member of the Disciples communion, preached a "powerful sermon" at Sandy River during those days of controversy which also contributed to the acceptance of Campbell's views by some of the people in that section.[98]

The members of Sharon who had been dismissed for communing with the Campbellites and entertaining Campbell's sentiments began worshipping in Liberty meeting-house, which seems to have ceased being a place of regular Baptist worship after Sharon Church had been organized. Here in 1847 they constituted Liberty Church of the Disciples of Christ, with twenty-three members and S. H. Wootton and William Walton elders.[99] Upon his dismissal from Sharon Church, Walton identified himself with the Campbell movement. In 1838 he had been a subscriber for two years to Campbell's paper, the *Harbinger*.[100]

While Sharon Church was concerned with the controversy over doctrine, Spring Creek Church was involved in a controversy over polity. After Elisha Collins moved West, Spring Creek called as its pastor John T. Watkins of Cumberland. Although Watkins had been a member of the Sailor Creek mission society in 1817, he seems to have gone with the anti-missionary element which divided the Baptists in the 1830's. The James River Association had withdrawn fellowship from him at the time Spring Creek called him, a fact which seems not to have been known at Spring Creek. At the same time Spring Creek took the part of a member of Salem Church in Charlotte who had been dismissed and undertook to have him restored to membership. An investigating committee, of which Thomas A. LeGrand and Samuel Davidson were moderators and A. M. Poindexter clerk, studied the situation for the association and recommended that Spring Creek dismiss its pastor. Spring Creek defended its pastor, although it had declined to adopt his recommendation that it join an anti-missionary association, and its action before the Appomattox Association. In consequence the church was dismissed by the association in 1838, which expressed sympathy with the members disposed to keep good order and discipline in the church. The church suffered greatly during this period and at one time its male membership was reduced to three, James R. Whitehead, William Foster, and William Hunt. In 1840 the church sent Whitehead and Thomas G. Lindsey to the association asking restoration to membership, a request which was granted.[101]

Another divisive force among the Baptists was the Union Baptist movement. It had begun in Prince Edward by 1843, when Sharon Church appointed committees to confer with two of its members and advise them that they had broken the rules of the church by communing with the Union Baptists.[102] A Union Baptist church was organized through the instrumentality of the Rev. James W. Hunnicutt, the leader of the movement, in eastern Prince Edward about this time. The deed to the property, indented November 2, 1847, refers to the church recently organized and the house of worship recently built by general subscriptions and donations. The land was conveyed by Joseph Phillips and Louisa D. Phillips, his wife, to Richard S. Marshall, Jacob McGehee, Henry Tucker, and Henry M. Vaughan, trustees of the Union Baptist Church. This place of worship was Union meeting-house, located on the Burkeville road about two miles east of Rice. It was free for other denominations to use when not occupied by Union Baptists.[103] The Union Baptist movement in Prince Edward was short-lived. A decade later it was no longer in existence. Pisgah Church was organized in this meeting-house in 1857 and continued to worship there for a number of years.[104]

Baptists in earlier days did not limit their church meetings to the consideration of the business and financial affairs of the church and to cases of church discipline. They also raised questions concerning matters of faith, practice, and Scriptural interpretation. These were discussed, and if they could not be answered to the satisfaction of the members, they were referred to the association for an answer. In 1824 Welch Tract referred two questions to the Appomattox Association: Does the eighteenth chapter of Christ's Gospel by Matthew contain the root of all gospel discipline? Shall an offending member of a Gospel Church, who, when cited before the church, acknowledges his fault, begs forgiveness, and promises to forsake the practice for which he was cited be excommunicated? The answer to the first question was no, that the passage applied to fraternal disputes; the answer to the second question was that a church could retain a member who asked forgiveness, although in some cases when repentance could not "wipe off the dishonor done the cause of God" the person should be excommunicated.[105] At Sailor Creek Church it was the practice to raise the question at one meeting and have the discussion which looked to formulating an answer at the next. In replies to questions the church concluded in 1804 that the poor should be helped by the church and in 1806 that the head of family should, if he and his family had been invited to a place and dancing was introduced, leave with all his family.[106] In 1831 Sharon Church answered yes to the question "is not the washing of the Saints' feet one of those good works which ought to be followed by the followers of Christ?"

Some questions were referred by the association to the churches; in 1829 Sharon Church answered a query concerning the course to adopt in obtaining a presbytery for the ordination of a minister that no definite course was prescribed in the Bible and that consequently the procedure was a matter of choice for the church and concluded that "in all ordinary cases this church will conduct the ordination of her ministers through a presbytery sent by the association of which she is a member so long as that association shall continue to act only as an advisory council to the churches of which she is composed . . . ."[107]

The history of Methodism in Prince Edward County begins, insofar as can now be determined, with the preaching of Robert Marten (Martin ?) in 1786 in the section between the Courthouse and Moore's Ordinary and Briery Church. The next year a revival spread through Cumberland and the lower part of Prince Edward through the preaching of the Rev. Hope Hull, a Methodist minister. Organized work by the Methodists in Prince Edward began with a quarterly meeting in June, 1788, in McGehee's barn, between the Courthouse and Briery Church. The Rev. Thomas Conner was presiding elder at this meeting, and there were several ministers assisting. This meeting, at which many fell to the floor and lay prostrate, others cried out and prayed for mercy, and still others testified that God for Christ's sake had forgiven their sins, was the beginning of a revival in that community. Young people, both boys and girls, would walk miles to preaching. A large church was gathered by the Methodists at McGehee's barn, and societies were organized, according to John Hatchett, who attended the first quarterly meeting at McGehee's barn, in several other places, of which he names only one, George Cardwell's home, which was near his and where there was circuit preaching. Hatchett's father, also named John, and two of his sisters joined the church at McGehee's barn in 1788. Hatchett mentions the O'Kelly schism, which divided the Methodist Church in the 1790's, O'Kelly's followers being known first as Republican Methodists and later as Christians. (This was the Christian Church which combined with the Congregationalists in 1931 to form the Congregational-Christian Church and should not be confused with the Christian Church by which the Disciples of Christ, founded by Alexander Campbell, are known.) The schism does not seem to have affected Prince Edward Methodists, but some of the Methodists in Charlotte followed O'Kelly.

By 1798, when Hatchett joined it, the Methodist Church in that section was called Mt. Pleasant, and it continues to bear that name. The Rev. Pemberton Smith was the circuit preacher in that year. The next year Christopher Mooring and James Paterson "rode the circuit," and a class was organized at the Rev. William Spencer's schoolhouse, where there was preaching every two weeks. When Spencer moved to Lunenburg in 1804, the place of meeting was moved to the home of the elder John Hatchett, where the son continued to reside and taught school about 1805.[108]

The church which had been organized in McGehee's barn acquired its first property in 1792, when Abraham Foster conveyed to John Redd, Josiah Jackson, John McGehee, George Smith, and Benjamin Hodnett, trustees, one acre on the west side of Bush River, "with free liberty and use of the spring," for the use of the Methodist Church, "especially for its members in Prince Edward County and the congregation of that church in the neighborhood."[109]

The camp meeting was introduced into Virginia by the Methodists in Brunswick County in 1803.[110] Its popularity spread rapidly; in 1804 a camp meeting was advertised to begin Friday, September 7, at Sandy River Church and to continue "five, maybe six days." John Robertson, Clement Read, Edward Almand, John Hardin, and Archibald McRobert were expected to preach during the meeting, as were "many ministers of the Gospel from adjoining counties."[111]

Bishop Francis Asbury, in company with Bishop Richard Whatcoat, took the opportunity afforded by the meeting of the Virginia Conference at Edmund Taylor's in Granville County, North Carolina, in 1805 to visit Methodists of Southside Virginia; the two bishops included Prince Edward in their itinerary as they went to the conference.[112]

In 1807 John Early's ministry included Prince Edward. His *Journal* indicates no contact with Mt. Pleasant Church and the societies in that vicinity but instead a concentrated effort in the western part of the county. On Monday, June 15, 1807, he preached at Prospect to a "goodly number of Christians and some sinners." His mention of the name of the place and the presence of numerous Christians in the congregation suggest that a Methodist church had already been organized there. On this visit, as on the others he mentions in his *Journal*, Early stayed in the home of Robert Venable, to whom he was devoted. The next day he preached at Walkers Church, where he was not favorably impressed with the religious situation: "Three of four professions preach there. Some preach Jesus and some preach for the devil or contention. A few Christians, many hypocrites. Some poor formal professors that say they hope they have got religion. God pity them." Here he spent the night with "Brother Gray." Early does not appear from his *Journal* to have preached at Walkers Church again.

Early was forthright in his approach. In August, 1807, while on his way to Walker's (the home of John Meriwether Walker near Clover Hill in the extreme western end of Prince Edward, now Appomattox), he stopped at a home in Prince Edward "to see if God lived in the hearts of the people." It was the home of a widow where two young women were living together. "Their answer was as though they never heard of God for the devil had a palace there and one of them asked me, if I wanted a wife without a fortune, to court her. I told her the devil would have her here and in hell hereafter." After Early told them of the awful consequences of neglecting God, one apologized for her rudeness. When Early reached

Walker's on this visit, Mrs. Walker, *née* Susan Christian, gave him "a beautiful Virginia homespun coat." On his way from Prospect to Walker's on this trip, Early preached in an arbor at Andrew's old field. His pungent comment on this service is typical: "Christians shouted aloud for joy, sinners trembled and rolled in the dirt. The Presbyterians stood and looked." His comments on the Baptists, when he had contact with them, were equally sharp.

Beginning August 20, 1807, Early began a camp meeting at Prospect in which he was assisted by the presiding elder and several other preachers. The meeting began on a Friday and continued until Tuesday. People pitched tents in which they stayed during the meeting. It was a "powerful, awful, happy, solemn time." There were fifty conversions, with nineteen joining the Meethodist society there.

Early's *Journal* mentions several other visits to Prospect during the rest of 1807, to W. Gray's, to John Andrews', and to Walker's. Frequently on this circuit he included a visit to Pinea Ford's in Charlotte when going from Prospect to Walker's near Clover Hill.[113]

The Prospect Church acquired land for its place of worship in 1820 from Robert Venable, who conveyed it to the trustees of the church, Charles Venable, William Johnson, David Anderson, Jesse Bradley, and Samuel Venable. The trustees were to erect a meeting-house for the use of the Methodist Episcopal Church on this land. The site of this building, which burned in 1860, is now included in the cemetery. The present church was built in 1859.[114]

A few miles west of Prospect was another center of Methodist worship. At Wesley Chapel, on Jonna Gray's land, Lorenzo Dow preached each year in the early part of the nineteenth century. About 1814 the Methodists built a log meeting-house about three and one-half miles east of Gray's to which was given the name Olive Branch. The land on which the building stood was bought in 1829 from Benjamin and Mary W. Boatwright; the Olive Branch trustees were the Rev. William Johnson, the Rev. James McNeal, Edwin Gray, Thomas Andrews, Joel Elam, John C. Owen, Charles W. Wilkerson, James Martin, and Charles Venable. The first pastor was named Blunt; he was assigned about 1827.

A new church was built at Olive Branch in 1859, on the site of the present building.[115]

The Prince Edward circuit became a separate charge in 1831. In 1831 John Early, then presiding elder of the Lynchburg

District, planned the organization of a Methodist Church in Farmville. A building was erected in 1832 on the lot still occupied by the Farmville Methodist Church, and the following year a class was organized there by the Rev. William B. Rowzie, then pastor of the Prince Edward circuit. From the organization of this class until the Farmville Church became a separate station in 1838, Farmville was a regular preaching appointment on the Prince Edward circuit.[116]

There were four other Methodist houses of worship in antebellum Prince Edward:

Good Hope Meeting-house, near the intersection of the Jamestown road and Lockett's road, which had been built in 1816 when Thomas Goode and his wife, Elizabeth, sold the land on which it stood and a path to the spring to Robert Venable, Charles Venable, William Johnson, Samuel Venable, Joseph Goode, John Baldwin, and David Anderson, trustees, for the use of the Methodist Episcopal Church.[117]

An unnamed church, on a lot thirty-five yards square, where Lillious D. Womack's line crossed the road, conveyed in 1825 by Womack to James Bigger, Matthew M. Dance, Joseph Redd, John Clark, and Elbert Redd, trustees.[118]

Bethesda Methodist Church, of which Samuel Venable, James Moss, David Anderson, Charles Venable, William Johnson, and John Baldwin were the original trustees. The church was standing when the land was conveyed, apparently given, in 1830 by Merit B. Allen and his wife, Lucy Farrar Allen, to the trustees.[119]

A church near Prince Edward Courthouse, on land sold in 1840 by Nathaniel A. Venable and his wife, Catherine Venable, of Lunenburg County, to John A. Scott and Joseph Redd, trustees. The land adjoined Rowland Anderson's "improved lot." Six years later Redd conveyed the lot to a new group of trustees, John W. Redd, Elbert F. Redd, Beverly S. Scott, Branch O. Scott, Nathan G. McGehee, Frederick A. Ford, Samuel T. Clark, Henry J. Venable, and Edwin S. Redd, but for the same purpose expressed in the earlier deed, the use of the Methodist Episcopal Church.[120]

Methodist history in Prince Edward has been featured by revivals. One of the most notable took place in 1837, when John Wesley Childs was the minister. The revival followed recovery from a fractured shoulder Childs suffered when his horse threw him in March; he was confined for six weeks as a result (after the first ten days, which he spent at a home near the scene of the accident) at the home of John Wesley Redd, where he boarded his family while he was on the Prince Edward circuit. Childs used this period of confinement to prepare for the revival, discussing spiritual affairs with all who visited him and praying with them. During this period he preached twice at Redd's. The revival began when Childs resumed his active ministry and spread throughout the circuit from church to church. At the second quarterly conference, in July, between sixty and seventy made professions of faith, and it is estimated that there were some 500 conversions in the Methodist churches of the county during the year.[121] The Farmville Church was greatly strengthened as a result of this revival. Three of the converts, James W. Dunnington, Henry Y. Jenkins, and Abram Z. Venable, became and long remained pillars of the church. Many stores in the town closed during the revival (no doubt for the day services). The church grew to such an extent that a new church was built in 1839 to accomodate the members.[122] It must have been especially gratifying to Early to note the rapid growth of this church; undoubtedly he took pardonable pride in the church when it entertained the Virginia Conference in 1840, of which he was secretary and Bishop Waugh president.[123]

Another important revival was held in the Farmville church in 1847. In this revival Howell E. Warren was converted, and he has left an account of his experience. It was his custom to sit near the back of the church, and he frequently left before the service ended. Warren had inclinations to join the church, but there sat in front of him a man who led in prayer, in whom he had little confidence; the presence of this man deterred him from making a profession. One night, during prayer, he moved to the front, and while the congregation was singing after the prayer, he had the minister stop the hymn and he offered a prayer. When he sat down, he "felt an unusual degree of love for all people and to very intense degree to all Christians." Thirty years later he remembered some faces "which seemed alight with the glory of God." Both he and his wife joined the church at that revival.[124]

The controversy with the Baptists over the occupancy of Sandy River Church about 1832-34 suggests that there may have been a Methodist society at Sandy River at that time, and the fact that Matthew M. Dance preached there during the 1820's lends support to the suggestion.

There was worship at Wesleyan Church at Meherrin in 1852.[125]

Mt. Pleasant in 1848 and subsequent years had three classes for the religious instruction of its members. Members of classes were enjoined to observe the Friday before each quarterly conference as a day of fasting or prayer "for the prosperity of Zion and for us your ministers." John D. Southall was minister in 1848, and Thomas I. Bayton was helper. Class leaders were John Thompson, Edwin J. Redd, and Robert J. Smith. Nathan G. McGehee and John W. Redd were stewards, the latter being recording steward. The class book of the period contains a list of the board of trustees: John W. Redd, chairman, George W. Redd, treasurer, Samuel F. McGehee, secretary, Frank D. Redd, Robert J. Smith, Edwin J. Redd, Charles E. Redd, Joseph T. Redd, and John A. Redd.[126]

During this period there were usually two appointments to the Prince Edward circuit. In 1838, when the circuit was in the Lynchburg District, J. W. Childs and J. L. Rhea were appointed to it and J. Powers was assigned to the Farmville church.[127] In 1847, when the circuit was in the Randolph-Macon District, Southall and Bayton were assigned to Prince Edward and J. C. Garlick to Farmville.[128] In 1856 M. M. Dance is listed as supernumerary in Prince Edward.[129] The churches in Prince Edward were listed in the Farmville District in 1859, with William H. Christian as presiding elder, Frank Stanley as the appointee for Farmville, and D. J. C. Slaughter and William E. Allen appointees for the Prince Edward circuit.[130]

The Bible Society of Virginia was chartered in 1814.[131] The work of this organization had a special appeal in Prince Edward and received considerable support. In 1835 William M. Atkinson, agent of the society, visited Prince Edward and from Saturday, June 27, until Sunday, July 5, held meetings in the interest of the society at Sandy River Church, College Church, Farmville, The Grove, Prospect, Walkers Church, Buffalo, Spring Creek, Bethlehem, and Briery.[132] He thus reached each denomination in the county. In 1849 the Prince Edward Bible Society was described as one of the best organized in the state, enjoying the support of the entire community. It was reported as sharing in "the noble offering to France recently made." Life members of Virginia Society in Prince Edward were the Rev. E. Ballantine, Mrs. B. A. Ballantine, Rev. Isaac Cochrane, Rev. M. M. Dance, Rev. S. Field (Farmville), R. W. H. Goodrich, William P. Jackson (Farmville), Henry M. Jackson, Rev. J. H. C. Leach, D.D., Mrs. J. M. McNutt (Farmville), Miss C. B. Martin, Rev. William C. Scott, S. D. Stuart (Marble Hill), John Thompson, Thomas T. Tredway, C. R. Vaughan, Henry J. Venable,

Andrew R. Venable (Farmville), Mrs. H. E. Watkins, Rev. S. B. Wilson, and Branch Worsham, Jr.[133] The next year collections for the society amounting to $194.91 were reported from Prince Edward; there were two new life members, the Rev. George A. Baxter, D.D., and Henry Carrington Venable (Farmville). A. Biglow, Farmville, was reported as the Bible depository for Prince Edward. A new society had been organized in the county, the Bible Society of Hampden-Sydney College and Union Theological Seminary, auxiliary to the Bible Society of Virginia.[134]

The county Bible society still maintained a depository in Farmville in 1857. That year contributions in the amount of $34.37 were reported. New life members in the county were the Rev. R. L. Dabney, the Rev. Michael Osborne, the Rev. Benjamin M. Smith, the Rev. Benjamin F. Stanton, and the Rev. A. Wiles (Farmville).[135] The Bible society was still functioning after the War Between the States. The Prince Edward auxiliary to the Virginia Bible Society held its annual meeting February 14, 1874 in the Farmville Baptist Church, with the Rev. H. H. Hawes presiding. The report of the secretary, W. F. Farrar, "showed great good accomplished during the year."[136] The 1875 meeting was held in the Farmville Presbyterian Church.[137] That congregation in 1880 gave $10 to the state society.[138]

The foreign mission movement stimulated the interest of the churches in many other activities, notably the establishment of colleges and theological seminaries and in the founding of denominational journals. Interest in Sunday Schools was also quickened by the mission influence, and following the formation of missionary societies there developed in the churches a concern over social problems, which in those times were limited to two major issues, temperance and slavery.

The earliest Sunday School in the county of which this writer has found a record was that at Spring Creek Baptist Church, reported to the Appomattox Association in 1834.[139] The Baptists in Farmville organized a Sunday School in 1835, the year before they constituted their church.[140] Sharon Baptist Church organized a Sunday School in 1842, and Sailor Creek in 1843.[141] There was a Sunday School at the Farmville Methodist Church by 1853.[142] A Sunday School was organized at Buffalo Presbyterian Church in 1839.[143] College Church had Sunday Schools for both white and colored in 1860.[144]

CHAPTER XI

Of Social and Moral Concern

THE results of intemperance make it not surprising that the churches became concerned about indulgence in strong drink in this era of awakening social consciousness. Two cases from Prince Edward are examples. One leading citizen, who has figured prominently in this account, became so addicted to drink that he was unable to devote the proper attention to his business and in consequence was reduced to want. His wife's brother educated his oldest son, whose promise and achievement merited the aid.[1] Another Prince Edward citizen of prominence began drinking and when on a spree would beat his wife. After removing from the state, he placed in trust for her benefit certain pieces of property, to be conveyed to her if he should ever beat her again.[2]

The earliest indication in Prince Edward of the practice of abstinence from the use of alcoholic beverages is found in that revealing entry in Richard N. Venable's diary for December 9, 1791: "Went to Ginning's Ordinary found him and his company drunk. Spent the evening like a stranger."[3] A few years later, when Venable and Benjamin Latrobe made a survey of the Appomattox River to determine ways in which to improve navigation, the latter wrote that "Mr. Venable and myself are water drinkers, the rest drink grog."[4]

The first temperance society in Virginia and in the South and the second in the United States was organized by Abner W. Clopton at Ash Camp Baptist Church in Charlotte in 1826. Clopton's concern for temperance developed when he observed the practice of total abstinence by Daniel Witt, a young minister who assisted Clopton and studied under him from about the first of 1825 until the first of 1827. Witt came to Prince Edward in 1827 and became pastor of Sharon Church that year.[5] Eight years after Clopton had organized the temperance society at Ash Camp, there was one in Spring Creek Church, of which he had been pastor when it was Welch Tract. The Rev. Philip Matthews led a group in Rocks Baptist Church to establish a new church, Matthews, at Walkers Church when opposition to their plan to organize a temperance society developed.[6]

269

Interest in the temperance movement spread. A petition from Prince Edward, signed by 255 people with the names of James N. Jackson, William Willis, and C. C. Read at the head of the list, asked the Virginia legislature "to free the sons of Virginia from the demoralizing traffic in alcoholic liquors." The petition noted the promptness with which the colored population yielded to the temptation to drink and advised the legislature that it would be "an act of wisdom to stop the traffic." The petition, presented January 8, 1839, was rejected.

A problem arose in Farmville when the Prince Edward County Court construed an act of 1832 as denying it the privilege of refusing to issue a license to sell liquor to an applicant in an incorporated town. This left the way wide open for irresponsible and undesirable persons to open barrooms. W. L. Morton and others petitioned the General Assembly in 1841 to require retailers of alcoholic beverages to obtain a recommendation from the town trustees before they were issued a license. And the next year the trustees themselves, in a petition signed by Clement C. Read, president, and Joseph E. Venable, clerk, asked the legislature to require those who would sell strong drink in the town to get a license from the County Court in the same way retailers in the rest of the county did, by first obtaining a certificate of good moral character from the Court.[7] This situation may explain the interest in temperance demonstrated at the Fourth of July celebration in Farmville in 1843, described in one of the toasts as the first temperance rally in Farmville.

Whiskey and other alcoholic beverages were generally sold in the stores. The Court issued licenses to those who were regarded as of good moral character.[8] The widespread use is indicated in a special license granted James Morton to retail spiritous liquors at Hampden-Sydney College during exhibitions of students at vacation time in 1786.[9] Church records show that over-indulgence in strong drink was subject to church censure and even dismissal. On the other hand, wine and whiskey were used as medicines; in 1859 R. T. Harding, writing to Hezekiah Harding about the threat of an individual to present their store at Moore's Ordinary for selling French brandy by the bottle, advised that he was able to prove that he had bought it on the advice of Dr. H. A. Vaughan and Dr. Wootton.[10]

Slavery had given concern to thoughtful people in the American colonies in colonial times. John Woolman advocated abolition in Quaker meetings which he attended and won considerable support, although he aroused opposition. In Virginia, in 1789, the Baptist General Committee, consisting of representatives of the district associations, passed a resolution holding "that slavery is a violent deprivation of the rights of nature and inconsistent with a republican government and therefore recommend it to our bretheren to make use of every legal measure to extirpate this horrid evil from the land; and pray Almighty God that our honorable Legislature may have it in their power to proclaim the great Jubilee, consistent with the principles of good policy."[11] As the churches took more interest in the problem, slavery became a social, as well as an economic, concern.

In Prince Edward the number of slaves continued to increase. A census, taken by militia districts in 1782, has been preserved for seven of the ten districts. According to these returns, Peyton Randolph, with eighty-one slaves, was the largest slaveowner in the county at the time; others with more than twenty slaves were George Walton, sixty-four; Robert Walton, thirty-three; Richard Bibb, thirty; Joseph Moore, twenty-nine; John Holcombe and Francis Watkins, twenty-eight each; Peter Johnston, twenty-six; Henry Watkins and Josiah Chambers, twenty-five each; Philemon Holcombe, twenty-three; Peter LeGrand, twenty-two; John Watson, twenty-one; Elizabeth Venable and David Walker, twenty each. Many persons owned fewer than twenty; the section in which they were least numerous was in the territory of Captain Dick Holland's company, in a part of the section of the county now Appomattox; of twenty-three heads of families listed, only six owned slaves, none with more than four and three with one slave each[12] The 1860 census showed about 7,341 slaves and 465 free Negroes in Prince Edward. There were 4,035 whites.[13]

The traffic in slaves continued throughout this period, although the importation of slaves from Africa was stopped in 1808. Slaves were sometimes mortgaged to secure the debts of their owners; fourteen Virginia-born slaves were sold under a deed of trust at James Morton and Company's store on June 9, 1804, to satisfy a debt owed by their master to the store; other such sales are recorded.[14] Negroes were sometimes sold at the death of their master in settlement of the estate.[15] When Richard K. Randolph disposed of his Prince Edward holdings to move to Rhode Island about 1810, he advertised eighty-nine Negroes for sale (along with 4,440 acres on Spring Creek); among them were skilled workers: a young and healthy blacksmith, a wheelwright, a good cooper and carpenter.[16]

There were dealers in slaves, who bought and sold them; they would carry slaves in companies, or droves, as they were described. Two dealers carrying a company of slaves were murdered in Prince Edward in the 1830's.[17] A runaway Negro, taken up in Petersburg in January, 1828, told the jailor that he had been bought by a slave dealer at Prince Edward Courthouse in the summer of 1827 and that he ran away from him the next day, when they were in Powhatan.[18]

Slaves continued to run away; when they were taken up, they were lodged in the county jail. The jailor advertised their apprehension, together with a description and such other information as he could get from them, including the name of the owner which they gave him.[19] Slaves ran away from their Prince Edward owners, too. Watkins Dupuy in 1811 advertised for a runaway, last seen in Richmond and supposed to be lurking there.[20] A slave bought by Nathaniel E. Venable from Nathan Wells ran away in 1833; Venable thought he might be working as a boatman on the James River.[21] Asa Dupuy in 1821 advertised for a runaway, a good wheelwright and rough carpenter belonging to General John Purnall; he anticipated, on the basis of threats made by the slave, that he would try to get to Ohio or some other free state.[22] Four years later George Abbitt of Prince Edward advertised for a runaway whom he thought might be near Cartersville, in the neighborhood in which he was raised; as he had relatives who were free, Abbitt thought he might have obtained "free papers."[23]

Patrols continued to operate; these usually consisted of a captain with from four to six men who usually patrolled their district for a period of three months.[24]

Estate appraisals in the will books of the period show the valuation of slaves, but they did not always bring the price at which they were appraised. John Watts sold three slaves for his brother William in 1789; a girl, referred to in the phrase of the day as a wench, valued at £40 brought £30; a boy about fourteen valued at £35 brought £26:5; and a boy about nine or ten valued at £30 brought £22:10.[25] Laban Hawkins paid John Ligon £22:10 for a Negro woman in 1795[26] and the estate of Richard D. Pincham $80 for a Negro boy in 1808.[27] Ann Pincham, widow of Richard D. Pincham, agreed to sell Hawkins two slaves for £75 in 1809 and take in part payment a horse at $60.[28]

Most masters treated their slaves well and made good provision for their needs, although they required them to work. The motto of many masters was expressed by Thomas T. Tredway in a letter to his overseer: "The health of the hands is the first consideration always." Writing from Richmond while attending the session of the legislature when he was a delegate from Prince Edward in the winter of 1856, Tredway observed that the change of weather from the "long cold, dry spell" to the "warm, damp one" would be apt to produce colds and pneumonia; he thought his Negroes were well provided with shoes, each having two good pair; he cautioned his overseer to see that "they keep themselves dry-shod." If necessary the overseer was to get leather, thread, and shoe tacks and have the shoes mended.[29] In another letter Tredway advised that he was sending "a parcel of yarn socks to be distributed among my folks."[30] When Tredway went to the "Springs" for a stay of a few weeks in 1856, he instructed his overseer to send for Dr. Terry if any of the Negroes should become seriously sick.[31] Through his correspondence with John Woodall Tredway demonstrated a continuing concern for the welfare of his slaves and affection for them; "Remember me kindly to all my Negroes," he wrote in one letter.[32]

A natural leadership among the Negroes was recognized. Thomas T. Tredway, in one of his letters from Richmond, asked his overseer to "tell Ben I should be sorry to hear any bad report about him or any of the folks," adding that he thought Ben would do his duty. Ben and Pompey were mentioned for special salutations. This letter also revealed a consideration for the feelings of Negroes whose families had been broken up, although it was cloaked in caution:

"Let it be known to some of the Negroes so old Rachel at my father's can hear it that I have seen her son Titus & that he is very well & has a good home."[33]

Another indication of affection for and interest in the slaves found expression in recording the dates of birth (or age of the slave when he was purchased and his birth date was not known) and death of slaves in the family Bible. The Bible which contains the records of the family of William Weaver also contains the records of his slaves.[34]

Some masters were, in the opinion of others, altogether too lenient in the management of their slaves. Charles Woodson felt that not only was the owner's interest neglected by such leniency, but the slave's too. "Intercourse, trading and dealing with slaves is too generally practiced and indulged in by free people and in many cases by whites of exceptionally general character," he wrote. He saw such practices as an evil which "has done more mischief to the slave population and the morals of both slaves and free, the interests of slave owners, and consequently agricultural prosperity than any other cause." Because these practices rendered the slave largely independent of the master and careless and inattentive in the performance of his duties, they were destructive of the master's interest; because they encouraged the slave to spend his nights in roving and debauchery, the practices made him incompetent for work the next day and ended "too frequently in actual disease and destruction of life." They also resulted in severe treatment of the slave for inattention to duty and slovenly work. The laws covering the problem were good, Woodson thought, but "interested avarice defies their execution."[35]

Slaveowners who owned more Negroes than they could work profitably on their own farms and in their own homes were accustomed to hire out the surplus slaves. Some farmers who did not own enough slaves to do all the work they needed done would hire slaves. Merchants and craftsmen were likely prospects to hire some Negroes,[36] and sometimes there were innkeepers who did not own enough slaves to do all the work required around the tavern. R. L. Saunders at the Farmville *Journal* printing office advertised to hire a good gardener and field hand, "sober, honest, industrious," in 1852; in the same year G. W. A. Raine who was then operating the Eagle Hotel in Farmville wanted to hire one or two good female servants accustomed to serving in the house and a No. One cook."[37]

The construction of public works also afforded an opportunity for masters to hire out Negroes whose work was not needed at home. The Richmond and Danville Railroad wanted to hire "a number of able-bodied Negro men" for construction work in building its line. It offered to hire them by the month or for longer periods at the option of the owner.[38] William Weaver hired one of his slaves to work on the Southside Railroad at $300 per year in 1864 and 1865 (prior to April 1, 1865).[39]

An important source of supply of Negroes for hire was from the executors of estates and the guardians of minor children who had inherited slaves but had no land on which to work them. The executors of Edward Dillon (Henry E. Watkins, Charles Morton, and John Gilliam) hired to Anderson and David Blanton a Negro girl in 1818 for that year; they paid $18 in cash for her work and agreed to provide the following clothing: two shifts of good oznaburg or homespun, a summer coat of the same material, good negro (black) cotton plain or homespun yarn cloth for winter clothes, a pair of stockings, a pair of "Double-Soaled" shoes, and a blanket.[40] Colonel Asa Dupuy, as administrator of the estate of Thomas Walton, hired out the slaves belonging to that estate in the 1820's; the highest amount received for the year's work of one of these slaves was $69; a man, his wife, and five children were hired out for $30 a year. The hire of eighteen slaves belonging to this estate yielded $352.05 in 1824.[41] The person hiring a slave provided his food as well as the clothing agreed upon. Richard Marshall, guardian of the orphans of Joseph Mottley, hired a man in 1827 to James Blanton for $63.25 for the year; Blanton was to provide summer clothing, consisting of a pair of pantaloons and two shirts of good German ozna[burg], a winter coat and pair of pantaloons of good "napt" cotton No. 5, a pair of double soled shoes, a pair of yard socks, a hat, and a blanket.[42] In 1841 William Walton hired a Negro man belonging to his niece and ward, Susan L. Farley, to Granville Nunnally. The slave was taken sick suddenly; Nunnally sent for his family physician, Dr. Wilson, who was not at home; he then called Dr. Lyle and later Dr. Chappell. All three physicians came "and by diligent attention that evening and night saved the life of sd. boy." To determine responsibility for paying the physicians, Thomas Hickson and William M. Womack were asked to decide whether the owner or the person hiring the slave was responsible for payment. They, "of opinion that sd. Nunnally acted promptly & with humanity," held that Walton, as guardian of the slave's owner, should pay.[43] This is an example of the medical care given slaves. One can imagine the consternation in the Nunnally household when it was found that a slave belonging to someone else, but in its care, was seriously ill.

The churches which owned slaves received their income from them by hiring them out. It has already been noted that Briery Church invested the funds contributed for the permanent support of the Gospel in slaves, the income from hiring them out the dividend on the investment. A slave belonging to Cumberland Church was hired in 1797 for £17:15 per year; a Negro woman was hired for £8 annually for a period of several years.[44] While concern was occasionally expressed about church ownership of slaves and the church's use of income derived from hiring them out for work, the practice was generally accepted. Slavery was legal, and it was in the South the prevailing labor system. As devout a minister as Daniel Witt did not, even after the ending of the system, consider it as sinful *per se,* although he did not regard it as profitable.[45] And as the abolitionists pressed the fight against slavery on moral and religious grounds, Southerners fought back with the same ammunition, justifying the holding of slaves on moral and religious grounds.

The slaveowner constantly faced risks, not only of loss by running away, but also from death. Two young girls belonging to Joseph Redd were poisoned from eating hemlock root which they mistook for angelica; one died almost immediately, the other was saved "by prompt and active medical treatment."[46] Dr. Owen lost two slaves when one of his men killed his wife with an ax because she did not have his bread baked when he came to his house for dinner; he was convicted and hanged.[47]

Slaves, for all the strictness of the patrols, had a certain amount of freedom in visiting neighboring plantations; they were required to have passes from their masters to leave the premises. There was considerable intermarrying among slaves on different farms. In such cases the man was permitted to visit his wife from Saturday afternoon until Sunday night. Children born to the couple belonged to the master of the mother.[48] In some instances the marriages of slaves took place in the parlor of the home of the woman's master, the ceremony being performed by a white minister. Afterward there was a party for the couple and their friends, with food in abundance and dancing until daybreak.[49]

The slaves had their parties, to which slaves from neighboring farms sometimes came. One of the most unique of slave parties was the "persimmon beer dance." Dr. William B. Smith of Cumberland has described such a dance which he saw at Samuel Poe's in the lower end of Prince Edward. The Negroes had brewed a barrel of persimmon beer and were given permission by their master to have a "beer dance." They began the party by singing "Whozen-John, who-za," of which the first stanza is

> "Old black bull come down de hollow,
> He shake [hi'] tail, you hear him bellow;
> When he bellow he jar de river,
> He paw de yearth, he make it quiver.
> Who-zen-John, who-za."

Those who could not get in the house watched from the outside, commenting on the dancers in the inimitable way of the slave, which some of us remember as characteristic of what is usually called "the

old-time colored person." Music was furnished by a banjo, and the
Negroes danced jigs and clapped "juber." The banjo-man had a long
white cow's tail tied with red ribbon around his head and hung down
his back; over this he wore a three-cornered hat, decorated with
peacock feathers, a rose cockade, a bunch of ripe persimmons, and
three pods of red pepper. In a way this headgear set the tone for the
evening. Two men clapped "juber" in rhythm with the banjo; a
fourth man was serving beer with a gourd; and two women were
baking larded persimmon dough in the great fireplace. One woman
held a torch light for the company. The others were dancing. As
they danced they sang a ballad set to "juber":

> "Juber up and Juber down
> Juber all around de town,
> Juber dis, and Juber dat,
> And Juber roun' the simmon vat."

When the bread was baked, supper was announced; the banjo-
player was served first, then the clappers and beer-server during the
dance, and lastly the beaux and their partners. Each had a loaf of
persimmon bread and a gourd of beer.[50]

But for all the outward pleasantness and gaiety and despite its
place in the economic system, thoughtful minds saw slavery as a
problem and were concerned about what to do. William Branch, Jr.,
who lived at Golgotha near Rice and was a teacher and lawyer, in
1819 published a book of 218 pages in the heroic couplet to which
he gave the title *Life*. In it he describes the development of an
individual from youth to age in the society with which he was
familiar. "Slaves near our offspring teach them to be slaves," he
wrote in criticism of the institution; his comment gives a different
estimate of the practice of permitting slaves to rear children from
that which has been preserved in nostalgic memories:

> "...................... the kidnapped brood,
> Robb'd of their rights and barr'd of every good;
> Barren of mind, and in their manners base,
> We foolish, o'er our infant nurseries place.
> The blooming charge oft leaves the mother's charms,
> To breathe infection in the bondman's arms;
> Oft the pert youngling quits the mother's side,
> To mess with slaves, to follow as they guide.
> He learns their jargon, all their maxims learns;

Contracts their habits; with their passions burns;
Becomes dishonest, flatters, truckles, steals,
Heirs all their fears, partakes their guilty meals;
Wise converse spurns, and deeds of heroes rise,
And every manly virtue basely flies.
Of taste deprav'd, and judgment prone to err,
His early habits lead him to prefer
The Black companions of his early days,
With all their sinful deeds and vulgar ways.
Nurs'd in corruption—neither wise nor bold,
He's rais'd for commerce—to be bought and sold;
Than self no other spring e'er moves his breast,
And all he craves is gewgaws, pelf, and rest.
Devoid of genius and bereft of pride,
No manly ardors through his bosom glide;
No sky-borne flight, no gen'rous view, no aim
At future grandeur, point him out to fame;
Dead to himself, his friends, his native land,
He haunts the sty, and loves the swinish band;
Thus rear'd by slaves, he ever lives a slave,
For crouching bondmen seldom rear the brave."[51]

What, indeed, was to be done about slavery? Emancipation was possible, and some slaveowners freed their slaves. A notable example was that of Richard Randolph of Bizarre, who freed his slaves by his will which was probated in 1797 and provided for them a part of his land in Prince Edward which has long been known as Israel Hill.[52] The experiment was not regarded as successful, however. In reply to an inquiry in the *Farmer's Register* for an acocunt of the settlement, James Madison of Prince Edward wrote under date of March 22, 1836, that freed Negroes, about 100 in number, were settled on small parcels of land, some ten to twenty-five acres to the family. As long as the habits of industry acquired in slavery continued, they increased in numbers and enjoyed some degree of comfort. When this had been lost, with the passing or becoming aged or infirm of the older people, a new race "began to be idle and vicious," and the settlement began diminishing in number instead of increasing and at that time had continued to decrease each year, although there was no emigration. Madison reported that they were idle, poverty-stricken, dissipated wretches, "a great pest and a heavy tax on the neighborhood." With so little industry and so much dissipation the women could not rear their children and in consequence prostituted themselves with the further consequence of having few children. The editor of the *Farmer's Register* (Edmund Ruffin) noted that there was a demand for the labor of these free Negroes and that their preferred employment was boating on the Appomattox River, "because it is nearest to idleness."[53]

Randolph's emancipation experiment was described as a failure by a correspondent of the Richmond *Whig* in 1875; then the traveler on the Atlantic, Mississippi, and Ohio, he wrote, will see west of Farmville "a few huts on exhausted lands occupied by a few descendants" of the emancipated slaves. Israel Hill in contemporary opinion was not a convincing argument for emancipation.[54]

Restrictions were placed on free Negroes as well as slaves. They were required to register in the clerk's office of the county in which they lived every three years and had to have the certificate of registration to secure employment.[55] The Prince Edward records have numerous entries of the registration of free Negroes. Some Negroes were born free, that is, of free women. Some of the registrations note that the persons registering were emancipated by Richard Randolph One such person registered as late as 1861, and was number 564 in the registry of free Negroes.[56] At least twice, in 1826 and in 1831, permits given free Negroes to keep guns were revoked; in the former year the constables were dircted to take guns from free Negroes and hold them, in the latter year the sheriff was charged with responsibility of notifying them of the order and of making the necessary examination to ascertain that free Negroes were not keeping guns.[57]

Dr. Francis J. Mettauer emancipated some of his slaves by will.[58] One could also emancipate slaves by deed of gift. John Chaffin gave to a Negro man his freedom in this way in 1803.[59]

No person in Prince Edward gave more serious consideration to the problem of what to do about slavery than John Holt Rice. To William Maxwell he wrote in 1827 that the problem was "to produce that state of the public will, which will cause the people to move spontaneously to the eradication of this evil." He mentioned the difficulty the church or a minister faced in commenting on this problem, because when anything was said, it touched "what are called the rights of property." So jealous were people on this point that a minister or the church could not "take a step without arousing the strongest opposition and producing the most violent excitement." He wrote to Archibald Alexander that it was impossible for any decision of the church regarding slavery to be caried into effect, since three-fourths of the members were women and minors and three-fourths of the rest were men in moderate circumstances and without political influence. Yet he believed that Virginia, if left "undisturbed by foreign influences," would eventually emancipate the slaves. On the other hand, the interference from the outside which was already being felt made him almost despair of the prospect of emancipation.[60]

Many leaders felt that emancipation in itself was not enough. They foresaw the greatest problems which would arise from a situation in which two different races lived side by side. They recognized the problems posed by the free Negro in their midst, and they saw that problem multiplied if the slaves were set free, to live as free men among the whites. The answer to the problem they saw is what was termed colonization, that is, the return of the Negroes to Africa. That, too, posed staggering problems, for the cost of transportation was heavy. The American Colonization Society was organized to encourage emancipation and the return of emancipated Negroes to Africa and to raise money to pay their fares to the section of the African coast chosen for settlement, the area which became the Republic of Liberia.[61]

Mrs. John Holt Rice, who had kept her slaves, which she had inherited from her father, after her husband's death until 1853 decided that she wanted to send them to Liberia before she died. Friends in New York raised $1,000 to purchase the husband of her principal serving woman (who was owned by another person), in order that the entire family might emigrate together. Mrs. Rice freed twelve slaves, who went to Liberia.[62]

Transportation was expensive, and funds were limited. In 1833 the Virginia Assembly appropriated $18,000 to apply to the transportation of "free persons of color" from the counties in which they lived. Prince Edward's share amounted to $214.30.[63] On the basis of the cost of transporting the Watson Negroes in 1857, this would have paid for the transportation of only three persons.

The emancipation of John Watson's Negroes and their settlement in Liberia shows clearly the problem which the slaveowner who wished to free his slaves and send them to Liberia faced in the way of expense. Also, the slaves represented a considerable investment, and few were able to bear the loss emancipation would entail. Many men with children felt their first duty to provide for their children; to emancipate their slaves would deprive their children of a considerable portion of their inheritance. Watson was a bachelor. In his will, dated October 24, 1854, and proved August 13, 1856, he freed all his slaves, "to take place as soon after my death as suitable arrangements can be made by my executors for their removal to Liberia. . . ." They were to be subject to the control of the executors until placed on board ship for Liberia. Watson also provided that money from the sale of land and property not left to relatives and money due him by bonds or otherwise be used to pay transportation of his slaves to Liberia and if there was any money left over it was to be divided equally among them; each person over fifteen would be given his share, and the share of each person under fifteen would be given to a relative "who will most likely take care of it for their benefit." Robert J. Smith, Joseph Dupuy, and William F. Scott were named executors, but Scott declined to serve. Some relatives attempted unsuccessfully to break the will. The itemized expenses show the cost of getting the Watson Negroes to Liberia:

Oct. 16, 1857: Paid Joseph Dupuy and R. J. Smith expenses to Richmond to buy clothing, contract with railroad and steamboat company for carrying Negroes $ 22.30

Nov. 2, 1857: Paid Joseph Dupuy expenses to Richmond when carrying [off] Negroes, and S. D. Watkins 9.35

Nov. 3, 1857: Paid expenses of 66 Negroes from Meherrin Depot to Richmond. 70.20

Nov. 4, 1857: Paid expenses of 66 Negroes in Richmond and to Norfolk. 133.25

Nov. 4, 1857: Paid Taylor and Isaacs for premium on $4,000 in gold for Negroes. 480.00

Nov. 4, 1857: Paid express agent for carrying $4,000 in gold Richmond to Norfolk. 4.00

Nov. 4, 1857: Paid hack hire in Norfolk. 50

Nov. 10, 1857: Paid William McLain agent for expenses 66 Negroes to Liberia. 3,850.00

Nov. 12, 1857: Paid 66 of Mr. Watson's Negroes $60 each when put on board vessel, to wit (here are listed all the Negroes, those to whom the money was given for themselves and those to whom it was given for someone else; usually it was given to a mother for children under fifteen, but in one instance it was given to a brother for his sister). 3,960.00

Nov. 12, 1857: Paid Joseph Dupuy and S. D. Watkins expenses eight days in Norfolk.   29.00

Nov. 12, 1857: Paid expenses 66 Negroes eight days in
Norfolk, per bill .... $ 186.40
Nov. 12, 1857: Paid Stephen D. Watkins, service in carry-
ing Negroes to Norfolk and expenses home........   25.00
Nov. 12, 1857: Paid Joseph Dupuy expenses Norfolk and
Richmond and then home........................   9.00
Nov. 25, 1857: Paid R. J. Smith for services, William P.
Baker's expenses carrying Negroes to Norfolk.......   63.00
Nov. 25, 1857: Paid William P. Baker services and part
expenses in carrying off Negroes..................   35.00
Apr. 8, 1858: Paid Mrs. Drusilla Smith for attending to
making Negroes' clothes.........................   64.00[64]

One of Watson's slaves, Caesar, aged about fifty-seven, did not
wish to go to Liberia. In 1858 he asked and received permission of
the Circuit Court to choose an owner and remain in this country.
When he came into the County Court with Robert J. Smith to register
as a free Negro, he was not given permission to reside in Virginia.[65]

The cost of sending Negroes to Liberia, as shown in the expense
account, explains why more were not sent there. Few people were
able to provide the expenses, nor could the colonization society raise
enough money to send many.

The churches during this period showed concern for the spiritual
welfare of the slaves. The church rolls of Sailor Creek and Sharon
Baptist Churches list many slaves among the members. Sailor Creek
in 1830 gave to Sharon permission to receive into its membership
without letters Negroes who belonged to the former church living in
the neighborhood of the latter. While most of the Negro members
belonging to Sharon lived in the vicinity of the church and many
belonged to its members, some lived at a distance. Among those
were a slave of Richard N. Venable of Slate Hill, one of Nathaniel
E. Venable of Longwood, three of Henry E. Watkins of The Home,
between Farmville and the Courthouse, several of James D. Wood
of Poplar Hill; one of James Dillon of Sandy Ford; some of Asa
Dupuy of Linden, near Meherrin, one of the estate of Alexander
Marshall near Meherrin (Marshall himself was a member of the
church prior to his death in 1829), and several belonging to the
Cumberland and Briery Congregations (Cumberland and Briery
Presbyterian Churches). The latter slaves may have been hired out
in the neighborhood of Sandy River meeting-house. In 1860 forty-
five Negroes were baptized into the membership of Sharon Church.[66]

Two charter members of the Farmville Baptist Church were Negroes.[67] Buffalo Presbyterian Church had slaves in its membership
during this period, as did Briery and College churches.[68] Slaves had
to secure permission from their masters in order to join the church.
A Cumberland master refused to give permission to one of his slaves
to join Sailor Creek Baptist Church because he did not think that the
slave knew what he was doing or realized the commitment becoming
a church member involved. There are other letters in which permission was given.[69]

The Rev. John D. Paxton, who became minister of Cumberland
Presbyterian Church in 1823, became greatly concerned because
most of his salary was paid from the income received from hiring
out slaves owned by the church and for whose religious instruction
little was done. Slaves attended his church, and sometimes he
preached especially for them. Mrs. Paxton received from her father
the gift of a family of house servants when they came to Prince
Edward; these were freed and sent to Liberia. Paxton sold his own
home and land at a sacrifice and moved his family to the free states.[70]
He preached at College Church and was asked to resign because of
his abolitionist activities. He once tried to hold a meeting of Negroes
in Prince Edward Courthouse, but the door was locked, and he was
refused entrance.[71]

The Methodists maintained a colored mission in Prince Edward
just before the war. No specific assignments were made in 1860 and
1861, the notation being made that the mission was to be supplied.[72]

There have been indications, observed especially in some of the
toasts drunk at the Fourth of July celebrations, of an interest in
affairs in other lands. The Prince Edward citizen was no isolationist.
During the terrible Irish famine in 1847 an Irish Relief Committee
was set up in Farmville with Beverly S. Scott, chairman, A. Vaughan,
treasurer, and Joseph W. Watson, receiver. Scott asked every minister in the county to give his congregations an opportunity to contribute to the relief fund. In April gifts of fifty-four bushels of corn
and a box of clothing were reported. The corn and flour contributed
were sold, and the proceeds, with cash gifts, were forwarded to the
state committee. In June $53.90 was sent; of this sum, $15.50 was
from the Briery Congregation. Some provisions and clothing were
sent to Ireland; the British government paid the freight charges. Some
of the contributions were used to relieve destitution in Scotland.[73]

When trouble struck nearer home, there was an even more

generous response in Prince Edward. In August and September, 1855, there was sent from the county $381.40 for the relief of sufferers in the yellow fever epidemic which raged in Norfolk that year. Contributions were received at the Farmers Bank of Virginia office in Farmville by A. Vaughan, cashier, who acted as treasurer for the collection in Prince Edward. F. N. Watkins wrote a letter accompanying the check, in which he advised the Howard Association, which conducted the appeal for funds, that the contribution from Prince Edward was to be divided between Norfolk and Portsmouth on the basis of population, adding that the people of Prince Edward "feel it a privilege and a duty to contribute."[74] T. T. Tredway sent directly to the treasurer of the State Relief Committee $85 raised at Buffalo meeting-house.[75]

There was concern for mental illnesses then. Treatment, of course, was not comparable with that available today, but Virginia maintained an asylum at Williamsburg. Sometimes the institution was full when a prospective inmate was brought, as was the case with a person who had been adjudged insane in Prince Edward about 1804. In such cases the guards who had carried the person to Williamsburg were required to return him to the magistrates who had conducted the examination; if necessary, the person returned was confined in the county jail. For taking the person from Prince Edward to Williamsburg and bringing him back again, Emanuel J. Leigh and John Chaffin were paid $40.[76]

People today should not think that the references to wickedness and immoral conduct by the church historians and in the church records noting disciplinary cases concerned trivial matters. Drunkenness for which men were cited before the church and for which they were sometimes expelled was not a social or an occasional drink. It was the state of intoxication which resulted from prolonged and continuing drinking. There were illegitimate births, which, if the mother were a member of the church, brought dismissal. In one such case in Prince Edward the infant died and the father and brothers of the mother buried the baby secretly. All four persons were excluded from the church, the mother for immorality, her father and brothers for their part in secretly burying the infant. Men, too, were excluded from church membership for immoral conduct, the immoral sometimes being qualified by grossly.[77] Fighting, too, was an object of church censure. Careful inquiry was made to determine who was blameworthy.[78]

One does not have to go to the church records to find cases of depravity. More was to be found outside the membership of the churches. At one point the moral code was so generally disregarded that one wonders if the conduct involved were regarded as coming under that code. The numerous references to mulattoes, whom a franker age than this was careful to distinguish, are evidence of the disregard of many white men and Negro or mulatto women for conventional moral standards. Such a condition cannot be dismissed by saying that the men were of a lower class or were not the leaders of the community. Men of standing and reputation were fathers of children by Negro or mulatto women.[79]

While the birth of mulatto children apparently aroused little concern, the responsibility of the natural father for the child born of an unmarried white woman was recognized. In 1858 the Prince Edward Court adjudged a man, upon the complaint of the woman, the father of an illegitimate male child and ordered him to pay to the overseers of the poor $15 per year for seven years "for the maintenance of said child"; he was put under a performance bond of $150.[80]

As exciting an experience as the Prince Edward Court experienced in the ante-bellum era grew out of a morals case. A Negro man, who belonged to Captain Thomas E. Davis, was charged with rape of a white married woman who lived near Prospect. He was brought to trial at the August term of Court in 1858, but the case was continued until September. In September because of the absence of one of the attorneys for the accused, the case was again continued. This was too much for the husband of the violated woman; when the decision to continue was announced, the dignity of the court, respect for the authority of the bench, the crowded courtroom were all, in his mind, subordinate to his determination to punish the prisoner. He leaped at the Negro with a drawn knife, evidently aiming to cut the prisoner's throat. He missed the throat, but slashed the cheek from ear to mouth. The accused started to run, but bleeding profusely, fell to the floor. For a few minutes there was pandemonium in the courtroom. As soon as order was restored, the wounded prisoner was taken to the courthouse yard where he received medical attention; he was then placed in jail under a strong guard. The attacker was arrested and placed under $1,000 bond. In October the case came up again and this time a decision was rendered; the accused was found guilty and was sentenced to transportation, a verdict "generally approved," according to a correspondent of the Richmond *Enquirer*. The value of the slave was fixed at $800.[81]

Then divorces were granted by the General Assembly of Virginia, and there remain several petitions from Prince Edward for divorce. A particularly sordid case involved the wife of a well-known resident who, six months after her marriage, bore a child admittedly begotten by her husband's brother. The petition for divorce implied that the woman's reputation prior to marriage was not good; and if either one of two dates of birth given for one of the sons of the woman and the man she married is approximately correct, he was born either two or four years before his parents were married. The petition for divorce implies that the woman lived in the house of the man she married for some time prior to marriage. There is no doubt, from contemporary records, that the father regarded the son as his child.

A Prince Edward woman asked for a divorce from her husband, because he had developed the habit of stealing and had married two other women, one in North Carolina, the other in Tennessee. Still another Prince Edward wife sought a divorce because her husband whipped her; the husband filed a counter petition that a divorce was contrary to his wish. He took the precaution of inquiring of competent legal counsel concerning his right to property which had been inherited by his wife. And there were other petitions which aired the marital difficulties of Prince Edward couples in the period between the Revolution and the War Between the States.[82]

The churches regarded the treatment of a wife as coming within the scope of their discipline; one case is on record that a church dismissed a man for grossly immoral conduct, which was described as denying to his wife "the necessary and common comforts of life, and contemptuous treatment" of his spouse.[83]

One of the complaints of the church historians of the post-Revolutionary period concerned the disregard for the Lord's Day. A growing concern was seen in the petitions for changing the day of holding court from Monday to a later day in the week, in order that lawyers and others who had business at court would not have to make preparation or to travel on Sunday. To the grand jury at the November, 1823, Court, William Randolph gave information that Thomas Read of Charlotte had permitted his ox cart and team, and Richard Simpson of Cumberland had permitted his ox cart, team and Negroes, "to labor in Jamestown" on Sunday, November 9.[84]

Concern for religious practices did not exclude concern for man; in fact, underneath all these social and moral concerns was an interest in man's spiritual welfare.

CHAPTER XII

The Flowering of a Civilization

THE economy of Prince Edward during the period between the Revolution and the War Between the States was characterized by progressiveness and vision. As soon as the unsettled conditions of the immediate post-Revolution period became more stable and the ratification of the Constitution gave promise of a sound Federal government, people gave increased attention to building personal fortunes and to promoting the prosperity of the community.

A group of Prince Edward men figured prominently in the organization of the Virginia Yazoo Company, which in 1789 received from the Georgia legislature a grant of 7,000,000 acres of land within these bounds: beginning at the mouth of Bear Creek on the south side of the Tennessee River and up said creek to its head, thence in a due west course to the Tombigbee River or Twenty Mile Creek and down same to the latitude of thirty-three degrees; along said latitude to the Mississippi River and up the Mississippi to the northern boundary of Georgia; along said boundary to the Tennessee River and thence to the beginning. For this vast tract, which covered what is now the northern part of the state of Mississippi, the company agreed to pay $93,741. The company actually paid a little over $1,500 in two payments and within the time limit offered to the Treasurer of Georgia the remainder of the purchase price due.[1] That official declined to accept payment, and Patrick Henry, David Ross, Abraham B. Venable, William Cowan, and Francis Watkins on behalf of themselves and the Virginia Yazoo Company prepared a petition to the Georgia legislature asking it to honor the contract, which they had complied with and regarded as binding upon both parties, by confirming the grant which had been made to the company.[2] Georgia did nothing, and suit was instituted by the company and the South Carolina Yazoo Company in the United States Supreme Court to compel compliance with the contract. Late in 1793, Congress passed an amendment to the Constitution to the effect that "the Judicial power of the United States shall not be construed to extend to any suit in law or equity, commenced or prosecuted against one of the United States, by citizens of another State, or by citizens or subjects of any foreign state." Thus the suits of the companies against Georgia were abated. The Virginia Yazoo Company made no attempt to settle the land it had sought to purchase and withdrew the payment it had made.[3]

That summary of the Virginia Yazoo Company does not tell the interest and concern which were felt in Prince Edward. Four entries in the diary of Richard N. Venable between August 3 and October 10, 1791—two years after the grant had been made and apparently just after the offer of final payment had been refused, mention discussion of the Yazoo business: August 3—to Francis Watkins'— consulted of the Yazoo business; September 10: Z. Cox came yesterday [to Prince Edward Courthouse] and talked most on Tennessee and Yazoo companies—a junction is proposed; in evening with John Watts, Cox, A. B. Venable at Francis Watkins' discussing the business, nothing resolved; September 11: forenoon, same business with Z. Cox to New London, nothing resolved; October 10: preparing papers at F. Watkins' for Yazoo company. A year later, on October 8, 1792, Venable noted that he and Abraham B. Venable met David Ross and his son, James N. Ross, at Francis Watkins' where "the subject of Yazoo prospects employed our attention."[4] No wonder so much time was spent in discussing the Yazoo Company's situation; it was a speculative venture, but one which promised to make fortunes for the stockholders. An extensive and attractive tract had been secured for a sum which, considering the size, was little more than nominal; the appeal of that part of the country to settlers promised sales at handsome profits. When Georgia declined to go through with the grant, the hopes of the stockholders in the Virginia Yazoo Company were blighted.

Francis Watkins, the Prince Edward clerk, was treasurer of the Virginia Yazoo Company; his account book for the period 1789-91 gives the names of a number of stockholders, with these from Prince Edward: Patrick Henry, John Watts, Francis Watkins, John B. Scott, who was also agent of the company; Abraham B. Venable, Robert Watkins, Martin Smith, Richard N. Venable, and Adam Calhoun. Among the stockholders from neighboring counties were William Cowan of Lunenburg, Willis Wilson of Cumberland, Joel Watkins and Paul Carrington of Charlotte. Stockholders present at a meeting of the company on July 25, 1795, were Francis Watkins, director, Patrick Henry, John Watts, Abraham B. Venable, William

Call (of Richmond), John B. Scott, and David Ross of Richmond, for himself and also as attorney in fact for Wade Hampton.[5]

It should be noted that the Virginia Yazoo Company was not involved in the case which created so much controversy and reached the United States Supreme Court. That case grew out of a subsequent grant by the Georgia legislature, in 1795, to four companies, of 35,000,000 acres for $500,000; when it was learned that every member of the Georgia legislature, except one, who voted for the grant had been bribed either by gift of money or stock in one of the companies, the matter became a scandal, and the grant was repudiated. The Supreme Court held that the annulment of the grant violated the obligations of a contract and was therefore void. The issue got into Congress after Georgia, in 1802, ceded its western lands to the Union, and John Randolph of Roanoke broke with Jefferson and Madison over the matter; Randolph led the opposition to a compromise which would permit the companies to make a profit and was able to prevent its adoption as long as he was in Congress.[6]

A project nearer home and one of great importance to the entire county was the navigation of the Appomattox. The river had been used from the earliest settlement as an avenue of transportation, but the need of improving the channel and of keeping it clear for navigation was recognized as necessary if the river was to be used regularly.

In 1787 the General Assembly named seven trustees "to clear, improve, and extend navigation of the Appomattox River from Banister's Mill as far up the river as they judge practicable, and have sufficient depth and width of water to navigate boats, batteaus or canoes, capable of carrying six hogsheads of tobacco." The work was to be financed by subscriptions, which the trustees were authorized to receive; tolls were to be charged, not in excess of those charged on the Potomac, to provide the expenses of maintenance and to yield a dividend on the subscriptions. John Holcombe was the only trustee from Prince Edward (the others were John Pride, Joseph Michaux, John Archer, Joseph Jones, Everard Meade, and Richard Crump). They and their successors were incorporated as the Appomattox trustees.[7]

Work under these trustees did not proceed satisfactorily; in 1790 the legislature, noting that "the dispersed situation of the trustees . . . has greatly retarded and impeded navigation . . ." named John Morton, John Archer, and Edward Munford trustees to put into effect the act of 1787.[8] The next year Morton entered into and acknowledged bond to receive subscriptions for opening the Appomattox River.[9] Five trustees, none from Prince Edward, were added in 1792 in an act clarifying the authority of the trustees.[10]

There was criticism of this plan, for all the changes and clarification. A petition from Prince Edward, presented to the Assembly in 1795, called it inadequate and proposed that the plans adopted for the James and Potomac Rivers be enacted for the Appomattox because it would be the "most cheap, expeditious and effectual" arrangement. Signers of the petition were Phil. Holcombe, Jr., C. Scott, James Daniel, Brett Randolph, Jr., George Booker, Andrew Johnston, Josiah Perkinson, Nathaniel Price, Richard N. Venable, John Cunningham, Xr (Christopher) Dejarnatt, George Redd, Charles F. Nash, George Moore, Paul M. Cunningham, James Franklin, Miles Fergusson, Laban Hawkins, John Tabb, Jacob Cunningham, William Brooks, William Bailey, Marten Saylor, Hezekiah Morton, Thomas Walthall, Charles Jones, and David Sims.[11]

The petition bore fruit in the incorporation of the Upper Appomattox Company with the same responsibilities as were given the Appomattox trustees in 1787, except that the river was to be made navigable for boats with a capacity of eight, instead of six, hogsheads of tobacco. The trustees of the company were Everard Meade, Joseph Eggleston, William Murray, Francis Anderson, John Wiley, Peter Johnson [sic], Charles Allen, Ryland Randolph, Edmund Harrison, Alexander M'Rae, Drury Jones, John Johns, James Morton, Charles Scott, Richard N. Venable, John Epperson, Nelson Patterson, John Archer, John Royal[1], John Finney, Edward Munford, Peter F. Archer, Francis Eppes, Henry Skipwith, Buller Claiborne, Joshua Chaffin, John Nash, Jr., Samuel Carter, James Wade, John L. Crute, Roger Atkinson, Jr., James Watt, George Markham, John Purnall, and Samuel Allen. Of these trustees, Johnston, Charles Allen, Randolph, Morton, Scott, Venable, Nash, Carter, Wade, Crute, and Purnall were from Prince Edward. The trustees could appoint five superintendents to take charge of the work of clearing the river and a treasurer, whose bond was fixed at $50,000. The trustees had to live within twenty miles of the river; their term was two years. Stock in the company was sold at $100 per share; the limit could be fixed by the trustees at the amount necessary "to carry out the purposes of this act."

Tolls were fixed for produce and goods carried on the river: a pipe or hogshead of wine over sixty-five gallons—63 cents; hogshead of rum or other spirits, 50 cents; hogshead of tobacco, 42 cents; casks between thirty-five and sixty-five gallons, one-half the rate for pipe or hogshead; barrels at one-fourth the rate; smaller casks according to the quality and quantity of content of wine or spirits; bushel of wheat, peas, beans, or flaxseed, two cents; bushel of Indian corn, other grain, or salt, one cent; barrel of pork, twenty-one cents; barrel of beef, fifteen cents; barrel of flour, ten cents; ton of hemp, flax, potash, or manufactured iron, $1.05; ton of pig iron or castings, thirty-five cents; ton of copper, lead, or other ore except iron ore, eighty-three cents; ton of stone or iron ore, seventeen cents; hundred bushels of lime, fifty-three cents; cauldron of coals, seventeen cents; hundred pipe staves, eight cents hundred hogshead staves or pipe or hogshead heading, five cents; hundred barrel staves or barrel heading, four cents; one hundred cubic feet of plank or scantling, thirty-five cents; one hundred cubic feet of other timber, twenty cents; every hundredweight of all other commodities or packages, five cents. The profits from the tolls were to be used to clear and keep in repair canals, locks, and other works to aid navigation and to pay dividends to the stockholders, when there was an "overplus."

Owners of milldams were given eighteen months to build locks through the dams or canals around them. They were required to provide constant attendance for the locks.[12]

The number of trustees was reduced to thirteen in 1797.[13]

In 1796 the noted engineer Benjamin Latrobe made an inspection of the Appomattox, apparently as a consulting engineer for the Upper Appomattox Company. Among those who accompanied him was Richard N. Venable.[14]

The work was proving more costly than anticipated. For example, the superintendents and the work crew found a stretch of one and one-half miles of rocks which proved quite expensive to clear. The money gave out when the work was within three miles of Petersburg, a distance of 130-140 miles "as the stream meanders." Since a considerable portion of the capital had been invested in slaves to do the work, it was deemed inadvisable to sell them until the work had been completed. Accordingly in 1801 the superintendents of the company, Joseph Eggleston, Edward Munford, Abraham Venable, and Edmund Harrison, petitioned the legislature to authorize the state treasurer to buy up to twenty-five shares of stock to provide the necessary funds to complete the project.[15] The petition was granted with a proviso: the treasurer could subscribe twenty-five shares whenever the trustees received subscriptions for 100 new shares. The state had already subscribed for some shares in the company.[16] It was then the practice for the state to aid projects in internal improvements by subscribing to stock in the company chartered to make and to maintain the improvement.

The work made it possible for boats carrying 250-300 bushels of wheat to use the river except in dry seasons.[17]

In a letter to the Governor, Joseph Jones wrote in November, 1801, that he had been to see the canal a few days before and that it had been built about three-fourths of a mile below Atkinson's mill, some four miles "from where they intend the basin to be in the Corporation of Petersburg."[18]

At this time Joseph Eggleston was president of the Upper Appomattox Company, and Thomas Munford was clerk.[19]

For the company's fiscal year September 1, 1802 to August 31, 1803, boats on the Appomattox carried 13,029 barrels of flour, 10,301 bushels of wheat, 220 hogsheads of tobacco, and seventy bushels of Indian corn on which tolls amounting to $1,601.32 were paid.[20]

Stockholders held meetings from time to time. One such meeting was held December 12, 1798, at Chinquapin Church in Amelia County. Three resolutions contain the principal business: a fifth requisition on stock subscriptions was set at $20 per share, to be paid by March 1, 1799; the treasurer was directed to enforce indiscriminately the collection of all arrears on stock subscriptions; and the superintendents were authorized to remove all dams which did not have safe locks or slopes for the passage of boats after June 1, 1799. The notice of the resolutions was signed by Edmund Harrison, Edward Munford, Richard N. Venable, Francis Eppes, John Archer, John Royall, and John Wily and attested by Thomas Pride, clerk.[21] It was then general practice for subscribers to pay for the stock to which they subscribed in installments, as called for by the company.

Stockholders' meetings were held in different places: at James Townes' October 2, 1800;[22] at Prideville September 14, 1804, notice of which was signed by Richard N. Venable, Joseph Eggleston, and Edward Munford;[23] at Prideville June 14, 1805, for the election of trustees; at that meeting payment of $25 per share on the new stock subscription was called for;[24] again at Prideville June 7, 1806, where the fourth requisition was made for payment on the stock;[25] at Paineville May 9, 1807;[26] at Amelia Courthouse August 22, 1816, notice of which was given by Thomas A. Morton, Edward Munford, Richard N. Venable, and John Grammer;[27] at Amelia Courthouse November 21, 1821, notice being given by Morton, Venable, Grammer, and William S. Archer;[28] at the Eagle Hotel, Farmville, August 11, 1857, the notice being signed by S. D. Morton, clerk.[29]

There was a fall of water of over 100 feet from the canal at Petersburg, divided into falls of twelve, fourteen, and twenty feet; to encourage manufacturing the company offered mill sites along this stretch of the canal where water power was available. As managers of the company, Edward Dillon, John Grammer, Edward Munford, Richard N. Venable, and Thomas A. Morton met in Petersburg April 2-3, 1813, to sell these lots. At that time the clerk of the company was Daniel E. Allen of Petersburg. That three Prince Edward men should be among the five managers shows the interest of the county in Appomattox navigation.[30]

The state of Virginia in 1820 subscribed an additional $15,000 in stock of the Upper Appomattox Company to enable it to complete some work in improving navigation. For a second time an extension in time was granted the company to pay back to the Commonwealth money borrowed to carry on its work; the first was a five-year extension in 1814; the second, granted in 1820, was for three years. A third extension, this time for four years, was granted in 1822.[31] In 1827 the superintendents of the company, Thomas A. Morton, Richard N. Venable, James Madison, and Nathaniel J. Venable, asked for an extension of time to repay $4,500 which had been borrowed from the state; the company had planned to pay the money, but the destruction of the aqueduct over Old Town Creek made necessary the outlay of funds to replace it.[32]

It seemed almost impossible to get the Appomattox River in proper navigable condition. At a public meeting in Farmville on January 23, 1835, the "present state of navigation" was regarded "precarious, uncertain, and inadequate"; following the report of the State Engineer's estimate of the cost of improving navigation at $74,718.70 from Petersburg to Farmville and at $10,276.20 from Farmville to Planterstown, a resolution was passed asking that the capital stock of $85,000 be authorized.[33] The legislature did more than the petition asked; it authorized a capital stock increase of $100,000, to provide at all times a depth of two feet of water from Farmville to Petersburg and of eighteen inches from Farmville to Planterstown. Such depths would be maintained by the construction of locks in lateral canals below Farmville and by wing dams and gates above.[34] In 1839 an increase in capital of an additional $20,000 was authorized.[35] The superintendents of the company in 1835 were all Prince Edward men: Richard N. Venable, James Madison,

Nathaniel E. Venable, Thomas A. Morton, Samuel W. Venable, Jr., W. L. Venable, and James D. Wood; they petitioned for authority to construct a tow path along the river to Petersburg.[36]

The project to make the river navigable to Planterstown, a Buckingham town, would extend the navigation some distance upstream above Farmville; that town, however, remained the head of navigation on the Appomattox; some forty batteaux of from five to seven tons' capacity were engaged in the river transportation.[37] In 1840 Smith, Blanton and Company entered into an agreement with Brightwell and Company under which the latter employed two boat hands named Billy Patterson and Stephen hired by the former from Robert Gillaspie at the wages and consideration in clothing the former had engaged them for and bought from the Smith, Blanton firm the new boat it had bought from C. Crenshaw at the price Smith, Blanton had promised to pay for it. Brightwell agreed to do all the boating of Smith, Blanton, agreeing to give the refusal of one boat on both the downstream and upstream trips to Smith, Blanton, who in turn agreed to give Brightwell the refusal of all their freight at the prices agreed to.[38]

During this period the company was prospering; a dividend of $10 per share on the old stock was declared in 1847.[39]

Merchants were proud to own a boat which would carry eight to ten hogsheads of tobacco from the towns on the upper Appomattox to the basin at Petersburg. The wharf at Farmville was behind the Randolph tobacco warehouse; hogsheads of tobacco were rolled downhill to the wharf, and sometimes one got away from the men and rolled into the river.

Boats were manned by a captain and two deck hands; the captain would guide the helm; the deck hands would propel the boat by putting a pole on the river bottom and shoving it as they walked up and down a plank on each side of the boat. Many of the boatmen were the free Negroes who lived on Israel Hill, four of whom were mentioned in a description of Appomattox navigation by one who remembered it; they were Phil John, Curtis White, Alfred Booker, and Billy Ballou, all of whom were described as much respected and trusted.[40] Free Negroes and mulattoes who operated boats were required to carry a certificate from some respectable white man certifying the truth of the manifest of their cargo and the right of the free Negro or mulatto to the property.[41]

An example of the vicissitudes of river traffic is related in the experience of a man who shipped a cargo of tobacco from Farmville to Petersburg during the unusually dry summer of 1849; the boat was stranded on shoals about midway its trip where no mails could reach it; it remained on that sand bar a month. Finally, after a heavy rain, the boat was lifted off the bar and came safely to Petersburg. The owner was compensated for his anxiety, for he had heard nothing of his boat or cargo during the interval; the drought so reduced the crop that the price of tobacco increased by fifty per cent by the time the tobacco reached market.[42]

The plan of navigation included a scheme to link the Appomattox and the Staunton Rivers. In 1806 the legislature authorized a survey of a route for a navigable canal from the head of Buffalo River to the head of Little Roanoke River in Charlotte; Creed Taylor, Isaac H. Coles, Joseph Wyatt, Richard K. Randolph, Samuel Carter, Charles Scott, and William B. Banks were named commissioners to select a route and make a report to the next Assembly.[43] At the next session the time for making the report was extended;[44] this seems to have ended the matter for the time being. Six years later a petition was presented the legislature asking that Buffalo be cleared for navigation from the Appomattox to Samuel Carter's mill and that that section of the stream be made a public highway. The petition was signed by Moses Tredway and many others, including James Madison, Peyton Randolph, Alexander Marshall, Larkin Anderson, Drury Lacy, Jesse Michaux, Richard N. Venable, and Samuel Carter; it was unusual since it also bore the signatures of two women, Judith Randolph and Elizabeth Price.[45] An act of Assembly provided that the stream be declared a public highway as soon as it was pronounced navigable by two commissioners appointed by the Prince Edward Court.[46]

In response to petitions from Charlotte and Prince Edward, the General Assembly in 1825 chartered the Junction Canal Company which was authorized to improve the navigation of Buffalo and Little Roanoke Rivers, to construct canals, and to open, improve, and keep in repair a road from the upper navigation of one to the upper navigation of the other for a short portage. A capital stock of $30,000 was authorized. Trustees named for the company were Thomas A. Morton, James Madison, Nathaniel E. Venable, Samuel Carter (all from Prince Edward), Clement Carrington, Sr., John Morton, Henry A. Watkins, Nicholas Edmunds, John Marshall, John Clarke of Halifax, John Sims, James Bruce, John Wimbish, Edward Carrington, and John Randolph.[47]

While the building of the Southside Railroad ended navigation of the Appomattox around Farmville, it continued downstream; the Upper Appomattox Company was in existence and operating from Clementown Mills to Petersburg in 1882, when it was authorized to enlarge its canal and locks to a channel forty feet wide and five feet deep. In the same year the company was allowed to pay the state for its stock in the company in bonds of the Commonwealth. For five years immediately following the War Between the States the company paid a dividend, but in 1882 had paid none since that five-year period. Yet the only concession it asked of the state was release from payment of interest for two years following the panic of 1873--74.[48]

The last boat to bring a cargo to Farmville came up the river from Amelia County in 1878. George M. Robeson and L. M. Blanton moved their foundry equipment by flatboat to Farmville, where they established the business which has now become the Farmville Manufacturing Company. There was one dam across the river between their starting point and their destination; the flatboat was lifted by a company of men over the dam at Stony Point Mills.[49]

River transportation provided a stimulus to the establishment of towns in Prince Edward. The first town chartered in Prince Edward was not on the river, however. Alexander LeGrand in 1795 petitioned the General Assembly to establish a town on a tract which he owned near Hampden-Sydney College in "a healthy and pleasant part," which he thought "would be a proper place for an inland town."[50] The legislature granted his request; it authorized the trustees (John Purnall, James Morton, James Allen, Josiah LeGrand, Baker LeGrand, Charles Allen, Sr., and Ryland Randolph) to lay off twenty-five acres in half-acre lots with convenient streets; the lots were to be sold at auction, and the purchaser was required to erect a dwelling at least sixteen feet square, with brick or stone chimney, within five years after purchase or forfeit his lot. To this town was given the name Germantown.[51] The name survives in a road leading to its site.

Not only were the owners of land at advantageous sites for towns along the Appomattox interested in the development of towns; the people generally wanted towns established from which they could ship their produce to market and to which goods could be shipped conveniently from the outside world. A petition was presented to the General Assembly November 29, 1796, asking that a town be established on the land of John Townes at Buffalow [*sic*] Falls on the Appomattox in Prince Edward; it was signed by many people, among those from Prince Edward being Robert Goode, Christopher Walthall, William Worsham, Richard Marshall, Waddill Armes, Anderson Wade, Richard Waddill, Reps Osborne Childress, Edward Redford, Richard Phillips, Robert Foster, William McGehee, Walthall Marshall, Richard Bradshaw, John Cunningham, William Wooton, Paul M. Cunningham, and Sterling Smith. The petition was reported as reasonable,[52] and on December 14, 1796, the establishment of the town was authorized; Abner Watkins, Robert Goode, George Eggleston, Josiah Perkinson, Christopher Walthall, William Worsham, Richard Pincham, Thomas Gibson, and John L. Crute were named trustees. In the usual terms, the trustees were authorized to lay off twenty-five acres of John Townes' land in half-acre lots with convenient streets. This town was to be called Jamestown.[53]

A little over a year later, on January 15, 1798, the legislature established another town on the Appomattox in Prince Edward; this was Farmville, and the trustees, Charles Scott, Peter Johnson [*sic*], John Randolph, Jr., Philip [*sic*] Holcombe, Jr., Martin Smith, Blake B. Woodson, and Creed Taylor, were authorized to lay off fifty acres of the land of Judith Randolph into half-acre lots with convenient streets.[54]

Of the two river towns Farmville enjoyed a more vigorous growth than Jamestown; the latter had its warehouse, its stores, its girls' school, its taverns, its church; but there is no record that it ever expanded beyond its original twenty-five acres. Farmville was chartered as a town in 1833; under the charter, the seven trustees were elected by the freeholders;[55] David Bruce and fifty-seven others petitioned the legislature to grant a charter to the town.[56] The act which granted the charter also enlarged the town by taking into its limits six to eight acres of the estate of the late Abraham B. Venable.[57] Two years later the trustees (then James Madison, president of the board, Frederick Hobson, James Dupuy, Clement C. Read, James B. Ely, Thomas Hickson, and David Bruce) petitioned that twenty-five acres of the estate of Judith Randolph and forty acres of Josiah Chambers' land be added to the town. Madison, as trustee of Chamber's, certified that he believed it would be to Chambers' interest for his land to be sold as town lots; and Hobson, as trustee for the sole heir of Judith Randolph (her son, John St. George Randolph), expressed a similar opinion.[58] In 1836 the legislature approved this request and, following Hobson's suggestion, named special commissioners to sell the property since both Chambers and Randolph were persons of unsound mind; James Madison, Thomas A. Morton,

Nathaniel E. Venable, James D. Wood, Henry E. Watkins, William
S. Morton, Samuel Lyle, and William Wilson were named commissioners for Randolph; and Tazewell S. Morton, James M. Jackson,
A. Z. Venable, George Daniel, Charles Thackston, George R. Mottley, Edmund Wiltse, and John Rice, commissioners for Chambers.[59]
It was later discovered that title to the Randolph land was not vested
in the heir, but in Henry St. George Tucker, surviving executor of
Judith Randolph. In 1846 Tucker was authorized to give deeds to
purchasers of lots in that addition.[60] The Farmville trustees in 1839
were authorized to apply to the Prince Edward Court for a writ of
ad quod damnum to fix any damages which might remain unsettled
for owners of land over which the trustees conducted water for the
municipal supply. They were also authorized to erect a prison, to
appoint and regulate weighmasters of tobacco, to lay out a public
square and erect public buildings, to manage and control all springs
of water in the town, and to lay off a lot for a public cemetery.[61]

In 1845 Farmville was the fourth tobacco market in Virginia
with two warehouses; it also had ten tobacco factories, seven or eight
stores, a branch of the Farmer's Bank of Virginia, a newspaper
printing office, and one Presbyterian, one Methodist, and one Baptist
church.[62] A fire on January 28, 1858, did much damage in Farmville, destroying several buildings and a quantity of timber ready for
use. It was started when an "old hostler" went to a stable loft for
provender, carrying a candle which set fire to the straw. The timber
loss was sustained by the builder of the "new tavern," and the
people got up a "proposition" the next morning "to reinstate him,"
which received a gratifying response from the citizens.[63]

Martin's *Gazetteer* of 1835 listed Prince Edward Courthouse,
Farmville, Jamestown, and Sandy River Church as the larger places
of Prince Edward; smaller places were Burkesville, Carter's Store,
Hermitage (in what became Appomattox), Marble Hill, Merriman's
Shop (the present Pamplin), Moore's Ordinary, Prospect, and
Walkers Church. Kingsville and Londonderry (not far west of the
present Five Forks) should be added to the list.[64] Clover Hill, which
became the county seat of Appomattox County, was established as a
town by the act which created the new county.[65]

An inspection of tobacco was established at both Jamestown and
Farmville before the towns were authorized to be established; an
inspection was established at Townes' Warehouse, which was to be
built by the proprietor, John Townes, by an act passed December 8,
1796; an inspection was authorized at a warehouse which Judith

Randolph was to build on her land near Rutledge's Bridge in Prince Edward by an act passed January 8, 1798. The inspectors' salaries were fixed at $100 per year.[66] John L. Crute, Josiah Perkinson, William Worsham, and John Armes were recommended for appointment as inspectors of tobacco at Townes' Warehouse in 1797, and John Walthall and Daniel Ellington were appointed pickers of tobacco there.[67] In 1798 Crute, Armes, and John Childress qualified as inspectors of tobacco at Jamestown.[68] Charles Allen, Sr., Charles Allen, Jr., Francis Smith, and Abner Watson were recommended as inspectors at Randolph's Warehouse in 1799.[69] In 1800 Archer Allen and Charles Allen were named commissioners to superintend Randolph's Warehouse, and John L. Crute and Josiah Perkinson Townes' Warehouse.[70] John Purnall was appointed to secure scales and weights for Townes' Warehouse in 1798,[71] and Archer Allen was directed to examine the scales and weights of the tobacco inspection in Farmville in 1800.[72]

The inspectors at Farmville, on delivering their notes or an order in cases in which they did not issue notes, delivered the tobacco for transportation by wagon or batteau or canoe to Manchester or Petersburg. They were required to give a manifest for the tobacco showing the owner's name, the name of the skipper of the batteau or the driver of the wagon, with the marks, number, and weight of tobacco, and the name of the warehouse. Inspectors in Manchester or Petersburg were required to accept the tobacco according to the manifest; if upon examination it was found damaged or "embezzled," it was to be held, pending directions of the owner.[73]

About 1814 inspection was discontinued at both Jamestown and Farmville.[74] A petition, signed by William Routon, Thomas Berry, Osborne Lockett, William White, Edmund Booker, and others, asking that the inspection at Jamestown be revived, was presented to the legislature December 3, 1817, and was reported as reasonable. It noted that James Jackson, the proprietor of the warehouses there, was willing to repair them, and that the weights and scales had been kept in good order during the three years since the inspection had ceased.[75] The Farmville inspection was revived by a legislative act in 1817.[76] The inspectors resumed their work in March, 1818. During the following summer over 500 hogsheads of tobacco were inspected there, and Nathaniel Venable, Sr., Edward Redford, Richard Paulett and others petitioned that salaries of the inspectors be increased.[77] The salaries were raised to $250 per year, provided the inspection fees were sufficient to provide it.[78] By act of February 20,

1818, the legislature established an inspection of tobacco at the Farmville warehouse on the lands of William L. Venable, Edward Redford, Nathaniel E. Venable, and Thomas A. Morton. The inspector's salary was first set at $100 per year,[79] but it was raised to $250 in 1821.[80] Randolph's Warehouse was enlarged in 1820 by the construction of an additional building with a capacity of 100 hogsheads.[81]

The tobacco produced in Prince Edward (and throughout Virginia and North Carolina prior to the discovery of flue curing in 1839) was the dark-fired type. The curing process continued into the fall, and during the winter the leaves were stripped from the stalk and tied into bundles. These were packed into hogsheads on the farm, and the tobacco was prized. Each farm had its prize barn—the name has continued to designate certain barns to the present; in this barn was an upright post, to which was attached one end of a long pole; the other end of the pole was weighted with heavy weights; under the pole was a bar which rested on the top of hogshead. The top was placed on the hogshead when it was filled with tobacco; when the pole was weighted, the bar pushed the top of the hogshead down, packing the tobacco much tighter than it could be packed by hand; then the hogshead was refilled, the packing or prizing process repeated, and in this way the hogshead was filled until no more tobacco could be gotten into it. In later years a wooden screw was used to prize the tobacco. The tobacco was kept on the farm until spring or summer, when it was taken to market.[82]

Not all Prince Edward tobacco was sold in the Farmville and Jamestown warehouses. Much was taken directly to warehouses in Richmond, Manchester, and Petersburg; this tobacco was usually taken by wagon. The main road from Prince Edward to Richmond was known as the Genito road, from its crossing over the Appomattox at Genito mill; this road turned north from the main Farmville-Petersburg road (the present highway 460) at Flippen's Fork, a short distance from the Nottoway line; it continued north through Nottoway and Amelia, via New London, Deatonville, and Paineville.[83]

In 1819 John R. Cook and Company, James D. Wood, Edward Redford, and Venable and Company were tobacco dealers in Farmville. That year 1,090 hogsheads of tobacco, or over 1,000,000 pounds on the basis of the minimum of 950 pounds to the hogshead, were inspected in Farmville.[84] James Madison and James D. Wood were licensed as stemmers and manufacturers of tobacco at Farmville in 1823.[85] Patrick H. Jackson began the manufacture of tobacco after moving to Farmville in 1827. Richard S. Paulett entered the tobacco manufacturing industry in Farmville in 1844.[86] Joseph E. Venable and Company was another tobacco manufacturing firm in Farmville in this period; it did not manufacture tobacco during 1849 and may have closed its business then, as it stopped renting from James Blanton the building it had occupied at the beginning of that year.[87] About 1856 Farmville had a number of manufacturers of tobacco: Patrick H. Jackson, James M. Jackson and George W. Daniel; Merritt Steger; James W. Dunnington and Alexander Bruce; Clement C. Read; and Williamson and Venable.[88] The tobacco manufactory of Peters and Blanton in Farmville burned March 23, 1861.[89]

In the 1830's the French market for Prince Edward and Charlotte tobacco was "most gratifying."[90] In 1848 France ordered 2,300 hogsheads of Virginia tobacco, which was 800 less than was ordered for the year 1847. In the spring of 1848 lugs were bringing $2 to $3.25 per hundred and leaf $4 to $6.50.[91] Between October 1, 1831, and August 31, 1832, inspectors in Farmville passed 2,500 hogsheads and refused 1,569.[92] For the year ending September 30, 1848, 2,464 hogsheads were inspected in Farmville, and during the next year the number rose to 3,163.[93] Between 1853 and 1854, Farmville was the only Virginia market which did not show a decline in the number of hogsheads of tobacco inspected; the number there increased from 1,024 to 1,154. A drop in the number inspected at Richmond, Petersburg, Lynchburg, Clarksville, and Tye River accounted for the decline in the state of 3,444 hogsheads that year.[94] Thomas B. Rice, Edwin N. Price, James J. Rice, and Francis Anderson were inspectors at Randolph's Warehouse in 1853, and Joseph G. Williams, John W. Ritchie, and Granville F. Deshazor were inspectors at Farmville Warehouse.[95]

Throughout this period grist mills continued an important part of the Prince Edward economy. Wheat was a principal product of Prince Edward, and flour made from it and shipped out provided an important source of income. The thrifty farmer, too, undertook to provide enough flour from his own wheat to give bread to his family and his slaves throughout the year.

The Revolution did not stop the interest in building mills. Numerous applications were filed for appraisal of damages.[96] Permits were issued in 1778 to John Watson to erect a mill on Falling Creek on the site of Randolph's old mill and to John Mason to build on Mountain Creek after paying Rice Scott £12 damages.[97] Both Joseph

Moore and Thomas Redd advertised mills for sale in 1778; Redd's mill was on the Appomattox River or a tributary stream near the river; it was equipped with a large pair of Cologne stones and bolting cloths.[98] Elizabeth Venable received permission to build a mill on Harris Creek in 1780, and Daniel Clarke on the same creek in 1781.[99]

Inspectors of flour were appointed by the Court in 1781 for six Prince Edward mills: Philemon Holcombe, inspector at Nash's mill; Thomas Scott at Martin's mill; Joel Jackson at Watts' mill; William Penix at Randolph's mill; Nicholas Davis at Watson's mill; William Price at Bibb's mill; Archibald Tanner was subsequently named for Martin's mill.[100]

Upon the death of Jacob McGehee in 1783, ownership of his mill passed to his sons, William and Jacob.[101] Permits were issued to Jerusha Price, Tyree's branch, 1783;[102] John H. Overstreet on Little Buffalo and Richard Burks on Mill Creek, 1787;[103] John Dupuy on Buffalo, 1788;[104] John Cunningham on Spring Creek and John Clarke on Mill Creek, 1789;[105] Caleb Baker, Spring Creek, and Matthew Jackson, Bush River, 1791;[106] Joseph Mettauer, Shelton's Branch, Dudley Barksdale on Rocky Branch, John Booker on Bush River, and John Clarke, Jr., of the north fork of Sandy River, 1792;[107] James Allen, Jr., Hamlett's Branch, 1793;[108] John Phillips, Little Sailor's Creek; John Epperson and Ichabod Hunter, Appomattox River near the Cutbanks road, and Alexander LeGrand, 1795;[109] Thomas Gibson, on a branch on his land; James Dodson, on Shop Spring Branch; William Fore, on the Appomattox; Benjamin and Charles Allen, near Allen's Ford on the Appomattox; and Josiah Fowlkes, on William McGehee's mill creek; 1796;[110] Alexander Marshall and William Baldwin, on Big Nottoway River, 1797.[111]

Allen's mill posed a problem for John Randolph: he thought an "intolerable inconvenience" would "result from the plantation being made a perfect highway both across the river and to Allen's mill . . . Not a day or night but four or five strangers go through and as often the gates are left open." He had no objections to friends and acquaintances using the plantation road.[112]

Brett Randolph, Jr., and Ryland Randolph offered for sale in 1793 a mill on the Appomattox; it was fifty-four feet by twenty in size, with three floors, and had been built for a manufacturing mill, but had been used only as a toll mill and at the time was out of repair.[113]

S. W. Venable and Womack advertised for a miller to "attend" a manufacturing mill in 1806.[114]

John Ford's map of the county made in 1820 locates thirty-two mills and one burned mill, Fore's on Vaughan's Creek. The mills named were Lockett's and Ford's on Little Sailor Creek; Waddill's on Great Sailor Creek; Perkinson's, below the fork of Sailor Creek; Lockett's on Marrowbone Creek; Fowlkes on Leuse (Louse) Creek; Perkinson's, Scott's, and Ligon's on Sandy River; Haskins' on Mountain Creek; Marshall's on Camp Creek; Watkins' on Evans Creek; Fouk's [sic] on the north fork of Nottoway River; Purnall's on Bush River; Allen's on Briery River; Bell's on Mingo Creek; Wood's on Little Buffalo; Carter's on Buffalo; Dupuy's on a tributary of Buffalo; Tredway's, Womack's, and Cunningham's on Spring Creek; R. Venable's on Falling Creek; Glenn's on Harris' Creek; Jones,, Watt's, and Matthews' on Vaughan's Creek; Wright's on Plain Run; Union, Venable's, Morriss', and Trent's on the Appomattox.[115]

River navigation placed obstacles in the way of building mills. Those which already had dams across streams selected to be improved for navigation were required to build locks in the dams or canals around them. When a stream was declared a public highway by the legislature, the county court could not give permission for the construction of a dam across it.

When Thomas A. Morton wanted to build a mill in Farmville on the Appomattox, he had to petition the legislature for permission, which he did in 1836. Richard N. Venable appended a statement to the petition that he had no objection to building a dam for the mill if it did not interfere with navigation.[116] The legislature passed a law permitting Morton to apply to Cumberland Court for a writ of *ad quod damnum* (the legal phrase used for condemnation of property for mill purposes) to condemn up to one acre of the land of St. George Randolph opposite Morton's land on the Prince Edward side of the river. The Upper Appomattox Company was given the right to keep locks in Morton's milldam; if water was insufficient for both mill and company, the company had prior right to the water.[117]

The next year Robert, Joseph E., and Nathaniel J. Venable were given permission to build a milldam across the Appomattox near Venable's Ford on their property provided it was approved by the Buckingham Court; they were required to build locks in the dam or in the lateral canal around the dam to accommodate the passage of boats using the river above Farmville. The Upper Appomattox Company was given priority in the use of the water.[118]

In addition to manufacturing flour and meal, the mills also made feed for livestock. This was called shipstuff. In 1824 Josiah Perkinson ground 2,222 pounds of shipstuff for Edmund Booker, which he traded to David Blanton for twenty-eight gallons of whiskey, at the rate of five quarts of whiskey to 100 pounds of shipstuff.[119]

The earliest sawmills in the county to which reference has been found were those of Thomas S. Davis (1821) and James Wilson (1822).[120] James Cobbs of Darlington Heights advertised for sale in 1853, along with 400 acres of land in the lower end of Prince Edward on the Richmond and Danville Railway, a steam sawmill in operation on that property.[121] Watkins' sawmill at or near Meherrin burned "entirely up and also burnt everything appertaining to the mill" in late October, 1859. Watkins indicated his intention to rebuild as soon as possible on the same site. The fire was thought the work of an incendiary.[122]

Toward the close of the eighteenth century, Major James Morton became interested in finding coal in Prince Edward and made many attempts to locate veins; he was encouraged by finding many small veins and one vein about four feet thick and twenty feet deep. About 1833 John J. Flournoy found coal on his farm on Briery River about four miles south of the Courthouse. This coal was described by W. S. Morton in 1833 as being too small a development to estimate future prospects. He reported that a mass of black matter resembling dead coal had been found when he visited the project, but that Flournoy had found in digging deeper that good coal was constantly gaining in volume on the dead coal.[123] Three years later Dr. Morton was more enthusiastic; he felt that the area had "coal fields of incalculable value." On an expedition with several gentlemen he found several veins of dead coal on the Bizarre lands, with many lumps of good coal in them.[124]

Flournoy in 1837 applied to the legislature to charter a company to mine the coal on his property and transport it. He and his associates were incorporated as the Prince Edward Coal Company, with a capital from $5,000 to $50,000.[125]

Approximately a half-century after Flournoy's efforts to make coal-mining on his property a profitable venture, coal was mined on a limited scale at Slate Hill, between the Flournoy property and the Courthouse. Dr. J. D. Eggleston, Sr., and R. M. Dickinson leased the coal deposits on Slate Hill from Major Richard M. Venable of Baltimore, who then owned it. They provided coal to heat their own homes for one winter, hauling it from the Slate Hill pits in wagons.[126]

At the time of Flournoy's interest in coal, gold was being found and mined in Buckingham. In 1837 Thomas A. Morton, Charles Morton, and their associates were incorporated as the Farmville Mining Company to mine gold and other minerals in Buckingham.[127]

Howe reported that marl, coal, and copper ore had been found in Prince Edward.[128]

Local interest in minerals was so great that on July 23, 1836, the Mineralogical Society of Virginia was organized at Prince Edward Courthouse. Dr. W. B. Smith was chairman of the organization meeting, and Dr. B. F. Wilson secretary. The object of the meeting was to consider measures to develop a knowledge of the mineral wealth of Virginia. It urged every citizen to be his own geologist, to collect the minerals of his neighborhood, to have them analyzed, and to give their description and location. The meeting deplored the failure of every public institution in the country to teach analytical chemistry as a branch of learning. Those present waxed more enthusiastic and determined to cope with the problem; they decided to establish a school for the chemical analysis, assaying, and determination of the value of metals and minerals. The school would be at the graduate level, open to graduates of "respectable colleges"; those who lacked that standing could acquire the needed preliminary knowledge at Hampden-Sydney.

The meeting then organized the Mineralogical Society of Virginia, with Richard N. Venable as its president, Dr. W. B. Smith vice-president, and Dr. W. S. Morton secretary. It engaged John W. Draper, M.D., as its chemist and mineralogist, "an appointment drawing advantage from his knowledge of the geology and mining operation of South America." Draper had the endorsement of Dr. B. Turner, F.R.S., professor of chemistry in the University of London, under whom he had studied. Dr. Draper was directed to proceed with the organization of the school. The society was recommended, both in its object and its determination, to the people by D. L. Carroll, George H. Matthews, William A. Hughes, Thomas S. Flournoy, Charles Smith, F. N. Watkins, William I. B. Bedford, Samuel R. Simpson, Noble Snell, Samuel C. Anderson, James Madison, Samuel Branch, George A. Baxter, Stephen Taylor, W. Berkeley, and Henry N. Watkins.[129]

Draper was professor of chemistry and natural philosophy at Hampden-Sydney, 1836-39, before accepting a similar post at New York University. He is remembered in history as the father of modern portrait photography; he began his experiments in photography at Hampden-Sydney, and the camera which he used was preserved there. Draper was the first to photograph the human face with a camera with a lens.[130]

In addition to minerals, mineral springs have been reported in Prince Edward. Ryland Randolph reported in 1772 a mineral spring on one of his Bush River plantations, "hitherto used as a remedy in cutaneous and other (?) diseases."[131] On the Fears farm, now a part of the Prince Edward State Forest, were at one time a sulphur spring, an iron spring, and a pine spring.[132]

Two manufacturing enterprises were chartered in Prince Edward: the Farmville Manufacturing Company in 1847 to manufacture wool, cotton, hemp, flax, silk, and paper. Archer Vaughan, Thomas Hickson, James H. Wilson, Clement R. Barksdale, Edmund Wiltse, Fayette V. Morton, and Abraham T. Venable were appointed to superintend the sale of stock.[133] The Farmville Foundry Company was chartered in 1849 by Robert B. Cole, George W. Page, Howell E. Warren, B. M. Robertson, J. J. Rice, George King, William T. Rice, William A. Armistead, George W. Daniel, William G. Venable, James H. Wilson, William C. Flournoy, and James D. Ligon. The company was to cast iron and steel.[134]

James Blanton operated a carriage factory in Farmville for some time prior to 1846. He had closed his Farmville shop by May of that year, at which time it was apparently unoccupied.[135] W. D. Baber later made carriages in the shop. In 1852 Samuel A. Farrar and William J. Meador advertised that they manufactured "every description of riding vehicles and harness" in the shop formerly occupied by W. and J. Blanton and more recently by W. D. Baber. Farrar and Meador used the "best mountain seasoned timber and superior workmen." They also operated a blacksmith shop.[136] A popular carriage of those times was the coach, described by one who remembered them as the "old-fashioned terrapin-back carriage, swung on straps high in mid-air."[137] It made an impressive appearance, however, with its Negro driver on the high seat in front. Glasses could be raised and lowered. For some riders a disadvantage was the seat which faced backwards.[138] John A. Scott of Moilena had the first "modern" carriage one writer remembered, and A. D. Dickinson the first top buggy.[139]

Farmville boasted a piano factory in 1837, the only one south of Baltimore. George P. Knauff advertised "first rate" workmen and materials. He found in Farmville the advantage of low costs, and these he passed on to buyers in lower prices of "pianofortes."[140] He had probably been in the business for some time before this, for in 1835 he took I. deVlaming into the partnership of George P. Knauff and Company.[141] By 1842 he had discontinued the manufacture of pianos, for he announced that he was devoting all his time to tuning and selling pianos.[142]

Traffic on the Appomattox River from Farmville to Petersburg seems to have been limited to freight; perhaps the uncertainties of transportation which have been indicated made passenger traffic risky. Stage coaches provided public transportation facilities. One of the principal stage lines connecting Washington, D. C., and the South passed through Prince Edward. A mail stage from Fredericksburg via Cumberland Courthouse, Prince Edward Courthouse, Charlotte Courthouse, and Halifax Courthouse in Virginia, Milton, Greensborough [sic], Salem, Salisbury, and Charlotte in North Carolina, York Courthouse and Abbeyville Courthouse in South Carolina, Washington and Milledgeville (then the state capital) in Georgia, Montgomery and Demopolis in Alabama, to Natchez, Mississippi, was proposed in the United States Senate in January, 1823.[143] The line had gotten into operation before the end of the year. It may have replaced an earlier stage line which had not proved altogether satisfactory for the proprietors (whose names are not given in the advertisement) "to retrieve the character of the line and to insure the comfort and safety of the passengers" spared neither trouble nor expense in procuring "suitable carriages, good horses and skillful, accommodating and *sober* drivers." The italicized sober may be the clew to the necessity for "retrieving" the reputation of the line. The route, the shortest from Washington to the South, lay through "pleasant and healthy country," with "generally very good" accommodations provided at low charges; sufficient time for rest and refreshment was allowed. The stage left Fredericksburg every Tuesday at 5:00 A. M. and arrived at Halifax Courthouse every Friday afternoon; it left Halifax every Saturday at 5:00 A. M. and arrived at Fredericksburg every Tuesday morning. The distance between those points was 175 miles, and the fare for the trip was $14, at the rate of eight cents per mile.[144]

The stage line was operating three times weekly from Fredericksburg via Farmville, Prince Edward Courthouse, and Hampden-Sydney College in 1831; passengers from Richmond on Edwin Porter's Richmond, Scottsville, and Staunton mail coach could transfer to the line that served Prince Edward at George's.[145]

A new stage line was started from Petersburg to Farmville in 1834.[146] When Dr. Richard McIlwaine came as a student to Hampden-Sydney in 1848 he traveled by stage from his home in Petersburg and hired a conveyance to take him to the college. Conveyances from Burkeville (Burke's Tavern) to Hampden-Sydney were also available, and Dr. McIlwaine's father, Archibald Graham McIlwaine, a trustee of Hampden-Sydney, transferred from stage to private conveyance there. The trip consumed a day and a third of another day. When Dr. McIlwaine made the trip to Hampden-Sydney in January, 1850, he took a circuitous route, perhaps to get an opportunity to ride on a railroad; leaving Petersburg on New Year's day at 3:00 P. M. he went by rail to Richmond, where he spent the night; at 8:00 A. M. the next day he boarded the Lynchburg packet boat (on the James River canal) and went to Pemberton, which he reached at 6:00 P. M.; he stayed at the tavern until 1:00 A. M., awaiting the arrival of the stage, but instead of the stage, which had broken down, there came an open wagon, drawn by four horses; he rode twenty-two miles, to Cumberland Courthouse, for breakfast, and got to Farmville in time for dinner; there he hired a conveyance to take him to the college, arriving there at 5:00 P. M. January 3, two days and two hours after leaving Petersburg! The Hampden-Sydney catalogue stated that the college was two miles from Prince Edward Courthouse and seven from Farmville, both of which were connected by stage lines with Richmond, Petersburg, Lynchburg, and Milton, North Carolina, making the college "easily accessible from every quarter."[147]

Alexander Patteson of Clover Hill (the present old Appomattox Courthouse on the surrender grounds) operated the stage line from Richmond to Lynchburg. He and his brother Lilbourn started the line about 1811, three years before they bought Clover Hill. Lilbourn Patteson died in 1817, and Alexander continued its operation until his death in 1836.[148] Stages on this line ran three days weekly until 1833, when by direction of the Post Office Department it went on a six-day week schedule, leaving both places every day except Saturday and arriving every day except Sunday. It crossed only the extreme northwest corner of Prince Edward, by the owner's home, but passengers who left Richmond on Mondays, Wednesdays, and Fridays could connect with Peeks and Welford's line which served Farmville and Hampden-Sydney.[149]

During the year 1837 the Patteson estate accounts show an

income from the stage line of $14,742, of which $12,773 was received from passenger fares; the mail contract yielded an income of $1,500.[150] The inventory of Patteson's estate includes a jack for taking off wheels, two stage "polls" or tongues, one Troy stage-coach nearly new and appurtenances complete, including two double and two single trees at $400; one running stage-coach and appurtenances with one double and two single trees, $250; one stage-coach, Piedmont No. 29, not in use at the time, but "capable of service," $200; one Piedmont No. 1 coach, "not fit for much service," $85; one old and broken down coach, $50, twenty-four horses and three mules, one set of harness for four horses, and another for six. These items were in the listing of property in Prince Edward; in addition inventories of property in Campbell, Botetourt, Bedford, and Buckingham Counties were filed; some of this included equipment, and provisions for horses at inns in those counties.[151]

Taverns were found at frequent intervals along the roads. Stages stopped at them to change horses and to enable passengers to eat and rest. Some travelers chose to spend the night at taverns, although some of the stages seem to have traveled all night.

The innkeeper's obligation was set forth in the ordinary license bond (the following is Samuel Booker's, who received his license in 1789):

"He is to provide in his Ordinary good and wholesome meat and drink for travellers Bedds with clean sheets Stablage and pastrage for their Horses and do not suffer nor permit, any unlawful Gaming in his said Ordinary, nor on the Sabbath day suffer any person to Tipple nor drink any more than is necessary, then this obligation to be void or else to remain in force and virtue."

It was signed by the innkeeper, in this case Samuel Booker, and his security, George Redd, and was witnessed by Richard Watkins.[152]

Among those to whom ordinary licenses were granted in this period were John Queensberry, 1795, and Mackness Rowlett, 1797,[153] both in the neighborhood of the present Green Bay; James D. Cole, 1799, at French's Old Store;[154] Robert Flippen, 1800, who lived near the intersection of the Genito road and the Farmville-Petersburg road;[155] Anderson P. Miller, 1800, whose tavern in 1822 became Samuel D. Burke's,[156] which is still standing and is called Burke's Tavern; John East, January, 1801, and John Bibb, February, 1801, both in Farmville, the first ordinary licenses to be granted innkeepers in that town;[157] Elisha Betts, 1801;[158] Benjamin Dennis, January, 1801, the first license for an ordinary at Jamestown;[159]

George B. Hamner, 1801, at the Courthouse;[160] William Smith at Jamestown, 1802;[161] Peter Francisco, 1803;[162] Nancy Beazley, 1803, at John Purnall's store;[163] Peter Fore, William Ellington, and Benjamin Nunnally, 1804;[164] Absalom Farmer, at Clark's Store, Sandy River Church, Thomas A. Morton (renewed), and William Worsham, at the Courthouse, 1805;[165] John Williamson, 1806, at the Courthouse;[166] Maurice Langhorne, Jr., 1808, in Farmville;[167] William H. Worsham, 1809, French's Old Store;[168] Abner Nash, 1811;[169] George Foster, 1812;[170] Rowlett Perkinson, 1815,[171] between the present Green Bay and Miller's, later Burke's, Tavern; Alexander Patteson, at Clover Hill (Patteson was the operator of the Richmond and Lynchburg stage line), and Edmund Booker, at Jamestown, 1817;[172] Theodorick Love, Edward Redford, the latter probably at Farmville (Redford and Henry Turner received a joint license in 1816), and Francis Smith, at Farmville, 1818;[173] Peter B. Foster, in Edmund Booker's place and Samuel D. Burke, in Anderson P. Miller's place, 1822;[174] John Pearson, in William Worsham's place, 1823;[175] Moses Tredway, 1824,[176] in Farmville; George King, 1826, in place of Peter Foster, French's Old Store, which later became known as Kingsville;[177] William Penick, 1827, in Farmville;[178] James B. Ely, 1829, probably in Farmville;[179] William White, 1830, probably in Jamestown.[180]

In 1823 James Madison offered for sale the Farmville Tavern upon his decision to retire from public life.[181]

George R. Jeffress took over the operation of the Eagle Hotel (the Old Stand) in 1834;[182] subsequent operators of the Eagle Hotel were Colonel F. H. James, Thomas W. Epes (beginning in 1846), and G. W. A. Raine (in the 1850's). Epes advertised that his table was "constantly provided with the best season and country afford," his bar was stocked with the best liquors, and his stables afforded the best grain and provender and were attended by "experienced and attentive hostlers." Raine, who leased the hotel from W. C. Flournoy, also emphasized his table, his bar, and his stable.[183] In 1847 Colonel Joseph L. Carrington operated the Central Hotel in Farmville.[184]

While some visitors, like Mrs. Anne Royall in 1830, complimented the Farmville tavern,[185] John Randolph of Roanoke, who visited it on his way to Buckingham after he returned from Russia, was critical: in England the room would not have been considered fit for his servant; the walls were black, the bed and its furniture sordid, little furniture and some of that broken, no mirror, no fire irons. But Randolph at this time was ill; though he described his room as the "meanest" he had occupied in America, he went on to say, "Wherever I stop, it is the same."[186]

In 1783 the Prince Edward Court set these rates for inns: good West India rum, ten shillings the gallon; good brandy and whiskey, seven shillings, sixpence; wine, twenty shillings per gallon; French brandy, sixteen shillings a gallon; lodging, sixpence per night; dinner one shilling, sixpence; breakfast, one shilling, threepence; pasturage, sixpence per night; corn and oats, seven and one-half pence per gallon; and fodder, one pence per bundle.[187] In 1790 the price of dinner had gone up to two shillings, but the price of breakfast remained the same; lodging on a good bed with clean sheets had doubled and was now a shilling a night; West India rum was up to twelve shillings, but French brandy had dropped to twelve shillings. A greater variety of wines was offered: madeira at five shillings the bottle, Lisbon at three shillings, sixpence; claret at four shillings. Strong beer was two shillings the bottle, small beer fourpence. Corn and oats were sixpence per gallon.[188]

Not only travelers used the accommodations of the inn; nor did local people limit their patronage to the bar. When a group of Prince Edward citizens decided to honor John Randolph of Roanoke with a dinner, they chose John Pearson's tavern at the Courthouse for the affair on April 13, 1827. Randolph himself was unable to attend, but the dinner went as scheduled, probably because the committee received Randolph's regrets too late to change their plans. Dr. George W. Crump of Cumberland, Colonel Joseph Wyatt of Charlotte, and "a number of Revolutionary gentlemen" were invited guests. The committee arranging the dinner consisted of John James Flournoy, president, Peyton Randolph and Dr. Stephen C. Farrar, vice-presidents, Edward Booker, Henry E. Watkins, Samuel C. Anderson, Pugh W. Price, Dr. Reuben H. Dejarnett, and Jacquelin A. Berkeley. Randolph's letter regretting his inability to attend was read when the cloth was removed. Thereupon Flournoy proposed a toast to the better health of the honoree, which was drunk with enthusiasm. The thirteen regular toasts followed: to the people, the Constitution of the United States, the Constitution of Virginia, the memory of Washington, the memory of Jefferson, Madison (Randolph present might not have appreciated these two), John Randolph of Roanoke, Littleton Waller Tazewell, General Andrew Jackson, liberty of the press, agriculture, the surviving patriots of the Revolution, and Virginia. Numerous volunteer toasts were proposed, those offering them including Dr. S. C. Farrar to Dr. George W. Crump, who in reply proposed a toast to Virginia; Peyton Randolph to Colonel Joseph Wyatt, who offered a toast to the Constitution of Virginia in his reply; William Berkeley to Henry E. Watkins, who left early because of illness in his family; Jacquelin A. Berkeley; Nathaniel F. Cabell and Simon Hughes, both to the author of the Israel Hill resolutions—may he remain anonymous; Abraham W. Venable, to the memory of George Mason; Samuel C. Anderson; Henry Thweatt; Samuel Allen; Thomas Flournoy; Asa Dupuy; Branch J. Worsham; Edward Booker, Dr. Reuben H. Dejarnett, Joseph Dupuy, and James A. Dillon.[189]

From the meager indications available, it appears that there was no public postal service serving Prince Edward in the colonial period or in the early post-Revolutionary period. Reference has already been made to mail held for Prince Edward people in Petersburg and Warwick. In 1782 the route of expresses southward was changed, from early in that year going from Manchester (the present South Richmond) via Cumberland Old Courthouse, Prince Edward Court-house, Charlotte Courthouse, and Coles Ferry to Peytonsburg. The inference is that the route was for military expresses to the Southern army.[190]

In 1783 a petition from Prince Edward asked that county courts be authorized to levy about £20 annually "to hire a rider to convey all public dispatches, newspapers, and letters (frank) from the next adjacent county courthouse," in order to "save much unnecessary expense in the hire of expresses." The petition was signed by Charles Allen, Thomas Scott, Thomas Haskins, William Bibb, John Clarke, William Wootton, John Morton, Joseph Moore, Richard Foster, Charles Venable, Jacob Woodson, Francis Watkins, John B. Smith, John Nash, and Archibald McRobert.[191]

The new Federal government established a network of mail routes giving a much improved service and reaching practically every town. These routes were let by bids, submitted to the General Post Office in Washington. In 1802 route 47 provided a weekly mail service from Powhatan Courthouse to Halifax Courthouse, via Farms-ville [sic] and Prince Edward Courthouse; mail left Powhatan every Thursday at 10:00 A. M. and was scheduled to arrive at Halifax by 4:00 P. M. Saturday; it left Halifax at 10:00 P. M. Saturday, to arrive at Powhatan by 1:00 P. M. Tuesday. Route 50 provided weekly service from Richmond to Farmville, via Genito Bridge,

Amelia Courthouse, Painsville, Ligontown, and Jamestown. The schedule called for leaving Richmond at 8:00 A. M. on Wednesday and arriving in Farmville by 8:00 P. M. on Thursday; the return trip was scheduled to leave Farmville at 8:00 A. M. on Friday and arrive in Richmond by 8:00 P. M. Saturday.[192] Creed Taylor's advertisement in 1802 of his law practice in the Richmond district High Court of Chancery and the Federal court in Richmond gave his postoffice as Farmville.[193] Route 48 provided mail service every two weeks from Prince Edward Courthouse to New London, via Lester's Store and Campbell Courthouse in 1804.[194] The contracts for 1805 showed that this route, listed now as No. 49, was to provide weekly service; the schedule called for leaving Prince Edward on Friday at "4½" P. M. and arriving in New London by 3:00 P. M. Saturday; the mail was to leave New London Sunday at 4:00 A. M. and arrive at Prince Edward Courthouse by 9:00 A. M. Monday. The schedule for Route 47 was changed for the Farmville-Richmond trip; in 1805 the mail was to leave Farmville by 6:00 A. M. Monday and arrive in Richmond by 4:00 P. M. on Tuesday.[195] In 1805 there was a mail route from Prince Edward Courthouse via Hunter's Tavern to Lynchburg giving weekly service.[196]

Farmville and Prince Edward Courthouse were served by Route 31 in 1807, which provided weekly mail deliveries between Washington, via Fredericksburg, Cumberland, Charlotte Courthouse, Halifax, and Danville to Huntersville, North Carolina; the trip one way on this route required three days.[197]

Postage rates then were much higher than they are now. The distance carried and the size of the letter determined the cost. In 1816 postage on a single letter (a single sheet of paper) carried not more than thirty miles was six cents; from thirty to eighty miles, ten cents; from eighty to 150 miles, twelve and one-half cents; from 150 to 400 miles, eighteen and one-half cents; over 400 miles, twenty-five cents. Double letters went for double rates, triple for triple, and in proportion upward. Newspapers received more favorable rates; the rate on one paper was one cent up to 100 miles or within the state of publication, one and one-half cents when carried more than 100 miles or outside the state of publication. The rates on magazines and pamphlets was one cent up to fifty miles, one and one-half cents fifty to 100 miles, and two cents when over 100 miles.[198] It was then the custom for the recipient of the letter to pay the postage; under certain circumstances, however, the sender was expected to pay the postage; for example, Edmund Booker, as treasurer of the Jamestown

Female Seminary lottery in 1817, notified "adventurers" to send letters concerning the lottery postpaid.[199]

In 1819, connecting with the Farmville-Richmond route at Perkinsonville in Amelia County was a route to Charlotte Courthouse, Jennings Ordinary, Miller's Tavern (later Burke's), Moore's Ordinary, and Keyes', providing weekly service.[200]

Stage-coach operators were frequently successful bidders for the mail routes, the principal mail routes usually following the stage routes. The stage line established in 1823 from Fredericksburg to Halifax, via Farmville and Prince Edward Courthouse, and connecting at Halifax with stage lines into the deep South, was a mail stage.[201] Alexander Patteson was confronted with a problem when the government required him to increase the mail service from Lynchburg to Richmond from three times a week to six days a week in 1833; he was compelled to use the Manchester Turnpike, a toll road, in leaving and entering Richmond; although the mail was exempt from toll, the stage was not, paying $150 in tolls annually; doubling the service meant doubling the toll costs, and he sought relief for his stage line.[202]

Some of the other mail routes serving Prince Edward, with dates when bids were asked, were: Prince Edward Courthouse via Prospect to Concord, once a week, 1826;[203] Buckingham Courthouse via Farmsville, Prince Edward Courthouse, Moore's Ordinary, and Lunenburg Courthouse to Boydstown in Mecklenburg, once a week, 1827.[204]

In 1838 bids for a four-and-one-half year period (January 1, 1839 to June 30, 1843) were asked for the following routes serving Prince Edward: Fredericksburg to Farmville, in four-horse post coaches, three times weekly; Richmond via Jamestown to Farmville, twice weekly; Petersburg via Blacks and Whites, Nottoway Courthouse, Jennings Ordinary, Burkesville, and Sandy River Church to Farmville, three times weekly by stage, with offices not on the direct route to be supplied by post; Prince Edward Courthouse via Marble Hill, Meherrin Grove, and Keysville to Christiansville (the present Chase City), once a week; Farmville, via Prince Edward Courthouse, Midway Inn, Roanoke Bridge, Charlotte Courthouse to Milton, North Carolina, three times weekly in four-horse post coaches (a continuation of the route from Fredericksburg); Farmville, via Prospect, Walkers Church, Spout Spring, and Concord to Lynchburg, three times a week; Walkers Church via Wheelers Spring, Red House, and Reedy Spring to Concord, once a week; Clover Hill in a circuit to Bent Creek, Stone Wall Mills, and Oakville and thence to Clover

Hill, three times a week; Cumberland via CaIra and New Store to Clover Hill, twice a week; Cartersville, via Buckingham and Clover Hill to Lynchburg in four-horse post coaches, three times weekly[205]

In 1840 there were ten postoffices in Prince Edward: Marble Hill, Sandy River Church, Midway Inn, Farmville, Walkers Church, Prospect, Prince Edward Courthouse, Burkeville, Jamestown, and Clover Hill.[206]

The advertisement for bids for the period July 1, 1843 to June 30, 1847, substituted a route from Hallsboro via Jamestown to Farmville for the former route from Richmond. Merriman's Shop (the present Pamplin) appears as an office on the Walkers Church-Concord route.[207]

Trains were used to carry the mails after the Richmond and Danville and Southside Railroads were built through Prince Edward. The change in mail service opened two new postoffices in Prince Edward, one on each railroad, Green Bay and Rice's Depot.[208]

In 1855 J. W. Womack succeeded J. M. McNutt as postmaster at Farmville;[209] John Hughes, Jr., succeeded George Berry as postmaster at Green Bay in 1858.[210]

People in ante-bellum Prince Edward were not accustomed to getting their mail each day. Thomas T. Tredway sent a boy (slave) to the Prospect postoffice three times a week, on Tuesday, Thursday, and Saturday. When he was in Richmond attending the House of Delegates, he instructed his overseer to keep his father's mail until the elder Tredway sent for it. In good weather, if the horses were not working, the boy rode horseback. If the weather was bad, the instructions were to send a young man. A bag was kept to carry the mail in, and the boy the elder Tredway sent to his son's for the mail had his own mail bag.[211] Not all people sent for mail this often. In the William Weaver household in eastern Prince Edward, it was the custom to send to the postoffice, Rice's Depot after the railroad was built, once a week, on Saturday.[212]

Freight was also delivered by wagon before the days of railroads. In 1844 John N. Gordon of Richmond notified James Blanton at Farmville that he was sending him eight carriage springs and one box of merchandise by Thomas W. Daniel's wagon; the springs and merchandise had come to Richmond on the steamship *Pocahontas*, and Gordon held it a few days until he found a wagon going to Farmville by which he could send it.[213] It was a general practice to send by a neighbor who was sending or taking a wagon to Richmond or Petersburg for supplies. A "Memorandum for Mr. Scott to get some things at Petersburg" has been preserved: 3 dozen of all blades sortable 2 piggin alls, 3 dozen of sortable Shoe Taxs, one hundred 4d nails, one hundred 3d nails, one hundred 2d nails, 3 or 4 shoe knives, one pair of good shoes for me if to be had; on the reverse of the sheet is another memorandum: 1 or 2 shoe knives, 1 or 2 doz. aul blades sorted, 2 or 3 pegging aul blades, i or 2 doz. shoe Tacks sorted; 2 or 300 2 or 3d nails, 1 lb. or ½ lb. Green or Hyson Tea, 5 or 10 lbs. best coffee, i oz. or ½ oz. Cambrick Thread, 1 paper Ink powder, Silk for Girls Bonnetts, 1½ yd. plain neet Gause for Caps, Cap wire, 2 pair Large Gloves (women), 1 pair Shoes for Jesse, Cloth for coat and fore body of a Jacket, Lineing to face them, Trimmings—no body Lineing or pockets, Cap for Patsy at Milliners, Shirts for Self, 1 or 2 Negro Girls between 2 and 18.[214]

Travelers were asked to attend to personal business as well as fill memoranda of goods wanted. One unidentified visitor to Richmond carried a memo for Dr. Farrar, which included calling on Barret Walthall for a shirt, asking if he sent a journal to S. C. Anderson, and calling at the Farmers Bank to "ask of Docr Farrar's Bank A/c; he also was commissioned by H. N. Watkins to draw the dividend on his bank stock and get four single horse ploughs; Colonel Woodson gave him a letter to deliver to the auditor and Thomas W. McGlasson had business with the Register's (Land) office which he asked this Richmond-bound traveler to attend to; in addition there was a long list of goods to buy. One traveler, probably the same, carried on a trip to Richmond a memorandum to buy table ware and other household goods for Mr. and Mrs. Womack, as well as to have a glass frame minted and a mirror put in it, to have the hammer to a gun lock faced, and to have a watch repaired for this couple; he was also to get an eight-day clock and some books, including the latest edition of a Greek lexicon, for Mr. Dickinson; some cotton yarn and candles for Mrs. Dillon; a coffee pot for A. G. Green; pay James H. Dupuy's subscription to the *Family Visitor*; get two bushels of clover seed for Thomas Nelson; get Scott's family Bible, a leghorn hat, a barrel of Irish potatoes, and a half-bushel of clover seed for H. N. Watkins; A. B. Venable sent by him for purple and white cape broccoli seed, and early York and purple cabbage; James H. Dupuy gave a long memorandum of goods, including a barrel of herrings, two dagon moulds, iron, steel, sugar, a barrel of tar, salt, rice, tea, castor oil (just a bottle), cotton shirting, diaper material, and an oven lid; William J. Dupuy wanted coffee, spades, copperas, calomel (four ounces) and ipecac (two ounces); John P. Dupuy sent for "1 very fine pannel saw."[215]

Many travelers provided their own conveyances in those days. The most famous traveler ever to pass through Prince Edward was George Washington, who included the county in his Southern tour of 1791. On this trip, which was something of an official tour of the country, Washington traveled in his own carriage, usually stopping at taverns. On Sunday, June 5, he dined at the home of Colonel Isaac Coles in Halifax, who was the first representative from Prince Edward in Congress, and stayed there until Tuesday morning. He left Colonel Coles' at daybreak and ate breakfast at Charlotte Courthouse; there he had his horses shod. He reached Prince Edward Courthouse on June 7. Washington observed the land between Charlotte Courthouse and Prince Edward Courthouse to be of inferior quality, with few people living in sight of the road. He heard that the country off the road was thickly settled, and he concluded that the road, by keeping to the ridge, passed through the most indifferent land. Washington spent the night of June 7 at Prince Edward Courthouse, where a great throng of people awaited his arrival, "all," according to Richard N. Venable, "crowding the way where they expect him to pass, anxious to see the saviour of their country and the object of their love." The President left the Courthouse at light on the morning of June 8, traveled thirteen miles to Tredway's tavern where he ate breakfast; he dined in Cumberland that day. He found the road from the Courthouse to Tredway's thickly settled, although the land appeared thin, with a prevailing growth of pine.[216]

Washington's practice of rising early and traveling some distance before eating breakfast seems to have been general. John Randolph of Roanoke, traveling from his home in Charlotte to Washington in January, 1811, spent the first night of the journey at the home of a friend, Thomas T. Bouldin; the second at Moore's Ordinary, from which he went on to Miller's for breakfast.[217]

Still another famous traveler passed through Prince Edward in that era, but his journey was no triumphal procession. Aaron Burr, a former Vice-President of the United States, had been arrested on charges of treasonable acts against the United States. In the custody of Captain Perkins of the United States Army and six or seven other persons, Burr spent the night of Sunday, March 22, 1807, at Journey's tavern near Hampden-Sydney. On the next day the trip to Washington was resumed, via Cumberland; when the party reached

Fredericksburg, Captain Perkins received orders from President Jefferson to take Burr to Richmond,[218] where he was subsequently tried in the United States Court, Chief Justice Marshall presiding, and acquitted by a jury of which John Randolph of Roanoke was foreman.

In this era of an expanding economy merchants opened stores in every community. Political independence brought economic independence of the Scotch and English merchants who in colonial times dominated the Prince Edward trade. James Morton paid £5 for a merchant's license in 1787; he operated for many years a store near Hampden-Sydney College,[219] located on Wood's map (1820) at the intersection of the Five Forks and "back Hampden-Sydney road" and the road to Kingsville. Other early licensees were Richard Bibb, 1788, and Baker LeGrand, 1789.[220]

The two partnerships of John Chaffin, John Truly, Jr., and Jarratt Rison of Jamestown and Chaffin, Rison, and Benjamin and Saymur Wright at Farmville were dissolved in August, 1800. Chaffin, who lived at Jamestown, settled the accounts attendant upon the dissolution of these partnerships. In September, 1801, the partnership of Chaffin, Joseph Vaughan, and Benjamin Wright, which operated as Joseph Vaughan and Company of Farmville, was dissolved, Joseph Vaughan looking after the business of settling up.[221] Quin Morton is credited with building the first store in Farmville; the business was conducted by his son, Thomas A. Morton.[222] Robert Venable had a store near Prospect, mentioned as early as 1802.[223] Hart and Nimmo operated a store in the western part of the county in the period.[224] Smith, Lee and Company was doing business in Farmville in 1802; three years later George and William Smith are described as the surviving partners of the firm.[225] In the settlement of the estate of Nathaniel Venable, reference was made to two firms in which he had been a partner, Venable and Venable and Venable and Womack.[226] Carter and Booker were in the mercantile business in 1807, probably at or near Darlington Heights, where Love's store was located in 1820.[227] Anderson P. Miller had a store at his tavern in 1817; Samuel D. Burke worked in the store for him that year, and the next year was taken into partnership, the store becoming Miller and Burke. William White and Edmund Booker were merchants at Jamestown at the same time. Customers bought fabrics, rum, sugar, salt, pepper, tea, whiskey, molasses, nails, hats, saddle blankets, saddles, bridles, ornamental side combs, according to accounts of the period.[228] Other stores of the period were Venable and Madison, Thornton and Tredway (with William C. Thornton and Thomas Tredway in a partnership formed in 1823), and Joseph Dupuy, which was on the road from the Courthouse to Briery Church.[229] Nathaniel E. Venable and Samuel W. Venable in 1828 were partners in N. E. Venable and Company and with Samuel Lyle in the firm of Samuel Lyle and Company.[230] Two Farmville partnerships were dissolved in 1840; Jacob W. Morton continued the business formerly conducted by him and Samuel D. Morton; and Charles and Abraham Z. Venable dissolved the partnership of Venable and Venable, of which name there were several in Prince Edward's history.[231] The partnership of Owen R. and Henry Tucker had been dissolved prior to the latter part of 1839;[232] their store, if their places of residence give indication, was in the northeastern part of the county. Green and Omohundro were merchants at Londonderry in 1805; they sold their business to Charles Venable and James Martin in 1812.[233] There were stores at Sandy River Church. William and Samuel Mathews had a store at Walker's Church, and Kelso's Old Store was between Walkers Church and Merriman's Shop (now Pamplin).[234]

The panic of 1837 proved a temporary setback to the prosperity of the era. The leading mercantile firm of Thweatt and Miller, at Kingsville, failed as a result of the financial stringency of the times. Both partners, Colonel Henry Thweatt and Anderson P. Miller, lost considerable property as a result. The "large and new brick storehouse," with five rooms besides the cellar, and the frame storehouse with three rooms in which the firm carried on an extensive business seem to have belonged to Thweatt. The frame store had been successively occupied by James D. Wood, Thweatt and Miller, and Thweatt, Miller, and Hudson. Thweatt's home and farm of 407 acres at the store were sold; and Miller offered for sale his home and farm of 550 acres in Nottoway near Burkeville, a gristmill, a tannery, two other tracts in Nottoway and three tracts in Prince Edward, and thirty to forty Negroes to pay his liabilities; in addition to this he transferred assets of A. P. Miller and Sons to Giles A. Miller to protect the creditors of that firm. Asa D. Dickinson settled the accounts of Thweatt and Miller; he gave notice that he would be found on all business days except when he was in court in Colonel Thweatt's counting house.[235]

Two Farmville tobacconists, Patrick H. Jackson, and his uncle, James Madison, also lost heavily in the panic of 1837.[236] The mercantile firm of Steger and Nash (Merritt T. Steger and Thomas P. Nash) of Farmville failed during the same period of hard times.[237]

Among the Farmville merchants in 1852 were William G. Stratton, Chappell and Womack (William H. Chappell and J. W. Womack), Warren and Davis, Dunnington and Barksdale, Scott and Walton, Paulett and Carrell, Venable, Anderson and Flournoy, George King (pianos), A. P. Biglow (dry goods, books, pianos), B. M. Robertson, who advertised the closing of his business at the end of the year, McNutt and Anderson, J. W. and J. T. Morton, and Lockett, Womack and Company.[238] Morton and Dupuy had a store in Farmville in 1840, which sold, from an account that year, bleached domestic, linen, muslin, flannel, cambric, calico, lutestring ribbon, alpaca, rice cambric, and carpet binding.[239] Joel W. Womack and Company of Farmville was selling superfine flour manufactured by N. E. Venable and Company in 1842.[240] The firm of C. R. Barksdale and Company of Farmville was dissolved early in 1852 by the withdrawal of E. M. Barksdale. The partners, N. C. Read and the Barksdales, also dissolved their firm of Read and Barksdale in Richmond at the same time.[241]

John and Ezekiah Harding operated one of a chain of stores at Meherrin during the mid-nineteenth century. There was considerable demand for store buildings there in 1859; when John Harding inquired about renting John Thompson's storehouse, he was told that there were six applicants to rent the building ahead of him. One attraction was the possibility that the railroad depot might be built on the Thompson land. Wall closed out his store at Meherrin at the end of 1859, and Anderson Harding and James T. Staples planned to open a wholesale store in the Wall building in the spring of 1860.[242]

Rowland Anderson operated several stores in Prince Edward and Charlotte Counties; one was at Sandy River Church, another at Keysville.[243]

As one would suppose was the case in an agrarian society, much of the mercantile business was carried on on credit. Manuscript collections abound in statements of account rendered by merchants. Yet there were times when credit restrictions were applied. One Farmville merchant wrote a customer in 1849:

"It would afford me a great deal of pleasure to fill your orders when I have the honor of receiving them but the circumstances are such that it is entirely out of my power to do it. in the first place

I am not able to wait so long as it is necessary that I should wait under the circumstances that you labor under, for I know that your crop last year was a failure & feel confident that I shall have to wait on you for your last years dealings until you can make a crop. That a/c is near 40$ & Marys is some 17 to 20$. If you see you[r] way clear to pay & make arrangmts through Par I will send you such articles as you may want. All of this is plain brotherly talk & take it as such."[244]

A popular method of retailing was by peddling. These traveling merchants would carry through the country an assortment of goods; stopping at homes, they would display and sell their wares. Licenses were required of them; they could take out a license in one county which was good for the state, but they had to record the license in the county in which they sold goods.[245]

The increasing business of the area made it seem desirable to open a bank in Farmville. In 1832 a petition was signed by Nathaniel J. Venable and many others asking that a branch of one of the Virginia banks be opened there. The petition noted that each year nearly 5,000 hogsheads of tobacco, worth $300,000 to $400,000, were sold in Farmville, that there was a considerable annual trade in wheat and flour, that merchandise worth $100,000 was imported into Farmville annually, and that the town's commercial exchange amounted to half a million dollars a year.[246] A bill to establish a branch of the Bank of Virginia at Farmville was defeated 34-79 in the House of Delegates that year, Asa Dupuy, the Prince Edward delegate, voting against the proposal.[247]

The decision of the legislature did not satisfy the people. On January 20, 1834, there was a mass meeting at the Courthouse which unanimously instructed James Madison and John J. Flournoy to petition the Assembly, in the name of the meeting, for the establishment of a branch bank at Farmville. The petition was referred to a select committee. Another meeting was held, this one December 20, 1834, in Jeffries' tavern in Farmville, with Madison as chairman and Theodorick B. McRobert as secretary; on motion of Dr. J. T. Ligon, Madison and James H. Dillon were instructed to go to Richmond to carry a petition of the meeting for the opening of a branch bank. A year later (December 2, 1835) there was another meeting in Farmville, of which William B. Watkins of Charlotte was chairman and Abraham Z. Venable secretary, at which a petition to establish a bank in Farmville was endorsed; the petition was drawn up by

Nathaniel E. Venable, Thomas A. Morton, James Neal, Dr. William
B. Smith, and James Madison. Still another petition went to the
legislature before a branch bank was authorized; this one, signed by
Archibald A. Lyle, James D. Wood, and others, was presented on
December 22, 1836, and was reported as reasonable January 2,
1837.[248] On February 25, 1837, the legislature authorized the
Farmers Bank of Virginia to increase its capital by $1,010,000 and
to establish several branch banks, one of which was to be at Farmville and which was to have a capital of $200,000.[249] As of January
1, 1838, the Farmers Bank reported offices in Richmond, Norfolk,
Petersburg, Fredericksburg, Lynchburg, Winchester, and Danville,
with assets of $7,183,970.83, and aggregate profits on its operations
for the year of 13.13 per cent.[250] In February, 1839, the bank declared a dividend of 4½ per cent for the preceding half-year.[251] An
office in Farmville was reported at the beginning of 1840; the branch
had seven directors, three appointed by the Governor, and four
elected by the stockholders; those elected by the stockholders for 1840
were Clement C. Read, Jacob W. Morton, Tazewell S. Morton, and
John Dupuy; as the Governor deferred making appointments, the
full board was not reported.[252] The Governor's appointees for 1841
were James D. Wood, Edwin Edmunds, and Patrick H. Jackson, who
was described as a new director, indicating that the two former had
been gubernatorial appointees for the preceding year.[253]

In 1846 there was considerable controversy over the election of
directors. William C. Flournoy presented a slate at the stockholders'
meeting in Richmond, consisting of N. E. Venable, W. C. Flournoy,
James B. Anderson, and M. R. Flippen; it was rejected; then N. E.
Venable proposed his ticket: himself, F. N. Watkins, John Dupuy,
and Frank Anderson; finally the stockholders elected Venable,
Watkins, Flournoy, and J. W. Morton. Venable described the meet-
ing as "a most painful and disagreeable scuffle." Warning that a
hard fight was to come before the Governor, he urged Morton to
hold on to his place—"it is important to you and other interests."
The gubernatorial appointments went to Patrick H. Jackson, George
W. Daniel, and Clement R. Barksdale.[254] The next year James
Blanton and Joel E. Scott replaced Venable and Morton; and the
Governor named Monroe R. Flippen instead of Barksdale.[255] A.
Vaughan was cashier of the bank at the time.[256]

Among the subsequent directors were: 1849: Flournoy, Scott,
C. R. Barksdale, and Blanton (elected by the stockholders), Jackson,

Joseph B. Anderson, and Howell E. Warren (appointed by the Governor);[257] 1851: Flournoy, George O. Scott, A. D. Dickinson, W. H. Middleton (elected), Jackson, James B. Anderson, and Clement C. Read (appointed);[258] 1852: Flournoy, Scott, Dickinson, George W. Daniel (elected), Middleton, Francis P. Wood, and Read (appointed);[259] 1853: Read, C. C. Lockett, John Dupuy, James T. Spencer (elected), Jackson, John W. Wilson, and James B. Anderson (appointed);[260] 1855: Read, Spencer, John T. Thornton, W. W. H. Thackston (elected), Wilson, Middleton, and William A. Walton (appointed);[261] 1856: Read, Thornton, Thackston, James M. McNutt (elected), Walton, Henry S. Guthrey, Patrick H. Jackson (appointed);[262] 1857: Read, Thackston, McNutt, Stephen O. Southall (elected), Guthrey, Jackson, and William P. Elam (appointed);[263] 1858: Read, McNutt, Southall, William T. Rice (elected); J. J. Walker, Middleton, and Thomas L. Morton (appointed);[264] 1859: Read, Southall, Rice, C. D. Anderson (elected), Middleton, Morton, and Samuel B. McKinney (appointed);[265] 1861: Read, Charles D. Anderson, Thornton, and McNutt (elected).[266]

The Farmers Bank entered deposits on the left page of the depositor's bank book and the checks drawn on the right page. The two pages balanced; thus the first page in Edmund W. Hubard's bank book shows eight deposits totalling $5,142.99 and thirteen checks drawn on the account amounting to $5,142.99. Evidently the book was kept at the bank, or was balanced in this way from time to time upon presentation by the depositor.[267]

Bad checks were problems in those days also. R. T. Harding, who was working in the Harding store in Meherrin during the latter part of 1859, wrote his brother about a check given the store by a customer which "came back yesterday and with it a protest." A month later he reported an effort to get the matter settled, without success; he determined to give the person who had given the bad check another week and if it were not made good he would institute suit to collect.[268]

When the War Between the States began, there were at least three other banks in Farmville in addition to the branch of the Farmers Bank of Virginia. The Appomattox Savings Bank had been chartered in 1847 with a maximum capital of $50,000, by A. Z. Venable, F. N. Watkins, A. W. Millspaugh, S. C. Southall, Monroe R. Flippen, P. H. Jackson, E. Wiltse, B. M. Robertson, Archer Vaughan, Howell E. Warren, and C. R. Barksdale.[269] The Farmville

Savings Bank had been incorporated in 1860 with an authorized capital of $100,000 by John A. Dalby, William W. H. Thackston, H. E. Warren, Benjamin C. Peters, James B. Ely, Thomas B. Rice, John T. Thornton, and Beverly S. Scott.[270] Also incorporated in 1860 was the Planters Bank of Farmville with an authorized capital of $100,000 to $500,000, with a subscription of the minimum limit required before the bank could open. Superintendents of the stock subscription were Henry S. Guthrey, Walter H. Middleton, S. O. Southall, C. C. Lockett, James T. Gray, W. W. Forbes, Blake B. Woodson, John W. Wilson, Howell E. Warren, Thomas B. Rice, John J. Walker, James B. Hilliard, W. J. Eppes, Charles D. McKinney, and John P. Woodson. The bank was authorized to circulate paper to the value of three times the coin in its possession; whenever the coin reserve was reduced to less than one-third the value of the bank certificates outstanding, the bank could make no new loan or discount until the ratio of paper to coin was again three to one.[271]

The first indication of the activity of the insurance business in Prince Edward came in November, 1803, when the Board of Trustees of Hampden-Sydney insured the college buildings with the Mutual Assurance Society.[272] In 1805 that firm wanted to place a special agent in each judicial district; Creed Taylor was asked to recommend an agent for the Prince Edward district.[273] The Hardings carried insurance to cover the stock of goods in their Meherrin store in 1859;[274] in 1860 they took out a policy for $3,500 covering goods, wares, and merchandise, on which they paid a premium of $525; the company with which they took out this policy was the Caswell Mutual Fire Insurance Company of Milton, North Carolina.[275] When the Peters and Blanton tobacco factory in Farmville burned in 1861, the owners were reported to have had the building insured for $5,000; the loss was estimated at $12,000[276]

The county's first newspaper was the Farmville *Chronicle*, founded in 1832 when Theodorick B. McRobert moved the presses of the Scottsville *Aurora*, which he had founded in 1829, to Farmville. The minutes of the Appomattox Baptist Association for 1834 were printed in Farmville at the "Chronicle Office." The minutes of the 1837 session of the same organization were printed by the Farmville *Journal*. A. P. and Silas Biglow published the paper in succession to McRobert, and Alexander M. Cowan became publisher in 1848. It was called the Farmville *Republican* for a short time, but soon became the Farmville *Journal* again.[277]

Prince Edward people did not wait, however, until a paper was established in Farmville to begin reading the newspapers. The news and advertisements in the *Virginia Gazette* prior to the Revolution indicate some circulation in Prince Edward. In 1802 the *Virginia Argus* appointed Major James Morton its agent in Prince Edward to receive money due it, some of which was certainly for subscriptions.[278]

The Richmond *Enquirer* in 1858 published a list of its long-time subscribers. There were two people on the subscription list who had been subscribers since the first issue was published May 9, 1804; they were Judge Thomas Ruffin of Graham, Alamance County, North Carolina, and Moses Tredway of Hampden-Sydney College. Five others in Prince Edward were numbered among the older subscribers, and the dates of the beginning of their subscriptions were given: James Redd, Prince Edward Courthouse, May 31, 1819; J. H. C. Leach, Farmville, December 11, 1819; John W. Redd, Prince Edward Courthouse, November 27, 1821; W. Brightwell, Walkers Church, December 1, 1821; and W. T. Wootton, Green Bay, November 23, 1825.[279]

The growing nation and the expanding economy stimulated interest in internal improvements. In the early years after the War of 1812 there seemed little opposition to a Federal program of internal improvements; later, however, internal improvements became one item in the states-rights controversy, Southern Democrats opposing Federal participation in internal improvement projects. This did not include opposition to state participation, for the State of Virginia supported financially the construction of canals by subscribing to stock and making loans, and it, as well as localities, subscribed to railroad stock and turnpike stock. Before the issue of internal improvements became clearly drawn politically, a convention met at Charlottesville July 14-17, 1828, to consider such improvements for the state. Ex-President James Madison presided over the meeting, and Richard N. Venable of Prince Edward was a member of the committee of thirteen, along with ex-President James Monroe, Chief Justice John Marshall, and James Barbour to report measures they would recommend to the convention for endorsement. The recommendations concerned the James, Potomac, and Shenandoah Rivers and turnpikes from Richmond to the Southwest and to the Ohio River. Oddly enough, although Venable was on the committee, no recommendation concerning the Appomattox

was made. W. H. McFarland of Petersburg introduced a resolution
to the effect that a turnpike road or a canal between the waters of
the Roanoke and the Appomattox was of vital interest to the Southside and was entitled to the "early attention" of the General Assembly, but it was defeated.[280]

Although the principal concern in Prince Edward was with
Appomattox navigation, when the stock subscription to the James
River and Kanawha Canal was opened in 1835, Richard N. Venable,
Henry E. Watkins, James D. Wood, James Madison, and Samuel C.
Anderson managed the subscription at Farmville;[281] in Prince Edward
there were subscriptions to twenty-five shares, an investment of
$2,500, in that canal.[282]

A commercial convention met in Norfolk in November, 1838,
and in preparation for it there was a meeting in Farmville to act on
the invitation and to appoint delegates. Thomas A. Morton served
as chairman of the Farmville meeting, and James D. Wood as
secretary. It was resolved to accept the invitation of Norfolk to send
delegates, and Nathaniel E. Venable, Thomas A. Morton, Henry E.
Watkins, Asa Dupuy, William M. Womack, James D. Wood,
William C. Flournoy, Thomas L. Morton, Henry Thweatt, William
Matthews, Dr. William H. Chappell, Thomas Tredway, Francis N.
Watkins, Anderson P. Miller, William H. Venable, Clement C. Read,
and Tazewell S. Morton were named as delegates from Farmville
and Prince Edward. N. E. Venable, Wood, Flournoy, and Henry E.
Watkins and Venable were assigned to the committee on agriculture;
this committee proposed that the legislature aid "the diffusion of
agricultural instruction and knowledge" and the promotion of agricultural improvement. The convention, not surprisingly in its meeting place, named committees to seek the support of legislatures of
Virginia and North Carolina in inviting foreign manufacturers and
capitalists to establish agencies here and recommended to inland
merchants that they give preference to importers in Virginia and
North Carolina ports.[283]

William C. Flournoy was appointed a delegate from Virginia to
the Southern Commercial Convention which met in Richmond
January 31, 1856; J. T. Morton and H. A. Wood of Farmville also
attended the meeting.[284] Flournoy was one of three delegates from
the Fourth District appointed to attend the commercial convention
which met in Knoxville in August, 1857.[285]

In one of the periodic expressions of concern over the inadequacy of Appomattox navigation and of determination to improve it, James Madison and Nathaniel E. Venable called a meeting to be held at Farmville on January 21, 1834, to consider the problem.[286] A Prince Edward "Planter" endorsed their motives in an open letter to Madison and Venable, but he cautioned them that by restricting the object of the meeting to navigation of the Appomattox, they might be overlooking a better means of transportation for the section. He pointed out that although work had been done and money spent to improve the river for almost fifty years, it still did not provide a satisfactory means for transportation; "Planter" did not think river transportation on the Appomattox would ever prove satisfactory, because it was too small a stream and the water supply fluctuated too much; one day there might not be enough water in the river to float a small batteau, the next it might be in flood covering the valley. After classifying water transportation on the Appomattox as a delusion, he proposed a railroad from Farmville to Cartersville, to connect with the James River navigation system.[287]

The railroad idea was taking hold. In 1836 Willis Blanton, Samuel W. Venable, and many others petitioned the legislature to charter railroads from Petersburg to Farmville and from Farmville to Danville.[288] Both proposed railroads were authorized in 1837; the Farmville and Danville Railroad was to be incorporated when 3,000 shares of its stock had been subscribed, and the Petersburg and South-Western Rail-Road Company was to be incorporated when 5,000 shares of its stock had been subscribed. Stock subscriptions for the Farmville and Danville were to be opened at Farmville and Prince Edward Courthouse and for the Petersburg and South-Western at Farmville.[289] The same session of the Assembly directed the Board of Public Works to survey a route from Richmond to Farmville and thence to Danville and a route from Petersburg via Nottoway Courthouse to Farmville.[290] The survey for the latter road estimated that the 69¼ miles of railroad linking Petersburg and Farmville could be built for $900,364,41, including grading, masonry, superstructure (rails and ties), turn-outs, turning platforms, sidings, depots, water stations, and wood sheds (locomotives burned wood then). The survey, made by William H. Morrell, proposed a route by Burke's Tavern to Sandy River and down Sandy River, crossing the stream twice, then from the lower stretches of Sandy crossing Bush and following the Appomattox into Farmville to a point on Main Street near Phillips' tannery. The survey reported the Appomattox River

bend near Venable's mill so sharp that it would be necessary to cross
and recross the Appomattox or construct a curve with a radius of
600 feet; it was deemed more feasible to cross the river, since it
would save 3,000 feet in 6,200 feet and also expensive road building
along a rocky bluff.[291]

Neither railroad was constructed as proposed. But the interest
had not been lost. On May 7, 1846, a well-attended meeting was
held in the Methodist Church in Farmville to discuss railroad building. Delegates from Amelia, Buckingham, Charlotte, Chesterfield,
Cumberland, Lunenburg, Nottoway, and Richmond were in attendance as well as delegates from Farmville and Prince Edward. Representing Farmville were William H. Chappell, C. C. Read, William
C. Flournoy, G. W. Daniel, James Spencer, James Lyle, and W. F.
Carrington; the Prince Edward delegation consisted of S. C. Anderson, W. T. Wootton, H. N. Watkins, N. E. Venable, J. H. C. Leach
(who opened the meeting with prayer), R. S. Carter, John Thompson, B. S. Scott, J. H. Wilson, B. Allen, A. Dupuy, F. N. Watkins,
T. Clark, S. L. Graham, J. W. Redd, T. F. Venable, A. G. Green,
N. McGehee, H. Guthrey, J. B. Ely, J. A. Scott, B. J. Worsham,
William Elliott, W. C. Flournoy, W. H. Venable, A. S. Dillon, and
Thomas T. Tredway. Samuel C. Anderson was president of the
convention, and F. N. Watkins one of the secretaries. N. E. Venable
and W. C. Flournoy were named to the committee on business, which
recommended that the convention endorse the building of a railroad
from Richmond to Danville. Several substitutes, proposing specific
stretches to be included in the line, were proposed. The outcome of
the meeting must have been disappointing to the Farmville people;
for the substitute and rider adopted recommended that the line be
run through Nottoway to some point in Charlotte on the Staunton,
which might be extended westward, and that a new road be built
from the Amelia line (on the Appomattox) into Richmond. The
vote was 59 to 31, and it was by the same vote that a Flournoy
substitute, that a route from Richmond to Salem be surveyed, was
defeated.[292]

A second meeting on the Richmond-Danville railroad was held at
Charlotte Courthouse August 4, 1846. Prince Edward was repre-
sented by William C. Flournoy, Henry N. Watkins, N. G. McGehee,
Asa D. Dickinson, C. R. Barksdale, Samuel Allen, Edward F. Booker,
William P. Dickinson, Booker Foster, J. W. Brightwell, D. F.
Womack, William T. Carter, James H. Dupuy, Charles H. Hender-

son, R. S. Carter, and James W. Womack, a part of a considerably larger delegation named at a meeting held at the Courthouse July 20, of which Asa Dupuy was chairman and J. W. Brightwell secretary. The Charlotte Courthouse meeting endorsed a Richmond-Danville railroad by a vote of 79-43, Prince Edward voting 10 (its full vote) in favor. A proposal to endorse navigation of the Roanoke and its tributaries was defeated 36 to 79, Prince Edward voting 10 against. William C. Flournoy's resolution, prophetic since the Norfolk and Western years later made the proposal a reality, that a railroad be built from Tidewater to the Ohio River, did not receive a single vote, but had 109 votes, including Prince Edward's 10, cast against it.[293]

The Richmond and Danville Railroad Company was chartered by the legislature March 9, 1847, with a capital of $1,500,000, with the state subscribing 1,375 shares. No route was fixed; the road was to follow "the most eligible route."[294] Commissioners were promptly appointed to sell stock: William H. Venable, John A. Scott, Joseph E. Venable, Thomas J. Spencer, W. C. Flournoy, P. H. Jackson, F. N. Watkins, B. J. Worsham, and Samuel C. Anderson in Farmville and Prince Edward.[295] Later Henry N. Watkins, William T. Wootton, Daniel McCormick, Asa Dupuy, James H. Dupuy, Samuel D. Burke, and Edward B. Miller were named commissioners to sell stock in conformity with the charter.[296] As subscribers were slow to pay the requisitions, collectors were appointed in each county, Samuel D. Burke being named for Prince Edward.[297]

The first charter to the Southside Railroad Company was granted in 1846, but it provided for a railroad from Petersburg only to some point on Cox's road in Nottoway County east of Black's and White's tavern (Blackstone).[298] The Petersburg and Lynchburg Railroad Company was chartered in 1849, and the charter of the Southside Railroad was amended to permit it to build its line to connect with the Richmond and Danville at Burkeville; the state transferred its stock in the Petersburg and Roanoke Railroad to the Southside;[299] the stock amounted to $322,500.[300]

The Southside Railroad charter was amended a second time, this time in 1850 to permit it to extend its line to Lynchburg, on the Virginia and Tennessee Railroad. Stock already subscribed to the Petersburg and Lynchburg Railroad was ordered transferred to the Southside with the consent of the stockholders.[301]

In 1850 the trustees of Farmville were authorized to subscribe up to $30,000 to stock in the Southside Railroad, if three-fifths of the voters approved; the town was authorized to borrow money to pay for the stock and to levy taxes to pay the interest and redeem the principal.[302] In an election held June 17, 1851, the townspeople by a vote of 64 to 5 authorized the town to buy 200 shares of Southside Railroad stock.[303]

While the railroads were under construction, trains were run to stations near the construction, and were met by stages to take passengers to more distant destinations. On December 23, 1851, regular passenger service on the Richmond and Danville was inaugurated to Jetersville, where the train met Flagg and Company's line of stages for Burkeville, Farmville, Lynchburg, and Danville. Trains left Richmond at 8:00 A. M. on Tuesday, Thursday, and Saturday and the return trains left Jetersville at 11:30 A. M. The stage left Jetersville at 11:00 A. M. and on return met the "cars" there.[304] On February 19, 1852, passenger service was extended to Jennings Ordinary, where trains met Flagg's stages for Burkeville, Farmville, Danville, and Lynchburg. Servants (slaves) who traveled alone were required to have two passes, one to leave on file in the railroad office. A freight train ran from Richmond to Jennings Ordinary every Wednesday.[305] It was January 24, 1857, before train service was provided all the way from Richmond to Danville.[306] In June, 1854, passengers from Richmond to Lynchburg could transfer to the Southside Railroad at the Junction (Burkeville) and cover all but sixteen miles by rail; stage-coach accommodations were provided for the last sixteen miles of the trip at the Lynchburg end.[307] By August the railroad was within eleven miles of Lynchburg; passengers went five miles by stage and took the canal packet boat at Beaver Creek for the last six.[308] The Southside Railroad was completed in October, 1854.[309]

Southside receipts for the month of September, 1855, were reported to have been $27,178.31, an increase of $15,186.45 over the same month in 1854.[310] The Southside had a capital of $1,400,000, of which the state's interest amounted to $80,500; of the Richmond and Danville's capital of $2,000,000, the state's interest was $1,181,200.[311]

The winter schedule of the Southside provided for the mail and passenger train to leave Petersburg at 9:00 A. M. in the morning, arrive at the Junction at 11:55 A. M., and at Lynchburg at 4:40 P. M. A train left Lynchburg at 8:00 A. M., arrived at the Junction at noon, and at Petersburg at 3:10 P. M. The fare from Petersburg to Lynchburg was $5.[312]

Much of the iron for the Richmond and Danville rails was imported from England.[313]

Two locomotives for the Southside Railroad were made by Uriah Wells in his shop in Petersburg; the railroad had two passenger cars made in Springfield. In the construction of the Southside Railroad, the High Bridge over the Appomattox posed an engineering problem. The bridge was 3,400 feet long, sixty feet high at the abutments, and 100 feet high near the river. The engineer rejected the wooden piers generally in use in such construction because of danger of injury in a tornado. When the engineer decided to use brick, he could find no instance in which brick had been used for railroad bridge piers in the world; however, the examples of brick shot towers convinced him of the advantages of using this material; the High Bridge was the first railroad bridge in the United States to have brick piers.[314] Stone was also used in the construction of the piers. Much of it was quarried near the present High Rock Baptist Church (on Route 460) and hauled over a narrow gauge railroad track to the main tracks at the west side of Marrowbone Creek.[315] Many Irish workmen were employed in the construction of the Southside Railroad; they used to visit neighboring farms to buy butter and eggs.[316]

Weather presented problems in the early days of railroading. In January, 1856, there was an especially bitter cold spell; the Lynchburg train due in Petersburg Saturday evening, January 12, had not arrived by Tuesday, January 15; it was reported by telegraph from Farmville to be "stuck fast" at Pamplin's Depot.[317] A year later, during Cox' snow of 1857, trains on the Richmond and Danville could not begin running the day the line was opened to Danville, but had to wait two days.[318]

Miss Judith E. Woodall's description of her train ride on the Richmond and Danville in the late summer of 1852 has been preserved:

"I have been to see the cars and road 24 miles there was a very large crowd of people there they all road on the cars was the prettiest things inside I ever saw there was 5 trains they was as long as from hom hous [to] the stable they was crowded just as full as they could whole they want but 3 qurters of an hour going 12 miles and the same coming back when they came up in the morning they did not squeel until they got write a mong the people some of them was scard most to death. It scard me when they squeel sow I had the head ache for a little while but I soon got over It. I enjoyed my self

very well   Cousin was scard half to death I wish you could have
seen her and sister."[319]

This was one of the first, if not the first, trains to come into
Meherrin.

The coming of the first trains on both railroads attracted the
greatest interest, and great crowds assembled at the stations to see
them.[320]

S. H. DeBow, on a trip through Southside Virginia to look at
mineral lands in the section in 1858, went from Richmond to Farmville by train. His baggage was scarcely off the Richmond and
Danville at the Junction when the "Mountaineer" came in over the
Southside tracks. He described the lower end of Prince Edward
through which the railroad passed as the "piny barrens" and High
Bridge as "the bugbear of old maids and bachelors." Farmville was
"celebrated for tobacco, wheat, soil, men, destined to be celebrated
for its minerals."[321] The prophecy is yet to be fulfilled.

The railroad also brought express service to the various parts of
Virginia. In 1853 Parisen and King's Southern Express advertised
delivery of goods from New York to nearly all points in Virginia
within forty-eight hours. Merchandise was shipped from New York
to Virginia ports via the steamships *Roanoke* and *Jamestown* and
transferred to rail. J. W. Womack was agent for the express company in Farmville.[322]

The railroads also brought telegraph service to the towns and
stations along their route. The War Between the States was to give
great impetus to the use of this system of communication. The railroads appointed agents at the various stations. Benjamin F. Flippen
was the first agent of the Southside Railroad at Rice. As the locomotives used wood for fuel, and the fuel tenders were small, they
had to stop frequently for wood. The railroad contracted with people
to furnish wood, cut in proper lengths, at the different stations. The
boilers, too, on the early engines were small, and there were water
tanks constructed at comparatively frequent intervals along the
railroad. The Southside Railroad had four water tanks in Prince
Edward: at its crossing over Marrowbone Creek between Rice and
Moran, at Farmville, at Tuggle, and at Prospect.[323]

Compensation for railway rights of way was set by commissioners. John W. Redd, Henry S. Guthery, Albert G. Green, and
Thomas R. Marshall appraised the value of the land required for the
right of way for the Southside Railroad and set the price which was
paid. They began their work April 1, 1851. The railroad survey cut

through the farm of Joseph Phillips a distance of 3,900 feet; at the eastern entry into this farm the right of way was only eighty feet wide, but the width increased to 150 feet over the first 1,600 feet and then decreased in width to eighty feet at the western boundary of Phillips' farm. The railway took ten and one-half acres of this farm, for which Phillips was allowed $150. The railway right of way varied in width; it was 120 feet through the estate of Jack Raines, 130 feet through the farm of Vincent Phillips, 163 feet through the land of Edward Moring, and 204 feet through the land of William Bradshaw.[324]

Joseph A. Watson, Thomas R. Marshall, and William W. Watkins were the commissioners who fixed compensation for the land purchased for the right of way of the Richmond and Danville Railroad. They began appraisals of this land on January 24, 1854. The right of way sought by this road does not appear to have been as wide as that acquired by the Southside. Through the land of F. T. Wootton the average width of the right of way was 63.1 feet; in addition to the right of way the railroad bought from Wootton one and one-fifth acres of land for a station master's house and paid him $75 for the land acquired for both purposes.[325]

Interest in transportation extended to roads. The one improved road in the Prince Edward area promoted the commercial interests of Farmville as it led from Buckingham County to Farmville. The Farmville and Buckingham Plank Road Company was chartered in 1852 with a capital of $25,000. The road (evidently the right of way is meant by road in this place) was required to be twenty feet wide, and the width of the surface of plank eight feet. The plank road was built some distance out of Farmville, and the name survived long after the boards had decayed and mingled with the alternate mud and dust which the present generation remembers. An amendment to the act of incorporation, passed in 1853, gave permission to the company to extend the plank road to Midway Inn, if the Prince Edward Court approved.[326] This extension was not made.

The prevailing picture of ante-bellum agriculture is one of abusing the soil. A Prince Edward farmer blamed the "present degenerate state of agriculture in Middle Virginia" on grazing and injudicious plowing. The three-shift system was in general use, and few farmers had standing pastures. It was the practice to turn stock into the fields after harvest, there "to devour the scanty provision made by nature to improve the soil." These stubble fields were soon trampled and grazed to barrenness. This farmer was "pained at the number who plow up and down hill."[327]

There were notable exceptions to the prevailing picture; many Prince Edward farmers demonstrated great interest in agricultural progress. Edmund Ruffin was the leader in Virginia in the awakening interest in soil conservation and the improvement of crops, and his *Farmer's Register* was the manual of the progressive farmer of the 1830's. The number of his correspondents from Prince Edward and the quality of their reports and letters is evidence of interest in and practice of scientific farming methods as they were being developed then.

Dr. William S. Morton of Prince Edward was an early disciple of Ruffin in the use of marl for the improvement of soil. Dr. Morton had used "cement of calcareous pebbles" found in gullies on his farm to mend plastering, but he never thought of looking for marl in these gullies until he read Ruffin's "Essay on Calcareous Manures." Morton found on his own land beds of clay marl (land he described as once the bed of seas or lakes). In February, 1833, he reported that he had spread about 1,000 horse carts of marl on ten acres of land, nearly all of which was in second growth of trees and was regarded as exhausted; he proposed to put part in corn, part in cotton. Although he found the application of marl expensive and laborious, he was pleased with the results. The following December he reported that the corn and cotton on "gullied old field land" which had been marled were "quite respectable" and that four acres of tobacco which had been marled ripened earlier than tobacco on adjoining unmarled land.[328]

Morton continued his search for a better grade of marl than the clay he had found and used. He got his friend, George W. Dame of Hampden-Sydney College, to analyze one deposit; Dame reported that 100 grains included fifty-two grains of carbonate of lime, four of carbonate of magnesia, six of carbonate of soda, eight of oxide of iron, three of sulphur, four and one-half of copper, two of manganese, eight of silica, ten of alumine [*sic*], and two and one-half grains were lost.[329] Dr. Morton sent several samples of calcareous rocks to Ruffin in 1835; one sample, from Captain Branch's farm, was reported sixty-five percent carbonate of lime.[330] Dr. Morton also experimented with the use of gypsum (there was a "considerable bed of gypseous earth or mud" on his farm), and quoted Chaptel's *Agricultural Chemistry* on its preparation. He had used plaster nearly twenty years before he wrote in 1835; when he began using it, he paid at the rate of $35 per ton; although plaster sold in 1835 at $14-$16 per ton, farmers could not afford to use it extensively.[331]

During the next quarter century farmers were introduced to other fertilizers, such as Peruvian guano and superphosphate. Thomas T. Tredway in 1859 endorsed Rhodes superphosphate in a letter to its dealer, H. E. Warren of Farmville, as being as good as Peruvian guano for tobacco and wheat; Tredway was a cautious endorser, however; if he could be sure that Rhodes superphosphate would always be compounded as it was then, he would not use guano any more, but his "experience with artificial manures has resulted in the suspicion that manufacturers sometimes put out a valuable product to win favor, then a meaner one to make a profit. . . ."[332]

Tredway prepared his own tobacco plant bed fertilizer; it was his practice, when the stables were cleaned out in the spring just before his slaves finished plowing in the manure, to litter the stalls with tobacco stalks, which were saved for the purpose; before grass seed ripened, this manure was then removed and piled under shelter, where it was kept until the following spring, when it was used on plant beds.[333]

Any account of Prince Edward agriculture must place Charles Woodson in the first rank of farmers and experimenters in agriculture. A valuable horse died; most farmers would have assumed that grubs caused the death; but Woodson performed an autopsy and showed that the cause of death was bursting of the stomach as a result of eating too many dry oats after having been "carelessly starved." He also developed a treatment for a horse with colic: drench immediately with a quart or more of lukewarm soap suds, preferably from old soap, bleed freely and throw up a strong decoction of tobacco, milkwarm; if the horse recovers he should be allowed to rest until he regains his strength. For a swelling in horses with indication of sudden death, he recommended stabbing with a trocar or canula or knife four to five inches deep in a right line exactly half-way between the left hip bone and the lower end of the short rib, then turn the instrument a little forward to avoid striking the kidney; the instrument should perforate the large intestine; it was advisable to insert a tube or quill to let out the wind.[334]

Woodson urged "clemency and protection for the whole race of birds and mammals" for their part in destroying bugs, worms, and other insect pests.[335]

Woodson began his agricultural experiments early. When he was a boy, he proved that the prevailing practice of saving corn fodder was wasteful and unprofitable. Under the direction of his father, General Tarlton Woodson, he planted thirty-nine rows of corn, sixty hills long, five and one-half feet each way, with two stalks in every hill; it was cultivated in the usual way until it was time to pull the fodder. He then carefully pulled the fodder from each first and second row, leaving each third row with tops and fodder until entirely dry. Then, at the proper time as it was so judged, they cut the tops off each first row. There were then thirteen rows with fodder pulled and tops cut; thirteen with fodder pulled to one blade above the ear and the tops left until dry; and thirteen from which the tops had not been cut nor the fodder pulled. Each parcel of fodder was dried and kept separate; each lot of corn gathered and when dry shelled and weighed separately from each of the three groups of rows. The corn from the thirteen first rows (fodder pulled and tops cut) weighed considerably less than the corn from the second thirteen rows (fodder pulled), and the corn from the second group much less than the corn raised on the thirteen third rows (on which the fodder was not pulled nor the tops cut). The corn alone from the thirteen third rows weighed a few ounces more than both corn and fodder of the second set of rows and a few ounces less than the corn and fodder of the first set of rows. In another experiment Woodson found that stripping fodder from bottom of stalk to the top was the most unprofitable of all practices in harvesting corn.

Another experiment was carried out in wheat harvesting. He laid off two adjoining squares of wheat of equal size and equal quality; one square was harvested with a sickle about three days before it ripened; the grain was dried and kept separate. The other square ripened fully; it was harvested in the morning when damp with dew to avoid shattering. Woodson thought he saved every head in the two parcels. When both lots of wheat were perfectly dry they were threshed, cleaned, and weighed separately; the parcel harvested when ripe "weighed so much more as to astonish me." General Woodson told his son that he had tried the same experiment several times with wheat and once with barley, with similar results each time.[336]

From boyhood Woodson had also observed closely the growth of fruit trees. General Woodson, his father, planted an orchard of grafted apples and pears about 1784; the trees grew well until 1790, when some began to die. Young Charles dug up every piece of root of each tree which died between 1790 and 1800, observing that in no case did he find a root which had penetrated over one foot into the earth. He raised seedlings of young apple trees, dug them up when they were about the size of large goose quills, used them as stocks for hand grafting, and replanted them after grafting. He found that the tap roots of these small seedlings penetrated twenty-seven to thirty-six inches into the soil, but that if the tap root was cut, it "did not attempt to grow downward" and if it did, it was not strong enough to penetrate the subsoil. Woodson advocated the use of water spouts or suckers in grafting, never limbs from bearing parts. He found that by planting the seed of the most choice varieties of fruit in drills about six inches apart and with the trees eighteen inches apart they could be forced to bear fruit in four to five years. He warned against cutting stout limbs near the body of the tree in pruning in reporting that he "sometimes found pruning of infinite service." He also found it helpful to wash fruit trees with strong lye made from wood ashes and to whitewash the fruit trees with lime. Whitewashing them "prevents hares from biting them."[337]

Woodson developed a grape which attracted considerable attention, as also did Jacob Cunningham. A Dr. Norton of Richmand sent specimens of both to the *American Farmer*, and in reply to his inquiry about these grapes N. Francis Cabell wrote from Farmville in 1832 an account of them which he apparently had obtained from Samuel W. Venable. Venable, who had planted a two-acre vineyard about 1827 to determine the practicability of raising grapes "in sufficient abundance and suitable quality for making wine," had about forty stocks of the Woodson grape and about eighty of the Cunningham grape in his vineyard. Both grapes were Prince Edward natives and were supposed to be seedlings of the Bland, which had been generally and almost alone cultivated in early Prince Edward gardens and had been trained to grow on trees at old settlements; they had been discovered in the vicinity of farms where the Bland had been known to grow and were supposed to have grown from seed dropped by birds. The parent vine of the Woodson grape was then supposed to be over fifty years old and was then growing up an oak tree on high, dry soil. Cabell reported that this grape resembled the Bland except for the furze on the under side of the leaf. The Woodson vine was "highly prolific," some bunches in the Venable vineyard in 1832 weighing three pounds. The Woodson budded late, was rarely hurt by frost, was hardy on high, dry soil, and was not subject to rust. Its wine was considered good. It ripened October 10-15. The parent vine of the Cunningham grape was about twenty years old at the time and covered both sides and the top of an arched frame fifty feet long and twelve feet high in Jacob Cunningham's garden.

It was never pruned except for slips cut for propagation. In Venable's vineyard it was the most prolific vine except Woodson's. It also budded late and was rarely injured by frost. The grape ripened September 20 to October 10. The wine in body, smell, and flavor more nearly resembled Madeira than the wine of Woodson's grape. It was found difficult to root the Cunningham grape from slips, although Venable had some success in doing so; grafting was a more successful method of propagation, and the grape was easily propagated "with layers." Venable was successful with slips set out in November, but failed with those put out in the spring. There was a considerable distribution of the Cunningham grape through Virginia in 1828, 1829, and 1830.

The Venable vineyard was planted on a slightly declining hillside with a Southern exposure, the vines being planted twelve feet apart each way, with a sassafras pole seven feet high put by each vine. He had about 1,000 stocks, most of them obtained from Parmetier and Adlum; his most numerous varieties were Catawba, Constantia, Isabella, Schuylkill, Muscadel, Woodson, and Cunningham, all of which succeeded. His attempts to grow nearly forty foreign varieties failed, spring frosts proving destructive, and summer sun and rain burning and rotting the grapes which escaped the frost. Venable planted tobacco in his vineyard. He hoped to make from 500 to 1,000 gallons of wine in 1833.[338]

Charles Woodson's account of these varieties of grape differs in some points from Cabell's. He did not regard the Woodson grape as a seedling of the Bland, pointing out that the only resemblance between the two was in the brick-dust red or bright brown color. Woodson identified the grape which was named for him with a variety of wild grape which he had found from Goochland to the southern part of Prince Edward; the variety was not plentiful in that area, however. The fruit was about twice as large as the common black highland grape and the bunch much larger. The parent vine was found on the plantation of Henry Caldwell, which at the time Woodson wrote of the grape (1834) was owned by Isaac Read. Caldwell's son, James, told Woodson of the grape in 1794; it had been known then to the Caldwell family for several years. Since Henry Caldwell was an old settler, Woodson assumed that this vine antedated any Bland grapevine raised in the county. Woodson did not find the vine until 1806; it was north of Fort Creek, about a mile from its junction with Falling Creek. Woodson grafted a cutting of this grape on a thrifty bearing common wild grape vine in 1807;

the next year it yielded a basketful of bunches, and each succeeding year, except one, it had borne fruit when he wrote his account. He regarded the wine made from it the best he had tasted in Virginia and more like Madeira in color and flavor than any he knew.

The Cunningham grape, according to Woodson, was quite new in 1834. He first saw it in 1825, when it was a small vine, but it grew "astonishingly" in 1826. This grape Woodson did regard as a descendant of the Bland grape, for it was found in a corner of Jacob Cunningham's garden; there had been a Bland grape in the garden for many years. It resembled the Bland, although it was stronger and more vigorous. Woodson grafted some slips of the Cunningham grape on a vigorous native vine in his garden in 1826; eight years later the opposite ends of the vine were forty feet apart. He thought the Cunningham grape a superior wine grape.[339]

Henry N. Watkins found pruning and cultivating pear trees favorable to a blight. Observing that the ground around two pear trees at his grandfather's, where he was living in 1837, had been trampled by calves and horses and that they had been bearing fruit forty years and that four trees in a lot (adjoining the yard) which was sometimes cultivated were affected by blight (to the extent that two died), Watkins concluded that packing the ground about the trees was a factor in preventing blight. In 1821 he grafted about twenty pear trees; these he planted in a lot adjoining his yard and cultivated the lot for three years in tobacco; most of the trees were blighted. He then leveled the ground and included it in the yard; some of those most seriously injured by blight were enclosed with rails to protect them from calves which were permitted to graze in the yard. All twenty trees, except one, survived, and the survivors were in 1837 healthy; the one that died was in the cultivated garden. He recommended that pear trees be planted in rich soil, that they be plowed and worked for a few years, and then neither pruned nor plowed. He recommended ashes as a fertilizer, applied only on the surface and that small cattle be allowed to graze in the pear orchard.[340]

The farms of that day had extensive orchards; trees in many of these orchards remained until well within the memory of people now living. There was a variety of fruit: apples, peaches, pears, cherries, damsons, green gage plums, sometimes apricots. Then the chestnut was found at some homes as well as the walnut, which was often found growing wild.

Not only the extensive orchards give evidence of the fondness for fruit. In Prince Edward in ante-bellum times fifteen varieties of apple were developed, five of pear, two of peach, and four of grape. The apple varieties were: yellow winesap, developed on the farm of Thomas T. Tredway, a large yellow which kept all winter and was considered as good as the red winesap, a heavy bearer and a hardy tree; Gillespie sweet, on the farm of George Gillespie on Falling Creek, a fine cider apple, red with white dots, ripening in September, a heavy bearer; Arnold's cheese, on the farm of a Mr. Arnold, large, skin and flesh yellow, ripening in August and September; Cunningham's cheese, on the farm of Jacob Cunningham, rich-flavored, large, with red and yellow stripes, ripening in September; Prince Edward, on the farm of Mrs. Nancy Woodson (Brooklyn, near Prospect), large and showy, skin yellow with white dots, of high flavor, juicy, and a good keeper; Morton, on a Morton farm (otherwise unidentified), large, tender, juicy, white with a red cheek, ripening in August and September; Goosepen, on the farm of Henry E. Watkins, medium, red, sometimes striped, well-flavored and long keeping, a heavy bearer; Dicky Morton, on the farm of Richard Morton, medium, juicy, sweet, beginning to ripen about July 1; Price's cheese, on the farm of Captain Nathaniel Price, bright red cheek, ripening in September and keeping until December; Harvey's seedling, on the farm of Stephen Harvey near Prospect, large, showy, very red skin, juicy, keeping until March; Winter sweet, on the farm of Mrs. Nancy Woodson, laarge, striped, yellow flesh, rich, skeet, "keeps as well as the Limbertwig"; Venable's long keeping, on the farm of James Venable (Forest Green, near Prospect), medium, red, good flavor, keeps until July or August; Rosetta, also on the farm of James Venable, good-sized, fine flavor, keeps well, a "first rate cooking" apple; Black, on the farm of Mercer Brightwell near Prospect, large, deep red, almost black, high flavor, keeps well; Julia, on the farm of Henry J. Venable near Prospect, large, deep red on the sunny side, striped in the shade, yellow flesh, juicy, crisp, high flavored, ripening late in September and keeping until December.

Prince Edward's pear varieties were: Governor Allen, developed on the farm of Mrs. Nancy Woodson, large, covered with cinnamon russett, very juicy, rich, high flavored, ripening in October (named in honor of Governor Henry Watkins Allen of Louisiana); Jefferson, on the farm of Henry J. Venable, large, rusty, sweet juice, keeps all winter; three varieties of Woodson's seedlings, raised by Tarleton Woodson from the seed of the Vergalian pear: No. 1, large, juicy, vinous flavor, one of the best summer pears; No. 2, medium, melting, rich, and buttery; No. 3, medium, buttery, rich.

The two varieties of peach were Early Joe, developed on the farm of Joseph E. Venable, very early, rich-flavored, deep red cheek, and juicy white flesh; and Venable's extra early, developed on the farm of Nathaniel J. Venable near Prospect, a large and handsome freestone, melting and delicious, ripening a week to ten days before the Early Joe or Early Tillotson.

In addition to the Cunningham and Woodson grapes, there were also developed in Prince Edward the Davis grape, on the farm of Mrs. Martha Davis, large, black, juicy, sweet, ripening October 1; and the Spring Hill grape, developed in the Spring Hill nursery of Venable and Garden near Prospect, resembling the Morton seedling, with long, large, full bunches, hardy vine, a heavy and constant bearer, considered unsurpassed for eating, preserving, and making wine. The Cunningham grape according to this account, had large bunches, small black fruit, a hardy vine, and was very sweet. The Woodson grape was dark red, had large and full bunches, and was regarded as the best grape for making a dry wine.[341]

The first piece of farm machinery to come into general use was the threshing machine. In 1806 William S. Walton of Farmville advertised for sale "several threshing machines of the best kind" which would thresh seventy to eighty bushels a day and require only two horses and five hands.[342] These were rotary machines, and the horse was hitched to a shaft which he pulled around in a circle to furnish the power. Among the purchasers of Fox and Borland's Staple-tooth, spring-bed rotary threshing machines listed as references in an advertisement in 1838 was J. D. Wood of Prince Edward.[343] In an advertisement of the same machine in 1840 N. E. Venable and J. A. Scott were listed among the owners of the machine.[344] It was in this period when threshing machines were first coming into use that owners began the practice of threshing for others, taking their machines during season from farm to farm and threshing on a commission basis. There was at least one case in which a group of neighbors purchased a machine for their own use. The Rev. Daniel Witt (who farmed as well as preached), Thomas Clark, and William Weaver owned a machine together, which they used only on their own farms; it would be kept from one threshing season to the next on the farm of the person whose grain was the last threshed.[345]

While there are indications that the machine was coming into general use to replace the flail in threshing grain, it does not appear that the grain reaper, invented by Cyrus H. McCormick in Rockbridge County in 1831, replaced the cradle in Prince Edward very rapidly in harvesting wheat. Perhaps the supply of slave labor, which included experienced and expert cradlers, explains the absence of the machine on even the best farms. The art of cutting wheat with a cradle was known to older men remembered by this generation, and it was not an uncommon sight, as late as thirty to thirty-five years ago to see fields of wheat harvested with cradles, although binders had come into general use then, and custom harvesting was the prevailing practice, as it had been since the latter part of the nineteenth century. In addition to men skilled in the use of the cradle, there were men and women who were also skilled in tying the bunches of grain cut and dropped by the cradler and who followed him as he made his rounds.

In the steadily increasing interest in improving agricultural practices there were improvements made in the plows. When Thomas T. Tredway was in Richmond for the General Assembly of 1855-56, he attended a trial of the Watts new-pattern three-horse plows in competition with the Livingston plow. He was so much impressed by the performance of the Watts plow that he bought three and had them shipped to his Prince Edward farm. In the trial the Watts plow cut one-third more furrow than the Livingston, and it choked less than other plows in the trial field, a river bottom with weeds ten feet high. They were expected to arrive at Prospect on a Saturday, and the boy who went for the mail that day was to inquire at the depot in order that the cart might be sent for them at once. With the plows were twelve or thirteen loose points; Tredway had a shop on his farm at which the points could be repointed when necessary.[346]

Pests and poor growing weather from time to time plagued the farmer. Richard N. Venable noted on June 11, 1792, that the locusts, which had appeared May 2, had all gone. Evidently planting conditions were not favorable that year, for the entry in his diary for May 30 notes that very little tobacco had been planted.[347] Rust affected wheat and rye, tobacco, corn, and cotton as well; it was regarded as a disease and was observed not to appear until the fruit or other parts of the plant were full grown. A "Medico-Agriculturist" of Prince Edward County suggested that the bedding system might be the remedy for rust and mentioned the use of the dagon plow and coulter in preparing land.[348] Chinch bugs damaged the 1855 wheat crop.[349] Periodic droughts have appeared throughout the county's history. John Wright mentioned "the long drought" of 1755 and gave as one reason for the interest in religion in that year the "sword without the colony, famine within."[350] The year 1838 was a poor crop year; a report dated August 10 speaks of little rain since June 1; tobacco production was expected to be cut in half, and farmers who had not sold their 1837 crop were advised to hold it until the selling season in 1839 to take advantage of the almost certain high prices. The 1838 crop was late, plants were scarce that year, and a "great many" farmers had not planted their tobacco by August. The wheat crop was only a third as much as expected, and the corn crop, which earlier in the season had "bid fair to be the finest in years" had been seriously injured by drought and heat.[351] The year 1845 offered what was probably the shortest growing season on record; frost struck in Virginia as late as June 1 and came again in September. The June frost killed leaves on the trees.[352] A notable hail storm came August 7, 1854, when the ground was covered with solid hail at one time in the southeastern part of the county, near Moore's Ordinary; one hailstone measured five and one-half inches in circumference.[353]

There continued into this period the interest in blooded horses. During the season of 1796 *Herod*, an imported "handsome gray of elegant form," was at Bizarre, Richard Randolph's home in Cumberland just across the river from Farmville; *Herod* was the third of the name, his sire being of Lord Clermont's stud, his dam a daughter of *Conductor*. The season stud fee was $16, and enclosed pasturage was provided mares.[354] In 1802 *Quicksilver*, formerly owned by Colonel John Tayloe of Mount Airy, stood in Charlotte; he was exhibited at the Prince Edward District Court in April of that year. *Quicksilver* was described as the "best proportioned, best carriage, and carries the most lofty tail of any horse that was ever nicked and a number of his colts have the same carriage, points, and form." In color he was a dappled gray; his sire was the imported Hart's *Medley*, his dam's sire *Wildair*.[355] John Randolph, whose love of fine horses was one of the delights of his life, secured *Dragon*, once owned by the Duke of Bedford, for the 1804 season (March 1-August 1) and kept him at Bizarre; season stud fees for this horse were ten guineas and a dollar to the groom for each mare.[356]

In 1805 Thomas Haskins brought *Wrangler*, who belonged to

Colonel Miles Selden, to Prince Edward; *Wrangler* stood at Haskins' stable nine miles from the Courthouse and two miles from Elisha Betts' tavern (formerly Moore's Ordinary). The fee was £7 the season (March 10-August 10), twenty shillings of which was required as a down payment. Good, extensive, and enclosed pasturage was provided gratis, but Haskins assumed no responsibility for accidents or escapes. Grain, at market prices, would be fed mares at the request of the owner. *Wrangler* was bred by Sir Thomas Charles Bunbury. His sire was old *Diomed*, his dam Sir Charles Sedley's mare *Fleacatcher*, "decidedly the best mare of the day," whose sire was *Goldfinder*. *Wrangler's* performance record was as impressive as his pedigree: at three years old he won the sweepstakes at Alpaston in Sussex (England), at four he won at New Market (the second spring meeting), the Brighthelmstone sweepstakes of 300 guineas, and the four-mile heats at Bedford, open to all ages; at six he won the great Oatland stakes. He ran restive occasionally, and after 1800 this tendency increased; on this account he was sold and brought to Virginia.[357]

Richard D. Pincham of Prince Edward owned a "very beautiful and very valuable" horse, *Young Friday*, which stood at a stable near Cartersville during the season of 1805. In 1807, in the settlement of Pincham's estate, the executor advertised for sale, among other items, "one very likely stud colt, got by *Friday*, thought by good judges to be more valuable than his father," and among the Negroes Sam, "a noted hostler, and perhaps as good a groom as in the state."[358]

Sans-Culottes, who had stood at John Randolph's Middle Plantation on the Staunton River during the season of 1802, was "in or near Farmville," most probably at Bizarre, for the season of 1806; he was advertised as "believed to be inferior to no stallion in Virginia in form and action." *Sans-Culottes'* sire was *Old Celer*, and his dam's sire was the imported horse *Medley*.[359]

Richard K. Randolph advertised the imported horse *Mufti* for sale in 1807.[360]

Rinaldo, a stallion belonging to John Randolph of Roanoke, stood at Major (John) Rice's at Farmville during the 1833 season (February 14-July 14).[361]

In the 1830's Thomas Flournoy brought to Prince Edward a black Arabian stallion which had been bred in the stables of the Emperor of Morocco. In advertising for the 1837 season, Flournoy announced that that would be the last season his stallion would be in Virginia as he intended moving to Missouri; he changed his plans, however, settling again in Prince Edward "on the main road two miles south of Farmville." The *Arabian's* fourth season in America was in 1838. Flournoy charged a fee of $30 for the season if paid by July 1, $35 if not paid by then, and $50 to insure a mare, payable when it was ascertained she was with foal. The groom was paid $1 for each mare, and a fee of twenty-five cents per day was charged for caring for the mare; servants sent with mares were boarded free.[362] The stallion was presented by the Emperor of Morocco to the United States government through the consul at Tangier and was sold by Act of Congress February 28, 1835. Flournoy took his *Arabian* on a tour of the March courts, going to Buckingham, Nelson, and Amherst, and to Lynchburg after Amherst Court. The stallion was rather low, compared with the popular long-legged horses, but Flournoy agreed with John Randolph's characterization of the preference for tall horses as "a depraved leggy taste."[363] David Flournoy and Thomas T. Tredway purchased the *Arabian* for his seventh season in this country (1841), and he stood at David Flournoy's, four miles south of the Courthouse. The fees were reduced for this season: $30 the season ($25 if paid by July 15) and $40 to insure the mare; the dollar fee to the groom, the charge of twenty-five cents daily for care of the mare, and free board for servants sent with mares continued.[364]

The interest in blooded racing stock suggests interest in racing. This writer has found no evidence of racing or race-tracks in Prince Edward then, but there was racing in neighboring counties. Creed Taylor kept a horse belonging to Seymour Wright to race in 1794.[365] The Jockey Club Purse Race at Powhatan Courthouse seems to have been a popular event; in 1805 the prize for the first day's racing was the Jockey Club purse of £100, for the second day the proprietor's purse of £50.[366] Quin Morton's horse *Cow Driver* raced Daniel Willson's horse *Whipperwill* at Amelia Courthouse on a quarter-mile track July 12, 1804, the prize being $1,000.[367] There were race-tracks at Pridesville and Mansfield in Amelia.[368] Price's race-field in Charlotte was a popular track; in the races there in October, 1805, the first day's prize was an "elegant mahogany bedstead with curtains" and the third day's prize an "elegant gold watch."[369]

Mules came into use in Prince Edward in this period; the earliest reference this writer has found is the offer of a reward of $5 by Maurice Langhorne, Jr., for taking up and returning to him a pair of mules which strayed or were stolen from his lot in Farmville about September 1, 1809.[370]

Although farmers tried to raise enough feed for their teams and stock, sometimes they failed to do so and had to buy corn and hay. Creed Taylor bought two stacks from Mr. Venable in 1805; it amounted to six loads and a half, and its weight was estimated at 6,500 pounds.[371]

Among the proposals to improve agriculture was one by Benjamin F. Stanton of Prince Edward that the legislature or private individuals provide training in the making and use of farm implements. The Rev. Mr. Stanton was particularly critical of the care of implements by slaves and their awkwardness in a thousand other things; he mentioned that he had never seen a Negro raking wheat to tie into bundles who did not tread on the heads instead of the lower ends.[372] It was almost forty years later that a state agricultural college was established and still later before agriculture became a part of the public high school curriculum.

Put to more immediate use in promoting the progress of agriculture were agricultural societies. Henry E. Watkins of Prince Edward was elected a member of the Cumberland Agricultural Society in 1840.[373] In 1854 Watkins was elected a vice-president of the Southside Agricultural Society, of which James C. Bruce of Halifax was elected president.[374] The State Agricultural Society had 273 members in Prince Edward in 1856. Francis N. Watkins was commissioner to supervise the election that year of the three representatives from Prince Edward (on the basis of one additional representative for every 100 members over the first fifty) to the Farmers Assembly; life members of the society and every adult male member who could satisfy the commissioner that he had paid his annual dues of $1 were entitled to vote.[375] This assembly proposed the establishment at the University of Virginia of an agricultural department of three professorships, including one of veterinary surgery and practice.[376] Branch J. Worsham, B. S. Scott, and F. P. Wood were delegates from Prince Edward to the 1857 Farmers Assembly of the State Agricultural Society.[377]

The Virginia State Agricultural Society sponsored annual exhibitions, or fairs. In 1855 there were five judges from Prince Edward: H. G. Richardson was one of five judges of heavy draft horses; F. N. Watkins, one of five judges of Devon and Alderney cattle; A. D. Dickinson, one of five judges of long wools sheep; Francis P. Wood, one of five judges of straw and root cutters, corn shellers, and mills; and Philip A. Bolling, one of five judges of tobacco.[378] Prince Edward also furnished five judges for the exhibition in 1858, which was held in Petersburg. John A. Scott, was one of five judges of middle wools sheep of native stock and also one of five judges of rollers, clod crushers, and farm gates; Abram Carrington was one of five judges of swine; W. H. Anderson of Prospect Depot was one of five judges of horse powers, threshers, and separators; F. P. Wood, one of five judges of a miscellaneous assortment: deep-well pumps, water ram in operation, scoop or scooper, leveling instrument suitable for draining, churn, sausage cutter, washing machine, sewing machine, machine for shearing sheep, tide gate or model of tide gate; and James M. McNutt was one of five judges of blankets, cloth, shoes, and hats.[379] In 1860 the society's exhibition was held at the Hermitage Fair Grounds in Richmond. John A. Scott and F. P. Wood were judges of long-wool sheep of native stock, and A. R. Venable was a judge of wagons, carts, and harness.[380]

A tobacco marketing development claimed the disturbed attention of Prince Edward farmers in 1858, marking the beginning of a long-continuing concern about marketing practices and their effect upon the farmer's income. In May, 1858, W. Y. Sheppard opened a tobacco exchange at Thirteenth and Cary Streets, Richmond, for the sale of tobacco at auction. A number of Richmond commission merchants agreed to sell only on the exchange; if a customer who shipped tobacco to them for sale asked that it be sold in the public warehouse under the inspection system, his request would be disregarded. The inspectors at Shockoe, Public, and Seabrook's Warehouses in Richmond felt constrained to advertise, following the decision of the commission merchants, that they were continuing the "old custom" of selling tobacco through the inspection system and that the charge for selling, collecting, and remitting the proceeds of the sale remained the same, $1 per hogshead.[381] Prince Edward farmers were especially disturbed. The Bush and Briery Agricultural Club met at Moilena, the home of John A. Scott, on May 22, 1858; it adopted a preamble in which the apprehension that the establishment of the tobacco exchange would take control of the sale of tobacco away from the farmer and give it entirely to the commission merchant was made the basis of four resolutions: that members of the club would use commission merchants only at their own option as agents for the sale of their products, that they would not be compelled to sell through merchants against their will, and that their fellow tobacco growers be invited to join in this determination; that a committee be appointed to get all the information possible about the exchange and report to the next meeting; that the committee seek the cooperation of other clubs "in resisting the violation of the long established usage of this country and invasion of the rights of the planter"; that the Virginia State Agricultural Society be asked to cooperate in the effort to maintain the system of marketing tobacco through the established inspection. The committee named consisted of A. D. Dickinson, F. P. Wood, John A. Scott, P. H. Jackson, and Branch J. Worsham. Dickinson was secretary of the club.[382]

The tobacco growers of Prince Edward then held a meeting at the Courthouse on June 1: John W. Redd acted as chairman, and J. H. Knight as secretary. John A. Scott stated the purpose of the meeting, to take action in reference to the establishment of the tobacco exchange. Upon his motion, a committee of twelve, consisting of F. T. Wootton, John H. Knight, Edwin Edmunds, S. B. Scott, Thomas Clark, H. G. McCargo, David Womack, T. T. Tredway, Newton Cunningham, George W. Redd, Thomas Hickson, and Richard Scott, was named to draw up resolutions. While the committee was preparing the resolutions, A. D. Dickinson, John W. Wilson, and Joseph T. Morton of Richmond spoke. The committee report, presented by F. T. Wootton, went to the heart of the matter in its preamble: the exchange was established to abolish the sale of tobacco in the public warehouses and to substitute for the system of inspection, a long established and legally sanctioned practice which has given general satisfaction to planters, a system in which a board of trade, dominated by commission merchants and on which the farmers have no voice has control of the sales. This board could exclude the farmer from the privilege of selling his crops and levy a tax or commission to suit the interests of the board. The aim would be to force the farmer to deliver his tobacco to a commission merchant and sell on the exchange. The establishment of exchanges in the larger cities "has always excluded the grower from the privilege of selling produce as he thinks proper and forces him to employ an agent against his will," the committee held. The five resolutions were unanimously adopted: that they would resist the establishment of the exchange; that they would not sell on the exchange until the existing laws were amended and some other place of public sale provided; that they regard the assertion of the commission merchants that the dealers as a body demanded the exchange as erroneous; that they regard the merchants' resolution to sell only on the exchange and to disregard planters' instructions to sell at public warehouses an "unwarrantable and aggressive assumption of power" and they pledge not to employ as agent any merchant "who has entered into such a combination"; if the establishment of some other mode and place of selling is required, they would ask the legislature to establish a suitable place or places. Another resolution, presented by John A. Scott, that the planters would seek some other market than Richmond if they were forced to sell there on the exchange, was also adopted.[383]

H. G. Richardson, in a letter to the Richmond *Enquirer*, charged that the merchants were prejudiced against the inspectors because they realized that the inspectors were growing more popular as the "planters' true and reliable agents." The farmer was deprived of the services of his friend, the inspector, in the exchange, he observed. He then commended John Caskie, Gilmour, and the Messrs. Thomas, Richmond merchants who opposed the establishment of the exchange and who favored holding "to the established usages."[384]

The committee reported to the meeting of the Bush and Briery Club at the Clerk's Office on June 29 that its queries addressed to the proprietor of the exchange concerning sales practices there had gone unanswered; it reviewed the developments in the establishment of the exchange, reiterated the opposition earlier expressed to the exchange, and renewed the endorsement of the inspection system.[385]

Thomas T. Tredway's instructions for farm work in mid-August show that it was a busy season: fallow all the clovered land around the old settlement and the red lot around the old pea-patch cabin for wheat; fallow the hill which was in wheat and oats this year for rye, then all the highland around the house which was in wheat; keep tobacco in good condition, worked, wormed, suckered, and topped as fast as it will bear topping at eight leaves (top at eight until the last day of next week, then at seven).[386]

Livestock then was taken to market by driving. William Woodall, who kept a store at Jamestown, wrote in a letter to his brother John December 12, 1849, that he had a small drove of hogs to stay with him two nights last week; he sold some corn to their drivers to feed them and bought 500 pounds of pork.[387] The going was slow, for the beeves, sheep, and hogs could not be pushed hard; the driver had to consider conserving the weight of the animals as well as their health on the drive. For all the slowness and difficulty, the drove of stock, especially of hogs, was not an uncommon sight on the roads of Prince Edward until well after the building of the railroads.[388]

The farm through this period continued to be to a considerable extent a self-sustaining unit. Garden and orchard, cattle, sheep, and hogs provided food, and most farms had all. The farmer also tried to provide enough flour and meal for the needs of his family and his slaves, as well as of his livestock, from his production of wheat and corn, and oats and rye were raised to provide feed for stock. Sometimes, though, he was not able to raise enough food, and he had to buy it. Merchants did a rather large business in bacon, which they generally bought from Baltimore; with some merchants, the bacon trade was cash; as R. S. Paulett explained it, "when we order bacon from Baltimore we have to send our cheqe to pay for it before the bacon comes to hand."[389]

The typical Prince Edward farm also raised cotton for clothing. The home-grown cotton and the wool from the farm flock of sheep provided most of the clothing needs of the slaves and to some extent the clothing needs of the family. Wool and cotton were spun, woven on looms into cloth, cut out and made into clothing at home. The homespun was quite durable. In addition to the large cotton wheel, the household was likely also to have a small flax wheel. Carding machines, which could card six pounds of cotton a day, roving frames with a daily capacity of six pounds of cotton, and six-spindle spinning machines, which could spin six pounds of cotton daily were offered for sale in 1810. The carding and spinning machines cost $60 each, the roving frame $30. A demonstration of the machines was given at George N. Skipwith's in Cumberland; among those who saw them work and endorsed them were John Kelso of Prince Edward and Dr. T. Robertson of Farmville. Pugh W. Price of Prince Edward was one of the agents in Southside Virginia for the machines made by John George Baxter of Philadelphia.[390] Where there were several slave women, some were trained in spinning, making cloth, and sewing; but usually the mistress of the home was an expert in such matters, shared in the work, and exercised close supervision over it. Where there were no slaves, or the work of the few slave women was required in the field, the housewife herself did this work. Spinning and cloth making was woman's work from the dawn of history until the machinery of the Industrial Revolution made it more economical to buy cloth and to some extent ready made clothes than to make the cloth and clothes at home. The classic description of noble womanhood in Proverbs emphasizes the industry and the responsibility of the woman in spinning and making clothes. And there was told in Georgia, as an example of the industry of Mrs. Micajah McGehee (*née* Anne Scott of Lunenburg), who with her husband moved from Prince Edward to North Georgia in the 1780's, the story of how Mrs. McGehee spun the thread, wove the cloth, cut out the material, and made a petticoat—all in one day.[391] From fiber to garment between breakfast and supper, or even bedtime, was no small achievement.

Not only were much of the food and much of the clothing produced at home; the ladies made their own facial cream. An old Southside Virginia recipe for facial cream calls for one large cucumber grated and strained, to which were added equal parts of rubbing alcohol, glycerin, and rose water, and one lemon. "Shake well and keep corked," the directions concluded.[392]

Yeast was also made at home from hops; an unidentified Prince Edward resident found that one could substitute life everlasting (also called rabbit tobacco) for hops, using the dried leaves and flowers. He claimed that bread made with such yeast was not so likely to become sour as that made with yeast from hops, and he regarded its flavor as superior; he thought life everlasting's yeast-making qualities might be improved if it were cultivated, the leaves and flowers gathered when ripe, and dried in the shade.[393]

Although much work was done at home, especially if there were skilled slaves on the plantation, there were skilled craftsmen whose services were in demand. Some of the work a blacksmith did is shown on a bill of John Hurt to Laban Hawkins in 1807; upsetting an ax, mending an ax, making a bale for a kettle, shoeing horse around with old shoes "pinted" (for two shillings, sixpence), mending a staple, mending a shovel, putting a handle to a sod iron, making a screw-driver and tap, pointing nine rake teeth, shoeing sorrel horse around (four shillings), laying a coulter, mending two eyes for hill hoes, mending clivis, beating out three hoes, laying and upsetting a grub hoe, hooping a cart.[394]

Another important craftsman was the cooper, who made hogsheads in which tobacco was carried to market and barrels for flour and other commodities. William Woodall in 1839 asked his brother John if he could not "get Charles Cabbel to come up and set up 3 or 4 hogsheads for me" as he couldn't get a cooper in his neighborhood; "if it would be an inducement," he added, "tell him I will pay him as soon as the work is done."[395]

People sometimes had weaving done. A bill from Abraham McGehee to Laban Hawkins in 1813 contains the item: "Nancy for weaving 10¼ yards cloth—.86."[396] Other bills in manuscript collections include items for weaving, indicating that this was not an isolated instance. In 1852 William F. Farrar was advertising his tailor's shop on Main Street, opposite the Farmers Bank, in Farmville, emphasizing "particular attention to repairing and cutting."[397]

There was a fulling mill in Prince Edward in 1786 for the processing of cloth.[398]

Where there was no skilled cobbler among the slaves, the services of this worker were in demand. Laban Hawkins in 1806 billed John Rudd for eight pair of shoes, each pair for a different person, some of whom were members of the family and some apparently slaves, at two shillings the pair.[399] The low price suggests that Rudd furnished the leather.

The tanyard was a familiar industry in Prince Edward in those days. Martin Saylor and George King were partners in a tannery, under the firm name of Saylor and King, near the Courthouse. This partnership was dissolved October 17, 1809; King settled up the affairs of the firm,[400] and apparently continued the business, as John Wood's map of 1820 locates King's tanyard between the Courthouse and the present Kingsville. The industry gave the name Tanyard branch to the stream which flowed between the two villages. Wood's map also locates Mickle's tanyard on a branch of Falling Creek. This tanyard was evidently in operation in 1858, when it is one of the landmarks given in the dividing line between West Hanover and Roanoke Presbyteries.[401] One memoir of Farmville in its earlier period mentions Hill's tanyard near the spring "in the grass meadow" there.[402] Hides of cattle slaughtered at home were tanned at these yards and processed into leather for shoemaking. Old residents used to tell of the shoemaker going to different homes and making shoes for members of the family and slaves, remaining at one place until he had made enough shoes to outfit the household and then going to another home where his services had been engaged.

Another indication of concern for appearance in ante-bellum days was the advertisement of Crawley Mitchell, "barber and hair dresser" in Farmville in 1852.[403]

Materials for dress clothes were bought, as statements of merchants to their customers which include the better materials indicate. Charles Lewis, a tailor in Prince Edward in the 1820's charged $1 for making a pair of pantaloons; $4.25 for making a suit, evidently for a boy; $2.50 and $2 for making a coat; and $4 for making a frock coat.[404] During the latter part of the ante-bellum period men wore dress coats to church and to other gatherings; usually the coats were blue with brass buttons; black suits were also worn; ruffled shirts, white beaver hats, and pump-soled boots with high heels were popular items of men's dress.[405] The ladies used silk for their best dresses; younger women used colors, older women usually wore black silk. Men and women wore dusters when riding to protect good clothes.[406]

The cost of carpenter's work has been preserved in John Ford's bill to Laban Hawkins in 1808, obviously his statement for building a house:

Getting and putting on 4500 shingles @ 18/ per M. .£	4: 1: 0
hewing 561 feet @ 6/ per C.....................	1:13: 9
framing 16 1/6 squares @ 6/ per square..........	4:17
weatherboarding 7 ¼ squares @ 3/6 per square....	1: 5:10½
sheeting 6 ¾ squares @ 2/ per square...........	0:13: 6
casing 3 doors @ 9/ per door...................	1: 7
casing 2 windows @ 9/ per window..............	0:18
casing 2 windows @ 4/6 per window............	0: 9
putting on 4 cornerboards @ 9 d per board........	0: 3
putting on 2 large boards @ 1/ per board.........	0: 2
cornice and boxing 56 feet @ 1/ per foot..........	2:16
dressing joists.................................	0:12

£18:18: 1½[407]

It was during this period that most of the homes now regarded as old homes in the county were built. Periods of prosperity enabled some of the people to build residences of some beauty and pretentiousness. One has only to examine some of these old homes to find that a superior craftsmanship went into the work of construction, as well as quality materials. Handsome woodwork—paneling, door and window facing, staircases—was a feature of some of these homes; another handsome feature was the plaster centerpiece design in the ceiling. These centerpieces were made in molds of beeswax and were quite expensive. In the eastern part of the county, three of the larger old homes surviving were built in 1858; James S. Lockett added the imposing front to his home in that year; James D. Walthall built Sunnyside and Major James Watson Chatham in the same year.

When Chatham was wired for electricity in 1950, it was found that the studding was of three-by-fours, instead of the conventional two-by-fours. Other homes dating from the ante-bellum period are Walnut Hill (James D. Ligon), Rotherwood (Edwin Edmunds). Longwood (Nathaniel E. Venable), Kinderton (Abraham W. Venable), and Cork (Jesse Michaux). The imposing brick residences at Hampden-Sydney as well as the frame Estcourt there belong to this period, as do the brick town houses of Patrick H. Jackson (on Beech Street) and Richard S. Paulett (on High Street) in Farmville. There were not many brick houses in the county outside Farmville and Hampden-Sydney in this period. Sandy Ford, west of Farmville, survives, but Moilena, home of Peyton Randolph and later of John A. Scott, burned years ago, and Waverley, the Samuel Scott home, no longer stands. There was one stone residence in the county, built, according to the date on its chimney, in 1826 by P. L. Ligon, in the northeastern corner of the county; this is now in ruins, the chimney ends standing, but the other walls have fallen.[408]

The finest example of Prince Edward craftsmanship in home building is not to be found in the county. In this writer's opinion this example is to be found in Warrenton, North Carolina, and is the residence long known as the Eaton place and now the Mary Burwell Allen Memorial Parsonage for the Wesley Memorial Methodist Church. It is a brick structure, Greek Revival in style, of excellent proportions, and distinguished for beautiful workmanship. It was built for William Eaton, Sr., in 1843 by Jacob Holt, a Prince Edward native, who in the 1840's went to Warren County. Most of the fine ante-bellum homes of that county are credited to Holt, his brother Thomas, and Edward T. Rice, all Prince Edward men who spent several years in and around Warrenton engaged in building homes.[409] The Eaton place well merits its reputation as the show-place of Warrenton; it is one of the notable mansions of North Carolina.

It is not certain who was the first practicing physician to live in Prince Edward County. One of the earliest, if not the earliest, was Dr. Francis Joseph Mettauer, who came to this country as a surgeon with French troops during the Revolution. He bought a farm adjoining the glebe and Nathaniel Venable in 1784 and subsequently additional land.[410] He built up an extensive practice.[411] In 1797 Dr. Mettauer attended Governor Beverly Randolph of Cumberland; his bill to the Randolph estate includes an item of £2 for visit and attendance and pill. aperient on February 1, 1797, and another for £7:10 for visit and attendance February 2-6; other items for medicines are presented with pharmaceutical symbols.[412]

A set of instructions of Dr. Joseph Mettauer to a patient has been preserved:

"Take one pill out of No. 1 & No. 2 at night by going to bed, take two of No. 1 early in the morning continue them till used, but should you get very sick at the stomach take the vomit, do not take any pills for a day or two after taking the vomit and if you feel like getting well take no more pills but begin upon the Bitters. It is proper to bleed in the arm in a day or two when you begin to take the pills, bleed again when you break out with an itching. You are to take some gruel salt in it every morning early as often as the pills operates, and they operate to much take only one in the morning of No. 1. Your drink is to be toasted water used cool and some stockweed roots tea used cold. No drink cold water, no cyder brandy nor wine, eat no raw vegetables, no fish, eggs, milk nor fruit. rub your feet and hands with a little vinegar and tallow when they burn or feel cold. do not overheat yourself nor get wet or cold. the Bitters must be put in a quart bottle with a pint of water and half a pint of rum or whiskey, set it in the Sun for several days by sheaking now then, take a small wine glass full three times a day, when nearly all used fill them up again and set in the sun. You may drink cold water while using these Bitters and eat as common excepting fish.

"Jos. Mettauer
"March 19th 1808"[413]

It was during this period that inoculation for smallpox became widespread. In 1786 John Tabb of Amelia wrote William Watts that "symptoms of the small px on those now under inocluation appear this morning much more favorable than yesterday, and I - - - begin to expect my wife and her four daughters will have it lightly, the negroes are also greatly better."[414]

James Walker operated a hospital for inoculation for smallpox in Buckingham, about twenty miles distant from the courthouses of Buckingham, Prince Edward, Charlotte, and Campbell, six miles from Captain Flood's tavern and about the same distance from Captain Kelso's [in Prince Edward]. Board at $2 a week or $7 for the period of the inoculation was provided. The fee was a guinea for whites, fifteen shillings for blacks. The period in 1800 began

September 15, in 1802, which he advertised as his last, September 20.[415]

Dr. Thomas Robinson, a native of North Ireland, who attended the School of Medicine of the University of Pennsylvania 1803-04, practiced medicine in Farmville 1806-10.[416]

The great name in medicine in Prince Edward in this period, and one of the great names in American medicine, was that of Dr. John Peter Mettauer, son of Dr. Francis Joseph Mettauer and graduate in medicine of the University of Pennsylvania in 1809. His medical school has been discussed in another connection. He was the first physician in America to operate for the cleft palate, the first to employ iodine in the treatment of scrofula, one of the first to conceive the idea of curing vesicovaginal fistula, and one of the first to perform such major operations as amputation of shoulder, ligation of the carotid, and on the superior maxilla. Dr. Mettauer's work in differentiating three types of fever, synocha, typhoid, and typhus, has been called by Dr. Wyndham B. Blanton "one of his real contributions to medicine." He was the first to recognize typhoid fever as such. Dr. Mettauer was a frequent contributor to medical journals. Dr. George Ben Johnston praised the manuscript Dr. Mettauer prepared on general surgery, a treatise of some 3,000 pages. He maintained a hospital at his home.[417] Dr. Mettauer, Dr. Stephen C. Farrar, and Dr. William S. Morton attended Dr. John Holt Rice during his last illness.[418] Dr. Mettauer at times maintained an office in Farmville in addition to one at his home.[419]

Dr. Philip T. Southall of Jamestown was still sending out bills in pounds, shillings, and pence in 1819 and 1820. For a visit to Mrs. James Blanton on February 24, 1819, he charged twelve shillings. In 1832 Dr. John Spencer charged $2 for a visit during the day, $4 for a visit at night or in rain. Physicians then carried medicines with them; their bills included charges for them.   Dr. Southall in 1819 charged James Blanton four shillings sixpence for six laxative doses, three shillings for camp cathartic, and four shillings sixpence for fever mixture. Dr. Spencer's bill in 1832 included such items as six shillings for quinine, one shilling sixpence for turpentine, and the same amount for a "phial of vitriol." In 1839 the fee for a night visit was $5, although the charge for a visit in the rain remained $4.[420]

Dr. Mettauer's contributions to medical journals were not the only indications of professional interest among Prince Edward physicians. There was a Prince Edward Medical Society in 1855; in that year Dr. James Lyle was its representative at the national association in Philadelphia.[421] Dr. A. S. Dillon of Farmville was one of the delegates from Virginia to the American Medical Association meeting in Louisville, Kentucky, in 1859.[422]

Prince Edward was the home of a number of physicians during the latter part of the ante-bellum period. It has been mentioned that Dr. John Holt Rice was attended during his last illness by Dr. Mettauer, Dr. Stephen C. Farrar, and Dr. William S. Morton, who was living in Prince Edward in the 1830's when he contributed to the *Farmers' Register*. In the election of 1840 eighteen doctors voted in Prince Edward (eleven of them for Harrison). Dr. Joel W. Dupuy, Dr. Mettauer, Dr. Benjamin F. Terry, Dr. Sam V. Watkins, and Dr. Peyton R. Berkeley had the Courthouse as their address. Dr. William H. Chappell, Dr. George J. Smith, Dr. John T. Ligon, and Dr. B. F. Wilson could be reached at Farmville (Dr. Ligon's home was Aspen Hill, on the east side of Sandy River, near Rice). Sandy River Church was the address of Dr. R. H. Dejarnett, Dr. Robert S. Clark, and Dr. J. Vaughan. Dr. Thomas C. Overton, Jamestown; Dr. John R. McDearmon, Walkers Church; Dr. James Agnew, Burkeville; Dr. James H. Lacy, Marble Hill; and Dr. Merrit B. Allen, Prospect, were others. The address of Dr. Richard B. Tuggle who voted in Prince Edward is given as Nottoway County,[423] but in a reference to his marriage in 1845 he is said to have been of Prince Edward.[424] Dr. James Dillon and Dr. Goodrich Wilson practiced in Prince Edward earlier in the period.[425] Dr. William Britton, aged twenty-seven, of "high professional reputation and promise," died at Captain Henry Thweatt's in 1832.[426] Dr. B. Pryor was on the county Democratic committee in 1840, but he is not listed as "doctor" in the voting list. In 1856 Dr. James Lyle, Dr. James T. Spencer, and Dr. Benjamin C. Peters were practicing in Farmville.[427] After his graduation from the Medical College in Baltimore in 1849, Dr. Simeon Taylor Walton practiced for several years at Sandy River Church before moving to Keysville. His brother, Dr. James T. Walton, practiced dentistry there for a few years.[428] Two young men from Prince Edward were graduates of the Medical Department of Hampden-Sydney in Richmond during this period, Benjamin F. Lockett in 1848 and William H. Hughart in 1853.[429] There was a Dr. Puryear in the county in 1854.[430]

An early dental practitioner in Prince Edward was Dr. Monroe of Richmond, who in 1834 visited Brunswick, Lunenburg, Nottoway, and Prince Edward on a professional tour. He asked those who wished his services to leave their names at their county courthouse.[431]

Prince Edward also had one of the leading dentists of the day, Dr. William W. H. Thackston, who practiced in Farmville. Dr. Thackston was a member of the second class to graduate in dentistry in the United States, at the Baltimore College of Dental Surgery in 1842. He seems to have practiced for a time in Farmville before going to dental school, as the professional card of Drs. Smith and Thackston of Farmville for 1839 has been found. He was one of the organizers of the Virginia Society of Surgeon Dentists in 1842 and of the Virginia State Dental Society in 1870. He was a contributor to the *American Journal of Dental Science*.[432] Dr. Thackston charged Mrs. James Blanton $200 for making her a double set of teeth in 1850. His charge for extracting a tooth at that time was $1.[433] Some dentists of the period went to the homes of their patients, in response to calls, to render services, especially to pull teeth.[434]

Farmville had a drug store by 1842. In that year James Blanton's bill with William H. Chappell included saleratus, saltpetre, epsom salts, and ipecac; in 1814, Seidlitz powders, logwood, madder, bluestone, and nitric acid; and in 1847, blue pills, carbo-iron, quinine, antimonial merc. blistering ointment. Drug stores then did not limit their wares to pharmaceuticals; Blanton's account with Chappell in 1844 included a quire of letter paper and in 1847 three camel hair brushes.[435]

Patent medicines were an important stock in the drug trade by 1852; in that year Thomas Hickson of Farmville advertised George B. Green's "oxygenated bitters for dyspepsia, phthisic, asthma, general debility, nervousness, headache, and all diseases arising from derangement of the stomach"; Ayers cherry pectoral; Ruston Clark and Company's cod liver oil ("excellent for retarding the progress of consumption") and B. A. Fahnstock's vermifuge. Walter H. Middleton advertised at the same time Little's white oil, Udolpho Wolff's aromatic Schiedam Schnapps, Huchings vegetable dyspepsia bitters, and Dr. J. S. Houghton's pepsin. Hickson was also advertising such non-drug items as garden seeds, hops, and yeast powders.[436]

Eyeglasses have longed been used by Prince Edward people. William Watts was wearing spectacles in 1789.[437]

The American people have always been a migratory breed. Prince Edward was still a pioneer community when some of its people moved on to other places. The first minister in the county, the Rev. John Thomson, moved southward to Rowan County, North Carolina, in 1751, more than two years before Prince Edward was established. Others tarried only briefly also. The widow, Mary

Hanna, her son and daughter, moved from the county in 1765, as their certificate of membership in the Buffalo congregation indicates, supposedly to South Carolina.[438]

After the Revolution the migration from the county took many of its people to the new country opening up in the South and West, especially in Georgia and Kentucky. The lure of fresh land appealed to people of means and to people in humbler circumstances. Robert Lawson, whose rank as brigadier general in the Revolution and membership of the War Board of the Commonwealth during the Revolution and of the Council of State afterward gave him valid claim to be the county's most prominent citizen in the decade between the death of John Nash, Sr., and the coming to the county of Governor Patrick Henry, joined those who sought a new home in another state. Lawson seems to have first considered moving South. General, later Governor, Henry Lee, "Light Horse Harry" of Revolutionary fame, in 1787 gave Lawson letters of introduction to Pierce Butler and General Charles Cotesworth Pinckney of South Carolina and to William Few of Georgia. The letter to Butler introduced Lawson as a friend and fellow soldier "who intends to visit the Southern states . . . My worthy countryman to whom your marked civility will be gratifying to me." To Pinckney he was introduced as "well known to you in character"; Lee was "confident that the general will be happy in your circle." Lawson also carried a letter of introduction from George Mason to Charles Cotesworth Pinckney; Mason described him as "a very worthy and brave officer of our late Ar[my] General Lawson being a Member of our Assembly." Whether Lawson made his trip South is not known to this writer. In 1789 he moved to Kentucky, where he received a letter from General Adam Stephen addressed to him at Lexington, congratulating him on his safe arrival in the Territory of Kentucky, and voicing the expectation that Lawson would be elected to Congress.[439]

Alfred J. Morrison observes from the number of powers of attorney from Georgia recorded in the Prince Edward deed books prior to 1790 that there was a much more numerous emigation from Prince Edward to Georgia than to Kentucky.[440]

The pension declaration of Matthew Clark of Anderson District, South Carolina, relates that he served in the Revolution from Goochland, that after the Revolution he lived in Prince Edward for about ten years before moving to South Carolina.[441]

Micajah McGehee moved from Prince Edward to North Georgia, where he settled on Broad River, sometime between the birth of his son Abner in 1779 and the birth of his son Edward in 1786. There he achieved considerable success, as he owned good land and was a fine tobacco man—"he showed by his looks and ways he was a tobacco planter of the right sort." McGehee planted the first peach orchard in his section from which he made brandy. He built the first comfortable frame house and bought the first carriage on Broad River. For all his success—his income from his peach orchard alone was $1,600 a year—he made his children work, and for all the industry in the household, his home was a great place for dancing and good eating.[442]

William Bibb, sheriff in 1788 and 1789, moved to Georgia before the delinquent tax lands could be sold, thus creating a problem for his deputies.[443] Peter LeGrand had moved to Kentucky prior to 1805.[444] Joseph Venable, commonwealth's attorney for Prince Edward, moved to Shelby County, Kentucky, in 1810.[445] Another Prince Edward lawyer, William Watts, did not leave the state, but he did remove from Prince Edward, first to Botetourt County about 1787 and then to Campbell County prior to 1796; his address was New London in 1796.[446]

Not all the migrants went as well endorsed as Robert Lawson and not all prospered to the extent of Micajah McGehee. Some did not find conditions to their liking in the place of their first settlement and moved on. Elijah McGehee went to Kentucky in the 1830's, but finding land cheaper in Tennessee and esteeming the state of society better there than in Kentucky, he moved to Henry County, Tennessee. He found his Henry County farm a good place to raise corn, wheat, oats, and tobacco and enough cotton for home use. New Orleans was his tobacco market. In 1840 he wrote that the price of produce was low and that times were hard.[447]

As the line of settlement moved farther west, the migrants followed it. Josiah Walton settled at Hickory Grove, on the edge of Elkhorn prairie, in Warren County, Missouri, in the 1830's. He found the going rather hard. The interest rate on money loaned in his section was twenty per cent a year. At first he thought of returning to Virginia, but as his wife was satisfied to remain in Missouri he decided to stay there.[448] Daniel Witt made a tour of the West after attending the Baptist Triennial Convention in Philadelphia in 1844 and visited Walton; he was accompanied by the Rev. J. B. Jeter, and they preached several times in the community.[449]

The difficulties of moving were vividly described in two letters from William Woodall, who in 1853 moved from Jamestown where he had kept a store to a farm in Halifax County, to his brother John, who was then living near Moore's Ordinary. A summary of the letters tells of the vicissitudes of moving and getting settled in a new place a century ago:

Halifax County, Va., Oct. 21, 1853: Arrived here last Wednesday night a little before moon up. Last Tuesday night arrived Shattersburg about dark, tried to get room for wife and children, could only get a shanty where Davis and Webb used to keep a grocery; the chimney had fallen, so could have no fire. Catherine and the children had a little space about six or eight feet between the old counters; they were tired, but when they found out they were in Shattersburg they wanted to go on. I thought best to remain. Fed and watered teams, ate supper, then I took my "birth" in the wagon (suffering very much with my head) with all my money in my pocket. I slept an hour or two. McKeney sat up all night as guard, for I believe he was afraid to sleep. At two o'clock I roused up all hands, at four we took a warm breakfast on the old counter. I ate hearty of meat and corn bread and drank nearly a pint of strong coffee and was the pertest man on the road the whole day. I have eaten more bacon this week and corn bread than I have in the same length of time in many months. If I could keep traveling, I would get well. Had much fun and some vexation.

Found Mrs. Canady and family still in the house and no place to go. She was afraid I would put her out—poor widow with a passel of children. She blames her sons for not having provided a place for her. We are much pestered and crowded. Got hot fixing fences and gates. How I should like to have you living near me. All are well. Catherine looks a little worsted from the trip, the baby worried her a lot on the trip. Buck stood the trip very well though I was very attentive to him. I hope he will soon be well, the wound has nearly healed up.

Engaged ten barrels of corn at 2$, also engaged new corn but price not settled. Engaged as many shucks as I want, intending to feed mostly on them, as oats and fodder are scarce; wheat also scarce, expect to buy some on Monday, can't tell what I shall have to pay. Haven't seen any of the boys yet, don't know whether they have bought me any stock. Shall be in a fix about vegetables, none on this place.

November 13, 1853: Cold, rainy and snowy Monday after I got here, was driving a pin in a cellar frame and the ax flew off the helve and came down on the back of my hand, mangled it badly. Lost only one day from work, but suffered a lot. Had to sow wheat with it and that made it much worse. Edmund split his knee open with ax, has been confined in the house ever since, can't tell when he'll be able to walk about. I am quite unwell and nearly broke down.

Bought 12 Barrels old corn at 2$, some new at 2.50. Sellers are asking 3$—too high, won't pay it if I can help it. Bought a crop of shucks, expect to feed horses on shucks and meal. Oats too scarce and high for me to feed on.

Bought two cows, one giving milk, one soon will, at 12$ each. Also two sows at 6$ each, one has six pigs, the other will have pigs in a short time. So I have two cows and one calf, two sows and six pigs, soon to have another calf and another litter of pigs for 36$. Shall buy no more stock yet awhile, but fix fences. Want to buy a few sheep.

Bought three barrels of flour at 5$; $2.50 for salt. Only sowed ten bushels of wheat, paid 1$ a bushel for it. Paid 36$ for the two wagons. Had to buy two plows and a straw cutter, 11$. Now need cupboard or press, some bedsteads, cotton wheel and many other things that almost makes me sick to think of. My little money is slipping through my fingers like butter before the sun, and will soon be all gone.

Shall have to hire a hand. The plantation was injured this year more than the rest. You could leave home before breakfast and get here to supper. The stage passes my door twice a day, about day in the morning and about sunset.[450]

It was not all fun moving to a new home. And the adventure was a blend of prosaic routine, danger, expenditure of money, with the thrill of getting started in a new location.

James Mercer of Fredericksburg, writing to James Madison in 1786 about the recently established Fredericksburg Academy, thought his home town an ideal location for a school; comparing it with the locations of other institutions, he found Williamsburg "too gay" and Prince Edward "too rustic." Both are, he added, "the worse for want of the spice of competition." Richmond he thought had little interest in matters intellectual: "I see Richmond is only solicitous for instructing the heels and fingers."[451]

A half century later, however, friends of another institution just being launched saw in Prince Edward a society to be emulated. In the petition of a committee of the trustees of Richmond College to the Virginia Legislature for a charter for their institution, the importance of a college to the community in which it is located was an argument in favor of the establishment of their institution:

"Far from the subscribers be the desire of diminishing, in any measure, the usefulness of the excellent literary institutions already existing in the Commonwealth. They have no apprehension that the successful accomplishment of their scheme can exert an unfriendly influence on these seminaries. It is scarcely possible that colleges, founded and supported by individual munificence, can be multiplied to an injurious extent. The increase of their number, by augmenting the facilities for the acquisition of learning, and exciting a thirst for knowledge, and an honorable emulation, must contribute greatly to the intellectual and moral improvement of the community. To the correctness of this remark let the intelligence and respectability of the counties of Rockbridge and of Prince Edward bear testimony."

The trustees of Richmond College could make such an observation not only from a distant appraisal but from first-hand knowledge, for Daniel Witt, who had then been living in Prince Edward for thirteen years, was one of the charter trustees of the Richmond institution.[452]

Social life in the college community at Hampden-Sydney took its tone from the strictest standards of Presbyterianism. Dr. Richard McIlwaine has described a party at the home of President and Mrs. Lewis W. Green during his student days. There was neither dancing nor card-playing, and what were regarded as "innocent amusements" were not introduced. A boy did not even get a chance to take his girl to these parties; young ladies were escorted to them by their father or some other older male relative, who called to take them home at a stated hour. Chairs were placed along the walls of the reception room, and guests, after greeting the host and hostess, would seat themselves and engage in conversation—the entertainment of the evening.[453]

Meals, prayers, visiting, Bible reading, study, going to preaching featured the life of the college community. An entry in a diary kept by a person whose name is not in it shows a typical Sunday's activities:

Sunday, September 10, 1848: At Dr. Graham's. Did not get up early—headache. After breakfast prayers. Upstairs and read Bible and then heard Lucy say her prayers and catechism. To church, Dr.

Wilson preached; text, latter clause of Rev. 2:10. Excellent sermon. After dinner sat with mother in her room. Read part of one of Davies' sermons, then got my catechism a little. After supper to Seminary chapel;. Mr. Cocron [*sic*] preached, Matt. 24:32. Much affected by his preaching. Felt much for my impenitent brothers and sinners generally. Came back, prayed fervently, and felt happy. After going to bed read rest of Davies' sermon. Committed some in catechism and read Bible."

A week day saw these activities:

[Monday, September] 11: Up tolerably early and to breakfast. Mr. Penic [*sic*] had prayers. Afterwards upstairs and heard Lucy say her morning lessons. Then mended children's clothes. Made two pincushions, one for James Daniel, one for Beverly Watkins. After dinner practiced some [on piano]. Made two baby caps for Rose. After supper Judy Graham, James Daniel, and I walked out and got some chinquepins. When we came back Mr. Venable professor of math came and sat until nine o'clock. I played some on piano for him.[454]

The college students were fond of banquets; the Beta Theta Pi fraternity would sometimes have suppers in the cabin of "Aunt Rachel," whose husband, Davy Ross, was a janitor at the college. "Aunt Rachel" would prepare the meal, consisting of half a dozen kinds of meat, several cakes, ice cream, and jelly and serve it in style. Cigars were passed around after the meal, but no wine or liqueurs.

The community around the college reflected its influence. The planters in the neighborhood were usually "college-bred men of intelligence and culture," their wives "women of education and grace of person and manner." They had household servants, kept horses and carriages, and were known for their hospitality. Some were wealthy, and most of them were of independent means.[455]

This description of the college community society does not mean that all those who belonged to it started out in life handsomely endowed with this world's goods. Many achieved their means by application to business, industry, thrift, good management. A humble beginning was no barrier to social acceptance and economic opportunity. A family of the highest standing was that of John A. Scott of Moilena, one of the most prosperous farms in the county. In their time Moilena was a "mecca of those who loved gentle manners, graceful courtesies, a cordial greeting, a liberal hospitality and all the charms that gathered about a typical Virginia home of the olden day." When Mrs. Scott went to Moilena upon her marriage, she rode behind her husband on horseback and the young couple ate their first meal there from a plank on the head of a barrel.[456]

The restraint and refinement in social life was characteristic of other sections of the county. The churches—Baptist, Disciple, and Methodist, as well as Presbyterian—frowned upon worldly amusements, and there were many homes in which dancing and card playing were not indulged in. "Innocent" games, conversation, music provided entertainment at parties at these homes, and the refreshments were ample and delicious.

Such Puritan standards did not, of course, obtain in all Prince Edward homes. Dancing was permitted in some homes, and it was popular with the boys and girls. Most of the dancing was square dancing, with an occasional mazurka or waltz. Josh, a slave belonging to Mottley Fowlkes of Nottoway, furnished music for dances throughout the section, and one writer recalling his music said "no band ever furnished better." He called the figures for the square dances as well as played. Among the places at which Josh played for dances was Branch J. Worsham's home, Clover Hill, where Ned Price directed the dance.[457]

John Poole conducted a dancing school at Prince Edward Courthouse about 1784; his fee was 150 pounds of tobacco for instruction for six months, three days a month, and six shillings paid the first dance. The following patrons agreed to pay the fee for dancing instruction for their children: Miller Woodson, two children; Francis McCraw; Mary Price, two children; Metcalf DeGraffenreidt; John Woodson; Vincent DeGraffenreidt; John Hudson, Sary Walker, two children; John Ellis; Clement Vawter; and Joseph Lambert. Poole also gave dancing lessons in Cumberland about this time.[458]

The singing school was both an agency of instruction and a social affair in ante-bellum times. Frequently it was conducted in a church, the lessons scheduled to prepare the people to participate in the singing for the Sunday worship service. These schools were well attended. A bill bearing the name Abraham McGehee included an item for $4 for "two scholars to singing school," dated November 15, 1813. The singing schools were responsible for the excellent singing in the churches of that day. The singing school continued an honored institution of the Prince Edward rural communities for a number of years after the war. Charles E. Glenn conducted singing schools in the Prospect community in the postwar period.[459]

There seems to have been considerable social intercourse among the Randolphs when there were several of the family living in and near Prince Edward. In the 1790's it was the fashion, among friends of France in this country, to call each other "Citizen," after the custom in the French Republic. So Richard Randolph, Jr., passed on to Creed Taylor an invitation from "Citizen Ryland" [Randolph] "to dine with him at batchelor's Hall tomorrow. We all go. Suppose you come over to breakfast and go with us."[460] John Randolph addressed Creed Taylor as "Citizen" in a letter dated Bizarre, 16 Sept., 23d of Independence, and referred to the authentic report of "Citizen" Venable's intended resignation (Abraham B. Venable's decision not to stand for re-election to the House of Representatives).[461]

Perhaps eating was the major social diversion in ante-bellum Prince Edward. Food then was prepared in the kitchen, before open fireplaces and in ovens, pots, and skillets. Burning coals were put at different places on the hearth and food cooked on them. Breads were served in variety—cakes, biscuits, waffles, muffins—and rushed to the dining room hot from the kitchen, which was in a separate building from the dwelling.[462] At one home, at least, the family did not risk the walk from kitchen to dining room for the coffee; the walk would give it time to cool more than desired, so it was prepared on a trivet in the dining room fireplace.[463] Foods were not canned then, but preserves and pickles were made in abundance.[464]

When people in Prince Edward first began to put up ice is not known. Dr. William S. Morton mentions an ice house at Raines Tavern in Cumberland in 1835;[465] and Albert G. Green, advertising his Prince Edward farm for sale in 1860, mentions an ice house there.[466] Many farms had an ice pond, made by damming a small branch, from which ice was cut when it was sufficiently thick in winter. It was stored in pits, covered with leaves or pine tags. People who had ice houses kept milk and butter and other foods in them in warm weather. Those who did not usually had a box at the spring— water for most country homes then was gotten from a spring—in which milk and butter were kept.

When John Early visited Robert Venable's home on November 9, 1807, he "ate as good a watermelon there at that season of the year as I ever did in summer."[467] One wonders if Venable kept it, as some people have later kept melons until autumn, in a corn shock.

Weddings were important social events; they were usually held at the bride's home in ante-bellum days. An invitation to a wedding in 1859, reads:

Mrs. J. W. Morton

At Home

Wednesday, May 4, from 8 P. M. to 1 A. M.

Egbert Womack

Mattie H. Morton

Buffaloe.[468]

Girls married young in ante-bellum days. Family Bibles and other records show that many were only seventeen and eighteen when they married, and some were even younger. Men usually were older; the same records show that men in their thirties frequently married girls in their teens. There was one Prince Edward couple in which the man was forty when he married and the girl was eighteen. Brides then made much of their trousseaus; an important item, next to the wedding dress, was the second-day dress, for the festivities attendant upon a wedding were not limited to one day. The second day dress was usually of silk, as was the wedding dress.[469]

The customs relating to death were somewhat different from those of the present. No dealer carried coffins in stock then, as the country store did in the postwar period until a generation ago and as undertakers do now. When a person died, the measurements were sent to a cabinetmaker or carpenter in the neighborhood, and a coffin was made to specifications. In the Prince Edward Courthouse neighborhood, coffins were made in Cliborne's shop; in Farmville, John Doyne made coffins, thus launching his family in the undertaking business which it has continued to the fourth generation. A pole was used to take the measurement, notches indicating the length of the body. Neighbors shrouded the body and attended to the digging of the grave. Flowers were rarely used at ante-bellum funerals.[470]

In Prince Edward interment was generally in a family burying ground, though stones in the cemeteries at Buffalo and Spring Creek churches indicate that those church cemeteries were in use prior to the war. Funeral sermons were delivered in honor of the deceased who was a devout Christian. These were not eulogies, but real sermons which undertook to bring the hearers into a closer relationship with God. John Hatchett remembered hearing a funeral sermon preached by Robert Foster in 1784 and one by Thomas Grimes

(Crymes) in 1786.[471] The sermon which Daniel Witt delivered at the funeral of Elisha Woodfin, Jr., at Jamestown on September 4, 1859, was printed in a pamphlet of forty-two pages; the text was Romans 8: 28: "And we know that all things work together for good to them that love God, to them who are the called, according to his purpose." Dr. Witt developed the point that death is a solemn event; then he pointed out that "sometimes the dispensations of Providence are wrapped in gloom." He gave a detailed exposition of the text, making his sermon no mournful discourse nor a fearful warning, nor a eulogy of the deceased, but an interpretation of the love of God and how man demonstrated love for God and of the ways God works among men to accomplish His will.[472]

There was a friendly sympathy graciously expressed in time of sorrow. One of the tenderest is found in a letter of Francis Watkins to William Watts in 1790. Through Watts' brother Watkins learned of the death of Watts' young daughter. Watkins knew how to sympathize: "We have thrice felt the shock in my family nor ever been with anything so hard to overcome." But he offered the consolation of faith to the bereaved family: "There is a consolation greater than the distress and in times like this we should apply it."[473]

Family Bibles show the high rate of mortality among infants and children. Few homes escaped the loss of children in their early years. Epidemics of children's diseases, as scarlet fever, whooping cough, and measles, took heavy toll.

Fishing and seining were popular sports in Prince Edward. One of Dr. George W. Bagby's most delightful essays, "Fishing in the Appomattox," describes a day's fishing, with the fish supper that night, at the home of Evans relatives in Prince Edward, not far west of Farmville.[474] Seining was a favorite diversion on Easter Monday.[475]

Hunting, too, was popular; the hunter had to carry with him, along with his gun, his powderhorn, shot pouch, and ramrod.

Among the games of ante-bellum days were chumney, cat, and bandy. Chumney was similar to baseball, played with two teams, with batters, pitchers, catchers, and fielders. The pitcher tried to pitch a good ball, and the batter tried to knock the solid rubber ball out of sight. A runner had to be hit when in motion to down him, and to go around the ring, which was larger than a baseball diamond, twice was "a real accomplishment." It required four players to play "cat." Pitchers threw to batters, and the aim was to catch the batter out. Then pitcher and batter exchanged places. Bandy was played with hickory or dogwood sticks, used to try to force a small block of wood to the team's goal. It was a fast, rough game, and bones were sometimes broken. It was the only dangerous game of the day. Jumping, wrestling, boxing, running, kite-flying, marble-shooting, and skating—in season—were other sports for boys and young men.[476]

Some Prince Edward people went to resorts, though more for health, it would appear from the circumstances, than for pleasure. Samuel W. Venable was at Virginia Springs when he died suddenly, in 1821.[477] In 1839 Jacob W. Morton of Farmville, later of Buffaloe, went to White Sulphur Springs for a stay.[478] Thomas T. Tredway went to Alleghany Springs in Montgomery County for two or three weeks in August, 1856.[479]

Older men in the late ante-bellum period took snuff as a sneezer. Some had silver snuff-boxes. The box was opened with much dignity: "a pinch, a sniff, and a sneeze—followed by an old red or yellow bandanna which was vigorously applied to the nose and buried in the pocket again." The etiquette of taking snuff required that when the box was opened in company, it was offered to the old gentlemen present, "most of whom were sure to take a pinch." The practice of dipping snuff was unknown in the Prince Edward section, according to one writer of recollections. That writer had seen old ladies smoke, but had never seen one with a snuff-box.[480]

There is no more fitting close to the history of ante-bellum Prince Edward than William Mynn Thornton's description of Longwood as he remembered it in the 1850's:

"A broad, level lawn, shadowed by spreading trees, with grass growing long and thick and green up to their very trunks, and calves and colts grazing in the dappled shade; a big garden stretching away in the rear with democratic mingling of cabbages and roses and violets and onions and beds all abloom with the sweet old flowers of our grandmothers, and bushes loaded with curious fruits; and in the midst the old square house with its great wide hall and its high pitched rooms, dim and cool and fragrant and its floors polished like mirrors and slippery as ice itself; and the stately old lady, with delicate white cap and black silk gown, serenely beautiful in her honored age, with loving daughters to execute her orders and minister to her wants—this was Longwood."[481]

Peace and plenty form the dominant tone of that description, and peace and plenty were characteristic of ante-bellum Prince Edward. How soon was peace to be only a memory and plenty to be replaced by want!

CHAPTER XIII

The Nation Divided

THE nineteenth century saw the development of radically different attitudes toward slavery in the two sections of the United
States, North and South. At first slavery had been legal in the North,
but it did not prove there an advantageous system of labor. After the
Revolution, slavery was gradually abolished in the Northern states;
New Jersey, last of the states north of the Mason-Dixon line to
prohibit slavery, did not abolish the system until 1804.

The first notable victory for anti-slavery was the prohibition of
slavery in the Northwest Territory by the Ordinance of 1787, a
plan originated by Jefferson and actively supported by William
Grayson and Richard Henry Lee.[1] The second was the Constitutional
provision that the importation of slaves into the United States be
prohibited after 1808. Both these restrictions on slavery enjoyed
widespread support in Virginia, where there was at that time the
feeling on the part of many that slavery was wrong. Patrick Henry,
when representing Prince Edward in the Constitutional Convention
of 1788, pointed out the dilemma which Virginia and the South
failed to resolve: "Slavery is detested . . . we deplore it with all
the pity of humanity . . . Prudence forbids abolition . . . would
rejoice if all were emancipated . . . Emancipating is a local matter
not to be left to Congress."[2]

Virginia lost the opportunity to effect a gradual emancipation
when the House of Delegates defeated an amendment to a committee
report that it was expedient to make a legislative enactment concerning the abolition of slavery and indefinitely postponed consideration
of such matters. Thomas Jefferson Randolph, Jefferson's grandson,
had proposed a plan of gradual emancipation which led to the votes
on the committee report and amendments. In the parliamentary
maneuverings Asa Dupuy, delegate from Prince Edward, cast votes
which favored the retention of slavery. He did favor referring Randolph's plan to a select committee. When the committee's report,
that it was inexpedient to enact legislation concerning abolition, was
amended to read "expedient" instead of "inexpedient," Dupuy voted

for indefinite deferment of consideration of the amendment; that defeated 60-71, he was numbered with the majority in defeating the amendment (by a vote of 58-73); he opposed another amendment, which postponed further action until a "more definite development of public opinion," which passed 67-60; and when the original report as amended came to a vote, Dupuy was numbered with the opposition. It passed by a vote of 65-58.[3]

Meanwhile pressures were building up which complicated the problem. After the prohibition of the foreign slave trade, in which New England shipping interests had long been engaged, abolition sentiment spread rapidly in that area. And in the South, as John Holt Rice had pointed out, slavery became the more securely identified as a property interest. It was this intensified emphasis upon slaves as property that made the South increasingly sensitive to abolition pressures and propaganda. Anti-slavery sentiment, which came so near to abolishing slavery in Virginia in 1832, all but died out, or at least was effectively silenced by the pressure of public opinion.

Southern churchmen tended now to justify slavery as their brethren in the North voiced more strongly their opinion that the institution was un-Christian and immoral. The Methodist Church split in 1844 on the issue of permitting a bishop to own slaves, and the Methodist Episcopal Church, South, came into being as a result. The Baptists disagreed on the appointment of slaveowners as home missionaries, and the Baptist churches in the Southern states withdrew their support from the mission societies and the General or Triennial Convention to establish in 1845 the Southern Baptist Convention as the agency to carry on their missionary activities.

The slavery question got into politics. A delicate balance between free and slave states made them equally strong in the Senate, but the more rapidly increasing population in the North gave to the House of Representatives an increasingly anti-slavery tone. When a bill to appropriate $2,000,000 to conduct negotiations with Mexico during the war with that country was introduced in the House, David Wilmot of Pennsylvania offered an amendment which would prohibit slavery in territory acquired from Mexico. The amendment failed to pass, but it created concern in the South. Mississippi proposed a convention to meet in Nashville, Tennessee, in June, 1850, to consider ways to combat similar threats to the expansion of slave territory. A convention representing a part of the Fifth Congressional District was held in Farmville May 10 to elect two delegates to the Nashville meeting. William C. Flournoy, Samuel C. Anderson, Thomas T. Tredway, William T. Wootton, James H. Wilson, Branch J. Worsham, and C. R. Barksdale represented Prince Edward. As the Nashville meeting was to be bipartisan, a Democratic and a Whig delegate were chosen; William C. Flournoy was chosen the Democratic delegate, and John T. Thornton the Whig. That the matter was not regarded as too serious is indicated in the failure of both these men to attend the meeting. As a matter of fact, only one delegate from Virginia was listed in the news reports as attending.[4]

John Brown's Raid on Harper's Ferry, in which he captured the United States arsenal to get arms with which to equip slaves for an uprising, thoroughly alarmed Virginia. For the first time, it seems, Southerners realized the intensity of abolition feeling, the extremes to which some Abolitionists were willing to go. Not only did such action threaten property rights; it struck even closer in menacing the lives of family and friends. Suddenly the situation had become intolerable. Something had to be done.

Prince Edward Court adjourned early December 19, 1859. The large court day crowd assembled in the courtroom. The venerable and much respected Samuel C. Anderson addressed the assembly briefly, explaining the object of the meeting. He then moved that the meeting organize with Thomas T. Tredway as chairman and F. P. Wood, John H. Knight, and Henry Stokes as secretaries. Upon the passing of Anderson's second motion, Tredway appointed a resolutions committee of ten: John T. Thornton, William C. Flournoy, John H. Knight, Stephen O. Southall, F. P. Wood, Philip A. Bolling, Dr. F. B. Watkins, Branch J. Worsham, Abram C. Carrington, and A. R. Venable. While the committee was drawing up a report in another room, Colonel Farrar of Amelia and Professor Charles Martin of Hampden-Sydney addressed the meeting. Professor Martin identified himself with his neighbors and their cause when he said that he was born a New Englander, but that he was a Virginian by choice.

The resolutions take on added significance when it is remembered that some of the ablest and most distinguished members of the Virginia bar were on the committee which reported them. That fact indicates the seriousness which thoughtful Virginians attached to John Brown's attempted insurrection and the fears which it aroused in them. The content of the resolutions is an eloquent testimony to public feeling on the matter:

The people of Prince Edward intend to co-operate with their compatriots of Virginia and the other Southern states in this time of peril to the South and to the Union and to fulfill this duty if possible without dissolving the political bonds which connect the states of this Confederacy.

1. The invasion of Virginia by an armed band of conspirators from non-slaveholding states to incite a servile insurrection derives its main significance from being instigated and encouraged by predominant public sentiment.

2. We hail with hopeful appreciation the patriotic demonstrations in the North Atlantic cities, but we cannot forget that Northern conservatives are in the minority and that they have failed to restrain the destructive party.

3. Although the South has suffered injuries and insults from the North, we do not believe the South is justified in separating from the North at the cost of civil war; we value and cherish the constitutional union for its benefits, memories, and promise.

4. We look to the next election of a President as probably decisive of the fate of the union; if the Abolition or Black Republican party wins, the time may have come for the South, by proper regard to its interests and rights, to withdraw.

5. Without reference to the great struggle of 1860 and without delay, the Legislature and people of Virginia should prepare for the worst; we advise that they adopt the most efficient measures for trade with foreign countries and our own ports; the Legislature should aid this with liberal appropriations.

(Either there was an error in numbering, or the sixth resolution was omitted from the report found by this writer.)

7. The Governor's recommendation of prompt legislative provision for the thorough organization of the militia (especially for a well-armed body of younger men) is prudent and patriotic and ought to be adopted by the Assembly.

8. Regard for safety requires the prohibition of all peddling and itinerant exhibitions except by our citizens; vagrants should be punished by sentence to labor on public works and whipping upon trial by two justices of a county or a district.

9. The conduct of Governor Wise at Harper's Ferry and Charlestown in suppressing the attempted insurrection, in guarding the captured offenders from the just rage of the people, and in preventing

the intended rescue of convicts from the hands of the law merits cordial approval and entitles him to the thanks of the South.

10. We approve the Assembly's refusal to commute the punishment of Coppic (this case proves the wisdom of the law which withholds from the Executive power to pardon and commute punishment of criminals condemned to suffer death for such offenses).

11. Since the best laws and the best officers fail to reach all cases of offense, we advise the people of each district of the county to appoint a committee of vigilance to arrest and examine all suspicious persons, to hand them over to civil authorities for trial, and to expel them quietly from the county if believed dangerous, but not liable to legal conviction.

Anderson moved the adoption of the resolutions; three of the most eloquent lawyers, Thornton, Flournoy, and Bolling, spoke in support, and they were passed unanimously.[5]

A military convention was called to meet in Richmond January 10, 1860, to facilitate legislative action looking to the organization and arming of volunteer and militia companies in Virginia. Every commissioned officer of the militia was invited to attend.[6] A new military law was passed, effective March 30, under which every able-bodied male between the ages of eighteen and forty-five was required to register with the commander of the militia company in whose district he lived.[7] Prince Edward citizens were called to meet at the Courthouse on November 19, 1860, to form companies of "minute men" throughout the county. The call was signed by Norvell Cobb, Watson Cobb, F. P. Wood, H. G. Richardson, Thomas Hickson, W. A. Walton, J. T. Walton, and many others.[8]

Meanwhile one of the hottest political campaigns of the county's and nation's history was being waged.

The local campaigns went smoothly enough. Robert V. Davis, Richard W. Price, William T. Lee, Thomas B. Rice, Joseph T. Ligon, Robert C. Anderson, John P. Hughes, James E. Flippen, Richard B. Thackston, James T. Gray, James Whitehead, James S. Lockett, Charles A. Morton, Edwin J. Redd, James B. Ely, William T. Carter, Samuel S. Booker, Samuel B. Scott, John A. Dalby, and David F. Womack were elected justices of the county court in the May election.[9] William C. Flournoy was re-elected Commonwealth's Attorney , but he did not qualify; in a special election to fill the post held October 17, John T. Thornton was elected. He took the oath of office in November.[10] Henry B. Brightwell was elected to a second term as sheriff at the regular election.[11]

Colonel William C. Knight resigned as state senator from the district, and a convention was called to nominate a Democratic candidate to succeed him. A county Democratic meeting was held at the Courthouse September 17, 1860, of which John P. Hughes was chairman and William A. Walton secretary. On motion of William C. Flournoy the meeting recommended Asa D. Dickinson, then a member of the House of Delegates from Prince Edward, for the nomination, and the chair appointed a delegation of twenty-five persons, five from each district, to attend the district meeting.[12] As Dickinson was nominated to the State Senate, Prince Edward Democrats held another meeting October 15 and nominated Samuel C. Anderson for the House of Delegates to succeed Dickinson.[13]

A lack of local harmony was demonstrated early in 1860 in a petition that a portion of Prince Edward be attached to Nottoway. Robert S. Glenn, John Queensbury, Henry V. Miller, Ransom Chumney, James W. Morgan, Henry Hardaway, Littleton McC. Hudson, Adolphus T. Burk, Richard A. Stokes, and William L. Nelson asked that the portion of Prince Edward south of the Richmond and Danville Railroad from the Nottoway line to Clark's road and along that road to the Lunenburg line be detached and made a part of Nottoway; they represented that their business interests lay more with Nottoway and that they were more convenient to Nottoway Courthouse. A counter-petition, signed by John R. Cunningham and many others, was presented to the General Assembly on the same day, January 11, 1860. The counter-petition prevailed.[14]

It was the Presidential campaign which attracted attention and excited the keenest interest. Thomas T. Tredway was chosen elector for the Fourth District on the Democratic ticket[15] Because there was a split in the Democratic party, and the party in the state had not chosen which nominee to support, Tredway resigned as elector. To perform his duties he would have to decide for Virginia Democracy which ticket it should support, and that power belonged to the party in convention assembled for the purpose of making the choice. Tredway had no difficulty in selecting the nominee he would support, and he had no hesitancy in stating his intentions as a private member of the party; the ticket consisting of John C. Breckinridge of Kentucky for President and General Joseph Lane of Oregon for Vice-President was his choice.[16]

Prince Edward Democrats on July Court day held a meeting

over which George W. Daniel presided and of which Abraham B. Venable was secretary. Edmund W. Hubard reported on the course he had taken as a delegate at both the Charleston and the Baltimore conventions of the party that year. Hubard and Roger A. Pryor spoke in support of Breckinridge and Lane. Charles Irving made a speech endorsing the rival Democratic ticket, Stephen A. Douglas of Illinois and Herschel V. Johnson of Georgia. Asa D. Dickinson introduced resolutions endorsing the Breckinridge-Lane ticket and proposing that thirty delegates be sent to a state Democratic convention called by the state Democratic executive committee to meet in Charlottesville August 16. The first resolution was laid on the table until after the Charlottesville meeting, but the second was amended to provide that no delegates be sent to the Staunton convention called by Harman and Rives in the interest of Douglas' candidacy. The delegation named to the state convention consisted of Edwin Edmunds, F. T. Wootton, Colonel John Foster, Edward Clark, Samuel B. Scott, Major James Watson (from the Sandy River district), F. D. Redd, E. J. Redd, A. D. Dickinson, J. P. Fitzgerald, W. T. Carter, Richard H. Watkins (from the Courthouse district), Colonel P. A. Bolling, R. S. Paulett, P. H. Jackson, Egbert Womack, B. S. Scott, W. A. Walton (from the Farmville district), John A. Dalby, James Venable, Henry J. Venable, A. C. Carrington, Captain William Brightwell, John H. Knight (from the Prospect district), Thomas T. Tredway, John P. Hughes, Samuel F. Hunt, Colonel Francis Rice, Branch J. Worsham, and Newton Cunningham (from the Spring Creek district); to these were added the chairman and secretary.[17]

The Charlottesville convention endorsed Breckinridge and Lane, calling Douglas' nomination "pretended" because it was made after the delegations from Virginia and other states had withdrawn. Thomas T. Tredway was again named Democratic elector for the Fourth District, but this time the party in the state had chosen the ticket it recommended for support. A convention favoring the Douglas candidacy met in Staunton the same day of the Charlottesville convention.[18] Tredway again resigned as elector, but the state committee declined to accept it.[19]

John T. Thornton was elector for the Fourth District for the Constitutional Union party, which had nominated John Bell of Tennessee for President and Edward Everett of Massachusetts for Vice-President. Thornton and Tredway met at Lunenburg Courthouse October 8 and debated the issues in the campaign.[20]

The Prince Edward Democrats organized the county for the election. At their meeting on October 15, the secretaries (John H. Knight and John P. Fitzgerald) named vigilance committees for each precinct to get out the vote and distribute tickets: Farmville: G. W. Daniel, W. A. Walton, N. Cobb, J. W. Womack, F. P. Wood, B. S. Scott; Courthouse: H. S. Guthrey, R. B. Thackston, E. N. Price, J. W. Redd, F. D. Redd, A. J. Fowlkes; Marble Hill: W. T. Carter, G. W. Redd, Colonel H. D. McCargo, R. H. Watkins, R. L. Redd, Joseph D. Eggleston; Sandy River: F. T. Wootton, S. B. Scott, W. T. Wootton, John W. Foster, John H. Leigh, B. F. Flippen; Prospect: James Venable, John M. Harris, William Fergusson, Josiah Brightwell, W. Bradley; Darlington Heights: D. F. Womack, John P. Hughes, W. L. Womack, Charles T. Anderson, N. Cunningham, and G. W. Bell.[21]

Asa D. Dickinson, John T. Thornton, and John Hilliard were election commissioners in 1860.[22]

In that crucial election, Prince Edward cast 423 votes from Breckinridge, 374 for Bell, 65 for Douglas, and none for Lincoln.[23] Thornton was one of six Bell electors and Tredway was one of nine Breckinridge electors who were defeated in Virginia. The vote in Virginia was 74,701 for Bell, 74,379 for Breckinridge, 16,292 for Douglas, and 1,929 for Lincoln. When the electoral vote in the nation was counted, Lincoln received 180 votes, Breckinridge 72, Bell 39, and Douglas 12. All fifteen Virginia electral votes went for Bell, after the six Breckinridge electors who had been named as winners by the Governor's proclamation declined seats in the college, since they were "satisfied that they were not elected in fact."[24]

The outcome of the election was evident before the formal casting of the electoral votes. The people of Prince Edward, "without distinction of party," met at the Courthouse November 19; John A. Scott was chosen chairman and John P. Fitzgerald and Abraham B. Venable secretaries of the meeting. On motion of Stephen O. Southall, the chairman was asked to appoint a bipartisan committee of fifteen, representing every section of the county, "to draft and report suitable resolutions on the present aspect of federal relations" to a meeting to be held the Saturday after the first Monday in December. Scott named Samuel C. Anderson, Stephen O. Southall, Branch J. Worsham, John T. Thornton, Thomas T. Tredway, John H. Knight, Andrew R. Venable, Thomas E. Haskins, Dr. James H. Dillon, Thomas E. Perkinson, Dr. Alexander S. Dillon, R. J.

Mathews, W. T. Wootton, John W. Redd, and A. D. Dickinson, and the chairman and secretaries were added.[25] What their report was this writer has been unable to find.

In the midst of consideration of national affairs, the Court was asked to consider a matter of local concern. In December, 1860, W. E. Bradshaw, Benjamin F. Flippen, F. S. Williams, N. D. Mottley and others asked the Court "to re-arrange, alter, increase, or diminish the election districts" at its February session. Action then, on motion of Joseph T. Ligon, was deferred until the April Court; then the Court established separate polls for the Sandy River district at Green Bay and Rice's Depot, and discontinued Marble Hill as a separate voting precinct.[26]

Before the end of 1860 South Carolina had seceded; by early February, 1861, all the states of the lower South had joined South Carolina in leaving the United States. In January, 1861, the Virginia General Assembly called a convention to consider secession and designated February 4 as the day for the election of delegates. The convention was to have 152 members, chosen on the same basis as members of the House of Delegates.[27] John T. Thornton was chosen to represent Prince Edward in the convention.[28]

A few days after the legislature called a convention to consider secession, it authorized the county courts to arm such portion of the militia as they deemed expedient and to borrow money to finance the equipping of the militia.[29] The Prince Edward Court lost no time in acting upon the authorization; the bill was passed by the Assembly January 19; on January 21, the Court ordered the clerk to issue bonds of the county to the extent of $7,500, in sums of $100 each. The bonds were to be retired in three years, one-third each year, and interest was to be paid semi-annually at the Farmers Bank of Virginia in Farmville. A group of citizens appeared in court and bound themselves as sureties for the bonds: John T. Thornton, R. H. Watkins, John H. Knight, Charles E. Redd, H. Venable, J. P. Fitzgerald, B. J. Worsham, H. G. Richardson, T. E. Perkinson, Peyton R. Berkeley, T. T. Tredway, B. S. Scott, A. C. Carrington, P. H. Jackson, J. M. McNutt, J. T. Redd, J. A. Dalby, J. T. Gray, E. J. Redd, Edwin Edmunds, John A. Scott, and C. A. Price. Their names were directed to be inserted in the bonds.

Thornton, William J. Morrisett, E. G. Wall, and E. Wiltse were directed to sell the bonds and to invest the proceeds of the sale in arms, equipment, and munitions of war. Captains of the several volunteer companies in the county were given permission to sell $1,500 of the bonds and to apply the proceeds to the purchase of arms and equipment for their companies.[30]

The Farmville Guard evidently sold its quota, for $1,500 of the proceeds from the sale of the bonds, together with an additional subscription of $100, was appropriated for the purchase of arms for the company. Morrissett, who made the purchases for the Farmville unit, bought eighty minnie muskets from Tyler and Mitchell of Richmond. In a public demonstration described as the largest turnout in the company's history, the Guard exhibited its new weapons; at that time there were ninety-three members of the unit.[31]

Secession sentiment was strong in the county. The voters were called to meet at the Courthouse March 9 in a strong statement signed by Samuel C. Anderson, Frank D. Redd, James H. Martin, Robert C. Anderson, Theodorick B. McRobert, W. C. Trueheart, Henry L. Goode, B. Worsham, R. S. Hines, M. T. Hughes, Joseph M. Price, John P. Fitzgerald, H. S. Guthrey, R. B. Thackston, Joseph A. Watson, Robert L. Dabney, G. H. Gilmer, J. M. P. Atkinson, L. L. Holladay, J. W. Dunnington, B. C. Peters, J. W. Womack, J. A. Dalby, Joseph G. Williams, P. H. Jackson, Thomas Hutchison (Hickson ?), T. M. Noble, Egbert Womack, W. A. Walton, and James W. Womack, Jr.

The purpose of the meeting was to consider the "alarming condition of the country," but the statement expressed the opinion that the convention "should immediately detach the State from the Union," and proposed that the meeting instruct the delegate to the convention to move immediate secession. The statement noted that the President-elect (it was issued March 1, just before the inauguration March 4) "amidst all his intentional platitudes has carefully avoided uttering one word which could reassure the South." It condemned the bill then under consideration in Congress "to declare piratical war against the South without a moment's notice."[32]

The meeting was held, with Samuel C. Anderson serving as chairman and H. T. Parrish and H. Stokes as secretaries. Asa D. Dickinson, P. A. Bolling and John T. Thornton made strong secession speeches. The speakers represented each of the tickets polling votes in the election of 1860: Dickinson was active in support of Breckinridge, Bolling was one of Douglas' leading supporters, and Thornton had run as an elector on the Bell ticket. The meeting was studiously bipartisan; the chairman was a Democrat, the secretaries Whigs, and the committee, which reported resolutions favoring secession, consisted of three Democrats and two Whigs. When he called for a vote on the resolutions, Anderson asked each man present "to vote distinctly aye or no," in order that the sentiment of the county might be clearly known. There was shout of "Aye," but one "No" was heard. Dickinson then asked that any man present who dissented from the opinion expressed to vote no. The lone opponent to secession at this meeting in Prince Edward gained no support. "So," the Richmond *Enquirer* summarized the report of the meeting, "Prince Edward may be set down as perhaps the most unanimous county for immediate secession in the state."[33]

The Virginia Convention passed the Ordinance of Secession April 24, 1861, and decreed that it become effective as of that date if ratified by a majority vote in an election called for the fourth Thursday in May. Prince Edward's representative, Thornton, was one of eighty-eight voting for secession; there were fifty-five votes cast in opposition to Virginia's withdrawal from the Union. In the popular vote, those favoring secession numbered 125,950, those opposing, 20,373.[34] The day after passing the secession ordinance, the convention adopted the Constitution of the Provisional Government of the Confederate States of America.[35]

The convention redistricted the state for the Confederate Congress; Prince Edward was placed in the Fifth District, and Thomas S. Bocock was named by the convention representative to the provisional Confederate Congress from the district.[36]

Early in 1861 eight volunteer companies were organized in Prince Edward for Confederate service.[37] The cavalry company drew members from throughout the county. It was mustered into service as Company K, Third Virginia Cavalry. John T. Thornton was chosen captain, Peyton R. Berkeley first lieutenant, and H. I. Parrish, F. D. Redd, and Richard Stokes, second lieutenants.[38] Two infantry companies were recruited in Farmville. The Farmville Guard (Company F, 18th Virginia Regiment) was under the command of Captain Richard A. Booker, and the Randolph Guard, mustered into service June 12, 1861, was commanded by Captain Norvell Cobb. Charles D. Anderson was first lieutenant of the Farmville Guard, Charles H. Erambert second lieutenant, and Samuel B. McKinney, third lieutenant.[39]

On April 27, 1861, two Prince Edward companies were in Richmond: the Prospect Rifle Grays, with seventy-two men, under the command of Captain E. G. Waller; and the Farmville Guard, with ninety-six men, commanded by Captain Booker. The Prospect Company was armed with flint lock rifles, and the Farmville Guard with minnie muskets.[40] The Central Guard went from Prince Edward Courthouse and was mustered into service as Company I, 23rd Virginia Volunteers, at Richmond on May 22, 1861. Its muster roll states that it was the third company to leave Prince Edward; the newspaper account of the Prospect Rifle Grays and the Farmville Guard being in Richmond late in April indicates that they preceded it. Moses T. Hughes commanded the Central Guard; J. P. Fitzgerald was first lieutenant, Branch Worsham second lieutenant, and William G. Trueheart, third lieutenant.[41]

The company organized at Rice took the name "The Old Dominion Rifles"; it was mustered into service in 1861 as Company C, 53rd Virginia Infantry. Henry D. Dickerson was captain, Richard Miller first lieutenant, N. R. Mottley second lieutenant, and Richard Phillips third lieutenant.[42] A seventh company went out from Meherrin.[43] Three Prince Edward companies were issued equipment from the Richmond armory between April 1 and June 18, 1861: Captain R. A. Booker, eighty sets of accoutrements and 400 yards of webbing; Captain Henry D. Dickinson [sic]: fifty-one original percussion muskets and equipment and 2,600 cartridges, and later an additional 2,600 cartridges and 3,000 caps; and Captain Potts, 600 cartridges and 700 caps.[44] (It would appear that Potts was captain of the company which went from Meherrin; he is identified only as from Prince Edward in the list of equipment issued, but the captains of the other companies at that time are known, leaving only the Meherrin company.)

The eighth company from Prince Edward was organized at Hampden-Sydney. President J. M. P. Atkinson was captain of the company, John W. Jackson first lieutenant, Robert G. Temple second lieutenant, Tazewell M. McCorkle third lieutenant and W. W. Page orderly sergeant. The Hampden-Sydney company was attached to the 20th Virginia Regiment under Colonel John Pegram and was sent to join General Garnett's army in Pendleton County, now West Virginia. McClellan attacked the Confederates at Rich Mountain, and Colonel Pegram was forced to surrender July 11, 1861. General McClellan treated Captain Atkinson and the college company with great courtesy.[45]

While companies were being organized for active service, home guard units were being organized by older men. The Farmville *Journal* of April 25, 1861, published resolutions calling upon citizens in each district to form "associations to be called Home Guards." The Home Guard unit organized in Farmville at the time had as its officers J. W. Womack, captain, E. J. Erambert, first lieutenant, R. S. Paulett, second lieutenant, J. B. Hilliard, third lieutenant, and E. Womack, fourth lieutenant.[46]

The Randolph Guard was also in West Virginia, but the regiment to which it was attached was not in the Battle of Rich Mountain. It sustained a casualty, however, in the death of Lieutenant R. S. Brightwell who was killed when a wagon was upset over a precipice.[47]

The Prince Edward companies underwent successive reorganizations as the war progressed as a result of promotions, deaths, woundings, and resignations of officers. The cavalry company had four captains; Captain Thornton was elected lieutenant colonel of the Third Regiment in 1862 and Lieutenant Peyton R. Berkeley was chosen captain to succeed him. Thornton was killed in the Battle of Sharpsburg in Maryland, while commanding the regiment. Captain Berkeley resigned in 1863, and R. H. Watkins was chosen captain in his stead. Captain Watkins was disabled by wounds in 1864, and John H. Knight, who had been second sergeant when the company was mustered into service and had been chosen first lieutenant in 1863 succeeded Watkins as captain.[48]

After being wounded at Second Manassas, Captain Booker resigned as captain of the Farmville Guards and was succeeded by Z. A. Blanton. Booker then organized a company of reserves—men too old or incapacited for active service and boys too young—in Prince Edward and was elected its captain. The company was assigned to guard duty at High Bridge. There the 15th Virginia Regiment of Reserves was organized, and Booker was elected its colonel. After a time at High Bridge, the regiment was assigned to guard duty at the Richmond and Danville bridge over the Staunton River; subsequent assignments included Kinston, North Carolina; a second assignment at the Staunton River bridge; Richmond; Lynchburg, in anticipation of a raid by Sheridan; and Farmville, to protect the commissary stores. For men on inactive status, the Reserves got around.[49]

Captain Blanton was disabled by wounds at Gettysburg, and W. J. Morrisett succeeded him as captain. Captain Cobb of the Randolph Guard was promoted to major in 1862 and a year later to

colonel, in command of the 44th Virginia Infantry. He was succeeded as captain in May, 1862, by W. P. Walker, who was killed at
Chancellorsville. H. G. Richardson succeeded Walker as captain.
The Prospect company was re-organized May 1, 1862. A muster roll
of the re-organized company was prepared by A. B. Venable, first
lieutenant.[50] Moses T. Hughes resigned as captain of the Central
Guard in July, 1861, and was succeeded by John P. Fitzgerald.
Fitzgerald was promoted to major in June, 1863, and to lieutenant
colonel in November, 1863. Gustavus A. Bass, who was elected first
lieutenant when the company was re-organized in May, 1862, commanded the company in the Battle of Chancellorsville, which took
place in June, 1863; Bass was killed in the battle. William L.
Gutherie succeeded Bass as first lieutenant and was shortly thereafter made captain of the company. He was captured at Spotsylvania
Courthouse in 1864 and died in prison. N. E. Venable, who transferred from the Confederate Marines to the Central Guard in 1864,
was promoted to lieutenant and as such was commander of the company. Daniel A. Watson was later captain of the Old Dominion Rifles.

The account of the various re-organizations has given some
indication of the battles in which the Prince Edward troops took
part. It may be added that both the Farmville Guard and the Old
Dominion Rifles were in Pickett's Division, Longstreet's Corps, and
took part in Pickett's magnificent, but futile, charge at Gettysburg.[51]

Soldiers depended upon home sources for many supplies, including clothing. Cavalrymen furnished their own horses. Some soldiers
took a body servant with them; one of the duties of a cavalryman's
servant was to care for his master's horse. One of the servants who
accompanied his master to the wars was Peyton Coles, who belonged
to Nick Pamplin, who lived at the village named for his family.
"Uncle Peyton" lived in Prince Edward after the war to an advanced
age; as late as 1938 the writer had "Uncle Peyton" give reminiscences of his war experiences to a class in American history at the
Darlington Heights High School. Soldiers usually kept in contact
with their homes through letters and messages sent by soldiers going
on furlough and returning. Since the older companies were made up
of men from the same locality, this arrangement proved both satisfactory and convenient. A letter from Lieutenant N. R. Mottley of
the Old Dominion Rifles illustrates the soldier's dependence upon
home for supplies and upon his comrades for communication:

"Camp Page, Williamsburg, Aug. 22

"Dear Mama

"As Daniel [Watson] is going home today I thought I would write you a few lines though nothing of interest. The most of the boys are in good health. John Phillips has had two severe chills. Lawrence [Wingo or Finney] is up and about though not able to perform duty. Jim Flipin in in bad health, has been trying to get a furlough but did not succeed. Several others complaining though nothing much the matter, I hope. I am quite well myself at this time. Send me a pot of butter by Daniel and if it is convenient I wish you would get some grey cloth and make me a pair of panta-loons as my pants are worn out. I will send some money home in a few days as I expect to draw on the Southern Confederacy. Tell Sue to be certain to send those straps I asked her to make as to my other clothes they are very good. I send my Epauletts and a buckett by Daniel. I have not worn my Epauletts any worth speaking of since I left home. Shoulder straps are worn by all officers. Present my respects to all my friends. Give my love to all the Negroes. I must now close. Write soon and believe me as ever your devoted son

"N. Rich: Mottley

"P. S. Ma when you write back give me all the news and tell Sue she must answer my last letters as I have written several and have received no answer. Write soon.

"N. R. M."[52]

James R. Weaver, writing to one of his brothers from Camp Chaffin's Farm in 1864, asked him to get his mother to send him "some meat, to boil with peas. We draw peas very often but very seldom any meat," he explained.[53]

The problem of meeting the needs of dependent families of soldiers was as great in 1861 as it had been during the Revolution. In June, 1861, the county issued bonds in the amount of $12,500 to raise funds to provide for soldiers' dependents. Thomas T. Tredway, B. S. Scott, A. D. Dickinson, H. E. Warren, and James Venable were appointed to negotiate the bonds at par. Committees were appointed in each district to ascertain needs and provide for the wants of the families of soldiers: Prospect district, James H. Dillon, Thomas T. Tredway; Spring Creek district, Newton Cunningham and John P. Hughes; Courthouse district, George W. Redd and William T. Carter; Farmville district, C. C. Read and Beverly S. Scott; Sandy River district, Francis T. Wootton and Joseph Phillips. James W. Dunnington was treasurer of the county fund.[54]

The first government of the Confederate States was provisional until a permanent government could be elected. In the election November 6, 1861, Jefferson Davis of Mississippi was candidate for President and Alexander H. Stephens of Georgia for Vice-President. Wood Bouldin of Charlotte was presidential elector for the Fifth District, which included Prince Edward. There were two candidates for Congress from the district, Thomas S. Bocock of Appomattox and T. F. Goode of Mecklenburg. Bocock was elected; Colonel Goode, who was on active duty in the Army, declined the urging of his friends to enter into the canvass and waged no campaign. Davis and Stephens received the unanimous vote of the Electoral College, 109 votes, of which Virginia cast eighteen. Asa D. Dickinson was returned to the State Senate, and Thomas T. Tredway was elected to the House of Delegates from Prince Edward. When the Confederate Congress assembled in Richmond February 18, 1862, Bocock was unanimously elected Speaker of the House. Provision was made by which soldiers could vote in camp.[55]

Because of the shortage of metal to make small coins in the Confederacy, banks began issuing notes for small sums to meet this need. The Appomattox Savings Bank and the Farmville Savings Bank, both of Farmville, in 1861 issued notes in denominations of fifty cents and twenty-five cents respectively, which they would redeem in currency when presented in the sum of $5 or multiples. The grand jury at the November, 1861, term of Prince Edward Court presented both banks (J. H. C. Leach was president of the Appomattox Savings Bank, and H. E. Warren of the Farmville Savings Bank) for issuing notes in these denominations without authority in law. Samuel C. Anderson then entered a petition of *nolle prosequi,* which the Court overruled.[56]

As a result of the grand jury's action, two petitions concerning notes in small denominations were presented to the Legislature from Prince Edward. One, signed by J. W. Dunnington and many others and dated December 10, 1861, asked that issues of both banks in amounts under $5 be legalized. It cited the absence of silver and small gold coins. The second petition was signed by Howell E. Warren and other stockholders of the Farmville Savings Bank and asked for authorization to the bank "to issue notes of one dollar and under to supply the place of small gold and silver coins that can't be obtained."[57] The Assembly early in 1862 authorized banks to issue $1- and $2-notes in amounts not to exceed five per cent of the capital; a little later, they were authorized to issue notes in denominations of from $1 to $5, including fractional amounts, up to ten per cent of the bank's capital.[58]

Two other war measures were adopted in Prince Edward in 1861. Watkins Dupuy, commissioner of revenue, was directed to enroll all able-bodied, male, free Negroes in the public service.[59] J. Overby was appointed collector of the Confederate war tax for Prince Edward; H. T. Garnett was chief collector in Virginia.[60] The Confederate government collected taxes in supplies. R. B. Marye, major and quartermaster at the Quartermaster's Department office in Farmville, on July 4, 1864, gave a receipt of William Walton for 341 pounds of corn for the use of the Confederate States Army, to be returned in kind on or before September 1, 1864; and Major A. B. Garland of the Commissary Department on September 24, 1864, issued to Walton a receipt for 140 pounds of fodder which was fed to government mules "enroute from Blacks & Whites to Liberty, Va." on account of the Tax in kind.[61]

Samuel D. McDearmon was appointed district collector of the Confederate tax for Prince Edward and Appomattox in 1863.[62]

Coins became so scarce that Prince Edward County itself issued notes in small denominations to replace them. In May, 1862, the county issued notes to the total value of $10,000 in these denominations: $1,000 in notes of ten cents each; $750 in notes of fifteen cents each; $2,500 in notes of twenty-five cents; $1,000 in notes of thirty cents; $3,000 in notes of fifty cents; and $1,750 in notes of seventy-five cents each. The Court directed that a levy be laid to redeem one-third of the notes issued in that order in 1862, one-third in 1863, and one-third in 1864.[63] The Farmers Bank at Farmville was directed in May, 1863, to redeem notes issued under the order of May, 1862, up to $1.500 from money deposited in the bank to the credit of the county.[64]

Salt, too, soon became a rare commodity. Charles D. Anderson and Richard B. Thackston were appointed in May, 1862, to buy salt for the county, to enter into contract for its purchase and transportation, and to distribute it to the people according to the directions of the Court.[65] Howell E. Warren was agent for the distribution of salt in Prince Edward a year later, when he was directed to pay to James W. Dunnington, treasurer for the county, $2,500 out of money on hand derived from the sale of salt.[66]

Relief for needy families of soldiers was administered by committeemen in each district. In 1862 the Court fixed limits for expenditures for relief of these families for each district: Farmville, $1,064.36; Courthouse, $735.13; Sandy River, $915.53; Prospect, $829.84; and Spring Creek, $825.33.[67]

Some changes were made in the committee administering this program in May, 1863: Joseph T. Ligon replaced Joseph Phillips in the Sandy River district; R. S. Hines replaced George W. Redd in the Courthouse district; George W. Bell and Samuel S. Baker made a new committee in the Spring Creek district; James D. Crawley served in Prospect district; and James T. Gray and Thomas B. Rice were a new committee in the Farmville district.[68] A time of special need arose during a severe blizzard in the winter of 1863-64; neighbors responded to the challenge in carrying wood and other supplies to homes where there was need in what Dr. Richard McIlwaine called "the most complete exhibition on the spirit of the Christian religion and on the broadest scale I ever saw." McIlwaine was especially concerned for two homes, one in which were a mother and three children, the other in which were a widow and her soldier son who had returned home after losing a leg.[69]

Another opportunity to help came with the death of the Rev. Michael Osborne, who had been pastor of the Farmville Presbyterian Church; a native of New England, Osborne had not been sympathetic to the South; as a result he had to resign his pastorate, a development which caused hard feelings on his part. He died about a year later, and Dr. McIlwaine, who was supply pastor, called the attention of the church to the need of the former pastor's family, which was unable to buy food or pay the funeral expenses or the mortgage of $1,200 on their home. The people took up a collection which amounted to $4,000 and gave enough flour, corn, meat, and other supplies to last the Osbornes two years.[70]

Many refugees made Farmville their home during the war. They came from areas in which there was fighting and through which the armies were passing. The Randolph House register for the summer of 1862 showed a number of people there from Richmond and Winchester, and some from Warren, New Kent, and Caroline Counties, then scenes of hard battles and marching armies. Several guests registered as refugees: John H. Bocock of Georgetown, D. C., on October 17, 1861, and T. S. Dullers of Texas. The register, with its entries of guests from Savannah, Nashville, Missouri, Alabama, Memphis, and Texas, indicates that travel in the South during the early years of the war was not greatly restricted; some of these were soldiers, but there were women and children among the registrants from distant places.[71] Among the refugees was the Taliaferro family of Orange County, which subsequently settled in Farmville. Some Farmville people sought the security of the country during the war; H. E. Warren moved his family to the Edmund Lockett place on Marrowbone Creek, about two miles south of Rice, and James W. Dunnington took his family to Walnut Hill in Charlotte County.[72]

Elections were held on schedule during the war. In 1862 George W. Booker was elected sheriff, and Watkins Dupuy was re-elected commissioner of revenue.[73]

In the election of local officers in May, 1864, John P. Hughes, Edwin J. Redd, James T. Gray, William J. Porter, James S. Lockett, Robert C. Anderson, James J. Rice, John W. Jones, Richard A. Booker, William T. Carter, Richard W. Price, Charles A. Morton, Joseph T. Ligon, James Whitehead, John A. Dalby, Richard B. Thackston, Samuel B. Scott, Samuel S. Baker, John T. Johnson, and David F. Womack were elected justices. At their first meeting after the majority of those elected had qualified, Charles A. Morton was elected presiding justice.[74] Other officers elected were Branch J. Worsham, clerk; Stephen O. Southall, commonwealth's attorney; George W. Booker, sheriff; John R. Cunningham, commissioner of revenue; and Thomas J. Garden, surveyor. Branch Worsham was named deputy clerk.[75]

Bocock was returned to Congress from the Fifth District in 1864 and was re-elected Speaker of the House.[76] Asa D. Dickinson was returned to the State Senate in 1863 and in 1864 was chairman of the Senate committee which united with a committee of the House of Delegates in an Address to the Soldiers of Virginia, adopted March 9, 1864, which praised them for their valor and criticized the North for starting the war.[77]

The Confederate government operated a postal service; under it there were two routes out of Farmville, one via Cumberland to Cartersville, the other, three times weekly, to the Courthouse and Hampden-Sydney. There was also a route from Moore's Ordinary via Lunenburg Courthouse to Yatesville.[78] It will be observed that the postal routes now have railroad stations at their starting points. Mail service was interrupted, though, by enemy action. Early in 1864 the Federal troops robbed a postoffice during a raid. Some letters were later recaptured in their camp and were taken by Chaplain Cameron of the Confederate army. One of these letters was addressed to Mrs. Edwin Edmunds, Prince Edward Courthouse.[79]

A problem in communication was presented in the case of prisoners of war. One of the most efficient means was through the personals columns of newspapers. A letter would be inserted in the columns of a Southern paper with the request that a Northern paper copy it; prisoners or their friends would insert a personal in a Northern paper and ask that a Southern paper copy it. These requests were complied with, and the messages went through. Among the personal messages involving Prince Edward people were the following:

Farmville, Prince Edward County, Virginia, December 24, 1864. To M. W. R. New York. Your personal of Nov. 29th has relieved our anxieties very much; we have written frequently to Major Venable, and received one letter in the last few days written October 30. Let him know that we are all well; let us hear again before very long through this medium. Jane R. Venable. *New York News* please copy.

Prospect, Prince Edward County, Virginia, December 17, 1864. Mr. Edward B. Witt, Co. K, 3rd Virginia Cavalry, prisoner of war at Point Lookout, Maryland. My dear Husband: delighted to hear from you through personal, and reply immediately. Heard from you three times by flag of truce; received only one letter myself. Have written to you frequently. Sent boxes by flag of truce on 24th ult. Be of good cheer. All well and doing well, and join in much love. Reply soon. Your darling wife, Fannie. *New York News* please copy.[80]

Information wanted of Henry Norwood Vaughan, member 9th Virginia Cavalry, Company O. Captured October 11 or 12 on foraging expedition in Sussex County. Any communication relative to his whereabouts will be thankfully received by his father. Dr. Henry A. Vaughan, Moore's Ordinary, Prince Edward County, Virginia.[81]

It seemed to be the practice for comrades to notify members of the family of casualties. When Quentin Marshall of Company C, 53rd Virginia Infantry, died, Lawrence Finney of the same company wrote to his father:

"Mr. Marshall
"Dr Sir

"I am exceedingly sorry to inform you of the death of Mr Q. A. Marshall he died this morning at 2 o'clock

His friend
L. Finney

Chimborazo Hospt. July 28th/64

N. B. Mr. Quarles the wardmaster has his Pocket book and $10 $\frac{00}{100}$ in money $1 $\frac{50}{100}$ in stamps and other little things to numerous to mention which you can get on application his clothes & c.

L. Finey[82]

The inflation which scarcity of commodities and a paper currency brought to the Confederacy is familiar to every student of history. The Confederate government sought to curb this inflation by having commissioners set maximum prices for items which the government purchased. These prices were revised every two months. Among the prices fixed in September, 1863, by E. W. Hubard and Robert Gibboney, commissioners for Virginia, were: flour, $25 per barrel; bacon, $1 per pound; horses, $350 average price per head; good salt, $5 per bushel (fifty pounds); soap, forty cents per pound; tallow candles, $1 per pound; whiskey, $3 per gallon; brown sugar, $1 per pound; New Orleans molasses, $8 per gallon; coffee, $3 per pound; tea, $7 per pound; beef cattle, $16 per hundredweight (superior, $18 per cwt); cotton shirting, forty-two cents per yard; Army shoes, $10 per pair; wool socks for men, $1.25 per pair; mules, $300.[83]

Market prices a few months later were much higher. The Richmond market on March 15, 1864, quoted best family flour at $300 per barrel; bacon, $7 per pound; coffee, $12.50 per pound; Irish potatoes, $14 per bushel; molasses, $50 per gallon; whiskey, $100 per gallon; brown sugar, $10 per pound; salt, thirty-five cents per pound last sales; soap, $1.50 per pound; dried apples, $1.75 per pound; apples, $125 per bushel.[84]

Two months later the commissioners were still trying to hold the price line, setting the maximum the government would pay for flour at $22 to $28 per barrel; $3 per pound for bacon; $5 per bushel of dried apples; $8 per bushel of dried peaches; $3 per pound for brown sugar; $3 per pound for coffee; $7 per pound for tea; $25 per gallon of New Orleans molasses.[85]

These were not the peak prices. Flour sold in Farmville for $1,000 a barrel. Most of the commodities listed were almost impossible to obtain. Sugar was rare, and sorghum molasses was a substitute. Parched wheat, rye, or sweet potatoes were used to make coffee. Tea was hoarded for use in sickness; sassafras root tea took the place of tea in general use. To replace the rare flavoring extracts, emulsions of peach and other aromatic leaves were used. Medicine was hard to obtain, and some kinds could not be gotten; people had to fall back on herbs, both wild and cultivated, for medicines. The cost of clothing was so high that few could buy it, and fresh impetus was given to the spinning and weaving of cloth in the farm homes. Some older men and boys wore woolen caps and caps of skins—fox, raccoon, rabbit, or squirrel—in winter instead of hats. Salt could be obtained, no doubt because of the official set-up for its purchase, but it was scarce and had to be used sparingly.[86]

Illustrative of the worthlessness of Confederate money toward the end of the war is the request a soldier made that his partner not sell any more of his part of a stock of brandy for less than $150— or $3 in silver.[87]

So much emphasis has been given to military activity during the War Between the States that one finds it somewhat surprising to note business activity. Yet in 1863 the Farmville Insurance Company was chartered to write both fire and life insurance. The incorporators were James W. Dunnington, Howell E. Warren, Frank N. Watkins, Clement C. Read, James L. Hubard, Norvell Cobb, Stephen O. Southall, Richard McIlwaine, Christopher C. Lockett, Archibald Vaughan and their associates.[88]

The educators, too, were active during the war. A teachers' convention was held in Petersburg December 30-31, 1863, in which Prince Edward representatives played a leading part. Dr. J. M. P. Atkinson of Hampden-Sydney was chosen president; Dr. B. M. Smith of Union Seminary served on the Primary Department Committee, Professor Charles Martin of Hampden-Sydney on the Ancient Languages Committee, Professor A. Preot of the Farmville College on the Modern Languages Committee and Professor L. L. Holladay of Hampden-Sydney on the Natural Sciences Committee. Two resolutions introduced by Professor Martin showed educational statesmanship of a high order and unusual vision; one proposed that the General Assembly make an appropriation to provide for the education of disabled soldiers discharged from the Army; the other proposed the establishment of a Southern educational literature and the encouragement of the production of textbooks by Southern authors.[89]

The Board of Trustees of Hampden-Sydney College voted in 1862 that it had the right to change the investment of the college from United States bonds to Confederate bonds. Dr. Peyton R. Berkeley dissented from this view. The Board authorized the sale of its Virginia State bonds and $500 of Southside Railroad stock and the investment of the proceeds in Confederate bonds.[90] Later the college invested in cotton bonds of the Confederacy.

In the summer of 1864 the board asked the Secretary of War to exempt from military service students at the college who became seventeen years of age during the session.[91] How modern this request sounds!

In 1864 W. G. Venable of Farmville was designated a depositary for funding Confederate Treasury notes in Virginia; the chief quartermaster in each Army corps was also authorized to receive and fund Treasury notes.[92]

A General Hospital of the Confederacy was opened in Farmville in 1862, with a capacity of 1,200 to 1,500 beds. This hospital was used principally for chronic cases and for convalescents from hospitals in cities and those near the field of active operations. Dr. H. D. Taliaferro, a former surgeon in the United States Navy, was head of the hospital from its opening to the end of the war; Dr. Richard Peyton Walton was in charge of the First Division, Dr. Tufts of the Second, and Dr. James L. White, except for a period of active duty in the field and hospital duty at Lynchburg between January, 1864, and February, 1865, of the Third Division. Among the assistants to the division surgeons were Drs. Boatwright, Chandler, Mathews, Ladd, and Grayson in the Third Division, and Drs. Carter, Boykin, Russell, Hancock, and Tatum in the other divisions. Major R. B. Marye was in charge of the quartermaster and commissary departments. The First and Second Divisions were located in tobacco warehouses and factories; the Third Division was in new quarters on the north side of the Southside Railroad, just west of the then corporate limits, near the site of the present Norfolk and Western passenger station. The dispensary, of which L. W. Williamson was manager, the bakery, the commissary department, and Dr. White's office were on the south side of the tracks, opposite the Third Division.[93]

During the war there was much religious activity in the Confederate Army. Chaplains were encouraged in their work by General Lee and others of high rank. The example of General Stonewall Jackson helped make the religious atmosphere popular. As a result of the preaching of the chaplains there were numerous conversions. Sharon Baptist Church in 1863 received into membership Samuel E. Nunnally on certificate of Elder Andrew Broaddus, Army Missionary, who baptized Nunnally, and in 1864 received John C. Destin and Henry M. Borum on letter of P. H. Fontaine, Army chaplain.[94]

The Farmville Baptist Church in 1863 appointed a Committee on the Instruction of Slaves.[95]

Throughout the war the people maintained a loyal attitude and an optimistic outlook. The letter of Daniel Witt to a young soldier, John F. Walton, shows the attitude of Prince Edward people at the mid-war period:

"Mr. John Walton, Near Fredericksburg, Virginia

Sandy River, Aug. 22nd 1863

"Mr. John Walton

"My Dear Friend, I received your letter several days ago, & as Mr. Lockett is about to return to his company, I avail myself of the opportunity of dropping you a few lines by him. I am pleased to hear that your health is restored, & that you now have both the ability & inclination to resist the advance of our vile invaders. May the Lord crown with abundant success, the efforts of our brave young men, who, with self-sacrificing devotion, stand as a wall of fire between their country & their foes. Since you left us a few months ago, we have met with a series of unexpected disasters. The fall of Vicksburg & Port Hudson & the quick return of our own army from Pennsylvania caused a momentary shuddering, & cast a gloom over the face of the community for a brief season. We had been so used to victory for a long time, that we hardly knew how to receive the tidings of defeat. Perhaps we had grown too self-reliant & had forgotten that "God giveth the victory." If the recent reverses shall tend to quicken our sense of dependence upon the Almighty arm, & increase our confidence in that Providence which governs the world, the events which we now regard as misfortunes may be turned into real blessings. Victory is sometimes more disastrous than defeat:— it is always so when it begets a vain confidence in our prowess, & a contempt of the enemy we have to deal with. I think the Lord intends to teach us, in the late reverses, a more simple and strong reliance upon the resources of his adorable wisdom; & I expect in the next terrible conflict, which cannot be long deferred, a more signal triumph than we have ever had. Our enemy is certainly dispirited even in the hour of his success. He finds that the unconquerable spirit of the South remains unbroken; & he is still confronted with an army as firm & invincible as ever. His barren victories, like the fabled apples of Sodom, are turning to ashes on his life; & after the successes, which he thought would end the struggle, he finds the stupendous work of subjugation hardly begun.

Add to this, the growing disaffection at the North, with an increasing probability of foreign recognition, & we have a prospect before us as cheering as it has been at any time during the war. But whatever may be the signs of the times, the path of duty is plain before us—*we are shut up to the necessity of fighting on, until our savage foes shall let us alone, & acknowledge, bitter as the pill may be, our complete independence.* I do really believe, that the death of all of us, men, women, and children, is far more to be desired, than the doom which would await us as the conquered slaves of Yankeedom. May the Lord spare us that deep humiliation.

"We have just observed the day of fasting, humiliation, & prayer, appointed by our pious and excellent President. I trust that the spectacle of a nation on its knees, will move the Eternal mind—& "if God be for us, who can be against us?" We had a large & solemn assembly, who bore on their hearts & their prayers, a country threatened with destruction, & brothers and sons, in camp, field, & hospital, who are baring their breast to the storm of war, to preserve our civil & religious rights. You need not fear that you will be forgotten by the loved ones at home. They follow you with their fervent supplications on the painful march, & the perils of the battle field. And the daily & hourly prayer goes up to heaven, that our noble defenders may be spared, in life & limb, & be returned to us again, on some brighter, future day, when an honorable peace shall be achieved, & a permanent independence reward the sacrifices of these terrible times.

"My health has been feeble this summer; & I am afraid it will interpose an effectual barrier, for some time to come, to a compliance with your kind invitation to preach to you in the army. Nothing would give me greater pleasure. But it has pleased the Lord 'to weaken me in the way'; & while 'the will is present with me, how to perform that which I would, I find not.' Nevertheless I hope I may yet have the opportunity of complying with the wishes of yourself & friends, & will not neglect such an opportunity if it should occur. I greatly desire the religious welfare of our gallant men in the field. If any man in the world should be a christian a soldier is that man. In daily peril of his life, he should always be ready for whatever may befal him. A calm trust in God—a deep repentance for sin—a cordial committal of his soul to Christ—a constant preparation for eternity, ought to be his distinguishing & constant exercises. I trust, dear Johnnie, that you are no stranger to these pious

& ennobling impulses. May the Lord cover your head in the day of battle, & bring you back again to your friends, as sound in body, as I am sure you will be sound in morals, if it shall be the pleasure of the Lord you should come to the scenes of your earlier years.

"My wife & Mrs. Page send to you their love, & good wishes. The latter also sends some tracts, which after you have read, she desires you to hand to your comrades.

"Your father's family is in their usual health—so are the friends generally in this neighborhood. Edmund will give you all the news.

"I shall always be pleased to hear from you. You need not fear that you intrude upon me by writing to me at any time. When you have a leisure hour, let me have another letter. And now Good bye, my young friend. May the Lord bless you & keep you. Love to the boys, especially the Bruces.

"As ever Truly
D. Witt"[96]

Dr. James L. White wrote after the war that none in the Farmville community—hospital staff, citizens, refugees—"entertained any idea but the independence of the Confederacy would be established."[97] Dr. Richard McIlwaine wrote that until the first Sunday in April, 1865 (the date of the evacuation of Richmond and Petersburg) he never doubted the success of the Confederacy, so confident was he of the justice of the Southern cause and of the ability of the officers and the courage and endurance of the soldiers.[98] But the Court was getting ready for an invasion, although its measures implied, too, a confidence in Southern victory. In August, 1864, the magistrates were assigned the duty of preparing a record for the taking of evidence "of all outrages committed by the enemy in the county."[99]

War in all its fury of battle and pillage reached Prince Edward April 6, 1865. The day dawned ominously; after several days of pleasant weather, that Thursday morning was dark with a misty rain which lasted until noon.[100] But before the account of the fighting in and the troop movements through the county, a summary of the organization of the Confederate and Union armies which were engaged in Prince Edward may help the reader keep more clearly in mind the military action.

The Confederate First Army Corps, commanded by Lieutenant General James Longstreet, consisted of three divisions commanded by Major Generals George E. Pickett, Charles W. Field, and Joseph B. Kershaw and the artillery commanded by Brigadier General

Edward P. Alexander. The Second Army Corps was commanded by Major General John B. Gordon; it also consisted of three divisions, Rodes former division commanded by Major General Bryan Grimes, Early's division under Brigadier General James A. Walker, and Gordon's division commanded by Brigadier General Clement A. Evans; the corps artillery was under the command of Brigadier General Armistead L. Long. The Third Army Corps was commanded by Lieutenant General Ambrose P. Hill until he was killed April 2, 1865; its three divisions were commanded by Major Generals Harry Heth, Cadmus M. Wilcox, and William Mahone, and its artillery was commanded by Brigadier General R. Lindsay Walker. Anderson's Corps, commanded by Lieutenant General Richard H. Anderson, consisted of one division, Major General Bushrod R. Johnson's which on April 9 was commanded by Brigadier General William H. Wallace, and the artillery under Colonel Hilary P. Jones. The Cavalry Corps, commanded by Major General Fitzhugh Lee, consisted of three divisions, Fitzhugh Lee's, now commanded by Brigadier General Thomas T. Munford, Major General W. H. F. Lee's and Major General Thomas L. Rosser's; the artillery attached to the cavalry was commanded by Lieutenant Colonel R. Preston Chew. G. W. C. Lee's division was commanded by Major General G. W. Custis Lee, and Ewell's Reserve Corps was under the command of Lieutenant General Richard S. Ewell. The Engineer troops were under the command of Colonel Thomas M. R. Talcott. Certain rearrangements were made which were in effect on the fighting in and the march through Prince Edward. After Hill's death, the Third Army Corps was attached to Longstreet's command. Kershaw's division, from the First Army Corps, and G. W. C. Lee's division, with troops from the defenses around Richmond, were placed under the command of General Ewell.[101]

There were five major units of the Federal army participating in what Union officers called the Appomattox campaign: the Second Army Corps, commanded by Major General A. A. Humphreys;[102] the Fifth Army Corps, commanded by Brevet Major General Charles Griffin who had replaced Major General Gouvereur K. Warren only on April 1;[103] the Sixth Army Corps under Major General Horatio G. Wright.[104] These three corps belonged to the Army of the Potomac, which was commanded by Major General George G. Meade.[105] The Army of the James, commanded by Major General Edward O. C. Ord, included the Twenty-Fourth Army Corps under Major

General John Gibbon.[106] The cavalry under Major General P. H.
Sheridan was known as the Army of the Shenandoah.[107]

The Army of Northern Virginia, commanded by General Robert
E. Lee, in the winter of 1865 held the cities of Richmond and Petersburg and the defenses between those cities. Lieutenant General U. S.
Grant, commanding the United States armies, had since early 1864
been attacking Lee's army by flanking movements. From Spotsylvania County he had gradually worked southward during the year,
but had not been able to penetrate the defenses of Richmond. But
the Army of Northern Virginia could not indefinitely protect itself
and the key defenses from the flanking of much larger forces under
Grant. Federal troops got around the Confederates south of Petersburg and on April 1 in the Battle of Five Forks southwest of Petersburg smashed the southern anchor of the Richmond-Petersburg
defenses. Lee realized that his line was now untenable; the wary
chieftain withdrew his forces from south of the Appomattox around
Petersburg to the north bank; he pulled in the defenses from around
Richmond and between the two cities which Colonel Byrd had laid
out with such high hopes almost sevenscore years before. Meanwhile
he had notified President Jefferson Davis that he could not hold the
cities; the message had been delivered as the Chief Executive was at
worship in St. Paul's Church. Davis left the capital, going to Danville by train on the Richmond and Danville Railroad, which brought
him across the southeast corner of Prince Edward. He chose Danville
as his destination, because he expected Lee to take the army there.[108]
Lee's plan was to follow the same general route and effect a union
with General Joseph E. Johnston, a native of Prince Edward who was
in command of the Confederate Army which was then retreating
northward through North Carolina before a Federal army commanded by Major General William T. Sherman. Lee's plan was to
assemble the various units of his army at Amelia Courthouse. His
plans were delayed in execution because some of the bridges over the
Appomattox on roads leading to Amelia Courthouse could not be
used. When he did not find supplies awaiting him at Amelia, he lost
twenty-four hours "in endeavoring to collect subsistence" for men
who had been marching several days and nights with "neither rest
nor refreshment."[109]

Meanwhile units of the Federal army had been coming westward
and northwestward from Petersburg. When Lee was leaving Amelia
Courthouse on April 5, the Fifth Corps of the Army of the Potomac

and Sheridan's cavalry had reached Jetersville, to block his anticipated line of march. Lee changed his route and directed the line of
march to Farmville, to which he had ordered supplies from Lynchburg.[110] Late in the evening of April 4, Lee had issued orders for the
wagons of the Third Corps to move at dawn via Paineville, Deatonville, and Rice's Station to Farmville; orders had gone to Ewell's
wagon train to move at dawn on the Clementown road to Paineville
and from there via Ligontown to Farmville.[111] Thus the troops had
to use the same roads which were being used by the artillery and
wagon trains, and their progress was greatly impeded. From Amelia
Longstreet led the Confederate march, followed in order by Anderson, to whose command Pickett's Division was now assigned, Ewell,
and Gordon, who with W. H. F. Lee's cavalry, was protecting the
wagon train.[112]

Advance units of Ord's Army of the James reached Burkeville
on April 4. Grant figured that Lee was trying to reach Danville or
Lynchburg; he ordered Ord to destroy the bridges in the Confederate
front and to await orders at Burkeville, which he considered an
important point to hold. Ord determined to destroy one of the major
bridges in that section, the High Bridge of the Southside Railroad
over the Appomattox, and before daylight on April 6 sent two small
infantry regiments and his entire headquarters escort, all the cavalry
with him, under Colonel Washburn of the Fourth Massachusetts
Cavalry, with orders to make a reconnaisance when near the bridge
and if the bridge were not too strongly guarded to burn it and return
"with great caution" to Burkeville. Ord then sent his chief of staff,
General Theodore Read, to conduct the bridge-burning expedition,
after feeling a belated fear that the Confederate cavalry might attack
his expedition. Then, learning that Lee was headed toward Farmville, Ord sent another staff officer to warn Read that the Confederate
Army was in his rear and that he should return by way of Prince
Edward Courthouse. Read overtook Washburn; to examine the country, the cavalry went all the way to Farmville, then returned to the
infantry and headed for High Bridge.[113]

Longstreet reached Rice on the morning of April 6, just after
Ord's bridge-burners had passed. The Confederate corps commander
dispatched Rosser and his division of cavalry in pursuit. Hearing
that Ord was moving to Rice, Longstreet disposed his command for
action; Field's division was placed across the road Ord would come
up, with Mahone in support, and Wilcox on Field's right, with Heth

in support of Wilcox. Field and Wilcox were ordered to entrench, and the artillery was ordered in battery. The Confederate line was across the Burkeville road at its intersection with the road to Deatonville (the present crossroads on 460 at Pisgah Baptist Church) and Wilcox' position was where the business section of the present village now is.[114]

Meanwhile Rosser was joined by Munford and his cavalry division in pursuit of the Federal force sent to burn the High Bridge. They overtook the enemy on the road near the bridge, attacked, and defeated the Federals after a sharp encounter. Read was killed, and 780 Union soldiers were captured. But, as Fitzhugh Lee put it, "success was dearly bought," for the Confederates lost Brigadier General Dearing of Rosser's Division, Colonel Boston of the Fifth Virginia Cavalry, and Major James W. Thompson of the Stuart Horse Artillery.[115] Thus the threat of the raiding party to burn the bridge in front of the Confederates was ended.

The Federal Fifth Army Corps remained in position at Jetersville all day April 5; the Sixth Corps came up on the 5th and camped near Jetersville; the Second Corps also came to Jetersville, to assemble there the Army of the Potomac and the Army of the Shenandoah.[116] Lee had planned to march his army all the night of the 5th from Amelia, but Ewell's corps had only reached Amelia Springs by eight o'clock the morning of the 6th.[117] The Second Army Corps was moving toward Amelia Courthouse early on the 6th when its scouts discovered that the Confederate wagon train, guarded by a column of infantry, was moving rapidly toward Deatonville. The Second Corps changed its course to attack, and its artillery kept up a hot fire on the Confederate column and train. The Confederates got across Flat Creek before Major General Nelson A. Miles' First Division of the Second Corps could attack; Miles moved in line of battle for sixteen miles, preceded by skirmishers, to the right of and often in sight of the Confederate wagon train.[118] On the march from Jetersville the Fifth Corps was ordered to move north on the Pridesville road and on the right of the Confederates;[119] the Sixth Corps followed the road parallel to the Richmond and Danville Railroad to a road about a mile beyond the road which led to Deatonville; it then proceeded on the road parallel to and to the left of the Confederate line of march.[120] There was a continuing fight between the Confederate rear guard and the Second Corps.[121] And the Federal cavalry kept up a succession of attacks in a systematic fashion; General

Crook was ordered to attack the Confederate train; if it proved too strong at the point of attack, one of the divisions would pass him and attack farther on; if this point also proved strong, another division would pass and attack still farther on, with the aim of finding a weak spot on the line. The cavalry kept this up from near Deatonville to Sailor's Creek.[122] It is a tribute to the fighting qualities and the skillful command of the Confederates that the Federals were unable to penetrate their train in these successive attacks on the road to Sailor's Creek.

Some three miles west of Deatonville the road which the Confederates were following forks; one road turns to the right and follows Sailor's Creek northward; the other road crosses the creek and leads to Rice's Station. Longstreet took the road to Rice. Anderson, following the First Corps, halted at the fork, identified by some writers as J. Holt's, and repelled an attempt by Major General George Crook and Brevet Major General Wesley Merritt of Sheridan's cavalry to cut off the Confederate wagon train. When the head of Ewell's Corps, which had been about a mile in Anderson's rear, came up, it repulsed another attack by Crook and Merritt. Anderson also took the road to Rice, and Pickett's division, in Anderson's command, had crossed the creek when Gordon's corps reached the fork.[123] Kershaw, bringing up the rear of Ewell's corps, held the Federals off until the last of the wagon train had passed, the wagon train taking the road to the right and going toward Jamestown. Kershaw was directed to follow Custis Lee, who had followed the road to Rice; he did not know that Gordon, whose advance had come in sight before Kershaw's men left the fork, was to follow the wagon train and was accordingly surprised when he reached Sailor's Creek to find his rear menaced.[124]

Sheridan's tactics of the day paid off early in the afternoon, when Brevet Major General George A. Custer and his division, having crossed Little Sailor's Creek, moved by way of the Harper farm to the road over which the Confederates were moving. On this road, apparently just within Prince Edward, Custer found the weak spot Sheridan had been seeking all day, a wagon train between Mahone's division under Longstreet and Pickett's division under Anderson. He set fire to the wagon train and captured Huger's part of three batteries. About 400 wagons were destroyed.[125]

About two o'clock in the afternoon Anderson ordered B. R. Johnson to close to the right in consequence of the burning of the wagons and the occupation of the road in front of Anderson's corps. Johnson heard firing in Pickett's Division; as he closed to that unit he learned that the Federals occupied a commanding position on the road in front. General Wise ordered a charge, which two regiments carried out, but the other brigadier in Johnson's Division did not join in it. The enemy was driven from the crest of the hill in the Confederate front, and Anderson ordered Johnson to advance, as it appeared that they were driving the foe. Pickett moved by a right flank, connecting with Johnson's left, and Custis Lee by a left flank, connecting with Johnson's right. The Federal artillery opened fire as Johnson halted to bring up a brigade from the rear. The movement was resumed as firing in the rear and on the left flank was noted. The line was halted when it reached a lane beyond the field. At that point, Pickett rode up and asked Johnson to wait until he could connect with his left flank. Just then, the enemy broke between Pickett and Johnson; Johnson's men broke and moved rapidly to the west where they gained a road which took them to the advanced part of the army. Johnson reported to General Lee, who directed him to collect the scattered portions of Anderson's and Ewell's commands. Johnson reported that his losses were small.[126]

Fitzhugh Lee advised Ewell that a large force of Federal cavalry held the road in front of Anderson. Ewell and Anderson discussed two avenues of escape, one an attack on enemy in front, the other a dispersal through the woods to reach the road to Farmville. Ewell favored the latter course, Anderson the former; as Anderson knew the country and Ewell did not, the latter deferred to Anderson's judgment. Before dispositions were made, however, the enemy attacked the Confederate rear. Ewell and Anderson had no artillery— it was with the wagon train. Ewell's line lay across a small ravine, on the west side of Sailor's Creek; Custis Lee was posted on the left, with the Naval Battalion supporting his right, and Kershaw's division was put on the right. All of Lee's Division and a part of Kershaw's were behind a rising ground which gave some shelter from enemy artillery fire. Ewell's men were facing the creek they had just crossed to meet the attack from the rear. Kershaw, discovering that Gordon was not following his division, posted Humphreys' brigade under Colonel Fitzgerald and Gary's dismounted battalion under Lieutenant Colonel Barham in position near the house used as a hospital for Pickett's division (apparently the Hillsman house) to cover his crossing of the creek. When Kershaw reached the top of the hill on the other side of the creek, he was informed by Ewell that the enemy held the road in front of Anderson and that Ewell's corps was to hold off the enemy while Anderson cleared the road in his front. The enemy forced Humphreys' brigade and the dismounted battalion from their position across the creek to Kershaw's position. Then the Federals planted batteries near the hospital and swept Ewell's position. After a half-hour of artillery fire from that position, within a range of 800 yards from the Confederate position, the Federal infantry of the Sixth Corps advanced. Custis Lee and Kershaw repulsed several advances of the enemy, but Wright sent up fresh troops for each successive advance, working all the while to the left. Finally there came an advance which the Confederates could not resist. Just as the Federal commander thought his troops had been victorious, the Naval Battalion and the troops which had been defending Richmond made a counter attack upon the Federals to the great surprise of General Wright, but it was a last flash; the Confederates were quickly surrounded.

As the Sixth Corps attacked Ewell, Anderson made an attack which was repulsed in five minutes. The corps commanders then went to their commands. Ewell, on his return, found a strong line of enemy skirmishers advancing on his left rear, closing his only avenue of escape. Bullets were crossing each other from the front and rear over Ewell's troops and his right was completely covered. He surrendered himself and his staff to a cavalry officer who came in by the road Anderson left; Ewell sent Custis Lee a note notifying him that he (Ewell) had surrendered and suggesting that Lee surrender also, but he gave no orders as he was then a prisoner. Lee was captured before the messenger reached him; Kershaw was also captured. When Ewell left Richmond, his two divisions numbered 3,000 each; at Sailor's Creek 2,800 were captured, and 150 killed or wounded; he explained the difference of 3,000 by the fatigue of marching four days and nights, the last two days with nothing to eat; he had seen men eat raw fresh meat on the retreat. Ewell was taken to Wright's headquarters.[127] Thus ended the battle of Sailor's Creek, fought on the hill west of the creek around the point at which Prince Edward, Amelia, and Nottoway Counties meet.

Fitzhugh Lee was critical of the command at Sailor's Creek; he felt that the troops might have been more rapidly massed when the march was first interrupted and could then have cleared the enemy from the line of march before reinforcements came; he also thought that by moving toward the road Gordon took, the wooded, broken country would have protected them from harassment by the Federal cavalry; just before Ewell surrendered, Fitzhugh Lee urged again upon him this second alternative.[128] Humphreys credited Ewell with the intention of uniting with Anderson and fighting the cavalry which had attacked him or of going through the woods to another road to Farmville, but the Sixth Corps attacked before Ewell could do either. Humphreys put the Confederate losses in this battle at 6,000, 3,400 under Ewell and 2,600 under Anderson. He reported that of Ewell's command, only 250 of Kershaw's division escaped. The Sixth Corps lost 442 killed and wounded.[129]

The captured Confederates were taken to Burkeville and camped under guard at Inverness, then Mrs. Jeter's home, now the Agnew farm. Here they were on Sunday, April 9, when they heard the news of the surrender. They were later taken to City Point, where they were also in camp for several days; it was here that they heard of Lincoln's assassination. Then they were taken to prison at Point Lookout, Maryland.[130]

Humphreys arrived at J. Holt's fork about 4:30 P. M. on the 6th. He saw Ewell's Corps forming in line of battle on the other side of the creek, but he knew that Sheridan was pressing hard on the Confederates on the road to Rice, and he saw the entire Sixth Corps nearby. Humphreys accordingly continued with his Second Corps the pursuit of the Confederate wagon train and Gordon, maintaining a running contact with the Confederate rear for another three miles. The road for miles was littered with tents, camp equipment, baggage, battery, timbers, and wagons discarded by the Confederates. Gordon and his forces made a last stand near Perkinson's Mill on Sailor's Creek just before dark. Much of the fighting took place around the home of James S. Lockett; even now the house bears the scars of battle. The Second Corps captured in that engagement thirteen flags, four guns, and 1,700 prisoners; its losses were 311 killed and wounded.[131] Gordon found that the starved teams could not pull the loaded wagons through the mire of the lowgrounds on Sailor Creek, and many wagons, especially ammunition wagons, had to be abandoned.[132] Through this battle, which may appropriately be called the Battle of Lockett's Farm, the family of James S. Lockett remained in the basement of their home. The Locketts had cooked food for friends and relatives in the army whom they expected would pass, but the men did not have time to eat. The house was used as a hospi-

tal for the wounded of both armies. Lockett, his daughter, Miss Lelia
Lockett, and two colored boys, Branch and Henry Booker, helped
nurse the soldiers. The yard was a gruesome sight; blood over the
grass, and the dead lying against the trees. Those who died in the
hospital were buried in a plot nearby; Lockett kept a record of those
who died and notified their next of kin, as he had obtained this information from each wounded soldier. Most of the bodies were reclaimed by relatives.[133]

General Lee, waiting near the rear of Longstreet's Corps at Rice
for the arrival of Anderson and Ewell, heard from one of his staff
officers, Colonel Charles Scott Venable, a native of Prince Edward,
that the wagon train had been captured at Sailor's Creek. Lee asked
about Anderson and Ewell, wondering why he could not hear from
them. With General Mahone and Colonel Venable, he rode toward
the scene of the reported capture of the wagon trains. When they
got to the crossing of the river road overlooking Sailor's Creek (this
was evidently the fork at which one road led to Jamestown, the other
to Perkinson's mill; it is at the top of the hill which stretches eastward to the creek), they saw the evidence of the disaster which had
befallen the wagons: teamsters were hurrying on their teams, the
dangling traces jangling, worrisome evidence of wagons left behind;
fleeing infantrymen without guns, many without hats, all intent on
getting away from the evil which had come upon them; "with the
massive columns of the enemy moving orderly on." Lee straightened
in the saddle; as if talking to himself he said:

"My God! Has the army dissolved?"

Mahone mentioned the presence of his troops; as he placed his
division in position, he noticed the "retiring herd" crowding around
Lee as he sat on his horse, holding a Confederate battle flag.[134] Here
on a Prince Edward hill, in the gathering twilight of an April evening, took place what Lee's definitive biographer, Douglas Southall
Freeman, called the last rally of the Army of Northern Virginia.[135]

At eleven o'clock that night Mahone left the field, moving his
division to the High Bridge; by daylight of April 7 he had moved his
command across to the Cumberland side. Gordon and his men had
preceded Mahone across the Appomattox at the bridge.[136]

We left Longstreet at Rice on the morning of the 6th, his troops
lined up for battle across the Burkeville road. Ord, at Burkeville,
who had sent the bridge burners to the High Bridge early that
morning, heard from Sheridan that Lee's Army had gotten away

from him and was apparently headed for Burkeville. Ord put his Twenty-Fourth Corps into position to meet the expected Confederates; at noon on the 6th, finding that Lee was moving in another direction, he started his corps toward Farmville. When the corps' First Division, commanded by Brigadier General Robert S. Foster, reached Flippen's fork, Foster sent his Third Brigade under Colonel Dandy northward on the Genito road to meet, if possible, Sheridan and with the rest of his command moved on to Rice. It was late in the afternoon, and Foster disposed his command in line of battle when he found Longstreet across his line of march. He put his Fourth Brigade on the right, with the brigade's right resting at a house 200 yards to the right of the Farmville road, and the First Brigade on the left extending across the Southside Railroad a short distance beyond the Phillips house; he placed his battery to the left of the Farmville road. Under skirmish fire, he moved his line forward somewhat. Night stopped his advance before he could attempt to drive in the Confederate pickets.[137] The Federal Signal Corps established a station of observation in a tree near the line of battle from which the observers had a good view of the Confederate breastworks, the guns and movements of Longstreet's army.[138] That night Dandy, having made contact with Sheridan, rejoined Foster, and was placed in reserve in the rear of the Phillips house.[139] Merritt had come up with his cavalry late in the afternoon. He was critical of Ord: "it was soon apparent that the Army of the James was not operating with vigor against the enemy."[140]

That night Longstreet left his position at Rice and marched to Farmville, followed by Rosser's and Munford's cavalry. Foster, not discovering until daylight on the 7th that the foe he anticipated fighting had moved on, followed on the road to Farmville. He found a strong Confederate skirmish line entrenched on the hill on the west of Bush River(the road then crossed below the confluence of Briery with Bush), which his First Brigade dislodged with some cavalry assistance.[141]

Humphreys and his Second Corps took up the pursuit of Gordon early on the morning of the 7th. At 5:30 A. M., Brevet Major General Francis C. Barlow, commanding the Second Division of the Second Corps, in the van of the corps, started for the High Bridge. He sent the 19th Maine Volunteers ahead to secure the bridge for the corps' crossing. There this regiment engaged Mahone's rear guard, just as the Confederates had set fire to the road bridge over the river at that point and while the second span of the railroad bridge was burning. Three or four spans of the railroad bridge (Humphreys reported four spans, Barlow three) burned before the Federal soldiers could put out the fire. By 9:15 the Federal forces were crossing the Appomattox. Leaving High Bridge, one column of Confederates moved to the northwest, the other headed toward Farmville along the railroad. Barlow followed the Confederates along the railroad, only to find Farmville held by a strong Confederate force. Humphreys with Miles and DeTrobriand followed the Confederates moving to the northwest toward the old Richmond-Lynchburg stage road.[142]

On April 6 Lee had headquarters at Rice, from which he sent a message to President Davis that he would be in Farmville that night; he advised that Davis could communicate with him by telgraph to Meherrin and by courier to Lynchburg.[143] General Meade established headquarters at High Bridge on the 7th.[144]

Longstreet and the cavalry units following him reached Farmville on the morning of the 7th. Rations were distributed to the hungry Confederates, many of whom had had nothing to eat except raw or parched corn during the two days previous.[145]

The night of the 6th Secretary of War John Cabell Breckinridge, Quartermaster General A. R. Lawton, and Commissary General I. M. St. John stayed at the home of Patrick H. Jackson on Beech Street. When Lee got to Farmville on the morning of the 7th, he went to the Jackson home and had a conference with the three. Invited to have breakfast at the home, he declined, as he also did a toddy, but he drank a cup of coffee in a room which had been placed at his disposal.[146]

The Federal forces were pressing hard upon the Confederates at Farmville. There was fighting between Fitzhugh Lee's rear guard and the Union advance guard as they approached Farmville and in the streets of the town.

Lee moved his infantry to the north bank of the Appomattox and burned the bridge by which he had crossed. As the river was too deep to be forded, burning the bridge prevented the Federals, except Crook's cavalry, which forded the Appomattox with difficulty, from crossing the river on the 7th. The Confederate cavalry drove Crook back; he was recalled to the south bank of the river and was sent toward Prospect. That night the Confederates left the Cumberland hills overlooking Farmville; Lee assembled what was left after the disasters at Sailor's Creek and Lockett's Farm into a marching column again on the road to Appomattox Courthouse, with orders to march via Campbell Courthouse and through Pittsylvania to Danville. There were left now only two corps, Longstreet's and Gordon's; Since his stop at Rice on the 6th and Gordon's crossing of the river at High Bridge, Longstreet formed the rear guard of the remnant of one of the greatest fighting organizations of all history, Lee's Army of Northern Virginia. Fitzhugh Lee and the cavalry left Farmville about midnight and forded the Appomattox a short distance west of the town.[147]

After the Battle of Sailor's Creek, Wright and the Sixth Corps moved on to Rice. There they found that the Twenty-Fourth Corps had gone on to Farmville. Wright followed, massing his corps on the hills overlooking Farmville. Grant directed him to remain in that position until further orders. A foot bridge was built across the Appomattox for the infantry, and Grant had the pontoon train of the Twenty-Fourth Corps build a bridge across the river on which the artillery and trains crossed. On the 8th the Sixth Corps reached New Store.[148]

On the morning of the 7th, after its victory in conjunction with the Sixth Corps at Sailor's Creek the afternoon before, Sheridan's Cavalry resumed the pursuit of the Confederates. Lee still had the Union generals guessing, but they had forces enough to send men wherever they guessed he might go. Sheridan thought Lee might take the road to Danville; he sent Merritt with two divisions to Prince Edward Courthouse, to block that road should Lee take it. From the Courthouse Sheridan sent General MacKenzie with a division of cavalry from the Army of the James to make a reconnaisance to Prospect. When it was learned that the Confederates had crossed the Appomattox, Merritt left the Courthouse and camped at Buffalo Creek; orders were sent to Crook, who had followed the Confederates to Farmville, to recross the Appomattox, which he had forded with difficulty before the pontoon bridge was built, and camp at Prospect. On April 8 Merritt and MacKenzie were at Prospect, and Merritt and Crook moved on from Prospect to Appomattox Depot.[149]

The Signal Corps of the Army of the Potomac tried to open a line of signal communication between Rice and Prince Edward Courthouse, but it was unsuccessful because the necessary intermediate point was not accessible for some time after it was deemed desirable to open the line of signal communication.[150]

While the Federal cavalry and the Sixth Corps had been fighting at Sailor's Creek, the Second Corps fighting at Lockett's Farm, and the Army of the James moving from Burkeville to form a line of battle at Rice, Griffin and the Fifth Corps had marched through western Amelia County. Ordered to move north on the Pridesville road on the right of the army, the Fifth Corps continued via Paineville to the vicinity of Ligontown, covering thirty-two miles that day. It met only small cavalry detachments of the Confederates, but captured about 300 prisoners and "many wagons." Following instructions, Griffin started his men at five o'clock on the morning of the 7th via Rice for Farmville. As the head of his column was passing near the High Bridge, he received orders about 9:30 A. M. to pass to the rear of the Sixth Corps (moving from Rice to Farmville) and the Second Corps (then crossing the Appomattox at the High Bridge) and move as rapidly as possible to Prince Edward Courthouse. The Fifth Corps reached the Courthouse at 7:30 P. M. on April 7, after a march of twenty miles that day. That night at eleven new orders came: Griffin was to follow Gibbon's Twenty-Fourth Corps up the Lynchburg road at six the next morning, while the Second and Sixth Corps were following the Confederates on the north side of the Appomattox. The Fifth Corps reached the Lynchburg road at Prospect about noon on April 8 and followed the Twenty-Fourth Corps toward Appomattox. It was not an easy march, made slow and tedious by repeated and long halts of the Twenty-Fourth Corps. For the cautious Griffin, this restrained comment was criticism indeed. His corps was on the march until two o'clock on the morning of the 9th, when they bivouaced three miles from Appomattox Courthouse.[151]

On April 6-7 the Federal troops invaded another section of Prince Edward. On the morning of the 7th they reached Meherrin; the movement had begun from Burkeville Junction on the 6th; on that day, a stationmaster on the Richmond and Danville Railroad named Wilkinson went from Green Bay to Meherrin and reported that a detachment of Federal cavalry was on the way to the latter point; one of the railroad's Negroes reported of the camp that the "Yankee tents stretched for about one mile along the railroad." On April 8 the Federals ran a train from Burkeville to Meherrin.[152]

Grant reached Farmville early on April 7 and made his headquarters at the Randolph House. General Ewell, now a prisoner of war, had expressed to a kinsman, Dr. Smith, who was with Grant, the hope that Lee would surrender. Sheridan learned at Prince Edward Courthouse that seven trains of provisions and forage were awaiting the Confederates at Appomattox and headed for that station by forced marches. These two circumstances gave Grant the idea of opening a correspondence with Lee looking to surrender. Accordingly, at 5:00 P. M. on the 7th, he dispatched the first note to Lee, pointing out that the results of the week should show the hopelessness of further resistance and asking for surrender to shift responsibility for "needless shedding of blood." Lee's reply, which reached Grant before he left Farmville, differed on the hopelessness of resistance, but agreed in the desire to avoid "useless effusion of blood." Before Lee would agree to Grant's proposal, he would have to know the terms Grant would offer. The next day Grant replied. The correspondence led to the conference at the McLean house at Appomattox Courthouse.[153]

Prince Edward was devastated by the conquering army and the stragglers in its wake. The memory of the destruction of food and goods remained vivid in the minds of those who experienced it, even small children. Those old enough to remember people who lived through those hard days know well the wreck and waste which were the lot of practically every home and farm. Horses, livestock, poultry, provisions, valuables were carried off, and goods, furniture, and property were wantonly destroyed. Federal soldiers were responsible for some of the destruction, though, as Dr. W. W. H. Thackston put it, "as a rule, the conduct of Yankee officers and real soldiers was better, more creditable, and more honorable than expected; camp-followers, thieves, and plunderers invaded every house not protected by guards stealing and hunting for what they thought was concealed." Federal officers generally felt a sense of responsibility to maintain as much order as possible and to provide as much protection to civilians as possible. When a Federal officer saw the need or was asked, he placed a guard at a home, with strict instructions to protect the family from danger and the property from being plundered. Often the looting and pillaging had begun before the guard was placed.[154] Among the stories of plundering, there stand out stories of kindness on the part of Federal soldiers. One little girl in Prince Edward lived on a farm on the line of march from Sailor's Creek battlefield to Rice; in the pillaging there, every living animal and fowl, except a hen which had stolen a nest, had been carried off or killed; a detachment of Federal troops camped in the yard of this home and began cooking supper; this girl, then only four, got away from older members of the family to the front porch. The beef smelled good, and the child said so. The soldiers who heard her gave her enough for the family's supper that night.[155] People prepared food for the Confederates passing; Mrs. Richard McIlwaine had fifty persons to supper the day the army passed through Farmville and a dozen overnight guests. She hid twenty-two gold watches in balls of carpet rags for friends in the Confederate Army. Many people hid their jewelry, silver, and other valuables or sent them away.[156] Many who did not lost them to looters. Prince Edward was more fortunate than some counties through which the armies marched and in which there was fighting: none of the county records was destroyed. But there was scarcely a home in the county without some story of damage or loss during these troubled days. The experience was a harrowing one, and for some women, hitherto known for intelligence and piety, it was a time in which they lost their emotional balance or even, in Dr. McIlwaine's phrase, "drifted from their religious moorings."[157] It requires no psychologist to explain why.

To return to the military. Sheridan, Gibbon, and Griffin, with the cavalry, the Twenty-Fourth Corps, and the Fifth Corps pushed westward rapidly. On Sunday, April 9, Lee found the enemy across his line of march. Behind him Humphreys' Second Corps and Wright's Sixth were pushing hard upon his tired men. Discussion of surrender had begun soon after his army left Farmville. Now it seemed the one course to take. So Lee met Grant that Palm Sunday morning at Appomattox Courthouse, which twenty years before had been Clover Hill in Prince Edward; there they agreed upon terms of surrender, and formal surrender was made. There the battered and almost exhausted remnant of the once proud Army of Northern Virginia, but still glorious, even in defeat, laid down its arms.[158] And there the nation, whose beginning Prince Edward people had welcomed, in whose armies her sons had fought and for whose defense many of them had fallen, and in whose success the hope of her people had lain, died.

CHAPTER XIV

Reconstruction

THE ringing of church bells on the morning of Sunday, April 9, 1865, announced to Farmville the surrender of General Lee at Appomattox Courthouse.[1] The word spread rapidly. During the day the news was widely circulated by people traveling through the country.[2] Prince Edward had been occupied territory since the Federal army, pursuing the Confederates, had marched through on Friday, April 7. "Only those present can imagine the horrors of that miserable night," wrote Dr. J. L. White. "Closed doors were little protection from the swarm of the Federal host who crowded yards and streets and none at all from the horde of lawless thieves and boomers who followed." Martial law was established in Farmville on Saturday, April 8, and the town and vicinity were placed under military government with a provost marshal in charge and a strong garrison. Guards were placed over homes of those who applied for them. "Though prisoners in our own homes," to quote Dr. White again, "we felt less alarm and were more comfortable." The area was under military government, Dr. White recalled, "eighteen months or two years, and we had no freedom of action till the last bluecoat left."[3] Into Farmville on the morning military government was established came Colonel Richard A. Booker, lately commander of a regiment of home guards. On the advice of Dr. Boykin of the Confederate Hospital staff, Colonel Booker changed from his uniform to civilian clothes and presented himself at the Provost Marshal's office; he had little difficulty in securing a parole, and then he joined his family at the Randolph House.[4]

On the morning of Lee's surrender only a few of the regular congregation of the Presbyterian Church attended worship; the auditorium was crowded, however, with Federal soldiers whose conduct was "attentive and decorous." While troops were stationed in Farmville the congregation in that church continued to have that make-up.

The news of Lincoln's assassination, less than a week after Appomattox, was received with regret in the town. The presence there then of several thousand Federal troops had explosive possibilities, but there was no demonstration or violence. The day after

411

the news of Lincoln's death reached Farmville (probably Sunday, April 16, as he died on the morning of Saturday, April 15, after having been shot the evening before), the commandant of the post asked of Dr. Richard McIlwaine, the pastor, permission to use the Presbyterian Church for memorial services that day at eleven o'clock; permission was granted, and the service was held. The church was filled with soldiers, Dr. McIlwaine and one other person being the only Farmville people present; they heard nothing which might offend Southern feelings.[3]

During this period Federal troops were returning from Appomattox; a number of units passed through Prince Edward. The First Division of the Sixth Corps returned through Farmville on its way to Burkeville.[6] The Second Division of Sheridan's cavalry marched to Prospect on April 10 and on the next day escorted General Grant to Burkeville.[7] The Fifth Corps did not leave Appomattox until the 15th; it marched thirteen miles that day and camped that night, obviously at some point near the Prince Edward-Appomattox line. On the 16th it marched past Prospect to Farmville, a distance of seventeen miles, during the day. After spending the night in Farmville, the corps marched to Burkeville on April 17.[8] The Twenty-fourth Corps remained longest at Appomattox, as its commander, Major General Gibbon, was assigned the duty of settling matters subsequent to the surrender. It left Appomattox on April 17, marched past Pamplin, Prospect, and Farmville, and arrived at Burkeville on the 19th.[9] A detachment of Federal troops, a part of Ferrero's Division, on its way from Petersburg to Lynchburg, after drawing rations and forage at Burkeville, passed Prince Edward Courthouse on May 12 and camped at Pamplin that night.[10]

The Confederates were returning home, too. Those who were at the surrender at Appomattox were soon back. Those in Federal prison were not so fortunate. They had to wait release through regular channels. At Point Lookout they were released alphabetically; those whose names began with letters toward the beginning of the alphabet began the homeward trip fairly soon after the surrender. It was June 22, before those whose names began with "W" were released. When a prisoner of war was released, he took the following oath and parole:

"I do solemnly swear, in the presence of Almighty God, that I will henceforth faithfully support, protect and defend the Constitution of the United States, and the Union of the States thereunder;

and that I will in like manner abide by and faithfully support all acts of Congress passed during the existing rebellion in reference to slaves, so long and so far as not repealed, modified or held void by Congress, or by decision of the Supreme Court; and that I will in like manner abide by and faithfully support all proclamations of the President made during the existing rebellion, having reference to slaves, so long and so far as not modified or declared void by decision of the Supreme Court,—So help me God; and I give my solemn parole of honor (to be enforced according to military law,) that I will hold no correspondence with, or afford any aid and comfort to any enemies or opposers of the United States, save as an act of humanity, to administer to the necessities of individuals, who are in sickness or distress; and I solemnly declare that this Oath and Parole is taken and given freely and willingly, without any mental reservation or evasion whatever, and with full intention to keep the same."

He also took the following oath of allegiance, recorded here in the name of the soldier who through the years kept his copy:

"I, James R. Weaver of the County of Prince Edwd, State of Va., do solemnly swear that I will support, protect and defend the Constitution and Government of the United States against all enemies, whether domestic or foreign; that I will bear true faith, allegiance, and loyalty to the same, any ordinance, resolution or laws of any State, Convention, or Legislature, to the contrary notwithstanding; and further, that I will faithfully perform all the duties which may be required of me by the laws of the United States, and I take this oath freely and voluntarily, without any mental reservation or evasion whatever.

Jas. R. Weaver

"Subscribed and sworn to before me this Twenty second day of June A.D. 1865.

A. W. Brady
Maj. and Provost Marshal

"The above named has dark complexion, black hair, and Hazel eyes; and is 5 feet 5½ inches high."

After taking these oaths the prisoner of war received a Certificate of Release of Prisoner of War.

Head Quarters, Point Lookout, Md.
"Provost Marshal's Office, June 22nd 1865

"I hereby Certify, That Jas. R. Weaver Prisoner of War, having this day taken the Oath of Allegiance to the UNITED STATES is in conformity with instructions from the War Department hereby released and discharged.

"In witness whereof, I hereunto affix my official Signature and Stamp.

A. W. Brady

Maj. and Provost Marshal."[11]

Some persons thought it advisable to apply for presidential pardons,, which apparently could be issued by the Secretary of the Commonwealth. In the list of those to whom pardons were granted in August, 1866, was Dr. R. P. Walton, then of Prince Edward, who had been a surgeon in the Confederate Hospital at Farmville. Those who wanted such pardons were advised to apply in person to the Secretary of the Commonwealth or to give a written request to a friend to receive the pardon for him and deliver it to him in person. It was evidently considered important to have some papers, either of pardon or otherwise, showing allegiance to the United States government, in those difficult days.[12]

Many people, who had lost much or everything during the passing of the Federal troops, were in difficult circumstances. Many had to apply to the Federal authorities for aid. One of these was James S. Lockett, who sought food not only for his family, but also for the wounded soldiers left at his home after the battle which raged around it. Burkeville was the location of a principal military headquarters in this area, and it was to that village that Lockett and others from Prince Edward went to get food.[13]

The Federal forces took over the new wards of the Confederate hospital in Farmville; in addition to using them for hospital purposes, it made them a center for the distribution of food and other supplies to the Negroes of Prince Edward and other counties. This part of the hospital thus became the Farmville office of the Freedmen's Bureau, the agency which administered the government program for the recently freed slaves. About 1870, at the time the office of the bureau in Farmville was discontinued in Farmville, the hospital buildings of this ward were sold and, with one exception, were taken down.[14]

In the summer of 1865 it appeared that the normal processes of local government would be restored. An election was held and William T. Carter, James B. Ely, R. C. Anderson, James Whitehead, Richard W. Price, Edwin J. Redd, Samuel S. Baker, Richard B.

Thackston, Richard S. Paulett, James T. Gray, John A. Dalby, John P. Hughes, Charles A. Morton, David F. Womack, James J. Rice, Howell E. Warren, Robert V. Davis, Samuel B. Scott, and James S. Lockett were elected justices; they qualified in August before Branch J. Worsham, one of the election commissioners, by taking the oath prescribed by the Wheeling Convention of 1861. They were to hold office until August, 1868. Morton was chosen presiding justice. At the same session of Court, Branch J. Worsham qualified as clerk, Branch Worsham (the son) as deputy clerk, George W. Booker as sheriff, John R. Cunningham as commissioner of revenue, William H. Ewing as surveyor, and Stephen O. Southall as attorney for the commonwealth.[15]

The next month the Court set up patrols for each magisterial district with instructions to visit places suspected of having vagrants and others committing offenses; they were to report their findings to A. D. Dickinson, who in turn was directed to cooperate with the Provost Marshal and other military authorities in the county "to secure good order." In District One (Sandy River) the patrol was made up of Joseph T. Ligon, captain, William L. Clark, J. T. Johnson, Samuel Wootton, William J. McGehee, John Walton, P. S. Smithson, E. T. Clark, Charles Vaughan, William Farley, L. B. Walthall, John Southall, Stith Farley, Henry Harper, James Overton, George Bruce, Samuel Bruce, and Daniel A. Watson; the District Two (Courthouse) patrol included R. H. Watkins, captain, R. L. Shackleton, A. L. Bagby, William Booker, C. E. Redd, P. B. Sublett, R. S. Hines, James A. Bell, R. L. Redd, J. B. McGehee, George W. Fowlkes, and John H. Pearson; the District Three (Spring Creek) patrol consisted of William J. Rice, captain, Francis L. Elliott, Henry E. Elliott, Nat Thackston, D. Womack, John R. Cunningham, John W. Baker, James M. Dillon, Wiltshire Snead, Frank Womack, John F. Rice, Thomas W. Price, and John Gilliam; in District Four (Prospect) Edward N. Price, captain, William Hunt, George Elam, Robert Gilliam, Daniel P. Carter, Henderson Coleman, Adison Brightwell, Joseph Glenn, H. A. Allen, Mercer Brightwell, James Martin, and John J. Flournoy comprised the patrol; and the patrol for District Five (Farmville) was made up of J. W. Womack, captain, J. J. Bondurant, A. B. Venable, W. H. Richardson, Nat Morton, A. R. Venable, L. E. Agee, Drury Armistead, Thomas L. Robertson, Thomas L. Morton, William W. Evans, and William Daniel.[16]

New election officials, five commissioners and one conductor for each precinct, were named by the Court in August: Green Bay: Samuel B. Scott, Francis T. Wootton, Richard W. Scott, John T. Johnson, and Thomas O. Rowlett, commissioners, and H. A. Clark, conductor; Courthouse: R. C. Anderson, Edwin J. Redd, Richard Stokes, E. D. Redd, and William T. Carter, commissioners, and R. S. Hines, conductor; Spring Creek: D. F. Womack, S. S. Baker, G. S. Harper, John P. Hughes, and James Whitehead, commissioners, and Nathaniel Thackston, conductor; Prospect: Henry J. Venable, John O. Elam, Samuel S. Clark, Charles A. Price, and Robert V. Davis, commissioners, and Edward N. Price, conductor; Farmville: R. S. Paulett, C. C. Read, J. M. McNutt, George W. Daniel, and J. J. Rice, commissioners, and Edward T. Rice, conductor; Rice Depot: Joseph T. Ligon, Joseph Phillips, James A. Watson, Thomas E. Perkinson, and James M. Wootton, commissioners, and John W. Foster, conductor.[17]

In the new election of county officers, the people made no changes from their choice under the Confederacy. The same names which had appeared in the prewar and wartime lists continued in the list of those chosen in the first election after the war. From the old leadership both county and election officials were chosen; the patrols include many persons whose names are mentioned for the first time in these pages, but their family names are familiar; these were largely young men, and there were many Confederate veterans among them. From the election returns and the court appointments, it is evident that the people accepted defeat, but expected and intended to continue the direction of local affairs as though the defeat of the Confederacy were only an interlude in history which would not affect the routine of local government.

Some were disturbed of course. The widow of Colonel John T. Thornton shared the thinking of many Southern people of that dark day, that the only hope for Southerners lay in emigration to Mexico or Brazil. With five "promising boys," the oldest then about thirteen, Mrs. Thornton decided to leave the United States for one of these Latin American countries; she was dissuaded through the rather strenuous efforts of her pastor, Dr. Richard McIlwaine.[18]

The mingled mortification at defeat and determination to make the best of a bad situation are well set forth in a letter from Daniel Witt to his brother-in-law, Richard Gwathmey, in August, 1865:

"We have had a sad experience since I saw you last. In common with others, we have shared in the disappointment and mortification which must always attend the loss of independence, and the crushing of long cherished hopes. In addition to this, the storm of war swept right over us, leaving a wide scene of desolation in its track. There was no fighting on my farm; but we were within the hearing of the muskets, and could see the flashing of the guns. The line of battle, as the armies fought through this neighborhood, extended from the Appomattox river nearly to Sandy River church, a distance of about twelve miles. After the surrender the Union troops returned to this region, and remained amongst us for about six weeks. You can readily imagine the ruin they wrought, and the state of destitution to which our people were reduced. Our horses and provisions, of every kind, were taken off, in many instances leaving nothing for the inhabitants to subsist on. We suffered as much as most of our neighbors, more than some of them, but still a mericiful Providence sustains us, and we really have not suffered for the necessaries of life. I thought when the robbers left us that we were literally stripped of all our means of living; and have been astonished since to see how well we can live upon what at first seemed to be absolutely nothing. But we now have comparatively few to feed, and have as many comforts as we need, and are living in more quiet than we did before these troubles came upon us. An inscrutable Providence has appointed for us this portion; I receive it as the chastening of the Lord, and bow, with adoring submission, to the dispensation of that mysterious wisdom which I cannot, at present, understand. I suppose we shall understand it hereafter; and it will be time enough for us to know it when God becomes his own interpreter, and explains by the developments of his providence the secret purposes of his eternal mind.

"According to my view of things, it is more in mercy than in wrath to us, that the relation between master and slave has been broken down in the South. With the light which I now have upon the subject I do not yet see that the relation itself was sinful *per se.* It was certainly not profitable to me, and was attended with vast responsibilities and perplexing cares. I do not, therefore, regret the emancipation of my slaves on my own account. But what is to become of the poor, thoughtless, improvident creatures themselves? Their first idea of freedom is to live without labor, and many of them are strolling over the country without making any provision for their future, or even present, support. It seems to me that the curse still rests upon Ham, and thickens over him. In this I may be mistaken, as I have often been in other things.

"I know that we all are a proud, thankless and rebellious people. We have deserved every stroke which the chastening hand of God has inflicted upon us. But surely he has ordained that we should be humbled by a people distinguished by their disregard of constitutional law, and, many of them, of the common decencies of life. I am sure I have never seen, in the whole course of my life, such exhibitions of depravity as were made by the Union soldiers here. The question of allegiance is settled in my mind. I intend to deport myself as a loyal citizen; but really, I cannot feel that our persons or property are safe in such hands. We are now lying powerless at their feet, awaiting the disposal they may choose to make of us. What that may be, it is impossible for us to divine. I confess I see no gleam of light in the dark future as it presents itself to my view. But the Lord may have in store for us something we do not now apprehend. Let us wait and see what he will do. My trust is now, as ever heretofore, in him alone."[19]

God did provide, and people of that day pointed out as an evidence of divine care an unusually abundant "crop" of squirrels in the fall of 1865. Boys and men picked up the lead seals which were used on railroad boxcars and melted them down to make shot. These they used in hunting squirrels, and some almost destitute families are said to have subsisted largely on squirrels during that hard fall and winter.[20]

For a time matters moved smoothly enough. The Court in August, 1865, notified Cumberland Court of the need for rebuilding the bridge over the Appomattox at Farmville and the next month named R. S. Paulett, James B. Ely, and John A. Dalby commissioners to represent the county in building the bridge.[21] In August F. N. Watkins, S. O. Southall, John P. Fitzgerald, Abram B. Venable, Asa D. Dickinson, P. W. McKinney, and John C. Hamlett, Jr., took the oaths required of attorneys and qualified to practice law.[22]

In August, 1866, Stephen O. Southall was named professor of constitutional and international law, the law merchant and equity at the University of Virginia; he resigned as commonwealth's attorney in September, and the next month Philip W. McKinney was named his successor and qualified.[23]

The political parties were generally known by different names during much of the Reconstruction period; the Republicans were called Radicals, the Democrats Conservatives. It does not appear that the Radicals had become particularly active in Prince Edward in 1866, as none from the county was named a delegate to the party's convention in Philadelphia in September of that year; Campbell was the only Southside county represented among the delegates.[24] But in the Constitutional Convention of 1867-68, usually designated the Underwood convention from its dominating member, Edgar Allan, a native of England who had lived in the North long enough to win the nickname Yankee, and a Negro, James W. D. Bland, both Radicals, represented Prince Edward and Appomattox; the two counties were made into a district to elect a delegate to the House of Delegates just after the war, and Francis N. Watkins, a Conservative, was delegate from the district between the end of the war and the convention. For this period, too, Prince Edward was in a senatorial district which embraced in addition Chesterfield, Amelia, Cumberland, and Powhatan; Christopher C. McRae was state senator for this district.[25]

The Conservatives did not intend to take Radical domination without a fight. They held a meeting at the Courthouse January 21, 1868, with Colonel Richard A. Booker as chairman and McD. R. Venable as secretary. Colonel J. P. Fitzgerald read a circular letter from the State Central Committee on the subject of party organization. R. M. Dickinson offered resolutions that the Prince Edward Conservatives approve the plan of organization proposed by the state convention which had met in Richmond December 11, 1867, and pledge their cooperation in carrying the plan into execution; that R. H. Watkins, F. D. Redd, J. T. Ligon, P. S. Smithson, Dr. J. L. White, James Dinwiddie, Dr. J. W. Dillon, J. W. Jones, T. T. Tredway, and J. P. Hughes be named the county committee to select a party superintendent for the county; and that they add to their number and supply vacancies as they deemed advisable. F. N. Watkins, R. H. Watkins, J. P. Fitzgerald, and P. W. McKinney in addresses urged the "immediate and thorough organization of the party as the only means of saving the State from the degradation of Negro rule." T. T. Tredway was then chosen Conservative superintendent for Prince Edward.[26]

The state was redistricted for Congress in 1868, and Prince Edward was put into the Fifth District with Greene, Albemarle, Fluvanna, Nelson, Buckingham, Amherst, Appomattox, Bedford, Campbell, and Lynchburg. Allan and another Carpetbagger, Charles

H. Porter, were given in a news dispatch in April, 1868, as Radical candidates for Congress, and Adolphus W. Harrison of Nelson, a Conservative candidate. Each offered his record in the Constitutional Convention in support of his candidacy.[27] Robert Ridgway of Amherst County ran on the Whig ticket and was elected from the district, but congressmen from Virginia were not admitted to the Fortieth Congress. Ridgway was elected to the Forty-First Congress in July, 1869, and took his seat January 27, 1870,[28] with the first group of Virginia Senators and Representatives to serve in the national Congress since the Senators and Representatives serving in 1861 resigned when Virginia seceded. The state was again redistricted in 1872; Prince Edward was put in the Fourth District, with Petersburg, Dinwiddie, Brunswick, Mecklenburg, Lunenburg, Nottoway, Amelia, Greensville, Charlotte, Powhatan, and Cumberland.[29] Prince Edward has remained in the Fourth District ever since.

The Constitution drawn up in the convention of 1867-68 made radical changes in the set-up of local government. The Conservatives, even those who had been members of the convention, did not like the new instrument of government; those who were members of the convention circulated an address to the people urging that the Constitution be rejected because it "will not secure the ends of good government."[30] But the new Constitution prevailed. Under it Prince Edward again was given one delegate in the lower house of the state legislature; with Charlotte it constituted a senatorial district; and with Mecklenburg, Lunenburg, Charlotte, Amelia, Powhatan, Buckingham, and Cumberland it made up the Third Judicial Circuit.

One of the greatest changes made was in the county courts. The justices of the peace became township officials, and the county court was made to consist of one judge, learned in the law of the state, to be elected by joint vote of the two houses of the state legislature (the circuit court judge was chosen in the same way). The voters in the county were to elect a sheriff, a commonwealth's attorney (who served in both county and circuit courts), a clerk (who also served both courts), a treasurer, and a superintendent of the poor. The two latter were new officials created by this Constitution. A superintendent of schools for the county was to be appointed by the State Board of Education (the Governor, the Attorney General, and the Superintendent of Public Instruction) and was subject to Senate confirmation. Each county was to be divided into not less than three townships, and in each township the people were to elect annually one supervisor, one clerk, one assessor, one collector, one commissioner of roads, one overseer of the poor, one justice of the peace, and one constable; the terms of the justice and the constable were to be three years, and there were to be three such office holders in each district; in the first election one justice and one constable were to be elected for one year, one each for two years, and one each for three years. Local elections were set for the fourth Thursday in May, and the officials chosen were to take office on July 1. The supervisors of the townships constituted the county Board of Supervisors, which was directed to meet on the first Monday in December to audit the county books, regulate and equalize the valuation of property, fix county levies for the year and apportion them among the townships. The townships could be divided into as many school districts and road districts as needed. Each road district had an overseer, and each school district three trustees, each serving three-year terms, but at the first election or appointment one was to be chosen for one year, one for two, and one for three.[31]

Before the provisions of the Constitution went into effect in 1870, the military authorities of Military District No. One (in the Reconstruction organization, the South was divided into five military districts, of which Virginia was No. One) replaced the elected local officials with appointees of their own choosing. On January 22, 1869, Major General Stoneman, named Joseph Jorgenson, a carpetbagger, clerk of Prince Edward to replace the venerable Branch J. Worsham, who had held that office for forty-four years with a distinction and an attention to duty rarely equalled and never surpassed; Jorgenson qualified in March.[32] In the simple notation which Worsham made of the event one reads all the pathos of the removal of the man to whom the clerk's office had so long been almost life itself. "1869, Jan'y 26th, 4 o'clock in the evening, rec'd orders removing me from office as clerk, and I cease forthwith to do any official business. B. J. Worsham."[33] In April other Stoneman appointees qualified, to replace the elected officials: Samuel M. Page, commonwealth's attorney, and James Mickle, commissioner of revenue, who promptly proceeded to name his predecessor, John R. Cunningham, his assistant. No sheriff had been appointed, so George W. Booker qualified. At that time there was neither sheriff nor constable nor coroner in the county. The justices were removed, too, and replaced by only four: R. S. Hines, who was chosen presiding justice, W. S. Berry, Henry T. Owen, and John Carpenter. All except Carpenter qualified in April, 1869, when they took over their duties.[34]

Subsequently Benjamin M. Cox was appointed sheriff of Prince

Edward by the military authorities. In the fall of 1870 the Richmond *Enquirer* accused the "radical sheriffs" of robbing the Commonwealth, noting that in the short time they had been in office (some less than a year) they were defaulters to the amount of $241,719.24, while "our own sheriffs" (those elected by the people) were defaulters in the amount of $60,789.99. Cox' deficiency was reported as $2,653.62.[35]

The first county court with one judge held its first session April 18, 1870. Judge Francis N. Watkins, who had been elected judge of the Prince Edward County Court by the General Assembly, had taken the oath of office on April 15 before R. R. Howison, a notary public of Richmond. He promptly proceeded to fill county offices by appointment until successors to his appointees could be elected. Judge Watkins restored, for a brief period, the old order. Branch Worsham was appointed clerk, and upon his motion his father, Branch J. Worsham, was named his deputy; George W. Booker was appointed sheriff, the post to which he had first been elected in 1862; Philip W. McKinney was restored to his old position of commonwealth's attorney, from which he had been removed by the military authority. John R. Cunningham, who had been appointed commissioner of revenue for one year by the state auditor of public accounts, qualified and named as his assistant James Mickle, who had named Cunningham his assistant when he replaced him by military appointment. After Worsham had been appointed clerk, Jorgenson appeared in court and protested; he refused to deliver the clerk's office, books, and papers to Worsham unless delivery was demanded by authority of the Court. The Court which had appointed Worsham intended that he should be clerk; it demanded by its authority that Jorgenson deliver the office, keys, books, papers, and archives to Worsham. R. S. Hines was appointed keeper of the Courthouse.[36]

The appointees of Judge Watkins held office until the end of 1870. The terms of officials elected November 8, 1870, the first to be elected under the new Constitution, began January 1, 1871. Joseph Jorgenson was elected clerk, Henry R. Hooper sheriff, Edgar Allan commonwealth's attorney, Edwin J. Redd treasurer, and William Barbour, superintendent of the poor.[37] Thomas J. Garden was appointed sealer of weights and measures and was directed to apply to the Governor or to the superintendent of weights and measures for a full set of weights, balances, and measures for the use of the county.[38]

When Jorgenson resigned as clerk in October, 1871, Judge Watkins appointed Branch Worsham a second time;[39] in a special election,

November 17, 1871, Henry R. Hooper was elected clerk, his term beginning January 1, 1872.[40] William H. Wilkerson succeeded Hooper as sheriff.[41] In the election November 4, 1873, Samuel H. Bliss was elected treasurer, Wiltshire Cardwell sheriff, and Edgar Allan commonwealth's attorney. Judge Watkins was re-elected county judge in 1873.[42] When Cardwell moved from the county in 1874, Judge Watkins named Thomas H. Dickinson his successor,[43] thus continuing to follow his policy of naming a Conservative to office when he had opportunity.

The Board of Supervisors held its first meeting August 2, 1870, at the courthouse. At that time there were only four townships in the county, the former Prospect and Spring Creek districts having been combined as Buffalo township; the old Sandy River district was now Leigh township; and the former Courthouse district was now called Hampden township. All four supervisors were present at this first meeting: R. J. Matthews of Buffalo, who was chosen chairman; F. D. Redd of Hampden; W. H. Ewing of Leigh; and B. S. Hooper of Farmville.[44]

At the November, 1870, Court a petition signed by R. A. Marshall and over fifty other qualified voters in Leigh township asked for a division of the township. The petition was continued until the next day of court (November 22); as it had been posted thirty days at the courthouse and at the voting places in the township and as no opposition had been filed, the division was ordered. The dividing line began at Edmunds bridge on Bush River on the road from the Courthouse to Burkeville and continued on the southern boundary of the road to the branch of Sandy River nearest the church; at the middle of the stream the line crossed the road to its northern boundary and so continued to the Nottoway line; the area south of the line became Leigh township, the area north Lockett. On December 8 Judge Watkins in vacation appointed Frank W. Southall supervisor from Lockett Township.[45]

At this troubled period, Prince Edward experienced not only a change in its governmental organization; its county seat was moved from Prince Edward Courthouse to Farmville. The move to change the county seat had been launched not long after the military authorities had removed the elected officials and the Radicals had come into power. A petition asking for an election on changing the county seat was presented to the legislature in the fall of 1870; an election was set for the first Tuesday after the fourth Monday in May, 1871, or an earlier date designated by the Board of Supervisors, at which the people were to vote "for the present location" or "for the town of Farmville."[46] The act authorizing the election was amended a few months later to require Farmville, before becoming the county seat, to erect a courthouse, clerk's office, and jail within the corporate limits of the town on a lot of no less than one-half acre and no more than two acres. The buildings to be erected were subject to the approval of and acceptance by the Court. The Town Council of Farmville was permitted to borrow up to $13,000 at not more than ten per cent to build the county buildings, provided the voters of the town approved the issuance of bonds.[47] In April, 1871, the Farmville Council advised the Court that it had contracted with James B. Ely to buy a lot of not less than half an acre on the east side of Main Street between the Baptist and African Baptist churches and asked approval of the site for the courthouse, clerk's office, and jail. The Court gave its approval.[48]

The cornerstone of the new courthouse was laid October 20, 1871, by the Farmville Lodge of Masons. N. H. Champlin, Z. A. Blanton, R. A. Booker, F. D. Redd, and C. Zimmermann constituted the committee on arrangements. W. D. Rice was appointed by the Masonic Lodge to invite the Knights of Pythias to march in the procession. R. A. Booker, W. D. Rice, H. T. Parrish, N. H. Champlin, and J. R. Elam were appointed the reception committee, while the committee to prepare the contents of the box included H. T. Parrish, W. D. Rice, and S. W. Paulett. Dr. J. Lansing Burrows, then pastor of the First Baptist Church of Richmond, delivered the address at the ceremonies. His address treated the antiquity and honor of Masonry, justified secret fraternal orders, explained the appropriateness of having Masons lay cornerstones, and pointed out the relationship between Masonry and the Bible. Governor Gilbert C. Walker, Thomas F. Owens, Grand Master of the Masonic order in Virginia, and United States Senator Robert E. Withers, Deputy Grand Master of the Virginia Grand Lodge, were present.[49]

R. B. Berkeley, H. R. Hooper, and E. Wiltse were named commissioners at the February, 1872, Court to confer with the Farmville Council concerning the buildings erected for the county.[50] They recommended to the March Court that, since it appeared that a majority of the voters had chosen Farmville as the county seat and the town had erected buildings, it accept the conveyance of land and buildings, the clerk move the books and papers as soon as practicable, that the title to the real estate be vested in the Board of Supervisors, that the Farmville Town Council and the town officers be permitted to use the court room for meetings, that Henry J. Crute be appointed superintendent of buildings and grounds, and that notices of the change be printed under the supervision of the clerk and posted by the sheriff in each township. The Court accepted the recommendations and incorporated them in an order directing the removal of the county seat to Farmville. The last session of a county court at Prince Edward Courthouse was held March 19, 1872, 118 years, two months, and eleven days after the first county court had been held there; one week later, on March 26, the first session of the county court was held in Farmville.

The Court on March 26, 1872, directed that the voting precinct in Hampden Township hitherto known as Prince Edward Courthouse should henceforth be known as Worsham.[51] Later there was discussion of moving the county seat from Farmville to Worsham. In 1890 the Farmville Town Council sent Mayor W. W. H. Thackston, R. M. Burton, and O. T. Wicker to Richmond to oppose a bill pending in the legislature which looked to making Worsham the county seat. At its meeting in March, 1890, the Council passed a vote of thanks to the committee, Judge J. M. Crute, and P. H. C. Rice for their part in opposing the change.[52]

The town of Farmville, too, had its governmental organization changed during this period. Its affairs had been under the direction of a board of trustees. In 1870 the trustees were replaced by a mayor and nine councilmen.[53]

One innovation of the Underwood Constitution did not long survive. In 1875 constitutional amendments were adopted which abolished townships and their fairly numerous offices. The old name of magisterial district was restored for township, the hitherto existing townships being constituted districts, retaining the names, boundaries, and voting places. Thus one effort to model Virginia local government after New England failed. It was anticipated then that Buffalo District would be divided, but the prophecy was not realized for nearly a half-century, although it had, prior to the adoption of the Constitution, been two districts, Prospect and Spring Creek, sometimes called Darlington Heights.[54]

Early in the Reconstruction period Edgar Allan emerged as the leading politician in Prince Edward. Although influential in high circles in the Republican party, he was a highly controversial figure in the party in Prince Edward. He had come to Prince Edward as a private in the Federal army and had been left as a guard at Hickory Hill, home of Mrs. Henry Venable. He protected the family, contributed to the peace of the neighborhood, and exercised a remarkable influence over the freedmen. Thus he laid the foundation for his rise to political power. In the gubernatorial campaign of 1869 he was a principal lieutenant of Gilbert C. Walker, both in Walker's effort to secure the nomination by the more conservative wing of the Republicans and in the campaign against Henry H. Wells, who had been the military appointee. Walker carried the state, but the vote in Prince Edward was 1,430 for the Radical Wells to 920 for Walker.[55]

Prince Edward was firmly in the control of the Radicals. In 1872 General U. S. Grant received 1,185 votes in Prince Edward to 583 cast for Horace Greeley, candidate of the Democrats and Liberal Republicans.[56]

The Conservative party, which was made up of white people loyal to the Confederate tradition and opposed to domination of carpetbaggers (Northerners who had come South for political and economic advantage), Scalawags (white Southerners who had allied themselves politically with the Radicals), and Negroes, made a determined effort to recapture control of state and local governments in 1873. The Conservative ticket in the state consisted of James W. Kemper of Madison County for Governor, Robert E. Withers of Wythe County for Lieutenant Governor, and Raleigh T. Daniel of Richmond for Attorney General. The local Conservative ticket included P. F. Southall for state senator, Ligon (most likely Colonel Joseph T. Ligon) for the House of Delegates, and George Booker for sheriff. The Radical ticket included Robert W. Hughes for Governor, C. P. Ramsdell for Lieutenant Governor, Fultz for Attorney General, Edgar Allan for state senator and commonwealth's attorney, Tazewell Branch for the House of Delegates. W. P. Gilliam for sheriff, and S. H. Bliss for treasurer. An independent ticket proposed John Robinson for the State Senate, John A. Thompson for the House of Delegates, R. M. Dickinson for commonwealth's attorney, and E. J. Redd for treasurer.[57]

The Conservatives in Prince Edward set up an active and enthusiastic organization; J. P. Fitzgerald was party superintendent in the county, and William D. Rice was named county canvasser during the course of the campaign; the latter was subject to the call of the county and township party committees to attend meetings, make speeches, and secure speakers.[58] A Kemper Kampaign Klub was organized at the Courthouse on September 29, with John A. Dalby, president; G. B. Wright, R. S. Paulett, and Dr. J. L. White, vice-presidents; C. E. Madison, secretary, J. R. Cunningham, corresponding secretary; Z. A. Blanton, treasurer; and R. M. Burton, J. T. Gray, J. V. Rice, A. H. Porter, John Overton, O. T. Wicker, and John A. Scott, Jr., members of the executive committee. "Colonel Booker suggested money, and the stove was ornamented with filthy lucre." A barbecue was planned, and Captain Philip W. McKinney, Colonel W. R. Berkeley, W. D. Rice, and a Mr. Crawley made speeches.

The Radicals met in Farmville October 1 and nominated their ticket. Their candidate for Lieutenant Governor, C. P. Ramsdell, spoke.[59]

The Kemper Kampaign Klub met again October 6. A permanent committee, consisting of Colonel R. A. Booker, Judge F. N. Watkins, Colonel W. R. Berkeley, W. H. Kennedy, and Captain P. W. McKinney, was named to receive visiting speakers. The executive committee was enlarged by adding a number of citizens, whose specific responsibility was the solicitation of funds for the barbecue: Frank Redd, George Booker, Jr., Colonel Stokes, Captain Carter, John W. Jones, C. A. Price, J. F. Walton, John T. Johnston, S. W. Vaughan, W. E. Bradshaw, A. B. West, R. S. Hines, T. T. Tredway, William N. Hunt, John M. Gilliam, J. T. Phillips, and B. Carter. At this meeting J. A. H. St. Andrew pledged the support of the English settlers in the county to the Conservatives.

At a Conservative rally October 7 Judge Ould spoke and Judge Francis N. Watkins presided. The speaker praised the Conservative record, especially in the achievements of the new school system. He was described as "more than a match" for Ramsdell and other Radical leaders brought to Prince Edward in their effort to win the white vote.[60]

R. B. Berkeley, W. R. Berkeley, and P. W. McKinney were effective speakers for the Conservative cause, and they were extensively used in the campaign.[61]

The barbecue on October 24 was held in Scott's Grove on Farmville's Main Street, adjoining Z. A. Blanton's store. In the morning ex-Governor William Smith and Thomas S. Bocock addressed the crowd. General Kemper, the gubernatorial candidate, arrived in the afternoon and spoke, although he appeared tired. In the evening the band played *Dixie*, and Major John W. Daniel delivered an address in which the qualities of his eloquence, his rich, full, clear voice, his "almost faultless diction," his graceful gestures were demonstrated to fine effect. The length of the speeches of other days was recalled in his two-hour address, but so eloquent was he that it seemed a brief

speech. R. B. Berkeley followed Major Daniel. Although it was getting late, the crowd was in no mood to go home; the band and a
large company serenaded General Kemper, who was a guest at
Colonel W. R. Berkeley's. The candidate was too weary to appear,
so Major Daniel and the Berkeleys addressed the serenaders; "after
receiving the hospitalities of the house," the serenaders withdrew.

The candidate for Lieutenant Governor, R. E. Withers, also
addressed the Kemper Kampaign Klub in Farmville.[62]

In the election the Conservatives carried the state, but the Radicals rolled up impressive majorities in Prince Edward County. In
Virginia Kemper received 121,812 votes to Hughes' 93,666; the
Radical state ticket led in Prince Edward by 617 votes—1,527 for
Hughes to 910 for Kemper. The Radicals won the county offices, too;
Edgar Allan was elected state senator and commonwealth's attorney;
for the former post he received 1,388 votes to 892 for Southall and
151 for Robinson; for the latter, he defeated R. M. Dickinson 1,393
to 979. Tazewell Branch defeated Ligon for the House of Delegates,
1,376 to 907. Wiltshire Cardwell defeated Booker for sheriff 1,375
to 386; S. H. Bliss was elected treasurer over E. J. Redd, the incumbent, by the vote of 1,376 to 798.[63]

Defeat in 1873 seemed to take the zest for fighting out of the
Conservatives for the 1874 elections; one doughty warrior proposed
a convention to nominate a candidate to oppose H. R. Hooper for
clerk; he suggested F. H. Armistead, the deputy, "who has all the
duties to perform." But no Conservative opposition was raised against
Hooper or against the member of the House of Representatives from
the district, W. H. H. Stowell. Prince Edward voted against several
proposed amendments to the State Constitution relating to local
government: abolition of township offices of clerk, assessor, collector,
and superintendent of roads; the election of the commissioner of
revenue; and substituting magisterial districts for townships.[64]

In the 1873 campaign one of the Prince Edward speakers for
Kemper struck a note which proved prophetic of a political development to come. Speaking in Charlottesville, R. B. Berkeley declared
that the Radicalism of the South bore no resemblance to the Republi-
canism of the North.[65] Berkeley may not have been conscious of
doing it, but he was helping to pave the way for the coalition between
the Southern Democrats and Northern Republicans. It was this
coalition which made Rutherford B. Hayes President in 1877, and
the coalition based on roughly the same general lines has been a
powerful, sometimes dominant, influence since.

A coalition ticket was put up for Farmville town offices in 1875. It originated formally in the Republican mass meeting of May 6 and was made because of a split in the local Republican party. The idea seems to have been "Yankee" Allan's. The meeting began inauspiciously, no one being certain that a meeting would be held. When the people assembled in Town Hall, they found that no provision had been made for light, and someone found a paraffin lamp and tallow candles. Tazewell Branch presided over the meeting. Dr. W. W. H. Thackston, a Conservative who had been mayor in 1871-2, was nominated for mayor on what was called the fusion ticket to succeed H. R. Hooper. B. M. Cox, a Radical, was nominated sergeant, although John V. Miller, a Conservative, got twelve votes for the post held by John S. Holman, Radical. N. E. Venable, Conservative, was nominated treasurer, Edgar Allan presenting his name to succeed B. M. Cox. W. S. Berry, Radical, was nominated commissioner of revenue. A committee of seven was named to nominate the council members, to succeed the all-Radical council consisting of B. S. Hooper, Tazewell Branch, Edgar Allan, W. D. Evans, W. S. Berry, John S. Holman, B. M. Cox, John W. White, and Wiltshire Cardwell.[66]

The Conservatives met a week later to consider the fusion ticket proposed by the Republicans; E. T. Rice was chairman of their meeting, and J. R. Cunningham secretary. R. A. Booker withdrew as a candidate for mayor, but advocated a straight Conservative ticket because of the division of the Radicals. Captain H. G. Richardson said that he didn't object to a fusion ticket if the Conservatives could nominate their own men, but he wasn't "going to let Yankee Allan tell [him] who to vote for." Colonel J. P. Fitzgerald thought half a loaf better than none; he reminded the party that the Radicals had a clear majority and could elect an all-Negro ticket if they chose; he didn't want to run the risk of such a ticket when the fusion ticket proposed offered a Conservative mayor and treasurer, and several Conservative councilmen. Richardson replied to Fitzgerald that he had "no faith in weak-kneed Conservatives," that any man who would run on a Radical ticket was weak-kneed, and that Colonel Fitzgerald was getting weak-kneed. Captain Kennedy then moved approval of the fusion ticket "to save time." H. E. Warren opposed the ticket offered, but saw no use to put a Conservative ticket in the race because it had no chance of winning. The Conservatives on the ticket would protect property and would stick with the party, Captain F. D. Irving told the audience. Richardson then asked if Captain

Philip W. McKinney would serve if elected, and Dr. Russell replied that he had said he would. McKinney was one of the nominees for the council recommended by the committee; other Conservatives proposed for the Council were Dr. J. L. White, O. T. Wicker, L. C. Butler, and S. W. Paulett; Radicals proposed were B. S. Hooper, W. S. Berry, Jackson Patterson (colored), Richard Burton (colored); thus the Conservatives were offered a majority of one on the Council. When the chair called for the ayes and noes on Colonel Fitzgerald's motion to adjourn, "Young America, largely represented . . . in an apparent spirit of boyish fun" shouted "No"; when the youngsters were excluded from the voting and only the qualified voters permitted to express an opinion on the motion, it was passed 44 to 39.

The Conservatives met again May 18, with R. A. Booker as chairman and J. R. Cunningham as secretary, and appointed a committee to confer with the Radicals on the fusion ticket: W. D. Rice, chairman, J. H. Mottley, P. S. Smithson, A. H. Porter, A. J. Davis, J. V. Rice, and R. M. Burton.[67]

Rice presented the report of this committee, that the Radicals were determined to stick to the proposed ticket, at the Conservative meeting May 21, of which R. A. Booker was chairman and R. M. Burton secretary. The motion of Dr. Peter Winston to adjourn from a partisan meeting to a citizens' meeting carried. Some Conservatives left, and the re-organized meeting nominated a fusion ticket: Dr. Thackston for mayor, John V. Miller for sergeant, N. E. Venable for treasurer, E. T. Rice for commissioner of revenue; for councilmen six Conservatives—Dr. J. L. White, H. E. Warren, S. W. Paulett, A. J. Davis, O. T. Wicker, and P. W. McKinney—and three Radicals, all Negroes—William (Buck) Fuqua, John Coleman, and Richard Watson. R. A. Booker urged support of the ticket and W. D. Rice advocated "hearty co-operation between white and colored for the good of the town."[68]

The fusion ticket proposed by the Radicals won the election, Dr. Thackston receiving 356 votes for mayor; B. M. Cox 234 to 135 for John V. Miller for sergeant; N. E. Venable 351 for treasurer; W. S. Berry 284 to 41 for E. T. Rice for commissioner of revenue; the vote for the winning councilmen is given after the name: P. W. McKinney, 353; J. L. White, 352; O. T. Wicker, 342; S. W. Paulett, 338; L. C. Butler, 326; B. S. Hooper, 294; W. S. Berry, 289; Jackson Patterson, 242; and Richard Burton, 241.[69]

Thus fusion in Farmville antedated fusion on a nationwide scale which in 1877 resulted in the selection of Hayes as President over Tilden.

The county Radical convention on May 1, 1875, was outwardly harmonious, although some signs of lack of harmony were indicated. There were twenty-three delegates attending, of whom nineteen were Negroes; the four white delegates present were Edgar Allan, B. S. Hooper, B. M. Cox, and W. H. Wilkerson. John Goode, colored, of Lockett District, was temporary chairman, and B. S. Hooper was permanent chairman. With the exception of commissioner of revenue, there was only one candidate for nomination for each county office: H. R. Hooper for clerk, Edgar Allan for commonwealth's attorney, S. H. Bliss for treasurer, and W. H. Wilkerson for sheriff; they were nominated unanimously; J. L. Richardson was nominated for commissioner of revenue by a vote of sixteen to seven for J. E. Harris. Referring to successes by the Democratic party in the North, Allan told the convention that every colored man "should pray the Lord to save them from a Democratic government." Tazewell Branch, in defending his record in the House of Delegates, which was being criticized because of his record of absences from the sessions totalling twenty-three days, sounded a discordant note in proclaiming his independence from dictation and in protesting that his character had been reflected upon; he then stated that if setting himself right would break up the Republican party, he would break up the party tomorrow. His reference to the reflection upon his character no doubt referred to charges that he had been an accessory in what the Farmville *Mercury* called "no secret that money was offered the delegates to obtain a certain nomination." The editor of the *Mercury*, however, expressed the belief that Branch was superior to such political conduct, adding that the paper was "glad he has taken the matter up."[70]

The Radical split came out more openly at the Republican barbecue held in the woods between Worsham and Hampden-Sydney late in May. Over 700 attended the affair, of which N. M. Baker was chairman and E. J. Redd secretary. Edgar Allan spoke and blamed the dissension in the party on the ambitions for office of one or two individuals in whom the party had lost confidence; he charged them with responsibility for fusion with the Conservatives; R. S. Hines, an aspirant for the treasurership, was an especial object of attack in Allan's speech; when the civil rights bill was passed (which, among other things, forbade innkeepers to refuse to give accommodations to Negroes), Hines, according to Allan, took down his hotel sign, but when he became a candidate for office he put it up again. (This statement was in a later issue of the Farmville *Mercury* described as incorrect: Hines' "sign like Liberty in this section lies in the dust.") Other speakers at the barbecue were Goodwin of Petersburg, Tazewell Branch, DeMortie of Burkeville, and E. J. Redd. Richard Burys thanked the group on behalf of the English visitors present for the hospitality shown them. Buck Fuqua prepared the barbecue and lemonade, and there was an abundance of good whiskey and punch.[71]

The Radicals carried Prince Edward County in the election in which the fusion ticket won in Farmville: Allan was elected commonwealth's attorney by 1,253 votes to 790 for J. P. Fitzgerald; H. R. Hooper defeated J. R. Cunningham for clerk by a vote of 1,310 to 773; C. H. Bliss, Jr., won a three-entry race for sheriff, with 1,044 votes defeating his fellow Radical W. H. Wilkerson who got 756 votes and Conservative T. H. Dickinson who received only 186; S. H. Bliss was elected treasurer, defeating R. S. Hines 1,216 to 840; J. E. Harris ran for commissioner of revenue, despite his defeat for the Republican nomination in convention by James L. Richardson, but Richardson polled 1,189 votes to Harris' 686; the Radicals also elected the Board of Supervisors: S. W. Sellers, Leigh; C. H. Bliss, Farmville; E. J. Redd, Hampden; R. N. Wilkerson, Buffalo; and Edward Thompson, Lockett.[72]

Radical dissension moved in crescendo during the summer of 1875. On August 3 "Yankee" Allan, state senator and commonwealth's attorney, was tried before Dr. B. C. Peters and W. S. Berry, justices of the peace in Farmville District, on the charge of tampering with voting papers in such a way as to deprive five Negroes "of their right to vote for whom they please." He had been indicted by the grand jury at the July Court on the charge that he had furnished an illiterate elector with a ballot at the same time advising him that it contained a name different from that printed on it, "with intent," so the charge ran, "to deceive." S. F. Coleman, commonwealth's attorney of Cumberland County, was named by the Court to prosecute, and R. M. Dickinson was engaged by Allan to defend him. Allan pleaded not guilty to the charge. The case was continued in magistrates' court until September; all the magistrates in the county were summoned to attend, and eleven of the fifteen took their places on the bench. Coleman, the prosecutor, told the justices he had been misinformed about the witnesses who would testify and that he was satisfied the evidence would not sustain a prosecution; at his request, the accused was discharged. Allan then expressed to the magistrates his regret that the case was abandoned at that stage; he wanted "a full and free investigation." But as the justices, in this last reminder of the oldtime county court of justices, signed the order for his discharge, this effort of Allan's Radical enemies to discredit him crumbled.[73]

Though the formal charge against Allan of irregularities in an election was dismissed, the venom of his Republican enemies was not spent, nor were their fangs removed. The trial having failed, they imported the "portly and jovial" Joseph Jorgenson, the former clerk who had since left the county, and the "cherubic" W. L. Fernald in their effort to "crush" Allan. By late September the word was abroad that "King" Allan was king no longer. At the Farmville District Republican Convention September 30 Jorgenson and Fernald "open[ed] up the career of Allan in an edifying manner." Tazewell Branch denounced Allan as a disorganizer and mischief maker and called his opponent for the Republican nomination to the House of Delegates, Richard Burton, candidate of the Allan faction, "woefully deficient." When Allan tried to speak, he was shouted down. The attack on Allan leaped the county lines; the Fourth District's Representative, W. H. H. Stowell of Burkeville, saw advantage to himself in the dissension in Prince Edward; he had made an agreement to retire from the Congress at the end of his term which expired March 3, 1877, in favor of Allan, but it appeared now that he was "strong enough to do without his old ally," and he consequently broke his promise. The anti-Allan faction, led by H. R. Hooper, chairman of the convention, and Tazewell Branch, withdrew briefly to the clerk's office when Allan tried to speak; upon its return, the convention broke up.

When the Republican county convention assembled on October 1, Allan, as party chairman in the county, sought admission to the meeting; he was refused by H. R. Hooper, who was again convention chairman. Allan and his supporters then went to Lee Hall, where they held a "regular" convention. Resolutions were adopted calling the election of delegates at the meeting September 30 "pretended"; they criticized the conduct of that meeting as providing no opportunity for a fair expression of the public will and Tazewell Branch in particular; Branch's speech of two days before was labeled "unchristian and unrepublican," and the Allan convention went on record as desiring the election of Republican candidates but protesting that it could not support a candidate "who has publicly prayed to God that some Republican leaders 'may be driven from our midst and be forced to seek another home, perhaps across the briny ocean.'" Richard Burton and E. S. Sellers were nominated for the House of Delegates, one colored man nominating "Mas'r Allan," who preferred to continue in the upper house of the legislature. Burton was nominated by a vote of twenty to eight. It also named Allan chairman of the party county committee and N. H. Blue committee secretary.

The other convention, designated "Stowell's Convention," of which Hooper was chairman, unanimously nominated Tazewell Branch for the House of Delegates; E. S. Sellers' name was proposed, but he received no votes. Branch again lambasted Allan, calling him a "devil in human shape."[74]

After the convention, there was a mass meeting at the courthouse, of which C. Brown (colored) was chairman. Tom Harris made a bitter attack on Richard Burton, the Allan faction's nominee for the House of Delegates, calling the meeting two days before "an insult to every colored man." When Edgar Allan demanded that both sides be heard, Brown, the chairman, informed him he could hold a meeting afterward. Then Tazewell Branch spoke, making another attack on Allan. When W. L. Fernald arose to speak, there was a tumult, some calling for Fernald, some for Allan; in course of the argument, Joseph Jorgenson advised the audience to "act like white men"; he described the meeting as a Branch meeting and claimed that Allan had no right to speak. But a compromise, under which both Fernald and Allan spoke a half-hour, ended the dispute. Allan claimed his group was the regular group and the Branch faction the bolters, denouncing Branch for arrogance. Fernald took the opposite view, calling Allan the bolter and Branch the regular nominee.

The fighting was not confined to meetings. E. S. Sellers, smarting under the rebuff given him at the Branch meeting, rallied the Radicals of Leigh and Lockett Districts to his support, and continued his race. One Negro leader of Lockett District who had been a strong Burton supporter came to Farmville where he was royally treated by the Branch crowd; after having been plied with "sundry wet groceries," he switched his allegiance and joined the Branch faction. His defection was balanced by the defection of C. H. Bliss, Jr., from the Stowell-Branch faction to the Allan side.[75]

Despite the three-way factional split among the Radicals, Tazewell Branch was able to carry the election, topping, with a vote of

925, the 753 votes for Philip W. McKinney, the 247 for E. S. Sellers, and 236 for Richard Burton. A Prospect correspondent of the Lynchburg *Virginian* credited McKinney's defeat to Conservative apathy, but the Farmville *Mercury* disagreed: the defection of Burton's supporters (estimated by their leader, Edgar Allan, at 500) to Branch was the explanation.[76]

The Reconstruction era saw a political bitterness unequalled before or since in Prince Edward history. The bitterness of factional feeling in the Republican party has just been described. The Democrats were as bitter against the Republicans. As the Radical—carpetbagger, scalawag, and Negro—rule continued, the Democrats made even stronger efforts, some questionable, some looking to violence, to rid the county of the domination which they despised openly and of which, in their heart of hearts, they were ashamed. Desperation over failure to win control by the orderly process of elections led some to look to violence as the only means to overthrow the Radicals. Some of the Democrats saw their opportunity in an observance by the Negroes of "Union League and Emancipation" day in the early 1870's. Young and old white men who were good shots were stationed in second story windows near the corner of Main and Third Streets in Farmville with instructions to shoot white Republicans who were participating in the celebration in the street. Negroes were not to be harmed. The signal to start shooting was to be the beginning of a fight; to provoke the fight, two white men, Jim Miller and a man named MacPhearson, a son-in-law of Shelton Davis, dressed in calico dresses with long trains, and started to break through the column of the parade. The Negroes in the parade regarded this interruption as a joke and gave place to the two men dressed as women. Miller and MacPhearson were given no opportunity to start a fight by interrupting the parade; then Miller placed a chip on his shoulder and dared the Negroes to knock it off; he dared them to step on his train; but they laughed good-naturedly and refused to do either, backing away from the aggressive movements of Miller. The two pistol shots which Miller and MacPhearson were to shoot when the fight started were never fired, fortunately. Cooler heads and more cautious souls did not depend upon this reaction from the Negroes. Judge Francis N. Watkins secretly warned each white man who had been marked for destruction to keep out of the parade. It was the impression of Judge Watkins' son, Judge Asa D. Watkins, that Dr. Richard McIlwaine, Captain Philip W. McKinney, and others advised his father to warn the white Republicans.[77]

The Democrats found cleverness and strategem better and more effective weapons in their fight to gain control of Prince Edward. Many of the practices resorted to have been lost forever to the record of history, for many who took part in them went to their graves without revealing them. But one election official of the period did relate how the Democrats in Lockett District carried one election. B. J. Olgers was a native of The Netherlands who settled at Rice during the Reconstruction period. The cause of the Southern white people aroused his sympathy and enlisted his support. In due course he was made a judge of election. At this particular election, which he did not identify, he sat at the ballot box and put the ballots in. When he received a ballot from a Negro, he folded it twice; a white man's ballot was folded once. It was the plan, to which he was party, to distract the attention of the election officials during the day, during which confusion a white person was to stuff the ballot box with ballots marked for the Democratic candidates and folded once. The stuffing was not discovered until the ballots were counted and they were found to be in excess of the number of persons recorded as voting. It was then decided to discard enough ballots to make the number of ballots equal to the number of voters recorded as voting. Olgers proposed that he be blindfolded and draw out that number of ballots. The proposal was agreeable to the other election officials, so he promptly proceeded to pick out of the ballot box only those ballots which had been folded twice. As a result the Democrats won that election. But how, no one ever knew until Olgers chose to talk— to a select audience, of course.

Even under these circumstances, it was sometimes deemed necessary to apply some force. At one election, Calvin H. Bliss of Farmville, one of the leading Republicans of the county, came to Rice to make certain that the ballot box at that precinct would not be stuffed or if stuffed that Republican votes would not be discarded. When he got to the door of the room in which the election was being conducted, D. J. Weaver caught him by the collar and told him he had gone far enough. That was as far as Bliss got toward the ballot box.

Nor did the Democrats hesitate to buy votes at election time during that troubled period. It was one era in which even men of principle acted on the idea that the end justifies the means.[78]

The Radicals dominated Prince Edward during the greater portion of the Reconstruction period. The tide of national Democratic resurgence in 1876 was not enough to win a majority in Prince

Edward; Rutherford B. Hayes carried the county by a vote of 1,601 to 1,137 for Samuel J. Tilden, although Virginia went for Tilden by 38,000. The vote in the Congressional race was similar; the Radical Joseph Jorgenson received 1,588 votes to 1,128 cast for William E. Hinton, and Jorgenson carried the Fourth District by 6,600.[79]

During this period of Republican control, the first Prince Edward resident was sent to the House of Representatives since Abraham B. Venable, who retired from the House in 1799. Benjamin S. Hooper, who had been active in Radical politics, was elected in 1882 on the Readjuster ticket.[80] There was a temporary alignment in Virginia politics in the 1870's and 1880's. Readjusters favoring reduction or repudiation of the State debt, Funders favoring full payment.

Democratic hopes for carrying the Fourth District rose in 1884, but the death of the party's candidate, Rives, on the eve of the election resulted in the election of one of the Republican candidates, James D. Brady, over the other, Evans.[81]

In the election of State officials in 1885, the Republicans held their usual margin in Prince Edward. John S. Wise polled 1,614 votes in Prince Edward to 1,108 cast for General Fitzhugh Lee, who carried the state.

After the defeat of Democratic candidate Mann Page for Congress in 1886 by William E. Gaines, Republican, when the Democratic vote reached a low for the period in Prince Edward (Gaines 1,448, Page 561), the Democrats in the county began their climb to regain political control of the county.[82] In 1888 Benjamin Harrison carried the county in the Presidential election, getting a majority of 424 over Grover Cleveland. But the Democrats showed a gain of thirty-three votes over the election of 1885, and they carried the county in 1888 for the Democratic nominee for Congress, Edward C. Venable, a Prince Edward native then living in Petersburg, by the narrow margin of twenty-six votes.[83] The Republican split between John M. Langston and Judge Arnold probably contributed to Venable's success both in Prince Edward and the district. But Langston contested the election and was seated by the Republican majority in the House of Representatives; it was on the vote of seating Langston that the Democrats adopted the plan of withdrawing from the Hall of the House to avoid being counted as a part of the quorum when it was apparent that the majority party intended to seat its candidate on a strictly partisan vote and basis. This was the first of three cases in which the Republican majority in the House seated the Republican candidate from the Fourth District on contest. James F. Epes was elected to Congress as a Democrat in 1890 and 1892; as there were Democratic majorities in the House then he was not challenged. But with the return of Republican control of the House after the election of 1894, Robert T. Thorp of Mecklenburg successfully challenged the election of Democrats William R. McKenney of Petersburg in 1894 and Sidney P. Epes of Blackstone in 1896. Langston, who successfully challenged Venable's election, was a native of Louisa County, Virginia, who moved to Ohio, practiced law at Oberlin, and recruited troops for the Federal army. The president of the Virginia Normal and Collegiate Institution in Petersburg when he ran for Congress, he was the only Negro to represent Prince Edward in the national House of Representatives.[84]

Three Negroes represented Prince Edward in the House of Delegates during the Reconstruction period: Tazewell Branch (1874-77), W. D. Evans (1877-80), and N. M. Griggs (1883-84).[85] The county was also represented in the State Senate by three Negroes: James W. D. Bland (1869-70), John Robinson (1871-73), and N. M. Griggs (1887-90).[86]

Gradually the Democrats regained control of the county. Membership on the Board of Supervisors seesawed from the organization of that body, Conservatives or Democrats being elected on occasion from various districts. It was 1885 before a Democrat represented Prince Edward in the Virginia House of Delegates after the Underwood Constitution went into effect. William P. Dupuy holds that distinction.

In 1889 the Democrats nominated Philip W. McKinney for Governor. McKinney had been a wheelhorse of the Conservatives during the political dark age of the 1870's; he had been a leading Funder, serving as Presidential elector on the Funder (then Democratic) ticket in 1880. In the Democratic convention which met in Richmond in August, 1889, McKinney was nominated for Governor by Judge William Hodges Mann of Nottoway. He led on the first ballot, receiving 595 votes, including Prince Edward's eleven. The next day he was nominated unanimously.[87] For all the Republican strength in Prince Edward, McKinney carried his home county, through by a narrow margin; he received 1,067 votes to 1,018 cast for General William Mahone; McKinney carried Virginia by over 42,000.[88]

As Governor, McKinney settled the State debt satisfactorily, saving Virginia's fiscal credit. He also made the oyster laws effective in bringing in revenue. These his old schoolmate and long time friend, Thomas J. Garden, regarded as the outstanding accomplishments of his administration.[89]

On McKinney's return to his home in Farmville from the Governor's Mansion on January 2, 1894, he received a royal welcome. The Farmville Guard was his escort. The Farmville Silver Band led the parade from the station, then at the Main Street crossing of the railroad, to the Opera House, on the site of the present Municipal Building. As the procession moved along Main Street the band played *Home, Sweet Home.* Stores in the town were closed, and the students at the Normal School were dismissed to attend the affair. The large crowd, which had met the retiring Governor at the station, filled the Opera House. After a prayer by Dr. E. H. Harding, resolutions honoring McKinney were read by Major A. R. Venable, Jr. Dr. W. W. H. Thackston delivered the address of welcome. McKinney responded to the address with obvious emotion. Several colored people sat on the stage and took part in the program, which closed with the benediction offered by the Rev. J. W. Ware.[90]

Republicans held most county offices until 1891, when E. T. Clark was elected commissioner of revenue, T. H. Dickinson sheriff, and W. H. Ewing treasurer; they replaced, respectively, J. E. Harris, C. H. Bliss, Jr., and S. H. Bliss. A. D. Watkins was elected commonwealth's attorney.[91] In the election of 1893 the Democrats elected the county clerk, W. P. Gilliam, who had been nominated by a vote of ten to six over R. H. Watkins at the county convention at Worsham. H. R. Hooper, the incumbent, was nominated by the Republicans at their convention at Rice, but he withdrew. As an example of bitter partisan feeling in Reconstruction, the Farmville *Herald* commented on Hooper's announcement of withdrawal that though he "did not have (or could not have) the good will of any true Democrat, all bear the kindliest feelings for him in non-political life."[92]

During the 1890's the political scene in Prince Edward was complicated by the rise of the Populist party. The outgrowth of agrarian discontent with the discrimination against farmers by railroads in fixing freight rates, by industry and business in setting prices for the goods sold farmers and for the produce bought from them, the Populist movement gained considerable strength in farm areas. In Prince Edward they were particularly strong in the Rice area. One of the earliest indications of political activity by farmers as a group appears in 1874 when T. E. Chambliss of Brunswick, the "farmer's candidate" for Congress, spoke from the porch of Holman's hotel on August Court day.[93] The Populists made little impression in the voting in the Presidential election in 1892, when Prince Edward cast 1,311 votes for Republican Benjamin Harrison, 1,089 for Democrat Grover Cleveland, and only 51 for James B. Weaver, the Populist candidate.[94] But the next year the Populists carried the county. Colin Stokes, Populist, defeated incumbent R. M. Burton, Democrat, for the House of Delegates by 1,347 to 840; and the Populist candidate for Governor, Edmund R. Cocke of Cumberland County, received 1,264 votes in Prince Edward to 879 for the Democratic candidate (who was elected), Charles T. O'Ferrall. S. H. Bliss and J. E. Harris, Republican leaders, were given credit by some Democrats for the Populist victory. Bliss was said to have been quite influential with the Negro voters, and Harris, at that time chairman of the county Republican committee, was described as "one of the best Negro organizers in the black belt."[95] That the Republicans joined forces with the Populists is shown in the supervisor's race in Lockett District that year. W. H. Hubbard, who stated that he was a Populist, was nominated for the Board of Supervisors by the Republicans; after receiving the Republican nomination, he announced his candidacy as an Independent. Described as the Third party candidate, Hubbard received 167 votes to 127 for B. H. Carter, the Democratic candidate and incumbent; Carter contested the election; several witnesses testified that the bundle of tickets in the court was not the bundle put up from Rice. On opening the ballots the Court determined that B. H. Carter had been elected suprvisor by a majority of twenty votes; it then rescinded the qualification of Hubbard and permitted Carter to qualify for the office.[96] Two years later, Hubbard, running on the Populist ticket, defeated Dr. S. A. Bruce, Democratic nominee, by two votes for the Board of Supervisors. Thus the constitution of the Board of Supervisors after the 1895 election was three Democrats (R. M. Burton of Farmville, J. M. Venable of Hampden, and J. Walter Davis of Leigh), one Republican (G. W. Scott of Buffalo), and one Populist (W. H. Hubbard of Lockett). The Democrats won the county offices, re-electing W. H. Ewing treasurer over Republican S. H. Bliss by 1,058 to 794; A. D. Watkins (unopposed) commonwealth's attorney by a vote of 1,954; and T. H. Dickinson sheriff over Populist W. Macon Gilliam (who also had the Republican nomination) by 1,058 to 702; the Democratic candidate for commissioner of revenue, William L. Clark, brother of the incumbent Edward T. Clark, was elected over the Republican candidate, T. R. N. Cocks, and the Populist candidate, W. A. Barrow; Clark received 944 votes, Cocks, 610, and Barrow, 78[97]

An "Honest Elections" convention met in Farmville September 18, 1895, and nominated William Lancaster of Cumberland for the State Senate over Joseph X. Morton of Prince Edward by a vote of twelve to eight. The convention represented the Populists.[98] The Populist candidate, Colin Stokes, in that year defeated the Democratic candidate, R. M. Burton, for the House of Delegates.[99]

One explanation of the Democratic successes in the 1890's lies in the split in the Republican party, which from time to time opened like a wound which would not heal. In 1896 B. S. Hooper wanted to return to Congress and also to have his half-brother, George Richardson, named county chairman; in the Farmville District convention, where he started his effort, he ran into opposition from the Bliss-Harris-Bland faction; that wing was willing enough to pledge support to Hooper for Congress, but it was unwilling to give up Harris as county chairman. The meeting was so tumultous that a police officer had to be summoned to restore order. R. T. Thorp, who was supported by Pompey Bland of Prince Edward, won the Republican nomination. Hooper was unable to win the support of the county convention, which sent its delegates to the district convention uninstructed.[100]

The election of 1896 aroused more local interest than usual for a Presidential election. One reason was the split in the Democratic party over support of the nominee, William Jennings Bryan. The split affected Prince Edward as well as the nation. Loyal Democrats organized Bryan and Sewell clubs. Over thirty joined the club organized in Farmville on July 28; officers of the club were J. P. Fitzgerald, president, R. M. Burton, vice-president, J. L. Hart, secretary, D. T. Elam, treasurer, and J. M. Crute, J. F. Walton, and A. D. Watkins, executive committee.[101] A club was organized at Rice in August, with Dr. H. E. Watkins, president, B. H. Carter, first vice-president, J. Y. Phillips, second vice-president, E. T. Clark, third vice-president, and J. R. Weaver, secretary-treasurer. Leigh District Democrats endorsed the Bryan-Sewell ticket and joined with Farmville District in pledging support to Philip W. McKinney if he would be a candidate for Congress; both named Sidney P. Epes as second choice.[102] McKinney was not a candidate, so Prince Edward cast its eleven votes in the district convention for Epes, who was nominated. The district convention endorsed the national party platform, singling out for special approbation the leading and perhaps the most controversial of all the planks, that advocating the free coinage of gold and silver at the ratio of sixteen to one. The Farmville Bryan-Sewell club promptly added Epes to its name.

There was much speaking during the campaign. President R. E. Blackwell of Randolph-Macon College, while visiting in Farmville, was invited to speak by the "gold bugs," as Democratic opponents to the free coinage plank were sometimes called. After Blackwell had been speaking for an hour and a half, A. W. Drumeller asked Blackwell some questions; Blackwell was unable to answer some of Drumeller's questions, especially those relating to silver, so Drumeller answered Blackwell and turned the "gold meeting" into a "silver speaking."[103] Judge W. H. Mann of Nottoway, Judge Henry W. Flournoy of Richmond, and Judge L. D. Yarrell of Emporia were among the speakers for the Democrats in the campaign, while Edgar Allan, Jr., spoke for the Republicans, who were supporting McKinley. Allan followed the practice of his father in inviting those who wished to do so to come forward after the meeting and shake hands with him.[104] Judge A. D. Watkins, who spoke often in the county in support of Bryan, and C. M. Wallace, Jr., of Richmond were the speakers at the barbecue given by the Green Bay Bryan-Sewell club on September 26.[105]

An early indication of dissension within Democratic ranks came with the protest over the election of R. S. Paulett, W. G. Venable, and John A. Cunningham as delegates from Farmville District to the state convention; they were chosen by a majority of two in a meeting attended by only thirty-five persons and represented the "goldite" wing of the party. Dissidents protested inadequate notice of the meeting.[106] On August 24 eight citizens attended a meeting of the "Gold Democrats" at the Dunnington factory; Charles Bugg was elected chairman and J. A. Scott secretary; Bugg and W. G. Dunnington were named delegates to the state convention of their faction to be held in Richmond.[107]

When Bugg took the chair, as chairman of the Farmville District Democratic Committee, at a mass meeting of the party on October 6 and stated that he was unaware of the object of the meeting, J. L. Hart offered a resolution declaring the chair vacant since the chairman had become a bolter. Bugg resented the classification, declaring he was a Democrat by conviction and principle, not, taking a crack at many of those present, because his father had been one. Dr. Peter

Winston, a Bryan man, objected to the way in which the effort to remove Bugg was being handled. J. P. Fitzgerald offered a substitute motion, that Bugg be asked to resign because he could not conscientiously support the party nominees and platform. Dr. R. M. Bidgood was then elected chairman.[108]

The Populist party also endorsed Bryan as its candidate for the Presidency. This was as far as fusion with the Democrats went on the part of the Populists. Those of the Fourth District held a convention at Burkeville in August, of which Joseph X. Morton of Prince Edward was chairman, and nominated Colonel J. Thomas Goode of Mecklenburg for Congress to oppose Epes and the Republican nominee, R. T. Thorp.[109]

Bryan carried Prince Edward County by a narrow margin, 991 to 979 for William McKinley, the successful Republican nominee. John M. Palmer, the Gold Democratic nominee, received only 22 votes. R. T. Thorp, Republican, carried the county in the congressional election, receiving 1,146 votes to 1,031 cast for Democrat Sidney P. Epes. In the election 264 ballots were discarded because they had not been marked properly under terms of the law. Though close, the election was peaceable; the Farmville *Herald* attributed that characteristic to the closing of the saloons for the election.[110]

The Republicans continued divided; the statewide division between the Lamb and anti-Lamb (to which Edgar Allan belonged) factions affected Prince Edward. At their convention on October 9, 1897, they declared that they had no suitable candidate to offer for the House of Delegates in Prince Edward.[111] Not even the seating of Thorp on his contest of the election with Epes seemed to revive their flagging spirits; one reason the Republican majority in the House gave for unseating Epes was that some Thorp supporters had been prevented from voting in Prince Edward. The Republican mass meeting in Farmville on September 1, 1898, broke up in a big row; two sets of delegates to the county convention were named, one representing a faction led by Matt Grigg of Philadelphia, the other Pompey Bland's group. The county convention was unanimous on one point, the election of George Richardson as county chairman.[112]

They had an uproar when their speakers were given the opportunity to address the crowd on Court day, October 17, 1898. After Sidney P. Epes, Democratic candidate for Congress had spoken, the Republican program began. Noah Blue, representing the Negro candidate Jones, and Pompey Bland, representing the perennial Republican candidate, R. T. Thorp, rushed to the judge's bench; Blue got there first and claimed the privilege of calling the meeting to order and introducing J. E. Byrd, who had come from Petersburg to speak in behalf of Jones. Blue and Bland then engaged in a fight to settle the matter. That was too much for Judge Crute, of the County Court. He ordered the courtroom cleared and then gave permission to the Jones faction to proceed with their meeting. A majority of the Negroes came back into the room to hear Byrd, Bland being the only Negro leader in Farmville supporting Thorpe. Ross Hamilton, who had come from Mecklenburg County to speak in behalf of Thorp, spoke from the courthouse steps.[113] Prince Edward again went for Thorp in the election, giving him 833 votes to 657 for Epes, but Epes carried the district.[114]

The Democrats showed a gain in proportionate strength in Prince Edward in 1900, giving Bryan a vote of 843 to 574 for McKinley.[115]

Toward the end of the nineteenth century, the question of holding a convention to draw up a new instrument of government to replace the Underwood Constitution was raised. In an election on May 27, 1897, Prince Edward, as did Virginia, expressed opposition to such a convention.[116] But sentiment increased for it. In 1900 Prince Edward voted 647 for a constitutional convention to 583 against.[117] On February 16, 1901, Governor J. Hoge Tyler signed the bill passed by the General Assembly caling a convention. Dr. Richard McIlwaine, then president of Hampden-Sydney College, was chosen the delegate from Prince Edward. He had not sought the place, but, when asked by two farmer friends, who met him (separately) on the street in Farmville shortly after the bill had become law, if he would serve if elected, replied that he would if the people wanted him, but that he would make no canvass. He had no opposition and was elected on the fourth Thursday in May. The convention lasted twelve months; in its membership were eighty-eight Democrats and twelve Republicans. Dr. McIlwaine had made no commitments; accordingly he followed the practice of listening to both sides of a question and then forming his own opinion. He was chairman of the Committee on Education and Public Instruction and a member of the Committee on Corporations. He was in a way proud of the work of the education committee, expressing the opinion that the article on that subject drawn up for the new Constitution was "far ahead of the preexistent Constitution, but far behind what it should be." On the other hand, he was not satisfied with the article on

Suffrage with its "Understanding Clause." Describing it as "abhorrent" to him, he stated that he would not vote for it except as a compromise or "with the cordial and intelligent consent and approval of my constituents."[118]

Another question confronted the convention; how could it get its work accepted? It seemed risky to submit it to the vote of the people, since there was no way those who had been given the franchise by the Underwood Constitution could be prevented from voting in an election; as many of these were deprived of the vote by the suffrage restrictions in the new, they could be expected to vote against it, and it was possible, if not probable, that they could defeat it. The convention hit upon the plan of proclaiming their Constitution as the "organic law." Dr. McIlwaine returned to Prince Edward and spoke for two hours at the courthouse on Monday, April 21, 1902, on the work of the convention. A large audience came out to hear him. He expressed himself as favoring some features, opposed to some, but satisfied with the Constitution as a whole. The audience adopted unanimously a resolution endorsing his course and instructing him to vote in favor of putting the Constitution into effect by proclamation of the convention. Dr. McIlwaine complied with the instruction.[119] The new Constitution was proclaimed in effect by the convention which drew it up. Among its principal changes were the newly established qualifications for voters, which disfranchised illiterates, and the abolition of the County Court.

To qualify voters under the new constitution, which set up literacy requirements for voting, three registrars were appointed for each district: Buffalo: J. P. Glenn, Charles A. Morton, W. B. Binford; Hampden: R. E. Stokes, Samuel Lacy, George W. Redd; Farmville: A. R. Venable, Jr., W. H. Richardson, Peter Winston; Leigh: J. J. Gilliam, W. S. Dance, L. D. Jones; Lockett: B. H. Ligon, W. L. Clark, E. T. Bondurant. The period of registration was August 25-September 2. As a result of the new requirements for voting, the Negro vote in Prince Edward was substantially reduced.[120] The Farmville *Herald* estimated that not over ten per cent of that vote remained after the registration. Prior to the registration of 1902, Farmville District had cast 600 to 800 votes in elections; only 277 whites and forty Negroes in that district qualified in the 1902 registration.[121]

The new Constitution ended an institution Prince Edward had known from the beginning of its history, the County Court. The last session of the Prince Edward Court was held January 18, 1904, with Judge J. M. Crute presiding. Resolutions on the ending of the "long cherished and beloved system" and in tribute to Judge Crute were presented on behalf of the bar by Thomas E. Watkins, chairman, and J. S. McIlwaine, treasurer. For the most part the county paid little attention to the passing of the county court; only a few attended the last session; but Dr. Sears, of the Normal School, thought it well to give his classes a glimpse of a departing order, and he brought about 100 students to attend the session and afterward to inspect the jail.[122]

The possibility of Negro domination of local government, always a threat under the old suffrage law, was removed; control of State and local governments was assured to white men by the new instrument of government; and the aim of the majority of Virginia white men in their political activities since the military government had wrested control from them a generation before had been realized.

CHAPTER XV

The Churches After the War

THE end of the war and the emancipation of the slaves presented to the churches the issue of separate church organizations for Negroes. Heretofore they had belonged to the same churches as the white people. Freedom and the new independence stimulated in some the desire for separate churches.

Sharon Baptist Church took up the matter at the church meeting August 19, 1865. The roll of the Negro members was revised, and the colored members ascertained to be dead, those who had moved away, and those who could not be heard from were dropped. The Rev. E. S. Taylor was instructed to administer the Lord's Supper to the colored members of the church who lived in the neighborhood of Forest Church (near Meherrin) and to baptize the colored people in that community who desired membership in Sharon Church whom he considered worthy and report their names to the church to be entered on the rolls. When the question of a separate church for the colored members came up, they declined a separate organization and expressed the desire "to remain in connexion with this body upon terms heretofore existing."

Samuel Hines, a colored man, applied to the church for a license to preach in 1866, and F. T. Wootton, W. B. Rowlett, Dr. T. J. Owen, and J. T. Johnson were named a committee to hear him preach and report to the church. In July, 1866, the church reported 190 Negro members in a total of 361. It was not until after the war that the Negroes had family names, and the Sharon roll prepared in 1866 for the first time lists its colored members with their family names as well as their first names.

On October 21, 1866, after twenty-seven Negroes who had been baptized were received into the church, Sharon Church unanimously decided to have separate organizations for the white and colored members. Letters of dismissal were given to the entire colored membership to form a new church, for which the name Mt. Zion was selected; the Negroes forming the new church agreed to a church covenant which was read to them and adopted rules of decorum which were also read.[1]

There were two colored members of Pisgah Baptist Church in October, 1872, when a delegation of Negroes applied for membership. Dr. R. E. Bass and B. H. Carter were appointed a committee to confer with them; they brought back a favorable report, and the group was received. Negroes remained members until October, 1873, when they withdrew to form a church of their own, High Rock.[2] Although the Negroes withdrew from the white churches to form churches of their own, there remained between white and colored Baptists the bond of fellowship. One of the members of High Rock, Jim Haskins, was sexton of Pisgah Church in the 1890's and accordingly attended services with the white people. When the Lord's Supper was observed, he came down from the gallery and was served the bread and wine by the deacons, thus joining with the white Baptists in the communion.[3]

Since the colored people began organizing churches of their own, the following Baptist churches have acquired property for houses of worship in Prince Edward, the date being that of the deed:

Colored Baptist Church of Farmville: April 16, 1867: the lot known as the old Baptist Church lot of Farmville conveyed by P. W. McKinney, commissioner, W. T. Rice and his wife Mary, W. A. Armistead and his wife Fannie, G. B. Wright and his wife Sue A., and Fannie A. Rice to the church trustees; also a deed dated July 13, 1867, by which Thomas B. and Mary L. Rice conveyed a one-fifth interest in the lot which was known as the old Baptist Church or the Southside Institute, to William D. Evans, Ottaway Lipscomb, William Word, and Caesar White, trustees of the colored Baptist Church.[4]

Mt. Zion Baptist Church: May 26, 1870: Dr. Thomas J. and Louisa F. Owen to William L. Clark, John W. Foster, Carter Braxton, Samuel Hines, and George Scott, trustees, two acres of land on which Mt. Zion Church now stands on the west side of the road from Green Bay to Sandy River Church.[5]

Mercy Seat Baptist Church: November 14, 1870: A. R. Venable, executor of William H. Venable, deceased, to Samuel Brown, Dennis Evans, Maurice West, Elisha Jackson, and John Hill, trustees of the colored Baptist church near Prince Edward Courthouse, land at the fork of the road from Hampden-Sydney College to Charlotte Courthouse and the road to Prince Edward Courthouse.[6]

New Witt Baptist Church: August 29, 1873: M. J. Mattur to

Anderson Redd, Edward Jackson, Patrick Allen, John Redd, and Spot Saunders, trustees, one acre on the road from Redd's Shop to Keysville.[7]

Mt. Moriah Baptist Church: June 1, 1875: Peter Allen and wife to Gaskie Butler, William Snead, Wilson Goodhope, Peter Allen, and Henry Woodson, trustees, one acre on the road from Prospect to Farmville.[8]

Sulphur Springs Baptist Church: September 12, 1876: James M. and Harriet M. Richardson, to Phil Harris, Alex Scott, William Green, and Branch Wright, one acre on which the church is built.[9]

New Hope Baptist Church: December 24, 1877: P. W. Mc-Kinney, assignee, to Isaac Read, John R. Fowlkes, Alexander Smith, Peter Cary, Frank Cromwell, Joseph Moore, and Andrew Jeffress, trustees, one acre on the road from Worsham to Charlotte Courthouse.[10]

Triumph Baptist Church: August 27, 1878: Anderson Watkins to Hudson Baker, Joe Winslow, Henry Madison, Peter Morton, and Clem Carrington, trustees, adjoining P. W. Price and Dr. H. A. Watkins.[11]

Marble Hill Baptist Church: September 30, 1879: W. R. and Alice Barnes to Joe Booker, Thomas Crawley, and Henry Redd, trustees, land on the north side of the road from Marble Hill to James Booker's.[12]

High Rock Baptist Church: December 7, 1881: Abner and Elizabeth Ellett to the trustees (unnamed) of High Rock Baptist Church, one acre on the road near the High Rock. In 1898 George Washington, Abram Venable, W. R. Madison, J. H. Foster, and P. J. Perkinson were named trustees.[13]

Macedonia Baptist Church: April 26, 1883: S. M. Sheppard to James Young, Washington Woodson, and Jerry Ross, trustees, one-half acre on the public road.[14]

Monroe Baptist Church: December 1, 1883: George T. and Sarah Thornton to Stephen Brown, D. Hicks, N. White, R. Taylor, and Lucy Brown, trustees, land in the angle formed by two roads, one from Sandy River to Farmville, the other from Sandy River to Sandy River Church, near the river.[15]

Mt. Lyle Baptist Church: April 30, 1888: Willis and Delia Dupuy to Baxter White, Frank Lyle, and Henderson Cole, trustees, land on the road from Madisonville to Pamplin, commonly called Negro Hill.[16]

New Bethel Baptist Church: December 1, 1896: W. E. and Fanny H. Grant to John Eggleston, Morton Watson, and John Eggleston, Jr., trustees, land on the Farmville-Keysville road at the old Watson mill road.[17]

Calvary Baptist Church: March 31, 1897: E. T. and Pattie O. Miller to Hughes Fisher, William Scott, and Dennis Spencer, trustees, one and one-half acres on the south side of the road from Sandy River Church to Burkeville at the point the mill road crosses the Burkeville road.[18]

Peaks Baptist Church: January 1, 1899: L. P. Jones to William Mann, Edward Booker, Sam Hill, and Willie Jordan, trustees, the land and building known as Peaks Meetinghouse.[19]

Alabama Baptist Church: March 1, 1899: Amanda Randolph to Pompey Ford and Peter Winston, trustees, one square acre.[20]

Zion Hill Baptist Church: March 20, 1903: Jennie Redd to Wash Bell, Walter Brown, and James Redd, trustees, the lot with the building thereon on the west side of the Farmville road one-quarter mile from upper Briery bridge.[21]

First Rock Baptist Church: November 8, 1904: C. M. and E. E. Allen to A. Davenport, Fred Lockett, J. H. Thornton, John Woodson, Richard Wade, General Wooldridge, and Albert Woodson, trustees, two acres on the west side of the road from Prospect to A. J. Price's mill.[22]

Levi Baptist Church: October 7, 1905: Harvey and Bessie Stokes to James Knight, Samuel Wootton, and Noah Haulton, two acres on the south and east sides of the Levi Church lot.[23]

High Bridge Union Baptist Church: May 26, 1906: Thomas C. Fisher to Patrick Wiley, T. W. Greene, and Mathews Johnson, trustees, land three-fourths mile east of High Bridge.[24]

Calvary Baptist Church: January 5, 1906: heirs of W. P. Gilliam to Willis Watts and William H. Anderson, trustees, one acre; and September 3, 1914: W. H. Anderson and Willie Allen, trustees of the Silver Light Fountain No. 1325, subordinate fountain of the Grand Fountain of the United Order of True Reformers, to W. H. Anderson, Paul Watts, and J. E. Williams, trustees of Calvary Baptist Church, a lot on the south side of Walkers Church road, a part of the old Tredway farm.[25]

Union Baptist Church: June 9, 1916: R. B. Wilson, J. T. Clark, and L. D. Jones, trustees of Liberty Christian Church, to William Scott, James Knight, Doctor Hardy, Willie Irby, and E. L. Felton, trustees of Union Baptist Church, under an order of Circuit Court of January 24, 1916, the land originally sold to the trustees of Liberty Church by Rowlett Perkinson.[26]

Bethel Grove Baptist Church: February 20, 1928: J. Taylor and Helen O'Ferrall Thompson to T. B. Hicks, John Stokes, and Silas Tucker, trustees, land on the Green Bay-Farmville road.[27]

Abyssinia Baptist Church: April 8, 1929: T. C. and Louise C. Haskins to W. J. Neal, Spencer Wood, Lee Fears, Richard Langhorne, and W. H. Neal, trustees, lot near Meherrin.[28]

The dates given are not those of the church organization. In some instances, reference is made to the church already standing on the lot conveyed to the trustees. The establishment of some of these churches antedated the purchase of the land; Mt. Zion, for example, was organized four years before it acquired title to its property, and High Rock eight years.

The Baptist churches south of the James River constituted the Hasadiah Association in 1874. Its first regular meeting was held in Farmville in September, 1874, at which sixty ordained ministers and about seventy laymen represented the eighty-six member churches. The Rev. Henry Williams, Jr., of Petersburg preached the principal sermon in Powell's Grove on the Sunday of the session.[29] The Rev. Alexander Bates was at that time pastor of the Farmville Church; on the fourth Sunday in May, 1874, he baptized about fifty converts in the Appomattox River. [30] The Hasadiah Association met again in Farmville September 6-7, 1893, just about a year after a new Baptist Church building was dedicated (October 2, 1892). The Negro Baptists of Farmville were hosts to the State Baptist Sunday School Convention August 19-22, 1896, and to the General Association of Negro Baptists of Virginia in 1902. The General Association met again in Farmville in 1938, with the First Church and the Race Street Church, which was organized and ministered to for many years by the Rev. Jacob Randolph. The State Sunday School Convention met again in Farmville in 1932.[31]

Property for the Colored Methodists of Farmville was acquired in 1868 when John A. and A. C. Dalby sold to Talerand Branch, Booker Jackson, William Fuqua, Jacob Eppes, and William M.

Chappell, trustees of the colored Methodist Church of Farmville, lot No. 6 of the N. E. Venable survey on Main Street.[32]

As late as 1871 the Farmville Methodist Church (white) reported colored members: 69 in 1868, 95 in 1870, and 61 in 1871.[33] A church under the charge of the General Conference of the Colored Methodist Episcopal Church was organized in 1873, with the Rev. Charles Brown, who had been ordained by Bishop D. S. Doggett three years before, as pastor.[34] A revival at this church in 1875 continued for four to five weeks, with preaching and prayer meeting day and night; about 100 persons had made profession of faith when a report was made after four to five weeks of the evangelistic campaign.[35]

The trustees of the Negro Methodist Church in Farmville acquired in 1869 the property which had been bought in 1840 for a Methodist Church near Prince Edward Courthouse; it was conveyed to the same trustees who bought the lot in Farmville by J. W. Redd, B. S. Scott, S. T. Clarke, H. J. Venable, E. J. Redd, and R. S. Hines, trustees.[36] The Prince Edward circuit reported 105 colored members in 1868; in 1871 there was one colored member on the Mt. Pleasant-Mineral Springs charge and one colored member on the Prospect circuit. In 1891 the Farmville Methodist Church (white) reported one Negro member, the Prince Edward charge two, and the Prospect circuit one.[37]

Negro Methodists in the Prospect community acquired land on which to build a church in 1869. By deed dated September 9 of that year, William M. Jenkins sold to James Bruce, Henry Woodson, and Emmanuel Walker, trustees, a lot three-quarters of a mile west of Prospect Depot on the condition that a house of worship of the African Methodist Episcopal Church be built on it. Matthew Walthall was then pastor of the church.[38] In 1881 the church, whose trustees then were William Johnson and Landon B. Woodson, acquired a half-acre of land at Prospect by purchase from James D. and Amanda Crawley.[39] In two subsequent purchases the church acquired additional property in the village:

September 3, 1889: John R. Wilson and W. M. Gilliam, commissioners, to J. H. Jones, William Johnson, Emanuel Walker, Benjamin Brown, and Thomas Green, trustees, one acre at Prospect Depot on the railroad and adjoining the church for a parsonage and a church. This is the first instance the writer has found of the purchase of property for a home for its minister by a Negro congregation in the county.[40]

August 27, 1909: E. S. and W. R. Taylor and Alma A. Taylor, wife of E. S. Taylor, to Emanuel Walker, L. Watkins, Benjamin J. Brown, Henry Lee, H. Fleshman, John Ellis, and Landon Woodson, trustees, land adjacent to the A. M. E. Church parsonage on which to build a house of worship for St. James A. M. E. Church.[41]

Land for an African Methodist Episcopal Church near Pamplin was acquired in 1892, with the purchase of one-half acre on the public road "near the High Dump east of Pamplin City" from John and Ann Eliza Jennings by Barnett Saunders, Nat Shepardson, and Martin Watkins, trustees of the church.[42]

After the Presbyterian congregation stopped using the church at Jamestown, that old meeting-house was used by the Rev. Elnora F. Carter, a minister of the A. M. E. Zion Church. Revivals were being conducted there in the late 1920's under these auspices. The property was purchased in 1938, W. L. Vaughan and R. A. Johns, trustees of Jamestown Presbyterian Church, conveying the building and three-quarters of an acre of land (specifically excluding both the old and the new cemeteries) to Elnora F. Carter, now Brown, Willis Johnson, and Otey Palmer, trustees of St. Paul A. M. E. Zion Church.[43]

Negroes in the Prospect vicinity organized a Pentecostal Holiness Church, for which they acquired land for their building in 1936. W. D. and Mae Meredith Brisentine sold a lot on the Prospect-Venable Bridge road to Ike Davenport, J. R. Fleshman, and Willie Ellis, trustees, at that time.[44]

One feature of the Negro church program has been the emphasis upon the annual revivals. The time is in most cases fixed, the revival in a given church starting the same Sunday, usually in August, year after year. The revivals constitute a sort of annual homecoming occasion; many Negroes who have moved from the community, even to the Northern cities, make the week of the revival in the old church the occasion for a return to visit relatives and friends. The all-day services on the Sunday of the beginning of the revival include dinner on the church ground; it is an event long looked forward to.

In High Rock Church the long established custom of holding the church meeting on the Saturday before the fourth Sunday still prevails.

The postwar period saw the restoration of Episcopal worship in Prince Edward, the growth and extension of the denominations already in the county, and the coming of several new denominations.

The revival of the Episcopal Church took place among the

English immigrants who settled in what was called the Spring Creek colony a few years after the War between the States.

Bishop F. M. Whittle of the Diocese of Virginia visited the Spring Creek mission, as the Episcopal congregation of English immigrants was known, for a confirmation service November 8, 1874.[45] On the previous September 27, the Rev. Mr. Cooke of Petersburg had visited the mission and administered the sacrament of Holy Communion.[46] The establishment of a church organization among them received its greatest impetus from a visit made in February, 1874, by the Lord Bishop of Zanzibar, Dr. Tozer, to his old friend, Henry Jacob, who lived at Oak Grove. Bishop Tozer went north after his visit in Prince Edward and preached a special sermon in the interest of a church building for the colony; he raised $1,000 by this sermon and also persuaded some generous ladies to give an organ. Thomas Homer, then living at Oakland, gave a lot for the church from his tract. Several residents in the colony gave generously. When news of the undertaking reached England, the Rev. G. Lloyd Nash, vicar of the church at Tolpuddle, ancestral home of the Homer family, preached a special sermon, and every inhabitant "from the lord of the manor to the humblest laborer gave something." James MacLauren, who had lived briefly at Haverhill before going to New Zealand, sent a generous gift. Miss Trickett of England gave a marble font, and another English lady the altar cloth. Bishop F. W. Whittle of the Diocese of Virginia gave the prayer books. W. Wellington Webbe of New York donated books for the Sunday School library. Henry Jacob himself embroidered several lectern covers, which he presented. The prayer book for the clergyman was the gift of John Siddons of the colony, and the Bible for the clergyman's use was given by Webbe. Captain T. H. Butcher presented two "exquisitely carved chancel chairs from beams of oak from Cothele Hall, Devonshire." Upon Bishop Tozer's advice, a New York architect named Haight was selected to draw the plans for the church, which was constructed by Joseph Clark under the supervision of the building committee consisting of Henry Jacob, Thomas Homer, John Siddons, and T. H. Butcher. Jacob, an amateur woodcarver, made by hand the seats, the altar railing, and the reading desks. The account of the conse-cration of the building describes the east window as "really a fine work of art," and those who remember the quaint building which long gave an atmosphere of Old England to the Prince Edward countryside agree. Work on the church began in August, 1874, when

Mrs. Thomas Homer laid the memorial stone. The building was consecrated June 10, 1875, and was dedicated to St. Anne "in affectionate remembrance of Mrs. Annie Wyles, the wife of Tracy Wyles, who died in April, 1874." Bishop Johns conducted the service of consecration and made the address. Because he and the clergymen who accompanied him had to leave by train from Prospect, they did not have time to administer the sacrament of Holy Communion. But after the consecration service, the Homers entertained many guests at dinner at Oakland; after dinner a number of the Englishmen played a game of cricket. Henry Jacob was lay reader at St. Anne's after the church was erected, as he had been for the colony before (during the building of the church services were held at Oakland). He and John Siddons were trustees, and Homer was treasurer.. H. M. House was sexton.[47]

Regular worship at St. Anne's did not long continue. After a few years most of the English colony removed from Prince Edward, many returning to England. Occasionally thereafter services were held in the building, which in 1949 was declared the property of the Diocese of Southern Virginia; the building was taken down and removed to Appomattox, where it was reconstructed for the use of the Episcopal congregation there. The first service in the reconstructed church was held on February 12, 1950.[48] A small brick pillar reminds passers-by on the Hampden-Sydney-Prospect road that in the oak grove on the edge of the woods about a mile east of Five Forks was once located this church, the building of which attracted interest and received contributions from around the world.

Some of the English immigrants settled in and around Farmville, as well as in the Five Forks neighborhood. With their coming, Episcopal worship services were held occasionally in the town; in listing the services of the Farmville churches in 1873, the *Mercury* included this entry: "Episcopal, occasional services, Alfred Moth, Esq., Clerk to the Vestry."[49] Services were held in the courthouse for a time during this period.[50]

Among the ministers who conducted worship according to the Episcopal order in this era was the Rev. Dr. Anderson Wade, a native of Prince Edward, who was rector of Westover Parish in Charles City County. Dr. Wade held three services in the courthouse on Saturday and Sunday, April 17-18, 1875.[51]

The Episcopalians of Farmville met on May 19, 1879, in the home of L. M. Blanton and organized a church. They chose at that meeting Robert E. Hubard, Alfred Moth, L. C. Irving, James M. Johns, L. M. Blanton, Charles Bugg, and John Webb as vestrymen. The Rev. W. E. Webb, who, as rector of the parish, presided at the meeting, continued as rector until September, when he was succeeded by the Rev. Frank Stringfellow. The church in 1880 purchased the lot in the triangle formed by High, Buffalo, and St. George Streets, and erected the building which was consecrated in August, 1882, during the rectorship of the Rev. A. S. Lloyd. The name selected for the church was Johns Memorial.[52]

Since the War between the States the Presbyterians have organized four churches in Prince Edward.

Dr. Thomas E. Peck of the Union Seminary faculty began preaching, in February, 1862, in a church which belonged to the Methodists near the present Abilene. (This seems to have been the Methodist church built on land bought from Lillious D. Womack in 1825.) The building burned April 8, 1873, in a forest fire which destroyed the woods around the church. The Presbyterians worshipping under Dr. Peck's ministry, although not constituted into a church organization, asked permission of Roanoke Presbytery to move to the site of the burned church the "house known as Douglas Presbyterian Church," which had been used before the reunion of the Old and New Schools by the New School congregation which had split off from Briery. Permission was given, and the work of removal was promptly undertaken; the first service was held in the building August 17, 1873. In April, 1874, about twenty members of this congregation petitioned Roanoke Presbytery to be organized into a Presbyterian church; the organization was effected November 17, 1875, with eighteen members. Archer W. Womack and James A. Womack were elected and ordained ruling elders. This church continued the use of the name Douglas, by which the building in which it worshipped had been known on its former site. Dr. Peck was installed as pastor in 1877 and continued in that office until his death in 1893.[53] In 1894 the elders were T. C. Cary, clerk, A. W. Womack, J. W. Allen, and J. W. Womack, and the deacons were C. M. Rice and Frank Allen.[54] In 1890 Douglas Church secured a deed to the lot on which the church "now stands," A. J. and Pattie Price conveying to E. M. Rice, F. E. Allen, and Thomas Garnett, trustees, the land which had been sold on June 2, 1877, to the church by A. D. Dickinson, trustees.[55] The church acquired a nearby tract in 1918 for its present building; J. Flood and Lulie W. Morton conveyed this land to F. E. Allen, James W. Carter, and J. W. Singleton, trustees.[56]

When Dr. Richard McIlwaine was stated supply and pastor of the Farmville Presbyterian Church, 1862-70, he preached for the Presbyterians living near Jamestown in the old meeting-house there once a month. His successor, the Rev. H. H. Hawes, also preached at Jamestown, as did a number of students from Union Seminary. Dr. McIlwaine was enabled to do missionary work in the Farmville area during his pastorate there because of the availability of preachers to supply his pulpit when he was away. Dr. Benjamin M. Smith, Dr. Robert L. Dabney, Dr. Thomas E. Peck, all of the Union Seminary faculty, and the Rev. Samuel W. Watkins, who was then living near Farmville, preached for him when he was away from Farmville engaged in mission work.

Upon petition, West Hanover Presbytery sent a commission to constitute a Presbyterian church at Jamestown; the organization took place June 1, 1876, and F. W. Southall, who had been an elder in the Farmville Church, and Joseph X. Morton were chosen ruling elders and William L. Vaughan and Henry N. Madison deacons.[57] The building which was used by the Presbyterian congregation had been built as a free meeting-house, and the land on which it stood had been conveyed by J. Jackson to trustees in 1821; in 1827 Jackson sold his property at Jamestown to Dr. P. T. Southall; in 1884 the property belonged to F. W. Southall, and there was a question as to the title to the church. Upon the opinion of some lawyers that the deed to the trustees was void and with the approval and consent of "prominent people of other denominations" to Presbyterian occupancy of the building, F. W. and Ellen Southall conveyed the property to H. N. Madison, W. L. Vaughan, and T. E. Perkinson, trustees. The church was served by stated supplies until 1899, when the Rev. J. H. Davis, Jr., became pastor of Jamestown and Cumberland Churches.[58] About 1920, when the bridge over the Appomattox River was condemned and there was insufficient traffic to justify its repairs, the congregation decided to abandon the old building, since members living in Cumberland could no longer reach it and the location was inconvenient for only Prince Edward members. For several years services were held in the Beulah Christian Church, about three miles nearer Rice. In 1928 the Jamestown Church erected a building a short distance from Beulah Church on land conveyed by Mrs. M. S. Walthall and Jasper D. and Helen Vaughan Wilson.[59]

The Presbyterians in and around Meherrin organized a church

in 1882. A building was erected in 1894 and was dedicated on April 12, 1896, Dr. W. W. Moore of Union Seminary preaching the dedicatory sermon. At that time the Rev. Hugh Henry was pastor, John R. Morton, A. A. Haskins, and W. H. Ewing were ruling elders, and J. J. Owen, W. H. Priddy, and T. J. Baker were deacons. The land on which the church was built was sold by Ann J. Owen, George D. and Nannie Price to W. H. Ewing, John R. Morton, and A. A. Haskins, trustees, in 1893.[60]

The Davis Memorial Presbyterian Church at Prospect was organized March 25, 1911. The month before it had acquired the property on which it built its house of worship. The land was conveyed by R. A. and Sudie H. Davis to A. C. Allen, W. S. Garden, and J. S. Moore, trustees of the "Prospect Presbyterian Church," one of the conditions being that the church building be completed in two years.[61]

West Hanover Presbytery was divided on the eve of the War between the States, pursuant to action taken by the Synod of Virginia at the session of 1858. The presbytery was divided by a line beginning on the James River near Lynchburg and continuing downstream to Archer's Ford, thence eastward along the Norfolk and Western Railroad to Pamplin's Depot, thence along the county road by Mickle's tanyard to Buffalo Creek, up the creek to the road leading to Union Theological Seminary, and along that road between the Seminary and Hampden-Sydney College to the intersection of the road leading to Prince Edward Courthouse and along that road to the Courthouse and eastward along the Burkeville road to the line of East Hanover Presbytery (the Nottoway County line). The churches south of this line became affiliated with the new presbytery, which was called Roanoke. Its first session was held at Lynchburg April 14, 1859.[62] This was the last presbyterial division affecting the Prince Edward churches; according to the division of 1858, College (only about one hundred yards from the boundary), Farmville, Appomattox, Jamestown, and Davis Memorial Churches are in West Hanover Presbytery, and Buffalo, Briery, Bethlehem, Douglas, and Meherrin Churches are in Roanoke Presbytery.

The Presbyterian churches which were constituted prior to the War between the States continue to worship in the buildings they were using at the beginning of the war. The Farmville Church added a Sunday School auditorium in 1887 and an annex in 1922, at which time the interior was remodeled.[63]

The dissolution of Sailor Creek Baptist Church in 1867 left within the present area of Prince Edward none of the five Baptist churches which had been founded in the county during the eighteenth century. At a meeting August 17, 1867—the only meeting on record after the war—Sailor Creek Church, which worshipped in Jamestown meeting-house, authorized its clerk, James S. Lockett, to give letters of dismissal to members desiring them.[64] The Negro members joined churches of their own race, and the white members joined Pisgah Baptist Church, which was then worshipping at Union meeting-house, about two miles east of Rice. In 1881 the Pisgah congregation built a new church at Rice, within half a mile of the site of Rice's meeting-house where Sailor Creek Church had been organized a century before. The new church, on a commanding site overlooking the village of Rice, was dedicated August 4, 1881, the dedicatory sermon being preached by the Rev. Dr. William E. Hatcher, pastor of the Grace Street Baptist Church, Richmond. The land on which the church stood was conveyed by J. Y. and Hattie J. Phillips to L. B. Walthall, B. H. Carter, Dr. R. E. Bass, Dr. S. A. Bruce, and J. Y. Phillips, trustees.[65] Old Union meeting-house a few years later was taken down and by popular consent rebuilt as the two-room public school at Rice; it is still standing, opposite the present school there, and has been for some forty-five years used as a residence. The house of worship erected by Pisgah in 1881 was replaced in 1928 by a brick church erected on the same site.

One of the most significant events in Baptist history in eastern Prince Edward was the revival of 1869. Both Sharon and Pisgah Churches had felt the debilitating influences of war. The original church book of Pisgah had been destroyed by Federal soldiers passing through the community. Membership had declined greatly, at Pisgah from fifty-four in 1862 to twenty-nine in 1867, and at Sharon from 596 in 1864 to 171 in 1867, though withdrawal of the Negro members from the latter to establish a church for their own race accounts for a substantial part of the decline. In September, 1869, the pastor of the two churches, Daniel Witt, led both in a revival which not only added many members to both church rolls, but quickened the spiritual life of both churches. Among the converts were some destined to become pillars of these churches and to serve faithfully for many years, the last of them continuing active for over sixty-eight years. Baptismal services following the revival were held at Miller's mill-pond on September 25, 1869.[66] The revival is a testimony to the piety, the faith, and the industry of Daniel Witt;

while he lived two years more, the revival added a fittingly radiant glow to the twilight of his life's day.

Since the War between the States, five Baptist churches have been organized in Prince Edward. As the churches of an earlier time had their preaching stations in communities distant from the principal meeting-house for the convenience of members who lived too far to attend services regularly, the churches during the latter part of the nineteenth and earlier part of the twentieth century organized Sunday Schools in the outlying areas of their congregations. The community between Moran and Burke's Tavern was an area on the border of the territories served by Pisgah, Sharon, and Burkeville churches. The Burkeville Baptist Church was organized in 1874, and the next year ten members of Sharon Church were dismissed to join that church.[67]

The three churches encouraged the holding of services in this community; these services were first held in the Moran school in the late 1890's. In 1899 Adam and Lula G. Cook conveyed an acre of land to J. C. Moring, P. N. Jenkins, and W. V. Clements, trustees of the Moran white Baptist chapel. Among the ministers who preached in the community was Dr. George F. Bagby, pastor of the Farmville Church, 1891-99, and of Pisgah and Sharon 1899-1900. When a church was organized at the chapel on April 18, 1903, it was named Bagby Memorial in honor of Dr. Bagby, but the church is still popularly identified as Bagby Chapel. The charter members came from Pisgah, Sharon, and Burkeville churches. J. C. Moring, P. N. Jenkins, W. V. Clements, and W. T. Gibbs were the first deacons, P. N. Jenkins was the first treasurer, C. L. Elliott the first clerk, and W. Moseley Seay the first pastor.

The Rev. Dr. W. J. Shipman, pastor of Pisgah and Sharon churches, the Rev. W. Moseley Seay, pastor of the Burkeville Church, and F. L. Overton of Burkeville conducted the organization service of this church.[68]

The Mt. Nebo Baptist Church at Abilene was constituted November 29, 1903, by fourteen members of Ash Camp Church at Keysville. The new church elected T. B. Yeaman, J. W. Pankey, J. R. Pollard, and L. J. Yeaman deacons, John W. Allen clerk, and T. B. Yeaman treasurer. W. E. Warren became supply pastor when the church was organized, and John B. Williams was called to the pastorate in 1904. The church acquired the site on which its present house of worship was erected in 1906, J. W. Foster, Jr., and his wife conveying the land to J. W. Bagby, D. C. Allen, and J. W. Allen, trustees. Mt. Nebo is thus the second Prince Edward church to be organized from Ash Camp, which in turn had been organized from an old Prince Edward church, Mountain Creek.[69]

Bethpeor Baptist Church at Five Forks was the outgrowth of religious services held in that community for members of Spring Creek Church. Preaching services were being held there in 1904, and the chapel at that time was called Bethpeor. The land for the building was conveyed by J. S. Harris to C. O. Harris and G. W. Gilliam, trustees, in 1909, and the church was formally constituted in 1912. W. A. Pearson was first pastor of the church. In 1915 another church was organized from Spring Creek, Cullen in Charlotte County.[70]

The Baptists of Prospect and vicinity organized a church on June 21, 1925; the Rev. C. Edward Burrell, then pastor of the Farmville Church, was the moving spirit in the organization of the church, which took the name, Glenn Memorial, from Mrs. Lucy W. Glenn, donor of the land on which the house of worship was built. There were nineteen charter members, ten of whom came from Mathews Church at Hixburg, which in turn had been organized from Rocks Church, now in Appomattox County, but the first Baptist church organized in Prince Edward. The other nine came from Farmville, Concord, Hollywood, and Spring Creek churches. Hunter Wilkerson and Thomas H. Coleman were the first deacons, Wilkerson, Coleman, and Robert A. Brisentine were the first trustees, and Mrs. B. V. Wilkerson the first clerk and treasurer. Dr. Burrell was the first pastor.[71]

The Rev. Ralph N. Cullers took the initiative in organizing the Worsham Baptist Church. He began holding services in the old church building which had been built as the Constitutional Presbyterian Church and as a result the Worsham Church was organized in 1950. A lot a short distance south of the village, on which a church was built in the same year, was bought from Bessie B. Chernault and J. L. Chernault by J. D. Atchley, S. D. Bailey, Chester Lane, John Elder, and Burt Lane, trustees.[72]

In 1914 the Farmville Baptist Church replaced the meeting-house built in 1856 with a new church on the same site.[73] Spring Creek Church built a new house of worship, a commodious frame building, in 1922 a short distance from the old church which had been built in 1833 and on the same property.[74] This building burned April 29,

1944; it has since been replaced by a brick building, begun in 1948, completed in 1949 and dedicated October 22, 1950.[75] In the interval the congregation worshipped in the Darlington Heights School.

The Methodist churches in Prince Edward in 1868 belonged to the district sometimes called Farmville, sometimes Randolph-Macon. The Farmville Church, with ninety-six white and sixty-nine colored members, constituted a separate charge; it had one white local preacher and one colored local preacher. There were five churches, with 353 white and 135 colored members, on the Prince Edward circuit; there were two white and one colored local preachers on the circuit.[76] In 1870 the Prince Edward charge was divided; the Mt. Pleasant-Mineral Spring charge, with three churches, 166 white and 84 Negro members, remained in the Farmville District; the Prospect charge, with two churches (Prospect and Olive Branch) and 275 members, was assigned to the Lynchburg district. The Domestic Mission Board appropriated $150 to Wesleyan (Meherrin) and Mineral Spring that year.[77] In 1871 the Wesleyan Mission was transferred from the Mt. Pleasant-Mineral Spring charge, and George V. Ray was assigned its pastor; John S. R. Clarke was assigned to Mt. Pleasant and Mineral Spring; in that year Wesleyan and Mineral Spring together reported only twelve white members and one colored member. The Prospect charge reported three churches (Pamplin had been added to the charge) that year, 270 white members and one colored member.[78] The Rev. Alfred Wiles was the first pastor of the Prospect circuit. This charge remained in the Lynchburg District through 1890; in 1891 it was transferred to the Farmville District; that year it reported 533 white members, one colored member, and five churches (Prospect, Olive Branch, Pamplin, Piney Ridge, and Smyrna, which had been added to the Prospect Circuit in 1873). The Prince Edward Circuit reported in 1891 three churches, 288 white members, and two colored members.[79]

The decade of of the 1880's saw the organization of two Methodist churches in Prince Edward. Salem Methodist Church at Rice was organized in 1884 as the outgrowth of a Sunday School organized in the home of Mrs. Martha R. Watson the year before by A. W. Drumeller and a revival conducted at Rice by the Rev. J. S. Hunter of Farmville. There were fourteen charter members of the church. Property for the church building was acquired in May, 1884, through the conveyance by Edward B. and Fannie R. Witt of an acre on the road from Rice to Sandy River bridge to A. W. Drumeller, W. Henry

Hubbard, C. C. Wade, G. W. Davis, T. J. Davis, W. G. Venable, J. T. Gray, H. E. Barrow, and H. C. Paulett, trustees of the Farmville Quarterly Conference. Although the church property was vested in the trustees of the Farmville Quarterly Conference, the church was assigned to the Burkeville Circuit, and the Rev. J. B. Askew became the first pastor. The church has continued to be a unit of the Burkeville charge throughout its history.[80]

The property on which Beulah Methodist Church at Abilene is located was acquired in 1886 through the conveyance of the lot at the intersection of the County Line road and the Farmville road by E. H. and Sallie B. Jeffress to James H. Davis, John H. Daniel, Branch D. Waddill, Samuel F. Spencer, and George W. Redd, Jr., trustees, for the Methodist Episcopal Church, South. Beulah Church was assigned to the Prince Edward Circuit and with Mt. Pleasant and Wesleyan constituted the charge in 1891.[81]

Wesleyan Church in Meherrin acquired a lot in the village in 1912, conveyed to W. S. Dance, trustee, by George M. and Lena Owen, J. E. and Dora Mann, T. H. and Delia Vaughan, John D. Davis, C. P. and Bessie Capps, J. H. and Sunie Ward, Landon and Viena Priddy, Walker and Eliza Wilkerson, Wirt and Jennie Caldwell, Jackson and Mabel Donald, Ida May Price, MacFaden Price, Everette E. Price, Boyd Watson and Avis Owen, and T. H. Hatchett, guardian of the children of Virginia T. Hatchett, deceased.[82]

Construction of a new house of worship for the Farmville Methodist Church was begun in 1906, and the building was ready for occupancy in 1908.[83] The Olive Branch Methodist Church erected a new building in 1915, to which Sunday School rooms were added in 1924.[84] Prospect Methodist Church was remodeled in 1919.[85]

In 1881 the congregation of the Disciples of Christ worshipping at Liberty meeting-house moved their place of worship to Green Bay. The trustees of Liberty Church, Robert B. Wilson, A. H. Smith, Junius C. Rowlett, James T. Clark, and L. D. Jones, received a deed to the property from J. P. Fitzgerald, commissioner, in 1883. The present church was built about 1900, replacing the church which was erected when the lot was acquired in the village. The Rev. F. W. Berry became pastor of Liberty in 1881; he served until his death in 1931.[86] This ministry of half a century has the distinction of being the longest pastorate of any minister of any denomination in Prince Edward County. That the Rev. Mr. Berry should have preached his last sermon from the text from which he preached his first as pastor of Liberty is a coincidence.

A number of members of Liberty Church lived in the community north of Rice. For convenience of worship they organized a church, Beulah, and built a house of worship in 1894. The land, about two miles north of Rice on the Jamestown road, was bought from Jasper H. Wells and wife by the trustees of the church, S. T. Farley, R. H. Walton, E. T. Bondurant, J. A. Bondurant, and R. L. Walton.[87] After the deaths of the Rev. W. H. Rodgers, for thirty years the pastor, in 1943 and S. H. Bondurant, an elder, in 1944, the Beulah congregation disbanded in 1945, some of the members retaining their connection with the Disciples communion, others joining other churches of the community.

During this period the churches began building or buying homes for their pastors. The Farmville Baptist Church provided a home for the pastor in 1870; four years later it purchased the house at St. George and Beech Streets, which it apparently had been renting for the minister.[88] A parsonage was built for the presiding elder of the Farmville District of the Methodist Conference in 1874.[89] College Presbyterian Church bought Kinderton at Worsham from Branch Worsham in 1875 for use as a manse; the present manse adjacent to the church was built during the pastorate of the Rev. Edgar G. Gammon, 1917-24.[90] The Prospect Methodist Circuit acquired a parsonage in 1877, remodeling a store into a residence on the lot bought from James D. and Amanda M. Crawley by Joseph W. Gills, Thomas H. Crawley, Thomas H. Glenn, Joseph B. Glenn, George M. Gillespie, Robert N. Wilkerson, and W. E. H. Durphy, trustees. The present parsonage was built about 1929.[91] Johns Memorial Episcopal Church purchased a rectory at the northwest corner of High and St. George Streets in 1883. The Farmville Methodist Church built a parsonage on High Street in 1899; it was replaced by the parsonage which was built on Oak Street in 1948. The Farmville Baptist Church used the property acquired in 1874 as a pastorium until 1912; from 1912 until 1925 the pastorium was on Virginia Street; the pastorium on Buffalo Street was built in 1930.[92] In 1889 Pisgah and Sharon churches formed the Witt Union Field in an agreement to have the same pastor serve the two churches. Trustees of the two churches, L. B. Walthall, B. H. Carter, J. Y. Phillips, S. A. Bruce, and Robert E. Bass, representing Pisgah, and William L. Clark, Thomas H. Bruce, J. J. Gilliam, E. T. Clark, and D. J. Weaver, representing Sharon, bought a house and four acres of land at Rice from R. B. Bradshaw as a home for the minister.[93] Like the Prospect parsonage, the Baptist pastorium at Rice had been converted into a residence from a store. The present pastorium of the Witt Field was erected in 1925. Spring Creek Baptist Church bought sixteen and a quarter acres of land in 1916 for a pastorium, Elmer and Sophia Gibson conveying this land to E. D. Carwile, T. P. Singleton, and S. A. Wilkerson, trustees. The pastor's home of this church was completed in 1919 and was first occupied by a supply pastor, the Rev. W. W. Hamilton, Jr.[94]

Toward the close of World War I there was a marked interest in joint evangelistic efforts by all the churches in the community. At Rice in 1919, Baptist, Disciple, Methodist, and Presbyterian churches sponsored a revival for which the preacher was the Rev. W. R. Leckliter, a Baptist minister of Richmond; services were conducted in the Liberty Warehouse there. In 1920 the Baptist, Episcopal, Methodist, and Presbyterian Churches of Farmville sponsored a revival; the Rev. Charles F. Weigle was the preacher, and the services were held in the armory. The joint effort was revived in Farmville in 1936, the four churches sponsoring Holy Week services, which were held in the Methodist Church. That year the preacher was the Rev. B. R. Lacy, president of Union Theological Seminary; in 1937 the preacher was the Rev. John R. Sampey, president of the Southern Baptist Theological Seminary; the Rev. Arthur M. Sherman of the Forward Movement Commission of the Protestant Episcopal Church was the preacher in 1938; and in 1939 the Rev. J. J. Rives, then pastor of Centenary Methodist Church in Richmond, preached.[95] The churches of the Rice community began in 1935 the practice of holding annual revival services, a minister of the participating denominations, Baptist, Disciple (prior to the dissolution of Beulah Church), Methodist, and Presbyterian being invited in rotation.

This, too, was an era of greater Sunday School activity. The children appeared in public programs on Children's Day and at the Christmas tree; and the Sunday School picnic came into its own. At first these picnics were all-day affairs at the church; sometimes, as at Spring Creek in 1903, there was a program in connection.[96] Around 1900 it was the practice of the Farmville Baptist Sunday School to hold its annual picnic at Oakland, then the country home of W. P. Gilliam. The people rode out in wagons filled with straw, in buggies and carriages.[97] In later years the Sunday Schools began having their picnics at the lakes where those attending could engage in water sports which had become popular.

The Sunday Schools were not altogether social, however. They were seriously concerned with teaching the Word of God. The lessons of life with a spiritual interpretation had a profound influence in Prince Edward, and the instruction of some able teachers was long remembered. In the Buffalo community, for example, those who had been in the Bible class which Thomas T. Tredway taught at Buffalo Church long remembered and frequently quoted his injunction that it was better to break a bad promise than to keep it.[98] Churches organized Sunday Schools in the outlying areas of their congregation to serve those who could not get to church conveniently. Prospect Church, beginning in 1884, sponsored a Sunday School at Mt. Airy, the home of J. W. Gills, during the winter months for people in that community.[99] Pisgah Church during the first two decades of the twentieth century usually sponsored a Sunday School which met on Sunday afternoons in the Nile School building.[100]

The coming of German immigrants to the county about the beginning of the twentieth century brought two additional denominations to Prince Edward. Lutheran churches were founded at Meherrin and Farmville in 1904. St. Paul's Evangelical Lutheran Church purchased a lot near Meherrin in the fall of that year, adjacent to a mission established for work among the Negroes on land purchased six years before by the Missionary Board of the Evangelical Synodical Conference of North America for Missions among the Heathen and Negroes. On September 25, 1904, the Rev. R. C. Francke was installed as pastor of the Lutheran congregation in Farmville in a service in the Presbyterian Church. Shortly thereafter the Lutherans began the construction of a house of worship on Virginia Street; this building was dedicated on November 12, 1905, with preaching by the Rev. Messrs. Francke and Shooff, the later of Meherrin. J. Dodl, C. Sohre, and A. Kalow were leaders in the effort to organize the Lutheran Church at Farmville.[101]

The first Catholic church in the county was built near Meherrin, on a lot conveyed in 1912 by Fred and Ernestine Herzig to the Rt. Rev. D. J. O'Connell, Bishop of the Roman Catholic Diocese of Richmond. To this church was given the same name as that of the cathedral church of the diocese, Sacred Heart.[102] The first Catholic family to take up permanent residence in the county, insofar as this writer has been able to ascertain, was that of Peter Trear, who settled near Sandy River Church shortly after the War between the States.[103]

Catholic services had been conducted in Farmville for a number of years before St. Therese's Catholic Church was built on Buffalo Street in 1950. Prior to the erection of the church, on a lot conveyed by Horace and Lucile N. Adams to the Rt. Rev. Peter L. Ireton, Bishop of Richmond,[104] services were conducted in the Student Building of Longwood College, then the State Teachers College.

The Wesleyan Methodist Church built a house of worship on Bridge Street in Farmville in 1939, after the congregation had worshipped for several years in a building on Third Street near North. The church on Bridge Street was erected on a lot conveyed in 1937 by Carleton E. and Cora M. Swift to the Rev. T. H. Hill, the Rev. E. W. Jones, G. W. Hayworth, A. R. Tucker, and the Rev. E. L. Henderson, trustees of the North Carolina Annual Conference of the Wesleyan Methodist Connection, and C. E. Swift, J. C. Knapton and W. R. Cox, trustees of the Wesleyan Methodist Church of Farmville.[105]

After World War I ministers of the Church of God began preaching in Prince Edward. By the end of the decade of the 1920's they had gained for their faith a number of adherents. In the eastern part of the county, members of the Church of God used an abandoned store at Moran for their services for several years. This congregation purchased a lot on highway 460, about three miles east of Rice, in 1941; Mary F. Taylor and her husband, A. H. Taylor, conveyed it to Daniel O. Baggett, W. M. Lowman, and K. O. Perry, trustees of the Church of God of which A. J. Tomlinson was general overseer. A building was erected on this property in 1946.[106]

A lot on the old Farmville-Keysville road, near highway 15, was bought from Minnie Lee Newcomb by Charles McGuire, William Childress, and Edward Eggleston, trustees of the Church of God with headquarters in Cleveland, Tennessee, in 1939.[107] In 1948 Willie Johnson, Charlie Burrell, and A. H. Shipp, trustees of the Church of God, acquired from W. E. and Janie S. Chappell a lot on highway 15 and the old Farmville-Keysville road for a place of worship.[108]

Another religious group to make its appearance in Prince Edward was the denomination of Jehovah's Witnesses. The seed for this faith was planted by itinerant book salesmen who from time to time, especially after World War I, visited the county selling the publications of the International Bible Students Association. They were popularly called Russellites, from the name of the founder of their organization, Charles Tate Russell, who was also author of many of the books which they sold. The group won some adherents in Prince

Edward and in the 1930's opened a Kingdom Hall in Farmville. They have continued to stress the distribution of their publications, and members are to be found handing them out to passers-by on the streets as well as by house-to-house canvassing.

Mormon missionaries visited the county in 1895; two were in the Felden neighborhood in March. Although they were "extremely reticent as to their faith" and gave no indication of the intended length of their stay, they did say that they were "specially called to Prince Edward County" and at the end of a conversation would put a card or pamphlet into the hand of the person with whom they were talking as they said good-bye.[109] There is no record that these missionaries gained any converts.

The Prince Edward Bible Society, which had flourished at an earlier time, was re-organized in 1894 at a meeting at the Methodist Church of Farmville. Following a lecture by the Presbyterian minister, Dr. E. H. Harding, fifty-six joined the society. R. S. Paulett was president, Judge J. M. Crute secretary, and Charles Bugg treasurer. The society adopted the objective of furnishing Bibles to destitute people in the county.[110]

Farmville also had a Young Men's Christian Association early in the twentieth century. In 1905 it suspended operations because the quarters it then occupied were inadequate for gymnasium work. At that time the board of directors included F. M. Bugg, president; H. E. Barrow, first vice-president; P. W. Beckham, second vice-president; W. C. Fallwell, treasurer; W. T. Blanton, G. M. Robeson, Peter Winston, and S. D. Walton.[111]

It was not until after the War between the States that the practice became general in Prince Edward of having cemeteries at the churches. A few graves antedate the war in the Spring Creek cemetery, and there are several in the cemetery at Buffalo Church, especially in the older section. A grave was found underneath Sandy River Church when repairs were made to it several years ago; the interment was made many years ago, for no one living knew anything about the grave. There is an old cemetery in the woods behind the church, but the stones indicate use since the war. In 1890 Pisgah Church laid off a cemetery on two acres of land adjoining the church property, conveyed by J. Y. and Harriet J. Phillips to B. H. Carter, James S. Lockett, Robert E. Bass, J. S. Bradshaw, Joseph Y. Phillips, and S. A. Bruce, trustees.[112] Prospect Church also laid off a cemetery on land adjacent to the church, on which the earlier building had been located. In 1918 the Prospect Cemetery Association was organized by Mrs. Ida F. Glenn to take care of the burial-ground.[113] Olive Branch, Douglas, Jamestown, and Bethlehem are among the churches which have also laid off cemeteries. Hampden-Sydney has three burial-grounds, one designated the Seminary cemetery, one the College cemetery, and one the church cemetery. Liberty Christian Church at Green Bay maintains a cemetery. Many of the colored churches have cemeteries adjacent to the churchyard. The town of Farmville developed municipal cemeteries.

The beginning of organized women's work in Prince Edward churches belongs to the postwar period. There were two divisions of the work, one for the aid of local church projects, the other to support the missionary program. The assistance of the ladies was sought, however, before they had organized their own societies. When Pisgah Baptist Church decided in 1872 to move its place of worship from Union meeting-house to Rice, it asked the women of the congregation to give an entertainment or a supper for the benefit of the proposed new building.[114] In May, 1875, the ladies of the Farmville Baptist Church gave a festival which lasted several days. On the first day (Tuesday, May 25), they provided a "splendid supper"; the next day it was a "magnificent dinner of meats, entrees of every description, Brunswick stew, cakes, ice creams of all sorts, strawberries and other fruits." A similar dinner was given Thursday and continued through Friday (when they sent "an ample dinner" to the office of the editor of the Farmville *Mercury*) and Saturday.[115]

Some of the ladies of Pisgah Church on February 26, 1884, organized a Sewing Society for the support of foreign missions; it had an initiation fee of seventy-five cents and monthly dues of five cents. Mrs. J. Y. Phillips was chosen president, Mrs. J. C. Bland vice-president, treasurer, and buyer, Mrs. J. R. Weaver secretary, and Mrs. W. P. Bradshaw cutter. Other members were Mrs. S. A. Bruce, Mrs. J. A. Leslie, Miss Venona Carter, and Miss Lady Atkins. They made and sold for the benefit of their organization aprons (sold at prices from twenty to thirty cents each, usually twenty-five), bonnets (at twenty and twenty-five cents each), dresses (for $1), and underskirts (for sixty cents).[116] This Sewing Society became the Woman's Missionary Society.

About the same time the women of the Methodist churches were organizing. The Woman's Missionary Society of the Prospect Church was organized in 1889.[117] In 1939 this society, along with other women's societies in Methodist churches, became the Woman's

Society of Christian Service upon the unification of the Methodist
Episcopal Church, the Methodist Episcopal Church, South, and the
Methodist Protestant Church as the Methodist Church.

In Pisgah Church the Ladies Aid Society, for the support of local
church projects, was organized September 21, 1901, with Mrs. W. J.
Shipman president, Miss Delle Walton vice-president, Mrs. R. A.
Bradshaw secretary, Miss Bernice Bradshaw assistant secretary, and
Miss Mattie Bass treasurer. At the first meeting each member was
given ten cents to be used to make money for the church; the return
was $3.85. Thereafter this organization, as similar organizations in
other churches, gave entertainments of various kinds, readings, suppers—the oyster supper was a great favorite, lawn parties, tacky
parties, valentine parties, and plays, and held bazaars and rummage
sales to make money for the church. The lawn party was a major
community social event on summer evenings; people came to buy
ice cream which was available in a variety of flavors and remained
to converse with friends. The church grounds were lighted—it was
before the days of electricity—by candles in Japanese lanterns, and
lamps on the tables. During the history of the Pisgah Ladies Aid
Society (which covered more than thirty years), it raised and contributed to the church $3,244.[118]

CHAPTER XVI

Education After the War

The Colleges

THE educational institutions were left as destitute by the defeat of the Confederacy as the people. Confederate bonds in which Hampden-Sydney's funds had been invested were worthless. The people who had subscribed to the support of the college were not in a position in 1865 to pay their pledges. In July, 1865, the Hampden-Sydney trustees authorized the college president, Dr. J. M. P. Atkinson, to settle unpaid subscriptions as he deemed best and to convert into cash any commodities he might receive in payment of those subscriptions. He was also authorized to borrow money to pay the faculty during the period of suspension of the payment of interest on the state bonds, that interest to be pledged as security for the loan. As the scholarship funds were invested in state stocks which were not paying dividends and which could not then be converted into money, no student was received except on payment of tuition; this requirement was repealed in June, 1861.[1] Scholarships were available for students entering in September, 1866, when it was advertised that $300 would cover all necessary expenses, board, tuition, fuel, and washing, and $250 would cover expenses for students entering on scholarships. There were five members of the faculty that session: Dr. Atkinson taught moral science and political economy, Charles Martin was professor of Greek language and literature, Lewis L. Holladay of physical science, Walter Blair of Latin language and literature, and Colonel Delaware Kemper of mathematics. Private instruction in modern languages was available from a member of the faculty who had lived in Europe.[2]

In 1871 the students added to the commencement a diversion which was not consistent with the trustees' ideas of what constituted a "suitable exercise for young gentlemen of literary tastes and habits." The diversion was a tournament, and the trustees were sufficiently lenient to permit the "young gentlemen of literary tastes and habits" to go ahead with the tournament they had planned for

471

the Wednesday afternoon of Commencement week—the day after the
trustees had learned of the plan and had taken it under consideration.
So, on a field east of the college that June afternoon, fifteen knights
participated in the only tournament ever staged by Hampden-Sydney
men at their college up to that time—or since, to the knowledge of
this writer. Alexander Hall, knight of Buckingham, class of '72,
crowned the queen of love and beauty—a young lady whose name
was not recorded in the annals of the event. The next day the
alumni banquet was held, lasting from five in the evening until nine.
Fourteen toasts were proposed and responded to. The galleries of the
old chapel were assigned the ladies who came for the occasion, to
hear the speeches. At the end of the program, the company arose,
joined hands around the table, and sang *Auld Lang Syne*.[3]

Money was a pressing problem at Hampden-Sydney then, as it
was throughout the South. The office of general agent was abolished
in 1874; in his stead agents were to be appointed for various sections
to raise money, each of whom received ten per cent of the collection
for the college.[4] The next year Dr. Atkinson launched a campaign
for the college on the home ground; the response was generous and
heart-warming; College Church raised $4,000 for the college at the
outset of the campaign.[5] Before his death in 1883, Dr. Atkinson
raised $45,000 for the college endowment, a surprisingly large sum
for a college which had won no wealthy patron in an era when the
South was in the throes of Reconstruction. Dr. Atkinson also introduced courses in French and German into the regular curriculum
and established the chair of English and history, which was filled
by Dr. W. S. Currell.[6]

Dr. Richard McIlwaine was called to the college presidency upon
the death of Dr. Atkinson. During his administration, which continued until 1904, the college made the most extensive expansion of
its physical plant of its history. In 1883 the college buildings included the dormitory (Cushing Hall), the steward's hall, the president's house, and three professors' residences. None was in good
repair. The college library was small and was housed in a dormitory
room, but the two literary societies, the Union, founded in 1789, and
the Philanthropic, founded in 1805, had good libraries. Only the
physical science department had a lecture room. A well on the
campus provided the water supply. Gymnasium and athletic field
were lacking. Dormitory rooms were heated by fireplaces; it was
not unusual for a coal to roll on the wood floor and set fire to it. By

1904 the buildings and residences had been put in good repair. The Memorial Hall (later named McIlwaine Hall) had been built; this building had the chapel and chemistry laboratory on the first floor, six classrooms on the second, and two literary society halls on the third. Steam heat was installed in the buildings at a cost of $25,000, and an abundant water supply was provided. The old chapel (in Cushing Hall between Second and Third Passages) was made into "a commodious gymnasium and thoroughly equipped." The library had been expanded to 15,000 volumes. Death Valley (Venable Field) was developed as the athletic field, the gift of Major Richard M. Venable, who after the war practiced law in Baltimore. Major Venable also bought and gave to the college during the McIlwaine administration the old Union Seminary property, including the Seminary building which was renamed Venable Hall, and three professors' homes.[7]

For all the progress, however, Hampden-Sydney fell on hard times toward the close of the McIlwaine era. The removal of Union Seminary to Richmond was a blow to the college. Dr. McIlwaine had fought hard to keep the seminary in its old location and had made enemies of some of the influential leaders of the Synod of Virginia, who withdrew support from Hampden-Sydney. Enrollment fell off, and a general atmosphere of discouragement prevailed.[8] More than once was heard the proposal to move the college, and once it was proposed to merge it with Washington and Lee University. The diligent work, the persevering spirit, and the moving loyalty of such professors as Drs. J. H. C. Bagby (physics), W. H. Whiting, Jr. (Latin), Henry Clay Brock (Greek), James R. Thornton (mathematics), and J. H. C. Winston (chemistry) preserved not only the college, but its ancient spirit and its longtime devotion to the highest standards of scholarship. In adversity they did not despair, and all, except Professor Thornton, lived to see the college enjoy again the bright sunlight of prosperous days. Professors Bagby and Whiting served as acting presidents between the administrations of Presidents McIlwaine and J. Gray McAllister and the administrations of Presidents McAllister and H. Tucker Graham. The McAllister administration lasted three years (1905-08) and the Graham administration nine (1908-17).

Just before the end of the McIlwaine administration, a student disturbance added to the worries of the harassed and aging president. The trustees refused for the first time to permit two dances to be held at the intermediate celebration of the literary societies in February, 1903, and directed that no more germans be held in the college buildings. While the junior orator was delivering his address during the program on the evening of February 20, students began firing Roman candles, skyrockets, and popcrackers. The speaker did not notice the disturbance, but Dr. McIlwaine apologized to the audience and asked the members of the societies to end the disturbance. Dissatisfied students distributed circulars with the legend: "Rah-rah, rah — Look — No Dancing — Therefore No Intermediate Celebration — at Hampden-Sidney — Down with the Board." Thirteen students were brought before the faculty for the disorder.[9] A year later a student disturbance which led to trouble with the faculty was settled when the faculty agreed to expel no student and the offending students pledged to submit to other discipline cheerfully and to maintain order. The troubles were symptomatic of the sickness which was affecting the college.[10]

During Dr. Graham's presidency the H. Tucker Graham Gymnasium was built, and separate chairs of biology and modern languages, filled respectively by Dr. C. M. Clark and Dr. John A. Clarke, were established. Dr. A. W. McWhorter, professor of Greek, was acting president for two years after the resignation of Dr. Graham. It fell to Dr. McWhorter to direct the affairs of the college during World War I, when a unit of the Students Army Training Corps was trained at the college.

In 1919 Dr. Joseph Dupuy Eggleston, a former superintendent of schools in Prince Edward, a former State Superintendent of Public Instruction, and at the time president of Virginia Polytechnic Institute, accepted appointment as president of Hampden-Sydney. To his administration he brought a vigor and an inspiring leadership which infused new life into the institution. Electric lights were installed in the college buildings, current being furnished from the Farmville Municipal Plant; the dormitories were renovated; Bagby Hall was built and equipped for instruction and laboratory work in the physical sciences at a cost of $102,500;[11] Morton Hall, the present classroom building, was erected, the gift of Samuel Packwood Morton of Baltimore in honor of his ancestor, the Prince Edward patriot, Captain John Morton; an infirmary was provided. The enrollment increased from ninety to more than 300 during the Eggleston regime, and the faculty, which numbered eight when he came to Hampden-Sydney, more than doubled during the twenty years of his presidency.

Dr. Eggleston was succeeded upon his retirement in 1939 by Dr.

Edgar Graham Gammon, a former pastor of College Church. Shortly after Dr. Gammon became president, the present gymnasium was built. Then came World War II, which with its demand upon young men of college age for the manpower to fill the military forces threatened to close the college. A unit of the Navy officer training program, the V-12, was established at the college, with a Naval Reserve officer, Commander George Howe, in charge of the program. The V-12 program enabled the college to continue an uninterrupted operation through the war period.

A notable achievement of the Gammon administration has been the enlistment of alumni financial support through the Alumni Fund. The first alumni organization had been formed in 1840; the first annual meeting was held September 10 of that year in the College Chapel, with William H. Macfarland of Richmond delivering the address on the day after commencement. Robert C. Anderson of Prince Edward was first secretary of the society.[12] The Hampden-Sydney Alumni Association was organized in 1926, with Dr. Charles William Dabney who had been president of the Universities of Tennessee and Cincinnati and was a son of Dr. Robert L. Dabney of the Seminary faculty as president. Then a quarterly publication, *The Record*, was begun. In 1928, under the leadership of Dr. Dabney and Dr. Eggleston, the association engaged a full-time secretary, George L. Walker. Upon this solid foundation Dr. Gammon has built the Alumni Fund, which in 1953-54 secured $33,578 in gifts to the college; during the fourteen years of its existence, the Fund has raised over $450,000.[13]

Since World War II the Johns Auditorium has been erected and was opened for use in 1951. The name honors Dr. Frank S. Johns of Richmond, chairman of the Board of Trustees. Another achievement of the Gammon administration has been an increase in endowment past the $1,000,000 mark.

President Gammon in 1954 advised the board of his wish to retire at the end of the 1954-55 session, and a committee was appointed to recommend a successor. In January, 1955, announcement was made of the appointment of Dr. Joseph Clarke Robert, a native of Mississippi at the time president of Coker College, Hartsville, South Carolina, and a former associate professor of history and assistant dean of the Graduate School of Duke University, as president of Hampden-Sydney. Dr. Robert is the first president of the college to hold the degree of Doctor of Philosophy and is the fourth layman to hold the post (acting presidents are not included in this summary). Presidents Cushing, Maxwell, and Eggleston were his lay predecessors.

In 1865 Dr. William S. Morton, who had once lived in Prince Edward, the Rev. Samuel Davies Stuart, who had been pastor at Briery 1840-56, and Samuel C. Anderson ended their service on the Board of Trustees of the college. Prince Edward men serving at that time were Dr. Peyton Randolph Berkeley, Robert C. Anderson, Judge Asa Dupuy Dickinson, Captain Thomas E. Perkinson, Stephen O. Southall, Colonel Henry Stokes, Dr. Francis B. Watkins, and Thomas T. Tredway. Judge Francis N. Watkins began a second term of service on the board in 1866. Dr. Robert L. Dabney became a trustee in 1867. Later additions to the board from Prince Edward included J. P. Fitzgerald, W. R. Berkeley, R. B. Berkeley, P. W. McKinney, A. D. Watkins, Dr. Peter Winston, W. G. Dunnington,[14] Dr. P. A. Irving, and J. William Dunnington.

The large portion of the endowment of Union Theological Seminary which was invested in bank stock was totally lost in the defeat of the South; the remainder of the endowment, invested in state stock, paid no dividends immediately following the war. The seminary was kept open during that period by gifts from generous friends in New York and Baltimore and by contributions from churches and individuals in Virginia and Kentucky. Thus the seminary was able to give the necessary aid to all students who needed assistance during the first session after the end of the war. During that session the seminary had twenty-four students, more than the faculty had expected. There were four members of the faculty then: S. B. Wilson, professor of systematic and pastoral theology; R. L. Dabney, adjunct professor of theology and sacred rhetoric; T. E. Peck, professor of ecclesiastical history and church government; and B. M. Smith, professor of Biblical literature. Student expenses at the seminary then, exclusive of clothing and traveling expenses, amounted to $200 per session. In 1866 the seminary launched a campaign to raise $100,000 to replace its lost endowment. The appeal for support noted that the seminary, since its founding, had sent out over 400 ministers to fill pulpits at home and to serve as missionaries abroad.[15]

By 1869 the seminary had been placed in a favorable financial position.[16] During the decade after the war the seminary's endowment had been increased by $90,000, of which one-third was given by Cyrus H. McCormick of Chicago and another one-third by Henry Young of New York.[17]

The seminary continued to fill a large place in the Presbyterian churches of Prince Edward. Professors and students preached in their pulpits; without this ministry, some of the churches would have been destitute of preaching; instead, the congregations heard some of the ablest scholars and most promising ministers of the Southern Presbyterian Church. From Buffalo, George Hunt, long clerk of the session, would send his son John on Saturday afternoon either in a buggy or on horseback with an extra horse for the young theologue who was to preach the next day in the old church.[18] Theological students did most of the preaching for Jamestown Church during the earlier years of its existence. Dr. Peck supplied at Buffalo and was pastor at Douglas. Seminary students conducted Sunday Schools in the county, to leave a lasting influence upon those who sat under this ministry. Against this background of identification with and service to the Prince Edward community, the Union Theological Seminary observed its seventieth anniversary January 4, 1894, in the seminary chapel at Hampden-Sydney. A young professor, Dr. Walter W. Moore, gave the statistical report of the seminary's record. The Rev. Dr. Robert Burwell of the first class of the seminary gave reminiscences of the long-ago day when John Holt Rice was establishing the institution; and the great luminary of the Presbyterian Church of that era, the Rev. Dr. Moses D. Hoge of Richmond, delivered the commemorative address.[19]

Six months later the storm broke. Dr. W. W. Moore advocated the removal of the seminary from Hampden-Sydney to Richmond. A layman writing in the Farmville *Herald* promptly answered Dr. Moore's six points supporting his proposal. To the view that it was important for the seminary to be in or near a city so students could visit churches and Sunday Schools, "Layman" replied that four or five months of vacation should be enough for such visits. Dr. Moore pointed out that Hampden-Sydney lacked a water supply; "Layman" reminded him that a leading Richmond physician had condemned the water there, adding that the water at Hampden-Sydney was so pure that not more than two students at Hampden-Sydney had ever died of disease. Hampden-Sydney was without gas, said Dr. Moore, but Richmond's "flickering, fading, false gas lights" were the horror of the average student, according to "Layman." There were no pavements at Hampden-Sydney, but "Layman" thought there was sufficient sand "on which the D.D.'s may walk free of mud." Dr. Moore thought the distance of seven miles from the railroad made living more expensive; not so, rejoined "Layman"; after the student pays Walker Cralle a half-dollar for taking him to the Hill, he could get nowhere else the same fare for the same money. "Layman" agreed that the removal would be a "grand opportunity" for Richmond, but it would be the "death blow to all institutions of learning in Southside Virginia." If the seminary leaves, the college will follow, he argued, and then someone will put in a bid for the normal and that would go too. "Keep the Seminary students at least six months of the year at his books, in the lecture room, teaching country Sunday Schools, listening to peerless preachers on the Hill," he advised.[20]

Dr. McIlwaine in opposing removal quoted John Holt Rice's appraisal of Hampden-Sydney as the seminary site: "the place fixed on [is] peculiarly suitable . . ."[21] Dr. Moore replied to Dr. McIlwaine, correcting some of the things Dr. McIlwaine had thought he said. He told the people of Prince Edward that they could offer inducements to keep the seminary, since the board of trustees had taken only tentative action, and suggested that they follow Dr. McIlwaine's proposal that they help the seminary secure the improvements it desired. The main question, he observed, had not been discussed: the future of the Presbyterian Church on the Atlantic slope. Writing in the Farmville *Herald*, C. D. M. thought faster transportation to Hampden-Sydney would keep the seminary, noting that a railroad from Farmville there could be built for $25,000. He also mentioned the number of pulpits in the section filled by students and professors, the number of Sunday Schools taught by them, and the number of Prince Edward boys who had gotten an education there who would not have been able to get it had the seminary been located elsewhere.[22]

Thomas J. Garden joined the opponents of the move. Writing in the *Christian Observer*, he found nine objections to removal: the land had been given as a permanent site for the seminary and the endowments had been given to Union Theological Seminary in Prince Edward; the seminary was more prosperous than ever and was a good influence on the college; Hampden-Sydney was a charming place of residence; studying for the ministry gave students a passport to the best families of the community, a refining influence not to be found so much in cities; the seminary had a large library with a good stock of books; in ministers there students had the best models; the pure air and health of the Hill were proverbial, and there was an abundance of soft, clear water; students coming from the west by the Norfolk and Western could get to the Hill before they could get to Richmond; there were mail deliveries twice a day to Hampden-Sydney, and the village enjoyed communication facilities by telephone.[23]

In Green Bay Colonel Henry Stokes urged people to sign the petition calling for an election to authorize the county to subscribe to bonds to extend the Farmville and Powhatan Railroad by Hampden-Sydney to Charlotte by pointing out the importance of keeping Union Seminary in Prince Edward.[24]

Dr. Robert L. Dabney, a former member of the Seminary faculty who was then teaching at the University of Texas, also opposed removal. In the *Central Presbyterian* he characteristically minced no words. "Trivial, sensuous inducements," he described the city luxuries advocates of removal were talking about. The Church does not want the man who runs after such: "self-indulgent men are not fit for the work." Because country churches are the feeders, the chief aim of the Southern Presbyterian Church should be to provide pastors and missionaries for the country, thereby answering Dr. Moore's challenge to consider the future of the denomination in the East. Dr. Dabney illustrated his point by observing that Richmond was "prevalently a Baptist city," drawing upon the Baptist back country of the Tidewater counties.[25]

But the battle was going against Prince Edward, despite the stalwarts who rallied to its cause. "Five handsome sites" were offered in Richmond, two by Major Lewis Ginter, one of them, on Brook Road, being regarded as early as February, 1895, as the one which would be chosen. Plans for "a magnificent group of buildings" had then been drawn. Dr. Moore, an advocate of removal, and Colonel J. P. Fitzgerald of Farmville, who, so far as the newspapers of the time are concerned, had remained silent in the dispute, were among those named to the committee to select a site.[26] Before the end of the year the Brook Road site had been chosen, and its selection had been ratified by the Synods of Virginia and North Carolina. The executive committee of the seminary board had named a building committee.[27] Prince Edward was losing a beloved and useful institution. Removal from the Hampden-Sydney location took place in the fall of 1898, and the buildings on the Richmond campus were dedicated October 5, 1898.[28]

The Farmville College continued after the war under the ad-

ministration of President Arnaud Preot.[29] In 1869 S. F. Nottingham
was head of the school, which operated for nine months during the
1869-70 session, beginning October 21 and ending June 29. Board,
including lights, washing, and fuel and presumably the room, cost
$180 per session. Tuition in the academic department was $40 and
in the primary department $36; an additional fee of $18 was charged
for each foreign language, Latin, French, and Spanish. Piano and
vocal music was $45 extra, with an additional $9 charged for use of
the instrument. Art was also offered at an extra tuition fee, $50
for oil painting on canvas and $40 for drawing. Students had to
furnish their own towels and table napkins.[30]

By 1873 the Rev. Paul Whitehead had become president. There
were four professors for the session 1873-74: Whitehead taught moral
and mental philosophy, John Murray mathematics and natural
science, E. A. Allan languages, and Charles Hoffman music. There
were "competent ladies as assistants." Board had been reduced
slightly since 1869; it was in 1873 $170. Tuition was higher: in
English studies $50 in the collegiate courses, $40 in the introductory
and primary courses; languages were $20 each extra, or $30 for
two; tuition for instrumental music was $50, with a piano use fee
of $10; tuition for vocal music was $40 for the special class, $10 in
the regular class; extra fees for painting and drawing ranged from
$20 to $40. Students still had to furnish towels and table napkins.[31]
That year the panic—"sudden derangements of the circulation of
currency," it was described—affected the enrollment, but as business
activity resumed during the fall more students came after the
opening date.[32]

The first diplomas were given at the close of the 1873-74 session,
and an elaborate commencement season arranged from Sunday,
June 28, to Wednesday, July 1. The Baptist and Presbyterian
churches of Farmville suspended their Sunday service for the commencement sermon at the college, which was delivered by the Rev.
W. W. Bennett, editor of the Richmond *Christian Advocate.* Monday
evening there was a musical exhibition. Tuesday evening was the
time of the celebration of the M. P. S. and the literary society. The
graduation exercises were held Wednesday morning, and two young
ladies, Miss Lalla T. Saunders of Farmville and Miss Alice E. Custis
of Accomac County, received diplomas. For all the emphasis on the
education of women, however there were limits beyond which a
proper young lady did not go. One limit she did not transgress was
that of speaking in public. Neither Miss Saunders nor Miss Custis

delivered her address at the commencement. The Rev. William E. Judkins read Miss Saunders' salutatory address: "Mental Culture in Women"; and Miss Custis' valedictory, "The Advantage of a Liberal Education and How to Use it Practically in Life" was read by R. B. Berkeley. Between the reading of those papers, Whitehead announced the distinctions, and Dr. J. C. Granberry of Richmond held the audience "spellbound for an hour" with the literary address, "Esther, the Beautiful Queen." Wednesday evening a concert closed the commencement.[33]

Plans for enlarging the college were discussed at two meetings in May, 1875. At the first meeting over which the Rev. F. M. Edwards presided, John Murray told the group that the college was "totally inadequate to the demands on it."[34] At the second meeting it was decided to secure a charter for the college with a capital of $8,000 and authority to increase the capital of $50,000. Colonel W. R. Berkeley, President Whitehead, and W. D. Rice were appointed to draft the charter; and H. E. Warren, S. B. McKinney, J. H. Mottley, T. J. Davis, and Captain J. Womack were appointed to solicit subscriptions to the stock. Almost $2,000 was subscribed at the meeting. The figure $8,000 as the minimum capital seems to have been arrived at from Whitehead's report that an architect had estimated $8,000 as the cost of the proposed enlargement. H. E. Warren put the matter on the practical level by observing that every merchant was more or less benefitted by the college and should subscribe to the stock.[35]

A third meeting was held May 28 at which the charter proposed was approved; at this time the names of the officers and trustees were inserted in the charter: the Rev. Paul Whitehead, president; T. J. Davis, secretary-treasurer, and W. R. Berkeley, W. D. Rice, H. E. Warren, R. S. Paulett, F. N. Watkins, F. D. Irving, Charles Bugg, S. B. McKinney, Dr. Peter Winston, J. T. Gray, A. J. Davis, and Dr. W. W. H. Thackston, trustees.[36] In June, when nearly all the stock had been subscribed, Judge A. D. Dickinson of the Circuit Court granted the charter to the college.[37] Later in the month the trustees accepted the bid of Burton and Holt for $3,830 to build the new wing.[38] That year the faculty included Whitehead, Murray, Allan, Hoffmann, Mrs. V. M. Whitehead, music; Miss Bettie J. Powers, primary and introductory English; Mrs. A. G. Stewart, domestic department; and Miss Mary L. Bernard, matron.[39]

After Whitehead returned to the active Methodist ministry and was appointed to a pastorate in 1882, the Misses Carter of Mecklenburg County operated the school for two years.

The development of the public school system in Virginia after 1870 demanded more and better teachers than were available. The teacher shortage then was as serious a problem for the school system as it is now, probably more so. The George Peabody College was founded in Nashville, Tennessee for the special purpose of training teachers, and Dr. J. L. M. Curry, agent for the Peabody and Slater Funds for aid to education in the South, advocated the establishment of similar institutions in the Southern states. Dr. Curry's recommendation aroused the imagination of some in Farmville, notably Dr. W. W. H. Thackston, then mayor, and the Rev. James Nelson, then pastor of the Baptist Church. They led a movement to have a teacher training institution supported by the state located in Farmville.[40] On March 7, 1884, the Virginia General Assembly passed a law establishing a "normal school expressly for the training and education of white female teachers for public schools" at Farmville, on condition that the town would convey to the state the property known as the Farmville Female College. The legislature appropriated $5,000 to establish and continue the school and $10,000 annually toward the operating expenses and salaries of the staff. Each city of 5,000 population and each county were entitled to have one pupil (and one additional pupil for each member of the House of Delegates) receive free instruction in the school. W. H. Ruffner, J. L. M. Curry, John B. Minor, R. M. Manly, L. R. Holland, John L. Buchanan, L. A. Michie, F. N. Watkins, S. C. Armstrong, W. B. Taliaferro, George O. Conrad, W. E. Gaines, and W. W. Herbert were constituted the board of trustees.[41] Dr. Curry was chosen president of the board, and Judge Watkins secretary. Dr. William Henry Ruffner, who had been first superintendent of public instruction in Virginia, was chosen first president of Virginia's first normal school.

In 1887 Dr. Ruffner was succeeded as president by Dr. John A. Cunningham. After a ten-year administration, marked by growth, Dr. Cunningham died; he was succeeded by Dr. Robert Fraser, who held the post five years. During Dr. Fraser's administration, the school acquired the Richardson property across Spruce Street, and that street was closed at the school and made a part of the campus.

Dr. J. L. Jarman succeeded President Fraser in 1902. He continued in that post until 1946. During that period of forty-four years, the college continued to expand, acquiring a campus of twelve acres covering five blocks. The expansion under the Jarman administration included buildings, faculty, enrollment, offering. The school was granted the privilege of conferring degrees in 1916. Twice during Dr. Jarman's administration the name was changed: in 1914 from State Female Normal School (the S.F.N.S. so familiar to those whose memories go back to an earlier time) to the State Normal School for Women; and in 1924 to State Teachers College (the S.T.C. familiar to all except the very young).[42] Meanwhile four other State Normal Schools for the training of teachers had been founded in Virginia, at Fredericksburg, Harrisonburg, and Radford. These became State Teachers Colleges at the same time the Farmville institution did. All four were placed under the control of the State Board of Education. In the 1930's began another trend in name-changing, this time to leave out any suggestion of teacher-training. The Fredericksburg school became Mary Washington College, the Harrisonburg school Madison College. Dr. Jarman at Farmville and Dr. J. P. McConnell at Radford resisted the change. To both State Teachers College had a significance they were loath to give up in the names of the institutions both had served long and well.[43] But the changes in name seemed inevitable. After Dr. McConnell's administration, the Radford institution became Radford College, and after Dr. Jarman's death the Farmville State Teachers College became Longwood College in 1949, named for the historic home on the hill to the east of Farmville, which the college had acquired as a recreation center, largely as a result of the interest and vision of Mrs. Jarman.

Dr. Dabney S. Lancaster came to the presidency of the college in 1946 from the post of state superintendent of public instruction. To the college he has given a leadership which has invigorated it with new life. There has continued an expansion in buildings, in faculty, in student body. Jarman Hall, which replaced the old auditorium which was destroyed by fire, and the science building were erected during the Lancaster administration. There was widespread regret upon Dr. Lancaster's announcement in the spring of 1954 of his intended retirement at the close of the following session. Dr. Francis G. Lankford, professor of education at the University of Virginia, has been named Dr. Lancaster's successor.

During the greater portion of the college's existence as a teacher-training institution, one of the most popular courses was the two-year course leading to the normal professional certificate for elementary teachers. When the requirement of four years of college for the elementary teacher was instituted, this course was abandoned. Until about thirty years ago, it was also possible for a teacher to receive a certificate on the basis of summer school work only. The summer session was instituted to give teachers an opportunity to continue their studies, especially professional courses, as they taught. As early as 1895 the town of Farmville contributed to the support of the "summer Normal," and appropriations continued to be made from the town treasury for this purpose until as late as 1934.

The college has had a strong influence upon public education in Prince Edward. One source of this influence has been in the large number of teachers from Longwood (to use its present name) who have gone to teach in the county schools. Another source has been through the system of practice teaching by the students in these schools. The practice teaching program began in 1886 in the demonstration classes in the "model school" taught by Miss Clara Minor. After watching Miss Minor teach, the students themselves soon began teaching the groups under her supervision. This program developed into the Training School, first housed in one of the college buildings. In 1913 a separate building was erected for the Training School; it is now the Farmville Elementary School. Until 1937 the Training School not only provided all the elementary education facilities for the white children of Farmville, but maintained a high school department to which only girls were admitted. In 1924 the instructional program in the elementary schools at Rice and Worsham was carried on by student teachers, under the direction of supervisors; the student teachers taught in three-month shifts, three teachers instructing a grade during the session. Since 1937 practice teaching has been carried on in the Farmville Elementary School for prospective elementary teachers and in the Farmville High School, with which the College High School of the Training School was consolidated, for prospective high school teachers, under the supervision of the regular teacher for the grade or subject.[44]

Private Schools

The private schools for the instruction of children of prewar days continued through and after the war. One teacher who maintained a school through the war was Mrs. John T. Branch, whose home was about two miles east of Rice. After the war the release of men from military service brought more men into teaching, and they continued the predominant sex numerically in teaching until after the establishment of the public schools. Some of these private schools prepared boys and girls for college, giving what would now be regarded as advanced preparatory training. In some of these schools students studied Greek, as well as Latin, algebra, and geometry.[45] Robert C. Anderson advertised his classical school near Hampden-Sydney College for the 1866-67 session, at which students would be prepared to enter the lower college classes. The fee for board and tuition (lights extra) was $24 a month or $230 for the session from the first Monday in September to June 15, half payable in advance. He offered boarding accommodations in his family for eight to ten students.[46] Mrs. S. V. East conducted the Farmville Female School, for which tuition was $3 monthly for the 1868-69 session. In 1868 J. A. Scott opened a school for boys in the house formerly occupied by W. J. Morrisett; tuition for the ten-month session was $30 for English, $40 for ancient languages.[47]

Farmville had a number of private schools during this period; they were not established institutions, but rather classes conducted by a teacher to whom tuition was paid. Among the teachers of private schools were Elihu Morrisett, at whose school in the rear of the present elementary school he taught singing lessons on Saturdays; William P. Elliott, whose school was on Virginia Street; C. C. Bass and T. J. Garden taught in the Lee Hall factory, Bass also teaching in a building near the present elementary school; Clayton Manson, in a building at the rear of Dr. J. L. White's lot; the Messrs. Campbell; Robert C. Anderson; Miss Caroline Goodwin who had a school for girls in the basement of a home at the corner of High Street and First Avenue; Miss Janie Venable and Miss Belle McNutt, in a cottage in the back yard of the Thornton house, where Mrs. Riddle had taught; Miss Mattie Littleton and her sister, Mrs. J. H. Lewis; Miss Mollie Jackson; the Misses Walker; and Mrs. Moss.[48]

The most notable private school in Prince Edward had its origin in the planning of a group of citizens in and around Worsham. In 1874 they laid plans for opening a school at the old Courthouse, at first proposing the name Hampden Institute and hoping to secure James R. Thornton as principal. The plans were realized, the old courthouse was remodeled for school purposes, a new fence built around the grounds, and eighteen "scholars" assembled for instruction under the gifted teaching of Professor James R. Thornton. So auspicious was the beginning that the stockholders in the institution, which instead of Hampden Institute was called Prince Edward Academy, decided to apply for a charter which was granted by the

General Assembly. The stockholders elected a board of trustees in June, 1875, under the act of incorporation, among whom were A. D. Dickinson, J. M. P. Atkinson, Dr. J. D. Eggleston, Dr. J. P. Mettauer, Colonel W. R. Berkeley, and Colonel J. P. Fitzgerald. Dr. Eggleston was elected president of the board and Branch Worsham was elected secretary. Thornton was elected principal, and a resolution praising his efficiency was passed: "in one year he has placed the Prince Edward Academy in the front rank of classical schools." The incorporators were William R. Berkeley, Branch Worsham, R. S. Hines, A. J. Price, J. D. Eggleston, J. P. Smith, J. M. Venable, A. D. Dickinson, R. M. Dickinson, J. P. Fitzgerald, R. B. Berkeley, C. C. Bass, Richard Stokes, G. W. Cliborne, J. M. P. Atkinson, J. W. Bondurant, J. B. Price, J. J. Dickinson. In addition to Thornton, there were two other principals of the academy, Thomas Wharey and W. H. Whiting, Jr. The names of the principals indicate the excellence of the school, which prepared many students for Hampden-Sydney.[49]

One of the English settlers, J. S. Stanley-James, in 1875 opened the Stanley Park Academy at his home near Farmville, where he offered to accept several boys under fifteen years of age to educate with his children. His course included English (with special attention to grammar and writing), Latin, French, mathematics, and fencing. He offered to take a few boarders in his home. Stanley-James, who had been educated at Shrewsbury College, England, also offered private instruction for adults.[50]

A private school for girls was maintained at the home of Thomas T. Tredway after the war. In the 1870's there was at least one student from Buckingham County attending this school.[51]

Private schools were continued at Prince Edward homes for some forty years after the beginning of the public school system. An item in the news of May, 1893, from Overly noted that all the schools in the neighborhood had closed, except Miss M. E. Baird's private school at W. L. Vaughan's.[52] As late as 1912 and 1913 there was a private school at the home of E. D. Carwile between Darlington Heights and Madisonville.

The Rev. C. H. McDaniel and Miss M. W. McDaniel opened a private school for Negroes in Farmville March 29, 1897. Fifteen pupils made application prior to the opening, but the directors had no building. They engaged the public school building (the regular term there had apparently closed) and conducted a short session preparatory to a full session to begin in the fall. The McDaniels proposed for their school an eight-month session; tuition was $1.25 per month or $10 the session.[53]

Students in Other Schools

The presence of colleges for men and women in Prince Edward from an early time has meant unusual educational opportunity for the county's youth. For more than a century after its founding most of the young men of Prince Edward who went to college went to Hampden-Sydney, although some, as this history has mentioned, went to other institutions. After the founding of Richmond College in 1840 some of the Baptist families of the county sent their sons there.[54] In similar fashion some Methodist parents selected Randolph-Macon College for their sons.[55] The real beginning of a tendency for Prince Edward young men to go elsewhere to college began with the opening of a vocational college, the Virginia Agricultural and Mechanical College, now the Virginia Polytechnic Institute, at Blacksburg in 1872. The first session of this school attracted two young men of Prince Edward, Emmett D. Gallion and Samuel A. Wootton.[56] The number had tripled by the session of 1875-76, when Richard L. Booker, Henry L. Lockett, John J. Owen, Frank P. Price, Benjamin M. Smith, Jr., and Samuel W. Watkins were enrolled.[57] Since then the Blacksburg institution has grown increasingly popular with young men from Prince Edward. In the nineteenth century and prior to World War I the German universities had attained the educational and scholarly leadership of the world. A period of graduate study in one of those universities was the ambition of young men of scholarly inclinations from many lands. Some young men from Prince Edward were fortunate enough to study abroad; five studied at the University of Göttingen in the 1870's and 1880's: John R. Sampson of Hampden-Sydney, 1871; James E. Booker of Prince Edward, 1871; Charles W. Dabney of Hampden-Sydney, chemistry, 1878-80; Frank P. Venable, native of Prince Edward, but then living in Charlottesville, chemistry, 1881-82; and Addison Hogue of Hampden-Sydney, philology, 1884-85.[58]

Some Prince Edward parents also selected schools outside the county for their daughters as well as their sons. Hollins Institute, founded in 1842 and for many years under the direction of Charles L. Cocke, drew students from Prince Edward both before and after the War between the States. After Roanoke Female Institute (the present Averett College) was founded in Danville in 1859, it attracted some students from Prince Edward; one father, James S. Lockett, concerned over the turn of Confederate affairs with the loss of Petersburg and Richmond, went to Danville to bring home his daughter and the daughters of his neighbors in school there. They got back to Prince Edward to observe one of the keenest engagements of the closing days of the war take place on the Lockett farm and even on the lawn of the home, and father and daughter helped nurse the wounded. Both these schools appealed to the Baptist constituency; Hollins, though not formally Baptist, was headed by a Baptist and had many ties with the denomination.[59]

The Farmville Library

The Farmville Public Library had its origin in the activities of the Mothers Club of Farmville. In November, 1906, the club applied to the State Librarian for a model library for Farmville, which it hoped would be the beginning of a public library.[60] The next month the Mothers' and Children's Library Association of Farmville was organized with forty members.[61]

Public Schools

The Constitution drawn up by the Convention of 1867-68 established the public school system in Virginia in 1870. Administration of local school systems was committed to a county superintendent of schools and three trustees for each school district; in Prince Edward the school districts were the same as the townships. After 1872 the superintendent and all the district trustees in a county constituted the county school board, of which the superintendent was ex-officio president. Annual meetings between September 1 and 8 were required, but the superintendent was permitted to call meetings when he felt they were needed.[62]

The public school idea was not popular in Virginia; for many white people the system was not introduced under the proper sponsorship. Some of the difficulties in establishing a system of public free schools may be seen in the report to the superintendent of public instruction, Dr. W. H. Ruffner, by Dr. Benjamin Mosby Smith, first superintendent of public schools in Prince Edward:

"As to encouragements they are few, and of very mild type. I have induced a few most excellent men to act as trustees, and have reason to believe some few who were opposed to the system have had their views partially though slightly modified by the high character of the gentlemen who have accepted office as trustees, and the excellent character of many of the teachers, especially female. On the whole, the results have far exceeded my most sanguine expectations a year ago. [This was written in 1871, after the end of the first session.] We have abundant reason to take courage and persevere."

Thanks to the judgment and the perception of Dr. Smith in selecting trustees and teachers in whom the people had confidence, the public school system in Prince Edward got off to what was probably as good a start as possible.

For the first session there were twenty-two schools in Prince Edward, eleven for white pupils, eleven for Negroes; Dr. Smith reported that nine more schools were needed, however. Of the schools operated that year, three white and three Negro were in Buffalo District, three for each race in Hampden, one white and two colored in Farmville, one for each race in Lockett, and three white and two colored in Leigh. The school session was longest in Buffalo that year, the average length of operation having been 5.06 months; in Lockett the session was five months, in Hampden 4.97 months, in Leigh 4.8 months, and in Farmville 4.65 months, to give the county an average school year that first session of 4.92 months. The teachers were predominantly white—eighteen white men, eight white women, and one Negro woman, who taught in Farmville District. Average salaries for the men ranged from $36.58 per month in Leigh to $49.30 in Buffalo, for women from $27 in Leigh to $40 in Hampden, with the average monthly salary on a countywide basis for men $43.22, for women $33.08, and for all teachers $39.87. The State appropriated school assistance funds for each district: $1,066.75 for Buffalo, $844.90 for Hampden, $780.30 for Farmville, $334.05 for Lockett, and $467.50 for Leigh. The bulk of expenditures went for teachers' salaries; Buffalo paid its teachers $1,280 from public funds and $90 from other sources; Hampden $1,180 from public funds and $55 from other funds, Farmville $821 public funds and $9 other, Lockett $415 public funds and $35 other, and Leigh $745 public funds and $85 other. Other school expenses amounted to $132.10 in Buffalo District, $169.50 in Hampden, $140.22 in Farmville, $141.69 in Lockett, and $156.97 in Leigh. That first session Prince Edward public schools spent $4,441 for teachers' salaries from public funds, $274 for teachers' salaries from other sources, and $740.48 for other expenses necessary to operate the schools.

Prince Edward public schools enrolled 371 white pupils and 478 Negro pupils in 1870-71 out of a school population of 1,353 white and 1,751 Negro pupils. Thus only twenty-eight per cent of the children of school age of both races were enrolled in public schools. But seventy-four per cent of the white children enrolled were in average attendance and seventy-two per cent of the Negro children, though only twenty per cent of the white school population and only twelve per cent of the Negro school population were in average attendance. The teaching load, computed on the basis of enrollment, was thirty-one pupils, but it was only twenty-three of the basis of attendance; and the cost of tuition per pupil per month was $1.29 per pupil enrolled, $1.75 per pupil in attendance.

Of the 849 pupils enrolled in the county, 792 were in spelling classes, 842 in reading, 492 in writing, 405 in arithmetic, 233 in grammar, 254 in geography, and 44 in other studies.

The superintendent devoted forty-two days that session to public school work, traveled 367 miles on school business, had incidental expenses of $15, wrote 150 letters, examined thirty-five teachers and licensed thirty-four (teachers were then licensed to teach on the basis of their grades on an examination given by the county superintendent), delivered eight public addresses, held two meetings of the county school board, made twenty-two visits to schools; the trustees made forty visits to the schools.[63]

In the very beginning of the public school system, the public schools outdistanced the private schools in enrollment, although the eight-month session of the private schools was much longer than the public school session and the monthly tuition of pupils in private primary schools was $2.50 and in private classical schools $3.50. There were ten white private schools that year and one colored private school, with eleven white teachers and one colored teacher; the white schools enrolled 145 pupils and the Negro school twenty-three.[64]

At first buildings were rented for school purposes. The only property reported owned by a Prince Edward district board in 1870-71 was valued at $18 and was in Farmville District.[65] The first school for white children in Farmville was rented from J. H. Mottley for $10 per month. One of the first public school buildings in

Farmville was a frame building erected in 1875 by Scott and Davis. The colored Methodist Church was used as the first school for Negroes in Farmville and was rented for $10 per month. Charles V. Woodson, first teacher of the Farmville white school, and R. V. Watkins, teacher of the first Negro school there, were each paid $50 per month for a five-month session. In 1879 the Farmville District trustees bought a lot on Buffalo road for $160 for the white male and female schools and offered a contract to Burton and Davis to build a brick building with a tin roof for $1,835; the firm declined to accept the contract, but F. H. Twelvetrees accepted it for $1,850.[66]

There has been a succession of emphases in the school organization throughout the history of public schools. The first emphasis was the graded school, in which pupils were grouped by grades according to their educational status, instead of having a school in which all pupils, regardless of accomplishment, were together and classified according to the reading text (first reader, etc.) they were studying. The first graded school in Prince Edward was the Farmville colored school for the session 1878-79; William P. Ellett was principal; there were three teachers in the school that year and 120 pupils; the session was five months.[67] The Farmville white school, of which C. C. Bass was then principal, was reported as a graded school for the first time for the session 1880-81.[68]

Public school enrollment increased considerably during the first ten years the system was in operation. For the session 1880-81 there were 764 white and 984 Negro pupils in 27 white and 20 Negro schools. Average daily attendance, however, was comparatively low: 274 for the whites, 310 for the Negroes. The teachers continued to be predominantly white; of forty-seven teachers, only five were colored, two men and three women; the white teachers were evenly divided between the sexes, twenty-one men and twenty-one women.[69]

That session one of the earliest efforts in the professional training of teachers was reported. One teachers institute was attended by twenty-seven teachers, while some scheduled could not be held because of bad weather. The programs at the institutes consisted of the reading of essays on certain topics by teachers asked to prepare them, followed by a discussion in which the teachers attending participated; then Dr. Smith, the superintendent, gave his views on the topic presented.[70]

At this time there was developing among the Negroes a desire for more teachers of their own race in their schools. In 1882 a petition signed by five patrons of the Farmville colored school asked for the

appointment of a teacher of their own race when one as well qualified as the white teacher could be secured; the trustees replied that
no qualified Negro teacher had applied.[71]

The graded school idea was spreading in Prince Edward. Prospect, with two teachers, forty-two pupils, and M. R. Crawley as
principal, had a graded school in 1883-84, as did Meherrin, where
T. G. Massie was principal and there were two teachers and forty-
eight pupils.[72] The Rice's Depot school, of which R. C. Anderson
was principal, was on the graded school list in 1884-85.[73] The list of
Prince Edward graded schools had increased to eight in 1887-88:
Farmville (C. C. Bass, principal), Farmville colored (W. P. Nappur,
principal), Rice's Depot (R. C. Anderson, principal), near Prospect
(J. P. Glenn, principal), Worsham (J. D. Eggleston, principal—the
beginning of a long and distinguished connection with Prince Edward
education), Meherrin's Depot (J. J. Gallaher, principal), Green Bay
(Miss Ida Jones, principal), and Hampden colored (John H. Brown,
principal).[74]

During the 1890-91 session enrollment in Prince Edward schools
had increased to 3,101 (884 white, 2,217 colored), and there were
sixty-five schools, thirty-two white and thirty-three colored. Length
of term had not kept pace with the increase in enrollment and
schools; that year the average session in the county was 114 days—
5.7 months. Average salaries were considerably less than they had
been twenty years before, only $29.58 per month for men and
$25.51 for women. The proportion of Negro teachers had consider-
ably increased; there were now eleven colored men and twenty-two
colored women teaching in the system. The proportion of white
men had decreased markedly: that session there were only seven, and
there were twenty-five white women teachers.[75]

The next decade saw enrollment and schools increased. There
were 3,222 pupils (1,083 white, 2,139 colored) in eighty-three
schools (forty-two white, forty-one colored). The school term continued short: an average of 5.92 months for the county. Average
monthly salaries had come up slightly to $29.25 for men and $26.71
for women.[76]

The teachers institutes developed into county teachers organizations. Prince Edward had a teachers association in the spring of
1902, which met at the Farmville Normal School with addresses of
varied and practical interest: "Virginia and her Schools" by Dr.
Robert Frazer; "The Rural Schools of the South" by J. D. Eggleston,

then of Knoxville, Tennessee; "Public Education" by St. George Tucker; "Juvenile Ethics" by Dr. Linus Kline; "Current History" by Dr. B. Arnold; "Prince Edward County History" by Superintendent of Schools Thomas J. Garden; "Prince Edward Courthouse in Days of Yore" by Miss Sally B. Dickinson.[77] Later in the year J. D. Eggleston, Jr., was president and Miss Sally B. Dickinson secretary of the teachers association.[78] The colored teachers had an organization in 1904 with William H. Coleman president and Miss M. W. McDaniel corresponding secretary.[79] In 1905 the county teachers set up a reading course for professional and cultural improvement: Shakespeare's *Hamlet*, George Eliot's *Silas Marner*, White's *Elements of Pedagogy*, and McMuny's *General Methad.*[80]

At that time the county school board, consisting of all the district trustees, selected from the multiple lists approved by the State Board of Education, the textbooks to be used in the schools. The Prince Edward County board selected the following texts for the four-year period beginning August 1, 1898, and fixed retail (the first price listed) and exchange (the second figure) prices for them: Finch's Primer (30 cents, 18 cents); Merrill's Speller (16 cents, 10 cents); Glasse's Old Dominion spelling blanks (5 cents); for elementary readers the series *Stepping Stones to Literature*, grades one through seven, was chosen, at retail prices from 20 to 48 cents (12 to 30 cents, exchange); Warren Colburn's *Intellectual Arithmetic* (35 cents, 21 cents); White's first book, intermediate, *New Complete Arithmetic* (25, 27, and 50 cents; 10, 11, and 20 cents, exchange); Hyde's *Practical Lessons in the Use of English* (30 cents, 17 cents); Whitney and Lockwood's *English Grammar* (60 cents, 30 cents); Maury's *Elementary Geography* (45 cents, 23 cents); Maury's *Manual of Geography* ($1, 50 cents); Magill's *Stories from Virginia History* (50 cents); Smithey's *History of Virginia* (75 cents, 38 cents); Lee's *Primary History of the United States* (50 cents, 30 cents); Jones' *School History of the United States* ($1, 50 cents); Judson's *Young American* civics text (60 cents); the copy books were Heath's *Natural System for Vertical Writing* (grades 1-6, 6 cents; grades 7-8, 8 cents); Smithdeal's slant copy books (grades 1-6, 5 cents); Cutter's *Beginning Physiology* (25 cents, 12 cents); *Intermediate Physiology* (42 cents, 20 cents); *Comprehensive Physiology* (75 cents, 40 cents); Paul Bent's *First Steps in Scientific Knowledge* (60 cents, 30 cents) or in three books: No. 1 (30 cents, 15 cents), No. 2 (35 cents, 18 cents), No. 3 (30 cents, 15 cents); Webster's *Primary Dictionary*

(48 cents, 19 cents), *Common School Dictionary* (72 cents, 29 cents), *High School Dictionary* (98 cents, 39 cents), and *Academic Dictionary* ($1.50, 60 cents); Messervy's *Bookkeeping* (cloth, 80 cents, 50 cents; board, 65 cents, 40 cents); Thompson's *New Short Course in Drawing* (no price listed); Hall and Knight's *Algebra* (90 cents, 54 cents); Wentworth's *Plane and Solid Geometry* (90 cents, 55 cents); Tarr's First Book *Physical Geography* ($1.10, 66 cents); Gage's *Introduction to Physical Science* ($1, 60 cents); Steele's *New Chemistry* ($1); Waddey's *Composition and Rhetoric* ($1); Curry's *Southern States* ($1); Montgomery's *Leading Facts of English History* ($1.12, 67 cents); Myers' *General History* ($1.50, 90 cents); McCabe's Bingham's *Latin Grammar* ($1, 60 cents); McCabe's Bingham's *Caesar* ($1); D'Ooge's *Viri Romae* (75 cents, 45 cents).[81]

In 1904 the board appointed a committee of three trustees and three teachers to make the selections; it then passed a resolution protesting that Maury's geography cost more in Virginia than it did in some other states.[82] The multiple school list aroused dissatisfaction among patrons because of the high price of books and the poor arrangement made for purchasing them.[83]

The Prince Edward board opposed the appointment by the State Board of Education of five district inspectors and examiners (for teaching appointments) at salaries of $1,500 annually and expenses. It was an unwise and extravagant step, thought the Prince Edward trustees, according to resolutions drawn up by S. W. Paulett and E. G. McGehee. Division superintendents are better qualified to grade the examination papers of prospective teachers, they held. They also protested a regulation which gave graduates of the Normal School a second instead of a first grade certificate; such a policy "discredits the excellent work done at state institutions."[84]

The next organizational development in Virginia public schools was stimulated by J. D. Eggleston of Prince Edward who in 1905 was elected state superintendent of public instruction. He put into effect a plan under which the state would assist financially in supporting district high schools if the people and the localities would provide adequate buildings and matching funds to support the new schools. Farmville had had a high school for a number of years, but the schools in the other communities of the county were still "graded schools." The first meeting in the interest of getting a district high school was held in the Baptist Church at Rice, March 12, 1906. Superintendent of Schools J. H. Davis outlined the proposal that a building costing $1,000 be erected, one-half the cost provided by donations from the people and one-half from district school funds. The two-story building would have three classrooms on the first and a townhall on the second floor. The State Board of Education would provide $250 to supplement the principal's salary. Others who spoke at the meeting were Dr. Robert Frazer and James S. Thomas, examiner and inspector of the third school circuit.[85]

Green Bay citizens held a meeting April 6 to discuss the district high school plan. Superintendent Davis proposed consolidating three schools there and building a three-room school. To accomplish this required gifts from the community amounting to $500; the audience subscribed $300.[86] A citizens' meeting at Rice on May 1 decided to apply for the establishment of a district high school and laid plans to raise $1,000 for the building and $300 a year for five years to support a high school department.[87] Hampden District followed with a meeting at Worsham May 26 to consider raising the district school levy to twenty cents on the $100 property valuation and the consolidation of the Hampden-Sydney and Worsham schools to establish a district high school.[88]

The first district high school in Prince Edward established under the Ould high school law was at Green Bay. The new building, "a model of its kind for beauty of architecture and convenience of arrangement," was opened October 1, 1906, with a program on which State Superintendent of Public Instruction Eggleston, District Supervisor Thomas, and Judge A. D. Watkins took part.[89]

Meanwhile Farmville and Hampden Districts in a special election on September 11 had defeated a proposed increase in the school levy from ten to twenty cents, in the former district by 99 to 20.[90] At that time there were a county school levy of ten cents and district school levies of ten cents in Farmville, Hampden, and Leigh, fifteen cents in Buffalo, and twenty cents in Lockett.[91] In a special election February 28, 1907, Lockett District voted 44 to 11 to raise the district school levy from twenty to thirty cents.[92] Plans for establishing a high school at Rice followed immediately the authorization of an increase in the levy. A "beautiful site" of two acres across the road from the old school, on which it was proposed to erect a building costing $3,000 (to which the people were asked to subscribe $800) and which would have four classrooms on the first floor and a public hall on the second was secured.[93]

By the fall of 1907 all districts except Buffalo had high schools.

Leigh, which had been transporting to Green Bay by wagon pupils
from two other schools in 1906-07, closed a third school, the Ewing
School, in 1907 and added a third wagon. The two wagons in 1906-
07 had provided the first school transportation in Prince Edward.
At the beginning of the 1907-08 session, Hampden District consolidated four schools to form the Worsham graded and high school,
which used the old Clerk's Office, built in 1855. The two-room school
at Hampden-Sydney, the one-room schools at Felden, Throck, and
Worsham were consolidated to establish this school. On the first day
of the session one wagon ran, but a second wagon was added the
second day of the session. The faculty at Worsham that year consisted of P. Tulane Atkinson, principal, and Misses Mamie Fowlkes
and Edith Duvall. At the same time the district high school at Rice
opened with G. F. Somers as principal and Miss Bessie Gilliam
teacher. Buffalo planned that year to add a third room to the two-
room building at Prospect and open a district high school there.[94]

Few developments created more public interest in and enthusiasm
for the schools than the district high school establishment. The
rapidity with which the people of Prince Edward responded to the
opportunity indicates the popular favor with which the plan was
received.

Out of the movement to establish district high schools came the
organization in Prince Edward of citizens in the community to
support and help the schools. Two such organizations were formed
in October, 1907, the School Improvement League at Prospect, with
Mrs. R. J. Carter as president, and the Citizens School Improvement
League at Rice, with Mrs. B. H. Carter as president.[95] A Patrons
League was organized at the Farmville High School October 8, 1912,
with S. W. Watkins as president.[96] Later these organizations were
known as Community Leagues; and since the consolidation in 1933
of the Cooperative Education Association and the Virginia Branch of
the Congress of Parents and Teachers, they have become generally
known as Parent-Teacher Associations, although the usage "League,"
to designate the organization, has continued and is sometimes heard
today.

At the end of the fourth decade of Virginia public schools, Prince
Edward system had 2,858 pupils enrolled (976 white, 1,882 colored)
in eighty-four schools equally divided between the races. Farmville
and Hampden each boasted one brick building in 1910-11, but there
were even then fifteen log school buildings in the county—four of

Buffalo's twenty-one schools, eight of Hampden's fourteen, and three of Leigh's nine. The most amazing statistics for that session showed that only fourteen schools (of a total of eighty-four, remember) had toilets: two in Buffalo, four in Farmville, two in Hampden, three in Leigh, and three in Lockett. That year Buffalo had a district school levy of twenty-five cents, Farmville of ten cents, Hampden of twenty cents, Leigh of twenty cents, and Lockett of thirty cents.[97]

The interest in high school development seemed entirely confined to the white people. There was no comparable development of district high schools among the Negroes. In 1920-21 no colored high school teachers were reported in Prince Edward, but there were eight men and forty women reported as teachers in colored elementary schools. There were seven men and thirteen women teaching in the white high schools, and two men and thirty-eight women teaching in the white elementary schools that session, a half-century after the first public school session. Enrollment that year was 3,471. The average term in the white schools was 169 days, but only 131 in the Negro schools.[98] As early as 1885 a difference in term was noted, Farmville District having a session of eight and one-half months for its white schools and six months for its Negro schools.[99]

The administrative set-up for public schools was changed in 1922. The district school board was abolished, and in its stead a county school board with one representative from each district was established. No change at the time was made in the method of electing school board members; the commonwealth's attorney, the superintendent of schools, and a member appointed by the Circuit Court continued the electoral board. So in Prince Edward Judge A. D. Watkins, Superintendent T. J. McIlwaine, and Fred M. Bugg named the new board: W. B. Binford, Buffalo District; the Rev. Frederick Diehl, Farmville; E. G. McGehee, Hampden; J. H. Ward, Leigh; W. S. Weaver, Lockett; and T. R. N. Cocks, Prespect. McGehee was chosen chairman, and Mrs. Roberta H. Large was elected clerk of the board. In 1926 a new electoral board was constituted, all of the members being appointed by the Circuit Court. It consisted of P. T. Atkinson, who was elected chairman, E. S. Shields, and Bennett T. Taylor.[100]

At the same time further consolidations were being made. In 1922 all the white schools in Lockett District were consolidated at Rice, and within the next five years all white one-, two-, and three-room schools in the county, except the school at Meherrin operated jointly with Lunenburg County, had been consolidated into the six district high schools; Farmville, Prospect, Darlington Heights, Worsham, Green Bay, and Rice.

One impetus to the consolidation movement was the construction of splendid new brick school buildings in each district. A new high school building had been built in Farmville in 1912, and a new brick building had been built at Green Bay to replace the old building which had to be removed for the Norfolk and Western belt line in 1915. The countywide building program began with Prospect; in 1923 the General Assembly authorized the Prince Edward School Board to borrow up to $15,000 to build a school there and the Board of Supervisors to levy a special tax on the district to pay the interest on and create a sinking fund for the retirement of bonds issued to build the school. The building was erected the next year. Interest spread to other sections of the county, and in 1926 the legislature authorized the supervisors to levy up to fifty cents on the $100 valuation for a school tax to pay the interest and to create a sinking fund for the retirement of bonds issued for school purposes in each district. Lockett District voters approved the issuance of bonds in the amount of $40,000 and a special levy of forty cents to pay the interest and provide for their retirement on June 11, 1926. Construction of a new building began later and was completed in 1927. In the same year new buildings, financed by bonds, were erected at Worsham and Darlington Heights. A high school for Negroes was built in Farmville in 1926, which was named in honor of the distinguished Negro educator who as a boy lived in Prince Edward, Robert R. Moton, long president of Tuskegee Institute, Alabama. An annex, including auditorium and gymnasium, was built at the Farmville High School in 1926. An addition to the Green Bay school plant was erected in 1925.[101] The people were by no means unanimous in approving the issuance of bonds to provide these new buildings. During the past generation no more bitter political battles were fought in the county than those in the districts which voted on school bonds. Advocates and opponents worked hard to win support for their position, and feelings naturally ran high. In Buffalo District the first vote on bonds resulted in a tie, and the second election was carried in favor of bonds by only a small margin. Opposition centered largely around the increased taxation which would be required.

Prince Edward schools have suffered three disastrous fires since this building program began, all happening at an hour when the children were not in school. The Rice school was destroyed by a fire on Christmas morning, 1930, the older building of the Farmville High School burned April 21, 1936,[102] and the Prospect school burned on March 2, 1946.[103] The Rice building was replaced by a building of comparable size; a more commodious structure replaced the Farmville school; but as there was only an elementary school at Prospect when the building there burned, the destroyed building was replaced by a smaller plant.

In the 1930's there developed in Virginia a trend toward the consolidation of all high schools within a county into a county high school. This trend was strongly endorsed and warmly pushed by the State Department of Education in order to provide high schools with a fairly comprehensive curriculum. Naturally in the districts in which it was proposed to close the high school the trend was not viewed with unanimous approval, though in Prince Edward there developed some sentiment in favor of consolidation. Despite objections raised in the communities which stood to lose their high schools, the consolidation of high schools began in Prince Edward in the fall of 1941; that year the Rice and Prospect High Schools were consolidated with the Farmville High School, students from those localities being transported to Farmville, and Darlington Heights High School was consolidated with Worsham High School. The present status of consolidation was attained in 1947 when the Green Bay High School was consolidated with the Farmville High School.[104]

For the past decade and half, the status of Negro education has been of pressing concern in Virginia. It began with the suit of Newport News Negro teachers for equalization of their salaries with salaries of white teachers. The United States Supreme Court in 1939 held that discrimination in fixing salaries on the basis of race was unconstitutional under the Fourteenth Amendment. From equalization of salaries, the Negroes moved to ask equalization of school facilities and transportation to schools. There were also suits in which Negroes sought admission to hitherto exclusively white graduate and professional schools in Southern institutions supported by tax funds, and in each instance the United States Supreme Court held that facilities in Negro schools must be made equal to those of white schools in the same school division and that Negroes were entitled to admission to the graduate and professional schools. Prince Edward remained uninvolved for some time in the numerous cases of litigation. In 1939 an additional building had been erected at

Main, Barrow, and Ely Streets, in Farmville, near the brick school
erected in 1926, to accommodate the greatly increased student
body.[105] Some of the money from bond issues in the districts had
been used to improve the smaller Negro schools throughout the
county. Some schools had been built with funds provided by the
Federal government in the program to relieve the depression in the
1930's. During this period there was an increasing interest in securing a high school education on the part of Negro children, which
the increasing prosperity of the country made possible. Bus service
was steadily extended throughout the county for Negro pupils. This
trend was greatly accentuated during the World War II and postwar
period. The school administration in the county was aware of the
inadequacies of the Robert R. Moton High School facilities to accommodate the Negro youth of the county.

Plans were already under consideration to relieve this situation
when on Monday, April 23, 1951, the 450 students of the Moton
High School suddenly remained at home from school. For two weeks
only the teachers were in the classrooms. Application to attend the
Farmville High School on behalf of the students was made, but the
County School Board rejected the request. After refusing to attend
school for two weeks, the Negro pupils returned to the Moton High
School, but suit instituted in the federal court in the name of
Dorothy E. Davis vs. Prince Edward County by the National Association for the Advancement of Colored People asked both that
facilities of the Negro high school be equalized with those of the
white schools and that the Virginia segregation laws be declared
unconstitutional.[106]

The case, as was customary with those involving segregation in
the public schools, was heard by a special federal court of three
judges, in this case Judge Armistead M. Dobie of the United States
Circuit Court of Appeals for the Fourth Circuit, Judge Sterling
Hutcheson and Judge Albert V. Bryan of the United States District
Court of Eastern Virginia. The trial began in Richmond on Monday,
February 25, 1952, and continued through Friday, February 29.
Oliver W. Hill, attorney for the plaintiffs, and witnesses for the
plaintiffs contended that segregation breeds inferiority. John J. Brooks,
director of the experimental interracial New Lincoln School of New
York City, in his testimony told the court that segregation violates
democracy and is frustrating. M. Brewster Smith, chairman of the
Psychology Department of Vassar College, testified that neither race

nor color determined a person's learning ability, and Isidor Chein of New York, director of the Commission on Community Inter-relations of the American Jewish Congress, expressed the view that segregation fosters feelings of inferiority and insecurity. Another witness for the plaintiffs, Kenneth Clark, a Negro, assistant professor of psychology at the City College of New York, testified that segregation had "a corroding effect" on the Negro child.

T. Justin Moore, a Richmond attorney, and J. Lindsay Almond, Jr., attorney general of Virginia, conducted the case for the defendants. They presented a number of witnesses. The first, T. J. McIlwaine, superintendent of schools in Prince Edward, testified that the Moton High School was superior to the Worsham High School, but inferior to the Farmville High School; planned improvements for the Negro high school would make it superior to the white schools, he told the court. One of the points at issue were the comparative facilities for teaching science in the white and Negro high schools. McIlwaine admitted the inferiority of the science facilities in the Negro schools, a situation which he explained by saying that the demand for science courses was less in the Negro school. On the point of science facilities Dean Thomas H. Henderson of Virginia Union University testified for the plaintiffs that Prince Edward had spent the preceding year $18.75 per Negro high school pupil for science and vocational training in comparison with $53.07 spent for the same purposes per white high school pupil. Moore of the defense counsel told the judges that salary schedules, teacher load, and attendance figures for white and colored pupils in Prince Edward were substantially the same. Maurice R. Large, then chairman of the County School Board, denied on the stand that the board had given the "run-around" to Negroes seeking improvements to the Moton School. He also testified that a survey by the State Department of Education gave higher priority to the needs of the Farmville and Worsham High Schools for improvement than to the Moton High School, but that the board had determined to proceed with the improvements to Moton first. Then W. Irving Dixon, a Richmond architect, testified that plans for the Negro school would make it superior to the white schools of the county. Other witnesses for the defendant School Board included President Colgate W. Darden of the University of Virginia, who told the court that Negroes were making progress in a segregated school system and that the abolition of segregation would impair the opportunities for both races. Dowell

J. Howard, state superintendent of public instruction, also testified to the progress of the Negro in a segregated system. Dabney S. Lancaster, president of Longwood College and a former superintendent of public instruction, was another witness for the defendants. The last witness for the defendants was Henry E. Garrett, head of the Psychology Department of Columbia University; he took the position that "no reasonable man could defend segregation if it stigmatized a minority group"; however, he thought that given equal facilities, the Negro high school student would get a better education in segregated schools than in mixed schools. With his testimony the defense rested, and the five-day hearing was concluded.[107]

Judges Dobie, Hutcheson, and Bryan handed down their decision on March 7, a week after the hearing of the case had ended. They upheld one of the plaintiff's contentions and ordered relief granted on that, but they rejected the other. The special court found that the Negro school buildings, facilities, curricula, and means of transportation were "not substantially equal" to those provided white pupils, and it ordered the Prince Edward school authorities to equalize the schools "with all reasonable diligence and dispatch." On the other hand, it found that the laws which required separate but equal facilities did not hurt or harm children of either race; segregation is not founded, the judges held, on prejudice or caprice or some other measureless foundation, but is one of the ways of life in Virginia. In reaching a decision on this point, the special court accepted the decisions which upheld segregation on the separate but equal basis "as apt and able precedent."[108]

The plaintiffs, "disappointed" at the decision of the court, immediately decided to appeal to the United States Supreme Court.[109]

When the Prince Edward segregation case reached the Supreme Court, other cases involving the same issue had also been appealed to that court. The court heard all the cases; in addition to the Prince Edward case were cases from Clarendon County, South Carolina; Topeka, Kansas; Delaware; and the District of Columbia. Hearings on the appeals began December 9, 1952, and continued through December 11. The small chamber of the Supreme Court was filled to capacity at the beginning of the hearing; about half of the 300 were Negroes, while the crowd of 450 which had gathered in the corridor outside the chamber was predominantly Negro. All of the cases except the Delaware case had been appealed by the Negroes who in the lower courts had lost their suits to end segregation; in

Delaware the State Supreme Court had ruled segregation in the schools unconstitutional, and the school authorities were the appellants.[110]

Meanwhile the Prince Edward County School Board had proceeded with its plans to build a new Negro high school and to comply with the decree of the special court. Land south of Farmville, just off Route 15 on the road to Zion Hill Church, was selected as the site and purchased. The commodious and handsomely appointed new Robert R. Moton High School building was occupied in the fall of 1952. The building cost approximately $900,000.

A year after the case had been argued in the Supreme Court, the Richmond *Times-Dispatch* sent two reporters to Prince Edward to find out what the Negroes who were actually involved in the suit thought. The reporters visited only nineteen of the sixty-nine families involved, but they found that only five of the families contacted favored the abolition of segregation, six favored segregation, and eight were undecided or took a "middle ground."[111] The concern of some of these was not so much an integrated school system as it was an improvement of school facilities for Negro high school students, but in the planning of the National Association for the Advancement of Colored People, the Prince Edward suit was to be one of the test cases on segregation in the public schools.

From time to time a decision was expected. Finally, on May 17, 1954, the Supreme Court handed down a decision affirming the principle on which the decrees in the several cases involving segregation in the public schools would be based. In a unanimous decision read by Chief Justice Earl Warren the court held that segregation in the public schools is unconstitutional. It delayed until its fall term hearings on the decrees to be entered to put the decision into effect; these hearings have been scheduled for December 6, 1954. Thus the Prince Edward school system is involved in a case of the greatest significance; the principle already affirmed calls for a change in social standards which have prevailed in the county from its first settlement. It marks another step in the continuing effort to solve the problem of how the white and Negro races are to live together in the South—a problem foreshadowed when the Dutch slaver brought the first African slaves to Virginia in 1619, a problem which has given concern to the best thinkers and the ablest leaders the state has produced.

CHAPTER XVII

Building a New Economy

DEFEAT in the War between the States meant not only a political reconstruction imposed by the conquerors and a long, hard fight to redeem the Southern states and their localities from that rule; it meant, too, an economic reconstruction which involved making a fresh start on the ruins of the old economy. The difficulties which Prince Edward people faced in 1865 can scarcely be realized by people who do not remember those times. But picture, if you can, the plight of a people whose money was worthless, whose system of labor had been suddenly changed, who had lost by force and without hope of compensation a substantial investment, whose country had been ravaged, whose supplies had been stolen or plundered or destroyed. That was Prince Edward in 1865.

Even the vital statistics reflected the desolation of the county: for the year 1865 the number of deaths exceeded the number of births by 61; there were 172 deaths and 111 births.[1] In contrast there were 206 births and only 94 deaths reported in 1867 in Prince Edward.[2]

The first tide of immigration into Prince Edward after the war was from the North. The newcomers were not welcomed with the hospitality which had greeted visitors and strangers in more pleasant days. The object of the new immigrants, political and economic advantage, was understood and held in contempt. A number of Northern families settled in Prince Edward at this time, especially in and around Farmville.

Another type of immigration, which came a little later, was more cordially welcomed. These immigrants were from England, and their coming was regarded as bringing help for the economic recovery of the South. In the spring of 1868 two parties of English colonists arrived in Lynchburg, brought to this country under the auspices of the Virginia Immigration Society. Among these immigrants were several skilled mechanics, who found employment awaiting them. Contemporary with their arrival was the effort to arouse interest in Prince Edward in the English immigration.[3]

General John B. Imboden of Richmond and a Mr. Hazzard of London addressed the people of Prince Edward and Cumberland at a meeting in Farmville May 16, 1868, on the subject of immigration.[4]

Alfred Moth is said to have been the first of the English migration to settle in Prince Edward.[5] Most of the immigrants decided to farm, and many purchased farms in the county. Thomas Homer bought Oakland, which had been the home of Richard K. Randolph and the Berkeleys. Henry D. Jacob acquired Oak Grove, once the home of David F. Womack. Longwood, seat of Nathaniel E. Venable, passed into the hands of Wright Barber. Captain T. H. Butcher bought the farm on Spring Creek which had in earlier times been the home of Peter LeGrand. The Englishmen settled principally in the country between Hampden-Sydney and Five Forks, in what was called the Spring Creek colony, and in and around Farmville, as the few examples of their purchases indicate. One of the migration, Charles Bugg, decided not to farm on the advice of a friend, Dr. Benjamin C. Peters, who had settled in Farmville before the war; Dr. Peters warned against undertaking to farm in Virginia without experience. Bugg came to Farmville in 1869 and entered the grocery business; for a time he operated the Randolph House.[6]

Various organizations were formed, all with the purpose of promoting social intercourse among the settlers, of encouraging further immigration, and at least one to promote more friendly relations between the newcomers and the old residents. In 1873 there was the Southside Virginia Board of Settlers, with offices for the year located in Chase City; this board, from its officers, aimed to encourage migration from the North and from England. Judge R. W. Wright of Connecticut was president, and the Rev. J. Y. Ashenhurst of Ohio chairman of the executive committee. J. A. H. St. Andrew of England was deputy chairman of the executive committee. Charles Bugg and Alfred Moth were chairman and secretary of the standing committee on English colonies in Prince Edward and the neighboring counties, and Charles E. Madison and T. G. Sutherland were chairman and secretary of the committee on Canadian colonies.[7]

A British Society, primarily social in its function, was organized at a dinner at the Randolph House December 12, 1873; Henry Jacob was president, Charles Bugg first vice-president, Henry Bowler second vice-president, J. A. H. St. Andrew third vice-president, Charles E. Madison secretary, and the English and American Bank treasurer; the executive committee consisted of Alfred Moth, Edgar Allan,

Richard Powys, A. G. Powell, Thomas Armstrong, F. H. King, Thomas Homer, and T. R. Wylie.[8] The British Society decided to join with the Richmond committee in celebrating the Queen's birthday in 1874; at the same meeting, in Farmville, the society, "many of whose members intend to become United States citizens, disclaimed any intention of obtruding its political views on the people of the state"; it expressed a desire to promote the interests of Virginia "for whose institutions and people they entertain profound respect."[9]

In 1875 the Southside Virginia Immigration Society was organized, with its office in Farmville. Management was vested in an executive committee, which consisted of F. N. Watkins, president, J. A. H. St. Andrew, vice-president, Albert R. Hurd, treasurer, J. W. Womack, secretary, and J. S. Stanley-James, corresponding secretary. Judge Watkins appointed an organization committee representing both citizens and settlers: for the former, Dr. W. W. H. Thackston, N. E. Venable, Major H. R. Hooper, Captain J. W. Womack, W. D. Rice, J. A. Dalby, the Rev. Dr. R. L. Dabney, Colonel J. P. Fitzgerald, and Dr. Peter Winston; and for the latter, Charles Bugg, Albert Hurd, Jr., Alfred Moth, F. Harper Twelvetrees, Edgar Allan, J. S. Stanley-James, J. A. H. St. Andrew, Major A. G. Powell, and Dr. R. R. Stevenson. As no effort had been made to attract settlers since the panic of 1873, the executive committee decided to advertise in newspapers of New York, Pittsburgh, Baltimore, Indianapolis, Cincinnati, Des Moines, and other Northern and Western cities.[10]

Still later a Clarendon Association was formed, to ask for a post-office for the Spring Creek colony, which planned a town Clarendon at St. Anne's Church. The association also planned to lay off a public cemetery; it reserved ten acres for a Negro settlement. Thomas Homer was president, T. T. Tredway, R. C. Morton, T. H. Butcher, John Siddons, and Henry Jacob, vice-presidents, and C. W. Crawley, secretary.[11]

The English settlers undertook to recreate in Prince Edward English social life of the best sort. So, after the dinner which followed the consecration of their new church, they had a cricket game. Walter N. and Richard A. N. Powys, "mighty hunters and athletes in the old country," who bought "a fine plantation" five miles from Farmville, brought English game to Prince Edward. Walter Powys, whose prowess as cricketer and bowler was recorded in *Forest and Stream*, returned to England in the spring of 1874 to play for Cambridge in the University cricket match; on his return in the fall he brought thirty-two pair of English rabbits (similar to the Virginia hare) and two pair of English pheasants; half of the rabbits which he brought were of the peculiar breed of black rabbits, which he obtained from Hawkstone, Lord Hill's seat in Shropshire. These he turned loose on his Prince Edward farm. He planned to bring back on a later trip partridges and song birds. An English farmer did not look with favor on some of these importations: "Future generations," he was of opinion, "will curse the name of Powys for introducing the rabbit into Virginia."[12]

Not all the importations were game. Some brought blooded livestock. Neal Campbell, a Scotchman who settled in the Spring Creek colony in 1872, was gored to death in 1875 by the Alderney bull which he had brought over.[13]

When the Farmville British Association met on September 3, 1875, at Randolph House, the members dined on the traditional British fare of roast beef and plum pudding, and drank toasts in Bowler's ale. Officers elected at this meeting were Henry Jacob president, Charles Bugg, J. A. H. St. Andrew, and Thomas Homer, vice-presidents, and Alfred Moth, secretary and treasurer. The executive committee consisted of Edgar Allan, R. A. N. Powys, Thomas Armstrong, John Houston, John Webb, Robert Battersly, and Walter N. Powys.[14]

The Farmville *Mercury* of the period painted a bright picture of the life and activities of the English. Its publishers, St. Andrew, Madison and Company, in a promotion advertisement in 1873, described Prince Edward as "largely settled with wealthy Englishmen and Northerners whose aggregate purchases of goods reach an enormous total."[15] This was an obvious exaggeration, for the bulk of the white people, even then, was of the old stock, and more than half the total population was Negro. While there were some newcomers of means, there were also many less fortunately circumstanced. And the means of some who had come with money dwindled as they found farming an unprofitable venture. One of the English immigrants wrote home to a friend and patron asking the loan of $300 to buy a farm; the request was refused, with the advice that while it is "good to get a bit of land to work for yourself," it is a "bad plan to begin farming on borrowed money," and the immigrant "must be content to wait a year or two until you can save the money." That was in 1875.[16] In 1882 the same patron sent the same immigrant $50 to "clear his debt," but he was instructed not to pay the merchant until he got his deed and then to send the deed, after having it registered, to John B. Crenshaw of Richmond, a friend of the patron, who would keep it until he had repaid the loan.[17] Several of the English families remained in Prince Edward, but most of them returned to England. While they were in Virginia, the Englishmen kept faithfully the customs of home. Again in 1877 they celebrated the Queen's birthday, that year in Petersburg on May 24, with St. Andrew and Edgar Allan on the arrangements committee.[18]

The English had come, and many had gone, when the next significant migration reached the county. Early in 1898 it was reported that land around Meherrin was being bought and cultivated by Germans and people from other foreign countries.[19] Four years later a news item from Meherrin noted that "the German settlers continue to arrive" and mentioned the unloading of several cars of furniture during early March, 1902, and the moving in of four or five families.[20] Some Germans were settling in other parts of the county, too, and in 1904 Germans of the Lutheran faith organized two congregations, one at Meherrin, the other at Farmville. Scattered families of Germanic background or origin settling in other communities tended to become identified with the churches which had already been established; so in the eastern part of the county the Brandaus, the Franks, and the Schmidts became connected with the Methodists and the Cooks (Koche was the original spelling) with the Baptists.[21] These families had a more successful experience in farming than their English predecessors, and many of them have continued to prosper in Prince Edward.

About the time the German migration was under way, there came to eastern Prince Edward another group of newcomers. These were native Virginians, from Pittsylvania and Halifax Counties, and they came to Prince Edward to cultivate flue-cured tobacco when it was found that the soil in certain portions of the county was suitable for this variety of the ancient staple. For the first three decades of the twentieth century there was a fairly steady stream of migration from these counties in which the cultivation of flue-cured tobacco had been in progress since the discovery of the method of curing "yellow" tobacco in 1839. This group continues to form a sizable element in the population of eastern Prince Edward.

The last migration into Prince Edward belongs to the past decade and a half. It had its origin in East Tennessee, and a number of families from that section have moved into Prince Edward and adjacent counties;. here they have bought farms and have become identified with the life of the several communities in which they have located.

Migration for Prince Edward has not been a one-way movement. The emigration which has been in progress since the early settlement has continued through the years. People have been moving out as others have moved in; so Prince Edward shares with the rest of the nation the characteristic of being the home of a migratory people. Defeat in 1865, the consequent poverty, the trying Reconstruction were stimuli to many to go elsewhere to seek opportunity. Kentucky in the postwar years beckoned as it had in the post-Revolutionary era. Some found opportunity there, although hardships remained. J. J. Morgan went to Christian County, Kentucky, where he and his wife kept two toll gates, for which they were paid $450 a year. He wrote John Woodall: "If you have the money to run you the first year, come out here. You can do well. If you don't have that, you'll suffer as you never have if you come." Young men would get $16 to $26 a month—attractive wages for the times—in Kentucky.[22] Others went to other sections of the West and South. When the sugar producers of Louisiana were prospering in the late nineteenth century, many young men from eastern Prince Edward sought and found employment there. They had entree to that section through Ernest L. Monnot, himself a sugar planter who as a Confederate soldier had had a tour of guard duty at High Bridge and while there had met Miss Lelia Lockett, a daughter of James S. Lockett. Mr. Monnot and Miss Lockett were married in 1870. Through this connection came news of prosperity in the sugar country and of opportunities for young men.

The Negroes, too, began to seek employment opportunities in other sections. The bituminous coal fields in Southwest Virginia and West Virginia were opened to development in 1883. For some forty years thereafter they proved attractive to Negroes from Prince Edward, although the migration to West Virginia fell off markedly after World War I. They also sought employment in cities of the North: New York, Philadelphia, Jersey City, Newark, Baltimore, Washington. During World War I the Bethlehem Steel Works at Sparrows Point, Maryland, offered employment to many. Young women of that race, as well as the men, sought employment opportunities "up North" and found them in domestic employment. Many of these had been trained in housework by white matrons, who, after slavery, continued to take young colored girls into their homes and give thorough training in cooking, serving, and cleaning.

The end of the war emancipated the slaves in Prince Edward, and farmers had to find a new system of labor. Some slaves remained with their former masters as hired hands, continuing to live in their old quarters. For the work of these hired men in 1865 William Weaver paid in supplies, according to the receipt:

                                                    "November 13, 1865

"Received in full for our services the present year of William Weaver 22 barrels of corn 11 bushels wheat 13 gallons molases 1 bushel peas 1 gallon peach brandy"

The following signed by mark, all attested by Charles G. Weaver and R. H. Walton: Old man Ned, Old man Dick, Old man Cato, Archer, Ed, Sam, boy William Archer, girl Susan.

How the wages were arrived at is not certain; the wheat would grind into two barrels of flour.

In 1866 Weaver paid cash wages; on December 25 of that year four Negroes signed receipts (by mark) for payments for labor: Sam'l Rains for $80, Lucy Hines for $30, William Archer for $40, Charles Anderson for $40 and clothing for his wife and children. On the same day other payments were made: Cato Hines, $36; Samuel Rains, $29.50; Lucy Hines, $21; William Archer, $13.98.[23]

Fortunate was the farmer who had not sold his 1864 tobacco crop before the surrender at Appomattox and who had not had it destroyed by invading armies. These farmers must have been few, for this writer has been able to learn of only one in Prince Edward. They had something to sell for United States money when the war was over, and with the cash thus earned they were able to get a quicker start at rebuilding from the wreck of war. Most farmers, however, were not so fortunate; if they had not sold their 1864 crop, it, along with supplies of food and feed, was destroyed by the invader. This meant for many that there was no cash income until the beginning of the sale of the 1865 crop in the spring of 1866.[24]

It was not long, though, before there was some effort at improved farm practices. In the spring of 1869 William B. Wootton of Rice bought seed Norway oats from Vermont; his yield was six times as great as that of the common winter oat, and he regarded the Norway variety as "far superior to any other oat in this country." He offered the seed for sale at $5 per bushel.[25]

There was interest in livestock, too. The Messrs. Hurd just outside Farmville sheared a flock of 190 sheep in June, 1874, and got 850 pounds of wool; the fleece of a two-year old Merino ram weighed thirteen pounds.[26] Major A. R. Venable, Jr., went in for pigs at his Edgewood Stock Farm near Farmville. He advertised seventy pigs for sale in April, 1878: forty at $15 each; twenty, from imported stock, at $20 each; and ten, from imported premium boars and sows, at $50 each. To encourage interest in hog raising, Major Venable offered prizes to purchasers of his pigs who would exhibit at least five at the Virginia State Fair: $25 for the finest pig, $15 for the second, and $10 for the third.[27] P. S. Smithson advertised that the thoroughbred stallion, Young Revenue, would stand at his stables in Farmville during the 1873 season.[28] And there was encouragement of soil conservation practices; General James R. Slayton of New York, speaking at the Courthouse on March 9, 1875, pointed out a field on the nearby farm of Major A. G. Powell on which was a field of clover which in 1874 yielded two tons of hay to the acre and two years before had been bare.[29]

The arrival of a new insect pest was noted in 1875; it was the Colorado potato beetle, for which the best insecticide was Paris green.[30]

The economic order which emerged from the War between the States, in the victorious North as well as in the defeated South, put the farmer very much at the mercy of those from whom he bought and to whom he sold and of the railroad which carried his goods. He was not satisfied with the situation in which he found himself, and he and his neighbors formed organizations to promote his interests. One of the earliest farm organizations was the Grange. The first local grange in Prince Edward of which this writer has found record was the Prospect District grange, organized by Colonel D. S. Curtiss at Oakland, then the home of J. J. Homer, on December 17, 1873.[31] Other local units were organized shortly thereafter. The Bush and Sandy Grange was organized by J. W. Morton, state deputy, in February, 1874, at Sandy River Church. Colonel Henry Stokes was master, William Walton, overseer, H. W. Edmunds, lecturer, S. Spain, steward, R. R. Cralle, assistant steward, John F. Walton, secretary, Edwin Edmunds, chaplain, Dr. T. J. Owen, treasurer, Colin Stokes, gatekeeper, Mrs. F. L. Stokes, Ceres, Mrs. H. W. Edmunds, Pomona, Miss M. J. Stokes, Flora, and Mrs. M. W. Meredith, lady assistant steward.[32] The next month a grange was organized in Farmville by T. T. Tredway, deputy, with Walter H. Richardson, master, and A. W. Drumeller, C. R. Venable, Dr. H. E. Watkins, R. Hubard, Mrs. Colonel (J. T.) Ligon, Mrs. W. F. Anderson, and Mrs. Drumeller, officials.[33] Tredway organized the Liberty Grange in the Green Bay community in April, 1874; E. N. Wing was master and G. S. Wing secretary of this unit.[34] The next year a new grange was formed at Spring Mills (Redd's Shop) with James Gallagher as master, J. J. Riggins, overseer, and E. Shupe, treasurer.[35]

The granges showed concern in matters which affected farm life. The Prospect Grange in March, 1875, asked for a bridge over the Appomattox at Beazley's Ford.[36] In the same month the district grange, meeting in Farmville, "adopted both warehouses, leaving it discretionary with the seller to patronize either."[37] In other words, both Randolph's and Farmville Warehouse were put on the Grange's approved list. The battle which the Bush and Briery Agricultural Club had joined in 1858 over the marketing of tobacco was still going on in 1875, when the Farmville District Grange went on record as favoring the retention of public warehouses and the inspection system; it opposed converting public warehouses into private, because the selling charges would be increased, and accused the legislature of making such a transfer possible by delaying action on the matter.[38]

An example of the pressure which the manufacturer put upon distributors may be seen in Major A. R. Venable, Jr.'s, experience with the Farmer's Friend plow; the manufacturer fixed a selling price, which Major Venable thought too high; his agency was cancelled. At a meeting on Christmas Day, 1875, the Bush and Sandy Grange protested the imposition of "very arbitrary terms . . . on our respected agent and fellow patron"; and in a resolution members of the unit pledged not to buy a Farmer's Friend plow at any price from any dealer "except our agent." Public notice of that decision was signed by W. L. Clark, secretary of the grange.[39]

In 1878 the *Southside Sentinel* (Burkeville) reported satisfaction in Prince Edward that the Grangers were considering road laws and would propose amendments the next winter.[40]

T. T. Tredway was active in the grange; in the spring of 1874 he was appointed deputy for Prince Edward, Buckingham, and Appomattox; in January, 1875, he was elected overseer of the State Grange, and two months later he was elected district master.[41]

Another grange activity was the operation of a cooperative store; such a store seems to have been opened in Farmville about 1877;

one effect of its operation was the reduction of the price of sugar three cents a pound within six months; the store later closed, and in 1880 the price of sugar was reported as high as ever.[42]

The Farmers Union for Prince Edward, Cumberland, and Buckingham was chartered in 1886 with its principal office in Farmville and its purpose the manufacture of farming "utensils" and the operation of stores.[43]

The organization of farmers which did operate cooperative stores for a time during this period was the Farmers Alliance. Major A. R. Venable, Jr., was elected state business agent of the alliance in 1890, when an exchange was established in Richmond. W. A. Barrow attended the 1891 convention in Richmond as delegate from Prince Edward; he received an expense allowance of $12.30 for his trip.[44] The Farmers Alliance, Local No. 314, was organized at Rice May 11, 1889. The Alliance acquired property for a store in 1896, J. Y. Phillips and wife conveying a lot forty-four feet wide and 102 feet deep to Dr. H. E. Watkins and W. H. Hubbard, trustees.[45] For some time the Alliance operated a store on this property. Later it was leased on a long-term basis to J. R. Weaver and Sons, now the Weaver Company. The Farmers Alliance became connected with the Populist party in the 1890's.[46]

With the turn of the century there came to Prince Edward two developments in agriculture which were to contribute greatly to farm prosperity. One was the introduction of flue-cured tobacco in the eastern and a part of the southern section of the county. Cultivation of this type of tobacco spread in the 1850's after the discovery of the curing process. It had received decided impetus with the invention of the automatic cigarette machine which was put into use by the firm of W. Duke Sons and Company of Durham, North Carolina, about 1885. The machine made possible the mass production of cigarettes. In 1890 James B. Duke of the Duke firm led in the formation of the tobacco trust, the American Tobacco Company, which made possible better distribution of cigarettes as well as more efficient manufacturing processes. The flue-cured tobacco was one of the essential types in the cigarette blend, and there was an increasing demand for it. When it was found that the lighter gray soils of eastern and southern Prince Edward were admirably suited to the cultivation of bright tobacco, farmers began to produce the new variety. Since the curing particularly and the preparation for market required the services of experienced persons, farmers who were familiar with its cultivation were encouraged to move from Pittsylvania and Halifax Counties to make the crop in Prince Edward. Their coming gave rise to a new type of farm operation for Prince Edward, farming on shares. Since 1865, the farm operator and the help which he could hire had furnished the labor. Now the hired hand was gradually supplanted by the tenant.

A comparison of prices of flue-cured and dark-fired tobacco explains why farmers whose soil was adapted to bright tobacco built fireboxes and installed flues in their old curing barns. One farmer made fourteen curings of bright tobacco in 1901 which he sold for prices ranging from $20 to $31 per hundred;[47] another's first sales of his 1902 crop of fifty curings averaged $18;[48] in contrast, dark tobacco prices for the 1902 crop ranged from $2.50 per hundred for common lugs to $13 for the best long.[49] Danville and South Boston were the principal markets for the Prince Edward production of flue-cured tobacco in the early years of its cultivation.[50]

The cultivation and harvesting of the early flue-cured tobacco was not unlike that of the dark-fired. It was topped low, rarely over nine or ten leaves, and was primed when topped. The entire plant was harvested at one time, by splitting the stalk, cutting it below the leaves, and hanging it on the stick for curing. This type of tobacco was desirable for chewing tobaccos. The increased consumption of cigarettes increased the demand for a thinner, brighter leaf than that produced in Prince Edward. Farmers about 1930 began growing a different type of bright tobacco, varieties which were produced in the southern sections of the flue-cured belt. These varieties ripened gradually from the ground leaves upward and were harvested by pulling the leaves as they ripened and tieing them in bundles of two or three leaves on the sticks. When cured, these leaves were much thinner and brighter than the older type of flue-cured and were much more desirable for cigarettes. The plants were topped much higher, at twenty leaves or more. In 1934 the older type had its last good year; by 1936 the flue-cured production in Prince Edward was almost entirely of the cigarette type.

With the end of World War II there came a change in the fuel used for curing. Previously wood had been used exclusively. Since the curing process required continuing heat, at increasing temperatures, until it was completed, the use of wood meant constant attention, day and night. After the war farmers began to install oil burners in barns for the curing process. These were regulated by thermostats; the farmer could set the thermostat to provide a flow of oil to give the desired temperature and have a steady heat at that temperature until he changed it. Oil curers took much of the drudgery out of curing; the night-long vigils became memories for those who cured with oil.

About the time the cultivation of flue-cured tobacco was introduced into Prince Edward, dairying began on a small scale. One of the pioneer dairymen of the county, W. B. Gates, reported his experience during the period October 1, 1901, to October 1, 1902, in the Farmville *Herald*; so impressive was his report and so significant his experience that the Norfolk and Western Railway Company had 10,000 copies of the letter printed and distributed to encourage farmers to begin dairying. Gates reported that during that year he had milked nine Jersey cows, which came fresh all along during the year, some being dry a part of the time. He sold 1,611 gallons of cream, netting $1,204.67 from the sales. After deducting $160 which was spent for bran and cottonseed meal, he realized an average profit of $116 from each cow's production. He estimated that the skim milk fed to calves and pigs covered the cost of the rough feed and ensilage. He hired an extra hand at the annual cost of $150. Dairying, he advised, required personal attention. The farmer had to grow a lot of peas and clover, but these improved the soil. Dairying provided an abundance of manure for tobacco and corn land, and Gates used it also for top dressing grain and grass. It did not mean that lots were grazed too close. It was his practice to feed sorghum to the cows from September to December, then ensilage, straw, and hay until April, then rye for a while, pasturing the herd on broom sage the rest of the year.

The farmer going into dairying could expect a ready market: the demand for cream in Virginia was greater than the supply. A farmer with suitable buildings and fences and eight or ten cows would have to spend about $175 for a silo, separator, milk tester, cans, jackets, and ice-box in order to get started. Gates separated the cream immediately after milking; he passed the cream over an aerator to a cooler by which the temperature was reduced to about fifty degrees and then to the ice-box. Ice, he advised, was indispensable.[51]

From that beginning dairying has become a major farm enterprise in Prince Edward, especially in the eastern part of the county. The Guernsey breed became popular with Prince Edward dairymen during the 1920's. From H. E. Boswell, George Watts Hill bought the famous Guernsey bull, High Point Prince Maxim, and three daughters of that sire for $10,000 in 1930. High Point Prince Maxim was the foundation of the fine herd which Hill has developed at Quail Roost Farm, Durham County, North Carolina, and is considered probably the finest bull in the South. Each of the three cows in this purchase later made records of over 800 pounds of butterfat production in a year. In the consideration in this transaction, High Point Prince Maxim's selling price was $7,500, the selling price of the three cows $2,500[52]

Cream from these dairies was first shipped by train to Richmond. With the building of good roads dairymen found that trucks provided quicker service. It was in 1928 that a truck operated by E. C. Andrews began providing daily delivery of milk (by this time dairymen were shipping whole milk) from Rice to Richmond; about the same time dairymen around Burkeville and Green Bay also began shipping by truck.

To provide a local market for cream, the Farmville Creamery was established in 1906 through the efforts of A. F. Howard of Needham. G. M. Robeson was first president. The creamery board of directors bought cows to sell to suppliers. But the effort was premature; after two years the creamery suspended operations. It was re-opened in 1922 under the management of F. O. Jones. The present plant was built in 1938.[53]

In the decade following World War I, commercial orcharding was introduced into Prince Edward. Peach and apple orchards were set out in Leigh District, in the section between Burkeville and Meherrin. Peach orchards were planted in the Prospect section, where so many varieties of fruit had been developed in the antebellum period. These orchards proved successful ventures and continue an important factor in Prince Edward agriculture.

The cultivation of burley tobacco was introduced into the county in the late 1930's.

When the War between the States ended, the threshing machine was the only piece of what would now be considered farm machinery in use on Prince Edward farms. An improved thresher made its appearance not long after the war, a premium thresher and separator known as the Sweepstakes; it threshed, separated wheat from chaff, cleaned wheat for market, and stacked straw; as both power and thresher were mounted, the outfit was easily located to begin threshing. Major A. R. Venable, Jr., of Farmville advertised threshing with one of these machines at a moderate cost in 1873; about this time J. S. Bradshaw of Rice also bought a threshing machine of this type. Both machines enjoyed an extensive custom during harvesting seasons of the 1870's.[54] The threshing machine was generally replaced during the 1930's by the combine, which, as the name indicates, combined the operations of both binder and threshing machine. On some farms operators still use both binder and threshing machine, but these are now few. The binder had come into general use in wheat harvesting by World War I, its use having steadily increased over a period of years.

After the close of World War I there was some effort to introduce tractors on Prince Edward farms. Distributors would hold demonstrations of their machines to show how they worked and their advantages. But the tractor did not "catch on" with Prince Edward farmers at this time. A few bought the machines in the period of farm prosperity just after the war, but they were used on a limited scale. It was not until the late 1930's that they came into widespread use on Prince Edward farms; prior to this they were found principally on dairy farms. Their popularity on the eve of the outbreak of World War II and during and since that war has marked the mechanization of many farms. Most of the equipment is now powered by tractor, and the horse-drawn implements, except for the cultivation of row crops, principally tobacco, have become rare. The mechanization on Prince Edward farms which has taken place within the past decade and a half has been phenomenal.

During the past year another new practice has been introduced among Prince Edward farmers. In July, 1953, Booker H. Cunningham installed an irrigation system at Millbank, the farm of his father, H. C. Cunningham. Drawing upon the copious flow of the north fork of Spring Creek, he was able to provide an adequate water supply for all the crops on this farm and the garden as well. This was the first farm irrigation system to be installed in the county.[55]

Mechanization has been the answer to the steadily diminishing supply of farm labor. As long ago as 1883 a Prince Edward lady writing to a friend who was then living in Mecklenburg the news of the community attributed a neighbor's indisposition to his inability to get enough labor to farm like he wanted to.[56] Farm labor was reported scarce in 1905; when a writer for the Farmville *Herald* saw five men at work in the garden of T. Henry Glenn at Prospect in May of that year he thought it worth noting in view of the prevailing conditions.[57]

The marketing of tobacco, which aroused the concern of Prince Edward farmers when the Richmond tobacco exchange was opened in 1858, continued after the war to present problems. The inspection of tobacco was revived at Farmville Warehouse in 1870.[58] In the 1870's there were two inspectors appointed for each warehouse, one to represent the state, the other the owners of the warehouse. Inspectors at Randolph Warehouse in 1875 were R. A. Booker for the state, John R. Cunningham for the owners; and at Farmville Warehouse William T. Johnson for the state, and Edwin N. Price for the owners.[59]

The Farmville Tobacco Board of Trade favored the long-established inspection system. In resolutions unanimously adopted January 13, 1875, and signed by G. B. Wright president and C. C. Read secretary, the board announced its opposition to the repeal of the inspection laws; favored the appointment of two inspectors at each warehouse where tobacco was sold at public auction, one by the Governor, the other by the warehouse owners; and advocated repeal of the law permitting warehouse owners to convert from public (where there were inspectors) to private (where there were no inspectors) warehouses.[60]

The State Agricultural Society was also concerned about tobacco marketing conditions, and its president, Colonel William C. Knight, appointed to a committee to study the matter the following from Farmville: C. C. Read, representing the manufacturers; A. R. Venable, the commission merchants; and George W. Booker, the dealers.[61] A meeting of Prince Edward planters on November 16, 1875, of which R. W. Scott was chairman and B. H. Carter secretary, notified the agricultural society's committee of their endorsement of the Burkeville convention held August 11.[62]

A third warehouse was built in Farmville in 1875 "on the vacant lot west of the Presbyterian Church" by John R. Wilson, W. R. Berkeley, and Scott and Davis. The name Planters was given to this warehouse on its establishment, and George W. Harrison of Lunenburg and William Corson of Cumberland were named inspectors there by the Prince Edward court.[63]

By 1893 the Planters Warehouse had become the property of a corporation. At the annual meeting of the stockholders on May 22,

1893, S. W. Paulett was elected president, J. R. Martin secretary-treasurer, and S. W. Paulett, R. S. Paulett, W. P. Gilliam, E. T. Clark, C. T. Anderson, W. H. Richardson, R. M. Burton, H. E. Wall, and O. T. Wicker directors; and J. R. Whitehead and W. T. Johnson, inspectors.[64] J. R. Whitehead set a sales record at this warehouse on December 6, 1893, when he sold 239 piles of tobacco in one hour and forty minutes—over two piles a minute.[65] S. W. Watkins was chosen an inspector of tobacco at Planters Warehouse in 1895.[66] In 1897 this warehouse declared a dividend of eleven per cent.[67] Whitehead and Watkins were at this time inspectors at Planters; R. A. Booker and C. R. Morton inspectors at Randolph's; and R. W. Garnett and J. A. Armistead at Farmville. Garnett was later at Planters Warehouse, where he was succeeded in 1903 by C. M. Bass; John D. Watkins was the other inspector at Planters at this time. In 1902 G. H. Morris and S. W. Sheppard, succeeding W. E. Garnett, were inspectors at the Star Warehouse, Farmville.[68]

The panic of 1893 brought hard times which were keenly felt in 1896. A comparison of prices showed that the same items, including a barrel of flour, dry goods, shoes, a suit of clothes, a keg of nails, ten pounds of coffee and ten pounds of sugar, which cost $50.14 in 1873 cost only $31.07 in 1896. If the comparison had ended there, the farmer at least would have had no complaint. But in 1873 he could sell 120 bushels of corn at seventy-five cents a bushel and receive $90; he could pay for the bill of goods chosen for comparative prices and have $39.86 left over. In 1896 he could get only twenty-five cents a bushel for his corn, so he would have to sell 130 bushels to get $32.50, enough to pay for the same goods and leave him $1.43. The merchant, too, had ground for complaint; in 1873 he made a profit of twenty-five per cent on the sale, and the farmer's purchases in the list would have yielded him a profit of $12.53; in 1896 his profit had been cut to eight per cent, on the same goods amounting to $2.48[69]

Against that background it is not surprising that there were complaints about the prices farm products were bringing. There were some directed against the Farmville tobacco market, to which W. P. Gilliam, at the time president of the Tobacco Board of Trade, replied:

"When such farmers as the Bondurant Brothers, Tom Carter, Hester Walton, Warren Fuqua, Bob Carter, and a great many others I could name, come to market, they bring good tobacco, they get good prices, they go home satisfied. You never hear them grumbling about low prices. Why? Because they attend to their own business and you don't see them in town every day finding fault and croaking, or sitting around public places continually."[70]

At this time other officers of the Tobacco Board of Trade were E. L. Morris, vice-president; F. M. Bugg, secretary; A. W. Drumeller, timekeeper; T. B. Hawkins, S. W. Paulett, and G. A. Dunlop, arbiters.[71] In 1902 the duties of treasurer had been added to Bugg's position, and a new office, that of bonded inspector, held by R. W. Garnett, had been added; also added were the inspectors of sales, S. W. Watkins and J. M. Venable; and W. H. Hubbard had replaced Hawkins in the trio of arbiters.[72]

The Tobacco Board had more to worry it, though, than the criticism of farmers. A more powerful pressure was directed against it from the opposite direction. The board had charged tobacco buyers a tax of four cents on each hundred pounds of tobacco bought to cover certain market expenses and for promotion. In 1903 the board relieved the buyer of this fee and increased the cost of selling tobacco from ten to fourteen cents per hundred. A mass meeting of farmers was held December 5, 1903, to discuss the increased cost of selling on the Farmville market. J. X. Morton was president of the meeting, and E. G. McGehee secretary; a permanent organization, the Tobacco Growers Protective Association, was set up, with Major J. R. Morton president, W. D. M. Stokes vice-president, and W. L. Clark secretary. W. P. Gilliam explained the position of the board of trade, but the farmers named a committee consisting of Ponsford Butcher, William Anderson, E. E. Hundley, and E. T. Bondurant to ask the board to reconsider the increase in selling charges.[73] The board may have undertaken to restore the tax on buyers, for in 1904 buyers for the American Tobacco Company and the Imperial Tobacco Company announced that they would not pay the charge.[74] Final action on the four-cent fee came in 1905, when the board repealed the duty; it followed the announcement of A. B. Willingham, Jr., buyer for the American Tobacco Company, that he had been instructed not to pay the fee and not to buy any tobacco on the market if it were not repealed. The American was then the tobacco trust, controlling approximately eighty per cent of the tobacco manufacturing industry in the United States; the board, "unwilling to run off the American" which afforded "the market's sharpest competition" bowed to the ruthless power of monopoly and repealed the fee.[75]

The farmers' organization, however, continued. Similar protective associations were formed in Charlotte and Cumberland, and a corresponding committee consisting of J. D. Shepperson of Charlotte, E. T. Bondurant of Prince Edward, and H. N. Madison of Cumberland was named to invite farmers to send delegates to meet in Farmville March 12, 1904, to organize a state association.[76] The Prince Edward association adopted broad goals, prepared by a committee consisting of E. T. Bondurant, H. E. Richardson, Lindsay B. Walthall, J. C. Hamlett, and H. A. Stokes: farmers should work for higher yields and work fewer acres; should diversify crops and raise enough food and feed at home; should transact business on a cash basis; should join the association; should avoid rushing tobacco to market; and should buy fertilizer in clubs.[77]

The meeting of delegates from various parts of Virginia was held, and the Farmers Association of Virginia was organized in Farmville; J. D. Shepperson was elected president; Major J. W. Flood of Appomattox, E. T. Bondurant, and Wesley Irby of Nottoway were named vice-presidents; W. D. M. Stokes secretary and W. L. Clark treasurer, both of Prince Edward. The executive committee of the association was authorized to set a minimum scale of prices, and members were asked to agree not to sell below that scale, provided fifty per cent of the white growers in the dark-fired belt joined the organization. Members were encouraged to sell their tobacco either in the barn or by samples, instead of through warehouses.[78]

The dark-fired tobacco growers of Virginia were encouraged by the experience of growers in Tennessee and Kentucky;[79] they, too, had organized, and their organizer, John Allen, spoke in Farmville November 6, 1905; there the grower prized his tobacco (in Virginia this ancient practice had by this time been abandoned and sales were made in the winter), and the association sold it.[80] The Virginia group appointed the J. E. Johnston Company of Farmville, of which E. L. Morris was manager, to rehandle, order, and prize tobacco for the association; H. M. Vaughan of the firm of I. N. Vaughan and Company of Richmond was named selling agent of the association.[81] The association in 1906 proposed to all merchants known to make advances on tobacco that they sign an agreement allowing the owners of the tobacco to sell by the method they preferred. J. F. Walton and Company, Duvall Son and Company, C. M. Walker's Sons, Paulett and Bugg, Charles Bugg and Son, the Farmville Commercial Company (subject to the approval of A. E. Cralle), (all of Farmville) and W. H. Hubbard, Bradshaw Brothers, and J. R. Weaver and Sons (all of Rice) signed the agreement with the proviso "as long as our interests are duly protected."[82]

A fourth warehouse, the Star, was operating in Farmville in 1905, with George W. Redd of Prince Edward and P. A. Grigg of Buckingham as inspectors.[83]

Saturday sales on the Farmville market were discontinued after January 1, 1907.[84]

In addition to the Farmville market, there were also warehouses in operation at Meherrin and Rice. On February 12, 1898, sale of 35,000 pounds of tobacco was reported at Meherrin; construction of a second warehouse was progressing rapidly, and there was interest in improving the old warehouse there.[85] The tobacco market at Rice originated in the effort to establish a market for flue-cured tobacco in Farmville. One warehouse operated for a number of years, closing when the Tri-State Tobacco Growers Association, to which it was leased, ceased operations in 1926. A second warehouse to which was given the name Liberty was built at Rice in 1919 and operated during the 1919-20 sales season. Farmville had a warehouse for the sale of flue-cured tobacco during the season 1927-28, which was operated by H. H. Hubbard, T. W. Bruce, and W. H. Price, properietors of the Randolph Warehouse. The Farmville bright tobacco market sold 684,866 pounds of tobacco at an average of $17.08.

The cultivation of burley tobacco in Prince Edward and adjacent counties reached such volume during World War II that a burley market was established at Farmville in 1944. Prior to the opening of this market, Prince Edward producers of burley tobacco had to sell their product at Abingdon, Virginia, or more distant markets in Eastern Tennessee and Western North Carolina. During the 1945-46 season almost 300,000 pounds of burley tobacco were sold in Farmville at an average of $39.69. This market has since been discontinued. A market for sun-cured tobacco was also operated for a time in Farmville, to accommodate local producers of that type of tobacco; in 1947-48, approximately 100,000 pounds of sun-cured were sold in Farmville.

The high prices paid for tobacco during and immediately after World War I ended temporarily concern over marketing methods. But in stimulating production those prices meant that efforts to provide more favorable methods for the farmer would be renewed when supply exceeded demand and prices dropped. That time was not long in coming, and after the substantial decline in farm income for the year 1920 a new organization of tobacco growers was discussed and launched. This was the Tri-State Tobacco Growers Association, organized to market both flue-cured and dark-fired tobacco. The organization operated certain warehouses, to which members delivered their tobacco. Upon delivery, members received payment of one-third the total sale price of the tobacco, and the balance was to be paid in subsequent installments. Members entered into five-year contracts to deliver their tobacco to the association. There was considerable interest in Farmville in the organization of the association, and the Town Council asked the business men of Farmville to help in enrolling members; the Chamber of Commerce appropriated $500 toward the expenses of a picnic and rally in the promotion of the association at Serpell Heights on July 20, 1922. Over 5,000 people attended the picnic. After the first year of operations the efficiency of the association began to diminish, and there was growing dissatisfaction. After four years of operation, the tri-state association ceased to function in 1926.

Low prices, complicated by poor crops resulting from unusually severe droughts in 1930 and 1932, prompted the dark-fired growers to make another attempt to organize a cooperative marketing venture. The Virginia Dark-Fired Tobacco Growers Marketing Association was organized in 1932, with two Prince Edward men in key positions: N. B. Davidson as president, and B. T. Taylor as general manager. Taylor died three months after his election as general manager and was succeeded by Thomas B. Hall. Farmville was selected as headquarters of the association, and its publication, *The Tobacco Grower*, was published in Farmville by the *Herald*. Randolph Warehouse has been operated for the association since 1932, and since 1938 Middle or Farmville Warehouse has also been a marketing place for the association. The present building of the Farmville Warehouse was erected in 1924 by J. N. Carter, for many years its operator. The Planters Warehouse, of which Joel Watkins was long proprietor, and which is now operated by Joel Watkins, Jr., continues as an independent warehouse.[86]

Among the agencies inaugurated by the Franklin D. Roosevelt administration in its depression recovery program was the Agricultural Adjustment Administration, which put into operation a program of crop reduction, with benefits paid to farmers participating in the program. In the case of flue-cured tobacco, acreage allotments for 1934 were fixed at seventy per cent of the average annual acreage on the farm during the three years preceding, and production quotas in pounds were also set for farms. Prince Edward crops under the agricultural adjustment program were the two types of tobacco, wheat, and corn and hogs. Committees for each crop were set up to supervise the program in the county. During the first year of operation the flue-cured tobacco committee consisted of W. S. Weaver, chairman, S. H. Bondurant, and R. E. Jenkins; the dark-fired tobacco committee of B. E. Taylor, chairman, D. C. Morris, and W. H. Price; the wheat production control committee was made up of W. H. Glenn, Robert Harris, and C. M. Redd; and the corn-hog committee of T. C. Hix, Robert Harris, and J. G. Hudson. Local committeemen for the program during its first year of operation (1934) were J. H. Allen, J. W. Redd, O. L. Vassar, E. N. Cunningham, J. D. Carter, J. D. Wilson, W. L. Vaughan, W. W. Vaughan, Robert Harris, A. M. Bolton, W. C. Glascock, and J. J. Gilliam. With the introduction of the Triple-A program began the practice of measuring the land in crops under production control and the issuance of marketing cards, which a farmer must have to sell without penalty a crop for which allotments have been established. This program has been changed from time to time since the AAA was declared unconstitutional by the United States Supreme Court; it is now the Agricultural Stabilization and Conservation program, and is directed at the local level by a county committee and district committees; D. C. Morris is the administrative official of the program in Prince Edward.

Federal aid to agriculture on the local level began in 1914 with the introduction of the farm demonstration service and the employment of county farm agents jointly by the United States Deepartment of Agriculture Extension Service and the local government. C. W. Mason was the first county agent in Prince Edward. In 1925 R. B. Crawford became county agent; he resigned in 1927 and was succeeded by E. F. Striplin who has since held that post. Home demonstration work was begun in Prince Edward in 1917 by Miss Claudia Hagy. Among her successors have been Miss Mary B. Settle, Miss Helen Alverson, Miss Courtney Farrar, and the present agent, Mrs. Frances W. Gee. The farm and home agents in the earlier period of their work organized a variety of clubs among boys and girls: corn clubs, calf clubs, pig clubs, poultry clubs, and the like, depending upon the youth's project and special interest. This multiplicity of clubs was supplanted by the 4-H Club, into which the youth program was coordinated. Striplin set up a county advisory board to promote improved farming practices. In 1935 this board included T. B. Hix, Prospect; F. C. Wilson, Farmville; H. E. Hamilton, Pamplin; J. H. Allen, Farmville; W. E. Chappell, Meherrin; G. W. Palmer, Green Bay; S. C. Coleman, Green Bay; J. T. Bruce, Rice; R. E. Jenkins, Burkeville; N. B. Davidson, Farmville; J. B. Wall, Farmville; F. O. Jones, Farmville; E. S. Shields, Farmville; W. A. Watson, Jr., Farmville; J. L. Bugg, Farmville; H. L. Bradshaw, Rice; W. L. Vaughan, Rice; J. R. Glenn, Prospect; W. C. Chick, Prospect; D. C. Morris, Darlington Heights; O. L. Vassar, Keysville; J. H. Ward, Meherrin; J. S. Shackleton, Meherrin; and R. B. Crawford, Farmville.[87]

The federal farm program also brought to Prince Edward the soil conservation service, which provides advice in formulating farm plans for advantageous utilization of the land and for soil conservation.

When Prince Edward was settled and for many years thereafter, the low grounds were considered the most desirable farm lands. A gradual filling up of the stream beds has changed this estimate, and most of the low grounds along the larger streams in the county have been abandoned for cultivation. As long as navigation of the Appomattox made it necessary to keep that stream free of obstructions, the tributary streams did not fill up and make their low grounds more subject to overflow. After navigation of the upper Appomattox was abandoned and the Upper Appomattox Company no longer kept the river clear of obstruction, steps were taken to provide for cleaning the rivers in Prince Edward. In 1886 the supervisors were authorized by the legislature to levy a tax of fifteen cents per acre of low grounds subject to overflow from Bush River, Buffalo (to Bell's mill), Spring Creek, and the north fork of Spring Creek (to Womack's mill) to be spent in keeping those streams free of obstructions.[88] The supervisors were permitted in 1890 to levy a tax of twelve cents an acre on Sandy River low grounds to finance cleaning that stream.[89] The legislature two years later authorized the supervisors of Prince Edward, Buckingham, and Cumberland to levy a twelve-cent tax on low grounds on the Appomattox for a similar purpose[90] In 1902 the legislature declared several Prince Edward streams as public highways: Briery, from the bridge between Worsham and Redd's Shop to its mouth; Bush, from Falkland farm to its mouth; and Sandy, from the southern boundary of Wing's farm to its mouth; a year later the Prince Edward supervisors were given authority to declare any stream in the county a public highway. When a creek or river was declared a public highway, the owners of the land along the stream were required to keep the streams clear and free of obstruction; the county court appointed overseers to inspect the streams in April and October, to notify landowners who had not cleaned the streams of their failure to perform their duty, and to clean the streams at the landowner's expense if he did not do so after being notified.[91] The supervisors in 1903 declared as public highways Buffalo from its mouth to W. E. Anderson's and C. R. Watson's land; Spring Creek to Ben Woodson's line; the north fork of Spring Creek to Womack's mill; and Fort Creek. C. C. Carter was named overseer for Spring Creek and Fort Creek and for Buffalo upstream from Martin's bridge.[92] Among the items ordered paid by the supervisors in 1906 were several relating to cleaning streams: J. E. Garrett, inspecting creek, $8; cleaning out creek at W. M. Morton's, $1; at Thomas A. Bolling's, $2, and at Mrs. Bettie Ligon's, $1.[93] In time this practice was abandoned. Occasional efforts were made thereafter to clean the stream beds. M. L. Hardy, then superintendent of the county poor farm, cleared Bush River of obstruction, removed sand bars, and straightened that stream in places when its bed was dry in the summer of 1930. One of the projects of the first federal works relief program in the county in the winter and spring of 1934 was the cleaning of Spring Creek. As an example of the extent and the rapidity with which stream beds were filling, Spring Creek at the bridge near Frank E. Allen's was some five or six feet below the bridge about 1890;[94] when the Civil Works Administration project began in 1934 the water was washing the sleepers of the bridge. The cleaning project, in which hammocks and other obstructions were removed from the bed of the stream between the bridge and the confluence of Spring Creek and Buffalo, lowered the level of the water by about a foot.

Several of the Farmville ante-bellum tobacco dealers and manufacturers continued their businesses after the war. Among them were C. C. Read, P. H. Jackson, C. W. Blanton, and R. S. Paulett.[95] Three factories were enlarged in 1873; C. W. Blanton added a story to his plant, R. S. Paulett more than doubled the facilities of his factory by erecting a large three-story building adjoining; and another story was added to the old Vaughan factory, in 1873 owned by Colonel W. R. Berkeley and occupied by W. P. Gilliam.[96] About this time C. C. Read handled the largest volume of tobacco of any Farmville tobacconist. A little later C. W. Blanton was in first place in the local tobacco industry, but first rank was soon taken by the Dunnington firm. In 1876 Walter G. Dunnington became associated with his father, James W. Dunnington, in the tobacco business established in 1870; in the succeeding years he built up the firm into one of the major dealers in dark-fired tobacco. Dunnington represented both the Italian and the Austrian Tobacco Regie, the former until his death in 1922, the latter until World War I. He also represented tobacco interests in many other foreign countries, especially Norway; on one day in 1902 a train of thirty cars loaded with tobacco consigned to Norway left Farmville.

Two new tobacco factories were built in Farmville in 1896 and in 1898; in the earlier year W. P. Gilliam rebuilt the Lee Hall factory; in the latter, the Pauletts built a five-story brick structure to replace the frame factories which had burned. The Paulett factory had a steam redrying capacity of 10,000 to 18,000 pounds daily and an air drying capacity of 1,000,000 pounds daily.

Among the other tobacco dealers in Farmville during the last quarter of the nineteenth century were B. L. Anderson, George B. Wright, A. W. Drumeller, C. M. Walker, E. L. Morris, J. R. Cunningham, and J. L. Putney. Only two independent tobacco dealers, the Dunnington Tobacco Company and J. L. Putney and Company, remain in Farmville. Since the death of W. G. Dunnington in 1922, his son, J. William Dunnington, has been the active head of the Dunnington Tobacco Company; Walter G. Putney has managed the Putney firm since the death of his father, J. L. Putney.[97] In 1891 J. B. Ragland began the manufacture of cigars in Farmville, continuing in this business for several years.[98]

Another industry using the product of Prince Edward farms was the tomato cannery opened at Rice in 1891, which engaged in a successful packing business for a number of years. Under the management of W. B. Gates, it processed the High Bridge brand of tomatoes, and the label carried a picture of a train crossing the High Bridge.[99]

The banking business in Prince Edward also had to make a fresh start after the war. In February, 1866, the Virginia General Assembly chartered the Planters Savings Bank with a maximum capital of $50,000 and William T. Rice, P. H. Jackson, H. E. Warren,

N. Cobb, and William G. Venable as incorporators.[100] The act of incorporation was re-enacted in April, 1867, with a maximum capital of $100,000 authorized.[101] Under the re-enactment the present Planters Bank and Trust Company began business. H. E. Warren was named president of the bank and William G. Venable cashier. In 1871 the name was changed to the Planters Bank of Farmville.[102]

In 1873 there were three other banking institutions in Farmville: the English and American Bank, the Farmville Insurance and Banking Company, and the Commercial Savings Bank.

The English and American Bank's advertisement described a banking business of the time: in carrying on a general banking business, it issued certificates of deposit, sold checks on principal cities, made and remitted collections at fair rates, and had a savings bank feature. The banking hours are conspicuous in their contrast to today's hours of 9:00 A. M. to 2:00 P. M. The English and American Bank received savings deposits in amounts from twenty-five cents upward between 5:00 and 8:00 P. M. on Saturday evenings, and discount day was Monday, 8:00 A. M. The interest paid on savings was six per cent. Charles Bugg was president of the bank, W. W. H. Thackston vice-president, and Alfred Moth cashier; the directors were R. M. Dickinson, J. G. Cannon, N. E. Venable, H. R. Hooper, O. T. Wicker, W. W. H. Thackston, Edgar Allen, Thomas Homer, Charles Bugg, Charles Van Voorhis, S. H. Bliss, and A. G. Powell.[103] In 1873 N. E. Venable was elected vice-president of the bank; F. D. Redd was elected a director to succeed Charles Van-Voorhis, and W. E. Bradshaw was chosen a director to succeed J. G. Cannon. Moth had been employed in the banking firm of Glyn Mills, Halifax and Company of London.[104]

The Commercial Savings Bank advertised a general banking business also. F. N. Watkins was president of this bank, and John H. Knight cashier. W. R. Berkeley, T. J. Davis, John A. Dalby, J. P. Fitzgerald, S. B. McKinney, and C. M. Walker were the directors; W. L. Lancaster was named a director in 1873 to succeed John A. Dalby. The bank declared a semi-annual dividend of eight per cent, with six per cent paid to the stockholders and two per cent paid into the surplus fund.[105]

The Farmville Insurance and Banking Company was organized in 1872. This firm conducted both a banking and an insurance business; it was organized to give the people of the section "safe and reliable insurance" and to "keep in our own midst, for the use and upbuilding of our people, the vast sums annually sent abroad for insurance." In 1873, $100,000 of the authorized capital of $500,000 had been paid in. William D. Rice was president, Samuel B. McKinney vice-president, and J. Henry Mottley secretary; the directors were J. W. Dunnington, Richard S. Paulett, Samuel B. McKinney, Dr. James L. White, Charles McK. Walker, Colonel Joseph T. Ligon, Captain Francis D. Irving, Thomas J. Davis, Major A. Reid Venable, Jr., Captain H. G. Richardson, William D. Rice, Captain Z. A. Blanton, and James T. Gray. J. W. Womack was the local insurance agent of the company.[106] New directors listed in 1874 were W. R. Berkeley, Dr. Peter Winston, J. P. Fitzgerald, and P. W. McKinney.[107]

The growth of the Farmville Insurance and Banking Company, despite the panic of 1873, was substantial. Assets as of the first of 1873 after one year's operation were $109,096.15; they had increased to $112,369.66 by January 1, 1874. In 1874 the company had agencies in Virginia, North Carolina, and Texas and declared a semi-annual dividend of nine per cent—six per cent to the stockholders, three per cent to the reserve fund. By 1875 assets had increased to $218,289.29; during the year the company was admitted to do business in Maryland, naming H. G. Stewart and Company of Baltimore agent in that state. For 1875 the company reported a gross income of $86,697.26, with expenditures for losses and operating expenses of $54,188.65. Assets at the beginning of 1876 amounted to $250,716.39, with a paid in capital of $200,000.[108] The growth of the business encouraged an over-expansion in distant areas, and the company failed sometime prior to 1887.[109]

The Planters Bank in 1873 also advertised a general banking business, with interest paid on time deposits, loans negotiated, checks sold on principal cities, and collections made. H. E. Warren was president, W. G. Venable cashier, and J. W. Dunnington assistant cashier; J. T. Spencer, E. Wiltse, B. L. Anderson, H. G. Richardson, C. W. Blanton, T. J. Davis, and the officers were the directors.[110]

Although the panic of 1873 was one of the major depressions and financial crises in the nation's history, the Farmville banks weathered it successfully. Early in October, shortly after the "late convulsion in New York and elsewhere," the English and American Bank announced that it had "no panic on hand at present"; the Planters and Commercial Savings Banks were reported as "rapidly realizing their assets" and the word was given that "all will be serene again shortly." The stockholders of the Commercial Savings Bank met October 14 and received a complete and detailed statement of the bank's condition and the result of the failure of some important banking houses upon its business. The statement showed home and foreign bills amounting to $97,484.98; cash on hand and in banks not closed, $16,902.68; property, $775; capital paid up, $30,000; surplus, $42,961. The bank's resources amounted to $145,-651.67, with $88,731.87 due depositors and other banks, leaving an excess of assets over liabilities in excess of $56,000. The bank carried on a "limited business" during the critical period, making no new loans for a time. It was fortunate in that it was due only $5,136.67 from banks which had to suspend business.[111]

Another Farmville financial institution which came through the financial stringency of 1873 so successfully that a similar firm was organized in January, 1874, was the Building Fund Company of Farmville. In its annual report for 1873 the firm reported assets of $14,686.01 and no liabilities. Its receipts amounted to $9,660.61, of which $9,109 was from payment of installments; disbursements amounted to $9,519.70, of which $9,228 was paid for the redemption of seventy-two shares. Dr. Peter Winston was president, and W. M. Davidson was secretary-treasurer; directors were Dr. Winston, H. E. Warren, J. W. Womack, H. G. Richardson, J. J. Walker, R. M. Burton, and W. D. Rice.[112]

The similar firm was the Prince Edward Building Association; Colonel William R. Berkeley was president, Alfred Moth, secretary-treasurer, and Charles Bugg, B. S. Hooper, J. T. Ligon, F. D. Irving, N. E. Venable, and A. Hurd were directors. The first installment payment was called for January 29, to be loaned out on that day.[113]

In 1875 the English and American Bank was enjoying a profitable business; in April of that year it declared an annual dividend of fifteen per cent. New directors at this time included W. L. Fernald, Albert Hurd, and J. S. Stanley-James.[114] It was during this period, probably upon the departure from the county of many of the English settlers, that this bank discontinued business.[115]

The Farmville Building and Trust Company was organized in 1878. In 1893 the firm reported assets of $57,961.59, of which $54,057.27 was in loans; it declared a dividend of nine per cent that year and announced that it could have paid ten per cent if the town of Farmville had not assessed the company over $300 for taxes. Dr. J. L. White was president, J. R. Martin was secretary-treasurer, Judge A. D. Watkins attorney, and Judge J. M. Crute, O. T. Wicker, and Ben Holman trustees; and Dr. White, R. M. Burton, H. E. Wall, H. C. Paulett, W. T. Doyne, H. C. Crute, and J. B. Wall were directors.[116]

When the panic of 1893 brought a crisis in financial circles, there were two banks in the county. R. M. Dickinson was now president of the Commercial Savings Bank, and John H. Knight was still cashier; the bank had a capital of $19,950.[117] R. S. Paulett had succeeded to the presidency of the Planters Bank upon the death of H. E. Warren in 1878; W. G. Venable was still cashier, and T. L. Morton was assistant cashier; the directors were H. E. Barrow, Colin Stokes, C. W. Blanton, R. M. Burton, B. L. Anderson, and T. J. Davis.[118] During this depression the Commercial Savings Bank failed; it closed its doors August 1, 1893, and its assets were turned over to W. G. Venable, trustee, for equitable distribution to its creditors. This was the first bank failure in Virginia in the panic of 1893 and was attributed to the small investment in its capital stock, the stringency of the times, and the difficulty of collecting debts; an estimate at the time indicated that assets amounted to approximately sixty per cent of the liabilities, which were thought to be about $50,000. The Planters Bank at the same time had resources of $271,545.61, with loans and discounts amounting to $136,147.39, checking deposits of $83,070.32, and time deposits of $108,846..32.[119] The closing of the Commercial Savings Bank and the general difficulties prompted the Planters Bank to put into effect stricter regulations; after August 15 it would pay only $50 or a smaller amount in currency to depositors and would not pay more than $50 on checks; it would, however, on presentation of the check certify it as good. The bank was forced to this restriction on business because banks in New York, Philadelphia, Baltimore, Washington, Richmond, Lynchburg, Danville, and Staunton declined to furnish the Planters Bank currency against its balances with them.[120]

W. G. Venable as trustee of the Commercial Savings Bank liquidated its assets and paid them to the depositors; in March, 1895, payment amounting to twenty-four per cent of the deposit was made.[121] When the bank closed, there was on deposit $3,006.01 of license tax receipts to the credit of W. H. Ewing, county treasurer. He sued to recover this sum, but got only $1,143.28, which was turned over to the state; in consequence, the legislature in 1898, when it was reported that nearly all the bank's assets had been distributed, directed the auditor to accept from Ewing or his sureties bonds of the state and all unpaid coupons at their face value in satisfaction of the balance due the state treasury.[122] What seems to have been the last payment to depositors amounted to two per cent and was made in September, 1898, by R. H. Watkins, receiver.

For eight years the county had only one bank, although the Farmville Building and Trust Company was in operation; this firm advertised as its business: "Old Debts liquidated—New Homes Secured—Young Men Started in Business—Money Received on Time Deposit." To secure a loan, the customer was charged a fee of five shares—$5; a loan of $1,000 repaid in eight years cost the borrower $440 in interest; on this loan, the plan called for monthly payments of $15. Dr. J. L. White and John R. Martin were for many years president and secretary-treasurer, respectively; in 1902 H. E. Wall was vice-president;. E. Scott Martin, assistant secretary-treasurer; R. M. Burton, appraiser;and A. E. Cralle had succeeded Benjamin Holman as one of the three trustees, J. M. Crute and O. T. Wicker still serving in that capacity; in 1896 Dr. White, Burton, H. E. Wall, H. C. Crute, J. B. Wall, W. T. Doyne, and H. C. Paulett were directors; A. E. Cralle and E. L. Morris had succeeded Doyne and Paulett in 1902. H. E. Wall succeeded to the presidency upon the death of Dr. White in 1909.[123]

In 1896 the Planters Bank had assets of $343,177.19 and paid semi-annual dividends of three and one-half per cent. In 1897 H. C. Crute, H. A. Stokes, and A. H. Porter were elected directors of the bank.[124] H. E. Barrow, H. A. Stokes, C. W. Blanton, R. M. Burton, B. L. Anderson, and T. J. Davis were directors in 1896; in 1897 J. M. Crute succeeded Blanton.[125] T. J. Davis succeeded R. S. Paulett as president of the Planters Bank upon the latter's death in 1902 and served until his death in 1905; he was succeeded by H. A. Stokes, who held the post until his death in 1919, and was in turn succeeded by E. S. Shields. Upon Shields' death in 1950, C. Willard Hart became president. W. G. Venable retired as cashier of the Planters Bank in 1906 and was elected vice-president; he was succeeded by his son, W. P. Venable, who had been assistant cashier for several years. Cashiers in succession to the younger Venable have been Walker Scott (1909-17), E. S. Shields (1917-19), John B. Overton (1919-22), C. Willard Hart (1922-50), and J. C. Bondurant (1950-). Other officers in 1954 are J. W. Dunnington, chairman of the board, J. N. Carter, vice-president, and C. H. Pritchard, Jr., assistant cashier. Directors in 1906 were H. A. Stokes, John J. Walker, W. T.

Clark, S. W. Paulett, A. E. Cralle, H. C. Crute, and H. E. Wall; during succeeding years H. D. Cobb, Walker Scott, J. W. Hazelgrove, E. S. Shields, James H. Clark, and the present directors, William W. Carson, Jr., J. N. Carter, C. J. Cox, J. W. Dunnington, J. H. Forbes, F. H. Hanbury, Jr., C. W. Hart, J. C. Garnett, M. R. Large, C. M. Smith, and Joseph A. Weinberg have been added to the board.[126]

The temporary organization of the First National Bank was effected on November 10, 1900, in the office of Burton and Otley as a result of the preliminary work of J. W. and W. T. Otley. At this meeting $30,000 in stock was subscribed in a few minutes. The temporary officers were Dr. Peter Winston president and A. G. Clapham cashier, with W. G. Dunnington, Dr. Winston, N. B. Davidson, J. M. Hamlet, John R. Martin, Clapham, and Thomas J. Davis temporary directors.[127] Permanent organization of the bank took place January 10, 1901, with N. B. Davidson as president, Clapham as cashier, and W. P. Gilliam, Dr. Peter Winston, Dr. J. M. Hamlet, John R. Martin, N. B. Davidson, T. J. Davis, and R. H. Lynn as directors;[128] in 1902 Lynn was vice-president, and J. F. Walton, E. S. Taylor, C. C. Fleming, and W. D. M. Stokes had been added to the board of directors.[129]

In 1903 the Planters Bank reported resources of $410,309.94 and the First National $307,510.08—quite an increase in bank resources over those reported seven years before.[130]

A bank was organized at Meherrin in 1905; known as the Prince Edward-Lunenburg County Bank, it had an authorized capital of $50,000 and paid four per cent interest on time deposits. Tucker K. Sands was president, W. C. Winn and H. B. Miller, vice-presidents, and E. T. Yeaman, cashier; the directors were Sands, F. E. Nolting, Winn, Miller, M. E. Gee, J. H. Price, T. C. Haskins, J. C. Miller, J. J. Owen, W. H. Ewing, John L. Yates, E. P. Wallace, G. S. Wing, and C. D. Epes.[131]

In 1906 the Prince Edward-Lunenburg County Bank reported assets of $56,657.76, the Planters Bank of Farmville $557,318.87, and the First National Bank of Farmville $459,519.93.[132]

On April 29, 1907, the Citizens State Bank was organized in the office of Garland and Martin; at that meeting E. Scott Martin was elected president, George M. Serpell vice-president, and W. D. M. Stokes, Dr. Peter Winston, E. J. Whitehead, J. E. Garland, Serpell, Robert K. Brock, and Martin directors. The bank opened for business July 11, 1907 with F. W. Hubbard as cashier.[133] This bank was consolidated with the First National December 17, 1909; officers of the bank after the merger were N. B. Davidson, president, A. G. Clapham, vice-president, V. Vaiden cashier, John A. Booker and F. W. Hubbard, assistant cashiers, and Davidson, J. L. Putney, J. F. Walton, Clapham, J. R. Martin, W. D. M. Stokes, Joseph E. Garland, E. Scott Martin, and E. S. Taylor, directors.[134]

Davidson continued as president of the First National Bank until his death in 1936, when he was succeeded by Joseph E. Garland, who still holds that office. Clapham, the first cashier, served until 1904, when he was succeeded by John W. Long (1904-08), and successive cashiers have been Volusko Vaiden (1908-19), W. B. Morris (1919-25), Gordon E. West (1925-44), and E. W. Sanford, Jr. (1944-). Others who served as directors of this bank include Dr. R. L. Hudgins, Bennett T. Taylor, Dr. J. W. Smith, R. B. Johns, Herbert L. Bradshaw, Gordon E. West, and the present board: Horace Adams, Joseph E. Garland, R. E. Garland, Dabney S. Lancaster, George A. Newman, W. G. Putney, E. W. Sanford, Jr., Dr. W. E. Smith, and Vernon C. Womack. Officers, in addition to Joseph E. Garland, president, and E. W. Sanford, Jr., cashier and trust officer, are R. E. Garland and W. G. Putney, vice-presidents, W. K. Carter, assistant cashier and assistant trust officer, and S. B. Spencer and Mrs. Lurline A. Wootton, assistant cashiers, and John H. Varner, manager of the farm service department.[135]

The third of Prince Edward's present banks, the Peoples National of Farmville, was organized July 11, 1908, at the Prince Edward Hotel. At the organization meeting Dr. W. E. Anderson, E. T. Bondurant, R. J. Carter, C. C. Cowan, W. J. Hillsman, J. D. Watkins, W. M. Duvall, W. H. Robertson, G. M. Robeson, R. H. Paulett, and J. L. Bugg were elected directors. The next month the officers were announced, Robeson president, Bondurant vice-president, Bugg cashier, and A. C. Ogburn, Jr., assistant cashier; R. B. Cralle was at that time added to the board of directors. In 1941 Bugg succeeded Robeson as president, and I. C. Glenn succeeded Bugg as cashier. Other directors include H. E. Richardson and A. W. Weaver, and the present directors: W. C. Fitzpatrick, F. G. Baldwin, F. C. Hubbard, W. H. Glenn, S. C. Newman, W. S. Weaver, J. L. Bugg, E. M. Whitlock, and Lester E. Andrews, R. H. Paulett is now an honorary director. In addition to Bugg and Glenn officers in 1954 include F. G. Baldwin and W. S. Weaver, vice-presidents, and J. M. Watkins and S. P. Glover, assistant cashiers.[136]

In contrast to the resources of $1,073,496.56 of the Prince Edward banks in 1906 were the resources of $3,861,531.56 in 1940. During Farmville's sesquicentennial year 1948, the three banks had resources of $9,412,237.64, an astonishing increase over an eight-year period, but evidence of a greatly expanded economy during the World War II period.[137] In the middle of the county's bicentennial year, the banks report resources of $12,584,574.65.[138]

Although Prince Edward has never been an industrialized area, there has often been demonstrated an interest in industrial development. This interest has borne fruit in the founding and development of a number of small industries, some of which have had only brief histories, while others have continued in existence. In 1874 S. R. Murkland built a brick kiln in Farmville with a capacity of 600,000 bricks.[139] In the same year F. H. Armistead and J. T. Spencer bought the tanyard in Farmville which had belonged to T. B. and J. J. Rice and continued the operation of a tannery.[140] Two other small industries began operations in 1875: G. R. Bickers opened the Farmville Boot and Shoe factory, to which the Grange promptly pledged its patronage;[141] and J. M. Johns, Jr., started the Farmville Cigar factory, which made two brands of cigars, "Pride of the South," a pure Havana cigar with a portrait of Lee on the label, and "Pride of Farmville."[142] There was a foundry in Farmville at this time also, which was sold at public auction on August 1, 1875, and was bought by John A. Dalby for $2,250; Dalby made arrangements to have the foundry operating early in 1876.[143]

A letter to the Farmville *Mercury* in 1875, signed *Quondam*, of Worsham, was prophetic of the type of industry which was to prove more stable. Quondam advocated the establishment in Farmville of an industry which could use raw materials available in Prince Edward. The large tracts of original forests on the ridges between Bush and Briery and Briery and Buffalo would yield enough hickory and white oak suitable for wagons and plows, sweet gum for hubs, birch and dogwood for awl handles and button moulds, heart pine and poplar for sash and blinds and other woodwork to employ a large skilled force in manufacturing. The correspondent called attention to a wagon made of native woods by J. M. Hart of Worsham which would "compare favorably with the best made."[144]

An industry of this type came to Prince Edward when G. M. Robeson and L. M. Blanton moved their foundry from Amelia County to Farmville in March, 1878.[145] The letter-head of the firm

that year described the business: "Geo. M. Robeson, Farmville Foun-
dry and Old Dominion Handle Works, Manufacturer of Agricultural
Implements and Farm Machinery, Repairs and Castings of All Kinds
Made Promptly, Steam Saw Mill and Planing Mill, Handles and
Woodwork for Plows, Cultivators and Trucks a Specialty. L. M.
Blanton, General Manager." The firm made two plow points for
twenty-five cents and a tobacco hogshead for $1.70.[146]

After a fire destroyed the foundry and handle works on January
2, 1880, the business was chartered in 1882 as a stock company
under the name of the Farmville Manufacturing Company; the
incorporators were G. M. Robeson, L. M. Blanton, Albert Hurd,
Charles Bugg, R. S. Paulett, A. R. Venable, Jr., W. W. H. Thackston,
J. M. Venable, S. B. McKinney, J. P. Fitzgerald, O. T. Wicker, N. E.
Venable, C. M. Walker, N. H. Champlin, and their associates.[147]
Two years later Fitzgerald, Robeson, and Blanton and their associates
were incorporated as the Farmville Lumber Company.[148] The manufacture of handles continued for many years an important activity;
gradually, however, the manufacture and sale of building supplies
supplanted both foundry and handle manufacturing. In 1898 the
Farmville Manufacturing Company advertised beaded ceiling at $10
per thousand feet, siding at the same price, flooring at $12 per
thousand, and palings at $3 per thousand.[149] The latter were widely
used in building yard fences at the time, both in town and at farmhouses; only a few paling fences remain now, but at the turn of the
century it was most popular type fence for lawns. F. B. Gilbert was
later associated with Robeson in the Farmville Manufacturing Company; the business was purchased in 1944 by Maurice R. Large and
Lester E. Andrews.[150]

Early in the twentieth century the Rice Manufacturing Company
was engaged in a similar business in Farmville. J. Y. Phillips in
1906 bought the interest of Thomas A. Gray in this business and
with C. C. Dillon operated the business, changing the name to the
Virginia Manufacturing Company; the firm manufactured doors,
windows, blinds, lumber, and building materials, and tool handles,
wheelwright supplies and hogsheads. It continued in business only
a short time.[151]

One specialized phase of the lumber business was the manufacture of hogsheads. In earlier days the cooper had done this work,
usually on the farm. At the Rice Warehouse a cooper's shop was
maintained to make hogsheads for shipping tobacco from the ware-

house to the buyer's factory. Farmville had a cooperage industry in 1909, the Stonewall Hogshead Company, on Third Street, east of Grosse's Branch.[152] In 1912 another cooperage industry, the Buffalo Shook Company, was founded in Farmville by N. B. Davidson and F. H. Hanbury. This industry continues in operation, manufacturing hogsheads, staves, headers, and liners, and in addition to the Farmville plant there is a branch mill at Amelia. The business is still operated by Hanbury, with whom are associated his sons, F. H. Hanbury, Jr., and B. B. Hanbury.

Two other firms utilizing forest products have since been founded in Farmville. Bennett T. Taylor of Prospect organized the Taylor Manufacturing Company in 1919; after fire destroyed its plant at the western end of Buffalo Street in 1924, the firm moved across the Appomattox River into Cumberland County, where it continues to carry on a building supply and construction business. After Taylor's death in 1932, the business was conducted by his elder son, B. T. Taylor, Jr., and since his death in 1945 it has been under the management of the younger son, Robert E. Taylor. The other building supply and construction firm is the Mottley Construction Company, operated by Robert W. Mottley for several years before the formation of a closed corporation under the same name in 1945 by Mottley, F. L. Elliott, and C. W. Glenn.

An unsuccessful venture was the Farmville Kitchen Cabinet factory, which was built in 1928. The plant went into production as soon as it had been completed, and on June 20, 1929, it was reported that the 100th cabinet had been completed. The Farmville Furniture and Cabinet Company was unable to weather the depression of the 1930's, and the manufacture of kitchen cabinets was abandoned after a short time.[153]

In the industrial survey made of Farmville in 1930 by the Virginia Polytechnic Institute, four industrial plants, Farmville Manufacturing, Taylor Manufacturing, Buffalo Shook, and Farmville Furniture and Cabinet Companies were reported as employing 150 workers and as having an annual payroll of $143,000. The volume of business amounted to $429,000, and the industries used $96,000 worth of raw materials.[154]

The practice of spinning and weaving at home continued after the war, but on a steadily and rather rapidly diminishing scale. The Misses Wooldridge of Appomattox County carried on a weaving business in their home and numbered Prince Edward customers among their clientele. As late as 1871 what an antique note is sounded in this message to a Prince Edward customer:

"Have seen the Miss Wooldridges, they have a shilling per yard for yarn counterpanes and ninepence for white ones. They can't weave yours until after Christmas, have as much as they can do until then—will weave yours immediately after."[155]

It was not long, though, before Farmville was talking of textile mills; it was anticipated that English cotton spinners might build a factory there.[156] The prospect, however, was never realized. In 1876 a venture was chartered with authority to carry on varied manufacturing enterprises; the Farmville Manufacturing Company was incorporated to manufacture cotton, woolen, paper, and other fabrics, as well as wood, iron, and agricultural implements, and lime.[157] This enterprise, too, failed to become a reality. For a few years after 1900 Farmville had a knitting mill which produced half hose for men, fine women's hose, and merino socks for children. The mill employed twenty-five hands, who could turn out on the twenty machines 120 dozen pair of hose daily. Children were employed for this work at wages of $2 to $3 weekly, but workers were hard to get. The earlier management of the knitting mill evidently failed in 1903. With the mill under new management, it was announced in November, 1903, that work would be resumed soon. The venture never proved profitable.[158]

There have been two fertilizer plants in Prince Edward. At Worsham W. P. Dupuy manufactured Tuckahoe tobacco fertilizer with an analysis of 2-8-2 in the 1880's.[159] In 1896 W. G. Dunnington and Walter H. Robertson began the manufacture of fertilizer in Farmville under the firm name of Virginia State Fertilizer Company. Its brands for tobacco in 1898 were "Dunnington's Special Formula for Tobacco," "Wat Dunnington's Austrian Tobacco Grower," and "Farmer's Reliance Special for Tobacco"; grain and grass brands were "Blood and Bone Phosphate," "V.S.F.Co.'s Dissolved Bone & Potash," and "Pure Bone Meal." From 1900 until 1904 Robertson manufactured fertilizer in Lynchburg, but in the latter year he returned to Farmville and continued fertilizer manufacturing there until 1909, when he moved to Norfolk. The Farmville industry was the beginning of the present Robertson Chemical Corporation of Norfolk. The Farmville factory was located between the Norfolk and Western Railway and the Appomattox River, near the present passenger station.[160]

Another industry founded in Farmville during this period was the ice plant, which began operation in 1906 on the town spring lot near the passenger station. This industry, which was developed by W. C. Newman, was within the next two decades to put an end to the practice of cutting ice on ponds and storing it in pits for summer use. As automobiles came into general use, people began to buy ice when they came to Farmville and carried it home. Later, as good roads made possible truck transportation, regular ice deliveries were made in various communities of the county. During the three-year period, 1921-24, Thomas A. Gray also operated an ice plant in Farmville, the Prince Edward Ice Company. Since W. C. Newman's death in 1929, his ice plant has been operated by his son, Sydnor C. Newman.[161]

Another change in the industrial scene has been the passing of the gristmill. The mill in Farmville, however, developed into one of the county's present industries. This mill, established in 1838 by Thomas A. Morton, was sold in 1852 to R. A. Davis, who in turn sold it to John A. Scott in 1870. Scott sold the mill in 1889 to S. H. Bliss; the Bliss family operated the mill, which was known as the Farmville Mills, until it was destroyed by fire in 1933. While in the Bliss ownership, the mill erected the adjoining grain elevator, with a capacity of 50,000 bushels, in 1923. After the fire, the mill was purchased by Sydnor C. Newman, J. W. Dunnington, and S. W. Watkins, Jr., who owned the Prince Edward Mills on Venable Street, which had been purchased after the death of Thomas A. Gray, who operated that milling business from 1915 until 1924. The new ownership erected a new mill on the site of the Farmville Mills and gave to it the name under which it continues to operate, the Prince Edward Mills. The new mill began operations February 23, 1934. Newman and Watkins subsequently purchased the Dunnington interest, and Watkins' interest was bought after his death in 1945 by Newman.

The widespread unemployment during the depression of the 1930's directed the attention of civic-minded people in Farmville to the need of a stable industry which would give work to people who wanted to work but could find no opportunity for employment. In a project similar to that which has been used since with notable success by Scranton, Pennsylvania, and has become internationally known as the Scranton plan for securing new industries, the effort was launched in Farmville to secure a branch plant of the Craddock-

Terry Shoe Company of Lynchburg. A citizens committee, launched by N. B. Davidson and J. Taylor Thompson, developed into the Prince Edward Industrial Development Company, which acquired and remodeled for use as a shoe factory a tobacco factory on the east side of Main Street north of the railroad crossing. The company offered this building to the Craddock-Terry firm as a branch plant and offered to deed it to the company when the company had paid out $750,000 in wages, if it paid out that amount within seven years. Craddock-Terry accepted the proposal; by July 20, 1934, its 106 employees were turning out 600 pair of Lion Brand shoes daily under the management of T. A. Allen, who continues as head of the Farmville branch. Five years and five months after the shoe factory opened, it had paid out in wages $759,983, and the Prince Edward Industrial Development Company conveyed the property to Craddock-Terry. The shoe manufacturers then began the erection of a four-story addition. Average daily employment in 1947 had reached 264; at that time over 550,000 pair of shoes had been made in that plant.[162]

For many years after the war there continued an interest in mining in Prince Edward; the conviction remained that the mineral resources were a potential source of wealth and that their development offered promise of prosperity. Iron was reported discovered on the Osborne farm near Prospect in 1874;[163] thirty years later iron ore described as of "fine quality" was discovered on the R. F. Allen farm near Felden.[164] In 1896 gold was found in two places in Prince Edward, on J. S. Carson's farm on Briery and on John R. Morton's farm on Bush River, where iron was also found. Gold found near Prospect in 1897 was assayed to be worth $20 per ton.[165] Gold was reported in Prince Edward in 1907, but the difficulty of its recovery from low grade ore dimmed the lure of fortune.[166]

Coal continued to attract interest. In 1875 John Richard Tonkin, an English mineralogist, reported considerable quantities distributed through the area. He thought that deposits were richer farther down, although he believed, on the basis of the thickness of the seams, that the quantity would not increase as the quality increased. It was his opinion that it would be profitable to work seams of two to three feet in thickness if the quality was good, and he also advised the working of outcrops, as had been done in the past. About the same time W. P. Patterson, an experienced miner, estimated that it would cost about $8 per day to determine the extent of the Prince Edward coal deposits.[167] But dreams of developing industries from working the mineral resources of the county have never been realized except in the case of kyanite at Baker's Mountain. Deposits do not appear to be large enough to justify the venture. In some instances the quality of the ore makes the cost of extracting the mineral prohibitive. Dr. J. H. C. Winston used to tell his chemistry classes at Hampden-Sydney that a certain lot near the college had $10,000 worth of aluminum (pre-World War II values) in it, but that it would cost as much and probably more to extract it from the ore in which it was present. That seems typical of much of Prince Edward's mineral resources.

The two railroads which had been built through Prince Edward prior to the war were in subsequent years consolidated into major systems. The Southside, the Norfolk and Petersburg, the Virginia and Tennessee (Lynchburg to Bristol), and the Virginia and Kentucky Railroads were consolidated into the Atlantic Mississippi and Ohio Railroad Company in 1870. Thus a continuous rail line traversed southern Virginia, from Norfolk to Bristol. The A. M. & O. was sold in February, 1881, and was re-organized as the Norfolk and Western Railroad Company. With the opening of the coal fields in Southwest Virginia and West Virginia at that time, the Norfolk and Western built lines into those areas and extended its lines to Cincinnati and Columbus, Ohio.[168] The Norfolk and Western was bought by a re-organization committee of bondholders in the fall of 1896 and was re-organized as the Norfolk and Western Railway Company.[169]

The management of the Richmond and Danville Railroad furnished the leadership for the consolidations and purchases which resulted in the organization of the Southern Railway System in 1894.

Many in Prince Edward, especially people in Farmville and through the central part of the county, felt the need of additional rail connections. The Farmville, Charlottesville, and Stanardsville Railroad Company was chartered in 1871 to build and operate a narrow gauge line from Stanardsville to Farmville; authority to extend the line southward from Farmville either to the Staunton River or to Keysville on the Richmond and Danville was granted. Farmville and Prince Edward were both given permission to subscribe to stock in the company.[170] In 1875 an election was authorized to be held in Farmville to determine whether the town should subscribe to the stock; Farmville's proposed subscription of $40,000 was conditioned on the subscription by Albemarle and Buckingham Counties of $100,000 each.[171] At a citizens meeting in the interest of the railroad, Colonel E. W. Hubard, its president, urged support of the subscription to the stock by the town. He reminded his audience of his effort years before to get the Danville railroad through Farmville and of the opposition of some of the principal citizens. At this meeting Colonel J. P. Fitzgerald, Captain Philip W. McKinney, and Edgar Allan spoke in favor of the stock subscription; H. G. Richardson and G. B. Wright spoke in opposition.[172] At a meeting shortly thereafter, Fitzgerald and McKinney again spoke in favor of the road, and W. R. Berkeley opposed the stock subscription; C. C. Read declined to express an opinion. The objections were principally on the basis of the increase in taxes the issuance of bonds to pay for the stock would entail. At the second meeting the vote was 172 to 111 in favor of the railroad.[173] When the issue was voted on in the election, the proposal that Farmville buy stock was defeated.[174] Charles M. Walker of Farmville was one of the directors of the proposed raildoad.[175] The charter of this railroad was revived in 1887, and subsequently the Orange and Keysville Railroad was organized under the charter granted the Farmville and Charlottesville Railroad Company.[176] The Orange and Keysville in 1890 began the acquisition of property for its right of way, and a stretch of road bed at and in the vicinity of Hampden-Sydney was graded.[177] Prince Edward voters at an election March 5, 1888, voted in favor of the county's subscription to stock in the Farmville and Charlottesville.[178]

As early as 1875 the construction of a narrow gauge railroad from Farmville to Hampden-Sydney was proposed.[179] Later in the year a meeting was held in Farmville to discuss the construction of a narrow gauge railroad to Hampden-Sydney, Chase City, Clarksville, and into North Carolina. G. R. Bickers was one of the leading proponents of the idea, and he, Colonel Fitzgerald, H. G. Richardson, and Edgar Allan spoke in favor of it. In November Colonel A. A. Drake of the New York banking firm of Drake Brothers and Company and Amasa W. Lyon, a retired New York merchant, attended a meeting to discuss this railroad.[180] Still another railroad was proposed to be built from Farmville southward by Hampden-Sydney; this was the Farmville and Staunton River Railroad, chartered in 1882, to be built from Farmville to some point on the river not above Brookneal.[181]

The Farmville and Powhatan Railroad, one of whose incorporators in 1884 was A. R. Venable, Jr., was built and operated trains into Farmville. The town was authorized to subscribe to $50,000 stock in the railroad, provided three-fifths of the voters approved the issuance of bonds for the purpose.[182] O. T. Wicker, R. M. Burton, W. H. Richardson, T. J. Davis, and Charles Bugg were named commissioners to condemn land for the right of way of the railroad in Prince Edward, and the acquisition of the right of way in Farmville began in 1889.[183] In 1894 it was proposed to extend the Farmville and Powhatan to County Line Crossroads, eight miles from Keysville, and then to Keysville to connect with the Richmond and Danville and the Oxford and Clarksville.[184] B. H. Carter, J. E. Ligon, C. S. Hamlett, Henry Stokes, and James W. Womack were appointed commissioners to condemn the right of way for the extension.[185] An election was held November 17, 1894, to decide whether the county should issue $50,000 in bonds to buy stock in the railroad to finance its extension. Talk of moving Union Theological Seminary from Hampden-Sydney had already begun, and some felt that the construction of a railroad to Hampden-Sydney was essential not only to keep the seminary, but also the college. Dr. Richard McIlwaine, Henry Stokes, Philip W. McKinney, J. P. Fitzgerald, S. W. Watkins, A. R. Venable, R. H. Watkins, and Dr. J. D. Eggleston endorsed the subscription to the stock by the county. When the vote was tallied, 718 were found in favor of the bond issue and 545 against; the results showed that thirty-three votes were lacking to give the bond issue the required three-fifths necessary for approval. Of the total vote, 367 ballots were cast by property owners in the county, and of these 185 favored bonds and 182 opposed.[186]

The Farmville and Powhatan provided rail connections for Richmond at Moseley and Chester. Daily a train left Farmville at 4:45 A. M., arriving at Moseley at 7:35 and at Chester at 10:02. The train left Chester at 11:15 A. M., Moseley at 1:45 P. M. and arrived at Farmville at 4:35 P. M. There was a mixed passenger and freight train leaving Farmville on Tuesdays, Thursdays, and Saturdays, and one arriving in Farmville on Mondays, Wednesdays, and Fridays. The winter schedule in 1896 provided only mixed trains, one leaving Farmville at 8:30 A. M., one arriving in Farmville at 6:31 P. M. daily except Sunday.[187] This was the period of the road's greatest success. By 1898 it was in receivership, Edgar Allan, Jr., being receiver and W. G. Venable trustee.[188] The Farmville and Powhatan was sold in 1905, the eighty-five-mile line from Farmville to Ber-

muda Hundred bringing $125,000.[189] The name was then changed
to Tidewater and Western. But complaints were mounting about
the service the road gave Farmville. In 1907 the Farmville *Herald,*
after reminding its readers that Farmville provided the first money
for the construction of the road, observed that the $50,000 subscribed
to stock "might as well have been dumped in the Appomattox" insofar as the good it had done Farmville was concerned. There had
"never been a train run in the interest of Farmville," ran the complaint, noting further that a resident of Cumberland or Buckingham
who came to Farmville via the Tidewater and Western would have
to spend a part of three days away from home in order to spend an
hour in Farmville stores during business hours. The complaint got a
measure of results when a special train was run to Farmville every
Thursday, arriving at 10:48 A. M. and leaving at 3:44 P. M.[190] By
the beginning of World War I operations of the Tidewater and
Western had ceased, and the track was sold to the United States
government for use in France during that war. Langborne M.
Williams of Richmond was named receiver for the Tidewater and
Western in 1917. The Virginia Supreme Court in October, 1917,
permitted the dissolution of the railroad company and the sale of
its property.[191]

Still there persisted interest in building a railroad to Hampden-
Sydney. In 1902 an election was held on the question of authorizing
the Board of Supervisors to issue $60,000 in bonds to subscribe to
stock in the Orange and Keysville. For some reason, never explained,
no election was held on the first day (May 27) set for the voting;
and when the vote was taken on July 1, the proportion was five to
one in opposition to issuing bonds; only one favorable vote was cast
at Rice, only four at Prospect, eight at Green Bay, and forty-two
in Farmville.[192]

Plans for building the Deepwater, as the Virginian was then
called, seemed to stimulate the revival of interest in 1905, for a
group of citizens, including W. G. Venable, A. D. Watkins, and
W. G. Dunnington, proposed building a railroad on the bed of the
Orange and Keysville five miles beyond Hampden-Sydney, within
"striking distance of the Deepwater now being built through West
Virginia and Virginia." Meetings were held, the first of which had
as its chairman R. K. Brock; Colonel R. T. Hubard, president of the
Orange and Keysville, and Kenner T. Crawley, president of the
Virginia Railway Company, endorsed the project, but that was the
end of the plan.[193]

The last effort to build a railroad in Prince Edward was success-ful. The Tidewater Railroad Company came along the border of the county from Abilene to Meherrin, at places within the county, on its route from Norfolk to the coal fields in the Princeton, West Virginia, area. Acquisition of land for the right of way began early in 1906, and construction followed. This was the railroad now known as the Virginian.[194]

The Norfolk and Western has engaged in three notable construc-tion projects in Prince Edward. The original High Bridge was one of the engineering marvels of the time. The four spans which were burned April 7, 1865, were repaired within a few months. The brick piers of the old bridge are still standing. The present bridge at this point was built in 1914. A little later the Norfolk and Western con-structed a belt line from Burkeville, via Green Bay, Meherrin, and Abilene, to Pamplin to provide a better grade for east bound freight trains. The right-of-way for the belt line was acquired in 1915.[195] The route follows a natural grade, much of it being along the divide between the watersheds of the Appomattox and Staunton Rivers. Prior to the construction of the belt line, the railroad used two en-gines on eastbound coal freights from Farmville to Crewe, the second usually being at the end of the train and called a "pusher."

About the time of the construction of the belt line, the Norfolk and Western installed an electric signal system to promote safety. The signal system, which indicated the presence of trains on a given section of track, replaced the system in which the railroad main-tained telegraph stations at intervals of a few miles. That system, known as the block system, prohibited a train from leaving a station if there was a train between that station and the next one in the direction the train was headed. The block system was put into effect in September, 1897, and as a result the railroad opened over fifteen new telegraph offices between Roanoke and Norfolk.[196] Offices were maintained in Prince Edward during the two decades this system was used at Moran, Rice, High Bridge, Farmville, Tuggle, Prospect, and Elam. After the electric signals were installed, telegraph offices were closed except at Rice, Farmville, and Prospect.

By this time, a new means of transportation was becoming popular. The first motor vehicle appeared in Prince Edward July 3, 1902, when J. F. Herman made the trip from Richmond to Lynch-burg. He had left Richmond the day before, spent the night at Powhatan, and reached Farmville a little after 10:00 A. M. After a

stop of a few minutes he went on to Lynchburg, arriving there about
4:00 P. M.[197] A few people bought cars during the next several years,
and in 1914 there was a boom in automobile sales in Prince Edward,
Henry Ford's Model T being the popular brand.[198] It was no question
then that the automobile had come to stay. With it came undreamed
developments in road-building, which belong in this account in the
history of government and its activities. With it, too, came two new
types of business, the garage, usually in connection with an automobile sales service, and the service station. After cars became
fairly well distributed, some stores installed gasoline tanks and added
the sale of gasoline and motor oil to their line of commodities. In
1922 J. C. Brickert opened the first drive-in service station in Prince
Edward County.[199] Since that time every community in the county
has seen the introduction of the service station into its business life.

Perhaps no period has seen as many material changes as the past
three-quarters of a century. A major factor has been the adaptation
of electricity to constructive uses; another has been the invention
and development of the gasoline motor. Eleven years after Edison
invented the incandescent light, electric lights were introduced in
Farmville, supplanting the street gas lights. Judge A. D. Watkins
presented the matter of electric lights to the Farmville Town Council
on December 4, 1890; later in the month a petition bearing ninety-
one signatures asked the Council to get electric lights for the town.
The Council approved the petition and then voted five to four in
favor of having electricity provided by a private concern; the five
favoring a private source of power were A. H. Porter, J. M. Crute,
John R. Martin, H. E. Barrow, and W. P. Gilliam; the four who
wanted the town to own its electric plant were C. W. Blanton, R. M.
Burton, H. E. Wall, and Thomas L. Morton. On December 29, the
Council granted a fifteen-year franchise to the Farmville Electric
Light, Heat and Power Company, of which C. M. Walker was president, for providing street lights; there were twenty arc lights of
1,200 candlepower each, to burn from dusk until light the next
morning (except on nights when the moon was shining)ʹ at $6.25 per
light per month. Blanton and Burton, advocates of town ownership
of its power plant, voted in opposition to giving the franchise. Before
a year had passed, the town had an opportunity to buy the light
plant. The company, of which Dr. Peter Winston was now president,
and J. M. Crute secretary, accepted the offer of $9,700 for the plant,
and the voters of the town approved, 192 to 17, a bond issue in the

amount of $10,500 to pay for the plant. The Council moved the plant to Randolph Street, between the Norfolk and Western Railroad and the Appomattox River, because of the convenience to water and coal. In 1892 the charges for electricity were set at fifty cents per light per month, on a twelve-month basis, or seventy-five cents per month, for a shorter period. Pollard and Moring built the first power plant for the town. John R. Martin was first superintendent of the plant. A new plant was built after the town voted, 91 to 7, in favor of a $15,000-bond issue for construction in December, 1904. Although it had been proposed as early as 1895 that the Farmville plant furnish lights for Hampden-Sydney College (and power to operate cars to and from the college to Farmville), it was not until 1909 that the Council approved furnishing current to Hampden-Sydney, if the college would build and maintain the transmission line to Farmville; the rate was eight cents per 1,000 watts during the college session and twelve cents the rest of the year, or $75 per month for 300 lights or fewer. Current from Farmville was not furnished Hampden-Sydney until after a contract made December 14, 1920, was approved. The next year the Council approved furnishing current to Prospect at a charge ten per cent over charges in Farmville provided a line would be built according to the specifications of the Light Committee. B. T. Taylor organized the Prospect Light and Power Company which constructed the line, and on May 19, 1923, at 4:15 P. M., power was turned on the Prospect line. In 1928 a power line was built to Rice, the applicants in that community furnishing the right of way for the transmission line.

The Council declined to sell the municipal plant to the Virginia Railway and Power Company (later the Virginia Electric and Power Company) in 1916. Later the Virginia Public Service Company made offers to buy the municipal plant, beginning in 1927. A later offer was rejected by popular vote, 199 for selling, 287 against, in 1931. The next year the Council sold the plant to the Knightly Light and Power Company, a subsidiary of the Virginia Public Service Company, and the subsidiary subsequently transferred the Farmville property to the parent concern. The Virginia Electric and Power Company finally acquired the Farmville plant when it purchased the Virginia Public Service Company in 1944.

Rural Prince Edward for the most part lacked the convenience of lights and water. Light was furnished by kerosene lamps; water came from well or spring. In some rural and village homes, light was furnished by acetylene gas, generated from carbide; usually the home with acetylene lights also had a power pump and tank for its water system. About the period of World War I private electric systems, with their own generating plants and storage batteries, began to replace the acetylene lights and electric pumps came into use. The generating plant could be run every week or two and charge the batteries sufficiently to provide adequate current for lights and for pumping water. Except for those families who lived along the power lines from Farmville to Hampden-Sydney, Prospect, and Rice, and the lines which had been built to the schools at Darlington Heights, Worsham, and Green Bay, people living in rural Prince Edward had no transmission line to furnish electric power until the Southside Electric Cooperative, organized under the Rural Electrification Administration, began building power lines through Prince Edward communities in 1938.

Farmville's water supply was at first furnished by springs and wells. There were two town springs, one, near the present passenger station, given by H. St. George Tucker, executor of the estate of Judith Randolph; the other, known as the Tanyard spring, was behind the present Longwood College. There were three pumps on Main Street, one near the Courthouse, one in front of Chappells, one near the present shoe factory; another well was near the Methodist Church and still another on Baptist Hill. Cisterns in which water was stored for fighting fires were located in various parts of town, and the fire fighting was done by bucket brigades. In 1887 the Farmville Water Company was chartered; incorporators were A. R. Venable, Jr., W. G. Dunnington, A. D. Watkins, W. G. Venable, Paulus A. Irving, and B. S. Hooper; the company was authorized to bring water into town from Bass' millpond on Little Buffalo and from springs and wells. In 1893 the Council granted W. P. Dupuy and J. C. Rawn a franchise to furnish water for fifteen years at a rate not over five cents per 100 gallons. There was to be sufficient force to raise the water thirty feet above the level of C. R. Morton's lot at the corner of Buffalo and Appomattox Streets. Water works were built in 1894 of stone from W. W. Jackson's sandstone quarry, of which some buildings had been built at Bizarre over a century before. A private firm, the Farmville Drainage and Power Company, was organized in 1900 by John R. Martin and John W. Otley to put in a sewer system. In 1911 the town bought out both the water company and the sewer company. During the period of the water company's franchise, there were complaints: not enough pressure for fighting fire, excessive charges, unpalatable water after hard rains.[201]

Plans were made to construct telephone lines in Prince Edward a decade after Alexander Graham Bell exhibited his invention at the Centennial Exposition in Philadelphia. The Farmville, Hampden-Sidney and Worsham Telephone Company was chartered in 1886 to acquire, erect, and maintain telephone lines in Prince Edward, Cumberland, Buckingham, and Charlotte Counties. J. P. Fitzgerald, J. M. Crute, W. T. Doyne, A. D. Watkins, Richard McIlwaine, J. R. Thornton, J. D. Eggleston, W. P. Dupuy, and their associates were the incorporators.[202] The first request for permission to operate a telephone exchange in Farmville was made by Dr. Peter Winston in 1897; shortly thereafter a telephone company (undesignated) was permitted to place poles on the street under the supervision of the Council's Streets Committee. S. P. Vanderslice was granted a franchise to operate a telephone exchange and system in Farmville in 1899; poles and wires were not to interfere with the poles and wires of the electric light company. The maximum charge for telephone service was set at $15 per year. Permission was given the American Telephone and Telegraph Company to maintain its lines along streets and highways in Farmville in 1898.[203]

Telephone lines were built through rural districts of the county as well as in Farmville. The Union Telephone Company, which was given a franchise to operate a telephone system in Farmville in 1902 on condition it would not compete with the Farmville Telephone Company, decided to extend its line from Darlington Heights to Farmville, via Five Forks, Prospect, and Hampden-Sydney. It asked for bids to furnish poles of chestnut, white oak, or cedar, not less than five inches in diameter and twenty feet long, except those to be placed where the line crossed the road which were to be twenty-two feet long; it also asked for proposals to plant the poles four feet deep at intervals of sixty yards along the public roads and to string the wires. By April, 1904, the line had been built from Darlington Heights to Five Forks.[204]

The Southside Telephone Company, organized July 22, 1903, also served rural areas. Dr. Peter Winston was president and treasurer, J. D. Eggleston, Jr., vice-president and general manager, and E. W. Venable secretary; K. T. Cralle and W. M. Holladay were directors. Eggleston provided the initiative which extended telephone service into many sections of the county; according to the Farmville *Herald,* "not until [he] stepped to the front did we hear the ring of the instrument or the familiar voices of our friends from afar." The Southside Company in 1903 was granted privileges similar to those granted the Union Telephone Company by the Farmville Council. The next year the Southside Company was given permission to put up the necessary poles and wires in Farmville to connect with the rural system.[205] By 1907 the Southside Company had over 300 miles of wire in Prince Edward, Cumberland, Amelia, Buckingham, Charlotte, and Lunenburg Counties. Officers of the company elected that year were A. D. Watkins, president; Dr. Peter Winston, treasurer; E. R. Booker, secretary. The directors then were R. H. Walton, Rice; Dr. W. M. Holladay, Hampden-Sydney; A. D. Watkins, Farmville; Dr. Winston, Farmville; R. E. Anderson, Farmville R. F. D.; R. B. Johns, Farmville R. F. D.; T. P. Shelton, Jetersville; A. S. Spencer, Rival; and W. B. Gates, Rice. Each director served as a supervisor for the company in his district to whom customers referred their telephone problems.[206]

John R. Martin leased the Farmville Telephone Company's system in 1904 and took charge of the company. R. B. Johns became manager of the system in 1908, continuing until it was sold in 1931 to the Southeast Public Service Corporation of Virginia, which became the Virginia Telephone and Telegraph Company. When the franchise was renewed in 1909 maximum rates permitted were $18 per year for residences and $30 per year for businesses. Permission to increase the rates fifty cents a month was given in 1920 because of high prices then. The Farmville Telephone Company received a thirty-year franchise to operate a system in Farmville in 1929.[207]

The rural telephone lines were allowed to fall into disrepair about the close of World War I. Service became so uncertain that many patrons discontinued their connections with the lines. It was a familiar sight at that time to see broken wires and fallen poles along the roads. With the complete breakdown in rural telephone service, the community centrals were discontinued, and telephone service in the country districts came to an end generally throughout the county. One rural line, in the Bethlehem Church community, was maintained by its patrons and continued to be used. The need for telephone service in the villages was recognized, and some stores secured telephones. Gradually this service was extended into homes in and around the villages of Prospect, Rice, Worsham, and Hampden-

Sydney, but telephone service in rural Prince Edward is not nearly so extensive now as it was in the decade before World War I.

The commission merchant, whose business had developed before the War between the States, continued to flourish after the war. He was the leading mercantile operator in the county prior to World War I. In Farmville the stores prior to the War of 1861-65 tended to specialize: there were groceries and hardware and dry goods and drug stores. The tendency continued after the war, and after World War I the chain store grocery entered the Farmville mercantile scene. The village stores have continued to be general stores, carrying a variety of merchandise: groceries, dry goods, shoes, feed, fertilizer, some farm implements, and sometimes household appliances. They have dropped one line of merchandise which many once carried, that of coffins and caskets, and have left that trade now exclusively to the undertaker. With the increasing mechanization of farms, the line of farm implements is diminishing, since it is necessary for a merchant carrying an extensive line of implements to provide a repair service with his sales service. Country stores once included in their stock whiskey and other liquors; toward the end of the nineteenth century they began dropping this line.[208]

The building of railroads, which ended stage-coach transportation, put an end to the business of operating taverns. In the villages boarding and rooming houses took the place of the inn, to provide accommodations for transients, principally traveling salesmen or drummers, as they were usually called, who traveled by train from place to place in calling on merchants. To reach stores not accessible by rail, they usually hired horse and buggy at a livery stable (another vanished business) and drove out to see their customers. In addition to transients these boarding houses accommodated more permanent guests, usually teachers and unmarried store clerks. The boarding house, too, has disappeared in most communities, and it is almost impossible for a teacher to secure such accommodations in the villages.

One of the oldtime inns developed into a hotel. The tavern at the corner of Main and Second Streets, Farmville, had become the Randolph House prior to the War between the States. It was completely renovated in 1907 by George M. Serpell, who bought it from the estate of R. M. Burton, and was formally opened as the Prince Edward Hotel on August 8, 1907. This hostelry has continued to operate under that name. Charles T. Chick bought the hotel from

Serpell in 1913 and operated it until 1935.[209] A popular hotel of the last century was the Farmville Hotel; the building, on Main Street near the Planters Bank, was taken down in 1901.

The county's largest hotel, the Weyanoke of Farmville, was opened October 20, 1925. It was built and is owned by the Farmville Hotel Corporation, stock in which was sold in a campaign in 1924 by the Hockenbury System of Harrisburg, Pennsylvania. J. C. Woolling was the first and longtime manager of the hotel.[210]

In this era of the opening of new businesses the Farmville Steam Laundry began operations in Farmville about 1894. It was owned by George W. Bragg; after he opened a laundry in Richmond in 1894, the Farmville laundry was managed by his brother, D. P. Bragg.[211] Henry Lindsey began the operation of the Farmville Steam Laundry in 1899; this business was purchased in 1927 by R. B. Crawford and W. T. Smith, who gave to it a new name, Kilkare Laundry; W. W. McClintic is now associated with Crawford in the operation of this business, which in 1928 moved into the section of Farmville on the Cumberland side of the Appomattox River.[212]

The earliest photographer in the county of whom there is record was J. M. Wood, who had a daguerrotype gallery in Farmville in 1852. In that year C. H. Erambert became an apprentice in the gallery, continuing as a photographer in Farmville for forty-two years.[213]

The Farmville *Journal* was continued after the War between the States by its publisher, A. M. Cowan. Dr. Peter Winston became proprietor and associate editor in 1867, and the next year T. W. Porter became associated with him. R. A. Booker bought the paper in 1869 and changed the name to the Farmville *News*. He sold it to A. B. Venable the next year, and the new owner gave the paper a new name, *The New Commonwealth*. J. G. Cannon became proprietor of the paper in 1872; the change which he made in the name amounted to only a slight modification: it was now the Farmville *Commonwealth*. J. A. H. St. Andrew, with whom Charles E. Madison became associated in the editorship of the paper, bought it in 1873 and renamed it the Farmville *Mercury*. The old name, the Farmville *Journal*, was subsequently revived, and it was known by this name during the editorships of L. Cushing Irving and Junius Wilson and W. E. Edwards. The *Journal* was sold to A. D. Watkins in 1893 for $230.

A new paper, the Farmville *Herald*, began publication November

15, 1890, under the editorship of R. B. Berkeley. It was established in connection with the Farmville Coal and Iron Company, which at the time was engaged in a vigorous promotion for Farmville. J. L. Hart bought the *Herald* in 1893 and later the *Journal.* Thus the *Herald,* in acquiring the older paper, became the successor to the journalistic tradition which began when Theodoric B. McRobert brought his newspaper from Scottsville to Farmville in 1832. Berkeley continued his connection with the *Herald* until his death in 1916 and did much of the writing which appeared in it during the years he was associated with it. After Hart's death, J. Barrye Wall, the present publisher, bought the *Herald* in 1921. Until 1927 the *Herald* was published on the first floor of the old Opera House, on the site of the Municipal Building; it then moved to its present quarters on North Street. Long a weekly, the *Herald* is now published twice a week.

Another Farmville paper at the turn of the century was the *Southside Sentinel,* published by J. S. McIlwaine. Publication of this paper was suspended in 1903.

L. C. Martin and A. B. Dodge began publication of the Farmville *Leader* in 1915; this paper was bought in 1927 by A. M. Potter, who subsequently consolidated it with another paper which he owned, the *Virginia Union Farmer* of Dillwyn, as the *Farmer-Leader.* George Borum bought the *Farmer-Leader* after Potter's death in 1934, selling it shortly thereafter to J. B. Wall, who consolidated it with the Herald.[214]

A significant postwar development on the economic front has been the mounting inflation. Price controls kept prices stabilized during World War II. After the removal of controls, prices moved upward. The outbreak of the Korean War gave a decided impetus to price increases; efforts to impose anti-inflationary measures came late and did not prove generally effective. Prices of some commodities have tended to decline since the end of that war. In other sections of this book prices of commodities at various times have been quoted. A comparison of prewar and postwar prices shows the fluctuation in the cost of certain staple commodities:

Commodity	1940 Price	1946 Price	1948 Price	1954 Price
Hamburger (pound)	15 cents	39 cents	49 cents	35 cents
Butter (pound)	33 cents	73 cents	72 cents	Butter not quoted; Oleo, 25 cents

Commodity	1940 Price	1946 Price	1948 Price	1954 Price
Sugar	46 cents (10 lbs.)	80 cents (10 lbs.)		$2.49 (25 lbs.)
Coffee (pound)	12 cents	36 cents	79 cents (2 lbs.)	$1.13 (1 lb.)
Canned peaches	25 cents (2 cans)	28 cents (1 can)	33 cents (1 can)	21 cents (1 can)
Flour	31 cents (12 lbs.)	60 cents (10 lbs.)	89 cents (10 lbs.)	53 cents (5 lbs.)
Pork and Beans	9 cents (1 can)	11 cents (1 can)	25 cents (3 cans)	17 cents (2 cans)[215]

It was not until after the close of World War II that the first radio stations in Prince Edward began operation. On September 19, 1946, the Southside Virginia Broadcasting Company was authorized to establish a 1,000-watt radio station to serve Blackstone, Crewe, and Farmville. Station WSVS, operated by the company, with Farmville studios in the Herald Building, went on the air April 6, 1947. WSVS currently broadcasts from its Crewe studios. The second station, WFLO, with studios at 118 Third Street, Farmville, presented its first broadcast August 17, 1947, operating on 870 kilocycles. W. Harold Gray was first manager; his successor in this post was James C. Wilson,[216] who in turn was succeeded by the present manager, John D. Wilson.

CHAPTER XVIII

Three Wars

POLITICALLY Reconstruction came to an end in Virginia with the promulgation of the new Constitution by the Convention of 1901-02 which had drawn it up. Conditions which made possible such a convention and such a constitution, the control of state and local governments by white men through the Democratic party, had become stabilized during the 1890's, and the new Constitution in effect confirmed and secured the control which after the most prolonged and bitter political war in the history of the State had been won.

Emotionally Reconstruction came to an end with the Spanish-American War. The wheels had been set in motion with the Southern Democrat-Northern Republican coalition which made possible the selection of Rutherford B. Hayes as President in 1877 and gained in return the withdrawal of federal troops from the South. From Hayes' administration, the growing influence of Southerners in national affairs helped spread the feeling that again the South was a part of the Union. When war against Spain was declared in 1898, the Southern demonstration of patriotism left no doubt that the onetime Confederacy was a loyal section of the United States.

A few members of the Farmville Guard on April 25, 1898, signed enlistment papers for two years' service in the United States Army. The Farmville Guard was shortly thereafter called to active duty. The Guard, with forty men in the unit, left Farmville for Camp Lee, Richmond, on Monday morning, May 16. The company assembled at the Armory at 4:00 A. M.; after a picture of the group had been taken, the men marched to the railroad station, where, despite the early hour (early rising was more prevalent then than it is now), a large crowd awaited them. The seriousness of the occasion was impressed upon soldier and observer as the Guard's chaplain, the Rev. T. McN. Simpson, offered prayer for each of the men leaving to serve his country. At Blackstone the Farmville Guard was joined by the Nottoway Grays to bring the strength of the company to sixty-seven. Captain J. Davis Allen, of the Farmville Guard, had gone to Richmond the day before to make arrangements for quartering the men on their arrival.[1] The combined units from Prince Edward and Nottoway were mustered into service May 27, 1898, as Company C of the Third Regiment. The regiment left Richmond June 5 for Camp Alger.[2] By September 1 it was announced that the Third Regiment would be mustered out of service and by the middle of the month, the hostilities over, the Guard was back in Farmville. The Farmville Chapter of the United Daughters of the Confederacy gave a "brilliant reception" to the Guard at Planters Warehouse on September 15; an "abundant supper" was served, and addresses were delivered by Dr. George F. Bagby, Dr. W. W. H. Thackston, and the Rev. W. B. Capers.[3]

The Farmville Guard, in which 115 men went out in 1861 to fight for the Confederacy and in which only twenty, some of whom were crippled, returned in 1865, was reorganized about a decade after the war with George W. Davis as captain. S. W. Paulett succeeded him in command of the company, serving for ten years or more, from the late 1870's until the late 1880's. S. W. Watkins succeeded Paulett in command of the company, serving two years when the company disbanded.[4] In the fall of 1892 the members of the Guard held a meeting and decided to reorganize the company. John R. Martin was chosen captain and J. Davis Allen lieutenant.[5]

When rioting broke out in the Pocahontas coal field in the spring of 1895 as striking miners tried to prevent other workers from going into the mines, Governor Charles T. O'Ferrall ordered the Farmville Guard to report to Major W. E. Simons, commander of troops at Graham (now Bluefield), Virginia. (The strike protested a reduction in pay.) Sixty-two men left Farmville May 4 on the midday train, arriving at Graham at 10:30 P. M. The Farmville company joined companies from Richmond, Lynchburg, Charlottesville, Salem, and Roanoke; a train of two baggage cars, seven passenger cars, and a flat car on which were loaded a Gatling gun and the three-inch cannon of the Richmond Howitzers was made up and took the troops to Pocahontas May 6. Over 100 troops were on guard duty daily. Troops sent to Pocahontas received $1 a day and rations.[6]

The Guard was used to preserve order during another strike; when employees of the Richmond Passenger and Power Company struck on June 17, 1903, for higher pay and a shorter work day, the Farmville company was among those ordered to Richmond to quell riots and to keep cars moving. That tour of duty lasted a month, the men returning July 18.[7]

Between the Spanish-American War and World War I the most spectacular activities of the Guard were participation in the inaugural parade for President Woodrow Wilson on March 4, 1913,[8] and service on the Mexican border during the difficulties between the United States and Mexico. The Guard left June 22, 1916, under the command of Captain H. H. Hunt, for a brief period of training in Richmond before going to the border and returned to Farmville March 1, 1917. On December 13, 1916, motion pictures showing soldiers on the border, including men from Farmville, were shown at the Opera House.[9]

Company captains during this period included R. B. Cralle, J. L. Bugg (1902-03), E. Scott Martin (1903-05), H. H. Hunt (elected in 1905 and for another period later), W. C. Duvall, and Frank S. Blanton.[10]

The Farmville Guard had been home from duty on the Mexican border only a little over a month when the United States declared war on Germany April 6, 1917, and entered World War I. Six days later the Guard left again, this time to guard tunnels, bridges, and coal mines at St. Pauls, Virginia.[11] A military unit was sent to guard the High Bridge upon the declaration of war.

The war had been in progress in Europe almost three years before the United States entered. Although the United States was neutral, public sympathy on a widespread scale was aroused for the Belgians by German treatment of those people. Prince Edward people shared in contributing to the relief of the Belgian people in 1914; in a letter dated January 2, 1915, J. P. Andre Mottu, Belgian vice-consul in Norfolk, thanked the people of Prince Edward and Farmville for a shipment of goods contributed to Belgian relief.[12] The pressing needs of victims of the ravages of war in Europe prompted the organization of a war relief association in Farmville of which Robert K. Brock was president in January, 1917.[13] At that time the association reported the need of hospital supplies and clothing. On March 11 a large crowd attended a public meeting at the Normal School auditorium, at which Brock and Dr. J. L. Jarman spoke on the needs of the war relief program.[14]

With the outbreak of war young men began to volunteer for military service. The Farmville armory was used as a recruiting station for the area. Several young men left Farmville May 14 for medical examination for the Navy.[15] But the United States could not depend upon volunteer enlistments to raise the number of men necessary for the armed forces. A selective service system was introduced; men between the ages of twenty-one and thirty-one registered for the draft on June 15, 1917.[16] Judge J. M. Crute was chairman of the draft board for Prince Edward, and Dr. W. E. Anderson and J. H. Lewis were members.[17] A total of 695 men from Prince Edward saw service in World War I; of these 100 were in the Farmville Guard, 438 went into service from the county, 146 natives of the county went into service from some point outside the county, and eleven were in the Student Army Training Corps at Hampden-Sydney.[18]

The Farmville company did not remain long on guard duty. It was transferred to Camp McClellan, Alabama, for training, Hunt in command. There the First, Second, and Fourth Regiments of the Virginia National Guard were consolidated, and in the consolidation Company A of Farmville and Company G of Petersburg were combined to form Company G of the 116th Regiment of the 29th Division; Winston B. Davis of Petersburg was commissioned captain of the consolidated company. In the new organization, the Guard went to France and took part in some of the hardest fighting in which American troops were engaged in World War I.[19]

The war brought shortages in some commodities. Sugar became both scarce and high in price. At times only a kind known as rainbow sugar from the variety of color of the grains was available. On November 10, 1917, only one store in Farmville had sugar for sale.[20] To conserve certain food supplies people were asked to observe meatless and wheatless days; in patriotic spirit people generally responded, and in many Prince Edward homes people ate only cornbread and had no meat one day in the week. In a voluntary fuel conservation program stores which used coal closed one afternoon each week during the winter of 1917-18.

A Red Cross chapter was organized in Prince Edward on August 31, 1917, through the efforts of Dr. T. G. Hardy and Colonel Henry W. Anderson. Robert K. Brock, who had been active in promoting war relief work in the county, was elected chairman, Mrs. J. L. Jarman vice-chairman, the Rev. C. P. Holbrook secretary, and J. L. Bugg treasurer. The executive committee consisted of the officers and W. S. Weaver, Rice;. E. S. Taylor, Prospect; Mrs. T. P. Singleton, Darlington Heights; E. S. Martin, J. L. Jarman, Mrs. R. B. Tuggle, Mrs. A. T. Gray, and Mrs. W. P. Richardson, all of Farmville. The membership committee, consisting of Dr. Jarman, Mrs. Gray, Mrs. Tuggle, Mrs. T. G. Hardy, and Miss Sue Flippen, enrolled a large membership in the county. Branches of the Prince

Edward chapter were organized in the various communities of the county, with the following chairman: Rice, W. S. Weaver; Meherrin, M. E. Gee; Darlington Heights, Mrs. T. P. Singleton; Prospect, T. J. McIlwaine and later W. C. Chick; Sandy River, W. B. Bruce; Abilene, Miss Annie McGehee; Felden, Miss Marie Allen; Hampden-Sydney, Miss Susie Venable; Five Forks, Mrs. Norvell Crute. There was also a branch among the Negroes of Farmville.

Mrs. J. L. Jarman was chairman of the Woman's Work Committee, which did an impressive amount of war work. Women throughout the county participated in the sewing and knitting to produce the articles and garments which the Red Cross chapter sent to the national organization for distribution. Over 21,000 surgical dressings were made, 825 hospital garments, 818 refugee garments, and 1,100 comfort kits; 248 sweaters and 286 pair of socks were knitted by Red Cross workers in Prince Edward. In addition to this work by the women, the Junior Red Cross, under the direction of Miss Ilma von Schilling, made 200 property bags, 145 garments, and 500 gun wipes.

When the Home Service Section of the Red Cross chapter was organized in 1918, Dr. J. M. Lear was named chairman and Miss Mary Dupuy secretary; Miss Dupuy was succeeded by Mrs. Roberta H. Large.

In the first Red Cross fund drive after the Prince Edward chapter was organized in the spring of 1918, $6,250 was raised, although the quota was only $2,800. Previous to the fund drive, the chapter had raised funds from contributions.[21] Ladies of the chapter went to the Farmville warehouses in December soliciting from farmers contributions of tobacco, which was selling at hitherto unprecedented prices, to be sold for the Red Cross.[22]

Intensive campaigns were put on during the war to sell government securities to finance the war. The campaigns to sell government bonds were known as Liberty Loan drives, and the bonds were popularly called Liberty bonds. Although the first two Liberty Loan drives were not conducted on the intensive scale of subsequent drives, it was reported late in October, 1917, that Liberty bonds to the value of $70,000 had been sold in Farmville.[23] The Third Liberty Loan campaign took place during the spring of 1918, and the Fourth was launched September 28, 1918. At the outset of the campaign on October 1, Dr. Douglas Southall Freeman of Richmond spoke at a public rally at the Normal School in the interest of the drive.[24] The Fifth drive did not take place until after the end of the war and was in consequence called the Victory Loan Drive; it was launched in Prince Edward April 23, 1919, with a visit to the county of the Carter Glass (named for the then Secretary of the Treasury) Trophy Train with its exhibit of captured guns, cannons, trench mortars, a German field kitchen, helmets, and gas masks. The train stopped on sidings of the Norfolk and Western Railroad; the train was open for visitors at set hours, and while it was at the station there was a program with speaking in the interest of the drive.[25] J. L. Bugg was county chairman of the third, fourth, and fifth bond drives, in each of which Prince Edward exceeded its subscription quota.[26]

A savings program for investment in government securities was also provided through Thrift and War Savings Stamps. The Liberty bonds had sold at a par value, and the United States paid interest on them. War Savings Stamps were redeemable January 1, 1923, at $5 each. The Thrift stamp cost twenty-five cents. This stamp was designed especially for school pupils; when twenty were accumulated, they could be exchanged for a war savings stamp. Prince Edward schools sponsored the sale of thrift and savings stamps, both to pupils and to persons not in school through the pupils.[27]

False reports of an armistice were responsible for a premature peace celebration in Farmville on November 7, 1918. Four days later the armistice was signed, and the fighting in World War I came to an end. All Prince Edward joined in the rejoicing. Eighteen of the men from the county had died in service, and many had been wounded. War had brought sorrow and anxiety to many homes and to many friends of men in service, and there was genuine relief that the fighting in Europe had come to an end. Farmville celebrated that night of November 11, 1918; whistles blew, bells were rung, the Silver Band assembled at the corner of Main and Third Streets and played, while a "throbbing, cheering mass" filled the streets.

But life is rarely with unmixed emotions. A widespread sickness, an "infectious and malignant fever" which took many lives, had added to the burdens of the Prince Edward populace during the last summer of the Revolution; so it was at the end of World War I, although the influenza epidemic was just beginning when the armistice was signed. Yet the Farmville *Herald's* news summary for 1918 added after an account of the victory celebration a sobering note: "Many influenza deaths are being reported."[28] The epidemic was to increase in intensity, reaching a peak in severity and mortality about the end of the year. Few families in the county escaped the disease, and there were numerous deaths.

The soldiers and sailors of the county received a formal welcome home on September 4, 1919. The festal occasion began with a baseball game between the Farmville and Green Bay High Schools at Farmville, the home team winning by a score of eight to two. The Silver Band gave a concert in front of the armory. There was a parade on Main Street, commanded by Lieutenant Walker Paulette. A supper at the Normal School for the returning veterans followed the parade, at which Judge A. D. Watkins was toastmaster. The Rev. J. T. Bosman offereed the prayer, and speakers included Judge J. M. Crute, J. Taylor Thompson, Captain S. W. Watkins, L. R. Richardson, Major Maxwell Robeson, Dr. C. E. Burrell, Dr. J. H. Cocks, and Dr. J. L. Jarman, who explained to the former service men the new organization which was being organized by their old comrades, the American Legion.[29]

A month after the armistice, on December 10, 1918, the Farmville Town Council appointed V. Vaiden, E. W. Sanford, and P. W. Beckham to request the Board of Supervisors to appoint a committee to work with them in the formulation of plans to erect a monument honoring the soldiers from the county in World War I. Nothing came of the effort, but early in 1925 W. W. Sale, adjutant general of Virginia, notified the town that the State Board on the Distribution of War Trophies had allocated a captured field piece to Farmville if the town would apply for it in ninety days and pay the freight on it. The council made application and guaranteed payment of freight; it then designated the American Legion post, which had been organized in Farmville and named for Jack Garland, one of the local casualties in the war, to place the trophy. This was done November 11, 1925, in formal ceremonies,[30] the cannon being placed at the intersection of High, Oak, and Appomattox Streets, where it remained until contributed to a World War II scrap drive.

The Farmville Guard was reorganized September 8, 1921, as Company G of the 116th Regiment of the Virginia National Guard, thus preserving the name of the company which had fought with distinction in France. Wallace J. Wilck was chosen captain of the company, and D. Walker Paulett first lieutenant on the reorganization. In March, 1922, Wilck resigned, and Paulett was named captain. Paulett resigned in 1924, and F. W. Wagoner, then town manager of Farmville, became captain. Wagoner served only a few months, and Paulett resumed the captaincy. The company was called to duty in 1932 during the strike at the Dan River Mills, Danville.[31]

The first half of the twentieth century saw American partici- pation in two World Wars. The second World War began with the invasion of Poland by Germany in September, 1939. A year later the possibility of American involvement made it advisable to in- crease the military forces of the United States. As in World War I, the principle of selective service was used to draft men into Army service, the other branches of the Armed Forces recruiting by volun- teer enlistments. The first registration, involving men between the ages of twenty-one and thirty-six, took place October 16, 1940, a day unseasonably and disagreeably cold.[32] In Prince Edward 1,580 men registered.[33] There were five subsequent registrations: July 1, 1941, when ninety-one men who had become twenty-one since the preced- ing October 1 registered;[34] February 16, 1942, when 837 men be- tween the ages of twenty and forty-four who had not previously registered filled out the Selective Service registration forms;[35] April 27, 1942, at which time 1,257 men forty-five to sixty-five regis- tered;[36] June 30, 1942, when 370 young men aged eighteen and nineteen registered;[37] and December 11-13, 1942, which was the registration period for boys who had reached their eighteenth birth- day since July 1.[38] After that registration young men were required to register at the county selective service office in the courthouse as they reached their eighteenth birthday. When the first drawing was held to select men to be called to service after the first registration, the number 158 was drawn; persons within the jurisdiction of each Selective Service Board holding that number were called for induc- tion, and Charles Staples Wilson, who held that number in Prince Edward, was the first person inducted in the Armed Forces under selective service from the county.[39]

The first Prince Edward Selective Service Board consisted of E. S. Shields, chairman, J. Hugh Gilliam, and W. S. Weaver. Dr. T. G. Hardy was examining physician, Irvine C. Watkins clerk, and Robert K. Brock appeal agent.[40] In 1942 Gilliam became chairman of the board, Shields continuing a member. Weaver resigned from the board in 1942 and was succeeded by Herbert L. Bradshaw. Watkins later resigned as clerk and was succeeded by John P. Meanley.

As plans got under way during the latter part of 1940 for in- creasing the Armed Forces, Prince Edward men who held reserve commissions in the Army began to be called to active duty.

The Farmville Guard, Company G of the Virginia National Guard, was called into active service February 3, 1941. The seventy- four men of the company were under the command of Captain D.

Walker Paulette, who had commanded the company most of the time since its reorganization after World War I. Other officers were Thomas Bloomfield, first lieutenant, and Walter Potter, Carl W. Dickhoff, and W. Henry Hubbard, second lieutenants. Until February 19 the company was quartered at the armory; its daily schedule began with reveille at 6:15 A. M. and included breakfast, 6:45; drill, 8:00-11:15; dinner, 12 M.; drill, 1:30-5:15; supper, 6:00. Evenings were free, except for those taking special training. The company then went to Fort George G. Meade, Maryland; there Captain Paulette was promoted to the rank of major and became executive officer and temporary commander of the First Battalion of the 11th infantry, and Bloomfield became captain of the company. When Bloomfield was transferred in June, 1942, to the 83rd Division, Potter was promoted to the command of the company.

With the prospect of National Guard mobilization for active duty, plans were made to organize home guard units, to be known as the Virginia Protective Force, in December, 1940. Company 74 was mustered into service February 14, 1941, at Farmville, five days before Company G left for Fort Meade, with fifty-one men and three officers, R. B. Crawford captain, Vernon C. Womack first lieutenant, and Morton L. Davis second lieutenant. The following December Womack became captain of the company, Davis first lieutenant, and W. T. Rice second lieutenant. Subsequent lieutenants wese Malcolm Ranson, William McClintic, and T. E. Gilmer. The name was changed from Virginia Protective Force to Virginia State Guard in 1943. As men were continually leaving the ranks of the State Guard company for service in the nation's Armed Forces, there was a large turnover in its ranks, and a continuing recruitment for the State Guard was kept under way. The State Guard was disbanded June 30, 1947.

Another local military company was organized for service during the war in Prince Edward, but it was never active. A unit of the Virginia Reserve Militia, the "Minute Men," was organized at Worsham in the summer of 1942 as a result of efforts of Dr. A. C. Fraser, who was elected captain. Men eighteen to sixty, who had a gun, a telephone, and a five-passenger car, were eligible to join.[41]

Two of the registrations for selective service, the calling of men with reserve commissions to active duty, the mobilization of Company G, and the organization of the Virginia Protective Force had all taken place before the United States actually entered war. Formal declaration of war against Japan followed by a day the Japanese

attack on the naval base at Pearl Harbor in the Hawaiian Islands
on December 7, 1941, and the declaration of war upon the United
States by Japan. Declarations of war against Germany and Italy
followed declarations of war by those governments on the United
States on December 11.

With the formal entry into war, civilian defense became an
important local activity. On December 20, 1941, the Farmville Town
Council conferred on Mayor W. C. Fitzpatrick extraordinary authority to make rules and regulations essential to a civil defense program
for the town. Subsequently a county civilian defense organization
was set up by the Defense Council, of which Morris G. Smith was
chairman. Fitzpatrick was named co-ordinator of civilian defense
for the county.

The civilian defense staff consisted of a variety of workers: air
raid wardens, auxiliary firemen, auxiliary police, messengers, demo-
lition squad, decontamination squad, medical assistants, nurses aides,
drivers. Their work, happily, was limited to blackouts and air raid
drills—all drills to prepare the people and to help them prepare
quickly and smoothly for possible air attack. Training was required
of all those participating in the program. A school for civilian defense workers in Prince Edward began at the courthouse March 2,
1942; W. E. Hill, of the State Division of Trade and Industrial
Education, was the teacher; altogether there were twelve sessions of
two hours each on Monday and Tuesday evenings in the course of
instruction in gases, bambs, and first aid; after the second meeting
of the class the group had to move to the high school because it
was too large to be accommodated in the courthouse. Instructional
methods included both lectures and films. There were several opportunities to put the training to the test during 1942: there was a
darkness to dawn blackout on June 17; a daylight air raid test
August 5, between 10:15 and 10:45 A. M.; a simulated air raid
during the blackout August 18-19 between 8:30 P. M. and 1:00
A. M.; a test blackout October 5. The complete cooperation of all
the people was usually secured in these drills and blackouts, but
during the daylight air raid test August 5 a customer in a Farmville
store forced a boy to go out on the street and closed the door of the
building on the lad. The customer was fined $5 for violating the
rules which required all persons except civilian defense workers to
remain indoors during the tests. Although the workers had been
participating in the tests during the summer, organization of the
Prince Edward civilian defense group was not completed until De-

cember 14, 1942. At a meeting then over 200 volunteer workers took the oaths prescribed for civilian defense workers and heard an appropriate address by Dr. Edgar G. Gammon, president of Hampden-Sydney.

An aircraft warning service began operating in the county before Pearl Harbor. In several communities of the county citizens watched for airplanes and reported each plane seen from the observation post. Dr. J. P. Wynne organized the service in Prince Edward, appointing ten chief observers and calling for 200 volunteers on May 28, 1941. The observation posts were manned twenty-four hours daily.

The call of many physicians and nurses to service with the Armed Forces, even before Pearl Harbor, and the prospect of future calls of more posed the problem of shortage of trained and skilled medical practitioners. Dr. H. B. Holsinger of Farmville joined the surgical staff of Evacuation Hospital No. 8 (the unit of the University of Virginia Medical School) with the rank of major in February, 1942. Six months later Dr. T. E. Knight of Farmville reported to Chicago for Army duty. Dr. A. M. DeMuth closed his Farmville office to become an Army dentist. Public health departments and Red Cross chapters cooperated to relieve the problem the shortage was creating by training women to give the sick much of the attention physicians and nurses had formerly been depended upon to give. This training was given through home nursing classes. Three of these classes were offered at Southside Hospital, under the sponsorship of the health department, beginning in October, 1941; the instructors were three registered nurses, Mrs. Dorothy Ramsey, Miss Elizabeth Payne, and Miss Charlotte Piper. Mrs. Ramsey taught a nurses' aide course at the hospital under the sponsorship of the Red Cross chapter in January-February, 1943; this course, which consisted of thirty-five hours of instruction and forty-five of practical experience, was designed to train women to help in the hospitals. Four persons, Mrs. Sam Glover, Mrs. R. B. Crawford, Mrs. Charles Rogers, and Miss Josephine Towler, completed the course and qualified for the work.

One of the major instructional programs of the Red Cross in the immediate prewar period and during the war was in first aid. The first aid course offered by the Prince Edward Red Cross chapter began February 29, 1940, about six months after the outbreak of war in Europe. The class was organized through the efforts of Mrs. S. M. Holton, Jr., then first aid chairman of the chapter. The Red Cross also organized classes and provided instruction in canteen, the feeding of groups of people in emergency situations. Mrs. Trent Gilliland taught the first canteen course offered by the Prince Edward chapter, classes beginning in April, 1942; Mrs. Arthur H. Irby was chairman of the canteen committee which sponsored the instructional program.

As in World War I, the Prince Edward Red Cross chapter during World War II made a notable production record. The making of surgical dressings was a regular activity for much of the war period; instruction in this work began August 3, 1942; from that time, until the project ceased with the need, workers with the Prince Edward branch made 474,896 surgical dressings. The production committee of the chapter, of which Mrs. J. W. Garnett was chairman, maintained a room on the second floor of the Burger Building on Main Street, Farmville, for the work of volunteers; the work directed by this committee resulted in the making of 4,280 garments, 1,556 knitted articles, and 825 overseas kits.

Activities of the chapter increased so greatly in wartime, some, such as home service, making so great demands that volunteer workers could not respond to all, that the chapter employed a full-time worker, Miss Annie Claire Bone, as its executive secretary. Through the courtesy of Leggett Brothers the chapter maintained offices in the Warren-Walker-Martin house on North Main Street, Farmville, where the Leggett store is now located. During the war the chapter had three chairmen: Mrs. B. T. Taylor, Mrs. Farrar Shelton, and the Rev. Philip A. Roberts. The chapter had a successful record in fund raising during the war. Each of five drives during the years 1942-46 reached or exceeded its goal; with total goals of $45,976, the chapter raised $53,403.61.

The blood donor program, in which volunteers contributed blood to be used in the service hospitals, began during the war. In Prince Edward the principal promoter was Dr. F. R. Crawford, who directed the efforts of the Farmville Lions Club to recruit donors. The Red Cross reported that 250 persons from Prince Edward were on its list of blood donors. Locally the blood donor program began in 1942.

The nature of war work in Prince Edward was greatly influenced by the location of Camp Pickett to the east of Blackstone in Nottoway, Dinwiddie, and Brunswick Counties. The Red Cross chapter sent books and magazines regularly to the reading rooms of the camp. Each week a group of ladies from Farmville worked in the hospital canteen there. A Gray Ladies Corps of the Prince Edward Red Cross chapter was organized in 1945 by Mrs. Edwin P. Lancaster; the sixteen members received their training at the Camp Pickett hospital.

No town in the immediate area of Blackstone had recreation facilities adequate to accommodate the soldiers in training at Camp Pickett when they were free from duty for a few hours. Consequently the men visited many of the towns and cities within a few hours' ride from the camp. To help the soldiers from Camp Pickett who came to Farmville, and many did, especially on week ends, the town opened a recreation center for service men on the second floor of the Capps Building on October 16, 1942. Mrs. Shelton Whitaker, the first director, was succeeded in July, 1943, by Mrs. James H. Flippen, who continued in charge until the center closed on February 1, 1945. H. L. Newbill was chairman of the policies committee of the center. A game room was provided, and Mr. and Mrs. H. N. Gordon redecorated and furnished a reading room as a memorial to their son, Ray, who was Farmville's first war casualty, and the Farmville Woman's Club contributed books. In addition to the opportunities for recreation always available, dances were held frequently. Volunteer hostesses assisted the director in the operation of the center. Local contributions provided funds for the operation of the center.[42]

The transient visitors from Camp Pickett were not the only personnel from the camp for whom accommodations had to be provided in Prince Edward. Many of the men stationed at the camp, particularly officers, brought their families with them and sought living quarters as near the camp as they could find. Blackstone, the camp's nearest municipal neighbor, could not begin to meet the need, and the house-hunting extended into the other towns and villages of Nottoway and Brunswick, Lunenburg, and Prince Edward as well. The demand was so great that practically every house and apartment available for rent in Farmville and a considerable section of Prince Edward were taken by these military families, and there were times when even in the county the demand for accommodations exceeded the supply. Soldiers' families found homes, during the stay of the husband and father at Camp Pickett, not only in Farmville, but in Green Bay, Prospect, and Rice as well.

Camp Pickett from the beginning of its construction provided employment for many workers from Prince Edward. Trucks transporting these workers picked them up in the morning and brought them home each evening. After the camp was opened, a number of people from Prince Edward worked in the offices and facilities of the camp; commuting to Camp Pickett was a daily chore for many from several Prince Edward communities.

Although Prince Edward was the home of no specially built war plant during World War II, eight Farmville firms had contracts to furnish their products to the government. The part which these firms in their diversified activity played was so representative of the industrial activity of small town industry that the Bureau of Co-ordination of Inter-American Activities selected Farmville to feature in its picture magazines for July, 1943, *En Guardia* and *Em Guarda*, respectively in the Spanish and in the Portuguese language, for circulation in Latin America.

The Buffalo Shook Company in the summer of 1943 was devoting its full time to manufacturing box shooks for the United States government and tobacco containers for the British government. The two governments for some time during the war period took the full production of this firm, which got its raw materials entirely from the forests of Prince Edward and neighboring counties. The box shooks were used to make cases for shipping shoes and munitions for the military forces. Logs were trucked from the forests in which they were cut to the Farmville plant, where they were sawed into box shooks.

The other three Farmville firms manufacturing lumber products were also actively engaged in production for war purposes. The Farmville Manufacturing Company had a sub-contract to furnish truck handles to firms making floor trucks on government orders; these were sold directly to the Army and the Navy for use in arsenals and supply depots. The source of the oak and hickory used in the manufacture of the handles was largely local. The manufacture of truck handles accounted for twenty-five per cent of the production of the Farmville Manufacturing Company. This firm also made plow handles, essential items in the production of food on American farms; production of this item ran to 700 dozen handles weekly in the summer of 1943.

The manufacture of trailer boxes in which Army vehicles were shipped was a major wartime activity of the Mottley Construction Company. This work began in April, 1943. In the summer of 1943 it was estimated that ninety-five percent of Mottley's production was for war work. In addition to the trailer boxes, Mottley made shell boxes, pallets which were used in Army depots for loading freight, millwork for defense housing, and lawn chairs for the Red Cross and for clubs at Camp Pickett.

Millwork for government camps and bases and war industry plants took ninety per cent of the production of the Taylor Manufacturing Company. Among the plants and bases for which Taylor supplied millwork were the New River Ordnance Works and New River Bag Loading Company, Dublin, Virginia; Hercules Powder Company, Radford; Fort Belvoir, Virginia; Camp Butner, North Carolina; Camp Pickett, Virginia; Alexandria Quartermaster Depot, Cameron, Virginia; Naval Air Station, Virginia; Air Force Technical School, Goldsboro, North Carolina; and the Arlington Hall Station Project of the Signal Corps, Arlington. For its work with the Arlington Hall project, Taylor shared in the award of the "E" Army-Navy Production award.

The Farmville branch of the Craddock-Terry Shoe Company devoted fifty per cent of its production to the manufacture of special shoes for the Navy. For the wearing qualities of these shoes as demonstrated in the fighting on Guadalcanal, Rear Admiral W. B. Young, chief of the Navy Bureau of Supplies and Account, issued a special commendation. The shoe was originated by Craddock-Terry, and the company received its first contract for the manufacture of this shoe in September, 1942. The Farmville factory also manufactured some Army shoes, beginning war work in July, 1942, but the demand for the Navy shoe was so great that the firm had to concentrate on producing this shoe. Some of these Navy shoes were shipped in boxes made by the Buffalo Shook Company. In addition to the Navy shoes, Craddock-Terry in Farmville also manufactured mining and heavy labor shoes, which accounted for an additional twenty-five per cent of production. Since these shoes went indirectly to war work, three-fourths of the production of the Farmville shoe factory was for war purposes.

Much of the scrap materials collected in Prince Edward for war purposes was handled by the Farmville Iron and Metal Company. During the war practically all this firm's business was involved in the war effort. Scrap iron, steel, aluminum, brass, and copper went directly into the manufacture of armament. The firm also bought scrap rubber and paper, essential items in the war eeconomy.

All the laundering for the Navy V-12 School at Hampden-Sydney and the headquarters company at the Cumberland Camp was done by Kilkare Laundry. During the summer of 1943 the laundry had to build an additional building, a cinder block structure across the road from the main plant, to take care of the Navy work. The laundry also did some of the dry cleaning for Camp Pickett.

W. C. Newman, Inc., had the contract to furnish ice to Camp Pickett. This contract required the firm to operate at full capacity the year round, although normally it had been manufacturing ice only during the summer months. In the summer of 1943 Pickett was requiring as much as ninety tons of ice daily, and shipments were made from the Farmville ice plant to the camp seven days a week. To meet the demand for ice during the summer, Newman had to buy ice from Lynchburg and Roanoke plants, but Camp Pickett was one of the few cantonments in the Eastern United States which received all the ice it needed during the critical summer of 1943. On a year-round basis, seventy-five per cent of the output of the Newman ice plant went to Camp Pickett.[43]

Prince Edward had no paper mills, but the cutting of pulpwood was a major business in the county during the war. The paper made of the pine pulpwood was used to make waterproof cartons in which food and repair parts for tanks and trucks were thrown overboard to be carried ashore by incoming tides at the time of invasions; it was also used to make the cartons in which blood plasma was packed. In addition to the containers, shell cases, smokeless powder, rayon, heavy-duty multi-walled sacks, medical supplies, plastics, paper for numerous military uses were also products of pulpwood. In 1941 Prince Edward ranked fifth among the counties of Virginia in the production of pulpwood with a yield of 33,600 cords. For the year ending June, 1943, Prince Edward had moved into third place in the production of this essential product. Prince Edward pulpwood was loaded at Farmville, Rice, and Prospect on the Norfolk and Western, at Abilene and Meherrin on the Virginian, and at Green Bay on the Southern for the factories, nine of which were in Virginia; some Prince Edward pulpwood went to the plant of the Halifax Paper Company at Roanoke Rapids, North Carolina. So essential was pulpwood considered to the war effort that pulpwood cutting was classified as one of the occupations in which workers were deferred by Selective Service.[44]

For all the interest in the development in Prince Edward's mineral resources for the past century and a quarter, the only mine which has been operated successfully on a commercial basis has been the kyanite mine on Baker's Mountain, in the southwestern corner of the county. During the war, kyanite from Prince Edward replaced kyanite from India in the manufacture of refracting material and super-duty fire-brick and fire-clays which are used in steel and alloy furnaces. Practically 100 per cent of the production of the mine on Baker's Mountain was taken by war industry, and its output was allocated by the War Production Board. Kyanite is an aluminum silicate, or coordination of aluminum oxide and silica. It appears in what geologists call the Wissachickon formation, a crystalline schist formed in the late pre-Cambrian age, but subjected to changes in later geologic periods. Kyanite-bearing rocks are found in several Central Virginia counties, the principal deposits being at Willis and Woods Mountains in Buckingham and Leigh's and Baker's Mountains in Prince Edward and especially at Baker's and Willis Mountains. At Baker's Mountain the kyanite content of the kyanite quartzite ranges from twenty to eighty per cent and is thought to average over forty per cent. It is found there as deep greenish-blue bladelike crystals and as needlelike masses of radiating crystals in the quartzite. During the war the mining of kyanite was carried on by the Kyanite Products Corporation, a subsidiary of the Miller Separation North American Corporation of New York. The ore was obtained by open set mining with a power shovel, which was then carried by truck to rolled grizzles, where it was crushed to two inches. The crushed material was carried by a 24-inch conveyor belt to a 200-ton storage bin. From the bin it was taken by belt to a log washer, where the clay was scrubbed and disintegrated. The material was then taken through a secondary crusher and crushed to one inch. In the next step in the process it was taken by elevator to rolls of less than one-fourth of an inch. Then it was put through washing classifiers and was washed and dewatered. (A new washing plant installed at the plant in July, 1943, doubled the production of the mine.) The washed material was taken to feed bins and was fed to the rod mill by a feeder belt. In the rod mill it was ground to minus thirty-five mesh, a size suitable for floatation. In the floatation process the material was graded up to eighty-eight to ninety per cent kyanite. After floatation the kyanite went through a drying process, which was followed by magnetic separation, in which iron was removed to one and one-half per cent. The material was then suitable for refractory use, a raw .35 mesh kyanite, which was the grade of much of the kyanite shipped from Baker's Mountain. It was also ground to specification there and calcined for special trades. The calcining process consisted of running the kyanite through an oil burner kiln, heated to 2,500 degrees Centigrade. Kyanite was shipped both in bulk and bagged from Pamplin, over the Norfolk and Western, and from Cullen, over the Virginian. In addition to its use as a component for refracting material and in fire-brick and fire-clays, kyanite was used in porcelain in sanitary and hotel ware, in glass house refractories, crucible furnaces, saggers, high-temperature cements, boiler furnaces, and cement kiln linings. The kyanite mine and operation was later sold to a group of local stockholders who operate it as the Kyanite Mining Corporation. The mine had been operated before the war, although operations had been suspended several years immediately before the defense program requirements led to its reopening by the McLanahan-Watkins Company, which sold the property to the Kyanite Products Corporation.[45] Since the war the mill has been rebuilt and modernized. In consequence of the improvement in facilities, completed in 1953, the mining firm produces a more uniform product and has a capacity of 2,000 tons monthly.[46]

On the home front, a shortage of certain essential commodities was a notable feature of World War II. An effort was made to enable all to share in the reduced supply through a rationing system. Efforts were made to reduce voluntarily consumption of some goods in which shortages were beginning to be felt, but without exception such efforts proved ineffective. The gasoline shortage was noticed in the summer of 1941, four months before Pearl Harbor, and gasoline stations, Prince Edward stations included, observed the "gasoline curfew" by closing at 7:00 P. M. on August 3; three weeks later many service stations began to remain closed on Sundays.

The first items to be rationed were tires and tubes for motor vehicles; when the rapid Japanese conquest of Malaya in December, 1941, cut off the source of the rubber supply, prompt steps had to be taken to conserve stocks on hand. The sale of new tires was prohibited December 11, 1941, and rationing of tires became effective January 5, 1942. Prince Edward had a Tire Ration Board consisting of Maurice R. Large, chairman, T. D. Smith, and J. A. Harper, with Harry C. Kayton as distribution officer. The first month's quota for distribution in the county consisted of nine casings and eight tubes for passenger cars, light trucks, and motorcycles and twenty casings and seventy-seven tubes for buses and heavy trucks. A wave of tire thefts swept the country as a result of rationing. Individuals began locking garages, and some began locking spare tires on the automobiles. On the night of January 20, 1942, thieves broke into the Farmville warehouse of the Standard Oil Company and stole thirty-eight new tubes, fifty new tires, 444 spark plugs, and three cases of cans of motor oil.

The next step in the rationing program began May 5, 1942, when sugar rationing became effective. There were two registrations for sugar rationing, one for trade and industrial users April 28-29, the other for individuals May 4-7. Trade and industrial users were allowed seventy per cent of their 1941 consumption, and individuals were allowed a half-pound per week. The rationing of gasoline followed hard upon sugar rationing; registration for gasoline rationing took place May 12-14, and rationing began May 15. Three days later ceiling prices went into effect on all commodities. The Tire Ration Board had now, with the rationing of sugar and gasoline, become the War Price and Ration Board, with responsibility for administering the rationing and price ceiling regulations in Prince Edward. Two other registrations for gasoline rationing took place during 1942, one July 9-11, the other November 5-7. At the latter, the registrant had to present his motor vehicle registration, his gasoline ration book number, and the serial number of each tire.

Requests in the fall of 1942 for a voluntary limitation of meat consumption to two and one-half pounds per week per person failed to prevent meat rationing, which went into effect in March, 1943. Coffee rationing began November 29, 1942, and canned goods went on the ration lists March 1, 1943. Mrs. F. R. Crawford was appointed food advisory rationing officer in charge of registration for War Ration Book No. 2, which took place in February, 1943. Registration for book number 3 took place June 1-10, 1943; application forms were distributed at the postoffices; the use of this book began September 12 for meats, fats, oils, butter, and cheese. Registration for ration book number 4 took place October 25-27. These books contained stamps for various commodities which were detached by merchants when purchases were made.

The gasoline shortage had become so serious in March, 1943, that the time during which the coupons were effective was extended to decrease the gasoline ration. In May a ban on pleasure driving was put into effect, but it was later modified to permit vacation travel.

Increasing responsibilities and duties attendant upon the rationing program made necessary an increase in the number of people connected with the county Ration Board. S. M. Holton, Jr., H. C. Padgett, and R. M. Russell were named the price panel in the spring of 1943. Mrs. J. B. Wall at the same time was named to the community service panel, to which Mrs. Grace N. Gordon and Miss Elizabeth Burger were subsequently added. T. A. McCorkle was appointed gasoline rationing officer, Mrs. F. R. Crawford food rationing officer, and Dr. W. E. Smith fuel oil rationing officer, with Mrs. J. H. Cocks his assistant. J. F. Lewis and H. A. Birdwell made up the trial panel. The clerical staff in January, 1944, included Mrs. Morton Davis, chief clerk, Miss Betty Baldwin, price clerk, Miss Miriam Price and Mrs. W. D. Southall, clerks.

Gasoline rationing ended with the surrender of Japan in August, 1945, which marked the end of actual fighting. Gradually other commodities were removed from the ration list. On October 23, 1946, price control was removed from all foods except sugar, syrups, and rice.

The short supply of foods gave emphasis to the need of conservation. Early in the war the drying and evaporating of fruit, practices once in vogue in Prince Edward but at the time of the war engaged in rarely if at all, were encouraged. A dehydrator was installed in the foods laboratory of the State Teachers College in 1943. Dehydration, however, did not prove popular. On the other hand, there was a marked interest in conservation by canning, and the public canneries opened in 1943 at each of the white schools in the county proved popular. The Department of Agriculture helped finance the establishment of these canneries, which were supervised by the teachers of vocational agriculture. The Farmville cannery, which opened June 10, 1943, in the basement of the high school, had typical equipment: three retorts, a twenty-five horsepower boiler, and four pressure cookers. This cannery had a daily capacity of 2,000 cans, and patrons canned 21,154 cans during the first season which closed in December. The canneries have continued to operate and are still widely used by people in the various communities.[47]

The federal government raised large sums to finance the war through the sale of securities, as it had during World War I. O. H. Whitten served throughout the war period, beginning in February, 1942, as chairman of the Defense (later War) Savings Bonds and Stamp Committee of Prince Edward. In the purchase of government securities, Prince Edward made a notable record, exceeding the quota in purchases each year and in each special drive. In 1941-42, against a quota of $421,500, sales amounted to $649,875; in 1943 the quota was $844,900 and sales were $1,202,516; the 1944 quota was $1,519,000 and sales that year were $1,811,291; against a quota of $1,000,000 for 1945 sales amounted to $1,383,876. For the entire period quotas amounted to $3,785,400 and sales $5,047,558.[48]

Salvage of scrap metals, rubber, and paper was a major activity on the home front. The Farmville Junior Chamber of Commerce was particularly active in the salvage drives. In the summer of 1942 the service stations of Farmville and vicinity collected about 200,000 pounds of scrap rubber. Scrap aluminum was collected that summer in a kitchen to kitchen canvass; a bin was placed in front of the courthouse, and donations of scrap aluminum were made there. The World War I trophy cannon was contributed to one of the scrap drives. Salvage of fats, silk, nylon, and tin cans began in December, 1943. Other salvage collections were held from time to time during the war. Vernon C. Womack was chairman of the county salvage committee.

In time World War II ended with victory for the United States and its allies. The cessation of fighting on the major fronts was observed in Prince Edward in a much more restrained way than the end of World War I. The end of a war might be an occasion for rejoicing, but for all too many this war had broken home circles and had brought sorrow. Hearts were heavy, which could not be lightened. Wild tumult was out of place. Consequently, on May 8, 1945, when the Allied forces had attained victory on the European front, the Baptist Church in Farmville remained open, and the ministers of the town conducted a successive series of services which over 800 people attended. A little over three months later, when war in the Pacific ended with the surrender of Japan on August 14, observance of the event took the form of a prayer and praise service at the Farmville Methodist Church that evening.

The American Legion, which had been organized for veterans of World War I, admitted veterans of World War II to its posts. The latter war stimulated the organization of another veterans' group, the Veterans of Foreign Wars; the Thomas Hardy Graham Post No. 7059 (the name honoring a casualty of the war) was organized in Farmville April 25, 1946, with John E. Harwood as commander.

Two months before the State Guard was disbanded, the Farmville Guard, Company G, was re-organized to continue its service as the local home guard unit with twenty-four men and three officers: John G. Bruce, captain; Robert J. Bradshaw, first lieutenant, and Irvin S. Gill, second lieutenant.[49] Robert J. Bradshaw succeeded to the captaincy in 1950.

When the Farmville Guard was reorganized after the War between the States, it used Cox' factory as an armory. Later the Opera

House served also as the armory, but in 1889 it was moved to the upper floor of J. B. Wall's store, which was rented for $100 per year. Proposals to build an armory were made in 1896, and one was erected on Third Street soon after. The present armory, on Main Street opposite the courthouse, was built in 1913-14 at a cost of $6,895 by R. S. Rice. It was inspected and accepted February 10, 1914. An effort was made to build a new armory in 1935-36, but a grant could not be secured from the Works Progress Administration for the project, and the matter was dropped. Early in 1955 work on a new armory on Longwood Avenue was begun.[50]

CHAPTER XIX

Public Affairs

TO bring the temperance issue up to date requires looking back into the nineteenth century for the background. By the twentieth century temperance had become more than a matter of social and moral concern, as it had been before the War between the States. Gradually it had become identified with politics, and the intimate political associations of the temperance movement during the first third of the twentieth century explain its treatment in the chapter on public affairs.

Temperance organizations, which before the war in Prince Edward had been connected with the churches, became larger and more influential after the war, cutting across church and denominational lines. A Council of the Friends of Temperance was organized at Prospect on September 1, 1875, by that organization's State lecturer, the Rev. W. W. Green. Officers chosen for the Prospect council were J. P. Glenn, president; T. H. Glenn, associate; T. W. Crawley, chaplain; S. B. Davis, secretary; J. P. Harvey, treasurer; R. M. Johnson, conductor; J. W. Davis, assistant conductor; G. W. Scott, inside sentinel; and C. P. Wilson, outside sentinel.[1] At the meeting of the Virginia Council of the Friends of Temperance in 1876, J. P. Glenn was chosen one of the district vice-presidents, representing District 29, the Prince Edward County area.[2]

Like the slavery issue of prewar days, there were economic aspects to the temperance question, though on a much more limited scale. Many country stores sold whiskey, and barrooms, some of which were connected with the stores, had replaced the tavern as the dispensary for alcoholic beverages in the community. A few licensed stills continued to operate after the war, and all went out of existence within a quarter century after the war. The product of these stills, usually brandy, was stored in barrels and kept until the tax was paid to the Collector of Internal Revenue or a deputy. J. M. Blanton of Cumberland paid an excise tax of $240 on the apple brandy produced at his still for the month of October, 1867.[3] One of the last of the brandy stills to operate in Prince Edward was on the farm of

William Bradshaw and his widow; its operation was discontinued about 1880. Brandy was distilled there on a custom basis;. a farmer would send his apples to the still to be made into brandy, as he would send his corn or wheat to a mill to be ground into flour. But when William Bradshaw's son, J. S. Bradshaw, decided to open a store at Rice in 1885, he announced that he would not sell alcoholic beverages. His refusal to sell liquor was regarded as an unusual step for a country merchant to take at that time.[4]

The pressures were steadily increasing to curb the sale of liquor. In 1892 Judge J. M. Crute of the County Court refused to grant any licenses for the sale of whiskey at Rice,[5] and early in 1893 the Farmville *Herald* described that place as "absolutely a temperance village."[6] Prior to "liquor license day" (April Court) in 1893, Judge Crute announced that before a license would be issued, he would require each applicant to prove his character and that his place of business was a suitable place by those living next to or near by that place of business.[7] That same month the Town Council of Farmville increased the license fee for selling liquor in the town from $125 to $500 a year in response to a petition from the Young Woman's Christian Temperance Union and the Rev. H. H. Mitchell, pastor of the First Colored Baptist Church. Mitchell's appeal was based upon his observation of the effect of drinking among people of his race:

"To the Mayor and Council of the Town of Farmville, Va.

"Gentlemen:

"I have been informed that a movement is on foot for the betterment of our town through the increase of the bar-room license. As pastor of the largest church (colored) in this community, I have some knowledge of the effect of the bar-room on my people in their homes. It is the cause of much of their poverty and family troubles. I have had frequently to step in as peace-maker, and can testify to special cases where even bloodshed has been prevented only by my presence. I heartily endorse the movement to make the license $1,000 for next year."

The Rev. James Cannon, pastor of the Farmville Methodist Church who was to become the leader of the prohibition forces in Virginia, and Dr. Peter Winston spoke in favor of the increase. Thomas L. Morton made the motion that the license fee be quadrupled; A. W. Drumeller seconded the motion; on the roll call, eight members of the Council (Morton, Drumeller, R. M. Burton, D. T.

Elam, A. H. Porter, J. R. Martin, W. P. Gilliam, H. E. Barrow) voted "aye"; only one (C. W. Blanton) voted "no." The community, however, was not nearly so favorable, many expressions of opposition from business men following the increase.[8]

The "first class saloon" of C. C. Jackson and Company (the firm of Jackson and Joseph Manoni) subsequently advertised that despite the high license it was still in business with "a complete stock of whiskies, brandies, wines, gin, rum, ale, porter, beer, tobacco, cigars." It also advertised "beer on draught," "North Carolina corn whiskies a specialty," and "mint juleps raging under the new law," as well as the sole distributorship for "Paul Jones' celebrated Kentucky whiskies" and "Belle of Nelson Kentucky whiskies." Business with C. C. Jackson and Company, the advertisement did not overlook noting, was strictly cash.[9]

Only five applications were presented for liquor licenses to the April, 1895, Court, all of which were approved: J. L. Richardson, agent, Farmville; C. C. Jackson and Company, Farmville; J. E. Harris, Prospect; H. N. Brightwell, agent, Prospect; and W. M. Richardson, Green Bay. In August a license was granted H. W. Wall at Meherrin.[10] In May, 1853, there had been fifteen dealers certified as being of good character, to whom the Court had no objection to the granting of liquor licenses: Hilliard and Hill, Paulett and Carrell, Carter and Franklin, Samuel Wheeler, Harvey and Wood, Anderson and Hines, Anderson, Hines and Company, E. Campe and Brother, E. H. Bass, John T. Rudd, Pigg and Fuqua, M. A. Hurt, John W. Davidson, J. S. Mickle, and Armes and Musgrove.[11]

The tightening of legal restrictions on the sale of liquors encouraged even then the illicit manufacture of strong drink. In March, 1897, a county constable, R. I. Orange, found a still near Sandy River Church and at it a quantity of low wines and mash; Orange arrested the two operators, men who had lately come from North Carolina, whose corn whiskies were a specialty of the Jackson saloon, to make this product to quench Prince Edward thirsts for stronger drink than that supplied by its springs and wells. United States officers moved in, and the still operators were held for the Federal Court grand jury. But Orange "and good citizens around Sandy River Church deserve credit for breaking up this bad lot," commented the Farmville *Herald*.[12]

All the while the temperance advocates were keeping up an intensive campaign which was both informational and persuasive.

In every community there were held programs similar to that presented at Pisgah Baptist Church, in which "The Bottle and its Influence" was featured. The sum of $27 was raised for the temperance cause at this program. Temperance lecturers made frequent appearances under the sponsorship of a temperance society; one of these lecturers was Miss Frances H. Ensign, who gave an illustrated lecture in the Farmville Methodist Church on March 15, 1897, under the auspices of the Young Woman's Christian Temperance Union.[13] This sort of campaigning continued through the first two decades of the twentieth century, until prohibition of the manufacture and sale of alcoholic beverages had become a national law through the Eighteenth Amendment to the Constitution.

But there were several battles yet to be fought before prohibition carried the day. In an election held February 26, 1900, in Farmville, 304 voted against licensing the sale of intoxicants, only 31 for; it was reported that many "drys" refused to participate in the election.[14] The General Assembly in 1901 declared it "unlawful for anyone to sell, barter or exchange spiritous, vinous, malt or intoxicating liquors in Farmville District" after May 1, 1901, except as provided; that provision authorized the Town Council of Farmville to set up a dispensary board to sell liquor in Farmville.[15] Two years later the legislature authorized an election at Green Bay on December 19, 1903, at which the voters of Leigh District were to decide whether to open a dispensary at Meherrin. In the event they favored establishment of a dispensary there, the board was to be composed of the supervisor from the district and two citizens appointed by the Circuit Court; the maximum salary of the manager of the Leigh District dispensary was fixed by statute at $50 a month.[16]

Establishment of the Farmville Dispensary was not readily accomplished. Farmville saloons were closed at 9:00 P. M. April 30, 1901, under the dispensary act. But the saloon keepers were fighting. The constitutionality of the dispensary act was argued before Judge George J. Hundley in Circuit Court on April 22,[17] and he subsequently handed down an order that the act was unconstitutional. This decision permitted the saloons to re-open, but it was appealed to the State Supreme Court. It was March, 1903, before the Supreme Court handed down its decision reversing Judge Hundley. The saloon keepers planned an effort to get the dispensary act repealed, and their petition secured over 100 signers, including many Farmville business people.[18] The saloons in Farmville were closed March

21, 1903; the opening of the dispensary planned for March 25 was delayed because of a question of legal standing of the board, one member's term having expired and the vacancy remaining unfilled.[19] The first dispensary board consisted of W. T. Clark, appointed to the one-year term, Dr. Peter Winston, appointed for two years, and Dr. R. M. Bidgood, named for three years.[20] A dispensary board consisting of W. T. Clark (appointed for one year), J. L. Richardson (two years), and G. M. Robeson (three years) was named by the Council on December 31, 1903, with instructions to open a dispensary as soon as possible. The Council appropriated $2,000 to get the dispensary started, and it opened January 14, 1904. Leigh District had voted in favor of a dispensary, so early in 1904 there were only two places in Prince Edward where liquor could be bought legally, the dispensaries at Farmville and Meherrin. The Meherrin board consisted of F. H. Kauffman, A. A. Haskins, and J. J. Holt.[21]

During the year 1904 the Meherrin dispensary received $7,434.95 from the sale of liquor and reported a profit of $1,397.50.[22] Sales increased in 1905 to $10,825.32; that year the board divided the profits: State of Virginia, $303.42; Leigh District schools, $910.26; Leigh District roads, $1,213.68.[23] The Farmville Dispensary's receipts during the year ending January 15, 1906, amounted to $15,565.[24] In 1907 the Farmville board declared a dividend payment of $10,000, divided thus: State, $1,250; Farmville District, $2,500; Town of Farmville, $6,250.[25]

At first the Farmville Council declined to pay a rebate on liquor licenses which had been paid for the year in which the dispensary was established. Subsequently in April, 1905, it refunded pro rata shares of the unearned liquor license tax to sellers of liquor: C. H. Bliss, $23.43; Hugh O'Gara, $58.93; O'Byrne and O'Byrne, $53.20; T. W. Vaughan, $54.26; and Joseph Manoni, $62.36.[26]

While the debate over the establishment of the dispensary was in progress, a unit of the Woman's Christian Temperance Union was organized in Farmville on June 5, 1902, at the Methodist Church. Miss Nettie Morton was president, Mrs. C. M. Walker vice-president, Miss Ruby Venable recording secretary, Miss Maud Gray corresponding secretary, Mrs. E. W. Ellington treasurer.[27]

Later members of the Dispensary Board were L. J. Verser, succeeding W. T. Clark in 1904; H. C. Crute, succeeding Verser in 1909; A. E. Cralle, in place of Crute, who declined to serve; W. E. Moore, succeeding Cralle, 1909; Moore was found to be ineligible

and E. L. Morris was named in his stead; E. R. Booker, in place of
G. M. Robeson, 1910; N. B. Davidson, successor to Booker, 1910;
J. L. Richardson, M. S. Crowe, and R. D. Miller composed the
board in 1915.[28]

Public sentiment was steadily growing in favor of greater restrictions upon the liquor traffic. Judge W. H. Mann, as state senator
from the district which included Prince Edward, had introduced a
bill under which the court not only had to be satisfied that the
applicant for a license to sell intoxicating beverages would keep an
orderly place and that police protection would be provided at the
place, but also that a majority of the voters in the district had to
favor the sale of liquor at the place for which the application was
made. When he ran for the gubernatorial nomination in 1905, his
opponents charged that he was a fanatic on the whiskey question.
Judge A. D. Watkins in a speech in Mann's behalf in Farmville that
year answered that charge by saying that if anything should be
restrained, it was the traffic in wiskey. "How can the father of a boy
support the whiskey traffic?" he asked. He then pointed out that if
Mann were a fanatic on the matter, so were most of his colleagues in
the legislature, for only fifteen votes were cast against the Mann bill
in the House of Delegates and only six in the Senate. The Mann
bill did not apply to places of more than 500 population or to
"watering places," the resorts.[29]

During the campaign of 1911 the Anti-Saloon League had two
questions it asked candidates for the Democratic nomination for
both houses of the General Assembly. Would they support an enabling act to provide for a state-wide vote on prohibition if twenty-
five per cent of the qualified voters asked for such a vote? Would
they support a bill to prohibit the shipment of alcoholic beverages
from "wet" areas to "dry" areas? That year Robert K. Brock and
W. H. Ewing had no opposition for the nominations for State Senate
and House of Delegates, respectively. Both answered both questions
in letters to Dr. J. D. Terry and W. H. Hubbard, both of Rice, who
constituted the committee of the Anti-Saloon League in Prince
Edward to ascertain the attitude of the candidates. Both Brock and
Ewing promised to support an enabling act, conditioned upon a
request of one-fourth of the voters; Brock added that he would
support such a bill, although he believed local option the best
approach to the problem. Neither candidate, however, would agree
to support the bill to prohibit shipment of liquor by a dealer in a

section in which the trade was legal to a customer in a section in which there was prohibition of alcoholic beverages.[30]

The General Assembly in 1914 repealed the laws establishing the dispensaries in Farmville and Meherrin, provided a majority of the qualified voters favored closing the dispensaries; an election was ordered to be held within six months of the passage of the bill (which took place on March 24, 1914), the judge of the Circuit Court being directed to set a date for the election and give thirty days' notice. Should a majority favor closing the dispensary, no license for the sale of liquor should be granted.[31] Now Judge Hundley who had held the dispensary act of 1901 unconstitutional appeared as the defender of the dispensary; after a hearing on July 1, 1914, he denied a petition asking him to set a date for the election authorized the previous March by the legislature.[32]

In an election September 22, 1914, Virginia voted in favor of state-wide prohibition. The Prince Edward vote was 640 in favor of prohibition, 205 against.[33] Prohibition of alcoholic beverages became effective in Virginia November 1, 1916.

On March 16, 1916, the General Assembly repealed the laws establishing dispensaries at Farmville and Meherrin, effective May 1, 1916, and directed that no more licenses to sell liquors be granted in Prince Edward.[34] The council had sent J. A. Davidson to appear before the committee of the legislature considering the repeal measure to oppose closing the dispensary before November 1, 1916,[35] when state-wide prohibition became effective, but his effort was ineffectual. After the bill had passed, the Farmville Council appropriated $300 to be used in a joint effort with Farmville and Leigh Districts to test the constitutionality of the law. J. T. Coleman of Lynchburg was selected to represent the town and districts in the action.[36] But the dispensaries closed April 29; on the last day of its operation receipts at the Farmville dispensary amounted to $1,324.70.[37]

In November, 1916, the town adopted an ordinance setting penalties for the sale and purchase of intoxicating liquors in the corporate limits and within a mile of them on the outside. Penalty for the first offense of selling was a fine of $10 to $100, and a fine of $100 to $500 and sixty days in jail for the second offense; the penalty for purchasing liquor was a fine of $1 to $10.[38] Nearly a year later Mayor S. W. Paulett noted a continuing decrease in crime and credited the trend to the "abandonment of the sale of whiskey and the rigid enforcement of the prohibition law."[39]

In time there developed in Prince Edward as elsewhere disrespect for the prohibition laws. Illicit corn whiskey was made in considerable volume in Prince Edward, and much time was spent by Sheriff John A. Clark and his deputies in raiding and destroying stills and in seeking out stores of the unlawful liquor. Moonshining (making illicit whiskey) and bootlegging (distributing it) became familiar terms in conversation as well as fairly frequent activities. Drunkenness again became a matter of concern, but instead of undertaking to combat it by the educational process of earlier years, there was now the demand for stricter enforcement of the prohibition laws. A combined disrespect for the prohibition law and desire for strong drink on a nation-wide scale resulted in a vote on the Eighteenth Amendment to the United States Constitution and the prohibition laws of Virginia. In the election which was held October 3, 1933, Prince Edward voted in favor of national prohibition by a small majority, 461 opposing repeal of the Eighteenth Amendment, 436 voting for repeal. On the issue of state prohibition, 472 voted in favor of continuing prohibition, and 438 voted for a system of state control of the sale of alcoholic beverages.[40] The vote in Virginia on both issues was contrary to the Prince Edward vote, and a convention met to confirm the popular vote by repealing the ratification of the Eighteenth Amendment. Robert K. Brock was a member of the convention, all members having been chosen for the state at large; R. B. Crawford was one of the state-wide nominees for the convention on the dry ticket.

Prior to the repeal of the prohibition laws, beer of 3.2 per cent alcoholic content was legalized, and an ordinance governing its sale in Farmville was adopted by the Council September 6, 1933.[41]

In consequence of the vote favoring the establishment of a system of state control, the Alcoholic Beverage Control Board was established by the General Assembly to manage the sale of liquor through a system of state stores. At its meeting June 12, 1934, the Farmville Council drew up a petition asking the establishment of a state liquor store in Farmville.[42] The petition was granted, and the store opened Tuesday, September 11, 1934, with J. G. Lancaster as manager.[43] Thus was established the present system governing the sale of alcoholic beverages and the only legal outlet for strong drink now in

Prince Edward. Farmville received $1,226.62 in the first distribution of ABC profits in August, 1935.[44]

Concern for moral conduct probably reached its height in Prince Edward in the period between the War between the States and World War I. Churches continued to give much attention to disciplining errant members, and law-making bodies demonstrated interest in requiring adherence to a rigid moral code. The Puritan emphasis seems to have been the result of the influence of what had in the days of the Established Church been called the dissenting sects, which made conduct as much a part of the religious expression as they made the tenets of faith and the distinctive emphases of the denominations. Combined with this influence was the experience of defeat in war and the poverty which followed in which all shared. Those who fought back at the hard conditions in an effort to regain economic security and wealth developed habits of industry and thrift (sometimes to the extreme) which regarded the spending of time in aught but labor and worship and the spending of money for anything except the necessities as sinful.

Not all held these rigid views, of course. When J. H. Newbill, pastor of Sharon Baptist Church in 1875 presented the resolution "that we regard the traffic in intoxicating liquors as injurious to the interest of the Church and the Redeemer's Kingdom, therefore [we] cannot tolerate the practice on the part of any of our members," action on it was deferred. A month later the resolution was amended "to refer to those who keep tippling houses or regular bar rooms" and as amended was unanimously adopted. At the same meeting Newbill introduced his resolution, Samuel A. Bruce introduced a resolution concerning dancing: "Whereas we believe dancing with the worldly to be unbecoming the professor of the Christian religion and inconsistent with the spirit of the New Testament Scriptures, therefore Resolved—that we do earnestly and sincerely protest the participation in the said amusement by our members." The anti-dancing resolution was unanimously passed, but one of the members, Erastus McGehee, who had been cited by the church for dancing defended the amusement and held that the church "was not scripturally authorized to enact rules against dancing." His position was accepted as satisfactory to the church.[45]

There were other matters involving conduct and morals to claim public attention. In 1872 the grand jury presented two men "for keeping and exhibiting a gaming table called chuck a luck, like the gaming table called Fairo bank."[46] Dr. J. L. White, when a member of the Farmville Town Council in 1875, raised the question about keeping prostitutes and others off the streets late at night and stated that the town sergeant wanted the help of the Council in suppressing this nuisance. P. W. McKinney and W. S. Berry held that the sergeant had adequate authority to deal with the problem, and Mayor Thackston assured the Council that he would have the law enforced.[47]

The Farmville Council enacted a strict code in 1900, aimed at promoting sound morals: sales of intoxicants at bars were prohibited between 10:30 P. M. Saturday and light the following Monday morning; barbers were specifically prohibited from keeping their shops open on Sunday, only apothecaries, livery stable keepers, dealers in ice, and keepers of ordinaries being permitted to carry on business on Sunday; a fine of $10 to $25 was fixed as the penalty for gambling; fines ranging from $2 to $25 were fixed for drunkenness on the street and disorderly conduct; a fine of $1 to $5 was the penalty for bathing nude in the Appomattox River within the corporate limits between 4:00 A. M. and 8:00 P. M.; spoken, written, drawn, or acted obscenity was punishable by a fine of $2 to $25; sleeping, by day or night, on the street or sidewalk, on porch or in doorway or in any place exposed to public view would draw a fine of $1 to $5; admission to barrooms was limited to prescribed hours and persons were to be excluded at closing time; barrooms were not permitted to use blinds, painted windows, curtains or other obstructions to view from the street and billiard tables and games of chance were prohibited in the saloons.[48]

Sunday was fairly rigidly observed as a day of rest. Stores remained closed throughout the day, but they did not observe holidays as they do now. Stores remained open on Christmas day in the villages until about the World War I period. In the 1870's it was the custom of one Farmville bar, Thad Harris', to treat all customers to free eggnog on Christmas morning between the hours of 6:30 and 7:30.[49]

The disciplines, however, were relaxing; church discipline after World War I became a forgotten practice, remembered only in historical accounts. The strict standards of Sabbath observance began too to become less strict. Moving picture houses took advantage of the depression of the 1930's to offer to show Sunday movies, beginning in Farmville in 1934, a portion of the receipts being designated for the relief of the needy. Allocation of that portion of income was of temporary duration, and soon Sunday movies became entirely commercial. After World War II athletic contests, especially baseball, to which admission fees were charged became acceptable Sunday afternoon practices.

Efforts to break down racial segregation began in Reconstruction. Congress passed a civil rights bill in 1875 prohibiting hotels from refusing to give accommodations to Negroes. That the law was not favorably received in Prince Edward has already been shown. In 1896 the United States Supreme Court in the now famous Plessy vs. Ferguson case (which originated in Louisiana) upheld racial segregation on the public carriers, provided equal facilities were provided. To some that did not go far enough. "Sufferer" wrote to the Farmville *Herald* in 1902 proposing that the Virginia legislature enact segregation laws for depots as well as moving trains; "filth of body, filth of tongue, bad whiskey and bad pipe odors" made conditions especially in the railroad stations at Meherrin and Burkeville "intolerable" and they were bad enough at Farmville.[50] But there were times at which certain white men apparently did not want segregation. "The fashion and beauty of African descent held a ball at Holman's hotel last Friday night . . . a number of white gentlemen, it is said, were present, mingled in the dance and enjoyed themselves greatly," ran the report of an event in 1873.[51]

Prince Edward has been relatively free of major crime, although some of the crimes committed in the county have attracted wide attention. The most celebrated murder case of the ante-bellum period was the murder of Charles T. Edie of Christianburg by Edward A. Langhorne of Lynchburg in Cushing Hall, Hampden-Sydney, where both were students, on January 27, 1857. Langhorne was tried and acquitted in Circuit Court the following March. In a sermon on the tragedy, developed on the text of Psalm 119:9, Dr. Benjamin Mosby Smith took occasion to criticize human standards which were contrary to divine: "Much of the vaunting and boasting about Virginia principles is wicked nonsense. Conduct is praised as becoming, or condemned as unbecoming, Virginians. But what shall it profit men if applauded for pleasing Virginians, they should be condemned for displeasing God?" The tragedy which inspired the sermon was the result of following the teachings of men instead of the Word of God. Beyond that point Smith did not feel called upon to go in expressing judgment upon the actors in the tragedy; one was dead, his body buried, his soul in "the presence of that Judge whose decisions we have neither the right nor the desire to question." The other had been tried, and, "whether righteously or not, the law has released him from its claims." Perhaps there was significance in his comment that he was "not called upon to say whether the cause of justice was upheld by the decision."[52]

An attempted lynching was frustrated in 1896 by the strength of the jail. Wax Price and Charles Childress were returning to their homes near Rice after selling tobacco in Farmville on November 11 that year. They were assaulted on the way that night, and Price was knocked out and robbed and Childress dealt a heavy blow. Elisha Johnson, a colored man, was arrested, charged with the crime, and committed to jail. On Sunday night, November 15, a small but determined mob tried to take Johnson from the jail. Unable to break into the jail, the members of the mob began shooting at Johnson, who was lying on his cot in the jail. He was slightly wounded, but saved himself from more serious injury and possibly death by rolling under his bed. The mob shot out the windows, shot the bedposts to Johnson's bed away and a large hole in the stovepipe. Subsequently Johnson confessed the crime and was sentenced to twenty years in the penitentiary.[53]

No murder in Prince Edward attracted more attention than that of Hall Carter by Thomas W. Price. Carter worked for Price, a neighbor, and the two were seen in Farmville on July 28, 1898, apparently on the best of terms. On the next morning, while Carter was eating breakfast in the Price home, Price shot him. The trial began August 17. Price claimed that the only witness was his wife, but a Negro, Spencer Hill, saw the murder and at once ran for Carter's father, Theodorick Carter. In his conduct of the prosecution of this case, Judge A. D. Watkins gave an unusual demonstration of tact and courtesy blended with a sense of duty. Mrs. Price was highly respected, but it was obvious that her testimony did not accurately describe the crime. The commonwealth's attorney wanted to get across to the jury this fact. Instead of condemning the witness, he graciously excused her: the testimony was not true, Judge Watkins told the jury, "but the recording angel when he wrote it down dropped a tear that blotted it all out, while angels standing by approved. God will not hold her responsible—she did what she could to save her husband's life." The jury on August 20 returned a verdict of guilty, and Price, who was then about seventy years of age, was sentenced to be hanged. The sentence was subsequently commuted to life imprisonment on account of his age.[54]

Two trials held in Prince Edward which attracted state-wide interest were on charges of crime not committed in the county. Solomon Marable was tried for the murder of Mrs. Lucy Jane Pollard of Lunenburg in 1896, and E. C. Wooldridge and Charles J. Forbes in 1905 on charges of having burned the home and outbuildings of Forbes' father, John S. Forbes, in Buckingham. Both Wooldridge and Forbes were acquitted.[55]

Robert Booker was hanged on May 18, 1906, for the murder of Charlie Brown near Rice on January 20, 1906.[56]

The last legal execution by hanging in Virginia took place in Prince Edward. Jesse Ruffin and Massie Hill, Negroes, were hanged February 15, 1907, for the murder of John Grubb, merchant at Tuggle and postmaster of the office known as Acteon there, which took place on the night of June 5, 1906. The store and postoffice had been robbed, Grubb had been murdered, and the building, with Grubb in it, was burned. Neighbors who came to the fire remembered having seen two strange Negroes loitering about the store during the day before. "Hurricane" Branch of Suffolk and his bloodhounds, a team often called to track persons suspected of having committed crimes, were called at once, and the dogs followed a trail to the Norfolk and Western bridge over Buffalo River at Farmville. Hope of solving the case ended with the trail. But nearly two months later, a Negro who had been lodged in jail in Emporia, Virginia, on a charge of vagrancy was heard talking in his sleep, making demands that his "part of the money" be given him. The cellmate told the jailor, who could learn nothing from the vagabond who had given his name as Willie Jackson. Later Jackson told his cellmate that he had killed a man, robbed a postoffice, and burned the house. The cellmate again told the jailor, and since the description fitted the Tuggle crime, Sheriff T. H. Dickinson was summoned to Emporia. Brought to Prince Edward jail, Jackson said that his real name was Massie Hill; in his confession, he implicated two other Negroes, William Ruffin and one called "Railroad Bill," whose name he did not know. Ruffin was arrested in Hertford County, North Carolina in August, and Governor R. B. Glenn of that state granted extradition papers. Ruffin, whose real name was Jesse instead of William, testified that only he and Hill were at Grubb's store and he did not know "Railroad Bill." Ruffin was taken to Lynchburg jail for safekeeping, and the night before Sheriff Dickinson was to bring him back to Farmville, he escaped with two other prisoners. Prince Edward offered a reward of $350 for Ruffin, "dead or alive." He was captured December 18 at Williamston, North Carolina, three months and two days after his escape from Lynchburg. Meanwhile it was learned that a person who was known as "Railroad Bill" had died August 15 at New River. Ruffin then implicated another Negro, John Brown, who was located in Montgomery, West Virginia. He was indicted January 7, 1907, on Ruffin's testimony, but upon his insistence that he had witnesses in West Virginia who could testify to his whereabouts at the time of the Grubb murder, his case was continued until January 11. Two detectives brought affidavits that Brown was working in West Virginia at the time of the murder, and he was released. Ruffin and Hill were tried and found guilty of first degree murder. They were sentenced to be hanged February 15. Testimony at the trial indicated that they had stolen $104 and had burned Grubb alive.

Before his execution, Hill devised his property to the Rev. E. A. P. Cheek, pastor of the First Colored Baptist Church of Farmville and told him and J. L. Hart, publisher of the Farmville *Herald,* that he had buried money and stolen watches under a church in North Emporia. Hart and Cheek went to Emporia, where they enlisted the aid of Edward E. Goodwyn, a prominent citizen of the town, and the pastor of the church under which Hill claimed to have hidden the money. (The church is located on West Atlantic Street, Emporia, Route 58, a short distance west of the intersection of that route with North Main Street and Route 301.) The four spent the night in digging under the church, covering every bit of ground under it, but found nothing. When they returned to Farmville and told Hill they could find nothing and asked why he deceived his spiritual adviser, he told them he wanted to have one good laugh before he died.

Ruffin was hanged first the morning of February 15, 1907; the rope broke with Hill, but he walked back up the steps to the scaffold; the same rope which had been used to hang Robert Booker the year before was brought out and put around Hill's neck; this rope broke too, but in fifteen minutes Hill was pronounced dead.[57]

Each of these three murder cases gave opportunity for the demonstration of the strong religious influence and atmosphere which prevailed at the time. Although Thomas W. Price had on his arrest given no visible sign of regret for killing Hall Carter and had even told Carter's father when he came to his house when told of the murder that he would kill him "if he didn't quit hollering," he broke down and wept on the day after his conviction, a Sunday. He asked a young lady to bring him a Bible with large print—the print in his was so small he could not read it with his aging eyes—and he expressed the belief that he had "found the light of the Savior's countenance."[58]

Following his conviction, Robert Booker made a confession of faith. In what was probably the strangest baptismal scene in Prince Edward history, he was taken from the jail on April 25, 1906, by Sheriff Dickinson, Police Officer Leslie Fogus, and Constable Bliss to the colored Baptist Church. Manacled and handcuffed, an officer holding each arm, he was seated before the pulpit. The choir sang *On Jordan's Stormy Banks I Stand*. The Rev. S. C. Hatcher, pastor of the white Methodist Church, read the Scripture. The Rev. Nelson Jordan offered prayer. While the pastor, the Rev. E. A. P. Cheek, prepared for the service, the choir sang *Shall We Gather at the River*. Then Booker answered satisfactorily the questions concerning his faith and Christian experience, at one point sobbing that he had seen nothing but trouble all his life and he was now glad it would soon be over. He was then immersed. Following his baptism, the ordinance of the Lord's Supper was observed; the man condemned to lose earthly life who had found assurance of a better and eternal life through faith partook of the bread and wine. Then manacled to the officers, he was taken back to jail to await the penalty prescribed by law.[59]

On the day Hill and Ruffin were to be hanged, a congregation assembled at their cells and held Christian services there. Before Hill's hanging, the Rev. E. A. P. Cheek of the colored Baptist Church and the Rev. S. C. Hatcher of the white Methodist Church, who had shared in the service at which the condemned Robert Booker had been baptized a few months before, offered prayer. Both Hill and Ruffin had received spiritual advice from ministers of their race. Ruffin was baptized in his cell by the Rev. Mr. Robinson of the A. M. E. Church on the day before his execution.[60]

Another Prince Edward case attracted wide attention, especially from its aftermath. A white woman was raped by a Negro near Farmville on December 7, 1938. Clarence Howard was identified as the person who committed the crime, was arrested, was tried in Prince Edward Circuit Court, and sentenced to death March 28,

1939. The case was appealed to the Virginia Supreme Court, which upheld the sentence in a four to three decision on the following October 9. Before the sentence was carried into execution, Governor James H. Price commuted it to life imprisonment on May 31, 1940. The commutation provoked strong criticism in the county, many feeling that the crime warranted the penalty and that the Governor had been influenced by a mistaken sentimentality. Prince Edward feeling was again strongly aroused when Governor William M. Tuck granted Howard a conditional pardon on March 4, 1949. Howard returned to Kentucky, whence he had come to Farmville and where he had friends who made strong efforts to save him during his trial. On July 11 following his release on conditional pardon he was arrested in Ashland, Kentucky, charged with armed robbery and attempted rape; on March 18, 1950, he was sentenced to life imprisonment on these charges in Boyd County, Kentucky.[61]

Roads, schools, and temperance constituted a major trilogy of public interest during the latter part of the nineteenth and the early part of the twentieth century. From the early settlements, the county courts undertook to maintain passable roads; public interest found expression in the frequent presentments by grand juries of road surveyors for failure to keep the roads under their supervision in order. In ante-bellum days the impassability of roads in winter was more or less accepted. Travel in that season was almost entirely limited to horseback because of the bad roads. With the coming of spring, when the March winds had dried out the winter mud, farmers began sending out wagons to haul tobacco to market and to bring in supplies. The farmer assumed responsibility for putting the road he used in order; ruts and holes on a stretch of road would be filled by the first farmer sending out a wagon in the spring. After the war increasing attention began to be paid to roads.[62] The Farmville *Mercury* of April 30, 1874, observed that "never in the recollection of the oldest inhabitant have county roads been in worse condition than now" and urged the Grangers to work for reform in the inadequate road law.[63]

Apparently little attention was paid the requirement that male citizens work the roads under the supervision of overseers for certain roads and sections of roads. In 1875 the county court appointed three persons in each district to lay off the district into road precincts and to allot workers for each precinct: Buffalo: T. T. Tredway, C. A. Price, George Hunt; Farmville: C. H. Bliss, Sr., T. F. Venable,

T. L. Morton; Hampden: W. P. Dupuy, J. Overby, R. S. Hines; Leigh: J. Nunnally, E. N. Wing, W. H. Ewing; Lockett: B. H. Carter, J. X. Morton, and J. W. Foster.[64]

An act of the 1879 legislature prescribed in some detail the management of the road system in Prince Edward. The core of this legislation required each male citizen between sixteen and sixty to work on the roads two days in each year, at the call of the overseer of roads for the sub-district in which he lived. This act made each magisterial district a road district; it required the supervisor to appoint a road commissioner for a term of one year and the two to appoint in turn one of the justices of the peace who with the supervisor and commissioner constituted the board of district road commissioners. Districts were to be divided into sub-districts, for each of which an overseer was appointed annually. The overseers were responsible for keeping roads clear and smooth, free of loose rocks, from gates unlawfully kept up, and other obstructions, of required width, well drained, and the bridges safe and in good order. District boards could direct the placement of sign boards. The district road commissioner was required to inspect the road twice a year. The supervisors fixed the rate at which taxpayers were credited with work on the road and for the use of teams, plows, wagons, and other implements.[65] In 1888 a change was made in the method of choosing the board of road commissioners for the district; the county court appointed two persons in each district to serve with the supervisor.[66]

The system of having the men work the roads two days a year did not prove satisfactory. Such working proved inadequate to keep the roads in good condition. The supervisors devised other means to work the roads. In 1894 they decided to try convict labor. Twenty convicts, "all able-bodied, healthy looking Negroes," arrived early in June of that year and on the 7th began work on the Hampden-Sydney road under the direction of J. Wyatt Crute, superintendent of the road force. The county had to provide rations and three guards, two for day duty, one for night. Twenty days later one of the convicts escaped; he was captured near Darlington Heights by N. T. Dillon, though not until he had discarded his striped outfit and had tried to run away entirely unclothed. In October the convicts were sent to Bedford from Prince Edward; not every one in the county thought it advisable to use them, some regarding "their presence baneful and demoralizing . . . on youth." Although the

county had to pay a fine of $50 for letting a convict escape while
working on the roads (R. M. Burton made a special trip to see
Governor Charles T. O'Ferrall, but was unable to persuade him to
remit the fine), it was estimated that convict labor saved the county
over $1,000.[67]

In 1895 the board of supervisors bought a Western Wheel Rever-
sible scraper for the county roads, after a demonstration contest
between that and the American Champion road machine on the road
south of Farmville. Four horses were required to pull the machine,
which cost $200.[68] Shortly after the purchase of the machine, W. W.
Swan was appointed superintendent of road construction at a salary
of $50 per month for the time he was actually engaged in work on
the roads. The force was directed to begin working the roads in
Farmville District, spending ten days there and work in order roads
in the other districts: Lockett, ten days; Leigh, ten days; Hampden,
ten days; and Buffalo, fifteen days. The supervisor in each district
was authorized to give instructions to the superintendent of the
force concerning the work.[69]

A longer period for road work in each district was provided in
1896. Work was to begin April 13 in Lockett District, with thirty
days, exclusive of Sundays, assigned to work the roads in that district; the roads in Leigh, Hampden, and Farmville were then to be
worked for thirty days each, and the roads in Buffalo for forty-five
days.[70]

The road force camped at places convenient for its work in the
various communities, the tents pitched on the roadside being familiar
sights to travelers.

The General Assembly in 1896 put all roads in Prince Edward
"under the general direction, care, and control of the board of supervisors," thus ending the system of road commissioners. The board
was permitted to levy road taxes, at a rate between five and twenty
cents on the $100 property valuation. The board was also authorized
to use vagrants and convicted criminals to work the roads. Supervisors were allowed $2 a day, with a maximum of $30 a year, for
inspecting the roads.[71]

In addition to the road force, the board employed citizens to
repair roads and bridges when the force was not available for that
work where needed. Until the state took over the upkeep of the
roads under the Byrd bill of 1932, the records of the supervisors
contain numerous authorizations to pay individuals for the work
which they did on roads and bridges.[72] One bill for such work

requested payment at the rate of $2 per day for double team and wagon, $1 per day for the workers, and $1.50 per day for the citizen who supervised the work.[73]

The macadam road was regarded as the best type of road in the early twentieth century. Such a road was built from Farmville to Hampden-Sydney about 1901-02.[74] The advantages of the macadam road were noted in a letter to the Farmville *Herald* by Dr. W. M. Holladay of Hampden-Sydney: the farmer who needed four horses to pull a loaded wagon to Hampden-Sydney could unhitch two and send them home when he reached the macadam, since two could easily pull over that road the load which required four on the typical road of the county. W. C. Dunkum, who operated the hack between Farmville and Hampden-Sydney and carried the mail between those points, used one horse on the macadam, instead of the two he had used before it was constructed. Dr. Holladay presented a petition signed by many in the Hampden-Sydney community and in the upper end of the county proposing a system of macadam roads to be built in each district. The petition also proposed the construction of a dirt road parallel to the macadam, to be used in good weather, since the macadam was damaged by use in such weather; purchase by the county of a rock crusher and steam roller to be used in building macadam roads; engagement of an experienced road engineer to lay off the roads and of a reliable and experienced road builder to construct them; an advisory road commission of five members; a permanent plan for keeping the roads in good repair; and issuance of bonds in the amount of $100,000 to $150,000 to improve the roads. J. D. Eggleston, Jr., was the moving spirit in the circulation of the petition.[75]

It should not be overlooked that during this stage of the agitation for improved roads, horses and mules provided the motive power for road transportation in Prince Edward. In 1902 a new vehicle made its appearance in Prince Edward. This first trip made by automobile through Prince Edward, on July 3 of that year, forecast a time when motor vehicles were to make greatly improved roads necessary.[76] But that time was yet in the future. It was about 1914 before many people in Prince Edward began to buy cars. That year Henry Ford's Model T was on the market at a price many could afford. And many bought. It was then evident that the automobile would not be a rich man's toy, but a vehicle many people would use for travel to church and to town, to visit kinsfolk and acquaintances, to make trips in even to Richmond and Petersburg and Lynchburg.

It was not so much anticipation of the needs of automobile travel as the satisfying of current horse-and-buggy, mule-and-wagon transportation requirements which pressed the battle for good roads in the first decade of the twentieth century. Merchants perceived the advantage of good roads in promoting travel to village and town. Farmers realized the saving in time and in horsepower (in its literal sense) good roads would mean to them. Meetings in the interest of good roads began to be held. One of the first in Prince Edward was held at Green Bay February 2, 1907, when Judge A. D. Watkins, G. S. Wing, and P. St. Julien Wilson, first state highway commissioner in Virginia, spoke. The meeting was not altogether business; a lamb and shoat barbecue followed the meeting.[77] Wing and Watkins appeared before the supervisors at their April, 1907, meeting; as a result of their plea for road improvements, the board decided to petition the Circuit Court for a special election to vote on the issuance of bonds in the amount of $100,000 to build macadam roads in the county, the proposal being to construct ten miles of such roads in each of the three districts, Hampden, Leigh, and Lockett, and fifteen miles in Buffalo.[78] The bond issue which was submitted to the people on July 30, 1907, proposed the issuance of $50,000 in bonds for roads. The issue was narrowly defeated, 227 voting against bonds, 212 for. A majority of the voters at Abilene, Worsham, Briery, Green Bay, and Rice favored the bond issue.[79]

In addition to the several stretches of macadam road which were built, Prince Edward experimented with two other types of roads. Both the mile of concrete road leading south from the old town limits of Farmville and the mile of sand clay road leading southwest from Mercy Seat Church were constructed as a result of the efforts of Dr. W. M. Holladay when a member of the Board of Supervisors.[80] In 1916 new bridges and approaches were constructed over Sandy, Bush, and Briery Rivers between Rice and Farmville.

The next development in road improvement plans was the advocacy of a system of good state highways. The increasing use of automobiles was responsible for this effort, for the distance which the automobile could cover in a relatively short time made a uniform state system preferable to the county systems, which varied from county to county. Meetings were held in the various communities in advocacy of good roads. Speakers representing the State Highway Commission as well as local proponents of a highway system were usually on hand to address these meetings.[81] Support for the system

grew, and in 1921 State Highway Commission surveyors were chart-
ing courses for highways through Prince Edward. The proposed
Route 10 led from Burkeville past Rice and Farmville and Prospect
to Pamplin. Construction began soon, and by the spring of 1922
the highway had been completed from the east to Farmville. For the
most part it followed the route of the old road, but there were some
changes. One feature of the new highway was to eliminate as many
grade crossings of railroads as possible, so the new highway was
built to the north of the Norfolk and Western from Burkeville to
Rice; underpasses were constructed at Rice and west of Farmville,
and as the highway continued westward to Pamplin it kept to the
north of the railroad from the underpass near Farmville to Concord,
eliminating many crossings in both Prince Edward and Appomattox
Counties. The huge earth-moving equipment available for road-
building now was not known then. After the rights of way had been
cleared, where necessary, the earth was broken by plows drawn by
teams, and was hauled to fills in scoops also drawn by teams. After
Route 10, the present 460, had been built, Route 15 was built, running through the county from north to south. These roads were
surfaced with gray soil originally, and many a Prince Edward field
was sacrificed to the good roads movement. It was not until the mid-
1920's that these highways were surfaced with asphalt. When the
highways had been built, men were employed to work regularly
designated stretches of highway. These caretakers dragged the gray-
soiled surfaces regularly with mule-drawn drags and cut growth
along the right of way.

After the highways were surfaced, some of the tributary roads
were also given an asphalt surfacing. Much of the surfacing of these
roads did not take place until after the state took over all the roads
in 1932. There has continued a steady effort at improving the roads:
the main highways have been widened, straightened, and otherwise
improved since they were first constructed in the early 1920's.
Gradually the other roads have been surfaced and improved, until
most of the public roads in Prince Edward are passable in all weather.

As the demand for good roads increased and the state highway
program got under way, the question of the best method of financing
such a program was raised. Many advocates of good roads proposed
the issuance of bonds; North Carolina had passed a bond issue of
$50,000,000 for roads in 1920 and had begun an extensive program
of road construction, concentrating upon connecting the county seats

of the state with concrete roads in the "courthouse to courthouse" plan. State Senator Harry Flood Byrd led the opposition to bonds and advocated instead a pay-as-you-go program of financing road construction and improvement through a tax on gasoline. The issue was referred to the people in the general election in November, 1923; the state voted against bonds, and Prince Edward, by a narrow majority, followed the state trend, 411 in the county opposing bonds, 394 favoring them. Opposition to road bonds was strongest in Prince Edward in the rural sections, and there was a good turn-out of voters in the rural precincts in contrast to considerable apathy in Farmville.[82]

After the War Between the States, the United States government resumed the conduct of the postal service in the South. The method of letting by contract the carrying of mails to postoffices not served by railroads was continued. Bids to serve three routes from Farmville were invited in 1876 for the four-year period July 1, 1877, to June 30, 1881. Mail service was to be provided six days weekly to CaIra, McRae's, and Cumberland Courthouse and three times a week to Curdsville, New Store, and Buckingham Courthouse. Daily service, except Sunday, was provided by the route to Worsham and Hampden-Sydney College. The schedule required the carrier to leave Farmville daily at 3:00 P. M. and to arrive at Hampden-Sydney by 5:00 P. M., to leave Hampden-Sydney at 9:00 A. M., arriving at Farmville by 11:00 A. M. Bond of $300 was required of the carrier on this route. A route from Meherrin served Double Bridges and Pleasant Grove in Lunenburg County twice a week.

Darlington Heights and County Line Crossroads were served by carrier twice a week from Keysville. The carrier left Darlington Heights on Wednesdays and Saturdays at 7:00 A. M., arriving at Keysville by noon; he left Keysville at 1:00 P. M., arriving at Darlington Heights by 7:00 P. M. The bond required with bids for this route was $400.[83]

During the last quarter of the nineteenth century the number of postoffices increased greatly, until each small community had its office. This was a convenience to the people, as it diminished considerably the distance they had to go for postal service. A carrier brought mail from the nearest railroad station. Among the offices in existence at the turn of the century were Beck (Moran), Nile, Overly, Travis, Mount Leigh, as well as Rice, Green Bay, and Meherrin in the eastern part of the county; Sanco, Felden (which before 1894 had been Cypress for a time and before that Redd's Shop), Millbank, along with Farmville, Worsham, and Hampden-Sydney in the central part of the county; and Acteon (Tuggle), Gardenia (established in 1893), Five Forks, Adelle, Tredways, Venna, Putneys, in addition to Prospect and Darlington Heights in the western part of Prince Edward. Gardenia, Five Forks, and Tredways had a daily mail service out of Prospect.[84] A daily route serving Sanco and Felden from Farmville was inaugurated in 1895.[85]

The day of the neighborhood postoffice was brief. In 1904 the rural free delivery was introduced into Prince Edward. An editorial in the Farmville *Herald* on the re-election of Robert G. Southall to Congress in 1904 noted that "your constituents realize you belong to the minority, can secure no pensions, no post office buildings, not many appointments, but they do believe you can secure your full share of free rural routes and they expect you to do that. . . ." The editor overlooked the need for better postal service for country people in assigning a reason for this desire which he thought prevalent in the Fourth District. As he saw it, the reason rural mail routes were desired was that Southall's constituents "want a slight 'whack' at the Treasury box and this seems the only avenue of approach to it."[86]

One of the first rural mail routes in Prince Edward was from Green Bay through the communities served by the Travis and Mount Leigh postoffices. Route delivery service began December 1, 1904, and on that day the Travis and Mount Leigh postoffices were closed.[87]

With the introduction of the rural free mail delivery, the outlying postoffices were closed, leaving in Prince Edward the present postoffices: Farmville, Darlington Heights, Green Bay, Hampden-Sydney, Meherrin, Prospect, Rice, and Worsham. As the routes were not restricted by county lines, many Prince Edward people are served by routes from postoffices in other counties: Burkeville, Keysville, Cullen, and Pamplin, and residents of Amelia, Nottoway, Cumberland, and Buckingham Counties are served from Prince Edward offices. There has been during the half-century of R. F. D. service in the county a re-arrangement and consolidation of routes from time to time, with the result that postoffice addresses of many people have been changed and there are fewer but longer routes serving the county.

When the county seat was moved to Farmville, the clerk's office was a room in the courthouse. In 1896 the Board of Supervisors erected a separate building for the clerk's office.[88] Two years later, in September, 1898, the board approved the building of a new jail;

it set no limit on the cost, naming R. M. Burton, J. M. Crute, and W. H. Thackston the building committee.[89] In March, 1902, the supervisors purchased an iron fence for the front of the courthouse yard at a cost of $215 and directed that it be put on a brick foundation set in concrete.[90]

During the Wooldridge-Forbes trial, quite a furor was raised over the condition of the jail. When it was postponed from the November, 1904, term to January, 1905, Judge Hundley announced from the bench that it had been reported to him that the Prince Edward jail was in terrible sanitary condition and called for the jailor to be brought into court to explain. Sheriff Dickinson said that he was sending for the jailor, and Judge Hundley cut him short with the statement "You are the jailor by law." The jailor, whose name was Matthews, came, but before he could testify Judge Hundley named a commission consisting of H. D. Flood, of the defense counsel for Wooldridge, R. T. Hubard, commonwealth's attorney for Buckingham, and J. L. Hart, to examine the jail. They reported the prison "unsanitary, ill-smelling, infected with vermin" and "bedding and floors filthy and unfit for human habitation." Judge Hundley then announced report of the further complaint that the prisoners were not fed well and stated that he would investigate that complaint since the Commonwealth paid amply well for feeding prisoners. Then he issued a rule against the Board of Supervisors. When Judge A. D. Watkins, commonwealth's attorney for Prince Edward, explained that the board had done everything it could to make the jail sanitary and that the presence of vermin was due to the kind of person incarcerated, Judge Hundley retorted that the complaints about the Prince Edward jail were the only ones of the kind he had ever heard on his circuit, and he ordered Wooldridge and Forbes sent to Buckingham jail, to be kept there until the trial in January.[91]

The supervisors presented a report to the court which affirmed their watchfulness over conditions in the jail and disputed the findings of the special commission. The jail, almost new, had been built in 1898 at a cost of $3,000; it contained four rooms, eighteen by eighteen with a twelve-foot pitch. Three rooms contained steel cages, each divided into two apartments and a corridor. There was an abundance of water available, provided by the water company which furnished the town of Farmville its supply. Each room was fitted with proper sinks. The interior was regularly whitewashed three or four times a year. A close examination had discloseed no vermin or bad odor, "except such odor incident to the character of the prisoners." The board further asserted that no reasonable complaint had been made to the board, that it was satisfied that "the sanitary arrangement of the jail and its keeping compares favorably with any jail in the state and in many cases is far superior." Then the board voiced the feeling that a "great injustice" had been done Prince Edward County. All five members of the board at that time—E. L. Dupuy, R. Lee Price, A. A. Haskins, L. J. Verser, and W. H. Hubbard, signed the report.[92]

The board also took its case to the people. All the members except Hubbard signed a letter which was published in the Farmville *Herald* expressing a "feeling of grievance that Prince Edward County had been done a great injustice by reason of the publication in various papers concerning the condition of the jail." [The Wooldridge-Forbes case had attracted statewide attention and was fully reported in the newspapers.] The board did not concur in the report of the investigating committee. Since no supervisor was present at the investigation of the committee, the board did not know on what evidence the report was based. The supervisors themselves could find no vermin, and the "ill smelling" was "no doubt due to the character of the prisoners and other natural causes which exist in all jails." The "unsanitary conditions" were "simply the opinion of three gentlemen who, so far as this board knows, are not experts." The supervisors then quoted the jail physician, "one of the most eminent physicians in this section of the country," that the jail was the source of no typhoid fever germ or other disease known to him. The supervisors admitted that the jail was not the most modern of prisons, but limited means did not permit them to erect such a jail. However, "so far as we can ascertain, all prisoners are furnished every comfort which can be reasonably expected."[93] With the report to the court and the public statement of the supervisors, the matter ended.

In 1933 the Farmville *Herald* proposed the building of a new courthouse for the county. It presented an architect's drawing of a proposed building, showing the suggested front elevation and the interior floor plan.[94] During the next five years sentiment crystallized in favor of a new courthouse, and Prince Edward voters, in a special election held in September, 1938, by a vote of 327 to 99 approved a bond issue of $75,000 for its building. The town of Farmville contributed $10,000 to the cost of the new courthouse, and the Public Works Administration of the federal government provided $50,681 toward the cost.[95] The contract for the new building was let December 28, 1938 to the Farmville Manufacturing Company.[96] Construction began shortly thereafter. The first term of Circuit Court held in the new courthouse was in November, 1939; it happened to be the last term of the Circuit Court of Prince Edward County over which Judge Robert F. Hutcheson, who had succeeded Judge Hundley in 1924, presided.[97]

This period has seen another change in the system of local courts. The system of magistrates' courts in each district was steadily losing the respect of the people. The title of justice of the peace or magistrate which had once been one of respect had lost much of its dignity. Throughout the state these courts were failing in their performance to administer justice wisely or to carry out their duties efficiently. In order to make the local courts more efficient and more worthy of public confidence, the magistrate's court was abolished, and a trial justice court for the entire county was substituted. This change became effective in 1934. John F. Lewis was named trial justice for Prince Edward by Judge Robert F. Hutcheson of the Circuit Court; Lewis first qualified for the office which he continues to hold on June 10, 1934.[98]

The costs of conducting the county's business years ago seems quite small when compared with current budgets. In 1893 the county's income was $12,305.11, and at the end of the fiscal year (September 1), there was a balance of $1,963.70. But annual salaries of county officials were also small: the county judge received $426, the clerk $812, the commonwealth's attorney $400, the sheriff $410, the commissioner of revenue $450, the superintendent of the poor $300, supervisors $200, members of the road board $250, and overseers of the poor $100; the treasurer's commissions amounted to $474.23. The largest items of expense to the county were for welfare: $1,598.64 for the support of the poor at the poorhouse, $1,522.40 for the support of the poor not at the poorhouse. Road expenditures were kept by districts; not a single district spent over $700 during the year on the upkeep of its roads. Buffalo, the largest district, spent $622.37; Farmville $255.38, Hampden $274.52, Leigh, $174.16, and Lockett $163.03. Teachers' salaries were the largest items of district expenses: Buffalo paid its white teachers $1,959.30, its colored teachers $1,350, and spent $265.42 for rent and fuel for schools; Farmville paid its white teachers $1,240, its colored teachers

$1,140, and spent $2,400.31 for rent and fuel; Hampden's white teachers received $1,665, its colored teachers $825, and spent on rent and fuel $410.10; Leigh's white teachers' salaries amounted to $1,380, its colored teachers' salaries $556.25, and it spent $247.02 on rent and fuel; Lockett paid white teachers $1,225, colored teachers $735, and spent $259.45 for rent and fuel. The state paid a substantial portion of the teachers' salaries: to Buffalo District $2,542.90, to Farmville $1,750.56, to Hampden $1,757.72, to Leigh $1,438.78, and to Lockett $1,290.05.[99]

Even these low operating costs did not go unprotested, for times were hard, incomes small, and values low. One complaint noted that George Gould objected to paying taxes on $10,000,000 of Jay Gould's estate of $82,000,000; yet Prince Edward farmers paid taxes on farms valued for taxation at $5,000 "which they can't sell for $2,500."[100] A citizens' meeting at Rice on February 23, 1895, considered the problem. Dr. H. E. Watkins was chairman of the meeting, and J. X. Morton secretary. After noting that the price of produce of all kinds was low, that producers could not support their families and pay their taxes at the current levels of income and tax rate, that salaries and perquisites of state and county officers had been set "when money was much lower than now," and that lands were assessed at figures considerably higher than actual values as shown "by recent sales and attempted sales," the meeting passed four resolutions: that assessors reduce valuations at least twenty-five per cent "to comply with the law requiring [lands] to be assessed at 'fair cash value'"; that salaries of state and county officials should be reduced twenty-five per cent (read this in the light of salaries paid in 1893); that whoever should be elected supervisor from Lockett District be requested to do all in his power to reduce the county's expenses; and that citizens in other sections of the county be asked "to take some action on taxation and the economical administration of county affairs."[101]

For the fiscal year ending June 30, 1954, Prince Edward County spent $1,399,155.72, including $311,933.26 for school construction (the R. R. Moton High School), $592,974,72 for the operation of schools (including the amount allocated by the state to Prince Edward schools) and $403,011.97 for general county expenses.[102]

During the earlier history of the county public health and public welfare were administered by the parish vestry. The vestry paid for the care of the indigent ill, and that was the extent of public health

History of Prince Edward County

service then. The overseers of the poor succeeded the vestry as the administrators of public welfare. In at least one case of unusual concern for public health the County Court acted. In March, 1829, on learning that Indians infected with smallpox, one of the most dreaded diseases of the time, were passing through the county, it commissioned Henry N. Watkins, James T. Price, William T. Wootton, Francis T. Wootton, and Thomas Scott to provide a hospital for them and such necessaries as they might need and secure physicians and nurses to attend them.[103]

When smallpox struck in 1882, the Board of Supervisors appointed physicians in each section to vaccinate the people: Dr. R. E. Bass in Lockett District, Dr. W. G. Eggleston in Hampden, Dr. Peter Winston in Farmville, Drs. Hix and Humphreys in Buffalo, and Dr. T. J. Owen in Leigh.[104]

Another epidemic of smallpox threatened in the winter of 1906, when some twelve or fifteen cases were reported in the Five Forks neighborhood, principally among the Negroes. At a special meeting the Board of Supervisors ordered all school pupils in that section of Buffalo District to be vaccinated as soon as possible by a competent physician; the chairman of the board was authorized to furnish "genuine vaccine" to physicians at cost and at the expense of the county; the board also agreed to pay the vaccination fee of ten cents for children of parents unable to pay it.[105] About three weeks later the board approved compulsory vaccination for the section in which the disease had been found and agreed to pay ten cents for each vaccination.[106] Three physicians were subsequently paid by the board for their services: Dr. J. F. Alsop of Prospect received $30 for vaccinating 300 people; Dr. J. L. White of Farmville $17.50 for vaccinating 139 people and for vaccine points and $5 for professional services rendered smallpox patients; and Dr. W. M. Holladay of Hampden-Sydney $110 for vaccinations and professional services to the patients.[107]

The supervisors also provided medical attention for the indigent. In 1875 Dr. J. D. Eggleston was paid $100 for medical services at the poorhouse in 1873 and 1874.[108]

Farmville physicians in 1890 were requested to furnish prescriptions to the needy ill at fifteen cents each, for which the council agreed to pay.

When several cases of smallpox were reported in Farmville in 1899, the council ordered all people in the town to be vaccinated within thirty days after the passing of the ordnance on February 27. The sections of the town in which there were cases of smallpox were quarantined on March 9. The town paid Dr. Peter Winston $20 for attending smallpox patients during the threatened epidemic. About this time the town of Farmville purchased the pest house from Prince Edward County. There were cases of smallpox in Farmville again in 1913; Dr. R. L. Hudgins attended the patients. The council appropriated $331.50 to cover the cost of vaccinating the people then.

The first step toward setting up a public health program in Farmville was taken in 1907 when Dr. W. E. Anderson was authorized by the council to establish a board of health. The council in 1912 appropriated $100 to the board to be used in destroying insect carriers of disease. The practice of sending samples of the town water to the State Health Department for analysis and examination was begun in 1916, when Drs. Peter Winston, J. R. Spencer, and Thomas G. Hardy composed the board.[109]

Public health work began in Prince Edward County just after the close of World War I. In 1919 the County Health Association engaged a nurse, Miss Mamie Rice, who continues at the time of this writing as public health nurse for the county; her principal activity at the beginning of this work was toward the correction of defects in school pupils. She also gave much attention to vaccination and immunization against diptheria. Three years later the Board of Supervisors, the County School Board, and the Town Council of Farmville assumed a share of the financial responsibility for the support of the public health program, and a sanitation officer, J. E. Enders, was employed. The first diptheria immunization clinic in this section of Virginia was held in Farmville in 1923. A growing interest in public health, encouraged by the founding of the Southside Community Hospital, led to the organization by nine counties, (Amelia, Appomattox, Buckingham, Charlotte, Cumberland, Lunenburg, Nottoway, Powhatan, and Prince Edward) of the Southside Health District, with headquarters in Farmville, in 1928. The director of the district was Dr. W. A. Brumfield. This health program was especially active in giving the toxoid to prevent diptheria, and in vaccinating against smallpox and typhoid fever. It also sponsored home nursing classes, taught by the public health nurses. Through the work of the health program, school sanitation in Prince Edward reached a high level, and the county was described by Dr. Brumfield in 1934 as leading the state in sanitation. When it is recalled that twenty-four years before the school statistics showed only one-sixth of the schools in the county with toilets, this appraisal represents real achievement. The public health program did much to secure the installation of septic tanks and sanitary privies at Prince Edward homes.

After five years of operation, the other counties withdrew support from the Southside Health District. With the conclusion of a public health program on a district basis, Prince Edward continued the work as the Prince Edward County Health Department, retaining Dr. Brumfield as health officer. After the death of Dr. Brumfield in 1938, Dr. James N. Dudley succeeded him as director of the health department. Since Dr. Dudley's resignation, Dr. John G. McNiel (1945-46) and Dr. H. E. Jenkins have held this post. J. E. Enders was succeeded as sanitation officer by J. W. Simmons in 1930. Joseph Ogburn Hart was appointed to the post in 1952, following Simmons' death.[110]

Dr. John Peter Mettauer maintained what would now be considered a hospital in connection with his medical school at Worsham.

In 1874 Dr. R. Randolph Stevenson, who had been a surgeon in the Confederate Army and after the war with English troops—"her Majesty's local forces"—at Halifax, Canada, located in Worsham. He established a sanatorium there, which was advertised in 1875 as "the only sanatorium in Virginia . . . for the treatment of chronic and acute diseases." Gynecology was a specialty. Among the advantages of the Stevenson sanatorium were the "elevated and salubrious" location "in the midst of a polished and refined society," the "quiet and retirement" afforded nervous patients, the reasonable cost of board, lodging, and medical attention, and the daily mail service from Farmville. Professor S. D. Gross, M.D., LL.D., D.C.L. (Oxon.), of Philadelphia was private referee and consulting surgeon and physician for the sanatorium, which had an honorary board of visitors: Dr. James Lyle of Farmville, Judge F. N. Watkins, the Rev. R. L. Dabney of Union Seminary, J. S. Stanley-James of Farmville, Charles Bugg of Farmville, Judge A. D. Dickinson, J. A. H. St. Andrew of Farmville, and Colonel J. P. Fitzgerald of Farmville.[111]

Dr. W. E. Anderson and others operated a sanatorium at the Farmville Lithia Springs about the turn of the century. Patients were housed in the rear wing of the house which stands at the foot of the hill on the Farmville-Cumberland road. Although the sanatorium was not in Prince Edward, it is identified with the county through its director, Dr. Anderson.

There was talk of opening a hospital in Farmville in 1913, and the council went so far as to appoint a committee consisting of E. L. Erambert, R. W. Noel, and R. B. Cralle to ascertain the cost of fitting up rooms in a building on North Street for the purpose. Subsequently the question of building a hospital was referred to the council's Poor and Health Committee, where it apparently died. Two Farmville physicians, Dr. W. J. Gills and Dr. T. G. Hardy, maintained hospitals in their homes.[112]

Desire to have good hospital facilities in the section continued. The General Assembly in 1923 passed an act authorizing Prince Edward or Cumberland or some contiguous county to establish a public hospital. The board of supervisors of either of the counties was authorized to propose an inter-county hospital upon petition of one-fifth of the qualified voters in two or more of the counties affected. The Circuit Court was authorized to submit a bond issue for a hospital to the voters in a special election and to appoint seven trustees of the hospital if the issue should be approved.[113]

This approach did not prove promising. But then it was learned that the Commonwealth Fund generously aided selected localities in the erection of hospitals. Mayor E. W. Sanford of Farmville was sent to New York in September, 1925, to confer with officials of the fund concerning the possibility of getting assistance to build a hospital in Farmville. A hospital committee, consisting of J. L. Jarman, E. S. Shields, and N. B. Davidson of the Lions Club and Drs. W. E. Smith, R. L. Hudgins, and T. G. Hardy representing the medical profession of the town and county, pushed the effort. They reported to the Town Council on September 22 the conditions for the establishment of a hospital by the Commonwealth Fund: the fund would pay two-thirds of the cost of establishment provided the town, county, or some other agency would provide the other third and the operating deficit. The Farmville council guaranteed to meet one-third of the operating deficit (which was estimated to amount to $2,666.66).[114] The General Assembly in February, 1926, authorized boards of supervisors of Prince Edward, Cumberland, Charlotte, Buckingham, and Nottoway Counties to contribute up to $5,000 toward the construction and equipping of the hospital and to appropriate annually up to $2,500 to support the hospital. At that time approximately $50,000 had been raised by private subscription; this was only $10,000 short of the $60,000 goal, which the Commonwealth Fund would match with a gift of $120,000 when raised.[115] The campaign

for funds was successful, the Commonwealth Fund made its gift, and
the Southside Community Hospital was built on a bluff overlooking
Buffalo River, a commanding site. The hospital opened November
18, 1927, and the first patient was a colored girl, Matilda Metzner,
whose hand had been crushed and had to be amputated. Since the
construction of the hospital there have been two notable expansion
projects. The first was the erection of a nurses' home on the hospital
grounds as a memorial to E. Scott Martin.[116] The second was the
construction of the Mettauer wing which was dedicated in 1954.
The name commemorates the distinguished medical career of Dr.
John Peter Mettauer; and the wing has increased the present capacity of the hospital to eighty-seven beds and eighteen basinets; the
potential capacity of the hospital with this wing is 103 beds. Central
facilities to accommodate a hospital of 150 beds have been installed.
Gifts from individuals and firms throughout the area supplemented
an allocation of funds made available under the Hill-Burton Act of
1946 which provides grants for hospital construction to make possible
the erection of the wing. The first campaign for subscriptions for
the wing was in 1949.[117]

Presidents of the hospital's board of managers have been J. L.
Jarman (1926-30), E. Scott Martin (1930-34), R. E. Garland, J. B.
Wall (1942-46), S. M. Holton (1946-47), O. H. Whitten, W. S.
Weaver, and W. C. Fitzpatrick. The superintendents have been Miss
K. Frances Cleave (1927-29), Miss Carolyn Sykes (1929-36), Miss
Susie L. Pannell (1936-38), A. D. Kincaid (1939-41), Miss Char-
lotte S. Piper (1941-42), Miss Anne Lunney (1942-43), Miss Mary
P. Routt (1943-46), John M. Cofer, and Joseph S. Stubbs, Jr., whose
title, in keeping with current hospital parlance, is administrator.[118]

An increasing social consciousness urged the opening of a new
mental hospital, or lunatic asylum as it was then called, to meet the
increased demand for hospitalization of this type of patient. Inadequate accommodations in the existing institutions made necessary
the arrangements which were made in a case in Prince Edward in
February, 1874. "A respected lady was committed to jail by three
justices as a lunatic, her friends declining to take care of her." There
was no room for her and many persons in a similar condition in the
asylum with the result that there were "many unfortunate lunatics
in our county jails." The judge ordered the sheriff "to give special
attention to her comforts."[119] In the agitation for a new state asylum,
Farmville put in its bid to be selected as the location. Two com-

mittees to promote Farmville as the site of the new institution were appointed at a meeting at the courthouse February 18, 1874: Colonel W. R. Berkeley, Captain P. W. McKinney, Captain F. D. Irving, Major H. R. Hooper, and W. D. Rice were appointed to draft a petition to the legislature offering a site for the asylum in the vicinity of Farmville; Berkeley, Hooper, H. E. Warren, and Dr. J. T. Spencer were appointed to look into the matter of selecting a site.[120] In March, 1875, it was reported that Farmville was not chosen as the site of the new asylum.[121]

Prince Edward had had an almshouse since 1828. This property was located near Douglas Church. In 1874 the Board of Supervisors selected a new site and bought a farm known as the Sulphur Springs property adjoining the B. S. Scott farm for the poorhouse.[122] Here farming operations were carried on under the direction of the super- intendent of the farm; indigent persons who had no one to care for them and were unable to care for themselves were placed at the farm and were cared for. Each year, usually just before Christmas, the supervisors paid an annual visit to the farm and inspected the property; they were entertained at dinner by the superintendent and his wife. When the supervisors made their annual visit in 1895 they saw a five-room tobacco barn with a shed room twelve by twenty feet, double tenement houses, and a porch to the superinten- dent's home, all of which had been built since their last official visit. During that year over a mile of wire fencing with cedar posts had been run. The inventory showed that on the farm were two mules, one horse, one set of double harness, one two-horse wagon, an ox cart, one mower, one gleaner (rake), two double and four single plows, one harrow, one drag, one single and one double shovel plow, six hoes, two wheat cradles, three cows, two yearlings, one calf, sixteen stock hogs, 3,000 pounds of pork, 140 barrels of corn with shucks from same, six stacks of oats, 5,000 pounds of fodder, one large rick of tops, and 6,000 pounds of tobacco. N. H. Garland, who was superintendent of the farm for many years, was managing it at that time. There were ten inmates of the almshouse that year.[123]

Among Garland's predecessors as superintendent of the poor was William Barbour, who qualified for the office in 1870.[124] Among his successors as superintendent of the poor farm were Frank C. Wilson and M. L. Hardy.

There were some indigent persons who were physically able to care for themselves or who had relatives who could minister to them but were unable to contribute to their support. For such persons the county made provision by allowing to each a small sum each month, usually $1 to $3, on the recommendation of the overseer of the poor of the district to the Board of Supervisors. The money was not paid to the indigent person; the overseer of the poor gave an order to a merchant to furnish the needy person with groceries in the stipulated amount each month. The merchant then presented his bill to the supervisors. In August, 1906, the board ordered the following accounts paid for "rations for paupers": A. Q. Bradshaw, $12; J. Sam Harris, $5; T. Henry Glenn, $17; R. W. Price, $3; E. S. Taylor and Co., $3; J. W. Porterfield, $8; A. G. Vaughan, $8; W. E. Chappell, $3; J. B. Farrar, $11; Stokes and Davidson, $6; and E. G. McGehee, $3.[125]

No provision was made for the wandering indigent; jail, as it had been the only place which could provide a haven for many lunatics when asylum accommodations were inadequate to the demand in the 1870's, was often the only haven for the wanderer, young or old, who got into some difficulty. The county jail was accordingly the place to which a twelve-year-old white boy, caught riding a freight train in September, 1906, was taken when delivered to the Farmville police by the conductor of the train who found him. At that, the lad was not treated as a man would have been who was caught using a freight train as a means of free transportation; the man would have been put off when found. Because it was night when this lad was found on the train, the conductor did not put him off in the dark but brought him to Farmville and handed him over to the police. The boy told the police that his home was in Dunn, North Carolina, and that he had been working in Bedford.[126] What became of him was not recorded.

This boy was unusually young to be on the road alone; there were, however, many older than he who made their way from place to place by riding freight trains and stopping at villages or farmhouses to beg a meal or a place to spend the night. The usual response was a blend of generosity and caution; if he sought food, it was given him plentifully, but he was not invited into the house; if lodging was his desire, he was directed to a tobacco storehouse or barn; it was not safe to have him in the home, and there was always the danger that he might strike a match if he smoked and set the stable on fire if he went there to sleep. The appearance of these unfortunates was usually enough to put the prudent person on guard;

and sometimes the appearance was such that it was frightening to women and children. Not infrequently in those days the tramp might be killed in trying to catch or leave a train or in some way be thrown from it in riding. If identification papers could be found by the justice of the peace or constable or coroner who investigated the case, some person mentioned in them would be notified and the body held to wait claiming; usually in such circumstances it was claimed. When no identification could be found, the last resting place would be a grave beside the tracks.

In addition to the provision made by the county by providing an asylum for the needy at the county farm and by providing food to others, a limited effort toward the relief of the poor was made by the churches. Such efforts were usually limited to indigent members of the church. When a charter member of Pisgah Baptist Church, a maiden lady, lost her home by fire in 1893, her brother-in-law agreed to board her for $4 a month; the church assumed responsibility for making the payment. Members of the church subscribed to the fund in amounts ranging from twenty-five cents to $1 per month; one pledge was for a half-bushel of meal monthly to her support. Others were the recipients of help from the church, sometimes in small cash donations, sometimes in supplies.[127]

The churches and fraternal organizations supported orphanages, and this project was among the most popular benevolences, if not the most popular, of those groups. Churches designated special Sundays for contributions to the orphanages, and gifts were larger on such days than usual. The Children's Home Society of Virginia carried on an extensive program for the placement of orphan children in homes, caring for them until a home could be found. After an address by the Rev. W. J. Maybee, superintendent of the society, in the Farmville Methodist Church on August 31, 1902, a local advisory board to the society was organized: Dr. Peter Winston, president; Mrs. R. B. Berkeley, secretary-treasurer; A. B. Armstrong, counsel; Mrs. Etta Whitehead, Mrs. C. M. Walker, Mrs. Portia Morrison, Judge J. M. Crute, and G. M. Robeson.[128]

Human needs were met in these ways in Prince Edward until the depression which started with the stock market crash in October, 1929. So many people were placed in needy circumstances by the loss of jobs and the low price of farm commodities, aggravated by near crop failures resulting from the droughts of 1930 and 1932, that the normal means of supplying the necessary wants of the poor proved inadequate. Following the drought of 1930 the Red Cross distributed flour to the needy in Prince Edward.

Measures adopted by the Franklin D. Roosevelt administration to combat the depression affected directly the Prince Edward community as they did every community in the United States. Upon his inauguration on March 4, 1933, President Roosevelt ordered a banking holiday in which all banks in the nation were closed. The holiday lasted only a few days, but only those banks in a sound financial position were allowed to reopen. The three banks in Farmville were permitted to reopen, and Prince Edward went through the depression, in striking contrast to many other counties in Southside Virginia and to many towns and cities throughout the nation, without a bank failure.

One of the first steps taken by the new administration was the inauguration of the National Recovery Administration, which administered codes providing for a reduction in working hours, to provide more jobs, and minimum pay, to insure an adequate wage. Some small businesses in particular objected to the minimum wage scale because of lack of resources; one sawmill operator in Prince Edward did not see how he could afford to increase the rate of pay at his mill which was then seventy-five cents a day. (Farm labor was paid $1 a day then, though an unusually good worker might receive $1.50 for a day's work, which began about sunrise and continued until sunset.) For all the objections to NRA, businessmen cooperated and were generally pleased with the result. A group of Farmville men in August, 1933, urged the town to subscribe to the NRA code. After learning from the League of Virginia Municipalities that the law did not apply to cities and towns and that no towns in Virginia planned to adopt the code, Farmville declined to agree to operate under the provisions. It did cooperate in spirit by setting a minimum wage of twenty cents an hour for common labor and by putting the police on an eight-hour day, the latter decision being contrary to the counsel of Chief E. D. Lipscomb who felt that a ten-hour day would provide better protection.[129]

To provide employment for young men, the Civilian Conservation Corps was established in the spring of 1933. The work of this agency was of particular significance to Prince Edward, for it was through it that the state forest was started and Goodwin and Prince Edward lakes were built. A camp for CCC workers was located in the Gallion forest, which was the nucleus of the present state forest in the southeastern section of the county. Emmett D. Gallion of Prince Edward, who had been a student at the Virginia Polytechnic Institute during its first session and was at the time of his death an employe of the General Land Office in Washington, bequeathed all his property by his will dated April 25, 1918, and probated December 1, 1919, to the state of Virginia to be used as a forestry reservation under the management of the State Forestry Commission; his money was left to be used for making improvements on the land left for the forestry reservation; the State Forester of Virginia was named executor of the estate.[130] The terms of the will were carried out, and the Gallion state forest near Green Bay came into being. The state began the expansion of the forest in the mid-1930's and began buying land extensively in Leigh District to be diverted from farm to forest. Members of the CCC worked at forestry improvement, planting seedlings, building roads and fire trails, and the two lakes, which have during the past decade and a half become popular for fishing and swimming, Goodwin Lake for white people and Prince Edward for colored. The old Miller home at Stone Knoll was taken down and rebuilt as a residence for the superintendent of the forest. Prince Edward not only provided employment for many young men in the CCC; many young men from the county found employment in the corps.

The Federal Emergency Relief Administration was set up in 1933 to administer the funds appropriated by Congress for relief. Virginia borrowed $16,000,000, and Farmville joined other municipalities in the state to get one-fourth of the sum allocated for city and town streets. This agency financed a variety of educational projects. Operation of a nursery school at the Farmville Training School was begun under FERA auspices in 1934. Prince Edward County applied for $15,072.71 of FERA funds at the beginning of 1935. The district FERA office was located in Farmville.

Many Prince Edward people were employed through the Civil Works Administration. Work on CWA projects began in the winter of 1933-34. Among the first projects in Farmville were the construction of a sewer line on Park Street, the extension of the water line on Ely Street to the cemetery, and the improvement of streets and walks. At other places in the county were improvement projects on school grounds.[131] One company of CWA workers cleaned out Spring Creek from Allen's bridge to the junction of Spring Creek with Buffalo; hammocks were cut and other obstructions removed from the stream bed with the result that the level of the water was lowered several inches. Under the supervision of the Prince Edward Health Department, CWA workers built many septic tanks at homes with private water supplies and 2,279 sanitary privies at Prince Edward homes.[132]

A nine-months' school session in 1933-34 was made possible in Prince Edward through a grant of CWA funds to cover the teachers' salaries for one month. (Prior to the depression the school session had continued nine months, but the stringency of the times made it necessary to reduce the session to eight months; in 1932-33 teachers were asked to teach for two weeks without pay in order to extend the term, but Superintendent of Schools T. J. McIlwaine felt that such a request was unfair to the teachers, and he would not ask them to render instructional services without compensation thereafter.)

Beginning in 1935 the work relief program was administered through the Works Progress Administration. Under this program much work was done on Farmville streets and sidewalks; several Negro schools in the county were rebuilt and improved; and an appropriation from this agency helped finance the construction of the present county courthouse. In June, 1935, there were 530 persons in Prince Edward working on relief projects.[133]

To help administer the relief program, to help determine the need of relief, and to help locate persons who needed the assistance the relief agencies provided, Prince Edward County and the town of Farmville employed a trained social worker in December, 1933.[134]

The need for a better organized welfare program than the old system of overseers of the poor could provide became recognized during the hard times of the 1930's. The federal government was making appropriations for direct relief in cases of need, conditioned upon matching appropriations by state governments. To administer this program, Virginia set up a new system for the administration of public welfare locally. In 1938 a board of public welfare, consisting of three members appointed by the Circuit Court, was authorized to be set up in each county, with the administration of the program committed to a superintendent of public welfare.[135] In addition to the superintendent there were to be case workers to investigate applications for aid and maintain contact with clients. The first Prince Edward Board of Public Welfare consisted of Mrs. Bennett T. Taylor, Edward Carter, and Herbert L. Bradshaw, the latter being elected chairman. Carter succeeded him in the chairmanship in

1948, and Robert B. Wilson, Jr., was appointed to the board following Bradshaw's death in 1949. Miss Carrie Bliss was named superintendent of public welfare for the county when the office was created, and she continues in that post. Wilson died in November, 1954, and W. T. Cook was named his successor.

Another change came in the abandonment of the poorhouse and the sale of the county farm. Sale of the farm was authorized by the Board of Supervisors on April 4, 1941; a month later it was conveyed by J. Ashby Armistead, chairman of the board, on behalf of the board to William Ireland, Jr.[136]

In colonial times Prince Edward paid a bounty for killing wolves, as the levies show, to rid the section of a dangerous beast. Because of the great damage done by crows and squirrels, Prince Edward was included in the counties in which each person required to file a list of tithables was required to produce before the justice taking the list five crows' heads or squirrel scalps for each tithable listed. The law, passed in November, 1769, was repealed for Prince Edward and some other counties in February, 1772.[137] Annoyance from predatory animals did not cease as the frontier moved westward. The Prince Edward Board of Supervisors was authorized in 1892 to pay bounties not in excess of $1.50 for each red fox scalp, seventy-five cents for each gray fox scalp, and fifty cents for each hawk, owl, mink, or weasel killed in the county; the measure was designed to protect poultry.[138]

While it appeared desirable to destroy predators, it also became necessary to provide protection for desirable game. An early effort in this direction was through setting up hunting seasons. An early law setting the season in 1878 forbade the killing, capture, or sale of partridges between February 1 and November 1, of pheasants between February 1 and August 1, of robins between April 1 and November 1, and of wild turkeys between February 1 and October 15. Possession of the bird was deemed *prima facie* evidence of violation of the law, which was punishable by a fine of $10, and imprisonment until it was paid.[139]

To enforce the laws setting hunting seasons and other laws concerning game, game wardens were appointed in 1918: N. T. Dillon and R. H. Wilkerson, Buffalo District; J. V. Foster and J. G. Shannon, Farmville; C. R. Morton and C. M. Redd, Hampden; T. V. Owen and J. P. Perkinson, Leigh; Adam Cook and W. H. Price, Lockett.[140]

After the Presidential election of 1896 Prince Edward continued in the Democratic column in national, state, and local elections. The State Democratic Committee in January, 1902, adopted the primary as the method for choosing nominees for United States Senator (these were still elected by the state legislature), the national House of Representatives, the State Senate, and the House of Delegates.[141] On July 17, 1902, a primary was held to select the Democratic nominee for Congress from the Fourth District. R. G. Southall of Amelia opposed Francis R. Lassiter of Petersburg for the nomination and won. With returns from only Briery precinct missing, Prince Edward voted 368 for Southall to 53 for Lassiter.[142] In the general election in November Prince Edward cast 442 votes for Southall to 38 for R. T. Vaughan, the Republican nominee, and four for Jones, the Negro candidate.[143] The picture has changed considerably from that of a few years before when Republican candidates got a majority of the Prince Edward vote; there was a change, too, in the volume of voting, with fewer than 500 participating in this election in contrast to the 2,451 who voted ten years before.

There were only three contests for the Democratic nominations for county and district offices in the 1903 primary. J. J. Owen defeated T. H. Bruce for nomination for the House of Delegates by a majority of 162; L. J. Verser won the nomination for supervisor of Farmville District over Major A. R. Venable by a majority of 146; and R. Lee Price defeated J. S. Harris and H. A. Glenn for the supervisor's post in Buffalo District. The Democratic committee, consisting of W. E. Anderson, chairman, J. J. Owen, J. Y. Phillips, W. H. Walden, and E. L. Dupuy, declared the unopposed candidates for the nominations the party nominees.[144] R. G. Southall spoke at a party meeting at the October Court; he thanked Prince Edward for giving him the largest majority in the primary of the preceding year of any county except his home county of Amelia and he urged the support of Judge W. H. Mann for the State Senate and J. J. Owen for the House of Delegates. F. T. Saunders who as an Independent was opposing Judge Mann also spoke.[145] There were only two contests on a countywide basis in the general election; Saunders against Mann for the Senate and A. D. Elam, Independent, in opposition to R. J. Carter for the office of commissioner of revenue. Mann won, getting a majority of 294 in Prince Edward, and Carter defeated Elam by 275 votes. Voters then chose many more officials than they do now; in the 1903 election, Prince Edward voters favored Mann to the State Senate and elected Carter commissioner of revenue, J. J. Owen to the House of Delegates, W. H. Ewing treasurer, T. H. Dickinson sheriff; A. D. Watkins commonwealth's attorney; the supervisors: L. J. Verser, Farmville; E. L. Dupuy, Hampden; W. H. Hubbard, Lockett; R. Lee Price, Buffalo; A. A. Haskins, Leigh; these are still elected by popular vote. In addition the voters in 1903 elected three justices of the peace from each district: R. A. Booker, J. L. Hart, and A. W. Drumeller, Farmville; R. F. Allen, B. A. Rodgers, N. W. Bell, Hampden; B. L. Carter, J. T. Morrisette, J. T. Mahan, Lockett; R. L. Terry, T. W. Crawley, B. F. Hunt, Buffalo; T. T. Pettus, S. D. Brown, R. B. Wilson, Leigh; overseers of the poor for each district: W. H. Burger, Jr., Farmville; Bedford Brown, Hampden; J. S. Bradshaw, Lockett; R. A. Davis, Buffalo; and E. A. Owen, Leigh; and a constable in each district: J. W. Anglea, Farmville; R. N. Jones, Hampden; J. M. Mottley, Lockett; R. L. Hubbard, Buffalo; no constable was elected in Leigh that year.[146]

Justices, overseers of the poor, and constables had been elected by popular vote since 1852. The office of justice of the peace was eliminated in Prince Edward with the establishment of the office of trial justice in 1934, and the office of overseer of the poor ended with the establishment of the county Board of Public Welfare in 1938.

Although a national election was coming, the old factionalism broke out again in the greatly weakened Republican party in the county in 1904. The Farmville postmastership seemed to be the bone of contention, one member of the George Richardson faction accusing J. E. Harris of the Harris-Bliss faction of turning that office over to a Democrat when he could not secure it for himself. But the Harris-Bliss element was in control, electing the delegates to the district convention and Harris to the county chairmanship.[147]

That year ex-Governor William E. Cameron of Petersburg and Judge L. D. Yarrell of Emporia opposed Southall for the Democratic nomination for Congress. Cameron, who had been elected governor on the Readjuster ticket, went to Lunenburg to speak in the campaign; he made his speech and defended his record against Southall's charge that Cameron had worked with the Republicans and never supported the Democrats until after 1900; but the fifty-mile trip proved too much for the aging candidate and four days after going to Lunenburg he was exhausted; he then withdrew from the race. Judge Yarrell decided to withdraw also, but after Southall charged him with being a resident of Washington, he changed his mind.

Prince Edward gave Southall a substantial majority in the primary September 5, but the vote was small, 275 to 27 for Yarrell.[148] In the general election Judge Alton B. Parker received 576 votes to 101 for Theodore Roosevelt, and Southall got 579 in contrast to the 82 cast for his opponent Alexander. But interest in politics was definitely on the wane, now that the Democrats were in certain control of the county. In the campaign of 1904 there was no political meeting, no canvass, no club, no barbecue in Prince Edward;[149] the Democrats were sure of victory, the Republicans resigned to defeat and split by factionalism, so the political leaders did not bother.

The primary campaign for the nomination for state offices in 1905 aroused much more interest in Prince Edward, and something of the old time spirit for politics was shown. For one thing, a Prince Edward man was a candidate for a major office. After Dr. Joseph W. Southall, the incumbent superintendent of public instruction, announced that he would not be a candidate for the office because his age would not permit him to wage an active campaign, J. D. Eggleston, Jr., superintendent of schools in Prince Edward, announced for the post.[150] This office had been made elective by the new Constitution, and this was the first opportunity the people had to name the head of the state school system. In June the school trustees of the county endorsed Eggleston's candidacy, and fourteen members of the district school boards signed the endorsement: S. W. Paulett, W. A. McCraw, John R. Morton, L. D. Jones, W. B. Gates, C. E. Kennedy, W. H. Walden, H. E. Barrow, E. G. McGehee, T. T. Pettus, James T. Clark, George Hunt, H. D. Kauffman, and G. D. Warriner. Captain Pettus at a later meeting of the county trustees praised Eggleston as the most efficient superintendent of schools during his thirty-three years of service as a school trustee and moved that resolutions expressing appreciation of Eggleston's services be adopted; he, Hunt, Paulett, Clark, and McGehee were appointed to draw up the resolutions. Joining the school board members in endorsing Eggleston's candidacy were E. J. Whitehead, county clerk; Sheriff T. H. Dickinson; A. D. Watkins, commonwealth's attorney; F. M. Bugg, member of the School Trustee Electoral Board; J. L. Hart, publisher of the Farmville *Herald*; Judge George J. Hundley; J. J. Owen, member of the House of Delegates; and W. H. Ewing, treasurer.[151]

Other state races aroused interest. Thomas S. Martin, chief of the state Democratic machine of the day, was being challenged for his seat in the United States Senate by Governor Andrew Jackson Montague. Martin, with the backing of the railroad interests, had defeated the popular ex-Governor, General Fitzhugh Lee, when the legislature elected a successor to Senator John S. Barbour in 1895. The campaign for the senatorial nomination was a machine-anti-machine contest. There were three candidates for the gubernatorial nomination, Representative Claude A. Swanson of Pittsylvania, who had been defeated for the same nomination four years before by Montague, Lieutenant Governor Joseph Willard, and Judge William Hodges Mann of Nottoway, who represented Prince Edward in the State Senate and was widely known and esteemed in the county. His candidacy would provoke interest in the campaign in Prince Edward.

When Willard spoke in Farmville early in June, he was introduced by J. Taylor Thompson; but when the Mann Democratic Club was organized in July, Thompson was elected its president, along with N. B. Davidson vice-president, J. E. Garland secretary, and W. T. Clark treasurer.[152] Dr. W. E. Anderson, county Democratic chairman, introduced both Judge Mann and Governor Montague when they spoke in Farmville in the interest of their candidacies. Judge Mann defended the law which bore his name under which over 700 saloons in the rural districts of Virginia had been closed and stressed the need of better school facilities.[153] When Thomas S. Martin spoke in Farmville in the interest of his senatorial candidacy, he was introduced by his senior colleague in the Senate from Virginia, the greatly esteemed John W. Daniel, "the lame lion of Lynchburg"; Daniel endorsed Martin's record in the Senate to the Prince Edward audience.[154] In the primary which was held August 22, Montague received 252 votes to 251 for Martin, Mann led the field of gubernatorial candidates with 262 votes to 166 for Swanson and 82 for Willard; neither of Prince Edward's choices for these nominations won in Virginia; Martin won the senatorial nomination, and Swanson the gubernatorial. But Eggleston defeated Hulvey for superintendent of public instruction, receiving in Prince Edward the flattering vote of 441 to 46. J. Taylor Ellyson, candidate for Lieutenant Governor, received 454 votes in Prince Edward to 81 for his opponent Cabell; Ellyson carried the state.[155]

The Republicans had candidates in the field for state offices in 1905; they held a meeting in Prince Edward September 18, which was addressed by J. C. Blair of Wytheville and W. C. Franklin of Appomattox. The Democrats sent a speaker into every precinct in the county: H. D. Flood of Appomattox, Francis R. Lassiter of Petersburg, and Robert G. Southall of Amelia spoke in Farmville October 24; J. Taylor Thompson at Prospect October 28; A. D. Watkins at Meherrin October 28, and on the same day R. K. Brock spoke at Darlington Heights and J. M. Crute at Rice; Brock also spoke at Worsham October 27 and at Green Bay November 4.[156] Although Prince Edward Democrats had preferred Mann in the primary, they gave Swanson a substantial vote in the general election November 7, giving him 530 votes to 137 for Judge Lunsford L. Lewis, the Republican nominee. Eggleston received 585 votes for superintendent of public instruction to 77 for Harmon, his Republican opponent, and other Democratic nominees received votes comparable to those given Swanson for Governor. J. J. Owen had no opposition for the House of Delegates, nor did E. J. Whitehead have opposition for the clerkship.[157]

The next year the Democratic nominee for Congress, Francis R. Lassiter, had no opposition, but the county committee urged the people to go to the polls to give him a good vote. The Democratic committee then consisted of W. H. Ewing, chairman; Prospect precinct: W. H. Walden, chairman, R. T. Carter, J. Spencer Brightwell; Spring Creek: S. N. Cunningham; Farmville: W. T. Blanton, chairman, P. H. C. Rice, F. M. Bugg, John F. Walton, J. E. Garland, H. E. Richardson; Worsham precinct: E. L. Dupuy, chairman, T. H. Dickinson, W. A. McCraw, E. W. Venable; Briery precinct: John R. Morton, chairman, George W. Redd, E. G. McGehee, W. E. Chappell, Samuel Lacy; Green Bay precinct: J. J. Owen, chairman, L. D. Jones, A. A. Haskins, J. J. Holt, F. H. Kauffman, J. A. Shackleton; Rice Depot precinct: A. W. Weaver, chairman, W. H. Hubbard, T. H. Bruce, J. S. Bradshaw, J. R. Weaver, E. T. Bondurant.[158]

Another spirited campaign was threatened when A. D. Watkins became a candidate for the post of judge of the circuit court in opposition to Judge George J. Hundley in 1905. J. Taylor Thompson, R. H. Watkins, G. S. Wing, W. Lancaster, Robert K. Brock, and J. M. Crute of the Prince Edward bar endorsed Watkins; but in January, 1906, just before the General Assembly which was to elect the judge met, Watkins withdrew, leaving Hundley unopposed.[159]

Local contests featured the primary campaign in 1907. W. H. Ewing did not run for re-election as treasurer, and three sought the nomination for that post: S. W. Watkins, a deputy treasurer, Robert J. Carter, commissioner of revenue, and Major A. R. Venable, Jr.

Another deputy, T. H. Bruce, declined to run; thanking his friends for offers of support, he stated that he would soon reach the age of threescore years and that the office would require his absence from home and loved ones "which to me are dearer than political honors." In the primary Watkins won, receiving 313 votes to 245 for Carter and 90 for Venable; Judge W. H. Mann was renominated for the State Senate, receiving in Prince Edward 362 votes to 270 for E. P. Wallace of Lunenburg. There were three contests for supervisors' posts; in Farmville District J. L. Hart defeated H. E. Wall 135 to 75; in Buffalo R. W. Fuqua defeated W. B. Binford 97 to 81; and in Lockett, in what was described as "probably the hottest fight" for a supervisor's post, R. H. Walton defeated W. H. Hubbard 68 to 53.[160] Hubbard contested the election, but as he failed to get his petition signed by fifteen persons, the case was dismissed.[161] In the general election there was no opposition to the Democratic nominees.[162]

There have been only two Congressional campaigns in the past half-century in which the candidates have had to make vigorous fights. In 1912 Walter A. Watson of Nottoway defeated Robert Turnbull of Brunswick for the Democratic nomination by a narrow margin. Prince Edward gave Turnbull a small lead over Watson, 318 to 309.[163] Watson easily defeated his opponent in 1914, Herzig. In Prince Edward the vote was 331 for Watson to 10 for Herzig.[164]

When Watson died in 1919 Patrick H. Drewry succeeded him and continued in the House of Representatives until his death in 1947 without ever becoming involved in a serious contest to hold his position. There was a hard-fought contest in the winter of 1948 to succeed Drewry, however. Three Democrats, Watkins M. Abbitt of Appomattox, Morton G. Goode of Dinwiddie, Robert W. Arnold, Jr., of Sussex, and one Republican, T. Robert Cocks, native of Prince Edward but then living in Lunenburg, aspired to the position. Abbitt won the election; Prince Edward cast 1,203 votes for him, 535 for Goode, 15 for Arnold, and 52 for Cocks.[165]

Some of the state primaries have had special interest. In 1917 Lieutenant Governor J. Taylor Ellyson, Attorney General John Garland Pollard, and Westmoreland Davis sought the Democratic nomination for Governor. Ellyson and Pollard were both identified with the Democratic "organization" headed by Senator Thomas S. Martin; both were also "dry," and the Anti-Saloon League, then led by Bishop James Cannon, Jr., who a quarter century before had been pastor of the Farmville Methodist Church and now with the league was a power in Virginia politics, could not endorse one in preference to the other; and both persisted in running. Davis was anti-machine and "wet." In Prince Edward the vote was 202 for Ellyson, 164 for Davis, and 160 for Pollard. In the state, however, Davis won the nomination, receiving 30,925 votes to 21,874 for Ellyson and 18,350 for Pollard.[166] When Westmoreland Davis opposed Claude A. Swanson for Democratic senatorial nomination in 1922, Prince Edward favored Swanson, who had been appointed to the Senate in 1910 to succeed John W. Daniel by Governor William Hodges Mann, by 455 votes to 248 for Davis.[167]

After the death of Senator Thomas S. Martin in 1920, the leadership of the Democratic machine ultimately devolved upon Harry Flood Byrd. Byrd's successful leadership of the fight against bonds for roads in 1922 put him in line for this unofficial position, and his election to the governorship in 1925 gave him the opportunity to make his leadership of the party in Virginia unquestioned. Prince Edward did not give Byrd a majority in the primary in which he sought the gubernatorial nomination; Byrd received 500 votes in the county in comparison with 561 cast for his opponent, State Senator G. Walter Mapp of Accomac.[168] Mapp's sister, Mrs. H. E. Barrow, was a resident of Farmville, and this tie made Mapp favorably known in the county; and one of the most popular and influential men in Prince Edward, S. W. Watkins, the county treasurer, supported Mapp; it was said that Watkins favored Mapp because of Byrd's opposition to the fee system, which then provided a substantial part of the income of county officials. After Byrd became Governor, he led in abolishing the fee system and in putting county officers upon a fixed salary, determined by the State Compensation Board. This procedure, which was designed to correct a system which had become abused, in turn became one of the most potent factors in strengthening to so-called Byrd organization in Virginia Democratic politics. Four years later, when Mapp was again a candidate for the gubernatorial nomination, Prince Edward supported the candidate upon whom the retiring Governor chose to cast his mantle, John Garland Pollard, who a dozen years before had been defeated for the nomination; in the primary Pollard, who won in the state, received 413 votes in Prince Edward, Mapp 129, and Rosewell Page six.[169]

The general election of 1929 attracted more interest than the primary. The year before Virginia had gone Republican in the presidential election as a result of the support of Herbert Hoover by Bishop Cannon and other leaders of the "dry" faction in Virginia; they had preferred Hoover because the Democratic nominee, Alfred E. Smith, had declared himself in favor of repeal of the Prohibition Amendment. There was the keenest interest to see whether the rank and file of the voters could be weaned permanently away from the Democratic party. The Republicans and anti-Smith Democrats nominated a professor of psychology at Washington and Lee University, William Moseley Brown, for Governor. When the votes were counted, the wandering sheep were found again in the Democratic fold; and Prince Edward, which had not defected to Hoover in 1928, voted 986 for Pollard to 235 for Brown. Pollard was a good selection to win back the voters, for he had an outstanding record as a "dry" leader.[170] The only other comparable state election since Reconstruction was in 1953, when the Republicans with their gubernatorial nominee, State Senator Ted Dalton, sought to repeat the Republican victory which gave President Eisenhower the electoral vote of Virginia. Prince Edward followed the state trend in both elections, voting 1,120 to 441 in favor of the Democratic nominee, Thomas B. Stanley,[171] who in the primary had carried the county by a vote of 838 to 194 for Charles R. Fenwick.[172]

The primary in which the gubernatorial nomination was at stake four years before provided a more interesting party fight. The "Byrd organization" was both challenged from without and divided within. Francis Pickens Miller of Albemarle was a candidate openly opposing the "machine." Two loyal members of the "organization," State Senator John S. Battle of Charlottesville and Horace H. Edwards of Richmond, who had been chairman of the state party committee, were also candidates. A fourth candidate, Remmie L. Arnold of Petersburg, was well known in business and fraternal circles. The "organization" backed Battle, and in the primary the lines held firmly, in contrast to the 1917 primary. The Prince Edward vote reflected the attitude of the state: Battle, 836; Edwards, 462; Miller, 337; Arnold, 89.[173]

The Presidential campaigns have only rarely created more than passing interest in Prince Edward since the county became safely Democratic after the new Constitution. Bryan carried the county for the third time in 1908, receiving 561 votes to 117 for William Howard Taft.[174] Woodrow Wilson had a good margin in 1912, with 564 votes to 44 for Theodore Roosevelt and 71 for Taft.[175] In 1916

Prince Edward voted 668 for Wilson to 108 for Charles E. Hughes.[176] James M. Cox carried the county 779 to 189 for Warren G. Harding in 1920.[177] John W. Davis polled 714 votes to 140 for Calvin Coolidge and nine for Robert M. LaFollette, the Progressive candidate, in 1924.[178]

When Alfred E. Smith, the Democratic Presidential nominee, came out in favor of repeal of the Eighteenth (Prohibition) Amendment in 1928, the "dry" forces were outraged. The Anti-Saloon League, of which Bishop James Cannon, Jr., was the leader in Virginia, committed its support to the Republican candidate, Herbert Hoover, and so great was the influence of the "dry" leaders that it carried Virginia into the Republican column. Another factor which increased the Republican vote in predominantly Protestant areas was opposition to Smith because he was a member of the Roman Catholic Church. Prince Edward, though influenced, was not swept into the landslide for Hoover. The county voted 700 for Smith to 501 for Hoover. It was the best vote a Republican Presidential nominee had received in the county since 1896. Virginia went Republican 148,657 to 126,908.[179]

The depression which began in 1929 helped swing the nation into the Democratic column in 1932, and it helped return Prince Edward to its accustomed Democratic majority. Franklin D. Roosevelt carried the county 970 to 196 for Hoover.[180] Four years later Roosevelt's popularity was at its peak, and Prince Edward joined the nation in giving him an even greater vote than it had given in 1932; the county voted 1,153 for Roosevelt to 253 for Alfred M. Landon.[181] The Democratic vote declined slightly in 1940 in Prince Edward, but it was still flattering to a man running for an unprecedented third term as President; 1,110 votes were cast for Roosevelt in Prince Edward to 313 for Wendell Willkie.[182] That trend continued four years later; Roosevelt received 1,063 votes to 425 for Thomas E. Dewey.[183] Much more portentous of a drifting away from the Democratic party than the vote was the resignation of W. S. Weaver as county Democratic chairman because he could not support the Democratic ticket. The trend had gained additional momentum by the election of 1948, when for the first time since 1892 the Democratic Presidential nominee did not receive a majority of the votes cast in Prince Edward. Harry S. Truman carried the county with 740 votes. But Thomas E. Dewey, Republican, and J. Strom Thurmond, running on the States-Rights Democratic ticket, received 456 and 510 votes respectively to give a total well in excess of Truman's vote. Henry A. Wallace, running on the Progressive ticket, got two votes in Prince Edward that year.[184] The trend noted as only small in 1944 and more impressive in 1948 carried the day in 1952, when it carried Prince Edward into the Republican column for the first time in a national election since 1892. Dwight D. Eisenhower received 1,359 votes to 926 cast for Adlai E. Stevenson.[185]

The Democratic control of the county since Reconstruction has limited local political contests to those within the party which are settled in the primary. The result has been that contests for county offices have been relatively few, although at times they have aroused the keenest interest among county people. There has been only one major contest for the nomination for clerk. Horace Adams, who was appointed clerk upon the death of E. J. Whitehead in 1907, was opposed by C. B. Cunningham in 1911; Adams won in the primary by a vote of 541 to 301[186] and has continued to serve in that post; he has now, after forty-seven years as clerk, the distinction of having held the office longer than any other person in the county's history and is the third clerk to have passed the forty-year mark, two of his predecessors, Francis Watkins and Branch J. Worsham, having served respectively forty-two and forty-four years. In the same primary E. L. Dupuy defeated W. W. Swan for the nomination for commissioner of revenue 504 to 331.[187]

J. Taylor Thompson sought the nomination for commonwealth's attorney in 1915, but he failed to unseat Judge A. D. Watkins who set the record for holding that post in Prince Edward, serving forty-seven years (1891-1938). The vote was 486 for Watkins, 380 for Thompson.[188]

Sheriff T. H. Dickinson was killed by a train at Pamplin September 30, 1915. His successor, T. H. Bruce, was chosen in the general election the following November. There were four aspirants for the post, and the vote was as follows: Bruce, 302; C. B. Cunningham, 215; H. H. Hunt, 149; and J. Stanley Moore, 141.[189]

The nomination for treasurer was warmly contended in 1935 when three candidates sought it: S. W. Watkins, Jr., the incumbent, won the nomination with 1,137 votes to 619 cast for W. S. Weaver and 116 for A. E. Cralle.[190]

There were two contests for county offices in 1939. E. L. Dupuy announced that he would not seek re-election to the office of commissioner of revenue, and Vernon C. Womack and Eugene Hardy

announced their candidacies for the Democratic nomination to succeed him; Womack won the nomination, receiving 920 votes to 836
for Hardy. In the same primary J. E. Glenn sought the nomination
for the sheriff's office, then held by John A. Clark; Clark received
1,110 votes to 645 for Glenn.[191]

Nomination for the seat in the House of Delegates has been
frequently contested in Prince Edward. E. T. Bondurant defeated
Dr. Peter Winston for the nomination in 1919 by a vote of 437 to
136.[192] When Bondurant did not seek re-election in 1925, W. Basil
Bruce, E. W. Sanford, and J. W. Hazelgrove of Cumberland were
candidates for the Democratic nomination. Bruce was chosen by a
plurality in the district of 194, the vote in Prince Edward being 515
for Bruce, 412 for Sanford, and 121 for Hazelgrove.[193] Two years
later Bruce was unsuccessfully opposed by W. D. Mason; the vote
in Prince Edward was 824 for Bruce to 296 for Mason.[194] E. W.
Sanford opposed Bruce a second time in 1933, this time successfully;
Sanford received 918 votes to 698 for Bruce in Prince Edward.[195]
Sanford was challenged in the Democratic primary in 1935 by W. A.
Watson, Jr.; the incumbent won, receiving 964 votes to 915 for
Watson in Prince Edward.[196] Watson opposed Sanford a second time
in 1941, but Sanford won by a vote of 1,309 to 1,000.[197] In 1942 in
the redistricting for membership in the House of Delegates, Prince
Edward and Charlotte were constituted a district. In the first primary after the change, in 1943, T. C. Coleman of Prince Edward
and John H. Daniel of Charlotte sought the nomination; Coleman
carried Prince Edward by a vote of 491 to 466, but Daniel received
in Charlotte an overwhelming margin to carry the district 2,246
to 518.[198]

In the past forty years there have been five contests for the
nomination to the State Senate from the district, in three of which
Prince Edward men have been involved. When Robert K. Brock
sought re-election to the State Senate in 1915, he was opposed by
George E. Allen of Victoria. Allen was elected, carrying Prince
Edward by a three-vote margin, 432 to 429.[199] Louis S. Epes of
Blackstone and R. M. Williams of Crewe opposed the incumbent,
George E. Allen of Victoria, for the nomination in 1919. Epes won
in the three-way race; in Prince Edward the vote was 204 for Epes,
175 for Allen, and 144 for Williams.[200] In 1927 E. T. Bondurant, a
former member of the House of Delegates from Prince Edward,
opposed Dr. E. L. Kendig of Victoria; Kendig won in the district,

but 664 Prince Edward voters cast their ballots for Bondurant to 476 for Kendig.[201] Four years later Hunter H. Watson of Crewe defeated Kendig; in Prince Edward Watson led by 687 to 648.[202] Robert K. Brock of Prince Edward was unopposed during his second period of service in the State Senate which lasted twelve years, 1936-47. George W. Palmer of Prince Edward and Copeland E. Adams of Blackstone in 1949 sought the Senate seat made vacant by the death of Dr. W. D. Kendig of Kenbridge; Palmer carried both the district and his home county, receiving 1,260 votes in Prince Edward to 243 for Adams and 3,647 to 2,961 for Adams in the district.[203]

Prince Edward, with the exception of the brief period between the end of the War between the States and the imposition of military government upon Virginia when it was in the same district with Appomattox, constituted a separate district for representation in the House of Delegates. In the redistricting in 1922 it was grouped with Cumberland, and the two counties were given one delegate. During the entire period Prince Edward and Cumberland constituted the district, it was represented by a Prince Edward man. In 1942 Charlotte and Prince Edward were put into the same district and assigned one delegate. In the senatorial redistricting in 1954 Prince Edward was put in the senatorial district with Charlotte and Halifax; thus the new district embraces the same counties which constituted the senatorial district when the Commonwealth of Virginia was established by the Constitution of 1776; the three constituted a senatorial district until the state was redistricted by the Convention of 1829-30.

Some of the hottest political fights in recent county history have involved nominations to the Board of Supervisors. Farmville District has been notably free of such contests in recent years; J. L. Hart was opposed in two campaigns; he defeated H. E. Wall 135 to 75 in 1907 and J. Ashby Armistead 182 to 159 in 1911.[204]

In Leigh District there have been three contests within the past generation. F. H. Kauffman, incumbent, defeated T. I. Hailey 50 to 23 in 1923.[205] When Kauffman announced that he would not seek re-election in 1931, H. E. Boswell and F. O. Priddy were candidates, Boswell winning by a vote of 117 to 72.[206] Twenty years later R. B. Wilson, Jr., who had been appointed to succeed George W. Palmer when the latter went to the State Senate, defeated W. T. Cook 86 to 54.[207]

Since 1907 there have been three contests in Lockett District. James T. Clark defeated W. B. Gates 83 to 60 for the supervisor's nomination in 1915.[208] W. Basil Bruce defeated H. J. Hubbard 74 to 62 for nomination for supervisor in 1923.[209] R. B. Walthall defeated T. E. Miller 164 to 60 in 1927.[210]

Hampden District has had four contests for the Democratic nomination for supervisor. R. E. Stokes, who had been appointed to the Board of Supervisors on the death of Dr. W. M. Holladay, sought the nomination for the next full term. W. A. McCraw opposed Stokes in the 1915 primary, defeating him 80 to 36.[211] Edward Carter defeated the incumbent, McCraw, for the nomination in 1931 by a vote of 131 to 112.[212] McCraw was unsuccessful four years later in his effort to regain his seat on the board, Carter winning 94 to 41.[213] In 1951 Charles W. Rice opposed Carter, but the incumbent was re-nominated 171 to 91.[214]

In Buffalo District, J. S. Harris opposed R. W. Fuqua for nomination for supervisor in 1911; Fuqua won by a vote of 151 to 72.[215] Fuqua defeated J. Stanley Moore in the 1915 primary 180 to 88.[216] In the primary of 1919 W. W. Swan defeated Fuqua for the nomination by a vote of 144 to 141.[217] Buffalo District was divided, the portion north and east of the road from Martin's Bridge near Hampden-Sydney to the Appomattox County line becoming Prospect District January 1, 1921. Swan continued to represent the portion south and west of the road which kept the old name. He had opposition twice; he defeated T. S. Elam 104 to 36 in 1931.[218] In 1939 Roach A. Watson defeated Swan 132 to 60.[219] Prospect District has lost only two opportunities to have a contest for the supervisor's post in its comparatively short history of thirty-three years. R. W. Fuqua was named supervisor for the district when it was created by the division of Buffalo.[220] In 1923 he defeated W. H. Glenn for nomination for the post 154 to 107.[221] Glenn was successful in his second effort for the nomination, defeating Fuqua by a vote of 198 to 159 in 1927.[222] J. H. Wilkerson opposed Glenn in 1935, but was defeated. Glenn receiving 146 votes for 125 for Wilkerson.[223] Four years later Wilkerson won the nomination over Glenn by the vote of 224 to 208.[224] Glenn regained his seat on the board in 1943, defeating Wilkerson 217 to 149.[225] The next contest for the supervisor's post in Prospect District came in 1951, when Glenn opposed W. W. Vaughan, who had been elected in 1947.[226] Vaughan won the nomination, defeating Glenn by a vote of 182 to 121.[227]

Democratic nominees for county offices have rarely faced opposition in the general election. In 1911 J. E. Harris announced opposition to E. L. Dupuy for commissioner of revenue. Harris was then Republican county chairman, and Dupuy was Democratic chairman (Dupuy held this post from 1907 until 1939 when he resigned and was succeeded by Robert K. Brock), so the campaign was in a sense a contest between the party battle commanders. But Harris withdrew before the election, leaving only the Democratic nominees in the race.[228] A dozen years later, Jabe Smith, running as an Independent, opposed Dupuy, but received only 40 votes in contrast to 696 cast for the Democratic nominee.[229]

When the proposal to hold a constitutional convention in 1922 was submitted to the people, Prince Edward voters overwhelmingly rejected it, only 53 favoring and 435 opposing it.[230] The proposal failed, and the Constitution drawn up and proclaimed by the Convention of 1901-02 continues, after having been amended several times, the fundamental law of the Commonwealth.

CHAPTER XX

These Attained High Rank

THE migrations from and into Prince Edward have already been discussed in this work. The difficulties the migrants met, and the success some attained have been mentioned. Some who came to Prince Edward prospered and won prominence. Some who went from the county to other sections accumulated wealth; some attained eminence in public life. Insofar as the county is concerned, however, there is much truth in the proverb, "A prophet is not without honor save in his own country." Of the governors of states Prince Edward has produced, not one native son has been elected to the governorship while residing in the county, and only one to the national House of Representatives and to the United States Senate, although several have been elected to those offices when living elsewhere.

Governors of States

Patrick Henry moved to Prince Edward after he had served his fifth term as Governor of Virginia and had declined election to a sixth. He had already made his great reputation as an orator, and his notable service in swaying Virginia into the camp of the revolutionists against the British Crown had already been rendered when he moved to the county in 1786. Prince Edward honored him with election to the Virginia House of Delegates and to the Constitutional Convention of 1788. In the convention he led the fight against ratification of the Constitution of the United States. He resumed the practice of law after settling in Prince Edward, and it was during this period that he reached his greatest fame and did his best work as a lawyer. After leaving Prince Edward he declined appointments as Secretary of State in Washington's Cabinet, as minister to France, and as Chief Justice of the United States Supreme Court.[1]

The only other Governor of Virginia to live in Prince Edward was Philip Watkins McKinney, a native of Buckingham County and graduate of Hampden-Sydney College who practiced law in Farmville after the War between the States. He has the distinction of having been the only resident of Prince Edward to be elected Governor of the state.[2]

Abner Nash was born either in Henrico County or at Templeton Manor, the home of his father, John Nash, on the Appomattox River when the land was in Amelia County. He was a boy of thirteen when the section became a new county, Prince Edward, and his father became a justice of the County Court and a member of the House of Burgesses, and an older brother, John Nash, Jr., became justice and sheriff. Another brother, Thomas Nash, was second King's Attorney for the young county. With such a background, it was only natural that Abner, who was named for his Grandfather Nash in Wales, should become interested in public affairs. When he attained his majority, he was elected to the House of Burgesses from Prince Edward and served three years. He was also a justice of the Prince Edward Court. He moved to Halifax, North Carolina, where he began the practice of law, and represented the town in the North Carolina House of Commons 1764-5 and Halifax County in that body 1770-1. He moved to New Bern and served in the State House of Commons 1777, 1778, and 1780, having been speaker in 1777. He was a state senator 1779-80 and president of the North Carolina State Senate in 1779. Nash was Governor of North Carolina 1780-1. After his term as Governor, Nash was elected to the Continental Congress in 1782 and was a member of that body at the time of his death in 1786.[3]

While Nash was attaining prominence as a leader in North Carolina during the Revolution, another young man who had lived as a youth in Prince Edward was winning fame in Georgia. George Walton was born either in Prince Edward or Cumberland County; his father died either shortly before his birth or not long thereafter, and Walton lived for a time with his uncle, George Walton, Sr., of Prince Edward. He was apprenticed to a carpenter, who gave him an opportunity to go to school. Moving to Savannah in 1769, Walton studied law and began practice in 1774. He was elected to the Continental Congress in 1776 and served until 1781. While in Congress he signed the Declaration of Independence, the only person who ever lived in Prince Edward to sign that document, and the Articles of Confederation, the first attempt at formal union of the thirteen original states. Walton served in each of the three branches of government: the legislative, as a member of the Continental Congress and as United States Senator from Georgia, November 16,

1795-February 21, 1796; the executive, as Governor of Georgia, 1779, 1780, and again in 1789; and the judiciary, as Chief Justice of Georgia 1783-86 and again in 1793.[4]

When William Bibb, sheriff of Prince Edward, moved to Georgia about 1790, there went with him two sons who were destined to become Governors of the state of Alabama. William Wyatt Bibb graduated in medicine at the University of Pennsylvania and served as Representative and United States Senator from Georgia. When Alabama was made a territory, Bibb was made territorial governor; when Alabama became a state, Bibb was chosen its first Governor, serving from March, 1817, until his death July 9, 1820. He was succeeded by his brother, Thomas Bibb, who served until 1821.[5]

Sterling Price had a solid Prince Edward background. His father, Pugh Price, was third of the name in the county. Sterling Price studied at Hampden-Sydney, wrote in the clerk's office under Branch J. Worsham, studied law under Creed Taylor. Price moved to Missouri in 1831, served as speaker of the lower house of the Missouri legislature and as a member of the House of Representatives. He was Governor of Missouri 1853-57.[6]

The term of Thomas Watkins Ligon, another native of Prince Edward, as Governor of Maryland was almost identical with Sterling Price's term in Missouri. Ligon was Governor of Maryland 1854-58. Thus for a second time two sons of Prince Edward were contemporary Governors of states. Ligon was named for his grandfather, Captain Thomas Watkins of Revolutionary fame. Educated at Hampden-Sydney and the University of Virginia and in law at Yale, Ligon practiced law in Baltimore and served two terms in Congress (1845-49) from Maryland before becoming Governor.[7]

Ligon's first cousin, Henry Watkins Allen, was another native of Prince Edward who became a Governor. After teaching in Mississippi, Allen was admitted to the bar and served in the Mississippi legislature in 1846. He later moved to Louisiana and was in the Louisiana legislature in 1853. He served as Governor of Louisiana 1864-66.[8]

Congressmen

Abraham Bedford Venable has the distinction of being the only native of Prince Edward to be elected to the House of Representatives and the United States Senate while a resident of the county. He was elected to the second Congress and to the third, fourth, and fifth Congresses, declining to seek re-election for the sixth Congress.

He was a member of the House of Delegates from Prince Edward when he was elected to the United States Senate, where he served briefly, December 11, 1803-June 7, 1804; he resigned to become president of the Bank of Virginia. The son of Nathaniel Venable, he was educated at Hampden-Sydney and Princeton.[9]

Two Bibbs, natives of the county, served in the United States Senate. William Wyatt Bibb, Alabama's first Governor, served in the House of Representatives from Georgia 1807-13 and in the United States Senate from Georgia 1813-16. George Motier Bibb went from Prince Edward to Kentucky after having been educated at Hampden-Sydney and the College of William and Mary. He served twice in the United States Senate, 1811-14, resigning in the latter year, and 1829-35, and twice as Chief Justice of the Kentucky Court of Appeals, 1809-10, 1827-28. George M. Bibb is the only Prince Edward native to serve in the Cabinet of a President of the United States; he was Secretary of the Treasury under President Tyler, July 4, 1844-March 3, 1845.[10]

The only Negro ever to serve in the United States Senate was born in slavery on a Prince Edward farm. Blanche Kelso Bruce was taught to read and write by his master's son. He was educated at Oberlin College and after the War between the States settled in Mississippi. He was elected to the United States Senate from Mississippi and served one term, 1875-81. Subsequently he was register of the Treasury 1881-91, 1897-98.[11]

In addition to Abraham Bedford Venable, William Wyatt Bibb, Sterling Price, and Thomas Watkins Ligon who have been mentioned as serving in the House of Representatives, and George Walton and Abner Nash in the Continental Congress, (Venable and Walton in the Senate also) several other sons of Prince Edward have been Representatives: John Coffee, who went with his father to Georgia in 1800, was a Representative from Georgia, 1833-36.[12] Thomas Stanhope Flournoy, a native of Prince Edward who moved to Halifax, was elected to Congress as a Whig for the term 1847-49.[13] In 1855 and again in 1863 he was a candidate for Governor of Virginia. At the same time Thomas Stanhope Flournoy went to Congress from Virginia, Abraham Watkins Venable went from the adjoining district in North Carolina. Venable moved to Granville County, North Carolina, in 1829, served in the House of Representatives 1847-53, in the provisional Confederate Congress, 1861, and in the Confederate Congress, 1862-64.[14]

Two sons of Peter Johnston, Jr., both born at Longwood, were elected to the United States House of Representatives from Virginia districts. Charles Clement Johnston was elected as a States-Rights Democrat to the Twenty-second Congress. During the term he was drowned near one of the docks at Alexandria June 17, 1832. His younger brother, Joseph Eggleston Johnston, after a distinguished military career, lived in Georgia. Moving to Richmond, Virginia, later, he was elected as a Democrat to the House of Representatives from that district in 1878. He did not offer for re-election two years later. President Grover Cleveland appointed Johnston commissioner of railroads in 1887, and he held this post until his death four years later.[15]

The Fourth Virginia District was "redeemed" in the election of 1888 by the election of Edward Carrington Venable, the Democratic nominee, to the House of Representatives. He served March 4, 1889-September 23, 1890, when he was unseated on the contest of the Republican nominee, John M. Langston. Venable was then living in Petersburg, having moved there in 1876.[16]

During the Reconstruction period, one man who lived in Prince Edward briefly and who supplanted Branch J. Worsham as clerk on military orders and was later elected clerk of the county, Joseph Jorgenson, served in the House of Representatives from the Fourth Virginia District, 1877-83.[17]

During the same period, a resident of Prince Edward, Benjamin S. Hooper, served in the national House of Representatives 1883-85.[18]

In more recent years, Clement Cabell Dickinson, a son of Judge Asa Dupuy Dickinson, has been a member of the House from Missouri. Altogether Dickinson served in the House longer than any other person from Prince Edward, a total of twenty years. Dickinson went to Missouri in 1872; he served in the House 1911-21, 1923-29, 1931-35.[19]

The Military

During the Revolution Robert Lawson of Prince Edward attained the rank of brigadier general; he entered the service from Prince Edward and returned to Prince Edward after the war, although during 1781 he was much in the county raising troops and collecting supplies.[20]

Francis Nash, fourth son of John Nash, Sr., as a young man settled in Hillsboro, North Carolina. He became clerk of Orange County in 1763, served in the North Carolina House of Commons from Orange and the borough of Hillsboro, and was a captain in Governor Tryon's army which fought and defeated the Regulators in the battle of Alamance in 1771. In 1774-75 he was judge of the court of the Hillsboro District. Like his brother Abner, he served in the Provincial Congress. In 1775 he became lieutenant colonel of the First North Carolina Regiment, Continental troops. The next year he became colonel, and in February, 1777, he was commissioned brigadier general. Wounded in the battle of Germantown October 4, 1777, he died three days later.[21]

In the Creek War John Coffee, the Prince Edward native who had gone to Georgia, served with the rank of general in the Georgia militia.[22]

Sterling Price was commissioned brigadier general for service in the Mexican War. After serving as president of the Constitutional Convention of Missouri in 1861 and major general of the Missouri State Guard in the same year, he joined the Confederate Army and was commissioned major general in 1862.[23]

Henry Watkins Allen was another Prince Edward native to attain the rank of general in the Confederate Army. He entered the service at the beginning of the war as a colonel and in 1864 was promoted to brigadier general.[24]

The most distinguished soldier from Prince Edward was Joseph Eggleston Johnston, born at Longwood February 3, 1807, the son of the younger Peter Johnston. Johnston prepared for the career of a soldier, graduating from the United States Military Academy in 1829, in the class with Robert Edward Lee, with whom he was to be associated in the War between the States. Johnston fought with distinction in the Mexican War; for gallantry and meritorious conduct at the battle of Cerro Gordo he was brevetted major and colonel and after the battle of Chapultepec was brevetted lieutenant colonel. By 1860 he had risen to the rank of brigadier general in the United States Army and was quartermaster general. Johnston resigned from the army April 22, 1861, was made a major general of Virginia forces four days later; in May he was commissioned brigadier general in the Confederate States Army, and on August 30 of that year was commissioned general, one of eight men to hold that rank in the Confederate Army. He was in command in the Peninsula, retreating to the vicinity of Richmond. After he was wounded at the battle of Seven Pines in June, 1862, he was unable to continue in command and General Robert E. Lee, then Jefferson Davis' military advisor, succeeded him. After Johnston had recovered, he was placed in command of armies in Tennessee and Mississippi in November, 1862. In December of the next year he was assigned to the Army of the Tennessee to reorganize it and take the offensive. Johnston accomplished the first part of the assignment, but retreated instead of going forward. He was relieved of command in July, 1864, just before his army reached Atlanta. After the capture of Atlanta by the Federal Army and Sherman's march to the sea, Johnston was again placed in command of this army in February, 1865, while it was retreating through the Carolinas. At the Benton place, just outside Durham, North Carolina, Johnston surrendered his army to Sherman April 26, 1865.[25]

Three Prince Edward men served as staff officers for famous Confederate generals. Charles Scott Venable, son of Nathaniel E. Venable of Longwood, was teaching astronomy at the University of South Carolina when the war began. He served as second lieutenant in the Congaree Rifles at Fort Sumter; he came to Virginia as a private in the Governor's Guards and fought at Manassas. He was then made aide to General Wade Hampton and a little later adjutant, with the rank of captain, to General M. S. Smith. While General Robert E. Lee was serving as military adviser to President Jefferson Davis, Venable became an aide to Lee, with the rank of colonel. He continued on Lee's staff until the surrender at Appomattox.[26]

Robert Lewis Dabney, adjunct professor of theology in Union Theological Seminary, is remembered as a preacher, theologian, and architect of lovely churches. He had a distinguished war record as chief of staff to General Thomas J. Jackson, the beloved "Stonewall," Lee's "right arm," 1862-63. Dabney held the rank of major.[27]

Andrew Reid Venable, Jr., son of Samuel Woodson Venable, Jr., served on the staff of the Confederate cavalry commander, General J. E. B. Stuart, as inspector general with the rank of major. After the war, Major Venable inaugurated the movement to erect the Stuart monument in Richmond.[28]

Another Confederate officer from Prince Edward who attained high rank was Dr. Simeon Taylor Walton, who moved from Sandy River Church to Keysville about 1855. Although a physician, he enlisted in the Keysville Guards and was chosen second lieutenant. Subsequently he was promoted to lieutenant colonel and was in command of his regiment when he was killed at Verdiersville in 1863.[29]

(Reference has been made in the chapter, "The Nation Divided," to the men who went into service from the county and attained high rank.)

Education

In addition to its long interest in and support of the educational institutions within its borders, Prince Edward has made significant contributions to education in the person of distinguished college presidents and professors. Charles William Dabney (1855-1945), born at Hampden-Sydney while his father, Dr. Robert L. Dabney, was on the faculty of Union Seminary, was president of two universities, the University of Tennessee, 1887-1904, and the University of Cincinnati, 1904-20. He was Assistant Secretary of Agriculture during Grover Cleveland's second administration.

Another Prince Edward native, Francis Preston Venable (1856-1934), a son of Charles Scott Venable, was a fellow student of Dabney at Göttingen and joined the faculty of the University of North Carolina as professor of chemistry in 1880. Venable became president of the University of North Carolina in 1900 and served fourteen years before returning to his great interest, the professorship of chemistry in that institution.

During the 178 years Hampden-Sydney College has been in Prince Edward, it has had only one Prince Edward native as its president. Joseph Dupuy Eggleston (1867-1953), son of the beloved physician of the same name who lived at Worsham, was born at Marble Hill. After graduating from Hampden-Sydney in 1886, he began teaching in the public schools. In 1891 he became superintendent of schools in Asheville, North Carolina, and remained in that post nine years. This was the period of the educational renascence in North Carolina, one of the most important developments in postwar Southern history. It was the era when Edwin Anderson Alderman was president of the University of North Carolina, from which he went to Tulane and subsequently to the University of Virginia, and when Charles D. McIver was laying the foundations of the Woman's College at Greensboro. In the year Eggleston left Asheville, Charles B. Aycock was elected Governor of North Carolina on the famous education platform and James Y. Joyner State Superintendent of Public Instruction. From such an environment Eggleston caught the vision and the ideal and imbibed the spirit. He brought to Virginia this spirit of educational evangelism, and it, blended with his own excellent abilities, made his short administration of the Prince Edward public school system (1903-05) outstanding.

Eggleston was elected Superintendent of Public Instruction in Virginia in 1905; his term of office began February 1, 1906, and he served through 1912, when he became chief of field service in rural education in the United States Bureau of Education. His leadership as Superintendent of Public Instruction was outstanding. He advocated industrial training, favoring the incorporation of this training in high schools along with academic education. He secured the passage of a law providing state aid for school libraries, the state paying $10 and the local school board $15 when the school or its friends raised $15 for the purchase of books. During his administration the program in health and physical education was introduced, including the examination of the sight and hearing of pupils and the notification to the parents of defects. Eggleston worked diligently to improve salaries of teachers and superintendents, and while he was state superintendent two additional normal schools were founded, those at Harrisonburg (now Madison College) and Fredericksburg (now Mary Washington College). He also introduced a state-wide reading course for teachers, a plan which had been used in Prince Edward during his superintendency. He was one of the leaders in the educational conference in Richmond in November, 1906, which 1,600 delegates from various schools and groups interested in education attended. Supervision was introduced during the Eggleston regime with the appointment of a supervisor of rural elementary education.

Two achievements of Eggleston as Superintendent of Public Instruction stand out and merit special consideration. One was the introduction in Virginia of farm demonstration work. Corn clubs were organized for boys, and canning clubs for girls. These were the forerunners of the 4-H clubs, and the girls' clubs also expanded into the home demonstration clubs for women. Eggleston's other notable work was in the establishment of district high schools throughout the state. From seventy-four in 1905-06 the number of high schools increased to 218 in the next session. The Mann Act of 1906 encouraged the establishment of high schools through the appropriation of funds for their operation, and the Williams Act of the same year permitted school boards to borrow from the Literary Fund for building schools. Eggleston vigorously worked for the establishment of high schools.[30]

In 1913 Eggleston became president of Virginia Polytechnic Institute, where he remained six years. Then, in 1919, he came to Hampden-Sydney College for an administration of twenty years, which has been briefly reviewed in an account of that institution.

John T. Doyne, a son of John Doyne of Farmville, had a distinguished career as an educator in Arkansas, serving as State Superintendent of Public Instruction and as president of the Lonoke State Teachers College in that state. Edwin Carter Wade, a son of Edwin G. Wade of Prince Edward and a graduate of Hampden-Sydney College, served as president of Bluefield College, Bluefield, Virginia, 1934-46.

The foremost Negro educator of his day and one of the ablest in American history grew to manhood in Prince Edward. Robert Russa Moton was born in Amelia County August 26, 1867; one of his earliest memories was the removal of his family to Pleasant Shade, the farm of Samuel Vaughan on Sailor's Creek in Prince Edward, where his father was employed. Moton's father had belonged to Dr. Alexander of Charlotte and after Dr. Alexander's death, about 1850, had been bought by John Crowder of Prince Edward. He was married to Emily Brown in 1866 in the Hillsman home in Amelia and in 1867 hired himself to Samuel Vaughan, working for him for some time before moving his family to Pleasant Shade. At Pleasant Shade young Robert as a small boy carried "Miss Lucy's" (Mrs. Vaughan's) key basket, a task regarded as a great honor among small Negro boys. Later another youthful ambition was realized when he became house boy and waited on the table at Pleasant Shade.

Moton's mother secretly taught him to read and write, because the family was under the impression that the Vaughans disapproved of education for Negroes. One day Mrs. Vaughan found mother and son reading together and expressed her pleasure in finding that Robert was receiving the rudiments of an education. When a public school was opened for Negroes in the community one fall, taught by a white teacher, John Morrisette, young Moton attended and was placed in the highest class. He continued working for the Vaughans, before and after school.

Another boyhood educational experience for Moton was the Sunday School maintained by Jamestown Presbyterian Church in the old meeting-house on Sunday afternoons for Negroes. It was taught by white men and women. Young Moton showed so much promise that Captain Frank W. Southall suggested to him that he go to a school in Alabama and study for the Presbyterian ministry. Moton belonged to Macedonia Baptist Church, however, and replied that he had rather be an ignorant Baptist than an educated Presbyterian.

As a boy he took as his model W. L. Vaughan, "Mr. Willie," the son of his employer. His best friends in boyhood were two white boys, Ernest Morton, a son of Joseph X. Morton of neighboring Plum Grove, and George Denny, whose father, the Rev. George H. Denny of Amelia, frequently preached at Jamestown and visited in the Vaughan home, and a colored boy, Lee Brown. Years later Moton was to be principal of Tuskegee Institute in Alabama at the same time George Denny was president of the University of Alabama.

Robert Moton worked for a time at a lumber mill in Surry, but an epidemic of malaria sent him home. At this time he might have gotten started on a political career, had it not been for the unwavering honesty of his mother. At a Negro picnic in Vaughan's woods he made a political speech of such effectiveness that his hearers urged him to run for the state legislature. Some white people promised to "fix" his age, for he was well under 21, although he might have passed for being older. His mother, however, refused to swear to any age except his right age and thus prevented his entry into political life at the time.

Then Edward D. Stewart, who had studied at Hampton Institute, came to the community to teach. Moton decided to pursue his education there. His fellow church-members gave him a farewell reception at Macedonia Church, the pastor, Armistead Burwell, taking part on the program.

In October, 1885, young Robert Moton put his trunk on a mule cart, took it to Rice, and there boarded the train for Hampton. On his graduation there in 1890 he became connected with the Institute, serving as commandant of students and attaining the rank by which he was long known in the community in which he had been reared, Major Moton. When Booker T. Washington died in 1915, Moton was invited to succeed him in the principalship at Tuskegee Institute.[31] Here he did a notable work and earned an international reputation as an educator and a leader of his race. Appropriately the Negro high school in Prince Edward bears his name, as do many Negro schools throughout the South. Moton died in 1940.

The distinguished teachers of the county include Charles Scott

Venable, who after serving on Lee's staff became professor of mathematics in the University of Virginia and was the author of widely used texts in that subject; Stephen O. Southall, who became professor of law at the University of Virginia in 1866; William Mynn Thornton, who became professor in the schools of mathematics and engineering in the University of Virginia in 1875. This was a unique contribution for any county to make to the faculty of the state university, for all three were ornaments of a faculty which yielded to none in the United States in distinction, ability, and achievement. To them may be added the names of James R. Thornton, professor of mathematics, James Henry Curry Winston, professor of chemistry, and Asa Dupuy Watkins, professor of English, all at Hampden-Sydney College; Miss Minnie Rice, professor of Latin at Longwood College when it was the State Normal School and the State Teachers College; Bernard Camillus Bondurant (August 13, 1870-August 19, 1909), professor of Latin in the University of Florida; his brother, William Walton Bondurant, professor of Latin in Austin College, Texas, 1902-06, and subsequently superintendent of the Texas Military Institute and head of the San Antonio Academy; the Elliott brothers, William Whitfield Elliott, professor of mathematics in Duke University, and Emmett Roach Elliott, professor of mathematics at Hampden-Sydney. Four Prince Edward men have served on the faculty of the Virginia Polytechnic Institute, Joseph X. Morton, professor of English and history; John R. Parrott, professor of engineering; Frank L. Robeson, professor of physics; and William Newton Cunningham, professor of engineering.

In the field of medical education, two men from Prince Edward have attained prominence in the post-Mettauer era. Dr. Paulus A. Irving was professor of diseases of children in the University College of Medicine, Richmond, 1907-10; Dr. Edward H. Richardson began the teaching of gynecology in the medical school of the Johns Hopkins University in Baltimore in 1910.

After serving as professor of history at Hampden-Sydney, Henry Read McIlwaine, a native of Prince Edward, became State Librarian, filling the post with distinction and greatly increasing the usefulness of the institution during his tenure, 1907-34.

Medicine

One of the major figures in the modern medical world is identified with Prince Edward through his residence, during a part of his boyhood, in Farmville. Walter Reed has a high place among the benefactors of mankind through his research and experiments in typhoid and yellow fever. As a boy he lived in Farmville, and his formal education began there, a Mrs. Booker being his first teacher. Reed was six years old when his father, the Rev. Lemuel Sutton Reed, came to Farmville upon assignment to the Prince Edward Circuit by the Virginia Methodist Conference.

Walter Reed was born at Belroi, Gloucester County, Virginia, September 13, 1851. Both his parents (his mother was Pharaba White) were natives of North Carolina. His stay in Farmville was comparatively brief, for Methodist ministers at that time were moved frequently, usually staying only one year on a circuit, rarely more than two years. In 1866 the Reeds moved to Charlottesville, and Walter Reed attended the University of Virginia. He graduated in medicine there in 1869 and took a second M. D. degree at Bellevue Hospital Medical College, New York, in 1870.

In 1875 Reed joined the Army Medical Corps as first lieutenant and assistant surgeon. Fifteen years later, after service which included an eleven-year stay at Fort Lowell in Arizona, he was transferred to Baltimore and there he studied, specializing in bacteriology, at the Johns Hopkins Hospital. In 1893 he was promoted to major and became professor of bacteriology and microscopy in the Army Medical School at Washington. His work here led to his appointment to the chairmanship of the committee which investigated the causes and transmission of typhoid in the Army camps in 1898. The committee's *Report of Origin and Spread of Typhoid Fever in U. S. Military Camps during the Spanish War of 1898* proved an important document in medical history and literature. It showed that flies played a major role in the transmission of the disease during the epidemic in the camps.

The year before the committee investigated the typhoid problem, Reed became interested in yellow fever. In 1900 he was named chairman of the committee which investigated the causes and mode of transmission of yellow fever from which many American soldiers in Havana were suffering. Reed's experiments required the use of humans, and two of the physicians working with him volunteered to become infected with the disease. The Reed committee proved that the mosquito, *Aedes aegypti*, carried the disease. As a result of these experiments, the scourge of the tropics was brought under control.

Dr. Walter Reed lived less than two years after the completion of his investigation of the cause and method of transmission of yellow fever. He neglected his own case of appendicitis until too late and died November 22, 1902. The Walter Reed General Hospital of the Army Medical Corps in Washington honors his contribution to medical science and his memory.[32]

Books

John Thomson set an example for the writing of books with the publication of his *Explication of the Shorter Catechism* by William Parks of Williamsburg in 1749. William Branch, Jr., kept the tradition going with the publication of *Life* in 1819. After the War between the States more books have been added to the products of Prince Edward. Dr. Robert Lewis Dabney wrote a biography of his wartime chief, Stonewall Jackson: *The Life and Campaigns of Lt. Gen. Thomas J. Jackson* (1866). This was the standard Jackson biography prior to the publication of Henderson's work. Dabney's *Syllabus and Notes on the Course of Systematic and Polemic Theology* was used for many years as the standard text in theology in Union Theological Seminary. He also wrote *The Christian Soldier* (1863), *A Memorial of Lt. Col. John T. Thornton* (1864), *In Defense of Virginia and the South* (1867), and *Sacred Rhetoric* (1871). Through his theology text he exerted a wide influence throughout the Southern Presbyterian Church not only during his lifetime, but for years after his death. Dr. Richard McIlwaine's autobiography, *Memories of Threescore Years and Ten*, was published in 1908. Its value to the student of Prince Edward history has been indicated by frequent references to it in this work. *The Realm of Personality* (1944), by Denison Maurice Allan, professor of philosophy and psychology at Hampden-Sydney, is a distinguished contribution to the psychology bookshelf; the text was originally delivered as the Sprunt Lectures at Union Theological Seminary, Richmond. Francis B. Simkins, professor of history at Longwood College, has attained prominence as a writer on Southern history. His history, *The South*, has been published in two editions, and his biography of "Pitchfork Ben" Tillman of South Carolina is regarded as one of the best studies of the Tillman era in Southern politics. John P. Wynne, also of the Longwood faculty, has written extensively in the field of education; his most recent book is *General Education* (1952). Agnes Meredith Bondurant is the author of *Poe's Richmond* (1942), an account of the

Virginia capital during the era when Edgar Allan Poe knew it. J. Barrye Wall, as editor of *Today and Yesterday in the Heart of Virginia*, 1936), a collection of historical accounts dealing with Prince Edward, Buckingham, and Cumberland Counties, has earned a lasting place in the literary history of Prince Edward. Through his encouragement of the writing of historical articles by publishing them in the Farmville *Herald* and in pamphlet form, he plays a major role in the preservation of the history of Prince Edward and the adjoining counties. Although Wallace Gould lived just across the Appomattox River from Farmville in Cumberland, he was more identified with Farmville than with the county of his residence. Mention of his volume of verse, *Aphrodite and Other Poems*, published in 1929, may appropriately be made here. Prince Edward's foremost historian is Alfred James Morrison (1876-1923), author of *The Beginnings of Public School Education in Virginia 1776-1860* and numerous articles in the historical quarterlies and the Farmville *Herald* and editor of Hampden-Sydney's *Dictionary of Biography* and *Calendar of Board Minutes, 1776-1876.* At his death Dr. Morrison left the manuscript of a projected county history, *Old Prince Edward: A Miscellany.*

CHAPTER XXI

The Pleasant Life

OF Southside Virginia Dr. Philip Alexander Bruce wrote in his review of Walter A. Watson's *Notes on Southside Virginia* that "the spirit of colonial times lingered there longest after Yorktown; the spirit of ante-bellum lingered there longest after Appomattox."[1] If one takes this to mean the spirit of enterprise which was a conspicuous characteristic of ante-bellum Prince Edward, it is an adequate appraisal. If one takes it to mean the persistence of the magnolias and moonlight fantasy, he is mistaken; it is not that at all. The enterprise displayed in ante-bellum times was demonstrated during and since Reconstruction; it had to be to accomplish recovery. The exigencies of the Reconstruction era intensified the pressures to industry and thrift. People had to work and to work hard to get a fresh start; they had to economize to make the little which could be earned cover the needs and if possible stretched to lay aside some savings for the future. But amid the industry and the thrift the tradition of gracious living and cordial hospitality continued to prevail, and these characteristics belong in what Dr. Bruce included in "the spirit of ante-bellum" times.

Into these characteristics of industry, thrift, gracious living, and hospitality was blended the Confederate tradition which was a dominant influence in the life of the county for many years after Appomattox. For some thirty years it was apparently dormant. Economic stability had to be regained, an abhorrent political situation had to be redeemed. Loyalty to the tradition, the ideal, demanded the attainment of a measure of security, the recovery of local and state government by those whom the new order undertook to replace.

The Confederate veterans of the county reorganized the Thornton-Pickett Camp on the evening of April Court Day (third Monday), 1895. It adopted the project of completing the roll of soldiers from Prince Edward who served in the Confederate army and of those who had gone into service from some other county, but were at the time resident in Prince Edward; the work was under the direction of Dr. Peter Winston, who was named historian.[2] The

news report does not mention the commander, but he was most likely
S. W. Paulett, who was one of the dynamic spirits in the preservation of Confederate history and who was commander of the camp
for many years before his death; E. G. McGehee succeeded Paulett.
The camp of veterans honored in its name the chivalrous John T.
Thornton, whose memory was greatly revered by his comrades of
the Confederate cavalry troop, and General George E. Pickett, under
whom so many of the infantrymen from Prince Edward served.
The veterans at a meeting June 15, 1896, decided to attend the
general reunion in Richmond June 30-July 2; the Farmville Guard
acted as an escort for the veterans; the Norfolk and Western ran an
excursion, the train leaving Farmville June 30, the round trip tickets
costing $1.55 and good until July 6.[3]

The reunions were great events in the lives of the ex-soldiers.
As many as were able attended as regularly as possible the general
reunions, although it meant trips to Atlanta, or Little Rock, Arkansas,
or Tulsa, Oklahoma; fairly frequently they were held in Richmond,
and sometimes in Washington, the city which had once been their
objective. The railroads ran excursions; it was quite a thrill to a
youngster to see car after car pass, filled with elderly men wearing
gray coats and gray hats. There were state reunions, too, but they
did not arouse the interest which the general and the local reunions
commanded. The local reunion gave an opportunity to meet comrades of the county, to enjoy the fellowship of friends of long standing who had shared the hard and heart-breaking experiences of war
and defeat, and to renew the Confederate spirit and the Confederate
tradition. The Thornton-Pickett camp reunions were held in Farmville, though on one occasion, in 1902, there was a reunion of
Company D, 18th Virginia Infantry, at Five Forks, with S. W.
Paulett and R. D. Miller booked as speakers—"enough to guarantee
against a single dull moment." Colonel George Cabell, formerly
major of the regiment, spoke too.[4] At the reunions in Farmville,
held usually in May, the day's program began with a parade, in
which the veterans participated, from Captain Paulett's crockery
store (immediately north of the present Leggett's) to the Confederate
monument at the Methodist Church. There were brief exercises and
the firing of a salute by the Farmville Guard. Then the crowd
gathered, in earlier years in the Opera House, in later years in the
Eaco (now the State) Theater for an appropriate address and other
entertainment. In 1925 the "other entertainment" included a group

of Southern songs by a girls' chorus directed by Miss Mary Jackson. Also present were Tom Booker of Amelia and his banjo, who delighted many an annual reunion of Prince Edward veterans. Booker was a capital entertainer; even as an old man, he had a fine, clear voice; he played his banjo with a charming vivacity; and he sang the old songs which the veterans had known and loved through the years. One thinks of the gray-bearded, gray-coated men who were sires and grandsires of those now living as persons of impressive, almost forbidding, dignity; but at their reunions they were an uninhibited lot. They did not hesitate to interrupt the program to call for songs they wanted to hear, and there was one they always called for. It had two "cuss-words" in it, and Tom Booker, gentleman of the old school, did not use "cuss-words" in the presence of ladies. So he characteristically asked permission of the ladies present to sing the song, and always that permission was graciously, even enthusiastically, given. So, in a never-to-be forgotten experience, Tom Booker would sing Innes Randolph's song of a harder, bitterer day, *I Ain't Never Been Reconstructed and I Don't Give a Damn.* The theater never echoed greater applause than that which broke forth as Booker twanged the last note on his banjo. Then the prizes awarded by the Daughters of the Confederacy for the best essays by high school history students on a designated topic were awarded. At the 1925 reunion Dr. Douglas Southall Freeman, editor of the Richmond *News Leader* and later, as the author of *R. E. Lee* and *Lee's Lieutenants,* to become recognized as one of the foremost authorities on Confederate history, delivered the address of the occasion. After the program, the Daughters of the Confederacy entertained the veterans at a dinner.

The organization of a chapter of the United Daughters of the Confederacy followed the reorganization of the Thornton-Pickett Camp. The Farmville chapter was organized March 19, 1896, with fourteen members at a meeting at R. S. Paulett's home. Mrs. Henry Edmunds was chosen president, Mrs. J. L. White vice-president, Miss Bettie Johnson corresponding secretary, Mrs. S. W. Watkins recording secretary, and Mrs. R. S. Paulett treasurer.[5]

At that time there was under way a major project for the perpetuation of the Confederate tradition. The Confederate Monument Association of Prince Edward County, Virginia, was organized at a meeting in Farmville August 30, 1895. The officers of the organization were S. W. Paulett, president, R. H. Watkins, first vice-president, A. W. Drumeller, second vice-president, Dr. Peter Winston, secretary, J. P. Fitzgerald, corresponding secretary, and John F. Walton, treasurer; the executive committee consisted of John A. Cunningham, chairman, Judge J. M. Crute, T. H. Glenn, Prospect, W. H. Ewing of Green Bay, B. H. Carter of Rice, the Rev. Richard McIlwaine of Hampden-Sydney, John C. Cunningham of Darlington Heights, John R. Martin, R. A. Booker, and A. R. Venable of Farmville.[6] The first benefit entertainment for the proposed monument was given by Miss Belle Johnson of November 28, 1895; it included vocal and instrumental music and recitations.[7] A year later (November 27, 1896) the newly organized U.D.C. chapter gave an oyster supper in Richardson's store for the benefit of the monument and cleared $102.[8] On February 14, 1896, C. H. Hasker of Richmond, who had been boatswain on the *Virginia* during her historic fight with the *Monitor* in Hampton Roads, the first battle between ironclad ships, gave an illustrated lecture on the Battle of Hampton Roads for the benefit of the monument. So impressed was the audience that President Cunningham asked him to repeat it the next night at the Normal School for the students.[9] On May 6, 1897, the Rev. Abner Hopkins, D.D., of Charles Town, West Virginia, delivered an address on the last week of the Army of Northern Virginia in Farmville; the proceeds went to the monument fund.[10] In a special act, passed in 1900, the Virginia General Assembly gave permission to the Prince Edward Board of Supervisors to contribute not more than $400 to the monument fund.[11] So in a variety of ways money was raised to place the monument to commemorate the valor of the Confederate soldiers at High and Randolph Streets.

Under auspices of the Farmville Chapter, U.D.C., the first Memorial Day observance in Farmville, or the first in many years, was held May 30, 1905. Confederate soldiers and others marched from the armory to the burying ground of the Confederate Hospital just over the river in Cumberland. The Rev. J. H. Davis offered prayer; Major A. R. Venable and J. Taylor Thompson spoke; Miss Nannie Nicholson recited *Somebody's Darling* and Miss Anna Richardson *The Conquered Banner*.[12] A few days later the U.D.C. distributed the crosses of honor at the reunion; there were not enough crosses to go around to all the veterans present, and plans were made to present crosses later to those who did not get them on June 3. At the reunion on May 31, 1906, crosses were presented to twenty-eight other veterans.[13]

In the difficulties of Reconstruction people made provision for entertainment and social life. The Berger family of Swiss bell ringers played at Lee Hall in Farmville in November, 1873.[14] In the same month, the Farmville College presented an elaborate musical program, including duets for two pianos, duet for piano and organ, piano solos, vocal solos, and vocal duets. Dances were popular in some circles.[15] The 1874 Christmas festivities in Farmville ended with a dance at the Randolph House New Year's night, 1875; Burger's band furnished the music; there was dancing until midnight, when an elaborate supper was served; and after supper dancing continued until almost dawn.[16] Another popular diversion of the time was the tournament, which was followed by a ball. One was held in a field on the J. B. Ely estate at Farmville on October 8, 1875; the knight of plume, Bertie Walker, won and crowned Miss Lelia Blanton, daughter of Dr. Hugh Blanton of Cumberland, queen of love and beauty. Colonel W. R. Berkeley delivered the coronation address, and the ball took place at the Randolph House, with the Lynchburg String band furnishing the music. There were so many guests at the supper that the resources of the hotel were taxed to provide for them.[17]

In the 1890's the dances were called germans; it was popular in Farmville for the young men to get up a german honoring the young ladies who were visiting in town. On July 31, 1896, a german was held at the Old Dominion Hotel; during the first half it was led by John Stokes and Miss Gertrude Ewing of Green Bay, during the last half by W. P. Venable and Miss Leath of Burkeville.[18] A month later (August 31) a german at the same place honored Miss Mary Read of New Bedford, Massachusetts, and Miss Anne Atkinson of Columbia, South Carolina, who were visiting in town.[19] When Mr. and Mrs. W. P. Venable (she was the former Miss Bessie Ritnour) returned from their wedding trip in early October, 1896, they were entertained from five to seven in the evening at a reception at the home of the groom's parents, Mr. and Mrs. W. G. Venable, and from nine in the evening until two in the morning at a german at the Old Dominion Hotel, the Lynchburg Italian band furnishing the music, and the bride and groom leading the dance.[20] Since 1896 was leap year, the Farmville girls decided to exercise the feminine prerogative the year affords; they gave a leap year german at the Old Dominion in November, for which the Farmville String Band furnished the music.[21]

Farmville had its German Club, organized September 26, 1904, at a meeting in Dr. C. B. Crute's office. The membership, numbering about twenty, elected R. L. Freear president, J. Taylor Thompson vice-president and J. L. Bugg secretary-treasurer. The first german was planned for September 30 in the armory.[22] Three years later the club gave a costume ball at the Hotel Prince Edward, music being furnished by Professor Dean's orchestra. Prizes were offered for the best costumes, and Miss Katherine Verser, as a shepherdess, won the prize for ladies, and R. L. Freear as George Washington the prize for men.[23]

Valentine's Day offered special opportunity for parties. Miss Mary Glenn entertained "The Jolly Revelers of '96," a Prospect social organization of the time, at a Valentine party at the home of T. H. Glenn. After the program, refreshments of ice cream, cake, fruit, and pickles were served in the dining room, which was decorated with ferns and a calla centerpiece. After refreshments came the games, a geographical contest and a darkey song shout.[24] Two years later, a Valentine party at Junius C. Rowlett's entertained the young people of Green Bay; there were "many games, followed by a bountiful repast." The same year the Ladies Aid Society of the Episcopal Church in Farmville held a Valentine party at the rectory for the benefit of the tower fund; young ladies served refreshments in the dining room, and in the back parlor there were an archery contest and a wheel of hearts; Dr. W. E. Anderson played the part of St. Valentine.[25]

Communities had their clubs for social and intellectual entertainment. At Hampden-Sydney, the College Hill Club, which had been founded in 1856 by members of the college and seminary faculties, was active in the 1890's. Then it included some members who were not members of the faculties. It was the custom for the host of the month to entertain the club at supper, and the members entertained in rotation. At the October, 1896, meeting Dr. H. P. Lacy was host, and Professor Henry R. McIlwaine and the Rev. Dr. James Murray discussed the Boers "at length and exhaustively."[26] Farmville had its "Oldest Citizens Club" in the 1870's. The annual dinner for 1874 was held February 3 at the residence of P. H. Jackson.[27] More than a dozen attended the 1875 dinner on February 11 at the home of E. I. Erambert, who, having settled in Farmville in 1819, was believed to have lived in Farmville longer than any other person at that time.[28] The founder of the club, Dr. B. C. Peters, entertained at dinner on December 31, 1875; the members then were Henry Y. Jenkins, who at eighty-four was the oldest, E. I. Erambert, P. H. Jackson, J. W. Womack, Dr. Peters, and Dr. W. W. H. Thackston; all except Jenkins attended the dinner, and in addition to the members there were over a dozen invited guests.[29] At the turn of the century the Buffalo Literary Society flourished in the neighborhood of Buffalo Church. At the March, 1903, meeting at the home of Mrs. N. J. Terry, the Adelle Band, consisting of Ray and Matthew Mickle, Will Brightwell, and Misses Ellen and Nannie Mickle, furnished music.[30] Thanksgiving that year was celebrated at the meeting at the home of George Hunt, which was decorated with jack-o'-lanterns, autumn fruits, and berries. Five children in costume—Mary Moore, Edward Cunningham, Ethel Binford, Margie Binford, and Vara Cunningham—gave "The Mock Dinner." Also on the program were three other children, Bessie Chilton, Julia Cunningham, and Alma Hunt, and Misses Nannie Hunt and Carrie Binford. The society did not end its meeting before singing "the old songs." Samuel N. Cunningham was president of the society.[31] At the meeting January 8, 1904, at B. F. Hunt's, Mrs. W. T. Cunningham and W. R. Brightwell rendered violin and piano music. Misses Nan Hunt and Lelia May Cunningham and Mrs. S. N. Cunningham were the program committee for the January 22 meeting at W. T. Cunningham's.[32]

Candy pulls—there was one at the home of T. H. Bruce December 3, 1896,[33] easter egg hunts—such as Miss Sallie Dunnington gave April 7, 1898,[34] hayrides—like the one some Farmville young people took to Dr. J. D. Eggleston's at Worsham on August 7, 1895,[35] were other forms of entertainment. More unusual was the smoker at which Dr. J. H. C. Bagby entertained the Hampden-Sydney seniors in the class of 1905 at his bachelor apartments on January 28 of that year; "by cordiality and genialness he soon put everyone at his ease and soon story and anecdote under the influence of choice smokables engaged and entertained the guests."[36] Also unusual was the party at which Major A. R. Venable, Jr., entertained his Sunday School class of young girls of the Farmville Presbyterian Church; they picked strawberries in his "patch," and then enjoyed them with cream.[37]

The hayride might be combined with a picnic, as some seminary students arranged for September 21, 1896, at Leigh's Mountain. With some young ladies of College Hill, they rode in a wagon to Colonel Henry Stokes', where they were joined by other young ladies. On the ride to the mountain, the students entertained the company with music. They left the wagon at the foot of the mountain and climbed the elevation on foot; they took pictures at the top of the mountain and then returned to the wagon to eat lunch. Then chinquapins and chestnuts abounded, and the picnickers had a fine time gathering these nuts. The chestnuts have disappeared from the Prince Edward scene, the victim of a blight some thirty years ago, and the chinquapin has become almost extinct in the county.[38]

A particularly festive occasion was an oyster supper given by John D. Branch on February 15, 1894; supper was served at eleven o'clock in the evening and games continued afterward until a late hour. Chaperones for the supper were Mr. and Mrs. B. H. Carter, J. L. Weaver, and B. J. Olgers. One of the popular tunes of the day, *There'll Be a Hot Time in the Old Town Tonight*, made quite a hit at Branch's party. And there was unusual excitement to enhance the normal good time: it was feared that one of the young ladies of the community was planning to elope, and her father thought she might take advantage of the opportunity attending this party afforded; so he got some of the young men who were guests to be on watch and prevent her elopement. The young lady did elope—but not from the Branch party.[39]

During the latter part of the nineteenth century elopements were much more frequent than now; perhaps it was because the business of getting the consent of the father of the intended bride was taken more seriously then; perhaps the father took the business of giving consent more seriously; perhaps he was less inclined to leave the success of his daughter's marriage to chance and was more inclined to approve only the prospective husband who measured up to the ideals he had set. At any rate, elopements then enlivened the gossip of the community and added excitement to the routine. The newspapers of the time published the news of such weddings as elopements. One Wednesday evening in April, 1875, a young couple left the young lady's home for the ostensible purpose of attending prayer meeting. A carriage awaited them, and they started for North Carolina. As a Keysville reporter put it, "a young gentleman of nineteen and a modest maid of fifteen, accompanied by a sister and gentleman friend of the young man arrived at Keysville in the wee small hours of last night, all hailing from Farmville. A refreshing cup of coffee at the LeFarge house sent them on their way rejoicing" although a horseman arrived with news that her friends were in pursuit. The couple reached North Carolina and were married, getting back to Farmville by Saturday.[40] Usually the family accepted the situation, and whatever estrangement resulted from an elopement was of comparatively short duration.

In one case in the county, however, the estrangement between father and daughter lasted for years, the father refusing to permit her to return to his home. The newspaper account of the elopement mentioned that the groom had been "paying attention" to the bride for some time. The next week the father of the bride wrote to correct any misapprehension on the part of any "distant friends" who were unaware of his feelings that he had permitted the man his daughter married to visit his home: "he has not been in my home in months, nor never will again as long as I live."[41] The son-in-law never visited that home again, nor did his wife until years after his death.

In contrast was another elopement, which took place in 1892, in which parental forgiveness was promptly given. It was a sleepless night for the bride's parents when they learned of her elopement; as the mother told the story in after years, the father, she supposed, "would have died if there hadn't been a little whiskey in the house." But morning came, the father hitched up the buggy, the mother took her "best bed quilt" in a hastily assembled collection of items essential to housekeeping, and they drove to the home of the groom's father to see the young couple. To the children who heard the bride's mother tell of the experience, it was an entertaining story; but a father's anxiety, a mother's generosity, and parental love shine through it with a warmly radiant glow.[42]

Marriage licenses of the type now used were introduced in 1852. Prior to that time the prospective groom gave his bond in a stated sum that the intended marriage with the young lady named would take place; the bond was also signed by a surety for the groom. The surety might be a kinsman of the groom or bride or a friend. A copy of the marriage bond of William Fuqua and Sally Morton gives the form and content:

"Know all men by these presents, that we, William Fuqua and Josiah Morton, are held and firmly bound unto His Excellency, Beverly Randolph, Governor of the State of Virginia, in the sum of fifty pounds, current money of Virginia, to be paid to the said Beverly Randolph, or his successors, to the which payment eventually to be made, we bind ourselves and each of our heirs, Executors,

Administrators, jointly and severally, firmly by these presents, sealed with our seals, and dated, this 14th day of December, 1789.

"The condition of the above obligation is such, that, whereas there is a marriage shortly intended to be solemnized between the above William Fuqua and Sally Morton (spinster), daughter of John Morton, that if there be no lawful cause to obstruct this said marriage, then the above obligation to be void, or else to remain in full force and virtue. Sealed and acknowledged in the presence of Richard Watkins,

> "William Fuqua (seal)
> "Josiah Morton (seal)"

Beginning in 1852, licenses were issued, and the names of the couple and their parents, their ages, and the occupation of the groom were entered into the marriage register. In addition to the marriage register, a register of births and a register of deaths were also required to be kept, beginning 1852. The register of births was abandoned in 1896; in 1912 the use of the birth certificate was introduced in Virginia, to take the place of the birth register kept in each county.[43]

One of the notable events of the Farmville community in the 1870's, 1880's, and 1890's was the fish fry held on the fourth Thursday in May at George Thornton's, a few miles west of Farmville; fried silver perch from the Appomattox, fried chicken, buttermilk, and ash cake constituted tempting fare. In 1893 Henry Jenkins and William Meador prepared the food. The boys indulged in quoits, boating, fishing, whist, and seven-up.[44]

"A most excellent Brunswick stew" at Walter Smith's near Prospect attracted several hundred young people from Prince Edward, adjoining counties, and greater distances July 25, 1894. Dancing followed the repast.[45]

Since World War I the most popular form of social entertainment has been the bridge party. The game supplanted whist and euchre in popularity as a game among those accustomed to play cards and has even displaced rook among those who enjoyed the zest of a card game but looked with disfavor on playing with cards which were associated with gambling games. The popularity of rook a generation and more ago among people who took this attitude led to its description as "preachers' bridge." While other card games have been introduced during the ascendancy of bridge, none has been able to supplant it in popular favor. Bridge clubs are probably the most numerous social organizations, not only in Prince Edward, but else-where. The parties are held in morning, afternoon, and evening, though playing in the two earlier periods is usually limited to the ladies. The refreshments, usually a "salad plate" or dessert, some-times a luncheon, fancy and inviting enough, are less elaborate than the suppers which interrupted the games at evening parties in the "gay Nineties."

As has been indicated in the chapter on churches in the postwar era, the benefit entertainments were also social events. Such was the Chinese tea given by the George Hudson Mission Band at Felden in July, 1895. Little girls in Chinese costume served rice, peanuts, crackers, and tea against background decorations of mats, chop-sticks, and lanterns. A jing-ling band—tin buckets, jewsharps, horns, tam-bourines, cornstalk fiddles, bells, accordions, harps, and stove-lifters were the instruments—provided entertainment. Ice cream, cake, and lemonade were sold.[46]

Sports as well as social affairs provided diversion. Farmville young men organized a baseball club in the summer of 1874, playing "scientifically and vigorously" each fair evening. Thus the great American sport was introduced to Prince Edward youth.[47] Boating then was also popular; some of the boys of Farmville built a flatboat on the river and organized a boat club.[48]

Skating was a popular sport in the nineteenth century. The late George Hunt used to tell of skating on Cunningham's millpond when it froze over. This was before the War between the States. The skaters used iron skates and cut the figure eight and other designs on the ice. Several winters of the 1890's saw some extremely cold weather; on January 16, 1893, the temperature in Farmville was recorded as fourteen degrees below zero, with ice during that spell thirteen inches thick on Buffalo and the Appomattox. This was said to have been the coldest weather remembered since 1833. Two years later the Appomattox was frozen over and skating on it was "greatly enjoyed."[49] The sport has apparently been forgotten in Prince Edward.

Before the war there had been much interest in blooded horses, but there is no indication of racing in Prince Edward, although there were tracks in neighboring counties. In the latter part of the nineteenth century, the interest in horses extended to racing. Dr. W. E. Anderson had a fine horse, Duke of Wellington, which won first prize in the gentlemen's running race at the State Fair in

Richmond October 10, 1893, Hugh A. Walker, a young man from
South Carolina who was then working in Farmville for the tobacco
firm of Allen and Company, riding. The next day Walker was
thrown by this horse and fatally injured. While Dr. Anderson and
W. P. Venable were on the way to South Carolina, accompanying
Walker's remains, the horse was ridden without his owner's knowledge by Graham Hobson and won the mile dash. Subsequently Dr.
Anderson offered Duke of Wellington for sale for $1,000.[50] The next
year at the Lynchburg Fair one of Dr. Anderson's horses was involved in another fatal accident, but this time the two horses were
killed. While jockeys were exercising Lady Grey, J. W. Bradshaw's
two-year old which had been sired by Jim Grey out of Lady Buford,
the two horses collided; a buggy shaft penetrated Lady Grey's heart,
and Dr. Anderson's horse was struck on the head and killed.[51]

So great was the interest in racing in and around Farmville that
the Farmville Riding, Driving and Park Association was chartered
in 1896. The organization purchased the Hurd race track, which
apparently had been in operation previously, for use as a race track
for the Farmville Agricultural and Mechanical Society's fair and for
the use of the association's members. The association had about
thirty stockholders, with W. G. Venable president, J. B. Wall vice-
president, T. P. Robertson secretary-treasurer, and A. A. Cox, J. S.
Whaley, W. W. Jackson, Dr. W. E. Anderson, and E. L. Morris
directors.[52] For the tournament and races held there October 7-8,
1897, the railroads and the hotels offered special rates. On the first
day were trotting, running, and bicycle races; on the second day
bicycle races and the tournament. Dr. Anderson was chief marshal,
A. A. Cox chairman of the racing committee, and H. V. Baldwin
chairman of the bicycle committee.[53] The affair was well attended;
the Farmville and Powhatan excursion brought 300 people. Colonel
C. M. Walker's horse won the two-forty trotting race, Wirt
Vaughan's horse the three-minute running race, and Dr. Anderson's
horse the running race; Empie Ritnour of Washington won the mile
bicycle race, H. V. Baldwin the half-mile, and R. L. Baldwin the
third bicycle race. Frank Epes won the tournament and crowned
Miss Louise Otley of Farmville queen. That evening in the Opera
House the coronation ceremonies took place, the Rev. J. J. Duncan
of Buckingham delivering the oration.[54]

The Riding, Driving, and Park Association continued in operation
several years. In 1906 the officers were J. J Walker president, John

R. Martin vice-president, E. R. Booker secretary-treasurer, and E. C. Wiltse, A. A. Cox, S. W. Paulett, W. M. Duvall, and Dr. R. E. Hamlet directors.[55]

Interest in racing was evidently limited, for in a description of races at Farmville on June 13, 1907, the report observed that the large crowd in attendance was "unusual for Farmville." Greatest interest focused upon the race between Clyde Bliss' Little Billy and A. A. Cox' Little Belle. Little Billy won by two seconds, making the mile in two minutes and twenty-five seconds. Other races that day were between W. C. Duvall's Conqueror and W. H. Burger's Crescent, one of these winning one heat, the other the other heat, and between Annie C. owned by W. J. Burton and Tom Fenton, owned by one of the Blantons of Cumberland.[56]

Accidents were not confined to races, and traffic accidents did not originate in the automobile age. In one week in 1894 three runaways were reported. When an old threshing machine frightened the horse, A. A. Cox had his left leg fractured, and Hunter Steger received painful thigh bruises. The horse of a man identified only as Anderson was frightened by a train as his driver was returning to Prospect from Farmville. When Charlie Dance was driving Miss Myrtis Davis from the Lithia Springs into Farmville, his double team ran away, dashed to the railroad and along the tracks to the car bridge where they fell and were with difficulty extricated from their dangling position and dragged from the bridge. Miss Davis jumped from the buggy as soon as the horses started to run and was not hurt.[57] A horse hitched to a wagon ran away on Main Street in Farmville; the wagon struck an electric light pole and was broken in two, only the front wheels remaining; these were demolished when they struck a fence as the horse took to a path on leaving the street. For all the damage to the wagon, the horse was not hurt.[58] There were hazards to horse and buggy travel, too, as those who have used that method of transportation well remember.

Hunting has continued a favorite diversion of Prince Edward people. Rabbits and quail have been the game most frequently sought; turkey hunting has it devotees, but wild turkeys have not been too plentiful in Prince Edward. There has been some deer hunting in the county. The Rev. F. W. Berry killed a fine doe on a hunt near Green Bay during the Christmas season of 1893; in the party, in addition to the minister, were J. J. Owen, Dr. H. E. Watkins, S. W. Watkins, Messrs. Morton, Priddy, and Jacobs.[59] In recent years there have been annual hunts in the area along Buffalo, Spring, and Falling Creeks; some of the stands are along the Hampden-Sydney-Five Forks road west of Martin's Bridge. Fox hunting, too, has its vogue. Three chases which took place in December, 1894, are recalled: one, starting from The Cedars, then the home of William Priddy, struck a trail on Captain Watkins' farm and caught the quarry in an hour; a second fox was caught on this hunt after another hour; but the third fox proved a cunning operator; horses and dogs became exhausted before they caught him. In another chase near Worsham that month the fox was caught in J. M. Venable's garden. And on Christmas day a fox trail was found near the Venable place; but the dogs got off on a deer trail and in a little while they were in Nottoway County; thirty-nine dogs and twenty hunters (on horseback) participated in that hunt.[60] In recent years the Virginia Fox Hunters Association has held field trials for fox hounds at Slate Hill, where J. M. Venable was the last of his family to live. Prince Edward boys and men have also hunted the opossum and the raccoon which are found in sufficient quantity in the county to provide sport for those who enjoy this type of hunting. For brief periods hunting is allowed in the Prince Edward State Forest during the season; sportsmen have come to look forward to these opportunities, especially for turkey hunting.

Fishing also has been a popular sport through the years. People still fish in the streams of Prince Edward; the Appomattox in the vicinity of High Bridge and Sandy River below the highway 460 bridge are favored spots. The lakes in the State Forest have been well stocked, and are a popular resort for anglers. During the past decade many farmers have built fish ponds and stocked them, usually with bass and bream. As long ago as 1875 the restocking of streams was under way; in October of that year, John H. Rose of the State Fish Commission put 101 black bass in the Appomattox at Farmville.[61] Fishing for flatback in the Appomattox, immortalized by George W. Bagby in his charming essay, had a long popularity. During the season of the flatback run in March, 1874, both banks of the Appomattox for a hundred yards or so below the mill dam at Farmville were lined with fishermen "for two days past," the Farmville *Mercury* of March 19, 1874, reported.[62]

Fifteen Farmville men, among whom E. W. Sanford was the moving spirit, organized a Gun Club in 1911; the first trap shoot was held June 21 of that year, with Sanford breaking twenty-three out of twenty-five.[63] In April, 1928, the first golf course in Prince Edward was laid off on the farms of N. B. Davidson and J. J. Marshall by the Farmville Golf Club, of which R. E. Garland was temporary president. J. W. Dunnington was elected president upon the permanent organization of this club, which at that time had seventy-five members.[64]

Also claiming the interest of the men are the civic clubs, of which the most active are in Farmville: the Lions Club, organized in 1924, with J. L. Jarman as first president; the Rotary Club in 1937, with R. B. Crawford as first president; and the Junior Chamber of Commerce in 1940, with S. A. Martin as president.

The ladies also have, in addition to the bridge clubs in many communities, the Woman's Club of Farmville, organized in 1920 with Miss Ilma von Schilling as first president; the Junior Woman's Club, organized in 1923 with Miss Elizabeth Lewis as president; and various garden clubs, of which the oldest is the Longwood Garden Club, organized in 1917, of which Mrs. Elliott R. Booker was first president.[65] In the county, there are home demonstration clubs in each community except Buffalo District. The county also has two chapters of the Daughters of the American Revolution, the Judith Randolph and Slate Hill chapters, as well as the Farmville chapter of the United Daughters of the Confederacy. A patriotic organization which has in its membership both men and women is the Prince Edward branch of the Association for the Preservation of Virginia Antiquities, of which Dr. J. D. Eggleston was first director.

Farmville for many years had a band which participated in parades and other public affairs. There was a Farmville Brass Band in 1874, which in March of that year gave "two grand concerts" in Lee Hall.[66] Well remembered by many today is the Farmville Silver Band, which was organized in October, 1891, by J. B. Ragland with eleven members; Ragland was leader and musical director until the summer of 1892, when he was succeeded by N. B. Davidson. In January, 1893, W. L. Skaggs of St. Mary's, West Virginia, was appointed director. Citizens of Farmville subscribed $150, the sum of $200 was borrowed from the Planters Bank, and the money was used to buy the instruments of the Bedford City Band.[67] Among the benefit entertainments held for the support of the band was an oyster supper on November 24, 1893, for which Mrs. W. G. Venable was chairman of the managing committee.[68]

By 1905 the movies had come to Farmville, to launch a type of entertainment still popular. "Lawrence G. Mercer's high class moving pictures" were shown at the Opera House on December 4, "the best machines and newest films" being used. A special feature was the "famous Britt-Nelson fight from start to finish." Each picture was "presented with accompanying sounds," although the day of "talking pictures" was two decades in the future, and there were "two illustrated songs by a good tenor." The Opera House continued to be the moving picture theater for Farmville until the Eaco Theater was built by the Educational Amusement Corporation (from which the theater got its unusual name) in 1922. The name was changed to State in 1940. The Lee Theater was built in 1935.[69]

The circus came to Prince Edward, too, to provide entertainment. John Robinson's "Great World's Exhibition" and "strictly moral circus" gave a performance in Farmville September 3, 1874; a "grand street pageant" and a menagerie were among the attractions.[70] This circus made later visits to Farmville in 1902 and 1906; the street pageant had become a "long street parade"; the menagerie continued a popular attraction; and in 1906 John Robinson's circus employed a minister to preach to the crowds who attended.[71]

Although the automobile did not give to the public generally a mobility for seeking diversion away from home until about the time of World War I, the railroads provided excursions which were well patronized. The Farmville Guard and the Silver Band arranged an excursion to Appomattox on July 12, 1894, round trip fare being $1; the train left Farmville about 8:45 in the morning and returned twelve hours later. In Appomattox those who made the trip saw a foot race, which Asa Jenkins won; saw the Farmville baseball team lose to Pamplin by the score of 8 to 2; in the afternoon heard a concert by the band, given in the courthouse; and watched a dress parade by the military company.[72] The Farmville and Powhatan ran excursions to Powhatan for the laying of the corner-stone of the Confederate monument there July 4, 1895; some 300 people made the trip by train from Farmville, and the excursion from the other direction brought 800 from Richmond and Manchester.[73] When the Confederate monument at Nottoway Courthouse was unveiled, the Norfolk and Western ran excursions.[74] The Farmville and Powhatan operated an excursion for the meeting of the Farmville District Conference of the Methodist Church at Grove Church, Sunnyside, July 26-28, 1898; round trip fare was $1.25, good for travel at any time between July 25 and July 30; if one went for one day only, the round trip fare was $1.[75] The Norfolk and Western operated excursions to the Jamestown Exposition in 1907, and many Prince Edward people took advantage of the opportunity to make the trip. The railroad operated excursions several times during the summer to Norfolk; in this way many people went to the beach for a few days. Excursions also came to Farmville, and many were operated for the colored people. On Sunday (August 18, 1895, seven coaches, all packed, arrived from Lynchburg; the excursionists, numbering about 750, went to the Lithia Springs for preaching. The next day, there was an excursion from Richmond, via the Southern to Burkeville and thence to Farmville, for a baseball game between the colored teams of Richmond and Farmville; the former won, 13-8.[76] Excursion rates from Farmville to Richmond and return in 1897 were $1.50; the train left Farmville at eight o'clock in the morning, Rice at 8:19 A. M., and arrived in Richmond at 11:15 A. M.[77]

While it is not recorded that an excursion was run for the occasion, "several of the Darlington Heights crowd" went to Washington for the inauguration of Theodore Roosevelt as President on March 4, 1905.[78]

The lecture, both educational and humorous, was a favorite form of entertainment in the period between the War between the States and World War I. Churches and other organizations sponsored them and shared in the door receipts; a well known and popular lecturer made the occasion quite profitable. Farmville had four such programs during the year 1875: in February, Professor Caskie Harrison of the University of Tennessee on "Spoons, Sparks, and Spinsters, or the Ethics of Courtship and the Science of Matrimony"; in April Judge F. R. Farrar of Amelia, widely known as "Johnny Reb," whose topic was "Lights and Shadows, or the Story of a Life"; Mrs. Henry Bowler gave a program of classical readings at the courthouse in October; and Dr. George W. Bagby and James P. Cowardin, both humorists, put in an appearance in November.[79] Dr. Bagby was one of the most popular lecturers of the time; he had Prince Edward connections, some of his Evans kin having lived not far west of Farmville.

One of the most popular entertainers of the period between the wars was a native of Prince Edward. Polk Miller, born at Grape Lawn, with his "Old South" quartet of Negro men were welcome performers wherever they went. Often they were in Prince Edward, at Farmville in 1893, 1902, and 1904, where they put on their show in the Opera House, at Rice in 1904 where the theater was the cannery.[80] Miller played the banjo and the quartet sang such beloved favorites of the time as "Old Dan Tucker," "The Mississippi Sawyer," "The Arkansas Traveler," "The Watermelon Song." Some were folk songs, some the popular tunes of an earlier time. Some were of Polk Miller's own composition. One of them is one of the choicest nonsense songs—a popular type in Miller's time—ever written. "The Huckleberry Picnic" was typical of Polk Miller's entertainment; it had a distinctive flair, a rollicking lilt, a gay turn, and elements of folk song blended with nonsense:

> I look down de river, erbout de crack o' day,
> An' I seed a big commotion a mile erway,
> De critters o' de fiel' an' de forest done come,
> De animals all collected for to have a little fun.
> Dar was de Badger an' de B'yar, de Fox an' de H'yar,
> De Otter an' de Coon, de Possum an' Baboon,
> De Mink an' Kangaroo, de Wolf an' Weasel, too;
> De Monkey an' de Owl was a settin' up a howl:

Chorus:

> Come jine de huckleberry picnic,
> It's gwine'ter take place today;
> I's on de committee for to 'vite you all,
> An' I ain' got long to stay-ay-ay-ay!
> Come jine de huckleberry picnic,
> I ain' got long to stay,
> I's on de committee for to 'vite you all,
> An' I ain' got long to stay,

> De fus' thing dey done was to sweep off de groun',
> Den dey all got ready for a big walk aroun';
> De Badger an' de B'yar, dey jump Jim Crow;
> De Fox an' de H'yar dey danced de heel an' toe;
> De Otter an' de Coon dey cut de pidgin wing;
> De Possum an' Baboon dey danced de Highlan' fling;
> De Wildcat an' de Owl both began to sing,
> An' de Billy Goat an' de Pig struck up a jig: Chorus.

> Long to'des noon de table was set,
> An' dey brought out evything to eat dey could get;
> De Badger an' de B'yar too hash francaise;

De Fox an' de H'yar took soup consumé;
De Otter an' de Coon took fish cream sauce;
De Possum an' Baboon took Simmons—a la frost;
De Pig got sick off o' canter melon vine;
De Goat got drunk off o' huckleberry wine;
De Mule had a fit, and de Groun' Hog died;
An' when dey was all chock full, de Hyena cried: Chorus.

Long to'des night dem varmints got sick,
An' dey sent for de ole Snake Doctor quick;
Like de railroad c'yars, his wings did hum,
An' de little varmints hollered: "Yarn' he come!"
He feel de pulse o' de Badger an' de B'yar,
Put Jimpson weed on de Fox an' de H'yar;
He started fo' to open de haid o' de Horse
When de little varmints hollered, "Hol' on, boss;
Tain' no use for to do like dat!
Dat ain' de place where de misery's at!"—
He tied de Monkey's tail wid a rope,
An' he look down his throte wid a mikerscope;
You ough to o' seen dat Monkey's tail—
I declar for gracious, it turn right pale!
He rub it, an' he rub it, but it warn no use,
An' he paint it all over wid pokeberry juice:
An' when dat monkey took'n died,
He turned right over an' softly sighed: Chorus.[81]

Polk Miller never failed to attract a crowd or to delight it. His entertainment was one of the premier attractions of his day. Mark Twain said that when Prince Henry of Germany missed Polk Miller's concert at Carnegie Hall, New York, he missed about the only thing originally and utterly American.[82]

Other companies of entertainers came to Prince Edward, to Farmville and the villages. Some were not so popular as Polk Miller and failed to attract the crowds. Dr. Blue Mountain Joe and his company of five came to Farmville one August day in 1896, hired the Opera House for a week or more of performances, and put on their first show August 24. The people did not turn out; the admission fees paid were not enough for Dr. Blue Mountain Joe to pay the rent for the theater or the bill for board and lodging at the Old Dominion Hotel. The hotel held the entertainers' trunks. As word of the plight of the company got around, sympathy was aroused. Local people held benefit performances; one was held September 4, another September 7; one of the most popular features of the benefits was R. D. Miller's singing of the war songs, "Old Deacon Jones," "Good Old Rebel," "I Am a Conscript," "Rally Around True Southern Hearts." Local talent raised enough to send Dr. Blue Mountain Joe and his company on their way.[83]

Among the most popular forms of entertainment in Prince Edward were the plays performed by local talent. They were given in each community, usually for the benefit of church or school, and usually ice cream was sold afterward, thus giving the audience opportunity to enjoy the performance in retrospect with friends as they ate the homemade ice cream. In the 1890's Farmville had a Paint and Powder Club which put on some successful performances. One of the plays it performed had a moral; "Arthur Eustace or a Mother's Love" was a "strong and thrilling" temperance drama. One season, with the assistance of the Farmville Guard, the Paint and Powder Club gave "Virginia," a Southern war drama at least three times in Farmville; an added attraction was the between-act "specialties" of that inimitable pair of Confederate veterans, Captain S. W. Paulett and Sergeant R. D. Miller.[84]

An ever popular feature of Prince Edward social life has been the anniversary or birthday party. For Dr. and Mrs. Benjamin Mosby Smith, their golden wedding anniversary on October 31, 1889 was more a public program than a social event. It was held in the Seminary chapel, attended by students of college and seminary, with colored friends in the gallery. Dr. and Mrs. Smith sat on the platform, Dr. Moses Hoge made an address, Dr. W. W. Moore offered a prayer, and Dr. H. C. Alexander offered the benediction.[85]

Such a celebration was unusual, however. Usually it took the form of a dinner or a reception. Such an affair was the party given by Miss Sue Edmunds to celebrate the eighty-seventh birthday of her mother, Mrs. Edwin Edmunds, on January 3, 1895. "The doors of Rotherwood never opened wider to welcome the coming guests, the hickory fires never gave out more of grateful warmth, kerchiefed housemaids never moved more quickly or served more noiselessly, floors never shone more with glare born of well-applied brush, bedspreads never glistened with purer whiteness, curtains never reflected more of winter comfort, tables never gleamed with richer polish, pictures never peeped more peacefully from out their frame houses, the brass fire-dogs never looked brighter, the family time-piece never ticked more gently. . . ." Seated in the parlor, Mrs. Edmunds received her guests. At two "an abundant and substantial dinner" was served. "The dessert table was decorated with fruits and flowers, exquisite embroideries, resplendent with glass and silver." Mrs. Edmunds sat at a small table on which was placed her birthday cake, which had been brought by her brother, Dr. W. T. Richardson of Richmond. Even here there was speaking; Major A. R. Venable, Jr., was toastmaster and announced the toasts; to the toast, "The day we celebrate," Dr. Richardson responded, speaking of his family's Protestant ancestors in France, Switzerland, and England, and their loyalty to the Presbyterian faith; the Rev. L. S. Reed responded to the toast, the Virginia country home; toasts were drunk to the guests, to the hostess, and, after Mrs. James L. White and Miss Emma Cabell Venable led the company in singing "Auld Lang Syne," to Mrs. Edmunds "in a glass of generous wine."[86]

The western part of the county had its family gatherings, too. On March 30, 1893, the Cunningham kith and kin from four counties gathered at Millbank to celebrate the sixty-ninth birthday of Mrs. Newton Cunningham. "The early hours of the day were spent by the younger people in croquet, hunting, chatting, and singing. Fathers and grandfathers clustered round the wood-pile to talk over their different businesses and no doubt to relate war experiences. The matrons were busy exchanging hearty greetings and snatches of personal history.

"At an hour calculated to make all glad to hear the welcome sound a large bell, mounted in the yard, called the wanderers home to a bountiful dinner, spread in the room which had once been 'great-great-grandfather's room.' This sumptuous meal had been prepared at the homes of the children who came, not empty-handed, to help enjoy the day. In the afternoon everyone gathered into the house to listen to such music as is seldom one's privilege to hear."[87]

A dozen years later, the same connection gathered again at Millbank on August 16, 1905, to celebrate the ninety-ninth anniversary of the birth of their ancestor, Newton Cunningham. Mrs. Newton Cunningham was no longer living, but her faithful servant for many years, Harriet Winston, served Brunswick stew from a big pot in the yard to the ninety-three descendants of Newton Cunningham who were present and other relatives and guests there for the occasion.[88]

Good food is a Prince Edward tradition. From breakfasts of white lake fish and spoon bread, or ham and eggs, or beefsteak, or fried chicken through hearty dinners to substantial suppers, the Prince Edward resident liked to eat well. He welcomed guests—kinfolk, preachers, delegates, friends—and in an older day it was not unusual for guests to drop in unexpectedly. It was quite all right for a traveler to stop at a friend's home for a meal or for a night, supper, and breakfast. Summer, especially, was a great time for visiting, and most homes had an abundance of company. It was not unusual to have two tables, one set after the other, to accommodate the guests.

On occasion there might be three; the writer remembers hearing one lady tell of a time at her father's home when there were so many guests that there had to be three tables and that they ate so heartily everything except the cabbage gave out before some of the children were served at the third table. An example of the meal served in honor of a guest may be found in the menu of the dinner given in March, 1917, by R. B. Tuggle of Farmville for A. E. Schwartz, president of the Schwartz Cigar Company of Poughkeepsie, New York: mockturtle soup, turkey, old ham, a variety of vegetables, condiments "of all kinds," crisp celery, loafed lettuce, plum pudding, and cheese.[89]

Christmas in Prince Edward was a time for feasting and family reunions. Oysters or quail were the Christmas morning breakfast staple. For dinner turkey with dressing and gravy and ham—a ham especially selected and kept for Christmas—both kinds of potatoes and salsify, several varieties of pickles filled the great table. For dessert there were fruit jelly and custard, one pitcher flavored with vanilla, one with lemon, and at least four kinds of cake—fruit cake, kept moist with brandy or wine since it had been baked weeks before; Rocky Mountain cake, beautiful with its decorations of fruits and nuts against a cocoanut background; cocoanut; and orange, with its unusual tang from the bit of orange peel grated in; there were pies, too, the delicious individual chess and cocoanut pies which melted in one's mouth. How the growing boy delighted to sample something of everything, even to the two flavors of custard! And there was no lack of family talk, of friends and kindred, of store and farm, of church and school, of Christmas toys, and tales and jokes to make the day gay.[90]

Yes, Prince Edward people liked to eat, and the bountiful and delicious meals make a great chapter in the social history. If one were to select one meal as symbolic of the Prince Edward family's delight in good eating and good company, it would be Thanksgiving dinner at the home of the Misses Addie, Susie, and Emma Venable at Hampden-Sydney. The meal began at three in the afternoon. After an appropriate blessing, "Miss Addie" ladled from the great white ironstone tureen oyster soup which would have delighted the taste of the most discriminating gourmet. Then came the main course, which, after the fashion of the day and section, included two meats, roast turkey with dressing and gravy and ham, cured over hickory wood, adequately aged, and baked with brown sugar. Vegetables, including Irish and sweet potatoes and salsify, added substance to the meal, and pickles—peach, pear, cucumber, and green tomato—and a salad added zest. Then came the desserts. "Miss Addie" from the head of the table served generous portions of plum pudding, made the more delectable by the hard sauce which was the invariable accompaniment; from the other end of the table, "Miss Susie" served vanilla ice cream, rich from the lavish use of cream and eggs, smooth as silk from the turnings in the hand freezer. The rolls, generously buttered, and the coffee would in themselves have made a memorable meal. The service, like the food, was flawless. Efficient waiters anticipated every desire. It was four or after before the meal was over. Then the guests, who had gathered from near and far, went into the sitting room, and the talk which had added to the pleasure of the dinner continued—that delightful and animated talk of friends and other days and even current affairs.

The sunlight faded early those November evenings, and all too soon it was time to leave. The signal came when Mrs. John Venable, the beloved "Aunt Bet" of academy and college students in the 1870's, 1880's, and 1890's, in her mid-nineties and the oldest of the company in the 1920's, decided that it was time for her to go. Miss Emma, youngest of the sisters, would drive Mrs. Venable to her home at The Maples. The other guests left then, too, but there remained the memory of a Lucullan feast and the consciousness that they had shared in an event which had caught and preserved the best and the finest of the social heritage which is Prince Edward's.[91]

APPENDIXES

APPENDIX 1

THE POPULATION OF PRINCE EDWARD

Virginia Gazette (Purdie & Dixon) June 24, 1770: In 1714 there were 1,040 tithables in the area which was then Prince George County. In the same area there were in 1770 26,412 tithables in eleven counties: Amelia, 4,903; Bedford, 1,772; Brunswick, 3,793; Charlotte, 1,655; Dinwiddie, 2,986; Halifax, 1,827; Lunenburg, 1,585; Mecklenburg, 2,185; Prince Edward, 1,620; Pittsylvania, 1,677; Prince George, 2,449.

It may be noted that Amelia then included Nottoway, Brunswick included Greensville, Charlotte and Prince Edward parts of Appomattox, Bedford included Campbell, a part of Appomattox, and a part of Franklin, Pittsylvania included Henry and Patrick and a part of Franklin.

THE FEDERAL CENSUS OF PRINCE EDWARD

(Summary 1790-1900 from the Farmville *Herald*, Jan. 11, 1907; 1910-50 from atlases.)

Year	Population	Year	Population
1790	8,100	1860	11,844
1800	10,962	1870	12,004
1810	12,400	1880	14,668
1820	12,577	1890	14,694
1830	14,107	1900	15,045
1840	14,069	1910	14,270
1850	11,857 (a	1920	14,767
part of Prince Edward had been		1930	14,520
included in the new county of		1940	14,922
Appomattox in 1845)		1950	15,398

In 1783 there were 3,020 inhabitants reported in Prince Edward, 1,552 whites, 1,468 blacks. (*Calendar of Virginia State Papers* 3: 552.)

In 1801 the total population was reported as 10,962 (census of 1800), with 5,921 slaves and 8,594 federal numbers (all whites and three-fifths of the slaves were counted to determine representation in Congress).

Free and slave population were reported (Richmond *Enquirer*, Feb. 2, 1851, for 1830, 1840, and 1850; July 23, 1861, for 1860):

Year of Census	1830	1840	1850	1860
Free white	5,039	4,923	4,174	4,038
Free colored	475	570	485	465
Slaves	8,593	8,576	7,192	7,341
Total	14,107	14,069	11,851	11,844

APPENDIX 2

THE PETITION FOR RELIGIOUS LIBERTY

(Manuscript Legislative Petition, Archives Division, State Library)

To the Honourable the President and House of Delegates of Commonwealth of Virginia to meet in Williamsburg the first Tuesday in October, 1776:

The petition of sundry of the Inhabitants of Prince Edward County respectfully showeth, that we heartily approve and chearfully submit ourselves to the form of government adopted at your last session: hoping that our United American states will long continue free & Independent. The last article of the Bill of Rights we also esteem as the rising sun of religious liberty, to relieve us from a long Night of ecclesiastic Bondage: and we do most earnestly request that you would go on to complete what is so nobly begun; raise religious as well as civil Liberty to the zenith of Glory, and make Virginia an asylum for free inquiry, knowledge, and the virtuous of every Denomination. Justice to ourselves and Posterity, as well as regard to the honour of the Commonwealth, makes it our indispensable Duty, in particular to intreat, That without Delay, you would pull down all Church Establishments; abolish every Tax upon Conscience and private Judgment; and leave each Individual to rise or sink according to his Merit, and the general Laws of the Land. The whole Amount of what we desire, is That our Honourable Legislature would blot out every vestige of British Tyranny and Bondage, and define accurately between civil and ecclesiastic Authority; then leave our Lord Jesus Christ the Honour of being the Sole Lawgiver and Governor in his Church, and every one in the Things of Religion to stand or fall to him; he being, in this respect the only rightful Master. And your Petitioners in duty bound shall ever pray. Sept. 24, 1776.

Richd Sankey	Douglass Baker	George Shilliday Jr.
Hugh Porter	William Nixson	Robert Reed
Charles Richey	James Nixson	Wm Hamersly
Saml Baker	Tho. Alexander	Jacob Neighbors
George Shilliday	Jno Hamilton	Dick Holland
John Caldwell	Joseph Ried	William Baldwin
Robert Johnston	Jno Farlin	William Baldwin Junr
John Cunningham	James Fraizer	Benjamin Baldwin
Saml Cunningham	Jno. McSwine	Wiliam Findley
James Graham	Samuel McSwine	Robt. Watson
James Harfield	James Parks	Nat. Porter
Andrew Baker	Ezekiel Parks	Francis Clark
Jno. Dun	Joseph Parks	Wm Mills
Daniel Hays	Tho. Scott	Wm Marshall
Wm Hay	William Scott	John Marshall
James McMahen	Wm Huston	John Willson
Jno McMahen	Ro. Martin	Joshua Bunkley
Manassa Mcfarland	James Ewing Senr	Charles Hagens
Saml Arbuckle	Samuel Ewing	Richd Groce
Wm Arbuckle	Wm Gillespie	Edward Clark
Jno Arbuckle	George Gillespie	Thoms Marshill
Saml Porter	Phillip McTaggart	Ben Marshill
Jno Black	Laurance Cook	Thos Paulet
James McCormic	James Gillespie	John Hunter

Alex Hunter	Robt Elliott	Frans Hays
Silas Wood	Andrew Elliott	John Caldwell Senr
Luke Palmer	Robt. Johnston	Jno. Caldwell Junr
Seymor Ketichin	Saml Johnston	Jno Caldwell
James Richardson	Wm Johnston	David Caldwell
Charles Wood	Jno. Thompson Senr	Thos. Caldwell
Paul Wood	Jno. Thompson Junr	James Caldwell
Alexr Hamilton	Andrew Thompson	George Caldwell
James Cunningham	Jno. Granter	Thos. Armstrong
James Ewing Junr	Jno. Thompson Blacksmith	Jno. Crockett
Samuel Ewing	Adam Calhoun	Thos. Craig
James McElroy	James Calhun	Robt Craig
William Smith	Jno. Caldwell	Robt Hanna
Partrick Galaspie	Jas. Read	Saml Hanna
Wm Galaspie	Caleb Baldwine	Robt Hanna
George Galaspie	Wm. Thompson	Jno. Armstrong
Saml Baker	Glover Baker	Andrew Dun
James Donnell	Robt Baker	Robt Dun
John Donnell	Henry Dawson	John Clark Sen
William Donnell	Thos. Graham	John Cleaton
John Porter Senr	Robt Black	Saml Marshall
Natt. Porter	Wm Black	Tho. Coplin
Wm Porter	James Black	Wm. Coplin
John Porter Junr	John Martin	John Coplin
John Morrison	Caleb Baker	John Coplin Jur
Saml Scott	Robt Hamilton	Willm Watson
James Morrison	Jas. Hamilton	Duglass Watson Jur
Samuel Cunningham Senr	Manassa McBride	Wm Dawson
John Cunningham	Wm McBride	James McMachin
Matthew Cunningham	Robt Steel	

The petition is endorsed:

Referred to Committee of Religion.

APPENDIX 3

NAMES OF PRINCE EDWARD VOTERS IN THE PRESIDENTIAL ELECTION IN NOVEMBER, 1840

It was the practice for many years for voters to declare publicly their choice of candidate in an election and to be recorded by name as voting for such a candidate. When Edmund W. Hubard of Buckingham was considering making the race for Congress in 1841, he made a careful survey of the prospects of a Democratic candidate. In reply to his request for information concerning Prince Edward, Branch J. Worsham, clerk and active in Democratic party affairs, sent him a list of the voters, their addresses, and how they voted in the 1840 Presidential election. The list has been preserved in the Edmund W. Hubard Papers and is now, with that collection, some 31,000 items in all, in the Southern Historical Collection of the University of North Carolina Library, Chapel Hill.

For Van Buren electors [Democratic]

Wm. Scott, Marble Hill
Jacob Waddill, Sandy River Church
Simeon H. Wootton, do [ditto]
Simon Hughes, Midway Inn
Edwin Edmunds, Farmville
Thomas Hines, Midway Inn
Benjamin P. Purke, Walkers Church
Charles H. Price, Farmville
Anderson Lumpkin, Prospect
*John Morton, Court House
Absalom Nunnally, Sandy River Church
William Pigg, Marble Hill
Charles Baldwin, Court House
Drury A. Smith, Farmville
Drury W. Calhoun, Court House
Doctr. Rd. B. Tuggle, Nottoway County
Capt. Nathl. Price, Court House
Col. John Rice, Farmville
Beverly S. Scott do
Robert Knight, Burkeville
Wm. J. McGehee, Sandy River Church
Richard Carter, Midway Inn
Capt. Adam Calhoun, do
*Jacob McGehee, Sandy River Church
Reps. J. Childress, James Town
Wm. H. Armistead, Farmville
Wm. Willis   do
Edwin B. Jackson, Burkeville
Fredk. A. Ford, Court House
Nathan Bell, Midway Inn
*B. U. Brightwell, Walkers Church
*Abraham Dunnivant, Burkeville
*Thomas Mohorn, Marble Hill
Nathl. Thackston, Court House
James Scott, Sandy River Church
George W. Daniel, Farmville
Thos. B. Purcell, Prospect
John J. Brightwell, Walkers Church
Wm. B. Walthall, James Town
Nathan A. Fowlkes, Burkeville
Wm. T. Smith, Sr., James Town
Wm. McGehee, Sandy River Church
*James Deshazor, do
*Capt. Paschal G. Leigh, do
Thomas Goode, James Town
Doctr. R. H. Dejernatt, Sandy River
    Church
S. E. Rodgers, do
Obadiah Hendrick, Marble Hill
Joshua Hines, do
Wm. J. Morgan, Prospect
*John W. Boatwright, Marble Hill

Thos. H. Almand, Farmville
Col. John Foster, Sandy River Church
Paschal E. Dunnevant, Burkeville
Wm. D. Taylor, Prospect
Francis Rice, Court House
John Lloyd, do
Patk. H. Jackson, Farmville
Doctr. Wm. H. Chappell, do
Wm. C. Flournoy, do
Wm. D. Pool, Marble Hill
Wm. Foster, Midway Inn
Thos. T. Tredway, Court House
Revd. Saml. L. Graham, do
Wm. Elliott, Burkeville
James T. Price, do
John B. Bigger, Senr, Midway Inn
Johnson M. Dungans, Burkeville
Drury D. Mays, address not known
Chs. Brightwell Junr, Walkers Church
Henry Tucker, James Town
Henry L. Goode, address not known
John Johnson, Prospect
*Capt. James W. Womack, Marble Hill
*Doctr. Thos. C. Overton, James Town
Carolus B. Featherston, Farmville
Col. George Dungans, Burkeville
*John E. Scott, Marble Hill
Wm. L. Womack, Midway Inn
Waller Wilson, Farmville
Wm. M. Womack, do
Thos. O. Rowlett, Sandy River Church
*Henry N. Watkins, Esqr., Court House
Charles Fore, Farmville
*Thos. Hickson, do
James Bigger, Midway Inn
*John Thackston, Farmville
*Reuben Brightwell, Walkers Church
Thomas Weaver, Sandy River Church
Matthew J. Fowler, Court House
James Moss, Prospect
Henry S. Guthrie, Esqr., Court House
Capt. Frs. S. Martin, do
*Francis T. Wootton, Esqr, Sandy
    River Church
Pettus Perkinson, Burkeville
George W. Bell, Marble Hill
Richard Crafton, do
Wm. H. Borum, address not known
Wm. T. Irvine, Court House
Joseph M. Price, do
James Bondurant, Farmville
Jesse B. Johnson, Court House

James S. Allen, do
Wm. Bradshaw, James Town
David Ellington, Burkeville
John B. Bigger, Midway Inn
Ebenezer Crafton, Marble Hill
John Perrin, Midway Inn
Revd. John Thompson, Marble Hill
Dabney Hudson, Sandy River Church
Saml. Watson, Marble Hill
Saml. Elliott, Burkeville
Pleasant Fowler, Court House
Wm. W. Watkins, Marble Hill
James Whitehead, Court House
John B. Morgan, Prospect
John Tuggle, Farmville
John Queensberry, Burkeville
Henry Willard, Court House
Revd. Chs. Venable, Prospect
Redford Fowlkes, Burkeville
Allen Watson, Court House
Wm. B. Rowlett, Sandy River Church
James B. Ely, Farmville
Paschal F. McGlasson, address not
  known
Frs. Thackston, address not known
Presley Waddill, Sandy River Church
*Majr. John Bigger, Midway Inn
Capt. Richd. Marshall, James Town
Capt. Lil. D. Womack, Midway Inn
Jesse W. Rowlett, Sandy River Church
James D. Shepherd, Court House
Thomas Tredway, Court House
Wm. M. Walton, Sandy River Church
Saml. F. Hunt, Court House
Dennis R. Fielder, Farmville
Samuel D. Booker, Mecklenburg Co.
Thomas Clark, Sandy River Church
Benjamin Loudon, do
Doctr. George J. Smith, Farmville
Thomas B. McGehee, Farmville
Doctr. John T. Ligon, Farmville
Moses Tredway, Esqr, Court House
Watson B. Cobbs, do
John H. Williamson, Sandy River
  Church
Saml. Thackston, Midway Inn
Clement C. Read, Esqr, Farmville
James M. Wootton, Sandy River Church
Richard P. Richardson, Prospect
Benjamin Thackston, do
Henry Day, Marble Hill
Doctr. Robert S. Clark, Sandy River
  Church
Jacob W. Holt, Burkeville

Robert Harden, Burkeville
Wm. H. Cary, Midway Inn
Josiah Brightwell, Walkers Church
Perry G. Noel, Marble Hill
James B. Morgan, Prospect
Robert V. Davis, do
*John P. Hughes, Court House
John T. Flippen, Burkeville
Joseph M. Rowlett, Sandy River Church
Wm. W. Moring, Burkeville
Wm. W. Anderson, address not known
Drury Y. Stokes, Burkeville
Caswell Moring do
Nathl. Hill, Prospect
Obadiah D. Jenkins, Walkers Church
Henry Y. Jenkins, Farmville
John Foster, address not known
Wm. Leneave, Burkeville
Wm. Elliott, Court House
*Benj. W. Womack, do
Jesse Meadows, do
Nathan Fowlkes, Burkeville
Thomas T. Totty, Farmville
Abm. Z. Venable, do
Wm. Nunnally, Sandy River Church
Wm. A. Chambers, Marble Hill
Washington S. Leneave, Burkeville
*John W. Redd, Esqr, Court House
Nathan G. McGehee, Marble Hill
Wm. Clark, Halifax Co.
*Joseph Phillips, Burkeville
Waddell C. Armes, James Town
Wm. E. Bradshaw, do
Edmund E. Self, Farmville
John Raines, Burkeville
Joseph G. Williams, Farmville
James Edwards, do
*Philip Marker, Burkeville
Saml. S. Hawkins, do
Sterling Spain, Court House
*Robert S. Carter, Marble Hill
Wm. Fowlkes, Marble Hill
Joseph Williamson, Sandy River Church
John Watson, Marble Hill
Thomas J. Price, Prospect
Benj. F. Flippen, Burkeville
John M. Harris, Prospect
*Capt. Wm. Carter, Marble Hill
Abner W. Mason, Farmville
L. G. Brown, Prospect
Jesse Watson, Court House
Thomas J. Redd, do
Elbert F. Redd, do
*Wm. S. King, do

674

History of Prince Edward County

*Joseph A. Watson, do
*Capt. James B. Carter, Midway Inn
Wm. Warden, address not known
Granville Nunnally, Farmville
*James Venable, Esqr, Prospect
Marcus Beard, Walkers Church
Edward B. Vawter, address not known
George W. Cliborne, Court House
*Capt. John T. Carter, Midway Inn
John R. Elam, Walkers Church
*Joel W. Womack, Esqr, Farmville
Luke B. Ellington, Burkeville
*Thomas F. Venable, Farmville
Joseph S. Rice, Midway Inn
Harwood Cary, Midway Inn
*Thomas H. Anderson, Court House
Sims Allen, do
*Joseph Redd, Esqr, Court House
*George O. Smith, Burkeville
Lemuel W. Carter, Court House
James Calhoun, do
Branch O. Scott, do
*Saml. W. Venable, Farmville
Taylor W. Nunnally, Sandy River
  Church
Wm Mullins, Court House
*James H. Wilson, Esqr, Farmville
*Royall F. Godsey, do
*Capt. S. D. McDearmon, Walkers
  Church
*Wm. T. Wootton, Esqr, Sandy River
  Church
*Capt. Luther C. Jeffries, Midway Inn
John W. Ritchie, Farmville
*Robert C. Anderson, Courthouse
John F. Rice, Midway Inn
J. B. Sharp, Marble Hill
James W. Dunnington, Farmville
Chs. A. Scott, Sandy River Church
*Capt. Joseph Wilson, Midway Inn
Amplias Tuggle, Farmville
Thomas E. Madison, Farmville
Richard D. Noel, Court House
John M. Pugh, Midway Inn
Branch J. Worsham, Court House
Nathl. E. Venable, Esqr, Farmville
*Saml. C. Anderson, Esqr, Court House
Capt. Saml. Watkins [no address given]
*John Raine, Clover Hill
Wm. Hill (R), Walkers Church
Richard Ferguson, do
Littleberry Jenkins, do
Edmund Conner, do
Wm. L. Wood, do

Josiah Paris, do
*Jesse Hughes, do
Barnet Hill, do
Thos Mitchell, do
Spencer Gilliam, do
Johnson Marsh, do
Clayton Gilliam, do
Nathan Marsh, do
Chs. W. Wilkerson, do
Thomas A. Andrews, do
Majr. Saml. Baldwin, do
Peter L. Legrand, Clover Hill
Jeremiah Sears, do
Robert Webb, do
Wm. Gregory, do
Davis Hill, Walkers Church
John Gunter, do
Saml. Mitchell Senr, do
Revd. Thomas A. Legrand, Clover Hill
Andrew B. Baker, Walkers Church
Henry Inge, Clover Hill
Nathan Grubbs, do
James Hill, Walkers Church
Alexander Beard, do
Chs. Brightwell Senr, do
Robert Thaxton, do
Jehue Simmons, do
James Jennings, do
Saml. B. Baldwin, do
Saml. D. Hill, do
Saml. England, do
John Gorden, Clover Hill
George W. Beard, Walkers Church
Martin Webb, Clover Hill
Danl. C. Glenn, Walkers Church
Wm. J. Moore, do
Thos. Wright, Clover Hill
Wm. B. Cawthorn, do
John Jennings, Walkers Church
Wm. Trent, Esqr, Clover Hill
Dabney E. Wooldridge, do
James Clark, address not known
Jacob Tibbs, Clover Hill
Wm. Thaxton, Walkers Church
David H. Thaxton, do
Wm. Fears, do
Robert Wooldridge, Clover Hill
John Sears, do
Saml. Brightwell, Walkers Church
Newton Cunningham, Prospect
Saml. A. Wright, Clover Hill
Jesse Bagley, do
Edwin Gray, Walkers Church
Henry Brightwell, do

Chs. A. Wooldridge, Clover Hill
Obd. Gordon, do
Pryor Wright Senr, do
Archd. A. Legrand, do
Thos. D. Williams, Walkers Church
Alexr. Moss, do
Josiah Shepherd, do
Obd. C. Jenkins, do
James Moseley, do
Shepard Thaxton, do
Josiah Brightwell, do
Wm. A. Swann, do
Coleman Ledbetter, do
David Walker, Clover Hill
Ben Shepherd, Walkers Church
Robt W. Martin, Clover Hill
Pryor D. Martin, do
Ro. B. Wright, do
Wm. B. Baker, Walkers Church
Danl. M. Sanders, do
Saml. S. Hill, do
John M. Cunningham, Prospect
Pryor B. Wright, Clover Hill
Benja. Baldwin, Prospect
John W. Flood, Walkers Church

Wm. Martin, Clover Hill
Revd. James McDearmon, Walkers Church
John C. Owen, do
Clabn. Inge, do
Majr. Robert Kelso, Walkers Church
Ro. Hill, Prospect
Capt. Wm. Brightwell, Walkers Church
Wm. Brizendine, do
Matthew Bagby, do
James Durrum, Clover Hill
James B. Durrum, do
Azariah Martin, do
Wm W. C. Durrum, do
Owen J. Godsey, do
Joel Elam Esqr, Walkers Church
Henry Dawson, do
Abner Moore, do
Wm. Hill, do
Capt. Josiah Cunningham, do
Wm. St. Clair, Clover Hill
Thomas Giles, do
Allen E. Baker, Walkers Church
Anderson Hill, do

For Harrison electors [Whig]

Doctr. John R. McDearmon, Walkers Church
John P. Davenport, do
Ebenezer Price, do
Samuel S. Baker, do
John Hill, do
Wilkerson Watson, do
Josiah T. Cheadle, do
James Hurt, do
Geo. B. Ewing, do
James M. Gilliam, do
Wm. H. Watt, do
Wm. Shorter, do
E. B. Farrar, do
Reuben Johnson, do
John B. Dupuy, Court House
Richard Woodson, Walkers Church
Charles U. Woodson, address not known
Samuel B. Davenport, Walkers Church
Thomas Hill, do
Samuel Walker, do
Willis Inge, Clover Hill
Eldridge B. Land, Walkers Church
Saml. Mitchell Jr., do
Saml. L. Venable, do
Saml. Allen, Court House

Anthony W. Gilliam, Walkers Church
Henry Hubbard, do
Philip Goode, do
Nathl. J. Venable, do
Wm. M. Jenkins, do
John W. Gilliam, do
George Mickle, do
John B. Davis, do
Ryland J. Matthews, do
John Mills, do
Wm. Matthews, Esqr, do
Chs. W. Gilliam, do
Benj. F. Hill, do
Saml. P. Lodge, do
Joel E. Mickle, do
Philip A. Watkins, do
John Dillon, Court House
Elisha B. Beach, do
Wilson Carter, do
John B. Baker, do
Wm. B. Beach, do
John J. Flournoy Esqr, do
Henry E. Watkins Esqr, Farmville
John Robertson, do
Col. Wm. S. Morton, do
M. H. Steger, do

Doctr. James Agnew, Burkeville
Wm. Berkeley, Court House
C. C. Burton, Farmville
Doctr Joel W. Dupuy, Court House
Wm. Maxwell, do
R. K. Watkins, do
Booker Foster, Sandy River Church
Capt. John Stevens, Court House
James D. Walthall, James Town
Frs. N. Watkins, Esqr, Farmville
James A. Lindsey, Prospect
Jacob R. Angel, Farmville
Sam C. Hooton, Farmville
Stephen Shepard, James Town
Peter Gibbs, do
Richmond Shepard, do
Wm. C. Rudd, Sandy River Church
Stephen R. Godsey, James Town
Lewis M. Carter, Farmville
Wm. J. Owen, Court House
Allen Cockreham, Burkeville
Jacob W. Morton, Farmville
Venable Crute, Sandy River Church
Thomas H. White, James Town
John H. Armstead, Farmville
John N. Robertson, do
Charles Thackston, do
Thos Stratton, do
John Dupuy, Esqr, do
Wm S. White, James Town
Thomas Branch, Burkeville
Thomas Vaughan Jr., Burkeville
Edmund Wiltse, Farmville
Saml. B. Bruce, Sandy River Church
James Mickle, Walkers Church
Doctr. B. F. Wilson, Farmville
Thos. Vernon, do
Christr. C. Phillips, Burkeville
Jared Todd, Court House
Malcom Currie, Farmville
Alex. Bruce, do
G. B. Wright, do
John M. Anderson, Court House
David Flournoy, do
Capt. Josiah M. Rice, do
Thos. G. Lindsey, Prospect
John P. King, Cumberland Co.
John G. Adams, Farmville
Wyatt Whitehead, Court House
Tazewell S. Morton, Farmville
Hugh F. Morton, Court House
John M. Price, do
Wm R. Wright, address not known
Thos S. Morton, Farmville

Joel B. Mottley, Burkeville
Wiltshire M. Lewis, Court House
Joseph Davidson, do
Creed T. Nunnally, do
Doctr. James H. Lacy, Marble Hill
Elijah H. Irvine, Court House
Abner P. Biglow, Farmville
J. W. Brightwell, do } joint tenants
Sam. Croxton
Green L. Wren, Midway Inn
Joseph Todd, Court House
Wm. D. Baker, Farmville
Thos. B. Phillips, do
Edward F. Booker, Marble Hill
Revd. Isaac Cockreham, Court House
Giles Harris, Prospect
Thomas Wise, Court House
James R. Harper, Burkeville
Doctr. John P. Mettauer, Court House
John Walthall, do
Jerh. Porter, Farmville
Wm. C. Bell, Midway Inn
Alexr Marshall, Sandy River Church
Albert G. Green, Marble Hill
Saml. M. Fuqua, address not known
Benj. C. Peters, Court House
John Shepherd, James Town
George W. Lockett, Esqr, do
Joel J. Scott, Court House
Price Parcils, Farmville
Doctr. Benj. F. Terry, Court House
Anderson Croxton, Marble Hill
James L. Dupuy, Court House
Matthew Lyle, Marble Hill
Jesse Thomason, Sandy River Church
W. E. Noble, James Town
Wm. Bryant, Court House
Peter Partin, Farmville
Wm. McCormack, address not known
John Rudd, Sandy River Church
Saml. G. Osborn, James Town
Christr. C. Lockett, Court House
Douglas Baker, do
Henry P. Davis, Prospect
Francis J. Mettauer, Court House
Matthew V. Rice, Farmville
B. M. Robertson, do
Benj. Overton, James Town
Nathl. Jackson, Court House
Wilson Woodrough, address not known
J. B. Lankford, Farmville
John V. Miller, address not known
Edward A. Carter, Court House
Robert Bowman, Marble Hill

John P. Womack, Court House
Wm. D. Nash, do
Tarlton Woodson, Prospect
Nathl. M. Mottley, James Town
Creed P. Harper, do
James R. Whitehead, Court House
Vincent Phillips, Esqr, Burkeville
Mimarah Noble, James Town
Thos. E. Perkinson, do
Wm. H. Price, Court House
Wm. Seay, do
Nelson K. Crute, Sandy River Church
Chs E. Chappell, Farmville
Wm. A. Armes, James Town
Mackness Ship, Burkeville
James D. Ligon, Sandy River Church
George R. Mottley, Farmville
Chs. A. Morton, do
Thos. Flournoy, Esqr, Charlotte Co.
John P. Binford, Court House
Thos. Lipford, do
John C. Mottley, James Town
Col. Saml. D. Burke, Burkeville
Thos. E. Scott, do
Francis T. Woodson, do
Alanson A. Ellington, do
Wm. A. Womack, Court House
Beverly Cox, do
David M. Wallace, Cumberland Co.
David Comfort, Charlotte Co.
John P. Hawkins, Farmville
Edward B. Miller, Burkeville
Joseph Berry, James Town
Doctr, Merrit B. Allen, Prospect
Doctr. Saml. V. Watkins, Court House
Thos. T. Morgan, do
Wm. F. Ellington, Burkeville
Obd. Childress, Court House
Joseph W. Davidson, do
Obd. Morton, Farmville
Armstead B. Waddell, address not known
Saml. T. Clark, Prospect
Abm. M. Venable, Walkers Church
Henry A. Walthall, Court House
Richd. G. Chappell, Farmville
Frs. H. Williams, Court House
Alexr. S. Dillon, Farmville
Capt. Nathl. Jones, Court House
Gordon McCune, do
Revd. Saml. Mills, do

Doctr. Peyton R. Berkeley, do
Henry A. Morgan, do
F. W. Smith, Farmville
James H. Dupuy, Marble Hill
John A. Cobbs, Court House
John McGehee, Sandy River Church
Benj. Oliver, Midway Inn
George W. Vaughan, James Town
Robt. G. Branch, Court House
Richard M. Dillon, Farmville
James D. Wood Esqr, do
Wm. H. Venable, do
Edward M. Booker, do
Jacob Price, Court House
Joseph E. Venable, Farmville
R. H. Burruss, Burkeville
Wm. P. Hunt, Charlotte Co.
Doctr. J. Vaughan, Sandy River Church
Edward J. Erambert, Farmville
James B. Mills, Court House
Isaac Read, do
Aaron J. Lindsey, Prospect
Edward T. Price, address not known
Thos. T. Craghead, Court House
John Brown, Farmville
Joshua Routon, Prospect
Col. John Clark, Sandy River Church
Watkins Dupuy, Court House
Benj. Spain, do
Matthew Carter, Prospect
George R. Jeffries, Farmville
David F. Womack, Court House
Thos. E. Haskins, Esqr, do
Thos. B. Rice, Farmville
Stephen B. Farrar, Court House
Charles C. Wade, Sandy River Church
Pleasant Baldwin, Walkers Church
Thos. M. Ewing, Court House
Meredith E. Hurt, address not known
Col. Henry Thweatt, Court House
Jonathan Penick, Farmville
John Long, do
Thomas B. Wootton, do
Edward Armes, Court House
Alpheus M. Jones, do
Joseph N. Daniel, Lunenburg Co.
John A. Scott, Esqr, Sandy River
  Church
Thos. W. Arms, Court House
Richd. Garrett, Sandy River Church

George O. Scott, Court House   Saml. J. Hurt,   do
Asa D. Dickinson, Esqr, do   Col. Asa Dupuy, Marble Hill
Edwin Y. Price, Farmville   Elisha B. Thweatt ⎱ joint tenants
Anderson E. Scott, Court House   James M. Johns   ⎰
Rowland Anderson, do   Pitts[ylvani]a County
Revd. George A. Baxter, do   Buck[ingha]m County

Mr. Worsham was meticulous in giving the proper militia rank to all officers
with the rank of captain and above; according to the practice of the time, he
designated justices of the county court and practicing attorneys as esquire. Ministers and physicians were also given their titles. Persons listed as residents of other
counties were qualified to vote in Prince Edward because they were freeholders
(property owners) in this county. Joint tenants in a piece of property were
entitled to one vote for the property. Among the less obvious abbreviations of
names are Obd. for Obadiah, Christr for Christopher, Jerh. for Jeremiah, Chs for
Charles, Frs for Francis, Archd for Archibald, Ro. for Robert, Clabn. for Claiborne.

Persons voting the Democratic ticket and marked by a star were active
party workers.

APPENDIX 4

THE COUNTY COURT: JUSTICES

At January Court, 1754: John Nash, Sr., David Flournoy, John Nash, Jr.,
George Walker, Joseph Morton, James Wimbish.

Commission, Nov., 1754: John Nash, George Walker, Charles Anderson,
Joseph Morton, James Wimbish, Abraham Venable, Joel Watkins, David Flournoy, John Nash, Jr., Thomas Scott, Samuel Ewing, Thomas Haskins.

Commission, Aug. 1757: John Nash, James Wimbish, Joel Watkins, David
Flournoy, John Nash, Jr., Thomas Scott, Samuel Ewing, Thomas Haskins, Robert
Hastie, James Scott, Peter LeGrand, John Leigh.

Commission, 1758: John Nash, James Wimbish, Joel Watkins, John Nash, Jr.,
Thomas Scott, Samuel Ewing, Thomas Haskins, Robert Hastie, James Scott, Peter
LeGrand, John Leigh, Henry Watkins, John Morton.

Commission, Oct., 1761: Abraham Venable, Abner Nash, Charles Venable,
Nathaniel Venable, Benjamin Haskins added to the commission.

Commission, Nov., 1766: John Nash, Abraham Venable, Joel Watkins, John
Nash, Jr., Thomas Scott, Thomas Haskins, James Scott, Peter LeGrand, John
Leigh, Henry Watkins, Peter Johnston, John Morton, Abner Nash, Charles
Venable, Nathaniel Venable, Benjamin Haskins, William Booker, Philemon
Holcomb.

July, 1776, qualified under Constitution of the Commonwealth of Virginia:
John Nash (formerly identified as Jr.), Thomas Scott, Thomas Haskins, Peter
LeGrand, Nathaniel Venable, Benjamin Haskins, William Booker, Philemon
Holcomb.

1776 (new commission): John Nash, Thomas Scott, Thomas Haskins, Peter
LeGrand, James Scott, Benjamin Haskins, William Booker, Philemon Holcomb,

John Morton, Thomas Flournoy, William Bibb, John Clarke, Jacob Woodson, John Watson, Robert Goode, Thomas Scott, Jr.

The date given is that on which the justice qualified:

Charles Allen, June, 1781.
William Wooton, June, 1781.
Richard Foster, Jan., 1782.
Joseph Moore, June, 1782.

Commission of May, 1785: John Nash, Jr., Thomas Scott, Thomas Haskins, Peter LeGrand, John Morton, Charles Venable, Benjamin Haskins, Philemon Holcombe, Thomas Flournoy, William Bibb, John Clarke, Jacob Woodson, John Watson, Joseph Moore, Charles Allen, Richard Foster, William Wooton, Richard Winn, Richard Bibb, James Allen, Sr., Thomas Watkins, Thomas Gibson.

Additions, June, 1787: John Holcombe, Samuel W. Venable, Tarlton Woodson, John Fontaine.

Additions, Nov., 1791: James Morton, Peter Johnston, John Lamkin Crute, William Price, Jr., Robert Kelso, John Purnall.

The date is that of qualification for the office of a magistrate:

July, 1795: Archer Allen, Samuel Carter, John Booker, Samuel Baldwin, Alexander Marshall.

Oct., 1798: Augustus Watson, Josiah Perkinson, Samuel Watkins, Edmund Lockett, Robert Venable.

Feb., 1805: Osborn Lockett, Thomas A. Morton, Thomas Scott (son of James Scott), Edward Dillon.

Jan., 1807: Jesse Wootton, Armistead Miller, Richard K. Randolph.

Feb., 1807: James Ming.

Dec. 1809-Sept., 1810: Thomas A. Morton, Nathaniel Price, Samuel Wootton, Francis Watkins, Jr., Charles Woodson, John James Flournoy.

Dec., 1810: Anderson P. Miller, Zachariah Rice, Rezen Porter, John Clarke.

Nov., 1811: John Booker.

May, 1816: William L. Venable.

Oct., Nov., Dec., 1816: Jesse Michaux, Samuel V. Allen, Asa Dupuy, John Booth, Moses Tredway, Jack Vaughan, James D. Wood, James Madison.

Aug.-Oct., 1821: Lillious D. Womack, William Doswell, William T. Wootton, William Mathews, Augustus Watkins, Thomas A. LeGrand, Thomas E. Haskins.

July, 1825: Joseph Redd, Henry Thweatt, Abraham L. Venable, Robert Venable, Jr., Vincent Phillips, James Wilson.

Mar., 1826: Henry E. Watkins.

Nov., 1827: Samuel D. Burke, Edmund Booker.

1830: James W. Womack, Thomas E. Perkinson, James McDearmon, Joseph Todd.

Dec., 1832: John Rice.

1833: Richard Booker, Paschal L. Ligon, William Trent, Thomas Flournoy, William S. Morton, Thomas C. Overton.

1836: Frederick Hobson, C. C. Read, Nathaniel Jones, John W. Redd, John A. Scott.

1840: John Dupuy, Joel W. Womack, James Venable, Joel Elam, Luther C. Jeffress, Henry S. Guthrie, James McDearmon.

Jan., 1841: Francis T. Wootton.

1843: Thomas Clark, David F. Womack, Newton Cunningham, James Cobbs, Benjamin W. Womack.

Oct., 1845: William Brightwell, Albert G. Green, Joseph E. Venable, Thomas H. Venable, George W. Clibourn, Clement R. Barksdale.

Branch J. Worsham prepared the following list of justices whose terms of office were terminated July 31, 1852, under the Constitution of 1850-1: John Clark, Jesse Michaux, Moses Tredway, Lillious D. Womack, William T. Wootton, Thomas E. Haskins, Henry E. Watkins, Joseph Redd, Vincent Phillips, Samuel D. Burke, Clement C. Read, Nathaniel Jones, John W. Redd, John A. Scott, Joel W. Womack, James Venable, Joel Elam, Henry S. Guthrey, Francis T. Wootton, Thomas Clark, David F. Womack, Newton Cunningham, James Cobbs, Benjamin W. Womack, William Brightwell, Albert G. Green, Joseph E. Venable, George W. Clibourn, Thomas H. Venable, Clement R. Barksdale.

Elected in 1852: Francis T. Wootton, John A. Scott, Thomas Clark, Giles A. Miller, Henry S. Guthrey, Thomas E. Haskins, John W. Redd, Robert S. Carter, Newton Cunningham, David F. Womack, John T. Carter, Thomas T. Tredway, William Brightwell, John A. Dalby, Charles A. Morton, Robert V. Davis, Joel W. Womack, Clement C. Read, H. E. Warren, Francis P. Wood.

1853:	William B. Baker.	1856:	James S. Lockett.
1854:	James Whitehead.	1858:	Samuel S. Baker.
1855:	Joseph T. Morton.	1859:	Edwin J. Redd.

Elected in 1860: Robert V. Davis, Richard W. Price, William T. Lee, Thomas B. Rice, Joseph T. Ligon, Robert C. Anderson, John P. Hughes, James E. Flippen, Richard B. Thackston, James T. Gray, James Whitehead, James S. Lockett, Charles A. Morton, Edwin J. Redd, James B. Ely, William T. Carter, Samuel S. Baker, Samuel B. Scott, John A. Dalby, David F. Womack.

Elected in 1864: John P. Hughes, Edwin J. Redd, James T. Gray, William J. Porter, James S. Lockett, Robert C. Anderson, James J. Rice, John W. Jones, Richard A. Booker, William T. Carter, Richard W. Price, Charles A. Morton, Joseph T. Ligon, James Whitehead, John A. Dalby, Richard B. Thackston, Samuel B. Scott, Samuel S. Baker, John T. Johnson, David F. Womack.

Elected in 1865: William T. Carter, James B. Ely, R. C. Anderson, James Whitehead, Richard W. Price, Edwin J. Redd, Samuel S. Baker, Richard B. Thackston, Richard S. Paulett, James T. Gray, John A. Dalby, John P. Hughes, Charles A. Morton, David F. Womack, James J. Rice, Howell E. Warren, Robert V. Davis, Samuel B. Scott, James S. Lockett.

Appointed by military authority, 1869: R. S. Hines, W. S. Berry, Henry T. Owen, John Carpenter.

The County Court of Justices was abolished by the Constitution of 1868 and replaced by a County Court of one judge; the new court held its first session April 18, 1870.

APPENDIX 5

THE COUNTY COURT: JUDGES

Francis Nathaniel Watkins (Apr. 15, 1870-Feb., 1880)
Joseph Marshall Crute (Feb. 7, 1880-Feb. 15, 1886)
Asa Dickinson Watkins (Feb., 1886-Dec., 1891)
Joseph Marshall Crute (Dec. 24, 1891-Jan. 28, 1904)

APPENDIX 6

THE CIRCUIT COURT

The order books of the District Court do not list the presiding judge. The oldest order book of the Circuit Court is called Superior Circuit Court Order Book and is for the years 1831-46. The judges of the Circuit Court since the September, 1831, term have been, with the dates of the first and last terms held by the judge:

William Leigh (Sept., 1831[1]-Sept., 1857[2])
Hunter H. Marshall (Mar. 1858[2]-Sept. 1868[3])
Philip A. Bolling (First orders signed Apr. 23, 1869, in vacation; Aug. 1869[4]-1870[5])
Asa D. Dickinson (Aug., 1870[5]-Mar., 1884[6])
Francis D. Irving (Sept., 1884[7]-Sept., 1891[8])
Samuel F. Coleman (Mar., 1892[9]-Mar., 1898[10])
George J. Hundley (Sept., 1898[11]-1923[12])
Robert F. Hutcheson (April, 1924[13]-Nov., 1939[14])
Joel W. Flood (Feb., 1940[15]-   )

---

[1] Circuit Superior Court Order Book, 1831-46: 1.
[2] Circuit Superior Court Order Book, 1847-58: 370.
[3] Chancery Orders, Circuit Court, 1859-72: 259.
[4] Chancery Orders, Circuit Court, 1859-72: 262, 263.
[5] Chancery Orders, Circuit Court, 1859-72: 330.
[6] Law Orders, 1870-94: 412.
[7] Law Orders, 1870-94: 413.
[8] Law Orders, 1870-94: 572.
[9] Law Orders, 1870-94: 577.
[10] Law Orders, 1894-1909: 48.
[11] *Ibid.*
[12] Law Orders 7: 311: Governor E. Lee Trinkle appointed Judge Turner Clement to preside over court June 19, 1923, on account of the illness of Judge Hundley.
[13] Law Orders 7: 390.
[14] Law Orders 10: 19-21.
[15] Law Orders 10: 42.

APPENDIX 7

COUNTY OFFICERS

Clerks

John LeNeve (Jan., 1754-Mar., 1783)
Francis Watkins (Apr. 1783-July, 1825)
Branch J. Worsham (July, 1825-Jan. 26, 1869)
Joseph Jorgenson (March, 1869-Apr. 18, 1870)
Branch Worsham (Apr. 18, 1870-Dec. 31, 1870)
Joseph Jorgenson (Jan. 1, 1871-Oct. 17, 1871)
Branch Worsham (Oct. 17-Dec. 31, 1871)

Henry R. Hooper (Jan. 1, 1872-June, 1893)
W. P. Gilliam (July 1, 1893-Jan. 2, 1895)
W. H. Thackston (Jan. 2, 1895-July 31, 1900)
E. J. Whitehead (Aug., 1900-May 4, 1907)
Horace Adams (May, 1907-   )

King's Attorneys

Clement Read (Jan., 1754-Dec., 1755)
Thomas Nash (Jan., 1756-Sept., 1757)
Clement Read, Jr. (Sept., 1757-Nov., 1770)
George Walker, Jr. (Nov., 1770-July, 1776)

Deputy Attorney General

George Walker, Jr. (July, 1776-1784)
Robert Lawson (1784-April, 1788)
(After 1785, Deputy Attorney for the Commonwealth)
Abraham Bedford Venable (April, 1788-May, 1789)
Joseph Venable (June, 1789-June, 1810)
Samuel L. Lockett (1810)

Commonwealth's Attorney

Henry E. Watkins (Oct., 1810-Apr., 1813)
Samuel Branch (Apr., 1813-June, 1846)
William C. Flournoy (1846-1860)
John T. Thornton (1860-62)
Stephen O. Southall (1864-66)
Philip W. McKinney (1866-April, 1869)
Samuel M. Page (April, 1869-April, 1870)
Philip W. McKinney (April, ——-Dec., 1870)
Edgar Allan (Jan. 1, 1871-Mar. 31, 1883)
Philip W. McKinney (Apr., ——-June 30, 1883)
W. G. Forbes (July 1, 1883-Feb. 15, 1886)
Philip W. McKinney (Feb. 22, 1886-June 30, 1887)
R. B. Berkeley (July 1, 1887-June 30, 1891)
Asa D. Watkins (July 1, 1891-Apr. 14, 1938)
Frank N. Watkins (1938-   )

Sheriffs

John Nash, Jr. (1754-56)
David Flournoy (1757)
James Wimbish (1758-9)
John Nash, Sr. (1760-1)
Joel Watkins (1762-3)
Thomas Scott (1764-5)
Thomas Haskins (1766-7)
James Scott (1768-9)
Peter LeGrand (1770-1)
John Leigh (1772-3)
Henry Watkins (1774-5)
John Morton (Jan.-Feb., 1776)
Charles Venable (Feb. 1776-7)
John Morton (1778)
Charles Venable 1779-81)

Benjamin Haskins (1782-3)
Philemon Holcombe (1784-5)
Thomas Flournoy (1786-7)
William Bibb (1788-9)
John Clarke (1790-1)
Jacob Woodson (1792-3)
John Watson (1794-5)
Charles Allen (1796-7)
Richard Foster (1798-9)
Tarlton Woodson (1800-1)
James Morton (1802-3)
John Purnall (1804-5)
William Price, Jr. (1806-7)
Robert Kelso (1808-9)
Archer Allen (1810-1811)

Samuel Carter (Feb., 1811-13)
John Booker (1814-5)
Samuel Baldwin (1816-7)
Jacob Woodson (1818-9)
Samuel Watkins (1820-1)
Edmund Lockett (1822-3)
Josiah Perkinson (1824-5)
Robert Venable, Sr. (1826)
James Morton (1827-8)
Osborn Lockett (1829-30.)
Thomas Scott (1831-2)

Robert Kelso (1833-4)
Nathaniel Price (1835-6)
Charles Woodson (1837)
John J. Flournoy (1838-9)
John Clark (1840-1)
Jesse Michaux (1842-3)
Asa Dupuy (1844-5)
Moses Tredway (1846-7)
Jack Vaughan (1848-9)
Lillious D. Womack (1850-1)
William T. Wootton (1852)

Hilary G. Richardson (July 1, 1852-June 30, 1854)
Newton Cunningham (1854-58)
Henry B. Brightwell (1858-62)
George W. Booker (1862-69)
Benjamin M. Cox (1869-70)
George W. Booker (April-Dec. 1870)
Henry R. Hooper (Jan. 1-Dec. 31, 1871)
William H. Wilkerson (Jan. 16, 1872-Dec. 31, 1873)
Wiltshire Cardwell (Jan. 1, 1874-Dec. 22, 1874)
Thomas H. Dickinson (Dec. 22, 1874-June 30, 1875)
C. H. Bliss, Jr. (July 1, 1875-June 30, 1891)
Thomas H. Dickinson (July 1, 1891-Sept. 30, 1915)
Thomas H. Bruce (Nov., 1915-Apr. 30, 1920)
John A. Clark (May, 1920- 1944)
James T. Clark (Mar. 17, 1944-)

Commissioners of Revenue

John Morton, Richard Foster (1786)
John Morton, Thomas Watkins (1787.)
John Morton, Charles Allen (-1792)
John Morton, John Booker (1792-6)
John Booker, Thomas Green (1796-1813)
Thomas Green, Samuel V. Allen (1813-4)
Thomas Green, Abner Nash (1816)
Thomas Green, John Booker (1818)
John Booker, John P. Green (1819-20)
John P. Green (1820-6)
James Foster (1826-39)
Watkins Dupuy (1839-64)
John R. Cunningham (1864-69)
James Mickle (1869-70)
John R. Cunningham (1870-71)
J. L. Richardson (July 1, 1875-June 30, 1883)
James E. Harris (1883-91)
E. T. Clark (1891-5)
W. L. Clark (1895-9)
R. J. Carter (1899-1907)
E. L. Dupuy (1908-39)
Vernon C. Womack (1940-)

Treasurers

> Edwin J. Redd (Jan. 1, 1871-Dec. 31, 1873)
> Samuel H. Bliss (1874-June 30, 1891)
> W. H. Ewing (July 1, 1891-Dec. 31, 1907)
> S. W. Watkins (1908-27)
> S. W. Watkins, Jr. (1927-45)
> J. W. Wilson, Jr. (1945-   )

APPENDIX 8

THE BOARD OF SUPERVISORS

(Compiled from the Minute Books of the Board of Supervisors)

Chairmen of the Board

> (The date is that of election)
> R. J. Matthews (Aug. 2, 1870)
> B. S. Hooper (July 28, 1871)
> C. H. Bliss (Oct. 10, 1873)
> F. W. Holman (July 27, 1885)
> W. H. Ewing (July 25, 1887)
> J. M. Venable (Aug: 30, 1889)
> R. M. Burton (Aug. 14, 1891)
> E. L. Dupuy (Sept. 12, 1903)
> A. A. Haskins (Jan. 6, 1908, declined to serve)
> J. L. Hart (Jan. 6, 1908)
> R. W. Fuqua (Apr. 23, 1915)
> F. H. Kauffman (Jan. 5, 1920)
> J. Ashby Armistead (Jan. 8, 1932)
> Edward Carter (Mar. 3, 1950)

Buffalo District

> R. J. Matthews (Aug. 2, 1870-June 30, 1871)
> George W. Scott (July 1, 1871-June 30, 1875)
> R. N. Wilkerson (July 1, 1875-June 30, 1877)
> George W. Scott (July 1, 1877-Dec. 31, 1903)
> R. Lee Price (Jan. 1, 1904-Dec. 31, 1907)
> R. W. Fuqua (Jan. 1, 1908-Dec. 31, 1919)
> W. W. Swan (Jan. 1, 1920-Dec. 31, 1939)
> Roach A. Watson (Jan. 1, 1940-Aug., 1950)
> T. D. Dillon (Sept. 7, 1950-   )

Farmville District

> B. S. Hooper (Aug. 2, 1870-June 30, 1873)
> C. H. Bliss (July 1, 1873-June 30, 1885)
> F. W. Holman (July 1, 1885-1887)
> P. C. Bolling (Oct. 11, 1887-June 30, 1889)
> R. M. Burton (July 1, 1889-July 18, 1903)
> L. J. Verser (Sept. 12, 1903-Dec. 31, 1907)

J. L. Hart (Jan. 1, 1908-Apr. 23, 1915, resigned to become postmaster of Farmville)
N. B. Davidson (Apr. 23, 1915-June 30, 1918)
J. Ashby Armistead (July 12, 1918-Feb., 1950)
James H. Clark (Mar. 3, 1950-Oct., 1954)
John G. Bruce (Oct., 1954-)

Hampden District

F. D. Redd (Aug. 2, 1870-June 30, 1871)
John M. Venable (July 1, 1871-June 30, 1875)
E. J. Redd (July 1, 1875-June 30, 1877)
John M. Venable (July 1, 1877-June 30, 1885)
F. D. Redd (July 1, 1885-June 30, 1889)
John M. Venable (July 1, 1889-June 30, 1899)
E. L. Dupuy (July 1, 1899-Dec. 31, 1907, resigned to become Commissioner of Revenue)
W. M. Holladay (Jan. 1, 1908-Dec. 31, 1913)
R. E. Stokes (Jan. 1, 1914-Dec. 31, 1915)
W. A. McCraw (Jan. 1, 1916-Dec. 31, 1931)
Edward Carter (Jan. 1, 1932-)

Leigh District

W. H. Ewing (Aug. 2, 1870-1872)
S. W. Sellers (Nov. 12, 1872-1882)
W. H. Ewing (July 25, 1882-June 30, 1891)
J. J. Green (July 1, 1891-June 30, 1893)
J. Walter Davis (July 1, 1893-Oct., 1895)
A. A. Haskins (Oct. 12, 1895-1910)
F. H. Kauffman (July 8, 1910-Dec. 31, 1931)
H. E. Boswell (Jan. 1, 1932-1944)
George W. Palmer (Feb. 5, 1944-Dec. 31, 1950, resigned to enter State Senate)
Robert B. Wilson, Jr. (Jan. 6, 1950-Nov. 24, 1954)
Hugh M. Jenkins (Dec., 1954-)

Lockett District

F. W. Southall (Dec. 1870-1875)
Edward Thompson (Nov. 16, 1875-June 30, 1877)
J. X. Morton (July 1, 1877-1882)
B. H. Carter (Oct. 10, 1882-June 30, 1887)
Anthony Green (July 1, 1887-June 30, 1889)
B. H. Carter (July 1, 1889-June 30, 1895)
W. H. Hubbard (July 1, 1895-June 30, 1901)
J. R. Weaver (July 1, 1901-Dec. 31, 1903)
W. H. Hubbard (Jan. 1, 1904-Dec. 31, 1907)
R. H. Walton (Jan. 1, 1908-Dec. 31, 1911)
W. H. Hubbard (Jan. 1, 1912-Dec. 31, 1913)
James T. Clark (Jan. 5, 1914-1920)
W. Basil Bruce (Dec. 22, 1920-Dec. 31, 1925, resigned to enter House of Delegates)
R. B. Walthall (Jan. 1, 1926-Dec. 31, 1947)
C. W. Gates (Jan. 1, 1948-)

Prospect District

    R. W. Fuqua (Jan. 1, 1921-Dec. 31, 1927)
    W. H. Glenn (Jan. 1, 1928-Dec. 31, 1939)
    J. H. Wilkerson (Jan. 1, 1940-Dec. 31, 1943)
    W. H. Glenn (Jan. 1, 1944-Dec. 31, 1947)
    W. W. Vaughan (Jan. 1, 1948-   )

APPENDIX 9

THE VIRGINIA GENERAL ASSEMBLY

The House of Burgesses

    John Nash, Charles Anderson (1754-8)
    Charles Anderson, Peter LeGrand (1758-61)
    Peter LeGrand, Abner Nash (1761-64)
    Peter LeGrand, Nathaniel Venable (1765-68)
    Thomas Scott, Peter Johnston (1769)
    Thomas Scott, Paschal Greenhill (1769-71)
    Paschal Greenhill, Peter LeGrand (1772-4)
    Peter LeGrand, William Bibb (1775)

The Revolutionary Conventions

    Robert Lawson, John Nash (March, 1775)
    Robert Lawson, William Bibb (July, December, 1775)
    William Watts, William Booker (May, 1776)

The House of Delegates

Compiled from *Register of the General Assembly of Virginia 1776-1918 and of the Constitutional Conventions* by Earl G. Swen and John W. Williams and *The General Assembly of the Commonwealth of Virginia 1919-39* by E. Griffith Dodson.

The county had two delegates 1776-1830. The dates note the beginning of the first session and the end of the last session of which the pair were members.

William Watts, William Booker (Oct. 7-Dec. 12, 1776)
William Booker, John Morton, Thomas Flournoy (May 5, 1777-Jan. 24, 1778)
John Nash, Robert Lawson (May 4, 1778-Dec. 19, 1778)
Thomas Flournoy, William Bibb (May 3-Dec. 24, 1779)
William Bibb, Robert Lawson (May 1, 1780-Mar. 22, 1781)
Joseph Moore, Thomas Flournoy (May 7, 1781-Jan. 5, 1782)
John Holcombe, James Allen, Robert Lawson (May-Dec. 28, 1782)
Robert Lawson, Richard Bibb (May 5-Dec. 22, 1783)
Richard Bibb, John Clarke, William Bibb (May 3, 1784-Jan. 7, 1785)
Richard Bibb, John Clarke (Oct. 17, 1785-Jan. 21, 1786)
John Clarke, Richard Bibb (Oct. 16, 1786-Jan. 11, 1787)
Patrick Henry, Robert Lawson (Oct. 15, 1787-Jan. 8, 1788)
Tarlton Woodson, Patrick Henry (June 23, 1788-Dec. 29, 1790)
John Purnal, Tarlton Woodson (Oct. 17-Dec. 20, 1791)
Peter Johns[t]on, John Purnall (Oct. 1, 1792-Dec. 12, 1793)

John Purnall, Tarlton Woodson (Nov. 11-Dec. 27, 1794)
James Wade, John Purnall, Thomas Molloy[1] (Nov. 10-Dec. 29, 1795)
John Purnall, James Wade, Jr.[2] (Nov. 8-Dec. 27, 1796)
Richard N. Venable, Charles Scott (Dec. 4, 1797-Jan. 25, 1798)
Peter Johnston, John Purnall (Dec. 3, 1798-Jan. 20, 1799)
Peter Johnston, Charles Scott (Dec. 2, 1799-Jan. 28, 1800)
Peter Johnston, Abraham B. Venable (Dec. 1, 1800-Jan. 29, 1803)
Abraham B. Venable, John Booker, Peter Johnston[3] (Dec. 5, 1803-Feb. 6, 1804)
Peter Johnston, John Booker (Dec. 3, 1804-Feb. 1, 1805)
Samuel Carter, Peter Johnston (Dec. 2, 1805-Feb. 6, 1806)
Peter Johnston,[4] John Purnall (Dec. 1, 1806-Feb. 10, 1808)
John Purnel (Purnall), Tarlton Woodson (Dec. 5, 1808-Feb. 18, 1809)
John Purnall, Archer Womack (Dec. 4, 1809-Feb. 1, 1810)
Peter Johnston, John Purnall (Dec. 3, 1810-Feb. 14, 1811)
Charles Woodson, John Purnall (Dec. 2, 1811-Feb. 21, 1812)
Henry E. Watkins, John Purnall (Nov. 30, 1812-Feb. 23, 1813)
Edward Booker, William Lindsey (May 17, 1813-Feb. 22, 1817)
John Clarke, John J. Flournoy (Dec. 1, 1817-Mar. 13, 1819)
Edward Booker, Henry E. Watkins (Dec. 6, 1819-Feb. 25, 1820)
Richard N. Venable, Asa Dupuy, Henry E. Watkins[5] (Dec. 4, 1820-Mar. 5, 1821)
Asa Dupuy, John Clarke (Dec. 3, 1821-Mar. 4, 1822)
Henry E. Watkins, Asa Dupuy (Dec. 2, 1822-Mar. 9, 1827)
Stephen C. Farrar, Asa Dupuy (Dec. 3, 1827-Mar. 1, 1828)
Asa Dupuy, Samuel C. Anderson (Dec. 1, 1828-Feb. 17, 1829)
Asa Dupuy, James Dillon (Dec. 7, 1829-Feb. 23, 1830)

From 1830 until 1865 Prince Edward had one delegate.

Richard N. Venable (Dec. 6, 1830-Feb. 19, 1831)
Asa Dupuy (Dec. 5, 1831-Mar. 21, 1832)
Henry E. Watkins (Dec. 3, 1832-Mar. 9, 1833)
Asa Dupuy (Dec. 2, 1833-Mar. 12, 1835)
James Madison (Dec. 7, 1835-Mar. 31, 1837, resigned)[6]
Nathaniel E. Venable (June 12, 1837-Mar. 19, 1840)
Samuel D. Burke (Dec. 1, 1840-Mar. 12, 1841)
James H. Wilson (Dec. 6, 1841-Mar. 26, 1842)
Samuel C. Anderson (Dec. 5, 1842-Feb. 22, 1845)
Samuel D. McDearmon (Dec. 1, 1845-Mar. 6, 1846)
Samuel C. Anderson (Dec. 7, 1846-Mar. 23, 1847)[7]
Benjamin W. Womack (Dec. 6, 1847-Apr. 4, 1848)
William T. Wootton (Dec. 4, 1848-Mar. 22, 1850)
William C. Flournoy (Dec. 2, 1850-Mar. 31, 1851)
William C. Flournoy, James H. Wilson, Stephen O. Southall[8] (Jan. 12, 1852-Apr. 11, 1853)
Stephen O. Southall (Dec. 5, 1853-Mar. 4, 1854)
Thomas T. Tredway (Dec. 3, 1855-Mar. 19, 1856)
Asa D. Dickinson (Dec. 7, 1857-Apr. 2, 1860)[9]
Richard A. Booker (Jan. 7-Apr. 4, 1861)
Thomas T. Tredway (Dec. 2, 1861-Mar. 15, 1865)

Prince Edward and Appomattox constituted a district 1865-67.

Francis N. Watkins (Dec. 4, 1865-Apr. 29, 1867)

Prince Edward had one delegate 1869-1923.

T. P. Jackson (Oct. 5, 1869-Mar. 31, 1871)
Joseph Jorgenson (Dec. 6, 1871-Apr. 2, 1873)

Tazewell Branch (Jan. 1, 1874-Apr. 4, 1877)
W. D. Evans (Dec. 5, 1877-Mar. 9, 1880)
N. H. Champlin (Dec. 7, 1881-Apr. 22, 1882)
N. M. Griggs (Dec. 5, 1883-Dec. 1, 1884)
W. P. Dupuy (Dec. 2, 1885-Mar. 6, 1890)
R. M. Burton (Dec. 2, 1891-Mar. 4, 1892)
Colin Stokes (Dec. 6, 1893-Mar. 5, 1896)
Asa D. Watkins (Dec. 1, 1897-Mar. 4, 1898)
John J. Owen (Dec. 6, 1899-Mar. 27, 1908)
W. H. Ewing (Jan. 12, 1910-Mar. 15, 1912)
Dr. Peter Winston (Jan. 14, 1914-Sept. 9, 1919)
E. T. Bondurant (Jan. 14, 1920-Mar. 29, 1923)

Prince Edward and Cumberland constituted a district represented by one delegate 1924-42. The dates are those of the term, sessions of the legislature having begun in January in alternate years beginning in 1904.

E. T. Bondurant (1924-5)
William Basil Bruce (1926-33)
E. W. Sanford (1934-1942, deceased)

Prince Edward and Charlotte have constituted a district represented by one delegate since 1944.

John H. Daniel, of Charlotte (1944-   )

---

[1] Purnall succeeded Molloy, deceased.

[2] It is not certain that this should be James Wade, Jr. The Journal of the House of Delegates for 1796 does not contain a list of members. In one of the votes, Wade is listed as Wade, Jr., in the others Wade. In the list of delegates in the Journal for 1795, he is listed as James Wade. Since it is possible that Jr. in the instance used could have been a clerical error or a misinterpretation of J. Wade and since there is only the one reference to indicate that James Wade, Jr., was a member of this session, this writer is inclined to think the Jr. put in by mistake and that James Wade, who served in the session of 1795 was a delegate again in 1796.

[3] Johnston succeeded Venable, who had been elected to the United States Senate.

[4] Peter Johnston was Speaker of the House, sessions of 1805-6, 1806-7.

[5] Venable succeeded Watkins.

[6] Madison resigned, and Venable was elected to succeed him.

[7] McDearmon was a delegate from the new county of Appomattox, 1846-7.

[8] Southall was elected to succeed Flournoy, resigned.

[9] Dickinson resigned to enter the State Senate.

The State Senate

District: Charlotte, Halifax, Prince Edward—

Paul Carrington (1776-7)	Gideon Spencer (1799-1802)
Walter Coles (1777-80)	Isaac H. Coles (1803-10)
Nathaniel Venable (1780-82)	Joseph Wiatt (Wyatt) (1811-13)
William Hubard (1783-6)	William Rice (1813-14)
John Coleman (1786-90)	John Hill (1815-18)
Paul Carrington (1791-4)	Howson Clark (1819-22)
David Clarke (1795-7)	Joseph Wyatt (1823-9)
George Carrington (1798)	

District: Charlotte, Lunenburg, Nottoway, Prince Edward—

Joseph Wyatt (1830-32)
Henry E. Watkins (1833-34)
Archibald A. Campbell (1835-6)

Louis C. Bouldin (1838-42)
William H. Dennis (1843-50)

District: Lunenburg, Nottoway, Prince Edward—

Thomas H. Campbell (1852-7)
William C. Knight (1859-61)

Asa D. Dickinson (1861-65)

District: Amelia, Chesterfield, Cumberland, Powhatan, Prince Edward—

Christopher C. McRae (1865-7)

District: Charlotte, Prince Edward—

James W. D. Bland (1869-70)

John T. Hamlett (1870-1)

District: Amelia, Cumberland, Prince Edward—

John Robinson (1871-3)
Edgar Allan (1874-7)
C. H. Bliss (1877-87)

N. M. Griggs (1887-90)
Joseph W. Southall (1891-8)
Asa D. Watkins (1899-1904)

District: Amelia, Cumberland, Lunenburg, Nottoway, Prince Edward—

William Hodges Mann (1904-9)
J. J. Owen (1910-11)
Robert K. Brock (1912-5)

George E. Allen (1916-9.)
Louis S. Epes (1920-3)

District: Amelia, Lunenburg, Nottoway, Powhatan, Prince Edward—

Louis S. Epes (1924-5)
Edwin Lawrence Kendig (1926-31)
Hunter H. Watson (1932-5)

Robert K. Brock (1936-47)
William D. Kendig (1948-9)
George W. Palmer (1950-5)

District: Charlotte, Halifax, Prince Edward—

The Conventions

Compiled from the Registers of the General Assembly.

Convention of 1776—William Watts, William Booker.

Convention of 1788, for considering the Federal Constitution—Patrick Henry, Robert Lawson.

Convention of 1829-30 (District of Charlotte, Halifax, and Prince Edward)— John Randolph of Roanoke (Charlotte), William Leigh and Richard Logan of Halifax, and Richard N. Venable of Prince Edward.

Convention of 1850-1 (District of Appomattox, Charlotte, and Prince Edward)— Willis P. Bocock and Thomas H. Flood of Appomattox and Branch J. Worsham of Prince Edward.

Convention of 1861 (Secession)—John T. Thornton.

Convention of 1867-8 (District of Appomattox and Prince Edward)—Edgar Allan and James W. D. Bland of Prince Edward.

Convention of 1901-2—Richard McIlwaine.

Convention of 1933 (to ratify or reject 21st Amendment to the Constitution)— Robert K. Brock (at large from Virginia).

Constitutional Convention of 1945 to amend Constitution for voting by members of the Armed Forces (see *Journal*)—Dr. W. J. Sydnor of Prince Edward (from Ninth Senatorial District).

APPENDIX 10

THE NATIONAL HOUSE OF REPRESENTATIVES

(List of members compiled from the *Biographical Dictionary American Congress, 1774-1949*; districts from the various statutes.)

District (Sixth): Charlotte, Campbell, Buckingham, Bedford, Franklin, Halifax, Henry, Pittsylvania, and Prince Edward Counties.

First Congress (1789-91): Isaac Coles of Halifax. (Coles became a Federalist in the division into parties, later a Democratic-Republican.)

Second Congress (1791-93): Abraham Bedford Venable of Prince Edward. Venable became a Democratic-Republican in the division into parties.)

District: Buckingham, Charlotte, Cumberland, Fluvanna, Prince Edward.

Third Congress (1793-5): Abraham Bedford Venable.

Fourth Congress (1795-7): Abraham Bedford Venable.

Fifth Congress (1797-9): Abraham Bedford Venable.

Sixth Congress (1799-1801): John Randolph of Cumberland (Democratic-Republican).

Seventh Congress (1801-3): John Randolph.

District: Buckingham, Charlotte, Cumberland, Prince Edward.

Eighth Congress (1803-5): John Randolph.

Ninth Congress (1805-7): John Randolph. (About this time Randolph became anti-Jeffersonian in politics.)

Tenth Congress (1807-9): John Randolph (now of Charlotte).

Eleventh Congress (1809-11): John Randolph.

Twelfth Congress (1811-13): John Randolph (anti-war with England).

Thirteenth Congress (1813-15): John W. Eppes of Buckingham (Democratic-Republican, pro war).

Fourteenth Congress (1815-7): John Randolph of Charlotte.

Fifteenth Congress (1817-9): Archibald Austin of Buckingham (only one party at this time: Democratic-Republican).

Sixteenth Congress (1819-21): John Randolph.

Seventeenth Congress (1821-3): John Randolph.

Eighteenth Congress (1823-5): John Randolph.

Nineteenth Congress (1825-7): John Randolph, elected, but resigned effective Dec. 26, 1825, without qualifying for House to enter the United States Senate.

  George W. Crump of Cumberland (Democratic-Republican), elected to succeed Randolph, took seat Feb. 6, 1826.

Twentieth Congress (1827-9: John Randolph.

Twenty-first Congress (1829-31): Thomas T. Bouldin of Charlotte (Democratic-Republican).

Twenty-second Congress (1831-3): Thomas T. Bouldin.

Twenty-third Congress (1833-5): John Randolph, died May 24, 1833.

  Thomas T. Bouldin (anti-Jacksonian), took seat Dec. 3, 1833, died Feb. 11, 1834, while addressing the House.

  James W. Bouldin of Charlotte, took seat Mar. 28, 1834 (pro-Jacksonian Democrat).

Twenty-fourth Congress (1835-7): James W. Bouldin.

Twenty-fifth Congress (1837-9): James W. Bouldin.

Twenty-sixth Congress (1839-41): John Hill of Buckingham (Whig).

Twenty-seventh Congress (1841-3): Edmund W. Hubard of Buckingham (Democrat).

1843: Fourth District: Buckingham, Campbell, Charlotte, Cumberland, Fluvanna, Lunenburg, Prince Edward.

Twenty-eighth Congress (1843-5): Edmund W. Hubard.

(Appomattox included in district.)

Twenty-ninth Congress (1845-7): Edmund W. Hubard.

Thirtieth Congress (1847-9): Thomas S. Bocock of Appomattox (Democrat).

Thirty-first Congress (1849-51): Thomas S. Bocock.

Thirty-second Congress (1851-53): Thomas S. Bocock.

1852: Fourth District: Amelia, Brunswick, Charlotte, Cumberland, Dinwiddie, Lunenburg, Mecklenburg, Nottoway, Petersburg, Powhatan, Prince Edward.

Thirty-third Congress (1853-5): William O. Goode of Mecklenburg (Democrat).

Thirty-fourth Congress (1855-7): William O. Goode.

Thirty-fifth Congress (1857-9): William O. Goode.

Thirty-sixth Congress (1859-61): William O. Goode, deceased July 3, 1859.
 Roger A. Pryor of Petersburg (Democrat), took seat Dec. 7, 1859.

(Confederate Congress: Fifth District: Appomattox, Brunswick, Charlotte, Halifax, Lunenburg, Mecklenburg, Prince Edward.

Thomas S. Bocock of Appomattox, who was Speaker of the Confederate House of Representatives.)

Fifth District: Greene, Albemarle, Fluvanna, Nelson, Buckingham, Amherst, Appomattox, Bedford, Campbell, Lynchburg, and Prince Edward (Richmond *Enquirer*, Apr. 17, 1868).

Forty-first Congress (1869-71): Robert Ridgway of Amherst (Conservative), deceased Oct. 16, 1870.
 Richard T. W. Duke of Charlottesville (Conservative), took seat Dec. 5, 1870.

Forty-second Congress (1871-3): Richard T. W. Duke.

1872: Fourth District: Amelia, Brunswick, Charlotte, Cumberland, Dinwiddie, Greensville, Lunenburg, Mecklenburg, Nottoway, Powhatan, Prince Edward, and city of Petersburg.

Forty-third Congress (1873-5): William H. H. Stowell of Burkeville (Republican).

Forty-fourth Congress (1875-7): William H. H. Stowell.

Forty-fifth Congress (1877-9): Joseph Jorgenson of Petersburg (to which place he had moved from Prince Edward) (Republican).

Forty-sixth Congress (1877-81): Joseph Jorgenson.

Forty-seventh Congress (1881-3): Joseph Jorgenson.

Forty-eighth Congress (1883-5): Benjamin S. Hooper of Farmville (Readjuster).

1884: Fourth District: Amelia, Brunswick, Dinwiddie, Greensville, Lunenburg, Mecklenburg, Nottoway, Powhatan, Prince Edward, Prince George, Sussex, and Petersburg.

Forty-ninth Congress (1885-7): James D. Brady of Petersburg (Republican).

Fiftieth Congress (1887-9): William E. Gaines of Burkeville (Republican).

Fifty-first Congress (1889-91: Edward C. Venable of Petersburg (Democrat), unseated on contest, Sept. 23, 1890.
 John M. Langston of Petersburg (Republican), took seat Sept. 23, 1890.

Fifty-second Congress (1891-2): James F. Epes of Blackstone (Democrat).

Fifty-third Congress (1893-5): James F. Epes.

Fifty-fourth Congress (1895-7): William R. McKenney of Petersburg (Democrat), unseated on contest, May 2, 1896.

Robert T. Thorp of Mecklenburg (Republican), took seat May 2, 1896.

Fifty-fifth Congress (1897-9): Sidney P. Epes of Blackstone (Democrat), unseated on contest Mar. 23, 1898.

Robert T. Thorp, took seat Mar. 23, 1898.

Fifty-sixth Congress (1899-1901): Sidney P. Epes, deceased Mar. 3, 1900.

Francis R. Lassiter of Petersburg (Democrat), took seat Apr. 28, 1900.

Fifty-seventh Congress (1901-3): Francis R. Lassiter.

Fifty-eighth Congress (1903-5): Robert G. Southall of Amelia (Democrat).

Fifty-ninth Congress (1905-7): Robert G. Southall.

1906: Surry added to district as constituted in 1884.

Sixtieth Congress (1907-9): Francis R. Lassiter.

Sixty-first Congress (1909-11): Francis R. Lassiter, deceased Oct. 31, 1909.

Robert Turnbull of Lawrenceville (Democrat), took seat Mar. 16, 1910.

Sixty-second Congress (1911-13): Robert Turnbull.

Sixty-third Congress (1913-15): Walter A. Watson of Jennings Ordinary (Democrat).

Sixty-fourth Congress (1915-17): Walter A. Watson.

Sixty-fifth Congress (1917-19): Walter A. Watson.

Sixty-sixth Congress (1919-21): Walter A. Watson, died Dec. 24, 1919.

Patrick H. Drewry of Petersburg (Democrat), took seat May 10, 1920.

Sixty-seventh Congress (1921-23): Patrick H. Drewry.

Sixty-eighth Congress (1923-5): Patrick H. Drewry.

Sixty-ninth Congress (1925-7): Patrick H. Drewry.

Seventieth Congress (1927-9): Patrick H. Drewry.

Seventy-first Congress (1929-31): Patrick H. Drewry.

Seventy-second Congress (1931-33): Patrick H. Drewry.

The State of Virginia at large.

Seventy-third Congress (1933-5): nine Representatives, including Patrick H. Drewry.

Fourth District: Amelia, Appomattox, Brunswick, Buckingham, Cumberland, Dinwiddie, Greensville, Lunenburg, Mecklenburg, Nottoway, Prince Edward, Prince George, Surry, Sussex, and Petersburg.

Seventy-fourth Congress (1935-7): Patrick H. Drewry.

Seventy-fifth Congress (1937-9): Patrick H. Drewry.

Seventy-sixth Congress (1939-41): Patrick H. Drewry.

Seventy-seventh Congress (1941-3): Patrick H. Drewry.

Seventy-eighth Congress (1943-5): Patrick H. Drewry.

Seventy-ninth Congress (1945-7): Patrick H. Drewry.

Eightieth Congress (1947-9): Patrick H. Drewry, died Dec. 21, 1947.

Watkins M. Abbitt of Appomattox (Democrat), took seat Feb. 26, 1948.

Eighty-first Congress (1949-51): Watkins M. Abbitt.

Eighty-second Congress (1951-3): Watkins M. Abbitt.

Eighty-third Congress (1953-5): Watkins M. Abbitt.

Eighty-fourth Congress (1955-7): Watkins M. Abbitt.

Appendix 11

THE PUBLIC SCHOOLS

Superintendents of Public Schools

(The date is that of the beginning of service.)

Benjamin M. Smith, Hampden-Sydney, 1870
T. W. Crawley, Prospect, July 1, 1882
L. C. Irving, Farmville, 1886
Thomas J. Garden, Prospect, 1890, died June 6, 1903
Joseph D. Eggleston, Worsham, June 27, 1903
John H. Davis, Farmville, July, 1905
P. Tulane Atkinson, Hampden-Sydney, July 1, 1909
Thomas J. McIlwaine, Hampden-Sydney, acting, 1918-19
Thomas J. McIlwaine, 1919.

THE COUNTY SCHOOL BOARD

From the establishment of the public school system in 1870 until 1922 the schools were under the jurisdiction of district school boards. The records of these boards have not been completely preserved, and it is therefore impossible to compile a complete list for this work. The Farmville District records have been preserved, and a complete list of the Farmville District School Boards, compiled from these records is given in Chapter XVI, note 63, of this work.

The lists of members of the county school board and of the school electoral board have been compiled from the Minute Book of the School Electoral Board through the courtesy and assistance of T. J. McIlwaine, superintendent of schools.

Buffalo District

W. B. Binford (1922-28)
W. W. Booker (1928-44)

J. B. Cooke (1944-52)
George D. Shorter (1952-)

Farmville District

Frederick Diehl (1922-31)
R. B. Crawford (1931-46)

Maurice R. Large (1946-54)
L. E. Andrews (1954-)

Hampden District

Edward G. McGehee (1922-33)
Thomas E. Gilmer (1933-34)
D. M. Allan (1934-36)
Thomas E. Gilmer (1936-41)

George L. Walker (1941-50)
Thomas E. Gilmer (1950-51)
Frank W. Spindler (1951-)

Leigh District

J. H. Ward (1922-51)

W. L. Boswell (1951-)

Lockett District

W. S. Weaver (1922-39)
W. L. Vaughan (1939-51)

B. C. Bass (1951-)

Prospect District

T. R. N. Cocks (1922-33)   T. Cook Hix (1941-)
T. Robert Cocks (1933-41)

The Chairmen of the County School Board

Edward G. McGehee (1922-25)   George L. Walker (1946-50)
Frederick Diehl (1925-31)   Maurice R. Large (1950-54)
W. S. Weaver (1931-39)   B. C. Bass (1954-)
R. B. Crawford (1939-46)

The School Electoral Board

The Commonwealth's Attorney (Asa D. Watkins) and the Superintendent
of Schools (T. J. McIlwaine), ex-officio, and one member appointed by
the Circuit Court; Fred M. Bugg (1922-23); Mrs. Genevieve Holladay
(1923-26).

Since 1926 (all members appointed by the Circuit Court):

P. Tulane Atkinson (1926-), chairman
E. S. Shields (1926-50)   B. C. Bass (1949-50)
B. T. Taylor (1926-32)   Dr. J. H. Cocks (1950-)
J. H. Payne (1933-48)   E. T. Bondurant (1950-)

APPENDIX 12

TOWN OFFICIALS OF FARMVILLE

Until 1870 trustees, who had a president and secretary, constituted the
governing board of the town. After 1852 the trustees were elected by popular
vote. Complete lists of the trustees are not available, but lists which have been
preserved are given here.

TRUSTEES:

1798 (named in charter): Charles Scott, Peter Johnston, John Randolph, Jr.,
Philemon Holcombe, Jr., Martin Smith, Blake B. Woodson, Creed Taylor.

1829: Charles Morton, W. L. Morton, James R. Allen, Moses Tredway,
Nathaniel E. Venable, James Madison.

1835: James Madison, president, Frederick Hobson, John Dupuy, Clement C.
Read, James B. Ely, Thomas Hickson, David Bruce.

1839: Clement C. Read, president, Abraham Z. Venable, Willis Blanton,
Edmund Wiltse, James B. Ely, George W. Daniel, Joseph E. Venable.

1841: Clement C. Read, John Dupuy, Edmund Wiltse, P. H. Jackson,
Thomas H. Almond, J. P. Hawkins, Joseph E. Venable.

After 1871 the governing body of Farmville consisted of the mayor and
council. The complete records of the Farmville Town Council have been preserved from 1888. Prior to 1888 lists of town officials have been found in newspapers, and those which have been found are given here. The lists since 1888
are complete; those since 1948 were furnished the writer by Mayor W. C. Fitzpatrick.

Dr. W. W. H. Thackston was Farmville's first mayor. [Order Book, 1870-4, Apr. 18, 1871.] 1873: Major H. R. Hooper, mayor; B. S. Hooper, T. Branch, Edgar Allan, W. D. Evans, W. S. Berry, John S. Holman, B. M. Cox, John W. White, W. Cardwell, council; B. S. Hooper, treasurer; Edgar Allan, clerk; J. W. Overton, chief of fire brigade; Farmville Fire Co.: Z. A. Blanton, captain; A. B. Jenkins, first engineer; F. H. Mottley, second engineer; W. B. Cowan, third engineer; Alert Hook and Ladder Co.: W. H. Kennedy, captain; A. T. Davis, first fireman; E. F. Hilliard, secretary; N. E. Venable, treasurer.

1874: Alert Hook and Ladder Co.: William H. Kennedy, captain; Richard Hawkins, foreman; LeRoy Verser, assistant foreman; H. A. Crute, secretary; N. E. Venable, treasurer.

Major H. R. Hooper, mayor; John S. Holman, town sergeant; B. M. Cox, deputy town sergeant, treasurer, clerk, and deputy town sergeant; William D. Evans, street commissioner; James Bland, lamplighter and scavenger; W. S. Berry, B. S. Hooper, overseers of the poor.

1875 (elected that year): W. W. H. Thackston, mayor; N. E. Venable, treasurer; B. M. Cox, sergeant; W. S. Berry, commissioner of revenue; Capt. P. W. McKinney, Dr. J. L. White, O. T. Wicker, L. C. Butler, S. W. Paulett, B. S. Hooper, W. S. Berry, Jackson Patterson, Richard Burton, councilmen.

The obituary of Dr. Peter Winston (Farmville *Herald*, Feb. 6, 1920) stated that he was the first mayor of Farmville elected on the Democratic ticket.

1882 (from the Farmville *Herald*, Apr. 1, 1898): Council: J. J. Walker, J. T. Gray, P. S. Smithson, J. V. Rice, A. H. Porter, R. M. Burton, L. J. Verser (became a member that year), J. P. Fitzgerald, W. G. Dunnington. (The name of the mayor that year was not listed.)

Mayors since 1888: W. W. H. Thackston, 1888-90; O. T. Wicker, 1890-6; R. M. Burton, 1896-8; W. T. Blanton, 1898-1911; H. E. Barrow, 1911-16; S. W. Paulett, 1916-20; J. A. Davidson, 1920-22; E. W. Sanford, 1922-34; W. C. Fitzpatrick, 1934-.

Clerks since 1888: J. R. Whitehead, 1888-98; E. J. Whitehead, 1898-1903; Joseph E. Garland, 1903-12; F. W. Hubbard, 1912-3; W. F. Fallwell, 1913, declined to serve; C. B. Cunningham, 1913-4, 1918-22; W. E. Moore, 1914-6; H. A. Stecker, 1916-7; Paul T. Boggs, 1917-8; Leslie Fogus, acting, 1918; H. B. Warriner, 1922-33; R. W. Catlin, acting, 1933; E. L. Dahl, 1933-51; William J. Gills, Jr., 1951-.

Treasurers (since 1922 the offices of clerk and treasurer have been combined): O. T. Wicker, 1888-90; John A. Scott, 1890-1900; S. W. Paulett, Jr., 1900-15; M. Stanley Crowe, 1915-7; F. W. Hubbard, 1917-9; Gates Richardson, 1919-20; H. B. Warriner, 1920-33; E. L. Dahl, 1933-51; William J. Gills, Jr., 1951-.

Sergeants: R. D. Miller, 1888-1910; F. W. Hubbard, 1910-2; Leslie Fogus, 1912.

Commissioners of Revenue: E. T. Rice, 1890-99; Herbert Rice, 1899-1901; P. H. C. Rice, 1901-12.

Commissioners of Streets: E. T. Rice, 1889-96; J. W. Beal, 1896-1900; J. S. Hart, 1900-7; P. A. Tucker, 1907-12. (The offices of sergeant, commissioner of revenue, and commissioner of streets were not authorized in the charter amendment of 1912.)

Attorneys: A. D. Watkins, 1893-1938; Frank N. Watkins, 1938-46; John A. Lancaster, 1946-.

Town Managers: F. W. Waggoner, 1922-5; R. B. Cralle, 1925-30; E. W. Sanford, acting, 1930; R. W. Catlin, 1930-41; George Crichton, 1941-2; R. B. Johns, 1942-6; James S. Hughes, Jr., 1946-50; Lewis Z. Johnston, Jr., 1950-.

Chiefs of Police: Leslie Fogus, 1900-18; E. D. Lipscomb, 1918-41; G. Ross Nolan, 1941-6; J. W. Crute, 1946-9; C. H. Smith, 1949-54; Otto S. Overton, 1954.

MEMBERS OF COUNCIL

W. T. Doyne, 1888-90; 1893-6; 1904-10.
R. M. Burton, 1888-96
J. M. Crute, 1888-91
A. D. Watkins, 1888-90
Thomas L. Morton, 1888-96
John R. Martin, 1888-93; 1900-4; 1906-10; 1911-16
Wiley P. Gilliam, 1888-93; 1896-1905
H. E. Barrow, 1888-96, 1904-11, 1916-8
L. J. Verser, 1888-90; 1893-8
H. E. Wall, 1890-2; 1893 (did not qualify); 1896-1908; 1911-2
A. H. Porter, 1890-6
Z. A. Blanton, 1890-2
A. W. Drumeller, 1891-6
D. T. Elam, 1892-9
C. W. Blanton, 1892-6
Charles Bugg, 1896-1900
J. B. Farrar, 1896-1902
A. E. Cralle, 1896-1904
N. B. Davidson, 1896-8, 1902-4, 1908-10, 1913 (failed to qualify); 1920-2
W. M. Duvall, 1896-8, 1904-12
E. L. Erambert, 1898-1918
W. E. Davidson, 1898-1902
Dr. W. E. Anderson, 1898-1908; 1910-2
E. L. Morris, 1899-1904; 1920-3
O. T. Wicker, 1902
E. C. Wiltse, 1902-4
S. W. Watkins, 1904-6
A. G. Clapham, 1904 (failed to qualify)
Walker Scott, 1904-10
W. C. Fallwell, 1905-10
Dr. William J. Gills, 1908-12
J. A. Armistead, 1910-2
William N. Wilson, 1910-1
R. B. Cralle, 1910-6; 1920-4
V. Vaiden, 1910-4; 1918-9
R. D. Miller, 1912-3
R. W. Noel, 1912-4; 1916-8

Harvey T. Miller, 1914-6
J. A. Davidson, 1914-20
J. E. Garland, 1914-6; 1932-48
R. H. Paulett, 1916-8
E. W. Sanford, 1916-20
P. W. Beckham, 1918-20
H. A. Barrow, 1918-28
E. Scott Martin, 1919-28
E. S. Shields, 1920-30; 1932-4
W. C. Duvall, 1920-8
W. C. Newman, 1920-2
Dr. R. L. Hudgins, 1920-2
Dr. L. D. Whitaker, 1920-30; 1932-8
C. T. Chick, 1922-6; 1928-32
F. G. Baldwin, 1922-4
R. J. Martin, 1923-4; 1925-32
E. R. Booker, 1924-8
W. J. Hillsman, 1924-6; 1930-2
J. W. Dunnington, 1926-46
F. S. Blanton, 1926-37
R. B. Johns, 1928-42
J. B. Wall, 1928-54
L. E. Hubbard, 1928-32; 1934-9
A. T. Gray, 1930-40
W. C. Fitzpatrick, 1932-4
W. J. Bloomfield, 1934-40
T. D. Smith, 1937-40
J. H. Gilliam, 1938-40
W. J. Sydnor, 1939-46
Maurice R. Large, 1940-
George A. Newman, 1940-8
H. C. Kayton, 1940-6
Sydnor C. Newman, 1946-
T. W. Bloomfield, 1946-
E. M. Whitlock, 1946-54
R. J. Martin, Jr., 1948-52
Morton L. Davis, 1948-
J. H. Forbes, 1952-
A. O. Lafoon, 1954-
C. J. Cox, 1954-

PRESIDENTS OF THE COUNCIL (who preside in the absence of the mayor)

R. M. Burton, 1890-6
Charles Bugg, 1898-1900
Dr. W. E. Anderson, 1900-4
H. E. Barrow, 1904-11
W. M. Duvall, 1911-2
E. L. Erambert, 1912-8

J. A. Davidson, 1918-20
H. A. Barrow, 1926-8
E. S. Shields, 1928-30
J. W. Dunnington, 1930-46
J. B. Wall, 1946-54
Maurice R. Large, 1954-

APPENDIX 13

SOLDIERS FROM PRINCE EDWARD IN WORLD WAR I

(The list may be found in Burrell, pp. 201-10. The grouping used by Dr. Burrell has been followed here.)

* Indicates death in service.

The Farmville Guard

H. H. Hunt, captain   John H. Cocks, first lieutenant

(These were the officers when the company went into service.)

J. Watson Anglea	J. W. Fers	Raymond Phillips
John W. Almon	George Fitzgerald	Charles W. Rafferty
S. Blanton Badgett	R. H. Foster	Lucius R. Reedy
Henry Bailey	John N. Garland*	Spottswood B. Robinson
J. E. Baldwin	J. E. Garnett	Robert B. Rodgers
Robert S. Baldwin	J. H. Gilliam	Bryant Sheppard
Otis Bowman	R. R. Gilliam	Emmett Sheppard
Charles Boyd	W. S. Gilliam	Joel Sheppard
Lloyd Bullock	J. W. Goodman	H. B. Schultz
Wirt Cardwell	Walker M. Gray	Blanchard Skillings
D. J. Carroll	Thomas Greenalls	Frank E. Slaughter
C. E. Chappell	Mebane Harper	Melvin T. Smith
Granville Chappell	L. L. Haymaker	Millard G. Smith*
Felix Cline	W. W. Hillsman*	Thomas F. Taylor
Fields Cobb	Goode Hundley	J. C. Terry
Alfred Coleman*	J. Ashley Hurt	Lawrie W. Thompson
J. Vernon Collins	Courtney Irving	W. H. Waters
W. C. Collins	Linwood Irving	Cunningham Watkins
Mack Cowan	John N. Irving	Stanley Watkins
Guy J. Crenshaw	Emerson Jarman	John W. Webster*
William H. Crenshaw	Joseph L. Jarman, Jr.	Sam Webster
Reuben Daniel	A. G. Kelsey	George W. White
W. P. Davis	Henry A. Kelsey	J. A. Whitlock
F. L. Dietrick	Finney Kernodle*	T. H. Whitlock
Harry Dix	Guy F. Lancaster	Carl Wilck
Herschel Dix*	James E. Lipscomb	Paul Wilck
R. C. Dodl	Joseph E. Lowe	Wallace J. Wilck
J. F. Dodson	Rupert F. Mann	Homer F. Wilkinson
W. D. Druen	Richard K. Marsh	T. H. Williams
J. F. Echols	Frank L. McIntosh	James L. Wilson, Jr.
Littleton Edmunds	Horace H. Moorefield	Henry Wood
Charles F. Eifert	D. W. Paulett	Ernest Woodall
Decker Emerson	T. A. Perrow	

In Student Army Training Corps at Hampden-Sydney from Prince Edward

Francis S. Allen*	K. Drummeller	J. W. Putney
Robert W. Bugg	T. J. Headlee	W. E. Smith
J. S. Q. Carson	J. A. Jones	J. M. Watkins
G. E. Coffman	R. C. Moore	

White Men Who Went Into Service from Prince Edward

William S. Addleman
Henry G. Allen
Paul T. Atkinson
Everett Bailey
James T. Baker
Nathan Baker
Paul S. Barrow*
John Barton
Charles D. Beck
Lee Berry
Norman Berry
W. R. Berry
K. C. Bliss
Owen H. Bliss
T. L. Bliss
John C. Bondurant
Rush W. Bondurant
Samuel W. Bondurant
William H. Bondurant
William T. Bondurant
J. E. Booth
Charles H. Borum
Oscar Borum
Robert M. Bradshaw
John W. Brandau
J. M. Brightwell
R. A. Brisentine
W. D. Brisentine
Willie Brooks
Charles R. Bugg
F. B. Cale
J. L. Calhoun
Baudie G. Carter
Jasper S. Carter
L. B. Carwile
Albert Casey
R. C. Cheadle*
Frank B. Chernault
Charles M. Clarke
John B. Cobb
H. W. Covington
M. B. Coyner
J. C. Crawley
T. H. Crenshaw
Charles B. Cunningham
Linwood Dalton
T. B. Daniel
W. M. Davis
W. M. Dickerson
Shirley E. Dowdy
L. W. Drummeller
Leon L. Duncan

Harry S. Durfee
Charles M. East
Russell East
Andrew J. Fears
H. T. Ferguson
John W. Ferguson
Sam. S. Flippen
J. N. Foster
Henry Fowlkes*
Roland S. Franklin
H. Leonard Fulcher
N. C. Gallier
Thomas H. Garnett
William Gaunce
N. I. Gibson
F. T. Glenn
H. A. Glenn
Isaac C. Glenn
I. Peyton Glenn
James S. Goodrich
Watson W. Gray
Ulysses O. Gunter
Harry E. Hamilton
Henry Hancock
Thomas G. Hardy
E. H. Herzig
W. Edward Hines
J. B. Holt
W. A. Holt
B. G. Hood
J. C. Hopkins
W. Eleazar Hughes
W. W. Hughes
Alfred E. Inge
L. P. Inge
Edward L. Jennings
Ernest L. Jennings
J. N. Jennings
R. W. Jones
G. W. Kennedy
W. F. Lee
Herman Levy
J. V. Lewis
Joseph H. Lewis, Jr.
R. F. Mann
Charles W. Mason
W. H. Mason
M. R. Mays
Thomas J. McIlwaine
Mark A. Moffett
R. E. Moffett
D. C. Morris

John A. Morris
William Conway Morris
Richard L. Morton
Finley M. Nelson
C. M. Noel
L. N. Oliver
Otto Oliver
F. L. Orange
J. J. Overton
Robert H. Phillips
G. D. Pickett
Haywood Pollard
M. M. Ponton
Joseph A. Poole
C. A. Price, Jr.
William R. Price
James G. Redford
Gates R. Richardson
Sam H. Rodgers
Joe E. Rogers
T. B. Scott
Willie M. Scott
G. E. Shorter
Frank C. Shultz
F. G. Shultz
L. D. Simpson
Nunnally Smith
L. A. Snow
Hutch Stowe
William T. Straley
C. L. Stuart
Phil B. Swan*
John D. Thomas
Oscar Thompson
W. E. Tomlinson
Pitzer S. Turns
James B. Vaughan
Cecil F. Walker
Charles T. Walker
Gene B. Walker
G. L. Walker
H. E. Walker
Robert E. Warwick
Thomas E. Webster
Howard F. Weaver
Sam M. Weaver
Harry E. Whaley
John H. Whaley
Lee C. Whaley
Oscar H. Whitten
James W. Wilson, Jr.
Alfred Wolter
S. N. Wood

White Men from Prince Edward Who Went Into Service from Some Other Place

Willie Adams
Ernest Allen
Jean Anderson
Charles Bates
Richard B. Bates
J. P. Bondurant
Eugene Budd
J. Spencer Burger
W. G. Carter
Leslie Carwile
Melville Childress
Robert T. Cocks
Morris Conway
Martin Covington
James Cowan
A. B. Crawley
A. L. Crawley
J. G. Crenshaw
Charles B. Crute
W. C. Davis
E. M. Dickerson
Berlin Driskill
A. R. Dunkum
J. H. Dunnington
W. G. Dunnington, Jr.
Wallace Duvall

Reid Edmunds
J. Watson Elliott
H. G. Farley
Pierce Farr
James D. Fowlkes
Everett Garber
Ernest Garland
Thomas D. Glenn
T. A. Gray, Jr.
Hunter C. Harris
Willard Hart
C. A. M. Hubbard
C. W. Hubbard
H. J. Hubbard
T. A. Hubbard
Robert Hundley
Jack Irving
Hanes Lancaster
Hatcher Layne
Stanley R. Legus
Hicks Ligon
Massie Lowe
Clarence F. Lynn
———— McGinnis
Dan A. McIntosh*
Henry L. Moore

Percy Moring
Cumfy Mottley
Bernard Oliver
Walter Overton
Walter A. Palmore
Thomas G. Price
Clyde V. Ranson
Robert Richardson
Walter Richardson
DeWitt Riggins*
J. Maxwell Robeson
Floyd Rosser
Joel Sheppard
Ed. Shorter
Henry C. Thompson
Elmer R. Tomlinson
T. A. Tweedy
A. E. Vaughan
Pettit Venable
Reginald Venable
W. A. Vernon
Frank Nat Watkins
Samuel W. Watkins, Jr.
Louis Whitlock
E. Dixie Williamson
Earle H. Young

Negroes Who Went Into Service from Prince Edward

Luther Allen
C. H. Anderson
J. N. Anderson
William H. Anderson
James Armistead
Fred Baker
John Baker
Willie Baker
Robert Baldwin
Charles Banks
Cavel Barksdale
Vernon Bartee
William Beasley
Leonard F. Bedford
Wesley Bedford
Eddie Berry
Willie Berry
Ernest L. Berryman
J. C. Berryman
Edward Beverley
Richard L. Biggers*
Philip Bland

Clarence Blanton
Thomas B. Blue
William Booker
Archer Brown
Charles W. Brown
Eddie Brown
Floyd Brown
Henry T. Brown
Howard Brown
Hunter Brown
John Brown
J. H. Brown
Lancaster Brown
Norvell Brown
Percy Brown
Royall Brown
R. W. Brown
S. J. Brown
Wesley Brown
Waverley Burr
James Carter
Berkley Carthorn

Roy Carthorn
Albert Casey
John Cheatham
Willie Clark
James Clarke
William Clarke
Paul Coleman
Joe Coles
Morton Couch
J. H. Cromwell
Emmett Crute
George Daniel
Walter Davis
Amos Dickerson
H. A. Dodson
James S. Doswell
Edgar Durphey
Champ Dupuy
Alfred Eggleston
Charlie Ellis
Paul Ellis
Willie Ellis

Willie Ellis
Johnny Evans
Tom Evans
Frank Farley
John L. Fears
Clinton Felton
Fletcher Felton
Edward Flagg
Lewis Flagg
Robert Flournoy
Spencer Flournoy
James Ford
William Ford
Solomon Fore
Henry Foster
Jeff Foster
Robert Foster
Sam Foster
Robert Fowlkes
W. L. Fowlkes
John Freeman
Peter Freeman
George Fultz
Frank Gales
John D. Thomas Gallier
James Gans
Wiley Ghee
John H. Giles
Floyd Glenn
John Goode
Reese Gordon
Ederick S. Green
Herbert Green
Horace Green
Laban Green
Lewis W. Green
Philip A. Green
Charles Harris*
Floyd Harris
Pompey Harrison
Randolph Harrison
Nathan Harvey
Charles Haskins
John Haskins
Vernon Haskins
Wiley Haskins
Walter Hayes
John S. Hendricks
Adam Hicks
James Hicks
Clarence O. Hilton
Philip A. Hilton
Richard A. Hilton
W. Sanders Hines

Simie Holley
J. W. Holmes
Johnny Hurt
Spencer Hurt
Walter S. Hurt
Clinton Jackson
Durvan Jackson
Emmett Jackson
J. M. Jackson
Lee Jackson
Ulysses Jackson
George James
Chester A. Jeffries
John Jeffries
Nelson Jeffries
Jim Jenkins
H. E. Johns
Albert Johnson, Jr.
C. T. Johnson
Clem Johnson
Elijah Johnson
George Johnson
Henry Johnson
Herman Johnson
Joe Johnson
Johnny Johnson
Matthew Johnson
Tom Johnson
Wiley Johnson
Alex Jones
Benjamin F. Jones
Champ Jones
Charles Jones
Eddie Jones
Henry Jones
Henry T. Jones
Jasper Jones
J. H. Jones
Nineveh Jones
Thomas Jones
John Henry Jordan
Homer Kelso
Willie Knight
Lightfoot Lacy
Robert Lacy
Armistead Lambert
Freebelle Lee
C. Henry Lewis
James A. Lewis
Bascom Ligon
G. H. Ligon
Herman Ligon
Frank Lile
Thaniel Lockett

Jesse Logan
George Lucas
Edward Marshall
John Marshall
Ned Marshall
Walter A. Marshall
Racey Matthews
T. H. Matthews
Clyde Mayo
Edward Miles
N. P. Miller
Vanderbilt Miller
Joe Moore
Every Morton
Floyd Morton
Fred Morton
Junius Morton
Taze Morton
William Morton
David E. Moseley
John C. Paige
Oscar Palmore
Joe Paschal
H. T. Patterson
Richard Payne
William Payne
George T. Pryor
James Pryor
Warren P. Pryor
Waverley Pryor
Harrison Randolph
Moses Randolph
Ulysses J. Randolph
Romeo Randall
Ed Redd
Frank James Redd
Frank J. Redd
Flan Redd
Henry A. Redd
James Redd
Sam Redd
Thomas Redd
James H. Reed
Sam Reed
John Richardson
John Robertson
C. H. Robinson
Robert Rux
Oakley H. Sanders
Albert Scott
Cleveland Scott
Edward Scott
Henry Scott
Lurtie Scott

Matthew Scott
Prudential Scott
Richard Scott
Richard Scott
Sam Simms
George Smith
John Smith
Vester Smith
Tom Stith
George Street
Fred Taylor
Robert Terry
Ellie Thomas
Warren P. Thompson
James Thornton
Henry Threatt*
Watt Threatt
Frank Topp

John P. Towns
John Trent
Sam Trent
McKinley Tucker
Jimmy Venable
Bennie Walden
Cleveland Walker
Dennis Walker
H. W. Walker
Wiley Walker
Norfleet Ward
Stardie Ward
Clem Warren
Emmett Warren
Branch Washington
Henry Watkins
Monroe Watkins
Alex Watson

Charles Watson
Edmund Watson
Truly Watson
Walter Watson
Harrison West
William Whit
Ed Williams
Harrison Williams
Hilary Wilson
John Wingfield
Edward Winston
Robert Winston
Percy C. Womack
Richard Woodson
Willie Woodson
Willie Young

Negroes from Prince Edward Who Went Into Service from Some Other Place

Claude M. Allen
Dorsey Anderson
Paul Anderson
Charlie Baker
Nelson Baker
John S. Bolden
Robert Booker
Wesley Booker
Willis H. Branch
Anderson Brown
Dominion Brown
Harvey Brown
Herbert Brown
Wayman Brown
Charles Cooper
Edward Davis
Henderson Davis
Jack Dupuy
W. D. Elam
Robert A. Ellis
Samuel Fowlkes
A. S. Green
Levi Green

Burnett Griggs
Norman A. Hairston
James Hall
Lindsey Hays
George Hill
Herbert Hines
Spencer Hurt
Arthur Jenkins
Ernest L. Johns
Cleveland Johnson
James Johnson
Mesles Johnson
Neal Johnson
Nelson Jordan, Jr.
Paige Lancaster
Paul Layne
Coley Lewis
Joe Ligon
Daniel Logan
William H. Logan
Sam Matthews
James Miller
Preston Miller

Haskins Moseley
Lafayette Munford
Olney Pryor
Munford Richardson
Lud Roberts
Sam Sims
Charles Terry
Alfred Thornton
C. H. Wade
Joseph Walker
Shirley Walker
Dick Ward*
Nat Ward
Harry Watkins
Pernell Watkins
Thomas Watts
Howard White
Burley Wilson
Jefferson J. Wilson
Leonard Wilson
Robert Womack
Clyde Woodson

APPENDIX 14

PRINCE EDWARD MEN AND WOMEN WHO WERE IN SERVICE DURING WORLD WAR II

(This list was compiled by the Farmville *Herald*, but it is not certain that it is complete. Researchers for the *Herald* compiled the information from as many sources as they knew to determine those from Prince Edward who went into service. The *Herald* assembled the service records of all who responded to the request for these records. J. Barrye Wall, publisher, has generously made the list available for publication in this work. The branch of service has been indicated for those who sent their service records to the *Herald*.)

William Howard Abel
Clinton Abernathy
Glen Wooden Abernathy, Army
Walter D. Abbitt
Billy Morgan Adams
Horace Adams, Jr., Navy
Willie Adams
David Cleveland Adkins
Herman E. Adkins
Charles Elkin Agee
Roger N. Alderson
Carrol McRee Allen, Army
Dayton Sherman Allen, Navy
Dayton Sherman Allen, Jr., Navy
Elizabeth L. Allen, Navy (Waves)
Fern Russell Allen, Army Air
Howard Bouldin Allen
Hugh Earl Allen
John Henry Allen, Jr., Army
Richard Thomas Allen
Robert Earl Allen
Roderick E. Allen, Army
W. B. Allen
Alexander Ward Allison
Joseph French Alsop, Navy Medical
Herman Amos
Alfred Walter Anderson, Jr.
Edwin Threatt Anderson, Jr.
Lawrence Eugene Anderson, killed in service
Nelson Laertees Anderson
Richard K. Anderson
William Anderson
Earl Wendell Andrews, Army
Everett Junius Andrews, Jr.
Flood Shields Andrews
Maurice Carl Andrews
James Ashby Armistead, Army
Lewis Edward Armistead

Melvin Lee Arrowood
Carl Jenett Atkins
Noel Leonard Atkins
Robert L. Atkins
Paul T. Atkinson, Jr.
William Elliott Atkinson
Cecil Gray Bailey, Army
Clyde Daniel Bailey, Army
Evelyn R. Bailey, Navy (Waves)
Lawrence Sylvester Bailey, Army
Raymond Louis Bailey, Army
Thomas J. Bailey, Navy
William Lofton Bagby, Army
James Edward Baker, Navy
William R. Baker
William T. Baker
Calvin Edgar Baldwin, Navy
Charles Baldwin
Coy Wilson Baldwin, Army
Frank Benjamin Baldwin, Marine Air
Harry William Baldwin, Army
Joseph Kyle Baldwin, Navy
Thomas Kyle Baldwin
Wallace Franklin Baldwin, Army Air
William Herbert Baldwin
John Albert Banton
Samuel Banton
Lawrence Davis Barksdale
Thomas Irving Barksdale
Robert W. Barlow, Jr.
Floyd Edward Barnes
Clarence William Barr
Charles Allen Barton
Charles Davis Barton
Charlie Denest Barton
George Allen Barton
Vernie Calvin Barton
Woodrow Daniel Barton
William Nelson Baskervill, Army Air

Robert Gates Bass, Navy
Fletcher Dillard Bates
Floyd Lee Bates
King Solomon Bates
Luther Richard Bates
Noland Almond Bates
Richard B. Bates
Richard E. Bates
Robert Lee Beard
William Cecil Beazley, Army
Charles Beverley Beck, Army
Thomas Moore Beckham, Army
George Michal Bedinger, Navy
John Franklin Bedinger, Navy
Neal Anderson Bedinger, Jr., Navy
Robert Hudgins Bedinger, Army
Frances Bonn Bell, Navy (Waves)
Leon Edwin Bell, Jr., Army
Joseph Nathan Bell
Robert Earnest Bell
William Washington Bell, Army
Samuel C. Bennett
Frank Wysong Berry, Army
Philip Willard Berry, Army
William Roland Berry, Jr., Navy
Thomas Bryant Billings, Army
William David Billings, Army Air
Frank Hite Birdsong
Joseph A. Birdwell, Army Air
Margaret D. Birdwell, Navy (Waves)
Edward Russell Blackburn
Clyde Howard Bliss, Army
Mason Langslow Bliss, Army
Thomas William Bloomfield, Army
John Melois Bohamon
Harold Norman Bollinger
Howard Odell Bollinger, Navy
Hastin Ray Bolt
Harry J. Bolton
Samuel Bolton
Elmo C. Bondurant, Army
Thomas Ogburn Bondurant, Army
George Edward Bonn
Elliott Read Booker, Jr., Army
George William Booker, Army
Robert Scott Booker
Dallas Booth
Mark J. Booth, Jr.
Milton Alfred Booth
Daniel Jones Boothe
Thomas DeWitt Boothe
William Lester Boothe
Hodges Swan Boswell, Navy
Allen Howard Bouldin, Army

James Wood Bouldin, Jr., Navy
Dennis Willard Bowen
James Calvin Bowen
Ernest Carol Bowen
James C. Bowen
Willie Henderlite Bowles
Carl Howard Bowman, Army Air
Corbett Lee Bowman, Army
George O. Bowman, Jr.
Henry Theodore Bowman, Navy
Robert Cornelius Bowman
Roland LeRoy Bowman
Curtis Lee Boyce
Steiner Boyd
Herbert Benjamin Brackett, Navy
Clyde Weaver Bradshaw, Army
Robert Julian Bradshaw, Army
Thomas Henry Bradshaw, Army
Wilbert Bradshaw
Crawford Bray
Edgar Lee Bray
Walter W. Bray
John Taylor Brickert, Army
Ernest Jackson Brightwell, Army
Edgar Platte Brightwell, Army Air
John Edward Brightwell
Robert Everett Brightwell, Army
Robert Allen Brisentine, Jr., Army
Pamelia Adele Weaver Brooks, Navy
  (Waves)
Thomas W. Brooks, Jr.
Anthony Brown, Jr., Army
Velmon Barnett Brown, Marines
James Thomas Bruce, Jr., Army Air
John Gilliam Bruce, Army
John Martin Bruce, Army Air
Robert Wootton Bruce, Army
Taylor Mottley Bruce, Army
Thomas Clark Bruce, Army
Thomas Wilson Bruce, Army Air
William Basil Bruce, Jr.
James Luckin Bugg, Jr., Army Air
Roland Pickett Bugg
James Spencer Burger, Jr., Navy
Robert Balland Burger, Army
John Harrison Burke
Joseph Clifford Burr
Richard Allen Burrell, Coast Guard
Charles Gervas Burton
Claude Wright Butcher
Leslie Hazelgrove Butcher
Archibald McDowell Bynum, Army
Addison Allen Calhoun, Army
Albert Hugh Calhoun

Henry Walker Calhoun
James Richard Calhoun
Frank Kenneth Campbell
Jennings, Earl Campbell
John Allen Campbell
Robert C. Campbell
Robert Meredith Campbell
Robert Carroll
Robert Owen Carroll
Charles B. Carson
Crote Carson
Ural Carson
William Elantha Carson
Woodrow Carson
Charles M. Carter, Marines
Cleveland Glenwood Carter
Earl H. Carter
Evelyn M. Carter
Horace Robert Carter
John Benjamin Carter, Marines
James Nat Carter, Jr., Army
Roy Walton Carter
William Marshall Carter, died in
    service
Albert Hearn Carwile, Army
Cornelius Tucker Carwile, Army Air
Hugh Elliott Carwile, Jr., Army
William Harwood Cary, Army
Curtis Samuel Case, Army
James Case, Army
Bland Bushby Cash
Edward W. Cash
John S. Cash
Richard B. Cash
Cecil Wallace Cason
Thomas J. Cawthorne
Richard Vernon Chambers, Army
Andrew Jackson Chandler, Army
Theodore Watson Chaney
Fred B. Chapman, Army
John James Chapman
Morris Chapman
Robert Woodrow Chapman
William Dabney Chapman, Army Air
Thomas Henry Chappell, Army
Connie Lee Cheek
Frank Edward Chernault, Navy
Lula M. Chernault, Army Air (WAC)
Charles Lester Chick
Milton Chick
Emmett Wingfield Childress
Henry Edward Childress
Herman Spencer Childress
Rafe Daniel Childress

William Clyde Childress
James William Childrey
George Robert Clark, Army
Raymond Ogdon Clark, Army
Richard Payne Clark
William Paulett Clark, Army Air
Frank W. Clarkson
Hubert Clair Clawson
Herbert E. Clevenger, Army
L. Earle Clevinger
Burley Cobb
John Beach Cobb, Jr.
Henry Walker Cocks, Navy
Randolph Lester Cocks
James Grant Cole
Anderson David Coleman
Jack Coleman
James Stuart Coleman
Joseph Benjamin Coleman
Ray Coleman
Thomas Clarence Coleman, Jr., Army
Berkley Lee Collins
Thomas Joseph Collins
Ernest Cook
Kermit Henry Cook
Marshall Clay Cook
Alfred Walker Covington
Arnold W. Covington, Jr.
David Blanton Covington, Army Air
Harold Phillips Covington, Navy
Herbert Witt Covington, Navy
Jack Covington
Moses German Covington
Oten Clay Covington, Coast Guard
Russell Lee Covington
Benjamin Ashley Cox
Francis E. Cox, Army
Harry Walker Cox
Talmadge Rush Cox
Thomas Marshall Cox, killed in action
Loel Bethel Craig
Robert Lauck Crawford, Army
James Clifford Crawley, Jr., Navy Air
James Edward Crawley
James Wilbur Crawley, Jr., Army
Thomas Edward Crawley, Navy
Henry Lafayette Crenshaw
Geoffrey Creyke, Jr., Navy
Richard Paulett Creyke, Army
Carl Jonah Crigger, Army
Burlass A. Crump, Army
Charlie Edward Crump
George Lee Crump
George Crump

Dorothy Crute, Army (nurse)
J. M. Crute, Jr.
James Ligon Crute
Joseph David Crute, Merchant Marine
William Joseph Crute, Army
Wyatt Crute, Army Air Force
Hugh Carleton Cunningham, Jr., Navy
Richard Cunningham
Walter Newton Cunningham, Army
Will Dillon Cunningham
Robert Anderson Daniel, Army
William W. Daubenspeck
Charles Lindbergh Davis, Navy
Fayette Henry Davis
Floyd Cain Davis, Navy
George Holman Davis
George R. Davis, Army
Herbert R. Davis
Hunter Wood Davis
Percy G. Davis, Jr.
Sam Davis
William Monroe Davis, Jr.
Wiltshire Cardwell Davis, Jr.
William F. Davis, killed in action
Kenneth T. Daye
Stewart Warren Dean
Anthony M. DeMuth, Army Dental
  Corps
Grady Clifton Detherage, Jr.
Eugene Walker Dickerson
George Raymond Dickerson
George R. Dickerson
Robert Lee Dickerson, Army
Carl William Dickhoff, Army
John Henry Dickhoff, Army
Merriweather Blair Dickinson
Thomas Newton Dillon, Navy
John Bennett Douglas
Flemstead Carlyle Dowdy
Herman Aubrey Dowdy, Army
Murray Christopher Dowdy
Otha Cleveland Dowdy
Rankin B. Dowdy
Ryland T. Dowdy
Thomas Earl Dowdy
Waverly Thurston Dowdy
Willie Wilson Dowdy
Zebulon Montgomery Downey
Henry T. Driggs
George Hall Driskill, Jr.
Javan Cornealous Driskill, Navy
Jesse Willard Driskill, Army
Mildred Effie Driskill, Army Air
Thomas Bernard Driskill, Army

Thomas Lee Driskill, Navy
James Dancer Druen
Karl Drumeller, Navy
James Henry Dudley, Naval Air
Harry G. Dugger, Jr.
James Manson Dugger, Navy
Merrill Yancey Dugger, Army Air
Robert H. Dugger, Jr.
Roy Wallace Duncan, Marines
Tulane Marvin Duncan, Army
Gamaliel Owen Dunkley, Army
Aubrey Robinette Dunkum
Hugh Holladay Dunkum, Jr.
Robert Juan Dunkum
Ellis C. Dunnavant, Jr.
William Clyde Duvall, Jr., Navy
Henry Eagles
James Louis Eagles
William Henry Eagles
Andrew Jackson East
Ben East
Claude Malcolm East, Jr., Navy
Edgar W. East, Jr.
James E. East, Jr.
John T. East
Walter Jackson East, Army
Harley C. Easter
Clarence V. Easter
Harold V. Easter
Lester Echols
Willard Echols
George Wilson Edwards
Paul Edwards
Paul George Edwards, Jr.
William Robert Edwards
Jessie Raymond Eggleston, Army
Edward Underwood Elam, Army
Elliott Fuqua Elam, Navy
James Abner Elam, Navy
Marcus Cleveland Elcan, Jr.
Johnnie Ewell Elder
Jesse R. Elleston
Allman Chester Ellington
Paul Bosher Ellington
Emmett Roach Elliott, Navy
Carroll Weaver Elliott, Army
Leonard Adams Elliott, Army
Vinton Astor Epperley, Coast Guard
E. G. Estes
John Mell Estes
William Gordon Estes
Everett Winston Farley
James Edward Farley
William Joseph Farley

Claude Edward Farrar, Army
Omah O. Farrar, Jr., Army
Sam Louis Ferguson, Army
Steven Howard Ferguson, Jr., Army
Alfred Finch, Army
Finneyberry Finch, Army
William Finch, Army
Raymond Finchum
John Malcolm Firth, Jr.
John Fischer
Richard Albert Fitzgerald
Thomas Eldridge Fitzgerald
George D. Flippen
Leroy Samuel Flippen
Oscar Fred Flippen, Army
Oscar Nash Flippen, Jr., Navy
William Lewis Floyd
Withers J. Floyd
James Edward Foley, Naval Air
James Henry Forbes
William Gray Fore, Army
Marion Jackson Foster, Army Air
Reid Martin Foster, Army
Thomas Raymond Foster, Navy
Willie Edward Foster, Jr.
Julian Graham Fowlkes, Army
John William Fox
George H. Frank, Jr.
Lee Roy Frank
William Edward Frank, Jr.
James Henry Franklin
George Edwin Frayser
Dannie Lee Fulcher
Paulus Ashby Fulcher, Marines
Thomas Julian Fulcher, Jr., Marines
Andrew Gain
Blair Cochran Gammon, Navy
Edgar Graham Gammon, Jr., Army Air
Louis Lee Garland, Army
Harry Nelson Garner
Richard Edwin Garnett, Army
Wilson Blanton Garnett, Army
William Bernard Garnett, Navy
Franklin Trent Garrett
Harold L. Garrett
Robert Gaunce, Navy
Vaiden Gaunce, Army
William Gaunce, Jr., Navy
Cyril Hamlin Gee
Samuel Rothmel Geyer, killed in action
Rither Anding Gibson, Army
Robert Linwood Gilbert, Naval Air
William Henry Gilbert, Army
Edwin Marvin Giles, Jr.

James Aubrey Gilliam, Army
John Hugh Gilliam, Jr., Army
Llewellyn Walker Gilliam, Army
Overton H. Gilliam
Robert Taylor Gilliam, Navy
Walter Gilliam
John Gills
William James Gills
Robert Carson Gilmer, Navy
Thomas Edward Gilmer, Jr.
Willie H. Glargon
James Meccellus Glascock, Army
Walter Clarence Glascock, Army
Aubrey Berryman Glasgow, Army
William Henry Glasgow
Donald Taylor Glenn, Army Air
Edward Paige Glenn
Jesse Morton Glenn
Reginald French Glenn
Robert Pinkney Glenn
Samuel Perkins Glover, Army
Holly Gobble
Marvin Shirley Godsey
Robert Fears Goodwin
William C. Goodwin
Jasper Lee Gordon, Army
Raeburn Francis Gordon, killed in service
Woodrow Wilson Gordon, Navy
Earnest McKinley Gowin
Louis Atkins Graham, Navy
Samuel Lyle Graham IV, Navy Air
Wilson Liberator Grainger
John Adkins Gray, Navy (chaplain.)
Sydney Gray
Thomas Asbury Gray
Calvin Garnett Greear, Army
Dwight Moody Green
Ira Lester Green, Navy
Louis Alvin Green
Robert Nelson Green
Paul L. Grier, Navy
Joseph Frank Hadel, Army Air
Ralph Haga
James Conrad Haire
Renwick Thomas Hall
Willie Franklin Hall
Francis Hamilton, Army
Herman Foster Hamilton, Army Air
Marshall Edwin Hamilton, Army
William Sidney Hamilton, Army Air
Clarence William Hamlett
Emerson C. Hamlett, Army
Kenneth B. Hamlett, Navy

Lewis Bohannon Hamlett
Lindy Lynn Hamlett
Milton Curtis Hamlett, Navy
Nelson C. Hamlett, Army
Thomas Wilson Hamlett, Army
James L. Hamner
Winfield S. Hamner, Jr.
Burton Blanton Hanbury, Navy
Fred Hall Hanbury, Jr., Navy
William Lafayette Hanbury, Navy
Robert Thomas Hancock
James Garland Hanes, Jr.
Wesley S. Hardiman
Willie G. Hardiman
Bernard Joseph Harding
Hunter Alexander Harding
Walter Cleven Harding, Army
Marion Lee Hardy, Jr.
Thomas Griffin Hardy, Jr., Navy
O. W. Harper, Navy
Alexander Harris
James Carlton Harris
John Mace Harris, Jr., Army
Thornton Harris
Tucker Harris
William Goodrich Harris, killed in
  service
William L. Harris, Army
Withers Coleman Harris
Howard Lent Harrison, Navy
Joseph Harrison
Eugene Lloyd Hartley
Floyd Allen Hartley
Richard Clifton Harvey
William Robert Harvey, Army
John Elliott Harwood
Paul L. Hass
Hildred Mason Hatcher
Raymond Lee Hatcher
Benjamin Edward Hayes
Albert Edward Herzig
Claude Swanson Herzig
Fred Lee Herzig
Thomas William Hicks
Richard Henry Hillsman
John Henry Hines
Cornelius Winfrey Hodges, Army
Edward Lester Hodges
Ernest Lee Hodges
James Dollace Hodges
Paul E. Hodges
Robert Lee Hodges
Frank Rowe Holman
Taz C. Holly, Army

Howard Holsinger
Hubert Burner Holsinger, Army
  Medical
F. Curtis Hubbard
Harvey Johnson Hubbard, Jr.
Henry Fielder Hubbard
Hilda V. Hubbard, Army Air (WAC)
Joseph Walker Hubbard
Linwood French Hubbard
Louis Edward Hubbard, Jr., Navy
W. Henry Hubbard, Army
William Roscoe Hubbard, Army
Archer Conrad Huddleston
Raymond E. Huddleston
Charlie M. Hudson, Army
James Donald Hudson, Navy
Alfred Laddie Hughes, Army
Clyde Preston Hughes, Navy
George Howard Hughes, Army Air
Paul Delbert Hughes
Travis Wilson Hughes, Army
Elizabeth E. Hundley
John Pride Hunt, III, Army Air
Benjamin Franklin Hurt, Army
George E. Hurt
James Hubbard Hurt, Army
Bernice Webb Humphries, Army Air
  (WAC)
Frank Oliver Huskey, Navy
Gene Huskey
Harris Huskey
Howard Donald Huskey
Roy Wesley Hutchins
Charles Ellis Hutchinson
Richard D. Inge
Arthur Samuel Irby
Calvin Irby, Army
Cecil William Irby
Joseph Edward Irby
Anna Estelle Jacobs
Edward (Jack) Jacobs
Edward Wayne Jacobs
Harold G. Jacobs
James Buford Jacobs
Willard Smith Jamerson, Army
George Harrison Jarratt
George Jarrett
Sammy Jarrett
Embrey Cornelius Jarvis
David Edward Jenkins, Army
Hugh Martin Jenkins
Raymond H. Jenkins
Milton Lee Jennings
Ben Irving Johns

Clyde T. Johnson, Army
Edward Russell Johnson
Granville Earl Johnson
Harry Everett Johnson
James Clyde Johnson, Army
James Frederick Johnson, Army
Jamie Johnson
Ned Johnson, Army
Oscar Singleton Johnson
Otis Glenn Johnson
Paul Johnson
Paul Otis Johnson, Army
Raymond E. Johnson
Robert Ennis Johnson
Wallace Charles Johnson
Walter Carroll Johnson
Walter William Johnson
Willard Edward Johnson
Charles Crute Jones
Eppa Sebron Jones
Guy Thomas Jones, Navy
Howard Trent Jones, Navy
Leo Glenwood Jones, Army
Oscar Gordon Jones, Army Air
Paul Dibrell Jones
Ray Preston Jones, Navy
Thomas William Jones, Army Air
Walter Bennett Jones
Walter Davis Jones, Jr., Army Air
John Archer Jordan
William Barrow Kayton, Army
Murl Tucker Keiser, Army Air
James Wallace Kelley
John Wesley Kelley
Marshall Lee Kelley, Army
James Gallie Kelly
Caleb Franklin Kelsey, Army
George Budd Kelsey, Army
Grover Clarence Kelsey, Army
Philander Kelsey, Jr.
Charles A. Kennedy, Jr.
Joseph Edward Kennedy, Army
William Irving Kennedy
Harold Lee Kernodle
Sydney Warren Kernodle
Everett Charles Kickler
James Marshall Kidwell
Raymond Kenneth King
Chester Henry Kirstein, Army
Frank Robert Kirstein, Army Air
Harvey Comman Knick
Thomas Estin Knight
Graham R. E. Koch, Army Air
Beryl Kromer, Army

Earl E. Kromer, Army
Kenneth Park Kromer, Army Air
Leland Kromer, Army
Alwyn Otis Lafoon, Jr.
Glenn LaForce
Henry Leslie Lam
Albert Earl Lamberth
C. T. Lamberth, Jr.
Albert H. Lancaster, Jr., Army Air
David Landman
Moses Landman
Rebecca Landman
Rex Large
Clarence Wiley Lawhorne, Jr.
Maurice Travis Lawhorne
James William Layne
Wilbur Calvin Layne, Army
James Fred Leatherwood
Lester Frank Leatherwood
Ruwis Glenn Leggett
Harold William S. LeGrand
Eugene A. Legus
William Stanley Legus
David LeWarne
Howard LeWarne
John Filmore Lewis, Jr.
Walter Charles Lewis
William Henry Lewis
Joseph Anderson Ligon, Jr.
Lee Chapman Lindsey
Robert Bruce Lindsey
Robert Earl Linkin
James Edward Lipscomb
Elwood Monroe Lloyd
George Thomas Lloyd
Jesse Thomas Long
Jewel Ray Loveday
James Thomas Lowe
James Lee Lowry, missing in action
Eddie Elisha Lucado
Roy Phillip Lucado
Robert Warren Lucado
Frank Herman Lynch
Wade Baldwin MacDonald, Navy
Charles Edward Magann
Lester Allen Magann
Lemuel Judson Mann, Army Air
Richard Gordon Mann, Navy
Wilson Trent Mann, Army
Edwin Randolph Marshall, Army
Harvey W. Marshall
James J. Marshall, Jr., Army
John Page Marshall, Army Air
Samuel Anthony Martin

Robert Beverley Mason, Army
Thomas Burton Mason, Army Air
Walter Sydney Mason
Benjamin Henry Massey
Joseph Noah Matthews, Army
James Leo Mazingo
Merian Raymond Meador
George Gibson Meadows, Army
John P. Meanley, III
Alfred Elmo Melton
Harold Milton Mercer
James Bristo Metcalf
Paul D. Metcalf, Army
Thomas Murray Metcalf
Woodrow Wariner Miller, Army Air
Howard Bass Mitchell, Army
John Carroll Mitchell, Navy
Robert Lee Mitchell
Tommie Wallace Mitchell
Aeneas Moore
Daniel Elwyn Moore
Dixie Whitehead Moore, Naval Air
Edward Lee Moore
George William Moore
Handy Moore
James Homer Moore
John Andrew Moore
Ray Atkinson Moore, Jr.
Robert Patrick Moore
William Emmett Moore
Henry Thomas Moorefield
Albert Hale Morris, Army
Charles Edward Morris, Army
Dudley Webster Morris
Edwin Henry Morris, Jr., Navy
Henry Hunter Morris
William Rodger Morris, missing in action
William H. Morris
Aubrey Trent Morrissett
Thomas William Morrissett, killed in action
Hubert Andrew Morton, Army
Lewis A. Morton, Army
Frank Bernard Moss
Alman Woodoroe Mottley
Alvin Cornelius Mottley
Charlie Swanson Mottley
Dale Lancaster Mottley, Army
D. Marvin Mottley
Levi A. Mottley
Wilbur Joseph Moyer, Army Air
Ira William McAllister
Willie Woodrow McChristian

Kenneth Lloyd McClenny, Army
Willie Mott McCormick
Henry Irving McCraw, Army
John William McFadden, Army
Russell Joseph McFadden
Alexander Perrow McGhee
James Stuart McGhee
Daniel Ashby McIntosh
Frank W. McIntosh, Jr.
Oscar Wicker McIntosh
Clyde Walter McKay, Army
Otis S. McKay, Army
Willis Horace McKay
Frank Preston McQuarry
Bernard Lukin Nash
William Bradford Neal, Navy
Robert Scott Nease, Army Air
John William Neathery
John M. Neff
Johnny A. Nelson, Army
Joseph Lee Nelson, Jr.
Calvin Leroy Nevin, Army
Henry Logan Newbill, II, Naval Air
James Newby
Richard Claiborne Newcomb
Charles Henry Newman, Jr., Army
Robert Thomas Newman, Army Air
Woodrow Pershing Newton
Cary Randolph Noblin, Army Air
Julian Corbett Noblin, Army
John Fulton Noel, Army
Richard David Noel, Navy
Winston Owen Noel, Army
Claude Perry Norton
Claude Swanson Nunn
Frank Clark Nunnally
John William Nunnally
Dewitt Talmage Oakes
Walter Oertel
John Edward Olgers
Raymond Watkins Olgers
Raymond Withers Olgers
Benjamin Lee Oliver
Benny Thomas Oliver
Harold Eugene Oliver
Henry Paul Oliver
John Everette Oliver
Neale Hudgins Oliver, Army Air
Elijah Walker Orange
Fayette Lawrence Orange
Guy Roy Orange
James Harty Orange
Marvin Habel Orange, Army
Francis Leigh Orgain, Marines

Lawrence Overby, Navy
James C. Overton, Army
James Watson Overton, Jr.
Walter Scott Overton, Jr., Army
Charles Clifton Owen, Army
Clyde Hagood Owen
John Havens Owen, Army
Thomas Venable Owen, Jr., Army
Arlie James Owensby, Army
Edith Ruth Owensby, Army (WAC)
Charles Elton Palmer
Norley Parton, Army
Glen W. Patterson, Navy
Hazel Cornell Patterson
Kemper Withers Patterson
David Walker Paulette, Army
Walter E. Paulett, Army
Douglas Lyle Paulson, Marines
Ernest Hardy Paulson, Army Air
Frank Penick Paulson
Edward Alfred Payne
Gordon R. Payne, Army
Oliver Ross Pearson, Jr., Navy
Raymond Clayton Pearson, Navy
William James Pearson, Navy
James O'Keefe Peery, Jr.
Walter Raymond Perrow
Neil Henry Pfansteil
Donald Baker Phillips, Army
Hoyd Edward Phillips, Army
M. Louise Phillips, Army (nurse)
Percy Bruce Phillips
Charles Bramel Pickett
Andrew Leiws Pickral, Army
Oscar Perry Pickral, Army
Walter B. Potter, Army
Robert E. Potts
Samuel L. Poulston
Richard Mason Powell
Sewell Ross Pressen, Jr., Navy
James Clifton Price
Ollie Jones Price
Roy Melton Price
Sterling Bolling Price, Army
Thad Young Price, Army
Wilfred Ashby Price, Army Air
William Lloyd Price
William Kenningham Priddy
Snell Bullard Prince
Blake Fuqua Putney, Army
Meriwether Y. Putney, Navy
Samuel Waverly Putney, Jr., Army
William Witt Putney, Marines
Robert Edward Quarles, Jr.

Garland Lee Queensberry, Navy
James Mawyer Queensberry
Isaac W. Rainey
James Holman Rand, Army
Emmett Alexander Ranson
Howard L. Ranson
Radford Bennett Hanson, Jr.
Russell Robert Ranson
Thomas Raymond Ranson, Army
William Edward Ranson
Thomas Henry Reamer, Jr.
Charles Thomas Redd, Jr.
John Elbert Redd, Army
Werner Bruce Redd, Navy
George L. Redmond, Army Air
Lawrence F. Redmond
Charles Sidney Reed
Frederick Venable Reed, Navy
Willie Carter Reid
David Robert Reveley, Navy
Richard Louis Reynolds
Roscoe Edward Reynolds, Navy
Charles William Rice, Army
Herbert F. Rice
William Thomas Rice, Army
Emory D. Rice
Bernard Carson Richardson
John Taft Rickman, Army
Ray Moore Rickman
Vincent T. Rickman
James Oliver Riddick, Army
Joseph A. Riddick
Barney Washington Riddle
Thomas Jefferson Riley
Jacob Wilson Roach, Navy
James Edward Roach
William Edward Roach
Arthur Robertson
George Dillard Robertson
Thomas Virgil Robertson
John Bowers Robinson
Kermit Fenton Robinson
James Roscoe Rogers
Philip H. Ropp, Navy
Johnnie Rolfe Rothgeb, Navy
Ralph John Rothgeb
Ulric O. Rothgeb, Army
Ralph Wick Routt, Army
Raymond John Routt
Arthur Samuel St. John
Robert Lee St. John
Spencer W. St. John
Dabney Henley Sandidge
Jane Cabell Sanford, Navy (WAVES)

Arthur Phillip Schultz, Army
Berman Mason Scott
Charles E. Scruggs, Jr.
Clarence Cecil Scruggs, Army
Curtis William Scruggs, Army
Eurtis Scruggs
George Edward Scruggs, Army
Isaac Walker Scruggs
James Roscoe Scruggs
Jack Sealey
Leo I. Searcey
Ellis Junior Shanks
Charles Richard Sheffield, Army
Earl Sheffield
Frank Budd Sheffield
George William Sheffield, Jr.
Patterson Shelton
Samuel Fletcher Shelton, Army
Frank Davis Shepard
Lucy K. Shields, Red Cross
Walter Dunnington Shields
George Deford Shorter
Howard Aubrey Shorter
Earnest Boyd Showalter, Army
Joseph Peter Shumate, Army
Daniel Earl Simmons
James Wood Simmons, Army
Kenneth Lee Simmons, Jr.
James Archer Simpson
John Daniel Simpson
Luther Leslie Simpson
George Henry Singleton, Army
Jessie William Singleton
Noland Stanley Skinner
Edward Daniel Slate, Navy
Claude Hardy Slayton
Russell Obey Slayton
Cornelius H. Smith, Army
Earl Hardy Smith, Army
Earl James Smith, Jr., Army
Frank Maynard Smith, Jr.
Geeder Smith
Grover Melvin Smith
Herman Edward Smith
Howard Irving Smith
Joseph Trent Smith, Army
Lee Bolton Smith
Lynwood Gordon Smith, Army
Morris Gilbert Smith, Jr., Army
Raymond Carl Smith
Robert Adams Smith, Army
Thomas Winfred Smith, Army
Colley Cornelius Southall
Fred Bernard Southall

Walter Delbert Southall, Navy
William Donnan Southall, killed in
action
James C. Soyars, Army
Noel Leonard Soyars
Fred Sparkman
Gerald York Sparkman
Claude Asa Spence
John Miller Spencer, Army Air
Willie Thomas Spencer, Army
Eugene T. Stamey, Navy
George Herbert Stanley
Robert Wilson Stanley
Holt Wilson Staples, Jr.
William Lewis Staples
Gordon Wilbur Staton
William Bernard Statzer
George Wingfield Stimpson
Allen Young Stokes, Jr., Army
Herbert Rieves Stokes, Army Air
Wake Sewell Stone, Jr., Marines
Erastas Fain Striplin, Jr., Navy
Norman Dobson Striplin, Navy
David Marshall Stuart, Army Air
Mathew Lee Tatum, Navy
James Edward Taylor
Percy Lee Taylor
Willie Ernest Taylor
Booker Terry
Samuel Curtis Thackston, Army
Irving Lee Tharp
Eugene Walker Thomas
Melvin Francis Thomas
Charles D. Thompson
Charlie Bailey Thompson
Charlie Willard Thompson, Army
Eddie Beutel Thompson
Floyd Samuel Thompson
Frank Knight Thompson, Army
Herman Lee Thompson, Army
Hillery Lee Thompson
Ivan Lanier Thompson, Army
J. Taylor Thompson, Jr., Army Air
Roy Dillard Thompson
Arnold Jackson Throckmorton, Army
Elijah Judson Throckmorton, Army
Holladay Nelson Throckmorton
Roy Washington Throckmorton, Navy
Emmett Tony
George D. Tony
Bettie Chapman Towler
Eugene Morris Towler
Ralph Harwood Towler
Frank Wilson Trainer, Army Air

Peter Edward Trainer, Army
Aubrey Clarence Trear
Joseph Peterfield Trent, Navy
Alexander C. Tucker
James Alton Turns
William Leslie Turns
M. P. Tynes, Jr., Navy
Edwin Booth Vaden
John H. Varner
Willis N. Varner
Basil Moorefield Vassar, Army Air
Reginald Levi Vassar, Army Air
Archie Willis Vaughan
Danny Irving Vaughan, Army
Edward Arto Vaughan
James Ralph Vaughan
Luther Rice Vaughan
Mason Knight Vaughan
Stanley Thomas Vaughan
John L. Venable, Army
Clinton Webb Verelle, Navy
Buck Vermilyes
Lancing Averett Viccellio
George Cleveland Waddell, Jr.
Olaf L. Waddell, Army
Harry Hodge Wagner
Harry W. Wakeman
Stuart Sydnor Walden, Navy
George Luther Walker, Jr.
Warren Monroe Walker, Jr., Army Air
Joseph Barrye Wall, Jr., Navy
Donald Henry Ward, Marines
Linton Briggs Ward, Navy
Carl Hanson Warwick
Frank Harrell Watkins, Jr.
William Forbes Watkins, Jr., Navy
David Lee Watson, Army Air
Leonard Melvin Watson, Navy
Samuel Elijah Watson, Navy
William Abner Watson, III, Army Air
Carlton Dalmore Wayne, Army
Dalton Norwood Wayne, Army
Charles Francis Weaver, Marines
Charles Ray Weaver, Navy
Henry Thomas Weaver
Robert James Weaver
William Henry Weaver
William S. Weaver, Jr., missing in
    action
Bernice Webb
Charles Winfred Webb
George Paul Webb, Army
Henry Melvin Webb
Joseph Allen Weinberg, Army Air

Clarence Johnson Welch
Mabel Grace Cunningham Welch,
    Navy (WAVES)
Paschal Ewart Welch, Army
Hugh Morgan Wells
William Bassett Wells, Jr.
Ernest Vincent West
Harvey Skelton Whitaker
Lloyd Durham Whitaker
Charles Ellwood Wilkerson, Army
Charles Leslie Wilkerson, Army Air
Edward Wilkerson
Fulton Ray Wilkerson, Army
Harry Flood Wilkerson, Army Air
Isaac Potter Wilkerson, Army
James Maxey Wilkerson, Naval Air
John H. Wilkerson, Jr., Army
John W. Wilkerson, Jr., Army
Milton C. Wilkerson
Robert N. Wilkerson, Navy
Walter Floyd Wilkerson, Army Air
Walter Russell Wilkerson, Army
William H. Wilkerson, Army
John Herbert Wilkes
Archibald Alexander Williams, Army
    Air
Chester Nathan Williams
George Bruce Williams
George Martin Williams, Army Air
James George Williams, Army
James Taylor Williams, Army
John Lyle Williams, Army
Leon Hutton Williams
Mark Byrd Williams, Army
Paul Harrison Williams
Robert Kyle Williams, Army
Russell Lowell Williams, Army
John Foster Williamson, Naval Air
Garland Davis Wilmoth
Charles Staples Wilson
David Spencer Wilson, missing in
    action
John Dennis Wilson
John Frank Wilson
Samuel Vaughan Wilson
William Archer Wilson
William Lockett Wilson
Dallas Cameron Wine
Lawrence Hornberger Wine
Oliver T. Wine, Jr.
Edward Henry Wingo
Carl Wiseman
Alfred Pershing Womack, Army
Emmett Barksdale Womack, Jr., Navy

George Edward Womack
George Henry Womack
Henry Bernard Womack
Hugh T. (Billy) Womack, Army
Jack Norman Womack, Army
Mary Clair Womack, Army (nurse)
Roy Marshall Womack
William Baker Womack
William Clyde Womack, Army
Wilson Howard Womack, Army
Woodrow Wilson Womack
George Douglas Wood
Harry Holladay Wood
John Earl Wood
Thomas Lester Wood
Richard Roller Wooling, Army

Walter Fisher Woosley
Shirley Lightfoot Wooten
Bernard Maynard Wooton
Curtis Woodrow Yates
Crawford Tafe Yeatts
Damon Hanley Yeatts
James R. Yeatts
Robert Lewis Yeatts, Navy
Roy James Yeatts
Cecil Gordon Young
Charles Herman Young
Francis Baldwin Young
Humphrey Baldwin Young
James Henry Young
John Richard Young
Woodrow Hudgins Young

APPENDIX 15

PRINCE EDWARD BICENTENNIAL COMMITTEE

Officers

J. Barrye Wall, Jr.........*Chairman*
J. M. Grainger.......*Vice-Chairman*

Miss Mary P. Dupuy......*Secretary*
Edward Carter............*Treasurer*

Board of Managers

P. T. Atkinson
M. H. Bittinger
Mrs. M. H. Bittinger
Mrs. E. T. Bondurant
Mrs. Grace Bradshaw
H. C. Bradshaw
Mrs. R. M. Bradshaw
Robert K. Brock
Mrs. J. L. Bugg
J. H. Clark
Edward Carter
R. B. Crawford

Mrs. Mildred D. Davis
W. L. Dickenson
T. D. Dillon
Miss Mary P. Dupuy
Dr. E. G. Gammon
C. W. Gates
Mrs. Grace Gordon
J. M. Grainger
Mrs. Cook Hix
Mrs. Roxie Jones
Dr. Dabney S. Lancaster
Miss Lillian Minkle
Mrs. William S. Morton

Dr. C. G. G. Moss
George W. Palmer
D. W. Paulette
Edward A. Payne
Dr. J. H. Smith
W. W. Vaughan
W. F. Watkins, Jr.
W. A. Watson, Jr.
John W. Wilson
R. B. Wilson, Jr.
Mrs. R. B. Wilson, Jr.
V. C. Womack

Executive Committee

Mrs. John G. Bruce
T. W. Brooks, Jr.
W. C. Fitzpatrick

Dr. D. S. Lancaster
J. B. Wall
V. C. Womack

District Chairmen

Buffalo...........Edward A. Payne
Farmville........Mrs. Grace Gordon
Hampden ....Mrs. Ruby Redd

Leigh.............Mrs. C. T. Redd
Lockett........Mrs. Grace Bradshaw
Prospect...........Mrs. Roxie Jones

Chairmen of Special Committees and for Events

Churches..Rev. Arthur Stevens
Education and Schools..................................T. J. McIlwaine
Finance...Edward Carter
Historical Research....................................Dr. C. G. G. Moss
Publicity...John C. Steck
Commemoration of Lee's Retreat.........................D. W. Paulette
"I Am An American Day"................................Mrs. Grace Gordon
Hospital Dedication....................................W. C. Fitzpatrick
Old Prince Edward Courthouse........Miss Mary Dupuy and Mrs. Ruby Redd
French's Episcopal Church..............................Mrs. J. L. Bugg
Final Event..V. C. Womack

Events

Jan. 25—200th year of Court observed with members of the county bar and court officers present, Circuit Court.

Jan. 28—Dinner, Hotel Weyanoke, Board of Supervisors entertained representative citizens from every section of county to discuss bicentennial observance.

February—Courses in local history and geography in public schools.

Feb. 18—Annual banquet, Judith Randolph Chapter, D.A.R.

March—National Symphony Orchestra.

April—Opening of Hillsman and Lockett houses, Sailor's Creek Battlefield, each Sunday afternoon.

April—Commemoration program of Lee's Retreat, Robert L. Scribner, Virginia State Library, speaker.

May—Longwood College May Day, bicentennial theme.

May 19—"I Am An American" Day; Charles L. Kessler, adjutant, Virginia Department, American Legion, speaker; Col. D. W. Paulette gave history of Co. G, 116th Infantry, Virginia National Guard.

June 8—Farmville High School Commencement, bicentennial theme, Educational History of Prince Edward, H. C. Bradshaw, speaker.

June 19—Annual meeting and picnic, Prince Edward Branch, Association for the Preservation of Virginia Antiquities, Sharon Baptist Church (Sandy River meeting-house).

July 11—Homecoming, Mt. Pleasant Methodist Church, and dedication of historical marker.

July 18—Homecoming, College Presbyterian Church.

July 25—Homecoming, Prospect Methodist Church.
     Homecoming, Briery and Meherrin Presbyterian Churches, at Briery Church.

Aug. 21—Bicentennial Program, Old Prince Edward Courthouse at the old Clerk's Office building, Worsham; speakers, Judge Joel W. Flood, Mrs. Mildred D. Davis, Richard W. Dupuy, H. C. Bradshaw.

Aug. 29—Dedication, Mettauer Wing, Southside Hospital, Dr. Wyndham Bolling Blanton, Richmond; Hon. Watkins M. Abbitt, Appomattox, Member of Congress, speakers.

Sept. 12—Dedication of marker near site of Episcopal Church at French's (Kingsville); James E. Kinard, Hampden-Sydney, speaker.

Oct. 6—Longwood Garden Club flower show, "Our Heritage of Beauty."

Oct. 15—Final Celebration:
  The parade planned had to be cancelled because of a storm, "hurricane Hazel."
  3 P. M., Historical program, Jarman Auditorium, H. C. Bradshaw, speaker.
  5 P. M., Tea, Longwood House.
  7 P. M., Banquet, Longwood College dining room, Hon. J. Lindsay Almond,
    Jr., Attorney General of Virginia, speaker.
  Bicentennial ball, Longwood College gymnasium.

Nov. 15—Closing date in historical essay contest, in three groups, college students
    ($150, first prize; $100, second prize; $50, third prize), high school students
    ($50, first prize; $25, second prize; $15, third prize), and elementary school
    students $15, first prize; $10, second prize; $5, third prize).

NOTES

CHAPTER I NOTES

1. Morgan Poitiaux Robinson: *Virginia Counties: Those Resulting From Virginia Legislation:* 43, 177 (hereafter cited as Robinson).
2. Robinson: 68.
3. William Waller Hening: *The Statutes at Large*, 1: 497. (Hereafter cited as Hening.) In 1656 Bristol Parish, which embraced the portions of Charles City and Henrico Counties south of the James River, was authorized to hold courts within the parish, commissioners (justices) residing within the parish constituting the court. Right of appeal to the county courts of Charles City and Henrico from the courts authorized for the parish was granted (Hening 1:424). In 1656 the place of the Charles City Court was moved to the south side of the James, as a result of a petition presented by Col. Abraham Wood and Anthony Wyatt on behalf of the residents of the county on the south side of the river. (Hening 1:426). This arrangement was so unsatisfactory to the Charles City people on the north side of the river that there was evidently talk of dividing the county. The act authorizing alternate courts on either side of the James directed that the county not be divided. It was enacted in response to a petition from the inhabitants north of the James. Each side of the river was directed to bear the cost of building its courthouse and jail for Charles City.
4. Robinson: 65, 189.
5. Hening 4:77-9; Robinson 75-7.
6. Hening 3:304-6.
7. Virginia Patent Book 14:89, Virginia State Library; Capt. H. T. Owen: "Early Settlers in Prince Edward County, Virginia," *Virginia Magazine of History and Biography* 22:94-6, 193-5, 305-7 (The article will be hereafter cited as Owen: Early Settlers and the magazine as *V.M.H.B.*); Prince Edward Deed Book 4:64. Reference to the patent book raises a point which may confuse the claim that Richard Jones was the first landowner in Prince Edward. One of the bounds of the Jones patent is "a corner of Lewis Bobbit's land and along his line east seventeen degrees north one hundred forty poles." A search of the index of the patent books shows no patent issued to Lewis Bobbit. William Bobbit of Prince George County received a grant of 254 acres on the west side of Rocky Run in Prince George County in 1725 (Patent Book 12:278); this was the only grant to a Bobbit found for this section, but there appears no connection with the Lewis Bobbit land. A deed by which David Greenhill conveyed 617 acres on Bush River in Prince Edward to Paschal Greenhill in 1768 confirms the location of the Jones patent in the area which became Prince Edward and also suggests the way in which Lewis Bobbit had acquired his land before the first patent to land in the area was issued. The land in the Greenhill transaction included 337 acres granted Richard Jones by patent Sept. 28, 1728, and 280 acres "never before granted and being the said tract of land bought by David Greenhill of Richard Jones." So Jones took up 280 acres adjoining his grant for which he never received a patent. Lewis Bobbit may have acquired his land in the same way. The boundaries to the land patented by Jones at no point include Bush River, although it is described as being on the south (east?) side of Bush River; the only watercourse mentioned as a boundary in the patent is a branch. The Greenhill deed, however, gives Bush River as a boundary, indicating that the land taken

up by Jones and never patented was bounded by the river. Another boundary in the Greenhill deed is Jones Branch, which was a tributary of Bush River.

8. Mss. Commission of the Peace for Amelia County (framed), in the Clerk's Office, Amelia; *Virginia Colonial Register:* 108; *Journals of the House of Burgesses of Virginia, 1727-40:* ix (hereafter cited as *Journals HB*); Amelia Order Book 2:141. For a summary of the career of Richard Jones, see Augusta B. Fothergill: *Peter Jones and Richard Jones Genealogies:* 254-7.

9. Virginia Patent Book 13:457; Owen, *V.M.H.B* 22:306; the date of the Williamson grant is erroneously given in this listing as 1730, undoubtedly a clerical or typographical error. This grant was located on the south side of Bush River, beginning at a sycamore where the second great branch above the hunting path flowed into Bush River. From the boundaries—northeast *to the county line* and along the county line northwest—this grant evidently lay on the south side of the Prince George-Brunswick line and this line formed a portion of the northern boundary of the land. It lay directly on Bush River.

   The Charles Williamson grant was included in a grant of 5,364 acres on Bush and Sandy Rivers in Amelia County to George Walker Feb. 5, 1753 (Mss. copy of patent, papers in suit of Francis Nash vs. James Watson, Package, April, 1819, Clerk's Office, Prince Edward County). This indicates that Williamson either conveyed his interest to Walker or that he abandoned his grant and Walker took it up. Also included in the Walker grant were the 1,258 acres granted Mathew Talbot Mar. 15, 1735.

10. Hening 4:467-8; Robinson: 43, 174.

11. Amelia Order Book 1:1.

12. Mss. Commission of the Peace for Amelia County (framed), Clerk's Office, Amelia.

13. Hening 3:258. See also for classification of tithable Hening 1:454 (1657-8); Hening 2:84 (1661-2), Hening 6:40-44 (1748).

14. Amelia Order Book 1:5.

15. Owen, *V.M.H.B.* 22:94-6, 193-5, 305-7.

16. Ibid. For the Booker grants, see Patent Book 15:177, 178. In view of the considerable discussion of the spelling of Sailor's Creek some twenty years ago, some readers may be interested in the spelling followed in this history. The oldest reference the writer has found to the stream is in the Booker patents in 1733; the spelling in both patents is Sailors. The next reference is in the Jefferson patent (see infra) in 1734, where the spelling is Saylors. The Amelia records prior to 1750 use the spelling Saylor's. After 1750, it is Sailor's. In the Prince Edward records it is Sailor's. The writer has chosen the oldest usage, which was consistently used in the Prince Edward records. There is no justification from the oldest records for Sayler's, which came into vogue in the 1930's. In this connection, the spelling *Boush* in the Amelia records for Bush River suggests a delightfully quaint pronunciation for that stream in the era when it was on the frontier.

17. Virginia Patent Book 15:222; Owen, *V.M.H.B.* 22:193.

18. Owen. *V.M.H.B.* 22:94-6, 193-5, 305-7.

19. Amelia Order Book 1:5.   20. Amelia Order Book 1:181.

21. Amelia Order Book 3:143.

22. Owen. *V.M.H.B.* 22:94-6, 193-5, 305-7.

23. Amelia Order Book 1:22.   24. Amelia Order Book 1:37.

25. Amelia Order Book 1:58.   26. Amelia Order Book 1:66.

27. Amelia Order Book 1:137. It will be noted in the lists of those directed to clear and work the roads that some of the landowners had not themselves settled on their holdings on the frontier, but that they had established "quarters" at which they located overseers with slaves and possibly some indentured servants to work the land. The slaves and indentured servants were designated

"hands," a usage which has continued in this section to the present to describe workers.

28. Amelia Order Book 1:184.   29. Amelia Order Book 1:175.
30. Amelia Order Book 1:132.   31. Amelia Order Book 1:138.
32. Amelia Order Book 1:175.   33. Amelia Order Book 1:185.
34. Amelia Order Book 1:182.   35. Amelia Order Book 1:212.
36. Amelia Order Book 1:222.   37. Amelia Order Book 1:226.
38. Amelia Order Book 1:248.   39. Amelia Order Book 1:265.
40. Amelia Order Book 1:311. This road followed approximately the route of the present highway 360, from the neighborhood of the present Burkeville via the present Green Bay and Meherrin to the neighborhood of the present Keysville.
41. Amelia Order Book 1:314. This road was the predecessor of the present road from Abilene to Farmville.
42. Amelia Order Book 1:316.
43. Amelia Order Book 1:352. This road led from the neighborhood of the present Burkeville into a road leading to Sandy River Church.
44. Amelia Order Book 2:1. This is the first order concerning roads in which most of those directed to clear or work the road were Scotch-Irish settlers in the Buffaloe Settlement. It is the second group of Scotch-Irish settlers listed in the Amelia Court records. The Sandy Ford was a few miles up the Appomattox from Farmville. The name still survives. The main branch of Spring Creek was probably the creek below the junction of two forks. The road cleared evidently ran parallel to Buffalo River.
45. Amelia Order Book 2:55. It is not clear that the road of which George Foster was named surveyor was in the present bounds of Prince Edward. The landmarks and locations are not positively identified with the county. The name Bush River road may have applied to the entire stretch of the road from Amelia Courthouse or from some other location to the river, and the point referred to may not have been in Prince Edward.
46. Amelia Order Book 2:57. George Moore's was Moore's Ordinary, which later became Meherrin.
47. Amelia Order Book 2:57-8.   48. Amelia Order Book 2:61.
49. Amelia Order Book 2:101. This is the only instance in which the writer has found a reference to Bush River Church. Since Sandy River Chapel, subsequently Church, was not far from Bush River, it is likely that Bush River was a clerical error for Sandy River Church.
50. Amelia Order Book 2:279.   51. Amelia Order Book 2:292.
52. Amelia Order Book 2:342, 343, 345.   53. Amelia Order Book 2:350.
54. Amelia Order Book 2:351.   55. Amelia Order Book 2:352.
56. Amelia Order Book 1:65.   57. Amelia Order Book 1:197.
58. Amelia Order Book 1:292.   59. Amelia Order Book 2:84.
60. Amelia Order Book 2:100. The location of this bridge, as well as of some other bridges, and of some of the early roads indicate that routes of travel kept closer to the Appomattox River than they do today.
61. Amelia Order Book 2:92.   62. Amelia Order Book 2:101.
63. Amelia Order Book 2:179.   64. Amelia Order Book 2:279.
65. Amelia Order Book 2:306. Prior to 1752, New Year's Day in England and its colonies was March 20. Consequently March 15, 1750, the date court met, was later in the year than October, 1750.
66. Amelia Order Book 3:64.
67. A family tradition, long current and accepted by both the American Clan Gregor Society and Americans of Royal Descent, identifies Thomas Mackgehee

of King William County, father of Jacob McGehee, as having been James Macgregor of the Scotch clan Gregor. Cf. Herbert Clarence Bradshaw: *The McGehee Family.* Mss.; Amelia Order Book 1:184.

68. J. D. Eggleston: "The Michaux Family"—Nash Excursus. *V.M.H.B.* 45:109-113. Reference is made to the will of Thomas Nash, John Nash's brother, dated September 8, 1732, and probated in Henrico at the June, 1737, Court, in which mention is made of the testator's father, Abner Nash of South Tenby, Wales, and in which property was bequeathed to Thomas and Mary Nash, children of John Nash. This article says John Nash was married before leaving Wales to Anne, said to have been the daughter of Sir Hugh Owen of Pembrokeshire. John Nash married secondly Elizabeth Fisher of Sussex County, Virginia. (Cf. *William and Mary Quarterly,* First Series, 11:269: "Sussex County Marriage Bonds": September 24, 1757. Col. John Nash Sen. of Prince Edward and Elizabeth Fisher, spinster, daughter of Charles Fisher, deceased. Witness: Mary Fisher.) The Nash Excursus identifies Elizabeth Fisher as the wife of John Nash, Jr. (*William and Mary Quarterly* will be hereafter cited as *W. & M. Quart.,* with the series indicated by the numeral in parentheses.)

69. Statement of the late W. S. Morton, Farmville, Va., to the author. Mr. Morton was a recognized authority on local history and genealogy.

70. Owen. *V.M.H.B.* 22:194-5.

71. William Henry Foote: *Sketches of Virginia.* First Series, pp. 102-3. (Hereafter cited as Foote.)

72. Amelia Order Book 1:24.   73. Amelia Order Book 1:30.

74. Amelia Order Book 1:239, 241. This was a chancery suit in which the parties came to an agreement, and it was dismissed.

75. Flournoy Rivers: "The Flournoy Family." *V.M.H.B.* 2:84, 195-9.

76. Robert L. Haycock: "Ancestors of Peter LeGrand, the Burgess, Prince Edward County, Virginia." *V.M.H.B.* 44:257-61; J. D. Eggleston: "The Michaux Family." *V.M.H.B.* 45:102-9, 411-9, 46:76-84; Owen. *V.M.H.B.* 22:94-6, 193-5, 305-7. *W. & M. Quart.* (1). 15:246-9. *Genealogy of the Venable Family,* prepared by Nathaniel Venable of Prince Edward, dated Dec. 25, 1790.

77. *W. & M. Quart.* (1). 25:268-74. Herbert Clarence Bradshaw: *The McGehee Family.* Mss.

78. Herbert Clarence Bradshaw: History of Farmville. The Farmville *Herald,* October 24, 1948. Prof. and Mrs. J. M. Grainger, present owners of Buffaloe, have collected a large and interesting assortment of Indian relics on their farm. Mrs. Grainger very kindly showed them to the writer when he was preparing the sesquicentennial history of Farmville, and the quoted passage was written from notes made at the time of the visit.

79. In describing the Grainger collection in the sesquicentennial history of Farmville, the writer deliberately avoided mention of the apparent Mayan influence in the piece of jewelry. He was then unaware of any connection between Indians of Mexico and Virginia. That the presence of Mexican jewelry would not be an impossibility is an impression gained from reading *The Spanish Jesuit Mission in Virginia, 1570-1572,* by Clifford M. Lewis, S.J., and Albert J. Loomis, S.J.

80. *V. M. H. B.* 14:289; *Travels and Works of Captain John Smith.* Edited by Edward Arber. 1:25, 51.

81. Amelia Order Book 1:73.   82. Amelia Order Book 1:102.

83. Amelia Order Book 1:184, 196. The Amelia Order Books mention no other resident of the area which became Prince Edward than Walker as vestryman or warden of Raleigh Parish.

84. Amelia Order Book 1:215. February, 1742, would be 1743 according to present reckoning.

85. Amelia Order Book 2:49.   86. Amelia Order Book 1:264.

87. Amelia Order Book 1:264.

88. Amelia Order Book 1:272. March, 1743, when Nash was recommended for appointment as justice, would be March, 1744, under current reckoning. Justices named in the July, 1744, commission were: Edward Booker, Charles Irby, Richard Booker, John Burton, John Nash, Abraham Green, James Clarke, Thomas Tabb, William Watson, Joseph Scott, John Hall, George Walker, Abraham Cocke, William Clement, Samuel Tarry, William Archer, Hezekiah Ford, William Booker, Henry Childs, Wood Jones, and Samuel Sherwin.

89. Amelia Order Book 2:2, 201.

90. J. D. Eggleston: "The Michaux Family"—Nash Excursus. *V.M.H.B.* 45: 109-13.

91. Amelia Order Book 2:34, 88, 175, 294, 350. Anderson's name is not included in any list of magistrates.

92. Hening 4:467-8.

93. Amelia Order Book 2:95.

94. *Journals HB*, 1742-9:305, 308, 328.

95. Amelia Order Book 2:142.

96. Hening 6:272.

97. Amelia Order Book 1:265.

98. Amelia Order Book 1:316, 352.

99. Amelia Order Book 2:203.

100. Amelia Order Book 2:141-2.

101. Foote, First Series: 103-7; John G. Herndon: "The Rev. John Thomson" (hereafter cited as Herndon: "Thomson"), *Journal of the Department of History in the Office of the General Assembly (Presbyterian Historical Society)* 20:153-4 (hereafter cited as *Journal P.H.S.*); J. D. Eggleston: "Buffaloe Settlement," *V.M.H.B.* 49:234-5.

102. Herndon: "Thomson." *Journal P.H.S.* 20:154, 156; 21:34-7.

103. Foote, First Series: 126.

104. Herndon: "Thomson." *Journal P.H.S.* 20:117, 140; 21:34-44. J. D. Eggleston: "Buffaloe Settlement." *V.M.H.B.* 49:234-6. Herndon follows Dr. W. H. T. Squires and Mrs. Augusta B. Fothergill in giving as authority for John Thomson's school in Amelia the statement of a Thomson descendant, the Rev. Vernon I'Anson, D.D. Dr. I'Anson, who was born in Petersburg in 1850, was not too far removed in time and generations from John Thomson to have received a reliable account from older members of the family. Dr. I'Anson was pastor, 1916-18, of Spring Creek Baptist Church, which is located near the place generally designated Thomson's home. The place is Cork, once home of Jesse Michaux and now home of G. E. Shorter. He could have learned of his ancestor's school from older people in the community during his Spring Creek pastorate. [Herbert Clarence Bradshaw: History of Spring Creek Baptist Church. Mss.]

105. Amelia Order Book 2:100.

106. Amelia Order Book 2:170, 372.

107. Amelia Order Book 2:148.

108. *Virginia Gazette*, November 7, 1754.

109. Amelia Order Book 2:266; 3:11.

110. Amelia Order Book 2:299.

111. Amelia Order Book 2:381.

112. Amelia Order Book 3:65.

113. Amelia Order Book 2:88-89.

114. Amelia Order Book 2:95; *Journals HB*, 1742-49:338, 339; March 15, 1748; in an account of Joseph Morton in James W. Alexander: *Life of Archibald Alexander*, p. 180, reference is made to Morton's pursuit of a horse thief for over 100 miles, "with success, although the fugitive had taken all imaginable means of concealing his course." No doubt this reference is to the Anderson-Morton exploits; it explains why their neighbors regarded it as worthy of more than the customary reward.

115. *Journals HB*, 1742-9:177 (March 7, 1745).

116. Amelia Order Book 1:321.

117. *Journals HB*, 1742-9:177.

118. Hening 5:375-7. It may be of interest to note that each of the counties mentioned bordered on the Appomattox River. Prince George and Amelia lay on the south bank, Henrico, Goochland, and Albemarle on the north bank. Dinwiddie had not been cut off from Prince George, nor Prince Edward from Amelia. Chesterfield had not been separated from Henrico, Cumberland from Goochland, or Buckingham from Albemarle. Powhatan was later to be cut off from Cumberland.

119. Hening 6:291-3.   120. Amelia Order Book 2:95.

121. *Journals HB*, 1742-9:341. (March 7, 1748.)

122. *Journals HB*, 1752-8:109. (November 6, 1753.)

123. Amelia Order Book 3:143.   124. *Journals HB*, 1752-8:122.

125. *Journals HB*, 1752-8:124.   126. *Journals HB*, 1752-8:125.

127. *Journals HB*, 1752-8:170.   128. Hening 6:379-80.

129. Robinson: 189.

CHAPTER II NOTES

1. Prince Edward Order Book (hereafter cited as Order Book) 1:1.

2. This conclusion is suggested from Anderson's offer of his kitchen as a jail (see *infra*), the central location of his ordinary, and the subsequent choice of the place as the location for the courthouse (see *infra*).

3. Order Book 1:1.   4. Amelia Order Book 3:141.

5. Order Book 1:1.   6. Order Book 1:6.

7. Order Book 1:8.   8. Order Book 1:20.

9. Order Book 1:19.   10. Order Book 1:23; 4:335.

11. Order Book 5:507.   12. Order Book 1:2.

13. Order Book 1:3.

14. Order Book 1:10. After the symbol for the pound, the first figure indicates the number of pounds. The second indicates the number of shillings, and if there is a third figure it indicates the number of pence.

15. Order Book 1:67.   16. Order Book 1:65.

17. Order Book 1:67, 108.   18. Order Book 1:22.

19. Order Book 1:42.   20. Order Book 1:102.

21. *Virginia Gazette,* November 7, 1754. Charles Anderson offered for sale in an advertisement in this newspaper two tracts, one of 3,000 acres on which Prince Edward Courthouse stood and a nearby tract of 1,000 acres. Anderson's attitude toward serving as a magistrate in Prince Edward remains an enigma. He participated actively in civic and public affairs and served in the House of Burgesses from 1754 until 1761. But he never served as a magistrate, although he ranked third in the first commission which has been preserved. Was it because he felt it improper to serve as a magistrate of the court which met at the place where he kept a tavern? Or did he feel that serving as a magistrate would be to his disadvantage, when such service would take him from his place of business at the busiest time? Thus far, this Charles Anderson's career has not been traced except for the period he lived in Prince Edward. He had contemporaries of the same name. See Prince Edward Order Book 1:33: in March, 1755, Charles Anderson and Charles Anderson, otherwise called We Charles Anderson, of Amelia County and Charles Anderson of Cumberland County came into court and confessed judgment to Messrs. Archibald Buchanan, John Bowman and Co., merchants of Glasgow, for £469:2:4 (469 pounds, two shillings, four pence) current money of Virginia. The career of Charles Anderson of Cumberland as an adult and his descendants have been fairly

well traced. So have the adult career and descendants of Charles Anderson of Amelia, who in the late 1790's moved to Kentucky. No such good fortune has attended research in the life of Charles Anderson of Prince Edward, except for the decade and a half he was identified with the site which became Prince Edward Courthouse.

22. Order Book 2:40.

23. Order Book 2:123

24. Order Book 2:286.

25. Order Book 4:7.

26. Order Book 4:10.

27. Order Book 4:45.

28. Order Book 4:64.

29. Order Book 4:240.

30. Order Book 3:3.

31. Order Book 4:82.

32. Order Book 4:247.

33. Order Book 5:196. *Virginia Gazette* (Rind), February 4, 1773.

34. Order Book 5:477.

35. Order Book 5:496.

36. Order Book 5:477.

37. Order Book 5:490.

38. Order Book 5:512.

39. Order Book 1:3.

40. Order Book 1:6.

41. Order Book 1:22.

42. Order Book 4:55.

43. Order Book 1:111, 156.

44. Order Book 1:3.

45. Order Book 1:6.

46. Order Book 1:10.

47. *Ibid.*

48. Order Book 1:13.

49. Order Book 1:23.

50. Amelia Order Book 3:143.

51. Order Book 1:66.

52. Order Book 1:101.

53. Order Book 1:138.

54. Order Book 1:166.

55. Order Book 2:41.

56. Order Book 2:79.

57. Order Book 2:122.

58. Order Book 2:207-8.

59. Order Book 2:263.

60. Order Book 2:326-7.

61. Order Book 3:86.

62. Order Book 4:7-8.

63. Order Book 4:78-9.

64. Order Book 4:174.

65. Order Book 4:248.

66. Order Book 4:335.

67. Order Book 5:89.

68. Order Book 5:193.

69. Order Book 5:347.

70. Order Book 5:463.

71. Order Book 5:489.

72. Order Book 3:127; 4:7-8. The levy for 1766 was set in November at nine pounds of tobacco per poll, to yield 12,429 pounds. Expenses increased to 16,575 pounds of tobacco, and in May, 1767, the levy, was increased to twelve pounds of tobacco per poll.

73. Order Book 1:8.

74. Manuscript, Clerk's Office of Prince Edward County. Copy furnished author by Mrs. Margaret H. (W. S.) Morton, Farmville.

75. Order Book 4:13.

76. Order Book 5:241.

77. Hening 7:395-6.

78. Hening 7:544.

79. Hening 8:39-41.

80. Hening 8:178-82.

81. *Journals HB*, 1766-69:246, 285.

82. Order Book 1:39.

83. Order Book 1:111, 113 ff.

84. Order Book 2:72.

85. Order Book 2:198.

86. Order Book 2:266.

87. Order Book 2:117.

88. Order Book 5:239.

89. Order Book 2:229.

90. Order Book 1:42.

91. Order Book 1:65, 67.

92. Order Book 3:45.

93. Order Book 2:12, 78.

94. Order Book 2:29.

95. Order Book 4:232.

96. Order Book 4:279.

97. Order Book 4:280.

98. Order Book 4:282.

99. Order Book 5:291.   100. Order Book 1:78.
101. Order Book 2:209.   102. Order Book 4:62.
103. Order Book 2:225.   104. Order Book 2:287.
105. Order Book 4:94, 100, 101.   106. Order Book 5:42, 89.
107. Order Book 5:455.   108. Order Book 3:15.
109. Order Book 5:236-37.
110. *Virginia Gazette* (Rind), May 27, 1773.
111. Order Book 5:282.   112. Order Book 2:301.
113. Order Book 2:302.   114. Order Book 1:122.
115. Order Book 1:136.   116. Order Book 2:291.
117. Order Book 3:127: These patrollers covered most of the county, if not all. Both Rices lived in the neighborhood of the present village of Rice, and it was from the meeting-house built by William Rice (of which Ike or Icay Rice was also a trustee) that the place took its name (see *infra*). The Bowmans lived near Sandy River Church. Baulding (Baldwin), Caldwell, and Bird were residents of the Buffaloe Settlement.
118. Order Book 1:2. This road was the predecessor of the road leading from the Worsham-Abilene road to Darlington Heights. How far it led westward is uncertain, since the exact location of William Watson's house is not known.
119. Order Book 2:103.   120. Order Book 3:95.
121. Order Book 4:1.   122. Order Book 4:2, 14.
123. Order Book 4:6. At the next session of the court (Order Book 4:14), a power of attorney from James French to Andrew French was recorded. The Frenches gave their name to the settlement now called Kingsville, but which had previously been called French's Store or French's Old Store.
124. Order Book 4:18.   125. Order Book 4:101.
126. Order Book 4:104.   127. *Ibid.*
128. Order Book 4:193.   129. Order Book 1:8.
130. Order Book 1:39, 59.   131. Order Book 2:42.
132. Order Book 2:86.   133. Order Book 2:95.
134. Cumberland Order Book, July Court, 1761. This Charles Anderson lived in Cumberland.
135. Order Book 2:109. The amount of the bond was left blank in the record.
136. Order Book 2:133.   137. Order Book 4:184, 240.
138. Order Book 4:241.   139. Order Book 1:138.
140. Order Book 2:166.   141. Order Book 2:51.
142. Order Book 2:116.   143. Order Book 3:127.
144. Order Book 2:157.   145. Order Book 3:88.
146. Order Book 5:293.   147. Order Book 5:89.
148. Order Book 5:293.   149. Order Book 5:331.
150. Order Book 5:346.   151. Order Book 1:83.
152. Order Book 2:86.   153. Order Book 4:80.
154. Order Book 4:91
155. Order Book 1:89, 139;2:95, 106, 114; 4:135, 156.
156. Order Book 2:40, 50, 206.   157. Order Book 2:95, 106.
158. Order Book 2:39.   159. Order Book 3:87; 5:177.
160. Order Book 5:139.   161. Order Book 1:22.
162. Order Book 1:120.   163. Order Book 1:161.
164. Order Book 2:114, 206, 211.

165. Order Book 2:114; 4:197. The sheriff was directed to pay Theodorick Carter £13:16 due Peter LeGrand for repairs to Briery bridge.
166. Order Book 2:286.   167. Order Book 1:36, 89; 5:177.
168. Order Book 2:40.   169. Order Book 2:39.
170. Order Book 2:40.
171. Order Book 1:22, 76, 115; 2:38, 73, 139, 213.
172. Order Book 1:34, 147.   173. Order Book 1:5.
174. Order Book 1:47.
175. Order Book 2:53, 139, 286; 4:31, 204. Simmons lived fifteen miles from the Courthouse (Order Book 4:244) in the Prospect neighborhood (Order Book 4:101).
176. Order Book 1:155. August Court, 1758: the clerk was directed to notify the Governor that Mr. Ewing had received a license to keep an ordinary since the last commission. Since there is no other reference to the issuance of a license to Ewing, the order suggests that the Order Books do not contain a complete list of ordinary licenses granted in the county.
177. Order Book 2:38.   178. Order Book 2:44, 120.
179. Order Book 2:73, 121.   180. Order Book 2:145.
181. Order Book 3:4.   182. Order Book 3:129.
183. Order Book 4:23, 137, 247.   184. Order Book 4:82, 257; 5:19.
185. Order Book 4:88.   186. Order Book 4:123.
187. Order Book 4:183.   188. Order Book 4:251.
189. Order Book 5:60, 177.   190. Order Book 5:90, 197.
191. Order Book 5:33.   192. Order Book 5:83, 465, 488.
193. Order Book 5:334.   194. Order Book 5:465, 496.
195. Order Book 4:57.   196. Order Book 4:292.
197. Order Book 1:30, 77, 104, 147; 2:2, 51, 81, 139.
198. Order Book 1:30.   199. Order Book 1:104.
200. Order Book 1:147.   201. Order Book 2:2.
202. Order Book 2:51.   203. Order Book 2:139.
204. Order Book 2:270.   205. See *supra*, note 36.
206. *Virginia Gazette* (Purdie & Dixon), Nov. 5, 1767.
207. Order Book 1:8. Orange County, North Carolina, formed in 1752, still preserves as treasured relics the standard weights and measures of colonial times. Since standards had not been provided in Prince Edward by May, 1757, the grand jury presented the Court for its failure to provide them. [Order Book 1:111.]
208. Order Book 1:38.   209. Order Book 1:144.
210. Order Book 2:41.   211. Order Book 1:58.
212. Order Book 1:53. The dates given here and subsequently are those of the commission.
213. Order Book 1:78.
214. Order Book 1:109. There is no reference to Anderson presenting a colonel's commission and taking the oath of office.
215. Order Book 1:53.   216. Order Book 1:78.
217. Order Book 2:1.   218. Order Book 2:260.
219. Order Book 1:53.   220. Order Book 1:58.
221. Order Book 1:80.   222. Order Book 1:167.
223. Order Book 2:105.   224. Order Book 2:165.
225. Order Book 2:177.   226. Order Book 2:260.
227. Order Book 4:1.   228. Order Book 4:135.

229. Order Book 4:219.   230. Order Book 4:269.
231. Order Book 2:154.   232. *V.M.H.B.* 19:297-98.
233. Hening 7:120-21.   234. *Journals HB*, 1752-59:484.
235. Order Book 1:169.   236. Order Book 1:170.
237. Hening 7:229. Cf. Order Book 1:159 for Holcomb's account.
238. *Journals HB*, 1770-72:35-6, 49.
239. Order Book 6:66. This list from the Order Book has been published in *V.M.H.B.* 21:88-9 as "Prince Edward in the French War" by Alfred J. Morrison.
240. Order Book 6:67.
241. Order Book 6:68. Jeremiah Penix, brother and heir-at-law of Edward Penix, filed for his claim.
242. Order Book 6:69.   243. Order Book 6:73.
244. Order Book 6:77.   245. *Journals HB*, 1752-58:361, 369.
246. *Journals HB*, 1758-61:18.
247. *Journals HB*, 1752-58:426; 1758-61:20, 27, 33, 37.
248. *Journals HB*, 1758-61:81, 107.   249. Hening 7:232-33.
250. Order Book 1:159.
251. *Virginia Gazette* (Purdie & Dixon) Feb. 21, 1771. Campbell's 1771 schedule of musters: Surry, Mar. 15; Prince George, Mar. 18; Chesterfield, Mar. 19; Cumberland, Mar. 21; Prince Edward, Mar. 22; Amelia, Mar. 26; Brunswick, Mar. 29; Dinwiddie, April 1; Sussex, April 5; Southampton, April 8; Isle of Wight, April 10; Nansemond, April 15; Norfolk County, April 22; Norfolk Town, April 24; Princess Anne, April 26.
252. *Virginia Gazette* (Purdie & Dixon), Mar. 5, 1772.
253. *Virginia Gazette* (Purdie & Dixon), Mar. 4, 1775.
254. *Virginia Gazette* (Purdie & Dixon), Feb. 24, 1774.
255. *Virginia Gazette* (Dixon), Mar. 4, 1775.
256. *Virginia Gazette* (Purdie), Aug. 25, 1775.
257. Hening 5:408-31.
258. Vestry Book of St. Patrick's Parish, Prince Edward County, Virginia. Photostat. 55-67. Since any two processioners named in a precinct could carry out the processioning, the names of some of those designated may not appear in the reports.
259. Vestry Book: 9.   260. Vestry Book: 68-82.
261. Vestry Book: 83-84.   262. Order Book 1:2.
263. Order Book 1:28.   264. Order Book 1:53.
265. Hening 6:441. This act setting the bounds of Bedford set the eastern boundary as the line running from the mouth of Falling River north, twenty degrees east, to intersect the line of Prince Edward County. A portion of Albemarle above the head of Falling Creek was added to Bedford.
266. Order Book 1:159; *Journals HB*, 1758-61:76. The area of the proposed addition was mentioned in neither of these references.
267. Order Book 3:60.   268. Order Book 1:2.
269. Order Book 1:42.   270. Order Book 1:102.
271. Order Book 1:113.   272. Order Book 2:20.
273. Order Book 2:55.   274. Order Book 2:85.
275. Order Book 2:164.   276. Order Book 2:181.
277. Order Book 3:1.   278. Order Book 3:25.
279. Order Book 3:59.   280. Order Book 4:327.
281. Order Book 5:57.   282. Order Book 5:267.

283. Order Book 5:269.

284. Order Book 5:283.

285. Order Book 5:250, 269.

286. *Virginia Gazette* (Rind), Feb. 25, 1773; (Purdie & Dixon), Apr. 8, 1773.

287. Order Book 1:63.

288. Order Book 1:68.

289. Order Book 1:125.

290. Order Book 4:325.

291. Order Book 1:159.

292. *Journals HB*, 1758-61:6.

293. Hening 5:326-44; 7:242; 7:278.

294. Hening 7:384, 645.

295. Hening 7:397-401.

296. Order Book 4:331-34.

297. Order Book 5:41.

298. Hening 7:622.

299. Order Book 1:102, 116.

300. Order Book 1:155, 167.

301. Order Book 2:80.

302. Order Book 2:119, 123, 138.

303. Order Book 2:122.

304. Order Book 2:2, 122, 170, 239.

305. Order Book 2:122, 218.

306. Order Book 2:239. Cf. Order Book 2:80, Feb. 16, 1761, for probate of Wimbish's will. He was included in the commission presented to the March, 1761, Court, after his death. Cf. Vestry Book: 15 for Hastie's removal.

307. Order Book 3:119.

308. Order Book 4:2.

309. Order Book 5:108.

310. Order Book 5:151.

311. Order Book 5:465.

312. Order Book 1:2.

313. Order Book 1:90, 109, 116.

314. Order Book 1:132, 155; 2:3, 21.

315. Order Book 2:26, 30, 65, 82.

316. Order Book 2:95, 102, 173, 216.

317. Order Book 2:294, 260; 3:1.

318. Order Book 3:46, 75.

319. Order Book 4:30, 63.

320. Order Book 4:212, 245.

321. Order Book 5:54, 73.

322. Order Book 5:284, 329.

323. Order Book 5:479, 492, 494.

324. Order Book 5:494, 495.

325. Order Book 5:479.

326. Order Book 2:119, 239; 3:119.

327. Order Book 2:30, 102.

328. Order Book 2:139.

329. Order Book 2:260.

330. Order Book 3:87, 117; 4:3, 63.

331. Order Book 4:269, 286.

332. Order Book 4:247.

333. Order Book 5:329, 493.

334. Order Book 5:100, 235.

335. Order Book 5:334, 379.

336. Order Book 5:495.

337. Order Book 1:10.

338. Order Book 1:39.

339. Order Book 1:67.

340. Order Book 1:73.

341. Order Book 1:89.

342. Order Book 1:126.

343. Order Book 1:128.

344. Order Book 1:133.

345. Order Book 1:163.

346. Order Book 2:20.

347. Order Book 2:44.

348. Order Book 2:50.

349. Order Book 2:105.

350. Order Book 2:145.

351. Order Book 2:162.

352. Order Book 4:2.

353. Order Book 4:71.

354. Order Book 4:82.

355. Order Book 4:108.

356. Order Book 4:247.

357. Order Book 4:322.

358. Order Book 5:14.

359. Order Book 5:63.

360. Order Book 5:200.

361. Order Book 5:331.

362. Order Book 1:1, 2.

363. Order Book 3:117; 4:1.

364. Order Book 1:66, 137, 153; 2:315; 4:249; 5:489.

365. Order Book 4:1.

366. Cf. Charles S. Sydnor: *Gentlemen Freeholders: Political Practices in Washington's Virginia* for the development of this theme. Dr. Sydnor's book is an amplification of his inaugural address as Harold Vyvyan Harmsworth Professor of American History at Oxford University.

367. Hening 7:517-30; 6:498.   368. Hening 6:496-97.

369. Mss. records in the Clerk's Office, Farmville, Va. Copied for the author by Mrs. Margaret H. Morton, Farmville.

370. *Journals HB*, 1752-55:viii, note 22. Since the third session of the 1752-55 Assembly began Feb. 14, 1754 (p. 175) and ended Feb. 23, 1754 (p. 185), before the Prince Edward election, it is difficult to see how Nash and Anderson could have attended this session as burgesses. The House of Feb. 18 requested the Governor to issue writs for the election of burgesses in Prince Edward and Sussex Counties (p. 178). *Virginia Colonial Register,* compiled by William G. and Mary Newton Stanard lists them as attending the session of Feb. 14, 1754 (p. 131).

371. *Journals HB*, 1752-55:234.

372. *Virginia Colonial Register:* 132, 133, 135, 137, 139, 141, 143, 145.

373. *Virginia Colonial Register:* 147, 149, 151, 153.

374. *Virginia Colonial Register:* 154, 158, 159, 161, 163, 165, 168, 169.

375. *Virginia Colonial Register:* 173, 175, 177, 179.

376: *Journals HB*, 1766-69:16.

377. *Virginia Colonial Register:* 181.

378. *Virginia Colonial Register:* 184, 186, 189.

379. *Virginia Colonial Register:* 192, 197.

380. *Virginia Colonial Register:* 200; *Journals HB*, 1773-76:164.

381. *Virginia Colonial Register:* 202.

382. *Virginia Colonial Register:* 205, 207.

383. *Virginia Colonial Register:* 209.

CHAPTER III NOTES

1. Order Book 1:3.

2. *Journals HB*, 1752-58:236.

3. *Journals HB*, 1752-58:240.

4. *Journals HB*, 1753-58:258.

5. *Journals HB*, 1752-58:264.

6. *Journals HB*, 1752-58:281.

7. *Journals HB*, 1752-58:283.

8. *Journals HB*, 1752-58:284.

9. Hening 6:504-7.

10. Order Book 1:59; Vestry Book of St. Patrick's Parish, Prince Edward County. 1755-1774:1. Photostat. Hereafter cited as Vestry Book.

11. Vestry Book: 4; Order Book 1:68. There is no reference to the election of Samuel Goode, but he took the oath of office Jan. 13, 1756, and is listed as attending a meeting of the vestry Mar. 8, 1757. Since the names of only 11 of the 12 chosen at the first election have been given previously, it is logical to assume that Goode was the twelfth vestryman in the first election.

12. Vestry Book: 4. Scott qualified Apr. 12, 1751 (Order Book 1:109) and Martin at the August Court, 1757 (Order Book 1:123).

13. Vestry Book: 5. Hastie qualified at November Court, 1757 (Order Book 1:135).

14. *Journals HB*, 1758-61:71; Hening 7:301.

15. *Journals HB*, 1758-61:85.   16. Hening 7:301-3.

17. Order Book 2:25.
18. Order Book 2:30.
19. Vestry Book: 8.
20. Order Book 2:134.
21. Vestry Book: 15.
22. Vestry Book: 25.
23. Vestry Book: 38.
24. Vestry Book: 45.
25. Vestry Book: 11.
26. Vestry Book: 12.
27. Vestry Book: 15.
28. Vestry Book: 18.
29. Vestry Book: 22.
30. Vestry Book: 24.
31. Vestry Book: 25.
32. Vestry Book: 27.
33. Vestry Book: 30.
34. Vestry Book: 33.
35. Vestry Book: 36.
36. Vestry Book: 37.
37. Vestry Book: 39.
38. Vestry Book: 43.
39. Vestry Book: 1, 3.
40. Vestry Book: 42.
41. Vestry Book: 41.
42. *W. & M. Quart.* (2) 2:276-8. "Rev. James McCartney" by A. J. Morrison.
43. Order Book 5:478. Cf. *W. & M. Quart.* (2) 2:276-8. Morrison noted that McCartney was traceable to 1774 in the Vestry Book and adds that it does not appear what became of him. He mistakenly supposes that McCartney was a Tory and left Prince Edward at the beginning of the Revolution.
44. Vestry Book: 43. The minister is called Oglesby in the former reference, Ogilvie in this.
45. Vestry Book: 2.
46. Vestry Book: 4.
47. Vestry Book: 8.
48. Vestry Book: 25, 26.
49. Vestry Book: 40.
50. Vestry Book: 21, 29.
51. Vestry Book: 26, 29.
52. Vestry Book: 5.
53. Vestry Book: 7.
54. Vestry Book: 10.
55. Vestry Book: 18.
56. Vestry Book: 20.
57. Vestry Book: 37, 42.
58. The term sexton has long survived in Prince Edward to designate the caretaker at a church. Janitor now seems to be rapidly supplanting it, except among older people.
59. The records of Raleigh and Nottoway Parishes for the colonial period are not known to be in existence. Their loss (or unavailability, if they do exist) makes it impossible to establish the dates of the building of Sandy River Chapel and Buffalo Church (or it may have started as a chapel, as did Sandy River). A search of the deed book indexes in Amelia for the period fails to provide any information on this subject.
60. Vestry Book: 11.
61. Vestry Book: 12.
62. See *infra*, note 137.
63. Vestry Book: 13.
64. Vestry Book: 14.
65. Vestry Book: 16.
66. Vestry Book: 14.
67. Vestry Book: 15.
68. Vestry Book: 17.
69. Hening 7:611-12. Since John Nash was undertaker of the church at French's, and Peter LeGrand the builder of the chapel, this leaves Sandy River Church as the one built by Thomas Wood. The letting of Sandy River Church Mar. 25, 1763, seems to refer to the building to replace the burned church.
70. Vestry Book: 17.
71. Vestry Book: 18-19.
72. Vestry Book: 22.
73. Vestry Book: 24. From this reference, it appears that Peter LeGrand and Christopher Ford built Sandy River Church to replace the burned church begun by Thomas Wood. This is a part of the church which stands today.
74. Vestry Book: 21. Thomas Nash evidently was associated with his father, John Nash, in building the "upper church" at French's.

75. Vestry Book: 20.   76. Vestry Book: 26.
77. Vestry Book: 38.   78. Vestry Book: 13.
79. Vestry Book: 19.   80. Vestry Book: 14, 15.
81. Vestry Book: 20.   82. Vestry Book: 2.
83. Vestry Book: 4.   84. Vestry Book: 3.
85. Vestry Book: 4.
86. Vestry Book: 7. The levy was first set at 23,520 pounds tobacco on Nov. 8, 1758. It was raised in Jan., 1759.
87. Vestry Book: 9.   88. Vestry Book: 11.
89. Vestry Book: 17.   90. Vestry Book: 16.
91. Vestry Book: 21.   92. Vestry Book: 23.
93. Vestry Book: 24.   94. Vestry Book: 27-8.
95. Vestry Book: 30.   96. Vestry Book: 33.
97. Vestry Book: 35.   98. Vestry Book: 37.
99. Vestry Book: 42.   100. Vestry Book: 46.
101. Vestry Book: 1, 11.   102. Vestry Book: 1.
103. Vestry Book: 2.   104. Vestry Book: 4.
105. Vestry Book: 5.   106. Vestry Book: 6.
107. *Today and Yesterday in the Heart of Virginia.* "Episcopal Churches," by Mrs. J. Luckin Bugg. Pp. 307-8. Mrs. Bugg gives a copy of the contract, dated Sept. 6, 1758, between Peter LeGrand and Robert Hastie (given as "Bastie"), who was evidently security for LeGrand, and the church wardens. James Wimbish and Thomas Scott.
108. Vestry Book: 8.   109. Vestry Book: 6.
110. Vestry Book: 11.   111. Vestry Book: 3.
112. Vestry Book: 45.
113. Vestry Book: 26. In 1763 the vestry directed the minister to hold services once every three months at the chapel and to divide the rest of his time equally between the two churches (Vestry Book: 18).
114. Vestry Book: 20. Claret seems to have been the favorite wine for communion. John Nash was paid eight shillings for claret used at Sandy River Church in 1759 (Vestry Book: 8).
115. Vestry Book: 2.   116. Vestry Book: 8.
117. Vestry Book: 12.   118. Vestry Book: 10.
119. Vestry Book: 33.   120. Vestry Book: 32.
121. Vestry Book: 34.   122. Vestry Book: 38.
123. Vestry Book: 21.   124. Vestry Book: 20.
125. For examples, cf. Order Book 1:127, 133; 6:41.
126. Order Book 1:126.   127. Order Book 1:146.
128. Order Book 3:2.
129. For a full treatment of the Old Side-New Side controversy, see Leonard J. Trinterud: *The Making of an American Tradition.* Hereafter cited as Trinterud.
130. Foote, First Series: 159-60, 182.
131. Foote, First Series: 126-30; J. D. Eggleston: *The Beginnings of Old Briery and Cumberland Churches:* 7; Powhatan Bouldin: *The Old Trunk:* 29-30.
132. Foote, First Series: 160, 182, 214.
133. Foote, First Series: 214-5; Alexander: *Life of Archibald Alexander:* 180-1. Foote and Alexander give the place of Morton's residence at the time as Little Roanoke Bridge in Lunenburg (later Charlotte). Morton, however, lived at Slate Hill in Prince Edward until 1755 (*Today and Yesterday in the Heart of Virginia:* 259), having been a magistrate of the county when

it was established. Since the Rev. Robert Henry was installed as pastor of Briery June 4, 1755 (Foote, First Series: 220; Second Series: 41), Davies' visit to Morton must have taken place very soon after his removal to Lunenburg, if Morton were living there at the time of the visit. It is possible, perhaps probable, that Foote and Alexander assumed that Morton was living at Little Roanoke Bridge when Davies visited him because he was living there when they knew of him. The shortness of the time which the circumstances would require between Morton's conversion to Presbyterianism, the organization of Briery Church, the calling of Henry including action by Presbytery on the call, and Henry's installation on June 4, 1755, lend support to the view that Morton was living at Slate Hill when Davies visited his home. Dr. J. D. Eggleston was evidently of the opinion that Morton was living in Prince Edward at the time of Davies' visit. In *The Beginnings of Old Briery and Cumberland Churches*, p. 10, in introducing the quotation from Alexander concerning Mr. and Mrs. Morton's first participation in a Presbyterian communion, Dr. Eggleston says: "Joseph Morton did not hesitate to go from Prince Edward to Cumberland to attend a church service."

134. James W. Douglas: *A Manual of the Members of the Briery Presbyterian Church, Virginia* (1828): 14-20. (Hereafter cited as Douglas.)

135. Foote, First Series: 220; Second Series: 49-50.

136. Foote, Second Series: 49.

137. Foote, Second Series: 53.

138. Foote, Second Series: 44.

139. *V.M.H.B.* 49:239-40, 243. J. D. Eggleston: "The Buffaloe Settlement."

140. *V.M.H.B.* 49:239. J. D. Eggleston: "The Buffaloe Settlement."

141. Prince Edward Deed Book 2:77. Indenture dated Oct. 14, 1761, from Samuel Cunningham of Prince Edward to John Caldwell, James Donald, John Cunningham, and William Watson, a little over three acres for five shillings. The site was only a short distance from the present Five Forks, not at the present location of the church.

142. Order Book 2:29. This date suggests that Sankey himself may have come to Prince Edward before Aug. 21, 1759. If he did not come until then, he was promptly and prominently identified with the place of worship of the Buffalo congregation and as its pastor. Eggleston (*V.M.H.B.* 49:239) states that Sankey and a large part of his congregation moved to Prince Edward between Aug. 21 and Oct. 9, 1759.

143. Trinterud: 147-8. Trinterud spells Sankey's name Zancky. See Trinterud: 70, 74, 82 for Sankey's ordination difficulties, after having been found to have plagiarized heretical writers in his ordination sermon.

144. Foote, Second Series: 75.

145. Cf. Prince George County Records, 1713-28, Part I: 58 for the oath of Robert Norden, a Baptist preacher, in 1715.

146. Order Book 2:34.

147. Douglas: 3-5; Foote, Second Series: 51-2, for removal of Henry to Steel Creek and New Providence Churches on Catawba River in North Carolina.

148. *V.M.H.B.* 16:205-6. Hanna Records, contributed by Edward A. Claypool, Chicago. The spelling Buffles (for Buffalo) is obviously a copyist's or typographical error, which could easily have happened, since the certificate seems to have been copied from the book, *The House of Hanna*, by Sarah A. Hanna. The initials R.D.M. are not known to this writer. *R* is very likely a misprint for *V*. If it is, then V. D. M. would mean *Verbi Dei Minister*— minister of the Word of God. Sankey's father-in-law, John Thomson, used it following his degree on the title page of his book, *Explication of the Shorter Catechism*. Sealing ordinances were the communion services. Mary Hanna is identified as the widow of John Hanna. Robert Hanna married Mary Parks (there was a family of this name in the Buffaloe Settlement).

They settled near Brooksville, Indiana, in 1804. Their Bible gives the birth-place of their children as Laurens District, South Carolina, to which the Hannas may have moved from Prince Edward in 1765.

149. Morgan Edwards: *Materials Towards a History of Baptists in the Province of Virginia*, Vol. 3, pp. 28-31. Manuscript. (Hereafter cited as Edwards.) George W. Beale: *Semple's History of the Rise and Progress of the Baptists of Virginia:* 263-4. (Hereafter cited as Beale's Semple.)

150. Photostat of petition, Amelia Clerk's Office; Amelia Order Book 1767-8: 350; Amelia Will Book 2:327 (John Hall). *W. & M. Quart.* (2) 17:289-90. It is interesting to note in this connection that Millisant Dejarnett's sister Ann and her husband, William Purnell (Purnall), became dissenters and joined Briery Presbyterian Church. For the connection between Nottoway Church and the Sandy Creek revival, cf. *The Teacher* (Sunday School Board of the Southern Baptist Convention), May, 1941: H. C. Bradshaw: "The Mother Church of Southern Baptists." It should be noted that the George Walton whose home was desired to be licensed as a place of worship for Baptists and George Walton who was one of the first elders of Briery Church were differ-ent persons. The former George Walton lived in Amelia, in the section now Nottoway. He was a son of John Walton and his wife who was Mary Sims of Hanover County. He married Elizabeth Jennings. The latter George Walton married Martha Hughes and lived in Prince Edward; he was a brother of Robert Walton of Cumberland. The George Waltons were prob-ably related, as both appear to have been descended from the Walton family of New Kent County. George Walton of Amelia had a brother named Sherwood, who may have been the Sherwood Walton, elder in Briery Church.

151. Edwards: 28-31. Elizabeth Dejarnett was the wife of Elias Dejarnett and the mother of John Thomas Dejarnett (Prince Edward Will Book 1:101). Ellington and Foster are on the list of tithables for 1769 for Prince Edward (Mss. list, Clerk's Office). A granite boulder bearing a bronze plate marks the site of Nottoway Baptist Church on the road between Burkeville and Victoria.

152. Beale's Semple: 272, 280. Rocks Church, which is still in existence, was located in the part of Prince Edward which became Appomattox County.

153. *Ibid.*

154. Prince Edward Deed Book 5:419. By 1777 William Rice's meeting-house had become a sufficiently well known landmark to give its name to a road leading to it (Prince Edward Deed Book 6:26).

155. Beale's Semple: 281.

156. Order Book 2:42. This is the only reference this writer has found to Joseph Rice's meeting-house.

CHAPTER IV NOTES

1. Hening 6:154-93.
2. Hening 6:351-3.
3. Hening 8:69-111. The thirty-pound abatement was continued for Amelia, Buckingham, Charlotte, Cumberland, and Lunenburg Counties.
4. *Ibid.*
5. Loose mss. sheet in Order Book 3, not dated.
6. *Journals HB*, 1770-72:20, 36, 285.
7. *Journals HB*, 1773-76:14, 35.
8. *Journals HB*, 1773-76:132.

9. *Virginia Gazette* (Purdie): Aug. 15, 1777.
10. Order Book 1:138.
11. *Virginia Gazette* (Purdie & Dixon): Oct. 15, 1772.
12. *Virginia Gazette* (Purdie & Dixon): Aug. 22, 1766.
13. Order Book 2:230.   14. Order Book 3:5.
15. Order Book 3:88.   16. Order Book 3:113.
17. Order Book 4:180.   18. Order Book 2:298.
19. Order Book 5:31.   20. Order Book 5:90.
21. Order Book 5:98.   22. Order Book 5:419.
23. Order Book 5:458.   24. Order Book 3:90, 92.
25. Order Book 4:221.
26. *Virginia Gazette* (Rind): Apr. 27, 1769.
27. Order Book 4:2.   28. Order Book 4:10.
29. Order Book 4:55.   30. Order Book 4:70.
31. Order Book 4:221.   32. Order Book 5:14.
33. Prince Edward Will Book 1:176.   34. Prince Edward Will Book 1:79.
35. Package No. 35 in Clerk's Office. Mss. List of Tithables between Bush and Buffalo Rivers taken by Thomas Scott, June, 1755; Mss. List of Tithables from Buffalo to the County Line, Mr. Ewing's list, 1755. Copied by Mrs. Margaret H. Morton and generously made available to the author by her. (From the 1760 list, Colonel Randolph was Col. William Randolph.)
36. *Virginia Gazette* (Rind): Oct. 27, 1768.
37. *Virginia Gazette* (Purdie & Dixon): Nov. 8, 1770; Dec. 13, 1770.
38. *Virginia Gazette* (Dixon and Hunter): Nov. 25, 1775.
39. *Virginia Gazette* (Rind): May 25, 1769.
40. Order Book 1:16.   41. Order Book 1:159.
42. Order Book 4:8.   43. Order Book 1:159.
44. *Virginia Gazette* (Purdie & Dixon): Aug. 22, 1766.
45. *Virginia Gazette* (Rind): Apr. 23, 1772. Wimbish probably delayed advertising, thinking he could find the man.
46. *Virginia Gazette* (Purdie & Dixon): Aug. 16, 1770; Nov. 8, 1770; Mar. 7, 1771; Aug. 1, 1771; Nov. 7, 1771.
47. Cf. note 43.
48. *Virginia Gazette* (Purdie & Dixon): Aug. 16, 1770; Mar. 7, 1771.
49. *Virginia Gazette* (Pinkney): Nov. 10, 1774.
50. *Journals HB*, 1773-76:192, 225.   51. Order Book 5:460.
52. Order Book 1:163.   53. Order Book 2:271.
54. Order Book 5: dated March. 16, 1772.
55. *Virginia Gazette* (Pinkney): Nov. 17, 1774.
56. *Virginia Gazette* (Purdie & Dixon): Mar. 18, 1773.
57. *Virginia Gazette* (Purdie & Dixon): Nov. 24, 1774.
58. Order Book 5:210.   59. Order Book 5:174.
60. Order Book 6:16.   61. Order Book 3:125.
62. Order Book 4:5, 230.   63. Order Book 5:514.
64. Order Book 5:509.
65. *Virginia Gazette* (Pinkney): Nov. 17, 1774.
66. Order Book 1:22.   67. Order Book 5:80.
68. *Virginia Gazette* (Purdie): Mar. 15, 1776; Feb. 7, 1777.
69. *Journals HB*, 1758-61:208, 211.   70. Hening 7:409-10.

71. Hening 7:591-4.   72. Order Book 1:131.
73. Order Book 2:153.   74. Order Book 2:315.
75. Order Book 4:82, 221.
76. Order Book 4:6; *Virginia Gazette* (Purdie & Dixon): July 18, 1766.
77. *Virginia Gazette* (Rind): Oct. 22, 1772; (Purdie & Dixon): Sept. 8, 1774.
78. *Virginia Gazette* (Purdie & Dixon): Aug. 12, 1773.
79. *Virginia Gazette* (Purdie & Dixon): Sept. 8, 1774.
80. Order Book 4:104, 211; *Virginia Gazette* (Purdie & Dixon): June 7, 1773.
81. Order Book 4:82.   82. Order Book 4:124.
83. Order Book 4:251.
84. *Virginia Gazette* (Purdie & Dixon): Dec. 22, 1768.
85. Order Book 4:151.   86. Vestry Book: 13.
87. Vestry Book: 38.
88. *Virginia Gazette* (Purdie & Dixon): Nov. 2, 1769.
89. Order Book 2:300; 3:50, 95; 5:413.   90. Order Book 4:335.
91. See note 89.
92. *Virginia Gazette* (Purdie & Dixon): Mar. 12, 1767.
93. Order Book 3:78, 81.
94. Mss. List of Tithables for Prince Edward County, 1769, Clerk's Office. Copied by Mrs. Margaret H. Morton and made available to the author.
95. *Virginia Gazette* (Purdie & Dixon): Jan. 8, 1767; Feb. 18, 1767.
96. George W. Graham, M.D.: *The Mecklenburg Declaration of Independence, May 20, 1775, and the Lives of Some of its Signers:* 103-5. Alfred J. Morrison quotes in *The Beginnings of Public School Education in Virginia 1776-1860,* p. 131, but, possibly through clerical or typographical error, gives the name of the teacher as William Cassell. The writer has found no reference to either a Capples or a Cassell in the Prince Edward records. The Brevard file at Princeton University (from which Brevard graduated in 1768) gives his preparatory school as Crowfield Academy, Rowan County, North Carolina, "though I don't know on what authority," Walter H. Everts, Jr., assistant to the secretary of the university writes the author. Since Brevard did not enter Princeton until 1766 and is said by Graham to have studied in Prince Edward in 1761 it is possible and probable that he studied in both schools. Brevard was author of the Mecklenburg Declaration of Independence of May 20, 1775. Adlai Osborne was the ancestor of the Adlai Ewing Stevensons, the first and grandfather having been Vice-President of the United States, 1893-97, the latter and grandson having been Democratic Presidential nominee in 1952. The unusual first name was handed down from this ancestor who traveled the long journey through the Carolina and Virginia frontier to study in Prince Edward in 1761 and who later made the still longer journey from North Carolina to Princeton to study.

    A recent correspondent (Davis Lee McWhorter, Bethel, N. C., in a letter dated Jan. 5, 1955), also quoting Graham, gives the name of Brevard's and Osborne's Prince Edward teacher as William Cupples. I think that Cupples was most likely the correct name, as it is found in early Prince Edward records (see p. 51 of this work). The book which I consulted is an amplification of an address made by Dr. Graham before the Scotch-Irish Society of America at Lexington, Va., June 21, 1895, which was published in Vol. 7 of the society's transactions. Later Dr. Graham revised and expanded his address, and it was published in several pamphlet editions. Mr. McWhorter may have referred to one of the earlier editions, not available to me, which explains the difference in spelling.
97. Letter dated Apr. 28, 1954, from Walter H. Everts, Jr., assistant to the secretary of Princeton University, to the author, places Wallace at the head of a list: "Those whose connection with the county (Prince Edward) is

certain." (The others belong to the Revolutionary and post-Revolutionary period.) William Heth Whitsett: *The Life and Times of Judge Caleb Wallace:* 6-15. Dr. Whitsett assumed that Samuel Wallace, father of Caleb Wallace, lived in Charlotte County, but was not certain. When Caleb Wallace went north (he studied for a time at Elizabethtown, N. J., before entering Princeton), he took with him a certificate from the Rev. Robert Henry and may therefore be regarded as a member of Cub Creek Church. Caleb Wallace may have lived for a time in Charlotte, studying under Henry who was a Princeton graduate, and may have joined Cub Creek Church then. Since Wallace's name does not appear in Douglas' Briery Manual, there is no ground for any theory that he may have been a member of Briery, although the Manual is not regarded as complete. It is interesting to note Dr. Whitsett's comment: "Judge Wallace is suspected to have been christened Caleb Baker Wallace, but never used the middle name." The Princeton records give this full name, thus confirming Dr. Whitsett's speculation. A brother of Caleb Wallace, Andrew, married Catherine Parks in the Buffalo community. They moved to Kentucky, where Andrew Wallace was instrumental in founding a Presbyterian church near Stanford, which was named Buffalo, "very likely in compliment to his wife and in memory of happy days in old Virginia," as Dr. Whitsett puts it. Not only his wife, but Andrew Wallace himself grew up in Buffalo Church in Prince Edward.

The close connection between the Virginia and Carolina frontier and Princeton is one of the most interesting aspects of the history of this period. It demonstrates the zeal for education, which in the Scotch-Irish catalogue of virtues ranked second to piety, among the Scotch-Irish which was communicated to their neighbors, especially those who had become Presbyterians. The author and some members of his family were having lunch at the Princeton Inn a few years ago and as they ate the discussion turned to the contrasting transportation between these times and those when students from Southside Virginia were going there to college. We were planning to drive back to Prince Edward that afternoon and evening and made the trip by shortly after midnight, including a short stop in Philadelphia. Then the journey by horseback required several days. One could not help but wonder if Wallace and others, like the Venable "boys" who went to Princeton a decade later, did not become homesick so far from the familiar scenes of home.

98. *W. & M. Quart.* (2) 1:126. "Notes Relative to Some Students at William and Mary 1770-78."

99. Vestry Book: 2.

100. Maurice Bear Gordon, M.D.: *Aesculapius Comes to the Colonies:* 39; Cf. Wyndham Bolling Blanton: *Medicine in Virginia in the Eighteenth Century* for references to Dr. Cabell's medical practice.

101. *Virginia Gazette* (Purdie & Dixon): Oct. 17, 1766.

102. *Journals HB,* 1766-69:42, 124-5, 128.

103. *Virginia Gazette* (Rind): May 12, 1768.

104. *Virginia Gazette* (Rind): May 31, 1768.

105. *Virginia Gazette* (Rind): June 16, 1768.

106. *Virginia Gazette* (Purdie & Dixon): Dec. 13, 1770.

107. Order Book 5:83 5.

108. Order Book 2:231.

109. Cumberland Will Book 2:23.

110. Prince Edward Will Book 1:346.

CHAPTER V NOTES

1. *Virginia Gazette* (Purdie & Dixon): July 18, 1766.
2. *Virginia Gazette* (Purdie & Dixon): June 20, 1766; Aug. 15, 1766; Aug. 29, 1766; Sept. 12, 1766; Oct. 10, 1766.
3. *Virginia Gazette* (Purdie & Dixon), Sept. 19, 1766.
4. Cf. note 1.
5. *Virginia Gazette* (Purdie & Dixon), Sept. 12, 1766.
6. *Virginia Gazette* (Purdie & Dixon), Oct. 17, 1766.
7. *V.M.H.B.* 21:206-7.
8. *Virginia Gazette* (Purdie & Dixon): July 18, 1766. This incident was related by Philanthropus (friend to man) of Prince Edward in a letter dated June 22. Were Philanthropus and Dikephilos, the correspondent who reported the Routledge murder so fully, the same? There are strong indications in their letters that they were.
9. *V.M.H.B.* 22:383-5. Notes on Richard Adams' letter of Sept. 30, 1771, to his brother Thomas. The notes quote the *Virginia Gazette* of May 30 and June 6, 1771, concerning the flood.
10. *Journals HB*, 1773-6, viii-x. Nicholas' notice in the *Virginia Gazette* of Feb. 4, 1773, and Lord Dunmore's letter of Mar. 30, 1773, to Lord Dartmouth in which the circumstances are described in some detail are published in this reference; p. 20 for reference to John Lightfoot as the Governor's special agent.
11. *Journals HB*, 1773-6:18-20.   12. *Journals HB*, 1773-6:29, 36.
13. *Journals HB*, 1773-6:24.
14. *Virginia Gazette* (Purdie & Dixon), Apr. 8, 1773.
15. *Ibid.*
16. *Journals HB*, 1773-6:12.
17. *Virginia Gazette* (Purdie & Dixon), Apr. 8, 1773.
18. Order Book 5:231, 235.
19. *Virginia Gazette* (Purdie & Dixon), Apr. 8, 1773. Cf. depositions of Greenhill and Daniel Jones.

CHAPTER VI NOTES

1. *Virginia Gazette* (Purdie & Dixon), July 18, 1766. Although the statement is general, the fact that Dikephilos was writing from Prince Edward indicates that this view was prevalent in the county.
2. *Virginia Gazette* (Rind) May 4, 1769. Blagrave's letter is dated Apr. 4, 1768, but it may be a misprint for 1769, since it was not published until May, 1769.
3. *Virginia Gazette* (Purdie & Dixon), August 4, 1774.
4. *American Archives*, 4th Series, Vol. 3:1023.
5. *American Archives*, 4th Series, Vol. 3:367, 387, 400.
6. *American Archives*, 4th Series, Vol. 3:1192-3.
7. *American Archives*, 4th Series, Vol. 3:1616-7.
8. *American Archives*, 4th Series, Vol. 4:848.
9. *American Archives*, 5th Series, Vol. 2:320.
10. *American Archives*, 5th Series, Vol. 2:321-2. These lists are described as copies of the originals in the War Office.

11. *V.M.H.B.* 17:305-7. Payroll of Capt. John Morton's company of Regulars, 4th Va. 1776. (Original in U. S. Pension Office.)

   Payroll, June 28-July 28, 1776, from Morton's account book: John Morton, captain; John Holcombe, first lieutenant; Obadiah Woodson, second lieutenant; Edward Wood, ensign; James Morton, sergeant; Samuel Anderson, sergeant; Charles Stagg, sergeant; Charles Anderson, sergeant; Robert Lorton, corporal; Thomas Hastie, corporal; William Wright, corporal; William Chambers, corporal; privates: Thomas Morton, William Johnson, Robert P. Smith, Isham Chaffin, William Ascue, John Smith, Benjamin Tuggle, Thomas Tuggle, George Daniel, Isham Jennings, William Gillespie, Philemon Southerland, Glover Baker, William Southerland, James Jennings, Edward Davidson, Thomas Peirce, Isham Brown, Anderson Woodson, David Davidson, John Lee, Thomas Walker, William Walker, Nathaniel Rains, Nathan Hampton, John Webster, John Thompson, Thomas Byrk, Nathaniel Durham, Archebald Wright, Jasper Pillow, Julius Newcum, George Taylor, Alexander Smith, John Fraser (corporal July 28-Aug. 28, 1776), Thomas Frazer, William Davidson, Michael Boas, Aaron Peak, Sandy Holman, Anderson Cocke (fifer July 28-Aug. 28, 1776). Stephen Collins, David Robertson, Thomas Baldwin, Thomas King, Abner Watkins, Francis Fore, William Bigger, William Fuqua, Parsons Anderson, Christopher Chaffin, John Spaulding, Moses Sharp, Peter Hales, Archebald Lee, Jonah Whitlock, John Cunningham, Joshua Foster, John Foster, Dudley Rutledge, William Walker, William McGehee, Samuel Martin, James Howerton, William Cary. Additional names, July 28-Aug. 28, 1776: Charles Davis, Thomas Williams, Mesheck Boas. Additional names in subsistence accounts: William Bird, William Hood, Alexander Garratt, Nathaniel Cunningham, Charles Leigh, John Woodson, Jacob Edmunds.

12. *V.M.H.B.* 22:184-5. Deposition of William Wright for military service.

13. Hugh Blair Grigsby: *The Virginia Convention of 1776:* 189, 206.

14. Hening 9:126-8.

15. Order Book 5:498. Cf. Hening 9:126-8 for content of the new oath.

16. Order Book 5:499.   17. Order Book 5:504.

18. Order Book 5:499.   19. Order Book 5:504, 505.

20. Order Book 5:504, 507, 514.

21. Mss. petition, Archives Division, Virginia State Library.

22. *V.M.H.B.* 18:35. "Virginia Legislative Papers" from originals in the State Archives.

23. *Calendar of Virginia State Papers* 8:122 (hereafter cited as *Cal. Va. State Papers*); *V.M.H.B.* 27:341. "Virginia State Troops in the Revolution" from State Auditor's papers now in the State Library.

24. *Cal. Va. State Papers* 8:113.   25. *Cal. Va. State Papers* 8:117.

26. *Cal. Va. State Papers* 8:171, 173, 179.

27. *Cal. Va. State Papers* 8:196 (June 10, 1776), 223 (June 25, 1776).

28. *Cal. Va. State Papers* 8:206, 225.   29. *Cal. Va. State Papers* 8:236.

30. *V.M.H.B.* 6:279.   31. *V.M.H.B.* 6:401.

32. *V.M.H.B.* 7:254.   33. *V.M.H.B.* 14:80.

34. *V.M.H.B.* 15:186.   35. *V.M.H.B.* 15:190.

36. *V.M.H.B.* 8:196.   37. *V.M.H.B.* 13:17.

38. J. T. McAllister: *Virginia Militia in the Revolutionary War:* 40 (hereafter cited as McAllister). Cf. pp. 60-1 for affidavit of John Cunningham, pp. 64-5 for affidavit of John Dupuy, pp. 65-6, for affidavit of Henry Dawson. Dawson has the year of service at Hampton as 1775, Cunningham and Dupuy as 1776. Since the affidavits were not made until 1832, it is easy to see how the exact year could have become confused in memory.

39. Hening 9:179-84.

40. Mss. petition of Nathaniel Venable, dated Aug. 31, 1777, Archives Division, State Library.
41. McAllister: 40. Wade Mosby's affidavit, dated Powhatan, Sept. 19, 1832, gives the year as 1777. Venable's petition suggests that the year may have been 1776. Cf. *The Kaleidoscope*, 1929, for an article by Dandridge Spotswood, in which he states that the Hampden-Sydney company wore purple hunting shirts.
42. Hening 9:337-49.					43. Hening 9:445-9.
44. McAllister: 40.
45. McAllister: 41. Cf. affidavits of John Dupuy (pp. 64-5), Henry Dawson (pp. 65-6), Charles Brightwell (p. 56), John Cunningham (pp. 60-1), John Simmons (pp. 90-1), George Gillispie (p. 68), and William T. Walker (pp. 95-6).
46. *Tyler's Historical and Genealogical Magazine* 9:241. "Continental Soldiers: Abstract of men raised under the former laws passed for raising soldiers for the Continental service, Nov. 1782." Mss. in State Library. Report of John Nash, county lieutenant for Prince Edward. (The magazine hereafter cited as *Tyler's Mag.*)
47. *Virginia Gazette* (Purdie): Nov. 7, 1777.
48. *Virginia Gazette* (Dixon & Hunter): Jan. 24, 1777.
49. McAllister: 41. Cf. affidavits of John Cunningham, William Morgan (pp. 80-1), John Dupuy, John Simmons, John Wiltshire (pp. 98, 127), David Anderson (pp. 53-4), John Maxey, Sr., of Powhatan.
50. Order Book 5:515; 6:38, 47.
51. Order Book 5:512.
52. Order Book 5:515.
53. Order Book 5:516. The original record omits a family name after Nathaniel, obviously a clerical omission. Venable has been inserted in pencil by a later reader, but whether or not Nathaniel Venable is the person is not known.
54. Order Book 5:524.					55. Order Book 5:526.
56. Order Book 6:1.					57. Order Book 6:2.
58. Order Book 6:7.					59. Order Book 6:10-1.
60. Order Book 6:20.					61. Order Book 6:38-9.
62. Order Book 6:43.					63. Order Book 6:47, 79.
64. Order Book 6:79.					65. Order Book 6:89.
66. Order Book 6:96.					67. Order Book 6:98.
68. Order Book 6:99.					69. Order Book 6:101.
70. Order Book 6:102.					71. Order Book 7:15.
72. *Tyler's Mag.* 19:168. Payroll of Capt. Thomas Watkins' troop of Dragoons. Photostat in Virginia State Library, copied by W. S. Morton. Thomas Watkins, captain; Philemon Holcomb, lieutenant; Samuel Venable, cornet; Thomas Munford, sergeant; privates: (the first name was undecipherable to Mr. Morton), Thomas Jones, Thomas Shelton, Charles Scott, Clement Carrington, Zachariah Lee, Isham Britain, Charles Price, Charles Williams, William Gordon, Benjamin Thackston, Robert Daniel, Christopher Holland, Samuel Smith, Edward Haskins, Francis Anderson, Farrish Marton, Asa Purnell, James Chappell, Lewelling Hudson, Bassett Stithe, James Daniel, Dudley Holt. Foote, First Series: 403.
73. Mss. legislative petition, dated Nov. 22, 1781, endorsed Dec. 19, 1781.
74. Order Book 5:508. Cf. Grigsby, *The Va. Conv. of 1776*, p. 102, for the story of the Prince Edward soldier who, when asked on his return from the South if he hadn't killed a British officer whom he might have taken prisoner, replied yes, but he hoped the Lord would forgive him as he hadn't tasted salt for a year.
75. Order Book 5:512.					76. Order Book 5:516.

77. Order Book 5:517-8. In some instances the names of the women are given, which furnished a clue to Revolutionary service records, but usually they are identified as "a poor woman whose husband is in Continental service."

78. Order Book 5:518-9.	79. Order Book 5:522.
80. Order Book 5:524.	81. Order Book 5:526.
82. Order Book 6:1.	83. Order Book 6:2.
84. Order Book 6:7.	85. Order Book 6:10-1.
86. Order Book 6:11-3.	87. Order Book 6:17.
88. Order Book 6:19-20.	89. Order Book 6:21, 36.
90. Order Book 6:39.	91. Order Book 6:41.
92. Order Book 6:44.	93. Order Book 6:47-8.
94. Order Book 6:50.	95. Order Book 6:54-5.
96. Order Book 6:70, 84.	97. Order Book 6:91.
98. Order Book 6:93, 98.	99. Order Book 6:89.
100. Hening 9:338-43.	101. Order Book 6:95.
102. Order Book 6:97.	

103. *Val. Va. State Papers* 2:553. Col. John Nash to Col. Davies, Oct. 19, 1781.

104. *Cal. Va. State Papers* 2:26. Robert Walton to Gov. Jefferson, Apr. 10, 1781.

105. *Cal. Va. State Papers* 1:579. Gen. Nathaniel Greene to Baron von Steuben, Feb. 15, 1781.

106. *Cal. Va. State Papers* 1:536. Maj. John Mazaret to Gov. Jefferson, Feb. 26, 1781.

107. *Cal. Va. State Papers* 1:522. Gen. Robert Lawson to Governor, Feb. 16, 1781.

108. *Cal. Va. State Papers* 1:540. Gen. Robert Lawson to Gov. Jefferson, Feb. 25, 1781.

109. *Cal. Va. State Papers* 2:79. Gen. Robert Lawson to Gov. Jefferson, May 1, 1781.

110. *Cal. Va. State Papers* 2:252-4. Gen. Robert Lawson to Gov. Nelson, July 26, 1781.

111. *Cal. Va. State Papers* 2:370-1. Gen. Robert Lawson to Col. Davies, Aug. 30, 1781.

112. *Cal. Va. State Papers* 2:454. Col. John Nash to Col. Davies, Sept. 17, 1781.

113. *Cal. Va. State Papers* 2:160-1.

114. *Cal. Va. State Papers* 2:248. John Brown, Com. Gen. to Gov. Nelson, July 25, 1781.

115. *Cal. Va. State Papers* 2:121. Maj. John Pryor, commissary general military stores to Col. Davies, May 26, 1781.

116. *Cal. Va. State Papers* 3:315-6. Harry Innes of Bedford, district commissioner, to Col. William Davies, Sept. 20, 1782.

117. *Tyler's Mag.* 8:253-4. Charles Allen's desposition of Revolutionary service.

118. *V.M.H.B.* 57:262-3. "The Old Town of Cobham" by A. W. Bohannon.

119. Order Book 6:96, 97. One of the most frequently related traditions of Prince Edward states that Tarleton sent a detachment of soldiers to the glebe, where the Rev. Archibald McRobert was living. They ripped open feather beds, broke mirrors, set fire to the house on leaving. As McRobert had fled the approach of the soldiers, the house was left to burn, but a sudden shower put out the blaze, as it was burning slowly. Because his home had been saved thus, he named the place Providence. (Cf. William Meade: *Old Churches, Families, and Ministers of Virginia*, vol. 1: 449; the account is based on information furnished by a correspondent of Bishop Meade.) Meade also gives a letter from McRobert to the Rev. Devereux Jarratt, dated *Providence, July 13, 1780.* As this was a year before Tarleton's raid, it

appears that the tradition as so often related is not altogether accurate, unless Bishop Meade or the person furnishing him the letter put the date-line, *Providence*, on it from knowledge that McRobert's home was known at a later time as Providence. The tradition is, like so many traditions, undoubtedly founded upon fact. A sudden rain may have prevented the destruction of the house from fire at some time previous to the writing of the letter, a circumstance which gave rise to naming the place Providence. Later and inaccurately informed story tellers probably credited Tarleton's men with starting the fire. The writer knows of at least two instances in which the destruction of Prince Edward homes was credited to burning by Federal soldiers when they passed through in 1865; upon mentioning the report to older persons who knew the circumstances, he was informed that the homes were destroyed by fire, but that Federal soldiers did not set the fire. So it may have been at Providence, the Jarratt letter indicating that the glebe bore the name a year before Tarleton passed through the county.

Another tradition concerns a reported visit of Tarleton to Slate Hill, seeking military supplies. Nathaniel Venable, who lived at Slate Hill, was county commissary, but he was not at home at the time. When threatened with being shot if she did not reveal her husband's whereabouts, Mrs. Venable said, "Go ahead and shoot. My husband's life is more valuable to his country than mine." It is also related that Mrs. Venable packed the military stores which were at Slate Hill in hogsheads and had them rolled into the back yard. Tarleton's men, assuming that they contained tobacco, paid no attention to them.

Howe relates that Joshua Davidson, who had been wounded in the sword arm at Guilford and had returned to Prince Edward to recruit soldiers armed with a squirrel gun, went to look at the enemy. He was surprised by a British dragoon, who called on him to surrender. Replying that he was not prepared to yield, Davidson shot him, raising his gun with his left hand. Asked later if he was satisfied with killing a single man, he replied "By no means. I reloaded my piece and went in pursuit; but my firing had excited such alarm, and Tarleton fled with such expedition, that I never could have overtaken him, or I would have had another shot." (Howe: *Historical Collections of Virginia*: 435.) Cf. The Hatchett narrative, note 123, for a similar story which is most likely a version of this. They are not identical, but are not contradictory. Hatchett, who does not identify the man who did the shooting, locates the incident at Briery bridge south of the Courthouse.

Another tradition connected with Tarleton's raid relates that he left two cut-glass decanters at Mt. Airy, the home of Capt. James Wade, who is described as a Tory. The decanters are said to have remained on the Wade sideboard until smashed by Federal soldiers when passing in April, 1865. The hitch in this story is the identification of Captain Wade as a Tory. There is no evidence to support that statement, and his subsequent election to the Virginia House of Delegates inclines one to think that he was not.

Only one Tory was certified from Prince Edward (Order Book 5:508). James Crosse, a native of North Britain and factor for Alexander Spiers John Bowman and Co. at their Prince Edward store was in January, 1777, certified to the Governor as "not having uniformly manifested himself a friend to this country."

It is also told that a dance was given for Tarleton's men at Travis, near Sandy River Church (and also Mt. Airy). One of his men remarked to a young woman of the community with whom he was dancing, "I have heard that Light-Horse Harry Lee is illiterate, that he can't read or write his name." Observing a scar left on the officer's neck by Lee's sword during an encounter in the South, the young lady, who was of patriot sympathies, replied, "At least he can make his mark." One finds the substance of this story related in several Southern communities about the Revolution.

120. *Cal. Va. State Papers* 2:195. Thomas Smith, deputy commissary general military stores to Col. Davies, July 1, 1781.

121. See note 119, reference.

122. *Cal. Va. State Papers* 2:311. Capt. Nathan Reid to Col. Davies, Aug. 10, 1781.

123. *A Short Narrative of the Life of John Hatchett:* 7. (Hereafter cited as Hatchett.) The booklet was published by The Farmville *Herald.* It contains Hatchett's account of his life. The manuscript was then owned by Mrs. Louise Leonard, Route 1, Petersburg, Va. and was edited for publication by Dr. J. D. Eggleston.

124. Mss. circular letter of Robert Lawson dated Prince Edward, Aug. 3, 1781. Robert Lawson papers, Duke University Library.

125. See note 110.

126. *Cal. Va. State Papers* 2:505-7. Brig. Gen. Robert Lawson to Governor Nelson, Sept. 29, 1781.

127. *Ibid.*
    Lawson described the sickness as an "infectious and malignant fever, which has carried off many inhabitants, prevails[ing] greatly in this county [Prince Edward] especially."

CHAPTER VII NOTES

1. *Cal. Va. State Papers* 3:3, 42.

2. *Cal. Va. State Papers* 3:7. Col. Christian Febiger to Col. Davies, Jan. 4, 1782.

3. *Cal. Va. State Papers* 3:67. Col. Thomas Posey to Col. Davies, Feb. 17, 1782; 3:71. Col. Thomas Posey to Col. Davies, Feb. 22, 1782.

4. *Cal. Va. State Papers* 3:116. John Morton to Col. Davies, Mar. 30, 1782.

5. *Cal. Va. State Papers* 3:174. John Morton to Col. Davies, May 21, 1782.

6. *Cal. Va. State Papers* 3:315, 399. John Nash to Col. Davies, Sept. 20, 1782, Dec. 16, 1782.

7. *V.M.H.B.* 38:263-4. Capt. John Morton's Revolutionary Account Book.
    Morton's payroll for Nov., 1781, included the following: Joseph Holt, David Irvine, Jesse Herd, John Buckley, John McLeroy, Casey Ascue, Charles Price, Zach Robertson, Matthew Chitwood, Lewis Buckner, William Smith, Josiah Legrand, David Morton, David Anderson, Joseph Bell, James Taylor, John Armstrong, John Richards, John Fraser, Henry Ligon, Samuel Morton, George Foster, Abrm Foster, John Penix, Ambrose Crawford, John Ligon, Thomas Clark, John Burks, Josiah Cunningham; for Dec., 1781: Abner Watson, William Price, Ben Vaughan, Joseph Fuqua, Simon Jackson, Jacob Morton, William Penick, Charles Price, Allen Chambers.

8. Order Book 7:299.

9. Mss. Legislative Petition, Archives Division, Virginia State Library.

10. Hening 9:140-5.

11. Order Book 7:3.

12. Mss. Legislative Petition of Benjamin Haskins, Archives Division, State Library.

13. *Cal. Va. State Papers* 4:377-8.

14. *Cal. Va. State Papers* 4:594-6; 433-4. Patrick Henry to Governor Randolph, May 4, 1788.

15. *Cal. Va. State Papers* 4:487-521.

16. Mss. Legislative Petition of Thomas Flournoy, Archives Division, State Library.

17. Hening 13:555. Request for this legislation had been made by William Bibb's deputies, John Watson and Richard Bibb. Mss. Legislative Petition, Archives Division, State Library.

18. Mss. Legislative Petition, Archives Division, State Library.

19. Order Book 7:48, 50.   20. Order Book 5:506.

21. Order Book 5:521.   22. Order Book 6:151.

23. Order Book 8:518; 9:13.   24. Order Book 9:94; 8:518.

25. Order Book 8:518, 354.   26. Hening 12:243-54.

27. Order Book 8:166.   28. Hening 12:253, 254.

29. Hening 12:258-60.   30. Order Book 5:498; 6:14, 47.

31. Order Book 6:43, 55.   32. Order Book 6:82, 92, 95.

33. Order Book 7:50.   34. Order Book 6:96.

35. Order Book 6:97.   36. Order Book 6:101.

37. Order Book 8:92, 111.   38. Order Book 8:76.

39. Order Book 8:356.   40. Order Book 10:323.

41. Order Book 8:167. The road dividing District One from District Two is the old road from Nash's on lower Bush River to the present highway 460 (a part of this road is still used and the remainder of its route may be traced to the river), thence along the present road to Green Bay to the old road leading to Meherrin which turned off the Green Bay road near "Lawyer Wing's" old place and thence along that road to Meherrin. The Roanoke road is the Farmville-Abilene road; Caleb Baker's seems to have been near the road connecting the Abilene road with the Darlington Heights road at Singleton's store. Fontaine's is the place now called Martin's, up the hill from Martin's bridge over Buffalo on the Hampden-Sydney- Five-Forks road; the dividing line between Districts Three and Four was this road from Buffalo River westward to the point it crossed the old county line on its way to Lynchburg.

42. Order Book 9:95.   43. Order Book 9:118.

44. Mss. papers, Package 158, Clerk's Office.

45. Order Book 8:473.   46. Order Book 7:169.

47. Order Book 8:479.   48. Order Book 7:75, 254.

49. Order Book 7:276.   50. Order Book 7:209.

51. Order Book 8:70.   52. Order Book 7:23.

53. Order Book 6:39, 78; 7:15, 264.   54. Order Book 8:187.

55. Order Book 8:328.   56. Order Book 7:264.

57. Order Book 10:10, 74.   58. Order Book 8:56.

59. Order Book 7:49.   60. Order Book 9:13.

61. Order Book 7:31.   62. Order Book 7:38.

63. Order Book 7:168.   64. Order Book 7:277.

65. Order Book 7:286.   66. Order Book 8:70.

67. Order Book 8:226.   68. Order Book 8:480.

69. William Wirt Henry: *The Life and Correspondence of Patrick Henry*, 2:330. (Hereafter cited as Henry.)

70. Order Book 7:113.   71. Order Book 7:170.

72. Order Book 7:219.   73. Order Book 7:261.

74. Order Book 7:289.   75. Order Book 8:117.

76. Order Book 8:151.   77. Order Book 8:220.

78. Order Book 8:227.   79. *Ibid*.

80. Order Book 8:370; 7:85.

81. *W. & M. Quart.* (2) 16:536. "Claims of Pensioners for Revolutionary and Military Services as Returned under the Act for taking the Sixth Census in

1840." Contributed by W. S. Morton. In the 1840's one pensioner was receiving $42.40 annually. Cf. Order Book 26:27.

Major John L. Crute's pension certificate was preserved by his grandson, J. M. Mottley, who permitted the writer to make a copy:

"To Whom It May Concern:

"Be it known that by an Act of Congress date of 3d day of March 1809, John Crute now a citizen of the State of Virginia was placed on the pension list of the United States at the rate of $13 per month to commence on the 28th day of Sept. 1808.

"Given under my hand and the seal of the War Office this 15th day of March, 1810.

"W. Eustis"

82. Order Book 8:260.

83. Order Book 5:505.

84. Order Book 5:523.

85. Order Book 6:3, 5, 9, 47, 55.

86. Order Book 6:98, 100.

87. Order Book 7:77, 127.

88. Order Book 7:146; 8:10; *Cat. Va. State Papers* 4:594-6.

89. Order Book 8:94, 226.

90. Order Book 8:398; Hening 13:555.

91. Order Book 7:50, 149.

92. Order Book 6:88.

93. Order Book 7:127.

94. Order Book 8:264. The name Fontaine is here, as elsewhere in the orders, spelled Fountain.

95. Cf. note 27.

96. Order Book 8:313.

97. Order Book 10:107.

98. Order Book 7:207, 258.

99. Order Book 9:94, 145.

100. Order Book 9:130, 198. Letter of Walter H. Everts, Jr., assistant to the secretary of Princeton University, to the author, Apr. 28, 1954, based on alumni files. Abraham B. Venable graduated from Princeton in 1780, Joseph Venable in 1782.

101. Order Book 8:38.

102. Order Book 6:95, 96, 102; 7:11.

103. Order Book 7:289.

104. Order Book 7:301.

105. Order Book 7:305.

106. Order Book 8:32.

107. Order Book 8:279, 368.

108. Order Book 8:396.

109. Henry 2:304-25.

110. Foote, First Ser.: 431-2; Henry 2:332-3. Henry follows Foote's account of the controversy.

In a letter to James Madison dated June 12, 1788 (Madison Papers 5:59, Library of Congress), John Blair Smith criticized Henry for what would now be called "dirty politics" in the campaign preceding the election of delegates from Prince Edward to the Convention of 1788. He accused Henry of misrepresentation of the Constitution and credited Henry with starting the opinion fairly prevalent in Prince Edward at the time in favor of Virginia remaining independent or entering into a "partial Confederacy or a foreign alliance."

111. Henry 2:332-3.

112. Hugh Blair Grigsby: *The Virginia Convention of 1776:* 152.

113. Henry 2:338-85.

CHAPTER VIII NOTES

1. Alfred J. Morrison: *The College of Hampden-Sydney: Calendar of Board Minutes: 1776-1876:* 7-12 (hereafter cited as *Cal. Bd. Min.*); Foote, First Ser.: 393-6. In giving the name of William C. Houston, one of Smith's advisers in the selection of the faculty, the writer follows Thomas J. Wertenbaker: *Princeton, 1746-1896.* Morrison gives his name as William Churchill Houston, Foote as William Charles Huston. Prince Edward Deed Book 5:325-8. Conveyance of 98 acres of land for five shillings by Peter Johnston to the trustees of Hampden-Sydney, dated April 20, 1775.

2. *Cal. Bd. Min.*: 13.

3. *Cal. Bd. Min.*: 15-7.

4. Foote, First Ser.: 397.

5. Foote, First Ser.: 398.

6. *Cal. Bd. Min.*: 18.

7. Foote, First Ser.: 398, 400; Freeman H. Hart: "A Precocious Youth," in the 1929 *Kaleidoscope.* Why the College was named for John Hampden and Algernon Sydney, English patriots in the Civil War and Restoration periods, has never been satisfactorily explained, to this writer's knowledge. Were they favorite heroes of Samuel Stanhope Smith?

8. *General Catalogue of Princeton University, 1746-1906:* 82, 88, 93, 94, 97, 98; *V.M.B.H.* 7:33.

9. *Virginia Gazette* (Dixon & Hunter): April 27, 1776.

10. *Virginia Gaztete* (Dixon & Hunter): Sept. 27, 1776.

11. Foote, First Ser.: 400.

12. Foote, First Ser.: 400-1.

13. Hening 9: 321-2; *Cal. Bd. Min.*: 23; *Virginia Gazette* (Purdie): July 4, 1777.

14. *Virginia Gazette* (Purdie): July 10, 1778.

15. Order Book 5: 508.

16. *Cal. Bd. Min.*: 22; Foote, First Ser.: 401.

17. Foote, First Ser.: 401.

18. *Cal. Bd. Min.*: 25.

19. Foote, First Ser.: 401-2.

20. Hening 9: 272-5.

21. *W. & M. Quart.* (2) 2: 211-2. Copy of advertisement in the *Virginia Gazette and Public Advertiser*, Oct. 26, 1782.

22. Foote, Second Ser.: 106.

23. Foote, First Ser.: 405.

24. Foote, First Ser.: 406.

25. *Cal. Bd. Min.*: 36-7. It may be that Smith gave only one notice of intention to leave, in July, 1789. The writer has followed Foote in mentioning the notice in 1788. Foote, it will be observed, gives different circumstances from those mentioned in the board minutes, so it seems likely that Smith twice gave notice. Foote states that Smith resigned in Sept., 1789. Smith did not leave Prince Edward immediately upon severing his connection with college; Richard N. Venable mentions visiting him at Prince Edward Courthouse on Aug. 3, 1791, when Smith talked to him of going to Philadelphia. Cf. *Tyler's Mag.* 2: 137: R. N. Venable's Diary.

26. Foote, First Ser.: 432.

27. *Cal. Bd. Min.*: 38.

28. Foote, First Ser.: 430; Freeman Cleaves: *Old Tippecanoe*: 6. There is a tradition that Harrison lived at Slate Hill when attending the college. One phase of the tradition, however, which has Benjamin Harrison placing his motherless son in the household there to be reared, is inaccurate; Mrs. Benjamin Harrison survived her husband and lived until after her son, William Henry, had joined the army, several years after his student days at Hampden-Sydney (Cleaves, p. 14).

29. Foote, First Ser.: 407; *Cal. Bd. Min.*: 44.

30. Foote, First Ser.: 407.

31. *Cal. Bd. Min.*: 49-50; Foote, Second Ser.: 280: "Domestic discipline had re-laxed, and many things were considered by parents and guardians as admiss-able, that, in previous years, had been intolerable."
32. *Cal. Bd. Min.*: 61; Foote, Second Ser.: 280.
33. *Cal. Bd. Min.*: 43.   34. *Cal. Bd. Min.*: 44, 53.
35. *Cal. Bd. Min.*: 57.   36. *Cal. Bd. Min.*: 63.
37. *Cal. Bd. Min.*: 61; Foote, Second Ser.: 280, 368.
38. *Ibid.*   39. Foote, First Ser.: 408.
40. Hening 11:392-3; Order Book 7:304; Mss. Legislative Petition, Archives Division, State Library.
41. Samuel Shepherd: *The Statutes at Large* 1:315-6 (hereafter cited as Shep-herd); mss. Legislative Petitions, Archives Division, State Library.
42. *Cal. Bd. Min.*: 34.
43. *Cal. Bd. Min.*: 43. This was the present Kingsville. Hampden-Sydney sold a part of the property to George King (for whom Kingsville was named) in 1825. Cf. *Cal. Bd. Min.*: 93, 96, 99.
44. *Cal. Bd. Min.*: 32. The rule dated from 1784.
45. *Cal. Bd. Min.*: 37; Richmond *Enquirer*: Sept. 12, 1820: an appeal for funds notes that the only public donations to the college were the gifts of land made in 1784 and 1794.
46. *Cal. Bd. Min.*: 45.
47. *V.M.H.B.* 42:304-8; 315-6: Major Edgar Erskine Hume: "Virginia Society of the Cincinnati's Gift to Washington College"; *Cal. Bd. Min.*: 56.
48. Mss. Legislative Petition of Board of Trustees, Archives Division, State Library; cf. *Cal. Bd. Min.*: 66 for division of students in 1812. Cf. Foote, Second Ser.: 396. Cushing Hall had been completed by 1825, and the first college building had been taken down by that time.
49. *Cal. Bd. Min.*: 85.
50. *Cal. Bd. Min.*: 88; Foote, Second Ser.: 388-9; 372: Cushing, after accepting the chair of Natural Philosophy and Chemistry in 1819, is called Hampden-Sydney's first professor. Prior to this teachers were called tutors.
51. *Cal. Bd. Min.*: 95.   52. *Cal. Bd. Min.*: 108.
53. *Cal. Bd. Min.*: 119.   54. *Cal. Bd. Min.*: 128.
55. Foote, First Ser.: 408.   56. *Ibid.; Cal. Bd. Min.*: 136.
57. *Cal. Bd. Min.*: 144.
58. Richmond *Enquirer*: May 5, 1835; Oct. 6, 1840.
59. Richmond *Constitutional Whig*: Oct. 18, 1827; Oct. 8, 1828; Richmond *En-quirer*: Sept. 20, 1831; Sept. 15, 1846.
60. Richmond *Enquirer*: June 1, 1851.
61. Richmond *Constitutional Whig*: Oct. 18, 1827.
62. *Today and Yesterday in the Heart of Virginia:* 56. "Hampden-Sydney Col-lege" by W. H. Whiting, Jr.
63. Richmond *Enquirer*: June 1, 1827. 64. Richmond *Enquirer*: July 25, 1828.
65. Richmond *Enquirer*: June 1, 1851.
66. Richmond *Constitutional Whig*: Oct. 15, 1828.
67. Mss. College Accounts of Year Beginning 1 November 1824. Edmund W. Hubard Papers. Southern Historical Collection, University of North Carolina Library. Apparently the student attended some sort of benefit or entertain-ment Jan. 15.
68. *Cal. Bd. Min.*: 140-1; Richmond *Enquirer*: Oct. 9, 1849; July 22, 1853; Aug. 15, 1854.

69. Richmond *Enquirer*, July 13, 1847; Richard McIlwaine: *Memoirs of Three-score Years and Ten:* 43 (hereafter cited as McIlwaine).
   McIlwaine says President Lewis W. Green and Prof. Charles Martin inaugurated the scholarship plan in 1848. Green did not come to Hampden-Sydney until 1849, and Martin advertised the plan in 1847. Credit apparently belongs to Martin.

70. *V.M.H.B.* 6:174-84; 288-96. "Trustees of Hampden-Sidney College" by J. B. Henneman.

71. Foote, Second Ser.: 253-4.   72. Foote, Second Ser.: 278-9.

73. Foote, Second Ser.: 366.   74. Foote, Second Ser.: 369.

75. Foote, Second Ser.: 332, 371; Mss. Legislative Petition, Archives Division, State Library. The petition proposed Moses Hoge as president and George A. Baxter, Drury Lacy, John H. Rice, Samuel B. Wilson, Samuel W. Venable, Conrad Speece, James Morton, Henry E. Watkins, Benjamin Harrison, William Wirt, Stephen Bovelle, Josiah Leake, William Hill, and Matthew Lyle as trustees.

76. Foote, Second Ser.: 372.   77. Foote, Second Ser.: 374-456.

78. Richmond *Enquirer*, Aug. 27, 1822.

79. Richmond *Enquirer*, Jan. 28, 1823. An advertisement gives notice that the next and third session begins first Monday in March next.

80. Richmond *Enquirer*, Jan. 21, 1822.

81. Richmond *Enquirer*, Jan. 19, 1828.

82. Foote, First Ser.: 502. "A law school of high standing in the area in which free thinking had no check . . . . influences source of uneasiness to the pious people of Cumberland and associated churches."

83. Richmond *Enquirer*, Jan. 19, 1828.

84. Richmond *Enquirer*, July 8, 1845; *Cal. Bd. Min.:* 134, note.

85. *Cal. Bd. Min.:* 134.   86. *Cal. Bd. Min.:* 136.

87. Richmond *Enquirer*, Oct. 16, 1849.   88. Richmond *Enquirer*, July 20, 1817.

89. Richmond *Enquirer*, June 23, 1818.

90. Mariah Crute (Mrs. Nathaniel Mottley) and Lucy Ann Marshall (Mrs. William Bradshaw) were students at the school in the early 1830's. Sons of both have told the writer of this period of their mothers' education and that William White conducted the school. Samples of White's handwriting remain; his caerography is one of the most beautiful for legibility, style, and distinctiveness the writer has ever seen.

91. Richmond *Enquirer*, Oct. 20, 1837.   92. Richmond *Enquirer*, June 19, 1832.

93. Richmond *Enquirer*, Jan. 31, 1833.
   Joseph Martin: *A New and Comprehensive Gazetteer of Virginia and the District of Columbia* (Charlottesville, 1835), p. 268 (hereafter cited as Martin's *Gazetteer*) mentions the female seminary at the Courthouse "which deserves the high reputation it enjoys. There were then 80 pupils, two principals, and five assistants. Instruction in science and languages was given by Hampden-Sydney College professors. The school's course required three years to complete.

94. *Acts of Assembly, 1838:* 171; Mss. Legislative Petition, Archives Division, State Library.

95. Richmond *Enquirer*, May 11, 1838.

96. Richmond *Enquirer*, May 8, 1840.

97. *Today and Yesterday in the Heart of Virginia:* 182-3. "Prince Edward Courthouse" by George L. Walker. Walker mentions two students, one Miss Williamson who married John Stewart of Richmond and was the grandmother of the late John Stewart Bryan, publisher of the Richmond *News Leader* and president of the College of William and Mary; the other, Laetitia Green, daughter of President Lewis W. Green of Hampden-Sydney,

and later wife of Adlai Ewing Stevenson, Vice-President of the United States, 1893-7, and grandmother of Adlai Ewing Stevenson, Democratic Presidential nominee in 1952.

Mr. Walker has Branch succeed Root in 1845. Since he did not mention Dame, it is not clear whether Root returned after Dame was principal or whether he left for Wisconsin prior to Dame's principalship.

98. Richmond *Enquirer, Mar. 7*, 1845.
99. *Today and Yesterday in the Heart of Virginia:* 183. "Prince Edward Courthouse" by George L. Walker; Richmond *Enquirer,* June 15, 1858.
100. Richmond *Enquirer,* May 19, 1835.
   In the list of advantages offered by Farmville in Martin's *Gazetteer* (1835): 268, a girls' school is mentioned. The Huestis school was thus promptly recognized.
101. Richmond *Enquirer,* July 10, 1835.
102. Richmond *Enquirer,* Oct. 20, 1837.
103. *Acts of Assembly,* 1839: 120-2.
104. Farmville *Herald,* July 2, 1897. The unidentified correspondent was a thorough researcher. He gave references to the Acts of Assembly and the county deed books. He then detailed the history of the school. The date of the laying of the corner-stone is printed 1836, but the context indicates that this is a typographical error for 1839.
105. Farmville *Herald,* Oct. 22, 1948. "History of Farmville" by Herbert Clarence Bradshaw. Cf. *Acts of Assembly 1899-1900:* 72 for closing Spruce Street from High Street to Chambers.
106. *Ibid.*; Farmville *Herald,* July 2, 1897.
107. Richmond *Enquirer,* July 25, 1856. Letter of "Vernon" of Cumberland County.
108. *Acts of Assembly 1859-60:* 462-3. 109. Foote, First Ser., 491.
110. Alfred J. Morrison: *The Beginnings of Public School Education in Virginia, 1776-1860:* 131-3. Cf. *Today and Yesterday in the Heart of Virginia:* 182; Hatchett: 7-9; 13. "Prince Edward Courthouse" by George L. Walker for the Ballantine school; Mr. Walker quotes the late Branch Rodgers, one of the pupils there.
111. *Rev. William S. White and His Times* (1800-73). An Autobiography edited by his son, Rev. H. M. White, D.D., p. 43. White taught on a fixed salary; his pupils were eight boys, nearly all classical "scholars" of the same grade of scholarship.
112. Cf. Morrison reference, note 110.
113. *Today and Yesterday in the Heart of Virginia:* 56. "Hampden-Sydney College" by W. H. Whiting, Jr.
114. *Today and Yesterday in the Heart of Virginia:* 183. "Prince Edward Courthouse" by George L. Walker.
115. *The Kaleidoscope,* 1925: 6-11, "Asa Dupuy Watkins" by W. H. Whiting, Jr.
116. Richmond *Enquirer,* June 18, 1840.
117. Related to the author by his grandfather, James R. Weaver, who attended this school.
118. *Acts of Assembly 1838:* 170.
119. Richmond *Enquirer,* Aug. 6, 1858.
120. Farmville *Herald,* Oct. 22, 1948. "History of Farmville" by Herbert Clarence Bradshaw.
121. *Ibid.*; *Acts of Assembly 1852:* 182. 122. Order Book 19:24.
123. Order Book 19:307; 20:518.

124. Order Book 21:267; mss. records, Clerk's Office, copy furnished the writer by Mrs. Margaret H. Morton.

125. Order Book 21:34.

126. Order Book 21:263, 279.

127. Order Book 21:615.

128. Order Book 22:218.

129. Order Book 22:308.

130. Order Book 22:537.

131. Order Book 23:45.

132. Order Book 23:275, 284.

133. Order Book 23:476.

134. Order Book 24:96.

135. Order Book 24:287.

136. Order Book 24:391.

137. Order Book 25:287.

138. Order Book 26:136.

139. Order Book 26:263.

140. Order Book 26:316.

141. Order Book 26:391.

142. Order Book 26:456.

143. Order Book 26:533.

144. Order Book 27:287.

145. Order Book 27:172, 184, 195.

146. Order Book 27:238.

147. Order Book 27:279, 287.

148. Order Book 27:389.

149. Order Book 27:405, 426.

150. Mss. record of meeting of board of School Commissioners of Prince Edward County, Clerk's Office; copy furnished the writer by Mrs. Margaret H. Morton.

151. Order Book 26:397 *et seq. passim.*

152. Order Book 27:267.

153. Order Book 27:426.

154. *Acts of Assembly 1828:* 13-6.

155. Mss. Memorial of Acting School Commissioners of Prince Edward County, Archives Division, State Library.

156. Richmond *Enquirer,* Nov. 2, 1838.

157. Richmond *Enquirer,* Oct. 24, 1843.

158. Richmond *Enquirer,* Oct. 7, 1845.

159. Richmond *Whig,* Oct. 28, 1845.

160. *Acts of Assembly 1845:* 28.

161. Richmond *Enquirer,* Nov. 26, 1850.

162. *A Calendar of Legislative Petitions Arranged by Counties: Accomac-Bedford.* Virginia State Library. Special Report. H. J. Eckenrode, Archivist. A 1051. Appomattox.

163. *Acts of Assembly 1845:* 29-31.

164. *Cal. Bd. Min.:* 55.

165. Mss. Legislative Petition, Archives Division, State Library.

166. *Ibid.;* Shepherd 3:183.

167. *Cal. Bd. Min.:* 75.

168. *Cal. Bd. Min.:* 86.

169. *V.M.H.B.* 49:157-73; 234-53; 326-38. Minute Book of the Buffalo Circulating Library, edited by Joseph D. Eggleston.

170. Cf. *General Catalogue of Alumni of Princeton University, 1746-1906;* Letter of Walter H. Evert, Jr., assistant to the secretary of Princeton University, to the author Apr. 28, 1954. Mr. Evert most graciously identified the students from Prince Edward from the files of the university for the author.

171. *V.M.H.B.* 43:239 note; *Biog. Dict. Cong.:* 1955.

172. *Southside Times* (Burkeville, Va.), Jan. 14, 1870. Letter from Cornelius Nepos, Deatonville, giving recollections of the Prince Edward bar when he was admitted to practice at the Prince Edward Circuit Court in 1850. "Cornelius Nepos," who appears to have been Judge F. R. Farrar, states that H. E. Watkins studied law at William and Mary. The *V.M.H.B.* note cited above (note 171) says that it "seems" Watkins studied law at William and Mary. "Cornelius Nepos" says Watkins graduated from Princeton with honors in the class of which Nicholas Biddle was valedictorian. He also states that "it is said" that Watkins was the only student at Hampden-Sydney for a few weeks in 1798.

173. *W. & M. Quart.* (2) 3:273. Register of Students William and Mary College 1827-81.

174. Richmond *Enquirer,* Aug. 2, 1853; July 17, 1855.

175. *V.M.H.B.* 21:322-3. "Two Students from Virginia at the University of Edinburgh" by A. J. Morrison. The information was obtained from Flournoy's notebook, later in the possession of Dr. J. P. Mettauer and subsequently of Dr. J. D. Eggleston, Sr., and Dr. J. D. Eggleston, Jr. The other student was Dr. James Jones of Nottoway, of the Hampden-Sydney class of 1791.

176. *W. & M. Quart.* (2) 10:310-1. List of Members of the Judge H. S. G. Tucker's Law Class in 1827-8 and in 1828-9.

177. *W. & M. Quart.* (2) 3:273; 4:132, 138. Register of Students William and Mary College 1827-81.

178. *Biog. Dict. Cong.:* 1460.

CHAPTER IX NOTES

1. Hening 12:648-53.

2. Henry 2:441.

4. *Biographical Dictionary of the American Congress 1774-1949*: 51. (Hereafter cited as *Biog. Dict. Cong.*)

5. *Biog. Dict. Cong.*: 55.   6. Hening 13:536.

7. Hening 13:331-2.   8. *Biog. Dict. Cong.*: 59, 64, 69.

9. *Cal. Va. State Papers* 6:140; *W. & M. Quart.* (1) 1:29.

10. *Cal. Va. State Papers* 9:74-87; *Virginia Argus,* Sept. 12, 1800.

11. *Cal. Va. State Papers* 9:125; *Virginia Argus,* Sept. 5, 1800; Nov. 11, 1800.

12. *Virginia Argus,* July 28, 1804; Sheperd 3:86.

13. *Virginia Argus,* Dec. 11, 1805.

14. Mss. letters Creed Taylor to Col. Read, Apr. 3, 1804; Thomas Read to Creed Taylor, Apr. 7, 1804; Creed Taylor to Col. Thomas Read, Apr. 19, 1804. Creed Taylor Papers, University of Virginia Library.

15. *Virginia Argus,* Aug. 15, 1804.

16. *Virginia Argus,* Dec. 5, 1804.

17. William Cabell Bruce: *John Randolph of Roanoke, 1773-1833,* 1:150, 153. (Hereafter cited as Bruce.)

18. Mss. letter, John Randolph to Creed Taylor, Sept. 16, 1798. Creed Taylor Papers.

19. Bruce 1:589-90; Richmond *Enquirer,* May 5, 1807.

20. Mss. letter, John Randolph to Edward Dillon, Jan. 1, 1809. Dillon-Polk Papers, Southern Historical Collection, University of North Carolina Library. Cf. mss. letter, John Randolph to Edward Dillon, Nov. 10, 1810 (same collection), *re* Mr. Johnston, who will be elected for Prince Edward, meeting Col. Monroe in the House of Delegates and the "strange appearance" and "difficult part" they will make and have.

21. Mss. letter, John Randolph to Edward Dillon, Jan. 11, 1807. Dillon-Polk Papers.

22. Bruce 1:590-2. Cf. Richmond *Enquirer,* Nov. 10, 1812: Madison carried Prince Edward 107 to 28 for Rufus King in the Presidential election.

23. Richmond *Enquirer,* Mar. 11, 1808; Mss. letter, Creed Taylor to Edward

Dillon, Mar. 29, 1808. Dillon-Polk Papers; cf. mss. letter, Creed Taylor to William B. Giles, Mar. 20, 1808, Creed Taylor Papers.

24. Bruce 1:592-5; Farmville *Herald*, Apr. 12, 1907: unsigned feature, "Patrick Henry and John Randolph in Prince Edward."

25. Petersburg *Intelligencer*, Apr. 23, 1813.

26. Richmond *Enquirer*, Apr. 9, Apr. 16, Apr. 30, 1816. (Cf. *Virginia Argus*, Jan. 29, 1802: Virginia had been redistricted in 1802, and Prince Edward, Charlotte, Buckingham, and Cumberland had been constituted District 17.)

27. Bruce 1:598.					28. Bruce 1:599.

29. *Biog. Dict. Cong.*: 121; Richmond *Enquirer*, Mar. 25, 1817.

30. Bruce 1:599.

31. *Biog. Dict. Cong.*: 127, 134, 141, 149. 32. Bruce 2:1.

33. *Biog. Dict. Cong.*: 162, 168.			34. Bruce 2:1-6.

35. *Biog. Dict. Cong.*: 175.				36. *Virginia Argus*, Aug. 1, 1807.

37. Richmond *Enquirer*, June 12, 1812: Address to the Freeholders of Charlotte, Prince Edward, Buckingham, and Cumberland, by John Randolph of Roanoke.

38. Richmond *Enquirer*, Nov. 10, 1812.

39. Richmond *Enquirer*, Mar. 20, 1816. 40. Richmond *Enquirer*, Feb. 20, 1816.

41. Richmond *Enquirer*, Oct. 10, 1816. 42. *Virginia Argus*, Aug. 8, 1808.

43. Richmond *Enquirer*, Sept. 4, 1816. 44. Richmond *Enquirer*, Feb. 22, 1816.

45. Petersburg *Republican*, Feb. 18, 1824.

46. Petersburg *Republican*, Feb. 24, 1824.

47. Petersburg *Republican*, Mar. 2, 1824; Richmond *Constitutional Whig*, Feb. 27, 1824.

48. Richmond *Constitutional Whig*, Feb. 24, 1824; Richmond *Enquirer*, Feb. 23, 1824.

49. Petersburg *Republican*, Aug. 3, 1824.

50. Petersburg *Republican*, Mar. 16, 1824.

51. Richmond *Enquirer*, Nov. 12, 1824. 52. Richmond *Enquirer*, Dec. 2, 1824.

53. Richmond *Constitutional Whig*, Jan. 2, 1828.

54. Richmond *Enquirer*, Jan. 9, Jan. 10, Jan. 12, 1828.

55. Richmond *Enquirer*, Sept. 6, 1828. 56. Richmond *Enquirer*, Jan. 17, 1828.

57. Richmond *Enquirer*, Nov. 11, 1828. 58. Richmond *Enquirer*, Nov. 14, 1828.

59. Mss. legislative petitions, Archives Division, State Library. The agitation for more equitable representation had begun earlier. In 1816, letters were published showing the more favorable representation in both Senate and House of Delegates in eastern counties. In Senate districts there was a range between 5,264 free whites and 13,630 federal numbers in the district of Elizabeth City, Warwick, and York on the one hand and 77,111 free whites and 87,963 federal numbers in the district of Botetourt, Washington, Montgomery, Russell, Greenbrier, Kanawha, Mason, Grayson, Cabell, Lee, Wythe, Monroe, Tazewell, Giles, and Scott Counties. The Prince Edward-Charlotte-Halifax senatorial district with 23,235 free whites and 47,701 federal numbers was almost what the average district should be, 23,000 free whites and 40,625 federal numbers. Cf. Richmond *Enquirer*, Sept. 4, Sept. 7, Sept. 14, 1816.

60. Richmond *Constitutional Whig*, Apr. 26, 1828.

61. Richmond *Constitutional Whig*, May 17, 1828.

62. *Acts of Assembly 1828*: 17.

63. *Register of the General Assembly of Virginia, 1776-1918, and of the Constitutional Conventions:* 245. (Hereafter cited as *Register General Assembly*.)

64. *Register General Assembly 1776-1918:* 130, 131; cf. Hening 9:128-9.

65. Cf. Henry Howe: *Historical Collections of Virginia:* 131. (Hereafter cited as Howe.)

66. Richmond *Enquirer,* Mar. 17, 1832. The electoral district was made up of Prince Edward, Buckingham, Charlotte, and Cumberland, the congressional district established in 1823; cf. Richmond *Examiner,* Mar. 20, 1832; Richmond *Enquirer,* Jan. 28, 1823.

67. Richmond *Enquirer,* June 1, 1832.   68. Richmond *Enquirer,* Apr. 3, 1832.

69. Richmond *Enquirer,* Oct. 16, 1832.   70. Richmond *Enquirer,* Oct. 2, 1832.

71. Richmond *Enquirer,* Oct. 26, 1832.

72. Richmond *Enquirer,* Nov. 13, 1832; July 24, 1832; Richmond *Constitutional Whig,* Nov. 12, 1832.

73. Bruce 2:16.   74. Richmond *Enquirer,* July 3, 1832.

75. *Biog. Dict. Cong.:* 175.   76. Richmond *Enquirer,* Mar. 21, 1834.

76. Richmond *Enquirer,* Mar. 21, 1834.

77. Petersburg *Intelligencer,* May 11, 1835.

78. Richmond *Enquirer,* May 5, May 12, May 19, 1835.

79. Richmond *Enquirer,* May 22, 1835.

80. Richmond *Enquirer,* May 26, June 2, 1835.

81. Richmond *Enquirer,* Feb. 20, 1836.

82. Richmond *Whig and Public Advertiser,* Dec. 15, 1840.

83. Richmond *Whig and Public Advertiser,* May 1, 1838; *Richmond Enquirer,* May 1, 1838.

84. Richmond *Enquirer,* Aug. 17, 1838.

85. *Biog. Dict. Cong.:* 195; Richmond *Whig,* Apr. 2, 1839. One infers from the newspaper reference that Wilson was Hill's adversary in the campaign.

86. Richmond *Whig,* Apr. 2, 1839.

87. Richmond *Enquirer,* Feb. 22, Apr. 8, 1840. Nathaniel E. Venable declined to be a candidate.

88. Richmond *Enquirer,* Mar. 27, 1840.   89. Richmond *Enquirer,* Feb. 27, 1840.

90. Richmond *Enquirer,* Sept. 15, 1840.

91. Proceedings of the Democratic State Convention held in Charlottesville, Va., Sept. 9-10, 1840. Pamphlet 3, Vol. 11, Virginia Pamphlets, Duke University Library.

92. Richmond *Whig,* Sept. 11, 1840.

93. Richmond *Enquirer,* Sept. 4, 1840; Richmond *Whig and Public Advertiser,* Sept. 21, 1840.

94. Richmond *Whig and Public Advertiser,* Oct. 18, 1842; Richmond *Enquirer,* Nov. 10, 1840, gave the results: For Van Buren: at the Courthouse, 252; at Walkers Church, 110; For Harrison: at the Courthouse, 292; at Walkers Church, 39.

95. Mss. "Names of Prince Edward Voters at the Presidential Election in Nov., 1840." Edmund W. Hubard Papers, Southern Historical Collection, University of North Carolina Library. The list is in the handwriting of Branch J. Worsham, who furnished the list, according to a letter in the Hubard Papers, in reply to Hubard's request for the information to aid his campaign in Congress. It was then voting practice for the voter to announce publicly his choice of candidates, and he was recorded as voting for that candidate.

96. Richmond *Enquirer,* July 31, 1840.

97. Richmond *Enquirer,* May 8, 1840.

98. *Biog. Dict. Cong.:* 203, 210, 217.

99. Richmond *Enquirer,* Mar. 9, 1843.

100. Richmond *Enquirer*, Feb. 22, 1840.
101. Richmond *Enquirer*, Feb. 15, 1842, extra.
102. Richmond *Enquirer*, June 6, 1843; cf. Richmond *Enquirer*, Aug. 30, 1859.
103. Richmond *Enquirer*, May 2, 1843.
104. Richmond *Enquirer*, Apr. 18, 1843.
105. Richmond *Whig and Public Advertiser*, Mar. 7, Mar. 14, 1843.
106. Whig State Convention, Pamphlet No. 60 in Virginia Pamphlets, Vol. 3, Duke University Library.
107. Richmond *Whig and Public Advertiser*, Nov. 17, 1848.
108. Richmond *Enquirer*, Mar. 21, 1845.
109. Richmond *Enquirer*, Apr. 29, 1845.
110. Petersburg *Intellinger*, May 2, 1844.
111. Richmond *Enquirer*, Mar. 14, 1848.
112. *Register General Assembly:* 166; Richmond *Whig and Public Advertiser*, May 1, 1849.
113. Richmond *Enquirer*, Jan. 22, 1847.
114. Richmond *Enquirer*, Feb. 9, 1847.
115. Richmond *Whig and Public Advertiser*, Jan. 26, 1847. The list of Prince Edward delegates was not given.
116. Richmond *Enquirer*, April 27, 1847; May 21, 1847. *Biog. Dict. Con.:*
117. Richmond *Whig and Public Advertiser*, Aug. 11, 1848.
118. Richmond *Whig and Public Advertiser*, Nov. 21, 1848.
119. Richmond *Whig and Public Advertiser*, Dec. 25, Dec. 29, 1848; May 8, 1849.
120. Richmond *Whig and Public Advertiser*, Feb. 18, 1851.
121. Richmond *Enquirer*, Feb. 28, 1851.
122. Richmond *Enquirer*, Oct. 28, 1851.
123. *Register General Assembly, 1776-1918:* 246.
124. Richmond *Enquirer*, Sept. 5, 1851.
125. Richmond *Enquirer*, Oct. 14, 1851.
126. Richmond *Enquirer*, Nov. 25, 1851.
127. Richmond *Enquirer*, Dec. 12, 1851; Jan. 20, 1852.
128. Richmond *Enquirer*, Nov. 25, Dec. 12, 1851.
129. Richmond *Enquirer*, Sept. 5, Dec. 12, 1851. Apparently the October election for state senators and delegates was held in the event the amended Constitution failed to pass.
130. Richmond *Enquirer*, Apr. 29, 1853.
131. Richmond *Enquirer*, Apr. 23, Aug. 13, 1852.
132. Richmond *Enquirer*, Nov. 5, Nov. 12, 1852.
133. Richmond *Enquirer*, Apr. 29, 1853; cf. *Acts of Assembly 1852-3:* 3. The Fourth District now consisted of Prince Edward, Nottoway, Dinwiddie, Petersburg, Brunswick, Amelia, Lunenburg, Charlotte, Mecklenburg, Cumberland, and Powhatan.
134. Richmond *Enquirer*, May 27, 1853.
135. *Biog. Dict. Cong.:* 246.
136. Richmond *Enquirer*, Dec. 16, 1853.
137. Richmond *Enquirer*, May 15, 1855.
138. Richmond *Enquirer*, Nov. 21, 1854.
139. Richmond *Enquirer*, Dec. 5, 1854.
140. Richmond *Enquirer*, Jan. 23, 1855 (quoting the *Farmville Journal.*)
141. Richmond *Enquirer*, Mar. 30, 1855.

142. Richmond *Enquirer*, June 1, 1855.
143. Richmond *Enquirer*, Aug. 11, 1855.
144. Richmond *Enquirer*, Mar. 30, Apr. 20, 1855.
145. Richmond *Enquirer*, June 1, 1855.
146. Richmond *Enquirer*, June 15, 1855. This reference is both interesting and perplexing. Each of the five men was an active member of Sharon Baptist Church of which Daniel Witt was pastor. It is not clear for what purpose these five employed Atkins to preach for them, unless they engaged him to preach to their slaves. Nothing in the Sharon Church records indicates that he was engaged by the church to preach.

This incident in the campaign of 1855 throws light on the references to "preaching politicians" and "politicating-preachers" in a letter of Daniel Witt to R. Gwathmey, his brother-in-law, dated July 4, 1855 (cf. J. B. Jeter; *Life of the Rev. D. Witt, D.D.*, pp. 198-200), which seemed to perplex Dr. Jeter. Of more general interest is Witt's impression of the campaign of 1855: "Have you any religion now amongst your people? The hurricane of political excitement has blasted everything of the sort in these parts. I have been an observer of things for many years, and do not recollect ever to have seen so much asperity and bitterness, and all manner of ill feeling, in the masses of people as I have seen in the late canvass."

147. Richmond *Enquirer*, Aug. 5, 1856.
148. Richmond *Enquirer*, Nov. 18, 1856.
149. Richmond *Enquirer*, Mar. 27, May 1, May 15, 1857. Asa D. Dickinson had been a Whig, but changed parties about the time the Whigs became identified with the Know-Nothings.
150. Richmond *Enquirer*, Mar. 31, 1857.
151. Richmond *Enquirer*, May 26, 1857.
152. Richmond *Enquirer*, June 2, 1857.
153. Richmond *Enquirer*, Oct. 22, 1858.
154. Richmond *Enquirer*, July 13, 1858, Dec. 10, 1858.
155. Richmond *Enquirer*, May 27, 1859.
156. Richmond *Enquirer*, Jan. 14, Jan. 21, Feb. 16, Apr. 1, 1859.
157. Richmond *Enquirer*, Feb. 16, Apr. 1, 1859.
158. Richmond *Enquirer*, Mar. 29, 1859.
159. Richmond *Enquirer*, Feb. 15, 1859.
160. Richmond *Enquirer*, June 3, June 24, July 1, July 8, 1859.
161. Richmond *Enquirer*, July 8, 1859; *Biog. Dict. Cong.*: 36. Goode died July 3, 1859.
162. Richmond *Enquirer*, Aug. 9, Aug. 23, Aug. 30, Sept. 23, 1859.
163. Richmond *Enquirer*, Oct. 21, Oct. 25, 1859.
164. Richmond *Enquirer*, Nov. 4, 1859; cf. George W. Bagby: *The Old Virginia Gentleman:* 99 (Fourth Edition). In "Fishing in the Appomattox" Dr. Bagby mentions a visit to Randolph House in Farmville, where Pryor and Goode were, on the night before election.

165. Order Book 9:159.
166. Order Book 10:40.
167. Order Book 11:76.
168. Order Book 11:261.
169. Order Book 11:573.
170. Order Book 12:187.
171. Order Book 12:420.
172. Order Book 13:347.
173. Order Book 15:2.
174. Order Book 15:562.
175. Order Book 16:436, 654.
176. Order Book 17:121, 132, 355, 418.
177. Order Book 17:590.
178. Order Book 18:329.
179. Order Book 18:645; 19:59.
180. Order Book 19:219, 410.

181. Order Book 20:110, 184, 372.
182. Order Book 20:551; 21:96.
183. Order Book 21:330.
184. Order Book 21:432, 617, 652.
185. Order Book 22:57, 286.
186. Order Book 22:428, 594.
187. Order Book 23:74.
188. Order Book 23:291.
189. Order Book 24:1.
190. Order Book 24:131, 227.
191. Order Book 24:316, 415.
192. Order Book 25:41, 150.
193. Order Book 25:260; 26:16.
194. Order Book 26:82, 154.
195. Order Book 26:220.
196. Order Book 26:337, 414.
197. Order Book 26:472.
198. Order Book 9:293—16:567, *seriatim.*
199. Order Book 16:634.
200. Order Book 17:501.
201. Order Book 26:100, 105.
202. Order Book 26:438.
203. Order Book 11:493.
204. Order Book 10:107.
205. Order Book 11:603.
206. Order Book 17:611; 18:55, 367.
207. Order Book 18:668, 674; 19:75, 361.
208. Order Book 21:435.
209. Order Book 24:222, 284 *et seq.*
210. Order Book 21:227, 238; 18:479; F. Johnston: *Memorials of Old Virginia Clerks:* 315-7. Worsham was elected clerk Aug. 15, 1825.
211. Order Book 12:213.
212. Order Book 18:345, 423.
213. Order Book 23:314.
214. Order Book 23:372.
215. Order Book 25:492.
216. Order Book 11:115, 134, 316.
217. Order Book 16:611; 18:55, 484.
218. Order Book 8:356; 11:316.
219. Order Book 11:403; 12:185.
220. Order Book 12:185.
221. Order Book 12:302, 496.
222. Order Book 12:503.
223. Order Book 13:431, 488; 14:109.
224. Order Book 16:319.
225. Order Book 17:5, 47, 48 (Pettus was in the lower district, Hill in the upper.)
226. Order Book 25:88, 143.
227. Order Book 24:39.
228. Order Book 9:81.
229. Order Book 10:57.
230. Order Book 10:71.
231. Order Book 11:113, 116.
232. Order Book 11:247; *Cal. Va. State Papers* 8:258.
233. Order Book 11:261.
234. Order Book 11:797.
235. Order Book 12:72.
236. Order Book 12:94.
237. Order Book 14:176.
238. Order Book 14:248.
239. Order Book 15:240, 402, 418.
240. Order Book 15:323, 370.
241. Order Book 16:467, 481, 492, 503, 540, 625; 18:419.
242. Order Book 16:625, 670.
243. Order Book 17:179, 198.
244. Order Book 17:443.
245. Order Book 18:407, 483, 499, 521.
246. Order Book 18:523.
247. Order Book 20:77, 107, 163.
248. Order Book 20:315; 21:174.
249. Order Book 21:213, 228, 344.
250. Order Book 21:569, 625.
251. Order Book 21:161.
252. Order Book 22:266, 305, 316, 418.
253. Order Book 23:24, 69.
254. Order Book 23:132, 157, 165, 173.
255. Order Book 23:408-9, 422, 448, 451.
256. Order Book 24:392, 411, 416.
257. Order Book 25:234, 259.
258. Order Book 26:52, 65.
259. Order Book 26:492; *Acts of Assembly 1852:* 64.
260. Order Book 26:495.
261. Order Book 26:497.
262. Order Book 26:492-3.
263. Order Book 27:63, 172.
264. Order Book 27:298, 377.
265. Order Book 27: 63 *et seq.*

266. Order Book 26:532.

267. Order Book 27:12, 63.

268. Order Book 27:386.

269. Order Book 27:390.

270. Order Book 27:24.

271. Order Book 27:77.

272. Order Book 27:114.

273. Order Book 27:181.

274. Order Book 27:279.

275. Order Book 27:181, 326.

276. Order Book 27:376, 385.

277. Order Book 10:320.

278. Order Book 11:116.

279. Order Book 15:346-7.

280. Shepperd 3:22-4.

281. Richmond *Enquirer,* June 24, 1807.

282. *Acts of Assembly 1812:* 3-6.

283. Richmond *Enquirer,* Dec. 27, 1815.

284. Mss. Tax Receipt of Laban Hawkins, Hawkins-McGehee Papers, University of Virginia Library.

285. Richmond *Enquirer,* Feb. 29, 1820.

286. Richmond *Enquirer,* Apr. 28, 1857.

287. Richmond *Enquirer,* Jan. 18, 1850.

288. Richmond *Enquirer,* Jan. 9, 1816.

289. Mss. Tax Receipt of Laban Hawkins, Hawkins-McGehee Papers.

290. Order Book 7:264.

291. Order Book 10:10, 19, 74.

292. Order Book 20:312-3.

293. Order Book 20:523, 570.

294. Order Book 22:317, 327, 331, 353, 407, 548; 23:9, 21, 24, 25, 54.

295. Order Book 26:65, 75, 77, 81-2.

296. Order Book 27:101, 104, 108, 138. The jail rebuilt in 1855 was the old stone jail now in ruins at Worsham, but well remembered by all except the present younger generation. While the jail was being rebuilt in 1855, prisoners from Prince Edward were kept in Cumberland jail. The jail ordered built in 1823, which was the new jail the roof and cornice of which were ordered painted in Oct., 1824 (Order Book 21:102), probably replaced the jail built in 1791 by Peter LeGrand (*Today and Yesterday in the Heart of Virginia,* p. 179: "Prince Edward Courthouse" by George L. Walker). Walker assumed that the jail built in 1791 was the one which burned in 1855, but there were two other jails built during that period. The debtors' prison was built in 1787, but how long it was used for the purpose is not clear. It was not until 1848 that imprisonment for debt was prohibited in Virginia, but in June, 1825, an order was entered directing that the necessary repairs be made to the debtors' room. It may have been that the separate prison for debtors, a structure of massive hewn logs, was used until the 1823-4 jail was constructed. The upper rooms of the 1823-4 jail were doubled sheathed with oak plank one and one-half inches thick crossed (one sheathing running vertically, the other horizontally). (Order Book 21:102.)

297. Order Book 16:366; Prince Edward Deed Book 5:323-5 (Smith conveyance); Prince Edward Deed Book 14:453.

298. Order Book 27:73, 83, 89, 128, 143, 144.

299. Order Book 27:225.

300. Order Book 11:248-52; 22:328-33.

301. Order Book 10:91.

302. Order Book 21:626.

303. *Acts of Assembly 1883-4:* 210-1.

304. Order Book 10:212, 213, 220.

305. Order Book 11:111.

306. Order Book 11:231.

307. Order Book 12:38, 43, 44.

308. Order Book 12:367.

309. Order Book 12:374, 376, 409, 415.

310. Order Book 26:569.

311. Order Book 20:523.

312. Order Book 21:241, 544, 589.

313. Order Book 21:708.

314. *Acts of Assembly 1827:* 37-9.

315. Mss. legislative petition, Archives Division, State Library.

316. *Acts of Assembly 1830:* 151.

317. *Acts of Assembly 1844:* 34; mss. legislative petition, Archives Division, State Library.

318. *Acts of Assembly 1846:* 39; mss. legislative petitions, Archives Division, State Library.

319. Mss. legislative petitions, Archives Division, State Library.

320. *Acts of Assembly 1847-8:* 27.

321. Mss. legislative petition, Archives Division, State Library.

322. *Acts of Assembly 1849-50:* 18. The problem of getting a separate voting precinct may explain, in part, the zeal of the people in the southeastern part of the county to get one of their section elected to the House of Delegates, which they accomplished in the election of William T. Wootton, an advocate of a separate voting place in that section, in 1848.

323. *Acts of Assembly 1850-1:* 223.   324. *Acts of Assembly 1852:* 36, 45.

325. Prince Edward Deed Book 26: 176.

326. *Ibid.*; Order Book 26: 489.   327. *Acts of Assembly 1852-3:* 365.

328. Order Book 27:398, 405, 411. The *Acts of Assembly* (e.g. *Acts of Assembly 1865-6:* 261) give the same list of voting places in Prince Edward for the years 1852-66, failing to give Rice and Green Bay and to drop Marble Hill, as decided by the Court in April, 1861.

329. Mss. legislative petitions, Archives Division, State Library.

330. *Acts of Assembly 1841-2:* 47.

331. Mss. legislative petitions, Archives Division, State Library.

332. *Acts of Assembly 1843-4:* 51.   333. Hening 12:532-8; 730-63.

334. Hening 12:704.   335. *Cal. Va. State Papers* 5:392.

336. *Cal. Va. State Papers* 7:   337. *Cal. Va. State Papers* 6:519-20.

338. *Cal. Va. State Papers* 9:56.

339. *Virginia Argus,* July 7, Nov. 28, Dec. 1, 1804.

340. *Virginia Argus,* June 22, 1805.   341. *Virginia Argus,* Dec. 4, 1805.

342. *Virginia Argus,* June 20, 1806.   343. *Virginia Argus,* Nov. 25, 1806.

344. *Virginia Argus,* July 1, 1807.   345. *Virginia Argus,* Dec. 11, 1807.

346. *Acts of Assembly 1807:* 5-9.   347. *Acts of Assembly 1808:* 9-13.

348. Order Book 18:479.   349. *Acts of Assembly 1852:* 51, 59.

350. Order Book 10:60, 68.   351. Order Book 11:307.

352. Order Book 12:46.   353. Order Book 13:301.

354. Order Book 15:232.   355. Order Book 16:145.

356. Order Book 16:357.   357. Order Book 16:498.

358. Order Book 17:475.   359. Order Book 18:330.

360. Order Book 19:34.   361. Order Book 20:376.

362. Order Book 21:353, 407.   363. Order Book 22:86.

364. Order Book 22:582.

365. Tyler's Mag. 11:264. Letter of John Randolph of Roanoke to Edward Booker, described as from Prince Edward and a well-known lawyer.

366. *Southside Times* (Burkeville), Jan. 14, 1870. Letter to the editor from "Cornelius Nepos," Deatonville. "Cornelius Nepos" was most probably Judge Fernando R. Farrar; Farmville *Herald,* Oct. 1, 1897. Letter from "Boy Then, Old Man Now." (Probably R. B. Berkeley.)

    There were several law partnerships during the ante-bellum period, usually of lawyers with offices in different places. George W. Read of Charlotte Courthouse and William C. Flournoy of Farmville dissolved the partnership of Read and Flournoy Apr. 30, 1845 after the creation of Appomattox County and the change in time for holding Superior Courts rendered "the requisite interchange and co-operation between them . . . impracticable." Thereafter

Read practiced in Charlotte, Halifax, and Mecklenburg Courts. Flournoy and Thomas S. Bocock of Appomattox then formed the firm of Fournoy and Bocock, with offices at Farmville and Clover Hill, for practice in Buckingham, Cumberland, Prince Edward, Appomattox, Charlotte, Lynchburg and the Campbell Superior Court. As Bocock was commonwealth's attorney of Appomattox County, the firm would not engage in criminal practice in that court, but Flournoy as an individual would (Richmond *Enquirer*, June 6, 1845).

Other partnerships were those of Anderson and Thornton (Samuel C. Anderson and John T. Thornton) with offices at Prince Edward Courthouse and Farmville, for practice in Prince Edward, Buckingham, Cumberland, Charlotte, and Appomattox (Richmond *Enquirer*, July 5, 1847); and Bolling and Hughes (P. A. Bolling and M. S. Hughes) with offices at Farmville and Prince Edward Courthouse and practice in Prince Edward, Cumberland, Charlotte, Buckingham, Nottoway, and Lunenburg (Richmond *Enquirer*, Jan. 10, 1860).

367. *Southside Times* (Burkeville), Jan. 14, 1870; Farmville Herald, Oct. 1, 1897.
368. Richmond *Enquirer*, Jan. 7, 1832. Letter from "Petitioner for the New County," Buckingham, Jan. 2, 1832. Cf. Richmond *Enquirer*, Dec. 16, 1824, for petition presented legislature for a new county to be called Fayette, to be formed from Buckingham, Campbell, Charlotte, and Prince Edward.
369. Mss. legislative petitions, Archives Division, State Library.
370. *Acts of Assembly 1844:* 38-41. Merryman's is the present Pamplin. One of the petitions (dated Feb. 16, 1839) proposed Clover Hill as the Courthouse and described it as now Rains, lately Patteson's.
371. Richmond *Whig*, Apr. 28, 1846. The presence of Major McDearmon in the House of Delegates from Prince Edward may have been a factor in part responsible for the establishment of Appomattox County.
372. Order Book 7:116, 248.   373. Order Book 7:203, 280, 281; 8:239.
374. Mss. Commission as Brigadier General of Volunteers, Nov. 1780, signed by Thomas Jefferson. Robert Lawson Papers, Duke University Library.
375. Mss. Commission appointing Robert Lawson, Esq., to Privy Council or Council of State, June 28, 1782. Robert Lawson Papers.
376. Order Book 8:33.   377. Order Book 8:57, 72, 84, 115.
378. Order Book 8:226, 239, 311, 345, 352, 395, 473.
379. Hening 13:344-56.
380. Order Book 11:9, 48, 59, 104, 138, 162, 361.
381. *Cal. Va. State Papers* 7:165.   382. Order Book 11:444, 492.
383. Order Book 11:532.
384. *Cal. Va. State Papers* 8:471. Thomas Underwood of Hanover applied to the Governor for appointment as commandant of the arsenal expected to be established in Prince Edward.
385. *Cal. Va. State Papers* 9:64.   386. Order Book 12:65, 137, 481; 13:195.
387. Order Book 13:269, 343.   388. *Virginia Argus*, Aug. 4, 1804.
389. Order Book 13:484, 485; 14:90, 142.
390. Order Book 15:58.
391. *Virginia Argus*, Dec 11, 1805; Order Book 15:92.
392. *Today and Yesterday in the Heart of Virginia:* 263.
393. Order Book 15:95.
394. *Today and Yesterday in the Heart of Virginia:* 255.
395. Order Book 15:106, 169, 208, 218, 222, 389.
396. Order Book 15:428, 481.   397. *Virginia Argus*, Aug. 22, 1807.
398. Order Book 16;383, 431.   399. Order Book 16:476, 488.

400. Order Book 17:89, 120, 177.   401. Order Book 17:280, 355.
402. Order Book 17:502-3.   403. Order Book 18:57, 89, 160.
404. Richmond *Enquirer*, Dec. 24, 1814.
     Capt. Josiah Penick's company was on active duty during the latter part of 1814 and the early part of 1815. The company was in the 7th Regiment of Virginia militia, commanded by Col. William Gray. William Bradshaw was drafted for service in Penick's company at Prince Edward Courthouse about Aug. 1, 1814 for a term of six months and was discharged at Camp Carter Feb. 23, 1815. (Affidavit of William Bradshaw Mar. 15, 1851, in application for bounty lands granted officers and soldiers by act of Sept. 28, 1850. National Archives. Photostat in possession of the writer.) Bradshaw received a warrant (No. 26,523) for 80 acres. Later he made application for an additional grant as provided by Act of Mar. 3, 1855. In this application he states that he was in service 14 days. (Affidavit, William Bradshaw, May 5, 1855, National Archives. Photostat.) This probably means that Capt. Penick's company was engaged in actual hostilities for two weeks. A private's pay in the War of 1812 was $8 per month, a sergeant's $11 (Carded Records, Thomas Weaver, National Archives Photostat in possession of the author). Weaver's record notes that he was transferred from Capt. Redd's detachment (Thomas Redd was captain of the Prince Edward artillery company in 1814) to Capt. Isaac Tinsley's company in the 8th Regiment, Virginia Militia, in which he was on the muster roll Aug. 28, 1814.
     Old residents of the Rice community have told me that the following persons in the neighborhood saw service in the War of 1812: Capt. Richard Marshall, Ensign John Foster, Radford Fowlkes, William F. Ellington, Caswell Moring, Thomas Weaver, and William Bradshaw.
405. Farmville *Mercury*, July 22, 1875. At that time, one member of the company, Peter Foster, was still living; he resided at Cumberland Courthouse; *V.M.H.B.* 23:321 mentions muster roll of cavalry in Hampden-Sydney College library. In service Sept. 1-Sept. 13, 1814, discharged at Bottom's Bridge. This note says the troop of cavalry under Henry E. Watkins, but the writer follows the roll published in the Farmville *Mercury*, which is supported by Order Book 17:502-3, which gives the same officers taking oath in Apr. 1813 as the published muster roll gives. Copy of the roll, dated Sept. 12, 1814: S. V. Allen, captain; W. L. Venable, first lieutenant; H. E. Watkins, second lieutenant; S. L. Lockett, cornet; A. Fuqua, P. Randolph, B. Foster, sergeants; J. J. Foster, H. N. Watkins, O. Morton, corporals; J. D. Wood, musician; privates: Len Anderson, J. R. Allen, M. B. Allen, Cary C. Allen, S. C. Anderson, W. B. Booker, Richard Booker, P. Boothe, Thomas Ellington, Pas[chal] Fowlkes, Peter Foster, Jennings Fowlkes, William Fleming, Frank Flippen, Thomas Goode, Joseph Goode, John Holcombe, Simon Hughes, Theo. C. Haskins, H. W. Holland, Thomas Jackson, Nathan McGehee, Nat Morris, Sam Morris, William Morton, J. F. Nash, Edwin Price, D. Peerman, A. Poe, James Price, B. H. Price, William Price, Ch. W. Price, William Philips, John Redford, Josiah M. Rice, St.C. Richardson, John Rice, James S. Smith, Sion S. Spencer, J. H. Thurston, H. H. Vaughan, John H. Venable, Nat. Venable, William Venable, Thomas Wilborne, William H. Walthall, Sam Worsham, Richard Woodson, Aug.[ustus] Watkins, John Williams, John A. Watson.
406. See notes 401 and 405.
407. Farmville *Herald*, Feb. 6, 1903. "Prince Edward County" by Frankie I. McKinney.
408. Order Book 18:286.   409. Order Book 18:405, 479, 484.
410. Order Book 19:34.   411. Order Book 20:80.
412. Order Book 20:423.   413. Order Book 21:588, 592, 609.
414. Order Book 21:695.

415. Mss. Roll of Officers of the 63rd Regiment of Virginia Militia. Col. John Foster Papers, in possession of Col. Foster's great-granddaughter, Mrs. J. Woodfin Hughes and lent by her to the writer; cf. Order Book 22:266.
416. Richmond *Enquirer*, Nov. 13, 1832.
417. Richmond *Constitutional Whig*, Nov. 22, 1832.
418. Order Book 19:24.   419. Order Book 19:188.
420. Order Book 23:130, 140.
421. Order Book 23:254, 271. For a number of years in this period the Order Books do not specify the rank of many militia officers qualifying.
422. Richmond *Enquirer*, Aug. 3, 1847.
423. Statement to the writer by the late James R. Weaver, who was born in 1844. He remembered "Drummer" Hines' performances at musters. Queries over a period of years have failed to disclose any other soldiers in the Mexican War from Prince Edward.
424. Order Book 27:104-5.   425. Order Book 27:260.
426. *Today and Yesterday in the Heart of Virginia.* "Prince Edward Courthouse" by George L. Walker. Walker quotes reminiscences of Thomas W. Hooper, who participated in one of the musters.
427. Foote, First Series: 405.
428. Mss. Hawkins-McGehee Papers, University of Virginia Library.
429. Richmond *Enquirer*, July 11, 1843.
430. Richmond Constitutional *Whig and Public Advertiser*, July 21, 1848.

CHAPTER X NOTES

1. William Meade: *Old Churches, Ministers and Families in Virginia* I: 449. (Hereafter cited as Meade); William W. Bennett: *Memorials of Methodism in Virginia:* 56-60 (hereafter cited as Bennett). Cf. Order Book 5:475 for death of the Rev. James McCartney. His will was presented for probate Aug. 21, 1775, Bettana McCartney, executrix.
2. The Vestry Book of St. Patrick's Parish ends in the year 1774. It is not known who succeeded Nathaniel Venable as clerk, but apparently, from the ending of the record, he terminated his work as clerk in 1774. The meeting of Hanover Presbytery at Slate Hill, Venable's home, in Feb., 1775, suggests that he had become a Presbyterian by that time. The Vestry Book was preserved by Venable's descendants, his great-great-granddaughter, Miss Adeline Carrington Venable, giving it to the library of the Virginia Theological Seminary in Alexandria. A photostat copy is now in the Archives Division of the Virginia State Library, Richmond.
3. Bennett: 56-60. The theology of McRobert and Jarratt is described in a letter from Grosset Davis, one of the founders of Methodism in Petersburg, to John Wesley, dated July 11, 1780. Davis found the doctrine of final perseverance unacceptable, although he welcomed the preaching of the doctrine of salvation by grace.
4. *V.M.H.B.* 6:176. "Trustees of Hampden-Sidney College" by J. B. Henneman. McRobert became a trustee of Hampden-Sydney in 1776, succeeding the Rev. Samuel Leake, deceased. It is not likely that he would have been chosen to this post before coming to Prince Edward. A. J. Morrison, *Cal. Bd. Min.:* 174, has McRobert becoming a trustee in 1775, obviously too early, since he does not appear either in the list of those chosen in February or among the five additions made in November. Meade 2:24 gives McRobert as minister of St. Patrick's in 1777 and 1778, noting that he was on the list of clergy as

minister of Dale Parish 1773-76 (Meade 1:448). It would appear that he came to St. Patrick's during 1776, after the list of clergy had been prepared for that year.

5. Meade 1:449. McRobert related his change of religious affiliation in a letter to his friend Devereux Jarratt in a letter dated Providence, July 13, 1780.

6. Meade 1:449.   7. Foote, First Ser.: 494.

8. Order Book 5:484.   9. Order Book 5:507.

10. Order Book 6:4.   11. Order Book 6:57.

12. Order Book 6:66.

13. Order Book 7:7. Richard Foster, who had taken the oath of vestryman in 1780, is recorded as taking it again in 1782.

14. Order Book 8:95. Foster and Holcomb were probably the last church wardens of the parish, as the vestry was dissolved about this time by act of the General Assembly.

15. Hening 9:440-1.

16. Prince Edward Deed Book 6:99. The vestry which sold the glebe in 1778 consisted of Thomas Scott, Benjamin Haskins, Thomas Haskins, John Nash, Peter Johnston, Peter LeGrand, Philemon Holcomb, and William Bibb. Cf. Meade 1:449.

17. Mss. legislative petition, Archives Division, Virginia State Library. It is interesting to find McRobert's name among the petitioners, since a few months before he had been licensed to perform marriages as an Independent.

18. Order Book 7:7.

19. William H. Whitsett: *The Life and Times of Judge Caleb Wallace:* 33.

20. Mss. legislative petition, Archives Division, State Library.

21. Hening 9:164-7.

22. Beale's Semple: 53. This law declared all marriages previously performed by dissenting ministers valid. In 1784 any minister licensed to preach under the rules of the denomination of which he was a member could be licensed to perform marriages.

23. Beale's Semple: 52; 96-8; Foote, First Ser.: 338, 430-1.

24. Foote, First Ser.: 348.

25. Mss. legislative petition, Archives Division, State Library. Only a portion of the names of the petitions has been preserved with the petition.

In reference to the decline of the Anglican Church in Prince Edward, Meade 2:31 quotes a letter from "a gentleman well versed in the history of the Presbyterian Church." This correspondent of Bishop Meade quite accurately reports some of the factors in the decline: the defection of the minister, to which he might have added the minister's active effort to supplant the Established Church with Independent congregations; character of others, presumably ministers of other denominations, but that should not be interpreted as a reflection on McRobert, whose character and evangelical outlook were notable; the rise of Hampden-Sydney College; and the falling off of certain families.

It is when Bishop Meade's correspondent brings in the Huguenot influence, through Mrs. Richard Woodson, *née* Ann Michaux, as a factor in the decline of the Anglican Church that he perpetuates a popular, but misleading concept. The Reformed Church of France, to which the Huguenots had belonged in that country, was Calvinistic in doctrine and polity. But the Huguenot settlers at Manakin established a church which was a parish of the Church of England. Those who went from the Manakin settlement to other sections were Anglicans. So we find David Flournoy and Peter LeGrand vestrymen of St. Patrick's Parish, as also was Mrs. Woodson's husband. Mrs. Woodson's sister, Easter, or Esther, Mary Michaux, married Alexander Cunningham of a Scotch-Irish Presbyterian family, but there is no indication of this couple's active identification with Presbyterianism in Prince Edward; a son, John Cunningham, later became a member of Buffalo Church. It was at least 1774 before Mrs. Woodson's son-in-law, Nathaniel Venable, became a Presbyterian, and the circumstances indicate that he was influenced to make this change in religious affiliation more by the preaching of Samuel Stanhope Smith than from any other cause; Venable's brother, James, was an active member and an elder at Briery Church at the time his brother became a Presbyterian, so his influence may have been a factor. If Bishop Meade's correspondent was looking for a feminine influence as a factor in the decline of the Established Church, he could have found it in Agnes Woodson, the wife of Joseph Morton (and sister of Richard Woodson).

The writer has found no contemporary evidence to indicate that Mrs. Richard Woodson was a Presbyterian or any to indicate that she was not. Meade's Prince Edward correspondent (Meade 2: 31-2) thought that she was a Presbyterian. Meade's *Old Churches, Families and Ministers in Virginia* was published in 1857. The recently published records of Hanover Presbytery (*V.M.H.B.* 63: 59) show that Abram Venable, most likely Nathaniel Venable's brother of that name who then lived in Prince Edward on the Appomattox, was among the elders attending presbytery at its session Aug. 25, 1756. Abram Venable's wife was Elizabeth Michaux, and it is positive that she was a Presbyterian when Archibald Alevander came to Prince Edward in 1792 (Alexander: 205-23 gives an account of his ministry in Prince Edward). Joseph Morten (*sic*) and John Morten (*sic*) were elders attending presbytery Nov. 17, 1756 (*V.M.H.B.* 63: 63). It may be noted here that James Venable, brother of Abraham and Nathaniel, married in 1757 Judith Morton, daughter of Joseph Morton and Agnes Woodson. This marriage may have been a factor in his becoming a Presbyterian.

It is true that the Flournoys in time and the Dupuys, who later settled in Prince Edward and were of Huguenot descent, became affiliated with Briery Presbyterian Church. But the change seems due more to the influence of the preachers there and their proximity to the church than to any atavistic hark back to the Reformed Church of their forbears in France. Another factor in the Dupuy affiliation with Briery was the marriage of James Dupuy and the daughter of William Purnall, who with his wife had become Presbyterian.

While the idea that the French Huguenots were influential in the rise of Presbyterianism in Southside Virginia because the Reformed Church of France is one of the groups holding to the Calvinistic system is a romantic idea, this writer has been unable to find adequate support for it from contemporary evidence. The Huguenots were at first Anglicans in religious affiliation upon their settlement at Manakin. As they spread out from that center, they carried with them their connection with the Established Church, but later, as dissenting faiths began to grow and to establish places of worship, some persons of Huguenot descent joined dissenting congregations convenient to them. Some became Presbyterians, other became Baptists, and one of the leading Baptist ministers of Buckingham, Rane Chastain, was of Huguenot descent. Still others became Methodists with the rise of that denomination. All this is said not to detract from the piety and loyalty to Protestantism of the Huguenots but in an effort to correct a popular misapprehension. They could express their piety and they could be true to their Protestant tradition in the Anglican faith as well as in any dissenting sect.

This passage in Meade has two glaring errors; one was the identification of Nathaniel Venable's father as Alvan Venable; he was Abraham Venable, sometimes written Abram. The other makes the other Woodson son-in-law, Francis Watkins, the county clerk, into Francis Hopkins. Was it poor proof reading? Or was the caerography of the Bishop's correspondent indecipherable?

Although the correspondent, as others have done, greatly over-emphasized the Huguenot influence in the decline of the Established Church, the affiliation of such men of influence and standing as Nathaniel Venable and Francis Watkins with the Presbyterian Church undoubtedly influenced others to sever their ties with the Church of England and to join a dissenting congregation, where, let it not be forgotten, the preaching and the ministry were calculated to appeal most strongly to the people of Prince Edward.

Meade 2:26 mentions one Prince Edward resident whose loyalty to the Episcopal Church continued through the period of its eclipse in Prince Edward. He was William Berkeley, former treasurer of Virginia, who came to Prince Edward about 1810-11 and took up residence on property which had long been in the family of his wife, Elizabeth Randolph. Berkeley continued to attend the conventions of the Episcopal Church. He worshipped with the Presbyterian congregation at Hampden-Sydney (his home was Oakland), and he was a trustee of Hampden-Sydney, but he always had it distinctly understood that he was an Episcopalian.

26. Hening 13:555-6.

27. Order Book 11:78.

28. Order Book 8:266-7. One account was Samuel Arbuckle's for £6:19:4; the other was Peter LeGrand's for £8:7:6.

29. Foote, First Ser.: 405, 412; Beale's Semple: 255.

30. Foote, First Ser.: 413; Beale's Semple: 256.

31. Foote, First Ser.: 169-73, 414, 415.

32. Foote, First Ser.; 414, 422. This is the first indication the writer has found of the demonstration of interest in religion by or for Negro slaves in Prince Edward.

33. Foote, First Ser.: 419, 496.   34. Foote, First Ser.: 419, 427.

35. Foote, First Ser.: 428.   36. *Ibid.*

37. *Today and Yesterday in the Heart of Virginia:* 315-47. "Presbyterian Churches" by J. D. Eggleston. Cf. Prince Edward Deed Book 17:12, 102. Alexander: 127-30; 175; Foote, Second Ser.: 75-7. (The last reference contains an account of Sankey's ministry in Virginia; of particular interest are a description of his personal appearance, an account of his frequent practice of preaching directly from his Hebrew Bible. He was considered an excellent Hebraist.) Foote, First Ser.: 435. Tyler's *Mag.* 2:137: Diary of Richard N. Venable, Aug. 3, 1791: At Prince Edward Courthouse. Went home with Rev. John Smith. He talks of going to Philadelphia." This was two years after his resignation as president of Hampden-Sydney.

38. Beale's Semple: 258-60; Foote, Second Ser.: 352-3; Alexander: 205-223.

39. *Today and Yesterday in the Heart of Virginia:* 315-47. "Presbyterian Churches" by J. D. Eggleston.

40. Foote: Second Ser.: 420-2. Martin's *Gazetteer* (1835): 268 states that there were more Presbyterians in Prince Edward than in any other county in Virginia.

41. *Today and Yesterday in the Heart of Virginia:* 315-47. "Presbyterian Churches" by J. D. Eggleston; J. D. Eggleston: *The Beginning of Old Briery and Cumberland Churches:* 15-60.

Burrell: 280-1 gives in full the petition of members of Hanover Church worshipping at Farmville to West Hanover Presbytery asking that the church be divided and that they be constituted a church at Farmville and that the same pastor serve both churches. The original petition was then in the hands of Mrs. Henry Edmunds. The petitioners were F. N. Watkins, M[artha] A. Watkins, C. R. Barksdale, Ed. M. Barksdale, John Dupuy, Ann Dupuy, William C. Flournoy (by F. N. W.), M[artha] W. Flournoy, M. R. Flippen, Caroline Flippen, William M. Womack, N. D. Price, M. T. Price, M[ary] E. Venable (by F. N. W., by permission), Mary C. Womack, Jacob W. Morton, Mary Jane Morton, William C. Chappell, A. W. Millspaugh, C. C. Read, A[nn] E. Read, Mary P. Venable, Charles T. Carrington, C. Scott Venable, E. G. Venable, Mary E. Venable, Sarah S. Venable.

42. Prince Edward Deed Book 26:363.

43. *Today and Yesterday in the Heart of Virginia:* 319-20. "Presbyterian Churches" by J. D. Eggleston.

44. *Today and Yesterday in the Heart of Virginia:* 342. "Presbyterian Churches" by J. D. Eggleston.

45. Foote, Second Ser.: 432.   46. Foote, Second Ser.: 436-8.

47. Foote, Second Ser.: 538-56.   48. McIlwaine: 42.

49. *Today and Yesterday in the Heart of Virginia:* 315-47. "Presbyterian Churches" by J. D. Eggleston.

50. Richmond *Enquirer,* Aug. 7, 1857. The church called Farmville in the news story may refer to nearby Appomattox Church, of which Dr. Leach was pastor.

51. *Today and Yesterday in the Heart of Virginias* 336. "Presbyterian Churches" by J. D. Eggleston.

52. *Today and Yesterday in the Heart of Virginia:* 332. "Presbyterian Churches" by J. D. Eggleston.

53. Prince Edward Deed Book 12:284-6. Walker's Church is given as one of the early places of Presbyterian worship among the Scotch-Irish settlers. Mc. Robert's Independent congregation worshipping at the old chapel is described as being in the vicinity of Walkers Church. This building was, as the deed shows, open to use by all denominations.

54. *Today and Yesterday in the Heart of Virginia:* 337. "Presbyterian Churches" by J. D. Eggleston.

55. Mss. letter, Thomas T. Tredway to John Woodall, Aug. 14. 1856. Mr. Hunt was probably Samuel F. Hunt.

56. Beale's Semple: 272; 281-2.

57. See *supra*, Chapter 3.

58. Beale's Semple: 272; 282. Mountain Creek Church is described as being located two and one-half miles northwest of Green Bay. John Wood's map of 1820 locates it on the road from Moore's Ordinary to Sandy River Church, at the intersection of a road leading to a road connecting the Sandy River-Moore's Ordinary road with the Courthouse-Briery Church road. Mountain Creek Church was near Haskins' Mill on Mountain Creek.

59. Order Book 8:37.

60. Records, Sailor Creek Baptist Church, 1802-67. The two books covering this period are now in the library of the Virginia Baptist Historical Society, University of Richmond.

61. Beale's Semple:255.

62. Minutes, Middle District Baptist Association, 1791.

63. Minutes, Middle District Baptist Association, 1797.

64. Records, Sailor Creek Baptist Church, 1802-67. This Simeon Walton was a son of the Simeon Walton who in 1791 had been on the committee to visit Liberty Church. The elder Walton had been one of the first members of Nottoway Church in 1769, was its pastor 1784-95, in succession to Jeremiah Walker, was clerk of the Middle District Association. He moved to Kentucky in 1795. He was a surveyor. Semple (1809 edition) states that he was at one time county surveyor of Amelia County. The author has in his possession the plat of a farm in Nottoway County, a portion of which is a copy of a survey made by Walton in 1794.

   The exact date Abner Watkins succeeded Robert Foster as pastor has not been determined.

65. Beale's Semple: 256, 261; Minutes, Middle District Baptist Association, Oct. 1804.

66. Minutes, Appomattox Baptist Association, 1805.

67. Herbert Clarence Bradshaw: History of Spring Creek Baptist Church. Mss. Information concerning the founding of Welch Tract was determined from

minutes of the Appomattox Baptist Association, 1815, and subsequent years, which was furnished by the Samuel Colgate Baptist Historical Collection, then in Hamilton, N. Y., where are to be found the only copies of the minutes of this association for the years between 1807 and 1823. Another important source of information for this mss. was an account written by Margaret L. Payne, now Mrs. J. L. Green of Arlington, largely from recollections of older members of the church; Mrs. J. H. Payne, mother of Mrs. Green, gave her daughter much of the information; Mrs. Payne was much interested in the history of Spring Creek and had obtained much data from the generation of members older than her own, whose memory went back to an early period of the church's history.

68. Records, Sailor Creek Baptist Church, 1802-7.

69. Record Book, Sharon Baptist Church, 1827-60. Photostat. The original of this first record book of Sharon Church is preserved in the library of the Virginia Baptist Historical Society; the photostat copy is kept by the church clerk, John H. Bruce, together with other records of the church. The charter members of Sharon Church were Simeon Walton, William Ligon, Elijah McGehee, Willis R. V. Crute, Thomas Clark, Francis T. Wootton, William Walton, Daniel Witt, Littleberry Clark, John G. Loudon, Thomson A. Waddell, Alexander Marshall, Sr., Alexander Marshall, Jr., Francis Marshall, George Eaton, Peter Nunnally, Absalom Nunnally, Allen Nunnally, Samuel H. Pettus, Noel Waddell, Jamaica Waddell, Elderson Waddell, Nelson H. Crute, Nancy Walton, Anna McGehee, Ann Ligon, Tabitha Wooton, Sarah Hamlin, Virginsia McGehee, Susan Crute, Nancy Loudon, Lucilla Waddell, Martha W. Clark, Michael Scott, Elizabeth Leigh, Mary A. Davidson, Maranda Hudson, Mary A. Hudson, Frances Rudd, Mary W. Walton, Mary Pettus, Mary Williamson, Nancy Nunnally, Mary Ford, Martha Rudd, Elizabeth Waddell, Elizabeth Davidson, Elizabeth Nunnally, Phebe Clark, Martha Fagg, Mary Rudd, Malitia Marshall, Sarah Dungans, Martha Williamson, Alcy Brooks, Sarah Marshall, Drucilla Leneave, Mildred Leneave, Kishandra Crute, Nancy Armes; three slaves appear also from the record to have been charter members: Mrs. Wade's Salley, Thomas E. Haskins' Silvey, and Benjamin Borum's Alsey.

70. Meade 2:25.

71. J. B. Jeter: *Life of Rev. Daniel Witt, D.D.*: 146-7.

72. Meade 2:25; Prince Edward Deed Book 20:544, 553 (trustees of the Baptist congregation were Simeon Walton, Littleberry Clark, Griffith Dickerson, John Rudd, Jr., and Willis R. V. Crute); cf. Prince Edward Deed Book 2:198 for deed of Royall and John Sutton Bowman to Thomas Scott and Richard Woodson, church wardens, in 1764. The Leigh deed (Deed Book 20:553) states that the church was built in part on his land, and he gave one-half acre to the Baptist trustees.

73. Minutes, Appomattox Baptist Association, 1834.

74. Farmville *Herald*, Oct. 22, 1948: History of Farmville by Herbert Clarence Bradshaw; Charles Edward Burrell: History of Prince Edward County, Virginia: 220-7 (hereafter cited as Burrell). The list of charter members was taken from a historical sketch of the church by Dr. Peter Winston: Benjamin M. Robertson, Mrs. E. R. Robertson, C. E. Chappell, Mrs. A. B. Chappell, Miss Mary Harwood, M. Grigg, Mrs. Edith Mann, Mrs. Jane Williams, Granville Nunnally, Mrs. Betsy Nunnally, Washington Nunnally, Mrs. Judith Nunnally, Jeremiah Porter, Mrs. Jeremiah Porter, Reuben Seay, Royall Godsey, Mrs. Delilah Godsey, Thomas J. Valentine, Shelton Davis, Mrs. Mary Davis. Mandy Porter, Samuel White (colored), Phil White (colored).

75. Mss. list of subscribers, from a copy in the possession of the author which was given to him by the Rev. Charles Edward Burrell, pastor of the church.

76. Farmville *Herald*, Oct. 22, 1948. History of Farmville, by Herbert Clarence Bradshaw.

77. Herbert Clarence Bradshaw: History of Pisgah Baptist Church, 1857-1917, based on a manuscript list in the library of the Virginia Baptist Historical Society and on Minutes, Appomattox Baptist Association, 1858. The *V.B.H.S.* manuscript gives the list of charter members as James N. Marshall, John Redford, John T. Woodson, Henry T. Phillips, Vincent Phillips, John E. D. Harper, William B. Phillips, Benjamin F. Flippen, Lucinda G. Redford, Catherine R. Redford, Adalade T. Redford, Mary A. Redford, Mary V. Woodson, Fannie E. Marshall, Josephine Bradshaw, Eliza Bradshaw, Ariadna T. Dickenson, Louisa M. Williamson, Harriet S. Phillips, Susan B. Harper, Mary A. E. Harper, Pamelia P. Phillips, Anne Jane Phillips, Lucy A. Bradshaw, Polly Bradshaw, Phebe Ellett, Missoura A. Williamson, Sarah M. Flippen, Nancy Mottley, Elizabeth Fowlkes, Phebe Fowlkes, Rebecca Fowlkes, Adalade Holt, Mary Clements, Rebecca Carter, Sarah Mottley, Martha M. Mottley, Elizabeth Woodson, and Sarah F. Redford. In the mss. the name Redford is, with one exception, spelled Radford, but the family name is elsewhere spelled Redford.

78. *Today and Yesterday in the Heart of Virginia:* 350. "Baptist Churches" by Herbert Clarence Bradshaw.

79. Minutes, Appomattox Baptist Association, 1827, 1828.

80. Records, Sailor Creek Baptist Church, 1802-67. The last recorded meeting of the church at Rice's Meeting-house took place on July 20, 1833; the church met at Jamestown in August, 1834; Farmville *Herald*, Jan. 14, 1893.

81. *Ibid.*

82. Minutes, Appomattox Baptist Association, 1834.

83. Thoedore Louis Trost, curator of the Samuel Colgate Baptist Historical Collection, Colgate-Rochester Divinity School, Rochester, N. Y., consulted minutes of early sessions of the Appomattox Association (the only copies known to this writer being in the Colgate Collection). In letters to the writer dated Oct. 12 and Oct. 19, 1954, Mr. Trost advised that Mountain Creek Church was last represented at the Appomattox Association in Aug., 1816, according to records available to him. Beale's Semple: 282 has Mountain Creek go out of existence after the organization of Sharon Church in 1827. The writer has consulted Appomattox Association minutes of 1823 and subsequent years (available in the Virginia Baptist Historical Society library, University of Richmond) and finds no reference to Mountain Creek Church in them. From the research of Mr. Trost and the writer, it is evident that Mountain Creek went out of existence several years prior to the organization of Sharon. However, five Negroes were received into the membership of Sharon Church from Mountain Creek after the organization of the former in 1827 (Sharon Baptist Church Records, 1827-60). It would appear that these persons had not affiliated with any church after Mountain Creek ceased to exist until they joined Sharon.

84. Beale's Semple: 282.

85. Minutes, Appomattox Baptist Association, 1856, 1857, 1858; Beale's Semple: 280, 281, note. The second meeting-house of Appomattox Church burned and the third was subsequently occupied by a Negro congregation. John Wood's map of 1820 locates Appomattox meeting-house on Walker's Church road, not far from Devil's Elbow on the Appomattox River and Venable's Mill on that stream.

86. Minutes, Appomattox Baptist Association, 1859.

87. Prince Edward Deed Book 14:539. The trustees do not seem always to have been members of the church of which they were trustees. Alexander Marshall, for example, was a member of Sailor Creek Baptist Church, in the list of those worshipping at Liberty, transferring from that church to Sharon when it was organized in 1827. Since he lived nearer Mountain Creek than to Liberty, he may have been earlier a member of Mountain Creek; the Sailor Creek records do not indicate how he became a member of that church.

The proximity of Liberty may have been a factor in the decline of Mountain Creek, rather than the organization of Sharon. The organization of Ash Camp Church in Charlotte by Henry Lester, a pastor of Mountain Creek, may also have drawn members from Mountain Creek.

88. Prince Edward Deed Book 16:386.

89. Prince Edward Deed Book 22:264.

90. Records, Sailor Creek Baptist Church, 1802-67.

91. Record Book, Sharon Baptist Church, 1827-60.

92. Minutes, Appomattox Baptist Association, 1834, 1835; Herbert Clarence Bradshaw: History of Spring Creek Baptist Church, mss.

93. Record Book, Sharon Baptist Church, 1827-60.

94. Records, Sailor Creek Baptist Church, 1802-67.

95. Record Book, Sharon Baptist Church, 1827-60.

96. Frederick Arthur Hodge: *The Plea and the Pioneers in Virginia:* 29-30; 67-70; 146; 266-7 (hereafter cited as Hodge).

97. Hodge: 69.

98. Hodge: 156, 182.

99. Burrell: 288. Dr. Burrell queried older members and church officials for information on the history of their churches when he prepared his history of the county in 1922 and included in his book the accounts which he received. Although he does not give his source for Liberty Christian Church, it seems likely, from his known practice, that he obtained this information from some member or officer of the church.

100. Mss. statement of account, dated June, 1838, for vol. 1 and 2, n[ew] series, *Harbinger,* A. Campbell. Walton Papers, a collection of manuscript letters, accounts, etc., lent to the author by Mrs. Lockett Walton (James Keith) Marshall, Marshall, Va., formerly of Farmville, a granddaughter of William Walton.

101. Herbert Clarence Bradshaw: History of Spring Creek Baptist Church, mss.

102. Record Book, Sharon Baptist Church, 1827-60.

103. Prince Edward Deed Book 25:292.

104. Herbert Clarence Bradshaw: History of Pisgah Baptist Church, 1857-1917, manuscript.

105. Minutes, Appomattox Baptist Association, 1824.

106. Records, Sailor Creek Baptist Church, 1802-67.

107. Record Book, Sharon Baptist Church, 1827-60.

108. Hatchett: 8-13. McGehee's barn was most likely John McGehee's. This John McGehee was a son of Edward McGehee of Cumberland; it was in this section that Edward McGehee owned an extensive tract which he divided into tracts of 700 acres each for several sons, one of whom was John. The other sons of Edward McGehee sold their land in this section and moved elsewhere, Micajah and William to Georgia and Mumford to North Carolina. The family of Micajah McGehee became Methodists in Georgia; his son Edward was a pillar of the Methodist Episcopal Church in Mississippi; Micajah's son Abner became a leading Methodist Protestant in Alabama, George Cardwell married Sarah McGehee, a daughter of Jacob McGehee and a first cousin of the John McGehee of this note. The Cardwells lived in Charlotte, prior to their removal to Kentucky. (Herbert Clarence Bradshaw: The McGehee Family, mss.)

109. Prince Edward Deed Book 9:272.   110. Bennett: 417.

111. *Virginia Argus,* Aug. 25, 1804.   112. Bennett: 477.

113. *V.H.M.B.* 33:166-9, 284-7; 34: 130-4, 238, 247, 304. "Diary of John Early, Bishop of the M.E. Church, South. 25 May 1807-8 June 1814." Bishop Collins Denny in his introduction to the diary mentions Parson Weems'

reference (in his biography of Washington) to one of Early's camp meetings at Prospect at which 1,000 people were converted. Bennett: 523 refers to the same incident, noting that "it is said" that such were the results. The writer has not been able to find any confirmation of the details of this tradition. The comparatively late date at which the Prince Edward Circuit was established inclines him to question its accuracy. Early does not mention it in his *Journal* for the years 1807-14. Weems, who originated the cherry tree episode in Washington's life, cannot be depended upon for accuracy.

114. Prince Edward Deed Book 17:139; Mss. History of Prospect Methodist Church, sent to the writer by Mrs. Bennett T. Taylor, Farmville.

115. Woodrow W. Wilkerson: *Olive Branch Church from 1805 to 1934.* Pamphlet lent to the writer by Miss Mildred Harvey, Prospect. Lorenzo Dow (Bennett: 455) passed through Virginia in 1803, returning in 1804 to labor "with great success in different parts of the state."

116. *Minutes of the Annual Conferences of the Methodist Episcopal Church for the Years 1829-1839.* New York, published by T. Mason and G. Lane for the Methodist Episcopal Church, 1840. p. 95. This reference was lent to the author by Miss Elizabeth Royer, librarian of the Theology Library, Emory University.

Farmville *Herald*, Oct. 22, 1948. History of Farmville by Herbert Clarence Bradshaw. There was made available to the writer in the preparation of the Farmville history "A Short Sketch of Farmville Methodism" by the Rev. James Cannon, Jr., 1892, from which this information about the Farmville church was obtained.

117. Prince Edward Deed Book 16:46.

118. Prince Edward Deed Book 10:270. Capt. Lillious D. Womack's post office in 1840 was Midway Inn and he was a member of Briery Presbyterian Church. These facts locate his home in the south central part of the county, and suggest that the church built on his land may have been the forerunner of the Beulah Methodist Church at Abilene. This was most likely the Methodist Church in which the present Douglas Presbyterian Church was organized. (See *infra.*, p. 456.)

119. Prince Edward Deed Book 20:306. Dr. Merrit B. Allen's post office in 1840 was Prospect, and he was a trustee of the Appomattox Constitutional Presbyterian Church. These facts suggest that the Bethesda Methodist Church was located in the Tuggle-Prospect area.

120. Prince Edward Deed Book 23:57; 25:145.

121. John Ellis Edwards: *Life of Rev. John Wesley Childs:* 166-80. This book was lent to the writer by Mrs. John Fennell Redd, who lives at Locust Grove, the home of her great-grandfather, John Wesley Redd, where Childs and his family lived during the two years (1837-8) he was on the Prince Edward Circuit.

122. See note 116.

123. Minutes, Virginia Conference of the Methodist Episcopal Church, South, 1870.

124. Mss. Journal of H. E. Warren, lent to this writer by Mrs. E. Scott Martin, Mr. Warren's granddaughter, when he was preparing the sesquicentennial history of Farmville published in the Farmville *Herald*, Oct. 22, 1948.

125. Mss. letter of Judith E. Woodall to Miss Jane B. Morgan, Walkers Church P. O., Prince Edward, Va., Sept. 13, 1852. John Woodall Papers, Duke University Library. Mrs. John Fennell Redd told the writer that she had heard that there was a Methodist Church at Sandy River which was moved to Meherrin. It was her impression that the building was taken down and moved. The writer has found nothing to indicate such a move, but it is possible that after the controversy with the Baptists over ownership of Sandy River Church the Methodist group worshipping there moved its place of worship to Meherrin.

126. Class Books of Mt. Pleasant Methodist Church, lent to the writer by Mrs. John Fennell Redd. Cf. Richmond *Enquirer*, Nov. 26, 1847, for the appointment of John D. Southall and T. J. Bayton to the Prince Edward Circuit.

127. Richmond *Whig and Public Advertiser*, Mar. 6, 1838.

128. Richmond *Enquirer*, Nov. 26, 1847.

129. Richmond *Enquirer*, Dec. 9, 1856.

130. Richmond *Enquirer*, Nov. 23, 1859. The circuits were in the Randolph-Macon District in 1857 (cf. Richmond *Enquirer*, Dec. 1, 1857).

131. *Acts of Assembly* 1812-3: 120.

132. Richmond *Enquirer*, June 19, 1835.

133. *36th Annual Report of the Bible Society of Virginia with Proceedings of the Annual Meeting held at the Second Presbyterian Church, Richmond, April 3, 1849* (hereafter cited as Bible Society Annual Report with year). Pamphlet, Duke University Library.

134. Bible Society Annual Report, 1850. 135. Bible Society Annual Report, 1857.

136. Farmville *Mercury*, Feb. 19, 1874. 137. Farmville *Mercury*, Mar. 18, 1875.

138. Bible Society Annual Report, 1880.

139. Minutes Appomattox Baptist Association, 1834.

140. Farmville *Herald*, Oct. 22, 1948. History of Farmville by Herbert Clarence Bradshaw.

141. See *supra*.

142. Farmville *Herald*, Oct. 22, 1948. History of Farmville by Herbert Clarence Bradshaw.

143. John B. Cunningham: History of Buffalo Presbyterian Church, mss. Cites George Hunt's history of that church, 1884, as the reference to the founding of the Sunday School at Buffalo.

144. *Today and Yesterday in the Heart of Virginia:* 336. "Presbyterian Churches by J. D. Eggleston.

CHAPTER XI NOTES

1. Foote, First Ser.: 530-1.

2. *Tyler's Mag.* 33:70. Based on deed of trust recorded in Amelia County dated June 4, 1794.

3. *Tyler's Mag.* 2:137. Diary of R. N. Venable.

4. Benjamin Henry Latrobe: *The Journal of Latrobe:* 16.

5. J. B. Jeter: *Life of Rev. Daniel Witt, D.D.:* 135-41.

6. Minutes, Appomattox Baptist Association, 1834.

7. Mss. Legislative Petitions, Archives Division, State Library.

8. Order Book 26:544. Certificate of good character given a number of Prince Edward firms, to whom the Court had no objection to issuing a license to sell wine and ardent spirits.

9. Order Book 8:162.

10. Mss. letter, R. T. Harding to Hezekiah Harding, Oct. 11, 1859. E. and J. Harding Papers, Duke University Library.

11. Beale's Semple: 105.

12. Mss. lists "of the number of souls" (or of "inhabitants") in the militia companies of Captains Williamson Bird, James Clark, Dick Holland, James Ligon, Thomas Moore, Watson, and Jacob Woodson in the year 1782. The list for

Watson's company's district is undated, but it is with the lists for 1782. Clerk's Office. Copied by Mrs. Margaret H. Morton and lent to the writer.

13. Richmond *Enquirer*, Apr. 2, 1861.
14. *Virginia Argus*, May 2, 1804; Nov. 21, 1804; Dec. 18, 1805; Richmond *Enquirer* March 18, 1806; Feb. 16, 1822.
15. Richmond *Enquirer*, Nov. 21, 1809.
16. *Virginia Argus*, Oct. 23, 1810. *Tyler's Mag.* 2:304, note: Richard K. Randolph's brother-in-law, William Berkeley, and the Berkeley family settled on Mrs. Berkeley's estate, held jointly with her brother, late in 1810 or early in 1811, when Randolph moved to Rhode Island.
17. Walter A. Watson: *Notes on Southside Virginia:* .192. Judge Watson relates an incident which his mother remembered. She and her uncle were going to Hampden-Sydney College commencement when they came upon the scene of the murder at Bell's Tavern where graves were being dug. The traders, father and son by the name of Kirby, were killed by an ax and a club, which were on exhibition on the tavern porch. They were headed south with a drove of slaves. The murders took place in the year 1833, 1834, or 1835, according to Mrs. Meredith Watson, Judge Watson's mother.
18. Richmond *Enquirer*, May 20, 1828.
19. *Virginia Argus*, Nov. 21, 1804; Feb. 9, 1805; Sept. 14, 1805; Oct. 19, 1805; Mar. 18, 1806. William Worsham, jailor, Prince Edward Courthouse, advertised runaways taken up and lodged in jail.
20. *Virginia Argus*, Dec. 30, 1811.   21. Richmond *Enquirer*, Feb. 21, 1833.
22. Richmond *Enquirer*, Sept. 28, 1821.   23. Richmond *Enquirer*, Aug. 26, 1825.
24. Order Book 26:439, 543; 27:3, 405. Cf. sundry levies through the years for payments for patrolling.
25. Mss. letter, John Watts of Prince Edward County to William Watts, Mar. 25, 1789. Watts Papers, University of Virginia Library.
26. Mss. deed of sale, Hawkins-McGehee Papers, University of Virginia Library.
27. Mss. receipt, Hawkins-McGehee Papers, University of Virginia Library; receipt signed by Richard A. Pincham for John Walthall, executor, Richard D. Pincham.
28. Mss. Hawkins-McGehee Papers, University of Virginia Library.
29. Mss. letter, Thomas T. Tredway to John Woodall, Feb. 9, 1856. John Woodall Papers, Duke University Library.
30. Mss. letter, Thomas T. Tredway to Mr. Woodall, Dec. 5, ——.
31. Mss. letter, Thomas T. Tredway to John Woodall, Aug. 14, 1856.
32. Mss. letter, Thomas T. Tredway to John Woodall, Dec. 15, 1855.
33. Mss. letter, Thomas T. Tredway to Mr. Woodall, Dec. 5, ——.
34. The William Weaver family Bible, now in possession of Mrs. Herbert L. Bradshaw, Rice.
35. *Farmer's Register* 2:248-9. Letter of Charles Woodson, Prince Edward County, July 9, 1834.
36. Mss. letter James L. Waddell, Moore's Ordinary, to Ezekiah Harding, Clover Station, Va., Nov. 12, 1857. Waddell wanted to hire several good workmen and was willing to pay a fair price. Harding Papers, Duke University Library. Cf. *Virginia Argus*, Sept. 22, 1802; Jan. 5, 1803.
37. Farmville *Journal*, Mar. 11, 1852.
38. Richmond *Whig and Public Advertiser*, July 18, 1848.
39. Mss. statement of William Weaver to Southside Division, Atlantic, Mississippi, and Ohio Railroad, dated 1872, for services of slave hired to Southside Railroad, in 1864 and until Apr. 1, 1865. Copy from original in possession of the writer. In this connection it is interesting to mention the recollection of Ned Pincham, an ex-slave, who lived in Prince Edward, that his master, Dr.

Philip T. Southall, at one time of Jamestown and later of Amelia County, hired out several slaves to work in the coal pits in Chesterfield County.

40. Mss. agreement, dated June 1, 1818. James Blanton Papers, Duke University Library.

41. *Today and Yesterday in the Heart of Virginia:* 346, "Presbyterian Churches" by J. D. Eggleston.

42. Mss. agreement, dated Dec. 27, 1826, James Blanton Papers, Duke University Library.

43. Mss. award of reference G. Nunnally and Wm. Walton Gdn, dated Farmville Jan. 14, 1842. Walton Papers, lent by Mrs. J. K. Marshall.

44. *Today and Yesterday in the Heart of Virginia:* 346, "Presbyterian Churches' by J. D. Eggleston.

45. Jeter: *Witt:* 207.   46. Richmond *Enquirer*, June 20, 1854.

47. Richmond *Enquirer*, Mar. 23, 1855.

48. Related to the writer by Morton Carter, who was born May 12, 1852, and is at this writing (the summer of 1954) still living in Prince Edward. His father, Patrick, belonged to William Weaver, his mother to Radford Fowlkes. After freedom his father, whose birth date is entered in the Weaver family Bible, continued to work for his former master; even then he spent only week ends with his family, his visit continuing from Saturday afternoon until early Monday morning. This arrangement did not seem at all odd to the children, "Uncle Morton" has told me. Morton Carter died in February, 1955.

49. Farmville *Herald*, Nov. 30, 1906. "A Friend," writing of the death of Edward Matthews, remembered that Matthews married Bettie, a slave belonging to the correspondent's father, in the parlor of the master's home in Worsham in 1859 and that the ceremony was performed by the Rev. R. L. Dabney, D.D.

50. *Southern Literary Messenger,* Vol. 5, No. 5:461-6 (Nov.-Dec., 1943), "A Persimmon Beer Dance in Ante-Bellum Virginia" edited by Jay B. Hubbell. The description is a reprint of a letter of Dr. William B. Smith to the *Farmer's Register* of Apr. 1, 1838 (Vol. 6:58-61). The "old black bull" brings back memories of a tale told me in boyhood by Joe Ross, who lived on my father's and my grandfather's farm and who had in his younger days lived on the farms of both my Great-Grandfather Weaver and my Great-Grandmother Bradshaw. There was a huge cherry tree on the farm road between the Norfolk and Western Railroad and the dwelling on my father's farm. The tree was a familiar landmark in the Rice neighborhood and also to regular travelers on the railroad for many years. It was under this tree, "Uncle Joe" used to tell me, that "the black cow" found shade. Long ago, the story ran, that cherry tree was the only tree in all that part of the country. Far away there lived a man who had a black cow. On a hot day, the cow, having no shade in the pasture, jumped the fence and started in search of shade. After a long journey, it found shade under this cherry tree. Was the black animal of "Uncle Joe's" tale the "old black bull" of the ancient song?

51. William Branch, Jr.: *Life:* 37-8; 42. *Life* was published by the Franklin Press, Richmond, in 1819.

52. *Today and Yesterday in the Heart of Virginia:* 153-4, "Prince Edward County" by Herbert Clarence Bradshaw.

53. *Farmer's Register* 4:3, 4.   54. Farmville *Mercury*, Sept. 23, 1875.

55. Shepherd 1:238-9.

56. Order Book 17:21 (1811); 22:525 (1831); 26:149 (1846); 27:424 (1861) contain records of the registration of free Negroes. Martin's *Gazetteer* (1835): 268 states that there were more free Negroes in Prince Edward than in any other county in the state. This leadership is explained by the location in the county of Israel Hill on which the Negroes emancipated by Richard Randolph lived.

57. Order Book 21:483; 22:525.   58. *W. & M. Quart.* (2) 7:97.

59. Order Book 13:246.   60. Foote, Second Ser.: 446-7.

61. James Madison, James Monroe, and John Marshall were among the early leaders in the American Colonization Society. In 1846 Henry Clay was president, and among the vice-presidents from Virginia were the Rt. Rev. William Meade, Bishop of Virginia, William Maxwell, a former president of Hampden-Sydney, William C. Rives, and James Garland. (Richmond *Enquirer*, Feb. 23, 1846.) In 1858 John Rutherfoord was president of the Virginia Colonization Society and General John H. Cocke of Bremo, Fluvanna County, a vice-president (Richmond *Enquirer*, Apr. 2, 1858) .

62. Foote, Second Ser.: 447.

63. Richmond *Enquirer*, April 30, 1833.

64. Prince Edward Circuit Court Will Book 2:67-74; 82-93.

65. Richmond *Enquirer*, Apr. 20, 1858; Order Book 27:255.

66. Record Book, Sharon Baptist Church, 1827-60. Locations are provided by the writer.

67. Farmville *Herald*, Oct. 22, 1948, "History of Farmville" by Herbert Clarence Bradshaw.

68. John B. Cunningham: History of Buffalo Presbyterian Church, Mss. lent by him to this writer; *Today and Yesterday in the Heart of Virginia:* 320, 336, "Presbyterian Churches" by J. D. Eggleston.

69. Mss. letters, Virginia Baptist Historical Society Library, University of Richmond.

70. Cal. Bd. Min.: 85-6, note.

71. *Today and Yesterday in the Heart of Virginia:* 334, "Presbyterian Churches" by J. D. Eggleston.

72. Richmond *Enquirer*, Dec. 4, 1860; Dec. 6, 1861.

73. Richmond *Enquirer*, Mar. 27, Apr. 21, June 15, July 30, 1847.

74. Report of the Howard Association of Norfolk, Va., to All Contributors Who Gave Valuable Aid in Behalf of the Sufferers from Epidemic Yellow Fever During the Summer of 1855. Pamphlet 90, Vol. 5, Virginia Pamphlets, 1841-59, Duke University Library. In the United States $157,237.72 was raised for the relief of Norfolk during the epidemic.

75. Richmond *Enquirer*, Oct. 16, 1855.

76. Shepherd 3:129.

77. Record Book, Sharon Baptist Church, 1827-60.

78. John B. Cunningham: History of Buffalo Presbyterian Church, Mss.

79. The references in records of the period to mulattoes confirm the reports which have been related and which identify mulattoes as children of specified white men. The parentage was often known to these colored persons, as well as to other people of the neighborhood. There have been cases in which there could be distinguished family resemblances between mulattoes and the legitimate children of the fathers of the mulattoes, as many older people have observed.

80. Order Book 27:251.

81. Richmond *Enquirer*, Sept. 24, Sept. 28, Oct. 22, Oct. 26, 1858.

82. Mss. legislative petitions, Archives Division, Virginia State Library.

83. Record Book, Sharon Baptist Church, 1827-60.

84. Order Book 20:609.

CHAPTER XII NOTES

1. George White, Editor: *The Yazoo Fraud* (1852): 12-3 (hereafter cited as *Yazoo Fraud*); mss. petition to Legislature of the State of Georgia, by Patrick Henry *et al.* Undated. Package 35, Loose papers, Clerk's Office.
2. Mss. petition to Legislature of the State of Georgia by Patrick Henry *et al.*
3. *Yazoo Fraud*: 13, and note.
4. *Tyler's Mag.* 2: 137-8. Diary of R. N. Venable. Did the papers to which Venable refers include the petition to the Georgia legislature asking it to live up to its bargain?
5. *V.M.H.B.* 20: 313-5. Notes by A. J. Morrison on the Virginia Yazoo Company from small volume of miscellaneous accounts of Francis Watkins, 1788-93. Cf. *American State Papers* (Gales and Seaton). *Public Lands* 4: 197-203.
6. Bruce 1: 180-5; *Yazoo Fraud*: 14, 22; cf. pp. 53-8 for speech of John Randolph on the 1795 grant.
7. Hening 12: 591-5.   8. Hening 13: 153.
9. Order Book 10: 15.   10. Hening 13: 568-70.
11. Mss. legislative petition, Archives Division, State Library.
12. Shepherd 1: 390-4.   13. Shepherd 2: 108.
14. Benjamin Henry Latrobe: *The Journal of Latrobe:* 1-22. Those making the trip down the river about June 12-17, 1796 were Latrobe, Richard N. Venable, Mr. Epperson (probably John Epperson, a trustee of the Upper Appomattox Co.), Mr. Wily (John Wily, treasurer of the company), and Mr. Anderson, who is identified only as "a country gentleman from the neighborhood of Mr. Venable." Anderson was extremely adept in managing a boat in rocks and rapids and was captain of the expedition; he must have been quite a person; Latrobe tells that on one occasion Anderson stripped and equipped only with a pipe which he smoked during the performance took honey from two beehives. As there were several Andersons in Prince Edward who could answer Latrobe's description, the writer is unable to identify him.
15. Mss. legislative petition dated Dec. 10, 1801, Archives Division, State Library.
16. Shepherd 2: 344.
17. Mss. legislative petition dated Dec. 10, 1801, Archives Division, State Library.
18. *Cal. Va. State Papers* 9: 224-5.
19. *Ibid.*; *Virginia Argus*, Aug. 29, 1800; June 23, 1802.
20. *Virginia Argus*, June 2, 1804.   21. *Virginia Argus*, Jan. 18, 1799.
22. *Virginia Argus*, Aug. 29, 1800; Sept. 2, 1800.
23. *Virginia Argus*, Sept. 1, 1804.
24. *Virginia Argus*, May 18, 1805; Sept. 25, 1805.
25. *Virginia Argus*, May 27, 1806: Eggleston, Venable, Munford, and John Wily signed the notice; Aug. 8, 1806.
26. *Virginia Argus*, May 9, 1807: meeting postponed from April 14.
27. Richmond *Enquirer*, Aug. 7, 1816.   28. Richmond *Enquirer*, Oct. 30, 1821.
29. Richmond *Enquirer*, July 27, 1847.
30. Petersburg *Intelligencer*, Apr. 2, 1813.
31. *Acts of Assembly 1818-9*: 56; *1812-3*: 94; *1821*: 39.
32. Mss. legislative petition, Archives Division, State Library.
33. Mss. legislative petition, Archives Division, State Library.
34. *Acts of Assembly 1834-5*: 182-3.   35. *Acts of Assembly 1839*: 101.
36. Mss. legislative petition, Archives Division, State Library.
37. Howe: 132.

38. Mss. agreement, James Blanton Papers, Duke University Library.
39. Richmond *Enquirer*, Aug. 31, 1847.
40. Farmville *Herald*, Aug. 31, 1906: "Farmville Then and Now: Remembrance of Rip Van Winkle 60 Years Ago." Unsigned. Martin's *Gazetteer* (1835): 268 states that about 40 batteaux, each manned by three men and with a capacity of five-seven tons, served Farmville.
41. *Acts of Assembly 1835-6*: 49. The law was passed Mar. 21, 1836.
42. Farmville *Herald*, Aug. 31, 1906. The unidentified author of the reminiscences describes this as his experience.
43. Shepherd 3: 268.   44. Shepherd 3: 322.
45. Mss. legislative petition, Archives Division, State Library.
46. *Acts of Assembly 1812-3*: 44-5.   47. *Acts of Assembly 1824-5*: 57-63.
48. *Acts of Assembly 1881-2*: 341-2; 463-4; 492-3.
49. Farmville *Herald*, Oct. 22, 1948: "History of Farmville" by Herbert Clarence Bradshaw, from the reminiscences of George M. Robeson.
50. Mss. legislative petition, Archives Division, State Library.
51. Shepherd 1: 425-6.
52. Mss. legislative petition, Archives Division, State Library.
53. Shepherd 2:30-1. The act which established Jamestown also established CaIra on Willis River, Ligontown and Clementown on the Appomattox.
54. Shepherd 2:121-2. The act which established Farmville also established Planterstown at the Cutbanks on the Appomattox in Buckingham County. Among the trustees of Planterstown were Robert Kelso and Stephen Pettus of Prince Edward.
55. *Acts of Assembly 1832*: 155-8.
56. Mss. legislative petition, Archives Division, State Library.
57. *Acts of Assembly 1832*: 155-6. The various additions to the town of Farmville are detailed in the Farmville *Herald*, Oct. 22, 1948.
58. Mss. legislative petition, Archives Division, State Library.
59. *Acts of Assembly 1835-6*: 374-5.
60. Farmville *Herald*, Oct. 22, 1948: "History of Farmville" by Herbert Clarence Bradshaw.
61. *Acts of Assembly 1839*: 172-3.   62. Howe: 432.
63. Richmond *Enquirer*, Feb. 2, 1858.
64. Farmville *Herald*, Nov. 23, 1906: "Prince Edward County Records 1836-54"; John Wood's Map of Prince Edward County, 1820, reproduced in *Today and Yesterday in the Heart of Virginia* (appendix). Cf. *Today and Yesterday:* 137-62, "Prince Edward County" by Herbert Clarence Bradshaw. Martin's *Gazetteer:* 268-9. All the places listed by Martin were given as post offices except Moore's Ordinary. Farmville, Jamestown, and Prince Edward Courthouse were post villages. Hermitage was described as being on a considerable eminence, with a beautiful view, between Vaughan's Creek and a mill creek, at the junction of the road from Charlottesville south and the Petersburg-Lynchburg road. Before 1835 the inspection of tobacco had been discontinued at Jamestown, and the place "had ceased to flourish." There were there then several dwellings, a house of worship open to all denominations, two stores, and one house of entertainment (tavern). At Prince Edward Courthouse were 21 dwellings, one tanyard, one coach manufactory, two flourishing academies, a large and handsome brick Presbyterian church one-quarter mile distant, a female seminary. In the immediate vicinity of Sandy River Church were a house of entertainment, a mercantile store, several mechanics, and one physician. Farmville's five tobacco factories employed 250 persons, two warehouses inspected 4,000-5,000 hogsheads of tobacco annually, and there were there 10 stores, two churches (Methodist and Presbyterian), two taverns, one print-

ing office, one female school, one cabinet-maker, two smith's shops, one wheel-wright, one boot and shoe factory, one saddler, one tanyard, two confection-eries, and two milliners and mantua-makers. The population was 800.

65. *Acts of Assembly 1844-5:* 38-41; Richmond *Daily Whig,* Nov. 11, 1845.

66. Shepherd 2:32; 127-8.   67. Order Book 11: 571, 591.

68. Order Book 12:70, 85, 93, 94.   69. Order Book 12:187.

70. Order Book 12:295.   71. Order Book 12:91.

72. Order Book 13:321.   73. Shepherd 2:127-8.

74. *Acts of Assembly, 1814:* 133. The index notes that an act to discontinue the inspection of tobacco at Randolph's Warehouse is recorded on that page, but that page and several others are missing from the volume available to the author (Duke University Law Library). For Jamestown, cf. mss. legislative petition presented Dec. 3, 1817, noting that the inspection there had not been kept up for three years past.

75. Mss. legislative petition, Archives Division, State Library.

76. *Acts of Assembly 1816-7:* 171.

77. Mss. legislative petition, Archives Division, State Library.

78. *Acts of Assembly 1819-20:* 93-4.   79. *Acts of Assembly 1817-8:* 196-7.

80. *Acts of Assembly 1820-21:* 109.

81. Order Book 19:335: John Randolph as trustee for John St. George Randolph was summoned to the April, 1820, Court to give bond to finish the additional warehouse.

82. The method of prizing tobacco was explained to the writer by his father, the late Herbert L. Bradshaw, who had seen the prizes in old barns when he was a boy and young man. Thomas T. Tredway in a letter to John Woodall mentions having the prizes repaired. John Woodall Papers, Duke University Library.

    The date of the discovery of the method of curing "yellow tobacco" was long set as 1852 (see *North Carolina: A Guide to the Old North State,* Federal Federal Writers Project: 73). Nannie M. Tilley: *The Bright Leaf Industry 1860-1929:* 24-6 shows that the process was discovered in 1839 by Stephen, a slave belonging to Abisha Slade of Caswell County, N. C. Miss Tilley, in the first chapter of her book, "Quest for Yellow Tobacco 1606-1865," (pp. 3-36) gives in detail the various leads to flue-curing tobacco. Readers of this work will be interested in Miss Tilley's references to a crude flue-curing process patented by J. Robinson of Charlotte Co. in 1809, in the description by an unidentified farmer of Charlotte in the late 1820's of a set of flues similar to modern flues, and in the experiments of Dr. Davis G. Tuck of Halifax County in the production of yellow tobacco in 1828 (Tilley: 18-20). See pp. 508 and 513 of this work for references to flue-cured tobacco culture in Prince Edward.

83. Related to the writer by his grandfather, the late James R. Weaver. The name Genito is still used to designate this road north from Flippen's fork on Route 460.

84. Mss. legislative petition, Archives Division, State Library.

85. Order Book 20:455.

86. Farmville *Herald,* Apr. 4, 1902. Jackson was a nephew of Col. James Madison, who influenced him to come to Farmville.

87. Mss. letter Joseph E. Venable & Co. to James Blanton, Dec. 14, 1848. James Blanton Papers, Duke University Library.

88. Farmville *Herald,* Sept. 14, 1906. "Rip" writes of 50 years ago.

89. Richmond *Enquirer,* Mar. 26, 1861.

90. *Today and Yesterday in the Heart of Virginia:* 152: "Prince Edward County" by Herbert Clarence Bradshaw; information from A. J. Morrison mss. *Old Prince Edward: A Miscellany.* When I wrote that account of the county

(winter of 1934-5), Morrison's mss. was in the Hampden-Sydney College library. Martin's *Gazetteer* (1835) 268 states that Farmville afforded the largest inspection of fine French tobacco of any market in the state.

91. Mss. letter of Preston & Eu......, Richmond, to James Blanton, Mar. 3, 1848. James Blanton Papers. Blanton's correspondent did not know the extent of the other tobacco orders.

92. Richmond *Constitutional Whig*, Sept. 14, 1832.

93. Richmond *Enquirer*, Oct. 16, 1849.   94. Richmond *Enquirer*, Aug. 8, 1854.

95. Richmond *Enquirer*, Aug. 9, 1853.

96. Order Book 5:497, 515, 517, 528; 6:77, 82, 83, 97.

97. Order Book 5:526; 6:4, 6.

98. *Virginia Gazette* (Purdie), Aug. 21, 1778; Oct. 16, 1778. Redd's mill was located on a "never failing stream."

99. Order Book 6:83, 96.   100. Order Book 6:93, 98.

101. Prince Edward Will Book 1:346.   102. Order Book 7:26.

103. Order Book 8:391, 392.   104. Order Book 9:65.

105. Order Book 9:85, 88.   106. Order Book 10:22, 63.

107. Order Book 10:193, 196, 203.   108. Order Book 10:330.

109. Order Book 11:265, 311. No location was given for LeGrand's mill.

110. Order Book 11:343, 347, 375, 441.   111. Order Book 11:497.

112. Mss. letter, John Randolph to Creed Taylor, Nov. 27, 1799. Creed Taylor Papers, University of Virginia Library.

113. *Virginia Gazette and Richmond and Manchester Advertiser*, Dec. 5, 1793.

114. *Virginia Argus*, July 30, 1806.

115. John Wood's Map of 1820. Cf. *Today and Yesterday*: 146 for list. The dates when permits were given to build some of these mills are known: Josiah and Thomas Perkinson, Sailor Creek, 1803 (Order Book 13:199); 1810 (Order Book 16:571); Osborn and Edmund Lockett on Rice's Creek, 1819 (Order Book 19:169): was this Marrowbone or Little Sailor Creek (there was a Lockett mill on each); Louse (Leuse) Creek was in "McGehee country" and was probably the name of William McGehee's mill creek, on which Josiah Fowlkes was given a permit to build in 1795 (Order Book 11:307, 311); William and Henry Ligon, Sandy River, 1801 (Order Book 12:366); Marshall's on Camp Creek was most probably Alexander Marshall's, who lived in that neighborhood; Marshall and William Baldwin received a permit to build on Big Nottoway River in 1797 (Order Book 11:497); Nathan Bell, Mingo Creek, 1818 (Order Book 19:77); John Dupuy, Buffalo, 1788 (Order Book 9:65), probably the Dupuy's mill on a branch of Buffalo; Samuel Carter, Buffalo, 1805 (Order Book 14:525); Thomas Tredway, Spring Creek, 1815 (Order Book 18:350); John Cunningham, Spring Creek, 1789 (Order Book 9:85); Peyton Glenn, Harris Creek, 1799 (Order Book 12:206); William Jones, Jr., Vaughan's Creek, 1807 (Order Book 15:541); James Watt, Vaughan's Creek, 1807 (Order Book 15:539); David F. Womack and William M. Carter, Spring Creek, 1831 (Order Book 22:531); the location of Womack's mill on a map of 1820, eleven years before the permit was issued to build it, raises a question. Since George Booker had sold the land for Buffalo Church in 1808, and the church is near the mill, the writer supposed that Booker sold the mill which he received a permit to build in 1792 (Order Book 10:196) to Womack; a search through the deed books failed to show any connection; Booker sold the mill to Quin Morton in the same year (Deed Book 9:191) and Morton sold the mill in 1794 to Richard Bibb (Deed Book 10:196); the writer could find no trace beyond Bibb. Pryor Wright, Sr. and Pryor Wright, Jr., Plain Run, 1812 (Order Book 17:315). Some mills had been sold between the time of building and 1820. Permits for some had possibly not been recorded. The writer acknowledges appreciation to Mrs. W. S. Morton for a list of mill applications and permits 1788-1832.

116. Mss. legislative petition, Archives Division, State Library.

117. *Acts of Assembly 1835-6*: 236-7.

118. *Acts of Assembly 1836-7*: 164-6; *1839*: 104. Time for building the dam was extended three years beyond the original two-year limit put on the permit.

119. Mss. statement, David Blanton in account with Edmund Booker. James Blanton Papers. The term shipstuff was generally used in the writer's boyhood for a certain grade of livestock food ground finer than bran. It could be purchased commercially, but the tags were labeled middlings.

120. Order Book 20:156, 218.

121. Richmond *Enquirer*, Sept. 27, 1853.

122. Mss. letter, R. T. Harding to Ezekiah Harding, dated Moore's Ordinary, Nov. 1, 1859. John and Ezekiah Harding Papers, Duke University Library.

123. *Farmers Register* 1:506. Letter of W. S. Morton, Farmville, Dec. 29, 1833. Morton states that "my father about 35 years ago made many efforts to find coal." For location of Flournoy's farm, cf. mss. legislative petition dated Jan. 28, 1837, Archives Division, State Library.

124. *Farmers Register* 4:473.

125. Mss. legislative petition, Archives Division, State Library; *Acts of Assembly 1836-7*: 208.

126. Related to the author by Dr. J. D. Eggleston, son of the Dr. Eggleston who was one of the lessees of the coal. As my informant remembered it, the coal had good heating properties. The lessees hauled the coal from the pits to their homes in wagons. Lack of better transportation made working the pits unprofitable. When Dr. Eggleston and Mr. Dickinson were digging for coal, Major Venable visited Slate Hill and came out to see how the digging was progressing. Dr. Eggleston asked him if he thought they would find coal there. "Yes, certainly," he replied. Dr. Eggleston, thinking the major would have some sound geological reason for his answer, asked "What makes you think so, Major?" "Why this land is so damned poor on top, there's bound to be something underneath," was Major Venable's reason.

127. *Acts of Assembly 1836-7*: 228.   128. Howe: 432.

129. *Farmers Register* 4: 315-6.

130. Donald Fleming: *John William Draper*. Chapter Two of this biography covers Draper's life in Virginia in Mecklenburg and Prince Edward. Chapter Three relates in considerable detail his early work in photography.

131. *Virginia Gazette* (Purdie and Dixon), July 30, 1772.

132. These springs were mentioned to the writer when he visited the farm in 1935, when it was still operated by members of the Fears family. I drank from the sulphur spring on that visit. The iron and pine springs were reported as having been practically filled up from lack of attention. If the writer may editorialize, those in charge of the forest should locate the springs while it is yet possible to do so, clean them out, and keep them in good condition.

133. *Acts of Assembly 1846-7*: 194.

134. *Acts of Assembly 1849-50*: 157-8.

135. Mss. letter of S. D. McDearmon, Clover Hill, to James Blanton, May 10, 1846. James Blanton Papers.

136. Farmville *Journal*, Mar. 11, 1852.

137. Farmville *Herald*, Oct. 29, 1897. Letter from "56 Years Old."

138. The writer remembers the coach which belonged to his great-grandfather, William Weaver. It remained in the old coach house until it was demolished when the building was blown over in a windstorm about 1930. The writer remembers that the upholstery was pink, but the original color may have faded to that shade.

139. Farmville *Herald*, Oct. 29, 1895. The "modern" carriage was most likely the two-seated buggy.

140. Richmond *Enquirer*, Jan. 19, 1837. 141. Richmond *Enquirer*, July 21, 1835.

142. Richmond *Enquirer*, Aug. 2, 1842. 143. Richmond *Enquirer*, Jan. 28, 1823.

144. Richmond *Enquirer*, Dec. 27, 1823.

145. Richmond *Constitutional Whig*, Apr. 8, 1831.

146. Richmond *Enquirer*, July 11, 1834. 147. McIlwaine: 41, 56-6.

148. *V.M.H.B.* 57:269-73: "Clover Hill" by Ethel Marion Smith.

149. Richmond *Enquirer*, Jan. 31, 1833. The advertisement is signed A. Patteson, proprietor, Richmond and Lynchburg Stage Line.

150. *V.M.H.B.* 57:272: "Clover Hill" by Ethel Marion Smith.

151. Prince Edward Will Book 8:4-9; cf. pp. 9-12 for inventory of property in other counties.

152. Mss. miscellaneous papers, Package 159, Clerk's Office. Dated Jan. 19, 1789. Booker's Ordinary was at or near Meherrin. Copy lent to the writer by Mrs. W. S. Morton.

153. Order Book 11:213, 532. 154. Order Book 12:206.

155. Order Book 12:221. 156. Order Book 17:274; 20:424.

157. Order Book 12:312, 335.

158. Order Book 12:325. Betts tavern was at Meherrin.

159. Order Book 12:326. 160. Order Book 12:364.

161. Order Book 13:3. 162. Order Book 13:197.

163. Order Book 13:345. 164. Order Book 14:66, 164.

165. Order Book 14:415, 500; 15:65; cf. 16:133.

166. Order Book 15:96: Williamson's tavern was located at the Courthouse on John Wood's map of 1820. Cf. Order Book 16:146.

167. Order Book 16:64. 168. Order Book 16:467.

169. Order Book 17:63. 170. Order Book 17:471.

171. Order Book 18:225. 172. Order Book 18:578, 598.

173. Order Book 18:403, 423; 19:83, 118: Redford was a tobacconist in Farmville at the time. Smith was one of the original purchasers of lots in Farmville. His heirs sold the tavern in Farmville in 1822 to Moses Tredway (Prince Edward Deed Book 18:355). The 1818 date is the first ordinary license granted Smith. Cf. Richmond *Enquirer*, Aug. 27, 1822; Smith advertised the tavern for sale to retire to his farm. It was described as a good prospect for boarders, as there was a flourishing law school near Farmville, and students there usually boarded in town.

174. Order Book 20:397, 424.

175. Order Book 25:644: John Pearson was in 1832 made keeper of the new courthouse; he bought the old courthouse building.

176. Order Book 20:656: Tredway bought the tavern in Farmville in 1822 (Deed Book 18:355) with the lot at Main and Second Streets, the present site of the Prince Edward Hotel, for $2,000.

177. Order Book 21:316. This succession of King through Peter Foster to Edmund Booker is confusing. King bought French's from Hampden-Sydney College in 1825. When Edmund Booker got his ordinary license in 1817 he was living in Jamestown, which he gave as his address as treasurer of the lottery for the Jamestown School. Cf. Richmond *Constitutional Whig*, Dec. 7, 1824, for Edmund Booker's tavern at Jamestown. William S. King and George King, executors of the estate of George King, deceased, offered for sale King's tavern, one mile north of Prince Edward Courthouse, on May 14, 1840; also for sale were fifteen acres of land and eight or ten "very likely" Negroes (Richmond *Enquirer*, Apr. 14, 1840).

178. Order Book 21:546: Cf. Farmville *Herald*, Aug. 25, 1905: reminiscences of "Aunt Laura" Gaulding, Negro centenarian living near Leigh's Mountain: "Marse Buck Penick kept tavern and after he went away Marse Moses Tredway." The records have Tredway succeed Smith as inn-keeper in Farmville.

179. Order Book 12:65: James B. Ely lived in Farmville.

180. Order Book 22:267: William White lived at Jamestown and at this time conducted the girls' school there. He was also identified with mercantile interests in Jamestown.

181. Richmond *Enquirer*, Sept. 19, 1823.

182. Richmond *Enquirer*, Jan. 18, 1834.

183. Richmond *Enquirer*, Nov. 6, 1846; when H. E. Warren first came to Farmville in 1845 to consider moving there and opening a store, Col. James was proprietor of the hotel. Merchants did not encourage Warren to move, but Col. James, an enthusiastic booster of Farmville, did. Cf. H. E. Warren's account of his life, mss. Farmville *Journal*, Mar. 11, 1852.

184. Richmond *Whig and Public Advertiser*, Jan. 15, 1847.

185. Farmville *Herald*, Oct. 22, 1948: "History of Farmville" by Herbert Clarence Bradshaw.

186. Bruce 2:6.   187. Order Book 6:81.

188. Order Book 9:236.   189. Richmond *Enquirer*, Apr. 20, 1827.

190. *Cal. Va. State Papers* 3:73. Col. Christian Febiger to Col. Davies, Feb. 23, 1782.

191. Mss. legislative petition, Archives Division, State Library.

192. *Virginia Argus*, Nov. 27, 1802.   193. *Virginia Argus*, July 21, 1802.

194. *Virginia Argus*, Apr. 28, 1804.   195. *Virginia Argus*, Dec. 29, 1804.

196. *Virginia Argus*, May 8, 1805.

197. Richmond *Enquirer*, Jan. 13, 1807. Route numbers changed from year to year. In 1807 the Richmond-Jamestown-Farmville route was 51; the Powhatan-Halifax route 52; the Prince Edward Courthouse-New London route was 53; the Prince Edward Courthouse-Lynchburg route 203 (Richmond *Enquirer*, Apr. 28, 1807).

198. Richmond *Enquirer*, Apr. 24, 1816.

199. Richmond *Enquirer*, July 20, 1817.

200. Walter A. Watson: *Notes on Southside Virginia*:54.

201. Richmond *Enquirer*, Jan. 28, Dec. 27, 1823.

202. Mss. legislative petition, Archives Division, State Library.

203. Richmond *Constitutional Whig*, Aug. 15, 1826.

204. Richmond *Constitutional Whig*, Aug. 11, 1827.

205. Richmond *Enquirer*, June 22, 1838.

206. Mss. Names of Voters in the Presidential Election, 1840. Edmund W. Hubard Papers, Southern Historical Collection, University of North Carolina Library. The list contains names and addresses of the Prince Edward voters who participated in the 1840 election. It was prepared by Branch J. Worsham, clerk. Postoffice addresses do not always indicate the exact location of the home. Thus Capt. Richard Marshall's address is Jamestown; he lived about a mile east of Rice (B. G. Bass' home is at the site of Capt. Marshall's). His brother-in-law, Joseph Phillips, lived about one quarter mile distant, across the road (and now across the railroad), but his address was Burkeville. William Bradshaw, Marshall's son-in-law, who lived three to four miles east of these places on upper Marrowbone Creek, near Flippen's fork, had Jamestown as his post office, and Vincent Phillips, brother of Joseph, and Thomas Branch, whose wife was aunt of the Phillipses and Mrs. Marshall, and lived to the west of Bradshaw and to the east of Marshall went to Burkeville for their

mail. The Rev. Isaac Cockreham's (Cochran) address was the Courthouse, while his near neighbors, John M. and Newton Cunningham, who lived across the north fork of Spring Creek from Highland Manse (later the home of Dr. Nathaniel Terry and W. P. Terry), at Millbank (now the home of H. C. Cunningham) and Dublin (and nearer the Courthouse than Cochran) had Prospect as their postoffice.

207. Richmond *Enquirer*, Jan. 10, 1843.

208. Related to the writer by his grandfather, James R. Weaver. The oldest mention of Rice's Depot which the writer has found is on William Bradshaw's application for bounty lands in 1855 (Photostat copy from National Archives).

209. Richmond *Enquirer*, Jan. 1, 1855.   210. Richmond *Enquirer*, Dec. 14, 1858.

211. Mss. letter, Thomas T. Tredway to Mr. Woodall, Dec. 5 (1855), John Woodall Papers.

212. Related to the writer by his grandfather, James R. Weaver.

213. Mss. letter, John N. Gordon, Richmond, to James Blanton, Farmville, Oct. 28, 1844. James Blanton Papers.

214. Mss. in miscellaneous papers, Walton vs. Scott file, Package 153, Clerk's Office. Lent to the writer by Mrs. W. S. Morton.

215. Mss. lent the writer by Mrs. W. S. Morton.

216. John C. Fitzpatrick, editor: *The Diaries of George Washington* 4:196-8; *Tyler's Mag.* 2:136: Diary of R. N. Venable. Venable seems to have been at Peytonsburg when Washington arrived there June 4, and to have gone on to Prince Edward Courthouse for Washington's arrival. He noted at Charlotte Courthouse "great anxiety" to see General Washington. Since neither Washington nor Venable notes (in his respective diary) the place he stayed at Prince Edward Courthouse, it may be supposed that he stopped at the tavern there. There is a tradition that a dance was given in his honor at the Courthouse, and a dress has been preserved in the Venable family, said to have been worn on the occasion by Miss Martha Venable.

217. Bruce 1:571. Bruce supposes that Randolph went to Miller's to avoid having to eat breakfast at an inn. Since Randolph noted simply Miller's, without adding ordinary, Bruce seems to have assumed that this breakfast was in the home of a friend. But Miller's was an ordinary, too, which is still standing and known as Burke's Tavern, from a later owner.

218. *Virginia Argus*, Mar. 27, 1807. William Journey received a license to keep an ordinary in 1799 (Order Book 12:119).

219. Order Book 8:355.

220. Order Book 8:479; 9:114.

221. *Virginia Argus*, June 29, 1802: these firms were obviously among the first in those towns.

222. Farmville *Herald*, Oct. 22, 1948: "History of Farmville" by Herbert Clarence Bradshaw.

223. *Virginia Argus*, Apr. 19, 1802; May 11, 1805.

224. *Virginia Argus*, Sept. 4, 1805.

225. *Virginia Argus*, Sept. 14, 1805; Farmville *Herald*, Oct. 22, 1948: "History of Farmville" by Herbert Clarence Bradshaw.

226. *Virginia Argus*, Jan. 10, 1806.

227. *Virginia Argus*, Sept. 5, 1806. John Wood's map of 1820. The reference to Carter and Booker's store gives it as the place where depositions of James Ming and others would be taken for evidence to be used in a suit. Since Ming lived in this community, the location of the store may be regarded as having been in that locality. Wood printed Lore instead of Love on his map. In this connection it may be noted that Richard Booker of nearby Grampian Hills married Sallie Carter Love.

History of Prince Edward County

228. Mss. accounts of Laban Hawkins with Anderson P. Miller (1817) and Miller and Burke (1818): and with William White (1817). Hawkins-McGehee Papers.

229. Richmond *Enquirer*, Jan. 16, 1818; Jan. 28, 1823; May 2, 1823; May 16, 1826; John Wood's map of 1820.

230. Richmond *Enquirer*, Feb. 9, 1828.

231. Richmond *Enquirer*, Mar. 3, 1840; Oct. 2, 1840.

232. Richmond *Enquirer*, Dec. 24, 1839.

233. *Today and Yesterday in the Heart of Virginia*: 148: "Prince Edward County" by Herbert Clarence Bradshaw: information from Morrison mss. *Old Prince Edward: A Miscellany*. Londonderry was near Buffalo Church, on the road from Five Forks to the present Route 460; Morrison says the name was given to this settlement about 1760.

234. *Acts of Assembly 1830*: 151; John Wood's map of 1820.

235. Richmond *Enquirer*, July 12, 1842; July 26, 1842; Jan. 14, 1843; Apr. 7, 1843.

236. Richmond *Enquirer*, Feb. 11, 1840; Farmville Herald, Apr. 4, 1902 (special edition).

237. Richmond *Enquirer*, Jan. 3, 1846. Merritt and Nash had failed several years before this date.

238. Farmville *Journal*, Mar. 11, 1852.

239. Mss. account Morton and Dupuy in account with Mrs. M. B. Eppes, Oct. 29, 1840, Edmund W. Hubard papers. Mrs. Eppes was the widow of John W. Eppes, John Randolph's political opponent. Eppes first married Maria Jefferson, Thomas Jefferson's daughter; after her death he married Martha Burke Jones, daughter of Willie Jones of Halifax County, North Carolina. Mrs. M. B. Jones was the mother-in-law of Edmund W. Hubard.

240. Richmond *Whig*, Sept. 15, 1842. 241. Richmond *Enquirer*, Jan. 16, 1852.

242. Mss. letters, John Harding, Meherrin Depot, to Ezekiah Harding, July 11, 1859; R. T. Harding to Ezekiah Harding, Nov. 1, 1859. John and Ezekiah Harding Papers. The Hardings had stores at Danville, Clover (Halifax County), and Pleasant Grove (Lunenburg County), as well as at Meherrin.

243. Related to the writer by his grandfather, James R. Weaver, nephew and namesake of Rowland Anderson.

244. Mss. letter of R. S. Paulett, Farmville, to Presley B. Paulett, Appomattox, May 11, 1849. John Woodall Papers.

245. Order Book 13:300 contains one of the numerous records of peddler's licenses. This license, issued by the Richmond Hustings Court to Jacob Lyon, was recorded at the Prince Edward Court of August, 1803. Peddlers were passing through the county as late as the writer's boyhood; he remembers a visit which one made to his father's farm about 1913 and the abundance of goods which he carried in his pack on his back. The things which the peddler whose visit I remember carried were mainly table covers, napkins, and other textile goods.

246. Mss. legislative petition, Archives Division, State Library.

247. Richmond *Enquirer*, Feb. 24, 1832.

248. Mss. legislative petition, Archives Division, State Library.

249. *Acts of Assembly 1836-7*: 69.   250. Richmond *Enquirer*, Jan. 11, 1838.

251. Richmond *Enquirer*, Feb. 28, 1839. 252. Richmond *Enquirer*, Jan. 11, 1840.

253. Richmond *Enquirer*, Jan. 14, 1841.

254. Mss. letter N. E. Venable to J. W. Morton, Jan. 14, 1846. James Blanton Papers. Richmond *Enquirer*, Jan. 21, 1846.

255. Richmond *Enquirer*, Jan. 22, 1847; Richmond *Whig and Public Advertiser*, Jan. 26, 1847.

256. Richmond *Whig and Public Advertiser*, Apr. 9, 1847. Resolutions of the board of the Farmville branch of the Farmers Bank of Virginia on the death of Monroe R. Flippen were signed by A. Vaughan, cashier.

257. Richmond *Enquirer*, Jan. 23, 1849. Joseph B. Anderson may be an error for James B. Anderson.

258. Richmond *Enquirer*, Jan. 24, 1851.

259. Richmond *Enquirer*, Jan. 31, 1852.

260. Richmond *Enquirer*, Feb. 8, 1853.   261. Richmond *Enquirer*, Jan. 16, 1855.

262. Richmond *Enquirer*, Jan. 22, 1856. The paper gives Patrick H. Johnson, an obvious error for Jackson.

263. Richmond *Enquirer*, Jan. 20, 1857.   264. Richmond *Enquirer*, Jan. 22, 1858.

265. Richmond *Enquirer*, Jan. 21, 1859.   266. Richmond *Enquirer*, Jan. 22, 1861.

267. Edmund W. Hubard's bank book in account with the Farmers Bank of Virginia, Farmville branch, 1857-61. Edmund W. Hubard Papers.

268. Mss. letter, R. T. Harding to Hezekiah Harding, dated Moore's Ordinary, Oct. 11, 1859; Nov. 28, 1859. John and Ezekiah Harding Papers. R. T. Harding dated his letters Moore's Ordinary, John Harding dated his Meherrin Depot, both in 1859.

269. *Acts of Assembly 1946-7:* 185. Cf. mss. legislative petitions of J. W. Dunnington, Howell E. Warren, *et al.* 1861 for existence of two savings banks.

270. *Acts of Assembly 1859-60:* 523. It would appear that this was the Farmville Savings Bank in existence in 1861 rather than a bank of the same name chartered in 1838 (*Acts of Assembly, 1837-8:* 178-9).

271. *Acts of Assembly 1859-60:* 256-8. The writer has found no source material indicating the opening of this bank. However information given me by the late Major D. Burton Blanton of Farmville is evidence that it opened and carried on business during the War between the States.

272. *Cal. Bd. Min.:* 56.

273. Mss. letter Christopher McRae to Creed Taylor, Mar. 1, 1805. Creed Taylor Papers. The writer has not learned who was recommended or whether an agent was appointed for the district at that time.

274. Mss. letter R. T. Harding, Moore's Ordinary, to Hezekiah Harding, Nov. 1, 1859. John and Ezekiah Harding Papers. Referring to the Watkins sawmill fire, Harding said that he looked every night for his home to take fire and burn; he kept the policy at his father's.

275. Policy of the Caswell Mutual Fire Insurance Co. to E. and J. Harding of Clover Depot, Halifax Co., Mar. 16, 1860 to Mar. 16, 1861. John and Ezekiah Harding Papers.

276. Richmond *Enquirer*, Mar. 26, 1861.

277. Farmville *Herald*, Oct. 22, 1948: "History of Farmville" by Herbert Clarence Bradshaw; *Today and Yesterday in the Heart of Virginia:* 11: "Farmville Newspapers" by Scott Hart.

278. *Virginia Argus*, Jan. 8, 1802.

279. Richmond *Enquirer*, June 18, 1858.

280. Richmond *Constitutional Whig*, July 26, 1828; Richmond *Enquirer*, July 25, 1828.

281. Richmond *Constitutional Whig*, Apr. 9, Apr. 16, 1832; Richmond *Enquirer*, Apr. 10, 1832.

282. Richmond *Enquirer*, Nov. 11, 1845.

283. Richmond *Enquirer*, Nov. 29, 1838.

284. Richmond *Enquirer*, Jan. 18, Feb. 1, Feb. 5, 1856.

285. Richmond *Enquirer*, July 17, 1857.

286. Richmond *Enquirer*, Jan. 18, 1834.

287. Richmond *Enquirer,* Jan. 28, 1834.

288. Mss. legislative petition, Archives Division, State Library.

289. *Acts of Assembly 1836-7*: 119-21; 121-2.

290. *Acts of Assembly 1836-7*: 100.   291. *Farmers Register* 5:60-2.

292. Richmond *Enquirer,* Apr. 3, May 22, 1846.

293. Richmond *Whig and Public Advertiser,* July 24, Aug. 14, 1846.

294. *Acts of Assembly 1846-7*: 108-9.   295. Richmond *Enquirer,* Apr. 27, 1847.

296. Richmond *Enquirer,* Sept. 21, 1847. 297. Richmond *Enquirer,* Oct. 16, 1849.

298. *Acts of Assembly 1845-6*: 92.   299. *Acts of Assembly 1848-9*: 106, 107.

300. *Virginia Historical Register* 2:113. 301. *Acts of Assembly 1849-50*: 56.

302. *Acts of Assembly 1850-51*: 63.

303. Mss. legislative petition, Archives Division, State Library.

304. Richmond *Daily Dispatch,* Jan. 24, 1852.

305. Farmville *Journal,* Mar. 11, 1852.

306. Richmond *Enquirer,* Jan. 27, 1857. Cf. issue of Dec. 28, 1855 for report that the Richmond and Danville had completed 139 of its 142 miles of track.

307. Richmond *Enquirer,* June 23, 1854.

308. Richmond *Enquirer,* Aug. 11, 1854.

309. *Today and Yesterday in the Heart of Virginia*: 187: "Norfolk and Western Railway" by R. R. Horner.

310. Richmond *Enquirer,* Oct. 12, 1855. 311. Richmond *Enquirer,* Dec. 28, 1855.

311. The figure representing the state's interest in the Southside Railroad is evidently a typographical error. The state stock transferred from the Petersburg and Roanoke Railroad to the Southside amounted to $322,500 (p. 329).

312. Petersburg *Intelligencer,* Feb. 21, 1856.

313. Richmond *Enquirer,* Aug. 11, 1854.

314. *Today and Yesterday in the Heart of Virginia*: 187: "Norfolk and Western Railway" by R. R. Horner.

315. Related to me by my father, Herbert L. Bradshaw, and others. My father used to point out to me the route of the narrow gauge to the main line of the railroad. There used to be several pieces of large rock lying around at the point the narrow gauge met the railroad, apparently left from the hauling; this point was on the hill west of Marrowbone Creek. Sailor Creek runs through the quarry, and water gave trouble there; as there was then no means of pumping it out, the quarry was abandoned years ago. The stones in the foundation of the home of Dr. S. A. Bruce, now the property of H. C. and C. W. Bradshaw, about a mile east of Rice, were gotten from this quarry. As a boy, the writer in company with B. Calvin Bass, now chairman of the Prince Edward County School Board, and J. Martin Bruce explored the old quarry.

        Other stone for the piers was quarried not far from the bridge.

316. Related to me by my grandfather, James R. Weaver, who remembered the visits made by these workmen to his father's home and to other homes in the community.

317. Richmond *Enquirer,* Jan. 18, 1856.

318. Richmond *Enquirer,* Jan. 27, 1857. The snow has been so named because Dr. Cox of Chesterfield County lost his life in it.

319. Mss. letter Judith E. Woodall to Miss Jane B. Morgan, Walkers Church, "politeness of Mrs. Brightwell," Sept. 13, 1852. John Woodall Papers. It begins "Dear Aunt . . ." The John Woodall family was then living near Meherrin, and the context suggests that Judith Woodall boarded the train at Meherrin.

320. Related to the writer by his grandfather, James R. Weaver, who as a boy

was brought by his father with other members of the family to see the first train come into Rice's Depot. I have been told by older people that the trip over High Bridge was regarded with fear.

321. Richmond *Enquirer*, June 15, 1858.

322. Richmond *Enquirer*, Aug. 9, 1853.

323. Related to the writer by people who remembered the earlier years of the railroads. One of the first business undertakings of the writer's grandfather, J. S. Bradshaw, was a contract to furnish wood to the Atlantic, Mississippi and Ohio Railroad. This was in the mid-1870's. The writer as a boy used to enjoy watching the trains stop at the Marrowbone Creek tank and take on water. The creek was dammed and water was pumped up the hill into the tank, a huge, round, wooden affair, built above the height of the engine.

324. Prince Edward Deed Book 26: 93-5.

325. Prince Edward Deed Book 26: 453.

326. *Acts of Assembly 1852:* 132-3; *1852-3:* 178, 181; *1861:* 215.

327. *Farmers' Register* 2: 352-3.   328. *Farmers' Register* 1: 5-7; 506

329. *Farmers' Register* 2: 154-5.   330. *Farmers' Register* 3: 516-7.

331. *Farmer's Register* 1: 700; 3: 540-2.

332. Richmond *Enquirer*, Feb. 25, 1859.

333. Mss. letter T. T. Tredway to John Woodall, Feb. 15, 1856. John Woodall Papers.

334. *Farmers' Register* 2: 250-1.   335. *Farmers' Register* 2: 351-2.

336. *Farmers' Register* 2: 609-10.   337. *Farmers' Register* 2: 249; 309-10.

338. *Farmers' Register* 1: 89-90.

339. *Farmers' Register* 2: 310. The differences between Woodson's and Cabell's descriptions of the Woodson and Cunningham grapes are interesting; the points on which they differ are matters of opinion, such as the origin of the grape (which was not definitely known) and the characteristics of the wine, a matter of taste.

340. *Farmers' Register* 5: 188.

341. Farmville *Mercury*, Apr. 1, 1875: List of fruits originated in Prince Edward (sent by a friend). The Woodson grape in this account is said to have originated on Dr. Benjamin F. Terry's place, Hard Times. This farm may have extended to the north side of Fort Creek to include the area in which Woodson found the grape growing in 1806 and which had been Henry Caldwell's, later Isaac Read's.

342. *Virginia Argus*, Jan. 21, 1806.   343. Richmond *Enquirer*, Mar. 13, 1838.

344. Richmond *Enquirer*, May 8, 1840.

345. Related to me by my grandfather, James R. Weaver, a son of William Weaver. Dr. Witt, Clark, and Weaver owned adjoining farms on Sandy River.

346. Mss. letter, T. T. Tredway to John Woodall, dated House of Delegates, Richmond, Dec. 5 (1855). John Woodall Papers.

347. *Tyler's Mag.* 2: 138. Diary of R. N. Venable.

348. *Farmers' Register* 2: 417-8.   349. Richmond *Enquirer*, June 26, 1855.

350. Foote, Second Ser.: 53. Letter of John Wright (pastor Cumberland Presbyterian Church) dated Aug. 18, 1755.

351. Richmond *Enquirer*, Aug. 17, 1838. Letter of "Cumberland" dated Aug. 10. Prince Edward is specifically included in the drought area. Cf. issue of Aug. 28, 1838: the drought extended from Warrenton, Va., into the northern part of North Carolina and was also in Maryland, New Hampshire, New Jersey, and eastern Pennsylvania.

352. Unidentified and undated newspaper clipping in the scrapbook kept by Miss

Adelle H. Walton of Rice; the scrapbook is now the property of the writers' mother, Mrs. Herbert L. Bradshaw.

353. Richmond *Enquirer*, Aug. 11, 1854.

354. Richmond and Manchester *Advertiser*, May 7, 1796.

355. *Virginia Argus*, May 5, 1802.   356. *Virginia Argus*, Feb. 15, 1804.

357. *Virginia Argus*, Oct. 10, 1804, Feb. 16, 1805.

358. *Virginia Argus*, Aug. 18, 1804; Jan. 30, June 10, 1807.

359. *Virginia Argus*, Apr. 18, 1806; Richmond and Manchester *Advertiser*, Apr. 2, 1802.

360. *Virginia Argus*, Nov. 2, 1807.   361. Richmond *Enquirer*, Apr. 5, 1833.

362. Richmond *Enquirer*, Mar. 11, 1838. 363. Richmond *Enquirer*, Mar. 24, 1840.

364. Richmond *Enquirer*, Feb. 18, 1841. It would be interesting to learn if any blood lines in Prince Edward horses today can be traced to these fine stallions.

365. Mss. letter Creed Taylor to Seymour Wright ,June 28, 1794. Creed Taylor Papers.

366. *Virginia Argus*, Mar. 7, 1804; Mar. 12, 1805.

367. *Virginia Argus*, June 23, 1804. The writer has not learned which horse won that race.

368. *Virginia Argus*, Sept. 19, 1804; Oct. 9, 1805.

369. *Virginia Argus*, Sept. 7, 1805.   370. Richmond *Enquirer*, Oct. 31, 1809.

371. Mss. letter Creed Taylor to ———, July 11, 1805. Creed Taylor Papers.

372. *Farmers' Register* 2: 379.

373. Mss. minutes, called meeting, Cumberland Agricultural Society, Nov. 13, 1840. James Blanton Papers.

374. Richmond *Enquirer*, June 23, 1854.

375. Richmond *Enquirer*, May 23, Aug. 8, Aug. 19, 1856.

376. Richmond *Enquirer*, Oct. 31, 1856.   377. Richmond *Enquirer*, Oct. 6, 1857.

378. List of Premiums Offered at the 3rd Annual Exhibition of the Virginia State Agricultural Society Oct. 30-31, Nov. 1-2, 1855. Pamphlet 182 in Vol. 9, Virginia Pamphlets, Duke University Library.

379. 6th Annual Exhibition of the Virginia State Agricultural Society to be held in Petersburg Nov. 2-5, 1858. Pamphlet 183, Vol. 9, Virginia Pamphlets, Duke University Library.

380. Richmond *Enquirer*, Sept. 14, 1860.

381. Richmond *Enquirer*, May 21, June 29, 1858.

382. Richmond *Enquirer*, June 1, 1858. 383. Richmond *Enquirer*, June 29, 1858.

384. Richmond *Enquirer*, June 11, 1858. 386. Richmond *Enquirer*, July 9, 1858.

385. Mss. letter, Thomas T. Tredway to John Woodall, Aug. 14, 1856. John Woodall Papers. This was Woodall's first year as Tredway's overseer, and Tredway wanted the work to go according to his usual practice. Writing from Richmond Dec. 5 (1855) he told Woodall that if he reminded him of anxiety about the health of his Negroes, it was not from distrust of him but "through my complete ignorance of your habits and ways."

387. Mss. letter, William Woodall to John Woodall, dated Jamestown, Dec. 12, 1849. John Woodall Papers.

388. Recollections of old residents, related to the writer.

389. Mss. letter, R. S. Paulett to Presley [Paulett], dated Farmville, June 28, 1858. John Woodall Papers. Cf. mss. statements of accounts.

390. Petersburg *Intelligencer*, July 6, 1810.

391. George Richardson Gilmer: *First Settlers of Upper Georgia:* 166.

392. Mss. recipe used by Miss Jimmy Prince, Emporia, Va., and given to the author by Miss Lucy Brittle, Miss Prince's niece. Miss Prince used this

recipe for many years and did not, in 1944, remember where she had gotten it.

393. *Farmers' Register* 1: 631.

394. Mss., Hawkins-McGehee Papers. Laban Hawkins lived in Prince Edward; John Hurt was probably the John Hurt who lived in Nottoway and had a mill on Ellis Creek.

395. Mss. letter, William Woodall to John Woodall, Apr. 12, 1839. John Woodall Papers.

396. Mss., Hawkins-McGehee Papers.   397. Farmville *Journal*, Mar. 11, 1852.

398. Order Book 8: 167. Cf. Chapter 7, note 41.

399. Mss., Hawkins-McGehee Papers.   400. Richmond *Enquirer*, Oct. 31, 1809.

401. *Manual of Roanoke Presbytery*, 1894.

402. Farmville *Herald*, Aug. 25, 1905. Recollections of "Aunt Laura" Gaulding, a centenarian living near Leigh's Mountain.

403. Farmville *Journal*, Mar. 11, 1875.

404. Mss. statement, David Blanton in a/c with Charles Lewis. James Blanton Papers.

405. Farmville *Herald*, Oct. 29, 1897. Letter of "56."

406. Farmville *Herald*, Feb. 25, 1898. Letter of "56," who noted that the last duster he saw in use was worn by Governor McKinney. The writer remembers that the late Mr. and Mrs. Walter S. Beattie (Mrs. Beattie after Mr. Beattie's death married H. L. Vaughan of Fairview, Nottoway County) wore dusters when they drove in their buggy from Elmwood to Pisgah Church for worship. This was as late as the early 1930's.

407. Mss., Hawkins-McGehee Papers.

408. Much of the data on the old homes was given the writer by old residents who remembered that era. Grateful acknowledgment is made to Mrs. Anne Atkinson-Chamberlayne for tracing for him through the deed books the ownership of the stone house. The last family to occupy it as a residence was that of the late Junius Farrar.

409. *North Carolina: A Guide to the Old North State*. Federal Writers Project. P. 476. The Eaton house was purchased a few years ago by G. G. Allen, a native of Warren County and associate of James B. Duke in the American Tobacco Company, later chairman of the Duke Endowment, and given to the Methodist Church for use as a parsonage as a memorial to his mother.

410. *W. & M. Quart.* (2) 7: 96-7; Prince Edward Deed Book 7: 118. Cf. Farmville *Herald*. Feb. 6, 1903: "Prince Edward County" by Frankie I. McKinney: after the battle of Yorktown, smallpox broke out among the troops, and the French troops, in an effort to prevent their contracting the disease, were brought to Prince Edward and camped on the glebe lands. Dr. Mettauer came with them and liked Prince Edward so much that he settled here. There is an old tradition that French troops camped at Kingsville, then French's, after the Revolution. Another tradition has Patrick Henry and Robert Lawson persuading Dr. Mettauer to settle in Prince Edward. Cf. *Today and Yesterday in the Heart of Virginia*: 369: "John Peter Mettauer" by Wyndham B. Blanton.

411. Mss. legislative petition, Archives Division, State Library.

412. Mss. statement, Account of Dr. Joseph Mettauer to the estate of Beverly Randolph, July 17, 1797. Sworn to before Samuel W. Venable, justice of the peace for Prince Edward County. Creed Taylor Papers. This was Governor Randolph's last illness.

413. Mss. found among the papers of James R. Weaver at his death in 1938 and copied then by the writer.

414. Mss. letter, John Tabb to William Watts, Apr. 23, 1786. Watts Papers.

415. *Virginia Argus*, Aug. 29, 1800; Sept. 22, 1802.

416. Farmville *Herald*, Oct. 22, 1948: "History of Farmville" by Herbert Clarence Bradshaw.

417. *W. & M. Quart.* (1) 19: 161-2; *Today and Yesterday in the Heart of Virginia:* 369-75: "John Peter Mettauer" by Wyndham B. Blanton. Among the pupils taught by Dr. Mettauer were, according to Capt. Richard F. Burke of Prince Edward Courthouse (*W. & M. Quart.* (2) 7: 99), Drs. Dillon, Oscar Wiley, Clem Fontaine, Johns, Francis Joseph Mettauer, Archer Mettauer, Munford Mettauer, and possibly Dr. Gregory. Blanton lists Dr. Philip S. Blanton (under whom his father, Dr. Charles A. Blanton, studied medicine), Drs. Oscar Wiley, Stephen C. and Richard E. Farrar, John Hobson Nelson, Dr. Mettauer's sons, Francis Joseph, Henry Archer, and Edward Mumford; Clem Fontaine, a Dr. Johns, and a Dr. Gregory. Cf. *W. & M. Quart.* (2) 7: 97: Dr. James Jones of Nottoway studied under Dr. F. J. Mettauer (Dr. J. P. Mettauer's father) before going to the University of Edinburgh to study.

418. Foote, Second Ser.: 435.

419. Mss. letter, Jno. P. Mettauer to Mrs. Martha H. Price, dated Prince Edward C. H.,, July 15, 1858. John Woodall Papers. Dr. Mettauer wrote Mrs. Price he had discontinued his professional visits to Farmville and did not expect to resume them, "certainly not during the present warm season."

420. Mss. statements of account, James Blanton Papers.

421. Richmond *Enquirer*, May 8, 1855. 422. Richmond *Enquirer*, Apr. 26, 1859.

423. Mss. list of voters in the Presidential election of 1840 in Prince Edward County, Edmund W. Hubard Papers. Southern Historical Collection. University of North Carolina.

424. *W. & M. Quart.* (1) 19: 189.

425. Farmville *Herald*, Oct. 22, 1948: "History of Farmville" by Herbert Clarence Bradshaw; see also references in this history to Dr. Wilson.

426. Richmond *Enquirer*, Mar. 20, 1832. 427. Farmville *Herald*, Sept. 14, 1906.

428. Walton family papers, used by the writer in preparation of his history of the McGehee family, mss.

429. Richmond *Enquirer*, Mar. 21, 1848; Mar. 18, 1853.

430. Richmond *Enquirer*, Jan. 13, 1854. 431. Richmond *Enquirer*, Mar. 6, 1834.

432. *The Bulletin of the Virginia State Dental Association* 29: 15-18. "Tribute to William W. H. Thackston in Dental Organization" by William N. Hodgkin. A copy of this, the October, 1951, issue of *The Bulletin* was sent to the writer by Dr. J. H. Cocks of Farmville.

433. Mss., James Blanton Papers.

434. Related to the writer by his grandfather, James R. Weaver.

435. Mss. accounts, James Blanton Papers.

436. Farmville *Journal*, Mar. 11, 1852.

437. Mss. letter, John Watts, Prince Edward, to William Watts, Jan. 26, 1789. Watts Papers.

438. *V.M.H.B.* 16: 205-6.

439. Mss. letters: Henry Lee to Pierce Butler, dated Richmond, Dec. 12, 1787; Lee to General Pinckney, same date; Lee to the Hon. William Few, Georgia, dated Richmond, Dec. 19, 1787; G[eorge] Mason to Hon. Charles Cotesworth Pinckney, Dec. 21, 1787; Adam Stephens to General Lawson, Lexington, Ky., 1789. Robert Lawson Papers, Duke University Library.

440. *V.M.H.B.* 20: 313. Morrison thought the reason for the migration to Georgia the fact that the Virginia Yazoo Company was so much a Prince Edward enterprise. It is doubtful if this was the reason, for much of the migration took place before the Virginia company was organized. Since the grant was never perfected, the company sold no land to settlers. Nor did the Prince Edward migrants go to that part of Georgia which the Virginia company wanted to acquire, the area which is now northern Mississippi.

441. *V.M.H.B.* 19: 419.
442. George Richardson Gilmer: *First Settlers of Upper Georgia:* 163-6.
443. Mss. legislative petition, Archives Division, State Library.
444. *Virginia Argus*, May 11, 1805.
445. Womack: *Buffalo:* 24-5.
446. Watts Papers: Letter of Thomas Madison to William Watts, Dec. 28, 1787, refers to Watts' being at his seat in Botetourt; letter of Thomas Scott to William Watts, New London, Feb. 4, 1796; Prince Edward Deed Book 11: 166: William Watts of Campbell County sells land in Prince Edward to Larkin Anderson. Watts died prior to Sept. 10, 1798; his widow continued to live in Campbell (Deed Book 11: 321).
447. Mss. letter, Elijah and Virginsea McGehee to James Blanton, Aug. 20, 1840. Blanton and McGehee married sisters, the former Nancy Walker, the latter Virginsea Walker, daughters of William Walker. In this letter they acknowledged receipt of the message of the death of "Father" Walker.
448. Mss. letters, Josiah Walton to Thomas Clark, Aug. 10, 1839; to William Walton, Dec. 12, 1840. Walton Papers. In the latter letter, he mentions ill health.
449. J. B. Jeter: *Life of Rev. Daniel Witt, D.D.:* 179; 184-6. The home of Josiah Walton is described as hospitable, and he is referred to in Jeter's journal of the trip as "our generous host." One can only conjecture the delight at having friends from Virginia visit the family on the frontier.
450. Mss. letters, William Woodall to John Woodall, Oct. 21, Nov. 13, 1853. John Woodall Papers.
451. *W. & M. Quart.* (1) 17: 217. Letter of James Maury, Fredricksburg, to James Madison, May 19, 1786.
452. *Religious Herald*, May 11, 1939: "Richmond's Benefits Cited in Old College Petition." The text of the petition and the list of trustees are included in this article.
453. McIlwaine: 55.
454. Mss. Journal, Edmund W. Hubard Papers. The writer of the journal is at no place identified. From the content, one learns that she was a young widow, who with her mother and daughter, Lucy, was visiting at Hampden-Sydney. She mentions Cousin Agnes Branch at the Courthouse, brothers Edward and William. Her father seems to have lived near Clarksville, Va., and she apparently lived at his home during her widowhood. She returned there Sept. 30, 1848.

    A letter of Mary Moore Smith, College Hill, Sept. 16, 1856, to "Dear Aunt Em" indicates a similar way of life. Thomas M. Bondurant Papers, Duke University Library.
455. McIlwaine: 64-5.
456. Farmville *Herald*, Nov. 1, 1901: Obituary of Mrs. Elizabeth A. Scott, widow of John Archer Scott.
457. Farmville *Herald*, Oct. 29, 1897: Letter of "56"; Frederick Johnston: *Memorials of Old Virginia Clerks:* 314-7.
458. Mss., Clerk's Office. Copy sent me by Mrs. W. S. Morton. There is no date on the subscription list for the dancing school at the Courthouse, but two other papers relating to Poole's activities as a dancing teacher are dated in March, 1784.
459. Mss., Hawkins-McGehee Papers. My grandfather, James R. Weaver, has told me of the singing schools at Sandy River Church which he attended. A silver cup, engraved "To Our Chorister," was given to Charles E. Glenn by one of his singing classes.
460. Mss. letter, Richard Randolph, Jr., to Creed Taylor, Jan. 28, 1795. Creed Taylor Papers.

461. Mss. letter, John Randolph to Creed Taylor, Sept. 16, 1798. Creed Taylor Papers.
462. Farmville *Herald*, Oct. 29, 1897. Letter of "56."
463. This was the William Weaver home, and the practice was related to me by my mother, who was his granddaughter.
464. Farmville *Herald*, Oct. 29, 1897. Letter of "56."
465. *Farmers' Register* 3: 516-7.
466. Richmond *Enquirer*, Sept. 15, 1860. The practice of cutting ice off ponds continued until about 30 years ago, when it could be gotten conveniently from ice plants. The ice was stored in pits and covered with dry leaves. In these pits it could be kept all summer.
467. *V.M.H.B.* 34: 249. Diary of John Early.
468. Womack: *Buffalo:* 5; Prince Edward Marriage Register 1: 4.
469. Farmville *Herald*, Nov. 1, 1901. The obituary of Mrs. John A. Scott relates that she was seventeen when she was married. William Bradshaw at the age of forty married Lucy Ann Marshall, aged eighteen, in 1834, according to family records.
   An early marriage was that of Thomas Clark and Agnes McGehee in 1779, when he was 18 and she 15. Their oldest daughter, Nancy, was 15 when she married Joseph Ligon in 1796; another, Lucy, was 16 when she married Silas Watkins in 1810; Sally Clark was 16 when she married Archibald Fuqua in 1801; the other Clark daughters, Elizabeth and Mildred, were both 23 when they married, the former David B. McGehee in 1809, the latter Jacob McGehee (son of William McGehee) in 1813, when he was 28. Mss. sheet, Register of Births and Deaths of the Clark family, lent to the writer by W. A. Garner of Roanoke, Va.; Herbert Clarence Bradshaw: The McGehee Family, mss.
   Some beautiful second-day dresses were long preserved in some families.
470. Farmville *Herald*, Feb. 25, 1898: Letter of "56"; *Today and Yesterday in the Heart of Virginia:* 44-5: history of the Doyne Undertaking Establishment. Perhaps the making of coffins by cabinetmakers began the long association of undertaking with the furniture business.
471. Hatchett: 8-9.
472. *A Sermon Preached at Jamestown, September 4th, 1859, at the Funeral of Elisha Woodfin, Jr.*, by Daniel Witt. Published by request. Richmond: Ellyson's Steam Presses. 130 Main St. 1860. The pamphlet containing the sermon was lent to the writer by Mrs. S. H. Bondurant of Rice.
473. Mss. letter, Francis Watkins to William Watts, July 31, 1790. Watts Papers.
474. George W. Bagby: *The Old Virginia Gentleman* (Fourth Edition): 91-9.
475. Farmville *Herald*, Feb. 25, 1898: Letter of "56."
476. Farmville *Herald*, Jan. 21, 1898: Letter of "56."
477. Alexander: 130.
478. Womack: *Buffaloe:* 2. Letter of Mrs. M. J. Morton to her husband, dated July 24, 1839, in which she hopes he is enjoying the water and mountain air and that the trip will do him much good.
479. Mss. letter, Thomas T. Tredway to John Woodall, Aug. 14, 1856. John Woodall Papers.
480. Farmville *Herald*, Oct. 29, 1897: Letter of "56."
481. *The Kaleidoscope*, 1901. The stately old lady was Mrs. Nathaniel E. Venable, *née* Mary Embry Scott, whose husband had built the house on the farm which his uncle, Abraham B. Venable, had bought from Peter Johnston when the latter moved to Abingdon in 1811.

CHAPTER XIII NOTES

1. Beverley B. Munford: *Virginia's Attitude toward Slavery and Secession:* 27-8; John Fiske: *The Critical Period in American History:* 205.
2. Jonathan Elliott: *Debates on the Federal Constitution* 3: 534-5.
3. *Journals of the House of Delegates of Virginia, 1831-2:* 93-4, 109-10 (on microfilm, University of North Carolina Library). The history of this debate over the advisability of considering the abolition of slavery is treated in Joseph Clarke Robert: *The Road from Monticello.*
4. Richmond *Enquirer*, May 21, Nov. 29, 1850. Samuel Hobson of Cumberland was first named Democratic delegate with Robert H. Glass of Campbell, alternate; Col. Thomas H. Flood of Appomattox was named Whig delegate with Dr. John R. McDearmon, also of Appomattox, alternate. Both Hobson and Flood declined to go, and Flournoy and Thornton were named delegates in their stead. Gen. W. F. Gordon attended from Virginia.
5. Richmond *Enquirer*, Dec. 26, 1859.   6. Richmond *Enquirer*, Jan. 6, 1860.
7. Richmond *Enquirer*, Apr. 20, 1860.   8. Richmond *Enquirer*, Nov. 16, 1860.
9. Order Book 27: 376, 385. All except D. F. Womack qualified in July for the term beginning Aug. 1; Womack qualified in September.
10. Order Book 27: 386, 390.   11. Order Book 27: 377.
12. Richmond *Enquirer*, Sept. 18, Sept. 21, Sept. 28, 1860.
13. Richmond *Enquirer*, Oct. 19, 1860.
14. Mss. legislative petition, Archives Division, State Library.
15. Richmond *Enquirer*, June 29, 1860. 16. Richmond *Enquirer*, July 10, 1860.
17. Richmond *Enquirer*, July 24, 1860. 18. Richmond *Enquirer*, Aug. 21, 1860.
19. Richmond *Enquirer*, Oct. 12, 1860. 20. Richmond *Enquirer*, Oct. 16, 1860.
21. Richmond *Enquirer*, Oct. 19, 1860. 22. Richmond *Enquirer*, Aug. 28, 1860.
23. Richmond *Enquirer*, Nov. 16, 1860. The writer's grandfather, James R. Weaver, once told him how the vote went in his neighborhood, to show how the split in the Democratic vote put Virginia in the Bell column. Two neighbors, Col. Joseph T. Ligon and Edmund Lockett, who were Whigs, voted for Bell; another neighbor, Thomas Clark, and William Weaver, my grandfather's father, were Democrats; in 1860 Clark supported Douglas and Weaver supported Breckinridge.
24. Richmond *Enquirer*, Nov. 30, Dec. 7, Dec. 18, Dec. 25, 1860.
25. Richmond *Enquirer*, Nov. 23, 1860.
26. Order Book 27: 398, 405, 411.   27. *Acts of Assembly 1861:* 24-7.
28. *Register General Assembly 1776-1918:* 248.
29. *Acts of Assembly 1861:* 35-6.   30. Order Book 27: 399, 404.
31. Farmville *Herald*, Sept. 7, 1895, quoting Petersburg *Express*, April 20, 1861.
32. Richmond *Enquirer*, Mar. 9, 1861. 33. Richmond *Enquirer*, Mar. 23, 1861.
34. *Acts of Assembly 1861:* Appendix: 3-5; Richmond *Enquirer*, June 18, June 22, 1861.
35. *Acts of Assembly 1861:* Appendix: 6.
36. Richmond *Enquirer*, June 22, July 11, 1861. (Richmond *Enquirer*, July 2, 1861: The Fifth District included Prince Edward, Brunswick, Mecklenburg, Charlotte, Halifax, Lunenburg, and Appomattox.)
37. Related to the author by James R. Weaver, of Co. D, 25th Battalion, Virginia Volunteers, and J. M. Mottley.
38. Burrell: 107-11; muster roll of Co. K, Third Virginia Cavalry published in the Farmville *Herald* Oct. 21, 1898, and recorded by court order, Dec. 1898: John T. Thornton, captain; Peyton R. Berkeley, first lieutenant, captain

1862-3; H. T. Parish, second lieutenant, later colonel 16th Virginia Infantry; F. D. Redd, second lieutenant; Richard Stokes, second lieutenant; E. N. Price, first sergeant; John H. Knight, second sergeant, first lieutenant 1863, captain 1864; R. B. Berkeley, third sergeant; Frank H. Scott, fourth sergeant; L. M. Penick, first corporal; R. W. Dalby, second corporal; A. B. Cralle, third corporal; Daniel I. Allen, fourth corporal; Drury L. Armistead, Henry A. Allen, Charles B. Anderson, Frank C. Anderson, H. Thweatt Anderson, Charles I. Anderson, Wesley W. Anderson, M. L. Arvin, James A. Baker, James A. Bell, Clifford A. Bondurant, Samuel J. Bondurant, John J. Bondurant, Samuel W. Bondurant, W. A. Binford, George Booker, J. Horace Booker, William D. Booker, A. A. Bragg, William Brooks, Samuel A. Bruce, William A. Bruce, John Chaffin, William T. Crafton, John R. Cunningham, Charles E. Clark, Charles W. Crawley, John M. Daniel, John P. Dickinson, R. M. Dickinson, W. P. Dupuy, Henry W. Edmunds, F. L. Elliott, T. L. Elliott, John W. Elliott, R. C. Elliott, William W. Evans, W. H. Ewing, John J. Ewing, Charles Flournoy, John J. Flournoy, Thomas Flournoy, Rolin (Rowland ?) Foster, George W. Foster, George Fowlkes, James D. Fowlkes, Lafayette Garrett, J. H. Guthrie, Johnson Harvey, W. J. Harvey, A. A. Haskins, lieutenant 1863; Thomas E. Haskins, John Z. Holladay, George Hunt, John C. Hunt, Joby Hunt, John Jenkins, E. T. Jeffress, Frank Jenkins, John S. Kelley, E. S. Lockett, Goodrich Ligon, R. V. Ligon, George Nicholas, Charles Martin, H. T. Meredith, lieutenant 1863; R. A. Miller, B. M. Moseley, W. H. Morton, Charles R. Moseley, F. J. Penick, Daniel Price, B. H. Ragsdall, C. E. Redd, John A. Redd, John H. Redd, Joseph T. Redd, J. Wesley Redd, R. L. Redd, W. M. Richardson, John D. Richardson, James C. Rowlett, Junius C. Rowlett, S. S. Rowlett, Edwin Scott, Lafayette Scott, Charles B. Spencer, James C. Spencer, N. B. Spencer, J. D. Spencer, L. A. Starling, P. B. Sublett, Nat. Thackston, A. K. Todd, W. C. Trueheart, Charles Venable, A. R. Venable, John F. Walton, L. D. Walton, R. H. Walton, R. H. Watkins, lieutenant 1862, captain 1863-4; Thomas Watson, Marcus West, Oscar Wiley, Jack C. Williams, James H. Wilson, Ed Witt, A. C. Womack, A. W. Womack, D. G. Womack, Eugene Womack, W. W. Womack, Frank L. Womack, Jimmy Womack, Willie W. Wootton, Samuel T. Wootton.

39. Farmville *Herald*, Oct. 22, 1948: "History of Farmville" by Herbert Clarence Bradshaw; Dec. 9, 1898: roster of Farmville Guards, presented to court for recording Dec. 1898: Richard A. Booker, captain; Charles D. Anderson, first lieutenant; Charles H. Erambert, second lieutenant; Samuel B. McKinney, third lieutenant; Chesley Wood, first sergeant; William C. Priddy, second sergeant; William H. Pettus, third sergeant; William G. Venable, fourth sergeant; James W. Womack, first corporal; Robert E. Warren, second corporal; C. D. Lindsay, third corporal; Samuel C. Price, fourth corporal; Peyton B. Anderson, William F. Anderson, Z. A. Blanton, later first lieutenant and later captain; George R. Boatwright, Charles H. Brimmer, Thomas H. Bryant, Robert M. Burton, Allison Brightwell, L. C. Butler, Joseph E. Chappell, Thomas A. Cliborne, George W. Cliborne, E. B. Coleman, Richard Crafton, J. J. Chernault, W. M. Davidson, C. H. Dowdy, J. S. Davis, W. C. Davis, E. P. Davis, A. L. Deaton, James H. Dunnington, Tom Dowdy, Pat Dougherty, J. T. East, Robert W. Elam, George W. Elam, George W. Erambert, J. T. Elam, Obediah East, J. W. East, John Eagles, Peyton Enroughty, A. L. Faris, George R. Flippen, A. S. Foster, B. F. Foster, S. B. Foster, A. J. Fowlkes, John M. Foster, James F. Foster, Robert Gilliam, George Gills, Henry G. Haines, B. J. Harvey, J. S. Harvey, B. A. Holt, T. A. Holt, W. V. Holt, R. M. Hawkins, H. H. Hooton, S. C. Hooton, A. M. Hughes, J. W. Hancock, J. S. Hart, Jeff Hawkins, Jett Hawkins, Henry Harvey, Elisha Hunt, Tobe Hudgins, Johnson Harvey, Jesse Harvey, N. H. Jackson, third lieutenant; Abram Jenkins, John Jenkins, transferred to cavalry company; Henry Jenkins, Tom Jenkins, John Jackson, Archer Jennings, Elihu Morrissett, T. L. Morton, Nat S. Morton, William H. Morton, H. C. Middleton, W. J. Morrissett, later lieutenant and captain; Eddie Miller, R. D. Miller, John

Moss, Rod Mayo, Wm. A. Miller, J. H. Minor, T. F. McKinney, W. J. Nash, Thomas J. Osborne, V. C. Overton, Richard H. Page, John H. Pearson, Samuel B. Partin, John E. Patteson, T. J. Paulett, H. A. Paulett, Samuel W. Paulett, Tom Price, E. T. Rice, Charles R. Richardson, Walter H. Richardson, John W. Ransom, Jesse Robertson, T. L. Robertson, J. J. Riggins, George M. Setzer, W. G. Stratton, W. F. Smith, William Smith, Joel W. Toney, William A. Tuggle, ——— Tompkins, Cicero A. Verser, Ed. Verser, Paul C. Venable, C. M. Walker, L. A. Warren, W. H. H. Walthall, Thomas Weaver, B. C. Wells, T. A. Wells, W. C. Wells, W. Archer Wilson, Abram N. Womack, Nathan B. Womack, W. T. Worsham, Tom Walden, Peter Wells, J. T. Wilkerson, O. T. Wicker, Edgar Wicker, John D. Walthall, Conrad Zimmermann.

Southern Historical Society Papers 23: 94-6 (from Farmville *Journal,* Nov. 29, 1895): muster roll of the Randolph Guard on leaving Farmville June 11, 1861: Norvell Cobb, captain June 11, 1861-May 1, 1862; promoted to major 44th Virginia, 1863 colonel 44th Virginia Regiment; W. P. Walker, second captain (killed at Chancellorsville); H. G. Richardson, third and last captain; W. T. Lee, first lieutenant; Robert L. Brightwell, second lieutenant; T. L. Gibson, third lieutenant; C. L. Carr, second lieutenant; W. H. Wilkerson, first lieutenant; L. Amos, second lieutenant; B. F. Farrar, first sergeant; R. V. Jenkins, second sergeant; H. W. K. Davis, third sergeant; John J. Cobb, fourth sergeant; S. Branch Hunt, first corporal; R. H. Amos, second corporal; A. W. Cade, third corporal; Robert Harvey, fourth corporal; A. B. Adams, Robert H. Armistead, Willie Allen, W. S. Amos, Wesley Allen, W. A. Armistead, A. S. Atkins, T. P. Bell, A. V. Baker, A. B. Bennett, J. T. Coleman, E. H. Cobb, M. C. Cousins, Henry Cobb, Henry E. Cox, A. W. Deshazor, W. P. Ellett, James Evans, E. R. Griggs, Norman Grigg, N. C. Garnett, John Hayes, C. A. Hollman, Robert H. Hubbard, Thomas Hubbard, L. B. Huddleston, S. H. Huddleston, F. O. Hurt, W. A. Holman, J. S. Kidd, J. T. Murdock, Thomas A. Moore, John A. Morton, C. C. North, Thomas North, Henry Perkins, John J. Phaup, W. R. Phaup, P. B. Pollard, John Pollard, William Pollard, N. C. Perkinson, J. R. Perkinson, Henry Patton, W. S. Robertson, A. J. Randlett, John J. Ransom, Sam T. Tuggle, F. W. Taylor, G. Simpson, Peter Thackston, Charles Winston, B. H. Woodson, V. Wheeler, John W. Womack, T. W. Wiley.

40. Richmond *Enquirer,* Apr. 27, 1861.

41. Farmville *Herald,* May 5, 1899: roll of Central Guard, presented to court for record April, 1899: Moses T. Hughes, captain; J. P. Fitzgerald, first lieutenant, captain, 1861-3; major 1863; lieutenant colonel of regiment 1863; Branch Worsham, second lieutenant; William C. Trueheart, third lieutenant; Nathaniel G. Jones, first sergeant; Henry Venable, second sergeant; Christopher C. Bass, third sergeant; Gustavus A. Bass, fourth sergeant, later first lieutenant; James H. Thackston, fifth sergeant; Henry W. Edmunds, first corporal (later joined cavalry company); Thomas R. Farrar, second corporal; George W. Cliborne, third corporal (later joined Farmville Guards), William L. Guthrie, third lieutenant 1862, first lieutenant 1863, captain 1863; John M. Booker, fifth corporal; J. D. Allen, John J. Allen, John R. Allen, Robert P. Anderson, Elisha S. Boatwright, Richard F. Burke, Henry C. Campbell, William H. Campbell, John A. Chappell, John Carter, Elijah F. Collins, John W. Cave, James A. Crisp, Jeremiah G. Daub, Fayette H. Davis, Richard A. Davis, Joshua Foster, Nelson H. Garland, first lieutenant 1862; John R. Hughes, Shadrach H. Hines, Thomas L. Hines, Samuel C. Hines, James H. Hailey, William Hamilton, Francis Hamilton, James Hamilton, Irby King, Drury Lacy, Matthew L. Meadow, Overton Meadow, William J. Morris, Elijah Morgan, T. W. Price, Joseph B. Price, Albert G. Rogers, T. H. Rogers, R. T. Rice, John F. Rice, Jr., F. S. Scott, Robert C. Thackston, John S. Watson, John M. Williamson, Benjamin A. Womack. The following subsequently joined this company: N. E. Venable, later lieutenant; C. R. Venable, William D. Allen, James J. Bigger, Archer L. Bagby, Robert Fitzgerald, John E. Campbell, Richard Crafton, Beverley Dupuy, George G. Fowlkes, James T.

Fowlkes, Minford Fowlkes, Darius Hash, John T. Hines, Stephen Hines, George R. Hughes, John F. Jones, William L. Meadow, James M. Morton, Nelson McGehee, James Phelps, John Reider, Robert K. Thackston, John S. Thackston, William A. Walton, James L. Waddell.

A mss. obituary of Booker Foster Hunt, a member of the Prospect Grays, in possession of the author's wife, a great-granddaughter of B. F. Hunt, states that the Prospect Company was the first to leave Prince Edward for Confederate service.

42. Mss. roster of Co. C, 53rd Virginia Infantry, prepared by J. M. Mottley, brother of Lieut. N. R. Mottley, with the assistance of former members of the company and given the writer in 1927 by Mr. Mottley. The roster: Henry Dickerson, captain, Richard Miller, first lieutenant, N. R. Mottley, second lieutenant, Richard Phillips, third lieutenant, ———— Arthur, Fin Wingo, Lawrence Wingo, Sandy Harper, Moses Harper, George Harper, Thomas Harper, Seth Harper, Henry Harper, R. A. Childress, James Flippen, Andrew Flippen, J. Y. Phillips, Joseph Holt, C. G. Weaver, W. S. Weaver, Buddie Fowlkes, Clem Crute, D. A. Watson (later captain), L. B. Walthall (later second lieutenant), John Ligon, Henry Phillips, Robert Phillips, F. H. Ritchie, E. T. Miller, George Brown, James Cambby, E. T. Clark, W. L. Clark, R. A. Price, Henry Borum, J. C. Destin, Phineas Ellington, E. G. Redford, Richard Vaughan, Thomas Blanton, John Overton, John Binford, ———— Marion, Samuel Nunnally (ugly Sam), Samuel Nunnally (drinking Sam), Leigh Ligon (later first lieutenant), R. B. Bradshaw, W. P. Bradshaw, Joel Sliford, G. A. Farley, William B. Farley, James Carter, Charles Wade, Thomas Ellett, Edward Williamson, Floyd Moring, J. S. Lockett, W. B. Bruce, Robert Bradshaw, Quentin Marshall, William Nunnally, Osborn Ligon, Joseph Walton, Jeter Witt. This is the roll of the men who left Rice's Station in 1861 in the original company. Others joined later.

43. Related to the writer by James R. Weaver and J. M. Mottley.

44. Richmond *Enquirer*, Jan. 7, 1862.   45. *Cal. Bd. Min.:* 149, note.

46. Farmville *Herald*, April 29, 1898.   47. Richmond *Enquirer*, July 19, 1861.

48. The reorganization data concerning the Prince Edward companies is summarized from the muster rolls given in the notes.

Capt. R. H. Watkins' letters to his wife during the period of his war service have been preserved and are now in the library of the Virginia Historical Society. They were given to that library in 1929 on condition that no one but members of the family have access to them for the next 50 years and were accordingly not available to this writer for research. However, Miss Mary P. Dupuy of Worsham, a granddaughter, is making notes from them, and it is to be hoped that their content of public interest may be made known before the half-century is completed.

49. Farmville *Herald*, Jan. 22, 1897.

50. The writer's notes from the mss. muster roll of the Prospect company were made in 1939, when he was engaged in research for the sesquicentennial history of Farmville. This roll, and also the muster roll of the Central Guard, was in the Hampden-Sydney College library. The writer noted from the Prospect roster the names of B. F. Hunt and Charles E. Glenn, his wife's great-grandfathers. When he went to Hampden-Sydney to copy the roll for this work, it could not be found, no doubt a victim of the fire which destroyed the Hampden-Sydney library since his research for the Farmville history. How he has regretted that he did not copy the entire roll when he first saw it! But he thought that it was as secure in the Hampden-Sydney library as it could be made.

51. Burrell: 115-20: Burrell used the several letters written by the late Capt. S. W. Paulett for the Farmville *Herald* in 1897 about his war experiences. One letter concerned the battle of Gettysburg. The Farmville Guards, of which Paulett was a member, lost seven killed, eight (of whom he was one) wounded, and the company was captured. The part of the Rice company in

the battle was told to me by my grandfather, James R. Weaver. He once told me that his older brother, William Semple Weaver, was a sergeant in the company and that during the charge every commissioned officer in the company was killed or wounded, leaving the sergeant as the person with the highest rank in the company on the field. My grandfather was not a member of the Rice company, but enlisted in Co. D, 25th Battalion, Virginia Volunteers, at the beginning of 1863; this company was assigned to guard duty in Richmond during the entire year 1863.

52. Mss. letter N. Richard Mottley to his mother, Mrs. Nathaniel Mottley. Copied in 1926 from the original in possession of J. M. Mottley.

53. Mss. letter, James R. Weaver to "Dear Brother," dated Camp Chaffin's Farm, Apr. 1, 1864, copied by the writer from the original in the Weaver papers.

54. Order Book 27: 418.

55. Richmond *Enquirer*, Oct. 1, Oct. 15, Oct. 29, Nov. 1, Nov. 15, Dec. 3, 1861; Jan. 10, Feb. 21, 1862.

56. Order Book 27: 429-30.

57. Mss. legislative petition, Archives Division, State Library.

58. *Acts of Assembly 1861-2:* 82-4; 85-6.

59. Order Book 27: 420.

60. Richmond *Enquirer*, Nov. 8, 1861.

61. Mss. receipts, Walton papers.

62. Richmond *Whig*, July 1, 1863.

63. Order Book 27: 441.

64. Order Book 28: 53.

65. Order Book 27: 441.

66. Order Book 28: 53.

67. Order Book 27: 441.

68. Order Book 28: 53.

69. McIlwaine: 208-9.

70. McIlwaine: 199-201.

71. Farmville *Herald*, July 9, 1897: recollections of Dr. J. L. White; Randolph House Register, 1860-63. The register is now in the University of Virginia Library.

72. Information concerning the Warren residence during the war from James R. Weaver, whose father's farm adjoined the Lockett place where the Warrens lived; information concerning the Dunnington residence from Mrs. W. G. Dunnington. Both are noted in the Farmville *Herald*, Oct. 22, 1948, "History of Farmville," by this writer.

73. Order Book 28: 2, 96.

74. Order Book 28: 114, 116, 118.

75. Order Book 28: 111.

76. Richmond *Whig*, May 2, May 3, 1864.

77. Richmond *Enquirer*, June 5, 1863; Mar. 15, 1864. In the gubernatorial race in 1863, Col. George W. Munford, Col. Thomas Stanhope Flournoy, Gen. William Smith, and W. L. Goggins were candidates. Goggins withdrew from the race (Richmond *Enquirer*, May 22, 1863); Smith won the election.

78. Richmond *Whig*, May 25, 1863.

79. Richmond *Enquirer*, Mar. 5, 1864.

80. Richmond *Enquirer*, Dec. 27, 1864.

81. Richmond *Enquirer*, Jan. 7, 1865.

82. Mss. letter, L. Finney to Mr. Marshall, July 28, 1864, preserved in the family Bible of Alexander Marshall (usually designated Jr. to distinguish him from his grandfather of the same name), which is now in possession of Mrs. Branch Clements.

83. Richmond *Whig*, Sept. 9, 1863.

84. Richmond *Enquirer*, Mar. 15, 1864.

85. Richmond Enquirer, May 16, 1864: the commissioners Hubard and Gibboney were assisted by William B. Harrison in setting these prices.

86. McIlwaine: 201-3.

87. Mss. letter, E.B.T. to "Dear Wife"; dated Camp 22nd Virginia Battalion, Jan. 17, 1865. E. and J. Harding Papers.

88. *Acts of Assembly 1862-3:* 93-5.

89. Richmond *Enquirer*, Jan. 4, 1864.

90. *Cal. Bd. Min.:* 150.

91. *Cal. Bd. Min.:* 152.

92. Richmond *Whig*, Mar. 25, 1864.

93. Dr. James L. White: *History of the Confederate General Hospital*, 1897. Pamphlet. Farmville *Herald*, July 9, 1897: account by Dr. White.

94. Sharon Baptist Church Record Book, 1860-85 (Second Book).

95. Minutes, Appomattox Baptist Association, 1863.

96. Mss. letter, Rev. Daniel Witt to John F. Walton, Aug. 22, 1863. Walton papers; cf. Jeter, *Life of Witt:* 203-5, for letter of Witt to R. Gwathmey, Apr. 1864, in which he expresses the conviction is struggling for its rights and his hope for Southern success.

97. Farmville *Herald*, July 9, 1897.

98. McIlwaine: 210.   99. Order Book 28: 116.

100. *The War of the Rebellion: A Compilation of the Official Records of the Union and Confederate Armies.* Series I. Vol. 46. Part 1, pp. 630-1. (Hereafter cited as *O. R.*, with Series I implied, the number following *O. R.* referring to the volume.)

101. *O.R.* 46, Part 1: 1267-76.   102. *O.R.* 46, Part 1: 673-4.

103. *O.R.* 46, Part 1: 839-41.   104. *O.R.* 46, Part 1: 906-8.

105. *O.R.* 46, Part 1: 604-5.   106. *O.R.* 46, Part 1: 1161-2; 129, 1174.

107. *O.R.* 46, Part 1: 1107-9; 121.

108. Jefferson Davis: *The Rise and Fall of the Confederate Government* 2: 668.

109. *O.R.* 46, Part 1: 1265.   110. *O.R.* 46, Part 1: 1265; 85-7; 121.

111. *O.R.* 46, Part 3: 1384.   112. *O.R.* 46, Part 1: 1265-6.

113. *O.R.* 46, Part 1: 1161-2; Part 3: 1383: telegram from the operator at Farmville to the Secretary of War or Gen. St. John, filed at 3:20 P. M., April 4 advising that the enemy reached Burkeville ten minutes ago. Cf. Part 1, p. 135: some units did not get to Burkeville until April 5.

114. James Longstreet: *From Manassas to Appomattox:* 611-2. (Hereafter cited as Longstreet.)

115. *O.R.* 46, Part 1: 1302; 1162. General Ord's report (p. 1162) has the battle two miles from the bridge; General Fitzhugh Lee's report (p. 1302) gives the location as near the bridge.

116. *O.R.* 46, Part 1: 85-7; 101; 75; 121.

117. *O.R.* 46, Part 1: 1294.   118. *O.R.* 46, Part 1: 712.

119. *O.R.* 46, Part 1: 840-1; 604.   120. *O.R.* 46, Part 1: 906; 604.

121. *O.R.* 46, Part 1: 604.   122. *O.R.* 46, Part 1: 1107.

123. Andrew A. Humphreys: *The Virginia Campaigns of '64 and '65:* 379-80 (hereafter cited as Humphreys); Fred W. Cross: *The Battle of Lockett's Farm*, typescript. Cross, military archivist, State House, Boston, Mass., has made the most exhaustive study of the battle between the Federal Second Corps and Gordon's Confederate command and the Confederate wagon train which were headed toward Jamestown. Mr. Cross made several visits to the field; after completing his monograph, he sent a copy of the typescript to Mrs. Mamie O. Garnett, who lent it to this writer. Cross gives a detailed discussion of the various identifications of the fork at which the Confederate line of march divided.

124. *O.R.* 46, Part 1: 1283-4.

125. Humphreys: 380; *O.R.* 46, Part 1: 1132; 1107.

126. *O.R.* 46, Part 1: 1290. Johnson's men seem to have gotten away by the road which leads by the present residence of W. L. Vaughan.

127. *O.R.* 46, Part 1: 1284; 1294-5; 906.

128. *O.R.* 46, Part 1: 1301-2.   129. Humphreys: 383-4.

130. Statement to the author by his grandfather, James R. Weaver, who was captured at Sailor's Creek; he was in Custis Lee's division.

131. Humphreys: 381.
132. John B. Gordon: *Reminiscences of the Civil War:* 429-30. General Meade regarded both engagements as aspects of one battle, the Battle of Salor's Creek. Generally, however, they have been distinguished, the fight some two miles upstream, where Prince Edward, Nottoway, and Amelia Counties meet, being designated the Battle of Sailor's Creek, and this, when given a name, Perkinson's Mill. Fred Cross suggests the name, Lockett's Farm, from the location of most of the fighting, and this writer follows Cross' nomenclature, in the hope that usage here may contribute to the adoption of the name, Lockett's Farm.
133. Reminiscences of Mrs. Mamie O. Garnett, *née* Lockett, related to the writer. To Mrs. Garnett, who as a little girl at the time sat on a sack of potatoes in the basement of her father's home during the fighting, the battle remained a vivid memory throughout her long life.
134. Longstreet: 614-5; the account in Longstreet quotes Mahone.
135. Douglas Southall Freeman: *R. E. Lee* 4: 85.
136. Longstreet: 615; Humphreys: 386.
137. *O.R.* 46, Part 1: 1180, 129. Longstreet's line was along the road which crosses the present 460 at the Baptist Church at Rice and goes through the village. My grandfather, J. S. Bradshaw, has told me that the Confederate breastworks were along the edge of the yard of my parents' home, opposite the church. He was a boy of twelve at the time, living about four miles from Rice; he remembered hearing the firing of the guns during this engagement. The house at the right anchor of the Federal line must have been the Olgers house or an earlier one on or near the site. The Phillips house on the left was in the oak grove near the railroad just east of Rice. That home burned, and the present house replaced it.
138. *O.R.* 46, Part 1: 1177-8.   139. *O.R.* 46, Part 1: 1180.
140. *O.R.* 46, Part 1: 1120.
141. *O.R.* 46, Part 1: 1180-1; Longstreet: 616.
142. *O.R.* 46, Part 1: 758-9; 674; Part 3, 622.
143. *O.R.* 46, Part 3: 1386. The site of Lee's headquarters at Rice has been pointed out to the writer as the field northeast of the present intersection of Routes 460 and 307.
144. *O.R.* 46, Part 3: 620.
145. Humphreys: 386; Longstreet: 616.
146. Dr. James L. White: *History of the Confederate General Hospital.* Dr. White was the son-in-law of P. H. Jackson, having married Miss Lelia Jackson in 1864. Freeman (*R. E. Lee* 4: 95), on the basis of a statement of Miss Mary Jackson, later Mrs. Gould, a granddaughter of Mr. Jackson, says Lee drank a cup of tea. The White account was written in 1897, and Dr. White's information was first hand. Cf. Farmville *Herald*, July 9, 1897, for Dr. White's reminiscences: Lee entered Farmville early on the morning of the 7th, ascertained whereabouts of Generals Breckinridge, Lawton, and St. John, who had spent the night, but not in sleep, at the P. H. Jackson home, had an interview with them. Lee remained a short while and had a Confederate cup of coffee, which was sent to his room; he subsequently parted from these men at the yard gate.
    Farmville *Herald*, Apr. 11, 1902: Mrs. J. L. White recalled that her family had entertained General Lee and other generals in the house in which "she now lives." Mrs. White remembered that General Lee declined a toddy offered him then.
147. Humphreys: 386-91; *O.R.* 46, Part 1: 1266, 1281, 1302; Fitzhugh Lee: *General* Lee: 385-6; Farmville *Herald*, July 17, 1896: recollections of Dr. W. W. H. Thackston.
148. *O.R.* 46, Part 1: 907-8, 101.   149. *O.R.* 46, Part 1: 1109.

150. *O.R.* 46, Part 1: 638.
151. *O.R.* 46, Part 1: 841; cf. p. 83. Griffin had been put in command of the Corps April 1. His newness in command explains the obvious caution of his report and his frequent references to orders. No brash brass hat he!
152. *O.R.* 46, Part 1: 1388; 1390; 85-7.
153. *Personal Memoirs of U. S. Grant* 2: 475, 478-86.
154. McIlwaine: 212, 214-5; Farmville *Herald*, July 17, 1896, recollections of Dr. W. W. H. Thackston; July 9, 1897, recollections of Dr. J. L. White; reminiscences of Mrs. Mamie O. Garnett. My grandfather, J. S. Bradshaw, has told me that a Federal officer placed a guard at his mother's home with instructions to shoot any soldier or straggler who moved to molest members of the family or property; the house had been pillaged before this, however; he remembered that a Federal soldier took his late father's watch from the mantel where his mother kept it, despite his mother's protest.

    The late Mrs. J. W. Wilson, *née* Jennie Bradshaw, told the writer that at the home of her father, William E. Bradshaw, near High Bridge, Federal soldiers went into the storehouse and poured out the bags of cotton on the floor; then they took the bung out of the molasses barrel and let the molasses pour over the cotton; then they caught up all the kittens on the place and threw them into the mess of cotton and molasses. This was an example of the destruction of goods for which the soldiers had neither use nor need.

    There was concern for the safety of people. Samuel W. Bondurant of Panola, near High Bridge, had a number of the girls and young women who lived near the roads over which the armies were expected to come stay at his home which was some distance from a road. They took refuge in the cellar during the passing of the armies.

155. Related to me by my Grandmother Bradshaw, *née* Ann Mildred Jenkins. Her father's (R. A. Jenkins) home was later the home of J. A. Bondurant, on the road between Sailor's Creek battlefield and Rice. Her older sisters were among those invited by Samuel W. Bondurant to take refuge at his home at this time.
156. McIlwaine:212-5.   157. McIlwaine: 212.
158. The losses to the Confederate Army may be seen in the small number of members of the 53rd Virginia Regiment at Appomattox for the surrender. The list is found in the Farmville *Herald* of Nov. 10, 1895, and was copied from the Norfolk *Pilot*, which published the list from a mss. furnished by W. F. Pumphrey. The regiment was in George H. Steuart's Brigade, Pickett's Division, Longstreet's Corps. At the surrender were William Gibson Carter, surgeon; Henry Edmunds, captain of Co. F, P. Leigh Ligon, first lieutenant, Co. C (the Rice's Depot company); A. B. Anoenon, first lieutenant Co. F; L. B. Walthall, second lieutenant Co. C, acting A.D.C.; A. T. Farmer, second lieutenant Co. C; R. C. Shell, second lieutenant Co. G; C. Bilharz, second lieutenant Co. I: privates in Co. B: John W. Tate, J. B. Aaron, W. M. Smith, A. J. Wells, C. D. Crowder; privates Co. C (the Rice company): E. T. Clark, W. L. Clark, J. S. Fowlkes, F. H. Richie, A. J. Warren, J. P. Phillips, H. T. Phillips, Benjamin Angle, William E. Wellborn, A. Scott, C. A. Wave, T. M. Ellett; privates Co. D: John Bishop, Joseph Prush; privates Co. E: A. D. Davis, R. D. Wright; Co. F: Sergeant John E. Henderson, Privates Isham Amos, John Brander, William R. Compton, A. Cumbie, T. J. Glascock, Joseph T. Gull, Hy. P. Hull, Robert S. Gull, John S. Hopkins, Alexander Miller, William B. Old, William H. Smith, Jonathan Sink, William L. Bennett, Joseph V. Crank, and R. T. Jones.

CHAPTER XIV NOTES

1. Farmville *Herald*, July 9, 1897, reminiscences of Dr. J. L. White; July 17, 1896, recollections of Dr. W. W. H. Thackston.
2. My grandfather, James R. Weaver, used to tell of a man who lived on the Rice-Burkeville road, just east of Dickerson's crossing (of the Southside Railroad) who was sitting in the door of his home on Sunday, April 9, 1865, when a passerby on horseback called excitedly that Lee had surrendered at Appomattox Courthouse. Quite unperturbed, with the manner of one who did not regard such an outcome as final by any means, the man called back from his home: "Have they heard from Lunenburg Courthouse yet?"—a double jibe at the reputation of that place for its fights and for the vigorous pro-secession spirit of that county which won for it the soubriquet, "The Old Free State."
3. Farmville *Herald*, July 9, 1897.
4. Farmville *Herald*, Jan. 22, 1897, letter of Col. R. A. Booker.
5. McIlwaine: 222.
6. *O.R.* 46, Part I: 102.
7. *O.R.* 46, Part I: 1120.
8. *O.R.* 46, Part I: 85-7.
9. *O.R.* 46, Part I: 1178.
10. *O.R.* 46, Part I: 147.
11. The two oaths and the certificate of release are on a four-page folder. The original of the one copied in this work is now in the possession of the author, a grandson of Mr. Weaver. My grandfather told me that the prisoners were released in alphabetical order.
12. Richmond *Enquirer*, Aug. 31, 1866.
13. Related to the writer by Mrs. Mamie O. Garnett.
14. Farmville *Herald*, July 9, 1897.
15. Order Book 28: 136-9.
16. Order Book 28: 147.
17. Order Book 28: 139.
18. McIlwaine: 216. Dr. McIlwaine does not name Mrs. Thornton as the person, but his description of her circumstances leaves no doubt about the identification.
19. Jeter: *Life of Witt:* 205-9.
20. Related to the writer by his grandfather, J. S. Bradshaw.
21. Order Book 28: 139, 147.
22. Order Book 28: 138.
23. Richmond *Enquirer*, Aug. 21, 1866; Order Book 22: 214, 223.
24. Richmond *Enquirer*, Aug. 31, 1866.
25. *Register General Assembly 1776-1918:* 189, 190, 250.
26. Richmond *Enquirer*, Jan. 28, 1868.
27. Richmond *Enquirer*, April 17, 1868.
28. *Biog. Dict. Cong.:* 316, 1739.
29. *Acts of Assembly 1871-2:* 258-9.
30. Richmond *Enquirer*, Apr. 21, 1868.
31. *Acts of Assembly 1869-70:* 617-25.
32. Order Book 28: 417.
33. Johnston: *Memorials of Old Virginia Clerks:* 314-7.
34. Order Book 28: 423-4; 427; 428. The last session in which the elected justices held court was March, 1869, (Order Book 28: 423) with Charles A. Morton presiding justice, William T. Carter, John O. Elam, R. A. Booker, and R. W. Price present. From this period comes one of the most delightful of Prince Edward stories. Branch J. Worsham was the hero. As clerk, he was directed "to qualify" one of the new appointees to office. "I'll swear him in," said Mr. Worsham, "but all hell can't qualify him."
35. Richmond *Enquirer*, Nov. 14, 1870.
36. Order Book 1870-74: 1-6.
37. Order Book 1870-4: 86, 89.
38. Order Book 1870-4: 41.
39. Order Book 1870-4: 226.
40. Order Book 1870-4: 253.
41. Order Book 1870-4: 264.
42. Order Book 1870-4: 566-7.
43. Order Book 1870-4: 634.

44. First Record Book, Board of Supervisors (hereafter cited as Supervisors' Record, the volume number following): 1.

45. Order Book 1870-4: 64, 68, 83.   46. *Acts of Assembly 1869-70:* 549-50.

47. *Acts of Assembly 1870-1:* 150-1; 175-6.

48. Order Book 1870-4: 147.

49. Minute Book, Farmville Lodge No. 41, A.F. & A.M., 1871. Little of what had been placed in the corner-stone could be salvaged when the building was removed for the present courthouse.

50. Order Book 1870-4: 282.

51. Order Book 1870-4: 287-9; Prince Edward Deed Book 30: 181.

52. Minutes Town Council of Farmville, entries of Feb. 18 and Mar. 11, 1890.

53. *Acts of Assembly 1869-70:* 457-62.   54. Farmville *Mercury*, Feb. 25, 1875.

55. Farmville *Herald*, Oct. 22, 1948: "History of Farmville," by Herbert Clarence Bradshaw; Farmville *Mercury*, Nov. 13, 1873; Farmville *Herald*, Nov. 4, 1904: obituary of Edgar Allan.

56. Farmville *Mercury*, Nov. 13, 1873.

57. Farmville *Mercury*, Oct. 2, Oct. 9, Nov. 6, 1873.

58. Farmville *Mercury*, July 10, Oct. 23, 1873.

59. Farmville *Mercury*, Oct. 2, 1873.   60. Farmville *Mercury*, Oct. 9, 1873.

61. Farmville *Mercury*, Oct. 16, 1873.   62. Farmville *Mercury*, Oct. 30, 1873.

63. Farmville *Mercury*, Nov. 6, 1873.

64. Farmville *Mercury*, Oct. 8, Oct. 29, Nov. 5, 1874.

65. Farmville *Mercury*, Oct. 16, 1873.

66. Farmville *Mercury*, May 13, 1875; Prince Edward Deed Book 30: 185: Dr. W. W. H. Thackston as mayor and Edgar Allan as clerk signed the deed on behalf of the town of Farmville conveying the courthouse property to the county in 1872. Cf. Farmville *Mercury*, Oct. 30, 1873, Aug. 6, 1874, for H. R. Hooper as mayor. In 1873 B. S. Hooper was treasurer, Edgar Allan clerk. In 1874 John S. Holman was town sergeant, B. M. Cox deputy sergeant, treasurer and clerk, W. S. Berry assessor, William D. Evans street commissioner, James Bland lamplighter and scavenger, W. S. Berry and B. S. Hooper overseers of the poor.

67. Farmville *Mercury*, May 20, 1875.   68. Farmville *Mercury*, May 27, 1875.

69. Farmville *Mercury*, June 3, 1875. The history of the coalition of Southern Democrats and Northern Republicans to elect Hayes over Tilden is detailed in C. Vann Woodward: *Reunion and Reaction.* Professor Woodward observes that leaders among the Democrats in the coalition had been Whigs before the war. In this connection it is interesting to note that Dr. W. W. H. Thackston, Farmville's fusion candidate for mayor, had been a Whig.

70. Farmville *Mercury*, May 6, 1875.

71. Farmville *Mercury*, May 27, 1875.

The civil rights bill passed by Congress and signed by President Grant became effective in March, 1875. It did not apply to barrooms and saloons unless they were connected with inns. Judge Asa D. Dickinson of Prince Edward used the bill to have some fun at the expense of his Negro waiter at the St. James Hotel, Richmond, when it went into effect. In the presence of a number of guests, he told his waiter that under the civil rights bill a member of the legislature could not tip him unless the waiter gave the same amount to a white person. The waiter demurred, but the judge did not sustain the demurrer. Farmville *Mercury*, Mar. 1, 1875, quoting the Richmond *Whig*. Cf. Farmville *Mercury*, June 3, 1875, for reference to Hines' sign.

72. Farmville *Mercury*, June 3, 1875.

73. Farmville *Mercury*, Aug. 12, Sept. 23, 1875. This is the last instance the

writer has found in which all the magistrates in the county were summoned to hear a case.

74. Farmville *Mercury*, Oct. 7, 1875.

75. Farmville *Mercury*, Oct. 7, Oct. 14, 1875.

76. Farmville *Mercury*, Nov. 11, 1875.

77. The account of this incident was written by Judge Asa D. Watkins who remembered it and was sent by him to Dr. J. D. Eggleston. Dr. Eggleston sent the writer a copy of Judge Watkins' account. In *Today and Yesterday in the Heart of Virginia*, p. 168, the story without names is related in Judge Watkins' account of Reconstruction.

78. These incidents were related to the writer by his father, Herbert L. Bradshaw. Mr. Olgers told the story of the election to my father. I find especially intriguing the role played by D. J. Weaver in the election mentioned. He was my Grandfather Weaver's youngest brother, one of the mildest and quietest of men. I never heard him raise his voice from his accustomed soft drawl and never heard of anyone who did. Perhaps it was the positiveness in his quiet manner which deterred Bliss from carrying out his mission.

79. Richmond *Weekly Dispatch*, Nov. 24, 1876.

80. *Biog. Dict. Cong.:* 386, 1327.

81. Richmond *Weekly Dispatch*, Aug. 9, 1889: from Judge Mann's speech nominating Philip W. McKinney for Governor.

82. Richmond *Weekly Dispatch*, Nov. 26, 1886.

83. Richmond *Weekly Dispatch*, Nov. 9, 1888; cf. issue of Aug. 9, 1889, for Mann's speech.

84. *Biog. Dict. Cong.:* 417, 428, 431, 450, 461, 1134, 1435, 1540, 1908.

85. *Register General Assembly, 1776-1918:* 195, 197, 199, 201, 204.

86. *Register General Assembly 1776-1918:* 192, 194, 209-10.

87. Richmond *Weekly Dispatch*, Aug. 8, 1889; Richmond *Whig*, Nov. 22, 1880: In the 1880 election electors on the Funder ticket in Virginia received over 96,000 votes, Republican electors 83,000, and the Readjuster electors 31,000.

88. Richmond *Weekly Dispatch*, Nov. 5, 1893: voting record of 1889.

89. *The Kaleidoscope*, 1899: "Philip W. McKinney" by Thomas J. Garden. When Garden taught at New Store, he roomed with McKinney.

90. Farmville *Herald*, Jan. 6, 1894.

91. Order Book 1882-90: 464, 475; Order Book 1891-98: 25-26.

92. Farmville *Herald*, Mar. 25, Apr. 15, May 13, June 3, 1893.

93. Farmville *Mercury*, Aug. 20, 1874.   94. Farmville *Herald*, Nov. 10, 1894.

95. Farmville *Herald*, Nov. 11, 1893; cf. issue of Apr. 13, 1895, for Harris' party chairmanship.

96. Farmville *Herald*, Apr. 15, June 3, June 24, 1893.

97. Farmville *Herald*, Feb. 23, Apr. 13, May 25, June 1, 1895.

98. Farmville *Herald*, Sept. 21, 1895.   99. Farmville *Herald*, Nov. 9, 1895.

100. Farmville *Herald*, Apr. 3, May 29, June 5, 1896.

101. Farmville *Herald*, July 31, 1896.   102. Farmville *Herald*, Aug. 28, 1896.

103. Farmville *Herald*, Sept. 18, 1896.

104. Farmville *Herald*, Aug. 21, Sept. 4, Sept. 25, 1896.

105. Farmville *Herald*, Oct. 2, 1896; cf. issues of July 31, Aug. 28, 1896.

106. Farmville *Herald*, May 29, 1896.   107. Farmville *Herald*, Aug. 28, 1896.

108. Farmville *Herald*, Oct. 9, 1896.   109. Farmville *Herald*, Aug. 28, 1896.

110. Farmville *Herald*, Nov. 6, 1896.

111. Farmville *Herald*, Apr. 3, 1896, Oct. 1, Oct. 15, 1897.

112. Farmville *Herald*, Feb. 18, Sept. 9, 1898.
113. Farmville *Herald*, Oct. 21, 1898.   114. Farmville *Herald*, Nov. 11, 1898.
115. Farmville *Herald*, Nov. 11, 1904.
116. Farmville *Herald*, June 4, 1897. No statistics on this vote were given in the newspaper.
117. Ralph Clipman McDanel: *The Virginia Constitutional Convention of 1901-02:* 158.
118. McIlwaine: 337-8; 373-5.
119. McIlwaine: 376; Farmville *Herald*, Apr. 25, 1902.
120. Farmville *Herald*, June 20, Aug. 8, 1902.
121. Farmville *Herald*, Sept. 5, 1902.   122. Farmville *Herald*, Jan. 22, 1904.

CHAPTER XV NOTES

1. Record Book, Sharon Baptist Church, 1860-85.
2. First Record Book, Pisgah Baptist Church (now in Virginia Baptist Historical Society library, University of Richmond). The Negro members who withdrew from Pisgah to form High Rock were William Griffin (baptized after the memorable revival of 1869), Robert Perkins, Jim Hogwood, Elisha Green, Thomas Morgan, Robert Morgan, Booker Foster, John Haskins, Ben Scott, Jack Scott, Mingo Morton, William Meade, three women bearing the surname Bradshaw, one woman with the surname Madison, one Leigh, one Foster (the corner of the page with the list of women members has worn off and their first names are missing), Mary Scott, Martha Branch, Martha Foster, Eliza Haskins, Jinny Vaughan, Silvia Scott, Indiana Morgan, Susan Jackson, Lucy Thompson, Mary C. Wiley, Sarah Robinson.
3. Related to me by my father, who remembered the occasions.
4. Prince Edward Deed Book 29: 66, 67.
5. Prince Edward Deed Book 30: 144. W. L. Clark and John W. Foster, of the trustees, were white men.
6. Prince Edward Deed Book 30: 81. No name is given in the deed, but this is the site of the present Mercy Seat Church. The date of organization given on the sign over the door of the church is the date of the deed.
7. Prince Edward Deed Book 30: 524. This church was named for the Rev. Daniel Witt, who had recently died.
8. Prince Edward Deed Book 33: 440.
9. Prince Edward Deed Book 33: 172. Sulphur Springs Church is between Elam and the Prospect-Five Forks road.
10. Prince Edward Deed Book 34: 119: The land conveyed in this deed was a part of the Midway Inn tract.
11. Prince Edward Deed Book 33: 308. Triumph Church, near Darlington Heights, is at the intersection of the roads from Darlington Heights to Keysville, Farmville, Five Forks, and Bethlehem Church.
12. Prince Edward Deed Book 33: 544.
13. Prince Edward Deed Book 35: 66; Law Orders, Circuit Court of Prince Edward County 1894-1909: 47. High Rock Church stands on Highway 460 between Rice and Burkeville. The high rock for which it was named was on the old road. As I remember it, the rock had broken and part had fallen over, but older people remember it when it stood upright, a landmark along the road. Morton Carter, now 102 years old, told me that he cut the first log for the building of High Rock Church.

14. Prince Edward Deed Book 35: 219. Macedonia Church is near Overly in the northeast corner of the county.

15. Prince Edward Deed Book 35: 459. The name of the church is not given in the deed, but the location of the site identifies it as Monroe Church.

16. Prince Edward Deed Book 38: 91. The new road does not pass this site, and the traveler from Pamplin to Madisonville misses one of the most superb views any public road in this section of Virginia offered, from the top of Negro Hill at Mt. Lyle Church.

17. Prince Edward Deed Book 46: 467.

18. Prince Edward Deed Book 44: 231. No name of the church is given in the deed, but from the description of the location of the site it is readily identified as Calvary Church.

19. Prince Edward Deed Book 49: 409. This church is north of Prospect. The meeting-house had been occupied four decades and more before by the congregation of Appomattox Baptist Church.

20. Prince Edward Deed Book 44: 581. Alabama Church is on the road from the Darlington Heights-Pamplin road to Rosser's mill.

21. Prince Edward Deed Book 58: 524. 22. Prince Edward Deed Book 51: 307.

23. Prince Edward Deed Book 51: 358. 24. Prince Edward Deed Book 57: 462.

25. Prince Edward Deed Book 56: 50; 67: 411.

26. Prince Edward Deed Book 64: 300. This is an ancient church site, home of Liberty Baptist Church prior to 1797; then a preaching station of Sailor Creek Baptist Church until 1827; and the first house of worship of the Disciples of Christ in Prince Edward County from which that congregation moved to Green Bay in 1881.

27. Prince Edward Deed Book 79: 569. 28. Prince Edward Deed Book 81: 86.

29. Farmville *Mercury*, Sept. 10, 17, 24, 1874. The first news item refers to the association as "recently organized."

30. Farmville *Mercury*, May 28, 1874. Bates died Dec. 24, 1906; he was regarded then as probably the oldest person in Farmville and was thought to have been over 90 (Farmville *Herald*, Jan. 4, 1907).

31. Farmville *Herald*, Oct. 22, 1948: "History of Farmville" by Herbert Clarence Bradshaw; Sept. 9, 1893; Aug. 28, 1896.

32. Prince Edward Deed Book 29: 121.

33. Minutes of the Virginia Annual Conference of the Methodist Episcopal Church, South, 1868: 51; 1870: 35; 1871: 39. (Hereafter cited as the Va. Meth. Conf. Annual.)

34. Farmville *Mercury*, Oct. 2, 1873. The discrepancy between the reference to the colored Methodist Church in the deed of 1868, the Negro members of the Farmville Methodist Church in 1871, and the newspaper reference to the organization of a colored Methodist Church in 1873 is not explained, unless it was that the colored Methodists had a separate house of worship prior to their formal separation from the organization of which they and the white Methodists were members.

35. Farmville *Mercury*, Mar. 4, 1875.   36. Prince Edward Deed Book 29: 280.

37. Va. Meth. Conf. Annual 1868: 51; 1871: 31, 32, 39; 1891.

38. Prince Edward Deed Book 29: 261.   39. Prince Edward Deed Book 35: 333.

40. Prince Edward Deed Book 38: 625.   41. Prince Edward Deed Book 55: 418.

42. Prince Edward Deed Book 40: 544.   43. Prince Edward Deed Book 95: 287.

44. Prince Edward Deed Book 93: 87.   45. Farmville *Mercury*, Oct. 15, 1874.

46. Farmville *Mercury*, Sept. 17, 1874.

47. Farmville *Mercury*, Feb. 19, June 23, 1874; June 17, 1875.

48. Richmond *Times-Dispatch*, Feb. 12, 1950.

49. Farmville *Mercury*, Oct. 30, 1873.

50. Farmville *Mercury*, Aug. 26, Sept. 9, 1875.

51. Farmville *Mercury*, Apr. 15, 1875.

52. *Today and Yesterday in the Heart of Virginia:* 310-1; "Episcopal Churches" by Mrs. J. Luckin Bugg.

53. *Today and Yesterday in the Heart of Virginia:* 338; "Presbyterian Churches" by J. D. Eggleston.

54. Manual of Roanoke Presbytery, 1894. No 17 of Vol. 8, Virginia Pamphlets, 1880-99, Duke University Library.

55. Prince Edward Deed Book 37: 454. This deed was evidently given to clear title to the property.

56. Prince Edward Deed Book 67: 430.

57. McIlwaine: 226; *Today and Yesterday in the Heart of Virginia:* 343; "Presbyterian Churches" by J. D. Eggleston.

58. Prince Edward Deed Book 36: 18; *Today and Yesterday:* 343-4.

59. Prince Edward Deed Book 81: 79, 80; Dr. J. D. Eggleston (*Today and Yesterday:* 344) noted that "in April, 1927, the congregation decided to sell the church building, and, in January, 1928, they decided to buy the Baptist Church, if it could be obtained as a reasonable price. This plan seems to have failed, because at the next meeting of the session, January 27, 1928, it was decided to choose a site and build a church. . . ." The plan was not to buy the Baptist Church property, but the Baptist Church building and rebuild it on the lot which was bought. Pisgah Baptist Church built its new brick building at this time and sold the frame structure which had been built in 1881 to make way for the new building. The plan of the Jamestown Presbyterian Church in this matter was carried out.

60. Manual of Roanoke Presbytery, 1894; Farmville *Herald*, April 17, 1896; Prince Edward Deed Book 41: 30.

61. Prince Edward Deed Book 58: 381.   62. Manual of Roanoke Presbytery, 1894.

63. *Today and Yesterday in the Heart of Virginia:* 342, "Presbyterian Churches" by J. D. Eggleston.

64. Record Books, Sailor Creek Baptist Church, 1802-67.

65. Mss. history Pisgah Baptist Church 1857-1917 by Herbert Clarence Bradshaw; Prince Edward Deed Book 34: 250; First Record Book Pisgah Baptist Church. The existing church records begin in 1869, noting destruction of the earlier book when the community was invaded in 1865.

66. Record Book, Sharon Baptist Church, 1860-85; first record book, Pisgah Baptist Church.

67. Record Book, Sharon Baptist Church, 1860-85. Burkeville Baptist Church was organized with 33 members Sun., Oct. 18, 1874, by a presbytery consisting of Rev. S. J. Atkins of Prince Edward and O. Ellyson (Farmville *Mercury*, Oct. 29, 1874).

68. Mss. account of Bagby Memorial Baptist Church given the writer by G. P. Nunnaly, church clerk, in 1935 for the history, "Baptist Churches," in *Today and Yesterday in the Heart of Virginia*; Prince Edward Deed Book 49: 367.

69. Mss. account of Mt. Nebo Baptist Church furnished the writer by O. L. Vassar, church clerk, in 1935; Prince Edward Deed Book 52. 447.

70. Farmville *Herald*, July 29, 1904; *Today and Yesterday in the Heart of Virginia:* 352, 357, "Baptist Churches" by Herbert Clarence Bradshaw; Prince Edward Deed Book 59: 123.

71. Mss. account of Glenn Memorial Baptist Church furnished the writer by Mrs. B. V. Wilkerson, church clerk, in 1935; Prince Edward Deed Book 76: 585.

72. Prince Edward Deed Book 115: 448; Minutes, Appomattox Baptist Association, 1953.

73. Mss. history Farmville Baptist Church 1836-1936 by Herbert Clarence Bradshaw.

74. Mss. history Spring Creek Baptist Church 1815-1940 by Herbert Clarence Bradshaw.

75. Dates verified from the church records for the writer by D. C. Morris, church clerk.

76. Va. Meth. Conf. Annual, 1868: 48, 51, 56.

77. Va. Meth. Conf. Annual, 1870. 23, 35.

78. Va. Meth. Conf. Annual, 1871: 31, 32, 38-9.

79. Va. Meth. Conf. Annual, 1890, 1891; Burrell: 266.

80. Burrell: 271; Prince Edward Deed Book 35: 623. The charter members of Salem Methodist Church were Mrs. Martha J. Hubbard, Mrs. Martha R. Watson, Miss Betty Wade, John T. Branch, Mrs. M. B. Price, J. W. Garrett, Mrs. V. C. Garrett, W. H. Hubbard, J. E. Hubbard, S. D. Hubbard, Miss Nannie B. Hubbard, Miss Mary Watson, Miss Lou Watson, Miss Anna Watson. Burrell gives the place of the organization of the Sunday School as the home of C. L. Overton, but at the time the Sunday School was organized it was the home of Mrs. Martha R. Watson, whose daughter Overton married.

81. Prince Edward Deed Book 37: 136. 82. Prince Edward Deed Book 72: 344.

83. Farmville *Herald*, Sept. 7, 1906; Oct. 22, 1948, "History of Farmville" by Herbert Clarence Bradshaw.

84. Woodrow W. Wilkerson: *Olive Branch Church 1805-1934*; brochure lent to the writer by Miss Mildred Harvey.

85. Mss. history Prospect Methodist Church furnished the writer by Mrs. Bennett T. Taylor.

86. Prince Edward Deed Book 35: 460; mss. history Liberty Christian Church by Robert B. Wilson, Jr., of Green Bay and furnished by him to the writer; Burrell: 288.

87. Prince Edward Deed Book 41: 313.

88. Mss. history Farmville Baptist Church 1836-1936 by Herbert Clarence Bradshaw.

89. Farmville *Mercury*, Aug. 6, 1874.

90. *Today and Yesterday in the Heart of Virginia:* 336-7, "Presbyterian Churches" by J. D. Eggleston; Farmville *Mercury*, June 3, 1875.

91. Mss. history Prospect Methodist Church furnished by Mrs. Bennett T. Taylor; Prince Edward Deed Book 33: 140.

92. Farmville *Herald*, Oct. 22, 1948, "History of Danville" by Herbert Clarence Bradshaw.

93. Record Book, Sharon Baptist Church, 1885-1920; second record book, Pisgah Baptist Church, now in the Virginia Baptist Historical Society library; Prince Edward Deed Book 38: 276.

94. Mss. history Spring Creek Baptist Church 1815-1940 by Herbert Clarence Bradshaw; Prince Edward Deed Book 63: 385.

95. Farmville *Herald*, Oct. 22, 1948, "History of Farmville" by Herbert Clarence Bradshaw.

96. Farmville *Herald*, Sept. 11, 1903.   97. Farmville *Herald*, Aug. 22, 1903.

98. Mss. history Buffalo Presbyterian Church by John B. Cunningham.

99. Mss. history Prospect Methodist Church furnished by Mrs. Bennett T. Taylor.

100. Mss. history Pisgah Baptist Church 1857-1917 by Herbert Clarence Bradshaw.

101. Prince Edward Deed Book 44: 181; 50: 123; Farmville *Herald*, Sept. 16, 1904, Nov. 17, 1905; Oct. 22, 1948, "History of Farmville" by Herbert Clarence Bradshaw.

102. Prince Edward Deed Book 60: 336; 67: 374.

103. Peter Trear was a native of Spain who came to the United States to fight in the Federal army during the War between the States. The United States recruited a number of soldiers in Europe for that war. After the war, Trear settled near Sandy River Church.
104. Prince Edward Deed Book 110: 285.
105. Prince Edward Deed Book 91: 122; Farmville *Herald,* Oct. 22, 1948, "History of Farmville" by Herbert Clarence Bradshaw.
106. Prince Edward Deed Book 96: 294. 107. Prince Edward Deed Book 94: 296.
108. Prince Edward Deed Book 112: 42. 109. Farmville *Herald,* Mar. 30, 1895.
110. Farmville *Herald,* May 5, 1894.   111. Farmville *Herald,* Oct. 6, 1905.
112. Prince Edward Deed Book 39: 157.
113. Mss. history Prospect Methodist Church sent to the writer by Mrs. Bennett T. Taylor.
114. First record book, Pisgah Baptist Church.
115. Farmville *Mercury,* May 27, 1875.
116. Record book, Ladies Sewing Society for Foreign Missions, Pisgah Baptist Church.
117. Mss. history Prospect Methodist Church sent by Mrs. Bennett T. Taylor.
118. Summarized from the record books of the Ladies Aid Society, Pisgah Baptist Church.

CHAPTER XVI NOTES

1. *Cal. Bd. Min.:* 153.   2. Richmond *Enquirer,* Aug. 17, 1866.
3. *Cal. Bd. Min.:* 158. The description of the commencement was quoted from the *New Commonwealth* (Farmville) of June 22, 1871.
4. Farmville *Commonwealth,* June 18, 1874.
5. Farmville *Mercury,* Dec. 23, 1875.
6. *Today and Yesterday in the Heart of Virginia:* 59, "Hampden-Sydney College" by W. H. Whiting, Jr.
7. McIlwaine: 347-50; cf. pp. 65-6 for literary society references; B. S. Oliver, long superintendent of buildings and grounds of the college, once told the writer of conditions when dormitory rooms were heated by open fires. The late Dr. W. H. Whiting, Jr., told the writer about the building of the Memorial Hall. Dr. McIlwaine had raised much of the money for the building in Baltimore, and some of the contributors offered to save the college the cost of an architect's fee by drawing plans for the building themselves. When the brick walls had been built, they began to spread, and iron bars had to be put in near the top of the walls to hold them in place.
8. *Today and Yesterday in the Heart of Virginia:* 60, "Hampden-Sydney College" by W. H. Whiting, Jr.
9. Farmville *Herald,* Feb. 27, 1903.   10. Farmville *Herald,* Feb. 19, 1904.
11. *Today and Yesterday in the Heart of Virginia:* 61-2, "Hampden-Sydney College" by W. H. Whiting, Jr.
12. Richmond *Enquirer,* Aug. 18, 1840.
13. The Honor Roll, Hampden-Sydney 14th Alumni Fund, June 1, 1953-May 31, 1954: 3, 4.
14. *V.M.H.B.* 6: 61, 81, 103, 111-4, 117, 127, 130-2, 358-62; 7: 186, 190-1.
15. Broadside, "Claims of Union Theological Seminary, Virginia, on Friends of Theological Education." Signed by B. M. Smith on behalf of the directors, May 17, 1866. Col. W. A. Morgan Papers, University of Virginia Library.

16. Farmville *Herald*, Sept. 16, 1898.
17. *The Commonwealth*, Feb., 1952, "Union Theological Seminary" by Ernest Trice Thompson.
18. Related to the writer by John Cunningham Hunt, son of George Hunt.
19. Farmville *Herald*, Dec. 23, 1893.   20. Farmville *Herald*, July 14, 1894.
21. Farmville *Herald*, July 21, 1894.
22. Farmville *Herald*, July 28, 1894. Was C. D. M. Charles D. McKinney ?
23. Farmville *Herald*, Aug. 18, 1894.   24. Farmville *Herald*, Sept. 15, 1894.
25. Farmville *Herald*, Oct. 5, 1896.   26. Farmville *Herald*, Feb. 2, 1895.
27. Farmville *Herald*, Nov. 9, 1895.
28 Farmville *Herald*, Sept. 16, 1898. Cf. *The Commonwealth*, Feb., 1952, "Union Theological Seminary" by Ernest Trice Thompson. Dr. Thompson related that in 1898 the building at Hampden-Sydney was heated by open fireplaces, the student had to carry his wood and coal, build his own fires; for his bath he had to pump his water, carry it to his room, heat it, and bathe in a wooden tub.
29. Farmville *Herald*, Oct. 22, 1948, "History of Farmville" by Herbert Clarence Bradshaw.
30. *Southside Sentinel* (Burkeville), Dec. 10, 1869.
31. Farmville *Mercury*, Sept. 18, 1873. 32. Farmville *Mercury*, Oct. 30, 1873.
33. Farmville *Mercury*, July 9, 1874.   34. Farmville *Mercury*, May 20, 1875.
35. Farmville *Mercury*, May 27, 1875.   36. Farmville *Mercury*, June 3, 1875.
37. Farmville *Mercury*, June 10, 1875. 38. Farmville *Mercury*, June 24, 1875.
39. Farmville *Mercury*, July 15, 1875.
40. Farmville *Herald*, Oct. 22, 1948, "History of Farmville" by Herbert Clarence Bradshaw.
41. *Acts of Assembly 1883-4:* 417-8.
42. Farmville *Herald*, Oct. 22, 1948, "History of Farmville" by Herbert Clarence Bradshaw; cf. Farmville *Herald*, Oct. 15, Dec. 17, 1897.
43. Dr. J. L. Jarman revealed his attitude toward changing the name of the college in a conversation with the writer.
44. *Today and Yesterday in the Heart of Virginia:* 68-9, "Training School"; Farmville *Herald*, Oct. 22, 1948, "History of Farmville" by Herbert Clarence Bradshaw.
45. The writer has a Liddell and Scott Greek Lexicon used by a great-uncle in the late 1860's in a Prince Edward school as well as an Andrews Latin Lexicon which had been used by his grandfather before the war and by this great-uncle at the time he was using the Liddell and Scott lexicon. That students used the standard lexicons of the classical languages in Prince Edward preparatory schools indicates the quality of work done in the ancient languages. The writer also has a Cooper's Virgil, used by the same great-uncle during those postwar school sessions.
46. Richmond *Enquirer*, Aug. 17, 1866.   47. Farmville *Journal*, Sept. 6, 1868.
48. Minnie V. Rice: History of the Schools of Farmville, mss. lent to the writer by Miss Rice in the preparation of the sesquicentennial history of Farmville.
49. Farmville *Mercury*, July 2, 1874; Feb. 2, June 17, 1875; *Acts of Assembly 1874-5:* 434-5. There is still living in Prince Edward a student who was taught at the academy by Professor Thornton: J. J. Gilliam, now (1954) 98 years of age and still living at Moilena, from which he used to ride horseback to Worsham to school.
50. Farmville *Mercury*, Aug. 12, 1875.
51. Related to the writer by the late Mrs. Hattie Gannaway Crute, who was a student at the school in the early 1870's. Mrs. Crute had lived at Edgewood,

her father's home in Buckingham, but was living at Sheppards when the writer knew her.

52. Farmville *Herald*, May 27, 1893.

53. Farmville *Herald*, Apr. 2, Aug. 27, 1897.

54. Before the War between the States, Richard Edward Booker, a son of Richard Booker of Grampian Hill, attended Richmond College. Two students in that institution in the decade following the war were Samuel B. Witt, whose father, the Rev. Daniel Witt, had been a trustee, and Thomas H. Bruce, who was later active in the public life of Prince Edward. Witt became a lawyer and was subsequently judge of the Hustings Court of Richmond. His love for his native county was proverbial. His friends used to tell of him that he said that most people wanted to go to heaven when they died but just take him back to Prince Edward. Justice John J. Crutchfield of the Richmond Police Court is said to have dismissed a Negro brought before him on a charge after the accused had told the court that he was from Prince Edward County. "If I send you up to Sam Witt, he'll turn you loose when he hears where you're from," the inimitable Justice John is related to have said in dismissing the accused. Also students at Richmond College in the early post-war years were two ministerial students who were members of Sharon Baptist Church, Vernon I'Anson, later pastor of Spring Creek Church, and Joel T. Tucker.

A son of Dr. Daniel Witt, James Witt, attended the Southern Baptist Theological Seminary, then in Greenville, S. C., during its first session, 1859-60; he died after the completion of his first year in the seminary.

The writer has not included in the text of the history the names of the students who attended these schools which were not obtained from the college catalogues, since he cannot be sure of the complete lists. Therefore he mentions in the notes those names of students obtained from other sources to give readers some indication of those who were educated in colleges outside the county.

It may be noted in this connection that Emmett Fox Hilliard, a son of James B. Hilliard of Farmville, was educated at Roanoke College and in law at the University of Virginia in the 1870's. Hilliard practiced law in Farmville and at one time was editor of the Farmville *Journal*; he is said to have been one of the most brilliant editors that newspaper ever had.

55. Among Prince Edward students who attended Randolph-Macon College in the 19th century were William Archer Price of Rice and Dr. Charles B. Crute of Farmville, whose father, Judge J. M. Crute, a native of Buckingham, had been educated there.

56. Catalogue of the Officers and Students of the Virginia Agricultural and Mechanical College, First Session, 1872-3. Pamphlet 19, Vol. 1, Virginia Pamphlets 1860-79, Duke University Library.

57. Catalogue of the Officers and Students of the Virginia Agricultural and Mechanical College, Fourth Session, 1875-6. Pamphlet 19, part 4, Vol. 1, Virginia Pamphlets 1860-79, Duke University Library. Samuel W. Watkins was a captain in the cadet corps that session, and Frank P. Price was a sergeant.

58. *V. M. H.B.* 31: 253. The Rev. J. E. Booker later lived at Hampden-Sydney, a beloved trustee for many years. Charles W. Dabney was a son of Dr. R. L. Dabney and was later president of the University of Tennessee and the University of Cincinnati and an organizer and first president of the Hampden-Sydney Alumni Association in 1926. Francis Preston Venable was born at Longwood, the son of Charles Scott Venable and grandson of Nathaniel E. Venable. He was living at Charlottesville, where his father was professor of mathematics at the University of Virginia, when he went to Göttingen; he became professor of chemistry at the University of North Carolina and at one time (1900-14) was president of that university.

59. Miss Sarah Catherine Weaver, a daughter of William Weaver, attended Hollins Institute prior to the war; she left during her second year in 1857 because of a fever epidemic. After the war Miss Pamelia Agnes Branch, a daughter of John T. Branch and later Mrs. A. Q. Bradshaw, and Miss Sallie Ligon, a daughter of Col. Joseph T. Ligon, attended Hollins.

In addition to Miss Lelia Lockett (later Mrs. Ernest Monnot of Louisiana), Miss Martha Susan Overton (later Mrs. Lindsay B. Walthall) attended Roanoke Female Institute. Mrs. Mamie O. Garnett told the writer of her father's trip to Danville to get her sister and some friends just before the armies reached Prince Edward.

60. Farmville *Herald*, Nov. 03, 1906.   61. Farmville *Herald*, Dec. 21, 1906.

62. J. L. Blair Buck: *The Development of Public Schools in Virginia, 1607-1952:* 65-70; *Acts of Assembly 1871-2:* 81-5.

63. First Annual Report of the Superintendent of Public Instruction for the Year Ending Aug. 31, 1871: 146, 151, 168, 184, 189, 191. Morton Carter, now 102 years old, has told the writer that he attended the first school operated for Negroes in Lockett District in 1870-1. He was then 18 years old, but it was his first opportunity to go to school. The teacher of the school was a white man, William B. Phillips.

The writer has not been able to locate the district records of any district except Farmville, and the complete minutes of the Farmville District School Board have been preserved and were in the office of the superintendent of schools when the writer used them in 1939 in preparing the sesquicentennial history of Farmville (Farmville *Herald*, Oct. 22, 1948.)

The following served as school trustees for Farmville District during the period of the district school boards: T. J. Davis (1870-82), W. D. Rice (1870-78), A. B. Venable (1870-2), [Dr. J. T. ?] Spencer (1872-4), N. E. Venable (1874-83), Dr. Peter Winston (1878-87), W. D. M. Stokes (1882-83, B. S. Hooper (1883-6), R. B. Berkeley (1883-7), S. W. Paulett (1886-1920), W. P. Gilliam (1887-94), Z. A. Blanton (1887-94), L. J. Verser (1894-1903), B. M. Cox (1894-1920), H. E. Barrow (1903-08), —— Jones (1908), N. M. Wilson (1908-11), Dr. W. E. Anderson (1911-22), Dr. J. H. Cocks (1920-22), and Mrs. Roberta H. Large (1920-22).

64. First Annual Report, Supt. Pub. Instr.: 194.

65. First Annual Report, Supt. Pub. Instr.: 184.

66. Minutes, Farmville District School Board, mss.

67. Ninth Annual Report, Supt. Pub. Instr.: xxv.

68. Eleventh Annual Report, Supt. Pub. Instr.: 20.

69. Eleventh Annual Report, Supt. Pub. Instr.: 7, 11, 14.

70. Eleventh Annual Report, Supt. Pub. Instr.: 57.

71. Minutes, Farmville District School Board, mss.

72. Fourteenth Annual Report, Supt. Pub. Instr.

73. Fifteenth Annual Report, Supt. Pub. Instr.

74. Eighteenth Annual Report, Supt. Pub. Instr.

75. Twenty-first Annual Report, Supt. Pub. Instr.: 14, 18.

76. Virginia School Report 1900-1: 282-3; 266-7.

77. Farmville *Herald*, Apr. 4, 1902. Miss Sally Bruce Dickinson was principal of the graded school at Worsham 1891-2 (Biennial Report Supt. Pub. Instr., 1891-2, 1892-3, p. 21).

78. Farmville *Herald*, Nov. 28, 1902.   79. Farmville *Herald*, Mar. 18, 1904.

80. Farmville *Herald*, Mar. 9, 1906.   81. Farmville *Herald*, Sept. 23, 1898.

82. Farmville *Herald*, Feb. 26, 1904.   83. Farmville *Herald*, Feb. 17, 1905.

84. Farmville *Herald*, Aug. 18, 1905.   85. Farmville *Herald*, Mar. 16, 1906.

86. Farmville *Herald*, Apr. 13, 1906.   87. Farmville *Herald*, May 4, 1906.

88. Farmville *Herald*, May 25, 1906.   89. Farmville *Herald*, Sept. 21, 1906.

90. Farmville *Herald*, Sept. 14, 1906.   91. Farmville *Herald*, Aug. 17, 1906.

92. Farmville *Herald*, Mar. 15, 1907.   93. Farmville *Herald*, Mar. 22, 1907.

94. Farmville *Herald*, July 5, Oct. 18, Oct. 25, 1907.

95. Farmville *Herald*, Oct. 18, Oct. 25, 1907.

96. Farmville *Herald*, Oct. 22, 1948, "History of Farmville" by Herbert Clarence Bradshaw.

97. Virginia School Report, 1909-10, 1910-11: 428, 498, 520.

98. Annual Report, Supt. Pub. Instr., 1920-1: 118, 121, 125.

99. Minutes, Farmville District School Board, mss.

100. Information from T. J. McIlwaine, from Minutes of School Trustee Electoral Board, of which he is clerk.

101. *Today and Yesterday in the Heart of Virginia:* 77-80, "Prince Edward Schools" by T. J. McIlwaine, superintendent of schools.

102. Farmville *Herald*, Oct. 22, 1948, "History of Farmville" by Herbert Clarence Bradshaw.

103. Date verified for the writer from School Board records by T. J. McIlwaine.

104. Farmville *Herald*, Oct. 22, 1948, "History of Farmville."

105. *Ibid.*

106. Farmville *Herald*, Apr. 27, May 1, 1951; Durham (N. C.) *Morning Herald*, May 18, 1954, Associated Press dispatch from Richmond summarizing developments in the case; New York *Times*, Mar. 8, 1952, p. 15, col. 8; Feb. 26, 1952, p. 29, col. 4.

107. New York *Times*, Feb. 26, 1952, p. 29, col. 4; Feb. 27, p. 52, col. 3; Feb. 28, p. 18, col. 2; Feb. 29, p. 21, col. 2, Mar. 1, 1952, p. 30, col. 3.

108. New York *Times*, Mar. 8, 1952, p. 15, col. 2.

109. New York *Times*, Mar. 9, 1952, p. 40, col. 1.

110. New York *Times*, Dec. 10, 1952, p. 1, col. 4.

111. Durham (N. C.) *Morning Herald*, May 18, 1954; Farmville *Herald*, July 30, 1954. The Supreme Court subsequently postponed the date for hearings on the decrees until Justice John M. Harlan had been confirmed by the Senate to succeed Justice Robert H. Jackson, who had died since the decision was handed down May 17, 1954, in order that a full court would hear the arguments and participate in the decision. The hearings are now scheduled for April 11, 1955. (See Addendum, page 829.)

CHAPTER XVII NOTES

1. Order Book 28: 209.   2. Order Book 28: 365.

3. Richmond *Enquirer*, Apr. 14, 1868.   4. Richmond *Enquirer*, Apr. 21, 1868.

5. Farmville *Mercury*, Mar. 18, 1875.

6. Farmville *Herald*, Oct. 22, 1948, "History of Farmville" by Herbert Clarence Bradshaw, from information given by Mrs. J. L. Bugg.

7. Farmville *Mercury*, Oct. 30, 1873.

8. Farmville *Mercury*, Nov. 20, 1873, Feb. 5, 1874.

9. Farmville *Mercury*, Feb. 12, 1874.

10. Farmville *Mercury*, Mar. 18, May 20, 1875.

11. Farmville *Mercury*, Sept. 9, 1875.

12. Farmville *Mercury*, Oct. 15, 1874, Apr. 15, 1875.

13. Farmville *Mercury*, July 8, 1875.   14. Farmville *Mercury*, Sept. 9, 1875.

15. Farmville *Mercury*, Oct. 16, 1873.

16. Mss. letter Joseph Sturge of Birmingham to "Dear John," Nov. 17, 1875, John Woodall Papers, Duke University Library. John was John Crisday.

17. Mss. letter Joseph Sturge to John Crisday, Pamplin's Depot, Va., July 19, 1882, John Woodall Papers. There is a third letter to John Crisday in the Woodall Papers, from Mrs. Emma Hodgetts, Hollywood, Eng., to "My dear son John, dated Nov. 27, 1884, advising him of deaths in the family.

18. Richmond *Enquirer*, May 25, 1877. Edgar Allan's identification of himself with the English is interesting. He was born in Birmingham in 1843, but had come as a boy to the United States, served in the Union Army, and did not belong to the postwar migration. He has been remembered in Prince Edward more for his Northern than for his English background. Allan would make an interesting psychological study. There is something pathetic about the man's striving for social recognition in a society which regarded him as a carpetbagger. This aspect of Allan's personality may explain why some of his fellow Republicans turned against him (jealousy may have been another reason) and in turn Allan's desire to form a coalition or fusion with the Conservatives (Democrats), as he did in the Farmville municipal election in 1875.

19. Farmville *Herald*, Feb. 18, 1898.   20. Farmville *Herald*, Mar. 14, 1902.

21. The writer was told by A. L. Cook, son of Adam Cook who was one of the group which came to Prince Edward, that the family name was originally spelled Koche.

22. Mss. letters of J. J. Morgan, Longview, Christian County, Ky., to John Woodall, July 15, 1868; Lucy A. (Mrs. J. J.) Morgan to "Dear Sister" Mar. 24, 1876. John Woodall Papers.

23. Mss. receipts, William Weaver Papers preserved by James R. Weaver and copied from them by the writer.

24. My grandfather, James R. Weaver, has described the difficulties of the times to me. His father, William Weaver, was one of the fortunate few whose tobacco was not destroyed by the invading armies. How it escaped, unless it was the isolated location of the prize barn, I do not know.

25. *Southside Times* (Burkeville), Dec. 10, 1869.

26. Farmville *Mercury*, June 11, 1874.

27. *Southside Sentinel* (Burkeville), Apr. 5, 1878. Major Venable was a member of the Executive Committee of the Virginia State Agricultural Society in 1881 and 1882. See Officers, Rules and Schedules of Premiums for the Fairs of 1881 and 1882. Pamphlets 150 and 151, Vol. 10, Virginia Pamphlets, 1880-99, Duke University Library.

28. Farmville *Commonwealth*, July 10, 1873.

29. Farmville *Mercury*, Mar. 18, 1875.   30. Farmville *Mercury*, June 24, 1875.

31. Farmville *Mercury*, Dec. 18, 1873. No officials were listed in the news account of the organization.

32. Farmville *Mercury*, Feb. 12, 1874.   33. Farmville *Mercury*, Mar. 20, 1874.

34. Richmond *Enquirer*, Apr. 21, 1874.   35. Farmville *Mercury*, May 6, 1875.

36. Farmville *Mercury*, Mar. 18, 1875.   37. Farmville *Mercury*, Apr. 8, 1875.

38. Farmville *Mercury*, July 8, 1875.   39. Farmville *Mercury*, Jan. 20, 1876.

40. *Southside Sentinel* (Burkeville), Apr. 5, 1878.

41. Richmond *Enquirer*, Apr. 21, 1874; Farmville *Mercury*, Jan. 21, 1875; Mar. 25, 1875.

42. Mss. letter, addressed to the Editor of the *Virginia Granger*, dated Cumberland, Mar. 30, 1880, in the handwriting of Walker B. Blanton. James Blanton

Papers, Duke University Library. The inference from this letter is that the Granger store, to which he referred was in Farmville.

43. *Acts of Assembly 1885-6:* 119-20.

44. Proceedings of the Fourth Annual Association of the State Farmers Alliance of Virginia, held in Richmond Aug. 18, 19, 20, 1891. Pamphlet 97 in Vol. 6, Virginia Pamphlets 1880-99, Duke University Library.

45. *Acts of Assembly 1920:* 101. The purpose of this legislative act was to authorize the Circuit Court to convey the property to the Farmers Educational Cooperative Union, as the Alliance had long ceased to exist.

46. W. F. Sheldon: *Populism in the Old Dominion* is the best study of this movement in Virginia known to the author.

47. Farmville *Herald,* June 13, 1902; the farmer was D. J. Weaver.

48. Farmville *Herald,* Nov. 7, 1902; the tobacco referred to in this news account was produced by C. G. Weaver.

49. Farmville *Herald,* Feb. 27, 1903.   50. Farmville *Herald,* Aug. 22, 1902.

51. Farmville *Herald,* Dec. 5, 1902; Jan. 23, 1903.

52. Information from W. W. Fitzpatrick, manager Quail Roost Dairy Farm, Rougemont, N. C.

53. Farmville *Herald,* Oct. 22, 1948, "History of Farmville."

54. Farmville *Commonwealth,* July 10, 1873; related to the writer by his grandfather, J. S. Bradshaw; I have heard my grandfather say that he and Major Venable had the only two machines of this type in Prince Edward County.

55. Farmville *Herald,* July 21, 1953.

56. Mss. letter Mrs. Bettie E. Bradshaw to Mrs. Nannie McGehee Garner, July 27, 1883, original in the possession of W. A. Garner of Roanoke, copied by the writer. The neighbor who couldn't get the help he wanted was John W. Foster.

57. Farmville *Herald,* May 26, 1905.   58. *Acts of Assembly 1869-70:* 513.

59. Farmville *Mercury,* Nov. 5, 1874.   60. Farmville *Mercury,* Jan. 21, 1875.

61. Farmville *Mercury,* Aug. 26, 1875.

62. Farmville *Mercury,* Nov. 25, 1875. The writer has not found a copy of the Burkeville resolutions or any indication of their content.

63. Farmville *Mercury,* Aug. 5, Aug. 19, 1875.

64. Farmville *Herald,* May 27, 1893.   65. Farmville *Herald,* Dec. 10, 1893.

66. Farmville *Herald,* Jan. 4, 1896.   67. Farmville *Herald,* May 21, 1897.

68. Farmville *Herald,* Jan. 11, Mar. 6, May 22, 1896; Sept. 17, 1897; Sept. 12, 1902; May 22, 1903; May 27, 1904. Cf. issue of May 15, 1896, for death of W. T. Johnson. Col. R. A. Booker transferred from Randolph to Farmville Warehouse in 1897.

69. Farmville *Herald,* July 9, 1897. Grover Cleveland was generally blamed for the hard times of the 1890's, much as Herbert Hoover has been in our time for the depression of the 1930's. My grandfather, J. R. Weaver, staunch Democrat that he was, used to depreciate for me the difficulties of that era by pointing out that two of the hired men on his farm during the mid-1890's were able to save enough money to buy farms of their own.

70. Farmville *Herald,* Dec. 11, 1896.   71. Farmville *Herald,* Dec. 12, 1897.

72. Farmville *Herald,* Nov. 14, 1902.   73. Farmville *Herald,* Dec. 11, 1903.

74. Farmville *Herald,* Sept. 2, 1904.   75. Farmville *Herald,* Oct. 6, 1905.

76. Farmville *Herald,* Feb. 19, 1904.   77. Farmville *Herald,* Mar. 4, 1904.

78. Farmville *Herald,* Mar. 18, 1804.

79. Farmville *Herald,* July 1, Oct. 28, 1904.

80. Farmville *Herald,* Nov. 10, 1905.

81. Farmville *Herald*, Jan. 26, Aug. 10, 1906.
82. Farmville *Herald*, Mar. 2, 1906.   83. Farmville *Herald*, July 14, 1905.
84. Farmville *Herald*, Nov. 30, 1906.   85. Farmville *Herald*, Feb. 18, 1898.
86. Farmville Herald, Oct. 22, 1948, "History of Farmville"; for an account of the organization of the Dark-Fired Tobacco Growers Association, see *Today and Yesterday in the Heart of Virginia:* 103-4, "Tobacco Growers Association" by Thomas B. Hall, General Manager.
87. *Today and Yesterday in the Heart of Virginia:* 97, "Farm Organizations" by E. F. Striplin, County Farm Agent, 96, "Demonstration Clubs" by Sourtney Farrar, Home Demonstration Agent.
88. *Acts of Assembly 1885-6:* 38, 347-8.
89. *Acts of Assembly 1889-90:* 992.   90. *Acts of Assembly 1891-2:* 874-6.
91. *Acts of Assembly 1901-2:* 351-2; *1902-3:* 279.
92. Farmville *Herald*, Nov. 20, 1903.   93. Farmville *Herald*, Sept. 21, 1906.
94. The late Frank E. Allen told the writer of the earlier level of the creek at the bridge near his home.
95. Farmville *Herald*, Oct. 22, 1948, "History of Farmville."
96. Farmville *Mercury*, Dec. 18, 1873.
97. Farmville *Herald*, Oct. 22, 1948, "History of Farmville."
98. Farmville *Herald*, Jan. 13, 1894.
99. Farmville *Herald*, Jan. 14, 1893. The writer has seen one of the labels used by the cannery, but does not know of the existence of any now. The cannery was located a short distance east of the railroad station, on the opposite side of the tracks from the present station.
100. *Acts of Assembly 1865-6:* 428.   101. *Acts of Assembly 1866-7:* 820.
102. *Acts of Assembly 1870-1:* 176-7.
103. *Southside Sentinel* (Burkeville), June 27, 1873; Farmville *Commonwealth*, July 10, 1873.
104. Farmville *Mercury*, Sept. 18, 1873; June 24, 1875.
105. Farmville *Commonwealth*, July 10, 1873; Farmville *Mercury*, Oct. 16, 1873.
106. Farmville *Commonwealth*, July 10, 1873.
107. Farmville *Mercury*, July 30, 1874.
108. Farmville *Mercury*, Sept. 24, 1874; Mar. 11, 1875; Jan. 13, 1876.
109. My grandfather, J. R. Weaver, has told me that his father, William Weaveer, accepted several shares of stock in the Farmville Insurance and Banking Company in payment of a loan he had made and that at first he considered it a splendid settlement as the company paid a dividend of 14 per cent; shortly after he acquired the stock, the company failed to pay dividends, and not long afterward the firm failed. Over-expansion in distant areas, beyond the reach of the home office to provide proper supervision, was regarded as the reason for the failure.
110. Farmville *Commonwealth*, July 10, 1873.
111. Farmville *Mercury*, Oct. 9, Oct. 16, 1873.
112. Farmville *Mercury*, Jan. 8, 1874.
113. Farmville *Mercury*, Jan. 29, 1874.
114. Farmville *Mercury*, Mar. 18, Apr. 15, 1875.
115. Farmville *Herald*, Oct. 22, 1948, "History of Farmville."
116. Farmville *Herald*, Apr. 29, 1893.   117. Farmville *Herald*, Jan. 7, 1893.
118. Farmville *Herald*, July 22, 1893.   119. Farmville *Herald*, Aug. 5, 1893.
120. Farmville *Herald*, Aug. 19, 1893.   121. Farmville *Herald*, Mar. 9, 1895.
122. *Acts of Assembly 1897-8:* 556.

123. Farmville *Herald*, Oct. 22, 1948, "History of Farmville"; Mar. 6, 1896.

124. Farmville *Herald*, Mar. 2, Apr. 6, 1895; Jan. 4, May 15, 1896; Jan. 8, 1897.

125. Farmville *Herald*, Mar. 6, 1896; Sept. 24, 1897.

126. Farmville *Herald*, Oct. 22, 1948, "History of Farmville"; Dec. 27, 1905; Apr. 27, 1906; Jan. 8, 1909; Statement of Condition, June 30, 1954, Planters Bank and Trust Company.

127. Farmville *Herald*, Nov. 11, 1900.   128. Farmville *Herald*, Jan. 18, 1901.

129. Farmville *Herald*, Mar. 28, 1902.   130. Farmville *Herald*, Nov. 27, 1903.

131. Farmville *Herald*, June 15, 1906.   132. Farmville *Herald*, Sept. 14, 1906.

133. Farmville *Herald*, May 3, July 12, 1907.

134. Farmville *Herald*, Jan. 7, 1910.

135. Farmville *Herald*, Oct. 22, 1948, "History of Farmville"; Statement of condition of First National Bank, June 30, 1954. Charles W. Gates and J. M. Johns, Jr., were elected directors of the First National Bank in Jan., 1955.

136. Farmville *Herald*, July 11; Aug. 14, 1908; Oct. 22, 1948, "History of Farmville; Statement of condition of Peoples National Bank, June 30, 1954.

137. Farmville *Herald*, Oct. 22, 1948, "History of Farmville."

138. Figures consolidated from statements of condition of the three banks as of June 30, 1954; resources of the banks separately on that date were as follows: First National, $4,914,963.33; Peoples National, $4,567,315.63; Planters Bank and Trust Co., $3,102,290.69.

139. Farmville *Mercury*, Aug. 6, 1874.   140. Farmville *Mercury*, Oct. 1, 1874.

141. Farmville *Mercury*, Sept. 9, Dec. 9, 1875.

142. Farmville *Mercury*, Jan. 13, Feb. 3, 1876.

143. Farmville *Mercury*, Aug. 5, 1875; Jan. 13, 1876.

144. Farmville *Mercury*, Feb. 18, 1875.   145. Farmville *Herald*, Apr. 30, 1909.

146. Mss. statement of account, George M. Robeson, Farmville Foundry and Old Dominion Handle Works, to Walker B. Blanton, Dec. 30, 1878, James Blanton Papers, Duke University Library.

147. Farmville *Herald*, Oct. 22, 1948, "History of Farmville"; *Acts of Assembly 1881-2:* 331.

148. *Acts of Assembly 1883-4:* 485-6.   149. Farmville *Herald*, Oct. 21, 1898.

150. Farmville *Herald*, Oct. 22, 1948, "History of Farmville."

151. Farmville *Herald*, Feb. 23, Aug. 3, 1906.

152. Farmville *Herald*, Apr. 30, 1909.

153. Farmville *Herald*, Oct. 22, 1948, "History of Farmville."

154. Industrial Survey of Farmville, Va., Engineering Extension Division, Virginia Polytechnic Institute: 14.

155. Mss. letter, L. J. Morgan to "Dear Sister," dated Appomattox C. H., Va., Nov. 29, 1871, John Woodall Papers, Duke University Library. This is the latest date at which the writer has found English currency used in prices in Virginia. It was 90 years after Yorktown and 82 after the United States was established. The old usages died hard!

156. Farmville *Mercury*, May 7, 1874.   157. *Acts of Assembly 1875-6:* 275-6.

158. Farmville *Herald*, Jan. 10, 1902; Oct. 30, Nov. 20, 1903; cf. Farmville *Herald*, Oct. 22, 1948, "History of Farmville."

159. Eighth Annual Report of the Commissioner of Agriculture of Virginia, 1885: 32-3, Pamphlet 54, Vol. 3, Virginia Pamphlets 1880-99, Duke University Library.

160. Farmville *Herald*, Oct. 22, 1948, "History of Farmville"; July 8, 1898.

161. Farmville *Herald*, Oct. 22, 1948, "History of Farmville"; cf. issue of Apr. 6, 1906, for announcement of the plans for the plant. The plant planned had

as president Dr. Peter Winston, as manager John R. Martin, as secretary-treasurer E. Scott Martin, and the officers and Dr. W. E. Anderson, H. E. Barrow, William Duvall, and Dr. (R. E. or J. M. ?) Hamlet as the executive committee, W. C. Newman, insofar as the writer can ascertain, owned and operated the ice plant from the beginning of its operations. The history of the business is outlined in an advertisement in the Farmville *Herald*, Oct. 22, 1948.

162. Farmville *Herald*, Oct. 22, 1948, "History of Farmville."

163. Farmville *Mercury*, Jan. 8, 1874.   164. Farmville *Herald*, Dec. 2, 1904.

165. Farmville *Herald*, June 5, 1896; Oct. 29, 1897.

166. Farmville *Herald*, Feb. 2, 1907.

167. Farmville *Mercury*, Mar. 18, Apr. 1, Apr. 22, 1875.

168. *Acts of Assembly 1869-70:* 181-6; *Today and Yesterday in the Heart of Virginia:* 189, "Norfolk and Western Railway" by R. R. Horner.

169. Farmville *Herald*, Oct. 2, 1896.   170. *Acts of Assembly 1870-71:* 295-6.

171. *Acts of Assembly 1874-5:* 47-8; Farmville *Mercury*, July 8, 1875.

172. Farmville *Mercury*, July 8, 1875.   173. Farmville *Mercury*, July 15, 1875.

174. Farmville *Mercury*, Aug. 12, 1875; the tabulation of the vote was not given.

175. Farmville *Commonwealth*, July 18, 1873.

176. *Acts of Assembly 1887*, extra session: 351; *Acts of Assembly 1897-8:* 497-8.

177. Prince Edward Deed Book 39: 312 (B. M. Smith and wife Mary to Orange and Keysville Railroad); 313 (J. D. Eggleston and wife Nannie to Orange and Keysville Railroad). The line of the road bed may be traced on the edge of the athletic field and at other places in the vicinity.

178. First Record Book, Board of Supervisors, entry for Aug. 30, 1889.

179. Farmville *Mercury*, Feb. 18, 1875.

180. Farmville *Mercury*, Aug. 26, Sept. 23, Nov. 11, 1875. This road never reached Prince Edward, but a line over most of the proposed route, Keysville via Chase City, Clarksville, and Oxford, N. C., to Durham, N. C. was built.

181. *Acts of Assembly 1881-2:* 273-5.

182. *Acts of Assembly 1883-4:* 290-2; *1887*, extra session: 297.

183. Prince Edward Deed Book 38: 325; 461-2.

184. Farmville *Herald*, Sept. 1, 1894.   185. Farmville *Herald*, Oct. 20, 1894.

186. Farmville *Herald*, Sept. 1, Nov. 10, Nov. 24, 1894.

187. Farmville *Herald*, June 5, 1896; Oct. 23, 1896.

188. Farmville *Herald*, May 21, 1898.   189. Farmville *Herald*, June 9, 1905.

190. Farmville *Herald*, Mar. 1, May 10, 1907.

191. Farmville *Herald*, May 18; Dec. 28, 1917: news summary for Oct. 28, 1917.

192. Farmville *Herald*, May 30, June 20, July 4, 1902.

193. Farmville *Herald*, Nov. 24, Dec. 1, 1905. The Virginia Railway Company had been chartered in 1902 to build a railway from Rosney, Buckingham County, the terminus of the Dillwyn branch of the Chesapeake and Ohio, to Danville (Farmville *Herald*, May 30, 1902).

194. Prince Edward Deed Book 51: 189 (Mrs. Bettie J. Friend to the Tidewater Railroad Company); Farmville *Herald*, Feb. 23, 1906, notices of requests for appointment of commissioners to condemn certain tracts for the railroad right of way: to Simon and Catherine Zirknetzer, A. W. and George McCormick, John Hoops, —— Hoops, George Call, Conrad Fisher, German Mission School or Lutheran Church property and D. H. Shoff, Clifford Shackleton and wife, and Elizabeth Lyman.

195. Prince Edward Deed Book 62: 245 (T. P. and Mabel D. Shelburne to Norfolk and Western Railway Co. for Burkeville to Pamplin low grade connect-

ing line) contains the first recorded conveyance of right-of-way, dated Apr. 3, 1915. "The Fortifications at High Bridge," *Norfolk and Western Magazine*, January, 1955, pp. 24-7, 60. A photograph of the bridge, taken a few weeks after the fire of Apr. 7, 1865, shows repairs being made to the four spans which had burned.

196. Farmville *Herald*, Sept. 17, 1897.   197. Farmville *Herald*, July 11, 1902.

198. The writer has heard that Dr. R. L. Hudgins was the first person in Prince Edward to own an automobile. Dr. J. D. Terry owned the first car in Rice, buying it about 1912.

199. Farmville *Herald*, Oct. 22, 1948, advertisement of Brickert Oil Co.

200. Farmville *Herald*, Oct. 22, 1948, "History of Farmville"; July 20, 1895; minutes of Farmville Town Council.

201. Farmville *Herald*, Oct. 22, 1948, "History of Farmville"; July 7, 1894; minutes of the Farmville Town Council; *Acts of Assembly 1887*, extra session: 243-4.

202. *Acts of Assembly 1885-6:* 71-2.

203. Farmville *Herald*, Oct. 22, 1948, "History of Farmville"; minutes of the Farmville Town Council.

204. Farmville *Herald*, Feb. 6, 1903; Apr. 15, 1904; minutes of the Farmville Town Council.

205. Farmville *Herald*, July 24, 1903; Oct. 14, Nov. 18, 1904; minutes of the Farmville Town Council.

206. Farmville *Herald*, Mar. 8, 1907.

207. Farmville *Herald*, Oct. 22, 1948, "History of Farmville"; minutes of the Farmville Town Council.

208. The stores of Prince Edward are so numerous that the writer will not undertake to list them. Many have been mentioned in other connections in this work. Particular attention was given to old mercantile firms of Farmville in the sesquicentennial history of the town, Farmville *Herald*, Oct. 22, 1948.

209. Farmville *Herald*, Aug. 10, 1906; July 5, Aug. 9, 1907; Oct. 22, 1948, "History of Farmville."

210. Farmville *Herald*, Oct. 22, 1948, "History of Farmville.

211. Farmville *Herald*, June 9, 1894.

212. Farmville *Herald*, Oct. 22, 1948, "History of Farmville."

213. Farmville *Herald*, May 1, 1894.

214. Farmville *Herald*, Oct. 22, 1948, "History of Farmville"; Farmville *Herald*, Nov. 20, 1903, for suspension of *Southside Examiner*; for changes in ownership during the period, see the Farmville *Commonwealth*, July 10, 1873; announcing sale of paper by J. G. Cannon to St. Andrew, Madison and Co.; Farmville *Mercury*, Jan. 8, 1874, announcing dissolution of partnership of St. Andrew, Madison and Co.; July 16, 1874, announcing ownership of paper by Southside Newspaper Co.; Aug. 13, 1874, officers of Southside Newspaper Co.; J. A. H. St. Andrew, Chase City, president; George W. Endly, Chase City, treasurer; W. J. Clinch, Chase City, secretary and business manager; and directors: Gen. Bradley T. Johnson, Richmond; Col. E. L. Hobson, Richmond; Col. B. W. L. Holt, Richmond; R. J. Farrar, Richmond; Col. W. R. Berkeley, Farmville; George W. Endly; Capt. S. P. Thrower, Mecklenburg; J. A. H. St. Andrew; Maj. W. J. Clinch. A. M. Cowan was office manager at Farmville.

215. Farmville *Herald*, Oct. 22, 1948, "History of Farmville," for comparative prives in 1940, 1946, and 1948 (for the two latter years the prices were quotations in August); July 23, 1954, prices from advertisements of grocery stores.

216. Farmville *Herald*, Oct. 22, 1948, "History of Farmville."

CHAPTER XVIII NOTES

1. Farmville *Herald*, Apr. 29, May 13, May 20, 1898. The men who went from Farmville with the Guard for service in the Spanish-American War were J. Davis Allen, captain, W. P. Venable, first lieutenant, W. E. Anderson, surgeon, J. E. Beach, sergeant, N. M. Gill, sergeant, B. S. Hooper, quartermaster sergeant, W. N. Cunningham, artificer; privates: J. C. Ellis, H. H. Mosley, S. A. Morton, E. W. Nichols, Howell Richardson, Walter Sclater, James F. Shields, H. W. Lucado, T. B. Pettus, Oliver White, William R. Berkeley, J. P. Thackston, B. R. Roberts, S. M. Anderson, J. V. Richardson, Willie Cox, H. A. Hardy, Floyd Morris, J. T. Owen, L. M. Southall, W. A. Talley, E. C. Wallace, R. J. Eubank, B. M. Davis, H. B. Smith, R. H. Roberts, W. J. Barrow, C. W. Gills, J. M. Worsham, J. W. Childress, H. E. Watkins, George B. Shepperson, F. W. McKinney.

2. Farmville *Herald*, May 27, June 10, July 1, 1898.

3. Farmville *Herald*, Sept. 2, Sept. 23, 1898.

4. Farmville *Herald*, May 20, 1898.

5. Farmville *Herald*, Jan. 7, 1893, news summary of 1892; Feb. 25, 1893.

6. Farmville *Herald*, May 11, 25, 1895.

7. Farmville *Herald*, June 20, July 24, 1903.

8. Farmville *Herald*, Jan. 2, 1914, news summary of 1913.

9. Farmville *Herald*, Dec. 29, 1916, news summary of 1916; Dec. 28, 1917, news summary of 1917; information given the writer by Col. D. Walker Paulett.

10. Farmville *Herald*, Oct. 22, 1948, "History of Farmville" by Herbert Clarence Bradshaw; Feb. 2, 1902; Jan. 9, Feb. 11, 1903; Aug. 18, 1905; H. H. Hunt was chosen first lieutenant in 1902 and served under both Captains J. L. Bugg and E. Scott Martin. J. E. Beach became lieutenant when Hunt became captain.

11. Farmville *Herald*, Dec. 28, 1917, news summary of 1917.

12. Farmville *Herald*, Dec. 31, 1915, news summary of 1915.

13. Farmville *Herald*, Jan. 12, 1917.

14. Farmville *Herald*, Dec. 28, 1917, news summary of 1917.

15. *Ibid.*

16. Farmville *Herald*, May 25, 1917.

17. Information given the writer by Col. D. Walker Paulett.

18. Burrell: 201-10.

19. Information given the writer by Col. D. Walker Paulett.

20. Farmville *Herald*, Dec. 28, 1917, news summary of 1917.

21. Burrell: 198-200.

22. Farmville *Herald*, Dec. 28, 1917, news summary of 1917.

23. *Ibid.*

24. Farmville *Herald*, Jan. 3, 1919, news summary of 1918.

25. Farmville *Heerald*, Jan. 2, 1920, news summary of 1919.

26. Burrell: 199.

27. A notebook kept by the writer when he was in the third grade of the Rice School, 1917-8 session, shows that in a contest there the "Blues" sold $7,214.70 in war savings and thrift stamps; the sales of the "Reds" are not recorded but the "Blues" won the contest. This notebook listed three wartime activities for student participation in that school: War Savings Stamps Service, Junior Red Cross, and Victory Boys.

28. Farmville *Herald*, Jan. 3, 1919, news summary of 1918; *Col. Va. State Papers* 2: 506, letter of Robert Lawson to Governor Nelson, Sept. 29, 1781.

29. Farmville *Herald*, Sept. 5, 1919.
30. Minutes Farmville Town Council, entries Dec. 10, 1918, Jan. 13, Feb. 10, Oct. 13, 1925.
31. Information furnished the writer by Col. D. Walker Paulett.
32. Diary of the writer, entry for Oct. 16, 1940.
33. Farmville *Herald*, Oct. 25, 1940.   34. Farmville *Herald*, July 4, 1941.
35. Farmville *Herald*, Feb. 20, 1942.   36. Farmville *Herald*, May 1, 1942.
37. Farmville *Herald*, July 3, 1942.
38. The writer has found no record of the number who registered Dec. 11-13, 1942. Selective service regulations at the time provided against giving out much information. For example, earlier it had been permissible to publish lists of persons called for induction, but the practice was stopped, for security reasons, in the summer of 1942. It is likely that publication of the number of registrants in December of that year was forbidden for the same reason.
39. Farmville *Herald*, Nov. 1, 1940.   40. Farmville *Herald*, Oct. 25, 1940.
41. Farmville *Herald*, Oct. 22, 1948, "History of Farmville." Information for the portion of the sesquicentennial history of Farmville was obtained from the Farmville *Herald* files for the period.
42. *Ibid.*
43. Farmville *Herald*, Aug. 6, 1943. This article and the two cited in the two notes subsequent to this were prepared by this writer when employed during the summer of 1943 by the Farmville *Herald*. Information was obtained in interviews with the managers of the firms mentioned.
44. Farmville *Herald*, Aug. 13, 1943.
45. Farmville *Herald*, Aug. 20, 1943; *Kyanite in Virginia*, Bulletin 38, Virginia Geological Survey.
46. University of Virginia *News Letter*, Nov. 15, 1954, "Virginia's Mineral Resources" by William M. McGill, State Geologist.
47. Farmville *Herald*, Oct. 22, 1948, "History of Farmville."
48. Typescript report dated July 21, 1946, of Virginia World War II History Commission, giving figures compiled by the War Finance Committee of Virginia, a subdivision of the United States Treasury Department. Lent to the writer by J. B. Wall, publisher, the Farmville *Herald*.
49. Farmville *Herald*, Oct. 22, 1948, "History of Farmville."
50. *Ibid.*

CHAPTER XIX NOTES

1. Farmville *Mercury*, Sept. 9, 1875.
2. Richmond *Weekly Whig*, Dec. 8, 1876.
3. Mss. receipt from Collector's Office, Internal Revenue, Fourth District of Virginia, Dec. 13, 1867. James Blanton Papers, Duke University Library.
4. Related to the writer by his grandfather, J. S. Bradshaw. He has told me that after making the announcement that he would not sell whiskey in his store, he received a letter warmly commending him for his position from his pastor, Rev. W. B. Haislip, and he credited his refusal to sell alcoholic beverages in his store as being an important factor in his election as a deacon of Pisgah Baptist Church in 1887. Joe Ross, a colored man who lived on my father's farm when I was a boy, had in his youth lived on the farm of my Grandfather Bradshaw's mother; he remembered well the still there and would recall with pleasure drinking the "low wine" which ran off from the

still while it was in operation. It was much better, he used to tell me, than the moonshine corn whiskey of those prohibition days.

5. Farmville *Herald*, Jan. 2, 1893, news summary of 1892, entries for Apr. 30 and Dec. 22.

6. Farmville *Herald*, Jan. 14, 1893. 7. Farmville *Herald*, Apr. 15, 1893.

8. Farmville *Herald*, Apr. 22, 1893. 9. Farmville *Herald*, July 29, 1893.

10. Farmville *Herald*, Apr. 25, Aug. 24, 1895.

11. Order Book 26: 544.

12. Farmville *Herald*, Mar. 12, 1897. Twenty-five years later I read in the Farmville *Herald* news of twenty-five years before the account of this incident and the conviction of the two men for "moonshining." To my father I expressed surprise that "moonshining," then coming into notoriety in prohibition days, had existed so long before. He told me that "moonshining" was nothing new; he also recalled this particular case. The wife of one of the convicted men was illiterate; she would come to my Grandfather Bradshaw's store and get him to write letters for her to her husband in the penitentiary.

13. Farmville *Herald*, Dec. 18, 1896; Jan. 8, Mar. 19, 1897.

14. Farmville *Herald*, Mar. 2, 1900.

15. *Acts of Assembly 1901*, extra session: 109-13.

16. *Acts of Assembly 1903:* 677-80.

17. Farmville *Herald*, Jan. 3, 1903, news summary of 1902.

18. Farmville *Herald*, Mar. 20, 1903. 19. Farmville *Herald*, Mar. 27, 1903.

20. Minutes, Farmville Town Council, Apr. 2, 1901.

21. Minutes, Farmville Town Council, Dec. 31, 1903, Apr. 12, 1904; Farmville *Herald*, Jan. 8, Mar. 25, 1904.

22. Farmville *Herald*, Feb. 10, 1905. 23. Farmville *Herald*, Jan. 19, 1906.

24. Farmville *Herald*, Feb. 26, 1906.

25. Farmville *Herald*, July 19, 1907; cf. *Acts of Assembly 1902-3*, extra session: 559: the profits of the dispensary were to be divided one-eighth to the state, five-eights to the town of Farmville, and one-fourth to Farmville District.

26. Minutes Farmville Town Council, Apr. 11, 1905, Oct. 12, 1906.

27. Farmville *Herald*, June 13, 1902.

28. Minutes Farmville Town Council, Apr. 12, 1904, Jan. 19, Feb. 9, May 14, June 10, 1909; Jan. 18, July 12, 1910; Apr. 13, 1915.

29. Farmville *Herald*, July 28, 1905.

30. Farmville *Herald*, May 20, June 2, 1911.

31. *Acts of Assembly 1914:* 390.

32. Farmville *Herald*, July 3, July 10, 1914.

33. Farmville *Herald*, Sept. 25, 1914. The vote by precinct on prohibition was (the first figure is the vote for, the second the vote against statewide prohibition): Prospect: 147-7; Abilene: 22-2; Spring Creek: 83-15; Farmville: 193-116; Green Bay: 48-21; Rice: 96-12; Worsham: 37-30; Briery: 14-2.

34. *Acts of Assembly 1916:* 380-1.

35. Minutes Farmville Town Council, Feb. 1, 1916.

36. Minutes Farmville Town Council, Apr. 11, 1916.

37. Farmville *Herald*, Dec. 29, 1916, news summary of 1916.

38. Minutes Farmville Town Council, Oct. 19, 1916.

39. Minutes Farmville Town Council, Sept. 11, 1917.

40. Farmville *Herald*, Oct. 6, 1933.

41. Minutes Farmville Town Council, Aug. 30, Sept. 6, 1933.

42. Minutes Farmville Town Council, June 12, 1934.

43. Farmville *Herald*, Aug. 31, Sept. 14, 1934.

44. Minutes Farmville Town Council, Aug. 13, 1935.

45. Second Record Book, Sharon Vaptist Church, 1860-85.

46. Order Book 1870-4: 271.   47. Farmville *Mercury*, July 15, 1875.

48. Minutes Farmville Town Council, Aug. 23, 1900.

49. Farmville *Herald*, Dec. 21, 1906, news of 32 years ago, from Farmville *Mercury*, Dec. 24, 1874.

50. Farmville *Herald*, Feb. 9, 1902; cf. issue of Feb. 21, 1896, letter urging the legislature to pass "the separate car bill."

51. Farmville *Mercury*, Nov. 27, 1873.

52. Richmond *Enquirer*, Jan. 30, Feb. 27, 1857; B. M. Smith: A Sermon Occasioned by the Death of Charles T. Edie, who was killed by Edward A. Langhorne at Hampden-Sydney College, Virginia, Jan. 27, 1857. Delivered in the College Church, Mar. 22, 1857. The sermon was published at the request of the Union Literary Society. The writer has been told that there was placed upon the prosecutor's table a container of clear fluid, supposedly water, at the trial. The prosecutor was said to have been highly susceptible to the influence of alcoholic beverages and it was later said that this liquid was such a drink. His drinks, during the course of his speech, became more and more frequent, and his speech dwindled from the high eloquence of its peroration into maudlin foolishness. My informant could not vouch for the accuracy of the story, but had heard it in family talk. She was related to both prosecuting and defense attorneys in the case.

53. Farmville *Herald*, Nov. 20, 1896.

54. Farmville *Herald*, Aug. 5, 12, 19, 26, 1897. Judge J. M. Crute presided at the trial, and the jury consisted of J. J. Owen, J. L. Weaver, W. M. Gilliam, C. A. Morton, W. R. Drumeller, S. A. Bondurant, J. F. Chaney, J. J. Gilliam, T. H. Bruce, F. H. Redd, J. N. Foster, and N. W. Scott. Judge and jury after the trial, and also Commonwealth's Attorney A. D. Watkins asked the Governor to commute the sentence to life imprisonment on account of the age of the convicted man; he was then about 67, and it was supposed that he would live only a short time. In 1923 Price was pardoned by Governor E. Lee Trinkle. Then 93 years old, he had made a good record as a prisoner, having cared for the bloodhounds at the State Farm during much of the time of his sentence. I remember hearing Judge Crute, at the time of the pardon, give his recollection of the trial and the case. One of the most pathetic circumstances was that Price when pardoned had no near relatives then living and no where to go. It is my recollection that he lived the remaining few months of his life at the State Farm. In telling of the case, Judge Crute said that he had sentenced to death more men than any other judge in Virginia, a total of 24, six of whom were sentenced at one term of Pittsylvania County Court, when he was presiding in the absence of the regular judge.

55. Farmville *Herald*, Mar. 20, 1896; Nov. 25, 1904; Jan. 13, Mar. 24, 1905.

56. Farmville *Herald*, Apr. 27, May 25, 1906. The murder of Charlie Brown took place on the farm of my grandfather, J. R. Weaver. I have heard members of the family tell that there were frequently fights among the colored people on the place on Saturday evenings, usually the result of drinking. My grandfather was frequently called to settle the disturbances. The troubles reached a climax when Booker killed Brown. I have been told of the sense of awed shock which both white and colored on the place experienced when they heard witnesses calling my grandfather, "Marse Jimmy, Robert's killed Charlie."

57. Farmville *Herald*, June 8, July 26, Aug. 3, Aug. 10, Aug. 17, Aug. 24, Sept. 14, Sept. 21, Sept. 28, Dec. 21, 1906; Jan. 11, Jan. 18, Feb. 15, 1907; General E. E. Goodwyn of Emporia has described to me the search which he shared in making for the money said to have been buried under the church there. He did not recall the name of the pastor of the church there at that time.

The story is related in *Today and Yesterday in the Heart of Virginia:* 175-6, "Last Hanging in Virginia" by Scott Hart.

58. Farmville *Herald*, May 5, Aug. 26, 1898.

59. Farmville *Herald*, Apr. 27, 1906. It should be noted that Booker's attorneys, Judge J. M. Crute and J. Taylor Thompson, made an effort to secure commutation of his sentence to life imprisonment. Governor Claude A. Swanson gave a respite of two weeks, which delayed execution from May 4 to May 18, but beyond that declined to go (Farmville *Herald*, May 4, 1906).

60. Farmville *Herald*, Feb. 15, 1907.

61. Abstract of Farmville *Herald* file on the Clarence Howard case, lent to the writer by J. B. Wall.

62. Related to the writer by his grandfather, J. R. Weaver.

63. Farmville *Mercury*, Apr. 30, 1874.   64. Farmville *Mercury*, May 13, 1875.

65. *Acts of Assembly 1878-9:* 235-42.   66. *Acts of Assembly 1887-8:* 161-2.

67. Farmville *Herald*, June 2, June 9, June 30, Oct. 13, Dec. 15, 1894; Jan. 19, 1895.

68. Farmville *Herald*, May 4, 1895.   69. Farmville *Herald*, May 18, 1895.

70. Farmville *Herald*, Apr. 17, 1896.   71. *Acts of Assembly 1895-6:* 711-2.

72. For an example of these payments, see the Farmville *Herald*, Aug. 17, 1906. There are numerous instances in the records of authorization of payments by the supervisors.

73. Farmville *Herald*, July 20, 1907.

74. Farmville *Herald*, Feb. 7, May 9, 1902.

75. Farmville *Herald*, Apr. 17, 1903.   76. Farmville *Herald*, July 11, 1902.

77. Farmville *Herald*, Feb. 8, 1907.   78. Farmville *Herald*, Apr. 19, 1907.

79. Farmville *Herald*, Aug. 2, 1907. Defeat of this bond issue accounts for the poor condition of Prince Edward roads in the period of good roads agitation. The good roads of Nottoway County in the years prior to the building of the state highways were in decided contrast to Prince Edward roads. When the state took over the upkeep of roads in 1932, Nottoway was one of four counties which originally declined to turn over its roads to the state, largely because they were in good condition. It did not remain outside the general practice long.

80. Related to the writer by the late Dr. J. H. C. Bagby.

81. My father used to tell that at one of the good roads meetings which was attended by several of the staff of the State Highway Commission Capt. S. W. Watkins, the Prince Edward treasurer, advocated good roads very strongly, emphasizing the ability to pay for them. He was followed by his brother, Judge A. D. Watkins, who remarked, "I just don't understand Sam. When you go to his office to collect a claim, he's as poor as a church mouse. But when company comes, he's as rich as a Jew." Judge Watkins was indulging in good natured ribbing, for he was as staunch an advocate of good roads as his brother.

82. Farmville *Herald*, Nov. 9, 1923.

83. Advertisement of Oct. 1, 1876, Inviting Proposals for Carrying the Mails of the United States in the State of Virginia July 1, 1877 to June 30, 1881. James M. Tyne, postmaster general.

84. This list has been compiled fro mreferences in the Farmville *Herald* during that period and from various lists of Prince Edward people and their addresses. In the *Manual Of Roanoke Presbytery*, 1894, the address of one elder, A. W. Womack, is given as County Line Cross Roads, of another, J. W. Womack, Abilene; Abilene is also given as the address of one of the deacons, C. M. Rice. See Farmville *Herald*, Feb. 4, 1893, for establishment of post office at Gardenia; July 28, 1894, for change of name of Cypress to Felden; the corre-

spondent related the remark of an old colored man when he was told that the name of Redd's Shop had been changed some years before to Cypress: "It's been Redd's Shop since I was borned, and I don't see haw it gwine be anything else."

In connection with mention of these offices, it may be of interest to some readers to mention the map of Prince Edward made by Henry Jacobs of Oak Grove, near Darlington Heights, in 1875. A map which he made was exhibited in Alfred Moth's office in Farmville in June. In December it was announced that he was preparing a map of Prince Edward under instructions from the Board of Supervisors on the scale of one inch to one mile; the price of a plain map was 82, or a colored map $2.50. (Farmville *Mercury*, June 10, Dec. 16, 1875.) Miss Elizabeth Singleton, who now lives at Oak Grove, owns the only copy of the Jacobs' map of which this writer knows.

85. Farmville *Herald*, Aug. 17, 1895.   86. Farmville *Herald*, Sept. 18, 1904.

87. Farmville *Herald*, Dec. 2, 1904.   88. Farmville *Herald*, Feb. 14, 1896.

89. Farmville *Herald*, Sept. 16, 1898.   90. Farmville *Herald*, Mar. 21, 1902.

91. Farmville *Herald*, Nov. 25, 1904.   92. Farmville *Herald*, Dec. 16, 1904.

93. *Ibid.*   94. Farmville *Herald*, Nov. 3, 1933.

95. Farmville *Herald*, Sept. 30, 1938.   96. Farmville *Herald*, Dec. 30, 1938.

97. Law Orders 10: 19, 21 (Clerk's Office).

98. Bond Book (Clerk's Office) 7: 201.   99. Farmville *Herald*, Aug. 19, 1893.

100. Farmville *Herald*, July 6, 1895.   101. Farmville *Herald*, Mar. 3, 1895.

102. Supervisors Record Book 8: 186 insert; Auditor's Report for Prince Edward County, 1954, Exhibit D.

103. Order Book 22: 57.

104. Supervisors Record Book 1 (no page number), entry Jan. 17, 1882.

105. Farmville *Herald*, Jan. 26, 1906.   106. Farmville *Herald*, Feb. 16, 1906.

107. Farmville *Herald*, Mar. 10, 1906.   108. Supervisors Record Book 1: 70.

109. Farmville *Herald*, Oct. 22, 1948, "History of Farmville" by Herbert Clarence Bradshaw.

110. *Today and Yesterday in the Heart of Virginia:* 119-20, "Southside Health District" by W. A. Brumfield; Farmville *Herald*, Oct. 22, 1948, "History of Farmville"; Nov. 7, 1952.

111. Farmville Mercury, Sept. 23, 1875.

112. Farmville *Herald*, Oct. 22, 1948, "History of Farmville."

113. *Acts of Assembly 1923*, extra session: 178-85.

114. Farmville *Herald*, Oct. 22, 1948, "History of Farmville."

115. *Acts of Assembly 1926:* 76.

116. Farmville *Herald*, Oct. 22, 1948, "History of Farmville."

117. Dedication Exercise, Mettauer Wing, Southside Community Hospital, Farmville, Va., Aug. 29, 1954 (brochure).

118. Farmville *Herald*, Oct. 22, 1948, "History of Farmville"; Dedication Exercise, Mettauer Wing (brochure).

119. Farmville *Mercury*, Feb. 19, 1874.   120. Farmville *Mercury*, Feb. 26, 1874.

121. Farmville *Mercury*, Mar. 4, 1875.

122. Farmville *Herald*, Dec. 21, 1906, news of 32 years before from the Farmville *Mercury*, Dec. 24, 1874.

123. Farmville *Herald*, Dec. 7, 1895.   124. Order Book 1870-4: 89.

125. Farmville *Herald*, Aug. 17, 1906; I remember well seeing my grandfather, J. S. Bradshaw, who was overseer of the poor for Lockett District from 1897 until 1932, writing orders to merchants in the district (he never issued such an order to his store) to furnish groceries to indigents in the amount approved

by the Board of Supervisors, usually during the period I remember of $2 per month.

126. Farmville *Herald*, Sept. 7, 1906.

127. Second Record Book, Pisgah Baptist Church.

128. Farmville *Herald*, Sept. 5, 1902.

129. Farmville *Herald*, Oct. 22, 1948, "History of Farmville.

130. Prince Edward Will Book 17: 343.

131. Farmville *Herald*, Oct. 22, 1948, "History of Farmville"; Jan. 4, 1935.

132. *Today and Yesterday in the Heart of Virginia:* 120, "Southside Health District" by W. A. Brumfield.

133. Farmville *Herald*, June 28, 1935.

134. Farmville *Herald*, Oct. 22, 1948, "History of Farmville."

135. *Acts of Assembly 1938:* 638-69.

136. Prince Edward Deed Book 96: 425. The deed is dated May 2, 1941.

137. Hening 8: 389-90; 596-7.   138. *Acts of Assembly 1891-2:* 637-8.

139. *Southside Sentinel* (Burkeville), Apr. 5, 1878.

140. Fourth Supervisors Record Book: 243.

141. Farmville *Herald*, Jan. 17, 1902.   142. Farmville *Herald*, July 18, 1902.

143. Farmville *Herald*, Nov. 7, 1902.

144. Farmville *Herald*, Sept. 25, Oct. 2, 1903.

145. Farmville *Herald*, Oct. 23, 1903.

146. Farmville *Herald*, Nov. 6, No. 27, 1903.

147. Farmville *Herald*, Mar. 4, 1904.   148. Farmville *Herald*, Sept. 9, 1904.

149. Farmville *Herald*, Nov. 11, 1904.   150. Farmville *Herald*, Jan. 20, 1905.

151. Farmville *Herald*, June 2, July 7, 1905.

152. Farmville *Herald*, June 9, July 21, 1905.

153. Farmville *Herald*, June 23, 30, 1905.

154. Farmville *Herald*, July 21, 1905.   155. Farmville *Herald*, Aug. 25, 1905.

156. Farmville *Herald*, Sept. 22, Oct. 21, 1905.

157. Farmville *Herald*, Nov. 10, 1905.   158. Farmville *Herald*, Nov. 2, 1906.

159. Farmville *Herald*, May 5, 1905; Jan. 5, 1906.

160. Farmville *Herald*, July 5, Aug. 2, 1907.

161. Farmville *Herald*, Aug. 23, 1907.   162. Farmville *Herald*, Nov. 8, 1907.

163. Farmville *Herald*, Sept. 27, 1912; Landon C. Bell: *The Old Free State II:* 92 has an interesting paragraph on this primary. Bell, pp. 75-98, gives some interesting sketches of the Congressmen who represented Lunenburg; many of these also represented Prince Edward, for 1843-61, 1872 to the present, the two counties have been in the same Congressional district.

164. Farmville *Herald*, June 16, 1914.   165. Farmville *Herald*, Feb. 20, 1948.

166. Farmville *Herald*, Aug. 10, 1917.   167. Farmville *Herald*, Aug. 4, 1922.

168. Farmville *Herald*, Aug. 7, 1925.   169. Farmville *Herald*, Aug. 9, 1929.

170. Farmville *Herald*, Nov. 8, 1929.   171. Farmville *Herald*, Nov. 6, 1953.

172. Farmville *Herald*, July 17, 1953.   173. Farmville *Herald*, Aug. 5, 1949.

174. Farmville *Herald*, Nov. 6, 1908.

175. Richmond *Times-Dispatch*, Nov. 6, 1912.

176. Farmville *Herald*, Nov. 10, 1916.   177. Farmville *Herald*, Nov. 5, 1920.

178. Farmville *Herald*, Nov. 7, 1924.   179. Farmville *Herald*, Nov. 9, 1928.

180. Farmville *Herald*, Nov. 11, 1932.   181. Farmville *Herald*, Nov. 6, 1936.

182. Farmville *Herald*, Nov. 8, 1940.   183. Farmville *Herald*, Nov. 10, 1944.

184. Farmville *Herald*, Nov. 5, 1948.   185. Farmville *Herald*, Nov. 7, 1952.
186. Farmville *Herald*, June 8, 1911.   187. *Ibid.*
188. Farmville *Herald*, Aug. 6, 1915.   189. Farmville *Herald*, Nov. 5, 1915.
190. Farmville *Herald*, Aug. 9, 1935.   191. Farmville *Herald*, Aug. 4, 1939.
192. Farmville *Herald*, Aug. 8, 1919.   193. Farmville *Herald*, Aug. 7, 1925.
194. Farmville *Herald*, Aug. 5, 1927.   195. Farmville *Herald*, Aug. 4, 1933.
196. Farmville *Herald*, Aug. 9, 1935.   197. Farmville *Herald*, Aug. 8, 1941.
198. Farmville *Herald*, Aug. 6, 1943.   199. Farmville *Herald*, Aug. 6, 1915.
200. Farmville *Herald*, Aug. 8, 1919.   201. Farmville *Herald*, Aug. 5, 1927.
202. Farmville *Herald*, Aug. 7, 1931.   203. Farmville *Herald*, Nov. 11, 1949.
204. Farmville *Herald*, Aug. 2, 1907; June 9, 1911.
205. Farmville *Herald*, Aug. 10, 1923.   206. Farmville *Herald*, Aug. 7, 1931.
207. Farmville *Herald*, Aug. 10, 1951.   208. Farmville *Herald*, Aug. 6, 1915.
209. Farmville *Herald*, Aug. 10, 1923.   210. Farmville *Herald*, Aug. 5, 1927.
211. Farmville *Herald*, Aug. 6, 1915.   212. Farmville *Herald*, Aug. 7, 1931.
213. Farmville *Herald*, Aug. 9, 1935.   214. Farmville *Herald*, Aug. 10, 1951.
215. Farmville *Herald*, June 9, 1911.   216. Farmville *Herald*, Aug. 6, 1915.
217. Farmville *Herald*, Aug. 8, 1919.   218. Farmville *Herald*, Aug. 7, 1931.
219. Farmville *Herald*, Aug. 4, 1939.
220. Fourth Supervisors Record Book: 380.
221. Farmville *Herald*, Aug. 10, 1923.   222. Farmville *Herald*, Aug. 5, 1927.
223. Farmville *Herald*, Aug. 9, 1935.   224. Farmville *Herald*, Aug. 4, 1939.
225. Farmville *Herald*, Aug. 6, 1943.
226. Seventh Supervisors Record Book: 272.
227. Farmville *Herald*, Aug. 10, 1951.
228. Farmville *Herald*, June 2, Nov. 10, 1911; see issue of Aug. 23, 1907, "Election Contest Dismissed," for first reference to E. L. Dupuy as county Democratic chairman.
229. Farmville *Herald*, Nov. 9, 1923.
230. McDanel: *Virginia Constitutional Convention of 1901-2:* 158.

CHAPTER XX NOTES

1. The best biography of Patrick Henry remains that written by his grandson, William Wirt Henry, although publication of the biography by Dr. Robert D. Meade, professor of history in Randolph-Macon Woman's College, Lynchburg, is expected soon. The Meade biography, the result of some ten years of research and writing, promises to become the definitive Henry biography. The writer of this work summarized Henry's career in a feature published in the Richmond *Times-Dispatch*, May 26, 1946, and it is from notes for this feature, largely from the Henry biography, that the information in this paragraph is contained.

2. The frequent references to Philip W. McKinney in the chapter on Reconstruction indicate the leading part which he played in Prince Edward in that period. He was born in Buckingham May 1, 1832, graduated at Hampden-Sydney in 1851, and died in Farmville, March 1, 1899.

3. *Dictionary of American Biography* (hereafter cited as *D.A.B.*) 13: 383-4; *Biog. Dict. Cong.:* 1607; *V.M.H.B.* 11: 80. All three authorities give Nash's birthplace as Prince Edward County, *D.A.B.* giving it as Amelia, later Prince

Edward. That authority gives the year as about 1740. *Biog. Dict. Cong.* gives an exact date, Aug. 8, 1740. Earlier in this work, the writer dated the removal of John Nash, the father, to his Templeton holdings about 1743 on the basis of Amelia records, especially that in which Nash was recommended for appointment to the Amelia Court with the same rank he held in Henrico (see page 13). It would seem an unduly long time for the Court to wait to make such a recommendation if Nash had been living in the county as early as 1740. The election of Abner Nash to the House of Burgesses in 1761 indicates that he was at least 21 years of age at that time. Since all three authorities are secondary sources, it would be interesting to learn on what authority they locate the birthplace of Abner Nash as Templeton. This writer thinks the matter merits further investigation, as the circumstances suggest that Abner Nash was born before his father moved from Henrico to Amelia, unless he lived temporarily at Templeton about 1740. The service of John Nash on an Amelia Grand Jury in 1737 (Amelia Order Book 1: 31) indicates that he was living there at the time, but subsequent references and lack of references indicate that he was living in Henrico later (Amelia Order Book 1: 42, for example). His high rank on the Henrico Court (fifth, if the Governor approved the recommendation of the Amelia Court) indicates that he was well established in Henrico before moving to Amelia. Francis Nash, whose birth is set in *D.A.B.* 13: 384-5 at about 1742, might have been born at Templeton, since the approximate date fits the time when it is certain John Nash was living in Amelia. Another factor which suggests that John Nash did not come to Templeton until about 1743 is that the Amelia Court did not prior to that time appoint him to perform any public duties, as he was subsequently asked to do. His first appointment as a road surveyor was in Oct., 1743 (Amelia Order Book 1: 248). Abner Nash died Dec. 12, 1786, in New York, while attending a session of Congress. For the Nash genealogy, see *V.M.H.B.* 45: 109-13.

4. *Biog. Dict. Cong.*: 1972-3; *D.A.B.* 19: 403-4; *W. & M. Quart.* (1) 15: 279: Abstract of power of attorney in Prince Edward: "Whereas Robert Walton, late of the county of Cumberland, in the colony and dominion of Virginia, gentleman, decd. by will recorded at Cumberland aforesaid, in 1749, nominated George Walton the elder now of Prince Edward County and Tucker Woodson now of Goochland County, Virginia, executors. By said will gave lands to sons and daughter, John Walton, Robert Walton, Sarah Walton since married to Thomas Watkins, and George Walton Jun. of Savannah, Ga. George Walton the younger desiring partition, and Robert of Charlotte, one of legatees, having undertaken to effect it, the deed empowers him to act. Acknowledged before Joseph Pearson, late of Charlotte County, now on the river of Savannah, Ga., May 1, 1772."

Cumberland Will Book 1: 15-17. In Robert Walton's will, dated Feb. 27, 1746 (1747, current reckoning), he made bequests to two sons, John and Robert, and his wife Mary, who was named executrix. The will also provided that "if my loving wife Mary is now with child," the Negroes willed to Robert should be equally divided between this child and Robert. Robert Walton added a codicil to his will Sept. 5, 1749, in which bequests were made to sons John and Robert, daughter Sarah, and "the child my wife now goes with." Tucker Woodson and George Walton (the latter of Prince Edward) were named executors in the codicil, instead of Mrs. Mary Walton. From the will and codicil the approximate dates of the births of the two younger children may be determined. It is likely that Sarah Walton was not born until at least six or seven months after the will was written, her birth probably taking place in the late summer or fall of 1747, since Mrs. Walton's pregnancy was not certain at the time the will was written. George Walton, the signer of the Declaration of Independence, was the expected child mentioned in the codicil, but since pregnancy was certain when the codicil was written, the birth of George Walton almost certainly took place within six or seven months after Sept. 5, 1749, either in the fall or winter of 1749-50 (under reckoning then it was 1749 until Mar. 19). Robert Walton's will was probated in

Cumberland June 25, 1750, evidence that his death took place before that time. It is not known whether George Walton the signer was born before or after the death of his father. The will book notes that probate was granted Mary Walton. A note inserted May 23, 1757, calls attention to a discrepancy between the will book and the minute book (order book), the entry in the will book being described as an error and corrected, the notation showing that George Walton (Sr.) and Tucker Woodson were given probate.

Guardian accounts for the children of Robert Walton are recorded in Cumberland Will Book 1: p. 395, account of John Hughes as guardian of Robert Walton, orphan of Robert Walton, 1760; pp. 396-8, account of George Walton, guardian of Sally Walton, orphan of Robert Walton, 1757-60; pp. 398-9, account of George Walton, guardian of George Walton, orphan of Robert Walton, 1757-60; p. 400, account of Tucker Woodson, guardian of John Walton, orphan of Robert Walton, 1758; pp. 406-7, account of George Walton, guardian of Sally Walton, 1760-1; pp. 408, 416-7, account of George Walton, guardian of John Walton, 1761 (he has taken Woodson's place as John's guardian); p. 416: account of George Walton, guardian of George Walton, 1762-3.

From the power of attorney it is obvious that George Walton, Jr., of Savannah, Ga., was the child Robert and Mary Walton were expecting when Robert Walton made his will Sept. 5, 1749.

There is disagreement about the place and time of Walton's birth. *V.M.H.B.* 11: 80 gives the place as Frederick County, Va. Two old collections of biographies of signers of the Declaration of Independence, Benson John Lossing: *Biographical Sketches of the Signers of the Declaration of Independence* (New York, 1848): 234-7 and (John) *Sanderson's Biography of Signers to the Declaration of Independence*, revised and edited by Robert T. Conrad, (Philadelphia, 1847): 828 give the same place and both give the year as 1740. A later work, Charles C. Jones: *Biographical Sketches of the Delegates from Georgia to the Continental Congress* (Boston, 1891): 168, gives Walton's birthplace as Prince Edward County, Virginia, and the date 1749. *D.A.B.* gives the year as 1741 and the place near Farmville, Prince Edward County, Va. *Biog. Dict. Cong.* gives the year 1750 and the place near Farmville, Cumberland County. From Robert Walton's will, it is obvious that the year of George Walton's birth was either 1749 or 1750. It is also obvious that the place was either Prince Edward or Cumberland. Since Robert Hughes lived in Cumberland, there is a presumption in favor of that county, certainly if George Walton was born before his father's death. If George Walton was born after his father's death, it is quite likely that his mother, whose maiden name was Mary Hughes, may have gone to the home of her sister Martha, who married George Walton of Prince Edward, for her accouchement. It is not improbable that she may have gone to her sister's home for the event even if her son was born before his father's death. Thus it seems that Prince Edward and Cumberland may claim Walton as a son, just as North Carolina and South Carolina claim Andrew Jackson— and under similar circumstances. George Walton died Feb. 2, 1804.

George and Matthew Walton, the latter a Representative from Kentucky 1809-11, are described as cousins in *Biog. Dict. Cong.* The writer has been unable to find the parentage of Matthew Walton, and *Biog. Dict. Cong.* does not give the place or exact date of his birth. There is the probability that he may have lived in Prince Edward, may even have been a native of the county. His marriage bond, for his marriage to Frances Watkins, a daughter of Henry Watkins, dated Jan. 25, 1791, is found in the Prince Edward records. There is then the strong probability that Matthew Walton should be listed in the chapter, "Those Who Attained High Rank."

5. *Biog. Dict. Cong.:* 846; *D.A.B.* 2: 235; *V.M.H.B.* 11: 80-1. The last reference cited gives the birthplace of the Bibb brothers as Amelia. The two former, which treat only William Wyatt, give his birthplace as Prince Edward, which it almost certainly was. Their father, William Bibb, was a member of the convention of 1775 from Prince Edward and of the House of Delegates from

the county in 1777. *Biog. Dict. Cong.* gives William Wyatt Bibb's birth date as Oct. 1, 1780; *D.A.B.* gives it as Oct. 2, 1781, both though at a time William Bibb was living in Prince Edward as he appointed a justice in 1776 and became sheriff in 1788. *D.A.B.* identifies Thomas as William Wyatt Bibb's brother, in mentioning him as successor in the governorship of Alabama; Thomas succeeded to the office by virtue of being president of the Alabama State Senate. H. T. Owen of Richmond (*V.M.H.B.* 18: 195-6) undertook to disprove the statement that the Bibbs were natives of Amelia by reference to the land book for 1782 and land grants.

6. *Biog. Dict. Cong.:* 1704; *V.M.H.B.* 11: 82; Farmville *Herald*, Nov. 30, 1906. Price was born Sept. 20, 1809, died in St. Louis Sept. 29, 1867.

7. *Biog. Dict. Cong.:* 1460; *V.M.H.B.* 11: 82. Ligon was born May 10, 1810, the son of James Ligon and Martha Watkins Ligon, died Jan. 12, 1881. See Richmond *Enquirer*, Aug. 10, 1853, for his nomination for Governor of Maryland on the Democratic ticket. My Grandfather Weaver, who remembered seeing Governor Ligon when he visited his brother, James D. Ligon, at Walnut Hill, told me that one of Ligon's relatives who was a prisoner of war in one of the Federal prisons in Maryland wrote to Governor Ligon in anticipation of getting some aid in being released. Governor Ligon got word back to his kinsman that he would like to help him, but that he was being closely watched under suspicion of being a Southern sympathizer and that he was therefore unable to help.

8. *D.A.B.* 1: 191-2; Farmville *Herald*, Nov. 30, 1906; *V. M. H. B.* 11: 82. The son of Dr. Thomas Allen and Ann Watkins Allen, Allen was born Apr. 29, 1820, died Apr. 29, 1866. He removed when a boy to Missouri with his father, later ran away from college to Mississippi, taught school, and studied law. He eloped with his wife, but was later reconciled with his father-in-law, who proved generous. Douglas Southall Freeman in the *D.A.B.* sketch praises Allen for the vigorous and effective measures he took as Governor of Louisiana; he regarded him as one of the ablest Southern administrators. The Prince Edward tradition that Allen and his first cousin Thomas Watkins Ligon played together as boys at their grandfather's home, Oldham, seems the product of imagination. The difference of 10 years in their ages makes one doubt that they were playmates, although of course they would have known each other when Allen was a small boy and Ligon in his teens.

9. *Biog. Dict. Cong.:* 1915. Abraham B. Venable was born at Slate Hill Nov. 20, 1758, perished in the Richmond Theatre fire, Dec. 26, 1811.

10. *Biog. Dict. Cong.:* 846; *D.A.B.* 2: 235. George M. Bibb was the son of Richard and Lucy Booker Bibb. He was born Oct. 30, 1776, died Apr. 14, 1859. *D.A.B.* gives Bibb's middle name as Mortimer. The writer follows *Biog. Dict. Cong.* in giving it as Motier.

11. *Biog. Dict. Cong.:* 904-5; *D.A.B.* 3: 180. Blanche K. Bruce was born Mar. 1, 1841, Died Mar. 17, 1898. The late Dr. J. D. Eggleston told the writer that he had heard that Bruce was born at Linden, home of Allen Watson, later of Robert E. Stokes, and now of G. L. Cox. *Biog. Dict. Cong.* gives his birthplace as near Farmville, Prince Edward County; *D.A.B.* as Farmville.

12. *Biog. Dict. Cong.:* 998. John Coffee was born in Prince Edward Dec. 6, 1782, died at his home near Jacksonville, Ga., Sept. 25, 1836. *V.M.H.B.* 18: 196 quotes a letter from H. T. Owen of Richmond: about 1872-3, someone stated that General John Coffee was born in Amelia County. Abram Venable of the Farmville *Journal* replied that John Coffee was born on Mill Fork of Vaughan Creek 12 or 15 years after the formation of Prince Edward. *Biog. Dict. Cong.* confirms Prince Edward as his birthplace and shows that he was born 28 years after the formation of the county.

13. *Biog. Dict. Cong.:* 1167. Thomas Stanhope Flournoy was born Dec. 15, 1811, died Mar. 12, 1883. He was educated at Hampden-Sydney. Flournoy was

defeated for re-election to Congress in 1848. He ran unsuccessfully for Governor of Virginia in 1855 and 1863.

14. *Biog. Dict. Cong.:* 1955. Abraham Watkins Venable was born at Springfield Oct. 17, 1789, the son of Samuel Woodson Venable, and died Feb. 24, 1876. He was educated at Princeton. Venable was defeated for re-election to Congress in 1852.

15. *Biog. Dict. Cong.:* 1381, 1382. Charles Clement Johnston was born Apr. 30, 1795, died by drowning June 17, 1832; Joseph Eggleston Johnston was born Feb. 3, 1807, died Mar. 21, 1891.

16. *Biog. Dict. Cong.:* 1955. Edward Carrington Venable was born Jan. 31, 1852, died Dec. 8, 1908.

17. *Biog. Dict. Cong.:* 1390. Joseph Jorgenson was born in Philadelphia, Penna., Feb. 11, 1844; was register of the land office in Walla Walla, Wash., 1883-6; and died in Portland, Ore. Jan. 21, 1888.

18. *Biog. Dict. Cong.:* 1327. Benjamin Stephen Hooper was born in Buckingham County, Mar. 6, 1835, died Jan. 17, 1898.

19. *Biog. Dict. Cong.:* 1083. Clement Cabell Dickinson was born Dec. 6, 1849, died Jan. 14, 1938. He was defeated for re-election in 1920, 1928, and 1934.

20. The career of Robert Lawson has been treated in some detail in earlier chapters of this work.

21. *D.A.B.* 13: 384-5.

22. *Biog. Dict. Cong.:* 998.

23. *Biog. Dict. Cong.:* 1704; Farmville *Herald*, Nov. 30, 1906.

24. Farmville *Herald,* Nov. 30, 1906; *Biog. Dict. Cong.:* 1704; *D.A.B.* 1: 191-2. Both Price and Allen went to Mexico; Allen died there in 1866, but Price returned to Missouri. They are examples of the migration of ex-Confederates to other lands during the difficult times for them immediately after the surrender of the Confederate armies.

25. *Biog. Dict. Cong.:* 1382; *D.A.B.* 10: 144-6. The most extensive biography of Joseph E. Johnston is by a kinsman, Robert W. Hughes. Johnston's unpleasant relations with Jefferson Davis have been explored and discussed by numerous writers on Confederate history.

26. *D.A.B.* 19: 245-6; Farmville *Herald*, Oct. 22, 1948, "History of Farmville." Charles Scott Venable was born Apr. 11, 1827, died Aug. 11, 1900.

27. *D.A.B.* 5: 20-1. Robert Lewis Dabney was born Mar. 5, 1820, in Louisa County, Va., died Jan. 3, 1898 in Texas.

28. Farmville *Herald,* Oct. 22, 1909. Andrew Reid Venable, Jr., was born in 1831, the son of Samuel Woodson Venable, Jr., and Jane Reid Venable. He died Oct. 15, 1909. There were two Major Andrew Reid Venables who were contemporary in Prince Edward. This Major Venable is usually designated Jr. The other Major A. R. Venable was a son of William Henry Venable (who was a son of Richard N. Venable) and lived at Hickory Hill.

29. Herbert Clarence Bradshaw: *The McGehee Family,* mss. Simeon Taylor Walton was the son of William M. Walton and Mary Wootton Walton of Osceola; he was born Mar. 24, 1829, and was killed in battle at Verdiersville, Nov. 27, 1863. Soldiers in his command said that when his body was brought back to camp, his commission as brigadier general was awaiting him. This statement has not been confirmed from records, but he was referred to as General Walton and it is said that he was the only person from Charlotte County to reach the rank of brigadier general in the Confederate Army. The magisterial district of Charlotte County which includes Keysville is named for him, as is the U.D.C. chapter at Keysville. Confederate veterans used to say also that because of the great need of surgeons in Confederate Army hospitals, Dr. Walton was urged to transfer to that branch of service, but he declined, expressing a preference for service in the field.

30. J. L. B. Buck: *The Development of Public School Education in Virginia, 1607-1952:* 140-62. This chapter contains a detailed account of the activities and service of J. D. Eggleston as superintendent of public instruction.

31. Robert Russa Moton: *Finding A Way Out.* Dr. Moton relates memories of his early life and the account of his ancestral background, pp. 4-50. Of particular interest is his account of his mother's ancestors, including the ancestor who was brought from Africa and sold into slavery in this country. White people tend to think that the Negro's knowledge of his ancestry goes back only to emancipation or the latter part of the slavery era, and in many cases this is true. In Dr. Moton's case, however, knowledge of ancestry to his immigrant African ancestor had been handed down in the family. Dr. Moton's mother in her latter years lived at High Bridge, and Dr. Moton visited her regularly. The writer recalls seeing Dr. Moton on some of these visits. His mother is remembered as "Aunt Emily Jeter."

32. Howard Atwood Kelly: *Walter Reed and Yellow Fever* (see pp. 3-6 for his boyhood and references to Farmville); *Today and Yesterday in the Heart of Virginia:* 377-80: "Walter Reed" by G. W. Jeffers. A popular account of Reed may be found in Paul DeKruif: *Microbe Hunters. D.A.B.* 15: 459-61 gives 1852 as the date of the Reed family's removal to Farmville; this is five years too early. The writer's notes on assignments to the Prince Edward Circuit and the Farmville Methodist Church from contemporary newspapers (Richmond *Enquirer*, Nov. 11, 1851, Nov. 5, 1852, Dec. 12, 1854, Dec. 9, 1856, Dec. 1, 1857, Nov. 23, 1859) show that the Rev. L. S. Reed was assigned to the Prince Edward Circuit in 1857 (the date given in Professor Jeffers' account). My notes do not include assignments for 1858, and Reed may have continued on the circuit that year. He was not assigned to Prince Edward in 1859. Walter Reed's teacher, Mrs. Booker, has not been positively identified; some information received by the writer in the preparation of his history of Farmville led him to think that she was probably the wife of George E. Booker who was associated with the Morrisettes in the Southside Institute. Walter Reed's life in Farmville was comparatively brief, probably not more than two years.

CHAPTER XXI NOTES

1. Landon C. Bell: *The Old Free State* I: 9. Quoted from *W. & M. Quart.* (2) 6: 358.

2. Farmville *Herald*, May 11, 1895.

3. Farmville *Herald*, June 19, June 26, 1896.

4. Farmville *Herald*, Aug. 29, Sept. 19, 1902.

5. Farmville *Herald*, Mar. 27, 1896.   6. Farmville *Herald*, Sept. 7, 1895.

7. Farmville *Herald*, Nov. 30, 1895.   8. Farmville *Herald*, Dec. 4, 1896.

9. Farmville *Herald*, Feb. 1, Feb. 21, 1896. The writer when a teacher in McGuire's University School, Richmond, boarded in the home of a daughter, Mrs. A. W. Via. Mrs. Via then had her father's drawings of the battle of the *Virginia (Merrimac)* and the *Monitor;* they were excellent.

10. Farmville *Herald*, May 14, 1897.   11. *Acts of Assembly 1899-1900:* 668.

12. Farmville *Herald*, June 2, 1905.

13. Farmville *Herald*, June 9, 1905; June 1, 1906.

14. Farmville *Mercury*, Nov. 20, 1873.   15. Farmville *Mercury*, Nov. 27, 1873.

16. Farmville *Mercury*, Jan. 7, 1875.   17. Farmville *Mercury*, Oct. 14, 1875.

18. Farmville *Herald*, Aug. 7, 1896. The newspaper account gave no more identification of Miss Leath of Burkeville. As there were several Misses Leath of Burkeville at the time, the identification is quite vague.

19. Farmville *Herald*, Sept. 4, 1896.   20. Farmville *Herald*, Oct. 9, 1896.
21. Farmville *Herald*, Nov. 15, 1896.   22. Farmville *Herald*, Sept. 30, 1904.
23. Farmville *Herald*, Sept. 13, 1907. The ball took place Sept. 6, 1907.
24. Farmville *Herald*, Feb. 21, 1896. Miss Mary Glenn is now Mrs. W. H. Glenn.
25. Farmville *Herald*, Feb. 18, 1898.   26. Farmville *Herald*, Oct. 30, 1896.
27. Farmville *Mercury*, Feb. 5, 1874.   28. Farmville *Mercury*, Feb. 18, 1875.
29. Farmville *Mercury*, Jan. 6, 1876.   30. Farmville *Herald*, Mar. 20, 1903.
31. Farmville *Herald*, Dec. 4, 1903.   32. Farmville *Herald*, Jan. 22, 1904.
33. Farmville *Herald*, Dec. 11, 1896.   34. Farmville *Herald*, Apr. 15, 1898.
35. Farmville *Herald*, Aug. 10, 1895.   36. Farmville *Herald*, Feb. 3, 1905.
37. Farmville *Herald*, May 26, 1905.   38. Farmville *Herald*, Sept. 25, 1896.
39. Farmville *Herald*, Feb. 24, 1894; long before I read an account of this party in the newspaper files, my father had told me of it. He was only a boy at the time, but he was invited to the supper. The music impressed him very much; it was the first time he heard *There'll Be a Hot Time in the Old Town Tonight*, now so familiar. When he learned that some of the young men were shouldering the responsibility of preventing an elopement, an exciting flavor was added which made this supper a memorable occasion.
40. Farmville *Mercury*, Apr. 15, 1875.
41. Farmville *Herald*, Dec. 8, Dec. 15, 1894.
42. Farmville *Herald*, Jan. 7, 1893, news summary of 1892, for news of the elopement. The mother's account of her daughter's elopement I have heard her tell.
43. The copy of the Fuqua-Morton marriage bond was sent to the writer by a descendant of the couple, the Rev. William J. Gammon, Mo. He had copied it from the original in the Clerk's Office, Farmville. The marriage bonds are rarely available now for inspection, but in Prince Edward there is in the Clerk's Office an index to the marriage bonds which provides the genealogical information most people are seeking. Also in the Clerk's Office are the registers of marriages, births, and deaths.
44. Farmville *Herald*, May 27, 1893; May 26, 1894.
45. Farmville *Herald*, July 28, 1894.   46. Farmville *Herald*, July 20, 1895.
47. Farmville *Mercury*, July 23, 1874.   48. Farmville *Mercury*, July 30, 1874.
49. Related to the writer by John Cunningham Hunt of Waco, Tex., a son of George Hunt; Farmville *Herald*, Jan. 21, 1893; Jan. 5, 1895; Jan. 4, 1896, news summary of 1895.
50. Farmville *Herald*, Oct. 14, Oct. 21, 1893.
51. Farmville *Herald*, Oct. 6, 1894.   52. Farmville *Herald*, Mar. 27, 1896.
53. Farmville *Herald*, Sept. 17, 1897.   54. Farmville *Herald*, Oct. 15, 1897.
55. Farmville *Herald*, June 29, 1906.
56. Farmville *Herald*, June 30, 1907. Tom Fenton's owner is identified only as Mr. Blanton of Cumberland; as there were numerous "Mr. Blantons" in Cumberland at the time, the identification is inadequate.
57. Farmville *Herald*, June 23, 1894.   58. Farmville *Herald*, July 30, 1895.
59. Farmville *Herald*, Jan. 6, 1894.   60. Farmville *Herald*, Jan. 12, 1895.
61. Farmville *Mercury*, Nov. 4, 1875.   62. Farmville *Mercury*, Mar. 19, 1874.
63. Farmville *Herald*, June 2, 1911; Jan. 5, 1912, news summary of 1911.
64. Farmville *Herald*, Jan. 4, 1929, news summary of 1928.
65. Farmville *Herald*, Oct. 22, 1948, "History of Farmville."
66. Farmville *Mercury*, Mar. 26, 1874. 67. Farmville *Herald*, Jan. 13, 1894.
68. Farmville *Herald*, Dec. 2, 1893.
69. Farmville *Herald*, Dec. 1, 1905; Oct. 22, 1948, "History of Farmville."

70. Farmville *Mercury*, Sept. 3, 1874. 71. Farmville *Herald*, Sept. 14, 1906.

72. Farmville *Herald*, June 30, July 14, 1894.

73. Farmville *Herald*, July 13, 1895.

74. Related to the writer by his grandfather, J. S. Bradshaw.

75. Farmville *Herald*, July 22, 1898. 76. Farmville *Herald*, Aug. 24, 1895.

77. Farmville *Herald*, Sept. 17, 1897. 78. Farmville *Herald*, Feb. 24, 1905.

79. Farmville *Mercury*, Feb. 11, Apr. 15, Oct. 28, Nov. 25, 1875.

80. Farmville *Herald*, Mar. 25, 1893; May 30, 1902; Apr. 15, July 15, 1904.

81. Unidentified clipping in Miss Delle Walton's scrapbook, now in the possession of the writer's mother, Mrs. Herbert L. Bradshaw.

82. Farmville *Herald*, May 30, 1902. 83. Farmville *Herald*, Sept. 11, 1896.

84. Farmville *Herald*, Oct. 30, 1896; Feb. 5, 1897.

85. Richmond *Daily Dispatch*, Nov. 3, 1889.

86. Farmville *Herald*, Jan. 12, 1895.

87. Unidentified clipping in the scrapbook of the writer's wife.

88. Farmville *Herald*, Aug. 25, 1905.

89. Farmville *Herald*, Dec. 28, 1917, news summary of 1917.

90. The writer has described here dinner at the home of his paternal grandparents: during the lifetime of his grandmother, it was the custom of children and grandchildren to have dinner together there Christmas day. My grandfather liked the flavor of lemon, which explains the two custards my grandmother served.

91. The writer has described here, also from vivid and happy memories, the pleasant experience of Thanksgiving dinners at the home of the Misses Venable. The last dinner I had there was Thanksgiving, 1929, my senior year at Hampden-Sydney College. An editorial in the Durham *Morning Herald*, Nov. 22, 1951, recalled these happy occasions. A niece of the Misses Venable, Mrs. Louisa Venable (W. E.) Kyle, wrote a more detailed account of these dinners for the Norfolk *Virginian Pilot*, of Nov. 22, 1953.

The writer is loath to conclude without relating a story told by P. Tulane Atkinson, one of the most delightful raconteurs of Virginia, about a Thanksgiving dinner at the Misses Venable's before this writer's time. It was their custom then to serve goose instead of turkey, and their father, Major Andrew Reid Venable (there were two of that name and title in Prince Edward and they were contemporaries; the other is usually distinguished by Jr.), was carving. The goose was tough—how this came to be I'll never know; the Major was having a hard time; he sawed this way and that, but it seemed impossible to get a slice of goose for the company. In desperation, he looked up at his daughter at the other end of the table and said, "Susie, darling, you've gone and killed my old playmate."

ADDENDUM

The United States Supreme Court handed down the decree in the segregation suit May 31, 1955. It referred the case to the special court in which it was originally heard, with instructions to put the decision ending racial segregation into effect, but permitting it to allow a reasonable time for compliance after taking into consideration administrative problems. On the evening of the same day, the Prince Edward Board of Supervisors met and voted unanimously not to approve a school budget for the 1955-6 session. It continued the levy of $2.90 on the $100 valuation, earmarking 50 cents of the levy to finance an appropriation of $150,000 for the upkeep of school property during the session. At both its April and May meetings, the board deferred action on the school budget and levy, pending announcement of the decree.

NOTES ON THE ILLUSTRATIONS

THE FRONTISPIECE

This portrait of Prince Edward Augustus, Duke of York and Albany, for whom Prince Edward County was named, and his older brother, Prince George Frederick, who became King George III, was painted by Richard Wilson. The original is now in the National Portrait Gallery, London, and is used in this work by permission of the Gallery. The painting originally included the portrait of the Rev. Francis Ayscough, tutor of the young princes. Prince Edward Augustus, second son and third child of Frederick Louis, Prince of Wales, eldest son of George II, was born in 1739. He died in 1767. Prince Edward was only fourteen years of age when the county was named in his honor. Dr. Ayscough was dismissed as tutor to the young princes not long after the death of their father in 1751. Consideration of this fact, in connection with the fact that he was originally included in the portrait and the size of the boys in the portrait, indicates that it was painted about three years before the county was named for the prince.

It occurred to the writer that a portrait of Prince Edward would make an appropriate frontispiece for this work. Where to find it was the problem, for the writer had never seen one. He then thought that perhaps the Metropolitan Museum of Art in New York might have catalogues of the holdings of the various art galleries and might be able to help. A letter of inquiry was sent to the Museum. About ten days later came a reply and with it the print of the portrait reproduced as the frontispiece. Mrs. Gertrude G. Vilaska of the Museum's Publicity Department wrote that this was the only portrait of Prince Edward which their lists contained, although they searched the catalogue of the major museums in this country and abroad. In reply to her regret that the only portrait of the prince she could find was that of him as a child, the writer replied that this was just what he wanted, since Prince Edward was only a boy when the county was named for him.

PATRICK HENRY

This portrait of Patrick Henry is a reproduction of a miniature painted on ivory in 1791 by Lawrence Sully. The writer was especially desirous of using this likeness, not only because it is the only portrait of Henry painted from life but because it was painted while he was a resident of Prince Edward.

Henry has the distinction of being the county's most famous resident. He moved to Prince Edward in 1786, after he had declined election to a sixth term as Governor of Virginia (the term was then only one year); he chose Prince Edward because Hampden-Sydney College (of which he was a trustee) was located here and would give him a better opportunity to educate his sons. The house in which Henry lived is no longer standing; it was located not far north of the present Appomattox Presbyterian Church. Henry resumed the practice of law after moving to Prince Edward, a practice he had abandoned in 1774. He was eminently successful, being one of the most sought after attorneys of his day. While living in Prince Edward, Henry began one of his most famous cases, representing the defendants in a suit brought by British merchants for the recovery of pre-Revolutionary debts. The defendants won in the lower Federal court, but the Supreme Court subsequently, after Henry's connection with the case, reversed the decision. While Henry lived in Prince Edward, he represented

831

the county in the House of Delegates and in the Constitutional Convention of 1788, where he led the opposition to the ratification of the Constitution of the United States. He lost, by a narrow margin, that fight, but won the concession of having a bill of rights added to the Constitution as amendments. Henry moved from Prince Edward to Long Island in Campbell County in 1792.

Patrick Henry was born in Hanover County May 29, 1736. He entered public life upon his election to the House of Burgesses in 1765 and soon won fame from his eloquent speech attacking the Stamp Act at that session. The foremost representative of upcountry thinking on political matters, he was regarded as a radical by the more conservative leaders of Tidewater. Yet he was a competent politician, more than able to hold his own in contests with the established leaders. As the break with England became more and more serious, Henry was identified with the group seeking independence. He boldly resisted Lord Dunmore on the occasion of the removal of the powder from the Public Magazine at Williamsburg. When the Commonwealth of Virginia was established, Henry was chosen first Governor by the legislature. He served three terms, 1776-79; subsequently he served two more, 1784-85. Ill health and heavy responsibilities added to the weight of his later years. He turned down offers from President Washington to become Secretary of State, Chief Justice of the Supreme Court, and Minister to France. Henry died June 6, 1799, at Red Hill, in Charlotte County, to which he had moved from Long Island in 1796.

The illustration used is from a print lent by the Richmond *Times-Dispatch*. It is the print which this writer secured from the Patrick Henry Memorial Foundation and sent to the *Times-Dispatch* with a feature published May 26, 1946.

RICHARD N. VENABLE

Richard Nathaniel Venable was the third son of Nathaniel Venable and his wife, née Elizabeth Woodson, of Slate Hill. Born in 1763, he was educated at Hampden-Sydney and Princeton, graduating at the latter in 1781. He studied law and practiced for a time in Pittsylvania County. Later he returned to Prince Edward and lived at Slate Hill. Venable was a member of the Constitutional Convention of 1829. Throughout his mature life, he was a leading proponent of internal improvements, and he consistently worked to improve the navigation facilities of the Appomattox River. He seems to have blended the home-loving characteristics of his oldest brother, Samuel Woodson Venable, and the interest in public service of the second son of the family, Abraham Bedford Venable, who served in the national House of Representatives and the United States Senate and as president of the Bank of Virginia. Richard N. Venable married Mary Morton. He died in 1838. A copy of Venable's portrait was lent for this work by Mrs. W. Emmett (Louisa Venable) Kyle, a great-great-granddaughter, of London Bridge, Virginia.

SAMUEL STANHOPE SMITH

Samuel Stanhope Smith was the moving spirit in the establishment of Hampden-Sydney College. Born in 1750, a son of Robert Smith who conducted a "log college" at Pequa, Pennsylvania, and Elizabeth Blair, Samuel Stanhope Smith graduated from Princeton in 1769. He is described by contemporaries as handsome, eloquent, polished, able. He came to Virginia to preach, serving as pastor of Briery and Cumberland Presbyterian Churches. Smith remained at Hampden-Sydney a little more than three years, going to Princeton as professor of moral philosophy in 1779. In 1783 he added the teaching of theology to his duties, and in 1789 he became vice-president of Princeton, assisting his father-in-law, President John Witherspoon. Smith succeeded his father-in-law as president of Princeton in 1795, serving until 1812. He received the M. A. degree from

Princeton in 1772; both Princeton and Yale conferred on him the D. D. degree and Harvard conferred on him the LL.D. degree. He was a member of the American Philosophical Society. Smith died in 1819. The portrait reproduced in this work was painted from life by Charles B. Lawrence. The print was furnished by the Department of Art and Archaeology of Princeton University through Mrs. G. P. (Florence B.) Tschebotarioff of the department. There is a copy of the portrait in the Hampden-Sydney library.

JOHN BLAIR SMITH

John Blair Smith was a younger brother of Samuel Stanhope Smith. A graduate of Princeton in the class of 1773, he came to Hampden-Sydney when it was opened under the superintendence of his brother as one of the first teachers. When the Hampden-Sydney students were organized into a company of volunteers during the American Revolution, Smith was their captain. Under him they saw service at Williamsburg in 1777 and at Petersburg in 1778. Smith succeeded his brother as president of Hampden-Sydney in 1779 and remained in that post ten years. He also succeeded him in the pastorate of Briery and Cumberland. He went to Philadelphia from Prince Edward in 1791, to become pastor of the Pine Street Presbyterian Church. In 1795 he became president of Union College, Schenectady, New York, and remained there until his death four years later. John Blair Smith was moderator of the General Assembly of the Presbyterian Church in 1798. He received the M. A. from Princeton in 1783 and the D. D. in 1795. The print of the portrait used in this book was lent by the Public Relations Office of Union College.

BRANCH J. WORSHAM

Branch Jones Worsham was born December 8, 1788. He began writing in the Prince Edward Clerk's Office in 1802 and recorded his first deed in April, 1803, when he was only fourteen. In 1809 he became deputy clerk of the Circuit Court and in 1810 deputy clerk of the County Court. In 1816 he became clerk of the Circuit Court and in 1825 he became clerk of the County Court, succeeding Francis Watkins in both positions. He served as clerk until he was removed by the general commanding Military District No. 1 ("Virginia was once her name," Innis Randolph wrote in his poem) in 1869. He was a member of the Constitutional Convention of 1850-51. He married Susanna Booker. He died May 26, 1873. Frederick Johnston in his *Memorials of Old Virginia Clerks* (1888) pays high tribute to Mr. Worsham: his office a model of neatness and correctness—Mr. Worsham loved it as he did few things in this world—guarded every paper with unwearying care; methods rigorously exacting—life governed by laws as unvarying as those of the Medes and Persians; convictions strong and opinions firm and fixed; knowledge of Virginia statute law as accurate as that of any lawyer of his day—his judgment as reliable—his opinion as valuable. Johnston has also given a description of the man: dignified bearing, classic and cleanly shaven face, well-dressed person, quiet yet impressive manner and relates that as a child he feared him although he greatly respected him. The portrait from which this illustration is taken appropriately hangs in the clerk's office. His penmanship is a model of neatness and clarity.

DR. JOHN PETER METTAUER

The date of Dr. Mettauer's birth is uncertain. He was a son of Dr. Francis Joseph Mettauer, who came to America with French troops in the Revolution and who settled in Prince Edward at the close of the war. Dr. John Peter Mettauer attended Hampden-Sydney, graduated in medicine from the University of Pennsylvania in 1809, and won an international reputation as a surgeon. He practiced at Prince Edward Courthouse and at the time also had an office in Farmville. He and his son, Dr. Francis Joseph Mettauer, conducted the Prince Edward Medical Institute which became the Medical Department of Randolph-Macon College. Dr. John Peter Mettauer was the first American surgeon to operate successfully for the cleft palate and for vesico-vaginal fistula. He died November 22, 1875.

JOHN HOLT RICE

The Rev. John Holt Rice, D. D., was born in Bedford County in 1777. He was a tutor at Hampden-Sydney, pastor of Cub Creek Church in Charlotte, and of the First Presbyterian Church in Richmond. He was the founder and first professor in Union Theological Seminary, which opened at Hampden-Sydney in 1823. Here he continued until his death in 1831. Rice married Anne Smith Morton, a daughter of Major James Morton of Prince Edward. He was at one time editor of the *Evangelical and Literary Review*. He had a keen concern for slavery and was a foremost advocate of colonization, that is, the emancipation of slaves in this country and sending them to Liberia.

DANIEL WITT

The Rev. Daniel Witt, D. D., was born in Bedford Nov. 8, 1801. He early became a Baptist minister and was one of the first missionaries sent out by the Board of Managers of the Baptist General Association of Virginia after its organization in 1823. For a time he studied theology under the Rev. Abner W. Clopton, M. A., M. D., of Charlotte County. In 1827 he was called to the pastorate of Sharon Baptist Church upon its organization at Sandy River Meeting-house in Prince Edward. Here he remained as pastor until his death in 1781. Dr. Witt shared in the organization of the Farmville Baptist Church in 1836, revived Nottoway Church near Burkeville in 1833, preached at Sailor Creek Church at Jamestown, and organized Pisgah Baptist Church in 1857. He was a charter trustee of Richmond College in 1840 and attended the meeting at which the Southern Baptist Convention was organized in Augusta, Ga., in 1845. He was married three times, first to Miss Mary C. Cocke of Cumberland, secondly to Miss Mary A. Woodfin of Cumberland, and thirdly to Mrs. Mary Ellen Garlick Temple of King William County. The photograph used here was taken during the last year of his life and was lent by the writer's mother, Mrs. Herbert L. Bradshaw.

HENRY E. WATKINS

Henry E. Watkins was one of the county's most eminent lawyers in his time. Born in 1782, the son of Francis Watkins, clerk of the court 1783-1825, and his wife, Ann Woodson, Henry E. Watkins was well educated, studying at Hampden-Sydney and Washington Academy and graduating from Princeton in 1801. He lived at "The Home" between Farmville and Prince Edward Courthouse, not far from Poplar Hill, home of his father and of his grandfather, Richard Woodson. He taught law to a number of students. Watkins served in the House of Delegates and in the State Senate. He became a Whig, which in Prince Edward reduced considerably his opportunity to be elected to public office as the county usually voted Democratic. He was a member of the Board of Trustees of Hampden-Sydney College. He married Agnes Woodson Venable, daughter of Samuel Woodson Venable. He died in 1856. The portrait reproduced in this book hangs in the court room of the Courthouse in Farmville.

DR. W. W. H. THACKSTON

Dr. William W. H. Thackston was born in Prince Edward Feb. 29, 1820, the son of Charles and Mary Lee Thackston. He married Mary Elizabeth Fowlkes. He studied dentistry at the Baltimore College of Dental Surgery, graduating in 1842 in the second class in the United States to graduate from a dental school. He practiced his profession in Farmville until his death in 1899. In 1842, when he began the practice of dentistry in Farmville, he organized the Virginia Society of Surgeon Dentists. In 1870 he organized and was elected first president of the Virginia State Dental Association. Dr. Thackston was mayor of Farmville in 1872. He was mayor in 1888, when the town records begin, serving until 1890. He died December 8, 1899. Dr. Thackston was known as "the Lord Chesterfield of the dental profession." The illustration is from a print given the writer by Dr. J. H. Cocks, Farmville.

PHILIP W. McKINNEY

Philip Watkins McKinney was born in Buckingham County May 1, 1832, the son of Charles D. and Martha Guerrant McKinney. He graduated from Hampden-Sydney in the class of 1851 and studied law under Judge John W. Brockenbrough in Lexington. He was captain of Co. K, 4th Virginia Cavalry, C. S. A. McKinney practiced law in Farmville and served for a time as Commonwealth's Attorney of Prince Edward County. He was active in Democratic politics throughout the Reconstruction period. He served as Governor of Virginia 1890-94. Governor McKinney was twice married, first to Miss Nannie Christian of Charles City County, secondly to Miss Annie Lyle of Farmville, daughter of Dr. James Lyle. He died Mar. 1, 1899.

ASA DICKINSON WATKINS

Judge Asa Dickinson Watkins readily qualifies as one of the most honored and beloved citizens of Prince Edward in recent years. An able lawyer, he was for forty-seven years Commonwealth's Attorney. He was born at Ingleside, June 5, 1856, the son of Judge Francis Nathaniel Watkins and Martha Ann Scott. His grandfather was Henry E. Watkins. He was educated at Hampden-Sydney College and the University of Virginia Law School. He was judge of the Prince Edward County Court 1886-91, a member of the House of Delegates 1897-98 and of the State Senate 1900-04. He was also a trustee of Hampden-Sydney, 1896-1932, and secretary-treasurer of the Board of Trustees of the State Normal School, now Longwood College. Judge Watkins married Miss Nannie Forbes. He died April 14, 1938. The portrait of which this illustration is a copy hangs in the Courthouse.

THE COURTHOUSE, 1832-72

This was probably the county's third Courthouse building. The first was erected shortly after the establishment of the county, the second in the 1770's, and this building in 1832. It continued as the county Courthouse until Farmville became the county seat in 1872, and the court and county offices were moved there. In 1874 Prince Edward Academy, a preparatory school for boys, was founded, and it occupied the abandoned county buildings at what had been Prince Edward Courthouse, but became Worsham in 1872. This photograph was taken when the Courthouse was used by the Academy; Dr. W. H. Whiting, Jr., was principal at the time the photograph was made. The original photograph is owned by Miss Mary Dupuy, who lent it to the writer. Charles H. Cooper, staff photographer for the Durham *Herald-Sun* papers, made the copy which is reproduced here. This building was taken down, and its bricks used to build the E. E. Hundley home, just south of Farmville on Route 15.

VENABLE HALL, HAMPDEN-SYDNEY COLLEGE

This dormitory, which also houses the College dining hall, was originally the Union Theological Seminary building. When the Seminary opened in the fall of 1823, it occupied a two-story brick building, forty by thirty-eight feet. In 1824 this building was ordered to be enlarged by adding a third story and twelve feet to the length. This was to be the east wing of a larger building, which was completed in 1831. The Seminary occupied this building until it was moved to Richmond in 1898. Major Richard M. Venable of Baltimore bought the Seminary property and gave it to the college, and the main building was named in his honor.

THE COURTHOUSE, 1872-1939

This building was the first courthouse in Farmville. It was built by the town as one of the conditions for moving the county seat to Farmville.

THE COURTHOUSE, 1939

Few regretted to see the former Courthouse replaced by this building. Not only was it inadequate for the county's needs, but it had neither architectural beauty nor notable historic associations to endear it to the people. The present courthouse was occupied in 1939.

THE CLERK'S OFFICE, 1855-72

This building served as the last clerk's office at Prince Edward Courthouse. It was built in 1855. Like the Courthouse, it was later used by the Prince Edward Academy. Still later it was used as the public school, and an addition was made to it on the north side to accommodate the students. After the present Worsham High School was built, this building was used for a time as a residence. It is now the property of Miss Mary Dupuy and Richard W. Dupuy. This building replaced the clerk's office built 1809-10.

THE CLERK'S OFFICE, 1896-1939

This building was located on the Courthouse grounds in Farmville, between the Courthouse and Main Street, to the north of the walk from the street to the Courthouse. The earlier clerk's office in Farmville was a room in the Courthouse occupied in 1872.

COLLEGE PRESBYTERIAN CHURCH

Located at Hampden-Sydney, this church was built in 1860 according to plans drawn by Dr. Robert L. Dabney, then professor of theology at Union Seminary. Its fine proportions and classic lines give to its simplicity of design a unique beauty.

THE ROTUNDA, LONGWOOD COLLEGE

This, the main or administration building of Longwood College, is on the site of the building of the Farmville Female Seminary, erected 1839-42. The town gave the Farmville College property to the State of Virginia in 1884 to secure the location of the first State Female Normal School for the training of public school teachers.

LONGWOOD HOUSE

The present building was built during the ownership of Nathaniel E. Venable, although the name of the place is identified with earlier owners, the Johnstons. Here lived Peter Johnston, Sr., and Peter Johnston, Jr., in a dwelling which is no longer standing. Confederate General Joseph Eggleston Johnston was born in the earlier dwelling in 1807. A beautiful description of Longwood was written by Prof. William Mynn Thornton of the University of Virginia in *The Kaleidoscope* of 1901. Colonel Charles Scott Venable of Lee's staff, later professor of mathematics in the University of Virginia, was a son of Nathaniel E. Venable and lived here, and Colonel Venable's son, Francis Preston Venable, long the distinguished professor of chemistry in the University of North Carolina and president of that university, 1900-14, was born here in 1856. The next owner after the Venables was Wright Barber, who belonged to the English migration of the 1870's. The Barbers sold Longwood to the State Teachers College as a recreation center in 1924, and the college took its name from this estate in 1949. The name Longwood is a corruption of the name Lochwood, which was given to the place by Peter Johnston, Sr., for his ancestral home in Scotland.

THE LOCKETT HOUSE

The front section of this house, shown here, was built in 1858 by James S. Lockett. The rear wing is much older and is thought to date from the 1790's. Although the place was named Piney Grove, it is almost never identified by that name. The Lockett House is located on a hill on the east side of Sailor's Creek, near the junction of the two forks bearing that name. This house has a place in history because in the creek lowgrounds and along the road between the house and the creek the Federal troops attacked the Confederate wagon train on April 6, 1865. The house still has bullet holes in its weatherboarding from this battle. The house was used as a hospital for the soldiers wounded in the battle, and Mr. Lockett was careful to get the name and address of each soldier and the name and address of the next of kin. Those who died were buried across the road from the house, and their relatives were notified. Every body, except one, has been removed from this burying ground by kinsmen. Because no food was left on his farm by the passing armies, Mr. Lockett had to go to Burkeville to apply to Federal officers for food for his family and the wounded soldiers at his home. Mr. Lockett's daughter, Mrs. T. W. Garnett, later lived here, and it is now the home of a grandson, T. H. Garnett. Mrs. T. W. Garnett, née Miss Mamie O. Lockett, remembered vividly the battle, and the writer had a most pleasant interview with her in the fall of 1948, the results of which were published as a feature in the Richmond *Times-Dispatch* of Dec. 5, 1948.

SHARON BAPTIST CHURCH

This building is the oldest church building, the only one remaining from colonial times, in Prince Edward County. It occupies the site of a chapel which was standing in 1744. At some time between 1744 and 1749 Sandy River Chapel became Sandy River Church. The vestry of St. Patrick's Parish ordered a new church to be built at Sandy River in 1761. Just before the building was completed in 1762, it burned. A contract was let for a new building in 1763, and it was completed in 1765. After worship of the Church of England ceased in Prince Edward after the Revolution, ministers of the various denominations preached in this building. Sharon Baptist Church was organized in Sandy River Church, which by that time had come to be known as Sandy River Meetinghouse, in 1827, and has occupied the historic building ever since. Dimensions for the church were set in 1761 as twenty-four by forty-eight feet, but later John Nash was allowed to build a pew there on condition he add as much space to the building as his pew would require. Measurements confirm the information given by old residents that the back part of the church, including the east wing, is the oldest part of the church. That wing measures twenty-four feet, three inches, in width, and the length of the back of the church, from the eastern end of the wing (southeastern corner) to the southwestern corner is fifty feet, two inches, enough to take care of the Nash pew. Two windows in the east end have been weatherboarded over, and a door has replaced them. A door on the southern side of the church has been boarded over. The present front (facing north) measures thirty-four feet, four inches across, and the west side is forty-eight feet, four inches. A different design for the cornice is noted on the east wing in the photograph.

KINDERTON

Built in 1824 by Abram Watkins Venable, Kinderton was later a part of the girls' school operated first by Eleazar Root, Jr., and later by Robert G. Branch. It was at one time the home of Branch J. Worsham. After Mr. Worsham's death, it served as the Manse for College Church at nearby Hampden-Sydney. Still later it was the home of Mr. and Mrs. George L. Walker and Mrs. Walker's sister, Miss Annie Belle Martin. Mrs. Walker and Miss Martin were granddaughters of Abram Watkins Venable. Walker was the first alumni secretary of Hampden-Sydney College and was for a time dean of the college. It is now the home of Thomas W. Carter. Kinderton is in Worsham, facing Highway 15.

FOREST GREEN

Forest Green, the property of Charles A. Garden, is near Prospect and may be seen by travelers on Highway 460 just before getting to Prospect from Farmville. It was earlier the home of James Venable, the second superintendent of schools in Prince Edward County.

BUFFALOE

Buffaloe, now the home of Prof. and Mrs. James M. Grainger, was built by Jacob W. Morton, a Farmville merchant. It is reached from the "back Hampden-Sydney road" from Farmville, and is near Little Buffalo Creek. Here the Graingers have found numerous and varied Indian relics, and these have been assembled into the most extensive collection of Indian relics in the county. A grandson of Jacob Morton, Egbert Hudson Womack, has written an interesting account of his ancestral lines in a brochure entitled *Buffaloe.*

GOLGOTHA

Golgotha was the home of one of Prince Edward's most brilliant men, William Branch, Jr. The son of Thomas Branch and Nancy Clement, Branch was born June 1, 1791. Although he had little formal education, he educated himself. In 1819 he published a book of 218 pages entitled *Life.* Written entirely in the heroic couplet, the book describes life from infancy to old age. Branch taught a school at Golgotha. In 1822 he was admitted to the bar and began the practice of law. He married on December 16, 1812, his first cousin, Jane Davis Booker, daughter of Edmund Booker and Mary Harwood Clement. Branch died Nov. 31, 1825. The Prince Edward Court and bar wore mourning in his memory for thirty days. Golgotha became a Phillips property after the Branch ownership, and still later was the home of Barnett H. Carter. After the Carter ownership, it belonged to John W. Bradshaw, and it is now the property of A. W. and W. S. Weaver. It is located on Highway 460 about two miles east of Rice.

BUFFALO PRESBYTERIAN CHURCH

This building were erected about 1808 (the land was purchased in that year). The earlier church was about 200 yards southeast of Crute and Turns store at Five Forks. The front of two Sunday School classrooms and a recessed porch is a much later addition. Before the addition was made, there was a separate session house near the church. The session house was bought by Samuel Newton Cunningham and was rebuilt as the ice house at his home, Millbank. The communion silver shown in the illustration was in use at Buffalo when the oldest members now living can first remember. It is probably the oldest communion service in regular use in a Prince Edward church.

GENERAL TARLTON WOODSON'S HOME

This home, which is near Prospect, is said to have been built in 1812 by General Woodson. It was called Brooklyn, probably in memory of Woodson's service during the Revolution on Long Island, where he was imprisoned by the British as a prisoner of war and where he met his future wife, Anne van der Veer. The property was given to him in 1776 by his father, Charles Woodson. General Woodson (who received his title as a militia officer) served in the House of Delegates and was a presidential elector in 1792. He encouraged his son, Charles, to experiment with farming operations when he was a boy. The home is remote and cannot be reached by automobile. It is now owned by Frank Shultz.

JAMESTOWN'S MAIN STREET, 1953

Jamestown was chartered in 1796 and was a thriving village during the years when the principal transportation means was the Appomattox River batteaux lines. Here were a girls' school, taverns, Townes' warehouse with tobacco inspection, stores, a church, and homes. This scene was taken from the edge of the churchyard looking down what was once the Main Street of Jamestown toward the river. The bridge over the Appomattox was condemned about 1920, and with its closing the road was abandoned, although it was used as a path for some years afterward. The writer remembers walking over it in the 1920's when going to the river to swim. The bridge could then be crossed on foot. At one of the stone piers, a flatboat had been overturned, and the water had washed out a hole in which the boys of the neighborhood went swimming. For some distance downstream one could wade, the water being only a little more than knee-deep, too shallow for swimming except in the hole by the boat. The freshets in the mid-1930's carried away the bridge. It was difficult to imagine, when this picture was taken, that this was once an important trading point for both Prince Edward and Cumberland Counties. The smaller undergrowth marks the route of the street.

JAMESTOWN CHURCH, 1937

The old church was the last survivor of Jamestown. A lonely sentinel, it kept watch over the site of the town for more than three-quarters of a century after the town had been abandoned, after the building of the Southside Railroad put an end to the river commerce. Jamestown Church seems to have been built as a free church, open for worship to all denominations. A Baptist missionary society was organized at Jamestown in 1817, but it is not certain that the meeting took place in this building. This church became the regular place of worship for Sailor Creek Baptist Church after a cyclone destroyed the earlier house of worship, Rice's Meetinghouse, in 1834. Sailor Creek Church dissolved in 1867. In 1876 a Presbyterian congregation was organized in this building and worshipped here until about 1920, when the closing of the bridge to vehicular traffic made it impossible for members living in Cumberland to get to church. A more central location for the remaining members, those living in Prince Edward, was sought and found some three miles nearer Rice. The old church was sold in 1938, although for several years before that revivals conducted by the Rev. Elnora Carter, a Negro minister, were held in the church. The photograph reproduced here was taken by the writer's wife on the last day of the year 1937. In 1953 the church had been taken down, only the sills remaining. These are all left at Jamestown as a reminder of a more prosperous past. This building was erected as a free church, and the land was conveyed by J. Jackson and wife in 1821 to William White, Elisha Woodfin, and Branch Walthall, trustees.

WOMACK'S MILL

This mill is located on the north fork of Spring Creek. Wood's map, made in 1820, locates it at this present site, but the county Order Books do not mention a license to David F. Womack to build a mill until October, 1831, when he and William M. Carter received such a license. (David F. Womack owned land in the vicinity.) T. P. Singleton, who acquired the land of David F. Womack, operated the mill for many years and it was known as Singleton's Mill. It is now the property of Emory Dillon and grinds twice weekly. Womack's Mill is one of the last remaining mills in the county.

ROTHERWOOD

Rotherwood was long the home of Edwin Edmunds and his family. It was originally Randolph property, being a part of the Randolph quarter on Bush River. Older residents have told the writer that the one-story wing, which was built of logs and weatherboarded over (at the right in the illustration) was used as the home of Peyton Randolph's overseers. After Peyton Randolph disposed of his Bush River holdings in the 1820's, this portion was acquired by Edwin Edmunds, while the adjoining portion, known as Moilena, was bought by John A. Scott. Moilena, an imposing brick home in which Randolph lived, burned many years ago. Thweatt Anderson and Samuel Bondurant bought Rotherwood after Mrs. Edmunds' death. Later J. B. Houpe lived there. The present owner is F. W. Shanabarger, who makes his home there.

OAKLAND

Oakland was another of the Randolph plantations in Prince Edward. About 1810 Richard K. Randolph moved from this estate to Rhode Island, and his brother-in-law and sister, Mr. and Mrs. William Berkeley, moved here. Berkeley had been treasurer of Virginia before moving to Prince Edward. It is not known who built the present dwelling at Oakland. Another dwelling on the farm at a greater distance from the road in a grove of oak trees is said to have been the earlier residence. Thomas Homer, one of the English immigrants of the Reconstruction period, lived at Oakland. Later the farm was acquired by Wiley P. Gilliam, the Farmville tobacconist. It is now the home of L. H. Stockton.

CORK

The present residence was built by Jesse Michaux, who lived at Cork for many years. Cork is the site of the Rev. John Thomson's home and school—the first school, so far as is known, within the bounds of Prince Edward. While living here, Thomson wrote the first book ever written in the county, *Explication of the Shorter Catechism*, which was published in 1749. It is now the home of G. E. Shorter.

BURKE'S TAVERN

This tavern has a long history. Anderson P. Miller received his first license to operate an ordinary in Prince Edward in 1800, and in 1822 Samuel D. Burke received a license to operate an ordinary in Anderson P. Miller's place. John Wood's map of 1820 places Miller's Tavern at this location, at the intersection of the road to Prince Edward Courthouse via Sandy River Church with the road leading to Moore's Ordinary (the present Meherrin). The tavern is in Prince Edward, barely within the Nottoway County line. Col. Burke gave to the location his name, Burkeville, and there was a postoffice here. It is strange now to see references to Burkeville, Prince Edward County. Older residents used to call the tavern "Old Burkeville." The name was transferred to the village which developed at the junction of the Richmond and Danville and Southside Railroads after they were built. W. B. Farrar is the present owner of Burke's Tavern.

CHATHAM

The two illustrations from the interior of Chatham are provided to show the excellence of workmanship in ante-bellum Prince Edward. Chatham, which is between Bush and Sandy Rivers on Route 460, was built in 1858 by Major James Watson. Later it was the home of Major Watson's daughter, Mrs. Sallie V. Overton, and her husband, C. L. Overton. After Mrs. Overton's death it was bought by Herbert L. Bradshaw, and it is now the property of his sons, H. C. and C. W. Bradshaw. The parlor ceiling centerpiece is quite elaborate, the design being worked around four birds. A smaller and less elaborate ceiling centerpiece is in the hall. Plaster centerpieces were molded in beeswax.

LOCUST GROVE (REDD)

This home, which is about 200 yards from Route 15 between Worsham and Keysville, was the residence of John Wesley Redd. The date of its building is not known, but Redd moved into it in 1815. Locust Grove was a saint's rest for the Methodist Church. Methodist pastors on the Prince Edward circuit made it their headquarters, and the Rev. John Wesley Childs boarded his family here during his year on the circuit, 1837. The Rev. J. S. R. Clarke is buried in the family cemetery. It is now the home of Redd's great-granddaughter, Mrs. John Fennell (Ruby Ranson) Redd. A unique feature of the house is a warming oven built in the chimney of the room on the south side of the house.

LOCUST GROVE (CRUTE-MOTTLEY)

Major John L. Crute built this home when he settled on this farm at the completion of his service in the Revolution. It remained in his family until this year, when his great-granddaughter, Mrs. W. K. Daubenspeck, sold it to W. T. Lindsey. After Major Crute's occupancy, it was the home of his daughter, Mrs. Nathaniel Mottley, and later of her son, J. M. Mottley. During the War Between the States, Mrs. Nathaniel Mottley was awakened one night by what she thought was her son, Lieut. N. R. Mottley, coming up the steps. She got up to open the door, only to find no one there. Shortly afterward, she received a message that her son had been killed the night she thought that she had heard him on the steps. The writer remembers with kindly regard J. M. Mottley, whose stories of old Prince Edward helped begin for him an interest in local history. It was in Mr. Mottley's library that he found William Branch, Jr.'s, poem, *Life*, from which he borrowed it to read for the first time. Mr. Mottley was the most generous of neighbors, and the writer has gathered many a bucket of fruit there. A familiar invitation came in summer, "Boy, your Pa loves thin-skin apples. Mine are ripe, so come on down to my house and get him a bucketful." In the fall, there was an abundance of walnuts to be shared with the neighbors.

PROSPECT METHODIST CHURCH

This church was built in 1859. The older church was located on land which is now a part of the cemetery at the church. The property was conveyed to the trustees of the church in 1820 by Robert Venable. Federal troops camped in the churchyard in April, 1865.

BRIERY PRESBYTERIAN CHURCH

This house of worship is said to be the third used by the Briery congregation. It was designed by the Rev. Dr. Robert L. Dabney, professor of theology in Union Seminary and was built about 1855. Dr. Dabney is said to have arranged the doors so that tardy worshippers had to enter in full view of the congregation. The older church, thought to have been built about 1824, was on land adjacent to the present building, and the first meeting-house, built about 1755 according to some, about 1760 according to others, was not far distant.

THE JACKSON-WHITE HOUSE

Built by Patrick H. Jackson, one of Farmville's early tobacco manufacturers, this house on Beech Street was a center of social life in the town. It has a place in history, for here General Lee stopped, as he was passing through Farmville April 7, 1865, for a conference with Secretary of War John C. Breckinridge, Quartermaster General Lawton, and Commissary General St. John, all of whom had spent the night there. It was Lee's last conference as commander of the Army of Northern Virginia with the Confederate Secretary of War. Lee declined an invitation to breakfast, but did drink a cup of coffee here. This was also the home of Dr. James L. White, who married Miss Lelia Jackson, a daughter of P. H. Jackson. Dr. White was a greatly beloved physician, whose memory is still cherished. This residence was later the home of Mrs. White's brother, W. W. Jackson, and his daughter, Mrs. Wallace Gould, who is better remembered as Miss Mary Jackson. It is now the home of Miss Florence Stubbs.

PANOLA

Panola was a Bondurant home, of Samuel Watson Bondurant and later of his son, Edward Taylor Bondurant, a member of the House of Delegates from Prince Edward, 1919-23, and an outstanding farm leader. Although Panola is near High Bridge, its fairly isolated location made it a place of refuge for some of the young ladies of the neighborhood when the armies came through in April, 1865. It is now the property of W. H. Burruss of Lynchburg.

LINDEN (WATSON-STOKES-COX)

This Linden is located on Route 15, just south of Briery River. It has been the home of Allen Watson, Captain Richard Stokes, and Robert E. Stokes. It is now the home of G. Linwood Cox. Dr. J. D. Eggleston told the writer that Blanche Kelso Bruce, only Negro to serve in the United States Senate, was born and raised on this farm. Bruce was senator from Mississippi, 1875-81.

LINDEN (DUPUY)

This Linden, which is near Meherrin, was the home of Colonel Asa Dupuy, and was given to him by his uncle, General John Purnall. In more recent years it was the home of J. S. Shackleton.

THE McKINNEY HOUSE

This was the home of Governor Philip W. McKinney. It is located at the corner of Garden and Beech Streets, Farmville. It is now the property of W. B. Bruce, Jr.

ASPEN HILL

Aspen Hill is on a hill above lower Sandy River. The front, shown in the illustration, was added by Dr. John T. Ligon to an older house. The windows in the older house were small, and the rooms dark. Dr. Ligon said he was tired of dark rooms, so he put plenty of windows in the new part of his house. Later Aspen Hill was the home of Dr. Ligon's daughter, Mrs. Bettie Ann Ligon. From her it passed to her nephew, John T. Clark, and it is now the home of Mr. Clark's widow, Mrs. Lucy V. Clark, and their son, Walton Clark. A fascinating feature of this home to the writer, when he used to visit it as a small boy, was the windlass on the back porch which was used to draw water from the spring some distance away.

INGLESIDE

Ingleside, on Route 460 at Bush River bridge, was the home of Judge Francis Nathaniel Watkins and later of his son, Dr. Henry E. Watkins. It was later the home of Dr. Watkins's daughter and her husband, John A. Clark, who was for many years sheriff of Prince Edward. A grandson of Judge Watkins, Samuel W. Watkins, county treasurer, 1927-45, later acquired Ingleside and made his home there for a short time before his death. Irvine Cabell Watkins, brother of Samuel W. Watkins, now owns Ingleside and lives there. Prior to the Watkins ownership, Ingleside was the home of James Allen.

THE RUDD-OWEN HOME

Earlier the home of John Rudd, this was later the residence of John J. Owen, State senator and assistant commissioner of agriculture in Virginia. It is now the home of his son, T. Venable Owen.

TRAVIS

For over a century and a quarter, this home near Sandy River Church has been occupied by four generations of the same family. Col. John Foster lived here for many years, as did his son, John W. Foster. It then became the home of his son-in-law and daughter, Mr. and Mrs. James T. Clark. It is now the home of their son-in-law and daughter, Mr. and Mrs. J. Woodfin Hughes. Still preserved here is Colonel Foster's family Bible. Colonel Foster (1787-1874) was unusually well-informed about matters of local and family history. His papers on the McGehee (his mother's family) and Foster families contain valuable information. Old residents used to tell of a dance which was held at Travis by Tarleton's men when they raided Prince Edward in the summer of 1781; Travis was then a tavern.

OAK GROVE

Oak Grove was the home of David F. Womack. H. D. Jacobs, of the English colony of Spring Creek, later lived here. It was then bought by T. P. Singleton, whose wife was a niece of David F. Womack, and he lived there for nearly half a century. It is now the home of Mr. Singleton's niece, Miss Elizabeth Singleton. Oak Grove is near Darlington Heights, on the road from Darlington Heights to Bethpeor Baptist Church.

WALNUT HILL

Walnut Hill was built by James D. Ligon, planter and lawyer. It was later owned by his grandson, Spencer Price, who sold it to W. B. Gates. It is now the home of Drewry A. Gates, a son of Mr. Gates. James D. Ligon was a brother of Governor Thomas Watkins Ligon of Maryland.

THE PAULETT HOUSE

This residence was acquired by Richard Singleton Paulett, a tobacco manufacturer and merchant of Farmville, in 1858. It is located at the corner of High and Venable Streets. It is now the home of Mr. Paulett's granddaughter, Mrs. W. J. Gills.

THE STAIRCASE AT MIDDLECOURT

One of the most beautiful staircases in Prince Edward is the winding stairway at Middlecourt, the home of President Edgar G. Gammon of Hampden-Sydney College. Middlecourt was built to be occupied by a professor in Union Theological Seminary and was for many years the home of Dr. Thomas E. Peck. Later it was the home of Dr. W. H. Whiting, Jr., long the greatly beloved and greatly respected professor of Latin at Hampden-Sydney College. It has been occupied by the Gammon family since Dr. Gammon became president in 1939.

CUSHING HALL

Cushing Hall was built in 1822, to replace the original college building at Hampden-Sydney. It is now one of the two dormitories at the college.

STONE KNOLL

The present building is the home of the superintendent of the Prince Edward State Forest. It replaced the residence which had once been occupied by Richard A. Miller, one of the largest slaveholders and wealthiest men in Prince Edward on the eve of the War Between the States. The giant holly trees which hide the house remain from the days when the Millers lived there.

SUNNYSIDE

This is one of several homes which were named Sunnyside in Prince Edward. This house was built by James Dabney Walthall in 1858 and was later the home of Robert Hester Walton. It is now the home of Fred G. Walton, a son of R. H. Walton.

SLATE HILL

The picture at the top of the page shows Slate Hill during its occupancy by the last of the Venables to live there. John M. Venable is seated in the chair, and his wife, who was Miss Bettie Edmunds of Rotherwood, is standing by one of the columns. Asa Dupuy Watkins, later professor of English at Hampden-Sydney College, is seated on the railing with his back to the column. The others are not identified. Mr. and Mrs. Venable, who had no children, took a number of Hampden-Sydney students during the last three decades of the nineteenth century to room and board at Slate Hill. A nostalgic account of Slate Hill in those days was related by Dr. Watkins in *The Kaleidoscope* of 1929. The stained glass windows, the ornamentation of porch and gable were added in a remodeling project by Major Richard M. Venable of Baltimore, who owned the place and was a brother of John M. Venable. They gave a distinctly Victorian appearance to the front of the dwelling which dates from the middle of the eighteenth century. The appearance of the rear portion, however, was in keeping with its antiquity. The Presbytery which brought Hampden-Sydney College into being met in the office at Slate Hill in 1775. The office was then in the yard; later it was moved and attached to the rear wing of the house, on the side which shows in the lower picture. The office has since been moved to Hampden-Sydney, where it occupies a place on the campus. Joseph Morton lived at Slate Hill prior to his removal to Charlotte (then Lunenburg) in 1755. Nathaniel Venable then moved to Slate Hill and lived there until his death in 1804. It was then the home of his son, Richard N. Venable, and was later owned by Richard N. Venable, Jr., William H. Venable, and the latter's brother, Richard M. Venable. The writer remembers Mrs. John Venable when she was in her 90's. In her black widow's mob and black dress, she was a regular attendant upon the worship services at College Church.

The lower photograph was taken in the spring of 1954. The boxwood which line the front walk had overgrown it, reminding one that they were shaped to arch the walk in Mr. and Mrs. John Venable's time. Slate Hill is now owned by McFarland Brothers.

CLOVER HILL

Clover Hill, at the top of the hill from Buffalo River on the Worsham-Darlington Heights road, was originally a Baker home. William Baker and his son, General Andrew Baker of the militia, lived there. It was later the home of Branch J. Worsham, so long clerk of Prince Edward court. It is now the home of V. C. Turman. Frederick Johnston described it as "a seat of liberal and refined hospitality," in writing of Mr. Worsham.

OAKLAND

Oakland, near Meherrin, was the home of the Methodist minister, the Rev. Matthew Mayes Dance.

MIDDLECOURT

See note on the illustration, The Staircase at Middlecourt.

PENSHURST

Like Middlecourt, Penshurst was built as a residence for Union Theological Seminary professors. It is east of the Seminary building. After it, along with the other Seminary property at Hampden-Sydney, was given to the college by Major Richard M. Venable, it was the home of three of the presidents of the college, Drs. J. Gray McAllister, H. Tucker Graham, and J. D. Eggleston. It is now the home of Dr. and Mrs. Graves H. Thompson. It was named for the birthplace of Algernon Sydney, one of the English patriots for whom the college is named.

FARMVILLE HIGH SCHOOL

The portion of the high school building shown here was built in 1937 on the site of the building erected in 1912 which burned in 1936.

R. R. MOTON HIGH SCHOOL

This building, the county high school for Negroes, was occupied in 1953. It bears the name of one of the foremost Negro educators, Robert R. Moton, president of Tuskegee Institute, who was reared in Prince Edward.

THE DEBTORS' PRISON

The Debtors' Prison at Worsham was built in 1787. Its restoration is a current project of the Prince Edward Branch of the Association for the Preservation of Virginia Antiquities. The stone jail, built in 1855, is now in ruins. The Debtors' Prison was built of huge hewed logs.

The county has had many jails for criminals. Following the temporary use of Charles Anderson's kitchen in 1754, the county built prisons at Prince Edward Courthouse in 1754, 1755, 1759, 1764, 1784, 1791, 1823, 1845, and 1855, and at Farmville in 1871-2, 1897, and 1939.

A MEMENTO OF WAR

When Robert D. Miller of Farmville was a prisoner of war at Point Lookout, Maryland (he had been captured at the Battle of Gettysburg), he made with his pocketknife fans from a discarded goods box. These fans he sold for $5.00 each to people from Northern cities who visited the prison to see the Rebel prisoners. They were so popular that he and the commandant entered into partnership, the latter securing yellow pine for the fans. The fan-making business prospered, and at one time Miller had seven men working on them. Some of the prisoners of war, less skilled than he, sold him rings and other pieces of jewelry to get money to buy items which were not furnished the prisoners. By the time of his release, at the end of the war, he had accumulated a substantial sum of money and some valuable rings. Not wishing to have these taken and fearing that the guards would not permit him to take them with him, Miller decided to smuggle them out in a New Testament which had been given him by a colporteur of the Maryland Bible Society. He cut the hole which is shown in the picture, put his money and some rings in it. When called on to declare his possessions when he was leaving, he held up the Testament and was passed by the guard. The Testament is now in possession of his son, Harvey T. Miller, of Farmville.

INDEX

Where it is possible to distinguish between persons of the same name, the writer has done so. This has not always been possible, however; it has been impossible to separate the several John Caldwells in every instance, except as distinguishing identifications have been given in the source materials; nor is it possible to distinguish always the two John Watsons of the Revolutionary period or the two James Scotts of the 18th century. At one point the distinction between John Nash, Jr., and John Nash, III, is not clear; usually the Jr. in the former's name was dropped after the death of his father in 1776 and John Nash, Jr., after that date refers to John Nash, III, but this was not always the case. Another case which should be mentioned is that of J. W. Womack; when only the initials were given it was not possible to know whether they referred to James W. Womack or Joel W. Womack, contemporaries, so entries under all three names are made in the index.

A

Aaron, J. B., 796
Abbeyville, S. C., 307
Abbitt, George, 272
Abbitt, Watkins M., 621, 692, 714
Abilene, 219, 456, 460, 463, 545, 559, 570, 596, 719, 742, 767, 817, 819
Abingdon, Va., 522, 788
Abolition, 193, 276, 279-82, 370-2
Abyssinia Baptist Church, 451
Accidents, 657
Accomac County, 201, 480, 622
Acetylene gas, 548
Acteon, 589, 599
Adams, A. B., 791
Adams, Copeland E., 627
Adams, Horace, 467, 534, 625, 682
Adams, John (President), 175, 176
Adams, John, 252
Adams, John G., 676
Adams, John Quincy, 184, 185, 186
Adams, Lucile N., 467
Adams, Philip, 253
Adelle, 599
Adelle Band, 651
Adultery, 31
Africa, 87, 90, 271, 280, 827
Agee, L. E., 415
Agnew Farm, 403
Agnew, James, 192, 357, 676
Agricultural Adjustment Administration, 523-4
Agricultural Stabilization and Conservation, 524
Agriculture, U. S. Department of, 524, 574
Ainslie, Peter, 259
Air Force Technical School, 569

Air Raid Test, 564
Aircraft Warning, 565
Akin, Hudson, 4
Alabama, 205, 307, 387, 498, 558, 632, 633, 640, 766, 825
Alabama Baptist Church, 450, 801
Alamance, Battle of, 52, 63, 635
Alamance County, N. C., 325
Albany Presbytery, 159
Albemarle Barracks, 116, 117
Albemarle County, 19, 41, 50, 96, 104, 155, 419, 542, 623, 691, 722, 726
Albemarle Old Courthouse, 124
Alcoholic Beverage Control Board, 584
Alderman, Edwin A., 637
Alderson, Benedict, 39
Alert Hook and Ladder Co., 695
Alexander, ———, 618
Alexander, Dr., 639
Alexander, Archibald, 75, 151, 152, 157, 158, 159, 166, 171, 244, 245, 249, 279, 761
Alexander, Edward P., 396
Alexander, H. C., 664
Alexander, James, 6
Alexander, Thomas, 670
Alexandria, 156, 634
Alexandria Quartermaster Depot, 569
Allan, Denison Maurice, 643, 693
Allan, Edgar, 419, 422, 423, 425-6, 428, 429, 431, 432, 433, 434, 435, 443, 505, 506, 507, 508, 528, 542, 682, 689, 695, 798, 809
Allan, Edgar, Jr., 442, 543
Alleghany Springs, 369
Allein's *Alarm to the Unconverted*, 243
Allen and Co., 656
Allen, Ann Watkins, 825

847

Commissioner of Revenue, 134, 139-40, 206-7, 210, 211, 388, 415, 421, 422, 431, 432, 439, 440, 616, 617, 625-6, 629, 683

Committee of Safety, 108-9, 139

Commodity Substitutes, 390-1

Commonwealth Fund, 607, 608

Commonwealth's Attorney, 206, 211-2, 374, 388, 415, 420, 421, 422, 423, 426, 428, 431, 432, 439, 440, 588, 617, 625, 682

Communion, 63, 71, 72, 74-5, 258-9, 447, 448, 454, 455, 591

Community League, 496

Company C. 53rd Virginia Infantry, 792

Company G, Virginia National Guard —see Farmville Guard

Compton, Edward H., 250

Compton, William R., 796

Concord, 314, 315, 597

Concord Baptist Church, 461

Concord, Battle of, 108

Confederate Bonds, 391, 392, 471

Confederate Cemetery, 648

Confederate General Hospital, Farmville, 392, 411, 414, 648

Confederate Money, 391, 392

Confederate Monument, 646, 647-8

Confederate Reunion, 646-7

Confederate States of America, 380, 384, 385, 390, 395, 416, 471, 488, 555

Confederate Veterans, 645

Confederation, Articles of, 140, 141

Confirmation, 454

Congaree Rifles, 636

Congregational-Christian Church, 262

Congregationalists, 248, 249

Congress, Confederate, 380, 385, 388, 633, 691

Congress, Continental, 110, 111, 115, 631, 633

Congress, United States, 140, 150, 178, 180, 181, 182, 183, 191, 194, 198, 201, 227, 287, 289, 317, 345, 359, 370, 379, 413, 419, 420, 437, 438, 440, 441, 443, 587, 599, 613, 616, 617, 620, 632, 633, 634, 671, 690-2, 798, 821, 826

Congressional District, 175, 193, 194, 200, 371, 376, 380, 419-20, 599, 616, 634

Connecticut, 164, 505

Conner, Edmund, 168, 674

Conner, Thomas, 262

Conrad, George O., 482

Conservatives—see Democrats

Constables, 25, 56, 208, 210, 211, 421, 611, 617

Constitution, Confederate, 380

Constitution, U. S., 141-3, 150, 174, 175, 194, 236, 287, 311, 412, 413, 580, 584, 689, 832

Constitution, Virginia, 1776, 59, 111, 112, 186, 187, 311, 312, 627, 678

Constitution, Virginia, 1830, 187

Constitution, Virginia, 1851, 198, 199, 200, 206, 210, 219, 222, 680

Constitution, Virginia, 1868, 420-1, 425, 428, 438, 444, 445, 488, 680

Constitution, Virginia, 1902, 444-5, 555, 618, 623, 629

Constitutional Presbyterian Church — see Presbyterians, New School

Constitutional Unity Party, 376

Continental Currency, 27

Convention, Commercial, 326

Convention, Constitutional, 1787, 141-2

Convention, Revolutionary, 59, 109, 110, 111, 112, 686, 689

Convention, Secession, 378, 380, 689

Convention, Virginia, 1788, 141-3, 370, 630, 689, 743, 832

Convention, Virginia, 1829-30, 187, 224, 627, 689, 832

Convention, Virginia, 1850-1, 156, 198, 689, 833

Convention, Virginia, 1867-8, 419, 420, 488, 689

Convention, Virginia, 1901-2, 444-5, 555, 629, 689

Convention, Virginia, 1933, 584, 689

Convention, Virginia, 1945, 689

Conversation, 363, 365

Convicts, 593, 594

Convict Servants, 89-90, 91

Cook, Adam, 460, 615

Cook Family, 508

Cook, Lula G., 460

Cook, John R. and Co., 300

Cook, Laurance, 670

Cook, W. T., 615, 627

Cooke, the Rev. Mr., 454

Cooke, J. B., 693

Cooking, 366

Coolidge, Calvin, 624

Cooper, 271, 351, 536-7

Cooper, Charles, 39

Cooperative Store, 512-3

Coplin, John, 671

Coplin, John, Jr., 671

Coplin, Thomas, 671

Coplin, William, 671

Copper, 291, 305

Coppic, 374

Cork, 354, 721, 840-1

Corn, 89, 120, 121, 122, 129, 283, 291, 292, 334, 342, 343, 346, 350, 360, 361, 362, 386, 524

Corn Fodder, 335-6

Ligon, Ann, 764
Ligon, Bettie Ann, 526, 843
Ligon, B. H., 445
Ligon, Goodrich, 790
Ligon, Henry, 5, 7, 46, 49, 50, 68
Ligon, Henry, 229, 741, 775
Ligon, James, 130, 227, 768, 825
Ligon, James D., 155, 168, 169, 173, 192, 223, 306, 354, 677, 825, 844
Ligon, John, 120, 121, 272, 741
Ligon, John (II), 792
Ligon, John T., 188, 196, 199, 321, 357, 673, 843
Ligon, Joseph, 3, 6
Ligon, Joseph (II), 252, 788
Ligon, J. E., 543
Ligon, Joseph T., 169, 212, 232, 374, 378, 387, 388, 415, 416, 419, 529, 530, 680, 789, 807
Ligon, Mrs. J. T., 512
Ligon, Martha Watkins, 825
Ligon, Nancy Clark, 788
Ligon, Osborn, 792
Ligon, P. Leigh, 792, 796
Ligon, Paschal L., 210, 354, 679
Ligon, R. V., 790
Ligon, Sallie, 807
Ligon, Thomas Watkins, 173, 632, 633, 825, 844
Ligon, William, 3, 48, 84, 120, 130
Ligon, William (II), 229, 253, 764, 775
Ligon, William C., 257
Ligon's Mill, 37, 303
Ligon's Rolling Road, 46, 49
Ligontown, 313, 398, 408, 773
Limbertwig Apple, 340
Lime, 291, 334
Lincoln, Abraham, 377, 403, 411, 412
Linden (Dupuy), 167, 282, 843
Linden (Watson-Stokes-Cox), 825, 842
Lindsay, C. D., 790
Lindsey, Aaron J., 677
Lindsey, Henry, 552
Lindsey, James A., 676
Lindsey, Thomas G., 260, 676
Lindsey, William, 217, 687
Lindsey, W. T., 841
Lion Brand Shoes, 540
Lions Club, 566, 607, 659
Lipford, Thomas, 677
Lipner, Henry, 118
Lipscomb, E. D., 612, 696
Lipscomb, Ottaway, 448
Liquor License, 137, 578, 579, 581, 583
Liquor Rates, 40, 311
Liquor Selling, 32, 579
Liquor Traffic, 585
Literary and Philosophical Society (H.S.C.), 155, 156
Literary Fund, 154, 168, 170, 638

Little Briery River, 6
Little Buffalo Creek, 11, 13, 208, 302, 303, 548, 838
Little Mountain Creek, 11
Little Nottoway River, 78
Little Roanoke Bridge, 74, 730, 731
Little Roanoke River, 5, 17, 20, 295
Little Rock, Ark., 646
Little Sailor's Creek, 302, 303, 400
Littlejohn, Joseph, 6, 27
Littleton, Mattie, 485
Livery Stable, 551
Livestock, 85-6, 103, 104, 349, 507, 511
Livingston Plow, 342
Llewelling, Freeman, 43
Lloyd, A. S., 456
Lloyd, John, 672
Lockett, Benjamin F., 357
Lockett, C. C., 323, 324, 391, 676
Lockett District, 431, 432, 434, 436, 440, 445, 489, 495, 497, 498, 593, 594, 596, 603, 604, 615, 617, 621, 627, 685, 693, 713, 807
Lockett, Edmund, 206, 207, 209, 388, 679, 683, 775
Lockett, Edmund (II), 393, 395, 789
Lockett, E. S., 790
Lockett, Fred, 450
Lockett, George W., 210, 676
Lockett, Henry L., 487
Lockett House, 714, 837
Lockett, James S., 212, 353, 374, 388, 403, 404, 414, 415, 459, 468, 488, 509, 680, 792, 837
Lockett, Lelia, 404, 509
Lockett, Osborn, 169, 181, 184, 186, 206, 209, 299, 679, 683, 775
Lockett, Samuel, 183
Lockett, Samuel F., 181
Lockett, Samuel L., 206, 223, 230, 682, 758
Lockett Township, 423
Lockett, Womack and Co., 320
Lockett's Farm, Battle of, 403-4, 407, 408, 795
Lockett's Mill, 303
Lockett's Mill (II), 303
Lockett's Road, 265
Locks, 93, 291, 292, 293, 296, 303
Locofoco, 195
Locusts (insects), 342
Locust Grove (Crute-Mottley), 841-2
Locust Grove (Redd), 767, 841
Lodge, Samuel P., 675
Log College, 73-4, 832
Logan, Richard, 186, 187, 689
London, 94, 505, 528
London, Bishop of, 74
Londonderry, 220, 298, 319, 780
Long, Armistead L., 396

Port Hudson, Miss., 393
Porter, Andrew, 136
Porter, A. H., 427, 430, 532, 546, 579, 695, 696
Porter, Charles H., 419-20
Porter, Hugh, 242, 670
Porter, Jeremiah, 676, 764
Porter, Mrs. Jeremiah, 764
Porter, John, 50
Porter, John, Sr., 671
Porter, John, Jr., 671
Porter, Mandy, 764
Porter, Nathaniel, 670
Porter, Natt, 671
Porter, Rezin, 168, 169, 190, 209, 229, 679
Porter, Samuel, 670
Porter, T. W., 552
Porter, William, 117, 216, 227, 228, 671
Porter, William J., 198, 388, 680
Porterfield, J. W., 610
Porter's Mail Coach, 307
Portland, Ore., 826
Portsmouth, 111, 284
Portugal, 182
Posey, Thomas, 128
Postal Service, 94, 307, 308, 312-5, 388, 598-9
Potash, 291
Potomac River, 141, 289, 290, 325
Potter, 6
Potter, A. M., 553
Potter, Walter, 563
Potts, Capt., 381
Poughkeepsie, N. Y., 666
Powder, Removal of, 108-9, 832
Powell, A. G., 506, 511, 528
Powell's Grove, 451
Powers, Bettie J., 481
Powers, J., 267
Powhatan (Indian), 12
Powhatan County, 74, 124, 127, 153, 205, 272, 419, 420, 605, 689, 691, 722, 738, 752
Powhatan Courthouse, 312, 345, 545, 660
Powys Family, 507
Powys, Richard A. N., 506, 507
Powys, Walter N., 506, 507
Preot, Arnaud, 391, 480
Presbyterians, 15-6, 28, 63, 65, 73-7, 96, 101, 145, 158, 159, 238, 239, 240, 242, 243, 244, 244-51, 253, 264, 363, 365, 456, 457-8, 477, 478, 479, 640, 643, 665, 731, 735, 760, 761, 762, 763, 773
Presbyterians, New School, 249, 250, 251, 456, 461
Presbyterians, New Side, 73-4, 75, 76
Presbyterians, Old School, 249-50, 456
Presbyterians, Old Side, 73, 76
(Presbyterian) Union, Act of, 249

President, Confederate, 394
President, U. S., 181, 235, 379, 413
Preston, Walter, 205
Price, A. J., 456, 486
Price, Benjamin H., 190, 758
Price, Charles, 738, 741
Price, Charles A., 378, 416, 427, 592
Price, Charles H., 672
Price, Charles W., 758
Price Control, 390-1, 553
Price, Daniel, 790
Price, Ebenezer, 675
Price, E. N., 377, 790
Price, Edward N., 415, 416
Price, Edward T., 677
Price, Edwin, 758
Price, Edwin N., 301, 518
Price, Edwin Y., 678
Price, Elizabeth, 295
Price, Everette E., 463
Price, Frank P., 487, 806
Price, George D., 458
Price, Ida Mae, 463
Price, Jacob, 677
Price, James, 217, 758
Price, J. B., 486
Price, J. H., 533
Price, James H., 592
Price, James T., 163, 185, 190, 191, 196, 604, 672
Price, Jerusha, 302
Price, John M., 676
Price, Joseph, 167
Price, Joseph B., 791
Price, Joseph M., 379, 672
Price, MacFaden, 463
Price, Mrs. M. B., 803
Price, Martha H., 786
Price, Mary, 365
Price, Miriam, 574
Price, M. T., 762
Price, Nannie, 458
Price, Nathaniel, 128, 159, 169, 172, 173, 188, 190, 206, 209, 215, 217, 229, 231, 247, 290, 340, 672, 679, 683
Price, Nathaniel D., 234, 762
Price, Nathaniel J., 195
Price, Ned, 365
Price, Pattie, 456
Price, Pugh, 115, 148, 632
Price, Pugh, Sr., 48, 86
Price, Pugh, Jr., 46, 56
Price, Pugh W., 311, 350, 449
Price, R. A., 792
Price, R. Lee, 601, 616, 617, 684
Price, Richard W., 212, 374, 388, 414, 610, 680, 797
Price, Samuel C., 790
Price, Spencer, 844
Price, Sterling, 632, 633, 635, 825, 826

The Spirit of

*★ *The challenge and strange, the impossible, as told by 38 famous* ★*

NEW YORK : HENRY HOLT & COMPANY

Adventure

the fascination of the

and the dangerous ＊＊

writer-adventurers.

Edited by Whit Burnett

First Edition

For

JOHN SOUTHGATE BURNETT,

explorer, at present,

of the Nissequogue,

Long Island,

N. Y.

Acknowledgments

The editor wishes to thank for their suggestions, help, and cooperation the authors in this book, their publishers or agents who granted their permissions, and for special help of other kinds: John Burt, of the Brookhaven National Laboratory, Long Island; Dr. Robert Cushman Murphy, of the American Museum of Natural History, New York; Hallie Southgate Burnett; Edith Tyler of the Emma S. Clark Memorial Library of Setauket, Long Island; Louis Paul, the author; Bernardine Kielty of New York; William L. Laurence of the New York *Times;* Henry D. Smyth, Chairman, Department of Physics, Princeton University, and consultant of the Manhattan District, United States Engineers; and Peter Freuchen. For specific material in the book the editor has acknowledged sources and copyrights at the bottom of the first page of each contribution.

Adventure Is a Human Need

This is a book of human excitement in which man, daring the utmost, has walked into the unfamiliar, challenged the elements, and, human and fallible, has fought out his personal battle with his fate and, in most cases, won. The word for all such shining deeds is one we know—Adventure. And we know it in the usual sense, as a bold undertaking in which hazards are to be met, and the issue, as the dictionary says, hangs upon unforeseen events.

In this assemblage of experiences, some so painfully true that their authors have had to overcome a natural reticence in telling of them, there is no lack of bold undertakings. And from the armchairs of those who will never plunge into the jungle or ride the seas, the word will spring to action: as readers we shall find the dictionary definition perfectly articulated.

But for the men who participate in the life of the verb, those who pit themselves against the unforeseen event, who voyage into places where man has never been before, into the air, the sea, the wilderness, the mountains, coping with conditions that man has not coped with in his usual life, for these men—pioneers, discoverers, explorers, dreamers, pirates, poets, sailors, men—the word perhaps was never quite so bookish or so clear.

What is an adventure?

To Maurice Herzog, on Annapurna, a peak higher than man had ever reached in his life on earth, that summit once attained was "fulfillment," the achievement of a freedom never before experienced and never thenceforth to be lost. In an act of will, which verged on the loss of life, he found himself. To this indomitable and persistent man of France adventure is a quality of the human spirit.

"The adventurer is within us," wrote William Bolitho, a wise commentator, some years ago, "and he contests for our favor with the social man we are obliged to be. . . . We are born adventurers, and the love of adventure never leaves us till we are very old; old, timid men, in whose interest it is that adventure should quite die out . . ."

Well, we are none of us quite that old. Certainly none of us who pick up a book with a normal curiosity as to what's inside, what its writer thinks, how its actors act, and what is in the book to evoke the unfamiliarity of the *place*. Man's normal curiosity dies slowly. And it is born very early. And it propels him, even at a crawl, to venture from the corner that he knows, across the room to the corner unfamiliar, and later out across the threshold. The one romantic universal in all adventurers is the desire to be, or go, someplace else—and there, of course, to subject his total self to the test of whatever it is that there awaits him.

No dull, incurious creature ever belonged to this courageous and heady band of men. No dullard ever was an adventurer. Many odd things else he might be, like the whalers around the factory ships in the Antarctic, odd and ill-adjusted men pursuing the whale and fortune, or like old mad Ahab earlier just pursuing the whale; a man may be a gambler with his fate; or even a pirate, like Captain Kidd; he may be 90 per cent mad, like Don Quixote; but he may never be found among the dull ones, the creature of a soft routine, ready-made comforts, and a predictable life.

If it is true the adventurer is within us, in some the trace is slight, vestigial. And such diminished fellows must take it out in fishing. Or growing a beard, for three days, hunting deer. Or, perhaps, in simply reading of the derring-do of others.

There is a Don Quixote in the breast of many of us, bidding us be up and away, lance in hand, mounted, riding off into the distance to meet the dragon of our destiny. There is also in our bosoms something of the romantic Don's companion—the fat and reasonable peasant, Sancho Panza, soberly submitting all such dream stuff to the proverbs of common sense and seeing a sheep as mutton rather than enchantment. Yet even Sancho Panza was talked into the journey by the lively-witted Don. Even realists appreciate the fact that a little jaunt, a change, will do a man no harm. The adventurer, deep within us, is sometimes sorely hedged about. And some of us are fashioned, as was Alphonse Daudet's Tartarin of Tarascon, with both the glorious Don and the dull peasant encased in the same body, and he who wants to slay a lion cannot kill a fly, he who'd roam the world must stay and pay the taxes—a pretty kettle of fish, as Daudet observed, when the Don Quixote in our bosom cries, "Cover yourself with glory," and the voice of Sancho Panza cries from the same throat, "Stay, and keep on your warm long underwear!"

No adventure worthy of the name ever took place in one's own back yard. And in view of the significance of the place, the scene, the unfamiliar, against which a man of adventure acts, some of these pieces are generously long, suffused with the atmosphere of their particular worlds so far from all familiarity. If, as Bolitho has said, "adventure must start with running away from home," surely no more classic example of this truth could be found than the case of Robinson Crusoe, so widely known for his stolid British qualities of endurance and his practical adaptation to colonial life on his "desert isle," but less well known (though here presented) for the early, tortuous ratiocination that went on inside him, so intuitively realized by Defoe, when young Robinson tried and failed to conquer the urge within him which made him seek his destiny at sea and so subject himself to the dire prediction of his father that if he ran away he would be "the most miserable wretch that was ever born."

Misery is a part-time diet of adventurers. But it is a transient fare; ahead are richer satisfactions. We have all run away once. Some who ran away returned like Juan Belmonte, who, as a boy of ten or eleven, left his poverty-stricken home in Seville to hunt those lions in Africa; but when he looked at the broad expanse of sea before him he lost heart and went back home again, Africa and its lions never achieved. Not all adventurers become great hunters. Belmonte became the world's greatest bullfighter. The thing dared, some venture into the uncertain, has launched many a man into the wider world. Fools, some were called; Columbus was a fool, they said; Lindbergh was a flying fool; such "fools" abound in the literature of human risk in strange surroundings. But the adventurers have skins for shedding other people's jibes. Their curiosity is stronger than their sense of what people may think; and something drives them toward their ends in the world, even, at times, against their reasoned judgment, with "an obstinacy that nothing can resist."

Vague propulsion sometimes, this desire to get away. Mrs. Fahnestock ran away to sea at fifty. There was always the frontier. In 1845 it was the West. And a man with all the privileges of cultured Boston could still feel an unbearable discontent with home, as the writer points out in "A Man Called Horse." To the West he went, to live a freer life, to test himself against a new set of conditions. And so it was with the restlessness in Europe that had driven hundreds of thousands to seek a strange and different life in America. Restlessness blew Columbus across the Atlantic, and earlier sent the Vikings on their rovings . . . today the West is farms, factories, and dust bowls; plane wings cast their shadows over the African jungles, and some now look to space as the next pioneer outpost.

Adventure is a human need. We recognize it as the daring thing which makes us bigger than our usual selves. Adventure is the curiosity of man to see the other side of the mountain, the impulse in him that makes him break his bonds with lesser things and frees him for a greater possibility. Few men live so quietly and so sheltered that they have not risked their necks at some time in their lives. But one risk is not the life of adventure. To put oneself in the way of almost constant risk in the satisfying of this odd hunger "for the well-nigh impossible" is something else again. And many of the people in this book are just such folk, whose way of life is hazard, the risk there, the chance taken, and the venture set in motion.

Much in this book has come from books written by the adventurers themselves, their words set down on the remote scene or after their return to their respectable base at home. There is also some fiction, since fiction is often the truest distillation of some phases of the human truth, the third person providing us with a deeper and more comprehensive interpretation of the adventuring spirit than if the story were told in the attitude-limiting, first-person singular.

On the other hand, an adventure truly experienced is something we should share as directly as communication allows, and no false modesty should blur the effect, however an I-account may exhibit an author's personal virtues. Most of these writers have been both frank with themselves and honest with their readers in the deepest possible personal sense. We think of Admiral Byrd, for months in the winter darkness of the South Pole, alone, near death, setting down his gravest thoughts, not quite certain whether he would live or die or, in his self-chosen solitude, lose his mind. And again we mention Herzog who was thanked, in print, "for being so well aware that one can put aside modesty (in writing his experiences) without becoming vain. If it were not so," wrote Lucien Devies, president of the Himalayan Mountain Committee, "then every advance of the spirit would go unrecorded. It takes courage to draw the veil from those moments when the individual approaches most nearly to the universal."

By their personalities, their actions, and the result of their struggles, each of these writer-adventurers has, in his individual way, defined adventure. None is overly precise; each was engaged *in* the thing itself. In these experiences the men and women have come to grips with final realities. They have looked into the baleful eye of death, "the old man in the long white nightgown," and stared him down, and pushed on past him, across an ocean, down into the crater of a volcano, up to the highest peaks on earth, under the sea, into the jungles, against strange tribes, in bitter cold or raging heat, and against many and devious elements and forces seemingly created to render man of less consequence than the element or the obstacle itself. But whatever it is that makes a man court danger and cope with it has prevailed. And this book, out of hundreds of books of the human spirit setting itself up in the face of its possible extinction, is a partial result.

Adventure is more than the particular word for it all. Adventure is an atmosphere and essence, a climate of the mind. It is the man plus the place and the event; a man out of the ordinary in daring, endurance, and vision, and a place out of our common ken, even perhaps out of this world. And the *place,* not least of all.

Readers will note a change in the temper of adventuring since the big-game-hunting, native-intimidating jungle trips of a few generations ago. Livingstone went into Africa with Bibles; when Stanley followed to find him he took guns and whips to drive the natives on ahead of him. The Gheerbrant group of four young men went into the jungles of the Amazon, practically unarmed, their important equipment being sound machines to record and play back native music. No one these days can get away with unsupported tales like the Baron Munchausen's; the Himalayan climbers, their hands freezing, photographed all the lesser peaks below them as evidence of their climb; a man who goes into a volcano nowadays doesn't simply tell of it, he brings back the photographs showing the lava spilling near his feet.

Science accompanies today's adventurers. Columbus just had wind. Oxygen cannisters went up the last steps of Everest, almost as important in the final assault as the men who carried them. The instrument panel of a modern plane, an alien forest to a groundling, is the heart chart of the pilot. If Byrd was snowbound at the Pole for months, at least he had a radio. Gheerbrant played Mozart to the Indians of the Upper Amazon. Instruments aid but do not determine whether an experience, or a life, is an adventure. The thing that does determine it is the man.

What is the criterion of adventure?

What is adventure?

I asked this of Peter Freuchen, the rugged, bearded, humorous Dane, back from Greenland, where he had seen the ice-clad world he had helped discover as a youth now converted into an aerial outpost of mechanical civilization.

"Well," said the Viking who had married an Eskimo, frozen off a foot in the Arctic, and had had adventures enough to fill many books, "adventure is not an act in line of duty. It is not something done for science, either. Adventure is a strange experience for its own sake."

And who goes on such a sortie? Are these *men apart,* a special sort? Men who know no fear and thus completely different from the rest of us?

"I do what I can to get away from those fellows who never get scared," said the Arctic explorer. "They are very dangerous men. They get you into all kinds of trouble—those fellows who are scared of nothing. They die soon. I am always scared."

Sixteen men died in futile attempts to scale Mount Everest. Perhaps those who almost reached the summit knew the ecstasy and vertigo of heights; we shall never know. Perhaps they knew the fear of death. *"Fear is the truth of time,"* writes the poet Richard Eberhart. *"If it is not now, it will come here-after. Death is waiting for the human creature."*

An adventurer worthy of the adventure is destined to succeed. He feels it, and we feel it with him. The best of them survive to tell about it. They are men of daring, but men of more than ordinary control and discipline. It is in the nature of a true adventurer to push on through. When he doubts, his destiny sits back on its haunches, watching warily. If he breaks, the charm is at once withdrawn. He sinks into the sea; the adventure is over. That one failed.

This is a book in which they did not fail, a book of man against the ultimate, testing his spirit against the elements of life, the forces of nature, the dangers and the mysteries of the unknown; man on the heights, in the depths, in contests with the sea, the air, the earth, facing the strangeness and hostility of other men, and faced with the enigma and adventure of his own none too predictable human self.

WHIT BURNETT

Contents

1 *Farewell, My Home*

Farewell, My House

Adventure Starts with Running Away from Home*

WILLIAM BOLITHO

✳✳ William Bolitho, an English journalist and writer (1890-1930), was born in Capetown, South Africa, of Dutch-English parentage. He crowded into his 40 years of life a great deal of personal adventure, beginning when the British burned out the family farm because they were fighting on the side of the Boers.

He was the only man to escape alive, out of 15 English soldiers in a Somme front cave-in in 1916. He was a Paris correspondent for the Manchester *Guardian* and special European correspondent for the New York *World* in the late 20's. The following quotation is from one of his best-known books, a collection of biographical studies analyzing the impulse to adventure in men and women. ✳✳

A feat, a danger, a surprise, these are bonbons which adventure showers on those who follow her cult with a single mind. Their occurrence even repeated does not constitute a life of adventure.

Here also we renounce utterly the comfort of Mr. Kipling, who believed commuting, and soldiering in the British Army, and buying English country houses, adventurous; and Mr. Chesterton, who was certain that a long walk on Sunday and a glass of beer set one spiritually in the company of Alexander, and Captain Kidd and Cagliostro. All this amiable misconception is as touching as the children's wish for a good pirate, for bloodshed in which no one gets hurt, and roulette with haricot beans. Tom Sawyer knew better. The adventurer is an outlaw. Adventure must start with running away from home . . .

* From *Twelve Against the Gods,* published by Simon & Schuster, Inc., and reprinted by permission of the publisher.

The Lure of Islands*

JAMES NORMAN HALL

✳✳ James Norman Hall (1887-1951) fell in love with literature and the sea at almost the same time in the small town in Iowa where he was born. It was not until his meeting with Charles Nordhoff, after his return to Paris from a German prison camp and after serving as machine-gunner with the Royal Fusiliers, 1914-1916, and pursuit pilot with the Lafayette Escadrille, that these two strains in his nature were brought together in a collaboration that led the two men to go to Tahiti where they wrote their best books, including the well-known *Mutiny on the Bounty*, 1932; *Men Against the Sea*, 1934; *Pitcairn's Island*, 1934; and numerous others. Hall's first book under his own name was *Kitchener's Mob*, 1916, and his last one, *My Island Home*, 1952, is an autobiography, from which the following extract is taken. ✳✳

Ever since boyhood the mere name, "island," has had a peculiar fascination for me. An inland birth was, doubtless, partly responsible for that; islands were far to seek on the prairies of Iowa, and yet they could be found, of a sort. A mudbank in the sluggish midstream of a prairie slough was enough; and if at the season of the spring rains I found one larger, with a tree or two, the roots undermined by the current, leaning across it, I asked nothing better than to halt there and moor my flat-bottomed skiff to the roots of one of the trees. Try as I would, though, I could not imagine the sea—any sea. The fact that the earth is three-quarters water was not a fact to me. Neither the evidence furnished by maps in school geographies nor the assurance of my elders convinced me; or, if I believed, it was only with the surface of my mind. Within was a solid core of doubt.

Until one wintry afternoon—it must have been around my tenth or eleventh year: a memorable day that stands out with the entrancing roundness and clearness of objects seen through the stereoscopic glasses our parents used to keep with the knickknacks on the parlor table. I remember the very weather of it: the fine, dry snow filling the wagon tracks in the frozen mud, sifting lightly along the board sidewalks, piling in drifts along the fronts of the store buildings, adding little by little to the grayness of a gray world. I was on my way to Mrs. Sigafoos' shop.

She kept a small "stationery and notions" store not far from the C.R. I. & P. railway station, and there she would sit by the window, a shawl pinned around her thin shoulders, keeping her rocker going when there was nothing to be seen out of doors, stopping it abruptly and peering out when someone passed . . .

Mrs. Sigafoos had a shelf of books: boy's books such as *Cudjo's Cave, Lost River,* and editions of the Henty and Alger books, all of which I read, taking great care not to soil them. There were also padded-leather editions of the poets: Bryant, Whittier, Longfellow, and Lowell, for birthday and school-graduation gifts . . .

There was another book on the shelf. I had noticed it before, but, somehow, it had failed to arouse my interest: *Typee,* by Herman Melville. It may have been the strange title that threw me off. On this afternoon I was tempted to take it down and open it.

Six months at sea! Yes, reader, as I live, six months out of sight of land; cruising after the sperm-whale beneath the scorching sun of the Line, and tossed on the billows of the wide-rolling Pacific—the sky above, the sea around, and nothing else!

Who does not remember some day in boyhood, such as this one of mine, preserved, fragrant, and memorable, between the covers of a book? *Typee* has my day safely hidden among its pages. There was a quality approaching the ideal in my experience; indeed, I cannot imagine anything lacking that might have made it more so. It was my first authentic entrance, in literature, to the world of islands; and what more fitting vantage-point or vantage-time could I have had for the experience than the back room of Mrs. Sigafoos' shop, in a little farming town on the prairies on the afternoon of a snowy winter day? For the first time I believed in the sea—emotionally, I mean. That opening paragraph spread it out before me as something not to be questioned, like the sea of land rolling away to the horizons that bounded my home town. But, as I followed Melville across it, in the imagination, to Nuku Hiva in the Marquesas Islands, I little realized that the first gossamerlike thread of Chance was being spun which was to take me to the South Pacific, with my friend Nordhoff, so many years later.

The Young Crusoe*

DANIEL DEFOE

✳✳ Daniel Defoe (1661-1731) is generally supposed to have based *Robinson Crusoe* upon the real adventures of one Alexander Selkirk. This section begins the adventure classic that has been read by every generation since it first appeared in 1719, detailing how a shipwrecked Englishman, with ingenuity and self-reliance, adjusted himself to 24 years of solitude on a jungle island. ✳✳

THE URGE TO SEE THE WORLD

I was born in the year 1632, in the city of York, of a good family, though not of that country, my father being a foreigner of Bremen who settled first at Hull. He got a good estate by merchandise and, leaving off his trade, lived afterward at York, from whence he had married my mother, whose relations were named Robinson, a very good family in that country, and from whom I was called Robinson Kreutznaer; but by the usual corruption of words in England we are now called, nay, we call ourselves, and write our name "Crusoe," and so my companions always called me.

I had two elder brothers, one of which was lieutenant colonel to an English regiment of foot in Flanders, formerly commanded by the famous Colonel Lockhart, and was killed at the battle near Dunkirk against the Spaniards; what became of my second brother I never knew, any more than my father or mother did know what was become of me.

Being the third son of the family, and not bred to any trade, my head began to be filled very early with rambling thoughts. My father, who was very ancient, had given me a competent share of learning, as far as house education and a country free school generally goes, and designed me for the law; but I would be satisfied with nothing but going to sea; and my inclination to this led me so strongly against the will, nay, the commands of my father and against all the entreaties and persuasions of my mother and other friends that

* From *Robinson Crusoe*, first published in 1719.

there seemed to be something fatal in that propension of nature tending directly to the life of misery which was to befall me.

My father, a wise and grave man, gave me serious and excellent counsel against what he foresaw was my design. He called me one morning into his chamber, where he was confined by the gout, and expostulated very warmly with me upon this subject. He asked me what reasons more than a mere wandering inclination I had for leaving my father's house and my native country, where I might be well introduced, and had a prospect of raising my fortune by application and industry, with a life of ease and pleasure. He told me it was for men of desperate fortunes on one hand, or of aspiring, superior fortunes on the other, who went abroad upon adventures, to rise by enterprise, and make themselves famous in undertakings of a nature out of the common road; that these things were all either too far above me or too far below me; that mine was the middle state, or what might be called the upper station of low life, which he had found by long experience was the best state in the world, the most suited to human happiness, not exposed to the miseries and hardships, the labor and sufferings of the mechanic part of mankind and not embarrassed with the pride, luxury, ambition, and envy of the upper part of mankind. He told me I might judge of the happiness of this state by this one thing, viz., that this was the state of life which all other people envied; that kings have frequently lamented the miserable consequences of being born to great things, and wished they had been placed in the middle of the two extremes, between the mean and the great; that the wise man gave his testimony to this as the just standard of true felicity, when he prayed to have "neither poverty nor riches."

He bid me observe it, and I should always find, that the calamities of life were shared among the upper and lower part of mankind; but that the middle station had the fewest disasters, and was not exposed to so many vicissitudes as the higher or lower part of mankind; nay, they were not subjected to so many distempers and uneasinesses either of body or mind as those were who, by vicious living, luxury, and extravagances on one hand, or by hard labor, want of necessaries, and mean or insufficient diet on the other hand, bring distempers upon themselves by the natural consequences of their way of living; that the middle station of life was calculated for all kind of virtues and all kind of enjoyments; that peace and plenty were the handmaids of a middle fortune; that temperance, moderation, quietness, health, society, all agreeable diversions, and all desirable pleasures, were the blessings attending the middle station of life; that this way men went silently and smoothly through the world, and comfortably out of it, not embarrassed with the labors of the hands or of the head, not sold to the life of slavery for daily bread, or harassed with perplexed circumstances, which rob the soul of peace and the body of rest; not enraged with the passion of envy or secret burning lust of ambition for great things; but in easy circumstances sliding gently through the world, and sensibly tasting the sweets of living, without the bitter, feeling that they are happy and learning by every day's experience to know it more sensibly.

After this, he pressed me earnestly, and in the most affectionate manner, not to play the young man, not to precipitate myself into miseries which Nature and the station of life I was born in seemed to have provided against; that I was under no necessity of seeking my bread; that he would do well for me, and endeavor to enter me fairly into the station of life which he had been just recommending to me; and that if I was not very easy and happy in the world, it must be my mere fate or fault that must hinder it, and that he should have nothing to answer for, having thus discharged his duty in warning me against measures which he knew would be to my hurt. In a word, that as he would do very kind things for me if I would stay and settle at home as he directed, so he would not have so much hand in my misfortunes as to give me any encouragement to go away. And to close all, he told me I had my elder brother for an example, to whom he had used the same earnest persuasions to keep him from going into the Low Country wars, but could not prevail, his young desires prompting him to run into the army where he was killed; and though he said he would not cease to pray for me, yet he would venture to say to me that if I did take this foolish step, God would not bless me, and I would have leisure hereafter to reflect upon having neglected his counsel when there might be none to assist in my recovery.

I observed in this last part of his discourse, which was truly prophetic, though I suppose my father did not know it to be so himself; I say, I observed the tears run down his face very plentifully, and especially when he spoke of my brother who was killed; and that when he spoke of my having leisure to repent, and none to assist me, he was so moved that he broke off the discourse and told me his heart was so full he could say no more to me.

I was sincerely affected with this discourse, as indeed who could be otherwise? and I resolved not to think of going abroad any more but to settle at home according to my father's desire. But alas! a few days wore it all off; and in short, to prevent any of my father's farther importunities, in a few weeks after I resolved to run quite away from him. However I did not act so hastily neither, as my first heat of resolution prompted, but I took my mother, at a time when I thought her a little pleasanter than ordinary, and told her that my thoughts were so entirely bent upon seeing the world that I should never settle to anything with resolution enough to go through with it, and my father had better give me his consent than force me to go without it; that I was now eighteen years old, which was too late to go apprentice to a trade or clerk to an attorney; that I was sure, if I did, I should never serve out my time, and I should certainly run away from my master before my time was out, and go to sea; and if she would speak to my father to let me go one voyage abroad, if I came home again and did not like it, I would go no more, and I would promise by a double diligence to recover that time I had lost.

This put my mother into a great passion. She told me she knew it would be to no purpose to speak to my father upon any such subject; that he knew too well what was my interest to give his consent to anything so much for my hurt, and that she wondered how I could think of any such thing after such a discourse as I had had with my father, and such kind and tender expressions as she knew my father had used to me; and that, in short, if I would ruin myself there was no help for me; but I might depend I should never have their consent to it; that for her part she would not have so much hand in my destruction; and I should never have it to say that my mother was willing when my father was not.

Though my mother refused to move it to my father, yet as I have heard afterward, she reported all the discourse to him, and that my father, after showing a great concern at it, said to her with a sign, "That boy might be happy if he would stay at home, but if he goes abroad he will be the most miserable wretch that was ever born. I can give no consent to it."

It was not till almost a year after this that I broke loose, though in the meantime I continued obstinately deaf to all proposals of settling to business, and frequently expostulating with my father and mother about their being so positively determined against what they knew my inclinations prompted me to. But being one day at Hull, where I went casually, and without any purpose of making an elopement that time; but I say, being there, and one of my companions being going by sea to London in his father's ship and prompting me to go with them, with the common allurement of seafaring men, viz., that it should cost me nothing for my passage, I consulted neither father nor mother any more, nor so much as sent them word of it; but leaving them to hear of it as they might, without asking God's blessing, or my father's, without any consideration of circumstances or consequences and in an ill hour, God knows, on the first of September, 1651, I went on board a ship bound for London. Never any young adventurer's misfortunes, I believe, began sooner or continued longer than mine. The ship was no sooner gotten out of the Humber but the wind began to blow and the sea to rise in a most frightful manner; and as I had never been at sea before, I was most inexpressibly sick in body and terrified in my mind. I began now seriously to reflect upon what I had done, and how justly I was overtaken by the judgment of Heaven for my wicked leaving my father's house and abandoning my duty; all the good counsel of my parents, my father's tears and my mother's entreaties, came now fresh into my mind, and my conscience, which was not yet come to the pitch of hardness to which it has been since, reproached me with the contempt of advice and the breach of my duty to God and my father.

All this while the storm increased and the sea, which I had never been upon before, went very high, though nothing like what I have seen many times since; no, nor like what I saw a few days after. But it was enough to affect me then, who was but a young sailor and had never known anything of the matter. I expected every wave would have swallowed us up and that every time the ship fell down, as I thought, in the trough or hollow of the sea, we should never rise more; and in this agony of mind I made many vows and resolutions, that if it would please God here to spare my life this one voyage, if ever I got once my foot upon dry land again, I would go directly home to my father and never set it into a ship again while I lived; that I would take his advice and never run myself into such miseries as these any more. Now I saw plainly the goodness of his observations about the middle station of life, how easy, how comfortably he had lived all his days, and never had been exposed to tempests of sea or troubles on shore; and I resolved that I would, like a true repenting prodigal, go home to my father.

These wise and sober thoughts continued all the while the storm continued, and indeed some time after; but the next day the wind was abated and the sea calmer, and I began to be a little inured to it. However, I was very grave for all that day, being also a little seasick still; but toward night the weather cleared up, the wind was quite over, and a charming, fine evening followed; the sun went down perfectly clear and rose so the next morning; and having little or no wind and a smooth sea, the sun shining upon it, the sight was, as I thought, the most delightful that ever I saw.

I had slept well in the night and was now no more seasick, but very cheerful, looking with wonder upon the sea that was so rough and terrible the day before and could be so calm and so pleasant in so little time after. And now lest my good resolutions should continue, my companion, who had indeed enticed me away, comes to me.

"Well, Bob," says he, clapping me on the shoulder, "how do you do after it? I warrant you were frighted, wa'n't you, last night, when it blew but a capful of wind?"

"A capful, d'you call it?" said I, " 'twas a terrible storm."

"A storm, you fool, you," replies he; "do you call that a storm? Why, it was nothing at all; give us but a good ship and searoom, and we think nothing of such a squall of wind as that; but you're but a fresh-water sailor, Bob; come, let us make a bowl of punch and we'll forget all that; d'ye see what charming weather 'tis now?"

To make short this sad part of my story, we went the old way of all sailors; the punch was made, and I was made drunk with it, and in that one night's wickedness I drowned all my repentance, all my reflections upon my past conduct, and all my resolutions for my future. In a word, as the sea was returned to its smoothness of surface and settled calmness by the abatement of that storm, so the hurry of my thoughts being over, my fears and apprehensions of being swallowed up by the sea being forgotten, and the current of my former desires returned, I entirely forgot the vows and promises that I made in my distress. I found indeed some intervals of reflection, and the serious thoughts did, as it were, endeavor to return again sometimes; but I shook them off and roused myself from them as it were from a distemper and, applying myself to drink and company, soon mastered the return of those fits, for so I called them, and I had in five or six days got as complete a victory over conscience as any young fellow that resolved not to be troubled with it could desire. But I was to have another trial for it still; and Providence, as in such cases generally it does, resolved to leave me entirely without excuse: for if I would not take this for a deliverance, the next was to be such a one as the worst and most hardened wretch among us would confess both the danger and the mercy of.

The sixth day of our being at sea we came into Yarmouth Roads; the wind having been contrary and the weather calm, we had made but little way since the storm. Here we were obliged to come to an anchor, and here we lay, the wind continuing contrary, viz., at southwest, for seven or eight days, during which time a great many ships from Newcastle came into the same Roads, as the common harbor where the ships might wait for a wind for the river.

We had not, however, rid here so long, but should have tided up the river, but that the wind blew too fresh; and after we had lain four or five days, blew very hard. However, the Roads being reckoned as good as a harbor, the anchorage good, and our ground tackle very strong, our men were unconcerned and not in the least apprehensive of danger, but spent the time in rest and mirth, after the manner of the sea; but the eighth day in the morning the wind increased, and we had all hands at work to strike our topmasts and make everything snug and close, that the ship might ride as easy as possible. By noon the sea went very high indeed, and our ship rid forecastle in, shipped several seas, and we thought once or twice our anchor had come home; upon which our master ordered out the sheet anchor, so that we rode with two anchors ahead and the cables veered out to the bitter end.

By this time it blew a terrible storm indeed, and now I began to see terror and amazement in the faces even of the seamen themselves. The master, though vigilant to the business of preserving the ship, yet as he went in and out of his cabin by me, I could hear him softly to himself say several times, "Lord, be merciful to us, we shall be all lost, we shall be all undone"; and the like.

During these first hurries, I was stupid, lying still in my cabin, which was in the steerage, and cannot describe my temper; I could ill reassume the first penitence, which I had so apparently trampled upon and hardened myself against. I thought the bitterness of death had been past and that this would be nothing too, like the first. But when the master himself came by me, as I said just now, and said we should be all lost, I was dreadfully frighted. I got up out of my cabin and looked out; but such a dismal sight I never saw: the sea went mountains high and broke upon us every three or four minutes. When I could look about, I could see nothing but distress round us: two ships that rid near us we found had cut their masts by the board, being deep loaded; and our men cried out that a ship which rid about a mile ahead of us was foundered. Two more ships, being driven from their anchors, were run out of the Roads to sea at all adventures, and that with not a mast standing. The light ships fared the best as not so much laboring in the sea; but two or three of them drove and came close by us, running away with only their spritsail out before the wind.

Toward evening the mate and boatswain begged the master of our ship to let them cut away the foremast, which he was very unwilling to do. But the boatswain protesting to him that if he did not the ship would founder, he consented; and when they had cut away the foremast, the mainmast stood so loose and shook the ship so much, they were obliged to cut her away also, and make a clear deck.

Anyone may judge what a condition I must be in at all this, who was but a young sailor and who had been in such a fright before at but a little. But if I can express at this distance the thoughts I had about me at that time, I was in tenfold more horror of mind upon account of my former convictions, and the having returned from them to the resolutions I had wickedly taken at first, than I was at death itself; and these, added to the terror of the storm, put me into such a condition that I can by no words describe it. But the worst was not come yet; the storm continued with such fury that the seamen themselves acknowledged they had never known a worse. We had a good ship, but she was deep loaded and wallowed in the sea, that the seamen every now and then cried out she would founder. It was my advantage in one respect that I did not know what they meant by "founder" till I inquired. However, the storm was so violent that I saw what is not often seen; the master, the boatswain, and some others more sensible than the rest, at their prayers and expecting every moment when the ship would go to the bottom. In the middle of the night, and under all the rest of our distresses, one of the men, that had been down on purpose to see, cried out we had sprung a leak; another said there was four feet of water in the hold. Then all hands were called to the pump. At that very word my heart, as I thought, died within me, and I fell backward upon the side of my bed where I sat in the cabin. However, the men roused me, and told me that I, that was able to do nothing before, was as well able to pump as another; at which I stirred up and went to the pump and worked very heartily. While this was doing, the master, seeing some light colliers, who, not able to ride out the storm, were obliged to slip and run away to sea, and would come near us, ordered to fire a gun as a signal of distress. I, who knew nothing what that meant, was so surprised that I thought the ship had broke or some dreadful thing had happened. In a word, I was so surprised that I fell down in a swoon. As this was a time when everybody had his own life to think of, nobody minded me, or what was become of me; but another man stepped up to the pump, and thrusting me aside with his foot, let me lie, thinking I had been dead; and it was a great while before I came to myself.

We worked on, but the water increasing in the hold, it was apparent that the ship would founder, and though the storm began to abate a little, yet as it was not possible she could swim till we might run into a port, so the master continued firing guns for help; and a light ship who had rid it out just ahead of us ventured a boat out to help us. It was with the utmost hazard the boat came near us, but it was impossible for us to get on board, or for the boat to lie near the ship side, till at last the men rowing very heartily and venturing their lives to save ours, our men cast them a rope over the stern with a buoy to it and then veered it out a great length, which they after great labor and hazard took hold of, and we hauled them close under our stern and got all into their boat. It was to no purpose for them or us after we were in the boat to think of reaching to their own ship, so all agreed to let her drive and only to pull her in toward shore as much as we could, and our master promised them, that if the boat was staved upon shore, he would make it good to their master; so, partly rowing and partly driving, our boat went away to the norward, sloping toward the shore almost as far as Winterton Ness.

We were not much more than a quarter of an hour out of our ship when we saw her sink, and then I understood for the first time what was meant by a ship foundering in the sea; I must acknowledge I had hardly eyes to look up when the seamen told me she was sinking; for from that moment they rather put me into the boat than that I might be said to go in, my heart was as it were dead within me, partly with fright, partly with horror of mind and the thoughts of what was yet before me.

While we were in this condition, the men yet laboring at the oar to bring the boat near the shore, we could see (when, our boat mounting the waves, we were able to see the shore) a great many people running along the strand, to assist us when we should come near; but we made slow way toward the shore, nor were we able to reach it, till, being past the lighthouse at Winterton, the shore falls off to the westward, toward Cromer, and so the land broke off a little the violence of the wind. Here we got in, and, though not without much difficulty, got all safe on shore, and walked afterward on foot to Yarmouth; where, as unfortunate men, we were used with great humanity, as well by the magistrates of the town, who assigned us good quarters, as by the particular merchants and owners of ships, and had money given us sufficient to carry us either to London or back to Hull, as we thought fit.

Had I now had the sense to have gone back to Hull and have gone home, I had been happy, and my father, an emblem of our blessed Saviour's parable, had even killed the fatted calf for me; for, hearing the ship I went in was cast away in Yarmouth Roads, it was a great while before he had any assurance that I was not drowned.

But my ill fate pushed me on now with an obstinacy that nothing could resist; and though I had several times loud calls from my reason, and my more composed judgment, to go home, yet I had no power to do it. I know not what to call this, nor will I urge that it is a secret, overruling decree, that hurries us on to be the instruments of our own destruction, even though it be before us, and that we rush upon it with our eyes open. Certainly nothing but some such decreed unavoidable misery attending, and which it was impossible for me to escape, could have pushed me forward against the calm reasonings and persuasions of my most retired thoughts, and against two such visible instructions as I had met with in my first attempt.

My comrade, who had helped to harden me before, and who was the master's son, was now less forward than I; the first time he spoke to me after we were at Yarmouth, which was not till two or three days, for we were separated in the town to several quarters; I say, the first time he saw me, it appeared his tone was altered, and, looking very melancholy, and shaking his head, he asked me how I did; telling his father who I was, and how I had come this voyage only for a trial, in order to go farther abroad.

His father, turning to me, with a grave and concerned tone, "Young man," says he, "you ought never to go to sea any more; you ought to take this for a plain and visible token, that you are not to be a seafaring man."

"Why, sir?" said I. "Will you go to sea no more?"

"That is another case," said he. "It is my calling, and therefore my duty; but as you made this voyage for a trial, you see what a taste Heaven has given you of what you are to expect if you persist. Perhaps this has all befallen us on your account, like Jonah in the ship of the Tarshish. Pray," continues he, "what are you, and on what account did you go to sea?"

Upon that I told him some of my story; at the end of which he burst out with a strange kind of passion.

"What had I done," said he, "that such an unhappy wretch should have come into my ship? I would not set my foot in the same ship with thee again for a thousand pounds."

This indeed was, as I said, an excursion of his spirits, which were yet agitated by the sense of his loss, and was farther than he could have authority to go. However, he afterward talked very gravely to me, exhorted me to go back to my father, and not tempt Providence to my ruin; told me, I might see a visible hand of Heaven against me; and, "Young man," said he, "depend upon it, if you do not go back, wherever you go, you will meet with nothing but disasters and disappointments, till your father's words are fulfilled upon you."

We parted soon after, for I made him little answer, and I saw him no more; which way he went, I know not. As for me, having some money in my pocket, I traveled to London by land; and there, as well as on the road, had many struggles with myself what course of life I should take, and whether I should go home or go to sea. As to going home, shame opposed the best motions that offered to my thoughts; and it immediately occurred to me how I should be laughed at among the neighbors, and should be ashamed to see, not my father and mother only, but even everybody else. From whence I have often since observed, how incongruous and irrational the common temper of mankind is, especially of youth, to that reason which ought to guide them in such cases, viz., that they are not ashamed to sin, and yet are ashamed to repent; not ashamed of the action, for which they ought justly to be esteemed fools; but are ashamed of the returning, which only can make them be esteemed wise men.

In this state of life, however, I remained some time, uncertain what measures to take and what course of life to lead. An irresistible reluctance continued to going home; and as I stayed a while, the remembrance of the distress I had been in wore off; and as that abated, the little motion I had in my desires to a return wore off with it, till at last I quite laid aside the thoughts of it, and looked out for another voyage. . . .

Huckleberry Finn*

MARK TWAIN

✳✳ Mark Twain (Samuel L. Clemens, 1835-1910) first published *The Adventures of Huckleberry Finn* in 1884 and it has been read by adults as well as children steadily ever since. This section precedes Huck's encountering Jim, the runaway slave, with whom the boy goes down the Mississippi River on a raft. ✳✳

. . . . He kept me with him all the time, and I never got a chance to run off. We lived in that old cabin, and he always locked the door and put the key under his head nights. He had a gun which he had stole, I reckon, and we fished and hunted, and that was what we lived on. Every little while he locked me in and went down to the store, three miles, to the ferry, and traded fish and game for whisky, and fetched it home and got drunk and had a good time, and licked me. The widow she found out where I was by and by, and she sent a man over to try to get hold of me; but pap drove him off with the gun, and it warn't long after that till I was used to being where I was, and liked it—all but the cowhide part.

It was kind of lazy and jolly, laying off comfortable all day, smoking and fishing, and no books nor study. Two months or more run along, and my clothes got to be all rags and dirt, and I didn't see how I'd ever got to like it so well at the widow's, where you had to wash, and eat on a plate, and comb up, and go to bed and get up regular, and be forever bothering over a book, and have old Miss Watson pecking at you all the time. I didn't want to go back no more. I had stopped cussing, because the widow didn't like it; but now I took to it again because pap hadn't no objections. It was pretty good times up in the woods there, take it all around.

But by and by pap got too handy with his hick'ry, and I couldn't stand it. I was all over welts. He got to going away so much, too, and locking me in. Once he locked me in and was gone three days. It was dreadful lonesome. I

* Reprinted from *The Adventures of Huckleberry Finn*, with use of trade name "Mark Twain" in arrangement with the publisher, Harper & Brothers, New York.

judged he had got drownded, and I wasn't ever going to get out any more. I was scared. I made up my mind I would fix up some way to leave. . . .

I FOOL PAP AND GET AWAY

"Git up! What you 'bout?"

I opened my eyes and looked around trying to make out where I was. It was after sunup, and I had been sound asleep. Pap was standing over me looking sour—and sick, too. He says:

"What you doin' with this gun?"

I judged he didn't know nothing about what he had been doing, so I says:

"Somebody tried to get in, so I was laying for him."

"Why didn't you roust me out?"

"Well, I tried to, but I couldn't; I couldn't budge you."

"Well, all right. Don't stand there palavering all day, but out with you and see if there's a fish on the lines for breakfast. I'll be along in a minute."

He unlocked the door, and I cleared out up the river bank. I noticed some pieces of limbs and such things floating down, and a sprinkling of bark; so I knowed the river had begun to rise. I reckoned I would have great times now if I was over at the town. The June rise used to be always luck for me; because as soon as that rise begins here comes cordwood floating down, and pieces of log rafts—sometimes a dozen logs together; so all you have to do is to catch them and sell them to the woodyards and the sawmill.

I went along up the bank with one eye out for pap and t'other one out for what the rise might fetch along. Well, all at once here comes a canoe; just a beauty, too, about thirteen or fourteen foot long, riding high like a duck. I shot head-first off of the bank like a frog, clothes and all on, and struck out for the canoe. I just expected there'd be somebody laying down in it, because people often done that to fool folks, and when a chap had pulled a skiff out most to it they'd raise up and laugh at him. But it warn't so this time. It was a drift-canoe sure enough, and I clumb in and paddled her ashore. Thinks I, the old man will be glad when he see this—she's worth ten dollars. But when I got to shore pap wasn't in sight yet, and as I was running her into a little creek like a gully, all hung over with vines and willows, I struck another idea: I judged I'd hide her good, and then, 'stead of taking to the woods when I run off, I'd go down the river about fifty mile and camp in one place for good, and not have such a rough time tramping on foot.

It was pretty close to the shanty, and I thought I heard the old man coming all the time; but I got her hid; and then I out and looked around a bunch of willows, and there was the old man down the path a piece just drawing a bead on a bird with his gun. So he hadn't seen anything.

When he got along I was hard at it taking up a "trot" line. He abused me a little for being so slow; but I told him I fell in the river, and that was what made me so long. I knowed he would see I was wet, and then he would be asking questions. We got five catfish off the lines and went home.

While we laid off after breakfast to sleep up, both of us being about wore out, I got to thinking that if I could fix up some way to keep pap and the widow from trying to follow me, it would be a certainer thing than trusting to luck to get far enough off before they missed me; you see, all kinds of things might happen. Well, I didn't see no way for a while, but by and by pap raised up a minute to drink another barrel of water, and he says:

"Another time a man comes a-prowling round here you roust me out, you hear? That man warn't here for no good. I'd a shot him. Next time you roust me out, you hear?"

Then he dropped down and went to sleep again; what he had been saying give me the very idea I wanted. I says to myself, I can fix it now so nobody won't think of following me.

About twelve o'clock we turned out and went along up the bank. The river was coming up pretty fast, and lots of driftwood going by on the rise. By and by along comes part of a log raft—nine logs fast together. We went out with the skiff and towed it ashore. Then we had dinner. Anybody but pap would 'a' waited and seen the day through, so as to catch more stuff; but that warn't pap's style. Nine logs was enough for one time; he must shove right over to town and sell. So he locked me in and took the skiff, and started off towing the raft about half-past three. I judged he wouldn't come back that night. I waited till I reckoned he had got a good start; then I out with my saw, and went to work on that log again. Before he was t'other side of the river I was out of the hole; him and his raft was just a speck on the water away off yonder.

I took the sack of corn meal and took it to where the canoe was hid, and shoved the vines and branches apart and put it in; then I done the same with the side of bacon; then the whisky jug. I took all the coffee and sugar there was, and all the ammunition; I took the wadding; I took the bucket and gourd; took a dipper and a tin cup, and my old saw and two blankets, and the skillet and the coffee-pot. I took fish-lines and matches and other things —everything that was worth a cent. I cleaned out the place. I wanted an ax, but there wasn't any, only the one out at the woodpile, and I knowed why I was going to leave that. I fetched out the gun, and now I was done.

I had wore the ground a good deal crawling out of the hole and dragging out so many things. So I fixed that as good as I could from the outside by scattering dust on the place, which covered up the smoothness and the sawdust. Then I fixed the piece of log back into its place, and put two rocks under it and one against it to hold it there, for it was bent up at that place and didn't quite touch ground. If you stood four or five foot away and didn't know it was sawed, you wouldn't never notice it; and besides, this was the back of the cabin, and it warn't likely anybody would go fooling around there.

It was all grass clear to the canoe, so I hadn't left a track. I followed around to see. I stood on the bank and looked out over the river. All safe. So I took the gun and went up a piece into the woods, and was hunting around for some birds when I see a wild pig; hogs soon went wild in them bottoms after they had got away from the prairie farms. I shot this fellow and took him into camp.

I took the ax and smashed in the door. I beat it and hacked it considerable a-doing it. I fetched the pig in, and took him back nearly to the table and hacked into his throat with the ax, and laid him down on the ground to bleed; I say ground because it *was* ground—hard packed, and no boards. Well, next I took an old sack and put a lot of big rocks in it—all I could drag—and I started it from the pig, and dragged it to the door and through the woods down to the river and dumped it in, and down it sunk, out of sight. You could easy see that something had been dragged over the ground. I did wish Tom Sawyer was there; I knowed he would take an interest in this kind of business and throw in the fancy touches. Nobody could spread himself like Tom Sawyer in such a thing as that.

Well, last I pulled out some of my hair, and blooded the ax good, and stuck it on the back side, and slung the ax in the corner. Then I took up the pig and held him to my breast with my jacket (so he couldn't drip) till I got a good piece below the house and then dumped him into the river. Now I thought of something else. So I went and got the bag of meal and my old saw out of the canoe, and fetched them to the house. I took the bag to where it used to stand, and ripped a hole in the bottom of it with the saw, for there warn't no knives and forks on the place—pap done everything with his clasp-knife about the cooking. Then I carried the sack about a hundred yards across the grass and through the willows east of the house, to a shallow lake that was five miles wide and full of rushes—and ducks too, you might say, in the season. There was a slough or a creek leading out of it on the other side that went miles away, I don't know where, but it didn't go to the river. The meal sifted out and made a little track all the way to the lake. I dropped pap's whetstone there too, so as to look like it had been done by accident. Then I tied up the rip in the meal sack with a string, so it wouldn't leak no more, and took it and my saw to the canoe again.

It was about dark now; so I dropped the canoe down the river under some willows that hung over the bank, and waited for the moon to rise. I made fast to a willow; then I took a bite to eat, and by and by laid down in the canoe to smoke a pipe and lay out a plan. I says to myself, they'll follow the track of that sackful of rocks to the shore and then drag the river for me. And they'll follow that meal track to the lake and go browsing down the creek that leads out of it to find the robbers that killed me and took the things. They won't ever hunt the river for anything but my dead carcass. They'll soon get tired of that, and won't bother no more about me. All right; I can stop anywhere I want to. Jackson's Island is good enough for me; I know that island pretty well, and nobody ever comes there. And then I can paddle over to town nights, and slink around and pick up things I want. Jackson's Island's the place.

I was pretty tired, and the first thing I knowed I was asleep. When I woke up I didn't know where I was for a minute. I set up and looked around, a little scared. Then I remembered. The river looked miles and miles across. The moon was so bright I could 'a' counted the drift logs that went a-slipping along, black and still, hundreds of yards out from shore. Everything was dead quiet, and it looked late, and *smelled* late. You know what I mean —I don't know the words to put it in.

I took a good gap and a stretch, and was just going to unhitch and start when I heard a sound away over the water. I listened. Pretty soon I made it out. It was that dull kind of a regular sound that comes from oars working in rowlocks when it's a still night. I peeped out through the willow branches, and there it was—a skiff, away across the water. I couldn't tell how many was in it. It kept a-coming, and when it was abreast of me I see there warn't but one man in it. Thinks I, maybe it's pap, though I warn't expecting him. He dropped below me with the current, and by and by he came a-swinging up shore in the easy water, and he went by so close I could 'a' reached out the gun and touched him. Well, it *was* pap, sure enough—and sober, too, by the way he laid his oars.

I didn't lose no time. The next minute I was a-spinning downstream soft, but quick, in the shade of the bank. I made two mile and a half, and then struck out a quarter of a mile or more toward the middle of the river, because pretty soon I would be passing the ferry-landing, and people might see me and hail me. I got out amongst the driftwood, and then laid down in the bottom of the canoe and let her float. I laid there, and had a good rest and a smoke out of my pipe, looking away into the sky; not a cloud in it. The sky looks ever so deep when you lay down on your back in the moonshine; I never knowed it before. And how far a body can hear on the water such nights! I heard people talking at the ferry landing. I heard what they said, too —every word of it. One man said it was getting toward the long days and the short nights now. T'other one said *this* warn't one of the short ones, he reckoned—and then they laughed, and he said it over again, and they laughed again; then they waked up another fellow and told him, and laughed, but he didn't laugh; he ripped out something brisk, and said let him alone. The first fellow said he 'lowed to tell it to his old woman—she would think it was pretty good; but he said that warn't nothing to some things he had said in his time. I heard one man say it was nearly three o'clock, and he hoped daylight wouldn't wait more than about a week longer. After that the talk got further and further away, and I couldn't make out the words any more; but I could hear the mumble, and now and then a laugh, too, but it seemed a long ways off.

I was away below the ferry now. I rose up, and there was Jackson's Island, about two mile and a half downstream, heavy-timbered and standing up out of the middle of the river, big and dark and solid, like a steamboat without any lights. There warn't any signs of the bar at the head—it was all under water now.

It didn't take me long to get there. I shot past the head at a ripping rate, the current was so swift, and then I got into the dead water and landed on the side toward the Illinois shore. I run the canoe into a deep dent in the bank that I knowed about; I had to part the willow branches to get in; and when I made fast nobody could 'a' seen the canoe from the outside.

I went up and set down on a log at the head of the island and looked out on the big river and the black driftwood and away over to the town, three miles away, where there was three or four lights twinkling. A monstrous big lumber raft was about a mile upstream, coming along down, with a lantern in the middle of it. I watched it come creeping down, and when it was most abreast of where I stood I heard a man say, "Stern oars, there! heave her head to stabboard!" I heard that just as plain as if the man was by my side.

There was a little gray in the sky now; so I stepped into the woods and laid down for a nap before breakfast.

The Sailor Boy's Tale *

ISAK DINESEN

** Isak Dinesen, the writing name of the Baroness Blixen, was born in Denmark in 1885, the daughter of Captain A. W. Dinesen, an adventurous naval officer who lived for three years as a trapper with the Indians in Minnesota and wrote on hunting under his Indian name of "Boganis." Miss Dinesen married her cousin, Baron Blixen, in 1914 and went to Africa, where they ran a coffee plantation and the Baroness began writing. Seven years later she got a divorce, ran the plantation herself with native help, and continued her writing, which included her remarkable African memoirs *Out of Africa,* and the odd and notable short stories included in *Seven Gothic Tales,* 1934, and *Winter's Tales,* 1942. ******

The barque *Charlotte* was on her way from Marseille to Athens, in gray weather, on a high sea, after three days' heavy gale. A small sailor boy, named Simon, stood on the wet, swinging deck, held on to a shroud, and looked up toward the drifting clouds, and to the upper top-gallant yard of the mainmast.

A bird, that had sought refuge upon the mast, had got her feet entangled in some loose tackle yarn of the halyard, and, high up there, struggled to get free. The boy on the deck could see her wings flapping and her head turning from side to side.

Through his own experience of life he had come to the conviction that in this world everyone must look after himself and expect no help from others. But the mute, deadly fight kept him fascinated for more than an hour. He wondered what kind of bird it would be. These last days a number of birds had come to settle in the barque's rigging: swallows, quails, and a pair of peregrine falcons; he believed that this bird was a peregrine falcon. He remembered how, many years ago, in his own country and near his home, he had once seen a peregrine falcon quite close, sitting on a stone and flying straight up from it. Perhaps this was the same bird. He thought: "That bird is like me. Then she was there, and now she is here."

At that a fellow-feeling rose in him, a sense of common tragedy; he stood looking at the bird with his heart in his mouth. There were none of the sailors about to make fun of him; he began to think out how he might go up by the shrouds to help the falcon out. He brushed his hair back and pulled up his sleeves, gave the deck round him a great glance, and climbed up. He had to stop a couple of times in the swaying rigging.

It was indeed, he found when he got to the top of the mast, a peregrine falcon. As his head was on a level with hers, she gave up her struggle and looked at him with a pair of angry, desperate yellow eyes. He had to take hold of her with one hand while he got his knife out and cut off the tackle yarn. He was scared as he looked down, but at the same time he felt that he had been ordered up by nobody, but that this was his own venture, and this gave him a proud, steadying sensation, as if the sea and the sky, the ship, the bird, and himself were all one. Just as he had freed the falcon, she hacked him in the thumb, so that the blood ran, and he nearly let her go. He grew angry with her and gave her a clout on the head, then he put her inside his jacket and climbed down again.

When he reached the deck the mate and the cook were standing there, looking up; they roared to him to ask what he had had to do in the mast. He was so tired that the tears were in his eyes. He took the falcon out and showed her to them, and she kept still within his hands. They laughed and walked off. Simon set the falcon down, stood back, and watched her. After a while he reflected that she might not be able to get up from the slippery deck, so he caught her once more, walked away with her, and placed her upon a bolt of canvas. A little after she began to trim her feathers, made two or three sharp jerks forward, and then suddenly flew off. The boy could follow her flight above the troughs of the gray sea. He thought: "There flies my falcon."

When the *Charolotte* came home, Simon signed aboard another ship, and two years later he was a light hand on the schooner *Hebe* lying at Bod, high up on the coast of Norway, to buy herrings.

To the great herring markets of Bod ships came together from all corners of the world; here were Swedish, Finnish, and Russian boats, a forest of masts, and on shore a turbulent, irregular display of life, with many languages spoken and mighty fights. On the shore booths had been set up, and the Lapps, small yellow people, noiseless in their movements, with watchful eyes, whom Simon had never seen before, came down to sell bead-embroidered leather-goods. It was April, the sky and the sea were so clear that it was difficult to hold one's eyes up against them—salt, infinitely wide, and filled with bird shrieks—as if someone were incessantly whetting invisible knives, on all sides, high up in Heaven.

Simon was amazed at the lightness of these April evenings. He knew no geography and did not assign it to the latitude, but he took it as a sign of an unwonted good will in the universe, a favor. Simon had been small for his age all his life, but this last winter he had grown and had become strong of limb. That good luck, he felt, must spring from the very same source as the sweetness of the weather, from a new benevolence in the world. He had been in need of such encouragement, for he was timid by nature; now he asked for no more. The rest he felt to be his own affair. He went about slowly and proudly.

One evening he was ashore with land leave, and walked up to the booth of a small Russian trader, a Jew who sold gold watches. All the sailors knew that his watches were made from bad metal and would not go, still they bought them and paraded them about. Simon looked at these watches for a long time, but did not buy. The old Jew had divers goods in his shop, and amongst others a case of oranges. Simon had tasted oranges on his journeys; he bought one and took it with him. He meant to go up on a hill, from where he could see the sea, and suck it there.

As he walked on, and had got to the outskirts of the place, he saw a little girl in a blue frock, standing at the other side of a fence and looking at him. She was thirteen or fourteen years old, as slim as an eel, but with a round, clear, freckled face, and a pair of long plaits. The two looked at one another.

"Who are you looking out for?" Simon asked, to say something. The girl's face broke into an ecstatic, presumptuous smile. "For the man I am going to marry, of course," she said. Something in her countenance made the boy confident and happy; he grinned a little at her.

"That will perhaps be me," he said.

"Ha, ha," said the girl, "he is a few years older than you, I can tell you."

"Why," said Simon, "you are not grown up yourself."

The little girl shook her head solemnly. "Nay," she said, "but when I grow up I will be exceedingly beautiful, and wear brown shoes with heels, and a hat."

"Will you have an orange?" asked Simon, who could give her none of the things she had named. She looked at the orange and at him.

"They are very good to eat," said he.

"Why do you not eat it yourself then?" she asked.

"I have eaten so many already," said he, "when I was in Athens. Here I had to pay a mark for it."

"What is your name?" asked she.

"My name is Simon," said he. "What is yours?"

"Nora," said the girl. "What do you want for your orange now, Simon?"

When he heard his name in her mouth Simon grew bold. "Will you give me a kiss for the orange?" he asked.

Nora looked at him gravely for a moment. "Yes," she said, "I should not mind giving you a kiss."

He grew as warm as if he had been running quickly. When she stretched out her hand for the orange he took hold of it. At that moment somebody in the house called out for her.

"That is my father," said she, and tried to give him back the orange, but he would not take it. "Then come again tomorrow," she said quickly, "then I will give you a kiss." At that she slipped off. He stood and looked after her, and a little later went back to his ship.

Simon was not in the habit of making plans for the future, and now he did not know whether he would be going back to her or not.

The following evening he had to stay aboard, as the other sailors were going ashore, and he did not mind that either. He meant to sit on the deck with the ship's dog, Balthasar, and to practice upon a concertina that he had purchased some time ago. The pale evening was all round him, the sky was faintly roseate, the sea was quite calm, like milk-and-water, only in the wake of the boats going inshore it broke into streaks of vivid indigo. Simon sat and played; after a while his own music began to speak to him so strongly that he stopped, got up, and looked upward. Then he saw that the full moon was sitting high on the sky.

The sky was so light that she hardly seemed needed there; it was as if she had turned up by a caprice of her own. She was round, demure, and presumptuous. At that he knew that he must go ashore, whatever it was to cost him. But he did not know how to get away, since the others had taken the yawl with them. He stood on the deck for a long time, a small, lonely figure of a sailor boy on a boat, when he caught sight of a yawl coming in from a ship farther out, and hailed her. He found that it was the Russian crew from a boat named *Anna,* going ashore. When he could make himself understood to them, they took him with them; they first asked him for money for his fare, then, laughing, gave it back to him. He thought: "These people will be believing that I am going in to town, wenching." And then he felt, with some pride, that they were right, although at the same time they were infinitely wrong and knew nothing about anything.

When they came ashore they invited him to come in and drink in their company, and he would not refuse, because they had helped him. One of the Russians was a giant, as big as a bear; he told Simon that his name was Ivan. He got drunk at once, and then fell upon the boy with a bearlike affection, pawed him, smiled and laughed into his face, made him a present of a gold watch chain, and kissed him on both cheeks. At that Simon reflected that he also ought to give Nora a present when they met again, and as soon as he could get away from the Russians he walked up to a booth that he knew of, and bought a small blue silk handkerchief, the same color as her eyes.

It was Saturday evening, and there were many people amongst the houses; they came in long rows, some of them singing, all keen to have some fun that night. Simon, in the midst of this rich, bawling life under the clear moon, felt his head light with the flight from the ship and the strong drinks. He crammed the handkerchief in his pocket; it was silk, which he had never touched before, a present for his girl.

He could not remember the path up to Nora's house, lost his way, and came back to where he had started. Then he grew deadly afraid that he should be too late, and began to run. In a small passage between two wooden huts he ran straight into a big man, and found that it was Ivan once more. The Russian folded his arms round him and held him.

"Good! Good!" he cried in high glee, "I have found you, my little chicken. I have looked for you everywhere, and poor Ivan has wept because he lost his friend."

"Let me go, Ivan," cried Simon. "Oho," said Ivan, "I shall go with you and get you what you want. My heart and my money are all yours, all yours; I have been seventeen years old myself, a little lamb of God, and I want to be so again tonight."

"Let me go," cried Simon, "I am in a hurry." Ivan held him so that it hurt, and patted him with his other hand.

"I feel it, I feel it," he said. "Now trust to me, my little friend. Nothing shall part you and me. I hear the others coming; we will have such a night together as you will remember when you are an old grandpapa."

Suddenly he crushed the boy to him, like a bear that carries off a sheep. The odious sensation of male bodily warmth and the bulk of a man close to him made the lean boy mad. He thought of Nora waiting, like a slender ship in the dim air, and of himself, here, in the hot embrace of a hairy animal. He struck Ivan with all his might. "I'll kill you, Ivan," he cried out, "if you do not let me go."

"Oh, you will be thankful to me later on," said Ivan, and began to sing. Simon fumbled in his pocket for his knife and got it opened. He could not lift his hand, but he drove the knife, furiously, in under the big man's arm. Almost immediately he felt the blood spouting out, and running down in his sleeve. Ivan stopped short in the song, let go his hold of the boy, and gave two long deep grunts. The next second he tumbled down on his knees. "Poor Ivan, poor Ivan," he groaned. He fell straight on his face. At that moment Simon heard the other sailors coming along, singing, in the by-street.

He stood still for a minute, wiped his knife, and watched the blood spread into a dark pool underneath the big body. Then he ran. As he stopped for a second to choose his way, he heard the sailors behind him scream out over their dead comrade. He thought: "I must get down to the sea, where I can wash my hand." But at the same time he ran the other way. After a little while he found himself on the path that he had walked on the day before, and it seemed as familiar to him, as if he had walked it many hundred times in his life.

He slackened his pace to look round, and suddenly saw Nora standing on the other side of the fence; she was quite close to him when he caught sight of her in the moonlight. Wavering and out of breath he sank down on his knees. For a moment he could not speak. The little girl looked down at him. "Good evening, Simon," she said in her small, coy voice. "I have waited for you a long time," and after a moment she added: "I have eaten your orange."

"Oh, Nora," cried the boy. "I have killed a man."

She stared at him, but did not move. "Why did you kill a man?" she asked after a moment.

"To get here," said Simon. "Because he tried to stop me. But he was my friend." Slowly he got on to his feet. "He loved me!" the boy cried out, and at that burst into tears.

"Yes," said she slowly and thoughtfully. "Yes, because you must be here in time."

"Can you hide me?" he asked. "For they are after me."

"Nay," said Nora, "I cannot hide you. For my father is the parson here at Bod, and he would be sure to hand you over to them, if he knew that you had killed a man."

"Then," said Simon, "give me something to wipe my hands on."

"What is the matter with your hands?" she asked, and took a little step forward. He stretched out his hands to her. "Is that your own blood?" she asked.

"No," said he, "it is his."

She took the step back again.

"Do you hate me now?" he asked.

"No, I do not hate you," said she. "But do put your hands at your back."

As he did so she came up close to him, at the other side of the fence, and clasped her arms round his neck. She pressed her young body to his and kissed him tenderly. He felt her face, cool as the moonlight, upon his own, and when she released him, his head swam, and he did not know if the kiss had lasted a second or an hour. Nora stood up straight, her eyes wide open. "Now," she said slowly and proudly, "I promise you that I will never marry anybody, as long as I live." The boy kept standing with his hands on his back, as if she had tied them there. "And now," she said, "you must run, for they are coming." They looked at one another. "Do not forget Nora," said she. He turned and ran.

He leaped over a fence, and when he was down amongst the houses he walked. He did not know at all where to go. As he came to a house, from where music and noise streamed out, he slowly went through the door. The room was full of people; they were dancing in here. A lamp hung from the ceiling and shone down on them; the air was thick and brown with the dust rising from the floor. There were some women in the room, but many of the men danced with each other, and gravely or laughingly stamped the floor. A moment after Simon had come in the crowd withdrew to the walls to clear the floor for two sailors, who were showing a dance from their own country.

Simon thought: "Now, very soon, the men from the boat will come round to look for their comrade's murderer, and from my hands they will know that I have done it." These five minutes during which he stood by the wall of the dancing-room, in the midst of the gay, sweating dancers, were of great significance to the boy. He himself felt it, as if during this time he grew up and became like other people. He did not entreat his destiny, nor complain. Here he was, he had killed a man and had kissed a girl. He did not demand any more from life, nor did life now demand more from him. He was Simon, a man like the men round him, and going to die, as all men are going to die.

He only became aware of what was going on outside him, when he saw that a woman had come in, and was standing in the midst of the cleared floor, looking round her. She was a short, broad old woman, in the clothes of the Lapps, and she took her stand with such majesty and fierceness as if she owned the whole place. It was obvious that most of the people knew her and were a little afraid of her, although a few laughed; the din of the dancing-room stopped when she spoke.

"Where is my son?" she asked in a high shrill voice, like a bird's. The next moment her eyes fell on Simon himself, and she steered through the crowd, which opened up before her, stretched out her old skinny, dark hand, and took him by the elbow. "Come home with me now," she said.

"You need not dance here tonight. You may be dancing a high enough dance soon."

Simon drew back, for he thought that she was drunk. But as she looked him straight in the face with her yellow eyes, it seemed to him that he had met her before and that he might do well in listening to her. The old woman pulled him with her across the floor, and he followed her without a word. "Do not birch your boy too badly, Sunniva," one of the men in the room cried to her. "He has done no harm, he only wanted to look at the dance."

At the same moment as they came out through the door, there was an alarm in the street, a flock of people came running down it, and one of them, as he turned into the house, knocked against Simon, looked at him and the old woman, and ran on.

While the two walked along the street, the old woman lifted up her skirt and put the hem of it into the boy's hand. "Wipe your hand on my skirt," she said. They had not gone far before they came to a small wooden house, and stopped; the door to it was so low that they must bend to get through it. As the Lapp woman went in before Simon, still holding on to his arm, the boy looked up for a moment. The night had grown misty; there was a wide ring round the moon.

The old woman's room was narrow and dark, with but one small window to it; a lantern stood on the floor and lighted it up dimly. It was all filled with reindeer skins and wolf skins, and with reindeer horn, such as the Lapps use to make their carved buttons and knife handles, and the air in here was rank and stifling. As soon as they were in, the woman turned to Simon, took hold of his head, and with her crooked fingers parted his hair and combed it down in Lapp fashion. She clapped a Lapp cap on him and stood back to glance at him.

"Sit down on my stool, now," she said. "But first take out your knife." She was so commanding in voice and manner that the boy could not but choose to do as she told him; he sat down on the stool, and he could not take his eyes off her face, which was flat and brown, and as if smeared with dirt in its net of fine wrinkles. As he sat there he heard many people come along outside and stop by the house; then someone knocked at the door, waited a moment, and knocked again. The old woman stood and listened, as still as a mouse.

"Nay," said the boy and got up. "This is no good, for it is me that they are after. It will be better for you to let me go out to them."

"Give me your knife," said she. When he handed it to her, she stuck it straight into her thumb, so that the blood spouted out, and she let it drip all over her skirt. "Come in, then," she cried.

The door opened, and two of the Russian sailors came and stood in the opening; there were more people outside. "Has anybody come in here?" they asked. "We are after a man who has killed our mate, but he has run away from us. Have you seen or heard anybody this way?"

The old Lapp woman turned upon them, and her eyes shone like gold in the lamplight. "Have I seen or heard anyone?" she cried, "I have heard you shriek murder all over the town. You frightened me, and my poor silly boy there, so that I cut my thumb as I was ripping the skin rug that I sew. The boy is too scared to help me, and the rug is all ruined. I shall make you pay me for that. If you are looking for a murderer, come in and search my house for me, and I shall know you when we meet again." She was so furious that she danced where she stood, and jerked her head like an angry bird of prey.

The Russian came in, looked round the room, and at her and her blood-stained hand and skirt. "Do not put a curse on us now, Sunniva," he said timidly. "We know that you can do many things when you like. Here is a mark to pay you for the blood you have spilled." She stretched out her hand, and he placed a piece of money in it. She spat on it. "Then go, and there shall be no bad blood between us," said Sunniva, and shut the door after them. She stuck her thumb in her mouth and chuckled a little.

The boy got up from his stool, stood straight up before her, and stared into her face. He felt as if he were swaying high up in the air, with but a small hold. "Why have you helped me?" he asked her.

"Do you not know?" she answered. "Have you not recognized me yet? But you will remember the peregrine falcon which was caught in the tackle yarn of your boat, the *Charlotte,* as she sailed in the Mediterranean. That day you climbed up by the shrouds of the top-gallantmast to help her out, in a stiff wind, and with a high sea. That falcon was me. We Lapps often fly in such a manner, to see the world. When I first met you I was on my way to Africa, to see my younger sister and her children. She is a falcon too, when she chooses. By that time she was living at Takaunga, within an old ruined tower, which down there they call a minaret." She swarthed a corner of her skirt round her thumb and bit at it. "We do not forget," she said. "I hacked your thumb, when you took hold of me; it is only fair that I should cut my thumb for you tonight."

She came close to him and gently rubbed her two brown, claw-like fingers against his forehead. "So you are a boy," she said, "who will kill a man rather than be late to meet your sweetheart? We hold together, the females of this earth. I shall mark your forehead now, so that the girls will know of that, when they look at you, and they will like you for it." She played with the boy's hair and twisted it round her finger.

"Listen now, my little bird," said she. "My great grandson's brother-in-law is lying with his boat by the landing place at this moment; he is to take a consignment of skins out to a Danish boat. He will bring you back to your boat, in time, before your mate comes. The *Hebe* is sailing tomorrow morning, is it not so? But when you are aboard, give him back my cap for me." She took up his knife, wiped it in her skirt, and handed it to him. "Here is your knife," she said. "You will stick it into no more men; you will not need to, for from now you will sail the seas like a faithful seaman. We have enough trouble with our sons as it is."

The bewildered boy began to stammer his thanks to her. "Wait," said she, "I shall make you a cup of coffee, to bring back your wits, while I wash your jacket." She went and rattled an old copper kettle upon the fireplace. After a while she handed him a hot, strong, black drink in a cup without a handle to it. "You have drunk with Sunniva now," she said; "you have drunk down a little wisdom, so that in the future all your thoughts shall not fall like raindrops into the salt sea."

When he had finished and set down the cup, she led him to the door and opened it for him. He was surprised to see that it was almost clear morning. The house was so high up that the boy could see the sea from it, and a milky mist about it. He gave her his hand to say good-by.

She stared into his face. "We do not forget," she said. "And you, you knocked me on the head there, high up in the mast. I shall give you that blow back." With that she smacked him on the ear as hard as she could, so that his head swam. "Now we are quits," she said, gave him a great, mischievous, shining glance, and a little push down the doorstep, and nodded to him.

In this way the sailor boy got back to his ship, which was to sail the next morning, and lived to tell the story.

The Bullfighter from Brooklyn*

SIDNEY FRANKLIN

✳✳ "None of us ever dreamed that my pa's hot temper would spawn a matador," says Sidney Franklin, the bullfighter from Brooklyn. At seventeen, already
in business for himself—the silk-screen poster business, an outgrowth of a talent
for drawing—young Sidney had a difference with his father, who wanted him to
go on with his schooling and not with his business; words followed; and then
oblivion. When Sidney picked himself up from the floor, he says, Pa was gone.
Sidney decided to take a trip himself. He planned a three months' jaunt to Havana and Mexico.

In Mexico City, again in the advertising business (now making posters for
bullfights and averaging an income of about a thousand dollars a week—and still
under twenty-one) some Mexicans said Americans didn't have the guts to be
bullfighters. This was all young Franklin needed. He was as quick to flare up as
his father. But words of a red-blooded man were not enough. When required to
prove his point, Sidney engaged himself for a course of bullfight lessons with
Rodolo Gaona, "the only matador who ever competed on equal terms with Joselito
and Belmonte," and entered the Mexico City arena to show what he could do.
Unfortunately, at the time of that appearance he had learned only how to use the
cape, and when the moment came for him actually to kill his bull Sidney hadn't
yet had the lesson which tells you how to hold the sword. He got the idea from
one of the fellows in the ring, however, and slew his first bull.

Young Franklin soon made up for his lack of knowledge of the kill. He found
himself an early-morning job in a slaughterhouse where he killed from two hundred and fifty to three hundred cattle, with a knife, every morning, six days a
week, for several months.

At the peak of his bullfighting career—for he was idolized, in time, not only
in Mexico, but in Mother Spain as well—Sidney Franklin was described by Ernest
Hemingway as "better, more scientific, more intelligent, and more finished a
matador than all but about six of the full matadors in Spain today and the bullfighters know it and have the utmost respect for him. . . . He is brave with a

cold, serene, and intelligent valor . . . one of the most skillful, graceful and slow manipulators of a cape fighting today."

Franklin, finally proficient in his art, was later to have triumphant appearances in the arenas in Seville, Madrid, Cadiz, and elsewhere, filling the stands and winning the highest honors.

But the section presented here from his adventurous autobiography *Bullfighter from Brooklyn* is of his early, novice days, and deals with the several months after his Mexico City debut, when, unable yet to be taken seriously as a bullfighter— partly because there had never been a bullfighter from America, let alone Brooklyn—Sidney decided to tour the provinces of Mexico and get experience and maybe make a little money to get his belongings out of pawn.

He encountered "Guimpty" Badillo, who was recruiting bullfighters and their equipages for such a tour, and Guimpty shipped them upriver to Villahermosa, the capital city of the state of Tabasco, which borders on Guatemala. In Villahermosa, after a deft performance in the ring, Sidney Franklin was taken quite seriously. His youth, white skin, and red hair, fascinated the populace. He was fêted; he engaged in a drinking bout for the Tabasco championship, and he laid out twenty sundry Mexicans who, much to his surprise (for next morning Sidney in jail could not remember the events) complained to the police. Franklin hadn't a mark on him. The Mexicans were generally embarrassed and since nobody wanted to see a good bullfighter languish in jail, it was decided that in between the fortnightly bullfights the American ought to be provided with some amusement of his own. The most suitable plan was to take Señor Franklin on fortnightly hunting trips into the interior. The idea was that of a distinguished citizen and a very wealthy one, Nicolas Browne, called Colás for short, the grandson of a Southern Colonel Browne, who, "not satisfied with the way our War Between the States turned out, uprooted his entire family and settled in what is now the Mexican state of Tabasco. The family owned three quarters of the state, and Colás himself owned the light and power plant, most of the buildings, the bull ring, theater, and the fifteen paddle-wheel steamers that plied the state's three rivers.

"Colás took one of the paddle wheelers out of service and reserved it for our exclusive use," says Franklin. "His suggestion was as good a plan as any to keep me out of trouble in the city. The interior was tropical jungle at its best." ✳✳

THE MAIDS AND MATRONS OF TABASCO

Colás Browne was a wonderful host. He always invited a few friends to come along on our two-week hunting trips, although we were never more than twenty on any one trip because the little rear paddle-wheeler had only twenty small cabins on the upper deck.

The lower level was a wide-open space. The tall, round wood-burning

boiler was amidships and cords of wood were stacked all around the sides
of the boat. We always had to keep our thirty to forty hunting dogs chained
to the side railing so they wouldn't dive overboard and take off after game
without warning. And their constant yapping, especially at chow time,
warned the wilderness of our progress.

We never took any food with us except a couple of barrels of salt and
a couple of barrels of hardtack. We stopped in likely places whenever we
felt like it and trapped or hunted and fished for whatever we ate. The
native crew gathered a wide variety of lush tropical fruits I never had
seen before. The hunt lost some of its zest for me because game was so
abundant. At times I was reluctant to bring a piece down because, lacking human contact, the animals were too trusting. But if I let an animal
go, someone else in our party was sure to pick it off. Every one of them
was a marvelous shot. Crocodiles of all sizes snoozed everywhere along
the river banks, and quite often we spotted nests of their eggs hatching
in the sand.

On one of the early trips we stopped at Colás' Zaragoza Hacienda, far
up the Tenosique River. We sidled to the river bank and, after tying up
the boat to a big tree, went ashore. Not far inland we came to what
must have been a charming house in its day. It wasn't very large as hacienda houses go. It had only ten rooms. But lack of constant care, jungle inmates, and the humidity had taken their toll. . . .

I didn't see any natives at the hacienda until our third day at Zaragoza.
We were eating out in the open in the shade of a tall mango tree when
a little dark-skinned girl sidled up to me and sat on the ground at my
feet. She was completely naked and when I seemed surprised, Colás told
me that no one in this region ever wore any clothes at all, not even a
fig leaf.

The girl couldn't have been more than five years old. She tugged at
my leg and pointed to the food on the table. She didn't speak Spanish
and I couldn't understand her Mayan dialect. But when I started to give
her a piece of venison, Colás warned me not to give it to her. "Give
her a bone if you want to," he said, "with very little meat on it."

"What's the idea, Colás?" I asked, surprised. "We've got plenty of meat
and she's not a dog."

He laughed. "Don't misunderstand me," he said indulgently. "These
natives aren't used to meat. They get it very rarely and I don't believe
this child's stomach is prepared for it. Meat spoils very rapidly in the
tropics and when these people get any, they slice it thin and hang it up

in the sun to dry. They make *cecina,* or jerky, out of it. That's the only way they can keep it. They never eat meat the way we do. They just keep a small piece of *cecina* in their mouth and suck on it until it disappears. Their diet is mostly made up of coconut, breadfruit, beans, corn, and fruit, and once in a while they have some fish. This heavy meat is likely to do the child more harm than good."

I watched enthralled while the little girl, like an animal, gnawed the bone I gave her. After that, every time we were anywhere near the house, she followed me around like a pet. I couldn't get rid of her. But after the fourth day other natives seemed to pop up out of the foliage at every turn. Colás told me that I was the fairest person ever to visit the region. I was very light and freckled and had a curly shock of flaming coppery-red hair. They never had seen anything like that before and it took them a few days to get to the point where they came and went freely whenever I was around. And it took me just as long to get used to people of all ages casually going about their daily chores with absolutely nothing on.

The natives lived in bamboo and palm-thatch *jacals,* or huts, covered lightly in spots with clay. The bare earth was their floor and it was packed so solid that I suspect they mixed some clay with it. Some of the floors appeared to be glazed.

When we were getting ready to return to Villahermosa, Colás told me that the child's mother wanted me to take the little girl with me as a gift. I laughed at the thought of such a thing. But Colás was serious.

"What would I be doing with a five-year-old girl?" I asked.

"That's not the point," he said. "Her mother believes in *la hiciste ojo* —believes that you gave her The Eye. That's the only way she explains the child's not being afraid of you. You remember that the child was the first one to come out of hiding, and now she follows you around like a puppy. And she refuses to eat except what you give her yourself. And around these parts they all believe implicitly in The Eye!"

"You don't mean to tell me, Colás," I said, "that these people give each other away as gifts just like that! They must consider themselves something more than animals!"

So he sent the caretaker of the house to see what he could do with the child's mother. She wouldn't come and speak to us herself. She was afraid I'd give her The Eye too. But she was adamant. The child would wither and waste away before her eyes, and she couldn't stand the thought of watching such a horrible thing without being able to do anything about it. Fortunately, however, we were able to sneak out of the district without the child.

We returned to Villahermosa late Saturday night before my second appearance in the bull ring. The fight went off even better than my first one. Guimpty Badillo wanted me to appear more often than every other Sunday. And as much as I would have liked the idea and the money, I knew the crowd would tire of me if I overdid things by appearing too often. So I insisted on appearing only every other Sunday, as stipulated in our contract. Besides, I was in love with our trips into the interior.

It was late in October when we returned from a trip to find the whole region near Villahermosa in flood. A four-day cloudburst had swamped the area. We had to go a short distance upstream to get ashore on a bank that was high enough to have escaped the water. By the time we got into town it was very late.

Early Sunday morning I went with my *cuadrilla* to the bull ring to watch the drawing for the bulls we were to fight that afternoon. Luckily the ring was on high ground. But when I saw the bulls in the corral, one in particular looked queer. No one told me anything out of the ordinary had happened and I thought that the funny-looking bull was a runt. Although he was about half the size of the others, he had an enormous pair of horns. They went straight out to the side and turned up toward the front. But the spread of those horns was wider than I could reach with both arms. And somehow all those animals looked different than the ones we had fought before. I didn't have the experience, then, to know what the difference was. But I was soon to find out.

The runt fell to my lot in the drawing. As I was the second matador on the bill, which meant I would dispatch the second and fourth bulls, Guimpty begged me to leave the runt for last place. If I took him on in second place, the crowd might get out of hand. So to please him I let him have his way.

Elias Chavez, "El Arequipeño," had done rather well with the first and third bulls, and my first went off fine, without a hitch. The crowd was in great spirits. Then my second bull, the fourth of the afternoon, came into the arena with a terrific rush. That was the runt. Momentarily, when the mob saw how small he was and with such terrific horns, they were stunned. But as they watched the runt's vicious charges around the arena, they began to change their tune. And while my *banderilleros* hesitated to begin the preliminary cape work, some drunk jumped down from the stands and climbed into the ring before anyone could stop him.

The runt had stopped his wild charges and just stood in the center of the ring pawing the ground and snorting. And everyone seemed hypnotized as we watched that crazy drunk stagger toward the bull. He didn't hesitate or fall but just staggered at an even pace straight across the ring. When the drunk reached the bull, who seemed just as flabbergasted as the rest of us, he flipped his hand right in the bull's snoot as casually as only a drunk can, and kept right on staggering all the way across the ring. But the moment he started to climb the fence, the bull suddenly came to life and shot toward him as though fired from a cannon. The drunk barely managed to fall into the runway as the bull crashed against the fence.

The riot that exploded from the stands was fantastic. Someone started to yell something and pointed at the bull. At the same moment Guimpty begged me to get into action to check the riot. I had noticed something peculiar about that runt's sack. It seemed lumpy, and I was sure it was getting longer as he charged around the arena.

It reminded me of the Spanish Granadina goats at Xochitl. They had such long udders that to keep them from dragging on the ground or from getting bruised by the animals' legs while running, they were held up by supporters. And while the bull galloped around the ring his sack appeared to be flying behind him, swinging freely from side to side; and, weirdest of all, it seemed to be stretching.

But I couldn't take time off to figure out what was the matter. The way that crowd was acting, anything might happen. So I stepped right into the bull's oncoming charge without waiting for the *banderilleros* to do the preliminary passes and dropped to my knees. I passed the bull five times on my knees and finished off in a grand swirl, or serpentina. I remained kneeling for a while and then slowly got up and walked toward the horses that had moved into position.

We finished the horseplay in grand fashion. The crowd had accepted the situation philosophically and the *banderilleros* went about placing the darts. Two pairs had been placed when a *banderillero* tripped and missed his mark on the third pair. He was so surprised for the moment that he made a dash for the fence. He just barely got over it when the bull jumped over right after him. And the way the bull's hind legs went over that fence, I knew he would land upside down.

The *banderillero* hadn't expected the bull to follow over the fence right after him and had hesitated a moment to catch his breath. In that moment the bull landed right on top of him. Lucky for him, though, the bull was upside down. In the mad scramble to get the *banderillero* out of there before the bull could right himself, someone in the front row started screaming, and the riot started all over again. But this time it sounded ominous.

I didn't know what it was all about because I was on the other side of the arena waiting for the bull to come in again from behind the fence. And when he came in, with the riot mounting in fury all the time, what a sight!

I didn't know what to do. I looked again to make sure I wasn't dreaming. Those enormous horns, the ones I sensed were wrong all the time, were twisted in the most grotesque manner possible. One was turned backward with the point toward his tail and the other was dangling loosely but held by wires. And when that crowd saw those wires, they really went to town!

There was nothing I could do now. The hundred soldiers on duty were absolutely impotent. They couldn't hope to cope with thirty-five hundred roaring madmen. And that's a funny thing about bullfight fans. They'll stand for almost anything. But they won't stand for a hoax. Nothing could hold them now. So they began, slowly at first and then gaining momentum, to tear up the seating planks of the stands. Before anyone could put a stop to it, they started to build bonfires. And once that wood caught fire, the whole ring burned furiously.

The only thing for us to do was to get out of there in a hurry. We didn't care to have that crowd take anything out on us. So without even stopping at the hotel to change clothing, we made a dash for Colás' paddle-wheeler, waiting for us just below the town.

Once on board and safely on our way, the *banderilleros* told me what had happened. It seems that the flood had messed up the shipment of bulls scheduled to appear. It was absolutely impossible for them to get to Villahermosa in time. And rather than postpone the fight, which was completely sold out, Guimpty had substituted some ordinary meat steers from the slaughterhouse for the ones that hadn't arrived. They had a tough time of it but finally selected the four we had used. But all four were castrated steers and only had bone stumps from having been dehorned long ago.

True to form, Guimpty had ordered the sacks cut from the hides of common meat bulls that already had been slaughtered. He was lucky to get them the same color. Then he filled them with stones and sand and ordered them sewn to the sackless animals we had used. Picking horns out of the bone pile, he had had them attached with screws and piano wire to the bone stumps on those four animals' heads.

The hair around the horns was matted with mud and tar to cover up what had been done. And it had been done well enough so that it couldn't be seen unless someone was really close. In the case of the runt, though, the fellow who did it must have been either an artist or endowed with a queer sense of humor. To make that runt appear older even though half the size of the others, Guimpty's man purposely selected the largest horns he could find. And, with the same reasoning, he also used the largest sack and filled it with bigger stones than the rest!

We paddle-wheeled down the Grijalva and then up the Usumacinta River in the direction of Guatemala. It took us two and a half days to get where we were going, stopping now and then to hunt. We went ashore at a place Colás called Paraiso or Paradise, on the border across from Guatemala. Word evidently had been sent ahead because the caretaker expected us and had rounded up some thirty-five horses for our use.

The ranch house was in the same style but twice as large as the ones on Colás' other haciendas. He had brought along enough saddles for everyone. We spent the morning of our first day picking horses and, after a lengthy preparation, started off into the jungle on horseback.

Pascacio the caretaker and several native boys went ahead, cutting a path with their machetes where needed. This was the real thing, like the pictures I had seen of dense tropical jungle. The weather never had been better. We didn't see much of the sun, though. The vegetation was so profuse and vines and moss hung so thickly that we could rarely see fifty feet ahead of us even in the clear. The plumage of the birds was fantastic in variety and color. Huge flocks of parrots screeched and whistled everywhere. As we rode along we watched the bands of capering monkeys chase each other through the trees.

We waded through several swamp areas where the water was up to our horses' bellies, and after a few hours of slow but steady progress we came out in a small clearing with several footpaths leading from it. Colás held a short confab in Mayan dialect with Pascacio and then came over to me.

"This is as far as we go," he said. "It's forbidden territory and, even though it belongs to me, the tribe that lives near here won't permit outsiders to come in unless specifically invited."

We all started to suggest other places but Colás quieted us. "All the rest of you except Franklin had better turn back and wait for me at the hacienda. Franklin and I have to wait for someone who's coming out from the village to meet us. Pascacio and the native boys will show you the way back."

There was quite a discussion, but in the end they turned back and left

Colás and me with one of the native boys. We got down off our horses to rest while we waited. How long? Colás didn't know. But while we were waiting, he began to discuss a wide variety of subjects with me. Every once in a while he vaguely hinted at something on his mind and then quite suddenly he came to the point.

"You've been seen in my company all through this region. Even though you never saw anyone, you were seen. And word reached me that the tribal chief in this sector wanted you to be the village guest for a week or so. He's been after me for some time now. That's why we came to this particular place on this trip. I couldn't avoid the issue any longer."

"Why can't we all be the guests of the village? Why only us, you and me?" I said.

"No, Franklin, it isn't even you and me. It's just you. No one else. They idolize white skin all around here and your combination of white skin and red hair has caused a terrific commotion. The chief explicitly requested you and you alone. And in these parts a request from a chief is a command. As soon as the runner comes out to meet us, you go ahead with him and I'll go back with this boy to the ranch house. I won't say anything about this to the others unless you want me to."

When he saw that I was disturbed and perplexed, he continued, "There's nothing to be afraid of. They'll treat you like a king and wait on you hand and foot. But there's one other thing. I don't know how you'll take it, but I believe they expect something of you."

"What could they want from me?" I wondered out loud.

"That's just it," he said. "Whatever takes place, just act like the man you are."

What he was trying to say suddenly hit me between the eyes. "Wait a minute, Colás," I said. "If you mean what I think you do, don't I have anything to say about it?"

"Look, Franklin," he said. "Don't be a child all your life! These people absolutely idolize your skin and your hair. They'll do anything they can to acquire some of it for themselves. No one could pay you a better compliment. You know yourself that Navarro is about as light as you are. Yet no one ever asked for him. You have no idea what this will mean to these people. If you don't spend a week with them I'll never be able to return to this sector as long as they're in it."

It wasn't long before the runner arrived. Colás assured me that he'd be back in this same place to pick me up so that we could get back to Villahermosa in time for my next bullfight. He tried to cheer me up, and joked as much as possible under the circumstances, but even though I tried, I couldn't see anything funny about the whole deal. We hesitantly wished each other good luck before starting in opposite directions.

The native runner must have been in his early twenties. He was naked except for a necklace of iridescent feathers. He seemed a nice sort and took the reins to lead my horse. Every once in a while he looked back to see how I was doing or maybe to make sure I was still there. He never smiled or showed the slightest emotion other than awed respect.

All during the trek I never saw anyone. But as the afternoon shadows deepened, I began to feel I was being watched from all sides. As we progressed, the jungle seemed to close in on me.

Then I realized I was hungry. When I took some bananas from my saddlebag, the runner quickly indicated I shouldn't eat and pointed ahead into the wilderness. I figured he meant I would eat when I got where we were going. And while I was trying to figure out what to do, I became conscious of faint sounds. At times they were like voices and then again they were like low, thundering rumbles. I couldn't make it out. I guess I could hear whatever it was when the wind was blowing in our direction or when the foliage wasn't too dense. And when I thought I'd lost the sounds altogether, we suddenly came out of the jungle and onto a plateau by a lake. And on the plateau was a native village.

There were about seventy bamboo and palm-thatch *jacals* spread over a fairly wide area. In the center was a large plaza and a little off to one side was one *jacal* larger than the rest. When we came out into the clear, no one was in sight and everything was quiet. It looked as though the whole place were deserted. Not even a dog was running loose. But as we approached the chief's *jacal* off the plaza, the natives poured out of everywhere. They kept a respectful distance and just stared at me in awed silence.

The chief and six older men greeted me and indicated I was to come inside his *jacal*. They were all naked except for their beautiful iridescent feather necklaces. The chief's necklace was double the width of the others and much more elaborate. There were a number of mahogany armchairs with seats and backs of woven grasses around a large table. They motioned me to a chair and surrounded me. They just stood around and fingered my hair, completely enthralled. Then, apparently satisfied, they led me to the lake. About twenty feet from the water's edge was a large *jacal* that looked as though it had just been made. When we went inside, they indicated that this was where I would stay during my visit.

We walked back to the chief's *jacal*. While we were away, the table had been set with large woven palm trays piled high with steaming leaf-wrapped parcels of food. The coverings were of banana, wild grape, and corn leaves. It was like a lottery, opening a wrapper and trying to guess if the parcel contained meat, fowl, fish, or fruit.

In the ten days I spent there, all the food served in the village was prepared in leaf wrappings in barbecue pits over hot stones covered with leaves and earth for twenty-four hours or more. And every bit of it was indescribably delicious.

The liquid drinks, when not water, were any number of fruit juices. The natives had lime, lemon, orange, guanábana, chico zapote, zapote and zapote prieto, pineapple, mango, papaya, granada and granada de la China, strawberries, cherries, tunas, chayote and chilacayote, banana, plantain, yam, breadfruit from which they made a sort of pancake, calabaza, all kinds of berries, namey, aguacate, and of course coconuts, wild grapes, and all kinds of nuts, and so many other fruits I can't remember half of them.

They made drinks from some fruits and mixed some with others. They made fruit pastes, dry and in marmalade or jam form. They used fruits to flavor meats, fowl, and fish. They served fresh fruit and fruit cooked in the pits. I never knew fruit could be prepared in so many delicious forms. And although they ate with me, they seemed to expect me to eat more than all of them put together. I was soon so stuffed just from tasting the wide variety of things they insistently offered that I could hardly move.

I had brought my hammock and mosquito bar along but they proved unnecessary. My *jacal* was furnished with several mahogany chairs, one large table, and several smaller ones. The floor was covered almost completely with *petates,* or palm mats, so finely woven that they appeared to be made of linen. A variety of animal pelts were placed here and there like scatter rugs.

They were experts at weaving things of palm, reeds, and grasses. And they did wonderful things with feathers and long hairs. They made me a bed that wasn't a bed at all, but a number of puma and wildcat pelts over which they threw a sort of blanket of the softest down. I never found out exactly what that blanket was made from, but it certainly was soft and smooth to the touch.

That first night I didn't get to sleep for the longest time. The strangeness of everything and my predicament kept me awake until the small hours. All the while a half-dozen girls, none of them more than sixteen, hovered over me and tried to anticipate my slightest mood. Finally, I undressed and slept in my swim trunks.

In a short while I awoke dreamily to find one of the younger girls standing over me and squeezing flower petals so that the essence would drop on me. Then she stroked it into my skin with the lightest touch of the finger-tips imaginable. When she saw I was awake, she ran to the others who were lying on petates on the floor. When I dozed off again, the same thing was repeated all over. But this time I motioned for the others to go outside. They seemed surprised but did as I wished.

I motioned to the one who remained that she continue with the flower petals. She did, without too much urging. She seemed delighted to do something that pleased me. It went from one thing to another in a game as ageless as time and yet as new as the present moment. Eventually, satisfied that everything was as it should be, she let me sleep. And I slept until awak-ened by more flower drippings. This time it was another girl. And that's the way it went. I never noticed the slightest sign of jealousy on the part of the men. In fact, they accompanied the women to the door and waited outside for them. I had no way of knowing what relationship existed be-tween any of them.

I bathed in the lake mornings and afternoons. A number of the natives always accompanied me and were excellent swimmers. Sometimes we played games in the open with crude rubber balls or with a shuttlecock of crude rubber with long feathers in it. We used rackets of various sizes made of reed or bamboo with palm or grass webbing. And the children were much like youngsters anywhere: curious and playful. Their greatest pleasure was for me to pat them on the head. I can't say anything about their behavior because, after all, this was a special occasion.

They walked with the natural grace of most primitive peoples. Their bodies were well proportioned and about average height by our standards. Their skin was dark, somewhat like the African Moors. It had a deep olive cast that's neither black nor white. Some were dark enough to make the uninitiate believe they were black. But that isn't so. They were more like a coconut brown.

Their features were fine. They had narrow noses and full lips. Their high cheekbones made their large, dark eyes appear oriental. The men wore their shoulder-length hair cut straight across the forehead, even with the eye-brows. The women, of course, used flowers to decorate their brilliant blue-black long hair. I saw a few of them with slightly wavy hair, but mostly it was as straight as a die.

Until the afternoon of the ninth day I had lost all sense of time. I slept, ate, swam, played ball games, or walked, and they anticipated my slightest whims. Then during the afternoon they began to bring all sorts of gifts and left them just outside the *jacal*. They all wished to touch my hair in return. I believe my scalp was massaged more that week than in all the rest of my life.

That night we had a feast and fiesta to end all fiestas. There must have been at least fifteen hundred people of all ages present. And people came from neighboring villages. They danced and sang and played games all night; and mountains of food were served. Everyone ate whenever he felt hungry. Every once in a while the chief would motion for me to go inside his *jacal*. Several women would be waiting. As soon as they saw me, all would leave but one. And the one who stayed wasted no time.

I didn't sleep all that night. And in the middle of the morning they brought my horse already saddled. Then we had a mass farewell with the whole tribe and everyone taking turns at running their hands through my hair. After that the chief signaled me to mount and with twenty natives well loaded down with baskets and nets full of gifts leading the way in single file, Indian fashion, I started back to meet Colás where I had left him ten days before.

2 This Watery World

The Long Journey*

JOHANNES V. JENSEN

✳✳ Johannes V. Jensen, born in Denmark on January 20, 1873, is the Danish Nobel Prize winner for his six-volume anthropological historical novel *The Long Journey*. The Preliminary Note and the section, "Columbus in the Trade Wind," are taken from this book. ✳✳

PRELIMINARY—ON COLUMBUS

Christopher Columbus came from Genoa, a Ligurian by birth, but we shall understand the roots of his nature if we regard him as a descendant of the Longobards, of people who had moved from Lombardy to the coast.

From what we know of Columbus he was of northern type, fair-haired and freckled, with blue eyes, the stamp familiar in the north among skippers and farmers. The immediately preceding generations of his family were established in the mountains above Genoa, their last stage on the way to the sea; peasants who through handicraft and contact with the port became seafarers. The great migrations had brought their ancestors from forgotten shores by the Baltic, straight through the countries of the Old World and all the turbulent centuries of the Middle Ages, as far as the Mediterranean— now Columbus was to carry the migration farther. The history of the Longobards, then, is the history of Columbus's past; in his blood, though the origin is forgotten, he inherits profound and powerful promptings from wandering forefathers.

But his spiritual garb is another. Christianity in the literal adaptation of the peasant had replaced the traditions of his race long before he was born, and had become a part of his race's nature. His father, an ordinary craftsman, named him after Saint Christopher, a common thing in those days with pious folk who looked to a patron they could understand, flesh of their

* From the one-volume edition, 1933, translated from the Danish by A. G. Chater. Copyright, 1924, by Alfred A. Knopf, Inc., reprinted by permission of Alfred A. Knopf, Inc.

flesh, and gladly committed their children to his protection. Everybody was called Christopher, but Columbus when at the summit of his responsibilities felt convinced of his successorship to the carrier of Christ. Therefore the legend of Saint Christopher in its natural interpretation, Christianity accepted in primitive fashion, belongs to the antecedents which went to form Columbus, it contains the taste of the race.

His feeling Columbus derived from early impressions of the Gothic, which is the form under which northern peoples have adopted the spirit of Christianity. It was an intensity of thought, which was rooted in the northerner's memories and extended them beyond the finite, that created the pagan-Christian myth of God's mother. In its nature the myth is purely northern; the name is all the Holy Virgin has left of her biblical origin. Christianity demanded soul, adoration, of the pagan, and he gave what he had to give, what to him was sacred, Woman as Virgin and Mother. He centered his religion upon a beautiful ancient devotion to Woman, and in her honor his imagination refashioned his forest and his ship into a cathedral. Columbus was a child of the Gothic; we must seek its genesis if we would know how his nature came about; we must go backward in the youth of the race to the prototype of the myth of God's Mother, the heart of the Gothic. Columbus inherited it in the form of universal longing: the eternal feminine; the Holy Virgin was the woman in his life. *Santa Maria* was the name of his ship.

Forces which point back to lost elements in his origin, but whose tendency was influenced from elsewhere, directed Columbus onward in search of a world he was never to find.

Deep-lying northern instincts were crossed and dominated by surface currents from the world that had shaped his consciousness, the southerner's world, the local stamp, the stamp of his time; he behaved now as an Italian, now as a Spaniard, always as a Christian; an inner illusory world stood between him and Nature, which he still regarded with the prejudiced eyes of his day, several realities one within another, like the heavens of that age, and all of them fairly independent of experience, in conformity with the contemporary *imago mundi*—and yet Columbus went clean through all imaginary realities and came out with a new one.

Pure and monumental was that quality in him which made this possible: courage, a complete dauntlessness which he had received as a heritage from ancestors who were conquerors and colonists and to generations of whom uncertainty and playing for high stakes had become the very form of their existence. Courage and endurance, the sailor's daring, inflexibility of purpose, are the clean line which runs through Columbus's character as a discoverer. He was a sportsman, and he was a man of genius, his motives rose superior to his age; where he regarded his voyage as a mission the elements were at work within him, he pressed on as though the whole of human nature had been pressing upon him. . . .

Only he in whom the past is stowed is freighted for the future. Columbus grows with the bearing of his exploit; we see, however, looking backward, that history passed through his heart. As he stands, he bears a bridge which joins widely separated worlds and epochs. He sets up a boundary between illusion and reality, not by what he thought but by what he was and what his passion gave an impulse to. . . .

We must . . . look on him as a man of his time, such as heredity and experience had made him; we must see what he saw with the eyes he had, as an adventurer, a visionary, a gambler, and a victim, with his brief glory and long renown, as skipper of the caravel which bore him with the rest of its medieval cargo—and which stranded upon that coast where he knocked and knocked and was not to be admitted.

COLUMBUS IN THE TRADE WIND

The Sargasso Sea, hundreds of leagues from land; three little ships lost on the boundless ocean, and their crews in despair.

The worst of their fright over this threatening new phenomenon, the masses of seaweed floating mile after mile in the ocean, had subsided; but it had been a hard trial. The first floating island of weed was taken for firm ground, land; it looked like a very low stretch of meadow lying flush with the water, and for a moment the idea that it might be land raised a flicker of hope, which was only to give way to deep disappointment and uneasiness— if it was not land, what could it be?

Soon the islands became so numerous that they formed a continuous carpet of weed over the whole surface of the sea as far as the eye could reach, and the Admiral kept straight ahead, while the crew cried out, in God's holy name, and implored the helmsman to fall off. Too late, they were already in the midst of the green, and look! she could sail through it without losing so very much of her way—for the present. But supposing the masses of weed got denser and they ended by sticking fast in them? That it was a sort of seaweed the Admiral convinced them all by having some of it fished up; but not any known kind of weed, and how could it grow here, how did it come here, many many leagues from land?

They need not be too sure that they were so very far from land, suggested the Admiral, sanguine of course as usual, and putting on a bold face just when the others looked blackest. But where could this land be? At any rate it was not to be seen for miles ahead or on either side, only a boundless pale-green expanse of tufted water with a false promise of meadows—so deceptive indeed that many believed in them. Might it not be supposed that sunken countries or submarine realms lay underneath here, from which all this grass had come loose and floated up? In that case it was dangerous; there must be shoals, at any moment they might run aground, and stranding so far from any coast would mean death. The Admiral's only reply to these complaints was to have soundings taken, and the lead ran out for hundreds of fathoms, all the line they had, and no bottom! If the pastures they were talking about lay below, then he must say they were a long way down; and the Admiral was cruel enough to add that *now* nobody would be likely to expect a cow to stick its head out of the sea from the meadows below or to see a church spire jutting out. Loud cries of pain drowned his words; the men were thrown from fright into terror. So deep! Why, there was no bottom at all here! So they *were* outside the world now and over the inconceivable abyss of Ocean. They had to prop each other up at the thought, and their eyes nearly dropped out of their heads. To be wrecked here, to sink and sink and sink. . . . But the Admiral asked them rather dryly if it wouldn't be all the same to them how much water they drowned in, a fathom or a mile, if it had to be: a heartless thing to say, and incautious. They roared—one man threw his cap at him. The Admiral turned his back on them, but came again and pointed with a great sweep of the arm out over the sea of weed that shone like gold in the dazzling rays of the sun: if they believed that all this splendor came from impossible submarine islands, then it was *his* belief that it was a presage of real islands, perhaps not so very far off, where the golden fields extended just as far as the seaweed here—floors of gold far and wide! And then they made a fuss like a pack of women over the trouble and risk of getting there—as if the islands wouldn't have been discovered and occupied long ago if there had been no danger in it!

Silence, not a sound; some of them were put to shame, others led into a new train of thought—it sounded wonderful, that about the gold. And the end of it was that they went on sailing; while bandying words they easily did a half-day's run. But the men stuck to their opinion. They passed through the weed right enough, but all the same it was an ominous sign that the sea was getting so thick. What if it thickened still more? They might sail in gruel, but in porridge any man would stick fast. And the Admiral's words had left a sting behind them: if he had more learning, it didn't give him the right to make fun of poor Christian men.

If, however, there were lamentations over the danger of getting stuck in the sea of weed, it was not long before the fact of their slipping so easily through it gave uneasiness. What would be the end of it? This everlasting breeze from the northeast! Why, it held for weeks, they never touched the sails, which stood day and night on the starboard tack, easy sailing, but what about it when they had to go the other way? How would they come home again? What kind of a wind was it anyhow? It had never been reported anywhere else that the wind held so long from one quarter; it could scarcely be interpreted otherwise than that there was a sucking from the opposite quarter, the one they were making for, like the wind that goes over a waterfall; it was from the *Abyss* the sucking came, they were in it now, and it was a desperate thing, it was tempting God and throwing away one's fair wind, which was of the kind the Evil One sends . . .

The Admiral shrugged his shoulders. Truth to tell, he did not understand himself why the wind held so long; it was a new thing in his experience, and every day he scanned the clouds and all other indications a seaman stores in his head and recognizes on later occasions; but these waters were strange to him, and nobody as yet could know how it was with this wind. There was every reason to be grateful for it though, if the crew had not been growing more anxious every day and scarcely to be managed in the long run.

Then it happened one day, the twenty-third of September, that the wind changed, they had a head-sea, and the crew could no longer maintain that there were no other winds in these seas but from the northeast; Columbus was saved for another space, and he it was who clasped his hands that evening in deepest gratitude to the All-bountiful, in spite of the fact that they had made no headway that day.

In his private meditations, divided between the Bible and the logbook, he could not help thinking that evening of Moses, who led his refractory people through so many real dangers, but whose most difficult task was to preserve them from their own imagination and instinct of self-destruction.

But all the complaints returned with renewed force when the wind changed again; once more every one could clearly see that all the waves were hurrying to the west, the whole sea was flowing that way, straight into the Abyss!

They now passed out of the Sargasso Sea, out into clear deep waves again, and if lately they had eyed the hated weed with furtive looks of woe, they now cast back inconsolable glances after it. For all the signs of land the Admiral had fabricated with his ready tongue while it was there, were vanished now. That seaweed showed the proximity of a coast had sounded right enough; but now? That crabs which they had found in the weed were a good sign, that birds and fish they had seen, which found food in it, also pointed to the nearness of land, of course—but now it was days ago, and still there was no land!

The men's heads were beginning to get a little addled: they saw sea monsters in every wave that curled, and huddled together in groups at night, afraid of the dark; they wept over the increasing heat, which left no doubt that they were approaching the scorching regions in the immediate neighborhood of the sun, where nothing can live, except salamanders; they would not escape with being turned as dark as the blackamoors in Africa, they would be completely charred, scorched up like flies, the whole ship would blaze up—in the name of the most merciful God, man, turn about before it is too late!

Other voices made themselves heard, and those of the soberest men on board, the officers themselves. The bottom could be seen of the ship's provisions, in a literal sense; in several places they had gone down through the cargo to the bottom of the ship; if they were to count on food for the same number of days back as they had sailed out, they would have to turn pretty soon. To this Columbus said nothing. In his own mind he looked forward to the hour when they no longer *could* turn back, when their food was exhausted to that extent; then there would be no other way than straight ahead, but he didn't say this.

The other complaints he took up, rather glad to be able to keep them alive, so that they might overshadow thoughts of the provisions; he went through them again with the crew, as often and as long as they liked, talking and talking, hollow-eyed, stiff with fatigue but indefatigable. It ended in a sort of permanent ship's parliament on board, where all, even the ordinary seamen, had a voice, and where the tone grew sharper and sharper. During these discussions all the theoretical side of the voyage was probed deeper and deeper, a kind of cross-examination which the Admiral accepted in good part, and which he spun out with a certain warmth, keeping an inner eye on the log the whole time.

All that Columbus had adduced again and again for fourteen years, before a commission of scholars in Portugal, and before a learned commission at Salamanca, had to come up, and he had to listen to the same arguments against him and refute them again as well as he could. Now how did he think he would reach the Indies by this crazy route which took him farther and farther away from them every day he sailed?

To put it briefly, if the earth was round . . .

Yes, but the earth wasn't round! Everybody knew that, everybody could see it, and it was heresy to assert the contrary, high treason against the Church and against God. Juan de la Cosa, who was the owner of the vessel and accompanied the exposition in that capacity, here acted as spokesman and displayed no mean biblical knowledge. Neither the Pentateuch nor the Prophets nor the Apostles said anything about the earth being a globe; besides, ordinary common sense told you it was an error; take the Deluge, for instance, how would it have been possible if the earth was not flat? All the water would have run off if it had been curved . . .

Storms of applause from the whole crew for Juan de la Cosa, who modestly withdrew into the crowd, and a malicious chorus of yelping at Columbus.

But now the Admiral took to both Latin and Greek against Juan de la Cosa, quoted utterances of Saint Augustine and compared them with things Aristotle had said, Strabo, Seneca, Pythagoras, Eratosthenes . . .

Aristotle . . . Juan de la Cosa nodded manfully, he had heard the name before, and knew that it carried weight, but he was not sure of his ground and the Admiral was given a chance of quoting at length all the reasons that had induced the ancients to assume the spherical form of the earth, the shadow it cast on the moon in an eclipse, the weightiest of proofs, which passed over the heads of the crew like the wildest moonshine. Juan de la Cosa, however, had understood it and came forward with an objection:

How was it possible that the earth cast a shadow on the moon, *even* if it was round? In that case the sun would have to pass right round the earth, *under* it so to speak . . .

COLUMBUS: That is just what it does.

JUAN DE LA COSA: Oh, I see. But then the earth must rest upon something, whether it is flat or round, a foundation; how can a heavenly body pass under that?

COLUMBUS: The earth has no foundation; it is a globe hanging freely in space.

Sensation. Suppressed passion here and there. All eyes hung upon Juan de la Cosa, who was quite distressed and looked at the Admiral with genuine sorrow, as he asked in a faltering voice how . . . how . . . the earth, weighing many hundred thousand quintals . . . hang freely in space, how could that be?

What is impossible to Almighty God? answered the Admiral with force. He who has set the spheres in motion and keeps them going, with sun, moon, and stars to give light and measure the day, should He not be able to keep the earth suspended in its place in space? *He* alone knows how!

Juan de la Cosa bowed his head and his forefinger went up to his breast, the sign of the cross made itself at the mention of the holy name of God. The crew followed his example, they felt as if they were in church, and the threatening conflict of opinion was resolved in a moment of solemn awe.

But the dispute blazed up again, and Juan de la Cosa obstinately insisted, on behalf of all, that *even* if the earth was round, which it was *not;* nay, even if hung freely in space, by the power of God, whose name be praised, then it was nevertheless an impossible thing they were trying to do. A globe *might* be so big that to us men it would appear to be flat in that part where one was situated, granted, and that must necessarily be the upper part; but if one left it, one would have to proceed along a slope which would get steeper and steeper, vertical at last, and then turn inward on the under side, always supposing that the spherical theory held, which, of course, was sheer nonsense, for how could water hang on a globe all the way round?

Applause. *Bravo! bravo!* they cried to Juan de la Cosa; and he was really brave, he looked the Admiral straight in the face as, with a bow to his superior, he resumed his place in the crowd.

The last question the Admiral left alone and seized on the first, pounced on it like a hawk:

We are sailing *downward* at this moment!

Pause, until his meaning dawned on them, then violent excitement; several men shrieked aloud and ran to the bulwarks to look, some instinctively laid hand on hilt. Juan de la Cosa turned pale, but pulled himself together and asked:

And how did the Admiral think of sailing upward again?

Everybody grasped at once the bearing of Juan de la Cosa's words, pictured the immense curve down which they were engaged in sailing, saw the impossibility of ever coming up it again and stood as though turned to stone . . .

In the midst of this consternation the Admiral was heard to laugh, a perfectly careless laugh at such a serious moment; he was making fun of them, the hell-hound, the cup was full, they wouldn't listen to him any more . . .

We are sailing *upward* also at this moment, said the Admiral mildly to Juan de la Cosa, and explained his meaning more precisely; if the earth was really round there could be neither up nor down at any given point, except in the direction that passed through the center of the earth and the zenith . . . But Juan de la Cosa shook his head, gave the Admiral an honest look, and shook his head, grieved for him, for his ship, and for them all.

The Admiral then changed his tone, laughed with his cavernous eyes, and made as though he accepted the others' view, since they were in the majority; suppose they were right and the earth was flat. But in that case it could not be surrounded by an abyss down which the water plunged, for then the seas would long ago have run off the earth, the Deluge would have been impossible, as Juan de la Cosa very rightly pointed out. If on the other hand the Ocean lay about the earth in a ring, the common conception, it by no means precluded the idea of sailing westward to the Indies, round behind instead of straight ahead, not on a globe but on a circle, halfway round the earth's disc, if they preferred it that way . . .

Chorus of all hands that Juan de la Cosa was right, angry exclamation against the Admiral for evidently trying to obscure the heart of the matter and avoid Juan de la Cosa's direct question: How were you to sail up the curve of the earth again, when once you had had the mad idea of sailing down it? Out with it!

THE ADMIRAL: Now it was *they* who all believed that the earth was round.

Yells and bawling, cries of shame and general howls; and so the lesson came to an end.

In a succeeding one the Admiral had to produce all his reasons and proofs of the existence of land westward in the Ocean, apart from the cosmic ones; an argument they had heard before and that every man in Spain and Portugal had heard before, until they cried for help at the very sight of Columbus; an old trite lesson which he actually repeated for positively the last time, in fluent Spanish but with an accent that betrayed the Italian. In other circumstances than these, where their lives were at stake, they would have taken a wild delight in him, a glorious fool to have on board, all the more glorious as he was so big, so tall, and so touched in the upper story; had they not hated him as they did they might even have pitied him, alone against all, far out at sea, doubly alone as a stranger among strangers, this queer fish who was getting old and made himself a laughing-stock by repeating and repeating, explaining and dogmatizing about the same things over and over again——

Such as: From time immemorial ["Time immemorial . . ." Diego mimicked him, with Italian accent, discreet tone, and all; aside, of course, but loud enough to amuse his neighbors]—from time immemorial there had been reports of a vanished land out in the Atlantic Ocean, Plato's Atlantis; opinions were divided as to whether it had been swallowed up by the sea or the way to it had been forgotten; the latter view was supported by rumors repeated through the ages of such lands or islands far to the west of Europe. Many were of the opinion that these were Paradise itself, the Lost Country, from which mankind had once been driven out and had never found the way back; the holy Brandanus had set out in search of them and had actually arrived at a happy isle in the Ocean, the abode of the Blest, as might be read in his legend; but since then the way had been lost again, it was eight hundred years since Saint Brandan's voyage. The legend had afterward been connected with the Canary Isles, wrongly of course; the islands must lie much farther out in the Ocean, at least twice as far as the Azores, which were also out of the question, and presumably more to the southward, possibly in the very direction which they were now sailing.

Now it was to be remarked that in another, more recent view the legend of these mysterious islands or continents far far to the west might be regarded as obscure but substantially correct reports of the east coast of India, which extended so far around the earth that perhaps there had been contact with it now and then by the other way, straight across the Atlantic. It was known that very large islands lay off the coast of India, like Zipangu, of which Marco Polo had sufficiently trustworthy accounts; these must then be the same as the Antilia or the Island of Brazil which the latest geographers, in anticipation of their discovery, had already marked on their maps, as for example the most learned and famous Toscanelli ["What kind of a fool was he?" from Diego], and as the distance between the west coast of Europe and the extremity of India was more or less known, the width of the Atlantic, that is, the distance to be deducted from the whole circumference of the earth, could be approximately determined; in the Admiral's opinion it was neither more nor less than the distance they had already sailed, so now the islands might appear any day [scornful snorts from Diego and the rest of the audience; how often they had heard this sanguine irresponsible tale!].

Well, well, if the geographical arguments were no more obvious to them than the cosmic, then they had the direct, tangible proofs, the missives to be taken up and felt which from time to time had been brought by the Atlantic and which must point to there being land on the other side. In the first place there were the reports of many people who had *seen* the islands, on very clear days, out in the ocean to the west of the Canary Isles ["Long-sighted people, I must say"—Diego]; that was as it might be. Personal evidence: Columbus himself many years before in Madeira had given shelter to a shipwrecked man who disclosed to him on his deathbed that he had been driven by a storm twenty-eight days out into the Atlantic on a voyage to England, and had there come upon islands the natives of which went about naked; afterward he had got a fair wind back to Europe but was so worn out that he died in Madeira, the last of a crew of seventeen ["A nice story that! Why didn't he stay in the islands? Weren't they worth it?"].

There was Pedro Correa ["Oh, *that* fellow"] who was able to tell Columbus about a remarkable piece of driftwood that had come ashore at Porto Santo, curiously dark wood and, be it noted, carved, though apparently not with iron tools. Still more remarkable: some big reeds had drifted up on the same shore, like a sort of grass on an extraordinarily large scale, almost as though they came from a country where everything was of supernatural size. ["Let's see them!"] Columbus himself might have had a chance of seeing them washed up with his own eyes; he had spent three years in Porto Santo and had himself observed many things there which indirectly pointed to lands in the west, curious cloud formations and appearances of the sky, on which, however, he would not lay stress. The reeds, on the other hand, had been sent to the King of Portugal, and there he had *seen* them. Martin Vincenti, a seaman of worthy credit ["I'd like to have him here"—Diego], had also found carved driftwood far to the west of Cape Saint Vincent.

But the most remarkable of all proofs was that reported from the Azores: there after westerly winds they had found boats washed up on the beach, hollowed out of a single trunk, evidently the craft of savages; and on Flores, one of the Azores, two corpses had been washed up, possibly these same savages; they were broad in face and did not resemble any known race of men. This one might almost call tangible proof of the existence of the Antipodes . . .

The Antipodes . . . here Juan de la Cosa coughed and ventured an observation. To a sober view the finding of the two corpses, if the account was to be relied upon, did not appear to him to convey any information about the Antipodes, since from what one knew about them they must have an entirely different appearance, scarcely confined to such a trifle as greater breadth of face. In the nature of things nothing definite could be known about the Antipodes, but it was obvious that beings who were to inhabit the under side of the earth, where the trees grew downward and the rain fell straight up in the air, must at any rate have suckers on their feet, like certain kinds of lizards, to stay where they were; in other respects also they were doubtless very different from Christians. It was not necessary indeed to go so far as the earth's poles or supports to find monsters; even in the heathen world, toward the outskirts of the earth, there was a great falling-off from the human form, if one might believe travelers and writings whose age entitled them to veneration. Not that he was himself a man of great reading, but still he had heard of the Arimaspians and of the Satyrs, and knew that beyond Arabia there were people with only one leg, on which they hopped around, and that very swiftly; that there were Amazons and men without a head but with a face in their stomach was also known. From this it appeared that the farther one traveled from the Christian world, the more men ceased to be created in God's image, and there seemed to be good grounds for supposing that those who dwelt farthest down were created in the image of quite another Person, if indeed one might include the Devil in Creation; in which case they had wings and were to that extent capable of keeping on the under side of the earth. Instead of supposing Paradise to lie in that quarter, it was more natural to imagine Hell there, even to an unenlightened view, since there was every reason to presume that the earth rested on fire or had fire in its depths, as could be seen by volcanoes; the fact that it grew hotter and hotter the farther one sailed to the south was an indication in the same direction, as all those present were in a position to confirm. Thus the two corpses at the Azores, in Juan de la Cosa's humble layman's opinion, did not tell them much about the Antipodes. The mention of them, on the other hand, suggested quite other and horrible ideas to the mind.

An uncanny silence fell upon the crew at Juan de la Cosa's rational words. Of course, the Admiral always made it appear to them that the only goal of their desires was to sight land, but it depended a good deal on what awaited them when they did reach land. Speechless resentment against the Admiral was reflected in their features at the thought of what Juan de la Cosa had pictured; they could not find words for their horror and abomination. Was it possible that he intended and had been intending all the time to sail them straight into Hell? Were they to lose their salvation as well as their lives? Had he sold their souls? Then let the Devil take him . . . The oath stuck in their throats, for if he was the foul fiend himself . . .

Ugly pause. Even Jorge, the wholly inarticulate, who sat on deck poking bits of salt pork into his mouth with his knife and audibly pulling the blade out again between his teeth, an old galley slave with scars on his ankles from the shackles and bare places on his scalp like an old horse chafed by the harness—even he gave an *Ouf!* and raised his pock-marked face, shaking a little with age, blinked and cocked his ear: What now, what made the

men so quiet? Unwholesome air, he had always found, when abuse died
away on men's lips! Could there be worse things in store for him than he
had already gone through, in his long, precarious life?

But Jorge was quickly reassured and shoved in another mouthful that
had been checked in the air on the point of his knife, for the Admiral was
evidently saying things that restored the men's breath and gave them back
the use of speech: the Admiral crossed himself so frankly and feelingly for
his own part at the mention of the Evil One and his abode that only the
most grudging could doubt his piety; assuredly *he* was not in league with
the Prince of Fire, far less was he that personage himself, so much would
have to be admitted.

A protracted exchange of opinions ensued on difficult theological problems. The Admiral did not hold the view that the Underworld was a place
which could be reached by any known route, at any rate not by sea; that
was out of the question, since water was an element hostile and opposed to
fire; the way thither was inaccessible to man, while alive; for such as died
without grace it was easy to find. Paradise, on the other hand, which was
commonly placed in Heaven, without more precise indication . . . well,
they had no priest on board, but even in the absence of one the holy articles
of faith and the revelation of the Scriptures should remain entirely undisturbed; however, even the Scriptures gave nothing that one might call definite observation of the position of the Kingdom of Heaven; but as we were
told that our first parents were driven from thence it was permissible to
suppose that it had lain and still lay somewhere on earth. In contradistinc-
tion to the Underworld we had an example in Holy Writ that men might
be taken up alive into Heaven, the prophet Elijah; although this happened
a long time ago it could not therefore be regarded as absolutely impossible
that it might take place again.

Shaking of heads among the Admiral's hearers, divided opinions, and an
uncomfortable feeling in their insides; as usual, the talk had an inconclu-
sive, unsatisfied ending. To many whose sole unhappy thought was their
abandonment in the midst of Ocean, the future appeared in a doubtful,
hopeless light; in truth, with all the various prospects suggested by the officers, the cry of *Land* could not come soon enough!

When at last it came, however, it swept aside all other thoughts . . .
Land, land!

It was from Martin Alonzo Pinzon the blessed cry came. He had just
closed the flagship in the *Pinta,* a comparison had been made of logs and
charts, apparently of a disquieting nature, when Martin Alonzo noticed

something like a low cloud or indication of land ahead to the westward, right in the sunset, a long way off, but with so unmistakably the character of a long, broken coastline that Martin Alonzo was not in doubt for a moment:

Land, land!

They all saw it, the Admiral saw it and immediately fell on his knees on the quarter-deck and began to thank God with hands raised high. Immense sensation, all troubles forgotten, wild joy all over the ship at the sight of the distant blessed streak of land; the men ran up the masts and down again, fell into each other's arms, were quite beside themselves.

Ay, a mad scene of confusion, until the Admiral in a powerful, solemn voice which penetrated from one end of the ship to the other, ordered all hands to be called on deck for divine service.

A gun was fired, and the *Niña* sailed up; the three ships sailed abreast in the falling darkness, and as the streak of land vanished in the great glow of the sunset, and the afterglow paled away and gave place to the first tiny twinkling stars, the hymn arose from the *Santa Maria,* from the *Pinta* and the *Niña,* three choirs of men's voices which united in one and cried out upon the sea and to the stars:

Salve Regina, Mater misericordiæ, vita, dulcedo, et spes nostra, salve.
   Ad te clamamus exsules, filii Hevæ.
Ad te suspiramus, gementes, et flentes in hoc lacrymarum valle.
Eia ergo advocata nostra, illos tuos misericordes oculos ad nos converte.
Et Jesum benedictum fructum ventris tui, nobis post hoc exsilium ostende.
   O clemens, o pia, o dulcis Virgo Maria.

Laughter in the Desolate Mid-Pacific*

THOR HEYERDAHL

✳✳ One hundred and one days adrift in the Pacific Ocean on a balsawood raft of fantastic construction, Thor Heyerdahl and five male companions crossed the ocean from Peru to the Tuamotu Islands in the South Pacific, reaching there on August 7, 1947, in one of the unique voyages in all history, a voyage designed to test the theory that Polynesian settlers of the South Pacific had arrived there in similar rafts from Peru in about 500 A.D. This selection is from the saga of the 45-foot raft *Kon-Tiki* (named after the Incas' great forerunner—the sun king who had vanished westward over the sea from Peru and appeared in Polynesia 1500 years ago) and consists of observations made on and around the forty-fifth day at sea. ✳✳

On the forty-fifth day we had advanced from the 78th degree of longitude to the 108th and were exactly halfway to the first islands ahead. There were over two thousand sea miles between us and South America to the east, and it was the same distance on to Polynesia in the west. The nearest land in any direction was the Galapagos Islands to east-northeast and Easter Island due south, both more than five hundred sea miles away on the boundless ocean. We had not seen a ship, and we never did see one, because we were off the routes of all ordinary shipping traffic in the Pacific.

But we did not really feel these enormous distances, for the horizon glided along with us unnoticed as we moved, and our own floating world remained always the same—a circle flung up to the vault of the sky with the raft itself as center, while the same stars rolled on over us night after night.

When the sea was not too rough, we were often out in the little rubber dinghy taking photographs. I shall not forget the first time the sea was so calm that two men felt like putting the balloonlike little thing into the water

* From *Kon-Tiki; Across the Pacific by Raft*, by Thor Heyerdahl. Translated by F. H. Lyon. Copyright, 1950, by Thor Heyerdahl. Published in the United States by Rand McNally & Company, Chicago, reprinted by permission of George Allen & Unwin, Ltd., Publishers, London.

and going for a row. They had hardly got clear of the raft when they dropped the little oars and sat roaring with laughter. And, as the swell lifted them away and they disappeared and reappeared among the seas, they laughed so loud every time they caught a glimpse of us that their voices rang out over the desolate Pacific. We looked around us with mixed feelings and saw nothing comic but our own hirsute faces; but as the two in the dinghy should be accustomed to those by now, we began to have a lurking suspicion that they had suddenly gone mad. Sunstroke, perhaps. The two fellows could hardly scramble back on board the *Kon-Tiki* for sheer laughter and, gasping, with tears in their eyes they begged us just to go and see for ourselves.

Two of us jumped down into the dancing rubber dinghy and were caught by a sea which lifted us clear. Immediately we sat down with a bump and roared with laughter. We had to scramble back on the raft as quickly as possible and calm the last two who had not been out yet, for they thought we had all gone stark, staring mad.

It was ourselves and our proud vessel which made such a completely hopeless, lunatic impression on us the first time we saw the whole thing at a distance. We had never before had an outside view of ourselves in the open sea. The logs of timber disappeared behind the smallest waves, and, when we saw anything at all, it was the low cabin with the wide doorway and the bristly roof of leaves that bobbed up from among the seas. The raft looked exactly like an old Norwegian hayloft lying helpless, drifting about in the open sea—a warped hayloft full of sunburned, bearded ruffians. If anyone had come paddling after us at sea in a bathtub, we should have felt the same spontaneous urge to laughter. Even an ordinary swell rolled halfway up the cabin wall and looked as if it would pour in unhindered through the wide-open door in which the bearded fellows lay gaping. But then the crazy craft came up to the surface again, and the vagabonds lay there as dry, shaggy, and intact as before. If a higher sea came racing by, cabin and sail and the whole mast might disappear behind the mountain of water, but just as certainly the cabin with its vagabonds would be there again next moment. The situation looked bad, and we could not realize that things had gone so well on board the zany craft.

Next time we rowed out to have a good laugh at ourselves we nearly had a disaster. The wind and sea were higher than we supposed, and the *Kon-Tiki* was cleaving a path for herself over the swell much more quickly than we realized. We in the dinghy had to row for our lives out in the open sea in an attempt to regain the unmanageable raft, which could not stop and wait and could not possibly turn around and come back. Even when the boys on board the *Kon-Tiki* got the sail down, the wind got such a grip on the bamboo cabin that the raft drifted away to westward as fast as we could splash after her in the dancing rubber dinghy with its tiny toy oars. There was only one thought in the head of every man—we must not be separated. Those were horrible minutes we spent out on the sea before we got hold of the runaway raft and crawled on board to the others, home again.

From that day it was strictly forbidden to go out in the rubber dinghy without having a long line made fast to the bow, so that those who remained on board could haul the dinghy in if necessary. We never went far away from the raft, thereafter, except when the wind was light and the Pacific curving itself in a gentle swell. But we had these conditions when the raft was halfway to Polynesia and the ocean, all dominating, arched itself round the globe toward every point of the compass. Then we could safely leave the *Kon-Tiki* and row away into the blue space between sky and sea.

When we saw the silhouette of our craft grow smaller and smaller in the distance, and the big sail at last shrunken to a vague black square on the horizon, a sensation of loneliness sometimes crept over us. The sea curved away under us as blue upon blue as the sky above, and where they met all the blue flowed together and became one. It almost seemed as if we were suspended in space. All our world was empty and blue; there was no fixed point in it but the tropical sun, golden and warm, which burned our necks. Then the distant sail of the lonely raft drew us to it like a magnetic point on the horizon. We rowed back and crept on board with a feeling that we had come home again to our own world—on board and yet on firm, safe ground. And inside the bamboo cabin we found shade and the scent of bamboos and withered palm leaves. The sunny blue purity outside was now served to us in a suitably large dose through the open cabin wall. So we were accustomed to it and so it was good for a time, till the great clear blue tempted us out again.

It was most remarkable what a psychological effect the shaky bamboo cabin had on our minds. It measured eight by fourteen feet, and to diminish the pressure of wind and sea it was built low so that we could not stand upright under the ridge of the roof. Walls and roof were made of strong bamboo canes, lashed together and guyed, and covered with a tough wickerwork of split bamboos. The green and yellow bars, with fringes of foliage hanging down from the roof, were restful to the eye as a white cabin wall never could have been, and, despite the fact that the bamboo wall on the starboard side was open for one third of its length and roof and walls let in sun and moon, this primitive lair gave us a greater feeling of security than white-painted bulkheads and closed portholes would have given in the same circumstances.

We tried to find an explanation for this curious fact and came to the following conclusion. Our consciousness was totally unaccustomed to associating a palm-covered bamboo dwelling with sea travel. There was no natural harmony between the great rolling ocean and the drafty palm hut which was floating about among the seas. Therefore, either the hut would seem entirely out of place in among the waves, or the waves would seem entirely out of place round the hut wall. So long as we kept on board, the bamboo hut and its jungle scent were plain reality, and the tossing seas seemed rather visionary. But from the rubber boat, waves and hut exchanged roles.

The fact that the balsa logs always rode the seas like a gull, and let the water right through aft if a wave broke on board, gave us an unshakable confidence in the dry part in the middle of the raft where the cabin was. The longer the voyage lasted, the safer we felt in our cozy lair, and we looked at the white-crested waves that danced past outside our doorway as if they were an impressive movie, conveying no menace to us at all. Even though the gaping wall was only five feet from the unprotected edge of the raft and only a foot and a half above the water line, yet we felt as if we had traveled many miles away from the sea and occupied a jungle dwelling remote from the sea's perils once we had crawled inside the door. There we could lie on our backs and look up at the curious roof which twisted about like boughs in the wind, enjoying the jungle smell of raw wood, bamboos, and withered palm leaves.

Sometimes, too, we went out in the rubber boat to look at ourselves by night. Coal-black seas towered up on all sides, and a glittering myriad of tropical stars drew a faint reflection from plankton in the water. The world was simple—stars in the darkness. Whether it was 1947 B.C. or A.D. suddenly became of no significance. We lived, and that we felt with alert intensity. We realized that life had been full for men before the technical age also—in fact, fuller and richer in many ways than the life of modern man. Time and evolution somehow ceased to exist; all that was real and that mattered were the same today as they had always been and would always be. We were swallowed up in the absolute common measure of history—endless, unbroken darkness under a swarm of stars.

Before us in the night the *Kon-Tiki* rose out of the seas to sink down again behind black masses of water that towered between her and us. In the moonlight there was a fantastic atmosphere about the raft. Stout, shining wooden logs fringed with seaweed, the square pitch-black outline of a Viking sail, a bristly bamboo hut with the yellow light of a paraffin lamp aft—the whole suggested a picture from a fairy tale rather than an actual reality. Now and then the raft disappeared completely behind the black seas; then she rose again and stood out sharp in silhouette against the stars, while glittering water poured from the logs.

When we saw the atmosphere about the solitary raft, we could well see in our mind's eye the whole flotilla of such vessels, spread in fan formation beyond the horizon to increase the chances of finding land, when the first men made their way across this sea. The Inca Tupak Yupanqui, who had brought under his rule both Peru and Ecuador, sailed across the sea with an armada of many thousand men on balsa rafts, just before the Spaniards came, to search for islands which rumor had told of out in the Pacific. He found two islands, which some think were the Galapagos, and after eight months' absence he and his numerous paddlers succeeded in toiling their way back to Ecuador. Kon-Tiki and his followers had certainly sailed in a similar formation several hundred years before but, having discovered the Polynesian islands, they had no reason for trying to struggle back.

When we jumped on board the raft again, we often sat down in a circle round the paraffin lamp on the bamboo deck and talked of the seafarers from Peru who had had all these same experiences fifteen hundred years before us. The lamp flung huge shadows of bearded men on the sail, and we thought of the white men with the beards from Peru whom we could follow in mythology and architecture all the way from Mexico to Central America and into the northwestern area of South America as far as Peru. Here this mysterious civilization disappeared, as by the stroke of a magic wand, before the coming of the Incas, and reappeared just as suddenly out on the solitary islands in the west which we were now approaching. Were the wandering teachers men of an early civilized race from across the Atlantic, who in times long past, in the same simple manner, had come over with the westerly ocean current and the trade wind from the area of the Canary Islands to the Gulf of Mexico? That was indeed a far shorter distance than the one we were covering, and we no longer believed in the sea as a completely isolating factor.

Editor's Note: To show that the world does move, and with it man, too, and that what one or several attempt and do another may even surpass, William Willis, a lone man on a balsa raft, beat the *Kon-Tiki's* 4000-mile, six-man venture some time before this book went to press by ending a 6000-mile drift from Peru and landing at Pago Pago, Samoa. The voyage took four months, roughly, and his avowed intention was to beat the *Kon-Tiki* travelers at their own game on their own route. Mr. Willis sailed from Callao, Peru, June 22, 1954, passed on by the *Kon-Tiki* terminal in the Taumotu Archipelago, which they reached at 4300 miles in 101 days; and debarked at Pago Pago, 6000 miles, on his 115th day, October 14, 1954. He had never been heard from until he was sighted off Samoa, the day he landed. He had invited his wife on the trip, but she declined. So he was accompanied only by a parrot and a cat. He is 61 years old. His wife lives in New York and on the next such trip, she says now, she'll go.

Youth *

JOSEPH CONRAD

✳✳ Joseph Conrad (1857-1924), English novelist, born in the Kiev section of Ukraine, then Poland, resolved to become a sailor the first time he saw the sea at the Lido in Venice. He was then a 13-year-old orphan. His father died after he returned from political exile by the Russian government when Conrad was 13; his mother died when he was eight. After a few years at the Royal Gymnasium at Kraków and later private tutoring, he tried to run away to sea in Trieste. At 16, with his uncle's consent, he went to work on a French boat out of Marseille. For 16 years he sailed as officer and commander of small wooden boats in the British Merchant Service and was naturalized a British subject in 1886. His most famous short story, *Youth,* he wrote in England on the day his son Borys was born in January, 1898, "in the evening, downstairs, in a twopenny note book, in pencil, by the light of a solitary candle." ✳✳

A NARRATIVE

This could have occurred nowhere but in England, where men and sea interpenetrate, so to speak—the sea entering into the life of most men, and the men knowing something or everything about the sea, in the way of amusement, of travel, or of breadwinning.

We were sitting round a mahogany table that reflected the bottle, the claret glasses, and our faces as we leaned on our elbows. There was a director of companies, an accountant, a lawyer, Marlow, and myself. The director had been a *Conway* boy, the accountant had served four years at sea, the lawyer —a fine crusted Tory, High Churchman, the best of old fellows, the soul of honor—had been chief officer in the P. & O. service in the good old days when mailboats were square-rigged at least on two masts and used to come down the China Sea before a fair monsoon with stun'-sails set alow and aloft. We all began life in the merchant service. Between the five of us there was

---

* From *Youth and Other Stories,* by Joseph Conrad, reprinted by permission of J. M. Dent & Sons, Ltd., London.

the strong bond of the sea, and also the fellowship of the craft, which no amount of enthusiasm for yachting, cruising, and so on can give, since one is only the amusement of life and the other is life itself.

Marlow (at least I think that is how he spelt his name) told the story, or rather the chronicle, of a voyage:

"Yes, I have seen a little of the Eastern seas; but what I remember best is my first voyage there. You fellows know there are those voyages that seem ordered for the illustration of life, that might stand for a symbol of existence. You fight, work, sweat, nearly kill yourself, sometimes do kill yourself, trying to accomplish something—and you can't. Not from any fault of yours. You simply can do nothing, neither great nor little—not a thing in the world—not even marry an old maid, or get a wretched six-hundred-ton cargo of coal to its port of destination.

"It was altogether a memorable affair. It was my first voyage to the East, and my first voyage as second mate; it was also my skipper's first command. You'll admit it was time. He was sixty if a day; a little man, with a broad, not very straight back, with bowed shoulders and one leg more bandy than the other, he had that queer twisted-about appearance you see so often in men who work in the fields. He had a nutcracker face—chin and nose trying to come together over a sunken mouth—and it was framed in iron-gray fluffy hair, that looked like a chin strap of cotton-wool sprinkled with coal dust. And he had blue eyes in that old face of his which were amazingly like a boy's, with that candid expression some quite common men preserve to the end of their days by a rare internal gift of simplicity of heart and rectitude of soul. What induced him to accept me was a wonder. I had come out of a crack Australian clipper, where I had been third officer, and he seemed to have a prejudice against crack clippers as aristocratic and high-toned. He said to me, 'You know, in this ship you will have to work.' I said I had to work in every ship I had ever been in. 'Ah, but this is different, and you gentlemen out of them big ships; . . . but there! I dare say you will do. Join to-morrow.'

"I joined to-morrow. It was twenty-two years ago; and I was just twenty. How time passes! It was one of the happiest days of my life. Fancy! Second mate for the first time—a really responsible officer! I wouldn't have thrown up my new billet for a fortune. The mate looked me over carefully. He was also an old chap, but of another stamp. He had a Roman nose, a snow-white, long beard, and his name was Mahon, but he insisted that it should be pronounced Mann. He was well connected; yet there was something wrong with his luck, and he had never got on.

"As to the captain, he had been for years in coasters, then in the Mediterranean, and last in the West Indian trade. He had never been round the Capes. He could just write a kind of sketchy hand, and didn't care for writing at all. Both were thorough, good seamen of course, and between those two old chaps I felt like a small boy between two grandfathers.

"The ship also was old. Her name was the *Judea*. Queer name, isn't it? She belonged to a man Wilmer, Wilcox—some name like that; but he has been bankrupt and dead these twenty years or more, and his name doesn't matter. She had been laid up in Shadwell basin for ever so long. You can imagine her state. She was all rust, dust, grime—soot aloft, dirt on deck. To me it was like coming out of a palace into a ruined cottage. She was about four hundred tons, had a primitive windlass, wooden latches to the doors, not a bit of brass about her, and a big square stern. There was on it, below her name in big letters, a lot of scroll work, with the gilt off, and some sort of a coat of arms, with the motto 'Do or Die' underneath. I remember it took my fancy immensely. There was a touch of romance in it, something that made me love the old thing—something that appealed to my youth!

"We left London in ballast—sand ballast—to load a cargo of coal in a northern port for Bangkok. Bangkok! I thrilled. I had been six years of sea, but had only seen Melbourne and Sydney, very good places, charming places in their way—but Bangkok!

"We worked out of the Thames under canvas, with a North Sea pilot on board. His name was Jermyn, and he dodged all day long about the galley drying his handkerchief before the stove. Apparently he never slept. He was a dismal man, with a perpetual tear sparkling at the end of his nose, who either had been in trouble, or was in trouble, or expected to be in trouble—couldn't be happy unless something went wrong. He mistrusted my youth, my common sense, and my seamanship, and made a point of showing it in a hundred little ways. I dare say he was right. It seems to me I knew very little then, and I know not much more now; but I cherish a hate for that Jermyn to this day.

"We were a week working up as far as Yarmouth Roads, and then we got into a gale—the famous October gale of twenty-two years ago. It was wind, lightning, sleet, snow, and a terrific sea. We were flying light, and you may imagine how bad it was when I tell you we had smashed bulwarks and a flooded deck. On the second night she shifted her ballast into the lee bow, and by that time we had been blown off somewhere on the Dogger Bank. There was nothing for it but go below with shovels and try to right her, and there we were in that vast hold, gloomy like a cavern, the tallow dips stuck and flickering on the beams, the gale howling above, the ship tossing about like mad on her side; there we all were, Jermyn, the captain, everyone, hardly able to keep our feet, engaged on that gravedigger's work, and trying to toss shovelfuls of wet sand up to windward. At every tumble of the ship you could see vaguely in the dim light men falling down with a great flourish of shovels. One of the ship's boys (we had two), impressed by the weirdness of the scene, wept as if his heart would break. We could hear him blubbering somewhere in the shadows.

"On the third day the gale died out, and by-and-by a North-country tug picked us up. We took sixteen days in all to get from London to the Tyne! When we got into dock we had lost our turn for loading, and they hauled us off to a tier where we remained for a month. Mrs. Beard [the captain's name was Beard] came from Colchester to see the old man. She lived on board. The crew of runners had left, and there remained only the officers, one boy, and the steward, a mulatto who answered to the name of Abraham. Mrs. Beard was an old woman, with a face all wrinkled and ruddy like a winter apple, and the figure of a young girl. She caught sight of me once, sewing on a button, and insisted on having my shirts to repair. This was something different from the captains' wives I had known on board crack clippers. When I brought her the shirts, she said: 'And the socks? They want mending, I am sure, and John's—Captain Beard's—things are all in order now. I would be glad of something to do.' Bless the old woman. She overhauled my outfit for me, and meantime I read for the first time Sartor Resartus and Burnaby's Ride to Khiva. I didn't understand much of the first then; but I remember I preferred the soldier to the philosopher at the time; a preference which life has only confirmed. One was a man, and the other was either more—or less. However, they are both dead, and Mrs. Beard is dead, and youth, strength, genius, thoughts, achievements, simple hearts—all die. . . . No matter.

"They loaded us at last. We shipped a crew. Eight able seamen and two boys. We hauled off one evening to the buoys at the dock gates, ready to go out, and with a fair prospect of beginning the voyage next day. Mrs. Beard was to start for home by a late train. When the ship was fast we went to tea. We sat rather silent through the meal—Mahon, the old couple, and I. I finished first and slipped away for a smoke, my cabin being in a deckhouse just against the poop. It was high water, blowing fresh with a drizzle; the double dock gates were opened, and the steam colliers were going in and out in the darkness with their lights burning bright, a great plashing of propellers, rattling of winches, and a lot of hailing on the pier heads. I watched the procession of headlights gliding high and of green lights gliding low in the night, when suddenly a red gleam flashed at me, vanished, came into view again, and remained. The fore end of a steamer loomed up close. I shouted down the cabin, 'Come up, quick!' and then heard a startled voice saying afar in the dark, 'Stop her, sir.' A bell jingled. Another voice cried warningly, 'We are going right into that bark, sir.' The answer to this was a gruff 'All right,' and the next thing was a heavy crash as the steamer struck a glancing blow with the bluff of her bow about our forerigging. There was a moment of confusion, yelling, and running about. Steam roared. Then somebody was heard saying, 'All clear, sir.' . . . 'Are you all right?' asked the gruff voice. I had jumped forward to see the damage, and hailed back, 'I think so.' 'Easy astern,' said the gruff voice. A bell jingled. 'What steamer is that?' screamed Mahon. By that time she was no more to us than a bulky shadow maneuvering a little way off. They shouted at us some name—a woman's name, *Miranda* or *Melissa*—or some such thing. 'This means another month in this beastly hole,' said Mahon to me, as we peered with lamps about the splintered bulwarks and broken braces. 'But where's the captain?'

"We had not heard or seen anything of him all that time. We went aft to look. A doleful voice arose hailing somewhere in the middle of the dock, '*Judea* ahoy!' . . . How the devil did he get there? . . . 'Hallo!' we shouted. 'I am adrift in our boat without oars,' he cried. A belated waterman offered his services, and Mahon struck a bargain with him for half a crown to tow our skipper alongside; but it was Mrs. Beard that came up the ladder first. They had been floating about the dock in that mizzly cold rain for nearly an hour. I was never so surprised in my life.

"It appears that when he heard my shout 'Come up,' he understood at once what was the matter, caught up his wife, ran on deck, and across, and down into our boat, which was fast to the ladder. Not bad for a sixty-year-old. Just imagine that old fellow saving heroically in his arms that old woman— the woman of his life. He set her down on a thwart and was ready to climb back on board when the painter came adrift somehow, and away they went together. Of course in the confusion we did not hear him shouting. He looked abashed. She said cheerfully, 'I suppose it does not matter my losing the train now?' 'No, Jenny—you go below and get warm,' he growled. Then to us: 'A sailor has no business with a wife—I say. There I was, out of the ship. Well, no harm done this time. Let's go and look at what that fool of a steamer smashed.'

"It wasn't much, but it delayed us three weeks. At the end of that time, the captain being engaged with his agents, I carried Mrs. Beard's bag to the railway station and put her all comfy into a third-class carriage. She lowered the window to say, 'You are a good young man. If you see John—Captain Beard —without his muffler at night, just remind him from me to keep his throat well wrapped up.' 'Certainly, Mrs. Beard,' I said. 'You are a good young man; I noticed how attentive you are to John—to Captain——' The train pulled out suddenly; I took my cap off to the old woman: I never saw her again. . . . Pass the bottle.

"We went to sea next day. When we made that start for Bangkok we had been already three months out of London. We had expected to be a fortnight or so—at the outside.

"It was January, and the weather was beautiful—the beautiful sunny winter weather that has more charm than in the summertime, because it is unexpected, and crisp, and you know it won't, it can't, last long. It's like a windfall, like a godsend, like an unexpected piece of luck.

"It lasted all down the North Sea, all down Channel; and it lasted till we were three hundred miles or so to the westward of the Lizards: then the wind went round to the sou'west and began to pipe up. In two days it blew a gale. The *Judea,* hove to, wallowed on the Atlantic like an old candlebox. It blew day after day: it blew with spite, without interval, without mercy, without rest. The world was nothing but an immensity of great foaming waves rushing at us, under a sky low enough to touch with the hand and dirty like a smoked ceiling. In the stormy space surrounding us there was as much flying spray as air. Day after day and night after night there was nothing round the ship but the howl of the wind, the tumult of the sea, the noise of water pouring over her deck. There was no rest for her and no rest for us. She tossed, she pitched, she stood on her head, she sat on her tail, she rolled, she groaned, and we had to hold on while on deck and cling to our bunks when below, in a constant effort of body and worry of mind.

"One night Mahon spoke through the small window of my berth. It opened right into my very bed, and I was lying there sleepless, in my boots, feeling as though I had not slept for years, and could not if I tried. He said excitedly——

" 'You got the sounding rod in here, Marlow? I can't get the pumps to suck. By God! it's no child's play.'

"I gave him the sounding rod and lay down again, trying to think of various things—but I thought only of the pumps. When I came on deck they were still at it, and my watch relieved at the pumps. By the light of the lantern brought on deck to examine the sounding rod I caught a glimpse of their weary, serious faces. We pumped all the four hours. We pumped all night, all day, all the week—watch and watch. She was working herself loose, and leaked badly—not enough to drown us at once, but enough to kill us with the work at the pumps. And while we pumped the ship was going from us piecemeal: the bulwarks went, the stanchions were torn out, the ventilators smashed, the cabin door burst in. There was not a dry spot in the ship. She was being gutted bit by bit. The longboat changed, as if by magic, into match-wood where she stood in her gripes. I had lashed her myself, and was rather proud of my handiwork, which had withstood so long the malice of the sea. And we pumped. And there was no break in the weather. The sea was white like a sheet of foam, like a caldron of boiling milk; there was not a break in the clouds, no—not the size of a man's hand—no, not for so much as ten seconds. There was for us no sky, there were for us no stars, no sun, no universe—nothing but angry clouds and an infuriated sea. We pumped watch and watch, for dear life; and it seemed to last for months, for years, for all eternity, as though we had been dead and gone to a hell for sailors. We forgot the day of the week, the name of the month, what year it was, and whether we had ever been ashore. The sails blew away, she lay broadside on under a weather cloth, the ocean poured over her, and we did not care. We turned those handles and had the eyes of idiots. As soon as we had crawled on deck I used to take a round turn with a rope about the men, the pumps, and the mainmast, and we turned, we turned incessantly, with the water to our waists, to our necks, over our heads. It was all one. We had forgotten how it felt to be dry.

"And there was somewhere in me the thought: By Jove! this is the deuce of an adventure—something you read about; and it is my first voyage as second mate—and I am only twenty—and here I am lasting it out as well as any of these men, and keeping my chaps up to the mark. I was pleased. I would not have given up the experience for worlds. I had moments of exulta-tion. Whenever the old dismantled craft pitched heavily with her counter high in the air, she seemed to me to throw up, like an appeal, like a defiance, like a cry to the clouds without mercy, the words written on her stern: 'Judea, London. Do or Die.'

"O youth! The strength of it, the faith of it, the imagination of it! To me she was not an old rattletrap carting about the world a lot of coal for a freight—to me she was the endeavor, the test, the trial of life. I think of her with pleasure, with affection, with regret—as you would think of someone dead you have loved. I shall never forget her. . . . Pass the bottle.

"One night when tied to the mast, as I explained, we were pumping on, deafened with the wind, and without spirit enough in us to wish ourselves dead, a heavy sea crashed aboard and swept clean over us. As soon as I got my breath I shouted, as in duty bound, 'Keep on, boys!' when suddenly I felt something hard floating on deck strike the calf of my leg. I made a grab at it and missed. It was so dark we could not see each other's faces within a foot—you understand.

"After that thump the ship kept quiet for a while, and the thing, whatever it was, struck my leg again. This time I caught it—and it was a saucepan. At first, being stupid with fatigue and thinking of nothing but the pumps, I did not understand what I had in my hand. Suddenly it dawned upon me, and I shouted, 'Boys, the house on deck is gone. Leave this, and let's look for the cook.'

"There was a deckhouse forward, which contained the galley, the cook's berth, and the quarters of the crew. As we had expected for days to see it swept away, the hands had been ordered to sleep in the cabin—the only safe place in the ship. The steward, Abraham, however, persisted in clinging to his berth, stupidly, like a mule—from sheer fright I believe, like an animal that won't leave a stable falling in an earthquake. So we went to look for him. It was chancing death, since once out of our lashings we were as exposed as if on a raft. But we went. The house was shattered as if a shell had exploded inside. Most of it had gone overboard—stove, men's quarters, and their property, all was gone; but two posts, holding a portion of the bulkhead to which Abraham's bunk was attached, remained as if by a miracle. We groped in the ruins and came upon this, and there he was, sitting in his bunk, surrounded by foam and wreckage, jabbering cheerfully to himself. He was out of his mind; completely and forever mad, with this sudden shock coming upon the fag end of his endurance. We snatched him up, lugged him aft, and pitched him head-first down the cabin companion. You understand there was no time to carry him down with infinite precautions and wait to see how he got on. Those below would pick him up at the bottom of the stairs all right. We were in a hurry to go back to the pumps. That business could not wait. A bad leak is an inhuman thing.

"One would think that the sole purpose of that fiendish gale had been to make a lunatic of that poor devil of a mulatto. It eased before morning, and next day the sky cleared, and as the sea went down the leak took up. When it came to bending a fresh set of sails the crew demanded to put back— and really there was nothing else to do. Boats gone, decks swept clean, cabin gutted, men without a stitch but what they stood in, stores spoiled, ship strained. We put her head for home, and—would you believe it? The wind came east right in our teeth. It blew fresh, it blew continuously. We had to beat up every inch of the way, but she did not leak so badly, the water keeping comparatively smooth. Two hours' pumping in every four is no joke— but it kept her afloat as far as Falmouth.

"The good people there live on casualties of the sea, and no doubt were glad to see us. A hungry crowd of shipwrights sharpened their chisels at the sight of that carcass of a ship. And, by Jove! they had pretty pickings off us before they were done. I fancy the owner was already in a tight place.

There were delays. Then it was decided to take part of the cargo out and calk her topsides. This was done, the repairs finished, cargo reshipped; a new crew came on board, and we went out—for Bangkok. At the end of a week we were back again. The crew said they weren't going to Bangkok—a hundred and fifty days' passage—in a something hooker that wanted pumping eight hours out of the twenty-four; and the nautical papers inserted again the little paragraph: '*Judea*. Bark. Tyne to Bangkok; coals; put back to Falmouth leaky and with crew refusing duty.'

"There were more delays—more tinkering. The owner came down for a day and said she was as right as a little fiddle. Poor old Captain Beard looked like the ghost of a Geordie skipper—through the worry and humiliation of it. Remember he was sixty, and it was his first command. Mahon said it was a foolish business, and would end badly. I loved the ship more than ever, and wanted awfully to get to Bangkok. To Bangkok! Magic name, blessed name. Mesopotamia wasn't a patch on it. Remember I was twenty, and it was my first second mate's billet, and the East was waiting for me.

"We went out and anchored in the outer roads with a fresh crew—the third. She leaked worse than ever. It was as if those confounded shipwrights had actually made a hole in her. This time we did not even go outside. The crew simply refused to man the windlass.

"They towed us back to the inner harbor, and we became a fixture, a feature, an institution of the place. People pointed us out to visitors as 'That 'ere bark that's going to Bangkok—has been here six months—put back three times.' On holidays the small boys pulling about in boats would hail, '*Judea*, ahoy!' and if a head showed above the rail shouted, 'Where you bound to?— Bangkok?' and jeered. We were only three on board. The poor old skipper mooned in the cabin. Mahon undertook the cooking and unexpectedly developed all a Frenchman's genius for preparing nice little messes. I looked languidly after the rigging. We became citizens of Falmouth. Every shopkeeper knew us. At the barber's or tobacconist's they asked familiarly, 'Do you think you will ever get to Bangkok?' Meantime the owner, the underwriters, and the charterers squabbled amongst themselves in London, and our pay went on. . . . Pass the bottle.

"It was horrid. Morally it was worse than pumping for life. It seemed as though we had been forgotten by the world, belonged to nobody, would get nowhere; it seemed that, as if bewitched, we would have to live for ever and ever in that inner harbor, a derision and a byword to generations of longshore loafers and dishonest boatmen. I obtained three months' pay and a five days' leave and made a rush for London. It took me a day to get there and pretty well another to come back—but three months' pay went all the same. I don't know what I did with it. I went to a music hall, I believe, lunched, dined, and supped in a swell place in Regent Street, and was back to time, with nothing but a complete set of Byron's works and a new railway rug to show for three months' work. The boatman who pulled me off to the ship said: 'Hallo! I thought you had left the old thing. *She* will never get to Bangkok.' 'That's all *you* know about it,' I said scornfully—but I didn't like that prophecy at all.

"Suddenly a man, some kind of agent to somebody, appeared with full powers. He had grog blossoms all over his face, an indomitable energy, and was a jolly soul. We leaped into life again. A hulk came alongside, took our cargo, and then we went into dry dock to get our copper stripped. No wonder she leaked. The poor thing, strained beyond endurance by the gale, had, as if in disgust, spat out all the oakum of her lower seams. She was recalked, new-coppered, and made as tight as a bottle. We went back to the hulk and reshipped our cargo.

"Then, on a fine moonlight night, all the rats left the ship.

"We had been infested with them. They had destroyed our sails, consumed more stores than the crew, affably shared our beds and our dangers, and now, when the ship was made seaworthy, concluded to clear out. I called Mahon to enjoy the spectacle. Rat after rat appeared on our rail, took a last look over his shoulder, and leaped with a hollow thud into the empty hulk. We tried to count them but soon lost the tale. Mahon said: 'Well, well! don't talk to me about the intelligence of rats. They ought to have left before, when we had that narrow squeak from foundering. There you have the proof how silly is the superstition about them. They leave a good ship for an old rotten hulk, where there is nothing to eat, too, the fools! . . . I don't believe they know what is safe or what is good for them, any more than you or I.'

"And after some more talk we agreed that the wisdom of rats had been grossly overrated, being in fact no greater than that of men.

"The story of the ship was known, by this, all up the Channel from Land's End to the Forelands, and we could get no crew on the south coast. They sent us one all complete from Liverpool, and we left once more—for Bangkok.

"We had fair breezes, smooth water right into the tropics, and the old *Judea* lumbered along in the sunshine. When she went eight knots everything cracked aloft, and we tied our caps to our heads; but mostly she strolled on at the rate of three miles an hour. What could you expect? She was tired —that old ship. Her youth was where mine is—where yours is—you fellows who listen to this yarn; and what friend would throw your years and your weariness in your face? We didn't grumble at her. To us aft, at least, it seemed as though we had been born in her, reared in her, had lived in her for ages, had never known any other ship. I would just as soon have abused the old village church at home for not being a cathedral.

"And for me there was also my youth to make me patient. There was all the East before me, and all life, and the thought that I had been tried in that ship and had come out pretty well. And I thought of men of old who, centuries ago, went that road in ships that sailed no better, to the land of palms, and spices, and yellow sands, and of brown nations ruled by kings more cruel than Nero the Roman and more splendid than Solomon the Jew. The old bark lumbered on, heavy with her age and the burden of her cargo, while I lived the life of youth in ignorance and hope. She lumbered on through an interminable procession of days; and the fresh gilding flashed back at the setting sun, seemed to cry out over the darkening sea the words painted on her stern, 'Judea, London. Do or Die.'

"Then we entered the Indian Ocean and steered northerly for Java Head. The winds were light. Weeks slipped by. She crawled on, do or die, and people at home began to think of posting us as overdue.

"One Saturday evening, I being off duty, the men asked me to give them an extra bucket of water or so—for washing clothes. As I did not wish to screw on the fresh-water pump so late, I went forward whistling and with a key in my hand to unlock the forepeak scuttle, intending to serve the water out of a spare tank we kept there.

"The smell down below was as unexpected as it was frightful. One would have thought hundreds of paraffin lamps had been flaring and smoking in that hole for days. I was glad to get out. The man with me coughed and said, 'Funny smell, sir.' I answered negligently, 'It's good for the health, they say,' and walked aft.

"The first thing I did was to put my head down the square of the midship ventilator. As I lifted the lid a visible breath, something like a thin fog, a puff of faint haze, rose from the opening. The ascending air was hot and had a heavy, sooty, paraffiny smell. I gave one sniff and put down the lid gently. It was no use choking myself. The cargo was on fire.

"Next day she began to smoke in earnest. You see it was to be expected, for though the coal was of a safe kind, that cargo had been so handled, so broken up with handling, that it looked more like smithy coal than anything else. Then it had been wetted—more than once. It rained all the time we were taking it back from the hulk, and now with this long passage it got heated, and there was another case of spontaneous combustion.

"The captain called us into the cabin. He had a chart spread on the table, and looked unhappy. He said, 'The coast of West Australia is near, but I mean to proceed to our destination. It is the hurricane month too; but we will just keep her head for Bangkok and fight the fire. No more putting back anywhere, if we all get roasted. We will try first to stifle this 'ere damned combustion by want of air.'

"We tried. We battened down everything, and still she smoked. The smoke kept coming out through imperceptible crevices; it forced itself through bulkheads and covers; it oozed here and there and everywhere in slender threads, in an invisible film, in an incomprehensible manner. It made its way into the cabin, into the forecastle; it poisoned the sheltered places on the deck, it could be sniffed as high as the mainyard. It was clear that if the smoke came out the air came in. This was disheartening. This combustion refused to be stifled.

"We resolved to try water, and took the hatches off. Enormous volumes of smoke, whitish, yellowish, thick, greasy, misty, choking, ascended as high as the trucks. All hands cleared out aft. Then the poisonous cloud blew away, and we went back to work in a smoke that was no thicker now than that of an ordinary factory chimney.

"We rigged the force pump, got the hose along, and by-and-by it burst. Well, it was as old as the ship—a prehistoric hose, and past repair. Then we pumped with the feeble head pump, drew water with buckets, and in this way managed in time to pour lots of Indian Ocean into the main hatch. The bright stream flashed in sunshine, fell into a layer of white crawling smoke, and vanished on the black surface of coal. Steam ascended mingling with the smoke. We poured salt water as into a barrel without a bottom. It was our fate to pump in that ship, to pump out of her, to pump into her; and after keeping water out of her to save ourselves from being drowned, we frantically poured water into her to save ourselves from being burnt.

"And she crawled on, do or die, in the serene weather. The sky was a miracle of purity, a miracle of azure. The sea was polished, was blue, was pellucid, was sparkling like a precious stone, extending on all sides, all round to the horizon—as if the whole terrestrial globe had been one jewel, one colossal sapphire, a single gem fashioned into a planet. And on the luster of the great calm waters the *Judea* glided imperceptibly, enveloped in languid and unclean vapors, in a lazy cloud that drifted to leeward, light and slow: a pestiferous cloud defiling the splendor of sea and sky.

"All this time of course we saw no fire. The cargo smoldered at the bottom somewhere. Once Mahon, as we were working side by side, said to me with a queer smile: 'Now, if she only would spring a tidy leak—like that time when we first left the Channel—it would put a stopper on this fire. Wouldn't it?' I remarked irrelevantly, 'Do you remember the rats?'

"We fought the fire and sailed the ship too as carefully as though nothing had been the matter. The steward cooked and attended on us. Of the other twelve men, eight worked while four rested. Everyone took his turn, captain included. There was equality, and if not exactly fraternity, then a deal of good feeling. Sometimes a man, as he dashed a bucketful of water down the hatchway, would yell out, 'Hurrah for Bangkok!' and the rest laughed. But generally we were taciturn and serious—and thirsty. Oh! how thirsty! And we had to be careful with the water. Strict allowance. The ship smoked, the sun blazed. . . . Pass the bottle.

"We tried everything. We even made an attempt to dig down to the fire. No good, of course. No man could remain more than a minute below. Mahon, who went first, fainted there, and the man who went to fetch him out did likewise. We lugged them out on deck. Then I leaped down to show how easily it could be done. They had learned wisdom by that time and contented themselves by fishing for me with a chain hook tied to a broom handle, I believe. I did not offer to go and fetch up my shovel, which was left down below.

"Things began to look bad. We put the longboat into the water. The second boat was ready to swing out. We had also another, a fourteen-foot thing, on davits aft, where it was quite safe.

"Then, behold, the smoke suddenly decreased. We redoubled our efforts to flood the bottom of the ship. In two days there was no smoke at all. Everybody was on the broad grin. This was on a Friday. On Saturday no work, but sailing the ship of course was done. The men washed their clothes and their faces for the first time in a fortnight, and had a special dinner given them. They spoke of spontaneous combustion with contempt, and implied *they* were the boys to put out combustions. Somehow we all felt as though we each had inherited a large fortune. But a beastly smell of burning hung about the ship. Captain Beard had hollow eyes and sunken cheeks. I had never noticed so much before how twisted and bowed he was. He and Mahon prowled soberly about hatches and ventilators, sniffing. It struck me suddenly poor Mahon was a very, very old chap. As to me, I was as pleased and proud as though I had helped to win a great naval battle. O! Youth!

"The night was fine. In the morning a homewardbound ship passed us hull down—the first we had seen for months; but we were nearing the land at last, Java Head being about one hundred ninety miles off, and nearly due north.

"Next day it was my watch on deck from eight to twelve. At breakfast the captain observed, 'It's wonderful how that smell hangs about the cabin.' About ten, the mate being on the poop, I stepped down on the maindeck for a moment. The carpenter's bench stood abaft the mainmast: I leaned against it sucking at my pipe, and the carpenter, a young chap, came to talk to me. He remarked, 'I think we have done very well, haven't we?' and then I perceived with annoyance the fool was trying to tilt the bench. I said curtly, 'Don't, Chips,' and immediately became aware of a queer sensation, of an absurd delusion—I seemed somehow to be in the air. I heard all round me like a pent-up breath released—as if a thousand giants simultaneously had said Phoo!—and felt a dull concussion which made my ribs ache suddenly. No doubt about it—I was in the air, and my body was describing a short parabola. But short as it was, I had the time to think several thoughts in, as far as I can remember, the following order: 'This can't be the carpenter—What is it?—Some accident—Submarine volcano?—Coals, gas!—By Jove! we are being blown up—Everybody's dead—I am falling into the afterhatch—I see fire in it.'

"The coal dust suspended in the air of the hold had glowed dull red at the moment of the explosion. In the twinkling of an eye, in an infinitesimal fraction of a second since the first tilt of the bench, I was sprawling full length on the cargo. I picked myself up and scrambled out. It was quick like a rebound. The deck was a wilderness of smashed timber, lying crosswise like trees in a wood after a hurricane; an immense curtain of soiled rags waved gently before me—it was the mainsail blown to strips. I thought, The masts will be toppling over directly; and to get out of the way bolted on all-fours toward the poop ladder. The first person I saw was Mahon, with eyes like saucers, his mouth open, and the long white hair standing straight on end round his head like a silver halo. He was just about to go down when the sight of the main deck stirring, heaving up, and changing into splinters before his eyes, petrified him on the top step. I stared at him in unbelief, and he stared at me with a queer kind of shocked curiosity. I did not know that I had no hair, no eyebrows, no eyelashes, that my young mustache was burnt off, that my face was black, one cheek laid open, my nose cut, and my chin bleeding. I had lost my cap, one of my slippers, and my shirt was torn to rags. Of all this I was not aware. I was amazed to see the ship still afloat, the poop deck whole—and, most of all, to see anybody alive. Also the peace of the sky and the serenity of the sea were distinctly surprising. I suppose I expected to see them convulsed with horror. . . . Pass the bottle.

"There was a voice hailing the ship from somewhere—in the air, in the sky—I couldn't tell. Presently I saw the captain—and he was mad. He asked me eagerly, 'Where's the cabin table?' and to hear such a question was a frightful shock. I had just been blown up, you understand, and vibrated with that experience—I wasn't quite sure whether I was alive. Mahon began to stamp with both feet and yelled at him, 'Good God! don't you see the deck's blown out of her?' I found my voice and stammered out as if conscious of some gross neglect of duty, 'I don't know where the cabin table is.' It was like an absurd dream.

"Do you know what he wanted next? Well, he wanted to trim the yards. Very placidly, and as if lost in thought, he insisted on having the foreyard squared. 'I don't know if there's anybody alive,' said Mahon, almost tearfully. 'Surely,' he said, gently, 'there will be enough left to square the foreyard.'

"The old chap, it seems, was in his own berth, winding up the chronometers, when the shock sent him spinning. Immediately it occurred to him—as he said afterward—that the ship had struck something, and he ran out into the cabin. There, he saw, the cabin table had vanished somewhere. The deck being blown up, it had fallen down into the lazarette of course. Where we had our breakfast that morning he saw only a great hole in the floor. This appeared to him so awfully mysterious, and impressed him so immensely, that what he saw and heard after he got on deck were mere trifles in comparison. And, mark, he noticed directly the wheel deserted and his bark off her course—and his only thought was to get that miserable, stripped, undecked, smoldering shell of a ship back again with her head pointing at her port of destination. Bangkok! That's what he was after. I tell you this quiet, bowed, bandy-legged, almost deformed little man was immense in the singleness of his idea and in his placid ignorance of our agitation. He motioned us forward with a commanding gesture and went to take the wheel himself.

"Yes; that was the first thing we did—trim the yards of that wreck! No one was killed or even disabled, but everyone was more or less hurt. You should have seen them! Some were in rags, with black faces, like coal heavers, like sweeps, and had bullet heads that seemed closely cropped, but were in fact singed to the skin. Others, of the watch below, awakened by being shot out from their collapsing bunks, shivered incessantly and kept on groaning even as we went about our work. But they all worked. That crew of Liverpool hard cases had in them the right stuff. It's my experience they always have. It is the sea that gives it—the vastness, the loneliness surrounding their dark stolid souls. Ah! Well! we stumbled, we crept, we fell, we barked our shins on the wreckage, we hauled. The masts stood, but we did not know how much they might be charred down below. It was nearly calm, but a long swell ran from the west and made her roll. They might go at any moment. We looked at them with apprehension. One could not foresee which way they would fall.

"Then we retreated aft and looked about us. The deck was a tangle of planks on edge, of planks on end, of splinters, of ruined woodwork. The masts rose from that chaos like big trees above a matted undergrowth. The interstices of that mass of wreckage were full of something whitish, sluggish, stirring—of something that was like a greasy fog. The smoke of the invisible fire was coming up again, was trailing, like a poisonous thick mist in some valley choked with dead wood. Already lazy wisps were beginning to curl upward amongst the mass of splinters. Here and there a piece of timber, stuck upright, resembled a post. Half of a fife rail had been shot through the foresail, and the sky made a patch of glorious blue in the ignobly soiled canvas. A portion of several boards holding together had fallen across the rail, and one end protruded overboard, like a gangway leading upon nothing, like a gangway leading over the deep sea, leading to death—as if inviting us to walk the plank at once and be done with our ridiculous troubles. And still the air, the sky—a ghost, something invisible was hailing the ship.

"Someone had the sense to look over, and there was the helmsman, who had impulsively jumped overboard, anxious to come back. He yelled and swam lustily like a merman, keeping up with the ship. We threw him a rope, and presently he stood amongst us streaming with water and very crestfallen. The captain had surrendered the wheel, and apart, elbow on rail and chin in hand, gazed at the sea wistfully. We asked ourselves, What next? I thought, Now, this is something like. This is great. I wonder what will happen. O youth!

"Suddenly Mahon sighted a steamer far astern. Captain Beard said, 'We may do something with her yet.' We hoisted two flags, which said in the international language of the sea, 'On fire. Want immediate assistance.' The steamer grew bigger rapidly, and by-and-by spoke with two flags on her foremast, 'I am coming to your assistance.'

"In half an hour she was abreast, to windward, within hail, and rolling slightly, with the engines stopped. We lost our composure and yelled all together with excitement, 'We've been blown up.' A man in a white helmet, on the bridge, cried, 'Yes! All right! all right!' and he nodded his head, and smiled, and made soothing motions with his hand as though at a lot of frightened children. One of the boats dropped in the water and walked toward us upon the sea with her long oars. Four Calashes pulled a swinging stroke. This was my first sight of Malay seamen. I've known them since, but what struck me then was their unconcern: they came alongside, and even the bowman standing up and holding to our main chains with the boat hook did not deign to lift his head for a glance. I thought people who had been blown up deserved more attention.

"A little man, dry like a chip and agile like a monkey, clambered up. It was the mate of the steamer. He gave one look and cried, 'O boys—you had better quit.'

"We were silent. He talked apart with the captain for a time—seemed to argue with him. Then they went away together to the steamer.

"When our skipper came back we learned that the steamer was the *Sommerville,* Captain Nash, from West Australia to Singapore *via* Batavia with mails, and that the agreement was she should tow us to Anjer or Batavia, if possible, where we could extinguish the fire by scuttling, and then proceed on our voyage—to Bangkok! The old man seemed excited. 'We will do it yet,' he said to Mahon, fiercely. He shook his fist at the sky. Nobody else said a word.

"At noon the steamer began to tow. She went ahead slim and high, and what was left of the *Judea* followed at the end of seventy fathom of tow rope—followed her swiftly like a cloud of smoke with mastheads protruding above. We went aloft to furl the sails. We coughed on the yards and were careful about the bunts. Do you see the lot of us there, putting a neat furl on the sails of that ship doomed to arrive nowhere? There was not a man who didn't think that at any moment the masts would topple over. From aloft we could not see the ship for smoke, and they worked carefully, passing the gaskets with even turns. 'Harbor furl—aloft there!' cried Mahon from below.

"You understand this? I don't think one of those chaps expected to get down in the usual way. When we did I heard them saying to each other, 'Well, I thought we would come down overboard, in a lump—sticks and all—blame me if I didn't.' 'That's what I was thinking to myself,' would answer wearily another battered and bandaged scarecrow. And, mind, these were men without the drilled-in habit of obedience. To an onlooker they would be a lot of profane scallywags without a redeeming point. What made them do it—what made them obey me when I, thinking consciously how fine it was, made them drop the bunt of the foresail twice to try and do it better? What? They had no professional reputation—no examples, no praise. It wasn't a sense of duty; they all knew well enough how to shirk, and laze, and dodge—when they had a mind to it—and mostly they had. Was it the two pounds ten a month that sent them there? They didn't think their pay half good enough. No; it was something in them, something inborn and subtle and everlasting. I don't say positively that the crew of a French or German merchantman wouldn't have done it, but I doubt whether it would have been done in the same way. There was a completeness in it, something solid like a principle, **and** masterful like an instinct—a disclosure of something secret—of that hidden something, that gift, of good or evil that makes racial difference, that shapes the fate of nations.

"It was that night at ten that, for the first time since we had been fighting it, we saw the fire. The speed of the towing had fanned the smoldering destruction. A blue gleam appeared forward, shining below the wreck of the deck. It wavered in patches, it seemed to stir and creep like the light of a glowworm. I saw it first and told Mahon. 'Then the game's up,' he said. 'We had better stop this towing, or she will burst out suddenly fore and aft before we can clear out.' We set up a yell; rang bells to attract their attention; they towed on. At last Mahon and I had to crawl forward and cut the rope with an ax. There was no time to cast off the lashings. Red tongues could be seen licking the wilderness of splinters under our feet as we made our way back to the poop.

"Of course they very soon found out in the steamer that the rope was gone. She gave a loud blast of her whistle, her lights were seen sweeping in a wide circle, she came up ranging close alongside, and stopped. We were all in a tight group on the poop looking at her. Every man had saved a little bundle or a bag. Suddenly a conical flame with a twisted top shot up forward and threw upon the black sea a circle of light, with the two vessels side by side and heaving gently in its center. Captain Beard had been sitting on the gratings still and mute for hours, but now he rose slowly and advanced in front of us, to the mizzen shrouds. Captain Nash hailed: 'Come along! Look sharp. I have mailbags on board. I will take you and your boats to Singapore.'

" 'Thank you! No!' said our skipper. 'We must see the last of the ship.'

" 'I can't stand by any longer,' shouted the other. 'Mails—you know.'

" 'Ay! ay! We are all right.'

" 'Very well! I'll report you in Singapore. . . . Good-by!'

"He waved his hand. Our men dropped their bundles quietly. The steamer moved ahead, and passing out of the circle of light, vanished at once from our sight, dazzled by the fire which burned fiercely. And then I knew that I would see the East first as commander of a small boat. I thought it fine; and the fidelity to the old ship was fine. We should see the last of her. Oh the glamour of youth! Oh the fire of it, more dazzling than the flames of the burning ship, throwing a magic light on the wide earth, leaping audaciously to the sky, presently to be quenched by time, more cruel, more pitiless, more bitter than the sea—and like the flames of the burning ship surrounded by an impenetrable night.

"The old man warned us in his gentle and inflexible way that it was part of our duty to save for the underwriters as much as we could of the ship's gear. According we went to work aft, while she blazed forward to give us plenty of light. We lugged out a lot of rubbish. What didn't we save? An old barometer fixed with an absurd quantity of screws nearly cost me my life: a sudden rush of smoke came upon me, and I just got away in time. There were various stores, bolts of canvas, coils of rope; the poop looked like a marine bazaar, and the boats were lumbered to the gunwales. One would have thought the old man wanted to take as much as he could of his first command with him. He was very, very quiet, but off his balance evidently. Would you believe it? He wanted to take a length of old stream cable and a kedge anchor with him in the longboat. We said, 'Ay, ay, sir,' deferentially, and on the quiet let the thing slip overboard. The heavy medicine chest went that way, two bags of green coffee, tins of paint—fancy, paint!—a whole lot of things. Then I was ordered with two hands into the boats to make a stowage and get them ready against the time it would be proper for us to leave the ship.

"We put everything straight, stepped the longboat's mast for our skipper, who was in charge of her, and I was not sorry to sit down for a moment. My face felt raw, every limb ached as if broken, I was aware of all my ribs and would have sworn to a twist in the backbone. The boats, fast astern, lay in a deep shadow, and all around I could see the circle of the sea lighted by the fire. A gigantic flame arose forward straight and clear. It flared fierce, with noises like the whir of wings, with rumbles as of thunder. There were cracks, detonations, and from the cone of flame the sparks flew upward, as man is born to trouble, to leaky ships, and to ships that burn.

"What bothered me was that the ship, lying broadside to the swell and to such wind as there was—a mere breath—the boats would not keep astern where they were safe, but persisted, in a pigheaded way boats have, in getting under the counter and then swinging alongside. They were knocking about dangerously and coming near the flame, while the ship rolled on them, and, of course, there was always the danger of the masts going over the side at any moment. I and my two boat keepers kept them off as best we could with oars and boat hooks; but to be constantly at it became exasperating, since there was no reason why we should not leave at once. We could not see those on board, nor could we imagine what caused the delay. The boat keepers were swearing feebly, and I had not only my share of the work, but also had to keep at it two men who showed a constant inclination to lay themselves down and let things slide.

"At last I hailed 'On deck there,' and someone looked over. 'We're ready here,' I said. The head disappeared, and very soon popped up again. 'The captain says, All right, sir, and to keep the boats well clear of the ship.'

"Half an hour passed. Suddenly there was a frightful racket, rattle, clanking of chain, hiss of water, and millions of sparks flew up into the shivering column of smoke that stood leaning slightly above the ship. The catheads had burned away, and the two red-hot anchors had gone to the bottom, tearing out after them two hundred fathom of red-hot chain. The ship trembled, the mass of flame swayed as if ready to collapse, and the fore topgallant mast fell. It darted down like an arrow of fire, shot under, and, instantly leaping up within an oar's-length of the boats, floated quietly, very black on the luminous sea. I hailed the deck again. After some time a man in an unexpectedly cheerful but also muffled tone, as though he had been trying to speak with his mouth shut, informed me, 'Coming directly, sir,' and vanished. For a long time I heard nothing but the whir and roar of the fire. There were also whistling sounds. The boats jumped, tugged at the painters, ran at each other playfully, knocked their sides together, or, do what we would, swung in a bunch against the ship's side. I couldn't stand it any longer, and, swarming up a rope, clambered aboard over the stern.

"It was as bright as day. Coming up like this, the sheet of fire facing me, was a terrifying sight, and the heat seemed hardly bearable at first. On a settee cushion dragged out of the cabin, Captain Beard, with his legs drawn up and one arm under his head, slept with the light playing on him. Do you know what the rest were busy about? They were sitting on deck right aft, round an open case, eating bread and cheese and drinking bottled stout.

"On the background of flames twisting in fierce tongues above their heads they seemed at home like salamanders, and looked like a band of desperate pirates. The fire sparkled in the whites of their eyes, gleamed on patches of white skin seen through the torn shirts. Each had the marks as of a battle about him—bandaged heads, tied-up arms, a strip of dirty rag round a knee —and each man had a bottle between his legs and a chunk of cheese in his hand. Mahon got up. With his handsome and disreputable head, his hooked profile, his long white beard, and with an uncorked bottle in his hand, he resembled one of those reckless sea robbers of old making merry amidst violence and disaster. 'The last meal on board,' he explained solemnly. 'We had nothing to eat all day, and it was no use leaving all this.' He flourished the bottle and indicated the sleeping skipper. 'He said he couldn't swallow anything, so I got him to lie down,' he went on; and as I stared, 'I don't know whether you are aware, young fellow, the man had no sleep to speak of for days—and there will be dam' little sleep in the boats.' 'There will be no boats by-and-by if you fool about much longer,' I said, indignantly. I walked up to the skipper and shook him by the shoulder. At last he opened his eyes, but did not move. 'Time to leave her, sir,' I said, quietly.

"He got up painfully, looked at the flames, at the sea sparkling round the ship, and black, black as ink farther away; he looked at the stars shining dim through a thin veil of smoke in a sky black, black as Erebus.

" 'Youngest first,' he said.

"And the ordinary seaman, wiping his mouth with the back of his hand, got up, clambered over the taffrail, and vanished. Others followed. One, on the point of going over, stopped short to drain his bottle, and with a great swing of his arm flung it at the fire. 'Take this!' he cried.

"The skipper lingered disconsolately, and we left him to commune alone for a while with his first command. Then I went up again and brought him away at last. It was time. The ironwork on the poop was hot to the touch.

"Then the painter of the longboat was cut, and the three boats, tied together, drifted clear of the ship. It was just sixteen hours after the explosion when we abandoned her. Mahon had charge of the second boat, and I had the smallest—the fourteen-foot thing. The longboat would have taken the lot of us; but the skipper said we must save as much property as we could— for the underwriters—and so I got my first command. I had two men with me, a bag of biscuits, a few tins of meat, and a breaker of water. I was ordered to keep close to the longboat, that in case of bad weather we might be taken into her.

"And do you know what I thought? I thought I would part company as soon as I could. I wanted to have my first command all to myself. I wasn't going to sail in a squadron if there were a chance for independent cruising. I would make land by myself. I would beat the other boats. Youth! All youth! The silly, charming, beautiful youth.

"But we did not make a start at once. We must see the last of the ship. And so the boats drifted about that night, heaving and setting on the swell. The men dozed, waked, sighed, groaned. I looked at the burning ship.

"Between the darkness of earth and heaven she was burning fiercely upon a disc of purple sea shot by the blood-red play of gleams; upon a disc of water glittering and sinister. A high, clear flame, an immense and lonely flame, ascended from the ocean, and from its summit the black smoke poured continuously at the sky. She burned furiously, mournful and imposing like a funeral pile kindled in the night, surrounded by the sea, watched over by the stars. A magnificent death had come like a grace, like a gift, like a reward to that old ship at the end of her laborious days. The surrender of her weary ghost to the keeping of stars and sea was stirring like the sight of a glorious triumph. The masts fell just before daybreak, and for a moment there was a burst and turmoil of sparks that seemed to fill with flying fire the night patient and watchful, the vast night lying silent upon the sea. At daylight she was only a charred shell, floating still under a cloud of smoke and bearing a glowing mass of coal within.

"Then the oars were got out, and the boats forming in a line moved round her remains as if in procession—the longboat leading. As we pulled across her stern a slim dart of fire shot out viciously at us, and suddenly she went down, head first, in a great hiss of steam. The unconsumed stern was the last to sink; but the paint had gone, had cracked, had peeled off, and there were no letters, there was no word, no stubborn device that was like her soul, to flash at the rising sun her creed and her name.

"We made our way north. A breeze sprang up, and about noon all the boats came together for the last time. I had no mast or sail in mine, but I made a mast out of a spare oar and hoisted a boat awning for a sail, with a boat hook for a yard. She was certainly overmasted, but I had the satisfaction of knowing that with the wind aft I could beat the other two. I had to wait for them. Then we all had a look at the captain's chart, and, after a sociable meal of hard bread and water, got our last instructions. These were simple: steer north, and keep together as much as possible. 'Be careful with that jury rig, Marlow,' said the captain; and Mahon, as I sailed proudly past his boat, wrinkled his curved nose and hailed, 'You will sail that ship of yours under water if you don't look out, young fellow.' He was a malicious old man—and may the deep sea where he sleeps now rock him gently, rock him tenderly to the end of time!

"Before sunset a thick rain squall passed over the two boats, which were far astern, and that was the last I saw of them for a time. Next day I sat steering my cockleshell—my first command—with nothing but water and sky around me. I did sight in the afternoon the upper sails of a ship far away, but said nothing, and my men did not notice her. You see I was afraid she might be homewardbound, and I had no mind to turn back from the portals of the East. I was steering for Java—another blessed name—like Bangkok, you know. I steered many days.

"I need not tell you what it is to be knocking about in an open boat. I remember nights and days of calm when we pulled, we pulled, and the boat seemed to stand still, as if bewitched within the circle of the sea horizon. I remember the heat, the deluge of rain squalls that kept us baling for dear life (but filled our water cask), and I remember sixteen hours on end with a mouth dry as a cinder and a steering oar over the stern to keep my first command head on to a breaking sea. I did not know how good a man I was till then. I remember the drawn faces, the dejected figures of my two men, and I remember my youth and the feeling that will never come back any more—the feeling that I could last forever, outlast the sea, the earth, and all men; the deceitful feeling that lures us on to joys, to perils, to love, to vain effort—to death; the triumphant conviction of strength, the heat of life in the handful of dust, the glow in the heart that with every year grows dim, grows cold, grows small, and expires—and expires, too soon—before life itself.

"And this is how I see the East. I have seen its secret places and have looked into its very soul; but now I see it always from a small boat, a high outline of mountains, blue and afar in the morning; like faint mist at noon; a jagged wall of purple at sunset. I have the feel of the oar in my hand, the vision of a scorching blue sea in my eyes. And I see a bay, a wide bay, smooth as glass and polished like ice, shimmering in the dark. A red light burns far off upon the gloom of the land, and the night is soft and warm. We drag at the oars with aching arms, and suddenly a puff of wind, a puff faint and tepid and laden with strange odors of blossoms, of aromatic wood, comes out of the still night—the first sigh of the East on my face. That I can never forget. It was impalpable and enslaving, like a charm, like a whispered promise of mysterious delight.

"We had been pulling this finishing spell for eleven hours. Two pulled, and he whose turn it was to rest sat at the tiller. We had made out the red light in that bay and steered for it, guessing it must mark some small coasting port. We passed two vessels, outlandish and high-sterned, sleeping at anchor, and, approaching the light, now very dim, ran the boat's nose against the end of a jutting wharf. We were blind with fatigue. My men dropped the oars and fell off the thwarts as if dead. I made fast to a pile. A current rippled softly. The scented obscurity of the shore was grouped into vast masses, a density of colossal clumps of vegetation, probably—mute and fantastic shapes. And at their foot the semicircle of a beach gleamed faintly, like an illusion. There was not a light, not a stir, not a sound. The mysterious East faced me, perfumed like a flower, silent like death, dark like a grave.

"And I sat weary beyond expression, exulting like a conqueror, sleepless and entranced as if before a profound, a fateful enigma.

"A splashing of oars, a measured dip reverberating on the level of water, intensified by the silence of the shore into loud claps, made me jump up. A boat, a European boat, was coming in. I invoked the name of the dead; I hailed: *Judea* ahoy! A thin shout answered.

"It was the captain. I had beaten the flagship by three hours, and I was glad to hear the old man's voice, tremulous and tired. 'Is it you, Marlow?' 'Mind the end of that jetty, sir,' I cried.

"He approached cautiously and brought up with the deep-sea leadline which we had saved—for the underwriters. I eased my painter and fell alongside. He sat, a broken figure at the stern, wet with dew, his hands clasped in his lap. His men were asleep already. 'I had a terrible time of it,' he murmured. 'Mahon is behind—not very far.' We conversed in whispers, in low whispers, as if afraid to wake up the land. Guns, thunder, earthquakes would not have awakened the men just then.

"Looking around as we talked, I saw away at sea a bright light traveling in the night. 'There's a steamer passing the bay,' I said. She was not passing, she was entering, and she even came close and anchored. 'I wish,' said the old man, 'you would find out whether she is English. Perhaps they could give us a passage somewhere.' He seemed nervously anxious. So by dint of punching and kicking I started one of my men into a state of somnambulism and, giving him an oar, took another and pulled toward the lights of the steamer.

"There was a murmur of voices in her, metallic hollow clangs of the engine room, footsteps on the deck. Her ports shone, round like dilated eyes. Shapes moved about, and there was a shadowy man high up on the bridge. He heard my oars.

"And then, before I could open my lips, the East spoke to me, but it was in a Western voice. A torrent of words was poured into the enigmatical, the fateful silence; outlandish, angry words, mixed with words and even whole sentences of good English, less strange but even more surprising. The voice swore and cursed violently; it riddled the solemn peace of the bay by a volley of abuse. It began by calling me Pig, and from that went crescendo into unmentionable adjectives—in English. The man up there raged aloud in two languages, and with a sincerity in his fury that almost convinced me I had, in some way, sinned against the harmony of the universe. I could hardly see him, but began to think he would work himself into a fit.

"Suddenly he ceased, and I could hear him snorting and blowing like a porpoise. I said:

" 'What steamer is this, pray?'

" 'Eh? What's this? And who are you?'

" 'Castaway crew of an English bark burnt at sea. We came here tonight. I am the second mate. The captain is in the longboat and wishes to know if you would give us a passage somewhere.'

" 'Oh, my goodness! I say. . . . This is the *Celestial* from Singapore on her return trip. I'll arrange with your captain in the morning, . . . and, . . . I say, . . . did you hear me just now?'

" 'I should think the whole bay heard you.'

" 'I thought you were a shore boat. Now, look here—this infernal lazy scoundrel of a caretaker has gone to sleep again—curse him. The light is out, and I nearly ran foul of the end of this damned jetty. This is the third time he plays me this trick. Now, I ask you, can anybody stand this kind of thing? It's enough to drive a man out of his mind. I'll report him. . . . I'll get the Assistant Resident to give him the sack, by . . . See—there's no light. It's out, isn't it? I take you to witness the light's out. There should be a light, you know. A red light on the——'

" 'There was a light,' I said, mildly.

" 'But it's out, man! What's the use of talking like this? You can see for yourself it's out—don't you? If you had to take a valuable steamer along this God-forsaken coast you would want a light too. I'll kick him from end to end of his miserable wharf. You'll see if I don't. I will——'

" 'So I may tell my captain you'll take us?' I broke in.

" 'Yes, I'll take you. Good night,' he said, brusquely.

"I pulled back, made fast again to the jetty, and then went to sleep at last. I had faced the silence of the East. I had heard some of its languages. But when I opened my eyes again the silence was as complete as though it had never been broken. I was lying in a flood of light, and the sky had never looked so far, so high, before. I opened my eyes and lay without moving.

"And then I saw the men of the East—they were looking at me. The whole length of the jetty was full of people. I saw brown, bronze, yellow faces, the black eyes, the glitter, the color of an Eastern crowd. And all these beings stared without a murmur, without a sigh, without a movement. They stared down at the boats, at the sleeping men who at night had come to them from the sea. Nothing moved. The fronds of palms stood still against the sky. Not a branch stirred along the shore, and the brown roofs of hidden houses peeped through the green foliage, through the big leaves that hung shining and still like leaves forged of heavy metal. This was the East of the ancient navigators, so old, so mysterious, resplendent and somber, living and unchanged, full of danger and promise. And these were the men. I sat up suddenly. A wave of movement passed through the crowd from end to end, passed along the heads, swayed the bodies, ran along the jetty like a ripple on the water, like a breath of wind on a field—and all was still again. I see it now—the wide sweep of the bay, the glittering sands, the wealth of green infinite and varied, the sea blue like the sea of a dream, the crowd of attentive faces, the blaze of vivid color—the water reflecting it all, the curve of the shore, the jetty, the high-sterned, outlandish craft floating still, and the three boats with tired men from the West sleeping, unconscious of the land and the people and of the violence of sunshine. They slept thrown across the thwarts, curled on bottom boards, in the careless attitudes of death. The head of the old skipper, leaning back in the stern of the longboat, had fallen on his breast, and he looked as though he would never wake. Farther out old Mahon's face was upturned to the sky, with the long white beard spread out on his breast, as though he been shot where he sat at the tiller; and a man, all in a heap in the bows of the boat, slept with both arms embracing the stem head and with his cheek laid on the gunwale. The East looked at them without a sound.

"I have known its fascinations since: I have seen the mysterious shores, the still water, the lands of brown nations, where a stealthy Nemesis lies in wait, pursues, overtakes so many of the conquering race, who are proud of their wisdom, of their knowledge, of their strength. But for me all the East is contained in that vision of my youth. It is all in that moment when I opened my young eyes on it. I came upon it from a tussle with the sea—and I was young—and I saw it looking at me. And this is all that is left of it! Only a moment; a moment of strength, of romance, of glamour—of youth! . . . A flick of sunshine upon a strange shore, the time to remember, the time for a sigh, and—good-by!—Night—Good-by . . . !"

He drank.

"Ah! The good old time—the good old time. Youth and the sea. Glamour and the sea! The good, strong sea, the salt, bitter sea, that could whisper to you and roar at you and knock your breath out of you."

He drank again.

"By all that's wonderful, it is the sea, I believe, the sea itself—or is it youth alone? Who can tell? But you here—you all had something out of life: money, love—whatever one gets on shore—and, tell me, wasn't that the best time, that time when we were young at sea; young and had nothing, on the sea that gives nothing, except hard knocks—and sometimes a chance to feel your strength—that only—what you all regret?"

And we all nodded at him: the man of finance, the man of accounts, the man of law, we all nodded at him over the polished table that like a still sheet of brown water reflected our faces, lined, wrinkled; our faces marked by toil, by deceptions, by success, by love; our weary eyes looking still, looking always, looking anxiously for something out of life, that while it is expected is already gone—has passed unseen, in a sigh, in a flash—together with the youth, with the strength, with the romance of illusions.

Sea of Glory*

FRANCIS BEAUCHESNE THORNTON

✳✳ Francis Beauchesne Thornton, literary critic of *The Catholic Digest* and author of two books of poetry, was a chaplain in the last war. He spent four years talking and writing to the families and friends of the four United States chaplains who played a dominant role in the episode in the icy seas off Labrador, an experience he developed, with its background, in *Sea of Glory*. ✳✳

PROLOGUE

The freighter rose and fell sluggishly at her pier, her spring lines alternately slack and tight. In the darkness beneath the flooring, down at the waterline of the rusty ship, there was a slap of the waves—one of the loneliest sounds that can haunt man's ears.

Floodlamps turned the New England night into a garish noon, a noon full of shadows, and full of the sound of winches, of screeching cranes and booms and of the shuffling cadence of weary troops, keeping step out of habit rather than from conscious desire.

One of the shadows the lights didn't reach hung near the stern of the freighter, almost obliterating her name—the *Dorchester*—but neither the glare of the light nor the kindness of the shadows could hide the fact that the vessel was old, and small, and probably slow—or that she would undoubtedly pitch and roll even in good weather, and would yaw crazily in heavy seas.

Soldiers climbing the gangplank looked at the *Dorchester* as though they had been cheated in a poker game even before the cards were dealt. One whose humor had not been erased by hours of standing and marching spoke over his shoulder to another man behind him.

"She'd fit in a funnel of the *Queen Mary*. She's no bigger than a lifeboat."

He was right. She was devoid of class. Whatever dignity she was to possess would have to go aboard her in the hearts and breasts of the soldiers using her as a ferry to the bloody fields of war. She had none of her own.

She was listed with Lloyds' at five thousand tons, and the symbols in the Register, when translated, meant that she was just another workhorse of the sea, intended to carry slow cargo in her holds. Only the exigencies of total war had forced her transformation into a troopship.

On this night in January, 1943, she was being loaded with troops at a Massachusetts port, her destination hidden in an envelope of secret orders, the seal of which would stay unbroken until she had lumbered into position in a convoy, hours out of sight of land.

Deckhands, fighting the winter cold in reefers close-collared against the wind, moved about her decks with the slow precision of veteran seamen. Lights atop the king posts and the bridge illuminated the open hatches through which was being lowered the gear and apparatus of war. The booms, swinging from ship to pier and back again, complained with the strident sound of steel rasping against steel.

The tide was running out and the freighter chafed at her moorings, moving in a short arc within the confines of her hawsers. The motion caused the gangplank to move back and forth too, the lower end, supported by small wheels, rolling unevenly on the floorboards of the pier.

Each enlisted man, his duffel bag on his shoulder, had to break step as he reached the gangplank. Sometimes a foot would be poised for the first step and then the plank would pull away like a hoydenish thing. Again it would move drunkenly the other way, forcing the soldier to quickstep to protect himself.

Historians could speak of this contrivance in later years as a bridge to man's victory against the forces of totalitarian evil. It was a narrow, unstable link between the known and the unknown, between the safety of the shore and home and the awful dangers of the sea. Each man, tired and cold as he was that January night, must have thought about it as he plodded up the incline and stepped upon the steel plates of the freighter's deck.

There were humble GIs and equally humble officers who made the crossing from the pier to the *Dorchester*. A nameless fear quickened the pulse of every one of them, whether they spoke of it or not.

Among their number, carrying duffel bags like the rest, but without the reassuring strength that comes from rifle or sidearms, walked four chaplains. Their names—Fox, Goode, Poling, and Washington—told nothing.

On that night in January, 1943, destiny was curtained off completely. One by one, the army chaplains judged the eccentric behavior of the plank, adjusted their strides to match it, and stepped aboard the freighter, never dreaming the contraption was also a gangplank to everlasting glory.

Fox was a Methodist, called to duty from a snowbound parish in Vermont. Poling, another Protestant, had quit a comfortable existence in upstate New York. Goode, a Jewish rabbi born in Brooklyn, was fresh from a synagogue in rural Pennsylvania. Washington, the man with the odd name, was a Catholic priest born and bred in industrial New Jersey.

They shared a cabin on the *Dorchester*—a cabin in name only, not much different from the sleeping quarters of the enlisted men—dreary, airless, and heavy with the stench of fuel oil and bilge slop.

Fox was one up on his companions. He had gone overseas in the First World War—that time as a fighting man—and he knew the dirty business at its worst.

"I've been through this before," he said, stowing away his belongings to save space in the cramped room. "But with all these green kids and civilian workers it won't be any picnic. We'll make it all right, though."

Young Poling let the words hang suspended in the stuffy air, as they hung in each man's mind, while his stomach adjusted itself to the ship's motion.

"I'm a pretty good sailor," he said finally, "but when I crossed before I wasn't responsible for anyone but myself."

Soldiers tramped through the companionway outside, down into the bowels of the *Dorchester*. Naked light bulbs showed them their quarters—bunks hastily built into the holds, four tiers high, six niggardly feet of space per man—just enough room for a night's sleep, or for that last, long sleep from which there is no awakening.

The scrape of hobnails on steel decks, the creaking of the booms, and the whole mad cacophony of sound that grew out of the process of packing hundreds of men into narrow confines almost drowned out Father Washington's words.

"At least you've been to sea," he laughed. "I can't swim well enough to paddle across a duck pond. How about you, Alex?"

Rabbi Goode thrust his hands out. The other chaplains saw that his fingers were crossed and they guffawed.

"The way I see it," said Goode, "is this. We'll be so doggone busy with the men we won't have time to think of ourselves. Let's go topside for a minute. Maybe we aren't handsome, but if they catch us there smiling as they come aboard maybe it will kid them along a bit."

So they went up, making wrong turns in the narrow passageways as landlubbers always do, emerging on the starboard side aft when they had expected to come out forward on the port side. They laughed at their mistake and crossed to watch the dogfaces coming aboard like ants toiling to the top of their hill to disappear suddenly at the summit.

The men's faces were bleak, as only fighting men's faces can be, shoving off for overseas, or moving out on a patrol when the high brass, warm and safe at the rear, sends up orders to bring in prisoners for questioning or to apply more pressure in a diversion to protect the next division on one's flank.

It's the eyes that tell the story. The healthy glint that is any man's birthright grows lackluster on the eve of battle or danger. The sockets become a little deeper, stretching the skin into shadowed crow's-feet. So it was with these men coming aboard the *Dorchester*. They could only guess at the future.

The port of embarcation camp had been one vast rumor factory. They were going to Africa. They were going to Northern Ireland. They were part of a secret movement destined for a landing up some Norwegian fjord. There was a vital plant to be destroyed—something about heavy water—it didn't make any sense, but they were going to pull the Limey's chestnuts out of the fire again.

On board the *Dorchester* it was worse. Scuttlebutt passed from mouth to ear and on again with the speed of light. It was Africa. No it wasn't. It was Greenland. The Nazis had executed their promised invasion of England and they'd all be thrown into the fighting somewhere in Cornwall the minute they hit land.

The sky pilots knew they were bound for Greenland . . . the godforsaken, ice-covered, glacier-tortured end of the world.

As preachers of the Word and as ministers to the sick of heart and body, the chaplains knew what life in a hurriedly thrown-together outpost on the Greenland coast could be. Worse than the front. There would be bitter cold, nights and days when the sun could be only a memory, far below the horizon, and there would be the monotony and the boredom and the bitterness and the grousing and the endlessness of time unsweetened by the music of a woman's voice.

Fox and Poling and Goode knew this better than the priest, since each had left a wife behind, but Father Washington understood well enough the heavy duty that lay on all four if they were to make life a little more bearable for the youngsters coming over the side, being herded by top kicks and ship's officers into the fetid compartments below. . . .

At Point Option—the preselected rendezvous off the Massachusetts coast —the *Dorchester* found herself the seventh and last ship of a small convoy. If she had had two or three more knots in her she might have been the

Lucky Seventh. As she didn't, she was placed smack in the middle of the convoy, much to the shame of her crew and the joy of her troops.

In January of 1943 the North Atlantic was perhaps the bitterest battleground of all the fronts. Allied shipping, under constant attack by wolfpacks of Nazi U-boats, was being sunk almost as fast as it could be built. Men-of-war and planes to combat the submarines were still in perilously short supply.

The newest destroyers went with the fleet to guard the carriers and battlewagons pounding Japanese islands in the far Pacific. The bulk of those that were left stood guard with the fast convoys to the United Kingdom or formed the screens for baby aircraft carriers to constitute the killer groups that played such a large part in the ultimate defeat of the U-boats.

For such as the lumbering *Dorchester* and her sisters there were only a few Coast Guard cutters, refitted yachts, and other make-do craft.

The GIs, watching the *Dorchester* take station that first morning out, saw that three Coast Guard cutters were their only escort. . . . If they joked and kidded and laughed, maybe the steely fingers of fear would loosen a little about their hearts.

There was reason for the fear.

Word seeped down from the bridge and the radio shack that "Sparks," although never daring to send off a word, had heard many a dot-and-dash code message while listening to the endless chatter that even a war doesn't shut off.

There were lots of kraut subs around and they knew, it seemed, where the convoys were, and they must have been talking back and forth among themselves about a rendezvous at some not-too-distant "torpedo junction." . . .

Rolling and yawing, the *Dorchester* beat her slow way northeastward, unmindful of the comfort of her precious cargo. The cutters watched their brood with endless devotion and the ship's bells beat out their muffled count.

Somewhere up ahead, well north of the great circle route, in the impatient wilderness of the ocean, destiny was altering the *Dorchester's* course to a rendezvous with history.

EPILOGUE

From where the four chaplains stood at the lee rail there was nothing to be seen except the ships of the convoy and their escorts, heading into the wind but bucking a current that seemed to be sliding southward off the shelf of Labrador.

On their last visit to the chart room Captain Greenspun had shown them exactly where they were, making a little dot on the map with the help of dividers and parallel rules.

An inch or so away—on the chart—the coast of Greenland seemed to be extending her peninsulate fingers in greetings, urging the little convoy on to safe haven.

After that everyone felt better for a day or so. Then word was bruited about that both Captain Greenspun and Lieutenant Arpaia had a feeling they were being followed by enemy submarines. They couldn't explain it. It was just their psychological radar.

Lookouts were doubled, and the man in the crow's-nest was relieved every hour so that his eyes wouldn't be tired or his faculties dulled by the numbing cold. A rough assignment it was, lookout on the ship's main deck. High above the bridge and deck a little roost no cozier than a barrel was fastened to the mast and in it the lookout stood, straining his eyes for signs of a snorkel tube, a torpedo's wake, or any other hostile movement. The rim of the crow's-nest hit him at the armpits. His face was lashed by the wind and sleet and snow.

When the boat rolled, which was most of the time, the main mast swung back and forth like a great inverted pendulum, and the sailor in the crow's-nest felt like a pea in a bucket that some small boy was swinging around his head.

The chaplains could sense that the men were worried. They knew that every man aboard the *Dorchester* had a mysterious feeling that the ship was in critical danger.

The month of January was torn off the calendar in the main mess, and the act made the trip seem interminable. The men thought they had been at sea two months now and began to doubt whether the skipper and the navigator knew where they were. At night, when most of the lights had been extinguished, there was the sound of sobbing from some of the youngsters who had never been away from home before and who, overnight, were expected to be grown men. It was a funny thing that even the toughest of the old-timers never mentioned the nocturnal weeping. Even the four sky pilots had no cure for such heartache.

On the evening of the second day of the new month one of the three Coast Guard cutters blinked a message across the water to the troopship.

We are being followed by a submarine.

Captain Greenspun alerted his officers. The PA system crackled with orders and the gun crews jumped to their guns. In the engine room, in response to the telegraph from the bridge, the *Dorchester's* machinery whined and labored, but the best it could do was to push the ungainly freighter along at ten knots.

Ten knots is incredibly slow. A man can run as fast for a short while. If you subtract the distance lost by constant zigzagging it is easy to see how helpless the *Dorchester* was, wallowing along in the winter seas.

The old man, pacing up and down the bridge, silent, troubled, deeply concerned for the safety of all the lives in his care, never seemed to rest. He had slept no more than three hours in midday since leaving port, and the quartermaster had to keep hot coffee going to the bridge in a steady stream to prevent the skipper from falling asleep.

Out of the overcast the next day came a slow, lumbering patrol plane bearing Canadian insignia on the undersides of her wings. She looked frail and antique, but nonetheless "Sparks" flashed her a message by blinker, giving the *Dorchester's* position and asking for assistance. Back came the stuttering light flashes:

Planes on duty elsewhere. Impossible to send any at this time.

That night the soldiers were sure that fate had kicked them squarely in the seat of the pants. They felt sorry for themselves and cursed the rust-bucket the government had given them for a transport. They wrote letters home in a blind rebellion against their miserable lot, against the bitter winds and the raw cold that made every minute on deck a trial. Many a letter was blurred by tears that wouldn't stay back.

Men ate in subdued anger and fear. They fell into the chow lines with their life jackets on, the strings securely fastened, and no one thought it strange or cowardly.

After the evening meal the tables were moved and the equipment cleared away, and the GIs had a party. Mess boys from Cuba and Puerto Rico brought out instruments. An old upright piano that had been lashed to a bulkhead was freed of its fetters, moved into the mess hall, secured again, and made to give forth music. There were hot rumbas and hotter jazz and, best of all, the old familiar, popular songs that any American kid over eight knows how to sing.

The four chaplains led the singing. When the lads were a little slow on suggesting the next tune, Fox or Goode or one of the others would slip in a request for a hymn. They seemed a little out of place sandwiched in between "Mademoiselle from Armentières" and "Everything's Up To Date in Kansas City," but the troops never let the chaplains down. They sang the hymns as lustily as they did the pop tunes. . . .

Although it seemed that every man could fairly taste submarines in the seething water behind them, the *Dorchester* plowed on that night of February 2 and the next day gained shelter behind the boom at St. John's, New-foundland.

The sun came out and while the freighter was tied up to the pier, safe from all danger, the GIs shouted at the few girls who wandered down to the docks, sang happily, and acted as if they had won the war already.

The chaplains, with special passes, went ashore to mail the letters written by the troops too late to go off in the regular pouches. In the Bachelor Officers' Quarters they shot the breeze with American officers from the Argentia base, with Canadian pilots, and with the skippers of the little Canadian corvettes with which the Dominion was battling bravely against the hordes of undersea craft that Admiral Doenitz and Hitler thought could win the war by strangulation.

They'd have been better off—in a way—if they'd stayed on board the *Dorchester*.

The news was bad. At sea, with little to go on, the four chaplains had guessed how bad it was. On shore, where men were closer to day-to-day operations, the picture in all its somber colors unfolded—threatening, bleak, blood-curdling.

To the four chaplains the word was passed that sinkings were averaging as high as a hundred a month. The landings in North Africa, the top-priority convoys to Montgomery in Tripoli, the big U.K. runs from New York to Liverpool—all these were extending the Allied sea power too thin. Subs, fitted with their snorkel tubes, able to remain submerged with only a device the size of a mackerel above the surface, were raiding convoys and cutting out the prize targets like cowboys roping fat heifers from a moving herd.

"The Murmansk run is pure poison," the chaplains were told. "Almost no one comes back from that. It's a little better on the runs to England but those ships are faster. That rust-bucket of yours can't be any bargain. Must be mighty slow."

Slow? Lord in Heaven, that she was, and the sky pilots knew it and had to go on acting as if it were the *Queen Elizabeth* or the *Wakefield*. There was nothing for them to do but put on an act and try to kid the soldiers along, and whenever there was any spare time or when they were getting the little bit of horizontal drill they needed each night they could pray to God for a safe landing in Greenland.

There isn't much else to do with an elephantine five-thousand-ton freighter whose engines couldn't turn up another knot if they were fed aviation gas.

The respite in port was too short to do anyone much good.

A little after the church bells of St. John's had marked eight o'clock in the evening the *Dorchester* quit the pier and passed out to sea, through the submarine boom at the harbor mouth.

The convoy moved on northeastward, through the strange white darkness of an Arctic night. Each ship, it seemed to the men at the *Dorchester's* rail, stuck up like a clay target in a shooting gallery, inviting a torpedo from any sub that was within miles of the wallowing convoy.

On deck the crew made last-minute moves to secure odd gear and to lash the canvas covers on the hatches. In the brittle silence of the northern night each sound seemed maddeningly loud, each noise a gilt-edged invitation to a sub commander. . . .

In the middle of the night some of the soldiers sleeping in the compartments farthest below decks heard the engine-room telegraph bells jingle, and after that the *Dorchester* moved through the water more slowly. Up on the bridge Captain Greenspun had ordered speed reduced because he was running into pan ice, and knew that at any minute an iceberg might loom ahead out of the harmless slush.

From here on into port in Greenland engines would run at half-speed, the propeller blades would turn even more slowly because of the new threat.

Strangely the slower speed brought a sense of relief, both on the bridge and among the men bunking in the holds. The old man, knowing that the knife-sharp edges of an iceberg could rip a U-boat as a can opener splits open a tin of sardines, figured no submarine would operate in such dangerous waters.

The chaplains congratulated each other. They knew about the ice and its double portent—of danger and of safety both—and they knew that probably by now the convoy had moved far enough to the north to come under the protecting umbrella of patrol planes flying off Greenland's runways.

The weather grew nastier with each passing hour. Long ground swells battered the stumbling *Dorchester,* and in between white-capped waves hammered malignantly against her bows and shook her to her keel plates. . . .

The Arctic night was beautiful but it was deadly. Like a toy being dragged by a loitering child the *Dorchester* made her way through the early hours of the darkness—a darkness overcast with an eerie glimmering of whiteness. It zigged and zagged and it seemed to stumble from one crest to another, being punished by each in turn, yet staggering slowly on.

Below decks the passage of time was a slow gnawing at the mind, a dull sawing on the raw and open nerve ends of the soul.

There seemed to be an apprehensive silence that brooded over the ship. Men in their bunks sensed it, their eyes wide and their muscles tense. With the cutting of the speed the screws no longer threshed half the time out of water. The silence of the Arctic night muffled the clank of the engines.

The ship's bells struck twice. It was one o'clock in the morning. They never sounded again.

A minute or so later a torpedo smashed into the *Dorchester,* well below the waterline amidships.

The stricken ship staggered from the explosion. Men lying fully clothed in their bunks were tossed to the decks like walnuts from an upset basket. Others were catapulted against the bulkheads.

Blackout lights went out instantly, plunging the entire ship into darkness and leaving the men to grope in terror as they fought their way topside.

The German submarine skipper had caught the freighter fair on his periscope's crossed hairs. The torpedo, running swift and true, ripped open the tender skin of the ship and exploded in all its fury in the engine room.

Steam lines burst, letting their vapor escape to kill and scald and torture the engineers and oilers. Fuel tanks split open, spewing their oily contents over the scene of terror, making each ladder and catwalk a place of peril.

A wiper, checking the bearings in the shaft alley, heard the explosion, felt the ship tremble, and died in a sudden tidal wave of water and oil.

A junior engineer, standing at the side of a boiler, was flung against the water jacket unconscious, and awoke to die in a searing, blinding burst of steam.

In thirty seconds a hundred men were dead, scalded, mutilated, or drowned like rats in a trap.

Soldiers scrambled toward the companionways, already leaning crazily as the *Dorchester* listed to port, and fought their way, cursing and screaming, to the windy deck.

Abandon-ship drills, lectures on survival in torpedoings and the military discipline so newly acquired by civilians-suddenly-turned-soldiers went by the boards. In each man's mind was the single thought of how to save himself. The mores and the teachings of civilization were cast aside as a snake sheds its skin in the spring.

Then out of chaos came brief signs of order as men conquered the fear that had short-circuited their thinking. Doctors and medics snatched up their kits and headed below, bucking the tide of men seeking the open decks. If they sensed their own danger they brushed it aside and went on to rescue the injured. Their flashlights stabbed feebly at the blackness of the holds, already reeking with the choking fumes of ammonia.

Far below them in the engine room a boiler blew up, mangling bodies already mangled by the torpedo's warhead.

Up above things were no better. Even before the *Dorchester* had re-covered from the first shock the skipper clawed for the siren lanyard to send off the six-blast signal agreed upon before the convoy quit home waters.

Three times the siren roared. The fourth blast died in the whistle's metal throat, a hollow, mocking cough.

Because of the freighter's list, lifeboats on the starboard side hung inboard, and men struggled to free them. Some were lowered, bumping crazily down the ship's sloping sides. Others broke away and fell free, hurtling down upon men who had jumped overboard in the first seconds of terror.

The wind meanwhile had chopped around to the northwest and some of the lifeboats, safely launched, were breached by heavy seas which filled them to the thwarts. Men on the troopship saw them disappear, spewing soldiers into the water. Everywhere there were the red lights of the life jackets, twinkling on the water like sparks of fire.

Life rafts went over the side as frantic men hacked at their lashings. Some bobbled away in the darkness before anyone could reach them. Others were so crowded with survivors that men died struggling to get a grip on their handlines.

Here and there about the deck battle lanterns flickered fitfully, doing little to pierce the blackness of the night.

Men shouted and men wept. Soldiers made their way out of the hold without their lifejackets and went back to get them, dying in the smothering holds.

The devout cried to God for help, while others cursed His name. Kids who should have been in bed back home, resting for a day in the fields or at foot-ball practice, called for their mothers. Some just huddled at the rail, already awash, like frightened sheep.

Hysteria compelled weak men to jump into the Atlantic with mad words upon their lips, but the bitter cold of the ocean stilled their cries as if the words thickened in their throats.

Through this scene of terror moved a few strong men, purposeful, calm, and seemingly unafraid.

A soldier who couldn't have been out of his teens cut away a rope that had tangled in the block of a davit, setting a lifeboat, crowded with men, free upon the surface of the sea.

Captain Greenspun was everywhere, encouraging the soldiers, helping the crew to launch anything that would float, and issuing the few commands there were left to issue on a floundering, mortally wounded ship.

Army surgeons and medics behaved as though participating in a briefing session on how to care for the wounded at sea. Injured men were brought topside, bandaged, and helped into lifeboats when these were available. Men who might have died lived because of their ministration.

And everywhere about the ship, in the terror-ridden interior and on the crazily tilted deck, the four chaplains moved along the men with helpful words, giving some the strength to live and some the courage to die.

Knowing that the life expectancy of a man in such frigid waters was somewhere between 18 and 40 minutes, the three men with crosses on their collars and the one with the Tablets of the Law on his, urged the soldiers to stay aboard as long as possible after the smallboats had been cast off.

"Take it easy, soldier. It will be all right."

Strange how such simple, meaningless words could still panic in a man's heart. Stranger still how they could inject starch into a coward's spine.

The *Dorchester* by now had lost all way and was lying dead in the water. Fitful winds plucked spume from the wave crests and whipped it into the faces of the men on deck.

Suddenly the ship shivered and men everywhere cried out.

"She's going down. She's going down. We'll be sucked under."

Even the GIs who had never seen the ocean until they embarked on the *Dorchester* knew the added danger that accompanies a ship's last plunge.

Like old wives' tales feeding on themselves, lurid stories of the swirling, sucking vortex created when a vessel went down had gone the rounds among the men. What had made it worse was the knowledge that the evil couldn't be exaggerated.

Now, in the blackness of the night, the terror was multiplied a thousand-fold.

The chaplains sensed the threat.

"Over the side, men, make it fast." The wind tore the words from their lips.

"Swim to the lifeboats," they cried. "Get away from the ship."

Men looked at the four chaplains with new wonder. They saw them move together as though that way they could be of greater help.

Soldiers lifted their eyes to them as if for a sign, some symbol to carry with them into the valley of death.

A man—more boy than man—made his way to the group at the rail.

"Padre, I've lost my life jacket. I can't swim. I'll . . ."

One of the chaplains tore off his own and put it about the boy's shoulders. "Take this. I'm staying. I won't need it."

The soldier tied the jacket's strings, mounted the rail, and slipped into the sea, now almost level with the deck.

Of the three hundred or so men who survived not one can remember which chaplain it was who first voiced the decision to stay with the ship.

Was it Father Washington, who couldn't swim across a duck pond? Was it Fox, survivor of one war and victim of another? Poling, heir to a great name in preaching, or Goode, the rabbi from the Pennsylvania Dutch country?

What does it matter now? If the first had not spoken, another would. Catholic, Jew, and Protestant; each proved that night that courage knows no distinction of creed, bravery no division of caste.

Violent squalls confused the dying moments of the freighter. Flares on the bridge revealed the deck, now awash, at an ugly slant. Men fought for places on the last raft, and the losers cursed and wept.

The four chaplains stood with arms linked, each one without a life jacket. Somewhere off in the seething seas four other men were cheating death, supported by the chaplains' gifts.

Icy waters reached their knees as their lips moved in prayer.

"Our Father which art in Heaven, Hallowed be Thy name. Thy kingdom come, Thy will be done . . ."

The troopship labored to rise from a trough and staggered on. Water sluiced along the sloping deck.

". . . *ego te absolvo a peccatis tuis, in nomine Patris, et Filii, et Spiritus Sancti . . .*"

A soldier, bleeding through his bandages, crawled to where the four were standing. His voice was barely audible.

"God bless you," he said, and crawled into the sea.

A wave breached clear across the tilted deck.

"Hear, O Israel, the Lord Our God, the Lord is one . . ."

For an instant the light of a flare cast an effulgence upon the four of them for all who were left aboard to see.

". . . forgive us our trespasses, as we forgive those who trespass against us . . ."

Once more the ship labored to breast the next wave. There was a great noise of water and air churning in the darkness.

The *Dorchester* fought to right herself, failed, and plunged beneath the surface.

Eyes Open Under the Sea*

PHILIPPE DIOLÉ

✳✳ Philippe Diolé was for a time a foreign correspondent and later editor of two Paris dailies. He is a young traveler and explorer who has sailed the entire length of the Niger alone in a canoe and has done undersea research for the French Navy. ✳✳

> *"I can only think of one experience that might exceed in interest a few hours spent under water and that would be a journey to Mars."*
>
> —WILLIAM BEEBE

I have no particular "stories" to tell.

Breaking the surface of the sea, roaming about in the deep waters of the ocean, going down slowly, eyes open, watching the flicker of mullet and the dance of castagnoles, chestnut substitutes in these liquid skies for butterflies —all this does not constitute a "story." But if I do not know any stories, I have perhaps lived a miracle, one which I want to talk about: I have traveled to another world in which "action is sister to the dream." I have swept away in the heart of the sea, at a depth of several fathoms, all my anxieties as a man. Worries of the moment, scientific curiosity, metaphysical doubts, have all been hurled into the sea and I do not regret it.

Like many others, I do not feel in perfect harmony with our age and the solitude of diving lulls and stays a deep-rooted dissatisfaction. Down below, where dream and action move silently forward, side by side, through the dense waters, man feels for a moment in tune with life.

Whether that is telling a story or not, I don't know. It is always possible to write an account of journeys on land. I have been from one end of Europe to the other and made almost a complete tour of Africa. Every country I have visited can be described: it is simply a question of landscape, people, distances. But for three years my life has been entangled in the life of the sea. The only period of my existence worth anything in all this time has been spent far from other men, beyond a curtain of crystal, with fish or under-water animals more foreign in appearance and habits than anything one might come across if one traveled to the ends of the earth. It was an adventure without incident, and it is not yet over. Probably it will end only with my death, for those who have once listened to the siren songs of the ocean bed never return to land.

Norbert Casteret, in his Pyrenean caves, my friend Guy de Lavaur, exploring Padirac, have both had adventures with quite a definite beginning, intervening incidents, and an end. You enter these subterranean grottoes, you go all over them, and you finally leave them. The explorer may find a river, chambers, stalactites, narrow passages filled with clay, obstacles to surmount. But once out in the open again he has only to relive his underground journey to make a tale of it.

But what am I to say, a sea explorer whose objective is never reached, and who has never seen the end of those marine vaults, one minute black with shadows, the next hacked with swords of light? Here and there I have managed to snatch fragments of knowledge, I have tried to use my eyes, to understand the meaning of what was before me, and to fit together where I could the pieces of a vague jigsaw of the sea.

But there is no need to organize expeditions to explore the sea. Anyone can start when he wants and go down where he wants. All he needs is a flask of compressed air, some goggles, a piece of lead around his waist. Excuses are not so easy to justify, for we are each judge of our own daring, alone witness of our fears and hesitations. There are often humble and unimportant victories over ourselves. I have known bitter March mornings when the flesh refused to advance into a sea that cut like ice. I have shivered, alone on a rock, while the rising sun climbed behind the tip of the Islettes, simply because I was determined to observe the underwater world through all its seasons and because it seemed especially important to me at that green and yellow moment of the Mediterranean dawn. But is that a story? It's not even an anecdote.

Dramatic incidents? Certainly, I know a few; but I am not even sure I shall describe them. They were mostly trifling dramas that were over in a few seconds. A pipe getting hooked onto a piece of jagged rock; air cylinders refusing to work in an underwater grotto; moments of animal panic when I couldn't wait to surface, desperate to see another human being. None of that is worth talking about and even Fargue, who perished at a depth of sixty fathoms, would probably have had nothing to tell if he had survived.

But divers do certainly have adventures. Only they are not what land dwellers usually understand by that word. The greatest, most exciting adventure is the mere act of being alive where, among men, only the drowned visit you. And of making yourself at home there, living a comfortable, peaceful existence.

One does not go straight into the sea. Between the air and the water a steel blade quivers. What people call the surface is also a ceiling: a mirror from above, watered silk from beneath. Nothing is torn on the way through. Only a few bubbles mark the diver's channel and behind him the frontier soon closes. But once the threshold is crossed, one can turn back slowly and look up: that dazzling screen is the border between two worlds, as clear to one as to the other. Behind the looking glass the sky is made of water.

Is this light spilling out in all directions, this pure and deep substance, really water? So much brilliance and clarity do not seem to belong to the green, frothing surface, the sticky and resilient element through which the swimmer has to strike his path. Once he has broken the surface, the diver who is properly ballasted has no more weight, no more resistance: an aerial softness transports him where he wills. Here the world is sweetness. There is not a place in his body, from head to foot, which is not relaxed. It is a pleasure to stretch out, to lie on one's back and to feel the perfect fluency of one's muscles. Dreams float very slowly up from the sea. Walled in silence and completely alone, the diver begins an interior monologue in the cell of his undreamed-of content.

At a depth of two or three fathoms all swell subsides. Not a weed moves. A carpet of sand gleams faintly in the cleft of a rock some yards farther down. A mysterious continent traces itself below me. I swim between the huge pages of an illuminated manuscript. Now I am dazzled by the purity of the light, the luminous beauty of the deep. A crystalline quality of light gives everything the purity of glass. The opened pages end in a maze of rocks, beyond which a flow of blue water narrows out of sight and then widens. Over them is stretched a thick sky on which I glide until I reach shapes that turn into submarine peaks, or cathedrals rising from the plains on summer mornings. Inspecting these summits, feeling the hard rock under their soft exterior of weed, gives one a respite before the final slide toward an invisible bottom. I swim around a sapphire steeple. Everything in front of me is blue, but if I look down, a whole purple universe seems to swing out of the depths. Shall I go down to the foot of this tower or forget about it? At twenty fathoms, everything is forbidding, congealed, and cold, and the sudden iciness stabs me. I don't know whether it freezes or paralyzes me: I feel it in me like a living thing, a disease. What have I come here for? To explore the sea? I already know all that can be seen in it. I have come down in pursuit of a mirage. I have yielded to the dizzy madness of tearing open this blue canvas and making for the very heart of the dream. The rock cod, motionless in the shadow of their holes, gaze at the passer-by without stirring. Gorgonia spread their huge fans, quite still in the breathless water. Who has spoken of jungles? Not a single evasive flurry, not a moving shadow, brings this palace without walls to life. Were blood to flow, for example, it would not stain the crystal purity, for it would look blue. What is this vague terror as from a chamber of horrors? The slightest touch makes me tremble. I have even forgotten what the sky looks like, the real sky in which men can breathe without equipment.

Such is the aspect that submarine life presents, for the most part, today. Twenty fathoms is a prudent and reasonable depth. Even ten years ago we were less daring.

To the swimmer, clear water alone is reassuring, and man's mistrust of water has always been awakened by sharp and concealing corners or slopes too rich in vegetation. Throughout history, the best divers have come from the clear-water countries—Greece, Italy, Polynesia. Bretons, who are such good fishermen, never dive and seldom even swim.

Our anxiety in the water is like the panic of a blind man, but, by wearing a diving mask, we can enjoy clear vision and rid ourselves of these phantoms. Yet there remains in all of us a more or less vivid memory of those legends which peopled the sea with monsters and shadowy catastrophes.

All these underwater terrors have not yet been dispelled. How many times have I seen a friend tremble when I touched him on the shoulder under water and he had not felt my approach; how many times have I not shuddered as something brushed against me! Our imagination goes on suspecting mysterious dangers, where in reality there is only a dark patch or a harmless creature more frightened than we are.

Fear, cruelty, incomprehension, leave a heavy mark on our first encounters with the water world. We go into the sea with all our land dweller's prejudices. On land, we participate in a hierarchy of emotions which excludes the sea creatures; the man who can't bear to see a rabbit killed will look on with a cold eye while the back of a live fish's throat is torn out with the hook which is caught in it. The death agony of all terrestrial things, from a horse to a hedgehog, wakes in us some feelings of sympathy and self-identification, some echoes of tenderness for the common fate of beast and man. This sense of pity which is so easily aroused remains indifferent to sea creatures; our clemency is unable to go further than the shore or to be extended to the living world beyond.

Yet life and death are the same on land and sea; the blood which flows there is just as red and, in its farewell to life, the flesh of the scalebearers should offer as pathetic a spectacle to our eyes as that which is covered by feathers or fur. But far from it; a fish to most of us is generally only an oblong sack of bones and scales. If it dies in convulsions, it dies at any rate in silence and makes a nice clean corpse with a minimum of blood and gut. So we conclude it feels nothing.

That is because we watch it die in the air; once on land, where it is so helpless, a fish loses even the means to express suffering. It's quite a different thing when the death throes take place in the water. The eyewitness soon finds that he is spectator of a drama as painful as that of the dying hind which tramples on its entrails. The true hunter's instinct is the same in both cases—to finish them off quickly. If this seems hard to believe, here is the opinion of an underwater fisherman, Bernard Gorsky, from his *Ten Meters Down.*

I shall always have a clear memory of a splendid specimen of over five pounds which I harpooned with a horizontal shot. In its struggle the corb tore itself free and disappeared in a large overhanging crevice. I reloaded and was about to go down again when the fish reappeared, completely disabled; unable to turn, it was coming up toward me, dragging its pale intestines; there was such an anguish in the position of the body, in the expression of the half-closed eyes, that I was frozen by it and it was with very mixed feelings that I fired my harpoon again.

For the first time in human history, man and fish are finding themselves face to face in the same water, breasting the same weed. I can remember the time when fish were less frightened for their lives and would come up to nose my harpoon. Now their education is complete; they know we are murderers and flee at sight. I believe we have missed a wonderful opportunity, a possible friendliness such as the birds gave to Saint Francis. For fishes, holiness wasn't even a requisite!

A leaden sky slowly thickens about me. I move with small strokes in this atmosphere, threatened by submarine night. I continue to go down, slipping over rays of sunlight half-strangled by shadow. A silky silence broken by the rhythm of my breathing, a comic gurgling, like pipe bubbles, accompanies my exploration of this endless blue silk.

I roll over on my side for the pleasure of lying on a bed made of water. At the same time I bask in my loneliness: the sea surface seems far away, no longer watered silk but a dazzle of stars behind a sash of mist. Someone overhead is throwing pearls into the sea. No, I am wrong; these pearls are born of my breath. Rainbow-colored bubbles climb at steep angles and break on the sky; there are fragments of gold everywhere. My own pattern of bubbles bears witness that I am still alive, that I have not foundered on the sea bed.

But can I convince others that I am alive? Am I sure of it myself? With the help of two steel bottles filled with air an idea keeps going in the heart of the sea, but how hazardously!

"We commit his body to the deep." The ritual phrase pronounced on board English ships when a corpse is thrown into the sea. I too am committed to the deep and similarly ballasted. Intoxication and dream cradle me. Reason still controls me, but, enticed by every kind of treachery, it is poised for mad flight to the sky, attracted by the slumbering phantoms of the deep. I am the sleeper of the sea, the drowned but conscious man drawn by the wires of dream into a dangerous monologue.

Now comes the worst stage: the liquid sky over me is blotted out and I know that it is no longer any use my looking for it. I recognize this grisaille in which every color is diluted. I am in the body of the sea. But the sea bed cannot be far off. I shall find land again, a false land rubbed away by water, but firm, almost reassuring. Points of brilliance dance in front of my eyes: phosphene. Oppressive majesty of the solitude in which I move, dazzled and blind. No more familiar fish or rocky labyrinths. I have never gone down so far before. Perhaps I have overestimated my resources and agony in lying in wait among these shadows writhing below. A sky of terrifying storm has taken possession of the sea. I remember an evening when we were flying toward the African coast and found it guarded by black columns. We twisted between the pillars of tornadoes, into open corridors like so many snares. The snare is here, in this crevice which I am now going to explore.

Why do I think of Saint-Exupéry? Because of the storm, the black sky, or because of the trap? The pilot of *Night Flight* also discovered the trap in an opening between cyclones, and he entered it as I am going to do, in spite of the distaste of that "I" who keeps watch, uneasy.

In my liquid sky I understand at last this fulfillment in insecurity that was Saint-Exupéry's constant fulfillment. It was studiously hidden from the eyes of land dwellers and only showed itself in his writing. He made it the excuse for his art. In public he only built card houses with his strong and supple hands.

Land of men. Sky of men. Now, sea of men. Slow conquests. These metal constructions, which are called ships, airplanes, or diving suits, are worth less than the flesh which inhabits them. Man alone is interesting: it is he who dares the tempest, the cyclone in which Fabien perished, the abyss into which I am thrusting.

One must try to give a name to those confused reflections. But perhaps the human weight, the feeling of one's body that comes from submarine adventure and which machines take away, is the greatest sensation that the sea affords. Strange human weakness: a new world opens and man seeks an intercessor, the intervention of some enchanter to soothe the low reaches of his soul and persuade him to acts of daring. The low or the highest? That is a question for eternal debate. I am a lonely man who hesitates on the edge of the abyss and it is less with the abyss that I deliberate than with myself. Hans Hass tells how, in the Caribbean Sea, at a moment of great pain, he recited Schiller's "Diver" to himself, over and over again. I am aware that the diver exploring the sea has recourse to almost every science: biology, optics, geology, chemistry, archaeology. But is poetry a driving force of oceanography? Perhaps. One day when I asked Philippe Tailliez to describe to me how things looked at a depth of thirty to forty-five fathoms he pondered a moment, looked at me, and said with a doubtful expression:

"It's not possible. You can't describe it."

Then he seemed to change his mind, and his face brightened.

"Wait," he said. "Have you a Rimbaud?"

I went at once to get him the book.

Reading *"Le Bateau ivre"* under his breath, he marked some lines with his nail. They were:

> *Lactescent with suspended stars, the poem*
> *Of the sea*

and

> *Kisses ascending to the eyes of seas, slowly;*
> *The blue and yellow waking of singing phosphors.*

Each of these images, radiated by strange lights, enabled him to evoke a distant world. Only a few more words were needed to reach depths no one had ever described. Thus poetic transcription was a stage toward knowledge of the abyss.

Describing the outside world, we in fact describe only ourselves and our interior feelings. Poetry is the medium through which we grope at expression. "Poets," Freud said, "are our masters in the exploration of the soul, for they are steeped in sources we have not yet made accessible to science."

The further man explores the world of water, the deeper does he become involved in human problems. That, at any rate, has been my experience. The sea has met my demands with incalculable generosity. Whether it was a question of searching for the remains of ancient Mediterranean civilizations, turning over in the sea the problems of life, or nursing those non-Cartesian sides to the soul which claim their own portion of happiness, it has never failed me.

Perhaps there is, in fact, more to be got out of the sea than food reserves and increased scientific knowledge; an element of reassurance, giving us back confidence and balance, a reminder of true values, a biological wisdom. "I think," Robert Gruss has written, "that diving in self-contained equipment has created a new race: Men of the Sea. They view it in its totality, they bear its weight, and try to learn its secrets. I have never considered diving as an ordinary distraction, or even as a sport. The moment the sea closes over me I feel some great thing is happening. I feel a kind of awe, without really knowing why." Unless it is because the ocean depths give us the chance of a new humanism. Yet I think that we have not quite reached that stage; I'm not very happy about the word. Is it really a humanism, this slow impregnation, this gentle and pervasive enlightenment, prerogative of the "men of the sea"?

Anyway, the name doesn't matter. It is the assurance we get from our life under water that counts. Just as there is no part of the diver's body which remains unexercised or unsoothed in the sea, so there is no part of his mind not brought into play. What possibilities lie ahead!

3 Climate of Adventure

Thule *

PETER FREUCHEN

✳✳ Thule was given its name by Peter Freuchen in 1910. Freuchen, who was born in Denmark in 1886, was then 24. The name, he says, comes "from *Ultima Thule,* which means, of course, north of everything and everybody." It was to be a trading post with the Polar Eskimos. It is located on the west coast of Greenland at the northern end of Melville Bay. In 1910 Freuchen was there with the Norwegian explorer, Knud Rasmussen, who had thought at first of calling their trading center Knudsminde or Knudshope "but we agreed," writes Freuchen, "such a name would be pretentious." ✳✳

REMEMBRANCE

The Eskimos are moving away from Thule these days. They are deserting their ancient settlement. I read in the papers that two spokesmen for the Thule Eskimos have gone to Copenhagen to ask the Danish government to move their village to the north, away from the deafening noise of the American airplanes. They can no longer remain in the place where their ancestors lived in isolation for centuries, because modern civilization has moved in and Thule in northern Greenland, not far from the North Pole, has been turned into one of the world's major airports.

My friends laugh at the Eskimos. "Do they have such sensitive nerves?" they ask me. "Does the sound of the engines hurt their delicate ears?" my friends inquire. "Perhaps the Eskimos will become used to it like the rest of us."

How little they understand. I was in Thule not long ago and I met all my old friends again. They had always lived a proud and carefree life, but when I saw them they were badly off. They had no meat left. I talked to my old

* From *Vagrant Viking, My Life and Adventures,* by Peter Freuchen. Translated from the Danish by Johan Hambro. Copyright, 1953, by Peter Freuchen, reprinted by permission of Julian Messner, Inc., New York.

friend Odark, the last of the North Pole Eskimos. He upholds the traditions in Thule, he defends the old customs of his tribe.

"Things are not like they used to be, Pita," he told me. "When we were young and strong we chased the bear, the seal, and the walrus ourselves. We got meat where we wanted it. Today," he snorted, "today the meat is sold for money! I have money enough. The king gives me more than I need, but I shall never stoop to buying my meat. I shall never pay my friends to feed my dogs.

"Do you remember when you first came to Thule, Pita? I fed your dogs and I fed them well. Today meat is put on the scales and every morsel is weighed. No longer does a man know how to chase a bear or catch a fish. He waits for the fish to come by itself and swallow a lazy hook. I have never caught any fish but the salmon I stabbed with my spear.

"Things are not like they used to be when you were young. Do you remember the house you built in Thule, Pita? The first house ever built here. Today there is a city of white men, and the noise they make has chased away all living things. No longer does the ice bear cross to Melville Bay, seals and walrus have left for happier hunting grounds, and the wild geese are gone. Life seems a heavier burden than death to me today, Pita. And death cannot be far away when our land is like it is today and when my friends take money for meat!"

Odark was my friend. When I first met him forty years ago he had just killed Uvisakavsik and married his wife. Odark had gone to the North Pole with Peary, he was respected and renowned. Denmark pays him twice the normal pension, and through the Explorers' Club he receives an annual sum from the United States. He is not without money, but he has no meat. Never has he paid for his meat and he will not do so in his old age. "Let my dogs fend for themselves," says Odark. He does not need them. There are no more animals to hunt. His legs are not themselves any more, he says—the legs that once walked to the Navel of the Earth because the white man wanted to see how it was made.

We bridged the years and talked of our youth. "Can you remember when we had to eat our dogs to fill our stomachs? And when we were stranded in the middle of Melville Bay, when the ice would not freeze and we had no food for five days and nights? But when we returned to Thule every man was our host and there was always too much to eat."

We were always on the move in those days when I spent years of my life in Thule with Navarana, my Eskimo wife. . . .

All that seemed to belong to an ancient past. When I last returned to Thule most of my friends were still there, and they tried to explain to me what had happened to them. During the war Denmark agreed to let the United States establish military bases on Greenland and at that time all supplies came from the United States in generous amounts. Denmark made only one condition: The American forces were to be withdrawn at the end of the war. This promise was never fulfilled.

When I was last in Greenland there were seven thousand American soldiers in Thule—or rather in Pitufik across the bay at the mouth of the wide valley stretching all the way to the ice cap. Hundreds of times we had gone up this valley, driven across the glacier and down to Cape York or Parker Snow Bay. And Pitufik used to be the place where the polar bears came ashore in fall. They are crafty animals, the bears. They knew the short cut across the peninsula to the south. They went up the valley, across the glacier, and down to Puisortok in the fjord behind Cape York where they would be sure of finding seals.

Sometimes they fell asleep on the way. Only half of the bears hibernate. If they are not fat enough they cannot remain idle for many months, but when they are well fed they can afford the luxury of sleeping all through the winter. Behind Pitufik they settled down by the glacier's edge. They knew their geography, the old bears. They picked a spot where the snow would cover them until the sun woke them up in spring.

There are no bears by Pitufik any more. There are seven thousand soldiers. . . .

The walrus does not enter the fjord any more. No animal is as sensitive to smells as a walrus. If a house is heated with coal the smoke is enough to keep the walrus far away. The white whales go out to sea now, the narwhales have not been heard snorting in Ugli for many years. The Eskimos have to go away, they must follow the animals.

No one is to be blamed. No one can say that one thing is more important than the other. Sentimental thoughts must be forgotten for they lead nowhere. But where he has dreamed the dreams of his youth, there a man wants to return. . . .

Only one way out is open to the Eskimos. They can move. They can go farther north and settle down once more. The cost of a move is nothing to the United States, which built the enormous airbase. And a move is no symbol of defeat to the Eskimos. They are used to it, for centuries they have followed the animals. Here in the extreme north they have been successful in their fight against the hardest climate in the world. They have proved their invincible strength by surviving centuries of isolation and by absorbing and digesting modern civilization in the shortest span of time that has ever elapsed between the stone age and the air age. The meeting of the two ages was like an explosion. The Eskimos had to learn in a single generation what has taken other parts of the world hundreds of years to learn. . . .

I was fortunate enough to experience their first awakening from the ancient ways of the stone age to the tempo of modern days. I learned their language, I married an Eskimo, and I lived for years with them in Thule. I heard the wise men tell their tales of days gone by. They gave me a happiness which was the foundation of my future life. Wherever I went in the world—Siberia or South America, Alaska, Hollywood or New York—I never forgot my first wife, Navarana, and her family and friends. Her influence and the life I lived for years in Thule stamped me forever.

MARRIAGE TO AN ESKIMO

During the first half of 1911* we carried on our trading activities while we waited for the first ship from the south to bring us mail and news, and during these months my Eskimo friends seemed to be concerned about my status as a single man. It was well known, of course, that Knud Rasmussen had left his wife behind in Denmark. It was equally obvious to my friends that I was not captured as yet, and they were determined to do something to remedy this state of affairs.

Our elderly Eskimo housekeeper, Vivi, was a romantic soul, and she tried to force her attentions on me. She was an efficient woman but a singularly unattractive one. When she tried one night by sheer force to make me share my bed with her, I knew it was high time for me to leave home for a while.

I set out on another trip, north this time, to visit Mayark, a great hunter who lived with his father, a wise old man called Sorqaq. The old man was no longer interested in hunting expeditions, but he still kept a number of excellent dogs which he loved to overfeed. Sorqaq did not understand me when I asked if he would be willing to sell me some of his famous dogs. He told me, instead, that I was a man to his liking and, therefore, he wanted the two of us to eat from the same seal as a symbol of brotherhood.

I had to ask Mayark, the son, for the dogs. They were being fed constantly, because his old father could never remember when they had their last meal, and as the meat all came from Mayark's supplies, I thought it logical to ask him to sell me some of the dogs.

"But how can I sell another man's property?" he asked me.

"You are keeping them, you supply their food, and your father does not need them," I told him.

* The author was then 25 years old.

"True enough, but one does not rob an old man of his pleasure."

Mayark interpreted my interest in the dogs in his own way. He declared that my desire to move fast with new dogs clearly showed my restlessness and need for a woman. He called out through the window for a girl to come inside and introduced me to Arnanguaq who was offered for the satisfaction of Peterssuak's desires. He assured me she was the best speciment in the settlement. She was shaped well enough, but dirty beyond measure and cross-eyed. With a completely impassive face she obeyed Mayark's orders and began undressing to show me what she had to offer. I tried to decline the honor in the least offensive way and told him that I had my own girl in Denmark and that she was coming by the first steamer to join me in Thule. He was not offended when I left him without taking the cross-eyed beauty with me.

The weather was turning warmer, and I went out to Saunders Island in the bay outside Thule, where I spent the next few weeks with my Eskimo friends hunting birds and collecting large stores of eggs. One morning I was awakened by shrieks of ecstasy coming from outside. The Eskimos had sighted the first whaler of the season—the *Upernadlit* they are called in Greenland, meaning those who arrive in spring. We had made arrangements for the first whaler from Scotland to bring us supplies and mail, so with great expectation I boarded the *Morning of Dundee*. The Eskimo women all streamed on board at the same time. I had felt duty bound to warn them against the dangers of venereal disease, which might spread to the whole tribe if they had anything to do with the crew, but they paid no attention to my words.

The captain invited me for dinner while he sent some of the men on shore to collect birds' eggs. From the bridge I watched them with a sinking heart, as I saw them mercilessly rob one and then another of my caches until there were none left.

I got our supplies and mail and made ready to leave. But our departure was delayed, because one of the Eskimo girls had lost her fur pants in the crew's quarters and was too bashful to come on deck without them. I began an investigation but the captain told me not to delay him with such a trifle. One of the men happily saved the situation by giving her my large red bandana which she put on like a diaper.

Back on shore I heard two elderly women discuss the episode, and I was relieved—at first—to hear them condemn the girl sharply.

"It's a scandal," one woman continued. "I've told her over and over again she should always keep on one of the legs of the pants to be on the safe side!"

My mail had brought me news from my beloved Michella who promised to join me, and I eagerly looked forward to summer and her arrival. I stayed quietly at home in Thule waiting for the ice to break up and the ship from Denmark to appear. We had no radio at that time, of course, and no news from the outside world, so I could do nothing but wait. The ice lasted until the end of July, then followed a few weeks when we could neither drive on the ice nor sail on the water. And every day an iceberg would appear on the horizon with its outline resembling a ship. We would race to the top of the nearest hill to make sure, but not until the end of August did our ship arrive.

I ran to my kayak and paddled out in my dirty hunting clothes as I had no time to change. When I got near the vessel I was disappointed not to see my girl on deck waving to me. She is keeping below deck, I thought, probably a little scared and shy. It never occurred to me that she might not have come.

I rushed on board. No Michella! Only a letter! One of those letters which are hard to write and, therefore, seem doubly clumsy. Michella was not coming—now or ever.

What did I care about the unloading of our supplies or listening to news? How could I worry about sending off our precious collection of furs? I was indifferent to the ship and the entire crew. In my disappointment, while the others worked and celebrated, I was grateful to be left alone.

There was one man who also suffered silently but for different reasons. He was the local missionary who had been found unworthy and had been ordered home. In his great zeal to spread the gospel he had concentrated on the Eskimo women. He had worked on them in the privacy of his own room, and they had evidently enjoyed the zeal of the strong young man. He had spread his seed, but not in the biblical sense, and the results were disastrous to him. His superior in Upernivik had ordered him home and had put him on board the ship. When Knud heard the story and realized that the man had no prospect of a livelihood on his return to Denmark, he interceded.

"If the church cannot take care of an erring sinner, we certainly can!" he announced. "The man will stay with us if Peter Freuchen does not object."

Why should I object? The man moved into our roomy house with his wife and four children. He was given work in the store, and I had more time to go hunting and traveling.

The ship went off again, bearing a curt reply from me to Michella. That settled the matter, I thought, and the episode could be forgotten.

I did not realize that a revolution was taking place in me. Slowly I was developing a great reluctance against ever going home. What did I have to return to? Here I was among the happiest people in the world. They could afford to buy everything they needed, and if they did not have foxes enough for payment, they could go out and get more. They lived in a peaceful, orderly society. No one interfered in other people's business, because Eskimos are the most tactful people in the world.

I had been stupid enough to make it known that my girl would arrive on the ship from Denmark. But nobody asked me any questions. They knew, of course, what had happened.

Inukitsork, who had a beautiful wife Tukumerk, thought to prove his friendship by one day offering her to me.

"I am going south. There will be some weeks of absence while I am bear hunting. My wife will be left in your house while I am gone."

But I had no use for his woman. I had been deeply wounded by Michella and I was too angry with all women to care about the beautiful Tukumerk. Her husband had told her to take good care of me, she explained to me, but my heart was like a stone and all her efforts were in vain. When her husband returned and discovered I had not enjoyed his wife in his absence, it was agreed among the Eskimos that my abstinence must be the result of some disease. But still they did not give up.

When the days turned darker again and the ice settled once more in fall, visitors arrived from the north to tell us of a great food shortage among the Eskimos there. If we would take knives and guns and ammunition up to them, they could carry on their hunting without interruption, to our mutual advantage. It was decided that I should go up to the northern part of our district and take supplies to keep the people from undertaking the long trading expedition themselves.

If they had to come down to Thule with their first few foxes, they would miss the best part of the hunting season. For the foxes always go away from their winter depots, with the first ice of the winter. They are smart animals, and in summer they store large numbers of auks for the winter. They bite off the heads of the birds, put them in tight neat rows, cover them with gravel and snow, and put stones on top. To avoid temptation the fox stays away from his secret cache until his hunger drives him back to his early fall depots.

I decided to go north immediately with a large supply of goods for the Eskimos. Before I left my friend Tatianguak came to see me.

"It has been noticed that Peterssuak travels without a woman," he said. "My wife, Ivalu, has relatives in the north and would like to visit them. She might conceivably be of some use on the trip. She may be of help in cooking and in drying clothes. Also the traveler enjoys his nights more when they are shared by a woman."

Since I had now decided to settle down for good and live like the Eskimos in every respect, I thought why not accept the offer. And Ivalu and I set out together across the Wolstenholme Fjord and into Granville Bay. Our conversation the first few hours was neither fluent nor romantic.

"Are you afraid of me, Ivalu?" I asked her.

"No pleasure is felt."

"Do you know the way across the inland glacier?"

"There is no desire to cross the glacier. It's cold and windy there."

"But we'll have to. There is no ice around the cape."

"Your words are wasted. Let men talk to men and keep their silence when they are with a mere woman."

I kept quiet but after a while the silence became oppressive.

"Are you afraid of me, Ivalu?" I asked her.

"Why should I be afraid? Please do not talk unless reasonable words are spoken."

A rather cold response, particularly since the temperature was thirty degrees below zero and the wind was sharp from the north.

I jumped off the sled once in a while and ran next to it in order to keep warm while the girl remained seated, freezing in dignified silence. Every time I asked her if she was cold, I got the same reply:

"Keep quiet. One thinks!"

I hoped she was thinking of me and the many nights we were going to spend together. Finally I asked her what she was thinking about.

"Meat!" she answered and I stopped the dogs to prepare a meal for us.

In the evening we arrived at the bottom of Granville Bay where we met an Eskimo family on its way to Thule. We spent the night in a cave there with them. There was no sign of surprise when they met me with the wife of a well-known Eskimo as my single companion. We ate our evening meal with them, and Ivalu proudly served them tea from my supplies.

We prepared our bed in the cave by placing a large mat of dried grass on the rock, then a sealskin, then a bearskin, and finally my sleeping bag. Ivalu had brought no bag of her own. We removed our fur coats and rolled them up as pillows, and finally we undressed. In such a sleeping bag the best way to keep warm is to be naked. There were two of us in my bag and it was not hard to keep warm.

Our trip lasted several weeks and I visited all the northern settlements I could reach and traded guns and ammunition, knives and other tools for furs until I had nothing left to give them. I was sincerely sorry the last night when I knew I had to return Ivalu to her husband the following morning.

And I was wondering just how to say good-by to her after all our days and nights together. I need not have worried.

Crossing North Star Bay in the evening, with Thule a short distance ahead, I had a hard time controlling the dogs as they were impatient to get home. When I finally had them in hand, I tried hesitantly to talk to Ivalu. There was no reply. I looked around to discover that she was no longer on the sled behind me. I could see her in the distance—a small dot on the ice close to shore. She had calmly jumped off the sled to take a short cut back to her husband, without a single word of farewell.

In the following months I turned more and more into an Eskimo. It happened every now and then that Ivalu returned to me for a night, but I cannot claim she was my only companion. When I was traveling around the district I followed the local custom and usually had a woman along for the sake of convenience. But subconsciously I was longing for a more personal and permanent arrangement.

One young girl in Thule had attracted my attention. Her mother had had two children by her first husband—Mequ, a girl, and a boy who had died with his father during a hunger period. The mother had married again and had a great number of children whom Mequ had to look after. Once in a while the girl visited our store. On one such visit I gave her some bread, and a few days later she returned with a pair of gloves she had made me. "A small token of gratitude for bread," she said and disappeared again. She was very shy and not used to speaking unless she was asked something, and nobody asked her anything.

Once when we were walking through the village we noticed Mequ outside her house, and Knud said to me: "She is the only girl in Greenland who is good enough and smart enough and pretty enough to marry."

I considered his words and the more I thought the more I realized he was right. Mequ had just changed from girl to woman, and she seemed to me an extraordinarily pure and fine person. There was a great shortage of women in Greenland at that time. Young girls were married off even before they were grown, and many men had already asked for Mequ's hand. So far the suitors had been turned away.

Finally one day during the winter Knud and all the men in our house were off on a hunting trip, and I was left alone with old Vivi. Not because she was afraid of any aggressiveness on my part but rather to have some company, she invited Mequ to stay with us during the night.

We undressed and went to bed, turning the lamp very low. Suddenly I was seized by an urge too strong for me to control. I threw off my furs and took

Mequ to my bed without a word. In the morning I told her I wanted to keep her with me forever. Instead of Mequ I decided to use another of her names. She agreed with everything I said and she moved into my house with me.

Thus Navarana and I were married.

Nine Hours Fast to a Fighting Whale*

ROBERT CUSHMAN MURPHY

✳✳ Robert Cushman Murphy, naturalist, born in Brooklyn, 1887, chairman of the Department of Birds at the American Museum of Natural History, New York, since 1942, and the leader of numerous naturalist expeditions into tropical and sub-Antarctic Atlantic waters, the Mediterranean, and other parts of the world, was launched into a scientific career when a young man through the long-range vision of his fiancée, who gave him up temporarily to a whaling boat. . . . "Toward the end of the year 1911," writes Dr. Murphy, "six months after I had received my bachelor's degree from Brown, my friend Dr. Frederic A. Lucas, then Director of the American Museum of Natural History, spoke to me about an opportunity of voyaging to the edge of the Antarctic in a New Bedford whaling and sealing vessel. The suggestion provoked an evening of lively discussion which related, however, to other naturalist-candidates. I was planning to be married in June, 1912, and my own eligibility for such a cruise never entered my head.

"The conversation was routinely reported by letter to Miss Grace Emeline Barstow, 'of the State of Rhode Island and Providence Plantations.' With characteristic forthrightness, she awakened me by a telegram, delivered in the middle of the next night. The message urged me to hold the seafaring option pending further consideration, and to hasten the latter by catching the first train to Providence. Her subsequent argument was that the projected voyage would serve as the best-possible launching of my career, and that we would be married immediately so as to have several months together before my departure.

"I was persuaded without undue difficulty, but she alone had the audacity to invite a conventional and aghast family to prepare for her early wedding with a youth who would thereafter disappear for a year or longer!

"Nevertheless, everything worked out in just that way. We were married on February 17, 1912, and on May 25 we departed by steamer for the Lesser Antilles in company with Captain B. D. Cleveland, master of the brig *Daisy*, and his wife. Following a memorable stay at Barbados, where the whaler had made port after a year's cruise under command of another captain, we all boarded the *Daisy* and voyaged to Dominica. On July 1, the matron and the bride left us, taking passage on the steamship *Guyana* from Dominica to New York. That point marks the opening of my log.

"Most Americans knew little, and thought less, of wars at the time I shipped on the *Daisy*. No torpedoes or bombs were a source of worry, but there was little solace as regards means of communication. Radio was merely something we had begun to hear about, air mail hardly that. Going to sea as I did meant leaving the world.

"Foremost among my jobs was writing the records of day-to-day experience in the logbook I kept for my courageous wife and also in a separate set of scientific notebooks. My model for the latter was the journal of the youthful Darwin of the *Beagle*, for which I felt, and still feel, an unbounded admiration. Average daily jottings exceeded a thousand words, so I returned to New York, after an absence of precisely a year, with about 400,000 words of notes." ✷✷

August 17. Barn swallows, bound from somewhere "up home" toward their winter range in South America, visited us at noon today and perched in the rigging while they preened their feathers thoroughly. The position was lat. 30° 31′ N., long. 58° 40′ W. This is, roughly, 360 geographic miles on the seaward side of Bermuda and more than a thousand miles from Cape Hatteras, Cape Cod, and Halifax, Nova Scotia, all of which are about equally distant. At seven o'clock in the evening, at least six of the birds were still sitting and snuggling along the royal brace.

August 18. A rainy Sunday morning. Several of the barn swallows spent the night with us. They had better be on their way swiftly, if they hope to reach land, because the *Daisy* supports no flying-insect fauna, except cockroaches far too big for swallows to eat.

A school of whales was announced after dinner. At first the Old Man and Mr. da Lomba thought they were only killers, but presently they were distinguished as sperm whales mingled with and surrounded by killers. The latter were jumping in a most spectacular display, and the whole area was white water.

The aggregation was approaching the brig, so we waited with sails aback until the whales, blowing furiously, came close. Then we lowered four boats and, from the mainmasthead, I had a superb view of the hunt and death.

Most landlubbers suppose—as I did formerly—that a Yankee whaleman captures his prey by maneuvering the boat somewhere near the whale and then throwing the harpoon at it. Nothing of the sort! The harpoon is not "thrown"; it is planted. It rarely leaves the hands of the boat-steerer until the boat has been beached on the whale's back. "Wood to blackskin," is the muttered or grunted order by which the boat-header holds his harpooner's eagerness in check while the craft is sailing, or being pulled, onto the whale.

At half-past one o'clock the first of our boats made fast. At that moment a tropic-bird flew into the field and for some minutes circled about, watching the boats and whales. The killers had disappeared. At quarter before two, another boat made fast and went shooting ahead, lowering sail immediately as the whale sprinted at the surface. Six minutes later the third boat planted its iron. By this time the first boat had lanced and waifed its whale. The fourth boat, Mr. Almeida's, was unlucky and never succeeded in making fast.

At the first signal of "fin out," the ship-tenders began to haul up from steerage and 'tween-decks the heavy fluke chains, cutting tackle, and other gear used during the flensing, and the helmsman endeavored to keep the brig to windward of the boats. Mr. da Lomba was, however, a mile or more upwind, and his boys consequently had the added labor of towing their carcass to the *Daisy*. They looped a bowline from the flukes around the loggerhead and bent backs to five oars, but at each stroke the blades seemed to drop into the same hole in the water. I think that their progress would have been livelier if they had followed the time-honored custom of towing their whale head first, but there seem to be differences of opinion about that. At any rate, it took Mr. da Lomba two hours to bring in his prize. By that time the blue sharks had followed their noses in from all directions and were clustering about our catches like hyenas around a dead lion. The water was alive with them.

It was late afternoon before Mr. Vincent's whale was finally lanced. All three of the animals taken were small, and the Old Man couldn't have had a more disgruntled expression on his mug if he had filled his mouth with sour pickles.

October 1. Lat. 07° 55′ N., long. 24 S. The fifth month of our pilgrimage begins. Brisk southerly or head winds, ending in a tumbling calm which is, of course, far more unpleasant than a dead calm.

At nine o'clock this morning a big sperm whale was sighted, going quickly to windward and blowing out conspicuous and regular spouts. While three boats were being lowered, he crossed our bow at close range and I had a superb view of him from halfway up the rigging. His progression was marked by a gentle rocking or pitching, the blunt junk and the hump on the afterback alternately rising and falling. The flukes did not break the surface at any stage of their stroke. The appearance of ease, smoothness, and speed was exceedingly impressive.

The first sign of the forward end on the upswing was usually the spout, which burst forth a split second before the tip of the snout was exposed. The spout was slanted in the direction of the whale's course, and it fountained out for at least two seconds, perhaps longer. Mainly condensed vapor, it included also a basal spray of water due to the fact that violent expulsion of the breath began before the spiracle had quite reached the open air. This is contrary to what the books describe to us.

When the snout was at its high point, possibly eighteen inches above the water, I could see the mound made by the dilated lips of the single nostril as air was sucked back into the lungs. Then the whole head rocked slowly down, the long back rose and leveled, and the gleaming but curiously crinkled and rubbery skin showed clearly. Finally, the angular hump pitched into view, for a moment exposing also several of the lesser knobs and notches that lie along the crest of the back between hump and flukes. When the hump was highest, the submerged junk was lowest, and vice versa.

In less time than it will take you to read this, of course, the whale was nearly out of sight. . . .

The boats returned empty-handed after an hour's chase.

The leverage of whaleboat oars is extremely powerful because each rower sits at the end of his thwart farthest from his oarlock. Midship oar, with its oarlock on the starboard gunwale, is the longest—eighteen feet. Bow and tub oars, respectively afore and aft of the midship oar, are shorter and of identical length. They both rest on the port gunwale. Harpooner and after (or stroke) oars, nearest bow and stern and both starboard, are the shortest of all and likewise identical. Thus one long and two shorts to starboard work against two of medium length to port. And how our boats skim and fly when they race all abreast toward the brig!

Getting through the doldrums and across the Equator is a tedious and discouraging process. I hope that the South Atlantic will turn out to be more exciting, and that we may sight South Georgia before Christmas. Sometimes, when I think of the endless weeks of our southward course, I become fearful of the return. Last voyage the *Daisy* spent seven months on the way between South Georgia and New Bedford.

October 2. Evidently we are once more on sperm-whale grounds. At half-past six this morning the boats were down after a big bull, but again in vain. In midmorning, however, a school was sighted and the lowering, hauling aback, and all other maneuvers were repeated.

The three boats became widely scattered, and one went so far out into the dim horizon that we lost sight of it for a time. However, each crew killed its whale. It was half-past three in the afternoon before we had the carcasses all alongside, and also before anybody had a dollop of grub beyond his early breakfast. Moreover, the meal was a quick and a poor one, and Mr. da Lomba got the cutting-in started without stopping for a bite.

All three whales were rather small, and the cutting-in was completed at night. Then mincing and boiling were begun, while the last whale was still being hacked and stripped by artificial illumination. Between half-past eight and nine o'clock in the evening we had supper in shifts. The meal was at least hearty—hash of salt beef, potatoes, and onions, sperm-whale steak, corn hoecakes, and tea. Work is to be continued through the night. . . .

October 10. Evening. This has been the most exciting day of my life. Even though the cabin lamp is a poor, dull flicker, I must pour my experiences onto paper while they are still fluid.

The morning broke gray and overcast, with a strong wind whipping the ocean. About eight o'clock a squall blew up, bringing a torrent of rain which was just at its height when a school of sperm whales rose a few ship's lengths to windward. The boats were at once cleared on the davits and all hands stood by. The rain presently slackened and the weather brightened enough for us to see at least two pods of whales spouting off our quarter, and others astern. When the order, "Lower away!" was shouted and echoed, I slid down into the mate's boat and took stroke oar, replacing a Dominican who remained with the ship-tenders.

Seeing that the spouts were fast pulling to leeward, we stepped the mast, after reefing, for the wind was brisk and the sea choppy. As soon as the whales had sounded, indicating that they were foraging and not alarmed, we zigzagged and jibed to hold our headway, while we lashed the line tubs to the thwarts, poured sea water over the rope, and put all gear in order. Then the blue waif at the *Daisy's* masthead signaled "whales up" and gave direction. Mr. da Lomba pulled the tiller sharply; once more we jibed and made off before the wind, with the other two boats running abreast of us on either side. By this time it was raining a deluge again and we were drenched to the skin.

While we were bearing down toward the school, which was now steaming at the surface in preparation for the next dive, two good-sized bulls popped up unexpectedly just ahead and we were whisked upon them. The nearer of the pair crossed our bow and, while its gray body glided along a little under water, Emiliano drove the iron into the whale's right side, just in front of the hump. As the beast leaped forward, his whole massive head breached above the surface and his flukes grazed the keel as he cleared us and dashed to windward, making the wet line groan when it tautened and began to rub round the loggerhead.

Sail was dropped, mast lowered, and rudder unshipped, while harpooner and mate changed ends, the latter forsaking the helm for the still more ticklish business of lancing.

Our whale's run was for only a short distance. Coming up with others of the school, he joined them, and we could see him lying calmly at the surface. We four oarsmen now hauled line, the boat-steerer holding the turn around the loggerhead and coiling slack in the stern sheets as it was paid in. We pulled as hard and as fast as we could and, when we neared the whale, a strange sight was presented through the curtain of rain. Our whale lay wallowing, the harpoon shaft projecting from his blubbery back; beyond him were three or four half-grown calves. On the near side lay a second bull, belly up, his jaw and most of his head out of water, and our harpoon line caught between two of his teeth.

Mr. da Lomba gesticulated frantically for the other boats to come up, and we waited silently but in a shiver of impatience. Before Mr. Vincent's boat could arrive, the bull which had fouled our line, and which had probably been puzzled by the obstacle, allowed it to slip from his jaw. We then hauled up on the whale to which we were fast and, when the keel pressed his side, the mate drove in the long keen lance to the socket. Within the same instant the hump hove up, the great flukes reared into the air, our bow went down with a jerk, and we shipped a couple of barrels of water as the whale sounded.

"Forty-barrel bull," said Mr. da Lomba.

Forty-barrel bull! I recalled then what the Old Man had told me long before, that no big sperm whale is likely to make as much excitement for a boat's crew as a lusty forty-barrel bull, enjoying the most active period of his watery life.

For a quarter of an hour we bobbed about quietly within a small area, the line snubbed round the loggerhead, Emiliano expressing the sentiment of all good boat-steerers by slackening it as little as possible and only at the last moment of safety. Then the expected burst of vapor appeared to windward, the lopsided head began to seesaw with the pointed hump, and we shot ahead on our sleigh ride.

The sun broke through the lowering clouds, thawing out our gooseflesh while we strained at the line and gradually gained on our unwillingly harnessed beast. But the whale had been goaded to alertness, and the lance puncture had been too far aft to affect his staying powers. Before we attained even pitch-poling distance, he sounded again, jerked us about, carried us back two miles before the wind, and then, without rising to the surface, plunged deeper, tearing the smoking line after him and soon exhausting the two hundred fathoms in the large tub. When the contents of the small tub began to follow, we were in a quandary. But in the nick of time one of the other boats sailed alongside; we bent on borrowed line, and saved our forty barrels.

In the middle of this fight into which I was putting all I had, I confess to a certain sympathy with the enemy. It seemed reasonable at least that after being pricked with the harpoon that still galled him, and pierced through with the horrible lance, the whale should wish to steer clear of us. This, however, was not at all the mate's idea of good form and fair play. Standing like an armed crusader in the bow of the boat, Long John da Lomba would scratch his head after the whale had sounded, and mutter, "I cain't understand what make that animile so goddam shy!"

Our status, I thought from time to time, was that of the tin can on a dog's tail. We annoyed the whale, but were otherwise pretty helpless.

Time flies with a fighting whale on one's hands. The sun climbed to the zenith and its pleasant beams alternated with cold showers while we sped over the rugged, white-capped Atlantic, wearing the skin off our palms in this yet-undecided tug-of-war. The whale battled nobly for his life. He tried sounding, spinning, and running all ways with respect to the wind. At one time he was towing three whaleboats, besides two drogue tubs, one of which is alleged to offer as much resistance as four boats. Watching one of these tubs dragged through the water at high speed made me marvel that the single tiny harpoon was not ripped from its anchorage in the blubber.

During a midday tempest, the roughest period of our chase, the whale pulled us cross-seas through the troughs and crests so that combers slopped over the gunwales. It was then that we kicked off our oilskin pants (I was the only man wearing shoes), so as to be unencumbered for swimming. Over and over again the bow was pulled completely under water, because a boat-steerer hates to slacken line. Three times we half-swamped and had to let the whale steal line while all hands bailed; indeed, the piggins and our sou'westers were employed thus more or less continuously.

I have a dreamlike mental background for the day's play—the choppy, spumy water and the varying sky, the heliotrope Portuguese men-o'-war that seemed to bob past us, the bright flying fish scared up, the inquisitive

Mother Carey's chickens that fluttered astern; and, focus of it all, straight ahead, the rocking, shiny back of our forty-barrel bull, with an impertinent little harpoon sticking there.

The brig appeared to shunt about magically, being now abeam, now close aboard off the bow, now nearly hull down astern. Fortunately we were moving mostly in wide circles, for otherwise we should have been towed out of sight and would have had to cut line. Time and again we slacked away and tried to give another boat an opportunity to sail upon the brute and plant a second iron, but he was all wariness. When the boats came ever so softly within three or four lengths, he would kick up his big flukes and be gone. Mr. da Lomba eventually shot a bomb lance into the whale's back, but the rubber-feathered end of it broke off and went whizzing over the sea, while the cylinder failed to explode. Three more bombs from a shoulder gun were likewise vainly spent and the mate concluded that the charges were watersoaked.

The turning point of the struggle came when the frantic whale once more fell in with a gam of his fellows. The calming influence of neighbors was soon apparent, for he allowed us to draw right toward him. We pulled ourselves through an acre of sperm whales, big bulls that we might have touched with oars, cows at arm's length, and tiny calves, ten or twelve feet long, with huge remoras clinging to their flanks. Such company lay unconcernedly awash all about us, but we paid it scant attention because it is quite sufficient to be fast to one sperm whale at a time.

"Shush, easy, easy boys," whispered Mr. da Lomba; "trim the boat; don't shift your quids."

We hauled softly along the length of another whale and, when our line was as short as a dog leash, the mate braced his thigh in the clumsy-cleat, raised his long, powerful arms, and buried the five-foot shank of the lance in blubber and flesh. The tortured whale quivered and sank. We peered tensely over the side of his dark hulk, knowing that the sounding would be brief and that he might rise beneath us. The mate pounded and pried the twisted lance shaft into a semblance of straightness.

"Stern all!" Up came the whale under our keel. While we just avoided capsizing, the lance struck home twice or thrice again through the froth before the whale got under way on another lap of his race. Then everything was repeated. Once more we were drenched. Again we bailed and hauled and slackened and hauled and bailed.

Finally, the second officer's boat, which had been back to the brig, transferred to us a case of dry bombs. Late in the afternoon, when we once more entered a troop of whales, the crucial opportunity was seized. A bomb was shot into the brute's lungs, where it exploded with a muffled crack. In his leap, he half-filled our boat with water for the last time, but he no longer had the breath to sound. His spout, formerly so thin and white, reflecting tiny rainbows in the rays of the low sun, now became first pink and then crimson and gouted.

"His chimney's afire!" said Mr. da Lomba, with a heartless chuckle.

Mr. Almeida's boat closed in with ours. Lances were thrust between the whale's ribs, held there, and churned, until the creature went into his ghastly flurry, all the while belching squids from his gullet until we floated in a slimy pool of their remains.

He died and turned fin out after giving us nine thrilling hours. We chopped a hole through one of his flukes, attached a line, and rested, weary but content, munching hard bread, drinking fresh water, and awaiting the arrival of the distant brig which, happily, was then to windward. After all the bluster of the day, the sun set in a calm sky. Mars, burning red, followed closely on the same track and was hanging like a lamp on the waters when the *Daisy* bore down and gathered us in.

Gentleman Adventurer*

JOHN A. HUNTER

✳✳ John A. Hunter, who has recounted many of his own adventures as a professional white hunter in *Hunter* (1952), is represented here with a story of one of the pioneer "race of giants" who helped settle Africa. ✳✳

COLONEL GROGAN

In the winter of 1899, Captain Dunn, a British officer stationed in Egypt, took a small native craft and went on a shooting and fishing trip along the Sobat River in the lower Sudan. He stopped to camp one night on the shore. South of him lay thousands of miles of jungle, swamps, and desert, unmapped and unexplored. Captain Dunn's astonishment may well be imagined when, the next morning, he saw coming out of this wilderness a small group of porters, clearly at their last gasp, led by a young Englishman with an unlit pipe in his mouth and a sporting rifle slung over his shoulder. The young man's face was swollen by mosquito bites, he was flushed with fever, and he was clearly unable to use one arm. The porters collapsed on the ground, but the stranger removed his pipe and bowed politely.

Their conversation has been recorded. It went like this:

Captain Dunn: "How do you do?"

The Stranger: "Oh, very fit, thanks. How are you? Had any sport?"

Captain Dunn: "Pretty fair. Have a drink? You must be hungry. I'll hurry on lunch. Had any shooting?"

But at lunch, the captain's English reserve gave way and he could not help blurting out, "Excuse me, but do you mind telling me where the devil you came from?"

"From the Cape," replied the stranger.

* From *Tales of the African Frontier,* copyright, 1954, by John A. Hunter and Daniel P. Mannix, reprinted by permission of the publishers, Harper & Brothers, New York.

The Cape of Good Hope lay four thousand miles to the south—four thousand miles of country full of cannibal tribes, wild beasts, and mountain ranges. It was generally considered well-nigh impassable. Captain Dunn may well have thought the young man delirious. Yet this was not the case. He had indeed made this amazing trek on foot, the first man in history to accomplish the feat.

The young man was Ewart S. Grogan, now Colonel Grogan, and I am proud to say he is a friend of mine. After his famous walk, he settled in Kenya and now has a magnificent farm near Taveta in the southern part of the colony. Although now in his eightieth year, the colonel is still as slim and straight as he was when he walked from the Cape to Cairo. A prominent figure in the government, he is equally famous for his great knowledge of African affairs and his biting wit. Although many stories could be told of him, I will confine this narrative to an account of his notable walk, which I consider one of the great feats of all time. I have based this story on the colonel's writings and he has been kind enough to fill in a number of details not mentioned in his diary of the trip.

The flip of a ha'penny started Ewart Grogan on his adventuresome career. His father, a prosperous land agent, sent the boy to Cambridge and, after graduation, young Ewart decided to become an artist. His father, nothing loath, sent the boy to one of the best art schools in the country. But as Grogan now admits, "After being at the school a while, I didn't particularly like the look of the kind of people who were artists." One day his bearded teacher held up a sketch the young man was working on and after examining it said impressively, "If you work for many years, living, dreaming, thinking nothing but art, art, art, then you may someday be a great artist." He waited for the young man to faint with joy.

"But I'm not sure that I want to be an artist," remarked Grogan. "I think that I'd rather be a policeman."

His teacher nearly exploded with rage. "I suggest you make up your mind," he snapped.

"Right you are," agreed Grogan. He pulled a ha'penny out of his pocket. "Heads, I become an artist. Tails, I become a policeman." He flipped the coin. It came down tails. "Sorry!" said Grogan politely. Getting his hat and coat, he left the studio, never to return.

Grogan did indeed become a policeman but it was a policeman of a somewhat special sort. The Matabele Uprising had broken out in South Africa, one of the numerous native wars with which the British Empire was constantly plagued during the Victorian era, and Grogan enlisted as a trooper. He joined a gun crew and served as Number Four man on a muzzle-loading seven-pounder. After the war Grogan returned to England so wasted by fever that the doctors thought he might never completely recover.

This was a sore blow to young Grogan, for during his tour of service in South Africa, he had met Cecil Rhodes and caught that remarkable man's dream of a British Africa, extending from Cape Town to the shores of the Mediterranean. Rhodes believed that the first requirement for linking the vast continent together was a railroad running down the spine of Africa, to open the interior to commerce. But was such a railroad possible? What mountain ranges would it have to cross, how many rivers, how many stretches of jungle and desert? Even more important, would it have to cut across areas already parceled out among nations hostile to Great Britain? It was Grogan's dream to make the long trek from the Cape to Cairo and map a possible route for the proposed railway.

However, the doctors told the young man that he must take a rest before even considering such an adventure. A long sea voyage was advised, and Grogan decided to go to New Zealand and stay with an old Cambridge chum who had settled there. During the voyage he studied books on engineering and surveying and by the time he arrived in New Zealand, he had a rough knowledge of the subject.

His friend had an extremely pretty sister named Gertrude Watt. She and Ewart Grogan fell in love. They planned marriage but Miss Watt had a guardian who did not approve of Ewart.

"Young man, you appear to be drifting down the river of life without a rudder," the pompous old gentleman told Grogan. "A girl in the position of my ward can expect to marry an outstanding man."

Grogan reflected, "If I were to walk from the Cape to Cairo, would you consider me sufficiently outstanding?"

The older man was not amused. "I can only suppose that you are either a fool or have decided to play one. The jungles of Central Africa are impassable. Stanley was able to get about only on rivers and he had to take an armed guard of six hundred men to fight off the native tribes. To traverse the continent you would need a small army."

"Oh, hardly that," remarked Grogan. "If you have a large group, you arouse suspicion. I believe a small party could get through without too much trouble." This, then, might be said to be the start of the famous walk. Grogan returned to England and a few months later sailed for South Africa in company with another young man named Arthur Henry Sharp, who had decided to come along part of the way.

I should like here to say a few words about the typical upper-middle-class young Englishman of the Victorian era, of which these two young men were fine examples. According to our modern standards, they were in many ways a pampered lot. It was taken for granted that they would attend the best schools and afterward go to a famous university. The problem of making a living was a minor one, for their parents were usually well off. They were a class born to command and to possessions. Yet there was another side to the lives of these young men which is now largely forgotten.

They were brought up under a code so strict that many today would regard it as just short of brutality. When still children, they were sent off to schools where the slightest infringement of the rules was punished by a cane in the hands of a master or a prefect. For a boy to shirk the roughest games or complain of the most savage bullying promptly condemned him as an effeminate sniveler. They were generally introduced to blood sports as soon as they could sit a horse or hold a gun, and for many of them the seasons of the year were divided up according to what animal it was appropriate to hunt or shoot. To many people this would seem a faulty upbringing, but most of the young men grew up from childhood knowing how to handle a gun, how to endure hardship and how to put their horses at the most difficult hedge without flinching.

When Grogan and Sharp left on their memorable trip, they were already first-class shots. The habit of command was strong in them, and in dealing with savage and unruly porters this ability was worth more than all the beads and trinkets in Africa. There was still another side to their nature, also typical of the time. Although they could take only the barest essentials on such a trip, they included several volumes of poetry as naturally as they included ammunition for their guns.

The two young explorers differed strikingly in appearance. The pictures of Grogan show him as a slender, clean-shaven youth who always seemed to have a pipe stuck nonchalantly in the corner of his mouth. Sharp wore the mustache and carefully trimmed whiskers so fashionable among the young men of the period. He was a quieter, more matter-of-fact individual than Grogan but with an almost equal love of adventure. For equipment they had a battery that consisted principally of two sporting magazine .303 rifles —weapons I would consider somewhat light for even the larger antelopes, but which in their hands served admirably for everything from ducks to elephants. Each man had a small tent, a camp cot, mosquito netting, and a few changes of clothing. Their medical equipment was a bottle of quinine and another of potassium permanganate for wounds. The bulk of their outfit consisted of boxes of beads and rolls of the brightly colored cloth called "Americani," manufactured in the United States and used as a standard form of currency among African tribes. They also took along cameras and surveying instruments. Although they had some supplies, they intended to rely mainly on their rifles to provide food for the expedition.

In February, 1898, the two young men arrived in South Africa and began their memorable trek. The beginning of the trip across the great, open plains of the veldt proved reasonably easy, yet it was here that they first encountered African big game. One afternoon while Grogan and Sharp were fishing, they were attacked by a buffalo. Grogan promptly dove into the stream in reckless disregard of the crocodile-infested waters. Sharp, who had no idea of the power of a buffalo, stood his ground. As coolly as though firing at a target on a rifle range, he put bullet after bullet into the oncoming bull. As he was using soft-nosed .303's, the odds were a hundred to one on the buffalo. But one of his shots broke the bull's jaw. The buffalo staggered and Sharp fired again, breaking the animal's fetlock. The buffalo rolled to within three yards of the young man who was then able to finish him off. As Grogan emerged dripping from the stream, Sharp said to him in tones of mild surprise, "I had no idea these animals could take so much punishment. Next time one charges me, I'll follow your example and get out of his way."

So far the young men had been able to travel by ox wagon and mule-drawn carts. But when they reached Salisbury in southern Rhodesia, there was no other means of transportation north except their own feet, and equipment had to be carried by porters. Generally, native porters refused to travel more than a few miles from their village. In each new district it was necessary to pay off the old group and hire a new batch. However, a few miles north of Salisbury, the young men were fortunate enough to hire some Watonga porters who had a taste for adventure. Four of these porters stayed with Grogan all the way to Cairo. He assured the porters that he would show them great mountains that spit fire and passes so high that water turned to stone. Grogan always claimed that the Watonga went with him mainly because they didn't want to miss the chance of being with such a talented liar.

The safari pressed northward until by April they reached Ujiji on Lake Tanganyika where Stanley had found Livingstone thirty years before. Tanganyika was now a German protectorate, but there were still a number of old Arabs in the town who had settled there in the days of Tippu Tib. Slavery had been abolished, but these elderly men were still being cared for by their old slaves who had refused freedom. Ahead of the young men lay a series of mountain ranges which the old Arabs assured them were impassable. But Grogan and Sharp determined to make the attempt. As there would be no game in the mountains, all food for the expedition would have to be carried by porters. They hired one hundred and thirty rough-looking local natives who said they were willing to go. Grogan and Sharp organized ten of their Watonga porters into a sort of tiny standing army to handle this wild crew and started across the range.

Trouble began almost immediately. The nights were so cold that the porters, used to the heavy heat of the lowlands, sat shivering around their campfires unable to get warm. The Watonga felt the change even more than the new porters. The expedition crossed a ridge seven thousand feet high, and the next morning two of the Watonga deserted. This was a particularly serious blow as Grogan and Sharp had looked on the Watonga as the noncommissioned officers of their little force.

The weather constantly grew worse. Every morning dawned with the mountains covered by a cold, dank mist. The men had to force their way through masses of mimosa bushes heavy with dew. Within a few minutes every man was as completely soaked as though he'd been under a shower. As the mist usually did not lift until afternoon, no one ever had a chance to get properly dried out. Sharp was bitten so badly by mosquitoes that his hands became infected and he could scarcely use them. Both he and Grogan began to have constant attacks of fever which they could not throw off because of the chill and constant wetting.

Then the ten Watongas who had served as guards deserted in a body. Sharp came down with blackwater fever. Grogan was semidelirious with malaria and running a temperature of 106.9. The two boys nursed each other and struggled on until they finally crossed the range and dropped down into a little valley on the other side. Ahead of them a new range of mountains stretched on, apparently endlessly, but in the valley was a small native village. Here they stopped—collapsed would be a better term—while their porters returned to Ujiji, leaving Grogan and Sharp with the last four of the Watongas.

They stayed in the village for several weeks. Grogan was in a "pitiable condition," as he wrote in his journal, and Sharp, although very little better, acted as nurse. Ahead of them lay unknown country, the first completely unexplored territory they had reached. "Our expedition was really only just beginning and yet there I was, dying before the trip had actually started," Grogan told me. For days the boy lay on his cot looking at that great sea of mountains ahead of him, some of the most magnificent scenery in all Africa. Somewhere beyond those ridges lay the great Kivu Lake and the volcanoes reported by earlier explorers who had come in from the East Coast. Whether or not it was possible to reach Kivu from the south still remained to be seen.

Grogan did not recover as rapidly as they had hoped. The intense, mucky heat of the valley seemed to augment his fever. At last it was decided to push on and see if he would not do better in the cool highlands. As he was too weak to walk, Sharp arranged to have him carried in a litter. A new group of porters was hired and the boys headed out across the valley toward the distant ridges.

I doubt if any other country in the world shows such sharp variations in climate as Africa. Central Africa is tropical but in the highlands a man can walk for days through great forests and swear that he is in Canada or Norway. Then, within a space of a few hours, he drops down into a valley full of palm trees and grass huts where elephants roam and the streams are full of crocodiles. By the next morning he may be crossing a desert where the only sign of life is an occasional lizard. That night he may reach a plateau region that closely resembles the English countryside—pleasant grasslands cut up by little streams flowing gently between green banks. In another day or two he may be floundering through papyrus swamps, being eaten alive by mosquitoes and listening to the bellow of hippos in the reeds around him.

In the next few weeks Grogan and Sharp passed through all these types of country and many more. They saw their first elephant. Grogan left his litter to stalk one big bull—he was still so weak that his porters followed him with the litter in case he fainted—but the elephant escaped. Then the expedition entered a well-inhabited, prosperous district. Great herds of cattle with enormous horns grazed on the mountain slopes, guarded by naked children who hardly came up to the beasts' bellies. In the lowlands were forests of banana trees, carefully cultivated. Women, nude to the waist, worked in the fields of peas and beans. As they approached the shores of Lake Kivu, Ngenzi, the king of the district, came out to greet them. He even accompanied them for several miles with his retinue as a gesture of friendship.

When the king had left, the young men proceeded to check their stores and discovered to their horror that the king had not departed empty-handed. Much of their precious clothing had been stolen, but this was a minor matter. A tin box had been taken, containing their sextants, artificial horizon, thermometers, and many of their records and photographs. In a few minutes much of the hard work of the last months had been lost and the value of the rest of the trip seriously curtailed.

The old chief foolishly hung about the outskirts of the safari, hoping for another windfall. The young men explained to him how important the missing articles were, but the chief professed complete ignorance of the whole affair. "There are many bad men in this country," he explained blandly. "I can't keep track of them."

Grogan and Sharp may have had many shortcomings, but indecision was not one of them. The astonished chief suddenly found himself looking down the muzzles of two rifles. Before he could protest, he was grabbed by the scruff of the neck and flung into the boys' tent. When his bodyguard moved in to rescue him, they were also confronted by the two steady guns. After thinking the matter over, the bodyguard decided to let the chief stay where he was.

After bitterly protesting his innocence, the chief finally asked to speak to some of his officials. He gave them a few orders and the men left, returning shortly with the boys' missing clothes. Grogan and Sharp demanded their records and instruments, but the chief denied all knowledge of them.

Then the explorers had an inspiration. The natives obviously cared little about the chief, but they were vitally interested in the welfare of their cattle. Leaving Sharp to guard the camp, Grogan took a small force of the porters and set out for the nearest village. There he and his men seized a herd of one hundred and ninety cattle and started driving them back to camp. Within a few minutes the alarm drums sounded and hundreds of armed warriors began to assemble on the hills. Through the guide-interpreter, the young men shouted to the warriors that they would return the cattle as soon as the contents of the tin box was returned.

The next morning the tribesmen sent in a deputation. "We have already returned your clothes and those were the only valuable things we took from you," they explained. "The other articles were worthless—you couldn't wear them, you couldn't eat them, you couldn't cook your food with them so we threw them down a crevice in the hills. They are gone for good, and even if you shoot the chief and take all the cattle in the country you can never get them back. Now please go away and leave us alone."

Brokenhearted and miserable, the boys could do nothing else. They could only make a resolve never to allow the instruments and records still remaining to get out of their sight even for a moment.

The expedition passed through the country of the Watusi, the giant men who average over seven feet in height and have for their slaves the Wahutu, the original inhabitants of the district. Although the Wahutu outnumbered their giant masters a hundred to one, they regarded them with almost superstitious awe and never questioned their authority. A few marches farther on, the young men saw their first pygmies, little men scarcely four feet tall who live on the borders of the giants' country.

So far Grogan and Sharp had been concerned about the natives' stealing from their porters. Now they ran into the problem of how to keep the porters from stealing from the natives. They passed through districts so poor that the porters could hire the local inhabitants to carry their loads for them. The average wage for a native at that time was three shillings a month (about seventy-five cents). For a few pennies the porters were able to employ helpers. Then as the safari passed through still more poverty-stricken areas, the substitutes hired substitutes, who in turn hired other substitutes until the load was finally carried by a small boy or a starving old man while the original porter and two or three "middle men" walked alongside like gentlemen of leisure. The young Englishmen did not feel it was their responsibility to interfere with this system as long as everyone was satisfied, but soon they received complaints from local chiefs that the idle porters were raiding villages, molesting girls, and looting houses. It must be remembered that one of the old foot safaris often stretched out for miles. The men were constantly stopping to rest, take snuff, chat, or readjust their loads. The safari seldom averaged more than ten miles a day and late-comers were usually dribbling into camp three or four hours after the main body. The two young Englishmen could not possibly patrol the entire safari.

Several of the looters, caught red-handed, were punished on the spot, the instrument of punishment being the terrible rhino hide whip known as the kiboko. But the looting and rape continued. The reputation of the expedition began to precede it. Instead of welcoming the travelers, the local inhabitants fled to the hills, taking their families and livestock with them as though before an invading army. Unable to buy food, Grogan and Sharp were once forced to cut enough bananas from a native plantation to feed the porters and themselves. "That was the only time in my life I ever commandeered food from natives," Grogan told me.

The young men decided that their half-wild porters would have to be put under some sort of discipline. The next day they forced the long, straggling line to close up, and that night kept the porters in camp instead of allowing them to bivouac in a village. The result was soon forthcoming. The whole body of porters deserted the next morning, leaving their loads scattered on the ground.

Grogan and Sharp started after them. They came on a small group and these Sharp stopped at the point of his revolver. Grogan kept on after the main body. Topping a little rise, he saw the deserting porters walking along below him. Grogan called to them to come back and one of the headmen, who had been a ringleader in the trouble-making, shouted an insult. Grogan fired, knocking off the man's head covering. The other porters found the bewildered expression on the headman's face so amusing that they burst into howls of laughter and returned willingly to camp. They gave no more trouble for several weeks.

On the other side of Lake Kivu, the expedition passed a number of great volcanoes, some of them still active, Grogan, who remembered how the Watonga natives had considered him a brilliant liar when he told them of the volcanoes, pointed out the smoking cones to the four who were still with him. "What do you think now?" he asked them.

"We still think you're a great liar, Bwana," said one of the boys cheerfully.

"But there are the burning mountains in front of you," protested Grogan.

"Bwana, there is no such thing as a burning mountain," said the boy confidently. "You put those there by magic in order to fool us."

Grogan gave up.

Many of the conelike peaks had never before been seen by white men. Grogan and Sharp mapped the district and named several of the unknown mountains. One of them was named Mount Watt by Grogan, in honor, needless to say, of the pretty young girl in New Zealand who had played so prominent a part in launching the expedition. . . .

In spite of illness, porter troubles, and geographical obstacles, the safari continued to push on, making fairly good time. Then the party reached the borders of Mushari, between Lake Kivu and Lake Albert Edward. Here they came to a halt.

Between them and the Mushari district lay several miles of old lava beds —black, rocky, sharp-pointed rivers of stone that formed a serious barrier to the barefooted porters. But the lava beds were little more than a detail. The local natives assured the young men that a nomadic, cannibal tribe had swept into Mushari from the Congo and was laying the whole country waste. Grogan and Sharp were not fools. They had no desire to walk into the center of a district torn by native wars. So they spent several weeks trying to find some way to go around the area. On their first attempt their native guide deserted them in a forest of impenetrable bamboo. They were miles from water and had a hard time making their way back to camp. They made a second attempt with another guide. He also deserted them, having first taken them to the top of a particularly unpleasant mountain. At this point Grogan lost his temper.

He decided to go directly over the lava beds and so through Mushari. "I didn't believe that there were any cannibals there and if there were, I no longer cared," he admits. "I was sick of listening to native lies and native deceits. I was told that it was impossible to cross the beds. I was told there was no water there and we would all die of thirst. I was told that the country was full of savage lions. Then all our porters claimed that they were sick. They hobbled around with sticks, swearing they were too weak to walk. Fortunately they had made themselves so unpopular with the local natives that they didn't dare be left behind and as soon as they saw we were determined to push on, they started making sandals for the trip over the lava and collecting water skins."

It was decided that Grogan would go on with a small force and Sharp would follow later with the heavier equipment and a small flock of goats which were needed as food, there being no game in the district and no way of preserving meat in the intense heat.

So at dawn one morning Grogan started out with his little force across the supposedly impassable lava beds. "It was very much like crossing the Aiguille-du-Dru glacier in Europe, with blocks of stone instead of blocks of ice," he told me. By late afternoon they had crossed the beds and reached the fertile country on the other side. They camped that night by a little pool of clear water, delighted at having so easily surmounted the barrier.

The next morning Grogan was astonished to see men and women who had been living in holes among the lava rocks like wild animals, come crawling out to beg for food. These wretched people told him that a few weeks before the Bareka, a cannibal tribe, had invaded the country and were killing and eating everyone they could catch. "At night we steal down to our grain fields and try to grab a few armfuls of the unripened grain," a shivering woman told him. "But the Bareka are watching the fields and each time they catch some of us."

Grogan fed the poor creatures, but he privately thought they were probably the victims of one of the innumerable tribal wars which were so common as hardly to attract comment. Like most Europeans, he regarded cannibalism as something of a myth. He managed to persuade one of the men to act as a guide across the district and started on.

The little party now passed through some of the most beautiful country of the entire journey. On the horizon a line of great volcanoes stood out against the sky like a Japanese painting. They walked along a well-defined path leading through green, rolling country, dotted here and there with groups of little grass huts squatting under stately trees. The emerald green of the banana plantations contrasted with the gold of the ripening grain fields, and in the distance lay vast rolls of purple hills.

As they neared the first of the grain fields, Grogan could hardly believe his eyes. Along the edges were scattered the remains of the natives who had been caught the night before by the cannibals. Cooking fires were still smoldering beside congealing pools of fresh blood. In a daze the little party kept on. Every few yards they passed a spot where trampled grass, a few torn bits of clothing, white bones, and the black ashes of a fire showed where one of the unhappy villagers had been captured. It was like walking through a huge abattoir set in the Garden of Eden.

As Grogan and his men topped a little rise, they were silhouetted against the sky for a few brief moments. Instantly they were seen by a group of the Bareka who were camped in one of the captured villages. The cannibals had not expected anyone to walk into the area in broad daylight and so had kept no watch. But after one astonished look, they leaped to their feet, grabbing up their spears and shields, and charged Grogan's party howling like wolves.

"What are they saying?" Grogan asked his guide.

"They say that they're going to kill and eat us," said the anxious guide.

"Indeed?" said Grogan. He unslung his sporting rifle from his shoulder and kneeling beside a clump of grass took steady aim. When the oncoming Bareka were within comfortable range, Grogan dropped the leader. The cannibals simply shouted the louder and came on. They knew about firearms and had expected to lose one man. But the firearms they had encountered hitherto were the muzzle-loading muskets of Arab traders. Grogan fired again and another Bareka fell. Now the yells grew less confident but still the raiders did not stop. Grogan dropped four more men in rapid succession. At last the Bareka broke and ran for cover, terrified by this strange new weapon that apparently never ran out of ammunition.

Reloading, Grogan led his party toward the now-deserted village. A cloud of vultures rose from the place as he approached. The Bareka and their families had been interrupted at breakfast. Their fires were burning and their cooking utensils still in place. Grogan and his men walked through the street of the empty village. They passed a string of human entrails drying on a stick, a pot of soup stewing over a fire covered with human fat, a partly gnawed thighbone with shreds of half-cooked meat attached, and a head with the top of the skull removed as though for a trepanning operation sitting on some hot coals. A spoon was still sticking in the sizzling brains. Nearby was a partly roasted hand, still impaled on the end of a long stick which had been used as a toasting fork. By the next fire was a child's head, partly skinned, with one cheek and one eye eaten, the other eye still in place and staring. The stench was incredible. Over the whole village floated a black blizzard of scraggly-necked vultures and carrion crows.

"I can only say that although my porters were hardly delicately minded, they went without food for forty-eight hours rather than touch so much as a yam growing in that accursed ground," Grogan recalls.

Grogan sent a runner back to warn Sharp not to attempt to cross the district but to find another route north no matter what the difficulties. Grogan and his party were by no means out of danger. He describes the next two days as the worst of his life. He and his men traveled fast, hoping to escape from the area before the Bareka could recover from their alarm. Every village through which he passed had been sacked and burned. "Skeletons, skeletons everywhere!" he wrote in his diary to describe this dreadful place. The next district had also been destroyed by the cannibals and even the next. The Bareka lived on human beings much as some other tribes lived on game animals and, when they had exhausted one area, moved on to the next.

Grogan and his men traveled from dawn to dark. They were afraid to stay on the trails and had to force their way through the jungles. Food became a major problem. Even drinking water was scarce as the streams were polluted with corpses.

While the party was skirting the edges of a papyrus swamp, they suddenly came on a small group of the Bareka. The raiders instantly charged, yelling with delight. Grogan dodged a spear and fired into them. One man dropped. The rest ran, leaving behind them two women and two small children. Grogan examined his captives. They were miserably thin. "Things are very hard with us," explained one of the women pathetically. "There are fifty people in our party, and in the last week our men have only been able to catch two people." Grogan took the women and children along with him, partly as guides and partly as hostages. Later Grogan shot some game and the starving cannibals fell on it like hyenas, though Grogan is convinced that they missed what was to them a "normal" flavor in their meat.

Grogan's party finally managed to win clear of the cannibal area and camped for several days until Sharp, who had come by a different route, managed to catch up to them with the main safari. Reunited, the two young men worked their way north along the shores of Lake Albert Edward to Uganda. Here they separated permanently. Sharp decided to go east, crossing what is today Kenya, and take ship at Mombasa for England. Grogan continued northward, following the course of the Nile toward Egypt.

Grogan was now completely on his own and it is hard to understand how he ever managed to get through those terrible miles of swamp and desert. He lived with fever. He was almost never free from the weakening effects of dysentery. In one place the only additional porters he could find were an old dervish prisoner with a broken leg, a small boy, and a criminal lunatic in chains. A few days later, while Grogan was away trying to shoot some food, the lunatic called in the local natives and carefully distributed all Grogan's equipment among them. Then he deserted. The honest natives waited until Grogan got back and returned his belongings to him. Grogan hired canoes and tried to go north by water, but the Nile was so blocked by masses of floating water plants called *sudd* that he had to abandon this plan. He spent one night with the Baris, a people who had been driven out of their country by the warlike Dinkas and lived on islands in the river made of the compressed *sudd*. The mosquitoes were so bad here that at night the Baris covered themselves with dung, leaving only a small opening for breathing, and slept as though encased in plaster casts. All through this district the mosquitoes were a constant nightmare. One of his porters who fell sick and could not drive them off was literally killed by them during the night. Once Grogan was driven to firing the dry reeds and he and his porters sat in the smoke to obtain a few hours of relief from the insects.

During this part of the trip Grogan had serious trouble with the natives only once. While passing through the Dinka territory, his group was surrounded by over a hundred of these giant people. The Dinkas averaged over six and a half feet and were stark naked. They wore their hair in a tuft, somewhat like the crest on a dragoon's helmet, which added to their height. At first these strange people seemed friendly. They crowded around the terrified porters, fingering their loads and trying to talk to them. All might have gone well if the porters had not lost their heads and bolted. Instantly the Dinkas attacked them, much as a dog will snap at anything running from it. One of the porters was speared. Two more went down under the Dinkas' clubs. Grogan was carrying a double-barreled rifle. He shot the Dinka chief and another man. At the same instant he was attacked by a giant Dinka swinging a club. Grogan took the blow on his arm and jammed the empty gun into the man's belly. The Dinka staggered back, giving Grogan a chance to reload. He shot the man and then fired into the thick of the yelling crowd. They sullenly drew back, leaving one of the porters dying and three more insensible from club wounds.

"I never expected to see England again," Grogan admits. However, he managed to get his hysterical porters together and went on, the Dinkas following. Once, Grogan stopped and shot two more of them. The rest withdrew to a safer distance but still continued to follow.

"Camp that night was hardly a cheerful place," Grogan said. "Exhausted as we were, we still had to post sentries. I had a bad cold and my arm was so stiff from the club blow that I could hardly use it. My cook was crippled with dysentery, one of my porters had an infected foot which almost prevented him from walking, and two of the porters who had been clubbed were delirious. We could not make a fire as there was no fuel in the area. I found that my last two tins of tobacco had gone moldy so I could not even enjoy a smoke. The mosquitoes were so thick that they took turns sitting on my empty pipe, waiting for a chance to bite me."

The next morning they went on. One of the porters who lagged behind vanished and was never seen again. Day after day the little party struggled north, sometimes through swamps where they waded in mud up to their chests and sometimes across stretches of waterless desert. All the porters were sick. They had to be prodded along at the point of a spear to keep them from lying down and dying. There was no sign of game and the last of the grain that the porters were carrying had given out. Grogan computed that in another four days' travel, he should reach the Sobat River where there should be hippo and possibly water birds. But could they last four more days? Grogan seriously doubted it.

Then, while plodding across the desert, Grogan saw ahead of him a long, thin stick swaying in the wind. It did not look like a tree. It was too tall for a reed. Hardly daring to believe the truth, Grogan realized it was the mast of a small boat. He had reached the Sobat. A few minutes later he met Captain Dunn, the owner of the boat.

From the Sobat, Grogan and his men went on by boat to Cairo. The news of his amazing feat had preceded him and in Cairo the young man went from dinner to dinner and from reception to reception. The four Watonga porters, who had stayed with Grogan all through the long trip from Nyasaland, were interested but not unduly impressed by the wonders of civilization. One day Grogan was out with his gunbearer when they saw a train speeding across the desert toward them. The gunbearer tapped Grogan on the shoulder, pointed to the oncoming train, and then casually handed him his elephant gun.

Grogan returned to New Zealand where he and Miss Watt were married. They traveled extensively in Europe and the United States, but like many another man, Grogan could not get Africa out of his blood. When the Boer War came, he promptly enlisted as a captain in the Fourth Royal Münster Fusiliers. An attack of malaria laid him low, and he was hospitalized next to another young man who was planning to go to Kenya after the war and start a timber concern. The two men formed a partnership and at the end of hostilities, traveled to Nairobi, then a city of tents. Here Mrs. Grogan joined her husband.

The young colony was racked by many troubles, not the least of them being the problem of administrating an area three times the size of the British Isles with a force of a few hundred white men. Grogan threw himself enthusiastically into politics. His methods hardly endeared him to the government, but they were effective. At one period a defect in the mining laws allowed a man to stake out a claim anywhere in the colony. Irresponsible men were laying out mining claims across the intended routes of main highways and valuable farming lands. After vainly pleading with the government to have the law altered, Grogan went out one evening and gravely pegged out a claim all around Nairobi. A special meeting of the alarmed council had to be called in the middle of the night to change the law as Grogan was threatening to start tearing up the main street with a pickax.

Grogan left Kenya to take part in the First World War during which he received his colonelcy and a D.S.O. In World War II, he acted as the West Coast liaison officer for the British forces. In his later years, the colonel decided to take up farming. He and Mrs. Grogan settled at Taveta, not far from the Tanganyika border. By an ingenious system of irrigation canals, he tapped the melting snows of Kilimanjaro and turned what was once one of the most barren and desolate stretches of bush country in all Kenya into one of the most prosperous farms.

There were many young men like Colonel Grogan in the England of fifty years ago. Today, I fear that they are a vanishing breed. The world is the poorer for their passing.

A Man Called Horse*

DOROTHY M. JOHNSON

✳✳ Dorothy M. Johnson was born in Iowa and grew up in Whitefish, Montana, on the Great Northern Railroad in the northwest corner of the state. In her childhood she absorbed many of the legends and stories of that part of the West. After graduating from the University of Montana, she worked as a secretary in Washington and Wisconsin and for the next fifteen years was a book and magazine editor in New York. In 1950 she returned to Whitefish, where she became news editor for the weekly Whitefish *Pilot,* later secretary-manager of the Montana State Press Association with the title assistant professor in the U. of M. School of Journalism. She is also Honorary Police Chief of Whitefish.

"Man's efforts—and sometimes his failure—to adapt to his environment fascinate me," she writes. "I have a theory that most of the white men who peopled the frontier West went there because they did not quite fit in back home. They were too rash or violent or ambitious or lazy or poor; they did not match the pattern. But the nineteenth century was a time of freedom for those who did not fit. They could always move westward. Sometimes they did not fit there either. Sometimes they found a strange but perfect world. And sometimes, like the captive Easterner in 'A Man Called Horse,' they achieved greatness." ✳✳

He was a young man of good family, as the phrase went in the New England of a hundred-odd years ago, and the reasons for his bitter discontent were unclear, even to himself. He grew up in the gracious old Boston home under his grandmother's care, for his mother had died in giving him birth; and all his life he had known every comfort and privilege his father's wealth could provide.

But still there was the discontent, which puzzled him because he could not even define it. He wanted to live among his equals—people who were no better than he and no worse either. That was as close as he could come

---

* From *Indian Country,* copyright, 1949, 1950, 1951, 1952, 1953, by Dorothy Johnson. Appeared in *Better Living.* Published by Ballantine Books, 1954, reprinted by permission of the author's agent, McIntosh & Otis, Inc., New York.

to describing the source of his unhappiness in Boston and his restless desire to go somewhere else.

In the year 1845 he left home and went out West, far beyond the country's creeping frontier, where he hoped to find his equals. He had the idea that in Indian country, where there was danger, all white men were kings, and he wanted to be one of them. But he found, in the West as in Boston, that the men he respected were still his superiors, even if they could not read, and those he did not respect weren't worth talking to.

He did have money, however, and he could hire the men he respected. He hired four of them, to cook and hunt and guide and be his companions, but he found them not friendly.

They were apart from him and he was still alone. He still brooded about his status in the world, longing for his equals.

On a day in June, he learned what it was to have no status at all. He became a captive of a small raiding party of Crow Indians.

He heard gunfire and the brief shouts of his companions around the bend of the creek just before they died, but he never saw their bodies. He had no chance to fight, because he was naked and unarmed, bathing in the creek, when a Crow warrior seized and held him.

His captor let him go at last, let him run. Then the lot of them rode him down for sport, striking him with their coup sticks. They carried the dripping scalps of his companions, and one had skinned off Baptiste's black beard as well, for a trophy.

They took him along in a matter-of-fact way, as they took the captured horses. He was unshod and naked as the horses were, and like them he had a rawhide thong around his neck. So long as he didn't fall down, the Crows ignored him.

On the second day they gave him his breeches. His feet were too swollen for his boots, but one of the Indians threw him a pair of moccasins that had belonged to the half-breed, Henri, who was dead back at the creek. The captive wore the moccasins gratefully. The third day they let him ride one of the spare horses so the party could move faster, and on that day they came in sight of their camp.

He thought of trying to escape, hoping he might be killed in flight rather than by slow torture in the camp, but he never had a chance to try. They were more familiar with escape than he was and, knowing what to expect, they forestalled it. The only other time he had tried to escape from anyone, he had succeeded. When he had left his home in Boston, his father had raged and his grandmother had cried, but they could not talk him out of his intention.

The men of the Crow raiding party didn't bother with talk.

Before riding into camp they stopped and dressed in their regalia and in parts of their victims' clothing; they painted their faces black. Then, leading the white man by the rawhide around his neck as though he were a horse, they rode down toward the tepee circle, shouting and singing, brandishing their weapons. He was unconscious when they got there; he fell and was dragged.

He lay dazed and battered near a tepee while the noisy, busy life of the camp swarmed around him and Indians came to stare. Thirst consumed him, and when it rained he lapped rain water from the ground like a dog. A scrawny, shrieking, eternally busy old woman with ragged graying hair threw a chunk of meat on the grass, and he fought the dogs for it.

When his head cleared, he was angry, although anger was an emotion he knew he could not afford.

It was better when I was a horse, he thought—when they led me by the rawhide around my neck. I won't be a dog, no matter what!

The hag gave him stinking, rancid grease and let him figure out what it was for. He applied it gingerly to his bruised and sun-seared body.

Now, he thought, I smell like the rest of them.

While he was healing, he considered coldly the advantages of being a horse. A man would be humiliated, and sooner or later he would strike back and that would be the end of him. But a horse had only to be docile. Very well, he would learn to do without pride.

He understood that he was the property of the screaming old woman, a fine gift from her son, one that she liked to show off. She did more yelling at him than at anyone else, probably to impress the neighbors so they would not forget what a great and generous man her son was. She was bossy and proud, a dreadful sag of skin and bones, and she was a devilish hard worker.

The white man, who now thought of himself as a horse, forgot sometimes to worry about his danger. He kept making mental notes of things to tell his own people in Boston about this hideous adventure. He would go back a hero, and he would say, "Grandmother, let me fetch your shawl. I've been accustomed to doing little errands for another lady about your age."

Two girls lived in the tepee with the old hag and her warrior son. One of them, the white man concluded, was his captor's wife and the other was his little sister. The daughter-in-law was smug and spoiled. Being beloved, she did not have to be useful. The younger girl had bright, wandering eyes. Often enough they wandered to the white man who was pretending to be a horse.

The two girls worked when the old woman put them at it, but they were always running off to do something they enjoyed more. There were games and noisy contests, and there was much laughter. But not for the white man. He was finding out what loneliness could be.

That was a rich summer on the plains, with plenty of buffalo for meat and clothing and the making of tepees. The Crows were wealthy in horses, prosperous and contented. If their men had not been so avid for glory, the white man thought, there would have been a lot more of them. But they went out of their way to court death, and when one of them met it, the whole camp mourned extravagantly and cried to their God for vengeance.

The captive was a horse all summer, a docile bearer of burdens, careful and patient. He kept reminding himself that he had to be better-natured than other horses, because he could not lash out with hoofs or teeth. Helping the old woman load up the horses for travel, he yanked at a pack and said, "Whoa, brother. It goes easier when you don't fight."

The horse gave him a big-eyed stare as if it understood his language—a comforting thought, because nobody else did. But even among the horses he felt unequal. They were able to look out for themselves if they escaped. He would simply starve. He was envious still, even among the horses.

Humbly he fetched and carried. Sometimes he even offered to help, but he had not the skill for the endless work of the women, and he was not trusted to hunt with the men, the providers.

When the camp moved, he carried a pack, trudging with the women. Even the dogs worked then, pulling small burdens on travois of sticks.

The Indian who had captured him lived like a lord, as he had a right to do. He hunted with his peers, attended long ceremonial meetings with much chanting and dancing, and lounged in the shade with his smug bride. He had only two responsibilities: to kill buffalo and to gain glory. The white man was so far beneath him in status that the Indian did not even think of envy.

One day several things happened that made the captive think he might some time become a man again. That was the day when he began to understand their language. For four months he had heard it, day and night, the joy and the mourning, the ritual chanting and sung prayers, the squabbles and the deliberations. None of it meant anything to him at all.

But on that important day in early fall the two young women set out for the river, and one of them called over her shoulder to the old woman. The white man was startled. She had said she was going to bathe. His understanding was so sudden that he felt as if his ears had come unstopped. Listening to the racket of the camp, he heard fragments of meaning instead of gabble.

On that same important day the old woman brought a pair of new moccasins out of the tepee and tossed them on the ground before him. He could not believe she would do anything for him because of kindness, but giving him moccasins was one way of looking after her property.

In thanking her, he dared greatly. He picked a little handful of fading fall flowers and took them to her as she squatted in front of her tepee, scraping a buffalo hide with a tool made from a piece of iron tied to a bone. Her hands were hideous—most of the fingers had the first joint missing. He bowed solemnly and offered the flowers.

She glared at him from beneath the short, ragged tangle of her hair. She stared at the flowers, knocked them out of his hand, and went running to the next tepee, squalling the story. He heard her and the other women screaming with laughter.

The white man squared his shoulders and walked boldly over to watch three small boys shooting arrows at a target. He said in English, "Show me how to do that, will you?"

They frowned, but he held out his hand as if there could be no doubt. One of them gave him a bow and one arrow, and they snickered when he missed.

The people were easily amused, except when they were angry. They were amused, at him, playing with the little boys. A few days later he asked the hag, with gestures, for a bow that her son had just discarded, a man-size bow of horn. He scavenged for old arrows. The old woman cackled at his marksmanship and called her neighbors to enjoy the fun.

When he could understand words, he could identify his people by their names. The old woman was Greasy Hand, and her daughter was Pretty Calf. The other young woman's name was not clear to him, for the words were not in his vocabulary. The man who had captured him was Yellow Robe.

Once he could understand, he could begin to talk a little, and then he was less lonely. Nobody had been able to see any reason for talking to him, since he would not understand anyway. He asked the old woman, "What is my name?" Until he knew it, he was incomplete. She shrugged to let him know he had none.

He told her in the Crow language, "My name is Horse." He repeated it, and she nodded. After that they called him Horse when they called him anything. Nobody cared except the white man himself.

They trusted him enough to let him stray out of camp, so that he might have got away and, by unimaginable good luck, might have reached a trading post or a fort, but winter was too close. He did not dare leave without a horse; he needed clothing and a better hunting weapon than he had, and more certain skill in using it. He did not dare steal, for then they would surely have pursued him, and just as certainly they would have caught him. Remembering the warmth of the home that was waiting in Boston, he settled down for the winter.

On a cold night he crept into the tepee after the others had gone to bed. Even a horse might try to find shelter from the wind. The old woman grumbled, but without conviction. She did not put him out.

They tolerated him, back in the shadows, so long as he did not get in the way.

He began to understand how the family that owned him differed from the others. Fate had been cruel to them. In a short, sharp argument among the old women, one of them derided Greasy Hand by sneering, "You have no relatives!" and Greasy Hand raved for minutes of the deeds of her father and uncles and brothers. And she had had four sons, she reminded her detractor—who answered with scorn, "Where are they?"

Later the white man found her moaning and whimpering to herself, rocking back and forth on her haunches, staring at her mutilated hands. By that time he understood. A mourner often chopped off a finger joint. Old Greasy Hand had mourned often. For the first time he felt a twinge of pity, but he put it aside as another emotion, like anger, that he could not afford. He thought: What tales I will tell when I get home!

He wrinkled his nose in disdain. The camp stank of animals and meat and rancid grease. He looked down at his naked, shivering legs and was startled, remembering that he was still only a horse.

He could not trust the old woman. She fed him only because a starved slave would die and not be worth boasting about. Just how fitful her temper was he saw on the day when she got tired of stumbling over one of the hundred dogs that infested the camp. This was one of her own dogs, a large, strong one that pulled a baggage travois when the tribe moved camp.

Countless times he had seen her kick at the beast as it lay sleeping in front of the tepee, in her way. The dog always moved, with a yelp, but it always got in the way again. One day she gave the dog its usual kick and then stood scolding at it while the animal rolled its eyes sleepily. The old woman suddenly picked up her ax and cut the dog's head off with one blow. Looking well satisfied with herself, she beckoned her slave to remove the body.

It could have been me, he thought, if I were a dog. But I'm a horse.

His hope of life lay with the girl, Pretty Calf. He set about courting her, realizing how desperately poor he was both in property and honor. He owned no horse, no weapon but the old bow and the battered arrows. He had nothing to give away, and he needed gifts, because he did not dare seduce the girl.

One of the customs of courtship involved sending a gift of horses to a girl's older brother and bestowing much buffalo meat upon her mother. The white man could not wait for some far-off time when he might have either horses or meat to give away. And his courtship had to be secret. It was not for him to stroll past the groups of watchful girls, blowing a flute made of an eagle's wing bone, as the flirtatious young bucks did.

He could not ride past Pretty Calf's tepee, painted and bedizened; he had no horse, no finery.

Back home, he remembered, I could marry just about any girl I'd want to. But he wasted little time thinking about that. A future was something to be earned.

The most he dared do was wink at Pretty Calf now and then, or state his admiration while she giggled and hid her face. The least he dared do to win his bride was to elope with her, but he had to give her a horse to put the seal of tribal approval on that. And he had no horse until he killed a man to get one. . . .

His opportunity came in early spring. He was casually accepted by that time. He did not belong, but he was amusing to the Crows, like a strange pet, or they would not have fed him through the winter.

His chance came when he was hunting small game with three young boys who were his guards as well as his scornful companions. Rabbits and birds were of no account in a camp well fed on buffalo meat, but they made good targets.

His party walked far that day. All of them at once saw the two horses in a sheltered coulee. The boys and the man crawled forward on their bellies, and then they saw an Indian who lay on the ground, moaning, a lone traveler. From the way the boys inched eagerly forward, Horse knew the man was fair prey—a member of some enemy tribe.

This is the way the captive white man acquired wealth and honor to win a bride and save his life: He shot an arrow into the sick man, a split second ahead of one of his small companions, and dashed forward to strike the still-groaning man with his bow, to count first coup. Then he seized the hobbled horses.

By the time he had the horses secure, and with them his hope for freedom, the boys had followed, counting coup with gestures and shrieks they had practiced since boyhood, and one of them had the scalp. The white man was grimly amused to see the boy double up with sudden nausea when he had the thing in his hand. . . .

There was a hubbub in the camp when they rode in that evening, two of them on each horse. The captive was noticed. Indians who had ignored him as a slave stared at the brave man who had struck first coup and had stolen horses.

The hubbub lasted all night, as fathers boasted loudly of their young sons' exploits. The white man was called upon to settle an argument between two fierce boys as to which of them had struck second coup and which must be satisfied with third. After much talk that went over his head, he solemnly pointed at the nearest boy. He didn't know which boy it was and didn't care, but the boy did.

The white man had watched warriors in their triumph. He knew what to do. Modesty about achievements had no place among the Crow people. When a man did something big, he told about it.

The white man smeared his face with grease and charcoal. He walked inside the tepee circle, chanting and singing. He used his own language.

"You heathens, you savages," he shouted. "I'm going to get out of here some day! I am going to get away!" The Crow people listened respectfully. In the Crow tongue he shouted, "Horse! I am Horse!" and they nodded.

He had a right to boast, and he had two horses. Before dawn the white man and his bride were sheltered beyond a far hill, and he was telling her, "I love you, little lady. I love you."

She looked at him with her great dark eyes, and he thought she understood his English words—or as much as she needed to understand.

"You are my treasure," he said, "more precious than jewels, better than fine gold. I am going to call you Freedom."

When they returned to camp two days later, he was bold but worried. His ace, he suspected, might not be high enough in the game he was playing without being sure of the rules. But it served.

Old Greasy Hand raged—but not at him. She complained loudly that her daughter had let herself go too cheap. But the marriage was as good as any Crow marriage. He had paid a horse.

He learned the language faster after that, from Pretty Calf, whom he sometimes called Freedom. He learned that his attentive, adoring bride was fourteen years old.

One thing he had not guessed was the difference that being Pretty Calf's

husband would make in his relationship to her mother and brother. He had
hoped only to make his position a little safer, but he had not expected to be
treated with dignity. Greasy Hand no longer spoke to him at all. When the
white man spoke to her, his bride murmured in dismay, explaining at great
length that he must never do that. There could be no conversation between
a man and his mother-in-law. He could not even mention a word that was
part of her name.

Having improved his status so magnificently, he felt no need for hurry in
getting away. Now that he had a woman, he had as good a chance to be
rich as any man. Pretty Calf waited on him; she seldom ran off to play
games with other young girls, but took pride in learning from her mother
the many women's skills of tanning hides and making clothing and preparing food.

He was no more a horse but a kind of man, a half-Indian, still poor and
unskilled but laden with honors, clinging to the buckskin fringes of Crow
society.

Escape could wait until he could manage it in comfort, with fit clothing
and a good horse, with hunting weapons. Escape could wait until the camp
moved near some trading post. He did not plan how he would get home.
He dreamed of being there all at once, and of telling stories nobody would
believe. There was no hurry.

Pretty Calf delighted in educating him. He began to understand tribal arrangements, customs, and why things were as they were. They were that
way because they had always been so. His young wife giggled when she told
him, in his ignorance, things she had always known. But she did not laugh
when her brother's wife was taken by another warrior. She explained that
solemnly with words and signs.

Yellow Robe belonged to a society called the Big Dogs. The wife stealer,
Cut Neck, belonged to the Foxes. They were fellow tribesmen; they hunted
together and fought side by side, but men of one society could take away
wives from the other society if they wished, subject to certain limitations.

When Cut Neck rode up to the tepee, laughing and singing, and called to
Yellow Robe's wife, "Come out! Come out!" she did as ordered, looking
smug as usual, meek and entirely willing. Thereafter she rode beside him in
ceremonial processions and carried his coup stick, while his other wife pretended not to care.

"But why?" the white man demanded of his wife, his Freedom. "Why did
our brother let his woman go? He sits and smokes and does not speak."

Pretty Calf was shocked at the suggestion. Her brother could not possibly
reclaim his woman, she explained. He could not even let her come back if

she wanted to—and she probably would want to when Cut Neck tired of her. Yellow Robe could not even admit that his heart was sick. That was the way things were. Deviation meant dishonor.

The woman could have hidden from Cut Neck, she said. She could even have refused to go with him if she had been *ba-wurokee*—a really virtuous woman. But she had been his woman before, for a little while on a berrying expedition, and he had a right to claim her.

There was no sense in it, the white man insisted. He glared at his young wife. "If you go, I will bring you back!" he promised.

She laughed and buried her head against his shoulder. "I will not have to go," she said. "Horse is my first man. There is no hole in my moccasin."

He stroked her hair and said, *"Ba-wurokee."*

With great daring, she murmured, *"Hayha,"* and when he did not answer, because he did not know what she meant, she drew away, hurt.

"A woman calls her man that if she thinks he will not leave her. Am I wrong?"

The white man held her closer and lied. "Pretty Calf is not wrong. Horse will not leave her. Horse will not take another woman, either." No, he certainly would not. Parting from this one was going to be harder than getting her had been. *"Hayha,"* he murmured. "Freedom."

His conscience irked him, but not very much. Pretty Calf could get another man easily enough when he was gone, and a better provider. His hunting skill was improving, but he was still awkward.

There was no hurry about leaving. He was used to most of the Crow ways and could stand the rest. He was becoming prosperous. He owned five horses. His place in the life of the tribe was secure, such as it was. Three or four young women, including the one who had belonged to Yellow Robe, made advances to him. Pretty Calf took pride in the fact that her man was so attractive.

By the time he had what he needed for a secret journey, the grass grew yellow on the plains and the long cold was close. He was enslaved by the girl he called Freedom and, before the winter ended, by the knowledge that she was carrying his child. . . .

The Big Dog society held a long ceremony in the spring. The white man strolled with his woman along the creek bank, thinking: When I get home I will tell them about the chants and the drumming. Some time. Some time.

Pretty Calf would not go to bed when they went back to the tepee.

"Wait and find out about my brother," she urged. "Something may happen."

So far as Horse could figure out, the Big Dogs were having some kind of election. He pampered his wife by staying up with her by the fire. Even the old woman, who was a great one for getting sleep when she was not working, prowled around restlessly.

The white man was yawning by the time the noise of the ceremony died down. When Yellow Robe strode in, garish and heathen in his paint and feathers and furs, the women cried out. There was conversation, too fast for Horse to follow, and the old woman wailed once, but her son silenced her with a gruff command.

When the white man went to sleep, he thought his wife was weeping beside him.

The next morning she explained.

"He wears the bearskin belt. Now he can never retreat in battle. He will always be in danger. He will die."

Maybe he wouldn't, the white man tried to convince her. Pretty Calf recalled that some few men had been honored by the bearskin belt, vowed to the highest daring, and had not died. If they lived through the summer, then they were free of it.

"My brother wants to die," she mourned. "His heart is bitter."

Yellow Robe lived through half a dozen clashes with small parties of raiders from hostile tribes. His honors were many. He captured horses in an enemy camp, led two successful raids, counted first coup, and snatched a gun from the hand of an enemy tribesman. He wore wolf tails on his moccasins and ermine skins on his shirt, and he fringed his leggings with scalps in token of his glory.

When his mother ventured to suggest, as she did many times, "My son should take a new wife, I need another woman to help me," he ignored her. He spent much time in prayer, alone in the hills or in conference with a medicine man. He fasted and made vows and kept them. And before he could be free of the heavy honor of the bearskin belt, he went on his last raid.

The warriors were returning from the north just as the white man and two other hunters approached from the south, with buffalo and elk meat dripping from the bloody hides tied on their restive ponies. One of the hunters grunted, and they stopped to watch a rider on the hill north of the tepee circle.

The rider dismounted, held up a blanket, and dropped it. He repeated the gesture.

The hunters murmured dismay. "Two! Two men dead!" They rode fast into the camp, where there was already wailing.

A messenger came down from the war party on the hill. The rest of the party delayed to paint their faces for mourning and for victory. One of the two dead men was Yellow Robe. They had put his body in a cave and walled it in with rocks. The other man died later, and his body was in a tree.

There was blood on the ground before the tepee to which Yellow Robe would return no more. His mother, with her hair chopped short, sat in the doorway, rocking back and forth on her haunches, wailing her heartbreak. She cradled one mutilated hand in the other. She had cut off another finger joint.

Pretty Calf had cut off chunks of her long hair and was crying as she gashed her arms with a knife. The white man tried to take the knife away, but she protested so piteously that he let her do as she wished. He was sickened with the lot of them.

Savages! he thought. Now I will go back! I'll go hunting alone, and I'll keep on going.

But he did not go just yet, because he was the only hunter in the lodge of the two grieving women, one of them old and the other pregnant with his child.

In their mourning they made him a pauper again. Everything that meant comfort, wealth, and safety they sacrificed to the spirits because of the death of Yellow Robe. The tepee, made of seventeen fine buffalo hides, the furs that should have kept them warm, the white deerskin dress, trimmed with elk teeth, that Pretty Calf loved so well, even their tools and Yellow Robe's weapons—everything but his sacred medicine objects—they left there on the prairie, and the whole camp moved away. Two of his best horses were killed as a sacrifice, and the women gave away the rest.

They had no shelter. They would have no teepee of their own for two months at least of mourning, and then the women would have to tan hides to make it. Meanwhile they could live in temporary huts made of willows, covered with skins given them in pity by their friends. They could have lived with relatives, but Yellow Robe's women had no relatives.

The white man had not realized until then how terrible a thing it was for a Crow to have no kinfolk. No wonder old Greasy Hand had only stumps for fingers. She had mourned, from one year to the next, for everyone she had ever loved. She had no one left but her daughter, Pretty Calf.

Horse was furious at their foolishness. It had been bad enough for him, a captive, to be naked as a horse and poor as a slave, but that was because his captors had stripped him. These women had voluntarily given up everything they needed.

He was too angry at them to sleep in the willow hut. He lay under a sheltering tree. And on the third night of the mourning he made his plans. He had a knife and a bow. He would go after meat, taking two horses. And he would not come back. There were, he realized, many things he was not going to tell when he got back home.

In the willow hut, Pretty Calf cried out. He heard rustling there, and the old woman's querulous voice.

Some twenty hours later his son was born, two months early, in the tepee of a skilled medicine woman. The child was born without breath, and the mother died before the sun went down.

The white man was too shocked to think whether he should mourn, or how he should mourn. The old woman screamed until she was voiceless. Piteously she approached him, bent and trembling, blind with grief. She held out her knife and he took it.

She spread out her hands and shook her head. If she cut off any more finger joints, she could do no more work. She could not afford any more lasting signs of grief.

The white man said, "All right! All right!" between his teeth. He hacked his arms with the knife and stood watching the blood run down. It was little enough to do for Pretty Calf, for little Freedom.

Now there is nothing to keep me, he realized. When I get home, I must not let them see the scars.

He looked at Greasy Hand, hideous in her grief-burdened age, and thought: I really am free now! When a wife dies, her husband has no more duty toward her family. Pretty Calf had told him so, long ago, when he wondered why a certain man moved out of one tepee and into another.

The old woman, of course, would be a scavenger. There was one other with the tribe, an ancient crone who had no relatives, toward whom no one felt any responsibility. She lived on food thrown away by the more fortunate. She slept in shelters that she built with her own knotted hands. She plodded wearily at the end of the procession when the camp moved. When she stumbled, nobody cared. When she died, nobody would miss her.

Tomorrow morning, the white man decided, I will go.

His mother-in-law's sunken mouth quivered. She said one word, questioningly. She said, *"Eero-oshay?"* She said, "Son?"

Blinking, he remembered. When a wife died, her husband was free. But her mother, who had ignored him with dignity, might if she wished ask him to stay. She invited him by calling him Son, and he accepted by answering Mother.

Greasy Hand stood before him, bowed with years, withered with unceasing labor, loveless and childless, scarred with grief. But with all her burdens, she still loved life enough to beg it from him, the only person she had any right to ask. She was stripping herself of all she had left, her pride.

He looked eastward across the prairie. Two thousand miles away was home. The old woman would not live forever. He could afford to wait, for he was young. He could afford to be magnanimous, for he knew he was a man. He gave her the answer. *"Eegya,"* he said. "Mother."

He went home three years later. He explained no more than to say, "I lived with Crows for a while. It was some time before I could leave. They called me Horse."

He did not find it necessary either to apologize or to boast, because he was the equal of any man on earth.

4 *The Personal Issue*

Killer of Bulls*

JUAN BELMONTE

✳✳ Leslie Charteris, who translated Juan Belmonte's book, *Killer of Bulls,*
wrote: "If, without ever having heard of Belmonte, you were told that a man who
was practically a cripple, who was certainly a physical wreck, could become the
greatest bullfighter in the world, would you not say that if he did it he would be
performing a miracle? But this is only what Juan Belmonte has done. He is a
genius, a creator, an idol, an institution . . . born on the 14th of April 1892 in
one of the poor quarters of Sevilla . . . a slum child . . . to become one of the
best-loved names in Spain . . ." ✳✳

FEAR IS MY COMPANION

On the day of a *corrida,* the beard grows faster. It's Fear. During the hours
before a fight, one is so keyed up that the whole organism is stimulated to
an abnormal acceleration of all its functions. I don't know whether a doctor
would confirm it, but there is no doubt in any *torero's* mind.

Fear. I know it so well. It is my constant companion.

It's not so hard to shake it off the night before. It never disturbs my sleep,
because I can keep my mind busy thinking about remote and unimportant
things. Since I haven't a great deal of imagination, I go to bed and pretend
that I'm watching a sort of fantastic film, always the same; and this mental
scarecrow is sufficient to shut everything else out of my mind until I fall
asleep.

But in the morning it's not so easy. Fear is there, sitting over me in the
bed, as soon as I open my eyes. Antonio knows it well. If no man can be a
hero to his own valet, it's even more hopeless for a *torero* to be a hero to his
mozo de espadas.

* From *Juan Belmonte, Killer of Bulls,* an autobiography as told to Manuel Chaves Nogales,
edited and translated by Leslie Charteris. Copyright, 1937, by Doubleday & Company, Inc., reprinted by permission of the publishers.

I don't know what happens to other *toreros*. I myself have to fight this specter of Fear in a fierce imaginary debate, while I lie there waiting until it's time to get up.

For a while I am master of myself again; but my nerves are on edge. I get angry with Antonio for the slightest reason and start to quarrel bitterly with him. Anything will do for an excuse. He knows what is happening and bows before the storm. Little by little he lures me into my costume. The hours go by until, shortly before it is time to go to the ring, my friends begin to arrive. As soon as the first one comes, however intimate a friend he may be, Fear has to be crushed out of sight. But the struggle goes on. To be courageous in the *corrida,* you must have conquered Fear before you go into the arena. And probably the thing that gives the final victory is nothing but the sordid necessity of making a living. I don't believe that any *torero,* even the most courageous, wouldn't be glad to back out at the last moment if someone would guarantee him an income without obligating him to fight. At any rate, there would be no professional bullfighters. Perhaps there would be occasional ones: there will always be men who are ready to gamble their lives on the impulse of the moment. But the professional bullfighter, who goes to the bullying almost every day like a carpenter going to his shop, or a painter going to his easel, wouldn't exist.

Nor would one fight if one had to contract for a *corrida* two hours before it started. One fights because the contracts are signed weeks or months before they have to be fulfilled, when the day is so far away that it seems unreal.

On one occasion I was putting on my costume when Antonio told me that there were some impresarios who wanted to see me—they were offering three contracts for different bull rings on very attractive terms. And yet I could only think of them as treacherous criminals.

"Throw them out," I said to Antonio.

And when he came back I went on: "Why didn't you throw them out in the beginning? Don't you know by now that I'm not going to fight any more this season?"

The impresarios took no notice of either of us, being old hands at the game. They waited calmly until I came back from the *corrida,* full of my own triumph. They caught me in the hall of the hotel as soon as I came in, and I signed all the contracts they wanted.

When I find myself in front of the bull, it's quite different. A bull gives you no time for introspection. All your faculties are taken up with watching it. In the arena there is only one moment to spare for self-examination—the few minutes which the matador has to himself while the *banderillas* are being placed. What he does afterward is the result of that moment of meditation. When he takes up the sword and *muleta,* he instinctively follows the sub-conscious form of a plan which he has worked out in detail long before. In front of the bull he has no doubts. The exercise is so absorbing, so vital, that in my opinion any faltering of decision before the horns of the bull is fatal.

BEGINNINGS OF A BULLFIGHTER

I don't know when it was that I really made up my mind to be a *torero.* As a matter of fact I already felt like a professional bullfighter, even if I didn't dare to call myself one. When people are talking about their childhood they are apt to make out that from the time they left their cradles they felt an ir-resistible urge toward whatever vocation has taken them to success, but I personally must confess that I never succeeded in making a definite decision about my future at any point in my hard-fought apprenticeship. It is true that I had a kind of diffused aspiration toward something which my vacillating temperament could not make up its mind to define. If this ambition was to be a *torero,* I myself didn't know it. I practiced bullfighting, as you might say, "just because"—because I was influenced by my surroundings, because it amused me, because the risk and adventure of that hazardous profession fitted in with my own instinctive leaning toward uncertainty and adventure —because, with the cape in my hands, I, who was such a small and insig-nificant person with a vast inferiority complex, felt myself so much superior to the other boys who were physically stronger than I. Afterward I have realized that there must have been some heroic power of will in me which braced me up and kept me thrusting on through all the doubts and false starts and failures of my adolescence. An inexhaustible energy drove me on without telling me where I was going. My ambition was like a bow bent to the horizon with no target in sight. . . .

I had no sympathy with the "official" bullfighting fraternity, and I left them severely alone. Instead of that, I fell in with a band of youths who used to meet and talk about bulls at a soft-drink kiosk which stood by the wall of the convent of San Jacinto.

I liked bulls and disliked bullfighters. The more enthusiastic I became about bullfighting, the less use I had for the conventional type of young *torero.* It may have been because my pride was hurt by the insignificant fig-ure I cut among those self-opinionated *aficionados,* who wouldn't even condescend to look at me; or it may have been genuinely caused by a revolu-tionary conception of the art of bullfighting which forced me to quarrel with all the time-honored, old conventions from the start. Probably in the beginning it was merely indignation, wounded vanity if you like, which drove me away from the accepted standards and the steps by which tradition decreed that the ladder of the profession must be climbed.

The art of bullfighting is so mature, so hidebound, so rigidly and exhaustively hemmed in by canons of immemorial antiquity, that the would-be *torero* has to submit to a code of immutable rules and an inexorable discipline for which I was quite unfitted. I realized this clearly from the very start. So far from being ready to bow to the ancient gospels, I believed that I was the prophet of a new revelation.

So I joined up with the lads of San Jacinto, who all had the same protestant and revolutionary attitude as myself. They were a wild lot who had broken heroically away from everything. They never went to the *tentaderos* to be put through their paces, they wore no pigtails, and they made no effort to catch the eyes of the impresarios in the cafés of the Calle Sierpes. They had no respect for reputations, they had no patrons, and they had no practical ambitions in life. They were embittered and rather cruel people, with a supreme contempt for everything they looked at. Bombita and Machaquito were at that time the greatest figures in bullfighting, but to us they were just clowns. We acknowledged only one master, and that was Antonio Montes: he was a legend that we elaborated lovingly, and on the strength of our vague references to him we came to believe that we were the unique apostles of his technique, which in our opinion was the only technique worthy of consideration. We were all firmly convinced that we fought in his style; and with that conviction we regarded with implacable disdain the bullfighters who were then at the summit of their popularity. . . .

These lads had a new way of practicing bullfighting. The customary thing for an *aficionado* to do was to go to *capeas** to get permission from the ranchers to try a pass or two at the trials, where their nervousness and inexperience provided plenty of entertainment for the assembled guests. To the brotherhood of San Jacinto this procedure seemed much too undignified. They went out into the country to fight the rancher's bulls without his permission, in defiance of the guards, the constabulary, and the whole majesty of the law. They were the enemies of all established order, the complete outlaws. As time went on they maintained the same anarchistic attitude toward life in general as they had toward bullfighting. I have had to send money and cigarettes to nearly all of them in prison, where they got themselves put away from time to time as dangerous extremists.

* Public bullfights held in the village, where the square is barricaded off and a bull is let loose for any amateur who fancies himself to try his hand.

It was my job to set out in the afternoon for the Tablada grazing lands to find out if there was any herd about which could be fought. It was a seven- or eight-mile hike across country, and one had to avoid meeting the guards, who had a well-founded distrust of all boys who came near the herd. Then I had to come back and give my friends an account of my explorations, and if there were indeed bulls in the enclosures the expedition was promptly organized. We met at our refreshment stand and fixed the time of our departure so that the moon would be well up when we reached the pastures. We had to take the footpaths to avoid encountering any of the Guardia Civil,* and we had to do without a proper cloak because that would have been evidence against us if we were stopped. We used a coat belonging to Riverito, whom we all acknowledged as the most proficient.

When we got to the corral we would separate a promising-looking bull—usually the biggest one we could find. For the most part they were inferior stock, bred for meat rather than fighting; and when we had laboriously separated the animal it would rarely charge without a lot of provocation or until after it had turned round a few times and decided that there was no other way of escape.

Riverito played it first, which was his privilege as the leader. The others patiently waited for their turn, and no one ever dared to butt in before his allotted time. When Riverito had finished, he would pass the coat to the next man, and so we would follow each other in strict order. The social grades of that band of anarchists were religiously respected. The best fighter took the coat first; the least expert was relegated inexorably to the last place. Everyone's position was tacitly recognized by the others, and there was never any other ranking among us than that of unanimously respected merit.

I started by being the last in order, and when all the others had had enough they handed the coat to me to do the best I could with it. Naturally this wasn't much.

But one night something happened that upset all the accepted rules of precedence. Following our custom of playing the largest animal we could find, we had separated a huge bull which attacked from the first moment instead of trying to get away like the others. Accustomed as we were to half-blooded stock which charged only when it was cornered, we were completely disconcerted by the vigorous attack of that mountainous bull which only had to see the shadow of a bullfighter to launch itself at him like a streak of lightning. In four or five rushes it put the fear of God into our

* One of the many kinds of Spanish police. Their job is principally to guard the highways and to act as police in villages that have no other police force of their own. They are also employed in the towns in times of civil commotion, for which reason they are always assigned to districts a long way from their homes.

party, and very soon it stood alone in the center of the enclosure with its head in the clouds and its horns goring at the moon, while the gladiators flattened themselves against the fence and urged each other to attract its attention in any direction except their own. But the truth was that nobody wanted to take it on, and the bull was the unquestioned master of the arena.

"Has this bull got us licked?" I thought. "Are we supposed to be fighting it or is it fighting us?"

I waited trembling for a few seconds—I don't know whether with fear or jubilation. It wasn't my turn to take the field, but none of my companions would make a move, and the bull was still waiting there. A few paces away lay the coat we were using, which had been lost in the debacle. I stretched out my arm. When I had the coat in my hand I straightened up and moved slowly toward the bull. It pawed the ground and watched me approach, measuring the distance, and at the exact moment it hurled itself at me like a hurricane; I stood firm and led it past me with the coat. It turned quickly, kicking up a cloud of dust, and again I made it pass me. I had hardly recovered my position when it was on me again. I felt its quivering mass brushing against my body. Again and again I led it past, until at last I gave it a *recorte* which left it rooted to the ground and staring at me as if it couldn't make out what had happened to it. I turned my back on it and carelessly threw down the coat for anyone else to play with who felt like it, and the ovation I was giving myself almost deafened me.

After that night I was never again the last to fight. When the leader of the band gave up the coat, I would step forward and take it over as if I were exercising an indisputable right. I had won the position in fair combat, and nobody questioned my superiority. Nevertheless, the truth is that I was never the absolute leader.

I lived for nothing but bullfighting. At home everything went from bad to worse, and poverty was gaining on us every day. My father was loaded down with children whom he hardly knew how to feed with his pitifully meager little business; and I, who was the eldest, pretended not to see the catastrophe which was overtaking my family. I was indifferent to anything but my passion for bullfighting and my loyalty to the brotherhood of young bullfighters to whom I had given myself up heart and soul. I suppose every adolescent young man who finds himself out of tune with his environment is liable to find absorption in some such mystical ideal, whether it be social, political, or artistic, in which he can find an outlet for all his frustrated energy; and I was no exception.

In the morning I would sometimes think bitterly about the plight in which

I was leaving my family, and I would go penitently to the stall and help my father with the greatest cheerfulness and every intention of mending my ways. But it wouldn't be long before one of the gang would drift along to look me up.

"We're going to the country tonight," he would remark casually. . . .

And with that I would be lost. I would think of nothing else but the chances of the coming night, its innumerable risks and the pleasure of overcoming them. The oddments stall, the troubles of my family, and even the alluring image of my sweetheart of the moment vanished from my mind like shadows.

I never felt any of that all-absorbing emotion with which love is supposed to fill a young man. Love for me was no more than a passing distraction; my sweethearts followed each other as night follows day, and left no more trace. Bullfighting was the only passion that dominated me. The girls of the quarter whom I courted in the dim patios of Triana pass through my memory like shadows on a screen and leave nothing but a vague recollection of their charms. I can recall little more than the sensual caress of their silk blouses and the penetrating scent of jasmines in their hair.

So I would leave my sweetheart without remorse, and at midnight the seven of us would set out along the road toward San Juan de Aznalfarache in search of the risk and adventure of the bulls. To cross the river we would prowl through the cornfields until we found a boat to borrow. We would push it out into the stream with the mud sucking around our ankles, put out the oars, and paddle jubilantly away. One of us would lean over the side and spit at the reflection of the moon in the rippling water and begin to sing some soft and haunting gypsy song which reached no further than the reeds along the bank where our wake whispered and curdled. Sometimes we would pass a barge, laden with melons, tied up in a bend in the stream while the bargee slept. We would help ourselves to a few of them and go on our way nibbling them contentedly, with the juice running down our chins.

When we reached Tablada the pasture would be bathed in the milky-blue light of the moon. As we approached the enclosure we would fall silent; the oars would move quietly with short, slow strokes until the boat grounded in the mud. One of us would get out first to reconnoiter, and if he reported that there was no one else in sight we would all disembark and wriggle through the barbed wire into the enclosure. We would move on cautiously, taking as much cover as we could among the bushes and cactus, until we heard the silence suddenly broken by the tinkling movement of a belled ox.

"There are bulls!" we would breathe triumphantly.

Then would come the hard labor of running all over the field, which bristled with thorns and thistles, in order to separate the bull which we wanted to play, tire it out, and drive it into a corner.

On some nights, when we were absorbed in the task of moving the herd from one side to the other, we would hear the hoofbeats of a mounted guard coming to look for us. Toward the guards we had an attitude of open insubordination. We tried not to let them surprise us; when they did, the most that our dignity would allow us to do was to withdraw, but we never ran. We simply carried out a strategic retreat, without putting ourselves out or losing any of our cockiness; and the guard, who didn't want any trouble either, contented himself with keeping up appearances and letting us go in peace.

Because of the inefficiency of the private guards, the Guardia Civil were ordered to join in the persecution of amateur bullfighters. One night I was keeping watch while my comrades were playing a bull, and I saw two suspicious shapes advancing toward me. I hid behind a tree and called to them to halt.

"Who are you?" I demanded.

The figures separated a little and continued to advance without answering.

"Take one step more and I'll shoot," I shouted, and at the same time I covered them with the old pistol barrels which I had bought in the Thursday market when I was going to be a lion hunter. I clinked a couple of coins together to make them think that the guns were being cocked, and saw that the two shapes flattened themselves hastily into the ground. Elated with my daring, I threatened them again.

"Stay where you are and keep still until we've gone. If one of you makes a move I'll roast him."

The two figures did not move. It seemed to me that they were whispering. I whistled to the others according to our code of signals for them to get away, and while they were making tracks for the boat I kept watch on the intruders. As my eyes gradually became accustomed to the darkness I began to make out their contours more clearly. Something gleamed in their hands and on their heads. When I discovered that the gleams came from the barrels of their Mausers and their shiny three-cornered hats, the blood froze in my veins. "If I start running now," I thought, "they'll kill me like a dog." I crept backward inch by inch, holding my breath; and when I thought I was at a safe distance I flew rather than ran to the boat where my companions were waiting for me.

A few nights later one of the Guardia Civil did put a bullet through a young bullfighter who was trespassing in exactly the same way as we were.

One night in the enclosure a bull caught one of the boys and left him stretched out unconscious on the ground. We picked him up and carried him toward the river bank. We were all as naked as the day we were born, having swum across the river and left our clothes on the other side. As it was impossible for the injured lad, who was still bleeding, to swim back, we had to tramp along the bank looking for a boat. We found one at last and began to carry our unfortunate comrade along to it. There were five of us besides the casualty.

The tide was out, and between the firm ground and the boat there was a broad belt of mud and reeds where our feet sank up to the ankles under the weight of our burden. We were moving forward slowly and laboriously when we saw a big full-grown bull with finely developed horns emerging from the river and coming toward us. It saw us and stood with its head up, looking at the strange procession. And then it let out a roar and lowered its head as if it were going to charge.

I believe that the first impulse that flashed through all our minds was to drop our friend and run for our lives. Fortunately the clay in which our feet were embedded paralyzed this instinctive reaction, and whether we liked it or not we stayed there huddled together with the boy on our shoulders. Something similar must have happened to the bull, for its feet were similarly stuck in the slime, checking the attack which it had begun. At that precise moment somebody spoke:

"Keep still! Do a Don Tancredo!"*

It was marvelous. Everyone stood still, as if frozen into marble, in the position in which the warning had caught him. Naked, immobile, crushed together, and holding up the inanimate body of our friend, we must have formed a most curious piece of sculpture. Fear gave us an amazing rigidity. One of us was caught with his arm raised, and thus he stayed, absolutely motionless, as if he had been cast in bronze.

The startled bull gazed at us fixedly. Then it stepped forward slowly, lashing its loins with its tail and only waiting for the provocation of the slightest movement. We stood like statues, impassively offering it our naked bodies bathed by the moonlight. The bull took a few more steps, looked more puzzled by that strange monument in living flesh which had been erected in its dominions. The damned brute took a century to convince itself. Again and again, whenever it seemed as if it were going away, it would turn round and look at us again; until at last after an eternity of time it finally turned its

* A trick sometimes performed in the bull ring, in which a bullfighter stands on a box in the middle of the arena when the bull is first let out. If he remains absolutely motionless the bull is supposed to sniff all around him and go away without attacking him. This practice, however, is not favorably viewed by insurance companies.

bored back on us, dragged its hoofs out of the mud one by one, and with maddening deliberation went its leisured way.

We breathed again when the doctor at the emergency hospital in Triana told us that our friend's wound was not serious. We explained that he had torn himself accidentally on a nail.

The season of 1913 was the most dramatic of my career. Arising from my debut in Madrid, a furious battle began between my enthusiasts and my detractors. Without boasting, I believe that that was one of the most impassioned periods in the history of bullfighting. The rings were filled with people who were hoping or fearing that a bull would kill me at any moment; and the seal of a prospective corpse, which the technicians had given me by refusing to believe that it was possible to fight as I did, raised the tension to such a height that the fever of the crowd was let loose on the slightest pretext.

I was to fight in Sevilla at the beginning of April; but the appointed day dawned rainily, and the other two matadors and I agreed that the *corrida* would have to be postponed because the arena was swamped. Those who were beginning to consider themselves defrauded because I hadn't been killed as quickly as their technical knowledge insisted that I ought to be, became angry and started a great scandal on this pretext, saying that the plain truth was that I had lost my nerve. They put forward the theory that I had gambled my life like a lunatic in my early fights, but that now I didn't care to take any more chances. Some days later the postponed *corrida* took place, and I managed to demonstrate that if I was frightened I was at least clever enough to conceal the fact.

The following day I fought again in Madrid, and that was my real consecration.

I went into the ring like a mathematician going to the blackboard to prove a theorem. At that time the art of bullfighting was governed by the picturesque axiom of Lagartijo which said: "You stand *there,* and either you move yourself or the bull moves you." I was there to demonstrate that this was not as self-evident as they thought. My theory was: "You stand there, and you don't move and the bull doesn't move you—if you know how to fight." At that time there was a complicated system of "territories of the bull" and "territories of the *torero,*" which in my judgment was quite superfluous. The bull has no territory, because it is not a reasoning creature and there are no surveyors to lay down its boundaries. All the ground belongs to the *torero,* the only intelligent being in the game, and it seemed natural to me that he should keep it.

Those who saw me defying what they considered to be cosmic laws threw up their hands and said: "He's bound to die. If he doesn't change his ground he'll be killed." I didn't change my ground, the bull took a long time to kill me; and the knowing ones, instead of resigning themselves to recognize that there might be quite a simple and logical explanation which they hadn't thought of, went into hysterics and began to call me an earthquake, a cataclysm, a phenomenon, and I don't know how many other absurdly exaggerated things. As far as I was concerned, the only phenomenon was their lack of comprehension. What the humblest *aficionado* knows today, twenty years later, couldn't penetrate the skulls of those who were then the authorities on bullfighting. This was my whole contribution to the art.

In my second *corrida* in Madrid, "Don Modesto," the most famous critic of the day, took my side and wrote that I was fighting as Lagartijo, Frascuelo, Guerrita, Espartero, Fuentes, Bombita, Machaco, and the Gallos had never fought. This bold assertion let loose a hurricane of passions of which I was the stupefied vortex. I was just a poor fellow who thought he knew the truth and said so. I was saying it in all the bull rings, proving it in front of the bulls, with the cape or *muleta* in my hands, without any artifice. I was no expert, I didn't know the job very well, I had none of the resources of experience, and in addition I was so ill that I could scarcely move. I dragged myself into the ring, almost unable to walk, opened the cape, and gave my lesson as best I could. That was all. But what a tumult it caused! Nobody believed that I was fighting with conscious artistry. It was easier for them to think that I was a smart-aleck, a reckless suicide whose philosophy was that it was better to risk being gored than to starve. Instead of the cautious and calculating courage which one must have to fight bulls, and which in reality was what I had, they credited me with the fabulous valor of a legendary hero and a superhuman with a contempt for life which in fact I have never had.

But their misunderstanding did me no harm. On the contrary, it was an advantage. And it serves to explain why the incorporation of my personal manner of fighting into the traditional art provoked this controversy, which if I put aside all false modesty I should call one of the most intense stages through which bullfighting has passed.

When I went out to fight for the second time in Madrid I was really ill. I could hardly stand on my feet. Old troubles that had never been properly cured had drained my energy until I was kept going by nothing but enthusiasm, the spiritual force derived from the impetus of my success. In the street I couldn't take a step. In the arena, on the other hand, the public rose from their seats with a lump in their throats when they saw me fight. I mention this in support of my thesis that bullfighting is more than anything else a spiritual exercise. In a predominantly physical activity, a physical wreck such as I was at that time could never have triumphed. If the fundamental thing in bullfighting were strength of body and not of spirit, I should never have achieved anything in my life.

Once when I was in North America, I was interviewed by a Yankee journalist who while we were talking did nothing but look me up and down and round about with an insistence and a stupefaction that were frankly annoying. At last he turned to the friend who was interpreting for us and said: "And is he really the king of bullfighters?" Again he stared at me impertinently, confronted me with a photograph of mine which he had, and repeated: "Are you sure that this is the king of bullfighters?" I realized his state of mind and became angry. I stood up to put an end to the interview and said to my friend: "Tell this fool yes, that I am the king of bullfighters, and he needn't go on staring at me. Tell him that we don't kill bulls with our fists; and if he can't understand that, tell him that bullfighting is a spiritual exercise, a genuine art. And kick him out."

In this way and in no other I was able to triumph in Madrid. But although I was so carried away by the thrill of success that I didn't notice it, some of my friends were terrified to see me in such bad physical condition. Fernando Gillis spoke to my manager, Antonio Soto, and they agreed that I should have to rest for a while and be placed under treatment. I was lucky enough to be taken in hand by an excellent doctor and enthusiastic *aficionado* by the name of Serrano, to whom I owe my health and perhaps my life. I shut myself up in Sevilla, where Serrano came to look after me, and in a few days he managed to patch me up a little.

Nevertheless it was not easy to withdraw from the duties of the popularity I had won. The complete rest which had been recommended to me was disturbed by the good spirits of a horde of friends and admirers who never left me in peace. Whether I liked it or not, they dragged me out on parties and excursions, kept me drinking with them, and generally wore me out as much as if I had been fighting. I was still besieged by eager impresarios, whose eagerness was really no greater than my own; and twenty days later, although I was still far from cured, I returned to the arena.

There was so much curiosity in Spain to see me fight that for a week I fought every day in a different place. I started in Alicante, where I couldn't kill any bulls because the first one caught me as I was giving it a pass. In spite of this wound, I went on fighting all the other days of the week. On Tuesday I was in Ecija, on Wednesday in Huelva, on Thursday in

Sevilla, on Friday in Cortegana, on Saturday in Osuna, and on Sunday in Badajoz. I felt that I simply could not go to Badajoz, and my manager telegraphed to say that I was sick; but early that morning we were visited by some police officers sent by the civil governor of Sevilla, to whom the governor of Badajoz had telegraphed saying that Juan Belmonte must fight there whatever happened, because the city had been invaded by thousands of strangers from all over Extremadura and Portugal, and he was afraid that there would be serious riots if I didn't fight. So I was forced to go there, although I did make the condition that I should take another matador to substitute for me, while I only undertook to try and appease the public by letting them look at me.

But one thing simply led to another. If I could appear at Badajoz on Sunday, why couldn't I show up at Pozoblanco on Monday? And so the chain went on. I still found enough strength to fight once more in Linares, but at the end of that *corrida* I finally collapsed.

I was only able to take a fortnight's rest. Dr. Serrano was furious when I talked about fighting, and my friends advised me to give it up; but I was involved with too many interested parties, and as soon as I was on my feet I myself wanted to go back at once to the ring. On the first of June I was opening my cape again in the bull ring at Málaga. I also fought in Antequera and Huelva, and on the eighth I went to Valencia.

At Valencia I was badly received. The spectators were shouting at me and insulting me from the beginning of the procession into the arena until the last bull was dragged out. Nothing I did would calm them; and that day I felt all the weight of the injustice of the mob laid on my shoulders. I couldn't make out why the Valencians had turned against me, and why they whistled at me that afternoon as vigorously as they had applauded me before. When the *corrida* was over I talked to the impresario about that inexplicable hostility.

"The thing is that they feel you're letting them down," he said. "They think that because you're supposed to be a phenomenon the managements are only giving you easy fights in which you can show off without too much trouble. There's a rumor that you've refused to take on some big and difficult *novillos* that they've got in the pens here."

"If that's the case," I answered, "tell them that I'll fight these bulls the day after tomorrow."

That same night I had to leave for Madrid, where I was fighting the following day, and as soon as the fight was over I went straight to the station and caught a train back to Valencia to satisfy the people there by tackling the heavy bulls that they wanted to put up against me. I duly fought the *corrida* and was applauded with the same enthusiasm as I had been booed two days before. The bullfighting public is like that.

Once more I went from the bull ring to the station, because the next day I had to fight again in Madrid. I was worn out, and on top of that I was racked with the pain of a wound which one of those bulls had given me in my hand. I couldn't close my eyes during the journey. I remember that toward eleven o'clock at night the train stopped at a station where I got out and tried desperately to find something that would ease the pain. One of my *banderilleros* went up to one of those parties of girls who used to go to the stations to enjoy the harmless romance of exchanging smiles with a few travelers whom they would never see again.

"Have you got anything that would help to ease a wound?" he asked. "It's for Juan Belmonte."

"For Belmonte? Where is he?"

"Over there."

I smiled weakly at the girls; and they must have been touched to see me in so much pain, for they ran off and came back before the train started again with all the specifics that they could find within half a mile of the station. Popularity has these delicious compensations.

I was almost out on my feet when I went into the arena in Madrid the next day. When they let out my bull I walked painfully toward it, planted my feet on the ground, and citing it more with my will than with my arms I gave it five smooth and slow veronicas which were perhaps the best I have done in my life, without moving an inch. The public roared with enthusiasm. At the end of a *recorte,* the bull rushed me and trampled on me, leaving me on the ground with my costume ripped to pieces. When I felt them pick me up and carry me away, I closed my eyes in blissful relief. All around me the crowd was cheering, but I heard the noise only as a confused murmur, infinitely far away. I was half-unconscious. They put me on the operating table in the infirmary, where I lay limply with my eyes shut and only a blurred awareness of what was going on around me.

When the doctor arrived and prepared his instruments and began to take off my clothes, I had even stopped thinking. I was peacefully asleep. They tell me that he went over me inch by inch in a tense silence, while I gave no sign of life.

"What's the matter with him?" asked my *mozo de espadas* anxiously.

"The matter with him," announced the doctor at length, "is that he wants some rest. He has gone to sleep, gentlemen. And that's the only treatment he needs."

They didn't let me go on enjoying the treatment. They put one of the attendants' trousers on me, and I had to get up and go on fighting. It was one of my triumphant afternoons. "Five veronicas without a fault!" gasped the technicians. To which my answer would have been: "Five days fighting without a wink of sleep!"

Mad Ahab and the Great White Whale*

HERMAN MELVILLE

✳✳ Herman Melville (1819-91) was born in New York City, a descendant of English and Dutch Colonial families; his father died when he was 12. His first voyage was as cabin boy to Liverpool when he was 18; returning, he taught school in upstate New York until he sailed on the whaler from which he jumped ship in 1842 at the Marquesas, about which he later wrote in *Typee* and *Mardi*. *Moby Dick*, generally considered his greatest work, appeared in 1851 and was dedicated to Nathaniel Hawthorne. Subtitled *The Whale*, it has been a fertile field of critical appreciation, not only for its realistic adventure quality but for its symbolism of the conflict between man and his fate in which the whale represents infinite evil and Ahab the opposing will of man. ✳✳

PRELIMINARY: ALL MEN LIVE IN WHALE LINES

. . . The whale line folds the whole boat in its complicated coils, twisting and writhing around it in almost every direction. All the oarsmen are involved in its perilous contortions; so that to the timid eye of the landsman, they seem as Indian jugglers, with the deadliest snakes sportively festooning their limbs. Nor can any son of mortal woman, for the first time, seat himself amid those hempen intricacies, and while straining his utmost at the oar, bethink him that at any unknown instant the harpoon may be darted, and all these horrible contortions be put in play like ringed lightnings. . . . For, when the line is darting out, to be seated then in the boat, is like being seated in the midst of the manifold whizzings of a steam engine in full play, when every flying beam, and shaft, and wheel, is grazing you. It is worse; for you cannot sit motionless in the heart of these perils, because the boat is rocking like a cradle, and you are pitched one way and the other, without the slightest warning; and only by a certain self-adjusting buoyancy and simultaneousness of volition and action, can you escape being made a

---

*From *Moby Dick*, based on the 18-month voyage that Melville took on the whaler *Acushnet* in the South Seas in 1841.

Mazeppa of, and run away with where the all-seeing sun himself could never pierce you out.

Again: as the profound calm which only apparently precedes and prophesies of the storm, is perhaps more awful than the storm itself; for, indeed, the calm is but the wrapper and envelope of the storm; and contains it in itself, as the seemingly harmless rifle holds the fatal powder, and the ball, and the explosion; so the graceful repose of the line, as it silently serpentines about the oarsmen before being brought into actual play—this is a thing which carries more of true terror than any other aspect of this dangerous affair. But why say more? All men live enveloped in whale lines. All are born with halters round their necks; but it is only when caught in the swift, sudden turn of death, that mortals realize the silent, subtle, ever-present perils of life. And if you be a philosopher, though seated in the whale boat, you would not at heart feel one whit more of terror, than though seated before your evening fire with a poker, and not a harpoon, by your side.

ALL EVIL IN THE WHALE

His three boats stove around him, and oars and men both whirling in the eddies; one captain, seizing the line-knife from his broken prow, had dashed at the whale, as an Arkansas duelist at his foe, blindly seeking with a six-inch blade to reach the fathom-deep life of the whale. That captain was Ahab. And then it was, that suddenly sweeping his sickle-shaped lower jaw beneath him, Moby Dick had reaped away Ahab's leg, as a mower a blade of grass in the field. No turbaned Turk, no hired Venetian or Malay, could have smote him with more seeming malice. Small reason was there to doubt, then, that ever since that almost fatal encounter, Ahab had cherished a wild vindictiveness against the whale, all the more fell for that in his frantic morbidness he at last came to identify with him, not only all his bodily woes, but all his intellectual and spiritual exasperations. The White Whale swam before him as the monomaniac incarnation of all those malicious agencies which some deep men feel eating in them, till they are left living on with half a heart and half a lung. That intangible malignity which has been from the beginning; to whose dominion even the modern Christians ascribe one-half of the worlds; which the ancient Ophites of the East reverenced in their statue devil;—Ahab did not fall down and worship it like them; but deliriously transferring its idea to the abhorred White Whale, he pitted himself, all mutilated, against it. All that most maddens and torments; all that stirs up the lees of things; all truth with malice in it; all that cracks the sinews and cakes the brain; all the subtle demonisms of life and thought; all evil, to crazy Ahab, were visibly personified, and made practically assailable in Moby Dick. He piled upon the whale's white hump the sum of all the general rage and hate felt by his whole race from Adam down; and then, as if his chest had been a mortar, he burst his hot heart's shell upon it.

It is not probable that this monomania in him took its instant rise at the precise time of his bodily dismemberment. Then, in darting at the monster, knife in hand, he had but given loose to a sudden, passionate, corporal animosity; and when he received the stroke that tore him, he probably but felt the agonizing bodily laceration, but nothing more. Yet, when by this collision forced to turn toward home, and for long months of days and weeks, Ahab and anguish lay stretched together in one hammock, rounding in mid-winter that dreary, howling Patagonian Cape; then it was, that his torn body and gashed soul bled into one another; and so interfusing, made him mad. That is was only then, on the homeward voyage, after the encounter, that the final monomania seized him, seems all but certain from the fact that, at intervals during the passage, he was a raving lunatic; and though unlimbed of a leg, yet such vital strength yet lurked in his Egyptian chest, and was moreover intensified by his delirium, that his mates were forced to lace him fast, even there, as he sailed, raving in his hammock. In a strait-jacket, he swung to the mad rockings of the gales. . . . Nevertheless, so well did he succeed in dissembling, that when with ivory leg he stepped ashore at last, no Nantucketer thought him otherwise than but naturally grieved, and that to the quick, with the terrible casualty which had overtaken him.

The report of his undeniable delirium at sea was likewise popularly ascribed to a kindred cause. And so too, all the added moodiness which always afterward, to the very day of sailing in the *Pequod* on the present voyage, sat brooding on his brow. Nor is it so very unlikely that, far from distrusting his fitness for another whaling voyage, on account of such dark symptoms, the calculating people of that prudent isle were inclined to harbor the conceit that for those very reasons he was all the better qualified and set on edge, for a pursuit so full of rage and wildness as the bloody hunt of whales. . . .

THE CHASE—FIRST DAY

That night, in the mid-watch, when the old man—as his wont at intervals—stepped forth from the scuttle in which he leaned, and went to his pivot hole, he suddenly thrust out his face fiercely, snuffing up the sea air as a sagacious ship's dog will, in drawing nigh to some barbarous isle. He declared that a whale must be near. Soon that peculiar odor, sometimes to a great distance given forth by the living sperm whale, was palpable to all the watch; nor was any mariner surprised when, after inspecting the compass, and then the dog vane, and then ascertaining the precise bearing of the odor as nearly as possible, Ahab rapidly ordered the ship's course to be slightly altered, and the sail to be shortened.

The acute policy dictating these movements was sufficiently vindicated at daybreak, by the sight of a long sleek on the sea directly and lengthwise ahead, smooth as oil, and resembling in the pleated watery wrinkles border-ing it, the polished metalliclike marks of some swift tide-rip, at the mouth of a deep, rapid stream.

"Man the mastheads! Call all hands!"

Thundering with the butts of three clubbed handspikes on the forecastle deck, Daggoo roused the sleepers with such Judgment claps that they seemed to exhale from the scuttle, so instantaneously did they appear with their clothes in their hands.

"What d'ye see?" cried Ahab, flattening his face to the sky.

"Nothing, nothing, sir!" was the sound hailing down in reply.

"T'gallant sails—!—stunsails! alow and aloft, and on both sides!"

All sail being set, he now cast loose the lifeline, reserved for swaying him to the main royal-mast head; and in a few moments they were hoisting him thither, when, while but two thirds of the way aloft, and while peering ahead through the horizontal vacancy between the main-topsail and topgallant sail, he raised a gull-like cry in the air, "There she blows!—there she blows! A hump like a snow hill! It is Moby Dick!"

Fired by the cry which seemed simultaneously taken up by the three look-outs, the men on deck rushed to the rigging to behold the famous whale they had so long been pursuing. Ahab had now gained his final perch, some feet above the other lookouts, Tashtego standing just beneath him on the cap of the topgallant mast, so that the Indian's head was almost on a level with Ahab's heel. From this height the whale was now seen some mile or so ahead, at every roll of the sea revealing his high, sparkling hump, and regu-larly jetting his silent spout into the air. To the credulous mariners it seemed the same silent spout they had so long ago beheld in the moonlit Atlantic and Indian Oceans.

"And did none of ye see it before?" cried Ahab, hailing the perched men all around him.

"I saw him almost that same instant, sir, that Captain Ahab did, and I cried out," said Tashtego.

"Not the same instant; not the same—no, the doubloon is mine, Fate reserved the doubloon for me. *I* only; none of ye could have raised the White Whale first. There she blows! there she blows!—there she blows! There again!—there again!" he cried, in long-drawn, lingering, methodic tones, attuned to the gradual prolongings of the whale's visible jets. "He's going to sound! In stunsails! Down topgallant sails! Stand by three boats. Mr. Starbuck, remember, stay on board, and keep the ship. Helm there! Luff, luff a point! So; steady, man, steady! There go flukes! No, no; only black water! All ready the boats there? Stand by, stand by! Lower me, Mr. Starbuck; lower, lower—quick, quicker!" and he slid through the air to the deck.

"He is heading straight to leeward, Sir," cried Stubb, "right away from us; cannot have seen the ship yet."

"Be dumb, man! Stand by the braces! Hard down the helm!—brace up! Shiver her!—shiver her! So; well that! Boats, boats!"

Soon all the boats but Starbuck's were dropped; all the boat sails set—all the paddles plying; with rippling swiftness, shooting to leeward; and Ahab heading the onset. A pale, death-glimmer lit up Fedallah's sunken eyes; a hideous motion gnawed his mouth.

Like noiseless nautilus shells, their light prows sped through the sea; but only slowly they neared the foe. As they neared him, the ocean grew still more smooth; seemed drawing a carpet over its waves; seemed a noon meadow, so serenely it spread. At length the breathless hunter came so nigh his seemingly unsuspecting prey, that his entire dazzling hump was distinctly visible, sliding along the sea as if an isolated thing, and continually set in revolving ring of finest, fleecy, greenish foam. He saw the vast, involved wrinkles of the slightly projecting head beyond. Before it, far out on the soft Turkish-rugged waters, went the glistening white shadow from his broad, milky forehead, a musical rippling playfully accompanying the shade; and behind, the blue waters interchangeably flowed over into the moving valley of his steady wake; and on either hand bright bubbles arose and danced by his side. But these were broken again by the light toes of hundreds of gay fowl softly feathering the sea, alternate with their fitful flight; and like to some flag staff rising from the painted hull of an argosy, the tall but shattered pole of a recent lance projected from the White Whale's back; and at intervals one of the cloud of soft-toed fowls hovering, and to and fro skimming like a canopy over the fish, silently perched and rocked on this pole, the long tailfeathers streaming like pennons. . . .

On each soft side—coincident with the parted swell, that but once leaving him, then flowed so wide away—on each bright side, the whale shed off enticings. No wonder there had been some among the hunters who namelessly transported and allured by all this serenity, had ventured to assail it; but had fatally found that quietude but the vesture of tornadoes. Yet calm, enticing calm, oh, whale! thou glidest on, to all who for the first time eye thee, no matter how many in that same way thou may'st have bejuggled and destroyed before.

And thus, through the serene tranquillities of the tropical sea, among waves whose hand-clappings were suspended by exceeding rapture, Moby Dick moved on, still withholding from sight the full terrors of his sub-merged trunk, entirely hiding the wrenched hideousness of his jaw. But soon the fore part of him slowly rose from the water; for an instant his whole marbleized body formed a high arch, like Virginia's Natural Bridge, and warningly waving his bannered flukes in the air, the grand god re-vealed himself, sounded, and went out of sight. Hoveringly halting, and dipping on the wing, the white sea fowls longingly lingered over the agitated pool that he left.

With oars apeak, and paddles down, the sheets of their sails adrift, the three boats now stilly floated, awaiting Moby Dick's reappearance.

"An hour," said Ahab, standing rooted in his boat's stern; and he gazed beyond the whale's place, toward the dim blue spaces and wide, wooing vacancies to leeward. It was only an instant; for again his eyes seemed whirl-ing round in his head as he swept the watery circle. The breeze now fresh-ened; the sea began to swell.

"The birds!—the birds!" cried Tashtego.

In long Indian file, as when herons take wing, the white birds were now all flying toward Ahab's boat; and when within a few yards began flutter-ing over the water there, wheeling round and round, with joyous, expectant cries. Their vision was keener than man's; Ahab could discover no sign in the sea. But suddenly as he peered down and down into its depths, he pro-foundly saw a white living spot no bigger than a white weasel, with won-derful celerity uprising, and magnifying as it rose, till it turned, and then there were plainly revealed two long, crooked rows of white, glistening teeth, floating up from the undiscoverable bottom. It was Moby Dick's open mouth and scrolled jaw; his vast, shadowed bulk still half blending with the blue of the sea. The glittering mouth yawned beneath the boat like an open-doored marble tomb; and giving one sidelong sweep with his steering oar, Ahab whirled the craft aside from this tremendous apparition. Then, calling upon Fedallah to change places with him, went forward to the bows, and seizing Perth's harpoon, commanded his crew to grasp their oars and stand by to stern.

Now, by reason of this timely spinning round the boat upon its axis, its bow, by anticipation, was made to face the whale's head while yet under water. But as if perceiving this stratagem, Moby Dick, with that malicious intelligence ascribed to him, sidelingly transplanted himself, as it were, in an instant, shooting his pleated head lengthwise beneath the boat.

Through and through; through every plank and each rib, it thrilled for an instant, the whale obliquely lying on his back, in the manner of a biting shark, slowly and feelingly taking its bows full within his mouth, so that the long, narrow, scrolled lower jaw curled high up into the open air, and one of the teeth caught in a row-lock. The bluish pearl-white of the inside of the jaw was within six inches of Ahab's head, and reached higher than that. In this attitude the White Whale now shook the slight cedar as a mildly cruel cat her mouse. With unastonished eyes Fedallah gazed, and crossed his arms; but the tiger-yellow crew were tumbling over each other's heads to gain the uttermost stern.

And now, while both elastic gunwales were springing in and out, as the whale dallied with the doomed craft in this devilish way; and from his body being submerged beneath the boat, he could not be darted at from the bows, for the bows were almost inside of him, as it were; and while the other boats involuntarily paused, as before a quick crisis impossible to withstand, then it was that monomaniac Ahab, furious with this tantalizing vicinity of his foe, which placed him all alive and helpless in the very jaws he hated; frenzied with all this, he seized the long bone with his naked hands, and wildly strove to wrench it from its grip. As now he thus vainly strove, the jaw slipped from him; the frail gunwales bent in, collapsed, and snapped, as both jaws, like an enormous shears, sliding further aft, bit the craft completely in twain, and locked themselves fast again in the sea, midway between the two floating wrecks. These floated aside, the broken ends drooping, the crew at the stern wreck clinging to the gunwales, and striving to hold fast to the oars to lash them across.

At that preluding moment, ere the boat was yet snapped, Ahab, the first to perceive the whale's intent, by the crafty upraising of his head, a movement that loosed his hold for the time; at that moment his hand had made one final effort to push the boat out of the bite. But only slipping further into the whale's mouth, and tilting over sideways as it slipped, the boat had shaken off his hold on the jaw; spilled him out of it, as he leaned to the push; and so he fell flat-faced upon the sea.

Ripplingly withdrawing from his prey, Moby Dick now lay at a little distance, vertically thrusting his oblong white head up and down in the billows; and at the same time slowly revolving his whole spindled body; so that when his vast wrinkled forehead rose—some twenty or more feet out

of the water—the now-rising swells, with all their confluent waves, dazzlingly broke against it; vindictively tossing their shivered spray still higher
into the air. So, in a gale, the but half-baffled Channel billows recoil from
the base of the Eddystone, only triumphantly to overleap its summit with
their scud.

But soon resuming his horizontal attitude, Moby Dick swam swiftly
round and round the wrecked crew; sideways churning the water in his
vengeful wake, as if lashing himself up to still another and more deadly
assault. The sight of the splintered boat seemed to madden him, as the
blood of grapes and mulberries cast before Antiochus's elephants in the
book of Maccabees. Meanwhile Ahab, half-smothered in the foam of the
whale's insolent tail, and too much of a cripple to swim, though he could
still keep afloat, even in the heart of such a whirlpool as that; helpless Ahab's
head was seen, like a tossed bubble which the least chance shock might
burst. From the boat's fragmentary stern, Fedullah incuriously and mildly
eyed him; the clinging crew, at the other drifting end, could not succor
him; more than enough was it for them to look to themselves. For so re-
volvingly appalling was the White Whale's aspect, and so planetarily swift
the ever-contracting circles he made, that he seemed horizontally swoop-
ing upon them. And though the other boats, unharmed, still hovered hard
by; still they dared not pull into the eddy to strike, lest that should be the
signal for the instant destruction of the jeopardized castaways, Ahab and
all; nor in that case could they themselves hope to escape. With straining
eyes, then, they remained on the outer edge of the direful zone, whose center had now become the old man's head.

Meantime, from the beginning all this had been descried from the ship's
mastheads; and squaring her yards, she had borne down upon the scene;
and was now so nigh, that Ahab in the water hailed her: "Sail on the"—
but that moment a breaking sea dashed on him from Moby Dick and
whelmed him for the time. But struggling out of it again, and chancing to
rise on a towering crest, he shouted, "Sail on the whale!—Drive him off!"

The *Pequod*'s prows were pointed; and breaking up the charmed circle,
she effectually parted the White Whale from his victim. As he sullenly swam
off, the boats flew to the rescue.

Dragged into Stubb's boat with bloodshot, blinded eyes, the white brine
caking in his wrinkles; the long tension of Ahab's bodily strength did crack,
and helplessly he yielded to his body's doom: for a time, lying all crushed
in the bottom of Stubb's boat, like one trodden under foot of herds of elephants. Far inland, nameless wails came from him, as desolate sounds from
out ravines. . . .

"The harpoon," said Ahab, halfway rising, and draggingly leaning on one bended arm, "is it safe?"

"Aye, sir, for it was not darted; this is it," said Stubb, showing it.

"Lay it before me; any missing men?"

"One, two, three, four, five;—there were five oars, sir, and here are five men."

"That's good.—Help me, man; I wish to stand. So, so, I see him! there! there! going to leeward still; what a leaping spout!—Hands off from me! The eternal sap runs up in Ahab's bones again! Set the sail; out oars; the helm!"

It is often the case that when a boat is stove, its crew, being picked up by another boat, help to work that second boat; and the chase is thus continued with what is called double-banked oars. It was thus now. But the added power of the boat did not equal the added power of the whale, for he seemed to have treble-banked his every fin; swimming with a velocity which plainly showed, that if now, under these circumstances, pushed on, the chase would prove an indefinitely prolonged, if not a hopeless one; nor could any crew endure for so long a period, such an unintermitted, intense straining at the oar; a thing barely tolerable only in some one brief vicissitude. The ship itself, then, as it sometimes happens, offered the most promising intermediate means of overtaking the chase. Accordingly, the boats now made for her, and were soon swayed up to their cranes—the two parts of the wrecked boat having been previously secured by her—and then hoisting everything to her side, and stacking her canvas high up, and sideways outstretching it with stunsails, like the double-jointed wings of an albatross; the *Pequod* bore down in the leeward wake of Moby Dick. At the well-known, methodic intervals, the whale's glittering spout was regularly announced from the manned mastheads; and when he would be reported as just gone down, Ahab would take the time, and then pacing the deck, binnacle-watch in hand, so soon as the last second of the allotted hour expired, his voice was heard. "Whose is the doubloon now? D'ye see him?" and if the reply was, "No, sir!" straightway he commanded them to lift him to his perch. In this way the day wore on; Ahab, now aloft and motionless; anon, unrestingly pacing the planks.

As he was thus walking, uttering no sound, except to hail the men aloft, or to bid them hoist a sail still higher, or to spread one to a still greater breadth—thus to and fro pacing, beneath his slouched hat, at every turn he passed his own wrecked boat, which had been dropped upon the quarterdeck, and lay there reversed; broken bow to shattered stern. At last he paused before it; and as in an already overclouded sky fresh troops of clouds will sometimes sail across, so over the old man's face there now stole some such added gloom as this.

Stubb saw him pause; and perhaps intending, not vainly, though, to evince his own unabated fortitude and thus keep up a valiant place in his captain's mind, he advanced, and eyeing the wreck exclaimed, "The thistle the ass refused; it pricked his mouth too keenly, sir; ha! ha!

"What soulless thing is this that laughs before a wreck? Man, man! did I not know thee brave as fearless fire (and as mechanical) I could swear thou wert a poltroon. Groan nor laugh should be heard before a wreck."

"Aye, sir," said Starbuck drawing near, " 'tis a solemn sight; an omen, and an ill one."

"Omen? omen?—the dictionary! If the gods think to speak outright to man, they will honorably speak outright; not shake their heads, and give an old wives' darkling hint.—Begone! Ye two are the opposite poles of one thing; Starbuck is Stubb reversed, and Stubb is Starbuck; and ye two are all mankind; and Ahab stands alone among the millions of the peopled earth, nor gods nor men his neighbors! Cold, cold—I shiver!—How now? Aloft there! D'ye see him? Sing out for every spout, though he spout ten times a second!"

The day was nearly done; only the hem of his golden robe was rustling. Soon, it was almost dark, but the lookout men still remained unset.

"Can't see the spout now, sir—too dark," cried a voice from the air.

"How heading when last seen?"

"As before, sir—straight to leeward."

"Good! he will travel slower now 'tis night. Down royals and topgallant stunsails, Mr. Starbuck. We must not run over him before morning; he's making a passage now, and may heave to a while. Helm there! keep her full before the wind!—Aloft! come down!—Mr. Stubb, send a fresh hand to the foremasthead, and see it manned till morning."—Then advancing toward the doubloon in the mainmast—"Men, this gold is mine, for I earned it; but I shall let it abide here till the White Whale is dead; and then, whosoever of ye first raises him, upon the day he shall be killed, this gold is that man's; and if on that day I shall again raise him, then, ten times its sum shall be divided among all of ye! Away now!—the deck is thine, sir."

And so saying, he placed himself halfway within the scuttle, and slouching his hat, stood there till dawn, except when at intervals rousing himself to see how the night wore on.

THE CHASE—SECOND DAY

At daybreak, the three mastheads were punctually manned afresh.

"D'ye see him?" cried Ahab, after allowing a little space for the light to spread.

"See nothing, sir."

"Turn up all hands and make sail! he travels faster than I thought for— the topgallant sails!—aye, they should have been kept on her all night. But no matter—'tis but resting for the rush."

Here be it said that this pertinacious pursuit of one particular whale, continued through day into night, and through night into day, is a thing by no means unprecedented in the South Sea fishery. For such is the wonderful skill, prescience of experience, and invincible confidence acquired by some great natural geniuses among the Nantucket commanders, that from the simple observation of a whale when last descried, they will, under certain given circumstances, pretty accurately foretell both the direction in which he will continue to swim for a time, while out of sight, as well as his probable rate of progression during that period.

The ship tore on; leaving such a furrow in the sea as when a cannon ball, missent, becomes a plowshare and turns up the level field.

"By salt and hemp!" cried Stubb, "but this swift motion of the deck creeps up one's legs and tingles at the heart. This ship and I are two brave fellows! —Ha! ha! Someone take me up, and launch me, spinewise, on the sea,— for by live oaks! my spine's a keel. Ha, ha! we go the gait that leaves no dust behind!"

"There she blows—she blows!—she blows!—right ahead!" was now the masthead cry.

"Aye, aye!" cried Stubb, "I knew it—ye can't escape—blow on and split your spout, O whale! the mad fiend himself is after ye! blow your trump— blister your lungs!—Ahab will dam off your blood, as a miller shuts his water-gate upon the stream!"

And Stubb did but speak out for well nigh all that crew. The frenzies of the chase had by this time worked them bubblingly up, like old wine worked anew. Whatever pale fears and forebodings some of them might have felt before; these were not only now kept out of sight through the growing awe of Ahab, but they were broken up, and on all sides routed, as timid prairie hares that scatter before the bounding bison. The hand of Fate had snatched all their souls; and by the stirring perils of the previous day; the rack of the past night's suspense; the fixed, unfearing, blind, reckless way in which their wild craft went plunging toward its flying mark; by all these things their hearts were bowled along. The wind that made great bellies of their sails, and rushed the vessel on by arms invisible as irresistible; this seemed the symbol of that unseen agency which so enslaved them to the race.

They were one man, not thirty. For as the one ship that held them all; though it was put together of all contrasting things—oak, and maple, and pinewood; iron, and pitch, and hemp—yet all these ran into each other in the one concrete hull, which shot on its way, both balanced and directed by the long central keel; even so, all the individualities of the crew, this man's valor, that man's fear; guilt and guiltiness, all varieties were welded into oneness, and were all directed to that fatal goal which Ahab their one lord and keel did point to.

The rigging lived. The mastheads, like the tops of tall palms, were outspreadingly tufted with arms and legs. Clinging to a spar with one hand, some reached forth the other with impatient wavings; others, shading their eyes from the vivid sunlight, sat far out on the rocking yards; all the spars in full bearing of mortals, ready and ripe for their fate. Ah! how they still strove through that infinite blueness to seek out the thing that might destroy them!

"Why sing ye not out for him, if ye see him?" cried Ahab, when, after the lapse of some minutes since the first cry, no more had been heard. "Sway me up, men; ye have been deceived; not Moby Dick casts one odd jet that way, and then disappears."

It was even so; in their headlong eagerness, the men had mistaken some other thing for the whale spout, as the event itself soon proved; for hardly had Ahab reached his perch; hardly was the rope belayed to its pin on deck, when he struck the keynote to an orchestra, that made the air vibrate as with the combined discharges of rifles. The triumphant halloo of thirty buckskin lungs was heard, as—much nearer to the ship than the place of the imaginary jet, less than a mile ahead—Moby Dick bodily burst into view! For not by any calm and indolent spoutings; not by the peaceable gush of that mystic fountain in his head, did the White Whale now reveal his vicinity; but by the far more wondrous phenomenon of breaching. Rising with his utmost velocity from the furthest depths, the sperm whale thus booms his entire bulk into the pure element of air, and piling up a mountain of dazzling foam, shows his place to the distance of seven miles and more. In those moments the torn, enraged waves he shakes off seem his mane; in some cases this breaching is his act of defiance.

"There she breaches! there she breaches!" was the cry, as in his immeasurable bravadoes the White Whale tossed himself salmonlike to heaven. So suddenly seen in the blue plain of the sea, and relieved against the still bluer margin of the sky, the spray that he raised, for the moment, intolerably glittered and glared like a glacier; and stood there gradually fading and fading away from its first sparkling intensity, to the dim mistiness of an advancing shower in a vale.

"Aye, breach your last to the sun, Moby Dick!" cried Ahab, "thy hour and thy harpoon are at hand!—Down! down all of ye, but one man at the fore. The boats!—stand by!"

Unmindful of the tedious rope ladders of the shrouds, the men, like shooting stars, slid to the deck, by the isolated backstays and halyards; while Ahab, less dartingly, but still rapidly was dropped from his perch.

"Lower away," he cried, so soon as he had reached his boat—a spare one, rigged the afternoon previous. "Mr. Starbuck, the ship is thine—keep away from the boats, but keep near them. Lower, all!"

As if to strike a quick terror into them, by this time being the first assailant himself, Moby Dick had turned, and was now coming for the three crews. Ahab's boat was central; and cheering his men, he told them he would take the whale head-and-head—that is, pull straight up to his forehead, a not uncommon thing; for within a certain limit, such a course ere that close limit was gained, and while yet all three boats were plain as the ship's three masts to his eye; the White Whale churning himself into furious speed, almost in an instant as it were, rushing among the boats with open jaws, and a lashing tail, offered appalling battle on every side; and heedless of the irons darted at him from every boat, seemed only intent on annihilating each separate plank of which those boats were made. But skillfully maneuvered, incessantly wheeling like trained chargers in the field; the boats for a while eluded him; though, at times, but by a plank's breadth; while all the time, Ahab's unearthly slogan tore every other cry but his to shreds.

But at last in his untraceable evolutions, the White Whale so crossed and recrossed, and in a thousand ways entangled the slack of the three lines now fast to him, that they foreshortened, and, of themselves, warped the devoted boats toward the planted irons in him; though now for a moment the whale drew aside a little, as if to rally for a more tremendous charge. Seizing that opportunity, Ahab first paid out more line and then was rapidly hauling and jerking in upon it again—hoping that way to disencumber it of some snarls—when lo!—a sight more savage than the embattled teeth of sharks!

Caught and twisted—corkscrewed in the mazes of the line, loose harpoons,

and lances, with all their bristling barbs and points, came flashing and dripping up to the chocks in the bows of Ahab's boat. Only one thing could be
done. Seizing the boat-knife, he critically reached within—through—and
then, without—the rays of steel; dragged in the line beyond, passed it, inboard, to the bowsman, and then, twice sundering the rope near the chocks
—dropped the intercepted fagot of steel into the sea, and was all fast again.
That instant, the White Whale made a sudden rush among the remaining
tangles of the other lines; by so doing, irresistibly dragged the more involved
boats of Stubb and Flask toward his flukes; dashed them together like two
rolling husks on a surf-beaten beach, and then, diving down into the sea,
disappeared in a boiling maelstrom, in which, for a space, the odorous cedar
chips of the wrecks danced round and round, like the grated nutmeg in a
swiftly stirred bowl of punch.

While the two crews were yet circling in the waters, reaching out after
the revolving line-tubs, oars, and other floating furniture, while aslope little
Flask bobbed up and down like an empty vial, twitching his legs upward
to escape the dreaded jaws of sharks; and Stubb was lustily singing out for
someone to ladle him up; and while the old man's line—now parting—
admitted of his pulling into the creamy pool to rescue whom he could—in
that wild simultaneousness of a thousand concreted perils—Ahab's yet-
unstricken boat seemed drawn up toward heaven by invisible wires, as,
arrowlike, shooting perpendicularly from the sea, the White Whale dashed
his broad forehead against its bottom, and sent it, turning over and over,
into the air; till it fell again, gunwale downwards, and Ahab and his men
struggled out from under it, like seals from a seaside cave.

The first uprising momentum of the whale—modifying its direction as
he struck the surface—involuntarily launched him along it, to a little distance from the center of the destruction he had made; and with his back
to it, he now lay for a moment slowly feeling with his flukes from side to
side; and whenever a stray oar, bit of plank, the least chip or crumb of the
boats touched his skin, his tail swiftly drew back and came sideways smiting
the sea. But soon, as if satisfied that his work for that time was done, he
pushed his pleated forehead through the ocean, and trailing after him the
intertangled lines, continued his leeward way at a traveler's methodic pace.

As before, the attentive ship having descried the whole fight, again came
bearing down to the rescue, and dropping a boat, picked up the floating
mariners, tubs, oars, and whatever else could be caught at, and safely landed
them on her decks. Some sprained shoulders, wrists, and ankles; livid con-
tusions; wrenched harpoons and lances; inextricable intricacies of rope;
shattered oars and planks; all these were there; but no fatal or even serious

ill seemed to have befallen any one. As with Fedullah the day before, so Ahab was now found grimly clinging to his boat's broken half, which afforded a comparatively easy float; nor did it so exhaust him as the previous day's mishap.

But when he was helped to the deck, all eyes were fastened upon him; as instead of standing by himself he still half-hung upon the shoulder of Starbuck, who had thus far been the foremost to assist him. His ivory leg had been snapped off, leaving but one short, sharp splinter.

"Aye, aye, Starbuck, 'tis sweet to lean sometimes, be the leaner who he will; and would old Ahab had leaned oftener than he has."

"The ferrule has not stood, sir," said the carpenter, now coming up; "I put good work into that leg."

"But no bones broken, sir, I hope," said Stubb with true concern.

"Aye! and all splintered to pieces, Stubb!—d'ye see it. But even with a broken bone, old Ahab is untouched; and I account no living bone of mine one jot more me, than this dead one that's lost. Nor White Whale, nor man, nor fiend, can so much as graze old Ahab in his own proper and inaccessible being. Can any lead touch yonder floor, any mast scrape yonder roof?— Aloft there! which way?"

"Dead to leeward, sir."

"Up helm, then; pile on the sail again, ship keepers! down the rest of the spare boats and rig them—Mr. Starbuck away, and muster the boat's crews."

"Let me first help thee toward the bulwarks, sir."

"Oh, oh, oh! how this splinter gores me now! Accursed fate! that the unconquerable captain in the soul should have such a craven mate!"

"Sir?"

"My body, man, not thee. Give me something for a cane—there, that shivered lance will do. Muster the men. Surely I have not seen him yet. By heaven it cannot be!—missing?—quick! call them all."

The old man's hinted thought was true. Upon mustering the company, the Parsee was not there.

"The Parsee!" cried Stubb, "he must have been caught in——"

"The black vomit wrench thee! Run all of ye above, alow, cabin, forecastle—find him—not gone—not gone!"

But quickly they returned to him with the tidings that the Parsee was nowhere to be found.

"Aye, sir," said Stubb, "caught among the tangles of your line—I thought I saw him dragging under."

"*My* line! *my* line? Gone?—gone? What means that little word? What death knell rings in it, that old Ahab shakes as if he were the belfry. The harpoon, too! Toss over the litter there—d'ye see it?—the forged iron, men, the White Whale's—no, no, no—blistered fool! this hand did dart it!—'tis in the fish! Aloft there! Keep him nailed. Quick! All hands to the rigging of the boats—collect the oars—harpooners! the irons, the irons!—hoist the royals higher—a pull on all the sheets!—helm there! steady, steady for your life! I'll ten times girdle the unmeasured globe; yea and dive straight through it, but I'll slay him yet!"

"Great God! but for one single instant show thyself," cried Starbuck; "never, never wilt thou capture him, old man—In Jesus' name no more of this, that's worse than devil's madness. Two days chased; twice stove to splinters; thy very leg once more snatched from under thee; thy evil shadow gone—all good angels mobbing thee with warnings: what more wouldst thou have? Shall we keep chasing this murderous fish till he swamps the last man? Shall we be dragged by him to the bottom of the sea? Shall we be towed by him to the infernal world? Oh, oh, impiety and blasphemy to hunt him more!"

"Starbuck, of late I've felt strangely moved to thee; ever since that hour we both saw—thou know'st what, in one another's eyes. But in this matter of the whale, be the front of thy face to me as the palm of this hand—a lipless, unfeatured blank. Ahab is forever Ahab, man. This whole act's immutably decreed. 'Twas rehearsed by me and thee a billion years before this ocean rolled. Fool! I am the Fates' lieutenant; I act under orders. Look thou, underling! that thou obeyest mine. Stand round, men. Ye see an old man cut down to the stump; leaning on a shivered lance; propped up on a lonely foot. 'Tis Ahab—his body's part; but Ahab's soul's a centipede, that moves upon a hundred legs. I feel strained, half-stranded, as ropes that tow dismasted frigates in a gale; and I may look so. But ere I break, ye'll hear me crack; and till ye hear *that,* know that Ahab's hawser tows his purpose yet. Believe ye, men, in the things called omens? Then laugh aloud and cry encore! For ere they drown, drowning things will twice rise to the surface; then rise again, to sink for evermore. So with Moby Dick—two days he's floated—tomorrow will be the third. Aye, men, he'll rise once more, but only to spout his last! D'ye feel brave men, brave?"

"As fearless fire," cried Stubb.

"And as mechanical," muttered Ahab. Then as the men went forward, he muttered on: "The things called omens! And yesterday I talked the same to Starbuck there, concerning my broken boat. Oh! how valiantly I seek to drive out of others' hearts what's clinched so fast in mine!—The Parsee —the Parsee!—gone, gone? and he was to go before: but still was to be seen again ere I could perish—How's that? There's a riddle now might baffle all the lawyers backed by the ghosts of the whole line of judges: like a hawk's beak it pecks my brain. *I'll, I'll* solve it, though!"

When dusk descended, the whale was still in sight to leeward.

So once more the sail was shortened, and everything passed nearly as on the previous night; only, the sound of hammers and the hum of the grindstone were heard till nearly daylight, as the men toiled by lanterns in the complete and careful rigging of the spare boats and sharpening their fresh weapons for the morrow. Meantime, of the broken keel of Ahab's wrecked craft the carpenter made him another leg; while still as on the night before, slouched Ahab stood fixed within his scuttle; his hid, heliotrope glance anticipatingly gone backward on its dial; sat due eastward for the earliest sun.

THE CHASE—THIRD DAY

The morning of the third day dawned fair and fresh, and once more the solitary night-man at the foremasthead was relieved by crowds of the daylight lookouts, who dotted every mast and almost every spar.

"D'ye see him?" cried Ahab; but the whale was not yet in sight.

"In his infallible wake, though; but follow that wake, that's all. Helm there; steady, as thou goest, and hast been going. What a lovely day again! were it a new-made world, and made for a summerhouse to the angels, and this morning the first of its throwing open to them, a fairer day could not dawn upon that world. Here's food for thought, had Ahab time to think; but Ahab never thinks; he only feels, feels, feels; *that's* tingling enough for mortal man! to think's audacity. God only has that right and privilege. Thinking is, or ought to be, a coolness and a calmness; and our poor hearts throb, and our poor brains beat too much for that. And yet, I've sometimes thought my brain was very calm—frozen calm, this old skull cracks so, like a glass in which the contents turned to ice, and shiver it. And still this hair is growing now; this moment growing, and heat must breed it; but no, it's like that sort of common grass that will grow anywhere, between the earthy clefts of Greenland ice or in Vesuvius lava. How the wild winds blow it; they whip it about me as the torn shreds of split sails lash the tossed ship they cling to. A vile wind that has no doubt blown ere this through prison corridors and cells, and wards of hospitals, and ventilated them, and now comes blowing hither as innocent as fleeces. Out upon it!—it's tainted. Were I the wind, I'd blow no more on such a wicked, miserable world. I'd crawl somewhere to a cave, and slink there. And yet, 'tis a noble and heroic thing, the wind! who ever conquered it? In every fight it has the last and bitterest blow. Run tilting at it, and you but run through it. Ha! a coward wind that strikes stark-naked men, but will not stand to receive a single blow. Even Ahab is a braver thing—a nobler thing that *that*. Would now the wind but had a body; but all the things that most exasperate and outrage mortal man, all these things are bodiless, but only bodiless as objects not as agents. There's a most special, a most cunning, oh, a most malicious difference! And yet, I say again, and swear it now, that there's something all glorious and gracious in the wind. These warm trade winds, at least, that in the clear heavens blow straight on, in strong and steadfast, vigorous mildness; and veer not from their mark, however the baser currents of the sea may turn and tack, and mightiest Mississippies of the land swift and swerve about, uncertain where to go at last. And by the eternal Poles! these same trades that so directly blow my good ship on; these trades, or something like them—something so unchangeable, and full as strong, blow my keeled soul along! To it! Aloft there! Where d'ye see?"

"Nothing, sir."

"Nothing! and noon at hand! The doubloon goes a-begging! See the sun! Aye, aye, it must be so. I've oversailed him. How, got the start? Aye, he's chasing *me* now; not I, *him*—that's bad; I might have known it, too. Fool! the lines—the harpoons he's towing. Aye, aye, I have run him by last night. About! about! Come down, all of ye, but the regular lookouts! Man the braces!"

Steering as she had done, the wind had been somewhat on the *Pequod*'s quarter, so that now being pointed in the reverse direction, the braced ship sailed hard upon the breeze as she rechurned the cream in her own white wake.

"Against the wind he now steers for the open jaw," murmured Starbuck to himself, as he coiled the new-hauled mainbrace upon the rail. "God keep us, but already my bones feel damp within me, and from the inside wet my flesh. I misdoubt me that I disobey my God in obeying him!"

"Stand by to sway me up!" cried Ahab, advancing to the hempen basket. "We should meet him soon."

"Aye, aye, sir," and straightway Starbuck did Ahab's bidding, and once more Ahab swung on high.

A whole hour now passed; gold-beaten out to ages. Time itself now held long breaths with keen suspense. But at last, some three points off the weather bow, Ahab descried the spout again, and instantly from the three mastheads three shrieks went up as if the tongues of fire had voiced it.

"Forehead to forehead I meet thee, this third time, Moby Dick! On deck there!—brace sharper up; crowd her into the wind's eye. He's too far off to lower yet, Mr. Starbuck. The sails shake! Stand over that helmsman with a topmaul! So, so; he travels fast, and I must down. But let me have one more good round look aloft here at the sea; there's time for that. An old, old sight, and yet somehow so young; aye, and not changed a wink since I first saw it, a boy, from the sand hills of Nantucket! The same!—the same!—the same to Noah as to me. There's a soft shower to leeward. Such lovely leewardings! They must lead somewhere—to something else than common land, more palmy than the palms. Leeward! the White Whale goes that way; look to windward, then; the better if the bitterer quarter. But good-by, good-by, old masthead! What's this?—green? aye, tiny mosses in these warped cracks. No such green weather stains on Ahab's head! There's the difference now between man's old age and matter's. But aye, old mast, we both grow old together; sound in our hulls, though, are we not, my ship? Aye, minus a leg, that's all. By heaven, this dead wood has the better of my live flesh every way. I can't compare with it; and I've known some ships made of dead trees outlast the lives of men made of the most vital stuff of vital fathers. What's that he said? he should still go before me, my pilot; and yet to be seen again? But where? Will I have eyes at the bottom of the sea, supposing I descend those endless stairs? and all night I've been sailing from him, wherever he did sink to. Aye, aye, like many more thou told'st direful truth as touching thyself, O Parsee; but, Ahab, there thy shot fell short. Good-by, masthead—keep a good eye upon the whale, the while I'm gone. We'll talk tomorrow, nay, tonight, when the White Whale lies down there, tied by head and tail."

He gave the word; and still gazing round him, was steadily lowered through the cloven blue air to the deck.

In due time the boats were lowered; but as standing in his shallop's stern, Ahab just hovered upon the point of the descent, he waved to the mate, who held one of the tackle ropes on deck, and bade him pause.

"Starbuck!"

"Sir?"

"For the third time my soul's ship starts upon this voyage, Starbuck."

"Aye, sir, thou wilt have it so."

"Some ships sail from their ports, and ever afterward are missing, Starbuck!"

"Truth, sir: saddest truth."

"Some men die at ebb tide; some at low water; some at the full of the flood—and I feel now like a billow that's all one crested comb, Starbuck. I am old; shake hands with me, man."

Their hands met; their eyes fastened; Starbuck's tears the glue.

"Oh, my captain, my captain!—noble heart—go not, go not! See, it's a brave man that weeps; how great the agony of the persuasion then!"

"Lower away!" cried Ahab, tossing the mate's arm from him. "Stand by the crew!"

In an instant the boat was pulling round close under the stern.

"The sharks! the sharks!" cried a voice from the low cabin window there; "O master, my master, come back!"

But Ahab heard nothing; for his own voice was high-lifted then, and the boat leaped on.

Yet the voice spake true; for scarce had he pushed from the ship, when numbers of sharks, seemingly rising from out the dark waters beneath the hull, maliciously snapped at the blades of the oars every time they dipped in the water; and in this way accompanied the boat with their bites. It is a thing not uncommonly happening to the whale boats in those swarming seas; the sharks at times apparently following them in the same prescient way that vultures hover over the banners of marching regiments in the east. But these were the first sharks that had been observed by the *Pequod* since the White Whale had been descried; and whether it was that Ahab's crew were all such tiger-yellow barbarians, and therefore their flesh more musky to the senses of the sharks—a matter sometimes well known to affect them—however it was, they seemed to follow that one boat without molesting the others.

"Heart of wrought steel!" murmured Starbuck gazing over the side and following with his eyes the receding boat, "canst thou yet ring boldly to that sight?—lowering thy keel among ravening sharks, and followed by them, open-mouthed to the chase; and this the critical third day? For when three days flow together in one continuous intense pursuit; be sure the first is the morning, the second the noon, and the third the evening and the end of that thing—be that end what it may. Oh! my God! what is this that shoots through me and leaves me so deadly calm, yet expectant, fixed at the top of a shudder! Future things swim before me, as in empty outlines and skeletons; all the past is somehow grown dim. Mary, girl! thou fadest in pale glories behind me; boy! I seem to see but thy eyes grown wondrous blue. Strangest problems of life seem clearing; but clouds sweep between. Is my journey's end coming? My legs feel faint; like his who has footed it all day. Feel thy heart, beats it yet?—Stir thyself, Starbuck! Stave it off—move, move! speak aloud! Masthead there! See ye my boy's hand on the hill? Crazed; aloft there! Keep thy keenest eye upon the boats:—mark well the whale! Ho! again!—drive off that hawk! see! he pecks—he tears the vane," pointing to the red flag flying at the main truck. "Ha! he soars away with it!—Where's the old man now? see'st thou that sight, oh Ahab!—shudder, shudder!"

The boats had not gone very far, when by a signal from the mastheads— a downward-pointed arm—Ahab knew that the whale had sounded; but intending to be near him at the next rising, he held on his way a little sideways from the vessel; the becharmed crew maintaining the profoundest silence, as the head-beat waves hammered and hammered against the opposing bow.

"Drive, drive in your nails, oh ye waves! to their uttermost heads drive them in! ye but strike a thing without a lid; and no coffin and no hearse can be mine:—and hemp only can kill me! Ha! ha!"

Suddenly the waters around them slowly swelled in broad circles; then quickly upheaved, as if sideways sliding from a submerged berg of ice, swiftly rising to the surface. A low rumbling sound was heard; a subterraneous hum; and then all held their breaths, as bedraggled with trailing ropes and harpoons and lances, a vast form shot lengthwise, but obliquely from the sea. Shrouded in a thin, drooping veil of mist, it hovered for a moment in the rainbowed air and then fell swamping back into the deep. Crushed thirty feet upward, the waters flashed for an instant like heaps of fountains, then brokenly sank in a shower of flakes, leaving the circling surface creamed like new milk round the marble trunk of the whale.

"Give way!" cried Ahab to the oarsmen, and the boats darted forward to the attack; but maddened by yesterday's fresh irons that corroded in him, Moby Dick seemed combinedly possessed by all the angels that fell from heaven. The wide tiers of welded tendons overspreading his broad white forehead, beneath the transparent skin, looked knitted together, as head on he came, churning his tail among the boats, and once more flailed them apart, spilling out the irons and lances from the two mates' boats, and dashing in one side of the upper part of their bows, but leaving Ahab's almost without a scar.

While Daggoo and Queequeg were stopping the strained planks; and as the whale swimming out from them, turned, and showed one entire flank as he shot by them again; at that moment a quick cry went up. Lashed round and round to the fish's back; pinioned in the turns upon turns in which, during the past night, the whale had reeled the involutions of the lines around him, the half-torn body of the Parsee was seen; his sable raiment frayed to shreds; his distended eyes turned full upon old Ahab.

The harpoon dropped from his hand.

"Befooled, befooled!"—drawing in a long, lean breath—"Aye, Parsee! I see thee again. Aye, and thou goest before; and this, *this* then is the hearse that thou didst promise. But I hold thee to the last letter of thy word. Where is the second hearse? Away, mates, to the ship! those boats are useless now; repair them if ye can in time, and return to me if not, Ahab is enough to die—Down, men! the first thing that but offers to jump from this boat I stand in, that thing I harpoon. Ye are not other men, but my arms and my legs; and so obey me. Where's the whale? gone down again?"

But he looked too nigh the boat; for as if bent upon escaping with the corpse he bore, and as if the particular place of the last encounter had been but a stage in his leeward voyage, Moby Dick was now again steadily swimming forward and had almost passed the ship, which thus far had been sailing in the contrary direction to him, though for the present her headway had been stopped. He seemed swimming with his utmost velocity, and now only intent upon pursuing his own straight path in the sea.

"Oh! Ahab," cried Starbuck, "not too late is it, even now, the third day, to desist. See! Moby Dick seeks thee not. It is thou, thou, that madly seekest him!"

Setting sail to the rising wind, the lonely boat was swiftly impelled to leeward, by both oars and canvas. And at last when Ahab was sliding by the vessel, so near as plainly to distinguish Starbuck's face as he leaned over the rail, he hailed him to turn the vessel about, and follow him, not too swiftly, at a judicious interval. Glancing upward, he saw Tashtego, Queequeg, and Daggoo, eagerly mounting to the three mastheads; while the oarsmen were rocking in the two staved boats, which had but just been hoisted to the side, and were busily at work in repairing them. One after the other, through the portholes, as he sped, he also caught flying glimpses of Stubb and Flask, busying themselves on deck among bundles of new irons and lances. As he saw all this; as he heard the hammers in the broken boats; far other hammers seemed driving a nail into his heart. But he rallied. And now marking that the vane or flag was gone from the mainmasthead, he shouted to Tashtego, who had just gained that perch, to descend again for another flag, and a hammer and nails, and so nail it to the mast.

Whether fagged by the three days' running chase, and the resistance to his swimming in the knotted hamper he bore; or whether it was some latent deceitfulness and malice in him: whichever was true, the White Whale's way now began to abate, as it seemed, from the boat so rapidly nearing him once more; though indeed the whale's last start had not been so long a one as before. And still as Ahab glided over the waves the unpitying sharks accompanied him, and so pertinaciously stuck to the boat, and so continually bit at the plying oars, that the blades became jagged and crunched, and left small splinters in the sea at almost every dip.

"Heed them not! those teeth but give new row-locks to your oars. Pull on! 'tis the better rest, the shark's jaw than the yielding water."

"But at every bite, sir, the thin blades grow smaller and smaller!"

"They will last long enough! pull on! But who can tell," he muttered, "whether these sharks swim to feast on the whale or on Ahab?—But pull on! Aye, all alive, now—we near him. The helm! take the helm; let me pass," and so saying, two of the oarsmen helped him forward to the bows of the still-flying boat.

At length as the craft was cast to one side, and ran ranging along with the White Whale's flank, he seemed strangely oblivious of its advance—as the whale sometimes will—and Ahab was fairly within the smoky mountain mist, which, thrown off from the whale's spout, curled round his great, Monadnock hump; he was even thus close to him; when, with body arched back, and both arms lengthwise high-lifted to the poise, he darted his fierce iron, and his far fiercer curse into the hated whale. As both steel and curse sank to the socket, as if sucked into a morass, Moby Dick sideways writhed, spasmodically rolled his nigh flank against the bow, and, without staving a hole in it, so suddenly canted the boat over, that had it not been for the elevated part of the gunwale to which he then clung, Ahab would once more have been tossed into the sea. As it was, three of the oarsmen—who foreknew not the precise instant of the dart, and were therefore unprepared for its effects—these were flung out, but so fell, that, in an instant two of them clutched the gunwale again, and rising to its level on a combing wave, hurled themselves bodily inboard again; the third man helplessly dropping astern, but still afloat and swimming.

Almost simultaneously, with a mighty volition of ungraduated, instantaneous swiftness, the White Whale darted through the weltering sea. But when Ahab cried out to the steersman to take new turns with the line, and hold it so; and commanded the crew to turn round on their seats, and tow the boat up to the mark; the moment the treacherous line felt that doubt strain and tug, it snapped in the empty air!

"What breaks in me? Some sinew cracks!—'tis whole again; oars! oars! Burst in upon him!"

Hearing the tremendous rush of the sea-crashing boat, the whale wheeled round to present his blank forehead at bay; but in that evolution, catching sight of the nearing black hull of the ship, seemingly seeing it in the source of all his persecutions, bethinking it—it may be—a larger and nobler foe; of a sudden, he bore down upon its advancing prow, smiting his jaws amid fiery showers of foam.

Ahab staggered; his hand smote his forehead. "I grow blind; hands! stretch out before me that I may yet grope my way. Is't night?"

"The whale! The ship!" cried the cringing oarsmen.

"Oars! oars! Slope downward to thy depths, O sea, that ere it be for ever too late, Ahab may slide this last, last time upon his mark! I see: the ship! the ship! Dash on, my men! Will ye not save my ship?"

But as the oarsmen violently forced their boat through the sledge-hammering seas, the before-whale-smitten bow ends of two planks burst through, and in an instant almost, the temporarily disabled boat lay nearly level with the waves; its half-wading, splashing crew, trying hard to stop the gap and bail out the pouring water.

Meantime, for that one beholding instant, Tashtego's masthead hammer remained suspended in his hand, and the red flag, half-wrapping him as with a plaid, then streamed itself straight out from him, as his own forward-flowing heart; while Starbuck and Stubb, standing upon the bowsprit beneath, caught sight of the down-coming monster just as soon as he.

"The whale, the whale! Up helm, up helm! Oh, all ye sweet powers of air, now hug me close! Let not Starbuck die, if die he must, in a woman's fainting fit. Up helm, I say—ye fools, the jaw! the jaw! Is this the end of all my bursting prayers? all my lifelong fidelities? Oh, Ahab, Ahab, lo, thy work. Steady! helmsman, steady. Nay, nay! Up helm again! He turns to meet us! Oh, his unappeasable brow drives on toward one, whose duty tells him he cannot depart. My God, stand by me now!"

"Stand not by me, but stand under me, whoever you are that will now help Stubb; for Stubb, too, sticks here. I grin at thee, thou grinning whale! Who ever helped Stubb, or kept Stubb awake, but Stubb's own unwinking eye? And now poor Stubb goes to bed upon a mattress that is all too soft; would it were stuffed with brushwood! I grin at thee, thou grinning whale! Look ye, sun, moon, and stars! I call ye assassins of as good a fellow as ever spouted up his ghost. For all that, I would yet ring glasses with ye, would ye but hand the cup! Oh, oh! oh, oh! thou grinning whale, but there'll be plenty of gulping soon! Why fly ye not, O Ahab! For me, off shoes and jacket to it; let Stubb die in his drawers! A most moldy and oversalted death, though—cherries! cherries! cherries! Oh, Flask, for one red cherry ere we die!"

"Cherries? I only wish that we were where they grow. Oh, Stubb, I hope my poor mother's drawn my part-pay ere this; if not, few coppers will now come to her, for the voyage is up."

From the ship's bows nearly all the seamen now hung inactive; hammers, bits of plank, lances, and harpoons mechanically retained in their hands, just as they had darted from their various employments; all their enchanted eyes intent upon the whale, which from side to side strangely vibrating his predestinating head, sent a broad band of overspreading semicircular foam before him as he rushed. Retribution, swift vengeance, eternal malice, were in his whole aspect, and spite of all that mortal man could do, the solid white buttress of his forehead smote the ship's starboard bow till men and timbers reeled. Some fell flat upon their faces. Like dislodged trucks, the heads of the harpooners aloft shook on their bull-like necks. Through the breach they heard the waters pour, as mountain torrents down a flume.

"The ship! The hearse!—the second hearse!" cried Ahab from the boat; "its wood could only be American!"

Diving beneath the settling ship, the whale ran quivering along its keel; but turning under water, swiftly shot to the surface again, far off the other bow, but within a few yards of Ahab's boat, where, for a time, he lay quiescent.

"I turn my body from the sun. What ho, Tashtego! let me hear thy hammer. Oh! ye three unsurrendered spires of mine; thou uncracked keel; and only god-bullied hull; thou firm deck, and haughty helm, and Pole-pointed prow—death-glorious ship! must ye then perish, and without me? Am I cut off from the last fond pride of meanest shipwrecked captains? Oh, lonely death on lonely life! Oh, now I feel my topmost greatness lies in my topmost grief. Ho, ho! from all your furthest bounds, pour ye now in, ye bold billows of my whole foregone life, and top this one piled comber of my death! Toward thee I roll, thou all-destroying but unconquering whale; to the last I grapple with thee; from hell's heart I stab at thee; for hate's sake I spit my last breath at thee. Sink all coffins and all hearses to one common pool! and since neither can be mine, let me then tow to pieces, while still chasing thee, though tied to thee, thou damned whale! *Thus,* I give up the spear!"

The harpoon was darted; the stricken whale flew forward; with igniting velocity the line ran through the groove—ran foul. Ahab stooped to clear it; he did clear it; but the flying turn caught him round the neck and, voicelessly as Turkish mutes bowstring their victim, he was shot out of the boat, ere the crew knew he was gone. Next instant the heavy eye-splice in the rope's final end flew out of the stark-empty tub, knocked down an oarsman, and, smiting the sea, disappeared in its depths.

For an instant the tranced boat's crew stood still; then turned, "The ship? great God, where is the ship?" Soon they through dim, bewildering mediums saw her sidelong fading phantom, as in the gaseous Fata Morgana;

only the uppermost masts out of water; while fixed by infatuation, or fidelity, or fate, to their once-lofty perches, the pagan harpooners still maintained their sinking lookouts on the sea. And now, concentric circles seized the lone boat itself, and all its crew, and each floating oar, and every lance-pole, and spinning, animate and inanimate, all round and round in one vortex, carried the smallest chip of the *Pequod* out of sight.

But as the last whelmings intermixingly poured themselves over the sunken head of the Indian at the mainmast, leaving a few inches of the erect spar yet visible, together with long streaming yards of the flag, which calmly undulated, with ironical coincidings, over the destroying billows they almost touched—at that instant, a red arm and a hammer hovered backwardly uplifted in the open air, in the act of nailing the flag faster and yet faster to the subsiding spar. A sky hawk that tauntingly had followed the main truck downwards from its natural home among the stars, pecking at the flag, and incommoding Tashtego there; this bird now chanced to intercept its broad, fluttering wing between the hammer and the wood; and simultaneously feeling that ethereal thrill, the submerged savage beneath, in his death gasp, kept his hammer frozen there; and so the bird of heaven, with archangelic shrieks and his imperial beak thrust upward and his whole captive form folded in the flag of Ahab, went down with his ship, which, like Satan, would not sink to hell till she had dragged a living part of heaven along with her, and helmeted herself with it.

Now small fowls flew screaming over the yet-yawning gulf; a sullen white surf beat against its steep sides; then all collapsed, and the great shroud of the sea rolled on as it rolled five thousand years ago.

An Underground Episode*

EDMUND WARE

Three figures leaned against the slanting rain—Alamo Laska, Nick Christopher, and the boy who had run away from home. They rested on their long-handled shovels and, as they gazed into the crater which by their brawn they had hollowed in the earth, the blue clay oozed back again, slowly devouring the fruits of their toil.

Laska, the nomad, thought of the wild geese winging southward to warm bayous. Nick's heart, under the bone and muscle of his great chest, swelled with sweet thoughts of his wife and child who lived in a foreign city across an ocean. The boy felt the sting of rain against his cheeks and dreamed of his mother who seemed lovely and far away.

It was Sunday. The regular deep-trench gang lounged in their warm boardinghouse and drank dago red, while out on the job the three men toiled alone. They breathed heavily, and the gray steam crawled upon their backs, for it was cold.

"Look at 'er filling in," growled Laska, "faster than a man could dig."

"Mud's get inna pipe," said Nick. "The Inspector make us tear him out if she fill any more."

Backed close to the edge of the crater stood a giant trench-digging machine. In the dusk it appeared as a crouched and shadowy animal—silent, gloomy, capable. But a broken piston had crippled its engines and they were swathed in tarpaulin.

A long gray mound stretched away from the crater opposite the machine. Buried thirty feet below the mound was the new-laid sewer pipe. From the bottom of the pit at the machine, the pipe ran a hundred yards horizontally under the surface, opening in a manhole. This hundred yards of new-laid pipe was the reason for the three men digging in the rain. They had dug eleven hours trying to uncover the open end of the pipe in order to seal it

* From *Story*, copyright, 1934, by Story Magazine, Inc. Reprinted by permission of Story Magazine, Inc., and the author's agents, Brandt & Brandt, New York.

against the mud. But rain and ooze and storm had bested them. The bank had caved, and the mud had crawled into the mouth of the pipe, obstructing it.

"It's getting dark fast," said Laska, "an' we're licked."

"We can't do nothing more," said the boy.

Nick Christopher scraped the mud from his shovel. He looked up into the whirlpools of the sky. "In a year I go old country. I see my wife. I see my kid."

"Nick," said Laska, "go over to the shanty and get a couple of lanterns and telephone Stender. Tell him if he don't want the Inspector on our tail to get out here quick with a gang."

Nick stuck his shovel in the mud and moved away across the plain toward the shanty.

The cold had crept into the boy. It frightened him, and in the darkness his eyes sought Laska's face. "How could we clean out the pipe, even when the gang got down to it?"

"Maybe we could flush her out with a fire hose," said Laska.

"There's no water plug within a mile."

Laska said nothing. The boy waited for him to reply, but he didn't. Picking up his damp shirt, the boy pulled it on over his head. He did not tuck in the tails, and they flapped in the wind, slapping against him. He looked like a gaunt, serious bird, striving to leave the ground. He was bare-headed, and his yellow hair was matted and stringy with dampness. His face was thin, a little sunken, and fine drops of moisture clung to the fuzz on his cheeks. His lips were blue with cold. He was seventeen.

Laska stared into the pit. It was too dark to see bottom, but something in the black hole fascinated him. "If we could get a rope through the pipe we could drag sandbags through into the manhole. That would clean her out in good shape."

"How could we get a rope through?"

"I dunno. Stender'll know." Laska walked over to the digging machine and leaned against its towering side. The rain had turned to sleet. "It's cold," he said.

The boy followed Laska, and went close to him for warmth and friendship. "How *could* we get a rope through?"

Laska's shoulders lifted slowly. "You'll see. You'll see when Stender gets here. Say, it's freezing."

After a long time of waiting, a yellow light flamed into being in the shanty, and they heard the muffled scraping of boots on the board floor. The shanty door opened. A rectangle of light stood out sharply.

Swart figures crossed and recrossed the lighted area, pouring out into the storm.

"Ho!" called Laska.

"Ho!" came the answer, galloping to them in the wind.

They heard the rasping of caked mud on dungarees, the clank of shovels, the voice of Stender, the foreman. Lanterns swung like yellow pendulums. Long-legged shadows reached and receded.

The diggers gathered about the rim of the pit, staring. Stender's face showed in the lantern light. His lips were wrinkled, as if constantly prepared for blasphemy. He was a tall, cursing conqueror. Orders shot from his throat, and noisily the men descended into the pit and began to dig. They drew huge, gasping breaths like mired beasts fighting for life.

The boy watched, his eyes bulging in the dark. Hitherto he had thought very briefly of sewers, regarding them as unlovely things. But Laska and Nick and Stender gave them splendor and importance. The deep-trench men were admirable monsters. They knew the clay, the feel and pattern of it, for it had long been heavy in their minds and muscles. They were big in three dimensions and their eyes were black and barbarous. When they ate it was with rough-and-tumble relish, and as their bellies fattened, they spoke tolerantly of enemies. They played lustily with a view to satiation. They worked stupendously. They were diggers in clay, transformed by lantern light into a race of giants.

Through the rain came Stender, his black slicker crackling. "They're down," he said. "Angelo just struck the pipe."

Laska grunted.

Stender blew his nose with his fingers, walked away, and climbed down into the hole. They lost sight of him as he dropped over the rim. The sound of digging had ceased and two or three men on the surface rested on their shovels, the light from below gleaming in their flat faces. Laska and the boy knew that Stender was examining the pipe. They heard him swearing at what he had found.

After a moment he clambered up over the rim and held up a lantern. His cuddy, gripped firmly between his teeth, was upside down to keep out the wet.

"Someone's got to go through the pipe," he said, raising his voice. "There's fifty bucks for the man that'll go through the pipe into the manhole with a line tied to his foot. Fifty bucks!"

There was a moment of quiet. The men thought of the fifty dollars and furtively measured themselves against the deed at hand. It seemed to the boy that he was the only one who feared the task. He did not think of the fifty dollars, but thought only of the fear. Three hundred feet through a rathole, eighteen inches in diameter. Three hundred feet of muck, of wet black dark, and no turning back. But, if he did not volunteer, they would know that he was afraid. The boy stepped from behind Laska and said uncertainly: "I'll go, Stender," and he wished he might snatch back the words; for, looking about him, he saw that not a man among those present could have wedged his shoulders into the mouth of an eighteen-inch pipe. He was the only volunteer. They had known he would be the only one.

Stender came striding over holding the lantern above his head. He peered into the boy's face. "Take off your clothes," he said.

"Take off my clothes?"

"That's what I said."

"You might get a buckle caught in a joint," said Laska. "See?"

The boy saw only that he had been trapped very cunningly. At home he could have been openly fearful, for at home everything about him was known. There, quite simply, he could have said: "I won't do it. I'm frightened. I'll be killed." But here the diggers in clay were lancing him with looks. And Laska was bringing a ball of line, one end of which would be fastened to his ankle.

"Just go in a sweater," said Laska. "A sweater an' boots over your woolens. We'll be waiting for you at the manhole."

He wanted so desperately to dive off into the night that he felt his legs bracing for a spring, and a tight feeling in his throat. Then, mechanically, he began to take off his clothes. Nick had gone clumping off to the shanty and shortly he returned with a pair of hip boots. "Here, kid. I get 'em warm for you inna shanty."

He thrust his feet into the boots, and Laska knelt and tied the heavy line to his ankle. "Too tight?"

"No. It's all right, I guess."

"Well—come on."

They walked past Stender who was pacing up and down among the men. They slid down into the crater, deepened now by the diggers. They stood by the partly covered mouth of the pipe. They were thirty feet below the surface of the ground.

Laska reached down and tugged at the knot he had tied in the line, then he peered into the mouth of the tube. He peered cautiously, as if he thought it might be inhabited. The boy's glance wandered up the wet sides of the pit. Over the rim a circle of bland yellow faces peered at him. Sleet tinkled against lanterns, spattered down and stung his flesh.

"Go ahead in," said Laska.

The boy blanched.

"Just keep thinking of the manhole, where you'll come out," said Laska.

The boy's throat constricted. He seemed to be bursting with a pressure from inside. He got down on his belly in the slush-ice and mud. It penetrated slowly to his skin and spread over him. He put his head inside the mouth of the pipe, drew back in horror. Some gibbering words flew from his lips. His voice sounded preposterously loud. Laska's voice was already shopworn with distance. "You can make it! Go ahead."

He lay on his left side, and, reaching out with his left arm, caught a joint and drew himself in. The mud oozed up around him, finding its way upon him, welling up against the left side of his face. He pressed his right cheek against the ceiling of the pipe to keep the muck from covering his mouth and nose. Laska's voice was far and muffled. Laska was in another world—a sane world of night, of storm, and the mellow glow of lanterns.

"Are you makin' it all right, kid?"

The boy cried out, his ears ringing with his cry. It re-echoed from the sides of the pipe. The sides hemmed him, pinned him, closed him in on every side with their paralyzing circumference.

There is no darkness like the darkness underground that miners know. It borrows something from night, from tombs, from places used by bats. Such fluid black can terrify a flame, and suffocate and drench a mind with madness. There is a fierce desire to struggle, to beat one's hands against the prison. The boy longed to lift his pitiful human strength against the walls. He longed to claw at his eyes in the mad certainty that more than darkness curtained them.

He had moved but a few feet on his journey when panic swept him. Ahead of him the mud had built into a stolid wave. Putting forth his left hand, he felt a scant two inches between the wave's crest and the ceiling of the pipe. There was nothing to do but go back. If he moved ahead, it meant death by suffocation. He tried to back away, but caught his toe in a joint of the pipe. He was entombed! In an hour he would be a body. The cold and dampness would kill him before they could dig down to him. Nick and Laska would pull him from the muck, and Laska would say: "Huh, his clock's stopped."

He thrashed with delirious strength against his prison. He felt the skin tearing from the backs of his hands as he flailed the rough walls. And some gods must have snickered, for above the walls of the pipe were thirty feet of unyielding clay, eight thousand miles of earth below. A strength, a weight, a night, each a thousand times his most revolting dream, leaned upon the boy, depressing, crushing, stamping him out. The ground gave no cry of battle. It did no bleeding, suffered no pain, uttered no groans. It flattened him silently.

It swallowed him in its foul despotism. It dropped its merciless weight upon his mind. It was so inhuman, so horribly incognizant of the God men swore had made it.

In the midst of his frenzy, when he had beaten his face against the walls until it bled, he heard a ringing voice he knew was real, springing from human sympathy. It was Laska, calling: "Are you all right, kid?"

In that instant the boy loved Laska as he loved his life. Laska's voice sheered the weight from him, scattered the darkness, brought him new balance and a hope to live.

"Fine!" he answered in a cracking yell. He yelled again, loving the sound of his voice, and thinking how foolish yelling was in such a place.

With his left hand he groped ahead and found that the wave of mud had settled, leveled off by its own weight. He drew his body together, pressing it against the pipe. He straightened, moved ahead six inches. His fingers found a loop of oakum dangling from a joint, and he pulled himself on, his left arm forward, his right arm behind over his hip, like a swimmer's.

He had vanquished panic, and he looked ahead to victory. Each joint brought him twenty inches nearer his goal. Each twenty inches was a plateau which enabled him to vision a new plateau—the next joint. The joints were like small deceitful rests upon a march.

He had been more than an hour on the way. He did not know how far he had gone, a third, perhaps even a half of the distance. He forgot the present, forgot fear, wet, cold, blackness; he lost himself in dreaming of the world of men outside the prison. It was as if he were a small superb island in hell.

He did not know how long he had been counting the joints, but he found himself whispering good numbers: "Fifty-one, fifty-two, fifty-three ..." Each joint, when he thought of it, appeared to take up a vast time of squirming in the muck, and the line dragged heavily behind his foot.

Suddenly, staring into the darkness so that it seemed to bring a pain to his eyes, he saw a pallid ray. He closed his eyes, opened them, and looked again. The ray was real, and he uttered a whimper of relief. He knew that the ray must come from Stender's lantern. He pictured Stender and a group of the diggers huddled in the manhole, waiting for him. The men and the manhole grew magnificent in his mind, and he thought of them worshipfully.

"Seventy-six, seventy-seven, seventy-eight ..."

The ray grew slowly, like a worthwhile thing. It took an oval shape, and the oval grew fat, like an egg, then round. It was a straight line to the manhole, and the mud had thinned.

Through the pipe, into the boy's ears, a voice rumbled like halfhearted thunder. It was Stender's voice: "How you makin' it?"

"Oh, just fine!" His cry came pricking back into his ears like a shower of needles.

There followed a long span of numbness. The cold and wet had dulled his senses, so that whenever the rough ceiling of the pipe ripped his face, he did not feel it; so that struggling in the muck became an almost pleasant and normal thing, since all elements of fear and pain and imagination had been removed. Warmth and dryness became alien to him. He was a creature native to darkness, foreign to light.

The round yellow disc before him gave him his only sense of living. It was a sunlit landfall, luring him on. He would close his eyes and count five joints, then open them quickly, cheering himself at the perceptible stages of progress.

Then, abruptly, it seemed, he was close to the manhole. He could hear men moving. He could see the outline of Stender's head as Stender peered into the mouth of the pipe. Men kneeled, pushing each other's heads to one side, in order to watch him squirm toward them. They began to talk excitedly. He could hear them breathing, see details—and Stender and Laska reached in. They got their hands upon him. They hauled him to them, as if he were something they wanted to inspect scientifically. He felt as if they thought he was a rarity, a thing of great oddness. The light dazzled him. It began to move around and around, and to dissolve into many lights, some of which danced locally on a bottle. He heard Stender's voice: "Well, he made it all right. What do you know?"

"Here, kid," said Laska, holding the bottle to his mouth. "Drink all of this that you can hold."

He could not stand up. He believed calmly that his flesh and bones were constructed of putty. He could hear no vestige of the song of victory he had dreamed of hearing. He looked stupidly at his hands, which bled painlessly. He could not feel his arms and legs at all. He was a vast sensation of lantern light and the steam of human beings breathing in a damp place.

Faces peered at him. The faces were curious and surprised. He felt a clouded, uncomprehending resentment against them. Stender held him up on one side, Laska on the other. They looked at each other across him. Suddenly Laska stooped and gathered him effortlessly into his arms.

"You'll get covered with mud," mumbled the boy.

"Damn if he didn't make it all right," said Stender. "Save us tearing out the pipe."

"Hell with the pipe," said Laska.

The boy's wet head fell against Laska's chest. He felt the rise and fall of Laska's muscles, and knew that Laska was climbing with him up the iron steps inside the manhole. Night wind smote him. He buried his dead deeper against Laska. Laska's body became a mountain of warmth. He felt a heavy sighing peace, like a soldier who has been comfortably wounded and knows that war for him is over.

Annapurna *

MAURICE HERZOG

✳✳ *Annapurna* was dictated mainly from the American Hospital just outside Paris, a book in which Maurice Herzog recounted the extraordinary feat of the French expedition as the leader of which on June 3, 1950, he and his fellow climber Louis Lachenal were the first men to achieve the summit of an 8000-meter mountain peak. That peak was Annapurna, 26,493 feet high, in the Himalayas.

There were nine members in the expedition, and it was largely for them, Herzog says, that he set down his record.

"In overstepping our limitations, in touching the extreme boundaries of man's world," he wrote in his book, "we have come to know something of its true splendor. In my worst moments of anguish I seemed to discover the deep significance of existence of which till then I had been unaware. I saw that it was better to be true than to be strong. The marks of the ordeal are apparent on my body. I was saved and I had won my freedom. This freedom, which I shall never lose, has given me the assurance and serenity of a man who has fulfilled himself. It has given me the rare joy of loving that which I used to despise. A new and splendid life has opened out before me.

"In this narrative we do more than record our adventures, we bear witness; events that seem to make no sense may sometimes have a deep significance of their own. There is no other justification for an *acte gratuit*." ✳✳

FROM CAMP V TO THE SUMMIT

On the third of June, 1950, the first light of dawn found us still clinging to the tent poles at Camp V, at 24,600 feet. Gradually the wind abated and, with daylight, died away altogether. I made desperate attempts to push back the soft, icy stuff which stifled me, but every movement became an act

* Translated from the French by Nea Morin and Janet Adam Smith. Copyright, 1952, by E. P. Dutton & Company, Inc., reprinted by permission of E. P. Dutton & Company, New York, and Jonathan Cape, Ltd., London.

of heroism. My mental powers were numbed: thinking was an effort, and we did not exchange a single word.

What a repellent place it was! To everyone who reached it, Camp V became one of the worst memories of their lives. We had only one thought—to get away. We should have waited for the first rays of the sun, but at half-past five we felt we couldn't stick it any longer.

"Let's go, Biscante," I muttered. "Can't stay here a minute longer."

"Yes, let's go," repeated Lachenal.*

Which of us would have the energy to make tea? Although our minds worked slowly we were quite able to envisage all the movements that would be necessary—and neither of us could face up to it. It couldn't be helped— we would just have to go without. It was quite hard enough work to get ourselves and our boots out of our sleeping bags—and the boots were frozen stiff so that we got them on only with the greatest difficulty. Every movement made us terribly breathless. We felt as if we were being stifled. Our gaiters were stiff as a board, and I succeeded in lacing mine up; Lachenal couldn't manage his.

"No need for the rope, eh, Biscante?"

"No need," replied Lachenal laconically.

That was two pounds saved. I pushed a tube of condensed milk, some nougat, and a pair of socks into my sack; one never knew, the socks might come in useful—they might even do as Balaclavas. For the time being I stuffed them with first-aid equipment. The camera was loaded with a black and white film; I had a color film in reserve. I pulled the movie camera out from the bottom of my sleeping bag, wound it up, and tried letting it run without film. There was a little click, then it stopped and jammed.

"Bad luck after bringing it so far," said Lachenal.

In spite of our photographer, Ichac's, precautions taken to lubricate it with special grease, the intense cold, even inside the sleeping bag, had frozen it. I left it at the camp rather sadly: I had looked forward to taking it to the top. I had used it up to 24,600 feet.

We went outside and put on our crampons,† which we kept on all day. We wore as many clothes as possible; our sacks were very light. At six o'clock we started off. It was brilliantly fine, but also very cold. Our super-light-weight crampons bit deep into the steep slopes of ice and hard snow up which lay the first stage of our climb.

Later the slope became slightly less steep and more uniform. Sometimes

* Lachenal, an ardent amateur climber, who had left his Chamonix post as mountain guide and ski instructor to join the expedition.
† Metal frames with spikes, fitting the boot soles, for use on hard snow or ice.

the hard crust bore our weight, but at others we broke through and sank into soft powder snow which made progress exhausting. We took turns in making the track and often stopped without any word having passed between us. Each of us lived in a closed and private world of his own. I was suspicious of my mental processes; my mind was working very slowly and I was perfectly aware of the low state of my intelligence. It was easiest just to stick to one thought at a time—safest, too. The cold was penetrating; for all our special eiderdown clothing we felt as if we'd nothing on. Whenever we halted, we stamped our feet hard. Lachenal went as far as to take off one boot which was a bit tight; he was in terror of frostbite.

"I don't want to be like Lambert," he said. Raymond Lambert, a Geneva guide, had to have all his toes amputated after an eventful climb during which he got his feet frostbitten.* While Lachenal rubbed himself hard, I looked at the summits all around us; already we overtopped them all except the distant Dhaulagiri. The complicated structure of these mountains, with which our many laborious explorations had made us familiar, was now spread out plainly at our feet.

The going was incredibly exhausting, and every step was a struggle of mind over matter. We came out into the sunlight, and by way of marking the occasion made yet another halt. Lachenal continued to complain of his feet. "I can't feel anything. I think I'm beginning to get frostbite." And once again he undid his boot.

I began to be seriously worried. I realized very well the risk we were running; I knew from experience how insidiously and quickly frostbite can set in if one is not extremely careful. Nor was Lachenal under any illusions. "We're in danger of having frozen feet. Do you think it's worth it?"

This was most disturbing. It was my responsibility as leader to think of the others. There was no doubt about frostbite being a very real danger. Did Annapurna justify such risks? That was the question I asked myself; it continued to worry me.

Lachenal had laced his boots up again, and once more we continued to force our way through the exhausting snow. The whole of the Sickle glacier was now in view, bathed in light. We still had a long way to go to cross it, and then there was that rock band—would we find a gap in it?

My feet, like Lachenal's, were very cold and I continued to wriggle my toes, even when we were moving. I could not feel them, but that was nothing new in the mountains, and if I kept on moving them it would keep the circulation going.

*In May, 1952, Lambert, with the Sherpa Ang-Tsering, reached 28,215 feet on Mount Everest, possibly the highest point up to then attained.

Lachenal appeared to me as a sort of specter—he was alone in his world, I in mine. But—and this was odd enough—any effort was slightly *less* exhausting than lower down. Perhaps it was hope lending us wings. Even through dark glasses the snow was blinding—the sun beating straight down on the ice. We looked down upon precipitous ridges which dropped away into space, and upon tiny glaciers far, far below. Familiar peaks soared arrowlike into the sky. Suddenly Lachenal grabbed me:

"If I go back, what will you do?"

A whole sequence of pictures flashed through my head: the days of marching in sweltering heat, the hard pitches we had overcome, the tremendous efforts we had all made to lay siege to the mountain, the daily heroism of all my friends in establishing the camps. Now we were nearing our goal. In an hour or two, perhaps, victory would be ours. Must we give up? Impossible! My whole being revolted against the idea. I had made up my mind, irrevocably. Today we were consecrating an ideal, and no sacrifice was too great. I heard my voice clearly:

"I should go on by myself."

I would go alone. If he wished to go down it was not for me to stop him. He must make his own choice freely.

"Then I'll follow you."

The die was cast. I was no longer anxious. Nothing could stop us now from getting to the top. The psychological atmosphere changed with these few words, and we went forward now as brothers.

I felt as though I were plunging into something new and quite abnormal. I had the strangest and most vivid impressions, such as I had never before known in the mountains. There was something unnatural in the way I saw Lachenal and everything around us. I smiled to myself at the paltriness of our efforts, for I could stand apart and watch myself making these efforts. But all sense of exertion was gone, as though there were no longer any gravity. This diaphanous landscape, this quintessence of purity—these were not the mountains I knew: they were the mountains of my dreams.

The snow, sprinkled over every rock and gleaming in the sun, was of a radiant beauty that touched me to the heart. I had never seen such complete transparency, and I was living in a world of crystal. Sounds were indistinct, the atmosphere like cotton wool.

An astonishing happiness welled up in me, but I could not define it. Everything was so new, so utterly unprecedented. It was not in the least like anything I had known in the Alps, where one feels buoyed up by the presence of others—by people of whom one is vaguely aware, or even by the dwellings one can see in the far distance.

This was quite different. An enormous gulf was between me and the world. This was a different universe—withered, desert, lifeless; a fantastic universe where the presence of man was not foreseen, perhaps not desired. We were braving an interdict, overstepping a boundary, and yet we had no fear as we continued upward. I thought of the famous ladder of St. Theresa of Avila. Something clutched at my heart.

Did Lachenal share these feelings? The summit ridge drew nearer, and we reached the foot of the ultimate rock band. The slope was very steep and the snow interspersed with rocks.

"Couloir!" *

A finger pointed. The whispered word from one to another indicated the key to the rocks—the last line of defense.

"What luck!"

The couloir up the rocks though steep was feasible.

The sky was a deep sapphire blue. With a great effort we edged over to the right, avoiding the rocks; we preferred to keep to the snow on account of our crampons and it was not long before we set foot in the couloir. It was fairly steep, and we had a minute's hesitation. Should we have enough strength left to overcome this final obstacle?

Fortunately the snow was hard, and by kicking steps we were able to manage, thanks to our crampons. A false move would have been fatal. There was no need to make handholds—our axes, driven in as far as possible, served us for an anchor.

Lachenal went splendidly. What a wonderful contrast to the early days! It was a hard struggle here, but he kept going. Lifting our eyes occasionally from the slope, we saw the couloir opening out on to . . . well, we didn't quite know, probably a ridge. But where was the top—left or right? Stopping at every step, leaning on our axes, we tried to recover our breath and to calm down our racing hearts, which were thumping as though they would burst. We knew we were there now—that nothing could stop us. No need to exchange looks—each of us would have read the same determination in the other's eyes. A slight detour to the left, a few more steps—the summit ridge came gradually nearer—a few rocks to avoid. We dragged ourselves up. Could we possibly be there?

Yes!

A fierce and savage wind tore at us.

We were on top of Annapurna! 8,075 meters, 26,493 feet.

Our hearts overflowed with an unspeakable happiness.

"If only the others could know . . ."

* Gully.

If only everyone could know!

The summit was a corniced crest of ice, and the precipices on the far side which plunged vertically down beneath us, were terrifying, unfathomable. There could be few other mountains in the world like this. Clouds floated halfway down, concealing the gentle, fertile valley of Pokhara, 23,000 feet below. Above us there was nothing!

Our mission was accomplished. But at the same time we had accomplished something infinitely greater. How wonderful life would now become! What an inconceivable experience it is to attain one's ideal and, at the very same moment, to fulfill oneself. I was stirred to the depths of my being. Never had I felt happiness like this—so intense and yet so pure. That brown rock, the highest of them all, that ridge of ice—were these the goals of a lifetime? Or were they, rather, the limits of man's pride?

"Well, what about going down?"

Lachenal shook me. What were his own feelings? Did he simply think he had finished another climb, as in the Alps? Did he think one could just go down again like that, with nothing more to it?

"One minute, I must take some photographs."

"Hurry up!"

I fumbled feverishly in my sack, pulled out the camera, took out the little French flag which was right at the bottom, and the pennants. Useless gestures, no doubt, but something more than symbols—eloquent tokens of affection and goodwill. I tied the strips of material—stained by sweat and by the food in the sacks—to the shaft of my ice ax, the only flagstaff at hand. Then I focused my camera on Lachenal.

"Now, will you take me?"

"Hand it over—hurry up!" said Lachenal.

He took several pictures and then handed me back the camera. I loaded a color film and we repeated the process to be certain of bringing back records to be cherished in the future.

"Are you mad?" asked Lachenal. "We haven't a minute to lose: we must go down at once."

And in fact a glance round showed me that the weather was no longer gloriously fine as it had been in the morning. Lachenal was becoming impatient.

"We must go down!"

He was right. His was the reaction of the mountaineer who knows his own domain. But I just could not accustom myself to the idea that we had won our victory. It seemed inconceivable that we should have trodden those summit snows.

It was impossible to build a cairn; there were no stones; everything was frozen. Lachenal stamped his feet; he felt them freezing. I felt mine freezing too, but paid little attention. The highest mountain to be climbed by man lay under our feet! The names of our predecessors on these heights raced through my mind: Mummery, Mallory and Irvine, Bauer, Welzenbach, Tilman, Shipton. How many of them were dead—how many had found on these mountains what, to them, was the finest end of all?

My joy was touched with humility. It was not just one party that had climbed Annapurna today, but a whole expedition. I thought of all the others in the camps perched on the slopes at our feet, and I knew it was because of their efforts and their sacrifices that we had succeeded. There are times when the most complicated actions are suddenly summed up, distilled, and strike you with illuminating clarity: so it was with this irresistible upward surge which had landed us two here.

Pictures passed through my mind—the Chamonix valley, where I had spent the most marvelous moments of my childhood; Mont Blanc, which so tremendously impressed me! I was a child when I first saw "the Mont Blanc people" coming home, and to me there was a queer look about them; a strange light shone in their eyes.

"Come on, straight down," called Lachenal.

He had already done up his sack and started going down. I took out my pocket aneroid: 8,500 meters. I smiled. I swallowed a little condensed milk and left the tube behind—the only trace of our passage. I did up my sack, put on my gloves and my glasses, seized my ice ax; one look around and I, too, hurried down the slope. Before disappearing into the couloir I gave one last look at the summit which would henceforth be all our joy and all our consolation.

Lachenal was already far below; he had reached the foot of the couloir. I hurried down in his tracks. I went as fast as I could, but it was dangerous going. At every step one had to take care that the snow did not break away beneath one's weight. Lachenal, going faster than I thought he was capable of, was now on the long traverse. It was my turn to cross the area of mixed rock and snow. At last I reached the foot of the rock band. I had hurried and I was out of breath. I undid my sack. What had I been going to do? I couldn't say.

"My gloves!"

Before I had time to bend over, I saw them slide and roll. They went further and further straight down the slope. I remained where I was, quite stunned. I watched them rolling down slowly, with no appearance of stopping. The movement of those gloves was engraved in my sight as something irredeemable, against which I was powerless. The consequences might be most serious. What was I to do?

"Quickly, down to Camp V."

Rébuffat and Terray* would be there. My concern dissolved like magic. I now had a fixed objective again: to reach the camp. Never for a minute did it occur to me to use as gloves the socks which I always carry in reserve for just such a mishap as this.

On I went, trying to catch up with Lachenal. It had been two o'clock when we reached the summit; we had started out at six in the morning, but I had to admit that I had lost all sense of time. I felt as if I were running, whereas in actual fact I was walking normally, perhaps rather slowly, and I had to keep stopping to get my breath. The sky was now covered with clouds, everything had become gray and dirty-looking. An icy wind sprang up, boding no good. We must push on! But where was Lachenal? I spotted him a couple of hundred yards away, looking as if he was never going to stop. And I had thought he was in indifferent form!

The clouds grew thicker and came right down over us; the wind blew stronger, but I did not suffer from the cold. Perhaps the descent had restored my circulation. Should I be able to find the tents in the mist? I watched the rib ending in the beaklike point which overlooked the camp. It was gradually swallowed up by the clouds, but I was able to make out the spearhead rib lower down. If the mist should thicken I would make straight for that rib and follow it down, and in this way I should be bound to come upon the tent.

Lachenal disappeared from time to time, and then the mist was so thick that I lost sight of him altogether. I kept going at the same speed, as fast as my breathing would allow.

The slope was now steeper; a few patches of bare ice followed the smooth stretches of snow. A good sign—I was nearing the camp. How difficult to find one's way in thick mist! I kept the course which I had set by the steepest angle of the slope. The ground was broken; with my crampons I went straight down walls of bare ice. There were some patches ahead—a few more steps. It was the camp all right, but there were *two tents!*

So Rébuffat and Terray had come up. What a mercy! I should be able to tell them that we had been successful, that we were returning from the top. How thrilled they would be!

I got there, dropping down from above. The platform had been extended, and the two tents were facing each other. I tripped over one of the guy-ropes

---

* Gaston Rébuffat, experienced Alpinist, and Lionel Terray, professionally a Chamonix guide and skier.

of the first tent; there was movement inside, they had heard me. Rébuffat and Terray put their heads out.

"We've made it. We're back from Annapurna!"

THE CREVASSE

Rébuffat and Terray received the news with great excitement.

"But what about Biscante?" asked Terray anxiously.

"He won't be long. He was just in front of me! What a day—started out at six this morning—didn't stop . . . got up at last."

Words failed me. I had so much to say. The sight of familiar faces dispelled the strange feeling that I had experienced since morning, and I became, once more, just a mountaineer.

Terray, who was speechless with delight, wrung my hands. Then the smile vanished from his face: "Maurice—your hands!" There was an uneasy silence. I had forgotten that I had lost my gloves: my fingers were violet and white and hard as wood. The other two stared at them in dismay—they realized the full seriousness of the injury. But, still blissfully floating on a sea of joy remote from reality, I leaned over toward Terray and said confidentially, "You're in such splendid form, and you've done so marvelously, it's absolutely tragic you didn't come up there with us!"

"What I did was for the expedition, my dear Maurice, and anyway you've got up, and that's a victory for the whole lot of us."

I nearly burst with happiness. How could I tell him all that his answer meant to me? The rapture I had felt on the summit, which might have seemed a purely personal, egotistical emotion, had been transformed by his words into a complete and perfect joy with no shadow upon it. His answer proved that this victory was not just one man's achievement, a matter for personal pride; no—and Terray was the first to understand this—it was a victory for us all, a victory for mankind itself.

"Hi! Help! Help!"

"Biscante!" exclaimed the others.

Still half-intoxicated and remote from reality I had heard nothing. Terray felt a chill at his heart, and his thoughts flew to his partner on so many unforgettable climbs; together they had so often skirted death, and won so many splendid victories. Putting his head out, and seeing Lachenal clinging to the slope a hundred yards lower down, he dressed in frantic haste.

Out he went. But the slope was bare now; Lachenal had disappeared.

Terray was horribly frightened, and he could only utter unintelligible cries. It was a ghastly moment for him. A violent wind sent the mist tearing by. Under the stress of emotion Terray had not realized how it falsified distances. "Biscante! Biscante!"

He had spotted him, through a rift in the mist, lying on the slope much lower down than he had thought. Terray set his teeth and glissaded down like a madman. How would he be able to brake without crampons, on the wind-hardened snow? But Terray was a first-class skier, and with a jump turn he stopped beside Lachenal, who was suffering from concussion after his tremendous fall. In a state of collapse, with no ice ax, Balaclava, or gloves, and only one crampon, he gazed vacantly around him.

"My feet are frostbitten. Take me down . . . take me down, so that Oudot can see to me."

"It can't be done," said Terray sorrowfully. "Can't you see we're in the middle of a storm . . . It'll be dark soon."

But Lachenal was obsessed by the fear of amputation. With a gesture of despair he tore the ax out of Terray's hands and tried to force his way down; but soon saw the futility of his action and resolved to climb up to the camp. While Terray cut steps without stopping, Lachenal, ravaged and exhausted as he was, dragged himself along on all fours.

Meanwhile I had gone into Rébuffat's tent. He was appalled at the sight of my hands and, as rather incoherently I told him what we had done, he took a piece of rope and began flicking my fingers. Then he took off my boots with great difficulty for my feet were swollen, and beat my feet and rubbed me. We soon heard Terray giving Lachenal the same treatment in the other tent.

For our comrades it was a tragic moment: Annapurna was conquered, and the first eight-thousander had been climbed. Every one of us had been ready to sacrifice everything for this. Yet, as they looked at our feet and hands, what can Terray and Rébuffat have felt?

Outside the storm howled and the snow was still falling. The mist grew thick and darkness came. As on the previous night we had to cling to the poles to prevent the tents being carried away by the wind. The only two air-mattresses were given to Lachenal and myself while Terray and Rébuffat both sat on ropes, rucksacks, and provisions to keep themselves off the snow. They rubbed, slapped, and beat us with a rope. Sometimes the blows fell on the living flesh, and howls arose from both tents. Rébuffat persevered; it was essential to continue, painful as it was. Gradually life returned to my feet as well as to my hands, and circulation started again. Lachenal, too, found that feeling was returning.

Now Terray summoned up the energy to prepare some hot drinks. He called to Rébuffat that he would pass him a mug, so two hands stretched out toward each other between the two tents and were instantly covered with snow. The liquid was boiling though scarcely more than 60 degrees Centigrade (140 degrees Fahrenheit). I swallowed it greedily and felt infinitely better.

The night was absolute hell. Frightful onslaughts of wind battered us incessantly, while the never-ceasing snow piled up on the tents.

Now and again I heard voices from next door—it was Terray massaging Lachenal with admirable perseverance, only stopping to ply him with hot drinks. In our tent Rébuffat was quite worn out, but satisfied that warmth was returning to my limbs.

Lying half-unconscious I was scarcely aware of the passage of time. There were moments when I was able to see our situation in its true dramatic light, but the rest of the time I was plunged in an inexplicable stupor with no thought for the consequences of our victory.

As the night wore on the snow lay heavier on the tent, and once again I had the frightful feeling of being slowly and silently asphyxiated. I tried, with all the strength of which I was capable, to push off with both forearms the mass that was crushing me. These fearful exertions left me gasping for breath and I fell back into the same exhausted state. It was much worse than the previous night.

"Rébuffat! Gaston! Gaston!"

I recognized Terray's voice.

"Time to be off!"

I heard the sounds without grasping their meaning. Was it light already? I was not in the least surprised that the other two had given up all thought of going to the top, and I did not at all grasp the measure of their sacrifice.

Outside the storm redoubled in violence. The tent shook and the fabric flapped alarmingly. It had usually been fine in the mornings: did this mean the monsoon was upon us? We knew it was not far off—could this be its first onslaught?

"Gaston! Are you ready?" Terray called again.

"One minute," answered Rébuffat. He did not have an easy job: he had to put my boots on and do everything to get me ready. I let myself be handled like a baby. In the other tent Terray finished dressing Lachenal whose feet were still swollen and would not fit into his boots. So Terray gave him his own, which were bigger. To get Lachenal's on to his own feet he had to make slits in them. As a precaution he put a sleeping bag and some food into his sack and shouted to us to do the same. Were his words lost in the storm? Or were we too intent on leaving this hellish place to listen to his instructions?

Lachenal and Terray were already outside.

"We're going down!" they shouted.

Then Rébuffat tied me on the rope and we went out. There were only two ice axes for the four of us, so Rébuffat and Terray took them as a matter of course. For a moment as we left the two tents of Camp V, I felt childishly ashamed at leaving all this good equipment behind.

Already the first rope seemed a long way down below us. We were blinded by the squalls of snow and we could not hear each other a yard away. We had both put on our *cagoules,* for it was very cold. The snow was apt to slide and the rope often came in useful.

Ahead of us the other two were losing no time. Lachenal went first and, safeguarded by Terray, he forced the pace in his anxiety to get down. There were no tracks to show us the way, but it was engraved on all our minds—straight down the slope for four hundred yards then traverse to the left for one hundred fifty to two hundred yards to get to Camp IV. The snow was thinning and the wind less violent. Was it going to clear? We hardly dared to hope so. A wall of seracs* brought us up short.

"It's to the left," I said, "I remember perfectly."

Somebody else thought it was to the right. We started going down again. The wind had dropped completely, but the snow fell in big flakes. The mist was thick, and, not to lose each other, we walked in line: I was third and I could barely see Lachenal, who was first. It was impossible to recognize any of the pitches. We were all experienced enough mountaineers to know that even on familiar ground it is easy to make mistakes in such weather. Distances are deceptive, one cannot tell whether one is going up or down. We kept colliding with hummocks which we had taken for hollows. The mist, the falling snowflakes, the carpet of snow, all merged into the same whitish tone and confused our vision. The towering outlines of the seracs took on fantastic shapes and seemed to move slowly around us.

Our situation was not desperate, we were certainly not lost. We would have to go lower down; the traverse must begin further on—I remembered the serac which served as a milestone. The snow stuck to our *cagoules* and turned us into white phantoms noiselessly flitting against a background equally white. We began to sink in dreadfully, and there is nothing worse for bodies already on the edge of exhaustion.

Were we too high or too low? No one could tell. Perhaps we had better try slanting over to the left! The snow was in a dangerous condition, but

* Pinnacles of ice.

we did not seem to realize it. We were forced to admit that we were not on the right route, so we retraced our steps and climbed up above the serac which overhung us. No doubt, we decided, we should be on the right level now. With Rébuffat leading, we went back over the way which had cost us such an effort. I followed him jerkily, saying nothing, and determined to go on to the end. If Rébuffat had fallen I could never have held him.

We went doggedly on from one serac to another. Each time we thought we had recognized the right route, and each time there was a fresh disappointment. If only the mist would lift, if only the snow would stop for a second! On the slope it seemed to be growing deeper every minute. Only Terray and Rébuffat were capable of breaking the trail and they relieved each other at regular intervals, without a word and without a second's hesitation.

I admired this determination of Rébuffat's for which he is so justly famed. He did not intend to die! With the strength of desperation and at the price of superhuman effort he forged ahead. The slowness of his progress would have dismayed even the most obstinate climber, but he would not give up, and in the end the mountain yielded in face of his perseverance.

Terray, when his turn came, charged madly ahead. He was like a force of nature: at all costs he would break down these prison walls that penned us in. His physical strength was exceptional, his will power no less remarkable. Lachenal gave him considerable trouble. Perhaps he was not quite in his right mind. He said it was no use going on; we must dig a hole in the snow and wait for fine weather. He swore at Terray and called him a madman. Nobody but Terray would have been capable of dealing with him—he just tugged sharply on the rope and Lachenal was forced to follow.

We were well and truly lost.

The weather did not seem likely to improve. A minute before we had still had ideas about which way to go—now we had none. This way or that . . . we went on at random to allow for the chance of a miracle which appeared increasingly unlikely. The instinct of self-preservation in the two fit members of the party alternated with a hopelessness which made them completely irresponsible. Each in turn did the maddest things: Terray traversed the steep and avalanchy slopes with one crampon badly adjusted. He and Rébuffat performed incredible feats of balance without the least slip.

Camp IV was certainly on the left, on the edge of the Sickle. On that point we were all agreed. But it was very hard to find. The wall of ice that gave it such magnificent protection was now ironical, for it hid the tents from us. In mist like this we should have to be right on top of them before we spotted them.

Perhaps if we called, someone would hear us? Lachenal gave the signal, but snow absorbs sound and his shout seemed to carry only a few yards. All four of us called out together: "One . . . two . . . three . . . HELP!"

We got the impression that our united shout carried a long way, so we began again: "One . . . two . . . three . . . HELP!" Not a sound in reply!

Now and again Terray took off his boots and rubbed his feet; the sight of our frostbitten limbs had made him aware of the danger and he had the strength of mind to do something about it. Like Lachenal, he was haunted by the idea of amputation. For me, it was too late: my feet and hands, already affected from yesterday, were beginning to freeze up again.

We had eaten nothing since the day before, and we had been on the go the whole time, but men's resources of energy in the face of death are inexhaustible. When the end seems imminent, there still remain reserves, though it needs tremendous will power to call them up.

Time passed, but we had no idea how long. Night was approaching, and we were terrified, though none of us made any complaint. Rébuffat and I found a way that we thought we remembered, but were brought to a halt by the extreme steepness of the slope—the mist turned it into a vertical wall. We were to find next day that at that moment we had been only thirty yards from the camp, and that the wall was the very one that sheltered the tent which would have been our salvaion.

"We must find a crevasse."

"We can't stay here all night!"

"A hole—it's the only thing."

"We'll all die in it."

Night had suddenly fallen and it was essential to come to a decision without wasting another minute; if we remained on the slope, we should be dead before morning. We would have to bivouac. What the conditions would be like, we could guess, for we all knew what it meant to bivouac above 23,000 feet.

With his ax Terray began to dig a hole. Lachenal went over to a snow-filled crevasse a few yards further on, then suddenly let out a yell and disappeared before our eyes. We stood helpless: should we, or rather would Terray and Rébuffat, have enough strength for all the maneuvers with the rope that would be needed to get him out? The crevasse was completely blocked up save for the one little hole which Lachenal had fallen through.

"Lachenal!" called Terray.

A voice, muffled by many thicknesses of ice and snow, came up to us. It was impossible to make out what it was saying.

"Lachenal!"

Terray jerked the rope violently; this time we could hear.

"I'm here!"

"Anything broken?"

"No! It'll do for the night! Come along."

This shelter was heaven-sent. None of us would have had the strength to dig a hole big enough to protect the lot of us from the wind. Without hesitation Terray let himself drop into the crevasse, and a loud "Come on!" told us he had arrived safely. In my turn I let myself go: it was a regular toboggan slide. I shot down a sort of twisting tunnel, very steep, and about thirty feet long. I came out at great speed into the opening beyond and was literally hurled to the bottom of the crevasse. We let Rébuffat know he could come by giving a tug on the rope.

The intense cold of this minute grotto shriveled us up, the enclosing walls of ice were damp and the floor a carpet of fresh snow; by huddling together there was just room for the four of us. Icicles hung from the ceiling and we broke some of them off to make more head room and kept little bits to suck—it was a long time since we had had anything to drink.

That was our shelter for the night. At least we should be protected from the wind, and the temperature would remain fairly even, though the damp was extremely unpleasant. We settled ourselves in the dark as best we could. As always in a bivouac we took off our boots; without this precaution the constriction would cause immediate frostbite. Terray unrolled the sleeping-bag which he had had the foresight to bring, and settled himself in relative comfort. We put on everything warm that we had, and to avoid contact with the snow I sat on the movie camera. We huddled close up to each other, in our search for a hypothetical position in which the warmth of our bodies could be combined without loss, but we couldn't keep still for a second.

We did not open our mouths—signs were less of an effort than words. Every man withdrew into himself and took refuge in his own inner world. Terray massaged Lachenal's feet; Rébuffat felt his feet freezing too, but he had sufficient strength to rub them himself. I remained motionless, unseeing. My feet and hands went on freezing, but what could be done? I attempted to forget suffering by withdrawing into myself, trying to forget the passing of time, trying not to feel the devouring and numbing cold which insidiously gained upon us.

Terray shared his sleeping bag with Lachenal, putting his feet and hands inside the precious eiderdown. At the same time he went on rubbing.

Anyhow the frostbite won't spread further, he was thinking.

None of us could make any movement without upsetting the others, and the positions we had taken up with such care were continually being altered so that we had to start all over again. This kept us busy. Rébuffat persevered

with his rubbing and complained of his feet; like Terray he was thinking:
We mustn't look beyond tomorrow—afterward we'll see. But he was not
blind to the fact that "afterward" was one big question mark.

Terray generously tried to give me part of his sleeping bag. He had understood the seriousness of my condition, and knew why it was that I said nothing and remained quite passive; he realized that I had abandoned all hope
for myself. He massaged me for nearly two hours; his feet, too, might have
frozen, but he didn't appear to give the matter a thought. I found new courage simply in contemplating his unselfishness; he was doing so much to
help me that it would have been ungrateful of me not to go on struggling
to live. Though my heart was like a lump of ice itself, I was astonished to
feel no pain. Everything material about me seemed to have dropped away.
I seemed to be quite clear in my thoughts and yet I floated in a kind of peaceful happiness. There was still a breath of life in me, but it dwindled steadily
as the hours went by. Terray's massage no longer had any effect upon me.
All was over, I thought. Wasn't this cavern the most beautiful grave I could
hope for? Death caused me no grief, no regret—I smiled at the thought.

After hours of torpor a voice mumbled "Daylight!"

This made some impression on the others. I only felt surprised—I had not
thought that daylight would penetrate so far down.

"Too early to start," said Rébuffat.

A ghastly light spread through our grotto and we could just vaguely make
out the shapes of each other's heads. A queer noise from a long way off
came down to us—a sort of prolonged hiss. The noise increased. Suddenly
I was buried, blinded, smothered beneath an avalanche of new snow. The
icy snow spread over the cavern, finding its way through every gap in our
clothing. I ducked my head between my knees and covered myself with
both arms. The snow flowed on and on. There was a terrible silence. We
were not completely buried, but there was snow everywhere. We got up,
taking care not to bang our heads against the ceiling of ice, and tried to
shake ourselves. We were all in our stockinged feet in the snow. The first
thing to do was to find our boots.

Rébuffat and Terray began to search and realized at once that they were
blind. Yesterday they had taken off their glasses to lead us down and now
they were paying for it. Lachenal was the first to lay hands upon a pair of
boots. He tried to put them on, but they were Rébuffat's. Rébuffat attempted
to climb up the chute down which we had come yesterday, and which the
avalanche had followed in its turn.

"Hi, Gaston! What's the weather like?" called up Terray.

"Can't see a thing. It's blowing hard."

We were still groping for our things. Terray found his boots and put them on awkwardly, unable to see what he was doing. Lachenal helped him, but he was all on edge and fearfully impatient, in striking contrast to my immobility. Terray then went up the icy channel, puffing and blowing, and at last reached the outer world. He was met by terrible gusts of wind that cut right through him and lashed his face.

Bad weather, he said to himself, this time it's the end. We're lost . . . we'll never come through.

At the bottom of the crevasse there were still two of us looking for our boots. Lachenal poked fiercely with an ice ax. I was calmer and tried to proceed more rationally. We extracted crampons and an ax in turn from the snow, but still no boots.

Well—so this cavern was to be our last resting place! There was very little room—we were bent double and got in each other's way. Lachenal decided to go out without his boots. He called frantically, hauled himself up on the rope, trying to get a hold or to wiggle his way up, digging his toes into the snow walls. Terray from outside pulled as hard as he could. I watched him go; he gathered speed and disappeared.

When he emerged from the opening he saw the sky was clear and blue, and he began to run like a madman, shrieking, "It's fine, it's fine!"

I set to work again to search the cave. The boots *had* to be found, or Lachenal and I were done for. On all fours, with nothing on my hands or feet I raked the snow, stirring it around this way and that, hoping every second to come upon something hard. I was no longer capable of thinking —I reacted like an animal fighting for its life.

I found one boot! The other was tied to it—a pair! Having ransacked the whole cave I at last found the other pair. But in spite of all my efforts I could not find the movie camera, and gave up in despair. There was no question of putting my boots on—my hands were like lumps of wood and I could hold nothing in my fingers; my feet were very swollen—I should never be able to get boots on them. I twisted the rope around the boots as well as I could and called up the chute:

"Lionel . . . Boots!"

There was no answer, but he must have heard for with a jerk the precious boots shot up. Soon after the rope came down again. My turn. I wound the rope around me. I could not pull it tight so I made a whole series of little knots. Their combined strength, I hoped, would be enough to hold me. I had no strength to shout again; I gave a great tug on the rope, and Terray understood.

At the first step I had to kick a notch in the hard snow for my toes. Further on I expected to be able to get up more easily by wedging myself across the runnel. I wriggled up a few yards like this and then I tried to dig my hands and my feet into the wall. My hands were stiff and hard right up to the wrists and my feet had no feeling up to the ankles, the joints were inflexible and this hampered me greatly.

Somehow or other I succeeded in working my way up, while Terray pulled so hard he nearly choked me. I began to see more distinctly and so knew that I must be nearing the opening. Often I fell back, but I clung on and wedged myself in again as best I could. My heart was bursting and I was forced to rest. A fresh wave of energy enabled me to crawl to the top. I pulled myself out by clutching Terray's legs; he was just about all in and I was in the last stages of exhaustion. Terray was close to me and I whispered:

"Lionel . . . I'm dying!"

He supported me and helped me away from the crevasse. Lachenal and Rébuffat were sitting in the snow a few yards away. The instant Lionel let go of me I sank down and dragged myself along on all fours.

The weather was perfect. Quantities of snow had fallen the day before and the mountains were resplendent. Never had I seen them look so beautiful—our last day would be magnificent.

Rébuffat and Terray were completely blind; as he came along with me Terray knocked into things and I had to direct him. Rébuffat, too, could not move a step without guidance. It was terrifying to be blind when there was danger all around. Lachenal's frozen feet affected his nervous system. His behavior was disquieting—he was possessed by the most fantastic ideas:

"I tell you we must go down . . . down there . . ."

"You've nothing on your feet!"

"Don't worry about that."

"You're off your head. The way's not there . . . it's to the left!"

He was already standing up; he wanted to go straight down to the bottom of the glacier. Terray held him back, made him sit down, and, though he couldn't see, helped Lachenal put his boots on.

Behind them I was living in my own private dream. I knew the end was near, but it was the end that all mountaineers wish for—an end in keeping with their ruling passion. I was consciously grateful to the mountains for being so beautiful for me that day, and as awed by their silence as if I had been in church. I was in no pain and had no worry. My utter calmness was alarming. Terray came staggering toward me, and I told him: "It's all over for me. Go on . . . you have a chance . . . you must take it . . . over to the left . . . that's the way."

I felt better after telling him that. But Terray would have none of it: "We'll help you. If we get away, so will you."

At this moment Lachenal shouted: "Help! Help!"

Obviously he didn't know what he was doing . . . Or did he? He was the only one of the four of us who could see Camp II down below. Perhaps his calls would be heard. They were shrieks of despair, reminding me tragically of some climbers lost in the Mont Blanc massif whom I had endeavored to save. Now it was our turn. The impression was vivid: we were lost.

I joined in with the others: "One . . . two . . . three . . . HELP! One . . . two . . . three . . . HELP!" We tried to shout together, but without much success; our voices could not have carried more than ten feet. The noise I made was more of a whisper than a shout. Terray insisted that I should put my boots on, but my hands were dead. Neither Rébuffat nor Terray, who were unable to see, could help much, so I said to Lachenal: "Come and help me to put my boots on."

"Don't be silly, we must go down!"

And off he went once again in the wrong direction, straight down. I was not in the least angry with him; he had been sorely tried by the altitude and by everything he had gone through.

Terray resolutely got out his knife, and with fumbling hands slit the uppers of my boots back and front. Split in two like this I could get them on, but it was not easy and I had to make several attempts. Soon I lost heart—what was the use of it all anyway since I was going to stay where I was? But Terray pulled violently and finally he succeeded. He laced up my now-gigantic boots, missing half the hooks. I was ready now. But how was I going to walk with my stiff joints?

"To the left, Lionel!"

"You're crazy, Maurice," said Lachenal, "it's to the right, straight down."

Terray did not know what to think of these conflicting views. He had not given up like me, he was going to fight; but what, at the moment, could he do? The three of them discussed which way to go.

I remained sitting in the snow. Gradually my mind lost grip—why should I struggle? I would just let myself drift. I saw pictures of shady slopes, peaceful paths, there was a scent of resin. It was pleasant—I was going to die in my own mountains. My body had no feeling—everything was frozen.

"Aah . . . aah!"

Was it a groan or a call? I gathered my strength for one cry: "They're coming!" The others heard me and shouted for joy. What a miraculous apparition! "Schatz . . . it's Schatz!"

Barely two hundred yards away Marcel Schatz,* waist-deep in snow, was coming slowly toward us like a boat on the surface of the slope. I found this vision of a strong and invincible deliverer inexpressibly moving. I expected everything of him. The shock was violent, and quite shattered me. Death clutched at me and I gave myself up.

When I came to again the wish to live returned and I experienced a violent revulsion of feeling. All was not lost! As Schatz came nearer my eyes never left him for a second—twenty yards—ten yards—he came straight toward me. Why? Without a word he leaned over me, held me close, hugged me, and his warm breath revived me.

I could not make the slightest movement—I was like marble. My heart was overwhelmed by such tremendous feelings and yet my eyes remained dry.

"It is wonderful—what you have done!"

* Of Paris, betimes manager of his father's tailoring establishment there.

5 *The Mood Recalled*

Alone *

RICHARD E. BYRD

✳✳ Rear Admiral Byrd (retired) was born in Virginia in 1888, the second of three sons of Richard Evelyn Byrd and Eleanor Bolling (Flood) Byrd, who traces her lineage to Henry of Navarre. The Byrds have been prominent figures in Virginia for three centuries. Richard Byrd was the youngest boy in Virginia Military Institute, but his entry into aviation was late—he was nearly 30 before he qualified as an aviator. As a traveler, he began early, and at 12 made a trip, alone, around the world. He became the nation's leading Antarctic expert, having led expeditions to those regions in 1928, 1934, 1939, and 1947; he flew over the North Pole in 1926 and over the South Pole twice, and mapped more than a million square miles of Antarctic territory. At 66 he became technical adviser for an expedition sent by the U. S. government to the Antarctic in 1955 to stay in that region until 1958. ✳✳

THE IDEA

Bolling Advance Weather Base, which I manned alone during the Antarctic winter night of 1934, was planted in the dark immensity of the Ross Ice Barrier, on a line between Little America and the South Pole. It was the first inland station ever occupied in the world's southernmost continent. My decision to winter there was harder, perhaps, than even some of the men at Little America appreciated. For the original plan had been to staff the base with several men; but . . . this had proved impossible. In consequence, I had to choose whether to give up the base entirely—and the scientific mission with it—or to man it by myself. I could not bring myself to give it up.

This much should be understood from the beginning: that above everything else, and beyond the solid worth of weather and auroral observations in the hitherto-unoccupied interior of Antarctica and my interest in these studies, I really wanted to go for the experience's sake. So the motive was in part personal. Aside from the meteorological and auroral work, I had no important purposes. There was nothing of that sort. Nothing whatever, except one man's desire to know that kind of experience to the full, to be by himself for a while and to taste peace and quiet and solitude long enough to find out how good they really are.

It was all that simple. And it is something, I believe, that people beset by the complexities of modern life will understand instinctively. We are caught up in the winds that blow every which way. And in the hullabaloo the thinking man is driven to ponder where he is being blown and to long desperately for some quiet place where he can reason undisturbed and take inventory. . . . For fourteen years or so, various expeditions, one succeeding the other, had occupied my time and thoughts, to the exclusion of nearly everything else. In 1919 it was the Navy's transatlantic flight; in 1925, Greenland; in 1926, the North Pole; in 1927, the Atlantic Ocean; 1928-30, the South Pole; and 1933-35, the Antarctic again. In between there was no rest. An expedition was hardly finished before I was engaged in putting a new one together; and meanwhile I was lecturing from one end of the country to the other in order to make a living and pay off the debts of the completed expedition, or else scurrying around to solicit money and supplies for a new one. . . .

I wanted something more than just privacy in the geographical sense. I wanted to sink roots into some replenishing philosophy. And so it occurred to me, as the situation surrounding Advance Base evolved, that here was the opportunity. Out there on the South Polar barrier, in cold and darkness as complete as that of the Pleistocene, I should have time to catch up, to study and think and listen to the phonograph; and, for maybe seven months, remote from all but the simplest distractions, I should be able to live exactly as I chose, obedient to no necessities but those imposed by wind and night and cold, and to no man's laws but my own.

✳✳ The next passages from Admiral Byrd's book *Alone* are the dramatic core of a personal experience "so personal," he has said, "that for four years I could not bring myself to write the book." He nearly died before the experience was over. "And," he adds, "since my sufferings bulked so large in it and since a man's instinct is to keep such things to himself, I did not see how I could write about Advance Base and still escape making an unseemly show of my feelings." His friends, however, prevailed over his hesitations, and in *Alone* Admiral Byrd told with singularly distinguished style how for five months he lived an almost Robinson Crusoe life in his underground "shack" with a temperature outside around 60° below zero, and how his spirits rose and fell with the routine of his work, with the occasional beauties of the Antarctic night, and how at times an unaccountable depression almost overwhelmed him, for which he could not wholly account, wondering whether it was due to diet, or the loneliness, or the fumes of a kerosene stove which had never worked quite properly. We pick up his narrative on May 31, his seventy-second day at his one-man hole in the ice, at Latitude 80° 08′ south, 123 miles by trail from Little America and the others in his expedition, on a continent of 4,500,000 square miles of ice, alone in a breeding ground of the world's weather in the "coldest cold on the face of the earth." ✳✳

THE BLOW

Snow was still falling on Thursday, the thirty-first of May. The morning was dreary and stagnant; the temperature about 5° above. The calendar warned: "Radio schedule." I went about the preparations methodically. Before me now are the messages which I dispatched to Little America that day. One was to Chief Pilot June and Navigator Rawson, reminding them to swing the planes for compass deviations. Another was to my wife [in Virginia], suggesting that she take up with my secretary, Miss McKercher, and my representatives in the United States ways and means of reducing the expedition's expenses.

Dyer took these messages down, then read them back. . . . We talked back and forth nearly an hour and a half. From my desk in the shack I could hear the engine in the tunnel; for some reason it started skipping. "Wait," I spelled out to Dyer.

Unhooking the lantern, I went into the tunnel. The air was thick with exhaust gases. Thinking the mixture was at fault, I bent over the carburetor and tinkered with the needle valve. This had little effect. I remember straightening up. And that was the last conscious act of mine that I do remember.

The next thing I recall, I was down on my hands and knees; and through the drowsiness, like an echo from far away, came an insistent notion that something terribly important ought to be done. What it was exactly my mind couldn't tell; and I felt helpless to do anything about it. I don't know how long I remained in that position. It may be that the cold aroused me. Anyhow, after a little while I crawled into the shack. The radio desk emerged from the blur, and then I remembered what I was supposed to do. I fumbled for the key and signed off, thinking how hard it was to spell out what I had to say. If any acknowledgment came, I did not hear it; for I couldn't get the earphones on.*

My actions thereafter are uncertain; I don't really know which were nightmare and which were fact. I remember lying on the bunk, fully dressed, and hearing, as if with surprise, the irregular beat of the engine in the tunnel and realizing that I must shut it off to escape asphyxiation. I rolled off the bunk and staggered to the door. Dizziness seized me, and my heart turned fantastic somersaults; but, as from a great distance, I could see the gray fumes of the exhaust smoke curling under the top sill; and the upper half of the tunnel, when I entered, was so foggy that I could not see as far as the alcove where the engine lay.

Very probably I dropped to my hands and knees, as I must have appreciated the necessity for keeping my head under the fumes and in the uncontaminated air near the floor. Anyhow, I was on my knees when I reached into the recess and threw the ignition switch. When I turned around, the light was gone in the doorway; this was puzzling until I recalled that the only light in the shack was the electric bulb over the radio desk, which burned only while the engine supplied current. Luckily the lantern was still burning on a box, where I had set it down before adjusting the engine. Pushing the lantern ahead of me, I crawled back to the shack and to the bunk.

Whatever did, in fact, occur during the rest of this last day in May, this I do know: that much of it was probably fantasy—a slow and wearying fantasy. Perhaps I did in truth roll off the bunk and try to replace the sheets on the register drum; else how to account for the vague recollection of seeing the glass frame on the floor some time in the afternoon. But the rest of it—the skyrocketing pain in my forehead and eyes, the nausea, the violent beating of my heart, the illusion of being a thin flame drawn between two voids—they could not have been real. Only the cold was real: the numbness in the hands and feet, creeping like a slow paralysis through my body. At least, I could cope with cold. I grasped for the throat of the sleeping bag and eased in.

Once the ticking of the clocks roused me out of the stupor. I have no sure memory of winding them; but, so strong was the compulsion of habit, I do remember thinking bitterly that they ought to be wound and that the register and thermograph sheets ought to be changed. Evidently I performed these tasks; for the instruments were still going next day; and the records,

---

* The radio log at Little America shows that twenty minutes or so elapsed between the time I said, "Wait" and the time I signed off, saying, "See you Sunday." This fixes approximately the interval I was in the tunnel.

now in the possession of the U. S. Weather Bureau, show that the sheets were shifted at 2:00 P.M., two hours late. My only distinct memory from that period was arousing and thinking that I was blind. My eyes were open, but I could see nothing. Then I realized that I must be facing the wall. The lantern was out (from lack of fuel, I learned presently), but a dim glow showed in the side of the stove.

There is nothing more panicky than the loss of sight. I shall never forget the agony in Floyd Bennett's voice when we pulled him, terribly smashed up, from the debris of our crash landing. "I'm done for," he whispered; "I can't see anything." His face was a smear of oil; when I wiped it away and he could see again, the expression that transfigured his face was beautiful.

It is painful for me to dwell on the details of my collapse, particularly as the affairs of Advance Base are now receding into the gentling haze of the past. The subject is one that does not easily bear discussion, if only because a man's hurt, like his love, is most seemly when concealed. From my youth I have believed that sickness was somehow humiliating, something to be kept hidden. But the consequences of this collapse were never to depart during the rest of my stay at Advance Base;* and my struggle against the one universal certainty played too large a part in my experience there to be omitted from this account.

I have a pretty clear idea concerning much that happened, almost too clear, in fact. I shall not, however, depend upon memory alone. During the days that followed, I set forth in the diary—as far as I was able—what I knew and remembered. How natural is the instinct which drives a man alone to pencil and paper, as if his destiny required the right last word and period.

The afternoon ran out its time; though my eyes would not stop aching and the pain would not quit my temples, just lying in the sleeping bag quieted the hammering of my heart. Gradually my mind cleared, and I tried to reconstruct the events preceding the episode in the tunnel. The exhaust vent over the engine, I decided, must have filled with rime, causing the poisonous gases to back into the tunnel. I was pretty sure that it was carbon monoxide. The instantaneous way I was struck down, the absence of any consciousness of suffocation bespoke these things, plus the symptoms—the splitting headaches, the nausea, the stabbing pains in my body and eyes, the hot and cold rushes of dizziness. What had saved me in the tunnel was

* Admiral Byrd was not to see another human being until August 11; and he did not leave Advance Base until two months and four days after that.—The Editor.

the fact of my being dropped as though poleaxed. Since monoxide rises, the
air at the bottom of the tunnel must have been all right; and the oxygen
entering my blood brought me around.

All this represented a mind groping for bearings. To know I had escaped
disaster in one form was only a preliminary step in the process of preparing
to avert it in another. The fact was manifest that I was helpless, at least for
the time being. I barely had strength to light the candle standing on the tin
ledge directly over my head. If so simple a movement could empty me of the
little strength that had returned, what chance did I have of bringing in food
and fuel from the tunnels, let alone attending to the instruments? I could
live many days without food. I could suck snow to quench thirst. But, ill
and weak as I was, I could not live long without heat; and the fuel tank had
to be filled every three days. Pondering such difficult matters was too much
for me; my mind went blank again. When I awakened and looked at my
wrist watch, the time was seven o'clock. I wasn't quite so weak, and my
body craved water.

So I drew the flashlight from the sleeping bag and propped it on the edge
of the bunk in order to direct the beam toward the stove. With this to guide
me, I slipped from the bunk, clinging to the side for support. Waves of dizziness swept from head to foot, but after a little while I was able to reach the
chair and push it toward the stove. A little water remained in the bucket on
the stove; I dipped it out with a can. The first few swallows my stomach
threw up; nevertheless, I persevered until I had at least a cupful down. Wondering why my teeth chattered so, I put my hand against the stove. It was
out—no longer than a few minutes, evidently, else the water would have frozen. *Thursday . . . Thursday . . . the day to fill the tank.* So the tank was
dry, as was the lantern; and if I wanted to have light and warmth, both must
be filled at once.

The notes which I jotted down a few days afterward insist this stranger
reeling in the dark acted with the utmost deliberation. Perhaps so. Between
the pain and the weakness it was hard for more than one thought to find a
lodgment. I managed to pull on my parka and mittens. Then I lifted the
empty tank from the stand. Holding it by the handle with one hand and the
flashlight with the other, I started into the tunnel. The nearest fuel drum—
by the grace of God equipped with a spigot—was only fourteen feet from
the door; but to make the distance I had to stop and put around my neck
the loop attached to the flashlight so as to free one hand with which to steady
myself. I walked slowly and uncertainly; as, years ago, I had walked for the
first time after being desperately ill of typhoid fever while on a midshipman
cruise to England.

The funnel lay on top of a barrel. I fitted it into the tank; and, while the tank was filling, I rested on a box. But, though I had the strength to lift the tank (it weighed about twenty-one pounds filled to the brim), I could not carry it far. After a few steps my heart was pounding, and the dizziness returned. I let go and slumped on the tool box, near the head of the tunnel. For how long? I really don't know. Long enough, anyhow, to be shaken by the cold. If I couldn't carry the tank, perhaps I could pull it, which was what I did—a few feet at a time. At least I remember doing that.

Inside the shack, I poured half a gallon or so of the precious stuff into a pitcher; this would do for the lantern. A lot spilled on the floor. Presently I succeeded in lifting the tank itself to the stand behind the stove. With that a feeling of relief possessed me for a moment. I could now hold off the cold for at least two days, and maybe three if I economized. Nevertheless, I didn't attempt to light the stove, dreading the effort and knowing that I ought to be in the bunk; but, craving light after the long darkness, I did light the lantern. The light was so cheery that I was encouraged to attempt an observation at 10:00 P.M. (Actually 8:00 P.M. my old time; for, a day or two previously, I had advanced my clock two hours, as an experiment in moonlight saving, so to speak.)

That was a mistake. I was able to climb the ladder all right, resting at every rung; I pushed the door back with my head, waited a moment, and then hobbled to the instrument shelter, feeling dizzy and utterly forlorn. I guessed the wind's velocity as being seventeen miles per hour (the register trace shows an actual wind speed of only seven miles), and noted the absence of aurora. But I was unspeakably weak and sick again when I reached the bottom of the ladder. I must sleep, I must sleep, something was saying inside me. In the escape tunnel I groped around until I found the box of Phenobarbital pills. With the box in my hand I stumbled to the hut. I got my parka, pants, and shoes off; but the shirt was beyond me. Using the chair as a step, I hung the lantern from its peg above the bunk, then climbed in, weighed down by a sense of complete futility.

The instant the candle died, the darkness dropped like a blow. Sleep was the great hunger; but it would not come, so cruel was the pain in my head and back and legs. As I lay there, the intimation came that I would not recover. Carbon monoxide poisoning is an insidious thing. Once the haemoglobin in the blood stream and the lungs is broken down, it takes the liver and spleen a long time to restore the oxygen-carrying material. Even with the best of hospital care this is a matter of weeks and sometimes months. For me the worst of the cold and the darkest part of the night were yet to come. The sun was nearly three months away. I could not persuade myself that I had the strength to meet it. To some men sickness brings a desire to be left alone; animal-like, their one instinct is to crawl into a hole and lick the hurt. It used to be so with me. But that night, as never before, I discovered how alone I was; and the realization evoked an indescribable desire to have about me those who knew me best. Remembering the meticulous preparations, the safeguards which I had thrown about myself, my soul was bitter with reproaches. My fort had become an ambush. Nothing within the power of the night or cold had made it so. My stupidity was to blame, and this I should have feared before the others.

Even in my stupor I seem to have recognized that the gasoline engine was not solely responsible. The engine dealt the blow which knocked me down, but long before then I had partially perceived a developing weakness. I remembered the notches I had taken up in my belt; the headaches and hurt in my eyes earlier in the month. Maybe the frost in my lungs was at fault. Maybe something was organically wrong with me. But I doubted that these by themselves could have depleted me so much. What reason I could muster indicted the stinking stove as the principal villain. Monoxide poisoning is not necessarily an instantaneous matter. It may be a gradual and cumulative process, brought about by intermittent exposure to the chemistry of the fumes. And the more I thought about the leaky joints in the stove, the more I blamed it.

But all this was shadowy in my mind that last night in May. I wavered between self-recrimination and hopefulness, between pain and an emptiness devoid of feeling. I knew that I was in a frightful mess, one that would involve my family, the expedition, and God only knew whom else. But it was hard to see what could be done about that. I lighted the candle, intending to write certain messages; but no paper was within reach. After a little while I blew out the candle. In my hand was the box of sleeping pills. I was reluctant to take one, not from squeamishness but from the fear that the drug would weaken me further. So, telling myself I would wait until four o'clock before resorting to the sedative, I put the box down. Sometime after three o'clock I drifted off into a dream of horrors.

DESPAIR

June 1 was a Friday. A black Friday for me. The nightmare left me, and about nine o'clock in the morning I awakened with a violent start, as if I had been thrown down a well in my sleep. I found myself staring wildly into the darkness of the shack, not knowing where I was. The weakness that filled my body when I turned in the sleeping bag and tried to throw the flashlight on my wrist watch was an eloquent reminder. I was Richard E. Byrd, United States Navy (Ret.), temporarily sojourning at Latitude 80° 08′ south, and not worth a damn to myself or anybody else. My mouth was dry and tasted foul. God, I was thirsty. But I had hardly strength to move. I clung to the sleeping bag, which was the only source of comfort and warmth left to me, and mournfully debated the little that might be done.

Two facts stood clear. One was that my chances of recovering were slim. The other was that in my weakness I was incapable of taking care of myself. These were desperate conclusions, but my mood allowed no others. All that I could reasonably hope for was to prolong my existence for a few days by hoarding my remaining resources; by doing the necessary things *very slowly* and with *great deliberation*. So long as he did that and maintained the right frame of mind, even a very ill man should be able to last a time. So I reasoned, anyway. There was no alternative. My hopes of survival had to be staked on the theory.

But you must have *faith*—you must have faith in the outcome, I whispered to myself. It is like a flight, a flight into another unknown. You start and you cannot turn back. You must go on and on and on, trusting your instruments, the course you have plotted on the charts, and the reasonableness of events. Whatever goes wrong will be mostly of your own making; if it is to be tragedy, then it will be the commonplace tragedy of human vulnerability.

My first need was warmth and food. The fire had been out about twelve hours; I had not eaten in nearly thirty-six. Toward providing those necessities I began to mobilize my slender resources. If there had been a movie camera to record my movements, the resulting picture could have been passed off as slow motion. Every act was performed with the utmost patience. I lifted the lantern—and waited. I edged out of the sleeping bag—and rested on the chair beside the stove. I pulled on my pants, hiking them up a little bit at a time. Then the shirt. Then the socks. And shoes. And finally the parka. All this took a long time. I was shaking so from the cold that, when my elbow struck the wall, the sound was like a peremptory knock at the door. Too miserable to stick it out, I retreated to the sleeping bag; half an hour later the chill in my body drove me into a fresh attempt to reach the stove.

Faintness seized me as I touched foot to the floor. I barely made the chair. There I sat for some minutes, not moving, just staring at the candle. Then I turned the valve, and with the stove lids off waited for the wick to become saturated with the cold, sluggish oil. Thirst continued to plague me. Several inches of ice were in the water bucket. I dropped it on the floor, bottom up. A sliver of ice fell out, which I sucked until my teeth rattled from the cold.

A box of matches was on the table. I touched one to the burner. A red flame licked over the metal ring; it was a beautiful thing to see. I sat there ten or fifteen minutes at least, absorbing the column of warmth. The flame burned red and smoky, when it should have been blue and clear; and, studying it, I knew that this was from faulty combustion and was one source of my misfortunes. This fire was my enemy, but I could not live without it.

Thus this never-ending day began. To describe it all would be tedious. Nothing really happened; and yet, no day in my life was more momentous. I lived a thousand years, and all of them were agonizing. I won a little and lost a lot. At the day's end—if it can be said to have had an end—all that I could say was that I was still alive. Granting the conditions, I had no right to expect more. Life seldom ends gracefully or sensibly. The protesting body succumbs like a sinking ship going down with the certificate of seaworthiness nailed fast to the wheelhouse bulkhead; but the mind, like the man on the bridge, realizes at last the weakness of the hull and ponders the irony. If the business drags out long enough, as mine did, the essence of things in time becomes pitifully clear; except that by then it is wadded into a tight little scrap ready to be thrown away, as the knowledge is of no earthly use.

My thirst was the tallest tree in a forest of pain. The escape tunnel was a hundred miles away, but I started out, carrying the bucket and lantern. Somewhere along the way I slipped and fell. I licked the snow until my tongue burned. The escape tunnel was too far. But in the food tunnel my boots had worn a rut eighteen inches wide and six inches deep, which was full of loose snow. The snow was dirty, but I scraped the bucket along until it was nearly full, then pulled it into the shack, a foot or so at a time.

Snow took a long time to melt in the bucket, and I could not wait. I poured a little into a pan and heated it with alcohol tablets. It was still a soggy mass of snow when I raised it to my lips. My hands were shaking, and the water spilled down the front of my parka; then I vomited, and all that I had drunk came up. In a little while I tried again, taking sips too small to be thrown up. Then I crawled on top of the sleeping bag, drawing a heavy blanket over my shoulders, hoping I should somehow regain strength.

Nevertheless, I was able to do a number of small things, in a series of stealthy, deliberate sorties from the bunk. I attended to the inside thermograph and register, changing the sheets, winding the clocks, and inking the pens. The outlet ventilator was two thirds filled with ice; I could just reach it from the bunk with a stick which had a big nail in the end. After every exertion I rested; the pain in my arms and back and head was almost crucifying. I filled a thermos jug with warm water, added powdered milk and sugar, and carried the jug into the sleeping bag. My stomach crawled with nauseous

sensation; but, by taking a teaspoonful at a time, I finally managed to get a
cupful down. After a while the weakness left me, and I felt strong enough to
start for the instrument shelter. I reached the hatch and pushed it open, but
could go no farther. The night was a gray fog, full of shadows, like my
mood. In the shack I lost the milk I had drunk. On the verge of fainting, I
made for the bunk.

I won't even attempt to recall all the melancholy thoughts that drifted
through my mind that long afternoon. But I can say truthfully that at no
time did I have any feeling of resignation. My whole being rebelled against
my low estate. As the afternoon wore on, I felt myself sinking. Now I became
alarmed. This was not the first time I had ever faced death. It had confronted
me many times in the air. But then it had seemed altogether different. In flying things happen fast: you make a decision; the verdict crowds you instantly; and, when the invisible and neglected passenger comes lunging into
the cockpit, he is but one of countless distractions. But now death was a
stranger sitting in a darkened room, secure in the knowledge that he would
be there when I was gone.

Great waves of fear, a fear I had never known before, swept through me
and settled deep within. But it wasn't the fear of suffering or even of death
itself. It was a terrible anxiety over the consequences of those at home if I
failed to return. I had done a damnable thing in going to Advance Base, I
told myself. Also, during those hours of bitterness, I saw my whole life pass
in review. I realized how wrong my sense of values had been and how I had
failed to see that the simple, homely, unpretentious things of life are the most
important.

Much as I should have liked to, I couldn't consider myself a martyr to science; nor could I blame the circumstances that had prevented staffing the
base with three men, according to the original plan. I had gone there looking for peace and enlightenment, thinking that they might in some way en-
rich my life and make me a more useful man. I had also gone armed with
the justification of a scientific mission. Now I saw both for what they really
were: the first as a delusion, the second as a dead-end street. My thoughts
turned to gall and wormwood. I was bitter toward the whole world except
my family and friends. The clocks ticked on in the gloom, and a subdued
whir came from the register at my feet. The confidence implicit in these unhurried sounds emphasized my own debasement. What right had they to be
confident and unhurried? Without me they could not last a day.

The one aspiration I still had was to be vindicated by the tiny heap of
data collected on the shelf in the escape tunnel. But, even as I seized upon

this, I recognized its flimsiness; a romanticized rationalization, as are most of the things which men are anxious to be judged by. We men of action who serve science serve only a reflection in a mirror. The tasks are difficult, the objectives remote; but scholars sitting in bookish surroundings tell us where to go, what to look for, and even what we are apt to find. Likewise, they pass dispassionate judgment on whatever we bring back. We are nothing more than glamorous middlemen between theory and fact, materialists jobbing in the substance of universal truths.

Beyond the fact that I had suffered to secure them, what did I know about the theoretical significance of the records in the escape tunnel, of the implications which might differentiate them from a similar heap of records gathered at Keokuk? I really didn't know. I was a fool, lost on a fool's errand, and that was how I should be judged.

At the end only two things really matter to a man, regardless of who he is; and they are the affection and understanding of his family. Anything and everything else he creates are insubstantial; they are ships given over to the mercy of the winds and tides of prejudice. But the family is an everlasting anchorage, a quiet harbor where a man's ships can be left to swing to the moorings of pride and loyalty.

The chill went out of the shack; and the heat from the stove, accumulating in a layer under the ceiling, wrapped the bunk as in a blanket. A little after six o'clock, as nearly as I could remember afterward, I sipped the last of the milk in the thermos jug. My body needed stronger nourishment, but I possessed nothing like the strength to cook a meal. I nibbled an Eskimo biscuit and a piece of chocolate, but my stomach was turning somersaults. So I got up and refilled the thermos jug with hot water and powdered milk, a really desperate task, as I had to cling to the table to keep from falling. The next several hours are a blank. Later, when I was able to make notes of what had happened to me, I could not remember anything at all. Perhaps I slept. When I looked at my watch again the time was about nine thirty. I was dazed and exhausted. The idea came to me that I ought to put out the stove to give myself a needed rest from the fumes; besides, there was no telling when I should have strength to fill the tank again. As I twisted the valve, the room went black. The next thing I knew I was on the floor. I pulled myself up by the stove. It was still warm; so I could not have been out very long.

I dropped into the chair, convinced that the end was near. Up till now I had been sustained by a conviction that the only way I could nullify my mistake and make reparation to my family was by transcending myself and surviving. But I had lost. I flung my arms across the table, and put my head down, spilling a cup of water I had in my hand. My bitterness evaporated, and the only resentment I felt was concentrated on myself. I lay there a long time, sobbing, "What a pity, what an infinite pity!" So my pride was gone as well. A Virginian, I was brought up to believe that a gentleman never gives way to his feelings. I felt no shame then, although I do now. Fear was gone, also. When hope goes, uncertainty goes, too; and men don't fear certainties.

The only conscious resolve left was to write a message to my wife—a last groping touch of the hand. Beyond the very personal things, I wanted her to understand why I had not tried to inform Little America of my plight (forgetting that it needed no explanation) and my reasons for going to Advance Base. There had to be that. Pencil and paper were on a shelf nearby. When I went to reach out, my arm would not come free; my sleeve had frozen in the spilled water. I wrenched it loose. The frenzy to write supplied its own strength. After the first few paragraphs my mind calmed. But I was too weak to write sitting up. My head kept jerking forward; and, now that the fire was out, the shack was unbearably cold.

The bunk was a continent's breadth away, and I had to cross an interminable plateau to reach it. Safe at last in the sleeping bag, I lay still many minutes, shivering and gasping for breath. Then I finished the letter; and, as I did so, I thought of the last entry in Scott's diary: "For God's sake, look after our people." I had often pondered that simple phrase, but only intellectually. That night I understood what Scott meant. It seemed a pity that men must undergo a cataclysmic experience to perceive this simplest of truths.

The lantern flicked and grew dim. I managed to light two candles which stood on a ledge over the bunk. Just as the second one flamed, the lantern went out. Then, after a while, I wrote a letter to my mother, and another to my children, a few messages, very brief, of instruction to Dr. Poulter and Charlie Murphy concerning the welfare of the expedition, and a final letter to the men at Little America. On the shelf was the green metal box which held my personal papers. I have had it for years. In this I stowed the letters to my family. The ensuing periods are not very clear. I may have lapsed into a coma. A sensation of freezing came; my next recollection is of hoisting myself into a sitting position and composing a message to Murphy regarding the disposal of my papers. This, with the other messages, I secured with a string to the nail from which the lantern usually hung.

Something approaching gratitude flowed into me. Over my head the two candles still burned. Both were red. One stood in a cracked china holder. The other was planted in its own tallow. I looked up at them, thinking vaguely that, when they went out, I should never again see anything so friendly. After a little while I doused the wicks against the wall. Presently another reaction set in. My mind wandered off into a vision of the past, in which I seemed to be wrestling again for the welterweight championship of the naval academy. An agonizing pain was in my body; I had given up all hope of winning; there remained only an insane determination not to bring shame to my mother in the gallery. It was vivid, and the reason it was vivid was that I was again in almost the same situation, except that the stakes were infinitely greater and the chances of winning even less. Then the same determination that had kept me fighting on to the finish that day again came surging back. I saw that, although I seemed absolutely washed up, there was a chance I was mistaken. Anyway, I would have another try.

About three o'clock on the morning of June 2, I had another lucid phase. I tried without success to force my body into sleep. The sleeping pills were on the shelf. The flashlight fingered the bottle. I took it down and dumped the pellets into my cupped palm. There were more than two dozen, white and round; they bespoke a lovely promise. I reached for the bottle. But then I stopped. It was impossible to go on like this. I should become a madman, shrinking from every shadow and touch of pain. I found a match and lighted a candle. An unused sheet of paper lay on the bunk, on top of the diary. I wrote:

The universe is not dead. Therefore, there is an Intelligence there, and it is all pervading. At least one purpose, possibly the major purpose, of that Intelligence is the achievement of universal harmony.

Striving in the right direction for Peace (Harmony), therefore, as well as the achievement of it, is the result of accord with that Intelligence.

It is desirable to effect that accord.

The human race, then, is not alone in the universe. Though I am cut off from human beings, *I* am not alone.

For untold ages man has felt an awareness of that Intelligence. Belief in it is the one point where all religions agree. It has been called by many names. Many call it God.

This was the gist of the philosophy which had come to me out of April's hush. Dousing the candle, I slipped into the bag and repeated the sentiments over and over again. Sleep came after a while. It was intruded upon by another nightmare in which I seemed to be struggling desperately to awaken and take charge of my faculties. The struggle went on interminably in a half-lighted borderland divided by a great white wall. Several times I was nearly across the wall into a field flooded with a golden light, but each time I slipped back into a spinning darkness. Instinct plucked at my sleeve: You must wake up. You must wake up. I pinched the flesh over my ribs. I pulled my long hair. Then the tension eased; I fell across the wall; and, instead of warm sunlight, I found myself in darkness, shivering from cold and thirsting for water.

June 2 was a Saturday and a prolongation of the melancholy events of the day before. I was as weak as ever, and just as certain that I was at the end of my tether. The anemometer cups rattled most of the day; drift sifted down the ventilator in a fine haze, and dripped in hot, pinging pellets from the stovepipe to the deck. From the register I learned that the wind was in the northeast and blowing about twenty miles an hour. I prayed for it to stay in that quarter, since it would mean a continuation of the warm weather. Although the temperature did drop to −19° in the evening, it was above zero part of the day. If the cold held off, I could do without the stove for long periods and give my system a chance to throw off the effects of the fumes. Altogether, I could not have been out of the bunk more than two or three hours during the day.

As before, I did what had to be done piecemeal, doling out my strength in miserly driblets, creeping rather than walking, and resting long intervals after each small effort. Toward the middle of the day I made several sorties into the tunnels, once after snow and three times after fuel. I relayed the fuel in a tin pitcher, which held about a gallon, since the stove tank was too heavy for me. Later, when the snow had melted, I mixed more milk in the thermos jug. My stomach would not hold anything more solid, although I did manage to down a cup of tea.

I have a vague memory of climbing the ladder to see what the day was like. This was the period of the moon; but, if it showed, I have no recollection of it; my mind remembered a depressing darkness and drift burning against the cheek. In the late afternoon, when the shack had warmed up, I shut down the stove. The thermograph trace shows a minimum temperature of −22° for the day—a really moderate reading. But the water which I had spewed up was frozen on the floor; a film of ice was creeping up the shack walls; and the slop pail was a solid, messy chunk of ice.

That night, as well as I could estimate, I slept seven or eight hours. Sunday morning brought another anguished struggle to awaken. Sunday meant a radio schedule with Little America and a lie about my condition which every pain-ridden fiber entreated me not to make. God knows where the strength came from to slide the thirty-five-pound engine into the shack, get it up on the stove, and push it back into the tunnel again, a distance of some forty feet, all told. It was my good fortune to find the tank nearly half full of gasoline. The last thing I did was to pick the rime out of the surface ventilator pipe with a spiked stick. The pipe was almost solidly clogged. No wonder the tunnel had filled with fumes during the last schedule.

By the Little America radio log, I was about twenty minutes late reporting. Dyer's voice was saying, "KFZ calling KFY," in the same crisp, matter-of-fact way; but the sound was a surpassing miracle.

It took only the pressure of a finger to work the key; I knew that code would not betray me. Some days before, Charlie Murphy had asked me to give him certain weather information. The data had been lying on my desk for nearly a week. I sent that. Then some of the camp officers took up certain aspects of the proposed spring operations. I am not sure that I wholly understood everything that was said, for the sickness was coming on again. My answers were a simple yes or no or, "Will think over." Finally Dyer's stately, "Thank you, sir. We shall meet you again Thursday," came through the confusion. I shut off the engine, utterly spent.

I have often been asked why I did not tell Little America what had happened. My answer is that it was too dangerous for the men to come to me. This conviction was so strong that I took it for granted. But I was no automaton. When contact was made and Dyer remarked at the outset, as he always did, "We hope that everything is well with you," it was hard to say "OK." But it would have been harder to say anything else. The intervening darkness, the cold, the rolling vacancies of the Barrier, and the crevasses were all immutable facts. Advance Base was my responsibility. It was unthinkable that willing men at Little America should be made to suffer.

That afternoon I may have been close to going out of my mind; the strain of preparing for the schedule had raised Cain with me. I know that I was in torment, and the notion that I was dying would not leave me. Sometime during the evening I came out of the delirium, thirsty and hungry. Along with some milk, I managed to down half a dozen salt crackers, the first solid food since Thursday morning. That night I slept a little longer, though my slumber was lighted by unspeakable nightmares. Monday I scarcely left the sleeping bag. The rest did me good: as did, perhaps, my keeping the fire out most of the afternoon. At night I got up and supped on malted milk, salted crackers, almonds, and dried apples soaked in warm water. A queer mixture, which I myself cannot explain otherwise than by a dim notion that of all the edibles in the shack, these were the only ones that my stomach would tolerate.

I still had no endurance. The pain came and went in my eyes and head and back. And I was always cold.

That night, as before, I ranged the whole broad reaches of hell before finding sleep. Next morning I had much less difficulty waking up, which heartened me. Indeed, matters went somewhat easier. I even managed to empty the slop pail in the food tunnel. In the afternoon I had strength enough to crank the phonograph. The song "In the Gypsy's Life" from *Bohemian Girl* was on the disc. I played that, then the drinking song in *Heidelberg*. And "Adeste Fidelis." It was magnificent to hear the sound of many voices throbbing in every corner of the shack. *You are on the mend,* an inner voice said; *you really have a chance. One in a hundred, perhaps, but still a chance.*

A Naturalist's Wife on Sufferance in the Subantarctic*

GRACE E. BARSTOW MURPHY

✳✳ Mrs. Murphy is the wife of Robert Cushman Murphy of the American Museum of Natural History, New York; and science and travel—sometimes taking their three children with them—have set the pattern of her life. Her latest book is *Your Deafness Is Not You*. Mrs. Murphy has lived since the age of ten in the shadow of deafness and for the past four years has been cut off wholly from the world of normal sound—a disability which has at no time impeded her social life, scientific life, travel, or her interests in the world around her. ✳✳

The Snares Islands in the subantarctic ocean south of New Zealand were discovered by Vancouver in 1791. He described them as a "very dangerous cluster of barren rocks, seven in number, twenty leagues from the South Cape of New Zealand." There had been almost nothing written about them before our sojourn there. Very few people, and no scientists, had ever stayed on them. In 1803 a man named Bass quite appropriately asked the King of England for fishing rights at the Snares, the Penantipodes, and the Bounty Islands. In 1810 Captain Keith of London, short of rations on his schooner *Adventure,* stranded three men there, providing them with an iron pot, a half-bushel of potatoes, and a quart of rice. These men lived on seals and birds and the potatoes they grew from their tiny stock. They collected thirteen hundred sealskins and built five huts made of sealskins. After seven years, Captain Coffin brought them off in the United States vessel *Enterprise.*

These are the only records of people living on these islands. Even sealers have but rarely visited them. Maori mutton bird hunters† used to go to them

* From *There's Always Adventure*, by Grace E. Barstow Murphy. Copyright, 1951, by Grace E. Barstow Murphy, reprinted by permission of the author and the publishers, Harper & Brothers, New York.

† Captain Cleveland's original log of the voyage of the *Daisy,* now in the Mystic Marine Museum, records that on November 9, 1912 ". . . at 5:00 P.M. calm lowered the dory down and shot a lot of mutton birds they being very good food maid into a stew."

for short seasons of collecting young birds in large numbers, which they smoked and then packed in bags made out of the giant kelp. Scientific parties have landed, choosing their weather, for three or four hours at a time. Guthrie-Smith, in *Joys and Sorrows of a Naturalist in New Zealand,* has a short chapter on the Snares Islands. They are so far from shipping lanes and lie in such dangerous seas that the New Zealand government built and equipped a Castaways' Hut on the largest island about 1887. There is no record of its having been needed until the night our party landed in November, 1947.

Think of being a woman in a party of naturalists on a subantarctic island! There were ten of us, nine men and I, for about two weeks of the southern spring. Bob, besides being on his regular job of studying oceanic birds, was creating the Subantarctic Exhibit for the Whitney Hall of Pacific Bird Life. Watching an exhibit planned, collected, preserved, and crated, from the ground up, should be a "must" for every woman married to a museum man. One's self needs to get under the skin of such jobs, sharing not only in the thrilling adventure but also in the driving urgency of the work. There is a story attached to my inclusion in an expedition going to such a place. Our New Zealand colleagues were at first far from enthusiastic at the idea of having a woman along. Our leader, Dr. Robert A. Falla, director of the Dominion Museum in Wellington, whom I had long known casually under the urban conditions of New York, wrote to stress the danger. He added that the captain did not dare take a woman.

I wrote back saying that after a long life one learns that many things are of more importance than mere danger. I pointed out that, as is now told in the *Logbook,** I had been partially responsible for Bob's career in oceanic birds. If I had not urged him to reverse his decision and go to South Georgia, saying we would marry before he left, his genius might easily have turned in another direction than birds of the ocean. Consequently, I longed to see those birds. I had said for thirty-five years that I could not die till I had seen Bob's ocean birds. This was my chance. So I wrote to the New Zealanders, following Bob's own request, and told them all about it, ending with: "As for roughing it, I have just been camping with one of my sons and three of my grandchildren, all sleeping on the ground. There is no roughing it that you can do which I can't take."

New Zealanders are an understanding people. They wrote that I might go. On my arrival in Auckland, however, they showed me movies of fearful antarctic storms and shipwrecks. Of course I did not turn a hair and kept a poker face when I saw them smiling at each other. I knew it would be a

* See *Nine Hours Fast to a Fighting Whale,* pp. 129-37.

hard trip, but it was my chance to see what South Georgia is like. There are no glaciers or snow at the Snares in summer, as in South Georgia, but the birds and beasts and gales are the same.

We ten met at Bluff, the southernmost town of New Zealand, a friendly little flower-filled town rolling downhill into its tight little harbor. We walked down the long wharf to *Alert*. It was low tide. The seventy-three-foot launch, owned by Captain Black and subsidized by the New Zealand government for our trip, lay far below the wharf. There was no ladder and no move was made to help me down. I handed Bob my purse and slung aboard. Not a word was said, but I had a definite feeling that a test had been set—and passed.

Alert danced and stood on her head across Foveaux Strait to Stewart Island. By holding on tight, we all managed to stay aboard. I was too busy to be sick, for I was watching albatrosses flying. They swooped and soared so close that I reached out my hand in instinctive thought to touch them.

Their flight is everything that has ever been written about it, including all the descriptions of their best biographer, my husband. It is the poetry of motion in excess of poetry and into a world where music alone can partially express its rhythm. Petrels run along the water, often flying with the contour of the ocean heavings. Man-o'-war birds fly high above one, so that a favorite occupation of mine has always been to lie on my back on soft-swelling Pacific bathing waters, watching the man-o'-war birds halfway between my eyes and heaven. But albatrosses! All levels are theirs. Now high, now low, now at sharp angles to the ocean, with one long, slender wing tip almost cutting the water, they express the joy of creation as does nothing else in nature. I am sure that when the Lord rested on the Seventh Day, he broke his rest a little and made the albatross as an expression of his feeling. No scientific research yet has explained to satisfaction their soaring flight with hardly a tremor of a wingbeat. . . .

We lay that first night in a beautiful landlocked harbor at Stewart Island. At dusk Cape pigeons, another of Bob's South Georgia birds, frolicked near the boat, with the charm that petrels always have and without the fear ingrained in birds nearer to civilization.

But the Snares were our objective—getting there our captain's problem. Though weather reports were not good, Captain Black decided to make a southward dash the second night, following a fascinating day ashore on Stewart Island.

We ran into heavy weather at once. Bob, in spite of having lived for nearly a year in a whale ship in the South Atlantic, says that he had never seen dirtier weather than that night south of Stewart. The wind blew a full gale of eight on the Beaufort Scale. *Alert* was not a pleasure boat. The bunks were narrow, hard, without combings, and, of course, with nothing so effete as sheets. We lay in our clothes in blankets and hung on. Several of the men said they were braced hand and foot all night. I woke up once to find half of me in mid-air across the cabin, but enough of me remained in my bunk to haul the rest back. Almost everyone was sick. I did well till thirst drove me across the cabin in the dark to the cup of drinking water I had placed with care in the washbasin to keep it from spilling. Thrown in every direction, I managed to get hold of the cup, taking a big draught before realizing that the green toilet soap had slipped into it and lay soaking. That was my finale.

The gales increased. We were forced to turn back to Stewart Island. Even had we made the Snares, there would have been no chance of landing. We anchored quietly in Pegasus Harbor, on the opposite side to Abraham's Bosom, where we had lain at anchor during our first night on *Alert*.

This third night we faced a second beating, everyone dreading it in that cheerful way in which people look at such things. The boys, Roland and Hugh, groaned but grinned.

This time we made the Snares! Bob came down in soaking sou'wester to awaken me and tell me how wonderful was the approach to the rocky islands.

I clambered up to majesty superb! There was a heavy northwest storm on. We anchored in rolling swells and pouring rain under spectacular cliffs that towered a straight four hundred feet above us. Their shape and appearance grew into one's eyes with as permanent impression as lens on film. White water poured between them and outlying rocks. Oceanic birds were everywhere. The majesty of the scenery seemed even more subtle than that of the Grand Canyon. The latter bursts into one's vision when one is comfortable and warm. The effect is instantaneous. These Snares cliffs seeped through and through one's being during the hours of a long, cold, rough, and miserable day. We did not even have food, for the exhausted crew of four slept beside the galley entrance.

Mr. Newcombe, of Internal Affairs, botanist and artist, handed me something hard and cold.

"Have an apple?" It was terrible.

I said, "Can't someone raid the galley?"

Mr. Baird, geodesist and weatherman, volunteered, returning in triumph with one plate of cold sausage and another plate of sweet coconut crackers. We shivered but laughed at the horrid combination, and did not leave a crumb.

Time dragged, but the scene was matchless. Fur seals played about us and clambered on the cliffs. We rolled and pitched at anchor in our little lee, with nothing between us and the South Pole. The islands make a semicircle facing south. Had gales grown heavier to crash us against the cliffs, no one could have survived. Had we been forced to run to sea, there would have been no place to go. The only shelter for landing is a tiny cove on the east side of the mile-and-a-half-long island—its entrance in the gale's track.

At four in the afternoon the winds moderated a little. It was essential to get ashore and start the work of settling. Bob Falla had said it would take ten hours to get the tents up and the work must start at dawn.

"And if it is raining?" said I.

"It will be terrible," said he—and later I knew why.

The unloading alone of all our material would take hours: our food supplies, tents, and all items of our living, with instruments of many kinds, boxes, lumber, formalin, and six large drums of drinking water.

It was imperative to get ashore. Bad as the weather was, it could grow worse and drive us back to Stewart. The work must not be lost.

The anchor was twisted from its twenty-fathom depth. Yet we did not start at once, for the curiosity of the naturalist is eternal. If he were stood up against a wall out-of-doors to be shot, his last words would be "By Jove, that bird makes a record," following it with his eyes, oblivious of the rifles.

So we crept up closer to the cliffs, to see the seals and birds. The walls were already so near one felt one could touch them. Their straight sides continued straight down into deep water. The dark seals and dark-brown rocks merged in similar color. Grass grew in the depressions of the rocks, and stunted trees clung high above us. Cape pigeons and South Georgia petrels flew about us. A skua passed—a big bird with ugly habits, which I came later to enjoy and like. The men spoke of its intelligence with admiration.

Immediate human needs could wait. Yet finally we left the gorgeous spot we will never see again, and edged along the restless coast, holding on with hands and feet to stay aboard. Jagged rocks foamed with the lashing of the waves. We steamed between two of these scenic wonders, without much space to spare on either side. I was taking comfort out of thought of our captain's knowledge of rocks and ledges and depths, and said to Bob Falla:

"Has Captain Black been here often?"

Bob Falla bit off crisp words: "He has never been to the Snares before."

He was navigating by the color of the water, which took on meaning even to my unpracticed eyes. I felt no fear, but instead the uplifted stimulus of danger. There was no spot for any landing in case of need. It did not take much imagination for the tales one had read about castaways to become graphic.

One of the worst aspects must be the ice-cold water. The thought of that pierced through me.

We reached the tiny inlet the men had shown me on the map. A dinghy was lowered. Bob Falla and Alister, our student sailor, went ahead to explore and then waved to us to follow. The cove was so narrow that Captain Black turned our small craft and backed in! Bob Murphy said later that not one skipper in ten thousand would have risked it. Yet anyone would trust Captain Black's judgment and his general knowledge of New Zealand waters and their habits.

The cove was smooth—amazingly, all motion stopped. We moored to gnarled daisy trees and rocks. The trees grew out of the ledge about eight or ten feet above the water. Until we were fast our men worked ceaselessly pushing us off the thick and heavy branches. New Zealand is full of scores of kinds of daisy trees belonging to the family Compositae. I had seen many late ones at Stewart and on the mainland covered with white flowers exactly like our field daisies.

Penguins leaped all about us, diving in and out of the water at so fast a clip as to cover distance almost as if they were flying. They look so much like porpoises that Bob said when he first saw them at South Georgia he thought he had discovered a new species of tiny porpoise. They gather in groups and play. They turn on their backs and wash their white shirt fronts. They need good scrubbing as they live in mud.

Sea lions and solemn penguins sitting on the rocks, exquisite Antarctic terns about us, slender gray gulls, the long, brown, restless kelp forever stirring, the evening flight of millions of mutton birds beginning over our heads, the angry seas outside our little cove bursting against the rampart cliffs, engrossed me with the beauty of such far-off, unknown surroundings. As the captain stopped a moment beside me, I burst out in rapture:

"Oh, have you ever seen a more beautiful spot?"

"Yes, HOME," said he, so that I jumped. "Those rollers are backing up in here. I can't let you sleep aboard tonight. I've got to run for it."

It was nearly six. At top speed, the landing of supplies was completed at eight, with the loss of one water drum. *Alert* rushed off to safety. We ten bedraggled people had been set down in rain and gales and cold and mud and darkness, with no way to get tents up or food unpacked that night.

The Castaways' Hut was hope incarnate. With its corroded roof and mud-filled interior, it fulfilled its purpose after waiting sixty years. Little did its builders guess in 1887 it would harbor a group of naturalists in 1947. Little did its builders dream that the ship's biscuit would still be edible, though far from enjoyable. The wax vestas did not light. They bore the label of R. Bell & Co. London. Estab^d. 1832. The reading matter included a water-spoiled novel: *Those Bad Blue Eyes*.

The boys cleaned out a few hundredweight of mud. Mr. Stead and the major, our two nonprofessional ornithologists, stretched a tarpaulin over the roof, and laid one on the floor. Duffle bags ranged the walls, both to keep them dry and to give us backs to lean against.

The ugly little hut, only about eight by twelve feet, was still half-filled with crates too big to move out that night or to open inside. The roof was so low that we could not stand up straight in it: people were shorter in the 1870's and '80's.

We ten filed in, lady first, of course, so that I drew one wall, a large crate at my knees, a large husband who is not at all a jackknife, and a duffle bag filled, apparently, with bricks.

While the men had been landing the stores, I had made sandwiches and tea in *Alert's* galley. Leftover sandwiches, chocolate out of my purse, Mr. Stead's fruitcake, and some cans of orange juice were all the food we had. Water seeped around the tarpaulin and dripped on us. Some blankets appeared, and we curled up "to sleep." Cramps were almost intolerable. I could think of just the one idea someone gave me before my first baby was born: "It has got to be over sometime." Bob had his problems and I could not lean on him even though I was jammed against him and between the hard wall, crate, and bag. I tried in vain to ease us both. I could not even grouse, for I was on the Snares on sufferance. Then, too, there was the consciousness of the privilege of being there, knowing at first hand what men experience in the field. To create our Snares group, Bob not only had to have expert knowledge of his complete environment in ornithology, botany, geology, photography, and so forth, but he also had to take whatever discomfort the environment presented, plus working fast at least sixteen hours a day.

A week later I read Bob's report of that ghastly night. He ended: "Grace was the only one who seemed to enjoy it."

The eon-long hours passed. At half-past four a little light came in through the door of the windowless hut. Enough men had stirred so that Bob and I could climb over the scrambled legs. Charlie Fleming, our geologist, helped me with a good strong hand.

As we stood upright outside, Bob said excitedly, "Look! The cove!"

It was a boiling caldron of breaking waves. *Alert* would have been dashed to tinder had she stayed. The long, wide strands of kelp, ranging from darkest brown to golden tan, were churned and twisted and brushed on and off the jagged rocks as the waves washed them every which way. It seemed to emphasize the fact that we ten were alone on an empty island, not knowing what storms might hold us there.

Alone! Of course not: Bob and I sat on a pinnacle of rock above a raging sea and watched the penguins. The biggest waves—so big and angry no human being could survive in them—rolled penguins in by the score. Sometimes these hardy birds catch and climb up the cliff. Sometimes they fall back into the terrific undertow of the powerful surge. They try again and again until they make a landing by using their strong feet and their flippers. They waddle off, clean and sleek and sure, as if they had not taken such a beating as few animals could survive.

Gales drove the rain across the strange forest that covers much of our island. No branch obstructs their path. Coarse, heavy, but beautiful leaves lie on one level, close growing, almost as evenly laid as is a man-made roof. This forest is undulating, smooth flowing, like grass-grown hills above the tree line back in normal climates. Were this not so, the gales would tear the leaves to ribbons, as I have seen our two great hurricanes do on Long Island, where gales are not expected. The trunks, too, have habits adjusted to the gales, for they lie half-supine along the muddy ground. If they tried to stand up straight like other trees, the weight of the wind across their tops would break them down. Penguins march among them to their rookeries, and great, sluggish sea lions wallow in the mud, preferring the few open spaces in the shade of trees, however.

When the others finally woke, Bob and I had our first lesson in the science of camping in mud. The whole island is deep, oozy mud. It is under the trees, around each clump of tussock grass, everywhere. No one at home ever saw such mud. It is dark and squashy and slippery. We wore high rubber boots or shoes all the time. We slipped and fell in mud. Its only good quality was its softness, which broke the very fall it caused.

"South Georgia was never like this," said Bob. "Of course there was mud, as there nearly always is where there are penguins, but there was plenty of dry ground, and plenty of clear fresh water."

The "fresh" water on the Snares was mahogany brown and smelled so horribly of penguin and sea lion that not even the hardiest man would wash a finger in it.

There was not a level spot for the tents. We could not set them up by the landing because of the sea lion wallows and the gale's sweep. Above the high grass hummocks the forest rises in a fearful mass of great trunks and tangled branches, all moss-covered, reaching out close over the underbrush of—

mud. Big ferns, stumpy things with long fronds, somewhat soften the horrible medley of the tortured, twisted trees.

The efficient New Zealanders finally chose the edge of the bush. Ground was partially leveled. Great heavy fern fronds, six feet and more long, were piled inches deep as flooring. Four commodious sleeping tents were pitched near each other. . . . The mess tent, built by the major and the boys, was a work of art. I used to write at its long table, which was flanked by benches. There was a fireplace at one end for cooking, the pots hanging on S hooks. Crates of food lined the sides. We took turns with the work and had good, hearty meals. The warm wood fire was a blessing.

Each morning we breakfasted on fried mutton birds' eggs. One is larger than two hen's eggs. We were not robbing the birds, for only those laid deep in the burrows are incubated. During the early part of the nesting season, the birds cannot always wait, so lay them outside, just as babies get born in taxicabs before reaching the hospital. I have picked up these doomed eggs on the path to our tent, for the mutton bird burrows are everywhere, all over the island. At dusk one may stroke the soft gray of these beautiful petrels, as they squat outside their doorway holes.

This path that I speak of was, of course, mud. The boys filled it frequently with fern stumps, which helped till the water found it could ooze up just as well as without them.

Bob and I did not know the ropes about flooring nor did we have enough bedding. We were freezing on our cots. I told Roland and Hugh and asked for some of the big fern fronds to put under our sleeping bags. Instead they broke out the castaways' casks, with the result that under my sleeping bag there were six complete sets of men's clothing, including heavy underwear, of the vintage of my grandparents. The cloth of the suits was a gay check. Bob extracted some of the castaways' underwear and put it on. I thought I might succumb to the same idea if I shivered much more. Most of this clothing was sent later to European relief—to war castaways.

Mr. Stead had been asking how I stood the mud and if it was repulsive to me. I told him I had no time to worry over it, and that Bob and I helped each other dress till we got our boots on and could stand up in it. The boys gave us a potato sack which made a very good rug.

There was a colony of penguins between Bob Falla's tent and ours. They marched past our doors all day. They kept up an endless chatter, so that Bob Murphy said the din at night of penguins and mutton birds was fearful. The latter, in their burrows, sounded like millions of crying babies. Some of the penguins were nursing their big chicks, which were covered with dark gray down, making them look as large as their sleek parents. Narrow flippers, not feathered, cannot successfully cover chicks. The urge to cover them is the same, however, as with feather-winged birds. The parent-pairs are very affectionate, caressing each other or even helping to scratch. One parent stood quietly with a flipper touching the breast of its mate, while the other was actively demonstrative. I was told the females are the aggressive ones. Sometimes a chick pushed between the parents, wanting food but getting scant attention.

Down beyond the mess tent and up the hill beyond the hut, a small colony of penguins had been enacting exactly the same drama Bob had seen in South Georgia long ago. Three adults, equidistant from each other, were guarding twelve muddy chicks. The new-hatched chicks were cared for by a whole adult apiece, but older ones were graduated into nurseries. The parents did not overlook the advantage of having baby sitters.

There was a skua by the penguins, and I went up to watch the great, dark, predatory gull. The skua was hungry. Moreover, it had two chicks over the rise of the hill among the rocks, and they were always hungry.

The handsome bird walked around the penguin colony. Twelve penguins had herded their offspring in a tight clump. As the gull approached, in greater nonchalance than it probably felt, despite its strength, the penguins stretched their necks and screamed at it. They were so excited they turned now and then to peck at the poor babies, like cross nursemaids in Central Park. The skua would walk up close, but be driven back. Three times, on long, strong wings, it landed in the middle of the fright-filled group. It did not get a chick, though once it filled its bill with gray down, then tried to spit it out disgustedly. The chicks were big, and their parents did not give the skua time to get a good grip to carry one off. When it finally left, the penguins settled down to rest, half-nodding to each other in a well-that-is-over way. It is not possible not to dramatize penguins. One watches the crowds of people on New York streets and is wearied, but one never wearies of watching penguins and interpreting their actions.

The skuas kept up their attack on my little colony, gradually getting every chick in it. The parents had grown used to me, so that each day I walked close to their rain-bedraggled, muddy babies, whose bones were soon scattered under their parents' eyes. Three disconsolate adults came to look at the deserted spot, and now and then a weak attempt was made to live there again.

A scramble over the rocks of several headlands brought me to a favorite perch on a cliff one hundred feet above the sea, where there were penguins in thousands. They rode in on the highest, roughest waves of the cliff-dashing sea. Their main avenue, which we called Penguins Broadway, stretched away over the hills, worn out of the black rocks. The coast was the wildest I had ever seen. The winds there blew cold. Unknown centuries of plodding little feet, each set carefully down after the other as would yours or mine be set on a steep path, had worn this wide way which leads across the open tussock-covered hill to the rookeries. When there was a depression, they jumped across, both feet together, and when there was a slight elevation, they jumped up, measuring the distance accurately. Coming down such a path or on cliffs was not as easy, as they slipped and slid long distances. Sometimes they stopped and perched comfortably on a level hummock or on rocks. Sometimes they lay on their stomachs on almost perpendicular rock slides. I watched one high above me on a hummock, head hidden behind the flipper. He looked like a black kitten with whiskers showing, his dark steel gray turned darker by the light.

The penguins seem to have four methods of progression: walking or hopping on land, swimming like ducks, or leaping like porpoises in the water. The hop is faster than their almost ludicrous walk, for their feet are so big and their legs so short they cannot get all of one foot in front of all of the other foot. When I sat quietly among them, as I frequently did, I could watch all their habits even to the flash of their transparent extra eyelids over their open eyes every two or three seconds. When they grow sleepy, their eyes close or blink. At other times they are wide open. A dignified penguin sat solemnly at my crossed feet one day. We seemed to discuss many matters of interest. Getting restless, I uncrossed my feet and my friend turned to leave. As instinctively as I would speak to you, my reader, I said:

"Oh, please don't go."

And he turned and stayed.

Beyond where I was sitting, between my rock and the next promontory, there was an almost level ridge, kelp-edged, nearly free of water at low tide but covered by a few feet at high tide. Here penguins had a playground. Some poured into the surf and were swept out to sea, while others were spun out of the pounding waves to struggle to dry rocks. One large group had a game of standing stock-still on the flat rock ledge waiting for a rousing roller. When it came, it sent them tumbling and scurrying. As it receded, they climbed on the same rock again, awaiting the next. It was their kind of surfboard riding. They played in groups at sea too. They rolled over in the water to polish their white shirt fronts and wash the mud off.

It is fortunate that penguins have the thick skins I helped Bob prepare. Their armor against the terrific buffeting on jagged rocks explains their survival. The coat of feathers is thick and deep, and the skin is tough. Under the skin is a heavy layer of fat like a fibroid mattress. It was my job to cut this fat off after the skins were roughed out. With scissors I cut off the hunks, and partly cleaned out the skull. It was back-tiring work sitting on the hard bench, yet, as I said:

> "Seeing a penguin inside out
> Is something to write home about."

As everyone's back ached in our chairless, comfortless existence, no one bothered about his own. Bob said it was the hardest living he had ever known anywhere in the world.

There was never a level spot for two successive steps and we all fell down in the mud so much that no one ever noticed it. Penguins fall forward, because their tails are supports. Humans fall backward. I took one tumble backward downhill, getting my hair full of mud and no way to wash it. I was restless for a bath, yet would not have cut the experience short one hour for the sake of one. Have any pioneers expected hot baths every day?

The whole place was so damp with the constant rain that it was hard to dry the bird skins, much less wet clothing. The branches of the trees felt muddy and damp.

Our twelve days drew to an end. Bob worked to the last moment, for, in spite of mud, he would have preferred twelve weeks rather than days in which to absorb the knowledge ready for him on our island. Yet enough had been done and collected so that the Snares Exhibit could be created in New York.

Captain Black came back. Bob said to him:

"Welcome to our island," and he answered:

"You are welcome to your island," implying that our island and its surroundings were far from his liking. *Alert* could not come into the rough cove, but found a lee for anchoring.

As I sloshed through the muddy path for the last time, the penguins climbing up in single file scampered, and I said out loud, "You'll have it all back soon, my darlings," and my mind shot ahead to the island as it would be again, with not a person on it: a dirge for us, and a paean for the birds and beasts, some of us agreed. I sat on the rocks watching till rain came on. . . . I was tired but very happy. I had learned far more than subantarctic natural history.

On the last night, as I lay in my narrow cot, I had a sudden horror over the wildness of that place. The twisted trees, their writhing trunks lying along the ground without the dignity of trees, made no rhythm or design in all the forest. Instead, they made a scrawling dissonance like a Dante's or a Doré's Hell. One could imagine them moving to engulf one, with filthy sea lions crawling on their bellies, adding to the horror. And over all, a loneliness of gales and desolation and adjustment to desolation. It would drive one mad to be left alone in such a place, in spite of respite of the friendly little penguins, the soft beauty of the terns and gulls, the majestic inspiration of pounding waves on fantastic rocks below huge cliffs. The Maori have a legend of a maiden condemned to exile alone on such an island. The night crying of the sea birds—to her, voices of the spirits—drove her insane.

The subantarctic is for a different race of men. It is breathless. It is magnificent. But it twisted me in two and pulled the parts through a needle's eye. The men I have spoken to about it say it is always so, that they felt it too. It seemed incredible that the day after we had left the Snares we saw flowers in the gardens of the tiny town of Oban on Stewart Island.

Mozart in the Jungle*

ALAIN GHEERBRANT

✳✳ "There is nothing we need invent," said Alain Gheerbrant, speaking as an editor of a French magazine to his artist friends, philosophers, and poets. "But we have everything to discover."

Gheerbrant was a young man but he had been in the French Army during the war, serving in North Africa, and after the war he had gone back to his first loves —anthropology, ethnology, medicine, editing.

To discover more about the world and its people, he organized an expedition (he was then only 28) and with two other young Frenchmen, Pierre Gaisseaux and Jean Fichter, and a young man, Luis Saenz, from Colombia, South America, he set out in 1948 to cross Venezuela to Brazil. In two years the four young men covered thousands of miles of the Orinoco and the Amazon in Indian dugout canoes, and, in hitherto-unexplored territories, learned some of the ways of life of primitive tribes which they approached, not with guns, but with music. ✳✳

We started off at dawn the following morning [September 11, 1949]. Until midday we went up the Orinoco and then, under the instructions of our guide, we turned to the right into a smaller river almost hidden in a tangled mass of vegetation. This was the Mataveni. We made our way up it for several hours through a network of grass, vegetation, and liana, and we came across nothing to indicate that any human being had ever been that way before. At last our guide told us to turn to the left and there, once again hidden behind vegetation, we found a small tributary of the Mataveni, the Fruta Canyon. We should certainly have passed by without noticing it had we been alone. The branches and the growth ahead of us now became denser and denser, and we had to shut off the outboard motor and go forward by paddling. Several more hours passed in this way and the course of the Fruta became almost lost to sight under the reeds and rushes of an immense marsh-

* From *Journey to the Far Amazon*, by Alain Gheerbrant. Translated by Edward Fitzgerald. Copyright, 1953, 1954, by Alain Gheerbrant, reprinted by permission of the publishers, Simon and Schuster, New York, and the Librairie Gallimard, Paris.

land with here and there a few trees jutting out. But at last we got through this terrain and found ourselves in a big lagoon skirted by forest. A column of smoke rose straight up into the sky ahead of us, hanging there almost motionless above the trees.

"That's where it is," said our guide.

As we came closer we heard the sound of strange music, long drawn out and monotonous. A new mass of vegetation rose up in front of us and for the time being we lost sight of the column of smoke we were making for. The two Guahibo Indians now put down their paddles, stood up in the canoe, and, using their hands as megaphones, gave out a long call. The faraway music stopped at once.

"They'll be here before long," they said.

A quarter of an hour passed and then from between the trees on the edge of the lagoon a canoe manned by a crew of three emerged and paddled toward us. When they came up they spoke to our Indians without taking any notice of us, and then they jumped into our canoe with their paddles and guided us through the tangled vegetation which concealed the landing place of their village. We landed at a sort of terrace. Tied up there were perhaps a dozen little canoes of the type that had come out to meet us. A well-kept path rose from the quay between three or four huts made of straw. There was not a soul about. In the background and apparently raised over the path, the roof of a large rectangular hut towered above the others.

Apart from this there was nothing around us or ahead but muddy ground disappearing into a jungle of branches and undergrowth—the advance guard of the forest at whose verge the little village had been founded.

While we were making fast our canoe, timid faces began to appear between the palm leaves which closed the entrances to the huts, and after a while men, women, and children came out and walked down toward us, until in the end the entire population was assembled on the quay, all huddled together and looking at us with a mute question:

"Why have you come here to us?"

I ran my eye over the crowd in search of a pith helmet.

"You'll easily recognize Mario," our Colombian host at Puerto Nariño had told us. "He always wears a pith helmet painted blue. He's so proud of it he'd never be seen without it."

I spotted my man almost at once. He was rather simian-looking and seemed ill at ease. His high social position was easily recognizable not only from his wonderful headgear but also from the fact that he wore a white shirt and white trousers infinitely cleaner than anything worn around him. The wrinkled little eyes he fixed on us looked malicious.

I made no sign that I recognized him. Since we had landed, our two Gua-hibos had been standing to one side apparently a little uncertain of their wel-come. Perhaps they feared the Piaroas would be angry with them for having introduced strangers into their midst during tribal celebrations. I now called one of them over and told him to tell the Piaroan chief, Mario, that I should like to shake hands with him and that I had brought a letter for him. While saying this I rather ostentatiously flourished the letter I had held in my hand since we landed. It was a letter from the Colombian authorities in the person of our friendly host at Puerto Nariño to Mario, Chief of the Piaroan Indians.

Mario now came toward us as though casually, but with a broad smile on his face. He was clearly flattered to think that I knew about him already, and he listened with a complacent air to the speech I delivered concerning the letter. It was written on letterhead notepaper and it had many paragraphs and a number of official-looking violet stamps. He read it, carefully put it away in his pocket, and then proceeded to give a free translation of its con-tents—no doubt with suitable embellishments—to his fellow tribesmen. It was a long discourse in the Piaroan tongue, and, of course, we did not un-derstand a word of it.

The scene remains in my memory as an excruciating parody of almost any official small-town reception anywhere—complete with unrehearsed mishap. During my own discourse there was a sudden startling splash behind me, followed by a general burst of laughter. Jean, who was the photographer of our expedition and wished to record the occasion for posterity, had stepped back a couple of paces to obtain a better view, and, having forgotten how close he was to the water, had fallen in, the whole six feet of him.

The following is the letter I had brought with me:

> Puerto Nariño,
> September 9th, 1949.

To Don Mario, Chief of the Piaroa tribe on the Rio Orinoco, or the Rio Mataveni, or the Rio Fruta:

My most esteemed Mario,

Receive with this letter my special greetings and good wishes for your health and that of your wife Mariano and your children.

The gentlemen whom I introduce to you herewith are on a special mission from my government with a view to making your acquaintance and that of your people, taking photographs of all interesting matters, and finding out what your problems and difficulties are in order that they may be remedied.

The government of Venezuela is equally interested in their expedition. Please do us the pleasure of receiving them as well as you are able, providing them with all possible facilities and accompanying them on their investigations. If you are unable to accompany them in person, please provide them with one of your tribes-men who can speak Spanish and who knows the neighborhood well.

I should have very much liked to come with them myself and greet you in person, but I have so much to do at the present time that I am unable to leave.

Please God we shall see you again soon at the mouth of the Vichada. You know already that this house is yours.

While awaiting the pleasure of seeing you again, allow me to remind you that I am,

> Your servant and your friend,
> Alvaro B. de C.
> Representative of the Government of the Republic.

When Mario's discourse was at an end I made a sign to Elie, who brought me a small packet we had prepared before landing. I undid it under the eyes of the assembled Piaroa Indians to reveal three lengths of striped cotton cloth which I handed to Mario, saying:

"Here is a little present for you and your children."

I waited in vain for Mario to thank me, but the cloth disappeared at once together with a group of women, of whom one was Mario's wife. I remem-bered what one of the brothers Solano had said: A present isn't a present to an Indian, but a payment for some service previously forgotten. In that case, where is the need for thanks?

While Elie and our two Guahibos were taking the things out of our canoe, we held a long conversation with Mario.

All this is very flattering, he said to us in effect, but what do you really want here?

We explained to him that we had heard about the celebrations of the Piaroa tribe. We were very much interested in them and would like to be present at them if that were possible.

"Celebrations?" he exclaimed. "What celebrations?"

"Oh come, Mario," I said. "You are having celebrations here, making music, and singing and dancing."

He continued to deny it, and his face expressed the greatest possible sur-prise, but I was not deceived.

"We heard your music only a little while back," I insisted. "It stopped only when we came into the lagoon and our Guahibos called out to attract your attention."

I told him that in any case we wanted to stay in the village for a few days at least. It was difficult for him to refuse us hospitality and a hut was placed at our disposal. We carried our things into it and slung our hammocks. Mario stayed with us, looking curiously at our heavy cases, which were painted with the French and Colombian colors. A number of other tribesmen joined him and soon there was quite a gathering in the little hut. We continued to question Mario about the Piaroa celebrations and about the strange music we had heard when we came into the lagoon. He smiled, equivocated, and evaded our questions as far as possible. From time to time he rapidly translated what we said to the other tribesmen, who all laughed with him in chorus, and watched us with growing curiosity.

We opened our cases and unpacked our recording apparatus, assembling the instrument and its loud-speaker. Pierre produced our albums of records. We said nothing further until everything was ready.

"You don't want to talk to us about your music," I said finally. "Very well, we'll let you hear ours."

And at full strength Pierre started up a Mozart symphony. All the Indians immediately fell silent. It was quite obvious that they were flabbergasted. Then we heard the sound of quick footsteps outside and the mat which covered the entrance to the hut was lifted as more and more Indians came in. They stood there in silence and listened without moving a muscle, their eyes glued on the strange apparatus from which the glorious sounds came. Before long the entire male population of the village must have been assembled in and around our hut. It was not so much the strange thing itself that impressed them as the music. Quite a number of them, Mario for example, had been to Puerto Ayacucho, and there they had heard the noises made by the local juke box, the American mechanical player to be found in all the cafés of South America. A nickel in the slot produces atrocious Tin-Pan Alley music from scratched records. But that was the full extent of their acquaintance with the white man's music.

When the symphony was over we began to talk again. Our audience was very attentive now. I explained to Mario that the world was very large and that there were many different kinds of white men in it, some of whom he had never met, and that these white men had all sorts of music that he had not yet heard. Then I began to talk about other kinds of music—music, for example, played on bone and wooden instruments carved by men who lived in forests in various parts of the world. When I began to approach the question I was anxious to broach again with him he pretended to be listening with only half an ear, and he took refuge in embarrassed smiles. But neither he nor any other of those present lost a word of what I was saying.

An old man had followed the scene wordlessly, crouched in a corner of the hut. Mario now went up to him and took him outside. After a moment or two all the others followed them and we were left alone. The last man had left the mat at the entrance open, and the darkness, for night had already fallen, made a rectangle of blackness. The village might have been deserted, for the only sound was the whine of mosquitoes and the rattling of wing cases as the elytrons crawled around in the grass at the edge of the lagoon. We made our hammocks ready for the night, a little disturbed at the sudden and unexplained departure of the Indians.

Some time passed and then suddenly we heard again the same deep trumpetlike sound we had heard from the distance when we came into the lagoon, but this time it was quite close and extraordinarily loud. Above the deep and throbbing bass notes which stirred our vitals like the rolling of a great organ, there was a clear high-pitched melody, soft and harmonious.

A dozen or so Indians came forward out of the darkness and entered our hut. They were hardly recognizable as our visitors of a little while before. They had taken off their shirts, and their brown backs shone with beads of sweat and their dark eyes gleamed with joy. They were playing a variety of trumpets and flutelike instruments, blowing away with all their might and keeping on the move the whole time. They did not stop when they came in but went on marching round the interior walls one behind the other. Mario brought up the rear, and when he saw the mixture of surprise and pleasure on our faces he looked even happier than his men. It was our turn to remain silent and listen, our turn to hear and admire strange music we had never heard before.

The last man in carefully closed the door of the hut and the musicians went on marching round and round still playing at the top of their bent. It seemed almost as though the sounds of their music were accumulating in the confined space of the hut as smoke gradually thickens and makes the air almost unbreathable after a while. And we were almost breathless now, but with emotion and delight.

We were witnessing something unique, living, unforgettable, and unknown. The first miracle had happened. Before our eyes was a collection of primitive instruments which, in all probability, no white man had ever had an opportunity of examining. The music produced from them in the hands of these Indians was astonishingly harmonious and impressive. Jean and I rushed to set up the microphones while Pierre started up the sound recorder.

Thanks to the music of Mozart—which, incidentally, was to render us many valuable services throughout the course of our expedition*—we were

* On April 19, 1950, M. Gheerbrant was visiting a village in the Sierra Parima mountains in unexplored territory between Venezuela and Brazil, a starved and barren highlands where "not once did we see either the chief Cejoyuma or his men eat anything but boiled worms with the remains of cassava, dry and several months old." Here, among Indians of the Maquiritare tribe,

able to begin recording Piaroan tribal music from the very first day of our arrival in the village on the Fruta Canyon.

When the music was finally at an end, which was some two hours later, we played back our discs and let the Indians hear what we had recorded permanently of their music. When the players had departed Mario remained with us for a while. He was very proud and quite moved, and his emotion had the effect of making him more talkative. He was now prepared to admit that his tribe were celebrating. In addition to the music there were, it appeared, special masks worn for the celebrations—"tigers," he called them. The celebrations took place on the village square between the large tribal hut and the small hut facing it across the square. When he finally left us we tried to sleep.

However, we did not sleep very much that night, for we were excited, partly by our arrival in this Piaroan village and partly by all the strange and unknown things we felt around us, hidden behind the walls of palm leaves, behind the great black trunks of the trees which formed the horizon around the village and the lagoon, behind the faces of these Indians, behind their expressions, their laughter, their fears and their enthusiasms, and, finally, in the very air itself, a strange humid atmosphere which seeped into our hut and around our hammocks, charged with a ripe-rotten odor both sour and sweet. It seemed to be the characteristic atmosphere of the Piaroan world.

The next morning Mario walked with me up the village street toward the square. The big hut on one side was the collective gathering place, the

---

the population of the village seemed to be transfixed by the power of music which Gheerbrant and his party played to them in a sound-recording and reproducing concert which began with a minuet by Rameau, a spirited march, the playing of one of the Maquiritares' own songs, and then "our beloved Mozart . . . Mozart seemed to exercise some magic influence on the Indians," Gheerbrant writes, and his music dissipated the last misgivings of the younger women, who came out of their huts in which they had concealed themselves since the white men's arrival, and "they sat down with the old woman who had first taken courage . . .

"In the music of Mozart there is a strange charm in the widest sense of the word, some magic influence to which no Indian could remain insensible," Gheerbrant adds. "On them as on us the music seemed to exercise a soothing influence: it relaxed the body and allowed the soul to expand gratefully. It was a sort of oxygen, the very gentlest of balms. It dissipated fears, melancholy, and the fatigues of the journey. It solaced our loneliness and gave us comfort in the primitive life we were leading. Above this somber countryside eternally closed around its secret the music placed a trembling forest of clear-toned violins that made the hairs of the skin move as the bluish cassava shoots moved in the wind on the hill slope. Such music did not stiffen the body nor clamp down a mask of fear on the faces of those who listened. It opened up the secret places of the heart; it made a thousand hidden voices surge up from the hidden center of things, a thousand colors, a thousand unsuspected forms. . . .

"I do not know if music is really the universal language people often say it is, but I shall never forget that it was the music of Mozart to which we owed the rare moments when the chasm which centuries of our evolution had dug between us, civilized white men of the twentieth century, and them, the barbarians of the stone age, was almost completely filled."

tribal hut, a sort of village hall. The small hut on the other side of the square was really hardly a hut at all. It had no window and no visible door: just a few palm leaves stacked loosely against the side to cover a dark hole. It was a sacred place, a sort of shrine. Mario pushed the loose palm leaves aside and we crawled through the hole one after the other on all fours.

My eyes gradually accustomed themselves to the semidarkness inside, and the first thing I saw was several men squatting silently around, their heads lowered to some mysterious task. A number of objects were on the floor around them and against the walls. The interior of the little hut was hardly more than ten feet across. We were in the sacristy, the holy of holies. It contained all the sacred objects of the traditional religious cult of the Piaroas. Religion is part of the warp and woof of their lives, and they are more profoundly imbued with religion than any other people I have met, either Indian or white. This hut was the material heart of their collective religious life, as this month of celebrations, with all its traditional observances, was the spiritual heart. The hut was the stronghold of the tradition that God had confided to men. And here the use of the term men is exclusive: women are not allowed to enter the holy of holies under pain of death.

Quite close to me a small bunch of herbs hung from the roof by a strip of liana and burned slowly away as incense does. As the spikes were consumed, a long white ash formed like a fine stalactite, and now and again the ash fell onto a small, flat stone on the floor beneath. This was niopo, the basis of the narcotic taken by the religious head, or *chamane,* of the tribe, to enable him to shake off the restraining bonds of his physical body and soar away into the spiritual world.

A man crouched motionless beside the stone, waiting to collect the ash as soon as it fell. Treated by fire and water and mixed with many other substances, it forms a deep brown mixture which is pounded in a special mortar by the sorcerer. The resulting powder is sniffed up into the nostrils.

Before the entrance, suspended about three feet above the ground, hung five strange objects made of palm, feathers, and wickerwork, and covered with painted clay. These were the ritual masks, the conic headgear of the *uani-mesa* or *ye-uiuini-kusa,* the "palm men" or "tiger-panthers." These were the five anonymous priests who would officiate in the tribal hut, their features hidden behind the palm fringe depending from this headgear, their bodies completely covered by long robes reaching to the ground and made of strips of vegetation. In this way no part of them would be seen apart from the hand which shook the maraca. At the top of the masks was a sort of ring protruding like the collar of a vase. A large bunch of scarlet macaw feathers about twenty inches long was fastened by a strip of liana to this ring. These feathers are the special sign of their office. The priests never wear them outside, but as soon as they enter the tribal hut to begin their sacred office they adjust it before their faces.

Mario crouched beside me and explained all these details one by one, talking fluently in a monotonous voice as though he were reciting a litany, the corners of his mouth and his eyes wrinkling in his constant little smile. Five pairs of eyes shone behind him in the darkness, staring at me, for I had taken out my notebook and was carefully sketching the details of the masks and spelling out their names as I wrote them down. The men began to smile broadly.

"The 'tiger-panthers' go out twice a day," Mario went on. "Each time they go out they dance and sing for two or three hours in the center of the tribal hut."

By my side willing hands were feeling amid a heap of green palm leaves. Apparently the Indians intended to show me something else. A number of wooden objects of tubular and conical shapes were produced. Some of them were made of large spirals of bark and the others seemed to be just plain pieces of bamboo wood tubes from which the pith had been scraped. They were the instruments on which the sacred music had been played the night before in our hut. Every evening during the month of celebrations the women all gather in the tribal hut. Through the walls they can hear the blowing of these instruments as the musicians march round and round the hut, as they had marched round and round us. While the instruments are being played the women are forbidden to leave the hut under pain of death. They do not know that the music they can hear is being played on instruments of bark and bamboo invented and manufactured by the men of the tribe from time immemorial. They are taught to believe that what they can hear through the palm-leaf walls of the tribal hut is the voice of the protective spirits of the tribe who have come down to earth to talk with the menfolk.

This is not fraud in the sense that we understand the word, and although the men know the truth this does not prevent them from establishing an intimate relationship between this and that instrument and this and that personage of their mythology, and for them too the voice of the instruments is the voice of the spirits. There is a pair of each type of instrument, and the two are of unequal length.

"The male and the female of each voice," Mario said.

But there is one exception to this rule, and they showed it to me. It was perhaps the strangest instrument of all. It consisted of a clay vase painted with esoteric designs, and in the bottom was a fragment of rock crystal. It was played, Mario explained, by alternately inserting two flutes, the one of dark wood and the other of light wood, and then playing them. The vase served as a sounding box and modified the tone of the flutes. I asked Mario what this instrument was called but he only laughed.

"All right," he said when I insisted. "It's called the devil's wife."

"Why?"

"Well, you know what the devil is, don't you? It's the evil spirit which is always on the lookout to do men harm. Now this spirit has a wife just like everyone else, and it's the voice of the wife that comes out of the vase."

For me this instrument was the most astonishing of all the treasures of the Piaroan tabernacle. No ethnographer had previously recorded anything of the sort throughout South America. I observed with keen interest that the strange designs on this vase were similar to those which had been found on the necks of certain Aztec vases discovered during excavations in Mexico. Here on the Upper Orinoco, we had come across the only known evidence of the survival of a pre-Colombian Mexican instrument. By what devious ways had the tradition arrived in these parts?

When I had finished sketching and taking down the details of the masks, I did the same for the musical instruments. Mario told me their names and the names of the various woods out of which they were made. When I picked up the base instrument which was known as "the devil's wife" in order to examine it more closely, the Indians looked at me rather anxiously. When I had finished and put it down carefully, they audibly sighed in relief.

"I'll tell you a story," said Mario. "One day, when there was a Piaroan village farther down, on the river Mataveni, quite close to the Orinoco, a white man came to us at the same time as you have come, at the beginning of the New Year celebrations. It was in the evening, the masks had just danced in the tribal hut, and the musicians were preparing to go out.

"This white man needed paddlers. He wanted to go into the forest to look for resin. He had a big *falca* something like yours. 'Give me men for my boat,' he said to the Piaroan chief. The chief said nothing, but he turned to two *muchachos* and told them to take down their hammocks and go on board the *falca*. But the *muchachos* didn't want to go off and work for the white man; they wanted to stay in the village for the celebrations. So after a while they deserted the white man, returned to the tribal hut, and slung up their hammocks again. The white man was very angry. He ran through the village searching for the men. He looked everywhere, but he couldn't find them, because as soon as they saw him coming they ran away and hid themselves in the forest. The white man broke into the sacred hut where the musical instruments and the masks were kept, and he flung everything out. He was so angry that he trampled on everything, smashing the instruments and the masks and tearing off the palm leaves and the feathers—all the things that women must never see. Apart from the two *muchachos* who had made good their escape, the whole village was assembled, men, women, and children.

" 'Kill that man,' said our chief. So all our men took their lances, their bows and arrows, and their blow pipes, and they fell upon the white man. He fled and fell into the water. Some pierced him with their spears and others fired their arrows at him.

"He managed to crawl out of the water, and he talked very differently now. 'Don't kill me,' he cried. 'Don't kill me.'

" 'Kill him,' our chief repeated, and this time they killed him.

"His *falca* was full of merchandise. It was worth thousands and thousands of pesos. There were cooking pots, bales of cloth for making dresses, trousers, and shirts, knives, matches, and glass pearls for making necklaces. There was everything there the whites sell us. But our Indians didn't want the things. The white man was a bad man and his goods were bad, so the Indians sank his boat in the river and gave everything to the fishes.

"Now you know why I didn't want to tell you anything about our celebrations, neither about the music nor the *uani-mesa*. We didn't know what you wanted here. You didn't want resin, and you didn't want rubber, and you didn't want cassava. So what did you want? We didn't understand. We were afraid you might have come to destroy our masks and our instruments, or buy them and take them away from us. Do you know what would have happened if you had taken away our music? The spirits would have killed us all because the music is their voice and it mustn't be heard anywhere else but here. So we should have had to kill you to save our own lives, but that would have been very dangerous. One mustn't kill white men; there are too many of them and they come back too quickly. That is why we were very worried yesterday evening."

Mario looked at me and smiled. Then he rose and, going to the entrance, drew back the palm leaves which hid the interior of the sacred place. Standing back, he indicated that his explanation marked the end of my visit. I went out into the village square and the palm leaves closed over the entrance behind me. The square was deserted. After the semidarkness of the little hut the full sunlight dazzled me, and after the talk in the confined space the silence outside was enormous. As I walked down the little path toward the waterside two girls went by. They had been to fetch water, and they carried earthenware pitchers on their heads. They smiled at me in a friendly fashion but with a certain timid reserve. Their long hair shone with the vegetable oil which had been used to dress it. It was done up in a quite complicated fashion and fastened with red and green strips of liana. Their cheeks were freshly painted in brilliant colors.

I entered our hut and made myself comfortable in my hammock to note down the details of what I had heard and seen. I realized that the confidence of the Indians must be won by their own methods of patience and passivity, that no attempt must ever be made to override their misgivings and their fears, and that one must never go too far at once if one hopes to penetrate into their spiritual world, which is not dead but merely hidden. But it hides itself more and more with the passing of time in order to escape the prying eyes of the white man who, since the days of Christopher Columbus, has sought to establish nothing but his own world over the whole universe. The Indians have sought refuge from him in the night, and yet they love the sun as all other men do.

6 *Vertigo*

The Plane and the Planet*

ANTOINE DE SAINT-EXUPÉRY

✳✳ A poet of the air, a man to whom flying was more than simply a faster movement from one point in space to another, Antoine de Saint-Exupéry left several books of his experiences as a French air pilot; but one, *Wind, Sand and Stars,* is unique in the literature of the air age. Born in Lyon, France, in 1900, young Saint-Exupéry grew up near one of the early French airports and fell in love with planes. His parents wanted him to enter the merchant marine. He was schooled in the classics in Switzerland and on his return to France entered the air service as a cadet and became an officer in Morocco. His first regular flights were from Toulouse to Dakar in 1926 when airplanes were not what they are today and when an engine in a plane, with hardly any warning, might fall out, leaving a pilot stranded on a mountain, in the sea, or in a wilderness of sand, the Sahara. Saint-Exupéry flew the French mails over routes across the most dangerous sections of the Air Mail Service established by the French in Northwest Africa, the South Atlantic, and South America, many times narrowly escaping death. His death occurred in a plane in 1944 while on a reconnaissance mission for the French Air Force.

It is the airplane, St.-X believed, which has unveiled for us the true face of the earth. "For centuries," he writes in *Wind, Sand and Stars,* "highways had been deceiving us . . . The plane has taught us to travel as the crow flies . . . A cruel light has blazed, and our sight has been sharpened. Scarcely have we taken off when we abandon these winding highways that slope down to watering troughs and stables or run away to towns dreaming in the shade of their trees. Freed henceforth from this happy servitude, delivered from the need of fountains, we set our course for distant destinations. And then, only, from the height of our rectilinear trajectories, do we discover the essential foundations, the fundament of rock and sand and salt in which here and there and from time to time life like a little moss in the crevices of ruins has risked its precarious existence.

"We to whom humble journeyings were once permitted have now been transformed into physicists, biologists, students of the civilizations that beautify the depths of valleys and now and again, by some miracle, bloom like gardens where the climate allows. We are able to judge man in cosmic terms, scrutinize him through our portholes as through instruments of the laboratory. I remember a few of these scenes . . ." ✳✳

The pilot flying toward the Strait of Magellan sees below him, a little to the south of the Gallegos River, an ancient lava flow, an erupted waste of a thickness of sixty feet that crushes down the plain on which it has congealed. Farther south he meets a second flow, then a third; and thereafter every hump on the globe, every mound a few hundred feet high, carries a crater in its flank. No Vesuvius rises up to reign in the clouds; merely, flat on the plain, a succession of gaping howitzer mouths.

This day, as I fly, the lava world is calm. There is something surprising in the tranquillity of this deserted landscape where once a thousand volcanoes boomed to each other in their great subterranean organs and spat forth their fire. I fly over a world mute and abandoned, strewn with black glaciers.

South of these glaciers there are yet older volcanoes veiled with the passing of time in a golden sward. Here and there a tree rises out of a crevice like a plant out of a cracked pot. In the soft and yellow light the plain appears as luxuriant as a garden; the short grass seems to civilize it, and round its giant throats there is scarcely a swelling to be seen. A hare scampers off; a bird wheels in the air; life has taken possession of a new planet where the decent loam of our earth has at last spread over the surface of the star.

Finally, crossing the line into Chile, a little north of Punta Arenas, you come to the last of the craters, and here the mouths have been stopped with earth. A silky turf lies snug over the curves of the volcanoes, and all is suavity in the scene. Each fissure in the crust is sutured up by this tender flax. The earth is smooth, the slopes are gentle; one forgets the travail that gave them birth. This turf effaces from the flanks of the hillocks the somber sign of their origin.

We have reached the most southerly habitation of the world, a town born of the chance presence of a little mud between the timeless lava and the austral ice. So near the black scoria, how thrilling it is to feel the miraculous nature of man! What a strange encounter! Who knows how, or why, man visits these gardens ready to hand, habitable for so short a time—a geologic age—for a single day blessed among days?

I landed in the peace of evening. Punta Arenas! I leaned against a fountain and looked at the girls in the square. Standing there within a couple of feet of their grace, I felt more poignantly than ever the human mystery.

In a world in which life so perfectly responds to life, where flowers mingle with flowers in the wind's eye, where the swan is the familiar of all swans, man alone builds his isolation. What a space between men their spiritual natures create! A girl's reverie isolates her from me, and how shall I enter into it? What can one know of a girl who passes, walking with slow steps homeward, eyes lowered, smiling to herself, filled with adorable inventions and with fables? Out of the thoughts, the voice, the silences of a lover, she can form an empire, and thereafter she sees in all the world but him a people of barbarians. More surely than if she were on another planet, I feel her to be locked up in her language, in her secret, in her habits, in the singing echoes of her memory. Born yesterday of the volcanoes, of greenswards, of brine of the sea, she walks here already half divine.

Punta Arenas! I lean against a fountain. Old women come up to draw water: of their drama I shall know nothing but these gestures of farm servants. A child, his head against a wall, weeps in silence: there will remain of him in my memory only a beautiful child forever inconsolable. I am a stranger. I know nothing. I do not enter into their empires. Man in the presence of man is as solitary as in the face of a wide winter sky in which there sweeps, never to be tamed, a flight of trumpeting geese.

How shallow is the stage on which this vast drama of human hates and joys and friendships is played! Whence do men draw this passion for eternity, flung by chance as they are upon a scarcely cooled bed of lava, threatened from the beginning by the deserts that are to be, and under the constant menace of the snows? Their civilizations are but fragile gildings: a volcano can blot them out, a new sea, a sand-storm.

This town seemed to be built upon a true humus, a soil one might imagine to be as rich as the wheatlands of the Beauce. These men live heedless of the fact that, here as elsewhere, life is a luxury; and that nowhere on the globe is the soil really rich beneath the feet of men.

Yet, ten miles from Punta Arenas there is a lake that ought to be reminding them of this. Surrounded by stunted trees and squat huts, as modest as a pool in a farm yard, this lake is subject to the preternatural pull of the tides. Night and day, among the peaceful realities of swaying reeds and playing children, it performs its slow respiration, obedient to unearthly laws. Beneath the glassy surface, beneath the motionless ice, beneath the keel of the single dilapidated bark on the waters, the energy of the moon is at work. Ocean eddies stir in the depths of this black mass. Strange digestions take their peristaltic course there and down as far as the Strait of Magellan, under the thin layer of grasses and flowers. This lake that is a hundred yards wide, that laps the threshold of a town which seems to be built on man's own earth and where men believe themselves secure, beats with the pulse of the sea.

II

But by the grace of the airplane I have known a more extraordinary experience than this, and have been made to ponder with even more bewilderment the fact that this earth that is our home is yet in truth a wandering star.

A minor accident had forced me down in the Rio de Oro region, in Spanish Africa. Landing on one of those tablelands of the Sahara which fall away steeply at the sides, I found myself on the flat top of the frustrum of a cone, an isolated vestige of a plateau that had crumbled round the edges. In this part of the Sahara such truncated cones are visible from the air every hundred miles or so, their smooth surfaces always at about the same altitude above the desert and their geologic substance always identical. The surface sand is composed of minute and distinct shells; but progressively as you dig along a vertical section, the shells become more fragmentary, tend to cohere, and at the base of the cone form a pure calcareous deposit.

Without question, I was the first human being ever to wander over this . . . this iceberg: its sides were remarkably steep, no Arab could have climbed them, and no European had as yet ventured into this wild region.

I was thrilled by the virginity of a soil which no step of man or beast had sullied. I lingered there, startled by this silence that never had been broken. The first star began to shine, and I said to myself that this pure surface had lain here thousands of years in sight only of the stars.

But suddenly my musings on this white sheet and these shining stars were endowed with a singular significance. I had kicked against a hard, black stone, the size of a man's fist, a sort of molded rock of lava incredibly present on the surface of a bed of shells a thousand feet deep. A sheet spread beneath an apple tree can receive only apples; a sheet spread beneath the stars can receive only stardust. Never had a stone fallen from the skies made known its origin so unmistakably.

And very naturally, raising my eyes, I said to myself that from the height of this celestial apple tree there must have dropped other fruits, and that I should find them exactly where they fell, since never from the beginning of time had anything been present to displace them.

Excited by my adventure, I picked up one and then a second and then a third of these stones, finding them at about the rate of one stone to the acre. And here is where my adventure became magical, for in a striking foreshortening of time that embraced thousands of years, I had become the witness of this miserly rain from the stars. The marvel of marvels was that there on the rounded back of the planet, between this magnetic sheet and those stars, a human consciousness was present in which as in a mirror that rain could be reflected.

III

Once, in this same mineral Sahara, I was taught that a dream might partake of the miraculous. Again I had been forced down, and until day dawned I was helpless. Hillocks of sand offered up their luminous slopes to the moon, and blocks of shadow rose to share the sands with the light. Over the deserted work yard of darkness and moonray there reigned a peace as of work suspended and a silence like a trap, in which I fell asleep.

When I opened my eyes I saw nothing but the pool of nocturnal sky, for I was lying on my back with outstretched arms, face to face with that hatchery of stars. Only half awake, still unaware that those depths were sky, having no roof between those depths and me, no branches to screen them, no root to cling to, I was seized with vertigo and felt myself as if flung forth and plunging downward like a diver.

But I did not fall. From nape to heel I discovered myself bound to earth. I felt a sort of appeasement in surrendering to it my weight. Gravitation had become as sovereign as love. The earth, I felt, was supporting my back, sustaining me, lifting me up, transporting me through the immense void of night. I was glued to our planet by a pressure like that with which one is glued to the side of a car on a curve. I leaned with joy against this admirable breastwork, this solidity, this security, feeling against my body this curving bridge of my ship.

So convinced was I that I was in motion that I should have heard without astonishment, rising from below, a creaking of something material adjusting itself to the effort, that groaning of old sailing vessels as they heel, that long, sharp cry drawn from pinnaces complaining of their handling. But silence continued in the layers of the earth, and this density that I could feel at my shoulders continued harmonious, sustained, unaltered through eternity. I was as much the inhabitant of this homeland as the bodies of dead galley slaves, weighted with lead, were the inhabitants of the sea.

I lay there pondering my situation, lost in the desert and in danger, naked between sky and sand, withdrawn by too much silence from the poles of my life. I knew that I should wear out days and weeks returning to them if I were not sighted by some plane, or if next day the Moors did not find and murder me. Here I possessed nothing in the world. I was no more than a mortal strayed between sand and stars, conscious of the single blessing of breathing. And yet I discovered myself filled with dreams.

They came to me soundlessly, like the waters of a spring, and in the beginning I could not understand the sweetness that was invading me. There was neither voice nor vision, but the presentiment of a presence, of a warmth very close and already half guessed. Then I began to grasp what was going on, and shutting my eyes I gave myself up to the enchantments of my memory.

Somewhere there was a park dark with firs and linden trees and an old house that I loved. It mattered little that it was far away, that it could not warm me in my flesh, nor shelter me, reduced here to the role of dream. It was enough that it existed to fill my night with its presence. I was no longer this body flung up on a strand; I oriented myself; I was the child of this house, filled with the memory of its odors, with the cool breath of its vestibules, with the voices that had animated it, even to the very frogs in the pools that came here to be with me. I needed these thousand landmarks to identify myself, to discover of what absences the savor of this desert was composed, to find a meaning in this silence made of a thousand silences, where the very frogs were silent.

No, I was no longer lodged between sand and stars. I was no longer receiving from this scene its chill message. And I had found out at last the origin of the feeling of eternity that came over me in this wilderness. I had been wrong to believe it was part of sky and sand. I saw again the great stately cupboards of our house. Their doors opened to display piles of linen as white as snow. They opened on frozen stores of snow. The old housekeeper trotted like a rat from one cupboard to the next, forever counting, folding, unfolding, recounting the white linen; exclaiming, "Oh, good Heavens, how terrible!" at each sign of wear which threatened the eternity of the house; running instantly to burn out her eyes under a lamp so that the woof of these altar cloths should be repaired, these three-master's sails be mended, in the service of something greater than herself—a god, a ship.

Ah, I owe you a page, Mademoiselle! When I came home from my first journeyings I found you, needle in hand, up to the knees in your white surplices, each year a little more wrinkled, a little more round-shouldered, still preparing for our slumbers those sheets without creases, for our dinners those cloths without seams, those feasts of crystal and of snow.

I would go up to see you in your sewing room, would sit down beside you and tell you of the dangers I had run in order that I might thrill you, open your eyes to the world, corrupt you. You would say that I hadn't changed a whit. Already as a child I had torn my shirts—"How terrible!"—and skinned my knees, coming home as day fell to be bandaged.

No, Mademoiselle, no! I have not come back from the other end of the park but from the other end of the world! I have brought back with me the acrid smell of solitude, the tumult of sand-storms, the blazing moonlight of the tropics! "Of course!" you would say. "Boys *will* run about, break their bones, and think themselves great fellows."

No, Mademoiselle, no! I have seen a good deal more than the shadows in our park. If you knew how insignificant these shadows are, how little they mean beside the sands, the granite, the virgin forests, the vast swamp-lands of the earth! Do you realize that there are lands on the globe where, when men meet you, they bring up their rifles to their cheeks? Do you know that there are deserts on earth where men lie down on freezing nights to sleep without roof or bed or snowy sheet? "What a wild lad!" you would say.

I could no more shake her faith than I could have shaken the faith of a candle-woman in a church. I pitied her humble destiny which had made her blind and deaf.

But that night in the Sahara, naked between the stars and the sand, I did her justice.

What is going on inside me I cannot tell. In the sky a thousand stars are magnetized, and I lie glued by the swing of the planet to the sand. A different weight brings me back to myself. I feel the weight of my body drawing me toward so many things. My dreams are more real than these dunes, than that moon, than these presences. My civilization is an empire more imperious than this empire. The marvel of a house is not that it shelters or warms a man, nor that its walls belong to him. It is that it leaves its trace on the language. Let it remain a sign. Let it form, deep in the heart, that obscure range from which, as waters from a spring, are born our dreams.

Sahara, my Sahara! You have been bewitched by an old woman at a sewing table!

Craters of Fire *

HAROUN TAZIEFF

✳✳ A geologist by training, Haroun Tazieff is a man of many frontiers: he has adventured under the sea as a diver-explorer; he has trudged across the Sahara; discovered and mapped deep underground caves as a speleologist; and since 1945 he has been in and out of many of the world's greatest and some of its newest volcanoes in Africa and elsewhere, watching eruptions, making notes, descending into craters, photographing bubbling pools of spilling-over lava, and gazing fascinated into fathomless depths, breathing fire and fumes in a deadly mixture. In venturing so close to the forces at the center of the earth we live on, Tazieff says he has sometimes had to wrench himself out of a "fear-laden ecstasy," as he wavered, spellbound, between "a sort of intoxication and the necessity to act." Before such forces and such depths, he says, "our intellectual cocksureness simply evaporates." ✳✳

A DESCENT INTO NIRAGONGO

For months, during which I had been exploring the [Belgian Congo] district all round Kituro and Muhuboli, I had been casting covetous glances at their gigantic neighbor, Niragongo. I had already climbed it, but all I had been able to see from the edge of the enormous caldron on its summit was vapor and smoke. Three or four attempts to get down into it had been made without success. It was regarded as settled that there *was* no going down into it: it was too steep and there was too much gas. . . . All the same, in looking round I had seen what seemed to be a possible way down the almost vertical walls, and in the five months that I had been living in the midst of volcanic emanations I had got to know what they were like. So long as one kept out of the immediate neighborhood of the vents emitting them—in other words, so long as they were diluted with water vapor and air—these fumes were not toxic to a fatal degree. As for the descent being declared

* Translated from the French by Eithne Wilkins. Copyright, 1952, by Haroun Tazieff, reprinted by permission of the publishers, Harper & Bros., New York.

vertical—it was all of fifteen degrees less than that! It was not so very long ago since my Savoyard friends and I had been climbing rock face of quite a different order! I was certain that I would at least be able to reach a promontory jutting out about half or two thirds of the way down. After that, nobody could know what it would be like . . .

I had no difficulty in persuading Tondeur, a friend from Coste, to rope up with me in a first attempt to make the descent. A big, broad-shouldered man, Tondeur seemed to have the steady hands and the cool head indispensable to such an undertaking. And so the thing was undertaken in June and went off in the following manner . . .

We were now in the dry season. In the noonday light the string of porters, balancing packages on their heads, wound their way along through the tall grasses waving in the wind. Ahead of us, nearly 10,000 feet up, rose the base of the mighty cone.

At an altitude of 6500 feet we came into the very dense, almost completely dark forest that covers the lower part of the mountain. The only way of advancing through this fiendishly tangled jungle was along the elephant tracks. We clambered over huge fallen tree trunks, and we crawled on all fours under trees whose fall had been stopped at half a man's height from the ground by scrub and creepers.

At first we kept plunging up to the knees in mud, that black *potopoto* in which nettles abound—and what nettles! Higher up the ground became drier and the incline sharper.

Four o'clock. We come out at last into a clearing amid the gigantic brambles. Here we shall pitch our camp, a tent for Tondeur and me, two wattle huts for the natives.

The men have already lit fires. The porters' beans are boiling in a big old aluminum saucepan, our boys' manioc is simmering on a second fire, and the white men's "chop" (food) on a third. Inside the huts there are yet more fires burning, sending up thick blue coils of smoke. All this damp wood smokes so much that it makes our eyes water—a foretaste of the acrid vapors we shall get our fill of in the crater.

Turning the last two hours of daylight to account, we make a quick push higher up the mountain. After coming out of the last thicket of brambles, we leave the forest behind. Henceforth the dominant note is rock. There are still some lobelias, tall candlelike things standing up on the black stone, and then, between 10,800 and 11,500 feet, there are only the bare cliffs, which are fluted by huge ribs of basalt radiating out toward the base.

The crater! Amid the vapors we see the route, the first few hundred feet of the descent. We establish the fact that it is impossible to get along the knife-edge ridge surrounding the caldron; so there is no other way to be considered. This route itself makes "recalls" by fixed rope quite out of the question; there is not the slightest ledge to which one can fix anything.

The night was cold and very damp. Humidity is the main characteristic of the high mountains along the Equator. The air is constantly saturated with moisture, to such a point that wherever the ground is not porous (and fortunately it is, on the volcanoes that are not too much eroded) it is transformed into a peat bog.

At nine o'clock in the morning we were back on the summit and once more staring down into the vast sinkhole. Part of the "floor" was visible today. The center seemed to be pierced by a wide shaft, the southeastern rim of which we could see; the other two thirds of the orifice were veiled from sight by a terrific column of vapor. At our feet the walls surrounding the sinkhole were made up of horizontal strata alternating with tuff and outflows, gashed by vertical *dikes* of hard rock. To the south, one of these dikes ran right up from the bottom to the crest on which we were standing. It seemed to me a magnificent climb—very "artificial," of course, necessitating the use of iron eye bolts and rope yokes—but certainly a climb up well worth doing some day. However, for the present it was a matter of first getting down.

Paya handed me the haversack. I got out the rope, that good old rope of mine that had not been used for years now. It was exciting to feel its precious suppleness against the palm of my hand, and its delightful smell, which always made me think of a little village store in Savoyard with loaves of bread, candles, string, galoshes, and materials, all jumbled up together and everything smelling of everything else. . . .

At that moment the worthy head keeper of the National Park at last realized that we had not come up to the top of the volcano to have a look over the edge in the usual tourist way, but that we really meant to do down. The day before when we had explained our plans to him, he had seemed to approve. Was it a misunderstanding? Was he playing for time? Whatever the cause, today he broke into cries of distress, explaining volubly that there was every reason why such a descent was impossible: the devils haunting the craters, the dangers of the tottering edges of the wall, and of poisonous gases, and above all the sacrosanct regulations of the National Park of which he was the authorized representative here.

On this last point I quelled his doubts by showing him an official letter with a grand printed letterhead, authorizing me to go wherever I wished to in the Park, so long as it was in connection with volcanology. The letter-head alone would obviously have done the trick, for the aged worthy knew no word of French. It was a waste of time trying to make him understand that the danger of the descent was merely apparent and that we would take it on ourselves to look after the devils: I could not set his mind at rest. So there were four faces furrowed with anxiety watching us as we roped ourselves together and cautiously began that "infernal" descent.

The three first rope-lengths (we had left fifteen yards between us) were easy. The only delicate operation was finding holds: whatever their shape and size, they generally gave way at once. Then we had to clear the first considerable stratum of tuff that we came to—those very fine yellowish volcanic ashes interspersed with blocks of various sizes. Fortunately this dust had agglomerized and become cemented by the action of rain water; the weight of the strata above had rammed it down and given this rock, once entirely unstable, a certain degree of solidity. By gingerly making use of the jagged places shaped by erosion, and sometimes cutting steps for ourselves as though in hard snow, we made headway without any real difficulties, though not without a certain amount of nervous tension. There was no chance of exchanging reassuring and encouraging remarks; and each of us knew that if one fell, he would bring the other down with him. On the other hand, the psychological effect of the length of hemp that turns two climbers into a "party" was very great: I would certainly not have risked the climb on my own.

A little while later we reached the famous promontory that Tondeur christened the "spur of hesitation," an enormous ledge measuring several cubic yards, embedded in a stratum of tuff. We picked our way round it with due care and could then see the rest of our route. It needed only a few seconds to set our minds at rest: although the lower part was steeper than the wall we had just come down, it looked no less practicable. The riskiest stage would certainly be crossing the two very wide strata of tuff. As for the outflows, they were very solid rock and offered enough holds for us to get across them, in spite of their being almost vertical.

Here we could sit down. We took the opportunity to have a snack. As we looked down, the floor of the caldron seemed much nearer to us now and we could distinctly see a plain of gray lava streaked with long black concentric fissures running round the big central shaft. It was from this shaft that the mighty column of smoke rose incessantly. Fortunately the wind was driving it away from us.

We had scarcely got going again when the wind changed, wrapping us in a sulfurous fog. We had equipped ourselves with gas masks. Tondeur stopped to put his on, but since what we were breathing seemed a very pale imitation of what I had more than once encountered on Kituro, I went on down with my nostrils disdainfully free.

We now had to swing toward the right in order to get across a stratum of tuff more than thirty feet deep, which luckily was not very steep. There we noticed some of those little "fairy chimneys" or "crowned columns" that the process of erosion cuts out of the soft rock under a protective mass of harder rock. The water draining from the cliff, or the rain, wears the soft rock away round the hard rock, so that the latter is soon left in relief, and when the ground keeps disappearing under the action of rain and storm washing it away, the rock is soon left standing out further and further from its immediate surroundings, a sort of hat on an embryo column that in several centuries may reach a height of sixty feet.* Here these stones were no larger than one's fist, or even smaller, and the chimneys were no more than a foot high.

A hard lava flow made us work our way back to the left, after which we had to go obliquely to the right to get across another stratum of light-colored, crumbling tuff. Then came a series of fairly thin superimposed layers of lava, evidence of a period when there had been a rapid succession of emissions of lava. All along our descent we could read in this way the history of the last centuries of the volcano's life: outflow, great explosion, big outflow, less concentrated outflows, explosion of less intensity, very big outflow, explosions . . . and so on.

And then there we were! We got a foothold on the summit of a heap of stones that had crumbled down and from there, without stopping to take precautions, we ran full tilt down on to the floor of the sinkhole. It had taken us over three hours.

Once we had unroped, we slapped each other on the back with great heartiness, exulting over our magnificent effort! Coming down, all in all, had been easy. But what really made us ecstatic was the thought that we were the first to get here and that we had done so after all the experts had declared the place inaccessible!

The vapors did not trouble us. Tondeur took off his gas mask. His brown eyes sparkled. The breeze blew a few stray locks of hair across his forehead.

The floor was composed of the type of lava known as "pillow" lava, very slightly rippled, the hollows filled up with volcanic sand of the same kind

---

* An analogous phenomenon is sometimes observed on glaciers, where drift-blocks protect the ice underneath from the heat of the sun, so that at the end of the summer these rocks are left perched on the top of a short column of ice.

as the tuff in the cliff face, which had collected at this lower level as a result of erosion and the action of rainfall.

There was no familiar object to give us any sense of scale. The walls
seemed vertiginous: the jagged cliff top was outlined against the sky far
above. Around us there was nothing but this sealed-off world, enclosed by
immense cliffs, only a section of its gray area appearing between the walls
and the fumes ceaselessly rising from the center.

We discovered a long volcanic crevasse. It was evident that liquid lava
occasionally gushed up out of it, for lumps of lava that had landed still in a
pasty state had piled up along the edges; some of them had even piled up
to a height of nearly a hundred feet.

Counting our strides, we set out for the central shaft: the distance up to
it seemed to be about two hundred yards. When we got to the edge of the
vast pit, we found it was impossible to see anything at all: it was completely
hidden in eddies of gray fumes.

From far above we heard shouts. We raised our heads. Tiny silhouettes
were making movements up there: our native companions had come to
look over the edge of the caldron and were hailing our reappearance and
the success of the enterprise.

We then gave our minds to working out the height of the surrounding
walls by various methods. Tondeur went back, counting his long strides as
far as the foot of the cliff, and I did some rough calculations of angles, starting from a base a hundred paces long—all quite approximate, of course.
Finally we worked out that six hundred to seven hundred and fifty feet
would probably be not too remote from reality.

Once again we arrived at the shaft. Lying flat on our bellies on the edge
of it, we strained our eyes in vain to see anything beyond a few vague outlines of gray rocks blurred by vapors. . . . Suddenly a sharp gust of wind
from the north swept the moving smoke screen aside for several seconds.
We got a clear view of the crater itself.

It was in the shape of a gigantic cylinder about a quarter of a mile in
diameter, the sides practically vertical. But it was the sight at the bottom,
about five or six hundred feet down, that was amazing: in its northwestern
quarter there was a lake of live lava, boiling away ceaselessly from the action of forces deep below; every now and then the elastic black skin covering
it burst and threw up fountains of cherry-red lava, while at the southern end
a tremendous froth of liquid fire lashed the banks with heavy scarlet waves.

This lake was the shape of a half-moon, a hundred yards long and a hundred and fifty yards across at the widest point.

While we were filming this extraordinary spectacle the lava suddenly overflowed the limits of the lake and we saw it moving on, swiftly and silently, a sort of long tongue that in a few moments had covered a surface of more than an acre. Then the vapors spread out again, once more hiding the depths of the crater from view. But by a stroke of good luck the wind came to our aid, and during the two hours that we spent there it cooperated in this way, enabling us to make a great many more observations.

In the southern prolongation of the lake half a dozen little cones jutted up, some yards in height, continually spitting out gases, vapors, and virulent jets of black smoke. Sometimes they puffed comparatively quietly, sometimes again with such violence that one felt inclined to believe some living creature in paroxysms of rage was blowing these jets up from below.

The zone of chief activity was in the western part of the depths. The rest was made up of that "dead" lava to which the celebrated American volcanologist Jaggar gave the name of *bench magma*. It formed a sort of gigantic staircase, each tread of which was a real cliff. Between these escarpments yawned abysses out of which slow fumes curled up.

I studied the surroundings of the shaft itself with impassionate attentiveness, hoping to be able to make out a way to go down it. But the examination did not reveal anything very promising. The only hope lay in having oneself let down, either *en rappel* or by means of a windlass, till one reached the top of a pile of debris heaped up against the eastern part of the wall, and then to make use of that debris to get down to the bottom. But in any case we were not equipped for an adventure of that kind.

The climb up the cliff round the caldron was, of course, much less difficult than the descent. It is always incomparably easier, in rock climbing, to go up than to go down; furthermore, this time we knew that it could be done.

The welcome we got from our faithful Negroes, patiently waiting at the summit, was in itself a heart-warming reward. They were all benumbed with cold at that altitude—11,400 feet—even though we were on the Equator.

THE RED SAUCEPAN BOILS OVER

One morning, round about five, after I had come back to Kituro, I was wakened by a strange noise. It was a kind of heavy thudding, such as might have been produced by a herd of antelopes galloping through the bush. Sitting on the edge of my camp bed, still half-asleep, I tried to make out what it was. Wasn't it rather more like the noise of a great fire? But the night, now paling into dawn, held no glimmer of a reflection apart from the usual red glare from the crater.

So then I decided it must be a strong wind. It seemed to be blowing from the northern foot of Kituro. By this time the daylight had increased and I watched, fascinated but slightly disturbed, the leaves fluttering in the thin scrub which separates my camp from the active zone. The trees stirred with mild indifference in the early-morning breeze.

I wondered fleetingly if it might be a herd of elephants stampeding, but the minutes passed with no sign of trees being broken. Besides, the noise was not moving, whereas elephants generally move with amazing speed. Turning my head, I saw that Paya and Kaniepala, squatting in the doorway of their wattle hut, were gazing steadily in the direction from which the sound came.

"You think something, Paya?"

He did not answer except by opening his eyes very wide and lifting his shoulders slightly, holding his open hands palm upward, away from his sides. It was perfect pantomime for: "I don't know."

There was no doubt about it, it could not be anything but some sort of volcanic upheaval. Would it not be better to strike camp and move back some distance? I thought of the chances of a new outburst, or a new fracture, accompanied by a local earthquake.

Perhaps . . . but if I wanted to be sure about it I would have to go and take a look.

Dressing in two minutes, grabbing the knapsack and Rolleiflex, I dashed off along the trail, followed by Paya carrying the ciné-camera and the instruments. The tall grasses, heavy with dew, sagged across the narrow track. The sticky, elastic threads of spiders' webs wrapped themselves round our bare legs and stuck to our faces the moment we stopped shielding them with our arms.

The further we pressed on, the louder the noise became. It was now rather like the furious escape of steam from some immense locomotive with pressure up.

The winding path had brought us out of the forest, to the fringe of the lava. We went a hundred yards further. The noise became deafening. Soon we discovered its cause: between the foot of Kituro and two great walls of agglomerate, stretching away to the north, was a line of little cones, five to ten feet high, of the kind technically known as spatter cones. And out of the top of each of them, forcibly expelled by the gases whistling up through the incandescent opening, pasty lumps of red lava were flying up into the air.

We made our way into the maze formed by the congealed lava, cautiously approaching these new phenomena. Did their appearance herald a recrudescence of activity?

The little cones, eight in number, were strung out along a yawning fissure, a good three feet wide, which had opened up in the shell of the "pillow" lava stretching northward from the foot of Kituro. Two of them seemed to be already extinct, but the others were blowing off with furious intensity. However, it was neither difficult nor dangerous to approach them, for the showers of clots they were throwing out were not too densely concentrated for one to dodge them, with a little agility. The most active cone must have been about seven feet high. Flaring gases were shooting out of the top; the temperature of these flames rose to 960° C., and my little pocket spectroscope revealed the presence of sodium, and possibly also of azote. The new fissure was only letting its gases escape at certain well-defined points, between which it was possible to lean over the black gulf—although of course it was hopeless trying to see anything down there.

But as I was going round one of these spatter cones, the one nearest to the volcano, I suddenly discovered, less than ten yards away from me, something that was really rather sensational: a kind of basin in which liquid lava was splashing about. It was already covered with a gray, elastic "skin," very like an elephant's hide, which showed that it was cooling down. This "skin" would swell up under the pressure of bubbles of gas escaping from the *magma,* become covered with ripples, rise higher and then fall back with a heavy "flop"; this agitation was caused by the terrific heavings of the lava immediately underneath it. At every instant the "skin" would give way at some point, yielding to the pressure of the gases, and a little burst of liquid ash and embers would go up like grapeshot.

I looked about for a higher point from which to observe this pool comfortably; from where I stood at the moment it was only just below the level of my eyes. Making a detour westward round it, I perched on a pile of large boulders, with sulfurous fumes being blown down on me by the prevailing wind. Once again I found myself wavering between a sort of intoxication and the necessity to act. I was worried lest I might not have time to get a thorough impression of this exceptional sight; on the other hand I was in a hurry to take measurements, observe, fix what I saw by getting it down in sketches and photographs.

Really, the thing hardly differed at all from the crucible of some gigantic blast furnace. . . . Only, here we were not in a factory; we had penetrated into the inmost secrets of the earth we live on. What was frothing about down there was much more than ore that had been melted by the will of man, in a vessel constructed by man. This was the very substance of the earth itself, chopping about with terrible placidity on the surface of a kind of well that I could feel in my very bowels was beyond all human measuring—fathomless indeed.

The mind finds it easy enough to imagine depths of ten, a hundred, or even a thousand miles. We talk quite lightheartedly about what goes on in the "discontinuity" of the center of the earth, some eighteen hundred miles below the surface we walk on. But if we all at once find ourselves in the physical presence of such abysses, our intellectual cocksureness simply evaporates: the might of Nature herself seizes us in her unreasoning claw. The panic lying in ambush just below the surface of the skin is not the same as the terror a soldier feels, flat on his face in a foxhole, with shells crashing steadily all around him; nor is it the terror of a man cowering behind a wall, inwardly praying for the bombs to fall and end the growling of the air squadrons overhead. Nor is it the same as the shudder the mountaineer feels when he has set out across a field of avalanches and at every step, tight-throated, glances anxiously upward to the heights. No, it is much less clearly defined than any of those terrors. The primitive fear that choked me as I sat by the little pool of lava was less clearly defined and perhaps more fundamental.

On the edge of the great crater, when the eruption was in full swing, I had never had such a chance as I had now to study my own reactions. Up there I had had to keep far too much on the alert, and all the jumping about I had had to do, because of the violence of the phenomenon, acted as something like an antidote. Here, on the other hand, the calm of this fiery pool, which barely rippled under the ponderous lungings from below, spoke to me in enigmatic terms of a mighty and mysterious power. I was spellbound and literally had to wrench myself out of this fear-laden ecstasy to make myself film the phenomenon. Paya, who had stayed on the other side, seemed equally fascinated.

His amazement was itself something of a miracle for anyone who knew the superb faculty the Negroes have for not being surprised by anything. My good, faithful Paya, who until he became my traveling companion had never known anything but his native countryside on the banks of the Lualaba, had in the course of a single year discovered the fire in the earth and the snow on the high mountains—snow being something for which his language has not even a name, so that he referred to it either as "salt" or as "flour," it didn't matter which. He had helped us build the first igloo just under the Equator, at an altitude of 16,400 feet. He had scorched the soles of his feet in the craters of volcanoes; he had visited lakes covered with hundreds of thousands of pink flamingos and prehistoric sites where men of the early Pleistocene age had hacked their tools and weapons out of the black obsidian lava. He had seen airplanes flying and landing and taking off, and had not been particularly astonished since, as he said, the white men had made them for that purpose. . . . In almost three years of living together with him I had not been able to catch him in a state of thorough amazement except once: and that was the first time we went to Nairobi, the pleasant capital of Kenya. It was just the time when everyone goes back to work after lunch, and the long lines of little English motor cars jammed the avenues, a state of traffic congestion unknown in our much more provincial towns in the Congo. These processions of motor cars made a stupendous impression on Paya! He jumped about in his seat, turning this way and that, and could not stop saying over and over: "Oh! Bwana! *Musululu ya motocara, musululu ya motocara!*" ("Oh, Master, how many cars! How many cars!") Although considerably less taken aback by the little pool of lava than by the procession of motor cars in Nairobi, Paya was looking at it with more than ordinary interest and also, I believe, with terror.

However, I was filming away, very sad at having nothing but an ordinary black-and-white film, when suddenly I saw the gray elephant hide swell up all over, remain for an instant in that state of turgescence, overbrimming the rim of the basin by some ten or twelve inches, and then all at once overflow in two streams, one on my left, one on my right, which poured away at a rate of more than twelve miles an hour.

It was so extraordinarily beautiful that for several seconds I wasn't even frightened! It seemed all right just to wait . . .

At first only some feet wide, the torrents swiftly spread out until one was about twenty feet across, the other sixty or more. The narrower one had cut me off from Paya, the other was spreading out toward the west.

"Run, Bwana! Run!" Paya was yelling at me.

Still, I had to film what was going on. I had to take advantage of the fact that the reel wasn't yet used up. I was two or three feet above the bed of the two new outflows, which might, of course, at any minute close behind me in a pincer-movement. I made a rapid calculation and decided that there would have to be a quite considerable addition of new *magma* before that happened. If there should be such an additional boiling over, I would still have time to escape on to the old wall of agglomerate which towered up some thirty paces behind me. It was a safe refuge where I would be able to hold out until the new outflows had formed a crust strong enough for me to walk over.

The film was finished! Two, just two more photographs. Then, swinging round, I beat a retreat to the wall. On the other side of the river of fire Paya ran along parallel with me, looking anxious. The lava had passed the wall and was trickling on beyond it, spreading wider, but its speed was now less than the speed at which a man walks. The further it spread out, the more it slowed down. . . . Just as well, too!

As soon as I had scrambled up on to my perch, I was reassured. There to the north was a second wall of agglomerate, of equally ancient date, which would provide me with a way out. The lava, which had seemed as liquid as water when the pool overflowed, was now no more than a viscous fluid. Its speed was no longer more than three or four miles an hour.

I had simply not had time to take the temperature at the beginning of the phenomenon. The color of the lava, which was yellowish, suggested it had been nearly 1100° C. Now it was bright cherry red, gushing out of the pit at 1030°.

Very quickly, as it came into contact with the air, a skin formed, at first dimming and then entirely veiling the brightness of the incandescent paste. Thirty yards or so away, the elastic skin had already hardened into a rigid crust, which was quite opaque. And yet underneath the molten lava was still flowing on, seeping through the cracks and now and then licking out over the fringe—at the sides and in front—in scarlet bubbles that became larger and larger until they too were covered with a rigid crust. This process made it possible for the new lava to keep on spreading further and further.

I made a detour northward round the eastern outflow and rejoined Paya. He seemed relieved. A warm surge of gratitude rose within me to see how concerned he had been as to my fate. Good old Paya with his friendly face under the white cap he was so proud of! Every fresh adventure did a little more to make the servant he had been in the beginning into a real friend.

By the next day the gaseous vents were quieting down. The pointed flames, like those of a gas burner, had made way for lazy bluish fumes that came drifting up from the orifices. The ejection of clots of lava had completely ceased.

However, activity began again several hours afterward.

At first I could not succeed in discovering any regular rhythm in these manifestations, but after several times an amazing regularity suddenly set in, which was maintained for forty hours: there was a paroxysm lasting about two minutes, followed by a seventeen minutes' lull. I could not find any explanation for this strict precision except some mechanism analogous to that which regulates geysers.*

It was several weeks before the new outflows, which had been steadily slowing up all along their front lines, could cover the surrounding area, and so I had plenty of time to become familiar with them.

So long as I had the wind at my back, it was possible to come up to within a pace of the front of the outflow. It was pretty hot, of course, but one could just stand it. . . . One day Paya and I made use of the lava in this way for frying our eggs.

Another day, while exploring "my" new outflows—for I had come to regard this volcano and all its manifestations as being my private property— I came upon an extraordinarily lovely sight.

The lava was moving on in its usual way, seeping along under the newly formed shell, which was constantly trying to hold it back. Here, however, the front had reached the upper edge of a sheer drop over rock, some fifteen or twenty feet deep, and the molten paste, after flowing gently to the edge of the cliff, suddenly plunged into the void in a cascade of fire—but in slow motion, which gave it a fantastic appearance. It did not *fall;* it was a viscous sheet descending like a curtain. Nevertheless, this vertical descent was too rapid for a crust to form on it. Only at the bottom a thin elastic skin dimmed the red of this strange drop curtain.

Two other flows, about six or eight feet wide, like the first, reached the same cliff, and went down side by side in two new cascades.

The light veil caused by the cooling process gradually thickened toward the base, where it became a gray blanket, though still plastic. Drawn along by the current of the paste below, it wrinkled up into transverse ripples, curling and twisting in a last fling of plastic freedom, and finally produced something resembling thick cables, bluish gray-black in color. I was seeing with my own eyes the formation of the celebrated *corded* or *ropy* lava that in Hawaii is called *pahoehoe* and in Iceland *helluhraun.* . . . Sometimes, however, this corded crust would split and the incandescent *magma* would

---

* The reader will be aware that geysers, which are only to be found in volcanic areas, are jets of hot water and steam that shoot up vertically, sometimes to a great height, at more or less regular intervals. They are probably due to pressure from the gases rising from the depths and escaping through a network of fractures. In certain places these gases cannot escape freely on account of a double hairpin bend, i.e., a bend that is Z-shaped, in which atmospheric water, or water from the underground water level, accumulates. These gases, however, keep on rising, gradually pushing the column of water up the terminal tube. When the liquid at the base has passed the second bend, the gases, the pressure of which is greater than that of the atmosphere combined with the weight of the liquid column, suddenly and violently pass through the water, sweeping it up into the air with them. This is the eruption of the geyser. After this violent discharge a period of calm sets in, during which the water again seals up the conduit, forcing the magmatic gases to accumulate behind it.

ooze out through the cracks. The cliff with the three cascades gave off a won-derful red glow. At eight paces I could only just stand the dazzling glare of the stuff trickling down there at a temperature of more than 1000° C. I had to fall back once, and then again, before the torrents that, once they found themselves again on even ground, suddenly lunged out at me with horrible tentacles. Over the top of the cliff the viscous lava came flowing on and on inexorably, with no sound but a faint hissing.

It struck me that here was the origin of the stories about dragons that are to be found in so many different mythologies, originating in so many different parts of the world.

The ancient Greeks saw the gluey lava of Etna, Stromboli, and Santorin. Is not the Hydra herself, ceaselessly renewed as she is, that crimson out-flow whose black shell hardens so that for a fleeting moment one hopes it is halted, only to see the burning heads reappearing here and there, snapping forward, still there in spite of every obstacle? The Japanese, the Chinese, all the nations of the Far East, also knew the horror of those hundred-headed monsters. The Scandinavians themselves saw them loom up, more appalling than ever, in the gloom of the Polar winter.

One morning I found myself face to face with one of these *bestes feu jetant,* to use Villon's words. Its flaming jaws were opened wide, motionless, straight opposite me. The scarlet throat emitted slow gasps. I saw the torrid mucus palpitating, while the sulfurous breath was exhaled in purple volutes. Pointed, mobile fangs ran along its lips of fire. At some moments its fury seemed to be allayed, or perhaps it was gathering strength for the next on-slaught; at such times the swollen tongue slid back into the throat and the canines that had been jutting toward their prey collapsed, inert. But it was only a moment before those atrocious jaws opened wide again, and the fangs darted forward. . . .

It was no more than the gaping orifice of a spatter cone, and I was a mod-ern geologist, right in the middle of the atomic age: there wasn't much chance for the supernatural to get the better of me. But what would my thoughts have been, what terror, what looming vague dread would have stirred in me at such an encounter if I had been a shepherd from the Campagna or a Sicilian sailor three thousand years ago, on the slopes of some Mediterranean volcano?

How should I have described it, telling the story afterward, but as a *dragon?*

Hymns and Head Dances*

KILTON STEWART

✳✳ Kilton Stewart is an odd fellow. Born in Utah, in a mountain valley near Salt Lake, where trout dart in the canyon streams and where the Indians used to catch and dry them, young Stewart early evidenced an interest in the dream side of man's life. He was a Mormon (member of the Church of Jesus Christ of Latter-Day Saints) and in his youth he went on a mission for the Church. Some time after his graduation from the University of Utah, he began a serious study of tests to find out "what kept primitive peoples primitive while other peoples advanced in the culture of modern man."

When he was 30 he was in the Philippines, where he decided to go into the mountain jungles with his mental tests to learn how man "dealt with the images he acquired before he had astronomy, mathematics, religion, and philosophy." He believed that modern research "has already proved that one type of help or interpretation of the dream, vision, or reflective thought makes man into a saint; another social policy makes him into a cannibal or a head-hunter . . . I wanted to find out how this came about, so the dangerous images man built up in his mind could be made to stop working against him."

These excerpts from his very latest book, *Pygmies and Dream Giants,* discovers Dr. Stewart, with a scared young native guide, halfway through the adventures in that book. Stewart had spent the night at a Philippine farmhouse which was also a trading post run by Manolo de Leon—in the mountains north of Manila— and that night they had talked a good deal about the head-hunters in the hills, the Ilongots, who had never been conquered by the Spaniards and were not yet a part of the Filipino political state since the American administration had confined them to their own territory with strict insistence that they take no more heads from the Lowlanders.

The next morning when Stewart and his boy Gabriel set out, Gabriel was still remembering Manolo's fearsome stories, for Manolo was suspicious of Stewart— no white man had ever come into those mountains except to seek gold. Gabriel, a high school pupil, part Ilongot, had agreed, as a means of "improving his English," to go along with Stewart to work the tests among the Ilongots. ✳✳

"THEY ARE GOING TO TAKE MY HEAD"

As we walked off the road onto the footpath leading to Ijah's rancho, Gabriel's steps dragged. It was difficult to explain to him why I wanted to collect the dreams of the Ilongots, why I wanted to give them mental tests and observe their ceremonies, and why the dreams of Lowlanders would not do as well. Manolo had raised some logical questions. Why was I more interested in the Ilongots' magical ceremonies than in their gold?

Each time we stopped to rest I attempted in vain to allay Gabriel's fears and put the gay smile back into his eyes. I expected him to turn back, but he could not do this without losing face. By evening I despaired of comforting him and decided that his fears would only be overcome when he found from actual experience that they were groundless.

That night we camped in a beautiful little grove of trees, where two streams came together in a rocky canyon. The climb from the valley had been delightful, and it was pleasant to be away from the Lowland heat.

Since noon I had left Gabriel alone with his thoughts, and we had scarcely exchanged a word. We made a tiny fire to boil our rice, and extinguished it before darkness fell. Ijah who, as our host, was taking us to his home, explained that we must not keep the fire burning at night, since there might be expeditions about in search of heads. Gabriel suggested that we each sit up half the night on guard, and I agreed to take the first half, but I could see that even after our hard day's hike he had got no sleep. When it was his turn to watch, I offered to continue instead, but he said he couldn't sleep anyway and insisted on taking over.

Ijah and the five younger men who were with him were sleeping soundly. Apparently they depended on the dogs to protect them from surprise attacks. I felt Gabriel's insistence on the watch was stupid, but I could not tell him so without offending him.

When I awoke the next morning, Gabriel looked hollow-eyed and still more tense. I fully expected him to refuse to go farther, but he did not suggest turning back. Again we trudged on in silence, but I was worried about him. He had the same brooding look in his eyes that I had seen at Bangued in the eyes of a lad who had run amuck and stabbed his schoolteacher.

Gabriel had given me his absolute confidence during the first few days of the journey. Now a suspicion that I had deceived him about the purpose of my mission was gnawing at him. I tried to talk to him, but he answered in monosyllables. If the Ilongots were like the Negritos, Gabriel's suspicion of me would be obvious to them, and his fear of them would be interpreted as unfriendliness. "Certainly Ijah will be afraid to attack us," I said, as we paused for breath. "Manolo told him that his group would be wiped out if he harmed us, and Ijah knows that his place could easily by found by the police."

"If they've cultivated all the land in the vicinity of their houses, they'll be ready to move anyway," said Gabriel. "Then they could take our heads and move off where the constabulary could not find them; and if we leave their group, Ijah will, as like as not, steer us to an enemy village which he wants wiped out anyway."

At last I asked Gabriel if he wished to turn back, but he could not admit that he did.

The sun was almost straight above us when we came in sight of the first Ilongot house. Ijah shouted and waved his arms. It was as though he had poked a stick into an ant bed. Barking dogs and shouting people poured out of the door and down the little causeway which led from the elevated entrance of the house to the steep mountainside on which it was built.

The house was a large, squarish, well-built structure, supported by the stumps of trees. The upper side was about six feet above the ground, but because of the slope of the mountain, the stumps on the lower side were some twenty feet high. The roof was thatched, and on all four sides it went up evenly from the eaves, without a gable, to within ten feet of the top. From that point on, two facing sides were left open for ventilation, while the other two continued to a peak, which formed a short gable extending out on each end to protect the open space. At each end of the ridgepole of the short gable, above the open space, a carved stick swept upward as though the ridgepole were continued out and up. From a distance the two carved sticks looked like the horns of a wild buffalo.

The various families which the house sheltered lived on a low platform extending about fifteen feet from the outside walls of the house. Cross walls divided the platform into stall-like compartments. A clay hearth in front of each compartment served the family within. In the center of the house was a large, square, open floor.

Our belongings were moved into a vacant stall reserved as a rule for visiting suitors. Gabriel immediately hauled out our horsehair and gave a generous portion to Ijah, asking him to distribute it according to custom. The gift was promptly returned in sugar cane and other foods. One look at the group made it obvious why horsehair was so treasured among them. It served as a part of the braided and woven designs on the handles of all their spears, knives, and other implements, on their betel boxes and baskets,

and on the arm bands and earrings, leg bands and girdles of the women.
The white color was thought to have a magical influence. . . .

The women and children of the household had no reticence about taking
our tests and drawing pictures, and like the men we had tested at Manolo's,
they came up to the American norms on all the tests but the Porteus Maze.
They were equally willing to tell their dreams, and recalled them in abundance.

I had never seen a more charming and friendly people. The women and
children had uncut hair like the men, but the women and the preadolescent
boys did not wear hair nets.

The women and girls were no less spontaneous and self-possessed than
the men. I concluded that they must have a splendid culture, so far as their
social relationships with one another inside the group were concerned. I
warmed toward them immediately and felt very much at home.

As the afternoon progressed, however, their attitude toward Gabriel
alarmed me. He was afraid of them and they knew it. Their gestures expressed contempt. I could see that Gabriel's fear was turning to hatred. He
remarked to me at dinner that the Lowlanders were right in calling the
Ilongots ignorant savages. I could see that he was contrasting his experience
and accomplishments with theirs, and I tried to convince him of the danger
of adopting a superior attitude. "We must make friends with them," I
urged. "We must amuse them with stories of the world that you know and
they don't. After all, they did not ask us to visit them."

After dinner I instructed Gabriel to ask the Ilongots about their dances.
"Tell them we will sing songs and show them dances from other places," I
said, "and that we would like to see their dances. We would also like to
know about their magical ceremonies and medical practices."

Dancing was the chief pastime of the Ilongots. They responded to our request at once, hauling out drums and gongs, and primitive instruments
which resembled the xylophone. Each of these had been made from a large
joint of bamboo, eight to ten inches in diameter. When the wood was still
green, the hard outer surface of the bamboo was slit into strings of various
lengths, left attached at each end. A little wedge or bridge was inserted at
each end of the slit to lift the string away from the wood. Then the instrument was allowed to dry, making the strings taut and tough. Each was
played by a woman, who struck the strings with slender strips of bamboo,
holding one in each hand. Her child, husband, or lover held the instrument.
There were also Panpipes—mouth organs made of bamboo tubes about a
half-inch in diameter which were cut at different lengths, getting shorter
and shorter, so that as they were passed along the lips and blown they

sounded the various notes of a scale. These, with bamboo nose flutes, which were blown by the men, completed the instruments of the orchestra.

The music was excellent. Gabriel, now more at ease, translated the songs and talked with the old men about the meaning of the dances. The most impressive dance was performed by the men, who, with arms outstretched, danced in a circle, whirling and turning like hornbills in flight, while their women danced in one corner, in no particular formation, as though they were birds hopping about on the ground.

Gabriel did some steps of the *Rigodón,* the state dance of the Filipinos, and demonstrated other dances he had learned in the Lowlands. I contributed a shaman's dance, imitating a trance state at the end of it. Even before I arose from the floor, I realized I had made a mistake. Either the rhythm of the dance, or the trance, had thrown the Ilongots into a state of excitement. As the young men swung to the floor for their next dance, Gabriel turned pale and trembled.

"I have heard my mother sing that tune," he whispered. "It is the dance they do when they are going to take a head. We should not have come here without soldiers. Ijah has brought us up here as sacrifices. I was sure of it this afternoon when we arrived. They have harvested the rice, but have not yet put it into their storehouse. This means that they have not yet taken a head to pay the *anitos* back for the life force they will receive from eating the rice. When it is ripe, they cut the rice stalk by stalk and stack it up on bamboo platforms to dry until they take a head."

I tried to convince Gabriel that we were in no danger, but as the young men darted past us again and again, I became less confident that the dance was merely a friendly social gesture. As the pace of the dancers quickened, my companion's terror increased.

"You must stop them," he sobbed at last. "Everyone is looking straight at me as he passes. You must stop them quickly. They are going to take my head."

The change in the dancers was indeed alarming. They looked dazed and had a piercing and set expression about the eyes. They were staring at Gabriel with a concentration that sent shivers down my spine. Unless I did something quickly, Gabriel would probably die of fear.

I stepped toward the dancers and clapped my hands loudly. Throughout the evening Gabriel and I had clapped at the end of each performance. Taken by surprise, the musicians ceased playing. The dance came to a standstill. There was only one thing left to do. I must sing a song that would quiet them.

Fortunately I had grown up in a religious community. I launched into

"Nearer, My God, to Thee." It worked like magic. At first they listened with interest to the music; then they moved their heads to and fro with the rhythm. Then one of them yawned and the others took it up as though it were contagious. Their eyes began to droop, and when I could see they were starting to resist the drowsiness, I changed to another hymn. The same sequence occurred again. At dawn I was still singing hymns. I was astonished to find that I knew so many.

Gabriel's nerve was broken. He looked at me gratefully when I insisted that he return to the Lowlands, and gave him the money to take him back to Bangued. I realized that if he spent another day here he would almost certainly run amuck. It was better to have no interpreter at all than to have one who awoke contempt and suspicion. Through Gabriel I arranged for one of the young men of the household to carry my pack and explain my drawings and games. The fee was to be a handful of horsehair every day. When the lad wished to go no further south, he was to hire for me, at the house where he left me, another assistant who knew the territory I was about to enter.

By concentrating on learning the language, in which Gabriel had been instructing me intensively since I first met him, I would soon be able to speak the dialect well enough myself to give the nonlanguage tests at least.

An hour after Gabriel left, I set out for a clearing higher in the mountain, which could be seen dimly across the canyon. I might have stayed on longer with Ijah, but the cut rice drying on the bamboo platforms under the banana-leaf thatch bothered me. Probably I could find ranchos where the grain had already been put away.

With me was the young man whom Gabriel had engaged, and a half-dozen of his friends. The trail led up the steep side of the canyon, then across some flats where the grass was so high that we walked through a tunnel. Here and there the country was cut by deep ravines, and we crossed them on huge roots and primitive suspension bridges of woven vines and rattan that made me dizzy. My guide carried my pack over these sections as though he were walking along a flat country road.

We arrived at the clearing shortly after noon. A shout brought men, women, and children around us in a moment. They appeared out of nowhere and greeted their friends from the neighboring village with shouts and peals of laughter. I was much more of a curiosity here than I had been the day before. Apparently I was the first white man some of them had seen. The diversion was welcome.

Soon everybody was playing with the puzzles and experimenting with pencil and paper. Again, their drawings were excellent. They also made high scores on the puzzles, and they were not shy about doing them nor apologetic when they made mistakes on the Maze.

I was again given the compartment usually occupied by the young men who came to the community house to court the women of the group. The three suitors who were there when we arrived made arrangements to sleep in the already crowded compartment occupied by the young men of the house.

The air circulated freely through the chinks in the bamboo walls and under the raised floor of my room. The heavy thatched roof made an effective screen against the afternoon heat. I lay idly listening to the confused sounds without, in which were mingled children's voices, the birdlike twitter of the young women as they vied with each other for the attention of their admirers, the growling of dogs, and the ever-present afternoon chorus of the cicadas.

I was happy. What did it matter that it might take me a year or two to work my way to Manila, if I could live with these free and spontaneously friendly people? A couple of months of intensive work on their language and I would be able to learn about their institutions, their kinship system, their economy, and their magical and shamanistic practices.

As the preparation of the evening meal progressed, the chorus of household and jungle sounds was pushed into the background of my attention by the savory odor of food. In a slice of reddish sunlight, filtering from the eaves diagonally across the house, were tiny particles of blue smoke. Through the chinks I watched a wrinkled old woman as she moved into the beam and was lost again in the shadows from which she had emerged. The sun's rays revealed an expression of great patience and concentration. I marveled that a human being could be so completely absorbed by the simple task of cooking. On the coals of her slow fire I could see a half-dozen bamboo cylinders, olive green at the top, where the fire had not scorched them, and shading downward from tan through mahogany red to black, where they were charred by the heat. Deftly she plucked one from the coals, tilted it above the glossy surface of a traylike leaf, and removed the cover, made of a larger cylinder of bamboo. From the creamy throat came a cascade of dazzlingly white rice grains.

The woman was an artist. When I came to the evening meal I saw that each kernel of rice was as perfect as a snowflake, and as fluffy. From other tubes, laid on a number of fires, appeared a wide assortment of exotic vegetables and meats, including a tender mauve banana blossom, bamboo shoots, pale green tips of rattan plants, small boiled bananas with cubes of sugar-cane pith, squash, and several leafy vegetables and roasted roots which were strange to me.

In the center of the heap of food appeared the hindquarter of a giant tropical porcupine, which the men had been turning on a spit beneath the house. I was already dizzy with the variety of colors and odors when an enormous leaf was slid before me and I was told to eat. Was this my food for the week? I was surprised when, at the end of an hour, I had stowed it all away.

My desire to sleep after the heavy dinner was frustrated by my assistant, who told the gathering about the songs I had sung in his clearing the night before. From the interest he raised, I realized I could not escape another evening of singing and dancing. Bamboo jugs were hauled from under the house. They contained fermented sugar-cane juice, which the Ilongots extracted from sugar cane by crushing the stalks in a primitive mill. . . .

FEAR TO THE POINT OF PANIC

On the previous night no wine had been served. Even so, the natives had appeared dangerously aggressive in their dance. I watched my new hosts now as they set out a dozen jugs before the fireplace of the oldest patriarch in the house. The young men who had come along with me were pleased at the prospect of an evening's drinking, but I was not.

As the contents of the first large jug was poured into coconut-shell cups, a foreboding of evil and danger, amounting to conviction, possessed me. The men produced their drums, and the old patriarch dug a battered bronze Chinese *gansa* from beneath his mats. It was very old and had a hoarse, deep ring. From among their possessions, the women brought out the bamboo mouth organs and xylophones.

Soon all the group were singing. The songs went round and round the room, each man taking a solo, which was then repeated in chorus. The excellence of the music and the warming effect of the wine picked up my spirits. The little mugs were circulated repeatedly.

Finally my turn came to sing. I had found earlier that the Negritos had liked the rhythm and the tune of "Jingle Bells." Now I tried it out on the Ilongots, with such great success that I sang it over and over again. At first the drums and *gansas* picked up the rhythm. Then, as I repeated it, the Panpipes, xylophones, and nose flutes came in. Before I finished, a chorus of voices joined me, supplying words of their own to the music.

The fires on the clay hearths flickered. In their rosy, shifting light, white teeth, brown eyes, and lithe, handsome bodies gleamed or grew shadowy with the rising and falling of the evening breeze.

It seemed to me that I had no reason to fear these pleasant people, overflowing with music and good will. Now that they had shown they could appreciate my song and even sing it with me, I felt more easy about them. Surely my foreboding of evil was groundless. Soon the pulsing rhythm of the gong and the drums lulled me to sleep. The Ilongots dissolved into flitting dreamlike figures.

I opened my eyes; the fitful puffs of wind, which earlier had fanned the fires into rhythmic bursts of light, had now grown into a strong, steady current of air sweeping down from the east. It had blown the opalescent pall of smoke from the room. The bodies of the Ilongots stood out in bold relief against the red glow of the fires. An oily perspiration, drawn out by exercise, covered their skin, giving them a metallic sheen. They were no longer human beings filled with good will. They were sinister animated figures of bronze.

All the younger men, including the lads from the near-by clearing, were dancing in a circle in the center of the room. They had only one face and one rhythm. The old men at their drums, and the women at their instruments on the edge of the dancing group, were tied into this rhythm by an invisible current. The slightest movement might hurl me into that mysterious vortex. I lay perfectly still, peering out from under closed lids, attempting to collect my thoughts. Fear to the point of panic had got hold of me, but I was not yet sure what I was afraid of. I needed time to decide which was the real world and which was the world of dreams.

I examined the sounds, colors, and shapes, and the quality of the dance movement. Suddenly I realized that they were singing the head-hunting song which had set Gabriel shaking the previous night. But now *I* was the object of that terrifying concentration. The rhythm of the dance had been set, its direction determined like an arrow in flight. And I was the target.

The benevolent old gentleman at the gong had undergone a mysterious transformation during the hours that I had slept. Now the hard lines of his face expressed cruelty and condemnation. Round and round moved the dancers, slicing the air with their broad-bladed head knives.

I could not accept the cadence of this ceremony as my destiny. The old men had known many men before and had controlled many situations similar to this. I would have to act differently from their previous victims. I would have to act now.

My body bounded from beside the hearth. I felt a roar in my throat, a sound such as I had never heard, which paralyzed the old man's hands above the gong and the hands of the men at the drums, and which froze the dancers.

For a moment even the flames stood still. Two long steps carried me to the center of that frozen circle of dancers. Before the old man or anyone else had found the will to act, my own body was doing a crazy, violent dance. A voice which possessed me—my own voice, yet not mine—was singing a crazy song. All around I saw the open mouths of the dancers, the women, the old men at the drums.

I watched the hard lines of the patriarch's face change from astonishment to surprise, and gradually relax into the good-humored expression of the day before. As my body bounced and my arms made motions which some-how were attached to that strange voice within me, the astonishment on the faces of the men turned into amusement. With the change in the audience, I felt my song and my dance changing. The bounce left my muscles. Soon I was dancing waltzes for them, as I had done the previous evening. As the blackness outside the windows gave way to sickly gray, I was again singing the doxology and "Nearer, My God, to Thee."

Roars of laughter gave way to snores, as the wine and the soothing re-ligious music anesthetized my audience. In the midst of a sleeping house-hold, where only the children's eyes peeped at me, I softly sang Brahms' "Lullaby" as a finale.

When sunlight flooded through the glassless windows of the large room, dispelling the mist from the sea of bright green treetops below the house, it was difficult to believe that the mad dance of the night before was not just part of some nightmare I had had. In the jungles and mountains a great gulf is fixed between the night and the day worlds. My mind would not cross it now, as I watched the women laughing and singing at their task of preparing the morning meal. But here, as at Ijah's house, I saw the cut rice stalks drying on bamboo platforms under the banana-leaf thatch.

The afternoon before, all the members of the household had drawn their picture of a man for me, and had done my puzzles. I would not be able to collect their dreams or give the other tests until I learned the language, and I would have to pick that up on the trail. If I moved on, spending only a night in each house until I knew more about these people, I would not lose the advantage of the element of surprise, and their feeling of curiosity would not have time to give way to other emotions. The squirt gun in my pocket, full of ammonia, felt comfortable now, rather than heavy.

I woke my boy and pointed south. He declined to go farther, but a lad of the house helped to pack my things. After breakfast he set out with me for another community.

White-Skinned Woman Among Cannibals *

OSA JOHNSON

✳✳ Osa Johnson was born Osa Leighty, in the small town of Chanute, Kansas, but her life of adventure began early: at 16 she happened to attend a talk by a tall, thin young man who had been to sea in the *Snark* with Jack and Charmian London and as a result of having encountered South Sea Islanders he had set himself up as Martin Johnson (of Independence, Kansas), traveler and lecturer, going about Kansas with a reel or two of motion picture films and some slides.

Whether, at first sight, Osa fell in love with the man she spent most of the rest of her life with, she was never quite clear, but a few weeks after that first lecture, she was Mrs. Osa Johnson and in 1917 not long after her marriage she was on board ship with him, out of California, bound for the land of cannibals to help him find fresh material for more lectures and more pictures, and not until many years later did she get a chance to settle down at home in one spot—in Africa— among lions, tigers, elephants, and rhinoceros. ✳✳

Captain Trask was a big man with a seamed, weathered face, a fine big nose, and an air of awe-inspiring authority. I admired him very much and was prouder than ever of my husband when I saw how much the captain liked him. They talked a lot of places and people that I knew nothing about, so I decided the best thing for me would be to listen and learn—and all the more so because it was apparent that the captain had put me down as little, soft, and generally useless. He had known Jack and Charmian London, and very pointedly every now and then—squinting at me under his heavy brows—he spoke of Charmian.

"There's a woman for you," he'd say. "She had the soft ways of a kitten and the heart of a lioness, and her beat never lived and never will."

"You're right there." Martin was thoughtful. "She was perfect for Jack. Never a squawk out of her; the best wife a man ever had."

"Aye," the captain nodded with another look at me. "A woman that's too soft and sweet is like tapioca pudding—fine for them as likes it." Then he said something about the barometer falling but I wasn't interested, and when I climbed into my berth that night I thought about snakes and cannibals and dried human heads and wondered miserably if the day would ever come when I would fail Martin. I fell into a troubled sleep and woke up in the act of pitching from my berth and landing on my shoulder. I tried to get to my feet and found that the floor had taken the angle of our cellar door back in Chanute, just as I had figured this out, the up part was down and the down part was up. Then I heard a groan. It was Martin.

"I wish I could die," he said.

I did everything I could for the rest of the night to help Martin be a little less miserable, then, when I saw it was morning, I scrambled into some clothes and went up on deck. It was wonderful, though I had to hang on like mad. It didn't seem possible there could be waves of such a size. They piled up and piled up, until finally there was one that curled and broke right where I stood. It hit me with the force of a sack of sand, and the next instant I found myself in a swirl of green water and foam, and being swept to the other side of the deck.

Stunned and limp as a half-drowned kitten, I felt myself being picked up by the back of my jacket; then heard myself roughly ordered below. It was Captain Trask and he was in a fury that I would show myself above deck on such a day.

"Why aren't you sick?" he thundered. "Sick and in your bunk and out of the way like other decent folk!"

"I don't want to be sick," I replied crossly as he pushed me ahead of him down the companionway. "And I don't like my bunk and just because you're a captain of a ship I suppose you think you can order everybody around, but I don't like being ordered around——"

We had reached the bottom of the swaying companionway. The captain was still scowling.

"Well, I'm ordering you right now to stay off that deck until the ropes are strung, understand? Whether you're washed overboard or not doesn't interest me. Whether I have to put back to pick you up does interest me. I can't afford the time. Now you get into your bunk and stay there!"

"Then what do I do about breakfast? Martin doesn't want any, but I'm starved, and if you think I'm going back to bed without any breakfast——"

Captain Trask squinted at me. "How about some hot cakes," he said, "and a lot of butter and syrup, maybe some pig sausages and fried potatoes and a couple of cups of coffee?"

"Wonderful!"

The captain grinned. "All right, sailor," he said. "Get into some dry clothes and you shall have breakfast with me."

When I found that everybody aboard was sick except the captain and me—and, I suppose, some of the crew—everything brightened, and especially when it became apparent that the captain now regarded me as a right and good companion for Martin. Nothing more than this could I ask of either heaven or earth, and cannibals and snakes became mere trifles to take in my stride. At least, so I thought.

All the way across the Pacific to Honolulu, to Samoa, to Pago-Pago and finally to Sydney, Australia, my confidence grew. The captain became jollier by the minute and even played deck games with us, and when, on parting at Sydney, he told Martin I was "all right," it seemed to me I ought to burst, I was so proud. It took a few cockroaches to lay me low.

It was several days later; we were on our way from Sydney to the Solomon Islands aboard a tramp steamer, and while I longed for the departed comforts and cleanliness of Captain Trask's ship, I did what I was sure Charmian London would have done under the circumstances; I wore a smile. The captain, crew, and ship were filthy and there were cockroaches everywhere, some no less than two inches long. The mess swarmed with them, and I saw Martin every now and then jounce them off his shoes and go right on eating. Doggedly, I did the same and derived a glum satisfaction out of telling myself that from matters such as these, probably one acquired that easy, well-traveled look.

It's one thing to be brave when you're awake; it's another when you're asleep. Something crossing my cheek that night startled me into instant wakefulness, and in the dim light I saw a roach scurry across my pillow, then heard it drop to the floor. I clenched my teeth against a scream; then suddenly was aware of a curious activity at the tips of my fingers. My hands lay at my sides on the sheet which was my only cover, and I found, on inspection, that roaches were nibbling at my fingernails. My screams must have been heard from stem to stern of the ship.

Martin, laughing, took me in his arms. "That's nothing," he said. "Wait till you get down to the Solomons. Those coconut crabs down there aren't polite enough just to give you a manicure; they take your fingers right off!"

The next few months were disappointing and anxious ones. In whalers, luggers, and merchants we sailed from island to island of the Solomon group and found many primitive blacks. We even found some that were said to be cannibals, but always Martin shook his head and pushed on. Often I found this difficult to understand. My imagination went no further than the savages we had seen. It was incredible to me that anywhere in the world there could be wilder, more vicious-looking people. Because our funds were so limited I knew we couldn't cruise about indefinitely, and Martin insisted that because our film was so limited we could use it only when he was satisfied he had found savages that were completely untouched by civilization. Then he pointed out that all of those we had seen so far had been under the firm control of the British government authorities. They were subdued, tamed. Nothing I could say would persuade him to the contrary. His mouth, tender and fine, could become very stubborn, and his eyes, usually gay and carefree, would take on a look of pure, hard steel.

There were those aboard the different boats we took, traders and the like, who couldn't understand Martin's not herding some of the more savage-looking natives together, giving them trade stuff and "staging" some scenes. It had been done, they said, but then as always, Martin was a patient, persistent artist who would never be satisfied with anything but the truth. It seems to me that everywhere he went he asked hundreds of questions. He made hundreds of notes, and finally his decision was made. Malekula, second largest island of the New Hebrides group, was, he learned, the subject of disputed ownership between the French and British, and this meant a lack of the usual patroling and discipline. If man in his savage and original state existed any place in the world, he existed here. Further investigation revealed that there were parts of Malekula that had never been explored by white men, and it was rumored that cannibalism and head-hunting were common practices.

We returned to Sydney where Martin searched out the captain of a small ship that was leaving in a few days for the upper part of the Hebrides group. Once aboard, and our destination and purpose made known, a storm of protest and warning broke around us. The captain himself came to us, bringing a copy of the *Pacific Island Pilot*.

"Now you listen to me, young fellow," he said, "I don't want to scare the little lady, but it says right here in the *Pilot* that the natives of Malekula are a wild and savage race, that they're treacherous and it's a known fact that they still practice cannibalism!"

Martin smiled. He was happier than he'd been in months.

"I've had some experience with savages," he said, "and with plenty of tobacco and trade stuff, we'll be safe enough."

A recruiter of blacks, heavy, scarred, and rough, and with, I suspect, a trace of black in his own veins, broke into the conversation.

"The captain's right, sir," he said to Martin. "Why, I wouldn't go onto that island for a thousand pounds; at least, not without a gunboat at my back."

"I'm afraid we don't happen to have a gunboat in our equipment," Martin grinned.

"If you go through with this, you'll find it's no joking matter," the captain growled.

"But, why should the natives hurt us?" I said, putting in my bit. "My husband is only going to take their pictures."

"Take their pictures!" the captain snorted. "When you two get close enough to them for that, you can tell each other good-by!" He drank noisily from a flask, then continued: "Pictures of them cannibals! Why, they're ugly as the devil's own brats—and that's what they are, devils! Savage, cruel, murderous black devils!" His voice thundered. "And what's more, I'll not go off my course to set you down on Malekula, understand? Not with a woman along! It would be murder, that's what, woman-murder, and I'll not be guilty of it!"

I couldn't even look in Martin's direction, for it was I—my coming with him—that hampered all his plans. Already we were in sight of Malekula. In length it was seventy-five miles or more, the recruiter told us, shaped like an hourglass and about thirty miles across its widest part.

"There's around forty thousand savages on that island," he continued. "Strong fellows too, especially among the Big Numbers, but much as I'm needing blacks, I'll get 'em someplace else."

Forty thousand savages on one island. I was staggered.

Martin's interest sharpened. "Strong fellows, you say, the Big Numbers?"

"The most powerful tribe on the island, and they've got a chief, Nagapate, that's a holy terror."

Martin prodded the recruiter with more questions and learned that the Big Numbers, who derived their name from wearing a huge pandanus fiber, occupied the greater portion of the north end of the island, and that by sufferance another tribe known as the Small Numbers was permitted to occupy a minor portion. The latter, he said, wore merely a bit of twisted leaf.

I could see from the way Martin looked off toward the blue-gray mass that was Malekula, that somehow he would contrive to get there. A smaller shape, separated from the big island, now appeared, and quickly Martin asked about it.

"That's the island of Vao," the recruiter said. "About a mile and a half across and maybe four hundred savages." He paused, with a look at me. A couple of tears had dripped off the end of my nose. "You know," he said,

"I think Vao would be the very ticket for you and the little lady here. Four hundred wild men would be about as many as you could get in that camera of yours anyhow, and from all reports, even though the British patrol boat circles the island every so often and could rake it from end to end with fire, I hear that those fellows on Vao still bury their old people alive and eat long pig."

"And how far did you say Vao was from Malekula?" Martin asked cautiously.

"About a mile," the recruiter answered, "and there's a French mission there, too, run by Father Prin."

Martin seized his hand. "A great idea," he shouted. "Great!"

The captain eyed us suspiciously as we debarked at Vao; he knew that we could get to Malekula from there with very little trouble. Then he shrugged. If we were reckless enough to risk being served up as "long pig" by the savages of Malekula, that was our lookout, not his.

Father Prin gave us a hearty, if puzzled, welcome. This dear soul who had worked among the savages of the small island for nearly thirty years was a volume in himself, and all the more so when one considered that the only discernible result of his labor, was a mere seventeen converts. I marveled at his patience and loved him for his faith.

The little mud and grass church, with its quiet images and dim altar, seemed strange and beautiful on this savage island. The priest's small three-room home adjoining it was a sanctuary of cleanliness and repose. It was here we rested and made our plans.

Father Prin gravely shook his head and confirmed the stories we had already heard of the cruelties practiced even on Vao. How much worse it must be on Malekula where even the most hardened recruiters feared to land, should, he said, be perfectly apparent to us. I could see reproach in his eyes as he looked at Martin, and worse, I could see that Martin himself was beginning to fear for me. Always me!

With evening the boo-boos (native drums) began to sound back in the bush of Vao, and suddenly Father Prin pointed from the window of his hut. Martin and I looked, and there at the edge of the clearing we saw peering at us men whose black faces were so seamed and hideous, it was hard to believe they were men at all.

"T-that thing through their noses," I heard myself asking in a squeaky whisper. "What's that?"

"Bone," Father Prin replied. "Human bone."

Martin drew me away from the window. "I don't know, darling," he said, "but I'm afraid I can't risk taking you to Malekula. You'll be safe here with Father Prin. Please, Osa, for my sake."

Suddenly I was in a rage, with every bit of fear burned out of me.

"If you go I'm going with you, Martin Johnson. That's what I came for and that's how it's going to be—the whole way. The whole way!" I repeated.

Seeing that I would not be swerved, the good priest gave us every help in his power, and a twenty-eight-foot whale boat together with a crew of five trustworthy Vao boys was put at our disposal. Before sunup the following morning we were stowing our cameras, film, and trade goods in the boat. Then, hoisting a small jib and a miniature mainsail, we pushed off for Malekula, with Father Prin giving us his blessings from the shore.

Following the good father's advice, we first landed at a small salt-water village on the Vao side of Malekula, where the natives, because of their accessibility, had learned to respect the British gunboats and to recognize authority beyond their own, and where we added three more boys to our crew. These boys, being Malekulans, would help us, Father Prin felt, to contact the bush people of the island. We then set sail for Tanemarou Bay, in the Big Numbers territory.

The trip along the rocky shore was not very reassuring so far as the aims of our little expedition were concerned, for only now and then did we catch a glimpse of the natives, and they vanished as we rapidly approached. This apparent timidity eased our fears for our personal safety, however, and when we reached the beach at Tanemarou, a strip of dazzling yellow sand separating the sea from the thick bush, we found it deserted, and stepped boldly out of the whale boat.

"How does this look to you, Kitten?" Martin asked. His eyes were dancing with excitement.

"Why—all right I guess," I answered doubtfully. Then trying to be funny, "But I thought somebody said something about forty thousand savages on Malekula."

"Don't worry, they're back there in the bush, plenty of them."

He pantomimed the boys to take the trade stuff out of the boat. Our one precious motion picture camera he handled himself.

"Looks like a kind of trail into the bush over there," I said. Then I stopped short. "Oh!" I said.

A lone savage had appeared out of the jungle. Our boys, seeing him, moved back toward the boat—and with good reason: he was the most horrible-looking creature I had ever laid eyes on. Coal black and incredibly filthy, his shock of greasy hair and heavy wool beard were probably the nesting place of every sort of vermin.

A gorget of pig's teeth hung around his neck; he wore a bone through his nose and he was entirely naked except for a large breech cloth of dried pandanus fiber. As he came nearer I saw that his deeply creviced face was horribly distorted. It made me think of a grotesque mask—one I had seen on a theater program in New York, I think—representing *Tragedie*. I moved closer to Martin.

The black spoke in a guttural *bêche-de-mer* that astonished me with its scattering of English words.

"My word! Master! Belly belong me walk about too much!" He pressed his hands dramatically to his stomach.

I looked at Martin incredulously. We had come to Malekula warned and forewarned of natives who dealt swift and savage death to intruders, to be met by a whining black with a stomachache!

We rocked with laughter—which doubtless was part relief—then I opened our kit and poured out a small handful of cascara tablets. Martin explained carefully to the gaping savage that he was to take part of them when the sun went down and the other part when the sun came up. The black listened with apparent intentness to the end of the instructions, then opened his slobbery mouth and downed all the tablets at one gulp.

During this little comedy, several more savages had slipped quietly out of the bush—I think I counted ten in all—each as horrible in appearance as their advance man with the stomachache, and each apparently as harmless. Martin lost no time in setting up his camera—which they dismissed after a casual inspection—and exposed perhaps a hundred and fifty feet of film. I could see he was measuring it carefully.

The savages were carrying on what to me was an unintelligible jabber. Our carriers began to show signs of nervousness and to edge toward the boat. Martin understood a little *bêche-de-mer* and, with an air of complete casualness as he busied himself with the camera, told me what was up.

"They're saying that their chief is back there in the bush. He's been watching our boat as we came around to the bay——"

"You mean—the big chief—the Big Numbers chief, Nag——"

Martin stopped me with a sharp gesture. "Don't speak his name," he cautioned. "Play dumb."

"But—if we could get him in the camera! Oh, Martin—if we could!"

"It would be worth the whole trip."

I saw how terribly he wanted to plunge into the bush with his camera, but that he was afraid because of me.

"I'll take some trade stuff and go ahead," I said as casually as I could. "I'm not afraid of these old natives and their stomachaches." I began gathering up some tobacco and calico. "Just a lot of big bluffs." I started toward the trail.

"Wait, Osa! I can't risk it. Not with you. I'll come back tomorrow."

I kept right on going.

"All right then, wait," he shouted after me. "I'll get one of these boys to lead the way."

Organized at length, with one of the Big Numbers men acting as guide, and our three carriers bringing up the rear with tripods, film, still cameras, and the bulk of the trade stuff, we plunged into the jungle.

After the glare of the beach I seemed suddenly blind, and slid and stumbled along a dark trail that was treacherous with hidden muddy streams and wet creepers. The heavy, steaming breath of the swamps pressed down on us with the weight of something dead, and in it was the ominous smell of rot and slime. Then we started to climb. Suddenly we were in the hot glare of the sun once more, and the slope was sharp and covered with brush and tough cane. We climbed for what seemed hours. A pulse beat hard in the roof of my mouth, my breath was like a knife in my chest and perspiration dripped from my hands.

"Tough going, Osa," Martin said several times. He was just behind me and I could hear him breathing hard.

I nodded but didn't speak; I didn't know what my voice would sound like. Then abruptly we came on a clearing; a sort of plateau, where our guide stopped us as if waiting for something

I began to look about me. Far below—we must have climbed at least one hundred feet—I saw the yellow strip of beach and our whale boat, a mere dot at the edge of the water.

Off across a sort of chasm I saw thin columns of smoke. Martin had drawn close and put his arm about me.

"You're a grand little sport," he said. "That climb was tough."

I couldn't say anything, I was so proud. Martin followed the direction of my gaze.

"Making stews of their enemies over there, what?" he said jokingly.

Just then there was a shuffling sound and we turned. A score of natives carrying guns had moved in behind us. I saw Martin's face tighten.

"Don't let them see you're afraid, Osa," he said quietly but firmly. "Leave the trade stuff on the ground and ease down the trail. I'll attract their attention with the camera, and that'll give you a good start."

I turned to obey, but the trail was cut off. By now there must have been a hundred armed savages in the clearing. From somewhere off in the bush came the low, pulsing beat of the *boo-boos*. I glanced at our three carriers. They had stooped to pick up our goods and were fixed in attitudes of terror. There was neither movement nor sound until a huge parrot—a raucous blade of color and noise—slashed across the clearing.

Then all heads turned, and there on the edge of the bush stood a figure so frightful as to be magnificent. His face, like those of the rest of the savages, was framed in a mass of greasy black hair and beard. A bone was thrust through the cartilage of his nose. He wore the large pandanus fiber clout, but there was a difference in his bearing—the difference of a man of conscious power. There was power in his height, in the muscles that rippled under his glossy black skin, in his great shoulders, in the line of his jaw. Two furrows, amazingly deep, lay between his brows, and his eyes showed intelligence, strong will, and cunning. Here was a chief by every right of physical and mental superiority. Here, I knew, was Nagapate.

He stared at us speculatively and moved slowly toward us. His men drew back slightly as he advanced. To my astonishment, at this moment, I heard the purr of the camera crank. Martin was photographing the chief's entrance.

"Remember, darling," his voice was low and quiet, "show no fear—smile —open up the trade stuff."

I shaped my face into what I hoped would pass for a friendly smile. Nagapate was coming straight toward me—was now within three feet.

"Hello, Mr. Nagapate," I said, and held some tobacco out to him. He barely glanced at it.

"Try the calico," Martin said. "Keep it up, sweet, you're doing fine. If we win the chief over everything will be all right. The others take their cue from him."

"Yes. Yes, I know," I said. "I'll try. I'll do my best."

I saw four rings on Nagapate's hands; one a signet ring with a distinct crest. I felt a shudder creeping up my spine, and wondered whether he removed the rings from the fingers of his victims before or after he cooked them.

"Try that piece of red calico," Martin urged, and I clung to the sound of his voice as to the one sane thing left in a world gone grotesquely mad.

"This is a very nice piece of calico," I said loudly and distinctly, holding out the bright cloth to Nagapate. "A very nice color. You would be very handsome in it. It would make a very nice shirt, I think."

Nagapate reached out, but instead of the calico he took my arm; his great hand felt like dry leather.

Martin's quiet voice cut through my terror: "Don't be afraid, Osa. He's just curious, that's all."

Curious! Apparently the whiteness of my skin puzzled the big black man. With guttural grunts he first tried rubbing it off with his finger. This failing, he picked up a bit of rough cane and scraped my skin with it, and was astonished, apparently, when it turned pink. Shaking his head, he then took off my hat and looked at my hair. It was yellow, and I suppose this also puzzled him. He parted it and peered down at my scalp, then he pulled it hard —then he turned me around, tilted my head forward and looked at the back of my neck.

"Try to get him interested in the trade stuff, darling. Put it in his hands." Martin's voice shook a little. I looked at him. The film continued to purr through the camera. He was turning the crank automatically.

I got some tobacco and pushed it into Nagapate's hands. He looked at it then dropped it. I saw Martin rapidly remove the camera from the tripod.

"He won't take it, Martin! What shall I do?"

"Keep cool, darling—and whatever you do, keep smiling."

My husband then stepped between Nagapate and me, and, forcing a grin, clasped the chief's hand and gave it a hearty shake. This puzzled the black tsar. Apparently the gesture was new to him. He didn't like it, and scowled.

Returning look for look with the kingly savage, Martin spoke casually to me: "Get on down that trail with the carriers, Osa, I'll follow. Do as I tell you and hurry."

Nagapate was not to be diverted, however, and caught me as I turned away. He took my hand and shook it just as Martin had shaken his. My relief was so great at what seemingly had turned into a friendly leave-taking, that I laughed and heartily returned the shake. This may have been a mistake. At any rate, when I tried to withdraw my hand, he closed his fist hard upon it, and then began experimentally to pinch and prod my body. I choked back a scream and looked wildly toward Martin. His face was bloodless and fixed in a wooden smile.

Then, unexpectedly, I was released. Nagapate grunted an order and the savages retreated into the bush. Apparently we had won. Martin sharply ordered the carriers to shoulder the apparatus and we dashed for the trail. Whether Nagapate then changed his mind or whether releasing us and then recapturing us was a sort of cat-and-mouse game with the savages, I never knew, but suddenly there was a sharper accent in the beat of the *boo-boos,* our carriers with the apparatus fled at top speed down the trail, and I found myself seized from behind. This time I abandoned all pretense at bravery and screamed my terror. On almost the same instant I heard Martin's voice shouting at me desperately to remember the pistol in my pocket, and then shouting at the blacks to release him. I saw that he also had been seized.

"Martin!" I cried. A savage raked his back with a thorn-bush branch. I turned sick and faint and knew vaguely that I was being dragged backward toward the bush. I screamed again and again. I am no clearer on what happened next than a person is clear on the seeming happenings of a nightmare. I only know that the natives were suddenly quiet and staring down toward the bay. The *boo-boos* were still, and Nagapate stepped once more into the clearing. I followed the direction of his scowling gaze and saw what had silenced them. A British patrol boat was steaming into the bay.

Martin tore from his captors and faced Nagapate.

"Man-o'-war—Man-o'-war—Man-o'-war!" he shouted, threateningly, and his gestures indicated that the patrol boat had come on our behalf.

Nagapate scowled at Martin, only half-believing him, but my husband held his ground, and reluctantly Nagapate grunted an order for our release. Then he withdrew with his men into the bush.

With a sob of relief I started on a run toward the trail, but Martin caught me and held me to a quiet walk until we were well out of sight of that fringe of bush where we knew Nagapate and his men were. Then began our race down the steep path.

Cane grass chopped at our faces. We fell and scrambled up again more times than I could count. In places there were sheer drops to the jungle below of hundreds of feet, but we never slackened for an instant. We both knew, without even speaking of it, that should the gunboat leave the bay, our recapture was certain. To reach our whale boat before that could happen was our only hope.

After what seemed hours, we came to a clearing above the bay and there saw the patrol boat slowly turning and steaming away! Then once more the sound of the *boo-boos*. Nagapate and his savages up on the plateau were also witnessing the departure of the gunboat, and without a doubt the *boo-boos* were the signal for our recapture.

Neither Martin nor I spoke. Dense jungle still lay between us and the beach. We plunged on, the increasingly rapid beat of the *boo-boos* driving us recklessly over the slimy, treacherous trail. Brush tore at our clothing and flesh, but we felt nothing, stopped for nothing. Other than my terror I was aware of but one thing, and that an intolerable thirst. Once I fell in the mud and slime of a morass, but more serious than this was the fact that we had lost our way. Martin pulled me out and held me close, slime and all.

My fall probably saved us, for instead of plunging farther from the trail in our panic, we stood a moment where we were, and, looking around us, discovered the trail only a few feet off. We plunged into it, and I led the way this time because my eyes were sharper than Martin's.

Added to the terrifying sound of the *boo-boos* now were the shouts of the savages. They couldn't have been more than a quarter of a mile behind us. Neither of us spoke, we just ran, with branches and vines like enemy hands clutching at us, but at last the jungle thinned. A few more steps and we were at the beach. The savages were now so close behind us that we could hear the slap of heavy sodden leaves on their bare flesh.

The glare of the sun was almost a physical impact after the deep gloom of the jungle, and the thick sand clogged our feet. Martin took my arm, and I felt his hand shake. Then our carriers ran forward to help us. Soon we felt hard-packed sand under our feet, then shallow water and next, with the hands of the Vao boys reaching out to us, we were dragged across the gunwales of the whale boat. I raised my head and looked back; Nagapate's men were just emerging from the bush. I collapsed in the bottom of the boat, and one of the boys put water to my mouth which I scarcely had the strength to drink. How long Martin and I lay there I don't know, but we were safely out at sea when again we lifted our heads. It was night.

The tropical storm through which we then fought is another story. It is enough to say that when the hard, cool rain first swept down on us I raised my face and hands to it and let it wash off the jungle slime; while Martin, whose exhaustion was no less than mine—for he had had to carry the heavy camera and film during our headlong flight—got to his feet and went to work, glad of the skill he had acquired in handling the *Snark*. My usefulness in what was doubtless a hazardous trip began and ended in bailing our small open boat and protecting our camera and film as best I could. Reaching Vao finally we were gratified to find that we—including our carriers—had clung doggedly to every piece of apparatus and even most of the trade goods, and that the camera and film were unharmed by water.

We had been back at Vao only a few days when the British patrol boat, the *Euphrosyne,* put in with a letter for Martin from the Resident Commissioner for the New Hebrides. It read:

Matanovot, 10th November, 1917

Dear Sir:

I have been endeavoring to find you with a view to warning you against carrying out what I understand to be your intentions. I am told that you have decided to penetrate into the interior of this island with a view to coming in contact with the people known as the "Big Numbers." Such a proceeding cannot but be attended with great risk to yourself and all those who accompany you. The whole interior of this island of Malekula is, and has been for a considerable time, in a very disturbed condition, and it has been necessary in consequence to make two armed demonstrations in the "Big Numbers" country in the last three years. For these reasons, on the part of the Joint Administration of this group, I request that you will not proceed further with this idea, and hereby formally warn you against such persistence, for the consequences of which the Administration cannot hold itself responsible.

Yours faithfully,
(Signed) M. KING

H.B.M. Resident Commissioner for the New Hebrides.

In any case I trust you will not take your wife into the danger zone with you.

M.K.

Editor's Note: The films were perfect, they were processed in Sydney, and in a few months "Nagapate's scowling face was looking from the screen on Broadway's Rialto, New York, and within a year," Mrs. Johnson has recorded, "his face had sent shudders around the civilized world."

South Peak*

SIR JOHN HUNT

✳✳ The "roof of the world," Mount Everest, the highest mountain on earth, with a peak of 29,002 feet, was conquered for the first time, as the world knows, by two men on May 29, 1953. One of the men was a New Zealander, who when he is not climbing mountains, raises bees in the Antipodes; and the other was a Sherpa mountain-climbing guide, Tenzing, who had been up Everest, partway, before.

Many men have been up Everest, partway, since more than 30 years ago the first attempt was made to conquer it. Eleven major expeditions have sunk their crampons in its icy slopes, and some of the climbers got within 1000 feet of the top, only to be forced back, their physical endurance unable to carry them further. Sixteen of the climbers lost their lives.

The day the present queen of England was crowned in London the world was electrified, on this of all days for England, with the first word from the Himalayas that a British group had reached the highest point on the globe.

The Everest conquest was the result of a well-planned expedition, calculated with a hope to eliminate as much of the risk of life as humanly possible through long consideration in advance of the problems the climb would present. The success, Sir John Hunt, the leader, felt, depended "primarily upon the human fact" and the cooperation of "every man in the team," the quality of the planning, and the value of the equipment in meeting the demands of the altitude, weather, and terrain.

Readers of the account of the climb in *The Conquest of Everest,* the book, have been struck with the thoroughness of the advance thinking involved in the expedition. The mountain was taken by assault with planning equivalent to that involved in a gigantic battle. The expedition profited from the lessons of past attempts that had failed. One of the lessons learned was that most other parties had

* From *The Conquest of Everest* by Sir John Hunt, with A Chapter On The Final Assault by Sir Edmund Hillary. Copyright, 1953, by Sir John Hunt. Reprinted by permission of the publishers, E. P. Dutton & Co., New York, and with additional acknowledgment to John Hunt: *"The Ascent of Everest"* based on the original dispatches from Brigadier Sir John Hunt and other members of the Everest Expedition to the *Times,* and published by Hodder & Stoughton, London, England.

made their final assault from a base too low down the mountain and thus had used up their strength, in the most dangerous altitude, over too long a sprint. The expedition had recourse to the latest scientific information and gadgets. Oxygen was utilized and even at one point they had a "walkie-talkie"—or would have had if the batteries had functioned. And they brought back photographs of all the peaks they could see from the top, far down in the world below them.

On November 5, 1952, the names of the men who were to constitute the expedition had been chosen. There were 13: a surgeon from Liverpool, a physicist with the British Ministry of Supply, a director of a travel agency in Blackpool, a bee-keeper from Auckland, New Zealand, and a primary-school teacher from Hastings, N.Z., a young man from the British War Office, a statistician who is ex-president of the Oxford University Mountaineering Club, a recent graduate of Cambridge, a schoolmaster and author, a doctor, a physiologist, and a camera-man—all, of course, men with a background of mountain climbing as a dream or a passion. To this group Colonel Hunt, the leader, added later the Sherpa climber, Tenzing.

On February 12, 1953, the main party and baggage sailed for India. On March 8 the whole expedition assembled at the capital of Nepal, Katmandu, elevation 4200 feet, and on March 10 set out on foot over Nepal's Himalayan watershed, with 350 coolies carrying 473 pieces of baggage weighing seven and a half tons—a 17-day walk to the monastery of Thyangboche, first base camp below the Everest group.

On May 1 Camp IV had been established at 21,200 feet.

On May 26 Tom Bourdillon and Charles Evans, constituting the first assault group, reached the south summit of Everest, higher than man had ever gone on the mountain before, but not the final peak, and returned to Advance Base on May 27.

On May 29 Edmund Hillary and Tenzing reached the summit of Everest.

On June 20 the main party reassembled in the Valley of Nepal at Katmandu.

The summit of Everest was to be attained by teamwork, and for the final assault Colonel Hunt selected two teams of two men each, each team leaving within a few hours of each other from a base camp 21,000 feet up the 29,000-foot mountain. One team consisted of Charles Evans and Tom Bourdillon and the other of Hillary and Tenzing.

Colonel Hunt preceded both potential summit parties with his Sherpa porter Da Namgyal, both men carrying supplies which they planned to leave for either of the advancing parties at a cache on the mountain around 28,000 feet.

As Colonel Hunt and Da Namgyal climbed, they were passed by the less heavily burdened Evans and Bourdillon, and at 27,350 feet Colonel Hunt had to stop, leaving his cache of supplies on a ledge there. His oxygen tube had frozen (as he discovered on the descent) making breathing nearly impossible, and his

Sherpa's strength had given out. "He had reached his limit," he writes, "and I was near enough mine."

As Colonel Hunt and Da Namgyal wearily started down the mountain without oxygen—for they left their own canisters as a reserve for the summit party—they could see, coming up toward the South Col, along the snows of Lhotse Face, the second assault party approaching to join them—"a pleasing sight." This was the party of Edmund Hillary and Tenzing. "I suddenly felt as though the strength was leaving me like water," Colonel Hunt records. "My knees gave way and I collapsed, a ridiculous figure, as they came up. Da Namgyal flopped down also while we were plied with lemonade from Tenzing's flask. Ed (Hillary) helped me toward the tents, but finding that I could not make the distance, hurried off to get his oxygen set. With a boost of six liters a minute, I soon revived—I remember very clearly what a full and free flow I was receiving—and we were able to complete the few remaining yards. I shall never forget their exceeding patience and kindness."

What happened to Bourdillon and Evans, and how this first team almost made the peak and then had to turn back and let the second team, Hillary and Tenzing, struggle on to the peak, and how others in the expedition backed the climbers with supplies and support, establishing the "top camp" No. IX at 27,900 feet, is told by Colonel (now Sir) John Hunt in these extracts from his book. ✳✳

THE FIRST ASSAULT

On reaching the ledge where we had first stood upon the southeast ridge of Everest at 27,200 feet, Tom Bourdillon and Charles Evans were feeling well and confident. They arrived there shortly after 9:00 A.M., having taken one and a half hours to climb 1300 feet; only about the same height had to be covered to reach the south summit. At this rate of progress—almost a thousand feet in one hour—they should have time to spare for the suspected difficulties of that final hidden ridge leading to Everest itself. Best of all, the closed-circuit [oxygen] sets were functioning well, despite the anxiety caused earlier that morning and the fact that Charles' apparatus had perforce been set at the low flow of two liters per minute. Only the weather was unfavorable, but even this was not a serious hindrance. They set off determined and full of hope.

But from this point onward the going became worse. The overlay of fresh snow called for greater care, covering the ledges and making for difficulty in getting a grip with their crampons on the hard surface beneath; they moved much more slowly. In two hours, indeed, they had not covered more than half the distance toward the South Peak. But they had now reached an important landmark. This was the Snow Shoulder, so noticeable a feature when seen from the top of the Geneva Spur. As Tenzing pointed out later, it is probably about the highest place reached during the attempt by himself and Lambert in the spring of 1952. Clouds were all around them, snow was falling and being blown off the ridge.

As they paused on this less steep ground, an awkward problem arose affecting the oxygen equipment. The soda-lime canisters which form a part of the mechanism of the closed-circuit apparatus have an average endurance of approximately three to three and a half hours. They had now been going at least two and a half hours, and the canisters in use might be expected to have at most a further hour of useful life. Each man was carrying a second canister, and it was now a question whether they should change to the fresh ones at this point. By doing so here, they would have the advantage of a fairly spacious resting place, and this did not appear to be available higher up; in fact, the ridge steepened very considerably from this point onward. Equally important was the fact that there is a tendency for the valves in the apparatus to freeze up after a new and cold canister has been connected. This had happened only three days before, when they had introduced new canisters at Camp VI on their way up to the South Col.* The risk would be better faced here than on top of the south summit, where a breakdown of this nature might have very serious consequences. Against these arguments was the objection that by rejecting the canisters in use they would be wasting the endurance of their oxygen equipment and would thus shorten their day. If I have gone into this problem in some detail, it is merely to stress what a dilemma it must have been for Charles and Tom, at 28,000 feet on the southeast ridge of Everest, hardly the most congenial place in which to consider and discuss such a nicely balanced problem, especially wearing oxygen masks.

They decided to change the canisters, and went on. Charles was now having trouble again with his set, resulting in rapid, labored breathing, which may or may not have been due to the new canister; he was making a tremendous and gallant effort to keep going. They arrived at the foot of the final steep rise, a great slope tilted abruptly at a high angle sweeping up toward the South Peak. The snow was unstable, a fragile crust overlying loose deep snow underneath, and Tom, who was ahead at this point, suspected its safety. Away to the left were rocks, bordering the South Face where it falls away toward the western brink of the South Col. They traversed across to these, half-expecting the slope to break away beneath them. The angle of the rocks was also steep and they were somewhat crumbling, but the strata dip favorably to the climber on this side of the mountain, and the ledges, small

* Depression in a mountain chain; a pass. South Col is a pass between the peaks of Everest and Lhotse.

though they were, tilted so as to provide accommodating holds. On and on, up those last 400 feet they climbed, very slowly now, Charles in considerable trouble with his breathing, but determined not to give up. Then quite suddenly the angle eased, and almost at once they found themselves standing upon the South Peak of Everest, at over 28,700 feet. It was one o'clock. Charles Evans and Tom Bourdillon had climbed higher on Everest by many hundreds of feet than anyone had ever climbed before. Better still, they had reached the highest summit so far climbed.

Clouds were all around them, obscuring the view, adhering like a banner to the tremendous eastern precipice falling away from the final ridge toward the Kangshung valley. But that final ridge was clear, and they were now gazing upon a problem which had intrigued all mountaineers and which we especially had all been longing to see. It was not encouraging. Viewed thus, end on, it is narrow and apparently rising steeply. On the left it falls sharply away to the edge of the rocks topping the west face of the mountain, which drops sheer 8000 feet into the Cwm* above our Advance Base. On the right, or east, is an even more abrupt precipice of even greater height, masked now by cloud. Huge bulges of snow hung over it from the crest of the ridge, cornices of Himalayan dimensions formed by the prevailing westerly wind.

Should they go on? For them here was a unique chance to climb to the top. But unless it were to be a one-way journey, it obviously depended on the factors of time and weather; the question of time was directly linked with that of their oxygen supply. Unless they had sufficient oxygen to last the traverse along the ridge both ways and also to descend the ridge by which they had climbed, it was not feasible. To estimate the time required to climb an unknown ridge, seen foreshortened in this way so that you cannot be sure the farthest visible point is the summit, is not easy. Charles reckoned that it might take three hours to the top, another two hours back to the South Peak. At that rate they would long since have exhausted their remaining oxygen supply and, even had they been able to return to the South Peak without it, they would not be back there until 6:00 P.M., with nearly 3000 feet to descend to safety. In fact, it was out of the question.

Yet it was with some reluctance that they turned to go down. Both were now very tired, emphasizing, if any further persuasion had been needed, the futility of going on toward the summit of the mountain. The trouble with Charles' set persisted and they stopped while Tom adapted it for use on the open-circuit principle—a remarkable feat this, at that height and after all they had done already. Later, they had to stop again and change back to closed-

* Cwm, pronounced "Coom," is an enclosed valley on the flank of a hill; i.e., Western Cwm is the bowl-like depression forming Everest's western flank.

circuit, as Charles had been receiving rather less benefit still. They did not fancy the small ledges on those steep rocks and took a chance now on the snow slope to the left, sinking deeply into it through the crust, but probably too tired to think of the possible consequences. The descent of 1500 feet to the Swiss tent took them about two hours. Their state of exhaustion is shown by the fact that, sound climbers as both of them are, they slipped on a number of occasions on the technically easy part of the ridge above this tent. It was about 3:30 P.M. when they arrived there.

Then they, like Da Namgyal and myself a few hours before, had to face the couloir. They, too, took the usual precautions, but they were understandably more groggy than we had been. Tom led down and had just reached the end of the rope and fixed his ax as a belay when Charles came hurtling down the slope from behind, to quote Tom, "like a bullet." As the rope tightened around Tom's ax it was wrenched out of the snow and Tom was dragged from his steps, sliding with gathering speed down the hard surface of the couloir. But the jerk on the rope as the ax checked it had slowed Charles' fall. Tom instinctively took the correct action, turning onto his stomach and jabbing the pick of his ax above him into the snow as a brake. They came to a stop, waited to recover, and started on down again.

On the Col, I was resting in the "blister" tent, talking to Tenzing. George Lowe suddenly put his head through the entrance. He was tremendously excited; he was jubilant. "They're up: by God they're up!" he shouted. This was indeed electrifying news, quite sufficient to banish the weariness of my own efforts that day. Everyone was overjoyed. The Sherpas, toiling up toward the top of the Geneva Spur behind Gregory and Lowe, were no less thrilled than ourselves. Indeed, perhaps more so, for they were under the impression that the peak rising from the South Col was in fact the highest point. They believed that Everest had been climbed. When they reached the tents, Ang Nyima turned to me and said in slang Hindi: *"Everest khatm ho gya, Sahib,"* which in equally slang English may be translated, "Everest has had it." For them the spectacle had been particularly dramatic. They had been watching our progress all that morning while they were crossing the slopes of the Lhotse Face, but Bourdillon and Evans had been hidden for some time by the clouds which now screened the mountain. At about one o'clock there was a break in the mists around the sharp snow cone of the South Peak and upon it, like insects on a wall, two little dots could be seen. They climbed steadily up that forbidding, impossibly steep-looking snow slope and soon disappeared over the top. It was as if they did not trouble to stop, intent on going farther to the utmost point beyond.

We spent an anxious afternoon, with a lurking uncertainty lest Charles and Tom might not return. The clouds completely obscured the ridge and the wind had increased in strength. At 3:30 P.M. there was a thinning of the cloud at the top of the couloir, and there they were. They came down slowly and we prepared to receive them. At 4:30 they approached the tents and we went out to meet them, burdened with their cumbersome equipment and bulky clothing, their faces frost-covered, looking like strangers from another planet. Both were utterly weary.

Later they told us the story I have just narrated: the story of the first ascent of the South Peak of Everest. It was natural that disappointment should have been among their feelings, to get so near the ultimate goal and then be denied it. Yet it must be remembered that they had achieved exactly what had been hoped of them. I had been insistent that the South Peak was the objective and that, by reaching it, they would provide invaluable information to the second summit pair; indeed, the two assaults were intended to be complementary. Their feat in climbing to over 28,700 feet and back in one day from the South Col was a magnificent effort, and a triumph also for the oxygen equipment on which such infinite pains had been taken. They had sighted that last part of the ridge and were able to describe it to Tenzing and Hillary. They had given us all, by their example, incalculable confidence in final victory.

With the second assault party and their extra stores safely arrived on the South Col, preparations were made for their departure next day up the southeast ridge.

First, the Sherpas who had accompanied them, bringing up these stores, got ready to go down. Da Namgyal decided to join them, in spite of his outstanding and exhausting effort that day, and Balu also left. They were a heroic little band, whose names deserve to be specially recorded in this story of the ascent of Everest: Dawa Thondup, approaching his fifties; Da Tensing, another veteran; Topkie, a mere boy who had sometimes exasperated us in the Icefall and the Cwm by his carelessness and his irritating cough, yet with the heart of a lion; Ang Norbu, sturdy and unshakable; the jaunty Annullu, whose pace was like that of "a fast Swiss guide." For all these men save Da Tensing, this was their second trip to the South Col during this expedition. Da Tensing himself had done exceptional, skilled, and strenuous work with Lowe on the Lhotse Face and had made yet another of his many journeys to Camp VII on the day the first assault party had gone up there. No praise is too high for them.

George Lowe had escorted them up and now asked to stay to assist in the "carry" of stores to the top camp. This I very gladly agreed to. Of the three special Sherpas accompanying this second party, the team to carry the stores up to Camp IX, only one now appeared likely to be fit to continue. This was Ang Nyima, already renowned among us for his work with Lowe in the early days of preparing the Lhotse Face. The other two, Ang Temba and Pemba, my orderly during the march-out, were both feeling ill on arrival. In the second support team, too, it would be necessary for the climbers to become porters.

We were overcrowded that evening at Camp VIII. The Pyramid was occupied by the four members of the second assault party, while we of the first party, having finished our effort, occupied the Meade, designed for two. The three remaining Sherpas of the second support team somehow managed to squeeze into the tiny "blister" tent. It was a terrible night. For Hillary it was "one of the worst nights I have ever experienced." For those of us whose third night it was on the South Col, packed like sardines, managing without oxygen and exhausted after climbing high on the mountain throughout that day, it was a nightmare. The thermometer indicated –25° C, and the wind, which had been strong all day long, now rose again to gale force. Pressed as we were against the walls of the tents, it was as if we had no protection at all. Constantly buffeted throughout the night, there could be no question of sleep. It continued hour after hour, adding greatly to our existing state of weariness. On the morning of May 27, there was no longer any doubt that the first assault party was in very poor shape indeed, especially, I think, Tom Bourdillon.

My diary for this day reads as follows:

"It was no surprise to find at about 8:00 A.M. that Ed's* party had not started. The wind was blowing like mad, so much so that it was a nightmare to go out of the tent. A scene of wild confusion reigned around Everest, which was shrouded in cloud with snow being torn from the southeast ridge. We huddled into the Pyramid and discussed the situation while Tenzing made some attempt to work the Primus—of the other Sherpas, only Ang Nyima showed any sign of life. A postponement of 24 hours was imperative; fortunately we have stockpiled enough to make this possible and the important thing is to keep up our strength by eating and drinking enough. For me, this is my third day spent on or above the Col, and I've had three nights of it. It is interesting to compare our condition with that of the Swiss who spent a similar period here last year, and who scarcely got down alive. Here are we, well supplied with food, fuel, and oxygen, sitting at 26,000 feet almost as if at base.

* Edmund Hillary.

"At about midday Charles [Evans] and Tom [Bourdillon] started off on their way down. Then Charles suddenly reappeared with the alarming news that Tom could not get up the slope to the top of the Éperon [Spur] and was in a critical state. Another of us must accompany him down if he were to get down alive. Here was another difficult decision. My post was here on the Col, to see the big assault safely launched and decide, if need be, on a further postponement or, possibly, a withdrawal. Yet I was supporting the first assault, and by sending either Greg [Alfred Gregory] or George [Lowe] would only weaken the second assault's chances. I decided I must go. So I rapidly packed, with much willing help, and plodded very slowly up the slopes of the Spur, Ed [Hillary] carrying my sack.

"Left Ed with parting instruction not to give in if avoidable, and promising to send up a reinforcement party. We (Charles, Tom, Ang Temba, and self) started slowly—so painfully slowly—down the couloir and across the big slopes beneath Lhotse. We halted frequently and for long intervals, for Tom, and to a less extent Ang Temba, were barely in control of their legs. I led, Charles brought up the rear. So it went on until, very nearly at the end of our strength (except, perhaps, Charles), we staggered down the last few feet to Camp VII. To our relief and delight, here we were met by Wilf Noyce and Mike Ward, who helped us in. Just as we were coming down the ice pitch above Camp, Temba slipped and fell into the big crevasse. He was held by Charles, and Wilf managed to remove his sack (he was upside down) and get him up. It is indicative of my state of exhaustion that I could not find strength to lift a finger throughout this incident."

Wilfrid Noyce's presence at Camp VII was very fortunate. Without him, Tom Bourdillon, Ang Temba, and I could not have managed for ourselves that evening; he looked after us like a nurse and prepared our supper. Moreover, he was halfway to the Col and, unbeknown to him, I had told Ed Hillary before leaving there that I would send up Noyce and three more volunteer Sherpas with further stores, in order to enable them to stay out yet another day of bad weather if necessary. I also had in mind that Noyce and one or more of these men might replace any casualties up there and thus take part in the second assault. So it was that Charles Evans, who found the energy to continue on down with Michael Ward to Advance Base the same evening, was to arrange for three men to come up and join Noyce here at Camp VII on May 28.

Tom and I descended to the Cwm next morning. On the way we met Charles Wylie with the three Sherpas. Wylie had rightly decided that they should not go up to the Lhotse Face unaccompanied, and he had also felt that this camp should be occupied until the return of Hillary's party. These roles he took upon himself: a great contribution to the sound conduct of the assault. It is typical of Charles that as he passed I noticed in his bulky load an assault oxygen bottle. This and other items of replenishment he had taken over from a fourth Sherpa who should have been with the party, but who had not been able to go beyond Camp V. He was, of course, climbing without oxygen.

We reached Advance Base in the early afternoon, our immediate task completed. There was nothing for us now to do but await the outcome of the second assault.

THE SUMMIT

SIR EDMUND HILLARY

Early on the morning of May 27, I awoke from an uneasy sleep feeling very cold and miserable. We were on the South Col of Everest. My companions in our Pyramid tent, Lowe, Gregory, and Tenzing, were all tossing and turning in unsuccessful efforts to gain relief from the bitter cold. The relentless wind was blowing in all its fury and the constant loud drumming on the tent made deep sleep impossible. Reluctantly removing my hand from my sleeping bag, I looked at my watch. It was 4:00 A.M. In the flickering light of a match, the thermometer lying against the tent wall read −25° C.

We had hoped to establish a camp high on the southeast ridge that day, but the force of the wind obviously made a start impossible. We must, however, be prepared to go on if the wind should drop. I nudged the uncomplaining Tenzing with my elbow and murmured a few words about food and drink, then callously snuggled my way back into my bag again. Soon the purring of the Primus and the general warming of the atmosphere stirred us into life and while we munched biscuits and drank hot water flavored with lemon crystals and heaps of sugar, Lowe, Gregory, and I discussed rather pessimistically our plans for the day.

At 9:00 A.M. the wind was still blowing fiercely, and clad in all my warm clothing I crawled out of the tent and crossed to the small Meade tent housing John Hunt, Charles Evans, and Tom Bourdillon. Hunt agreed that any start under these conditions was impossible. Ang Temba had become sick and was obviously incapable of carrying up any farther. So we decided to send him down with Evans and Bourdillon when they left for Camp VII about midday. Hunt decided at the last moment to accompany this party, owing to Bourdillon's condition, and Lowe and I assisted a very weary foursome to climb the slopes above the camp and then watched them start off on their slow and exhausting trip down to Camp VII.

All day the wind blew furiously and it was in a somewhat desperate spirit that we organized the loads for the establishment of the ridge camp on the following day. Any delay in our departure from the South Col could only result in increased deterioration and consequent weakness. The violent wind gave us another unpleasant night, but we were all breathing oxygen at one liter per minute and this enabled us to doze uneasily for seven or eight hours.

Early in the morning the wind was still blowing strongly, but about 8:00 A.M. it eased considerably and we decided to leave. However, another blow had fallen—Pemba had been violently ill all night and was obviously not capable of going on. Only one Sherpa porter, Ang Nyima, was left to carry for us out of our original band of three. Our only alternative was to carry the camp ourselves, as to abandon the attempt was unthinkable. We repacked the loads, eliminating anything not vitally necessary and having no choice because of our reduced manpower but to cut down vital supplies of oxygen.

At 8:45 A.M. Lowe, Gregory, and Ang Nyima departed, all carrying over 40 pounds each and breathing oxygen at four liters a minute. Tenzing and I were to leave later so that we could follow quickly up the steps made by the other party and so conserve energy and oxygen. We loaded all our personal clothing, sleeping bags, and air mattresses, together with some food, onto our oxygen sets and left at 10:00 A.M., carrying 50 pounds apiece.

We followed slowly up the long slopes to the foot of the great couloir and then climbed the veritable staircase hewn by Lowe in the firm, steep snow of the couloir. As we moved slowly up the steps we were bombarded by a constant stream of ice chips falling from well above us where Lowe and Gregory were cutting steps across to the southeast ridge. We reached the ridge at midday and joined the other party. Nearby was the tattered ruin of the Swiss tent of the previous spring, and it added an air of loneliness and desolation to this remarkable viewpoint. From here Lambert and Tenzing had made their gallant attempt to reach the summit after a night spent without sleeping bags.

It was a wonderful spot with tremendous views in every direction and we indulged in an orgy of photography. We were all feeling extremely well and felt confident of placing our camp high up on the southeast ridge. We heaved on our loads again and moved 150 feet up the ridge to the dump made by Hunt two days previously. The ridge was quite steep, but the upward-sloping strata of the rocks gave us quite good footholds and the climbing was not technically difficult, although loose snow over the steep rocks demanded care. The dump was at 27,350 feet, but we considered that this was still far too low for an effective summit camp, so somewhat reluctantly we added all this extra gear to our already large loads. Gregory took some more oxygen, Lowe some food and fuel, and I tied on a tent. Apart from Ang Nyima, who was carrying just over 40 pounds, we all had loads of from 50 to 63 pounds. We continued on up the ridge at a somewhat reduced rate. Despite our great burdens we were moving steadily, though very slowly. The ridge steepened onto a slope of firm snow and Lowe chipped steps up it for 50 feet. By 2:00 P.M. we were beginning to tire and started looking for a camp site. The ridge appeared to have no relief at all and continued upward in one unbroken sweep. We plugged slowly on, looking for a ledge without success. Again and again we hopefully labored up to a prospective site only to find that it was still at a 45-degree angle. We were getting a little desperate until Tenzing, remembering the ground from the previous year, suggested a traverse over steep slopes to the left, which finally landed us onto a relatively flat spot beneath a rock bluff.

It was two-thirty and we decided to camp here. All day the magnificent peak of Lhotse had commanded our attention, but now its summit was just below us. We estimated our height at 27,900 feet. Lowe, Gregory, and Ang Nyima dropped their loads on the site with relief. They were tired but well satisfied with the height gained, and to them must go a great deal of the credit for the successful climb of the following day. Wasting no time, they hurried off back to the South Col.

It was with a certain feeling of loneliness that we watched our cheerful companions slowly descending the ridge, but we had much to do. We removed our oxygen sets in order to conserve our supplies and set to work with our ice axes to clear the tiny platform. We scratched off all the snow to reveal a rock slope at an angle of some 30 degrees. The rocks were well frozen in, but by the end of a couple of hours' solid work we had managed to pry loose sufficient stones to level out two strips of ground a yard wide and six feet long, but almost a foot different in levels. Even though not breathing oxygen, we could still work quite hard, but rested every ten minutes or so in order to regain our breath and energy. We pitched our tent on this double level and tied it down as best we could. There were no suitable rocks around which to hitch our tent guys, and the snow was far too soft to hold aluminum tent pegs. We sank several of our oxygen bottles in the soft snow and attached the guys to these as a somewhat unreliable anchor. Then while Tenzing began heating some soup I made a tally of our limited oxygen supplies. They were much less than we had hoped. For the assault we had only one and two-thirds bottles each. It was obvious that if we were to have sufficient endurance we would be unable to use the four liters per minute that we had originally planned, but I estimated that if we reduced our supplies to three liters per minute we might still have a chance. I prepared the sets and made the necessary adjustments. One thing in our favor was that Evans and Bourdillon had left two bottles of oxygen, still one third full, some hundreds of feet above our camp. We were relying on this oxygen to get us back to the South Col.

As the sun set we crawled finally into our tent, put on all our warm clothing and wriggled into our sleeping bags. We drank vast quantities of liquid and had a satisfying meal out of our store of delicacies: sardines on biscuits, canned apricots, dates, and biscuits and jam and honey. The canned apricots were a great treat, but it was necessary first to thaw them out of their frozen state over our roaring Primus. In spite of the great height, our breathing was almost normal until a sudden exertion would cause us to pant a little. Tenzing laid his air mattress on the lower shelf half-overhanging the steep slope below and calmly settled down to sleep. I made myself as comfortable as possible half-sitting and half-reclining on the upper shelf with my feet braced on the lower shelf. This position, while not particularly comfortable, had decided advantages. We had been experiencing extremely strong gusts of wind every ten minutes, and whenever I received warning of the approach of such a gust by a shrilling whine high on the ridge above, I could brace my feet and shoulders and assist our meager anchors to hold the tent steady while it temporarily shook and flapped in a most alarming manner. We had sufficient oxygen for only four hours' sleep at one liter per minute. I decided to use this in two periods of two hours, from 9:00 to 11:00 P.M. and from 1:00 to 3:00 A.M. While wearing the oxygen we dozed and were reasonably comfortable, but as soon as the supply ran out we began to feel cold and miserable. During the night the thermometer read −27° C, but fortunately the wind had dropped almost entirely.

At 4:00 A.M. it was very still. I opened the tent door and looked far out across the dark and sleeping valleys of Nepal. The icy peaks below us were glowing clearly in the early-morning light and Tenzing pointed out the monastery of Thyangboche, faintly visible on its dominant spur 16,000 feet below us. It was an encouraging thought to realize that even at this early hour the lamas of Thyangboche would be offering up devotions to their Buddhist gods for our safety and well-being.

We started up our cooker and in a determined effort to prevent the weaknesses arising from dehydration we drank large quantities of lemon juice and sugar, and followed this with our last can of sardines on biscuits. I dragged our oxygen sets into the tent, cleaned the ice off them and then completely rechecked and tested them. I had removed my boots, which had become a little wet the day before, and they were now frozen solid. Drastic measures were called for, so I cooked them over the fierce flame of the Primus and despite the very strong smell of burning leather managed to soften them up. Over our down clothing we donned our windproofs and onto our hands we pulled three pairs of gloves—silk, woolen, and windproof.

At 6:30 A.M. we crawled out of our tent into the snow, hoisted our 30 pounds of oxygen gear onto our backs, connected up our masks, and turned on the valves to bring life-giving oxygen into our lungs. A few good deep breaths and we were ready to go. Still a little worried about my cold feet, I asked Tenzing to move off and he kicked a deep line of steps away from the rock bluff which protected our tent, out onto the steep powder snow slope to the left of the main ridge. The ridge was now all bathed in sunlight and we could see our first objective, the south summit, far above us. Tenzing, moving purposefully, kicked steps in a long traverse back toward the ridge and we reached its crest just where it forms a great distinctive snow bump at about 28,000 feet. From here the ridge narrowed to a knife-edge and as my feet were now warm I took over the lead.

We were moving slowly but steadily and had no need to stop in order to regain our breath, and I felt that we had plenty in reserve. The soft, unstable snow made a route on top of the ridge both difficult and dangerous, so I moved a little down on the steep left side where the wind had produced a thin crust which sometimes held my weight but more often than not gave way with a sudden knock that was disastrous to both balance and morale. After several hundred feet of this rather trying ridge, we came to a tiny hollow and found there the two oxygen bottles left on the earlier attempt by Evans and Bourdillon. I scraped the ice off the gauges and was greatly relieved to find that they still contained several hundred liters of oxygen—sufficient to get us down to the South Col if used very sparingly. With the comforting thought of these oxygen bottles behind us, I continued making the trail on up the ridge, which soon steepened and broadened into the very formidable snow face leading up for the last 400 feet to the southern summit. The snow conditions on this face were, we felt, distinctly dangerous, but as no alternative route seemed available, we persisted in our strenuous and uncomfortable efforts to beat a trail up it. We made frequent changes of lead on this very trying section and on one occasion as I was stamping a trail in the deep snow a section around me gave way and I slipped back through three or four of my steps. I discussed with Tenzing the advisability of going on and he, although admitting that he felt very unhappy about the snow conditions, finished with his familiar phrase, "Just as you wish." I decided to go on.

It was with some relief that we finally reached some firmer snow higher up and then chipped steps up the last steep slopes and cramponed on to the South Peak. It was now 9:00 A.M. We looked with some interest at the virgin ridge ahead. Both Bourdillon and Evans had been depressingly definite about its problems and difficulties and we realized that it could form an almost insuperable barrier. At first glance it was certainly impressive and even rather frightening. On the right, great contorted cornices, overhanging masses of snow and ice, stuck out like twisted fingers over the 10,000-foot drop of the Kangshung Face. Any move onto these cornices could only bring disaster. From the cornices the ridge dropped steeply to the left until the snow merged with the great rock face sweeping up from the Western Cwm. Only one encouraging feature was apparent. The steep snow slope between the cornices and the rock precipices seemed to be composed of firm, hard snow. If the snow proved soft and unstable, our chances of getting along the ridge were few indeed. If we could cut a trail of steps along this slope, we could make some progress at least.

We cut a seat for ourselves just below the south summit and removed our oxygen. Once again I worked out the mental arithmetic that was one of my main preoccupations on the way up and down the mountain. As our first partly full bottle of oxygen was now exhausted, we had only one full bottle left. Eight hundred liters of oxygen at three liters per minute? How long could we last? I estimated that this should give us four and a half hours of going. Our apparatus was now much lighter, weighing just over 20 pounds, and as I cut steps down off the south summit I felt a distinct sense of freedom and well-being quite contrary to what I had expected at this great altitude.

As my ice ax bit into the first steep slope of the ridge, my highest hopes were realized. The snow was crystalline and firm. Two or three rhythmical blows of the ice ax produced a step large enough even for our oversized high-altitude boots and, the most encouraging feature of all, a firm thrust of the ice ax would sink it halfway up the shaft, giving a solid and comfortable belay. We moved one at a time. I realized that our margin of safety at this altitude was not great and that we must take every care and precaution. I would cut a 40-foot line of steps, Tenzing belaying me while I worked. Then in turn I would sink my shaft and put a few loops of the rope around it and Tenzing, protected against a breaking step, would move up to me. Then once again as he belayed me I would go on cutting. In a number of places the overhanging ice cornices were very large indeed and in order to escape them I cut a line of steps down to where the snow met the rocks on the west. It was a great thrill to look straight down this enormous rock face and to see, 8000 feet below us, the tiny tents of Camp IV in the Western Cwm. Scrambling on the rocks and cutting handholds on the snow, we were able to shuffle past these difficult portions.

On one of these occasions I noted that Tenzing, who had been going quite well, had suddenly slowed up considerably and seemed to be breathing with difficulty. The Sherpas had little idea of the workings of an oxygen set, and from past experience I immediately suspected his oxygen supply. I noticed that hanging from the exhaust tube of his oxygen mask were icicles, and on closer examination found that this tube, some two inches in diameter, was completely blocked with ice. I was able to clear it out and gave him much-needed relief. On checking my own set I found that the same thing was oc-curring, though it had not reached the stage to have caused me any discom-fort. From then on I kept a much closer check on this problem.

The weather for Everest seemed practically perfect. Insulated as we were in all our down clothing and windproofs, we suffered no discomfort from cold or wind. However, on one occasion I removed my sunglasses to exam-ine more closely a difficult section of the ridge but was very soon blinded by the fine snow driven by the bitter wind and hastily replaced them. I went on cutting steps. To my surprise I was enjoying the climb as much as I had ever enjoyed a fine ridge in my own New Zealand Alps.

After an hour's steady going we reached the foot of the most formidable-looking problem on the ridge—a rock step some 40 feet high. We had known of the existence of this step from aerial photographs and had also seen it through our binoculars from Thyangboche. We realized that at this altitude it might well spell the difference between success and failure. The rock itself, smooth and almost holdless, might have been an interesting Sunday after-noon problem to a group of expert rock climbers in the Lake District, but here it was a barrier beyond our feeble strength to overcome. I could see no way of turning it on the steep rock bluff on the west, but fortunately another possibility of tackling it still remained. On its east side was another great cornice and running up the full 40 feet of the step was a narrow crack be-tween the cornice and the rock. Leaving Tenzing to belay me as best he could, I jammed my way into this crack, then kicking backward with my crampons I sank their spikes deep into the frozen snow behind me and lev-ered myself off the ground. Taking advantage of every little rock hold and all the force of knee, shoulder, and arms I could muster, I literally cram-poned backward up the crack, with a fervent prayer that the cornice would remain attached to the rock. Despite the considerable effort involved, my progress although slow was steady, and as Tenzing paid out the rope I inched my way upward until I could finally reach over the top of the rock and drag myself out of the crack onto a wide ledge. For a few moments I lay regaining my breath and for the first time really felt the fierce determination that nothing now could stop our reaching the top. I took a firm stance on the ledge and signaled to Tenzing to come on up. As I heaved hard on the rope Tenzing wriggled his way up the crack and finally collapsed exhausted at the top like a giant fish when it has just been hauled from the sea after a terrible struggle.

I checked both our oxygen sets and roughly calculated our flow rates. Everything seemed to be going well. Probably owing to the strain imposed on him by the trouble with his oxygen set, Tenzing had been moving rather slowly but he was climbing safely, and this was the major consideration. His only comment on my inquiring of his condition was to smile and wave along the ridge. We were going so well at three liters per minute that I was determined now if necessary to cut down our flow rate to two liters per minute if the extra endurance was required.

The ridge continued as before. Giant cornices* on the right, steep rock slopes on the left. I went on cutting steps on the narrow strip of snow. The ridge curved away to the right and we had no idea where the top was. As I cut around the back of one hump, another higher one would swing into view. Time was passing and the ridge seemed never-ending. In one place where the angle of the ridge had eased off, I tried cramponing without cutting steps, hoping this would save time, but I quickly realized that our margin of safety on these steep slopes at this altitude was too small, so I went on step-cutting. I was beginning to tire a little now. I had been cutting steps continuously for two hours, and Tenzing, too, was moving very slowly. As I chipped steps around still another corner, I wondered rather dully just how long we could keep it up. Our original zest had now quite gone and it was turning more into a grim struggle. I then realized that the ridge ahead, instead of still monotonously rising, now dropped sharply away, and far below I could see the North Col and the Rongbuk Glacier. I looked upward to see a narrow snow ridge running up to a snowy summit. A few more whacks of the ice ax in the firm snow and we stood on top.

My initial feelings were of relief—relief that there were no more steps to cut —no more ridges to traverse and no more humps to tantalize us with hopes of success. I looked at Tenzing and in spite of the balaclava, goggles, and oxygen mask all encrusted with long icicles that concealed his face, there was no

* Masses of drifted snow clinging to and overhanging the crest of a ridge.

disguising his infectious grin of pure delight as he looked all around him. We shook hands and then Tenzing threw his arm around my shoulders and we thumped each other on the back until we were almost breathless. It was 11:30 A.M. The ridge had taken us two and a half hours, but it seemed like a lifetime. I turned off the oxygen and removed my set. I had carried my camera, loaded with color film, inside my shirt to keep it warm, so I now produced it and got Tenzing to pose on top for me, waving his ax on which was a string of flags—British, Nepalese, United Nations, and Indian. Then I turned my attention to the great stretch of country lying below us in every direction.

To the east was our giant neighbor Makalu, unexplored and unclimbed, and even on top of Everest the mountaineering instinct was sufficiently strong to cause me to spend some moments conjecturing as to whether a route up that mountain might not exist. Far away across the clouds the great bulk of Kangchenjunga loomed on the horizon. To the west, Cho Oyu, our old adversary from 1952, dominated the scene and we could see the great unexplored ranges of Nepal stretching off into the distance. The most important photograph, I felt, was a shot down the north ridge, showing the North Col and the old route which had been made famous by the struggles of those great climbers of the 1920's and 1930's. I had little hope of the results being particularly successful, as I had a lot of difficulty in holding the camera steady in my clumsy gloves, but I felt that they would at least serve as a record. After some ten minutes of this, I realized that I was becoming rather clumsy-fingered and slow-moving, so I quickly replaced my oxygen set and experienced once more the stimulating effect of even a few liters of oxygen. Meanwhile, Tenzing had made a little hole in the snow and in it he placed various small articles of food—a bar of chocolate, a packet of biscuits, and a handful of candies. Small offerings, indeed, but at least a token gift to the gods that all devout Buddhists believe have their home on this lofty summit. While we were together on the South Col two days before, Hunt had given me a small crucifix which he had asked me to take to the top. I, too, made a hole in the snow and placed the crucifix beside Tenzing's gifts.

I checked our oxygen once again and worked out our endurance. We would have to move fast in order to reach our life-saving reserve below the south summit. After fifteen minutes we turned to go. We had looked briefly for any signs of Mallory and Irvine, but had seen nothing. We both felt a little tired, for the reaction was setting in and we must get off the mountain quickly. I moved down off the summit onto our steps. Wasting no time, we cramponed along our tracks, spurred by the urgency of diminishing oxygen. Bump followed bump in rapid succession. In what seemed almost miraculous time, we reached the top of the rock step. Now, with the almost casual indifference of familiarity, we kicked and jammed our way down it again. We were tired, but not too tired to be careful. We scrambled cautiously over the rock traverse, moved one at a time over shaky snow sections and finally cramponed up our steps and back onto the South Peak.

Only one hour from the top! A swig of sweetened lemonade refreshed us and we turned down again. Throughout the climb we had a constant nagging fear of our return down the great snow slope, and as I led down I packed each step with as much care as if our lives depended on it, as well they might. The terrific impression of exposure as we looked straight down onto the Kangshung glacier, still 10,000 feet below us, made us move with the greatest caution, and every step down seemed a step nearer safety. When we finally moved off the slope onto the ridge below, we looked at each other and without speaking we both almost visibly shrugged off the sense of fear that had been with us all day.

We were now very tired but moved automatically down to the two reserve cylinders on the ridge. As we were only a short distance from camp and had a few liters of oxygen left in our own bottles, we carried the extra cylinders down our tracks and reached our tent on its crazy platform at 2:00 P.M. Already the moderate winds of the afternoon had wrenched the tent loose from some of its fastenings and it presented a forlorn sight. We had still to reach the South Col. While Tenzing lit the kerosene stove and began to make a lemonade drink heavily sweetened with sugar, I changed our oxygen sets onto the last partly filled bottles and cut down our flow rates to two liters per minute. In contrast to the previous day, when we were working vigorously without oxygen at this camp, we now felt very weak and exhausted. Far below on the South Col we could see minute figures moving and knew that Lowe and Noyce would be waiting for our descent. We had no extra sleeping bags and air mattresses on the South Col, so reluctantly tied our own onto our oxygen frames. Then with a last look at the camp that had served us so well we turned downward with dragging feet and set ourselves to the task of safely descending the ridge.

Our faculties seemed numbed and the time passed as in a dream, but finally we reached the site of the Swiss Ridge Camp and branched off on our last stage down onto the great couloir. There an unpleasant surprise greeted us. The strong wind which had been blowing in the latter part of our climb had completely wiped out all our steps and only a hard, steep, frozen slope lay before us. There was no alternative but to start cutting again. With a grunt of disgust I chipped steps laboriously downward for 200 feet. Gusts of driving wind whirling down off the ridge tried to pluck us from our steps

Tenzing took over the lead and cut down another 100 feet, then moved into softer snow, and kicked a track down the easier slopes at the bottom of the couloir. We cramponed wearily down the long slopes above the South Col.

A figure came toward us and met us a couple of hundred feet above the camp. It was George Lowe, laden with hot soup and emergency oxygen.

We were too tired to make any response to Lowe's enthusiastic acceptance of our news. We stumped down to the Col and slowly ground our way up the short rise to the camp. Just short of the tents my oxygen ran out. We had had enough to do the job, but by no means too much. We crawled into the tent and with a sigh of sheer delight collapsed into our sleeping bags, while the tents flapped and shook under the perpetual South Col gale. That night, our last on the South Col, was a restless one indeed. The bitter cold once again made any deep and restful sleep impossible and the stimulating effects of our success made us so mentally active that we lay there for half the night reliving all the exciting incidents and murmuring to each other between chattering teeth. Early the following morning we were all very weak and made slow but determined preparations for our departure.

The 200-foot slope above the South Col was a great trial, and even when we commenced the long traverse down toward Camp VII we found it necessary to move very slowly and to have frequent rests. The upper part of the Lhotse glacier seemed very steep to us and as we came down the ice steps toward Camp VII our main wish was to rest. We were only thirty yards from the camp when a cheerful shout attracted our attention and there to greet us were Charles Wylie and several of the Sherpas, all looking fresh and strong and with the same question trembling on their lips. The hot drinks they pressed into our hands and their joyful acceptance of our news were a great stimulant in themselves and we continued on down the Lhotse glacier mentally if not physically refreshed.

As we approached Camp IV, tiny figures appeared from the tents and slowly drifted up the track. We made no signal to them but wearily moved down the track toward them. When only fifty yards away, Lowe with characteristic enthusiasm gave the "thumbs up" signal and waved his ice ax in the direction of the summit. Immediately the scene was galvanized into activity and our approaching companions, forgetting their weakness, ran up the snow toward us. As we greeted them all, perhaps a little emotionally, I felt more than ever before that very strong feeling of friendship and cooperation that had been the decisive factor throughout the expedition.

What a thrill it was to be able to tell them that all their efforts amongst the tottering chaos of the Icefall, the disheartening plunging up the snowy inferno of the Western Cwm, the difficult technical ice work on the Lhotse

Face, and the grim and nerve-racking toil above the South Col had been fully rewarded and that we had reached the top.

To see the unashamed joy spread over the tired, strained face of our gallant and determined leader was to me reward enough in itself.

7 Adventure "Manquée"

Captain Kidd*

JOHN S. C. ABBOTT

THE BUCCANEERS

After the discovery of the New World, Pope Alexander VI issued a proclamation dividing all the newly discovered lands, in both the East and West
Indies, between the crowns of Portugal and Spain, to the exclusion of all
other powers. This papal bull excited great discontent throughout all Chris-
tendom. France, England, and the Netherlands, the three remaining great
maritime nations, combined against Spain and Portugal. These courts would
give any man a commission to take a ship, fill it with armed men, and prey
upon the commerce of Spain and Portugal. There was no court to decide
upon the validity of prizes. The captors were responsible to nobody. They
decided for themselves whether the prize they had taken was their legitimate
booty. The whole spoil was divided among them according to their own
agreement.

Very soon all seas swarmed with these adventurers. They sailed in fleets. In
armed bands they landed and ravaged the coasts, battering down forts and
capturing and plundering cities. They did not deem themselves pirates, but
took the name of buccaneers. Though often guilty of great enormities, they
assumed the air of legitimate privateersmen. With heads high uplifted they
swaggered through the streets of England, France, and the Netherlands,
with lavish hand scattering their ill-gotten gold. They were welcomed at
every port they entered, for they proved very profitable customers. They sold
their booty very cheap. They purchased very freely, regardless of price. In
drunken frolics they had been known to scatter doubloons in the streets to
see men and boys scramble for them. The merchants all welcomed them,
not deeming it necessary to ask any questions for conscience's sake. Their
numbers became so great and their depredations so audacious that no ship
could sail in safety under any flag. The buccaneers were not careful to obtain

* Published by Dodd, Mead & Company, reprinted by permission of the publishers.

any commission. Assuming that they were warring against the enemies of their country, even when there was no war existing between the two nations, they ravaged the seas at their pleasure.

Generally their bands were well organized and under very salutary discipline. The following articles of agreement, signed by the whole crew, were found on board one of these ships:

"Every man is entitled to a vote in affairs of importance, and to an equal share of all provisions and strong liquors which may be seized. Any man who defrauds the company in plate, jewels, or money shall be landed on a desert island. If he rob a messmate, his ears and nose shall be slit, and then he shall be landed on a desert island. No man shall play at cards or dice for money. The lights are to be put out at eight o'clock at night. No woman is to be allowed on board. Anybody who brings a woman to sea disguised shall be put to death. No man shall strike another on board, but quarrels shall be settled on shore with sword or pistol.

"Anyone deserting or leaving his quarters, during an engagement, shall be either landed on a desert island or put to death. Every man losing a limb or becoming crippled in the service shall have eight hundred dollars. The captain and quartermaster shall receive two shares of every prize; the master, boatswain, and gunner, one share and a half, and all other officers one and a quarter. Quarter always to be given when called for. He that sees a sail first is to have the best pistols and small arms on board of her."

Thus it will be seen that these buccaneers were regularly organized bands, by no means ashamed of their calling. They were morally scarcely inferior to the robber knights and barons of the feudal ages, from whom the haughtiest nobles of Europe are proud to claim their lineage. They were not petty thieves and vulgar murderers. They unfurled their banners and waged open warfare on the sea and on the land, glorying in their chivalric exploits and ostentatiously displaying, in all harbors, the trophies of their wild adventures.

These freebooters assumed the most gorgeous and extravagant dresses. Their favorite ornament was a broad crimson sash, of bright scarlet, passing round the waist, and fastened on the shoulder and hip with colored ribbons. This was so arranged that it formed a belt into which they could thrust three or four richly mounted pistols. These pistols were often sold at auction, on shipboard, for two hundred dollars each. Cocked hats, with a showy embroidery of gold lace, formed a conspicuous feature of their costume.

The captain, in time of battle, was invested with dictatorial power. He could stab or shoot anyone who disobeyed his orders.

These buccaneers were generally Englishmen, Frenchmen, or Germans. Still, adventurers from all nationalities crowded their decks. The Spanish court remonstrated with the several governments of Europe against these outrages. France replied:

"The people complained against act entirely on their own authority and responsibility, not by any commission from us. The King of Spain is at liberty to proceed against them according to his own pleasure."

Elizabeth, England's termagant queen, with characteristic tartness replied:

"The Spaniards have drawn these inconveniences on themselves, by their severe and unjust dealings in their American commerce. The Queen of England cannot understand why her subjects or those of any other European prince should be debarred from traffic in the West Indies. As she does not acknowledge the Spaniards to have any title to any portion of the New World by the donation of the Bishop of Rome, so she knows no right they have to any places other than those of which they are in actual possession. . . ."

THE METAMORPHOSIS: MERCHANT INTO PIRATE— WILLIAM KIDD, CAPTAIN OF THE *ADVENTURE*

In the year 1695, the King of England, William III, summoned before him the Earl of Bellomont, who had been governor of Barbados, and whom he had recently appointed governor of New York, and said to him:

"The buccaneers have so increased in the East and West Indies, and all along the American coast, that they defiantly sail under their own flag. They penetrate the rivers, land in numbers sufficient to capture cities, robbing palaces and cathedrals and extorting enormous ransom. Their suppression is vital to commerce. They have possessed themselves of magnificent retreats in Madagascar and other islands of the Indian Ocean. They have established their seraglios and are living in fabulous splendor and luxury. Piratic expeditions are fitted out from the colonies of New England and Virginia; and even the Quakers of Pennsylvania afford a market for their robberies. These successful freebooters are making their homes in the Carolinas, in Rhode Island, and along the south shore of Long Island, where they and their children take positions among the most respectable in the community.

"The buccaneers are so audacious that they seek no concealment. Their ships are laden with the spoil of all nations. The richest prizes which can now be taken on the high seas are the heavily laden ships of the buccaneers. I have resolved, with the aid of others, to fit out a private expedition against them. We have formed a company for that purpose. By attacking the pirates we shall accomplish a double object. We shall in the first place check their devastating operations, and we shall also fill our purses with the proceeds of the abundant spoil with which their ships are laden."

This second consideration was doubtless the leading one in the movement. The king was in great need of money. His nobles were impoverished by extravagance. They were ready to resort to any measures to replenish their exhausted treasuries. This royal company was therefore organized, not as a national movement, sustained by national law, but as a piratic expedition against the pirates. The reclaimed treasure was not to be restored to its owners, nor to be placed in the treasury of the kingdom, but to be divided among the captors, as their legitimate spoil. And still the king was to give the commission in his kingly name.

The king informed the Earl of Bellomont that he was about to invest him with the government of New York, and wished him to suggest the name of some suitable person, who was familiar with the North American coast and the West Indian seas, to whom he could intrust the command of the frigate they were then fitting out. It so chanced that an illustrious Englishman, Mr. Robert Livingston, the first of that name who had emigrated to the New World, was then in London. The earl consulted with him. He was informed that just the man he needed had accompanied him from New York to London, leaving his family behind. He was a merchant, by the name of William Kidd, a man of tried courage and integrity.

In the last war with the French, Captain Kidd had commanded a privateersman and had gained signal honor in many engagements. He had sailed over all the seas frequented by the buccaneers, and was familiar with their haunts. The commission which the king gave to Captain Kidd is a curious document. It is here given abridged of its excessive verbiage:

"William the Third, by the grace of God King of England, Scotland, France, and Ireland, to our true and well-beloved Captain William Kidd, commander of the ship *Adventure*. Whereas divers wicked persons commit many and great piracies, robberies, and depredations on the seas, upon the coasts of America and other parts, to the hindrance of trade and the danger of our subjects, we have thought fit to give to the said William Kidd full authority to seize all such pirates as you may find on the seas, whether our subjects or the subjects of other nations, with their ships, and all merchandise or money which shall be found on board, if they willingly yield themselves. But if they will not yield without fighting, then you are, by force, to compel them to yield. We do also require you to bring, or cause to be brought, such pirates, freebooters, or sea rovers, as you shall seize, to a legal trial, to the end they may be proceeded against according to the law in such cases.

"We enjoin you to keep an exact journal of your proceedings, giving the names of the ships you may capture, the names of their officers and crew, and the value of their cargoes and stores. And we command you, at your peril, that you do not molest our friends or allies under any pretense of authority hereby granted. Given the 26th of January, 1695."

Captain Kidd at the same time received another document, which was called a commission of reprisals. This authorized him, as a privateersman, to take any French merchant ships he might chance to meet; for there was then war between France and England.

A ship was purchased, for thirty thousand dollars, called the *Adventure*. Of this sum, Captain Kidd and Mr. Livingston furnished three thousand each. The remainder was contributed by the Earls of Bellomont and Romney, Lord Chancellor Somers, the Lord High Admiral, The Duke of Shrewsbury, and Sir Henry Harrison. The king, rather ingloriously, paid nothing. He purchased his share in the enterprise by the royal patronage.

It seems that Captain Kidd was a man of high reputation at that time. It was a large amount of property to be intrusted to his hands; for the vessel and its outfit must have cost at least fifty thousand dollars. Mr. Livingston became Kidd's security that he would faithfully discharge his duties and account for all his captures. It is said that Kidd was not pleased with this arrangement, as he was very unwilling that Mr. Livingston should be his bondsman. He probably, even then, felt that it might prove an obstacle in his future course. The operations of the human mind are often inexplicable. He might wish to steal the ship and turn pirate on his own account. And he could not honorably do this while his friend was his bondsman. Such pressure was put upon him that he was constrained to yield.

Armed with the royal commission and in command of the *Adventure*, Captain Kidd sailed from Plymouth, England, in May, 1696. The frigate had an armament of thirty guns and a crew of eighty men. He was ordered to render his accounts to the Earl of Bellomont in New York. He sailed up the Narrows, into New York harbor, in July. His wife and children were in his home there. In crossing the Atlantic, Captain Kidd came across a French merchantman, which he captured. The prize was valued at but seventeen hundred dollars. This was considered a legitimate act of war.

Captain Kidd knew full well that the enemy he was to encounter would fight with the utmost desperation and that he might meet a fleet of piratic ships, or a single ship, more powerful in men and armament than his own. He therefore sent out recruiting officers through the streets of New York, to enlist volunteers. The terms he offered were that every man should have an equal share of every prize that was taken, after reserving for himself and the owners forty shares. With these offers he soon increased his crew to one hundred and fifty-five men.

Sailing from the harbor of New York, he made first for Madeira, to lay in a stock of wine. Then he directed his course to the Cape de Verde Islands, for a supply of salt and provisions. Having obtained these, he spread his canvas for a long voyage around the Cape of Good Hope, to the Island of Madagascar, on the eastern coast of Africa. This island had become renowned as one of the most important rendezvous of the pirates.

Madagascar is larger than Great Britain. The pirates, by aid of their fire-arms, their desperate courage, and their superior intelligence, had gained possession of a considerable portion of the island. The natives were an inefficient race, copper-colored, with long, black hair. The pirates had treated them with such enormous cruelty that the savages fled before them as if they had been demons.

In this retreat, so far distant from the abodes of civilization, the buccaneers had reared forts and built mansions which they had converted into harems. From their voyages they returned here enriched with the plundered commerce of the world, to revel in all sensual indulgence. They made slaves of their prisoners; married, in their rude way, any number they pleased of the most beautiful of the native females; "so that every one," writes one of their number, "had as great a seraglio as the Grand Seignior at Constantinople. At length they began to separate from each other, each living with his own wives, slaves, and dependents, like independent princes. As power and plenty naturally beget contention, they sometimes quarreled, and attacked each other at the head of their several armies. In these civil wars many of them were killed."

These reckless men used their power like tyrants. They grew wanton in cruelty. Nothing was more common than, upon the slightest displeasure, to cause one of their dependants to be tied to a tree and shot through the heart. The natives combined for their extermination. The plan would have succeeded but for betrayal by a woman. They trembled in view of their narrow escape and combined for mutual defense.

These ruffians assumed all the airs of the ancient baronial nobility. Their dwellings were citadels. They generally chose for their residence some dense forest, near running water. The house was surrounded by a rampart and a ditch. The rampart was so high that it could not be climbed without scaling ladders. The dwelling was so concealed, in the dense tropical forest, that it could not be seen until you were very near it. The only approach was so narrow that two could not pass it abreast. It was contrived in so intricate a manner that, to all not perfectly familiar with it, it was a perfect labyrinth, with cross-paths where one might wander for hours, lost in the maze.

All along these narrow paths, large and very sharp thorns, which grew in that country, were planted in the ground, so as to pierce the feet of the unshod natives. If any should attempt to approach the house by night, they would certainly be pierced and torn by those cruel thorns.

It was a long voyage to Madagascar. Before Captain Kidd reached the island nine months had elapsed since leaving Plymouth. Captain Kidd had expended all his money, and his provisions were nearly exhausted. Not a single prize had they captured by the way. This ill luck caused a general feeling of murmuring and contention on board. The most amiable are in danger of losing their amiability in hours of disaster. Rude seamen, but one remove from pirates, in such seasons of disappointment and chagrin become almost demons in moroseness.

One morning the whole ship's crew were thrown into a state of the most joyous excitement by the sight of three ships on the distant horizon. They had no doubt that it was some buccaneer, with two prizes, heavily laden with the treasures of the Orient. Suddenly all became very good-natured. Eagerly they prepared for action. They had no fear that the pirate, with his prizes, could escape their swift-sailing frigate. The supposed pirate was apparently conscious that escape was impossible; for he bore down boldly upon them.

Terrible was the disappointment. Captain Kidd, gazing upon the approaching vessels through his glass, exclaimed, with an oath, "They are three English warships."

Captain Warren was in command of the men-of-war. Meeting thus in mid-ocean, the two captains interchanged civilities, visited each other, and kept company for two or three days. It was in the month of February, 1696, that Captain Kidd, coasting along the shores of Madagascar, approached the harbor upon the island frequented by the pirates. Here he expected to find treasure in abundance. He had very decidedly exceeded his orders in leaving the waters of America for the distant shores of Africa and Asia. Triumphant success, which he was sanguine of achieving, might cause the disobedience of instructions not only to be forgiven but applauded. Failure would be to him disgrace and irretrievable ruin.

Again Captain Kidd and his crew were doomed to disappointment. It so happened that they arrived at the island at a time when every vessel was out on a piratic cruise. There was not a single vessel there. All were growing desperate. Captain Kidd had but very little money left, and nearly all his provisions were consumed. As hastily as possible he replenished his water casks and, taking in a few more stores, weighed anchor, and voyaged thirteen hundred miles farther east to Malabar, as the whole western coast of Hindustan was then called, from Cape Comorin to Bombay.

He came within sight of these shores in June four months after his arrival at Madagascar. For some time he cruised up and down this coast unavailingly. Not a single sail was to be seen on the boundless expanse of ocean. There was universal discontent and murmurings on board the *Adventure*. The situation of the ship's company was indeed deplorable. One half of the globe was between them and their homes. Their provisions were nearly all gone, and they had no means with which to purchase more. It was clear that unless Providence should interpose in their favor, they must either steal or starve.

And Providence did, for a time, singularly interpose. As they were one day sailing by a small island, called Joanna, they saw the wreck of a ship on shore. Captain Kidd took a boat and was rowed to the land, where he found that it was a French vessel. The crew had escaped, having saved quite a quantity of gold. The ship and cargo were a total loss. The Frenchman, so the narrative goes, loaned this gold to Captain Kidd. Perhaps he did. It is more probable that it was a forced loan. Captain Kidd had, as we have mentioned, a double commission, one against the pirates and the other a regular commission as a privateersman against the French. Had he captured the ship before the wreck it would have been his lawful prize. It is hardly probable that he had any scruples of conscience in seizing the doubloons when transferred to the shore.

With this gold he sailed to one of the ports on the Malabar coast, where he purchased food sufficient for a few weeks only. There was, at that time, in Asia, one of the most powerful nations on the globe, called the Mongols. The emperor, who was almost divinely worshiped, was titled the Great Mogul. His gorgeous palaces were reared in the city of Samarkand, in the province of Bokhara. This magnificent city, thirty miles in circumference, glittered with palaces and mosques of gorgeous architecture, constructed of white marble. The empire was founded by the world-renowned Gengis Khan and extended by the equally celebrated Tamerlane. The sails of Mongol commerce whitened all the East-Indian seas. Piracy then so abounded that this commerce was generally carried on in fleets under convoy. Upon this cruise of disappointment and anxiety, Captain Kidd passed several of the ships of the Great Mogul. He looked upon them with a wistful eye. They were merchantmen. With his force he could easily capture them. There could be no doubt that they contained treasure of great value.

There was loud murmuring among the crew. They could not understand those scruples of conscience which would allow them to plunder a few ship-wrecked Frenchmen and yet would turn aside from the rich argosies of the East.

But Captain Kidd, a respectable New York merchant, held in high esteem by the community, and who had been sent on this expedition expressly to capture and punish the pirates, was not then prepared to raise himself the black flag and thus join the robbers of the seas.

The struggle, in his mind, was probably very severe. He was daily grow-ing more desperate. Starvation stared him in the face. His crew was growing mutinous. He had reason to fear that they would rise, throw him overboard or land him upon some island, and then, raising the black flag of the pirate, scour the seas on their own account and join the riotous band defiantly es-tablished at Madagascar.

He had no doubt that the powerful company, who had sent him on this cruise, would overlook any irregularities in plundering wrong vessels and would make no troublesome inquiries into his mode of operations, if he would only bring them home an abundance of gold. On the other hand, should he fail, he would be dismissed from their service in disgrace, an utterly ruined man.

He had learned that the Great Mogul was about to send from the Red Sea, through the Straits of Babelmandel, a richly freighted fleet of merchant-men, under convoy, bound to China. The Straits are but about fifteen miles wide. Consequently there could be no difficulty in intercepting the fleet.

Captain Kidd had probably, in his silent thoughts, decided to turn free-booter. Though as yet he had divulged his secret to no one and had com-mitted no overt act, he had passed the Rubicon, and was in heart a pirate. The change was at once perceptible. He ran his ship in toward the shore and coasted along until he came in sight of a village of the natives, where herds were seen in the fields and harvests were waving and the boughs of the groves were laden with the golden fruit of the tropics. Doubtless he would have been glad to purchase these stores. But he had no money. He had reached that point in his career at which he must either steal or starve.

He sent several armed boats to the land and robbed the unresisting natives without stint. He was not a man to pursue half-measures. Having well revictualed his ship, he turned her bows toward the entrance to the Red Sea. Summoning his crew before him, he informed them of the change in his plans.

"We have been unsuccessful hitherto, my boys," he said, "but take courage. Fortune is now about to smile upon us. The fleet of the Great Mogul, freighted with the richest treasures, is soon to come out of the Red Sea. From the capture of those heavily laden ships we will all grow rich."

This speech was greeted with shouts of applause by the desperate men whom he had picked up in the streets of London and New York. He sent out a swift-sailing boat well manned to enter the Red Sea and run along its eastern coast on a voyage of discovery. The boat returned after an absence of a few days, with the rather alarming intelligence that they had counted a squadron of fifteen large ships just ready to sail. While some of them bore the flag of the Great Mogul, at the masthead of others floated the banners of England and of Holland.

England was in alliance with Holland, and on the most friendly terms with the Great Mogul. In the commission given to Captain Kidd by the king it was written:

"We command you at your peril, that you do not molest our friends or allies, under any pretense of authority hereby granted."

Captain Kidd must have pondered the question deeply and anxiously before he could have made up his mind to become an utter outlaw, by attacking a fleet composed of ships belonging not only to England's friend and to England's ally but also containing England's ships. Neither did he yet know how strong the convoy by which the fleet was guarded.

He, however, while weighing these thoughts in his anxious mind, sailed to and fro before the mouth of the strait, keeping a vigilant watch at the masthead. After the lapse of four days the squadron hove in sight, far away on the northern horizon. As the vessels approached, Captain Kidd carefully scrutinized them through his glass. His experienced eye soon perceived that the fleet was convoyed by two men-of-war, the one English, the other Dutch. This added to his embarrassment and greatly increased his peril in case he should attempt an assault.

The fleet was much scattered; for, strong in its guard, no danger was apprehended. Kidd's vessel was concealed from the general view behind a headland. His ship was a swift sailer, and he had an immense amount of canvas, which he could almost instantaneously spread to the breeze. There was a large, bulky Mongol ship, laden to the gunwales, slowly plowing its way through the waves, approaching the point where the pirate lay concealed. The guard ships were at the distance of several miles.

Captain Kidd darted out upon the galleon like an eagle upon its prey. He probably hoped to capture it, plunder it, and make his escape before the war vessels could come to its rescue. He opened fire upon the ship. But the convoy, instantly taking the alarm, pressed all sail, and bore rapidly down upon him, opening a vigorous fire from their heavy guns. Kidd could not think of contending with them. His chance was gone. He sheered off, and soon his cloud of swelling canvas disappeared beyond the southern horizon. The armed frigates could not pursue him. They were compelled to remain behind to protect the slowly sailing fleet.

Captain Kidd, embittered by constant failure, was now a disappointed, chagrined, exasperated, desperate man. He was ready for any enterprise, however atrocious, which would bring him money. He ran back to the coast of Malabar. Cruising along, he soon came in sight of a native vessel. Kidd captured it without a struggle. It was called the *Maiden,* belonging to some merchants of Aden, but was commanded by an Englishman by the name of Parker. The mate, Antonio, was a Portuguese, familiar with the language of the country.

There was nothing of value on board. Kidd, having resolutely embarked on a piratic cruise, impressed the captain, Parker, as pilot in those unknown waters. The mate he retained as an interpreter. Vexed in finding no gold and believing that the crew had concealed it, he treated them with the utmost cruelty to extort a confession of where they had hid the coin. They were hoisted up by the arms and beaten with terrible severity. But all was in vain. No amount of torture could bring to light gold which did not exist.

The pirate, having robbed the poor men of a bale of pepper and a bale of coffee, with a few pieces of Arabian gold, contemptuously turned them adrift bleeding and almost helpless in their exhaustion. After continuing his cruise for some time without any success, Kidd ran into a small port, on the Malabar coast, called Carawar. There were several English merchants residing in that place. The tidings had already reached them of the capture of the Aden vessel, the impressment of the English captain and the Portuguese mate, and the cruel treatment of the crew.

As soon as Captain Kidd entered the port, it was suspected that he was the pirate. Two English gentlemen, Mr. Harvey and Mr. Mason, came on board, and charged him with the crime, asking him what he had done with his two captives, Captain Parker and the Portuguese mate. Kidd assumed an air of injured innocence, denied that he had any knowledge of the event, showed them his commission from the king of England as the head of a company of the most illustrious nobles to pursue and punish the pirates. Triumphantly he submitted the question if it were reasonable to suppose that a man who enjoyed the confidence of the king and his nobles, and was intrusted by them to lead an enterprise so essential to the national honor, should himself turn pirate.

The gentlemen were silenced but not convinced. All this time Parker and Antonio the Portuguese were concealed in a private place in the hold.

There he kept them carefully guarded eight days, until he again set sail. Just after he had left the port, a Portuguese man-of-war entered. The English merchants communicated to the commander their suspicions. He immediately put to sea in search of the *Adventure,* resolved, should he overtake her, carefully to examine the hold, hoping to find the captives on board, or at least some evidence of their having been there.

The two ships met. Kidd was by no means disposed to have his vessel searched. A fierce battle ensued which lasted for six hours. Neither vessel was disposed to come to close quarters until the other was disabled. Kidd at length, finding the Portuguese ship too strong for him, spread all his sails and escaped. With his vast amount of canvas he could run away from almost any foe. Ten of his men were wounded in this conflict, but none killed.

Again these desperate men found it necessary to run into the land for provisions. They entered a small port called Porco. Here they filled their water casks and "bought," Kidd says, a sufficient number of hogs of the natives to victual the company. As it is known that Kidd had no money, it is probable that the swine were obtained by that kind of moral suasion which is found in the muzzle of a pistol and the edge of a saber.

This suspicion is confirmed by the fact that the natives, in their exasperation, killed one of his men. The retaliation was characteristic of the crew and the times. Captain Kidd brought his guns to bear upon the village. With broadside after broadside he laid their huts in ruins. The torch was applied, and in an hour the peaceful village was converted into smoldering ashes.

One of the natives was caught. They bound him to a tree, and then a whole boat's company, one after another, discharged each a bullet into his heart. Having achieved this exploit, which they probably thought chivalric, but which others may deem fiendish, Captain Kidd again spread his sails for a piratic cruise.

The first vessel he came across was a large Mongol ship richly freighted. Kidd gave chase, unfurling the French flag. The captain was a Dutchman, by the name of Mitchel. Seeing that he was pursued under French colors, he immediately ran up the banner of France. Captain Kidd at once spread to the breeze the flag of England. He was very exultant. He could lay aside the odious character of a pirate and seize the ship in the less disgraceful capacity of a privateersman. He exclaimed with an oath, "I have caught you. You are a free prize to England."

A cannon ball was thrown across the bows of the ship, and she was ordered to heave to. The ship was hailed in the French language, and someone replied in the same tongue. They were then ordered to send their boat on board. The boat came bearing the captain of the ship, who was a Dutchman, by the name of Mitchel, and a French gentleman by the name of Le Roy.

Kidd received them in his cabin, and upon inquiry ascertained that the ship and cargo belonged to Mongol merchants, that they had intrusted the command to a Dutch captain, as was not unfrequently the case in those days, and that the French gentleman was merely a passenger accidentally on board, passing from one port to another.

These tidings, to use a sailor's phrase, "struck him all aback." Holland, as we have mentioned, was England's ally. The Great Mogul was England's friend. Kidd must release the ship or confess himself a pirate and an outlaw and run the imminent risk of being hanged should he ever return to England. For a moment he seemed lost in thought, bewildered. Then his wicked mind, now rapidly descending into the abyss of sin and shame, rested in a decisive resolve.

Captain Kidd, with a piratic frown upon his brow, and piratic oaths upon his lips turned to Mr. Le Roy and said:

"Do you pretend that this is not a French ship, and that you are but a passenger on board?"

"It is so," Mr. Le Roy politely replied. "I am a stranger in these parts, and have merely taken passage on board this native ship, under Captain Mitchel on my way to Bombay."

"It is a lie," said the pirate, as he drew from his belt a pistol and cocked it. "This is a French ship, and you are its captain; and it is my lawful prize. If you deny this, you shall instantly die."

The features of Kidd, and his words blended with oaths, convinced Mr. Le Roy that he was in the hands of a desperate man, who would shrink from no crime. He was silent. Kidd then added:

"I seize this ship as my legitimate prize. It belongs to a French subject and is sailing under the French flag. I have a commission from his majesty the king of England to seize all such ships in his name."

It seems strange that Kidd, after the many lawless acts of which he had already been guilty, should have deemed it of any consequence to have recourse to so wretched a quibble. But the incident shows that the New York merchant, formerly of good reputation, still recoiled from the thought of plunging headlong into a piratic career. By observing these forms he could, in this case, should he ever have occasion to do so, claim the protection of the royal commission authorizing him to capture French ships.

Kidd took his prize, which he called the *November,* because it was captured in that month, into one of the East Indian ports and sold ship and cargo for what they would fetch. What the amount was, or how he divided it, is not known. Again he resumed his cruise. It was evident that he had become anxious to renounce the career of pirate, upon which he had barely entered, and resume that of privateersman. They soon came across a Dutch ship, unmistakenly such, in build and flag and rigging. The crew clamored for its capture; Kidd resolutely opposed it. A mutiny arose. A minority of the ship's company adhered to the captain. The majority declared that they would arm the boats and go and seize her.

The captain, with drawn saber in his hand, and pistols in his belt, and surrounded by those still faithful to him, stood upon her quarterdeck and said to the mutineers, firmly:

"You may take the boats and go. But those who thus leave this ship will never ascend its sides again."

One of the men, a gunner by the name of William Moore, was particularly violent and abusive. With threatening gestures he approached the captain, assailing him in the most vituperative terms, saying:

"You are ruining us all. You are keeping us in beggary and starvation. But for your whims we might all be prosperous and rich."

The captain was by no means a meek man. In his ungovernable passion he seized an iron-bound bucket, which chanced to be lying at his side, and gave the mutineer such a blow as fractured his skull and struck him senseless to the deck. Of the wound the gunner died the next day. Not many will feel disposed to censure Captain Kidd very severely for this act. It was not a premeditated murder. It was perhaps a necessary deed, in quelling a mutiny, in which the mutineers were demanding that the black flag of the pirate should be raised and which demand the captain was resisting. And yet it is probable that this blow sent Kidd to the gallows. Upon his subsequent trial, but little evidence of piracy could be adduced, and the death of Moore was the prominent charge brought against him.

Kidd ever averred that it was a virtuous act, and that it did not trouble his conscience. It was done to prevent piracy and mutiny. He also averred that he had no intention to kill the man. Had he so intended he would have used pistol or saber. In the ballad which, half a century ago, was sung in hundreds of farmhouses in New England, the lullaby of infancy, the event is alluded to in the following words:

> *I murdered William Moore, as I sailed, as I sailed,*
> *I murdered William Moore as I sailed;*
> *I murdered William Moore, and left him in his gore,*
> *Not many leagues from shore, as I sailed.*

The Dutchman had no consciousness of the peril to which he had been exposed. The two ships kept company for several days and then separated. Is it possible that all this time Kidd was hesitating whether to raise the black flag and seize the prize? It looks like it; for a few days after the Dutch ship had disappeared, quite a fleet of Malabar boats were met with, laden with provisions and other articles which Kidd needed. Unscrupulously he plundered them all. Probably he had no fears that tidings of the outrage would ever reach England. And even if a rumor of the deed were ever to reach those distant shores, he had no apprehension that England would trouble herself to punish him for a little harsh treatment of semisavages on the coast of Malabar.

A few days after this robbery a Portuguese ship hove in sight. Kidd's moral nature was every hour growing weaker. He could no longer resist the temptation to seize the prize. He robbed the vessel of articles to the estimated value of two thousand dollars, and let her go, inflicting no injury upon the ship's company.

For three weeks they continued to cruise over a sailless sea, when one morning, about the middle of December, an immense mass of canvas was seen rising over the distant horizon. It proved to be a native ship of four-hundred-ton burden. The ship was called the *Quedagh Merchant,* was very richly laden, and was commanded by an Englishman, Captain Wright. The wealthy merchants of the East were fully aware of the superior nautical skill of the English seaman and were eager to intrust their important ventures to European commanders.

Kidd unfurled the French flag, chased the ship, and soon overtook it. A cannon ball whistling over the heads of the crew was the very significant hint with which the ship was commanded to heave to. Kidd ordered the captain to lower his boat and come on board the *Adventure.* The captain obeyed and informed the pirate that all the crew were East Indians, excepting two Dutchmen and one Frenchman, and that the ship belonged exclusively to East Indian merchants.

Kidd took piratic possession of the ship. He had not the shadow of a claim to it on the ground of his commission as a privateersman. He landed the officers and the crew, in boatload after boatload, upon the shore, and left them to shift for themselves. One or two of the merchants who owned the ship and cargo were on board. They offered the pirate twenty thousand rupees, which was equivalent to about fifteen thousand dollars, to ransom the property. Kidd declined the offer.

His own ship, after such long voyaging, was leaky and much in want of repairs. The *Quedagh Merchant* was far superior to the *Adventure.* He therefore transferred all his stores to his prize. The torch was applied to the *Adventure,* and the ill-fated ship soon disappeared in a cloud of smoke and flame. Kidd, now a confirmed pirate, directed his course toward the great rendezvous of the pirates at Madagascar. Here the prize was valued at sixty-four thousand pounds, or about three hundred and twenty thousand dollars.

Still this strange man assumed that he was acting under the royal commission, in behalf of the London company; and these treasures were the legitimate plunder of a piratic ship. He therefore reserved forty shares for himself and the company. There were about one hundred and fifty men composing this piratic crew. Each man received about two thousand dollars. Kidd's portion amounted to nearly eighty thousand dollars.

In the pirates' harbor at Madagascar, Kidd found a large ship, the *Resolution,* belonging to the East India Company, which the captain, a man by the name of Culliford, with the crew, had seized and turned into a pirate. It was clearly Kidd's duty, under his commission, at once to attack and capture this piratic ship. When Captain Culliford saw him entering the harbor with his powerful and well-armed ship, he was terrified. The pirates had heard of Captain Kidd's commission and had not yet learned that he had turned pirate himself. Captain Culliford, with the gallows in vision before him, and trembling in every nerve, for there was no possibility of escape, sent some officers, in a boat, on board the *Quedagh Merchant,* to ascertain Captain Kidd's intention.

It was testified at the subsequent trial of Kidd, that he stood upon his deck and received with open arms the piratic officers as they came up over the ship's side, that he invited them to his cabin, where they had a great carouse in drinking and smoking; and that in the frenzy of drink he offered for a toast:

"May damnation seize my soul if I harm a hair of the head of any one on board the *Resolution.*"

It was declared that he received large presents of bales of silk from the piratic captain and sold him some heavy ordnance, with suitable ammunition, for two thousand dollars; and that he was on the most friendly terms with Culliford, exchanging frequent visits with him.

On the other hand, Kidd emphatically denied all these charges. He said, "I never stepped foot on board Captain Culliford's ship. When I entered the harbor and ascertained the character of the craft, I ordered my men to prepare for action. But the mutinous crew, who had already compelled me to resort to measures against which my soul revolted, peremptorily refused, saying that they would rather fire two shots into my vessel than one into that of Captain Culliford. The mutiny became so menacing that my life was in danger. The turbulent crew rifled my chest, stole my journal, took possession of the ammunition. I was compelled to barricade myself in the cabin. The mutineers held the ship, and being beyond all control, acted according to their own good pleasure. I was in no degree responsible for their conduct."

The captain's statement was not credited by the court. At the same time it was quite evident that he had lost the control of his crew. His testimony was, however, in some degree borne out by the fact that ninety-five of his men in a body deserted him, and joined the piratic crew of Captain Culliford. This would seem to prove conclusively that Captain Kidd was not sufficiently piratical in his measures to satisfy the demands of the mutineers.

For several weeks these guilty and wretched men remained in the "own place" of the pirates, indulging in every species of bacchanal, wassail, and sensual vice, amidst their palaces and in their harems. Their revelry could not have been exceeded by any scenes ever witnessed in Sodom or Gomorrah. There were between five and six hundred upon the island. They were continually coming and going. Some of them were so rich that they remained at home cultivating quite large plantations by slave labor. They amused themselves by hunting, and in the wide meadows and forests found abundant game. The arrival of a ship in the harbor was the signal for an universal carouse. They endeavored to magnify the charms of their women by dressing them gorgeously in silks and satins with glittering jewelry.

Often a pipe of wine would be placed upon the shore, the head taken out, and the community would drink of it as they pleased, as freely as if it were water. Drunken pirates reeled through the streets. Oaths filled the air. Knives gleamed, and pistols were discharged, and there were wounds and death. In the midst of all their revelry and wantonness and brawls, it is evident from the record we have of those days, that a more unhappy, wretched set of beings could scarcely be found this side of the world of woe. . . .

How far Captain Kidd entered into these godless carousals is not known. But it is not probable that he was then able to throw off all restraint, and become hail-fellow with these vulgar, degraded, profane wretches, whom in heart he must have despised. Neither is it probable that one accustomed to the society in which an honored New York merchant would move could so soon have formed a taste for the drunken revelry of the lowest and vilest creatures on earth.

It is evident that these men had occasionally reproaches of conscience, and some faint sense of their terrible responsibility at God's bar. Four of them decided one day to make a little artificial hell for themselves, that they might see who could stand its pains the longest.

A cloudless tropical sun blistered the deck with its blazing rays. The cabin was heated like an oven. In addition to this, they built a fire in the stove, till the iron plates were red-hot. They then with blaspheming oaths entered this furnace, and sprinkled brimstone upon the fire till the room was filled with its suffocating fumes. One of these wretches, apparently as fiendlike as a man could be, bore the pains of this little artificial hell for five minutes. None of the others could endure them so long. The Victor came out very exultant. One would have thought that the idea would have occurred to their minds that there was some considerable difference between five minutes and eternity.

Captain Kidd found himself abandoned by nearly all his crew. He remained in port only long enough to recruit sufficient men to navigate his ship, and then, spreading the sails of his stolen vessel, the *Quedagh Merchant,* he set out for the West Indies, with his ill-gotten treasure of eighty thousand dollars. The news of Kidd's piratic acts had been reported to the home government by the East India Company. Orders had accordingly been issued to all the governors of the American colonies to arrest him wherever he should appear. . . .

THE SENTENCE

—The Old Bailey, London, July, 1701
"William Kidd, the sentence that the law hath appointed to pass upon you for your offenses, and which this court doth therefore award, is, that you, the said William Kidd, shall go from hence to the place from whence you came, and from thence to the place of execution, where you shall be hanged by the neck until you are dead. And may the God of infinite mercy be merciful to your soul."

Kidd replied, "My lord, it is a very hard sentence. For my part, I am the most innocent person of them all. I have been sworn against by perjured persons."

Editor's Note: As history and Mr. Abbott's last-century account records, Captain Kidd was arrested in the West Indies, taken to Boston and thence to England, where he stood trial and, largely on account of his slaying of his own seaman, sentenced to be hanged, and was executed.

Don Quixote de la Mancha*

MIGUEL DE CERVANTES

✶✶ Often referred to as the first modern novel, *Don Quixote,* the conception of Miguel de Cervantes which started as a satire on the chivalrous, the amorous, and the literary styles of his day and ended as a vast panorama of Spanish life and manners, is the product of a writer who was himself an adventurer. Born in 1547, he died in 1616 after a life in which he sought glory as a soldier of the king and found prison and poverty easier to come by than fame. His first act as a soldier has been called quixotic, although that was not then the term for it— when, below deck, sick with fever, he might have remained safe and sound but insisted on getting up and being placed by the captain in the most dangerous position, commanding a longboat in the battle of Lepanto, October 7, 1570, where he received three infidel bullets in his chest and permanently maimed his left hand. *Don Quixote* was not published until his fifty-eighth year and was, he has said, "just what might be begotten in a jail," to which he had been sentenced for debts.

"The whimsy which seized Cervantes floated up from the depths of his being," writes Joseph Wood Krutch, in his penetrating essay on the author in his book *Five Masters.* "His own soul was far more bound up with that of Don Quixote than he imagined . . . How then could he ridicule Don Quixote without ridiculing himself, . . . or fail to sympathize with this man whose only fault was to find himself in a world which provided no opportunities for the exercise of the high and selfless principles which he wished to profess? . . . Despite the insanity which makes him persist in interpreting every commonplace event in terms of romance, the Don speaks nobly, and as he grows in stature, his page, Sancho Panza, grows with him. Conceived at first as no more than a simple-minded foil to his extravagant master, the latter grows wiser in one kind of wisdom as the Don grows wiser in another until, though the one is mad and the other a clown, they have come to represent the two types of human wisdom— that which knows how things really are and that which knows how they ought to be."

Since we overtake the noble Don and his peasant squire Sancho Panza in this book in the sixteenth chapter of their adventures, it might be well to say that at

* First published in Spain in 1605, the sequel in 1615.

that moment both were grievously suffering from ills of the body induced by their last adventure and that across the mind of Sancho had already passed some misgivings and doubts as to whether he had been wise, after all, in allowing himself to be talked into leaving his wife and family to accompany the bookish elderly gentleman from La Mancha on this unparalleled search for knightly adventures, even if his master ever lived up to his promised reward of "at least an island" at the end of his service as a knight's squire.

Their last stop had been no bed of roses. The roving eye of Don Quixote's bony horse, Rozinante, had observed some likely females among the pack-train animals of some camped Galician freight haulers and after romping among them creating havoc had got himself beaten by the freighters into practical insensibility. Whereupon the lean but fiery-eyed Don Quixote, spear in hand, fell upon the twenty hardy carriers, ably assisted by the squat and pot-bellied Sancho Panza, with the net result: a rain of pack-staves, catastrophe, the eminent Don stretched on the ground, his squire's ribs blue with blows, Rozinante, four legs in the air, altogether as sorry a set of errants as the sun ever set on.

Leaning on a bruised elbow and surveying the damage around him, Don Quixote, as usual, took hope.

"Notwithstanding this, I tell thee, Brother Panza," he said, "there is no remembrance which time does not obliterate, nor pain which death does not terminate."

The rueful peasant was forced to agree.

". . . If this mischance of ours were of that sort which might be cured with a couple of plaisters, it would not be altogether so bad, but, for aught I see, all the plaisters of a hospital will not be sufficient to set us rights again . . . What I wonder at is that my ass should come off scot-free where we (and Rozinante) have paid so dear."

"Fortune always leaves some door open in misfortune to admit a remedy," said Don Quixote. "This I say because thy beast may now supply the want of Rozinante, by carrying me hence to some castle, where I may be cured of my wounds. Nor do I account it dishonorable to be so mounted; for I remember to have read that the good old Silenus, governor and tutor of the merry god of laughter, when he made his entry into the city of the hundred gates, was mounted, much to his satisfaction, on a most beautiful ass."

"It is likely he rode as your worship says," answered Sancho, who could see that his master could not sit up, "but there is a difference between riding and lying athwart like a sack of rubbish."

He could hardly get up from the ground himself, but after sixty sighs and a hundred and twenty curses (the good book says) he endeavored to raise himself, but stopped halfway, bent like a Turkish bow, being wholly unable to stand upright: nevertheless he managed finally to saddle his ass, then heaved up Rozinante, who had no tongue to complain, fortunately, and at length settled Don Quixote crosswise on the ass, to whose tail he then tied Rozinante, and taking hold of the halter of Dapple, led them toward the highroad, where after a time he espied an inn, which, much to his sorrow and Don Quixote's joy, must needs be a castle, a dispute which lasted so long that they arrived there before its exact nature was determined, and Sancho, without further expostulation, entered it with his string of cattle. ✳✳

WHAT HAPPENED TO DON QUIXOTE IN THE INN, WHICH HE UNHAPPILY MISTOOK FOR A CASTLE

Looking at Don Quixote laid across the ass, the innkeeper inquired of Sancho what ailed him. Sancho answered that it was nothing but a fall from a rock, by which his ribs were somewhat bruised. The innkeeper had a wife of a disposition uncommon among those of the like occupation, for she was naturally charitable, and felt for the misfortunes of her neighbors; so that she immediately prepared to relieve Don Quixote, and made her daughter, a very comely young maiden, assist in the cure of her guest. There was also a servant at the inn, an Asturian wench, broad-faced, flat-headed, with a little nose, one eye squinting, and the other not much better. It is true, the elegance of her form made amends for other defects. She was not seven hands high; and her shoulders, which burdened her a little too much, made her look down to the ground more than she would willingly have done. This agreeable lass now assisted the damsel to prepare for Don Quixote a very sorry bed in a garret, which gave evidence of having formerly served as a hayloft. In this room lodged also a carrier, whose bed was at a little distance from that of our knight; and though it was composed of pannels, and other trappings of his mules, it had much the advantage over that of Don Quixote, which consisted of four not very smooth boards upon two unequal tressels, and a mattress no thicker than a quilt, and full of knots, which from their hardness might have been taken for pebbles, had not the wool appeared through some fractures; with two sheets like the leather of an old target, and a rug the threads of which you might count, if you chose, without losing one of the number.

In this wretched bed was Don Quixote laid; after which the hostess and her daughter plaistered him from head to foot, Maritornes (for so the Asturian wench was called) at the same time holding the light. And as the hostess was thus employed, perceiving Don Quixote to be mauled in every part, she said that his bruises seemed the effect of hard drubbing rather than of a fall.

"Not a drubbing," said Sancho, "but the knobs and sharp points of the rock, every one of which has left its mark. And now I think of it," added he, "pray contrive to spare a morsel of that tow, as somebody may find it useful—indeed, I suspect that my sides would be glad of a little of it."

"What! you have had a fall, too, have you?" said the hostess.

"No," replied Sancho, "not a fall, but a fright, on seeing my master tumble, which so affected my whole body that I feel as if I had received a thousand blows myself."

"That may very well be," said the damsel, "for I have often dreamed that I was falling down from some high tower, and could never come to the ground; and when I awoke I have found myself as much bruised and battered as if I had really fallen."

"But here is the point, mistress," answered Sancho Panza, "that I, without dreaming at all, find myself with almost as many bruises as my master, Don Quixote."

"What do you say is the name of this gentleman?" quoth the Asturian.

"Don Quixote de la Mancha," answered Sancho Panza: "he is a knight-errant, and one of the best and most valiant that has been seen for this long time in the world."

"What is a knight-errant?" said the wench.

"Are you such a novice as not to know that?" answered Sancho Panza. "You must know, then, that a knight-errant is a thing that, in two words, is cudgeled and made an emperor: today he is the most unfortunate wretch in the world, and tomorrow will have two or three crowns of kingdoms to give to his squire."

"How comes it then to pass that you, being squire to this worthy gentleman," said the hostess, "have not yet, as it seems, got so much as an earldom?"

"It is early days yet," answered Sancho, "for it is but a month since we set out in quest of adventures, and hitherto we have met with none that deserves the name. And sometimes we look for one thing and find another. But the truth is, if my master, Don Quixote, recovers of this wound or fall, and I am not disabled thereby, I would not truck my hopes for the best title in Spain."

To all this conversation Don Quixote had listened very attentively; and now, raising himself up in the bed as well as he could, and taking the hand of his hostess, he said to her, "Believe me, beauteous lady, you may esteem yourself fortunate in having entertained me in this, your castle, being such a person that, if I say little of myself, it is because, as the proverb declares, self-praise depreciates; but my squire will inform you who I am. I only say that I shall retain the service you have done me eternally engraven on my memory, and be grateful to you as long as my life shall endure. And had it pleased the high heavens that Love had not held me so enthralled and subject to his laws, and to the eyes of that beautiful ingrate whose name I silently pronounce, those of this lovely virgin had become enslavers of my liberty."

The hostess, her daughter, and the good Maritornes stood confounded at this harangue of our knight-errant, which they understood just as much as if he had spoken Greek, although they guessed that it all tended to compliments and offers of service; and not being accustomed to such kind of language, they gazed at him with surprise and thought him another sort of man than those now in fashion; and after thanking him in their innlike phrase for his offers, they left him.

The Asturian Maritornes doctored Sancho, who stood in no less need of plaisters than his master. The carrier and she, it appeared, had agreed to sup that night together; and she had given him her word that, when the guests were all quiet, and her master and mistress asleep, she would repair to him. And it is said of the honest Maritornes that she never made a promise but she performed it, even though she had made it on a mountain, without any witness; for she valued herself upon her gentility, and thought it no disgrace to be employed in service at an inn, since misfortune and unhappy accidents, as she affirmed, had brought her to that state.

Don Quixote's hard, scanty, beggarly, crazy bed stood first in the middle of the cock-loft; and close by it Sancho had placed his own, which consisted only of a rush mat, and a rug that seemed to be rather of beaten hemp than of wool. Next to the squire's stood that of the carrier, made up of pannels, and the whole furniture of two of his best mules; for he possessed twelve in number, sleek, fat, and stately—being one of the richest carriers of Arevalo.

THE GENTLE ASTURIAN

After the carrier had visited his mules and given them their second course, he laid himself down upon his pannels, in expectation of his most punctual Maritornes. Sancho was already plaistered and in bed; and though he endeavored to sleep, the pain of his ribs would not allow him; and Don Quixote, from the same cause, kept his eyes as wide open as those of a hare. The whole inn was in profound silence and contained no other light than what proceeded from a lamp which hung in the middle of the entry. This marvelous stillness, and the thoughts of our knight, which incessantly recurred to those adventures so common in the annals of chivalry, brought to his imagination one of the strangest whims that can well be conceived; for he imagined that he was now in some famous castle, and that the daughter of its lord, captivated by his fine appearance, had become enamoured of him, and had promised to steal that night privately to him and pass some time with him. Then, taking all this chimera formed by himself for reality, he began to feel some alarm, reflecting on the dangerous trial to which his fidelity was on the point of being exposed; but resolved in his heart not to commit disloyalty against his lady Dulcinea del Toboso, though Queen Guinevra herself, with the Lady Quintaniana, should present themselves before him.

Whilst his thoughts were occupied by these extravagances, the hour—an unlucky one to him—arrived when the gentle Asturian, mindful of her promise, entered the room, and with silent and cautious step advanced toward the couch of the carrier. But scarcely had she passed the threshold of the door when Don Quixote heard her; and sitting up in his bed, in spite of plaisters and the pain of his ribs, stretched out his arms to receive his beauteous damsel, who, crouching and holding her breath as she went, with hands extended, feeling for her lover, encountered the arms of Don Quixote, who caught first hold of her by the wrist and, drawing her toward him (she not daring to speak a word), made her sit down on the bed. On touching her garment, though it was of canvas, it seemed to him to be of the finest and softest lawn; the glass beads that encircled her wrists, to his fancy were precious oriental pearls; her hairs, not unlike those of a horse's mane, he took for threads of the brightest gold of Arabia, whose splendor obscures that of the sun itself; and though her breath doubtless smelled powerfully of the last night's stale salt fish, he fancied himself inhaling a delicious and aromatic odor. In short, his imagination painted her to him in the very form and manner of some princess described in his books, who comes thus adorned to visit the wounded knight with whom she is in love; and so great was the poor gentleman's infatuation that neither the touch, nor the breath, nor other things she had about her, could undeceive him. So far from this, he imagined that he held the goddess of beauty in his arms; and clasping her fast, in a low and amorous voice he said to her, "Oh, that I were in a state, beautiful and exalted lady, to return so vast a favor as this you confer upon me by your charming presence! but fortune, never weary of persecuting the good, is pleased to lay me on this bed, so bruised and disabled that, how much soever I may be inclined to convince you of my devotion, it is impossible; to which is added another still greater impossibility— the plighted faith I have sworn to the peerless Dulcinea del Toboso, sole mistress of my most recondite thoughts! Had not these articles intervened, I should not have been so insensible a knight as to let slip the happy opportunity with which your great goodness has favored me."

Maritornes was in the utmost vexation at being thus confined by Don Quixote; and not hearing or attending to what he said, she struggled, without speaking a word, to release herself. The good carrier, whom busy thoughts had kept awake, having heard his fair one from the first moment she entered the door, listened attentively to all that Don Quixote said; and suspecting that the Asturian nymph had played false with him, he advanced toward Don Quixote's bed and stood still, in order to discover the tendency of his discourse, which, however, he could not understand; but seeing that she struggled to get from him, and that Don Quixote labored to hold her, and also not liking the jest, he lifted up his arm, and discharged so terrible a blow on the lantern jaws of the enamoured knight that his mouth was bathed in blood; and not content with this, he mounted upon his ribs, and paced them somewhat above a trot from one end to the other. The bed, which was crazy, and its foundations none of the strongest, being unable to bear the additional weight of the carrier, came down to the ground with such a crash that the innkeeper awoke; and having called aloud to Maritornes without receiving an answer, he immediately conjectured it was some affair in which she was concerned. With this suspicion he arose, and lighting a candle, went to the place where he had heard the bustle.

The Asturian, seeing her master coming, and knowing his furious disposition, retreated in terror to Sancho Panza's bed, who was now asleep, and there rolled herself into a ball. The innkeeper entered, calling out, "Where are you, Maritornes? for these are some of your doings."

Sancho was now disturbed and, feeling such a mass upon him, fancied he had got the nightmare, and began to lay about him on every side; and not a few of his blows reached Maritornes, who, provoked by the smart, cast aside all decorum and made Sancho such a return in kind that she effectually roused him from sleep, in spite of his drowsiness. The squire, finding himself thus treated, and without knowing by whom, raised himself up as well as he could, and grappled with Maritornes; and there began between them the most obstinate and delightful skirmish in the world.

The carrier, perceiving by the light of the host's candle how it fared with her, quitted Don Quixote and ran to her assistance. The landlord followed him, but with a different intention; for it was to chastise the wench, concluding that she was the sole occasion of all this harmony. And so, as the proverb says, the cat to the rat, the rat to the rope, and the rope to the post: the carrier belabored Sancho, Sancho Maritornes, Maritornes Sancho, and the innkeeper Maritornes; all redoubling their blows without intermission: and the best of it was, the landlord's candle went out; when, being left in the dark, they indiscriminately thrashed each other, and with so little mercy that every blow left its mark.

It happened that there lodged that night at the inn an officer belonging to the Holy Brotherhood of Toledo, who, hearing the strange noise of the scuffle, seized his wand and the tin box which held his commission, and entered the room in the dark, calling out, "Forbear, in the name of justice; forbear, in the name of the Holy Brotherhood." And the first he encountered was the battered Don Quixote, who lay senseless on his demolished bed, stretched upon his back; and laying hold of his beard as he was groping about, he cried out repeatedly, "I charge you to aid and assist me"; but finding that the person whom he held was motionless, he concluded that he was dead, and that the people in the room were his murderers. Upon which he raised his voice still louder, crying, "Shut the inn door, and let none escape, for here is a man murdered!"

These words startled them all, and the conflict instantly ceased. The landlord withdrew to his chamber, the carrier to his pannels, and the lass to her straw: the unfortunate Don Quixote and Sancho alone were incapable of moving. The officer now let go the beard of Don Quixote, and in order to search after and secure the delinquents, he went out for a light, but could find none, for the innkeeper had purposely extinguished the lamp when he retired to his chamber; and therefore he was obliged to have recourse to the chimney, where, after much time and trouble, he lighted another lamp.

THE BALSAM

Don Quixote by this time had come to himself, and in the same dolorous tone in which, the day before, he had called to his squire, when he lay extended in the valley of pack-staves, he now again called to him, saying, "Sancho, friend, art thou asleep? art thou asleep, friend Sancho?"

"How should I sleep? woe is me!" answered Sancho, full of trouble and vexation; "for I think all the devils in hell have been with me to-night."

"Well mayest thou believe so," answered Don Quixote; "for either I know nothing, or this castle is enchanted. Listen to me, Sancho—but what I am now going to disclose thou must swear to keep secret until after my death."

"Yes, I swear," answered Sancho.

"I require this," said Don Quixote, "because I would not injure the reputation of anyone."

"I tell you I do swear," replied Sancho, "and will keep it secret until your worship's death; and Heaven grant I may discover it to-morrow."

"Have I done thee so much evil, Sancho," answered Don Quixote, "that thou shouldst wish for my decease so very soon?"

"It is not for that," answered Sancho; "but I am an enemy to holding things long, and would not have them rot in my keeping."

"Be it for what it will," said Don Quixote, "I confide in thy love and courtesy, and therefore I inform thee that this night a most extraordinary adventure has befallen me; and to tell it briefly, thou must know that a little while since I was visited by the daughter of the lord of this castle, who is the most accomplished and beautiful damsel to be found over a great part of the habitable earth. How I could describe the graces of her person, the sprightliness of her wit, and the many other hidden charms which, from the respect I owe to my lady Dulcinea del Toboso, I shall pass over undescribed! All that I am permitted to say is that Heaven, jealous of the great happiness that fortune had put in my possession, or, what is more probable, this castle being enchanted, just as we were engaged in most sweet and delightful conversation, an invisible hand, affixed to the arm of some monstrous giant, gave me so violent a blow that my mouth was bathed in blood, and afterward so bruised me that I am now in a worse state than that wherein the fury of the carriers left us yesterday, owing to the indiscretion of Rozinante. Whence I conjecture that the treasure of this damsel's beauty is guarded by some enchanted Moor, and therefore not to be approached by me."

"Nor by me neither," answered Sancho; "for more than four hundred Moors have buffeted me in such a manner that the basting of the pack-staves was tarts and cheesecakes to it. But tell me, pray, sir, call you this an excellent and rare adventure which has left us in such a pickle? Not that it was quite so bad with your worship, who had in your arms that incomparable beauty whom you speak of. As for me, what had I but the heaviest blows that I hope I shall ever feel in all my life? Woe is me, and the mother that bore me! for I am no knight-errant, nor ever mean to be one; yet, of all our mishaps, the greater part still falls to my share."

"What! hast thou likewise been beaten?" said Don Quixote.

"Have not I told you so? evil befall my lineage!" quoth Sancho.

"Console thyself, my friend," said Don Quixote, "for I will now make that precious balsam which will cure us in the twinkling of an eye."

At this moment the officer, having lighted his lamp, entered to examine the person whom he conceived to have been murdered; and Sancho, seeing him enter in his shirt, with a nightcap on his head, a lamp in his hand, and a countenance far from well favored, asked his master if it was the enchanted Moor coming to finish the correction he had bestowed upon them.

"It cannot be the Moor," answered Don Quixote, "for the enchanted suffer not themselves to be visible."

"If they do not choose to be seen, they will be felt," said Sancho: "witness my shoulders."

"Mine might speak, too," answered Don Quixote; "but this is not sufficient evidence to convince us that he whom we see is the enchanted Moor."

The officer, finding them communing in so calm a manner, stood in astonishment: although it is true that Don Quixote still lay flat on his back, unable to stir, from bruises and plaisters. The officer approached him and said, "Well, my good fellow, how are you?"

"I would speak more respectfully," answered Don Quixote, "were I in your place. Is it the fashion of this country, blockhead! thus to address knights-errant?"

The officer, not disposed to bear this language from one of so scurvy an aspect, lifted up his lamp and dashed it, with all its contents, at the head of Don Quixote, and then made his retreat in the dark.

"Surely," quoth Sancho Panza, "this must be the enchanted Moor; and he reserves the treasure for others, and for us only fisticuffs and lampshots."

"It is even so," answered Don Quixote; "and it is to no purpose to regard these affairs of enchantments, or to be out of humor or angry with them; for, being invisible, and mere phantoms, all endeavors to seek revenge would be fruitless. Rise, Sancho, if thou canst, and call the governor of this fortress, and procure me some oil, wine, salt, and rosemary, to make the healing balsam; for in truth I want it much at this time, as the wound this phantom has given me bleeds very fast."

Sancho got up with aching bones; and as he was proceeding in the dark toward the landlord's chamber, he met the officer, who was watching the movements of his enemy, and said to him, "Sir, whoever you are, do us the favor and kindness to help us to a little rosemary, oil, salt, and wine; for they are wanted to cure one of the best knights-errant in the world, who lies there sorely wounded by the hands of the enchanted Moor who is in this inn."

The officer, hearing this, took him for a maniac; and as the day now began to dawn, he opened the inn door and, calling the host, told him what Sancho wanted. The innkeeper furnished him with what he desired, and Sancho carried them to Don Quixote, who lay with his hands on his head, complaining of the pain caused by the lamp, which, however, had done him no other hurt than raising a couple of tolerably large tumors; what he took for blood being only moisture, occasioned by the pelting of the storm which had just blown over. In fine, he took his simples and made a compound of them, mixing them together and boiling them for some time, until he thought the mixture had arrived at the exact point. He then asked for a phial to hold it; but as there was no such thing in the inn, he resolved to put it in a cruse or tin oil flask, of which the host made him a present. This being done, he pronounced over the cruse above fourscore *paternosters,* and as many *Ave Marias, salves,* and *credos,* accompanying every word with a cross, by way of benediction; all which was performed in the presence of Sancho, the innkeeper, and the officer: as for the carrier, he had gone soberly about the business of tending his mules.

Having completed the operation, Don Quixote resolved to make trial immediately of the virtue of that precious balsam, and therefore drank about a pint and a half of what remained in the pot wherein it was boiled, after the cruse was filled; and scarcely had he swallowed the potion when it was rejected, and followed by so violent a retching that nothing was left on his stomach. To the pain and exertion of the vomit a copious perspiration succeeding, he desired to be covered up warm and left alone. They did so, and he continued asleep above three hours, when he awoke and found himself greatly relieved in his body, and his battered and bruised members so much restored that he considered himself as perfectly recovered, and was thoroughly persuaded that he was in possession of the true balsam of Fierabras; and consequently, with such a remedy, he might thenceforward encounter without fear all dangers, battles, and conflicts, however hazardous.

Sancho Panza, who likewise took his master's amendment for a miracle, desired he would give him what remained in the pot, which was no small quantity. This request being granted, he took it in both hands, and with good faith and better will, swallowed down very little less than his master had done.

Now the case was that poor Sancho's stomach was not so delicate as that of his master; and therefore, before he could reject it he endured such pangs and loathings, with such cold sweats and faintings, that he verily thought his last hour was come; and finding himself so afflicted and tormented, he cursed the balsam and the thief that had given it to him. Don Quixote, seeing him in that condition, said, "I believe, Sancho, that all this mischief hath befallen thee because thou art not dubbed a knight; for I am of opinion this liquor can do good only to those who are of that order."

"If your worship knew that," replied Sancho, "evil betide me and all my generation! why did you suffer me to drink it?"

By this time the beverage commenced its operation, with such sweatings, faintings, and shivering fits, that not only himself, but all present, thought he was expiring. These pangs lasted nearly two hours and left him, not sound like his master, but so exhausted and shattered that he was unable to stand. Don Quixote, feeling, as we said before, quite renovated, was moved to take his departure immediately in quest of adventures, thinking that by every moment's delay he was depriving the world of his aid and protection; and more especially as he felt secure and confident in the virtues of the balsam. Thus stimulated, he saddled Rozinante with his own hands, and pannelled the ass of his squire, whom he also helped to dress and afterward to mount. He then mounted himself and, having observed a pike in a corner of the inn yard, he took possession of it to serve him for a lance. All the people in the inn, above twenty in number, stood gazing at him, and among the rest, the host's daughter, while he, on his part, removed not his eyes from her, and ever and anon sent forth a sigh which seemed torn from the bottom of his bowels: all believing it to proceed from pain in his ribs—at least those who the night before had seen how he was plaistered.

Being now both mounted and at the door of the inn, he called to the host, and in a grave and solemn voice said, "Many and great are the favors, Signor Governor, which in this your castle I have received, and I am bound to be grateful to you all the days of my life. If I can make you some compensation, by taking vengeance on any proud miscreant who hath insulted you, know that the duty of my profession is no other than to strengthen the weak, to revenge the injured, and to chastise the perfidious. Consider, and if your memory recalls anything of this nature to recommend to me, you need only declare it; for I promise you, by the order of knighthood I have received, to procure you satisfaction and amends to your heart's desire!"

The host answered with the same gravity, "Sir Knight, I have no need of your worship's avenging any wrong for me; I know how to take the proper revenge when any injury is done me: all I desire of your worship is to pay me for what you have had in the inn, as well for the straw and barley for your two beasts, as for your supper and lodging."

"What! is this an inn?" exclaimed Don Quixote.

"Ay, and a very creditable one," answered the host.

"Hitherto, then, I have been in an error," answered Don Quixote; "for in truth, I took it for a castle; but since it is indeed no castle, but an inn, all that you have now to do is to excuse the payment; for I cannot act contrary to the law of knights-errant, of whom I certainly know (having hitherto read nothing to the contrary) that they never paid for lodging, or anything else, in the inns where they reposed; because every accommodation is legally and justly due to them in return for the insufferable hardships they endure while in quest of adventures, by night and by day, in winter and in summer, on foot and on horseback, with thirst and with hunger, with heat and with cold; subject to all the inclemencies of heaven, and to all the inconveniences upon earth."

"I see little to my purpose in all this," answered the host: "pay me what is my due, and let me have none of your stories and knight-errantries; all I want is to get my own."

"Thou art a blockhead, and a pitiful innkeeper!" answered Don Quixote: so, clapping spurs to Rozinante and brandishing his lance, he sallied out of the inn without opposition and, never turning to see whether his squire followed him, was soon a good way off.

The host, seeing him go without paying, ran to seize on Sancho Panza, who said that, since his master would not pay, neither would he pay; for being squire to a knight-errant, the same rule and reason held as good for him as for his master. The innkeeper threatened, if he did not pay him, he should repent his obstinacy. Sancho swore by the order of chivalry which his master had received, that he would not pay a single farthing, though it would cost him his life; for the laudable and ancient usage of knights-errant should not be lost for him, nor should the squires of future knights have cause to reproach him for not maintaining so just a right.

Poor Sancho's ill luck would have it that among the people in the inn there were four cloth-workers of Segovia, three needle-makers from the fountain of Cordova, and two neighbors from the market-place of Seville, all merry, good-humored, frolicksome fellows; who, instigated and moved, as it appeared, by the selfsame spirit, came up to Sancho and, having dismounted him, one of them produced a blanket from the landlord's bed, into which he was immediately thrown; but perceiving that the ceiling was too low, they determined to execute their purpose in the yard, which was bounded upward only by the sky. Thither Sancho was carried; and being placed in the middle of the blanket, they began to toss him aloft, and divert themselves with him as with a dog at Shrovetide. The cries which the poor blanketed squire sent forth were so many and so loud that they reached his master's ears; who, stopping to listen attentively, believed that some new adventure was at hand, until he plainly recognized the voice of the squire: then turning the reins, he galloped back to the inn door, and finding it closed, he rode round in search of some other entrance; but had no sooner reached the yard wall, which was not very high, when he perceived the wicked sport they were making with his squire. He saw him ascend and descend through the air with so much grace and agility that, if his indignation would have suffered him, he certainly would have laughed outright.

He made an effort to get from his horse upon the pales, but was so maimed and bruised that he was unable to alight; and therefore, remaining on horseback, he proceeded to vent his rage by uttering so many reproaches and invectives against those who were tossing Sancho that it is impossible to commit them to writing.

But they suspended neither their laughter nor their labor; nor did the flying Sancho cease to pour forth lamentations, mingled now with threats, now with entreaties; yet all were of no avail, and they desisted at last only from pure fatigue. They then brought him his ass, and wrapping him in his cloak, mounted him thereon. The compassionate Maritornes, seeing him so exhausted, bethought of helping him to a jug of water, and that it might be the cooler, she fetched it from the well. Sancho took it, and as he was lifting it to his mouth stopped on hearing the voice of his master, who called to him aloud, saying, "Son Sancho, drink not water; do not drink it, son; it will kill thee: behold here the most holy balsam" (showing him the cruse of liquor), "two drops of which will infallibly restore thee."

At these words, Sancho, turning his eyes askance, said in a louder voice, "Perhaps you have forgot, sir, that I am no knight, or you would not have me vomit up what remains of my inside after last night's work. Keep your liquor, in the devil's name, and let me alone." He then instantly began to drink; but at the first sip, finding it was water, he could proceed no further, and besought Maritornes to bring him some wine: which she did willingly and paid for it with her own money; for it is indeed said of her that, although in that station, she had some faint traces of a Christian.

When Sancho had ceased drinking he clapped heels to his ass, and the inn gate being thrown wide open, out he went, satisfied that he had paid nothing and had carried his point, though at the expense of his usual pledge, namely, his back. The landlord, it is true, retained his wallets in payment of what was due to him; but Sancho never missed them in the hurry of his departure. The innkeeper would have fastened the door well after him as soon as he saw him out: but the blanketeers would not let him, being persons of that sort that, though Don Quixote had really been one of the knights of the Round Table, they would not have cared two farthings for him.

A Chance for Mr. Lever*

GRAHAM GREENE

✳✳ This short story introduced in America, through the pages of *Story*, the now widely known writer Graham Greene (born October 2, 1904). He is a distant relative of Robert Louis Stevenson, has traveled a good deal in America, Mexico, and Africa, and is the author of *The Heart of the Matter, The End of the Affair,* and other novels. ✳✳

Mr. Lever knocked his head against the ceiling and swore. Rice was stored above, and in the dark the rats began to move. Grains of rice fell between the slats onto his Revelation suitcase, his bald head, his cases of tinned food, the little square box in which he kept his medicines. His boy had already set up the camp bed and mosquito net, and, outside in the warm, damp dark, his folding table and chair. The thatched pointed huts streamed away toward the forest and a woman went from hut to hut carrying fire. The glow lit her old face, her sagging breasts, her tattooed, diseased body.

It was incredible to Mr. Lever that five weeks ago he had been in London.

He couldn't stand upright; he went down on hands and knees in the dust and opened his suitcase. He took out his wife's photograph and stood it on the chop box; he took out a writing pad and an indelible pencil: the pencil had softened in the heat and left mauve stains on his pajamas. Then because the light of the hurricane lamp disclosed cockroaches the size of blackbeetles flattened against the mud wall, he carefully closed the suitcase. Already in ten days he had learned that they'd eat anything, socks, shirts, the laces out of your shoes.

Mr. Lever went outside; moths beat against his lamp; but there were no mosquitoes; he hadn't seen or heard one since he landed. He sat in a circle of light carefully observed. The blacks squatted outside their huts and watched him; they were friendly, interested, amused, but their strict attention irritated

Mr. Lever. He could feel the small waves of interest washing round him, when he began to write, when he stopped writing, when he wiped his damp hands with a handkerchief. He couldn't touch his pocket without a craning of necks.

Dearest Emily, he wrote, *I've really started now. I'll send this letter back with a carrier when I've located Davidson. I'm very well. Of course everything's a bit strange. Look after yourself, my dear, and don't worry.*

"Massa, buy chicken," his cook said, appearing suddenly between the huts. A small, stringy fowl struggled in his hands.

"Well," Mr. Lever said, "I gave you a shilling, didn't I?"

"They no like," the cook said. "These low bush people."

"Why don't they like? It's good money."

"They want king's money," the cook said, handing back the Victorian shilling. Mr. Lever had to get up, go back into his hut, grope for his money box, search through twenty pounds of small change: there was no peace.

He had learned that very quickly. He had to economize (the whole trip was a gamble which scared him); he couldn't afford hammock carriers. He would arrive, tired out after seven hours of walking, at a village of which he didn't know the name and not for a minute could he sit quietly and rest. He must shake hands with the chief, he must see about a hut, accept presents of palm wine he was afraid to drink, buy rice and palm oil for the carriers, give them salts and aspirin, paint their sores with iodine. They never left him alone for five minutes on end until he went to bed. And then the rats began, rushing down the walls like water when he put out the light, gamboling among his cases.

I'm too old, Mr. Lever told himself, I'm too old, writing damply, indelibly, *I hope to find Davidson tomorrow. If I do, I may be back almost as soon as this letter. Don't economize on the stout and milk, dear, and call in the doctor if you feel bad. I've got a premonition this trip's going to turn out well. We'll take a holiday, you need a holiday,* and staring ahead past the huts and the black faces and the banana trees toward the forest from which he would come, into which he would sink again next day, he thought, Eastbourne. Eastbourne would do her a world of good, and continued to write the only kind of lies he'd ever told Emily, the lies which comforted. *I ought to draw at least three hundred in commission and my expenses.* But it wasn't the sort of place he'd been accustomed to sell heavy machinery in; thirty years of it, up and down Europe and in the States, but never anything like this. He could hear his filter dripping in the hut, and somewhere somebody was playing something (he was so lost he hadn't got the simplest terms to his hand), something monotonous, melancholy, superficial, a twanging of palm fibers which seemed to convey that you weren't happy, but it didn't matter much, everything would always be the same.

Look after yourself, Emily, he repeated. It was almost the only thing he found himself capable of writing to her; he couldn't describe the narrow, steep lost paths, the snakes sizzling away like flames, the rats, the dust, the naked, diseased bodies. He was unbearably tired of nakedness. *Don't forget . . .* It was like living with a lot of cows.

"The chief," his boy whispered, and between the huts under a waving torch came an old stout man wearing a robe of native cloth and a battered bowler hat. Behind him his men carried six bowls of rice, a bowl of palm oil, two bowls of broken meat. "Chop for the laborers," the boy explained, and Mr. Lever had to get up and smile and nod and try to convey without words that he was pleased, that the chop was excellent, that the chief would get a good dash in the morning. At first the smell had been almost too much for Mr. Lever.

"Ask him," he said to his boy, "if he's seen a white man come through here lately. Ask him if a white man's been digging around here. Damn it," Mr. Lever burst out, the sweat breaking on the backs of his hands and on his bald head, "ask him if he's seen Davidson?"

"Davidson?"

"Oh hell," Mr. Lever said, "you know what I mean. The white man I'm looking for."

"White man?"

"What do you imagine I'm here for, eh? White man? Of course white man. I'm not here for my health." A cow coughed, rubbed its horns against the hut, and two goats broke through between the chief and him, upsetting the bowls of meat scraps; nobody cared, they picked the meat out of the dust and dung.

Mr. Lever sat down and put his hands over his face, fat, white, well-cared-for hands with wrinkles of flesh over the rings: I'm too old for this.

"Chief say no white man been here long time."

"How long?"

"Chief say not since he pay hut tax."

"How long's that?"

"Long, long time."

"Ask him how far is it to Greh tomorrow."

"Chief say too far."

"Nonsense," Mr. Lever said.

"Chief say too far. Better stay here. Fine town. No humbug."

Mr. Lever groaned. Every evening there was the same trouble. The next town was always too far. They would invent any excuse to delay him, to give themselves a rest.

"Ask the chief how many hours——?"

"Plenty, plenty." They had no idea of time. "This fine chief. Fine chop. Laborers tired. No humbug."

"We are going on," Mr. Lever said.

"This fine town. Chief say——"

He thought: if this wasn't the last chance, I'd give up. They nagged him so, and suddenly he longed for another white man (not Davidson, he daren't say anything to Davidson) to whom he could explain the desperation of his lot. It wasn't fair, that a man after thirty years' commercial traveling should need to go from door to door asking for a job. He had been a good traveler, he had made money for many people, his references were excellent, but the world had moved on since his day. He wasn't streamlined; he certainly wasn't streamlined. He had been ten years' retired when he lost his money in the depression.

Mr. Lever walked up and down Victoria Street showing his references. Many of the men knew him, gave him cigars, laughed at him in a friendly way for wanting to take on a job at his age ("I can't somehow settle at home. The old warhorse you know . . ."), cracked a joke or two in the passage, went back that night to Maidenhead silent in the first-class carriage, shut in with age and ruin and how bad things were and poor devil his wife's probably sick.

It was in the rather shabby little office off Leadenhall Street that Mr. Lever met his chance. It called itself an engineering firm, but there were only two rooms, a typewriter, a girl with gold teeth and Mr. Lucas, a thin, narrow man with a tic in one eyelid. All through the interview the eyelid flickered at Mr. Lever. Mr. Lever had never before fallen so low as this.

But Mr. Lucas struck him as reasonably honest. He put "all his cards on the table." He hadn't got any money, but he had expectations, he had the handling of a patent. It was a new crusher. There was money in it. But you couldn't expect the big trusts to change over their machinery now. Things were too bad. You'd got to get in at the start, and that was where—why, that was where this chief, the bowls of chop, the nagging and the rats and the heat, came in. They called themselves a republic, Mr. Lucas said, he didn't know anything about that, they were not as black as they were painted, he supposed (ha ha, nervously ha ha); anyway this company had slipped agents over the border and grabbed a concession: gold and diamonds. He could tell Mr. Lever in confidence that the trust was frightened of what they'd found. Now an enterprising man could just slip across (Mr.

Lucas liked the word slip, it made everything sound easy and secret) and introduce this new crusher to them: it would save them thousands when they started work, there'd be a fat commission, and afterward, with the start . . . There was a fortune for them all.

"But can't you fix it up in Europe?"

Tic, tic went Mr. Lucas' eyelid. "A lot of Belgians; they are leaving all decisions to the man on the spot. An Englishman called Davidson."

"How about expenses?"

"That's the trouble," Mr. Lucas said. "We are only beginning. What we want is a partner. We can't afford to send a man. But if you like a gamble . . . Twenty per cent commission."

"Chief say excuse him." The carriers squatted round the basins and scooped up the rice in their left hands. "Of course. Of course," Mr. Lever said absent-mindedly. "Very kind, I'm sure." He was back out of the dust and dark, away from the stink of goats and palm oil and whelping bitches, back among the Rotarians and lunch at Stone's, "the pint of old," and the trade papers; he was a good fellow again, finding his way back to Golders Green just a little lit; his masonic emblem rattled on his watch chain; and he bore with him from the tube station to his house in Finchley Road a sense of companionship, of broad stories and belches, a sense of bravery.

He needed all his bravery now; the last of his savings had gone into the trip. After thirty years he knew a good thing when he saw it, and he had no doubts about the new crusher. What he doubted was his ability to find Davidson. For one thing there weren't any maps; the way you traveled in the Republic was to write down a list of names and trust that someone in the villages you passed would understand and know the route. But they always said "Too far." Good fellowship wilted before the phrase.

"Quinine," Mr. Lever said. "Where's my quinine?" His boy never remembered a thing; they just didn't care what happened to you; their smiles meant nothing, and Mr. Lever, who knew better than anyone the value of a meaningless smile in business, resented their heartlessness, turned toward the dilatory boy an expression of disappointment and dislike.

"Chief say white man in bush five hours away."

"That's better," Mr. Lever said. "It must be Davidson. He's digging for gold?"

"Ya. White man dig for gold in bush."

"We'll be off early tomorrow," Mr. Lever said.

"Chief say better stop this town. Fever humbug white man."

"Too bad," Mr. Lever said, and he thought with pleasure: my luck's changed. He'll want help. He won't refuse me a thing. A friend in need is a friend indeed, and his heart warmed toward Davidson, seeing himself arrive like an answer to prayer out of the forest, feeling quite biblical and *vox humana*. He thought: Prayer. I'll pray tonight, that's the kind of thing a fellow gives up, but it pays, there's something in it, remembering the long agonizing prayer on his knees, by the sideboard, under the decanters, when Emily went to hospital.

"Chief say white man dead."

Mr. Lever turned his back on them and went into his hut. His sleeve nearly overturned the hurricane lamp. He undressed quickly, stuffing his clothes into a suitcase away from the cockroaches. He wouldn't believe what he had been told; it wouldn't pay him to believe. If Davidson was dead, there was nothing he could do but return; he had spent more than he could afford; he would be a ruined man. He supposed that Emily might find a home with her brother, but he could hardly expect her brother—— He began to cry, but you couldn't have told in the shadowy hut the difference between sweat and tears. He knelt down beside his camp bed and mosquito net and prayed on the dust of the earth floor. Up till now he had always been careful never to touch a floor with his naked feet for fear of jiggers; there were jiggers everywhere, they only waited an opportunity to dig themselves in under the toenails, lay their eggs, and multiply.

"O God," Mr. Lever prayed, "don't let Davidson be dead; let him be just sick and glad to see me." He couldn't bear the idea that he might not any longer be able to support Emily. "O God, there's nothing I wouldn't do." But that was still an empty phrase; he had no real notion yet of what he would do for Emily. They had been happy together for thirty-five years; he had never been more than momentarily unfaithful to her when he was lit after a Rotarian dinner and egged on by the boys; whatever skirt he'd been with in his time he had never for a moment imagined that he could be happy married to anyone else. It wasn't fair if, just when you were old and needed each other most, you lost your money and couldn't keep together.

But of course Davidson wasn't dead. What would he have died of? The blacks were friendly. People said the country was unhealthy, but he hadn't so much as heard a mosquito. Besides you didn't die of malaria; you just lay between the blankets and took quinine and felt like death and sweated it out of you. There was dysentery, but Davidson was an old campaigner; you were safe if you boiled and filtered the water. The water was poison even to the touch; it was unsafe to wet your feet because of guinea worm, but you didn't die of guinea worm.

Mr. Lever lay in bed and his thoughts went round and round and he couldn't sleep. He thought: you don't die of a thing like guinea worm. It makes a sore on your foot, and if you put your foot in water you can see the eggs dropping out. You have to find the end of the worm, like a thread of cotton, and wind it round a match and wind it out of your leg without breaking; it stretches as high as the knee. I'm too old for this country, Mr. Lever thought.

Then his boy was beside him again. He whispered urgently to Mr. Lever through the mosquito net, "Massa, the laborers say they go home."

"Go home?" Mr. Lever said wearily; he had heard it so often before. "Why do they want to go home? What is it now?" but he didn't really want to hear the latest squabble: that the Bande men were never sent to carry water because the headman was a Bande, that someone had stolen an empty treacle tin and sold it in the village, that someone wasn't made to carry a proper load, that the next day's journey was "too far." He said, "Tell 'em they can go home. I'll pay them off in the morning. But they won't get any dash. They'd have got a good dash if they'd stayed." He was certain it was just another try-on; he wasn't as green as all that.

"Yes, massa. They no want dash."

"What's that?"

"They frightened fever humbug them like white man."

"I'll get carriers in the village. They can go home."

"Me too, massa."

"Get out," Mr. Lever said; it was the last straw; "get out and let me sleep." The boy went at once, obedient even if he was a deserter, and Mr. Lever thought: sleep, what a hope. He lifted the net and got out of bed (barefooted again: he didn't care a damn about the jiggers) and searched for his medicine box. It was locked, of course, and he had to open his suitcase and find the key in a trouser pocket. His nerves were more on edge than ever by the time he found the sleeping tablets and he took three of them. That made him sleep, heavily and dreamlessly, though when he woke he found that something had made him fling out his arm and open the net. If there had been a single mosquito in the place, he'd have been bitten, but of course there wasn't one.

He could tell at once that the trouble hadn't blown over. The village— he didn't know its name—was perched on a hilltop; east and west the forest flowed out beneath the little plateau: to the west it was a dark unfeatured mass like water, but in the east you could already discern the unevenesses, the great gray cotton trees lifted above the palms. Mr. Lever was always called before dawn, but no one had called him. A few of his carriers sat outside a hut sullenly talking; his boy was with them. Mr. Lever went back inside and dressed; he thought all the time, I must be firm, but he was scared, scared of being deserted, scared of being made to return.

When he came outside again the village was awake: the women were going down the hill to fetch water, winding silently past the carriers, past the flat stones where the chiefs were buried, the little grove of trees where the rice birds, like green and yellow canaries nested. Mr. Lever sat down on his folding chair among the chickens and whelping bitches and cow dung and called his boy. He took "a strong line"; but he didn't know what was going to happen. "Tell the chief I want to speak to him," he said.

There was some delay; the chief wasn't up yet, but presently he appeared in his blue and white robe, setting his bowler hat straight. "Tell him," Mr. Lever said, "I want carriers to take me to the white man and back. Two days."

"Chief no agree," the boy said.

Mr. Lever said furiously, "Damn it, if he doesn't agree, he won't get any dash from me, not a penny." It occurred to him immediately afterward how hopelessly dependent he was on these people's honesty. There in the hut for all to see was his money box; they had only to take it. This wasn't a British or French colony; the blacks on the coast wouldn't bother, could do nothing if they did bother, because a stray Englishman had been robbed in the interior.

"Chief say how many?"

"It's only for two days," Mr. Lever said. "I can do with six."

"Chief say how much?"

"Sixpence a day and chop."

"Chief no agree."

"Ninepence a day then."

"Chief say too far. A shilling."

"All right, all right," Mr. Lever said, "a shilling then. You others can go home if you want to. I'll pay you off now, but you won't get any dash, not a penny."

He had never really expected to be left, and it gave him a sad feeling of loneliness to watch them move sullenly away (they were ashamed of themselves) down the hill to the west. They hadn't any loads, but they weren't singing; they dropped silently out of sight, his boy with them, and he was alone with his pile of boxes and the chief who couldn't talk a word of English. Mr. Lever smiled tremulously.

It was ten o'clock before his new carriers were chosen; he could tell that none of them wanted to go; and they would have to walk through the heat of the middle day if they were to find Davidson before it was dark. He hoped the chief had explained properly where they were going; he couldn't tell; he was completely shut off from them, and when they started down the eastward slope, he might just as well have been alone.

They were immediately caught up in the forest. Forest conveys a sense of wildness and beauty, of an active natural force, but this Liberian forest was simply a dull green wilderness. You passed, on a path a foot or so wide, through an endless back garden of tangled weeds; it didn't seem to be growing round you so much as dying. There was no life at all, except for a few large birds whose wings creaked overhead through the invisible sky like an unoiled door. There was no view, no way out for the eyes, no change of scene. It wasn't the heat that tired so much as the boredom; you had to think of things to think about; but even Emily failed to fill the mind for more than three minutes at a time. It was a relief, a distraction, when the path was flooded and Mr. Lever had to be carried on a man's back. At first he had disliked the strong bitter smell (it reminded him of a breakfast food he was made to eat as a child), but he soon got over that. Now he was unaware that they smelled at all; any more than he was aware that the great swallowtailed butterflies, which clustered at the water's edge and rose in green clouds round his waist, were beautiful. His senses were dulled and registered very little except his boredom.

But they did register a distinct feeling of relief when his leading carrier pointed to a rectangular hole dug just off the path. Mr. Lever understood. Davidson had come this way. He stopped and looked at it. It was like a grave dug for a small man, but it went down deeper than graves usually do. About twelve feet below there was black water, and a few wooden props which held the sides from slipping were beginning to rot; the hole must have been dug since the rains. It didn't seem enough, that hole, to have brought out Mr. Lever with his plans and estimates for a new crusher. He was used to big industrial concerns, the sight of pit heads, the smoke of chimneys, the dingy rows of cottages back to back, the leather armchair in the office, the good cigar, the masonic handgrips, and again it seemed to him, as it had seemed in Mr. Lucas' office, that he had fallen very low. It was as if he was expected to do business beside a hole a child had dug in an overgrown and abandoned back garden; percentages wilted in the hot, damp air. He shook his head; he mustn't be discouraged; this was an old hole. Davidson had probably done better since. It was only common sense to suppose that the gold rift which was mined at one end in Nigeria, at the other in Sierra Leone, should pass through the republic. Even the biggest mines had to begin with a hole in the ground. The company, he had talked to the directors in Brussels, were quite confident: all they wanted was the approval of the man on the spot that the crusher was suitable for local conditions. A signature, that was all he had to get, he told himself, staring down into the puddle of black water.

Five hours, the chief had said, but after six hours they were still walking. Mr. Lever had eaten nothing, he wanted to get to Davidson first. All through the heat of the day he walked. The forest protected him from the direct sun, but it shut out the air, and the occasional clearings, shriveled though they were in the vertical glare, seemed cooler than the shade because there was a little more air to breathe. At four o'clock the heat diminished, but he began to fear they wouldn't reach Davidson before dark. His foot pained him; he had caught a jigger the night before; it was as if someone held a lighted match to his toe. Then at five they came on a dead black.

Another rectangular hole in a small cleared space among the dusty greenery caught Mr. Lever's eye. He peered down and was shocked to see a face return his stare, white eyeballs like phosphorus in the black water. The black had been bent almost double to fit him in; the hole was really too small to be a grave, and he had swollen. His flesh was like a blister you could prick with a needle. Mr. Lever felt sick and tired; he might have been tempted to return if he could have reached the village before dark; but now there was nothing to do but go on; the carriers luckily hadn't seen the body. He waved them forward and stumbled after among the roots, fighting his nausea. He fanned himself with his sun helmet; his wide, fat face was damp and pale. He had never seen an uncared-for body before; his parents he had seen carefully laid out with closed eyes and washed faces; they "fell asleep" quite in accordance with their epitaphs, but you couldn't think of sleep in connection with the white eyeballs and the swollen face. Mr. Lever would have liked very much to say a prayer, but prayers were out of place in the dead, drab forest; they simply didn't "come."

With the dusk a little life did waken: something lived in the dry weeds and brittle trees, if only monkeys. They chattered and screamed all round you, but it was too dark to see them; you were like a blind man in the center of a frightened crowd who wouldn't say what scared them. The carriers too were frightened. They ran under their fifty-pound loads behind the dipping light of the hurricane lamp, their huge, fat carriers' feet flapping in the dust like empty gloves. Mr. Lever listened nervously for mosquitoes; you would have expected them to be out by now, but he didn't hear one.

Then at the top of a rise above a small stream they came on Davidson. The ground had been cleared in a square of twelve feet and a small tent pitched; he had dug another hole; the scene came dimly into view as they climbed the path: the chop boxes piled outside the tent, the siphon of soda water, the filter, an enamel basin. But there wasn't a light, there wasn't a sound, the flaps of the tent were not closed, and Mr. Lever had to face the possibility that after all the chief might have told the truth.

Mr. Lever took the lamp and stooped inside the tent. There was a body on the bed. At first Mr. Lever thought Davidson was covered with blood, but then he realized it was a black vomit which stained his shirts and khaki shorts, the fair stubble on his chin. He put out a hand and touched Davidson's face, and if he hadn't felt a slight breath on his palm he would have taken him for dead; his skin was so cold. He moved the lamp closer, and now the lemon-yellow face told him all he wanted to know: he hadn't thought of that when his boy said fever. It was quite true that a man didn't die of malaria, but an old piece of news read in New York in '98 came back to mind: there had been an outbreak in Rio and ninety-four per cent of the cases had been fatal. It hadn't meant anything to him then, but it did now. As he watched, Davidson was sick, quite effortlessly; he was like a tap out of which something flowed.

It seemed at first to Mr. Lever to be the end of everything, of his journey, his hopes, his life with Emily. There was nothing he could do for Davidson, the man was unconscious, there were times when his pulse was so low and irregular that Mr. Lever thought that he was dead until another black stream spread from his mouth; it was no use even cleaning him. Mr. Lever laid his own blankets over the bed on top of Davidson's because he was so cold to the touch, but he had no idea whether he was doing the right, or even the fatally wrong, thing. The chance of survival, if there was any chance at all, depended on neither of them. Outside his carriers had built a fire and were cooking the rice they had brought with them. Mr. Lever opened his folding chair and sat by the bed. He wanted to keep awake: it seemed right to keep awake; he opened his case and found his unfinished letter to Emily. He sat by Davidson's side and tried to write, but he could think of nothing but what he had already written too often: *Look after yourself; don't forget the stout and milk.*

He fell asleep over his pad and woke at two and thought that Davidson was dead. But he was wrong again. He was very thirsty and missed his boy. Always the first thing his boy did at the end of a march was to light a fire and put on a kettle; after that, by the time his table and chair were set up, there was water ready for the filter. Mr. Lever found half a cup of soda water left in Davidson's siphon; if it had been only his health at stake he would have gone down to the stream and drank, but he had Emily to remember.

There was a typewriter by the bed and it occurred to Mr. Lever that he might just as well begin to write his report of failure now; it might keep him awake; it seemed disrespectful to the dying man to sleep. He found paper under some letters which had been typed and signed but not sealed. Davidson must have been taken ill very suddenly; Mr. Lever wondered whether it was he who had crammed the black into the hole; his boy perhaps, for there was no sign of a servant. He blanced the typewriter on his knee and headed the letter, *In Camp near Greh.*

It seemed to him unfair that he should have come so far, spent so much money, worn out a rather old body to meet his inevitable ruin in a dark tent beside a dying man when he could have met it just as well at home with Emily in the plush parlor. The thought of the prayers he had uselessly uttered on his knees by the camp bed among the jiggers, the rats and the cockroaches made him rebellious. A mosquito, the first he had heard, went humming round the tent. He slashed at it savagely; he wouldn't have recognized himself among the Rotarians. He was lost and he was set free. Moralities were what enabled a man to live happily and successfully with his fellows, but Mr. Lever wasn't happy and he wasn't successful, and his only fellow in the little stuffy tent wouldn't be troubled by Untruth in Advertising or by Mr. Lever coveting his neighbor's oxen. You couldn't keep your ideas intact when you discovered their geographical nature. The Solemnity of Death: death wasn't solemn; it was a lemon-yellow skin and a black vomit. Honesty is the Best Policy: that he saw quite suddenly was palpably false. It was an anarchist who sat happily over the typewriter, an anarchist who recognized nothing but one personal relationship, his affection for Emily, Mr. Lever began to type: *I have examined the plans and estimates of the new Lucas crusher . . .*

Mr. Lever thought with savage happiness: I win. This letter would be the last the company would hear from Davidson. The junior partner would open it in the dapper Brussels office; he would tap his false teeth with a Waterman pen and go in to talk to M. Golz. *Taking all these factors into consideration I recommend acceptance . . .* They would telegraph to Lucas. As for Davidson, that trusted agent of the company would have died of yellow fever at some never accurately determined date. Another agent would come out, and the crusher. . . . Mr. Lever carefully copied Davidson's signature on a spare sheet of paper. He wasn't satisfied. He turned the original upside down and copied it that way, so as not to be confused by his own idea of how a letter should be formed. That was better, but it didn't satisfy him. He searched until he found Davidson's own pen and began to copy and copy the signature. He fell asleep copying it and woke again an hour later to find the lamp was out; it had burned up all the oil. He sat there beside Davidson's bed till daylight; once he was bitten by a mosquito in the ankle and clapped his hand to the place too late: the brute went humming out. With the light Mr. Lever saw that Davidson was dead. "Dear dear," he said. "Poor fellow." He spat out with the words, quite delicately in a corner, the bad morning taste in his mouth. It was like a little sediment of conventionality.

Mr. Lever got two of his carriers to cram Davidson tidily in his hole. He was no longer afraid, of them or of failure or of separation. He tore up his letter to Emily. It no longer represented his mood in its timidity, its secret fear, its gentle, fussing phrases, "Don't forget the stout," "Look after yourself." He would be home as soon as the letter, and they were going to do things together now they'd never dreamed of doing. The money for the crusher was only the beginning. His ideas stretched further now than Eastbourne, they stretched as far as Switzerland; he had a feeling that if he really let himself go, they'd stretch as far as the Riviera. How happy he was on what he thought of as "the trip home." He was freed from what had held him back through a long pedantic career, the fear of some conscious fate that notes the dishonesty, notes the skirt in Piccadilly, notes the glass too many of Stone's special. Now he had said Boo to that goose.

But you on the other hand who are reading this, who know so much more than Mr. Lever, who can follow the mosquito's progress from the dead, swollen black to Davidson's tent, to Mr. Lever's ankle, you, I say, may possibly believe in fate, a kindly fate tender toward human frailty, ready to give Mr. Lever three days of happiness, three days off the galling chain, as he carried back through the forest his amateurish forgeries and the infection of yellow fever in the blood. The story may very well confirm your faith in that loving, merciful omniscience if it has not been shaken by personal knowledge of the drab, empty forest through which Mr. Lever now went so merrily, where it is impossible to believe in any spiritual life, in anything outside the nature dying round you, the shriveling of the weeds. There are two opinions about everything; it was Mr. Lever's favorite expression, drinking beer in the Ruhr, Pernod in Lorraine, selling heavy machinery.

The Fifty-first Dragon*

HEYWOOD BROUN

Of all the pupils at the Knight School, Gawaine le Cœur-Hardy was among the least promising. He was tall and sturdy, but his instructors soon discovered that he lacked spirit. He would hide in the woods when the jousting class was called, although his companions and members of the faculty sought to appeal to his better nature by shouting to him to come out and break his neck like a man. Even when they told him that the lances were padded, the horses no more than ponies and the field unusually soft for late autumn, Gawaine refused to grow enthusiastic. The Headmaster and the Assistant Professor of Pleasaunce were discussing the case one spring afternoon and the Assistant Professor could see no remedy but expulsion.

"No," said the Headmaster, as he looked out at the purple hills which ringed the school, "I think I'll train him to slay dragons."

"He might be killed," objected the Assistant Professor.

"So he might," replied the Headmaster brightly, but he added, more soberly, "We must consider the greater good. We are responsible for the formation of this lad's character."

"Are the dragons particularly bad this year?" interrupted the Assistant Professor. This was characteristic. He always seemed restive when the head of the school began to talk ethics and the ideals of the institution.

"I've never known them worse," replied the Headmaster. "Up in the hills to the south last week they killed a number of peasants, two cows and a prize pig. And if this dry spell holds there's no telling when they may start a forest fire simply by breathing around indiscriminately."

"Would any refund on the tuition fee be necessary in case of an accident to young Cœur-Hardy?"

"No," the principal answered, judicially, "that's all covered in the contract.

* From *The Collected Edition of Heywood Broun,* copyright, 1941, by Heywood Hale Broun. Published by Harcourt, Brace and Company, Inc., New York, reprinted by permission of Harcourt, Brace and Company, Inc.

But as a matter of fact he won't be killed. Before I send him up in the hills I'm going to give him a magic word."

"That's a good idea," said the Professor. "Sometimes they work wonders."

From that day on Gawaine specialized in dragons. His course included both theory and practice. In the morning there were long lectures on the history, anatomy, manners, and customs of dragons. Gawaine did not distinguish himself in these studies. He had a marvelously versatile gift for forgetting things. In the afternoon he showed to better advantage, for then he would go down to the South Meadow and practice with a battle-ax. In this exercise he was truly impressive, for he had enormous strength as well as speed and grace. He even developed a deceptive display of ferocity. Old alumni say that it was a thrilling sight to see Gawaine charging across the field toward the dummy paper dragon which had been set up for his practice. As he ran he would brandish his ax and shout "A murrain on thee!" or some other vivid bit of campus slang. It never took him more than one stroke to behead the dummy dragon.

Gradually his task was made more difficult. Paper gave way to *papier-mâché* and finally to wood, but even the toughest of these dummy dragons had no terrors for Gawaine. One sweep of the ax always did the business. There were those who said that when the practice was protracted until dusk and the dragons threw long, fantastic shadows across the meadow Gawaine did not charge so impetuously nor shout so loudly. It is possible there was malice in this charge. At any rate, the Headmaster decided by the end of June that it was time for the test. Only the night before a dragon had come close to the school grounds and had eaten some of the lettuce from the garden. The faculty decided that Gawaine was ready. They gave him a diploma and a new battle-ax and the Headmaster summoned him to a private conference.

"Sit down," said the Headmaster. "Have a cigarette."

Gawaine hesitated.

"Oh, I know it's against the rules," said the Headmaster. "But after all, you have received your preliminary degree. You are no longer a boy. You are a man. Tomorrow you will go out into the world, the great world of achievement."

Gawaine took a cigarette. The Headmaster offered him a match, but he produced one of his own and began to puff away with a dexterity which quite amazed the principal.

"Here you have learned the theories of life," continued the Headmaster, resuming the thread of his discourse, "but after all, life is not a matter of theories. Life is a matter of facts. It calls on the young and the old alike to face these facts, even though they are hard and sometimes unpleasant. Your problem, for example, is to slay dragons."

"They say that those dragons down in the south wood are five hundred feet long," ventured Gawaine, timorously.

"Stuff and nonsense!" said the Headmaster. "The curate saw one last week from the top of Arthur's Hill. The dragon was sunning himself down in the valley. The curate didn't have an opportunity to look at him very long because he felt it was his duty to hurry back to make a report to me. He said the monster, or shall I say, the big lizard?—wasn't an inch over two hundred feet. But the size has nothing at all to do with it. You'll find the big ones even easier than the little ones. They're far slower on their feet and less aggressive, I'm told. Besides, before you go I'm going to equip you in such fashion that you need have no fear of all the dragons in the world."

"I'd like an enchanted cap," said Gawaine.

"What's that?" answered the Headmaster, testily.

"A cap to make me disappear," explained Gawaine.

The Headmaster laughed indulgently. "You mustn't believe all those old wives' stories," he said. "There isn't any such thing. A cap to make you disappear, indeed! What would you do with it? You haven't even appeared yet. Why, my boy, you could walk from here to London, and nobody would so much as look at you. You're nobody. You couldn't be more invisible than that."

Gawaine seemed dangerously close to a relapse into his old habit of whimpering. The Headmaster reassured him: "Don't worry; I'll give you something much better than an enchanted cap. I'm going to give you a magic word. All you have to do is to repeat this magic charm once and no dragon can possibly harm a hair of your head. You can cut off his head at your leisure."

He took a heavy book from the shelf behind his desk and began to run through it. "Sometimes," he said, "the charm is a whole phrase or even a sentence. I might, for instance, give you 'To make the'—No, that might not do. I think a single word would be best for dragons."

"A short word," suggested Gawaine.

"It can't be too short or it wouldn't be potent. There isn't so much hurry as all that. Here's a splendid magic word: '*Rumplesnitz.*' Do you think you can learn that?"

Gawaine tried and in an hour or so he seemed to have the word well in hand. Again and again he interrupted the lesson to inquire, "And if I say '*Rumplesnitz*' the dragon can't possibly hurt me?" And always the Headmaster replied, "If you only say '*Rumplesnitz,*' you are perfectly safe."

Toward morning Gawaine seemed resigned to his career. At daybreak the Headmaster saw him to the edge of the forest and pointed him to the direction in which he should proceed. About a mile away to the southwest a cloud of steam hovered over an open meadow in the woods and the Headmaster assured Gawaine that under the steam he would find a dragon. Gawaine went forward slowly. He wondered whether it would be best to approach the dragon on the run as he did in his practice in the South Meadow or to walk slowly toward him, shouting *"Rumplesnitz"* all the way.

The problem was decided for him. No sooner had he come to the fringe of the meadow than the dragon spied him and began to charge. It was a large dragon and yet it seemed decidedly aggressive in spite of the Headmaster's statement to the contrary. As the dragon charged it released huge clouds of hissing steam through its nostrils. It was almost as if a gigantic teapot had gone mad. The dragon came forward so fast and Gawaine was so frightened that he had time to say *"Rumplesnitz"* only once. As he said it, he swung his battle-ax and off popped the head of the dragon. Gawaine had to admit that it was even easier to kill a real dragon than a wooden one if only you said, *"Rumplesnitz."*

Gawaine brought the ears home and a small section of the tail. His schoolmates and the faculty made much of him, but the Headmaster wisely kept him from being spoiled by insisting that he go on with his work. Every clear day Gawaine rose at dawn and went out to kill dragons. The Headmaster kept him at home when it rained, because he said the woods were damp and unhealthy at such times and that he didn't want the boy to run needless risks. Few good days passed in which Gawaine failed to get a dragon. On one particularly fortunate day he killed three, a husband and wife and a visiting relative. Gradually he developed a technique. Pupils who sometimes watched him from the hilltops a long way off said that he often allowed the dragon to come within a few feet before he said *"Rumplesnitz."* He came to say it with a mocking sneer. Occasionally he did stunts. Once when an excursion party from London was watching him he went into action with his right hand tied behind his back. The dragon's head came off just as easily.

As Gawaine's record of killings mounted higher the Headmaster found it impossible to keep him completely in hand. He fell into the habit of stealing out at night and engaging in long drinking bouts at the village tavern. It was after such a debauch that he rose a little before dawn one fine August morning and started out after his fiftieth dragon. His head was heavy and his mind sluggish. He was heavy in other respects as well, for he had adopted the somewhat vulgar practice of wearing his medals, ribbons, and all, when he went out dragon hunting. The decorations began on his chest and ran all the way down to his abdomen. They must have weighed at least eight pounds.

Gawaine found a dragon in the same meadow where he had killed the first one. It was a fair-sized dragon, but evidently an old one. Its face was wrinkled and Gawaine thought he had never seen so hideous a countenance. Much to the lad's disgust, the monster refused to charge and Gawaine was obliged to walk toward him. He whistled as he went. The dragon regarded him hopelessly but craftily. Of course it had heard of Gawaine. Even when the lad raised his battle-ax the dragon made no move. It knew that there was no salvation in the quickest thrust of the head, for it had been informed that this hunter was protected by an enchantment. It merely waited, hoping something would turn up. Gawaine raised the battle-ax and suddenly lowered it again. He had grown very pale and he trembled violently. The dragon suspected a trick. "What's the matter?" it asked, with false solicitude.

"I've forgotten the magic word," stammered Gawaine.

"What a pity," said the dragon. "So that was the secret. It doesn't seem quite sporting to me, all this magic stuff, you know. Not cricket, as we used to say when I was a little dragon; but after all, that's a matter of opinion."

Gawaine was so helpless with terror that the dragon's confidence rose immeasurably and it could not resist the temptation to show off a bit.

"Could I possibly be of any assistance?" it asked. "What's the first letter of the magic word?"

"It begins with an 'R,' " said Gawaine weakly.

"Let's see," mused the dragon, "that doesn't tell us much, does it? What sort of a word is this? Is it an epithet, do you think?"

Gawaine could do no more than nod.

"Why, of course," exclaimed the dragon, "reactionary Republican."

Gawaine shook his head.

"Well, then," said the dragon, "we'd better get down to business. Will you surrender?"

With the suggestion of a compromise Gawaine mustered up enough courage to speak.

"What will you do if I surrender?" he asked.

"Why, I'll eat you," said the dragon.

"And if I don't surrender?"

"I'll eat you just the same."

"Then it doesn't make any difference, does it?" moaned Gawaine.

"It does to me," said the dragon with a smile. "I'd rather you didn't surrender. You'd taste much better if you didn't."

The dragon waited for a long time for Gawaine to ask, "Why?" but the boy was too frightened to speak. At last the dragon had to give the explanation without his cue line. "You see," he said, "if you don't surrender you'll taste better because you'll die game."

This was an old and ancient trick of the dragon's. By means of some such quip he was accustomed to paralyze his victims with laughter and then to destroy them. Gawaine was sufficiently paralyzed as it was, but laughter had no part in his helplessness. With the last word of the joke the dragon drew back his head and struck. In that second there flashed into the mind of Gawaine the magic word *"Rumplesnitz,"* but there was no time to say it. There was time only to strike and, without a word, Gawaine met the onrush of the dragon with a full swing. He put all his back and shoulders into it. The impact was terrific and the head of the dragon flew away almost a hundred yards and landed in a thicket.

Gawaine did not remain frightened very long after the death of the dragon. His mood was one of wonder. He was enormously puzzled. He cut off the ears of the monster almost in a trance. Again and again he thought to himself, "I didn't say *'Rumplesnitz'!"* He was sure of that and yet there was no question that he had killed the dragon. In fact, he had never killed one so utterly. Never before had he driven a head for anything like the same distance. Twenty-five yards was perhaps his best previous record. All the way back to the Knight School he kept rumbling about in his mind seeking an explanation for what had occurred. He went to the Headmaster immediately and after closing the door told him what had happened. "I didn't say *'Rumplesnitz,'"* he explained with great earnestness.

The Headmaster laughed. "I'm glad you've found out," he said. "It makes you ever so much more of a hero. Don't you see that? Now you know that it was you who killed all these dragons and not that foolish little word *'Rumplesnitz.'"*

Gawaine frowned. "Then it wasn't a magic word after all?" he asked.

"Of course not," said the Headmaster, "you ought to be too old for such foolishness. There isn't any such thing as a magic word."

"But you told me it was magic," protested Gawaine. "You said it was magic and now you say it isn't."

"It wasn't magic in a literal sense," answered the Headmaster, "but it was much more wonderful than that. The word gave you confidence. It took away your fears. If I hadn't told you that you might have been killed the very first time. It was your battle-ax did the trick."

Gawaine surprised the Headmaster by his attitude. He was obviously distressed by the explanation. He interrupted a long philosophic and ethical discourse by the Headmaster with, "If I hadn't of hit 'em all mighty hard and fast any one of 'em might have crushed me like a, like a—" He fumbled for a word.

"Eggshell," suggested the Headmaster.

"Like a eggshell," assented Gawaine, and he said it many times. All through the evening meal people who sat near him heard him muttering, "Like a eggshell, like a eggshell."

The next day was clear, but Gawaine did not get up at dawn. Indeed, it was almost noon when the Headmaster found him cowering in bed, with the clothes pulled over his head. The principal called the Assistant Professor of Pleasaunce, and together they dragged the boy toward the forest.

"He'll be all right as soon as he gets a couple more dragons under his belt," explained the Headmaster.

The Assistant Professor of Pleasaunce agreed. "It would be a shame to stop such a fine run," he said. "Why, counting that one yesterday, he's killed fifty dragons."

They pushed the boy into a thicket above which hung a meager cloud of steam. It was obviously quite a small dragon. But Gawaine did not come back that night or the next. In fact, he never came back. Some weeks afterward brave spirits from the school explored the thicket, but they could find nothing to remind them of Gawaine except the metal parts of his medals. Even the ribbons had been devoured.

The Headmaster and the Assistant Professor of Pleasaunce agreed that it would be just as well not to tell the school how Gawaine had achieved his record and still less how he came to die. They held that it might have a bad effect on school spirit. Accordingly, Gawaine has lived in the memory of the school as its greatest hero. No visitor succeeds in leaving the building today without seeing a great shield which hangs on the wall of the dining hall. Fifty pairs of dragons' ears are mounted upon the shield and underneath in gilt letters is "Gawaine le Cœur-Hardy," followed by the simple inscription, "He killed fifty dragons." The record has never been equaled.

Mounted Warrior*

GOTTFRIED AUGUST BUERGER

✳✳ Gottfried August Buerger, a German classicist, took his *Munchausen* from the book by Rudolf E. Raspe. Although Raspe, the original author of *Munchausen*, was a German professor, he first published his book in English, Buerger's translation being the German version of the book. Then, Ulrich L. Steindorff translated Buerger's book back into English. Such a roundabout way of presenting the Baron seems perfectly in keeping with his wandering spirit, whose fictional characterization is probably only an amplification of the essential nature of his prototype, the Baron Karl Friedrich Munchausen, who was alive and noted throughout Germany for his genius as a teller of tall tales when Buerger (1747-94) was writing—translating the Baron's adventures into his native German and enabling the tales to find their way into the libraries of the Continent and the rest of the world. ✳✳

THE BARON MUNCHAUSEN

Modesty forbids the common soldier to attribute to himself great deeds and victories, the glory of which is usually credited to the officers, regardless of their true qualities or—awkward as it may seem—to kings and queens who smell powder on review days, never see a camp that is not staked for pleasure, nor a phalanx except at parades.

I lay no claims, therefore, to the honor won in our greater engagements with the enemy. We all did our duty, which, in the language of the patriot, the soldier, and the gentleman, is a very comprehensive word, a word of great import, although the idle busybodies at home have but a very poor idea of its true meaning. Having, however, command of a squadron of hussars, I had to make several expeditions where everything was left to my own ingenuity and courage. My success, I can justly and fairly credit to the brave fellows whom I led to conquest and victory.

* From the translation from the German by Ulrich L. Steindorff Corrington. Copyright, 1933, by Ulrich L. Steindorff.

Once, when driving the Turks into Oczakow, we of the vanguard had a very hot day. My fiery Lithuanian* almost brought me into a scrape. I had to reconnoiter quite some distance ahead and saw the enemy moving against me in a cloud of dust, which left me rather uncertain as to their actual number and real intentions. To wrap myself in a similar cloud of dust would have been a common trick but would have neither advanced my knowledge nor served the purpose for which I was commissioned. I let my flankers spread to the right and left and stir up all the dust they possibly could. I myself led straight against the enemy in order to inspect them a little closer. I was right. They stood and fought until the fear of my oncoming flankers made them take to their heels. Now was the time to fall upon them with all our might. We broke them entirely and drove them in terrible defeat back to their bastions and through the fortress, far beyond our most sanguinary expectations.

Since my Lithuanian was so extraordinarily swift, I was the foremost in the pursuit, and when I saw the enemy fleeting nicely through the opposite gate I thought it advisable to stop in the market place and call my men to rally. I stopped, but my friends, imagine my surprise when I could discover neither my bugler nor any of my hussars. "Are they scouring the streets or what has become of them?" I asked myself. They could not possibly be far off. They must soon catch up with me. Thus I walked my panting Lithuanian to the well in the market place and let him drink. He drank so greedily and with a thirst so unquenchable that it did not seem natural to me. When I turned my head to look for my men, what do you think, my friends, I beheld?—The whole hind part of the poor animal, croup and legs, was missing, nearly cut off. The water ran out as fast as it came in, without refreshing him or doing him any good. How it happened, remained a complete mystery to me until at last my orderly came galloping through the opposite gate and told me, over-flowing with felicitations and curses, what had occurred. When I had rushed

---

* This superb Lithuanian horse [the Baron elsewhere relates] a horse no money could have ever bought, I got because I had an opportunity to be invited to the most wonderful estate of Count Przobobowsky in Lithuania and after tea tarried with the ladies in the drawing room while the gentlemen were in the yard inspecting a young thoroughbred which had just arrived from stud. Suddenly we heard a cry for help. I ran downstairs and found the horse so wild and rebellious that nobody dared approach or mount him. The most resolute horsemen stood dismayed and aghast. Their faces were shadowed with fear when I, with one leap, sat on his back, taking the horse by surprise, and then worked the scared animal with my best equestrian skill into peace and obedience. To demonstrate this fully to the ladies and to spare them any unnecessary anxiety, I forced the horse to jump with me through one of the open windows into the salon. I circled the room several times in pace, trot, and gallop until I finally made him mount the tea table and repeat all the gaits docilely in miniature, which amused the ladies immensely. My good stallion performed so amazingly well that he broke neither cup nor saucer. This feat put me in such favor with the ladies and the Count that he asked me in his courteous way to accept the young horse as a gift and to ride it to conquest and victory in the campaign against the Turks, which was soon to open under the command of Count Munnich.

in pell-mell with the flying enemy, they had suddenly dropped the portcullis and thus severed the hind part from my horse.

At first said hind part, he asserted, wrought havoc among the enemy, who blindly scrambled for the gate, by pounding them with his hoofs, and then he meandered victoriously through the meadows, where I probably would still find him.

Instantly I turned and in a gallop, fast beyond belief, my half of the horse carried me to the pastures. To my great joy I found the other half and to my surprise I saw him passing his time in a better fashion than any master of ceremonies could have ever designed for a headless entertainment. Briefly said, the miracle-sire was strutting before the dames of the pasture whose admiration made him forget all the grief he had suffered. Little wonder that he did not miss his head. But it will amaze you, my friends, that the new generation of horses was lacking likewise brains and all, which their mothers thought quite fashionable.

Being sure beyond a question of a doubt that both halves of my horse were still fully alive, I sent for our farrier. Without losing time he sewed the two parts together with young laurel shoots. The wound healed perfectly. Something, however, happened that was most befitting such a glorious stallion. The shoots took root in his body, grew up, and formed a bower above me so that I could enjoy many an honest ride in the shade of my own and my horse's laurels.

By the bye, this encounter with the enemy caused me another trifling inconvenience. I had thrashed the enemy so vehemently and so incessantly that my arm was swinging automatically long after they had disappeared. As I did not like to pummel myself nor my innocent men, I was forced to wear my arm in a sling for almost a week, just as if I had been severely wounded.

You will believe, my friends, a man who was able to ride a horse like my Lithuanian when he tells you of another equestrian feat or rather of aerial acrobatics, although it might sound somewhat fabulous. We besieged, I do not recollect what town. The generalissimo was very anxious to find out the happenings in the fortress. It seemed impossible to sneak through the sentries and entrenchments, and moreover there was nobody capable of performing such a task. In my courage and eagerness to serve, I stepped almost too hastily beside a big cannon which was just being fired, and—bang!—I jumped on the ball in order to be carried into the fortress. When I was halfway through the air some serious doubts arose in my mind. "Hmm," I thought, "you might get in there but how do you intend to get out? What will happen to you in the fortress? Won't they recognize you instantly as a spy and string you up? Honor forbid such an end!" Upon these and similar reflections, I decided to take advantage of a cannon ball aimed from the fortress at our camp. I jumped over and, although I did not accomplish my mission, returned safely to our lines.

As good and ready a jumper as I was, my horse always equaled me. Neither gullies nor gates ever prevented me from taking the straightest path. One day I was coursing a hare who cut across the turnpike. A carriage with two beautiful ladies rolled along and passed between me and the hare. My stallion jumped right through the open window and did not leave me even time to doff my hat and apologize.

Another day I was jumping a morass which was wider than I expected. In mid-air I swung my horse about to let it take a better run. But even the second time I jumped too short and landed close to the edge where I sank up to my neck in the bog. Helplessly I would have drowned if I had not grabbed my hair and pulled myself and the horse, which I clasped tightly with my knees, through the strength of my arm, out of the morass.

8 *Frontiers*

THE VISIONS AND THE CALCULATION

The First Pile

CORBIN ALLARDICE
and
EDWARD R. TRAPNELL

✳✳ Corbin Allardice, who in 1946 was director of the Public Information Service, U. S. Atomic Energy Commission, New York Operations Office, and Edward R. Trapnell, associate director, Division of Public and Technical Information Service, U.S.A.E.C. Washington, compiled the first narrative history of the first self-sustaining nuclear chain reaction. It was based on the personal recollections of more than a dozen of the 42 scientists present in a calculated adventure in which few of the spectators were altogether certain of the outcome of what they were about to witness. This section is presented here through the permission of the authors and the Technical Information Division, Oak Ridge, Tennessee. ✳✳

On December 2, 1942, man first initiated a self-sustaining nuclear chain reaction and controlled it.

Beneath the West Stands of Stagg Field, Chicago, late in the afternoon of that day, a small group of scientists witnessed the advent of a new era in science. History was made in what had been a squash-rackets court.

Precisely at 3:25 P.M., Chicago time, scientist George Weil withdrew the cadmium-plated control rod and by his action man unleashed and controlled the energy of the atom.

As those who witnessed the experiment became aware of what had happened, smiles spread over their faces and a quiet ripple of applause could be heard. It was a tribute to Enrico Fermi, Nobel Prize winner, to whom, more than to any other person, the success of the experiment was due.

Fermi, born in Rome, Italy, on September 29, 1901, had been working with uranium for many years. In 1934 he bombarded uranium with neutrons and produced what appeared to be element 93 (uranium is element 92) and element 94. However, after closer examination it seemed as if nature had gone wild; several other elements were present, but none could be fitted into the periodic table near uranium—where Fermi knew they should have fitted if they had been the transuranic elements 93 and 94. It was not until five years later that anyone, Fermi included, realized he had actually caused fission of the uranium and that these unexplained elements belonged back in the middle part of the periodic table.

Fermi was awarded the Nobel Prize in 1938 for his work on transuranic elements. He and his family went to Sweden to receive the prize. The Italian Fascist press severely criticized him for not wearing a Fascist uniform and failing to give the Fascist salute when he received the award. The Fermis never returned to Italy.

From Sweden, having taken most of his personal possessions with him, Fermi proceeded to London and thence to America where he has remained ever since.

The modern Italian explorer of the unknown was in Chicago that cold December day in 1942. An outsider, looking into the squash court where Fermi was working, would have been greeted by a strange sight. In the center of the 30-by-60-foot room, shrouded on all but one side by a gray balloon cloth envelope, was a pile of black bricks and wooden timbers, square at the bottom and a flattened sphere on top. Up to half of its height, its sides were straight. The top half was domed, like a beehive. During the construction of this crude-appearing but complex pile (the name which has since been applied to all such devices) the standing joke among the scientists working on it was: "If people could see what we're doing with a million-and-a-half of their dollars, they'd think we are crazy. If they knew why we are doing it, they'd be sure we are." . . .

Three years before the December 2 experiment, it had been discovered that when an atom of uranium was bombarded by neutrons, the uranium atom sometimes was split, or fissioned. Later it had been found that when an atom of uranium fissioned, additional neutrons were emitted and became available for further reaction with other uranium atoms. These facts implied the possibility of a chain reaction, similar in certain respects to the reaction which is the source of the sun's energy. The facts further indicated that if a sufficient quantity of uranium could be brought together under the proper conditions, a self-sustaining chain reaction would result. This quantity of uranium necessary for a chain reaction under given conditions is known as the critical mass, or more commonly, the "critical size" of the particular pile.

For three years the problem of a self-sustaining chain reaction had been assiduously studied. . . .

At Chicago during the early afternoon of December 1, tests indicated that critical size was rapidly being approached. At 4:00 P.M. Zinn's* group was relieved by the men working under Anderson.† Shortly afterward the last layer of graphite and uranium bricks was placed on the pile. Zinn, who remained, and Anderson made several measurements of the activity within the pile. They were certain that when the control rods were withdrawn, the pile would become self-sustaining. Both had agreed, however, that should measurements indicate the reaction would become self-sustaining when the rods were withdrawn, they would not start the pile operating until Fermi and the rest of the group could be present. Consequently, the control rods were locked and further work was postponed until the following day.

That night the word was passed to the men who had worked on the pile that the trial run was due the next morning.

About eight-thirty on the morning of Wednesday, December 2, the group began to assemble in the squash court.

At the north end of the squash court was a balcony about ten feet above the floor of the court. Fermi, Zinn, Anderson, and Compton§ were grouped around instruments at the east end of the balcony. The remainder of the observers crowded the little balcony. R. G. Nobles, one of the young scientists who worked on the pile, put it this way: "The control cabinet was surrounded by the 'big wheels'; the 'little wheels' had to stand back."

On the floor of the squash court, just beneath the balcony, stood George Weil, whose duty it was to handle the final control rod. In the pile were three sets of control rods. One set was automatic and could be controlled from the balcony. Another was an emergency safety rod. Attached to one end of this rod was a rope running through the pile and weighted heavily on the opposite end. The rod was withdrawn from the pile and tied by another rope to the balcony. N. Hilberry was ready to cut this rope with an ax should something unexpected happen, or in case the automatic safety rods failed. The third rod, operated by Weil, was the one which actually held the reaction in check until withdrawn the proper distance.

Since this demonstration was new and different from anything ever done before, complete reliance was not placed on mechanically operated control rods. Therefore, a "liquid-control squad," composed of Harold Lichtenberger, W. Nyer, and A. C. Graves, stood on a platform above the pile. They were prepared to flood the pile with cadmium-salt solution in case of mechanical failure of the control rods.

Each group rehearsed its part of the experiment.

* The Canadian-born Walter H. Zinn, of Columbia University.
† Herbert L. Anderson, Fermi's associate.
§ Arthur H. Compton, University of Chicago.

At nine forty-five Fermi ordered the electrically operated control rods withdrawn. The man at the controls threw the switch to withdraw them. A small motor whined. All eyes watched the lights which indicated the rods' position.

But quickly, the balcony group turned to watch the counters, whose clicking stepped up after the rods were out. The indicators of these counters resembled the face of a clock, with "hands" to indicate neutron count. Nearby was a recorder, whose quivering pen traced the neutron activity within the pile.

Shortly after ten o'clock, Fermi ordered the emergency rod, called "Zip," pulled out and tied.

"Zip out," said Fermi. Zinn withdrew "Zip" by hand and tied it to the balcony rail. Weil stood ready by the "vernier" control rod which was marked to show the number of feet and inches which remained within the pile.

At 10:37 A.M. Fermi, without taking his eyes off the instruments, said quietly: "Pull it to 13 feet, George."

The counters clicked faster. The graph pen moved up. All the instruments were studied, and computations were made.

"This is not it," said Fermi. "The trace will go to this point and level off." He indicated a spot on the graph. In a few minutes the pen came to the indicated point and did not go above that point. Seven minutes later Fermi ordered the rod out another foot.

Again the counters stepped up their clicking, the graph pen edged upward. But the clicking was irregular. Soon it leveled off, as did the thin line of the pen. The pile was not self-sustaining—yet.

At eleven o'clock, the rod came out another six inches; the result was the same: an increase in rate, followed by the leveling off.

Fifteen minutes later the rod was further withdrawn and at eleven twenty-five was moved again. Each time the counters speeded up, the pen climbed a few points. Fermi predicted correctly every movement of the indicators. He knew the time was near. He wanted to check everything again. The automatic control rod was reinserted without waiting for its automatic feature to operate. The graph line took a drop, the counters slowed abruptly.

At 11:35 A.M. the automatic safety rod was withdrawn and set. The control rod was adjusted and "Zip" was withdrawn. Up went the counters, clicking, clicking, faster and faster. It was the clickety-click of a fast train over the rails. The graph pen started to climb. Tensely the little group watched, and waited, entranced by the climbing needle.

Whrrrump! As if by a thunder clap, the spell was broken. Every man froze

—then breathed a sigh of relief when he realized the automatic rod had slammed home. The safety point at which the rod operated automatically had been set too low.

"I'm hungry," said Fermi. "Let's go to lunch." . . .

They were back on the squash court at 2:00 P.M. Twenty minutes later the automatic rod was reset and Weil stood ready at the control rod.

"All right, George," called Fermi, and Weil moved the rod to a predetermined point. The spectators resumed their watching and waiting, watching the counters spin, watching the graph, waiting for the settling down and computing the rate of rise of reaction from the indicators.

At two-fifty the control rod came out another foot. The counters nearly jammed, the pen headed off the graph paper. But this was not it. Counting ratios and the graph scale had to be changed.

"Move it six inches," said Fermi at three-twenty. Again the change—but again the leveling off. Five minutes later, Fermi called: "Pull it out another foot."

Weil withdrew the rod.

"This is going to do it," Fermi said to Compton, standing at his side. "Now it will become self-sustaining. The trace will climb and continue to climb. It will not level off."

Fermi computed the rate of rise of the neutron counts over a minute period. He silently, grim-faced, ran through some calculations on his slide rule.

In about a minute he again computed the rate of rise. If the rate was constant and remained so, he would know the reaction was self-sustaining. His fingers operated the slide rule with lightning speed. Characteristically, he turned the rule over and jotted down some figures on its ivory back.

Three minutes later he again computed the rate of rise in neutron count. The group on the balcony had by now crowded in to get an eye on the instruments, those behind craning their necks to be sure they would know the very instant history was made. In the background could be heard William Overbeck calling out the neutron count over an annunciator system. Leona Marshall (the only girl present), Anderson, and William Sturm were recording the readings from the instruments. By this time the click of the counters was too fast for the human ear. The clickety-click was now a steady brrrrr. Fermi, unmoved, unruffled, continued his computations.

"I couldn't see the instruments," said Weil. "I had to watch Fermi every second, waiting for orders. His face was motionless. His eyes darted from one dial to another. His expression was so calm it was hard. But suddenly his whole face broke into a broad smile."

Fermi closed his slide rule——

"The reaction is self-sustaining," he announced quietly, happily. "The curve is exponential."

The group tensely watched for 28 minutes while the world's first nuclear chain reactor operated.

The upward movement of the pen was leaving a straight line. There was no change to indicate a leveling off. This was it.

"O. K., 'Zip' in," called Fermi to Zinn who controlled that rod. The time was 3:53 P.M. Abruptly the counters slowed down, the pen slid down across the paper. It was all over.

Man had initiated a self-sustaining nuclear reaction—and then stopped it. He had released the energy of the atom's nucleus and controlled that energy.

Right after Fermi ordered the reaction stopped, the Hungarian-born theoretical physicist Eugene Wigner presented him with a bottle of Chianti wine. All through the experiment Wigner had kept this wine hidden behind his back.

Fermi uncorked the wine bottle and sent out for paper cups so all could drink. He poured a little wine in all the cups, and silently, solemnly, without toasts, the scientists raised the cups to their lips—the Canadian Zinn, the Hungarians Szilard and Wigner, the Italian Fermi, the Americans Compton, Anderson, Hilberry, and a score of others. They drank to success—and to the hope they were the first to succeed.

A small crew was left to straighten up, lock controls, and check all apparatus. As the group filed from the West Stands, one of the guards asked Zinn: "What's going on, Doctor, something happen in there?"

The guard did not hear the message which Arthur Compton was giving James B. Conant at Harvard, by long-distance telephone. Their code was not prearranged.

"The Italian navigator has landed in the New World," said Compton.

"How were the natives?" asked Conant.

"Very friendly."

Man in a Skyrocket*

WILLIAM BRIDGEMAN

and

JACQUELINE HAZARD

✳✳ William Bridgeman is an ex-Navy pilot who, after 9000 flying hours fighting Japs in the Central Pacific and later ferrying planes across the ocean to others, found that after World War II life on the ground was not, for him, going to be altogether satisfactory. Something was missing. Flying, or the urge toward it, he came by naturally. His father had been a pilot of an old World War I crate for a barnstorming flying circus; as an ensign in the Navy young Bridgeman's first official duty at the U. S. Naval Air Station at Pearl Harbor was as officer of the day—on December 7, 1941. He went into the air as a bomber pilot, and for three and a half years was with Miller's "Reluctant Raiders" in the Pacific.

A pioneer in the testing of supersonic planes on the research project initiated through the vision of General Hap Arnold, Bridgeman was entrusted after the War with breaking in the experimental Skyrocket, a swept-wing turbojet and rocket-engine plane built by Douglas for the Navy in cooperation with the National Advisory Commission for Aeronautics.

The Skyrocket cost $12,000,000 and engaged the best efforts of 150 designers, engineers, and draftsmen for three years before it reached its first flight. Bridgeman began his test flights in the Skyrocket in 1949. It was a plane vastly different from anything the Navy pilot had ever handled. Its speeds necessitated long conditioning in pressure clothing and learning how to breathe at heights and speeds never hitherto attempted by man. On one test trip the windshield frosted over and he nearly lost his life; on others the buffeting the plane took as it approached and passed the sound barrier proved experiences unlike anything in traditional aeronautics. In attempting to pass and repass records for speed after attaining Mach 1, or the speed of sound, "bugs" developed in handling the plane which required test after test to overcome, flight after flight resulting in a struggle with the plane and the elements miles above the earth, and the inevitable jettisoning of the propellant, ("bleeding away in the seas of the sky") and a dead-stick landing on the bottom of a dry lake in California at terrific speed.

On official Flight No. 26, dropped into the sky for the third time from a B-29 bomber (at an altitude of 34,000 feet) the Skyrocket achieved an altitude of 63,000 feet and a Mach number of 1.72, and beat the Air Force's X-I by 200 miles an hour, and was thus officially the fastest airplane in the world.

But neither the Navy, the engineers, nor Bridgeman was quite satisfied that that was as much as could be got out of the plane, and Bridgeman was to make two more, and final record-setting flights, one in an attempt to push the Mach speed number up to Mach 2, or twice the speed of sound, and the last flight to reach an altitude higher than the plane had ever previously reached.

These two flights, he tells of here. ✳✳

Along the road the Joshua trees, angular-trunked with branch-arms held up like the warnings of scarecrows in a field, stood in irregular lines back into the gray sand. The irritation I had first felt when Carder singled me out to fly the new program was gone. In its place was a feeling of pride that I should be entrusted with the assignment.

Still this was something unknown. They were trying for speeds and heights nobody had ever attempted. Here there would be no one to tell you what to expect. I would be alone. And I thought of excuses to turn it down.

During the war I had picked up a book in Honolulu by a French pilot, Antoine de Saint-Exupéry, and I remembered the words: "There is no liberty except the liberty of someone making his way towards something." No matter what arguments I set up against the advisability of these new flights, I knew I would accept them. This was the kind of freedom the French flyer talked about that subconsciously I had sought all along, and here before me was a big chunk of it. All I had to do was take it. Here was the choice: going toward something, freedom—or security and stagnation. One or the other, the two were incompatible; there was no compromise. Find out, move, reach out. If I turned down this "freedom" I knew that later the knowledge that I had would never leave me alone.

MACH 2: TWICE THE SPEED OF SOUND

There she was, a celebrity now, the crew, members of a midnight cult, priming her for the big flight in their cumbersome, hooded uniforms.

I was at the height of conditioning as I approached the fueling scene, half out of the pressure suit, followed by the specialist Stum. I was determined to get everything out of her this time, to get it over with. There was nothing to fear. The roll had been conquered and no structural damage had resulted from it. She sat snug in the belly of the mother ship, gleaming iridescent white with her new skin of lacquer. Today was the culmination of three years' work.

The fueling was completed. The engineers came up one by one to offer some last-minute word, the equivalent of "Good luck." "See you after the flight" . . . "We'll discuss it afterward"—optimistic references to the future. Stum finished fussing with the helmet and thumped the top of it with his hand. The 29 fired up her engines, taxied out, and we were airborne.

I am no longer embarrassed by my need for the Dixie cup. It has become an established part of the flight. When it drops out, Everest, in his chase plane, familiar with the sight, calls, "Dixie cup away."

Thirty-five thousand feet. I acknowledge Jansen's salute. Twenty minutes later my hands are gripping the wheel.

"Two . . . one." The shaft of light, a sensation I am accustomed to meeting. Today the pullout is smooth, without any loss of rocket-seconds. How practiced I have become! How easily I control the power pouring from the four tubes. The tension I have felt waiting in the bomber has left me and the action of performing the job well acts as an exaggerated salve. Even the constant adjustment in the climb is an effortless series of practiced movements. How well she responds to my hand.

At the top I will push her over sharply and let her go. I am really going to put it to her . . . with the added acceleration at the pushover, she should do it.

Piercing up through the minus-80-degree sheer air, I hit 64,000 feet in a matter of seconds—the top of the hill. Now! She eats up 3000 feet while my hand moves the wheel. Over the top, right down into it. No gradual rocket-second devouring arc, but over the top like a roller coaster. Straight down in front of me I push the wheel and the limitless blue brilliancy ahead slides away and out of the silver windows the curve of the horizon moves up in its place.

And quietly she begins to "roll." The thing that had me on the edge of my parachute three long flights ago I take as a matter of course. And now, .25 G, just the other side of zero G where you beat gravity, where a pencil on the cockpit floor will float in mid-air. I glue the white needle to the figure .25 on the accelerometer. Let's see what you can do with *this*, baby! She accelerates into the hypersonic zone at one third of a mile a second.

The roll! I can't ignore it. It sets in more firmly as she plunges deeper into the pushover. *Well, let it, damn it. We're going this trip. She can take it.* Without changing the condition she protests against, I grip the wheel. Nothing is going to jar her loose from the .25 holding steady on the accelerometer. There is nothing she can show me that is going to stop me. Hunched over the wheel, I hang on.

Harder she rolls, harder and faster. The flat horizon line flips wildly through the squinting slit windows. I fight the crazy gyration with the ailerons. They are no weapons. They are feathers in a wind storm. Still, they are the only weapons I have. The flipping is so fast that I cannot get in phase against it with the ailerons. She has turned on me! I am making it worse with the ailerons and panic floods up into my chest and throat. I am almost sick with it as I fight a force so great now that my frantic flailings against it are pathetically puny.

There has got to be a way to bring order out of this. I release my hands from the aileron control and try to get in phase with the roll that snaps me violently back and forth in its teeth, flipping me over on my side level with the horizon, then instantly back in the other direction. A dog beating a cat against the ground. I do not fight it now, but wait to allow the crazy accelerated, windshield-wiper-like, flipping of the Rocket to neutralize so I can jump in and hold my strength against it. *Now.* I missed it. *I'll get it this time. I'll get it now.*

The action has a meager effect on the force that has grabbed us, but it is positive. It is a glimmer of control and I am somewhat retrieved from total despair. The wheel is a ridiculous toy against the thing that has hold of the ship. *Why don't they give me something to fight with, for God's sake?* A toy in my hands to fight the whole goddamned sky that has turned on me. One hundred and eighty pounds against a new world full of enraged energy. The frail weapons of my arms ache with the futile exertion put upon them.

I turn my back on the ridiculously matched contest long enough to glance at the Machmeter. It is building fast: 1.79, 1.80, 1.81, 1.82, 1.83, 1.84, 1.85.

That is the answer! That is the reason. No-man's-land. She's going. It is a justification.

I am aware of the face-plate that separates my eyes from the panel before me. Coatings of steam from my breath rapidly appear and disappear on the glass and the terrible sound of my lungs gasping and heaving air in and out vibrates like wind in a barrel through my ears. Despite all the activity I am aware of the terrible, animal-frightened sound.

Into this isolated, hopelessly vulnerable world that is myself and the Skyrocket comes another kind of faraway unreality—the voice of Al Carder, high and thin, crackling through my helmet.

"Has he started to descend yet, Chuck?" From his position on the floor 13 miles down, the project coordinator has been able to follow my white vapor trail in the climb. Then the Skyrocket reaches air that is too thin to condense.

I am swallowed up by the sky. It is an easy matter to get lost in the sky.

Yeager's voice, lost from me somewhere out there, "No. He was still climbing when his vapor trail disappeared and he left me."

"Any idea of his position, Chuck?"

"Last time I saw him he was fading away over Barstow."

It is like hearing voices of people standing over you when you are half-conscious. You are unable to answer. I would like to say something memorably glib, but I cannot.

My hands and face are wet with perspiration. Rivulets of stinging sweat drop into my eyes. How curious that a man can sweat in minus-80-degree-below-zero temperature.

If a horse is throwing you, you can let yourself be thrown. You can get away from the beast. But not this thing. I am part of it. Until she wears out the tantrum, I have no alternative but to go where she takes me.

Still doggedly I hold the needle on .25 G. The horizon of gyrating, half-blue, half-brown, is gone now and in its place is solid brown earth in a half-circle spin, spinning half around and respinning back again. A corkscrew at Mach 1.87 down toward the ground. Beyond the thickening fog of my face-plate there is no sky. It is all flat, hard earth that I head for.

I am losing the battle. To hang on longer is stupidity. A decision must be made. Cut off her energy! That will surely stop this horror. Behind me I feel for the switch that will turn off the 6000 pounds of thrust. I click it forward.

She shudders and decelerates into the wall, but the wild ride *continues* as if no change had been made. It doesn't alter her furious action. It is with terrible surprise I realize that the loss of power has no effect upon her condition.

The lake is 40 miles behind me and getting further and further away as the Skyrocket carries me far from my only port. To enter a turn back to the lake is impossible. I cannot force her into a bank. She won't leave her path! And now over my eyes the frost on my face-plate has thickened into a heavy white curtain and I can no longer see the gyrating, whirling bottom below me.

My cramped cockpit world has moved into my helmet. All that exists now is the white frost on the face-plate, the violent thrashing of the plane, and the feel of the wheel under my fingers. In the silent ship the terrible, convulsive breathing is my only companion.

A blind man in an out-of-control Rocket plunging, through low-pressure areas that can burst my body like a balloon, toward the ground at a speed twice as fast as a bullet in flight.

Altitude. It is the only road left to me, the only way I can go now. It is the margin, the delayer. In altitude there is some security. Time to think. With all the strength I am able to summon I pull back on the wheel and inflict a radical directional change on the downward-screaming ship. Bent upward into the big, safe sky by the tremendous force of the tight pull-up, I am sucked down into the pressure suit and my lower jaw is grabbed wide open like a man screaming for his life, and I know that I am moving away from the awful brown that I was headed into. It's soft blue before me now.

And now like a black night diluted slowly by the incipient water-color dawn, the gyrating falls away. I feel it fade away. It has stopped. All of the violence and horror is gone. The Rocket has changed back into a silent, gentle, featherlike missile, whooshing straight up in a steep climb.

She is controllable but I am blind. The windshield wiper! I remember with a flood of thankful discovery the windshield wiper that had been installed after the last flight at Al Carder's insistence. Thank God for Carder and the ridiculous little rubber lever that I move manually to clear away the frost.

Without power and bent into the steep climb, she will start shuddering into the first warnings of stall. The indicated air speed is the dial that commands my regained sight. It is sinking fast. *Fly her now, Bridgeman; she's all yours again.* Once more I am a pilot. I drop the nose a bit to pick up speed. Now I roll her over, drop the long nose, pulling positive G, and pull her on through. The Skyrocket is turned back in the direction of home. My ship again.

The chase pilots have lost me. Right now I am incapable of worrying about getting the rest of the way home. At this moment I am overwhelmed with relief that the Skyrocket is once more something I can understand and she is heading in the right direction.

The last few minutes have left my body still in a state of emergency despite the abrupt cessation of the nightmare. My legs and arms shake uncontrollably.

Sometime during the pushover I re-enter the altitude where my vapor trail forms again. Carder has seen it. From the ground it appears like an erratic corkscrew furrowed by my wild path. The jumble over the radio starts as Carder sees it with alarm.

"Chuck, can you see the vapor trail again? Can you get over there?"

Weakly I hear the sound of help coming and I wonder absently how I am going to explain this one to Carder. And why did I hang on so tenaciously to that .25 G? As I sit here trembling, guiding the empty Rocket sapped as dry of energy as I am, I remember the moments just passed.

Holy God! Not once did I think of the escape lever. Is it possible that I would have let her take me right into a 40-foot hole in the ground?

"Yeah, Al, I can see it. I'll be on him in a couple of minutes."

"That's a crazy-looking trail he's dragging. How does he look, Chuck?"

Chuck is coming. The now-obedient Skyrocket decelerates out of the supersonic zone down through the tender .9, emitting her usual shudder. The once-awesome shudder makes me smile weakly.

"Hold on. I haven't found him yet." The warm, competent, Southern softness of Yeager's steady voice is soothing as the first inhalation of fine sourmash whisky. "Now I've got him. He's pretty far away but he seems to be all in one piece."

"Bill," Carder calls to me now, "how are you doing?"

There it is! I can see the lake bed far below me and ahead. Just a few more minutes. "Shut up, will you?"

Beside me Chuck Yeager's silver F-86 slides in close and cozy.

"Hi, hotshot." A friend to see me home. I lift my hand to him. He is silent as he follows my glide path down. He knows. It is all I can do to follow the precise maneuverings necessary to get the still-hot little ship onto the lake bed. Even without power she'll land nearly a third again as fast as the F-86.

After a respectable length of time Chuck says, "I thought you were going to Arizona for a while there, Buddy."

With a great deal of effort I am able to answer. "I thought so too."

FIFTEEN MILES ABOVE THE EARTH

There was no horseplay this morning, no labored wisecrack. My associates were vaguely ill at ease when they greeted me. I suppose it was because I was more preoccupied than usual. The crew picked up the mood. They waited for me to open any conversation and they were more attentive than usual. Before I could ask for anything it was right there. I was grateful for the silence. Horseplay takes time and effort; it breaks the chain of thought. There had been other mornings when I had restrained myself from cutting a well-meant joke with, "Shut up." It was sometimes awkward and taxing to be obliged to make the effort of a retort.

The hoses had been withdrawn from the Skyrocket and the last lacing had been adjusted on the "corset." Everything was in order. George received his okay to take off and the big bomber began to jog along the runway.

This flight will be discovery. I will know a thing I have never known be-fore. Mixed with the clinical thoughts of how to handle the ship and the familiar counterpoint of the fear syndrome, today there is expectancy. Ad-venture. Before, the flights have been carefully controlled. Today I am going to let her go as far as she will. It is up to her.

Time! It will begin in ten seconds. A new road. The chase plane at this end checks in and stands by. Silence connects me now to the three chase planes, the men who wait on the ground, the mechanics in the hangar—clus-tered around loud-speakers as if for the last game of the World Series—the control tower, and Jansen who holds the pickle in his hand ready to count off the ten remaining seconds of security that I have snug in the womb of the mother ship. Now!

"Four . . . three . . . two . . . one," I hold the cold wheel in my bare hands and lean forward, *"Drop!"*

Four buttons down. One, two, three, four, and four gigantic blow-torches rumble into life. Mathematical at the beginning. A formula of numbers. Breathe air on the count of 1001, blow it out at 1005. Around the corner, feel it, at G. Going up. The numbers on the dials, .85 on the Machmeter. Hold it! Everest's voice in the F-86 counting, "One is good, two is good, three is . . . good." The report from the chase plane fades into distance. It is faraway and barely audible now, . . . "He's got all four!"

The needle on the indicated air speed falls off as the number .85 holds on the Machmeter. Change the numbers on the dials now. The needles slide up and down and around—.85 becomes Mach 1, she bumps into the quiet area and the high-drag rise of the shock waves. The larger altimeter hand winds up to 42,000, 43,000, reeling off the altitude. No pushover. Straight up. All the way, bending back a little more, a little more. The only world I am aware of is the world of dial eyes in front of me. The perpendicular light on the newly installed angle-of-attack instrument creeps up steadily as I move the stabilizer trim switch. *Zut . . . zut. Zut . . . zut,* pointing her nose higher, a little bit higher.

I follow the plan of the aerodynamicists in the Testing Division at Santa Monica. It looks like it is going to work after all. Five dials. A constant check as they all speak at once. Indicated air speed, Mach needle, angle-of-attack light, the rocket-seconds that remain, and the reeling off of the altimeter hand. Reeling off 57,000, 58,000, it rapidly reels back every 1000 feet I climb through.

In the thin air, actually, she does not want to fly but miraculously she does; she is held by a fantastic power that takes over. A ball atop a slim stick, she maintains an uncanny balance in the unresisting, weak air. She is going up at such speed that in reality she is close to stall. We are buoyed on a pivot that keeps us in balance. Although I am acutely aware of this circumstance, I am not alarmed by it. I am reluctant to believe she will not continue to fly.

Fifty-nine thousand, 60,000, reeling off 61,000. I have left the world. There is only the ship to identify myself with, her vibrations are my own, I feel them as intensely as those of my body. Here is a kind of unreality mixed with reality that I cannot explain to myself. I have an awareness that I have never experienced before, but it does not seem to project beyond this moment. Every cell, fluid, muscle of my body, is acutely awake. Perception is enormously exaggerated—black is blacker, white is whiter. Silence is more acute. It is the tender edge of the unknowable. And with this adrenalin-inflicted state floats the feeling of detachment.

It is an incompatible set of emotions I experience. Fear seems to be independent, a ghost sitting on my shoulder. And although it is most surely there, I am anesthetized to its warnings. I am without anxiety. I am powerless to anticipate what will happen the next moment. Time is now. Nothing but this experience is significant now. The rocket pressures are meaningless, the world of figures and equations that a second or two ago held such urgency have no reality in the face of *this* reality. I have the unshakable feeling that no matter what the instruments read, it will have no effect on the power that is making this ship fly. An independent, supernatural kind of power she has. She is alive with her own unknowable and unmovable power. I have complete faith, a faith that wraps me like a warm blanket now, that she will not be interrupted in this freedom.

Sixty-two thousand, 63,000 feet reeling off, reeling off the climb. The left wing is dropping! I respond automatically with no alarm, a robot racking in aileron against the dipping wing. I watch the eyes in front of me. The instruments stand out brighter—64,000 feet on the altimeter, reeling away . . . the Mach number . . . the rocket-seconds left to spend. Gently the wayward wing eases down again. Aileron full throw against it. No response this time. No effect. The wing keeps on going down. I kick the rudder against it but, of course, the rudder is locked. Seventy thousand feet. Check the Mach number: 1.4. I know I must bring her nose down. I am reluctant to reduce the altitude but I must; she will surely roll otherwise. Now slowly the aileron control comes back and I can once more return the ship to the nose-high altitude. *Zut, zut,* the pole-nose moves up. Seventy-five thousand feet. Again the wing dips. I ease the pole down once more and bring the wing level. It is a matter of easing her along the steep path tenderly. Give a little and grab a little. Seventy-six thousand feet registers on the dial and the rockets sputter off.

From hours of rehearsal my hand automatically hits the stabilizer switch for the pushover. It is with elation I feel the great force that shoves her over the top at .5 G. Even without the rockets she still has enough power to climb higher. Next time I will convert this energy to more altitude. In the arc she picks up a couple of thousand feet. The altimeter stops its steady reeling and swings sickly around 80,000 feet. The altitude is too extreme for the instrument to function.

Eighty thousand feet. It is intensely bright outside; the contrast of the dark shadows of the cockpit is extreme and strange. It is so dark lower in the cockpit that I cannot read the instruments sunk low on the panel. The dials on top, in the light, are vividly apparent. There seems to be no reflection; it is all black or white, apparent or nonapparent. No half-tones. It is a pure, immaculate world here.

She levels off silently. I roll to the right and there it is. Out of the tiny window slits there is the earth, wiped clean of civilization, a vast relief map with papier-mâché mountains and mirrored lakes and seas. The desert is not the same desert I have seen for two years; it is a pale brown hole bordered by dwarf mountains that run into other dwarf mountain chains that plait into other chains down to the Gulf of California and the Republic of Mexico. The coastline is sharply drawn with little vacant bays and inlets, a lacy edge to the big brown pieces of earth that dissolve into grays and the glimmer of lake puddles cupped in mountaintops and back to brown, gray, and finally the enormous black-blue of the Pacific. A globe-world in a planetarium, the earth curves to the south.

It is as if I am the only living thing connected to this totally strange, uninhabited planet 15 miles below me. The plane that carries me and I are one and alone.

There is a world down there and it must be revisited. There is the turn back to the place where the field is a pinpoint on the globe under me. The only way back from the springboard I am on has to be from memory, automatic. This, now, is the payoff for my preflight conditioning, for the drills, for the memorizing of steps back. Without this conditioning I am sure at this moment that I would not be able to return quickly enough from the euphoric state that holds me.

Following the steps mechanically, I am able to enter the turn. I am on my descent and slowly I return to what I knew before. Again I hear myself laboring for oxygen inside the helmet, and the world under me comes gradually into focus as something identifiable with life. At 15,000 it is comfortingly familiar. I take the face-plate out of the helmet and breathe air again, deeply, and I am back, fully returned to time and dimension and the brief span that is allowed me.

Transition to a New Age*

U.S. WAR DEPARTMENT

✳✳ The fact that this War Department release has quotation marks its entire length is because all the quoted matter in it was written by William L. Laurence, of the New York *Times,* and constitutes parts of several reports he prepared for the War Department prior to his departure to serve as the only official eyewitness of the use of the bomb over Japan. The final version of the release, however, is a composite rewrite job freely using the material he prepared, thus somewhat qualifying the authorship here. ✳✳

THE NEW MEXICO TEST, JULY 16, 1945

"Mankind's successful transition to a new age, the Atomic Age, was ushered in July 16, 1945, before the eyes of a tense group of renowned scientists and military men gathered in the desertlands of New Mexico to witness the first end results of their $2,000,000,000 effort. Here in a remote section of the Alamogordo Air Base 120 miles southeast of Albuquerque the first man-made atomic explosion, the outstanding achievement of nuclear science, was achieved at 5:30 A.M. of that day. Darkening heavens, pouring forth rain and lightning immediately up to the zero hour, heightened the drama.

"Mounted on a steel tower, a revolutionary weapon destined to change war as we know it, or which may even be the instrumentality to end all wars, was set off with an impact which signalized man's entrance into a new physical world. Success was greater than the most ambitious estimates. A small amount of matter, the product of a chain of huge specially constructed industrial plants, was made to release the energy of the universe locked up within the atom from the beginning of time. A fabulous achievement had

* Reprinted from *Atomic Energy for Military Purposes,* copyright, 1945, by Henry D. Smyth, chairman, Department of Physics, Princeton University, and consultant, Manhattan District, U.S. Engineers. Published by the Princeton University Press, 1945, reprinted by permission of H. D. Smyth.

been reached. Speculative theory, barely established in prewar laboratories, had been projected into practicality.

"This phase of the Atomic Bomb Project, which is headed by Major General Leslie R. Groves, was under the direction of Dr. J. R. Oppenheimer, theoretical physicist of the University of California. He is to be credited with achieving the implementation of atomic energy for military purposes.

"Tension before the actual detonation was at a tremendous pitch. Failure was an ever-present possibility. Too great a success, envisioned by some of those present, might have meant an uncontrollable, unusable weapon.

"Final assembly of the atomic bomb began on the night of July 12 in an old ranchhouse. As various component assemblies arrived from distant points, tension among the scientists rose to an increasing pitch. Coolest of all was the man charged with the actual assembly of the vital core, Dr. R. F. Bacher, in normal times a professor at Cornell University.

"The entire cost of the project, representing the erection of whole cities and radically new plants spread over many miles of countryside, plus unprecedented experimentation, was represented in the pilot bomb and its parts. Here was the focal point of the venture. No other country in the world had been capable of such an outlay in brains and technical effort.

"The full significance of these closing moments before the final factual test was *not* lost on these men of science. They fully knew their position as pioneers into another age. They also knew that one false move would blast them and their entire effort into eternity. Before the assembly started, a receipt for the vital matter was signed by Brigadier General Thomas F. Farrell, General Groves' deputy. This signalized the formal transfer of the irreplaceable material from the scientists to the Army.

"During final preliminary assembly, a bad few minutes developed when the assembly of an important section of the bomb was delayed. The entire unit was machine-tooled to the finest measurement. The insertion was partially completed when it apparently wedged tightly and would go no farther. Dr. Bacher, however, was undismayed and reassured the group that time would solve the problem. In three minutes' time, Dr. Bacher's statement was verified and basic assembly was completed without further incident.

"Specialty teams, comprised of the top men on specific phases of science, all of which were bound up in the whole, took over their specialized parts of the assembly. In each group was centralized months and even years of channelized endeavor.

"On Saturday, July 14, the unit which was to determine the success or failure of the entire project was elevated to the top of the steel tower. All that day and the next, the job of preparation went on. In addition to the apparatus necessary to cause the detonation, complete instrumentation to determine the pulse beat and all reactions of the bomb was rigged on the tower.

"The ominous weather which had dogged the assembly of the bomb had a very sobering effect on the assembled experts whose work was accomplished amid lightning flashes and peals of thunder. The weather, unusual and up-setting, blocked out aerial observation of the test. It even held up the actual explosion scheduled at 4:00 A.M. for an hour and a half. For many months the approximate date and time had been set and had been one of the high-level secrets of the best-kept secret of the entire war.

"Nearest observation point was set up 10,000 yards south of the tower where in a timber and earth shelter the controls for the test were located. At a point 17,000 yards from the tower at a point which would give the best ob-servation the key figures in the atomic bomb project took their posts. These included General Groves, Dr. Vannevar Bush, head of the Office of Scien-tific Research and Development, and Dr. James B. Conant, president of Har-vard University.

"Actual detonation was in charge of Dr. K. T. Bainbridge of Massachu-setts Institute of Technology. He and Lieutenant Bush, in charge of the Mili-tary Police Detachment, were the last men to inspect the tower with its cosmic bomb.

"At three o'clock in the morning the party moved forward to the control station. General Groves and Dr. Oppenheimer consulted with the weather-men. The decision was made to go ahead with the test despite the lack of as-surance of favorable weather. The time was set for 5:30 A.M.

"General Groves rejoined Dr. Conant and Dr. Bush, and just before the test time they joined the many scientists gathered at the Base Camp. Here all present were ordered to lie on the ground, face downward, heads away from the blast direction.

"Tension reached a tremendous pitch in the control room as the deadline approached. The several observation points in the area were tied in to the control room by radio and with twenty minutes to go, Dr. S. K. Allison of Chicago University took over the radio net and made periodic time an-nouncements.

"The time signals, 'minus 20 minutes, minus 15 minutes,' and on and on increased the tension to the breaking point as the group in the control room which included Dr. Oppenheimer and General Farrell held their breaths, all praying with the intensity of the moment which will live forever with each man who was there. At 'minus 45 seconds,' robot mechanism took over and from that point on the whole great, complicated mass of intricate mechanism was in operation without human control. Stationed at a reserve switch, however, was a soldier scientist ready to attempt to stop the explosion should the order be issued. The order never came.

"At the appointed time there was a blinding flash lighting up the whole area brighter than the brightest daylight. A mountain range three miles from the observation point stood out in bold relief. Then came a tremendous sustained roar and a heavy pressure wave which knocked down two men outside the control center. Immediately thereafter, a huge, multicolored, surging cloud boiled to an altitude of over 40,000 feet. Clouds in its path disappeared. Soon the shifting substratosphere winds dispersed the now-gray mass.

"The test was over, the project a success.

"The steel tower had been entirely vaporized. Where the tower had stood, there was a huge sloping crater. Dazed but relieved at the success of their tests, the scientists promptly marshaled their forces to estimate the strength of America's new weapon. To examine the nature of the crater, specially equipped tanks were wheeled into the area, one of which carried Dr. Enrico Fermi, noted nuclear scientist. Answer to their findings rests in the destruction effected in Japan today in the first military use of the atomic bomb.

"Had it not been for the desolated area where the test was held and for the cooperation of the press in the area, it is certain that the test itself would have attracted far-reaching attention. As it was, many people in that area are still discussing the effect of the smash. A significant aspect, recorded by the press, was the experience of a blind girl near Albuquerque many miles from the scene, who, when the flash of the test lighted the sky before the explosion could be heard, exclaimed, 'What was that?'

"Interviews of General Groves and General Farrell give the following on-the-scene versions of the test. General Groves said: 'My impressions of the night's high points follow: After about an hour's sleep I got up at 0100 and from that time on until about five I was with Dr. Oppenheimer constantly. Naturally he was tense, although his mind was working at its usual extraordinary efficiency. I attempted to shield him from the evident concern shown by many of his assistants who were disturbed by the uncertain weather conditions. By 0330 we decided that we could probably fire at 0530. By 0400 the rain had stopped but the sky was heavily overcast. Our decision became firmer as time went on.

" 'During most of these hours the two of us journeyed from the control house out into the darkness to look at the stars and to assure each other that the one or two visible stars were becoming brighter. At 0510 I left Dr. Oppenheimer and returned to the main observation point which was 17,000 yards from the point of explosion. In accordance with our orders I found all personnel not otherwise occupied massed on a bit of high ground.

" 'Two minutes before the scheduled firing time, all persons lay face down with their feet pointing toward the explosion. As the remaining time was called from the loud speaker from the 10,000-yard control station there was complete awesome silence. Dr. Conant said he had never imagined seconds could be so long. Most of the individuals in accordance with orders shielded their eyes in one way or another.

" 'First came the burst of light of a brilliance beyond any comparison. We all rolled over and looked through dark glasses at the ball of fire. About forty seconds later came the shock wave followed by the sound, neither of which seemed startling after our complete astonishment at the extraordinary lighting intensity.

" 'A massive cloud was formed which surged and billowed upward with tremendous power, reaching the substratosphere in about five minutes.

" 'Two supplementary explosions of minor effect other than the lighting occurred in the cloud shortly after the main explosion.

" 'The cloud traveled to a great height first in the form of a ball, then mushroomed, then changed into a long, trailing chimney-shaped column and finally was sent in several directions by the variable winds at the different elevations.

" 'Dr. Conant reached over and we shook hands in mutual congratulations. Dr. Bush, who was on the other side of me, did likewise. The feeling of the entire assembly, even the uninitiated, was of profound awe. Drs. Conant and Bush and myself were struck by an even stronger feeling that the faith of those who had been responsible for the initiation and the carrying on of this Herculean project had been justified.' "

"General Farrell's impressions are: 'The scene inside the shelter was dramatic beyond words. In and around the shelter were some twenty-odd people concerned with last-minute arrangements. Included were Dr. Oppenheimer, the director who had borne the great scientific burden of developing the weapon from the raw materials made in Tennessee and Washington, and a dozen of his key assistants, Dr. Kistiakowsky, Dr. Bainbridge, who supervised all the detailed arrangements for the test; the weather expert, and several others. Besides those, there were a handful of soldiers, two or three army officers and one naval officer. The shelter was filled with a great variety of instruments and radios.

" 'For some hectic two hours preceding the blast, General Groves stayed with the director. Twenty minutes before the zero hour, General Groves left for his station at the base camp, first because it provided a better observation point and second, because of our rule that he and I must not be together in situations where there is an element of danger which existed at both points.

" 'Just after General Groves left, announcements began to be broadcast of the interval remaining before the blast to the other groups participating in and observing the test. As the time interval grew smaller and changed from minutes to seconds, the tension increased by leaps and bounds. Everyone in that room knew the awful potentialities of the thing that they thought was about to happen. The scientists felt that their figuring must be right and that the bomb had to go off but there was in everyone's mind a strong measure of doubt.

" 'We were reaching into the unknown and we did not know what might come of it. It can safely be said that most of those present were praying—and praying harder than they had ever prayed before. If the shot were successful, it was a justification of the several years of intensive effort of tens of thousands of people—statesmen, scientists, engineers, manufacturers, soldiers, and many others in every walk of life.

" 'In that brief instant in the remote New Mexico desert, the tremendous effort of the brains and brawn of all these people came suddenly and startlingly to the fullest fruition. Dr. Oppenheimer, on whom had rested a very heavy burden, grew tenser as the last seconds ticked off. He scarcely breathed. He held on to a post to steady himself. For the last few seconds he stared directly ahead and then when the announcer shouted, "Now!" and there came this tremendous burst of light followed shortly thereafter by the deep, growling roar of the explosion, his face relaxed into an expression of tremendous relief. Several of the observers standing back of the shelter to watch the lighting effects were knocked flat by the blast.

" 'The tension in the room let up and all started congratulating each other. Everyone sensed "This is it!" No matter what might happen now all knew that the impossible scientific job had been done. Atomic fission would no longer be hidden in the cloisters of the theoretical physicists' dreams. It was almost full grown at birth. It was a great new force to be used for good or for evil. There was a feeling in that shelter that those concerned with its nativity should dedicate their lives to the mission that it would always be used for good and never for evil.

" 'Dr. Kistiakowsky threw his arms around Dr. Oppenheimer and embraced him with shouts of glee. Others were equally enthusiastic. All the pent-up emotions were released in those few minutes and all seemed to sense immediately that the explosion had far exceeded the most optimistic expectations and wildest hopes of the scientists. All seemed to feel that they had been present at the birth of a new age—The Age of Atomic Energy—and felt their profound responsibility to help in guiding into right channels the tremendous forces which had been unlocked for the first time in history.

" 'As to the present war, there was a feeling that no matter what else might happen, we now had the means to insure its speedy conclusion and save thousands of American lives. As to the future, there had been brought into being something big and something new that would prove to be immeasurably more important than the discovery of electricity or any of the other great discoveries which have so affected our existence.

" 'The effects could well be called unprecedented, magnificent, beautiful, stupendous, and terrifying. No man-made phenomenon of such tremendous power had ever occurred before. The lighting effects beggared description. The whole country was lighted by a searing light with the intensity many times that of the midday sun. It was golden, purple, violet, gray, and blue. It lighted every peak, crevasse, and ridge of the nearby mountain range with a clarity and beauty that cannot be described but must be seen to be imagined. It was that beauty the great poets dream about but describe most poorly and inadequately. Thirty seconds after, the explosion came first, the air blast pressing hard against the people and things, to be followed almost immediately by the strong, sustained, awesome roar which warned of doomsday and made us feel that we puny things were blasphemous to dare tamper with the forces heretofore reserved to the Almighty. Words are inadequate tools for the job of acquainting those not present with the physical, mental, and psychological effects. It had to be witnessed to be realized.' "

Operation in Space*–I

KENNETH W. GATLAND
and
ANTHONY M. KUNESCH

THE ARTIFICIAL SATELLITE

Whereas it would be possible for a pilotless rocket to escape from the earth and reach the moon, or even the nearer planets, the same cannot yet be said of a man-carrying space ship. The power requirements are so great, principally because of the extra propellant that must be carried for the return flight, that nothing short of an applied form of atomic energy will ever be adequate. It is a sobering thought that even when such theoretically promising chemical propellants as oxygen/hydrogen, fluorine/hydrogen and fluorine/hydrazine have undergone full development, they will still not be sufficient to propel a space ship from the earth's surface on any two-way interplanetary journey.

Scientists and engineers all over the world have given a great deal of thought to finding an answer to this problem—to the possibility of producing lighter rocket structures, for example, or by methods of improving step-construction† whereby the vehicle is lightened progressively as it proceeds

* From *Space Travel, an Illustrated Survey of Its Problems and Prospects,* by Kenneth W. Gatland and Anthony M. Kunesch, members of the British Interplanetary Society. Published, 1953, by the Philosophical Library, reprinted by permission of Philosophical Library, Inc.

† Stage, or step, as applied to step rocket, as in a two-stepper, three-stepper, or multistep or multistage rocket, means the principle of joining one rocket to another. The power in the first, or lower, rocket is started first and carries the combination of two or three rocket vehicles on its take-off and some distance beyond; when the first rocket has reached its top speed the first rocket then separates from the other two, is jettisoned to earth, and the remaining part (or parts) of the rocket ship speeds on at an accelerated speed, that of the second rocket's speed added to the first; at the terminal velocity of the second rocket, the third rocket step takes over, adding its speed increment to the accelerated second step, etc. In theory the space ship of the future could be constructed of two, three, or even as many as five or more separate rockets, technicians say.—The Editor.

under thrust. However, although these economies will undoubtedly be applied in future space vehicles, they have always been recognized as being a long way short of the complete answer.

Then, as sometimes happens in scientific work, two people working independently hit upon an idea which overnight revolutionized the entire conception of the Interplanetary Project.*

Whereas all previous investigators had conceived the interplanetary vehicle as a giant streamlined space ship designed to make the round flight directly in one stage, the new theory advanced the use of a number of smaller rockets, none of which travel the full distance, but depend instead on a carefully planned sequence of operation, rather like runners in a relay team.

In the eyes of the uninitiated the proposal, known as Orbital Technique, is certain to outstrip fiction, relying as it does on relays of satellite rockets to build up a store of propellant for refueling purposes in a circular orbit outside the earth's atmosphere; nevertheless, it is based on well-established scientific theory.

The principle of satellite rockets is very simple. A good analogy may be obtained by tying a stone to a piece of string and whirling it round in a circle; the stone keeps traveling in a circle because the inward tension in the string balances the outward centrifugal force produced by the stone's motion. In exactly the same way a body circling the earth at the right speed would remain at a constant distance from the surface in a state of equilibrium. This time the outward centrifugal force would be balanced by the invisible but very powerful pull of gravity. Moreover, once the satellite had been given its initial speed, it would never lose it again, since there is no air resistance in the vacuum of space. It would stay out there forever without using any power and could never fall down—any more than could the moon which remains in its orbit for exactly the same reason. It is important to realize that the satellite would not stay up because it is "beyond the pull of gravity," as is sometimes stated. The pull of gravity (like the tension of the string in the analogy) is essential to prevent it from flying off into space. Thus a rocket guided into the correct circular path around the earth could shut off its motors once it had reached the required speed and remain orbiting the earth forever in perfect safety. The satellite could be established at any distance, but for technical reasons it would be easier to place it as near the earth as possible—as long, of course, as it was outside the atmosphere and thus immune from air resistance. . . .

* K. W. Gatland, "Rockets in Circular Orbits," *Journal of the British Interplanetary Society* (March, 1949).
   H. E. Ross, "Orbital Bases," *B. I. S. Journal* (January, 1949).

THE LAUNCHING SITES

In selecting a suitable launching site, a number of factors have to be borne in mind.

1. Range and points of impact of jettisoned tanks and steps.

2. If, as is probable, the launching site is so located that boosters, etc., will fall back into the sea, the track of the main shipping routes should not lie anywhere near the dropping areas.

3. Access to site, whether by sea or by rail, should be easily possible in view of the large quantities of materials required.

4. Minimum inclination of orbit relative to the plane of the Equator, to obtain maximum benefit from the earth's rotation.

5. Weather conditions, which may rule out a site that otherwise would be quite suitable.

When it is borne in mind that the 12½-ton V-2 rocket took several hours to prepare for launching, the problems of fueling and servicing a 500-ton, three-step rocket can be appreciated. The operation would probably take at least 24 hours to complete and postponement due to the sudden emergence of bad weather would be costly and possibly dangerous.

6. Owing to the probability, when launching large numbers of these satellite rockets, that one or more will go seriously off-course due to some defect, automatic cutoff will have to be employed; this will prevent any possibility of the rocket (still weighing several hundred tons) or of the jettisoned steps falling on to a populated area. For this reason, it would be advisable to clear an area of 50 miles' radius from the site, on to which any rocket malfunctioning at an early stage could be ditched. In the case of a failure in the third step, however, little could be done unless it occurred very soon after separation from the second step, as the range of the step could vary from approximately 1700 miles (in the case of failure occurring shortly after leaving the second step) to the extreme case in which the motor fails at the point of reaching the transfer orbit, when (due to the fact that the velocity increment could not be added for transferring to the final 500-mile orbit) the step would continue to circumnavigate the earth in its elliptical transfer orbit undergoing a fractional loss of height each time it "grazed" through the upper fringes of the atmosphere at its nearest approach. This would continue until eventually the rocket encountered denser air, where, due to its comparatively light construction and lack of streamlined form, it would undergo violent deceleration and heating effects which would destroy it.

The debris would come down as a shower of pieces spread over a wide area, the motor, pump, and miscellaneous air bottles being the most dangerous items.

Island launching sites in the Pacific, particularly on the Christmas Island group, would be high on the list of suitability with some 4500 miles of ocean extending to the Galapagos Islands. These islands are located near the Equator approximately 2° north latitude, and the firing lane would cross no major shipping routes. However, due to the vast distances in the Pacific, the material supply lines would be rather extended.

A position on the East Africa coast in Kenya would give an adequate firing lane extending across the Indian Ocean to the Dutch East Indies. The supply position would be better than for the previous example but the dropping area would straddle a number of shipping routes.

Brazil would present some possible sites on or near the Equator with a clear stretch of the South Atlantic in which to drop tanks and steps, extending into the Gulf of Guinea.

A large and highly trained organization will be required, with extensive radar-tracking coverage, and capable of operating with a high degree of accuracy. The launching techniques will follow closely those already used for existing high-altitude rockets.

THE TAKE-OFF

We are standing some paces from the main control room—a large concrete blockhouse. In front of us brilliantly illuminated by batteries of arc lamps, stands the satellite rocket, towering 130 feet above the concrete launching apron like some gigantic obelisk. Final adjustments have been made and the erection Gantry is being moved away; the bustle and flurry of the past 24 hours dies away and the scene is set for man's greatest venture.

As the floodlights are switched off we realize that dawn is approaching; the sky is already tinged with orange, Venus the "Morning Star" can still be seen, a pinpoint of light near the waning moon. In the west climbing rapidly to the zenith there is a small starlike object—the latest unmanned satellite equipped as a homing beacon. Suddenly, a siren sounds from the roof of the control room: 10 minutes' warning—everyone under cover—we turn to enter the control room, taking a final glance upward at the delta-winged third step, where the crew are already in position on their acceleration couches.

Inside the control room the radio operators are maintaining contact with the ships and observation stations stretched out in a vast chain across the

Pacific. Apart from official shipping no other vessel will be found in a 500-mile belt of sea stretching 2000 miles eastward of the launching site; similarly no aircraft will be permitted to fly over the area. These precautions have been taken as a purely routine measure chiefly against the remote possibility of the spent rocket steps causing damage.

Five minutes to "zero" and all is ready. Two minutes now and the firing crew begin to show the strain of their vigil—the atmosphere in the blockhouse seems hot and uncomfortable and beads of sweat appear on the faces of the men who will monitor the flight.

Another minute passes slowly by and for the hundredth time each man glances at the instruments in his special care. A single error can mar the whole venture, and the responsibility bears heavily on the firing officer on whose judgment may depend the lives of the three crewmen should the trajectory veer from the preselected path. The firing button is, in effect, a "dead man's" control and should the firing officer release his pressure on it a signal will automatically be transmitted to the rocket, which will instantly cut the motors and jettison the boosters; simultaneously, control will be passed to the pilot of the third step whose job it will be to glide the winged rocket back to earth, aided by its motor. The decision to terminate the flight must be made in a matter of seconds, for failure of the rocket to maintain its correct path would mean that the vehicle may not reach its correct orbit, which may seriously jeopardize the crew.

One minute to firing and on the television screen the rocket stands alone on its concrete apron silhouetted against the dawn. All signs of life have departed: humanity could be a million miles away.

Thirty seconds to go and the "count-off" begins: 29-28-27 . . . 20 and the ignition button is pressed—19-18—and on the screen there is a wisp of vapor dropping from the motors of the first step: 13-12—and the wisp of vapor becomes a tongue of flame shooting down in the blast pit. Around the edge of the concrete apron the vents, carrying the hot exhaust gases, are discharging vast quantities of steam from the cooling water. In the control room the firing officer checks the telltale lights on the ignition panel—all motors firing satisfactorily! 7-6-5—disconnect fueling lines; the automatic valves snap shut—the rocket is now using propellant from its own tanks: 3-2-1 "FIRE!" The pumps rapidly speed up and the motors build to full thrust. The noise, despite the "soundproofed" blockhouse, is unbearable—the ground trembles. As we watch the TV screen the mighty vehicle stirs, then rises majestically, balanced on the incredibly bright cascade of flame, which appears to splash off the edges of the blast pit. In the first second the rocket lifts nine feet and seems to build up speed very slowly; ten seconds later it is 1000 feet from the ground and accelerating more swiftly; in another ten seconds it will start turning toward the east to take advantage of the earth's rotational velocity.*

One minute after take-off and the vehicle, now nearly eight miles high, is traveling at over 1200 mph and inclined at an angle of 50°. The crew are beginning to feel the increasing acceleration which seems to press them down into their couches as by a giant's hand.

The first step of the rocket will continue to fire† for another minute, by which time the vehicle will be over 60 miles away from the launching site at a height of 36 miles and traveling at over 6000 mph.

It is now full sunlight—but sunlight such as this is never seen on earth; without the atmosphere to scatter light, the sun appears as a blinding white disc surrounded by a flamelike corona; in the blackness of space the stars are piercing points of light.

After the first step of the spent rocket is jettisoned the second step will continue to accelerate the vehicle; the inclination of the trajectory is now only 12° and thus the retardation due to gravity is reduced to a fraction of the initial figure.

In the meantime the empty first step continues to climb under momentum before it falls back into the Pacific nearly 400 miles from the take-off point, its descent being retarded by a number of drogue parachutes.

The second step, firing for two minutes, accelerates the vehicle to 13,600 mph after which the manned step continues alone. The second step which is jettisoned 360 miles from the take-off point at a height of 65 miles falls back into the sea nearly 12 minutes after "zero," having covered a distance of 1800 miles.

The third step§ accelerates for another five and one-fourth minutes to obtain a final velocity slightly in excess of 18,000 mph—this figure includes the increment of 1000 mph imparted by the earth's rotation.

In the control room we have watched the radar screens trace out the path of the rapidly accelerating rocket and seen how the radar stations along the path have handed over to new stations further on as the rocket gets out of range of the first positions.

As we emerge from the control room the sun is just appearing above the

* This amounts to approximately 1040 mph at the Equator.
† The first and second rockets use liquid oxygen and hydrazine as propellant giving an exhaust velocity of 1.86 miles per second.
§ Nitric acid and hydrazine with an exhaust velocity of 1.74 miles per second are employed for the third step.

horizon, but to the men in the satellite rocket, now under free-fall conditions, it is climbing rapidly to the zenith as they approach the South American coast.

Over now the vast forests of Amazonia the rocket is still climbing under momentum; to the north can be seen the Caribbean and the United States. Ahead stretches the broad expanse of the Atlantic where less than 500 years before Magellan was setting out on the first circumnavigation of the world —a three-year journey! As Africa is approached the time draws near for the final burst of firing which will place the rocket in the required orbit.

The vehicle is carefully aligned before this final period of acceleration with the aid of certain bright stars used as sighting points; these are focused on to photocells by means of small telescopes. Steering jets are used to bring the vehicle into the correct altitude.* Then the motors fire again and the journey is over.

Once in the orbit the tension is relaxed and the men have a chance to look about them; nearby floats the instrument rocket identified a short hour before as a speck of light near the zenith. In less than an hour, as they circle the earth, the men will be looking down on the brown speck of land in the middle of the Pacific that had been their starting point such a short time ago.

They will not be left in peace for long for down below on one of the other sites the supply rockets are about to be launched.

These pilotless rockets would be controlled in much the same way as the manned vehicles and would be placed as close together as possible in the orbit. There must inevitably be a certain amount of dispersion, due to the impossibility of starting or cutting out rocket motors within a split second of the required schedule. When they arrive, it will be necessary for the crew members to run out lines from a small winch to the freighter rockets. This will involve the use of miniature hand-operated rocket units which will assist the crew to maneuver in space.

* A space ship may well be constructed within the next few years, astronauts say, the only problem being that of cost, which would probably have to be met by the government. The space ship, from which further explorations into space might be made, probably would be stationed further from the earth however than the 300 to 500 miles estimated by Gatland and Kunesch; most astronauts agree a serviceable distance would be 1075 miles, a figure used by Wernher von Braun, formerly German rocket technician and now technical director of the U. S. Army Ordnance Guided-Missile Development Group, Redstone Arsenal, Huntsville, Alabama. At 1075 miles from the earth, the space station, needing no further power and becoming a satellite moving around the earth in its own orbit, would circle the globe once every two hours, or 12 rotations in 24 hours, permitting, with good optical instruments, observations of all parts of the globe roughly equivalent to observations, they say, from a plane at about 4000 feet above the earth.—The Editor.

The first task would be the provision of an elementary "space station" and material store which would act as a scientific base and later for preparing Operation Luna.

The latter project following closely upon the establishment of the space station would require an interorbital vehicle of totally different characteristics from those employed between earth and orbit. For the initial stage of the operation a manned vehicle, designed to circumnavigate the moon, would be erected in the orbit, using material ferried out by the freighter rockets. . . . In the nose would be the crew cabin, a large sphere 15 feet in diameter; this would be carried into the orbit in sections, and when assembled it will be pressurized.

Also contained within the cabin would be radio, radar, and all the control equipment required for the voyage.

The main structure of the space ship, formed from triangulated longerons and braces bolted together, provides support for the two bays of propellant capsules which total 48. These capsules are similar to the containers used for carrying up material, and each houses five tons of propellant. In operation, propellant is taken from these capsules by pipelines, which run inside the main longerons, and thence into a common manifold leading to the pumps. The propulsion unit is composed of five motor and pump units (obtained from the empty freighter rockets) giving a total thrust of 25 tons.

Departing from the base orbit, the vehicle—which has a starting weight of 260 tons—will accelerate very slowly (initially at 3.1 feet per second) until it has reached a speed some 200 mph less than escape velocity, an increment of 6700 mph. Due to the minute rate of acceleration it will take more than 34 minutes to achieve this velocity.

The astronauts coasting away from the earth on a parabolic orbit then climb out from the cabin and with their safety lines attached proceed to cast off the propellant capsules exhausted during the prolonged period of acceleration. If the luxury of an automatic release mechanism can be afforded, the crew will be spared this task—but otherwise it would be no more different from moving about in space in the base orbit.

As the space vehicle proceeds from the earth its velocity is continually being reduced by the earth's gravitational pull until a point is reached, some 217,000 miles from the earth's center, at which the gravitational pull of the smaller (but now much nearer) moon* is equal to that of the earth. The space ship crossing this point with a speed of a few hundred miles per hour would then start falling at a steadily increasing rate toward the moon. The vehicle would now be turned through 180° by use of small steering jets and

* The moon's gravitational pull is approximately one sixth that of earth's.

as soon as it approached the moon, after traveling for four and one half days, its motors would again start firing—this time to reduce its velocity in order to enter a circumlunar orbit.

In addition to the crew, the vehicle would carry a payload consisting of telescopes, instruments, and radio and radar transmitters (which might be powered by a small solar generator). Air, water, and food supplies would allow a stay of 14 days in the orbit.

Operation in Space*–II

MARTIN CAIDIN

✳✳ Martin Caidin, author of two books on jets, rockets, and guided missiles, is former associate editor of *Air News* and *Air Tech* magazines, and at present a technical specialist with the New York State Civil Defense Commission. ✳✳

ON THE MOON

When the first men descend from their space ship to the surface of the moon, they will be faced with two weeks of life on a dishearteningly inhospitable, strange, lifeless, and even terrifying world. To avoid the tremendous heat on the surface during the two-week "moon-day" period, the space ship will probably land in the "night" half of the satellite. Even under these conditions there will be considerable illumination across the rocky world, a garish, green-tinted light reflected from the distant earth.

Because no atmospheric dust, air, or water vapor exists to refract and distort light waves, the magnificent panorama of space with uncounted stars gleaming in a jet-black sky will always be visible to the spacemen. The full earth will appear as a brilliant, swollen ball in the skies, of a size several times larger than the moon appears to us. Even during the day, when the sun casts its painful brilliance across the surface, the horizon will terminate in the absolute blackness of space instead of in the familiar diffusion of light so familiar on the earth. A searing ball of flame in the sky, the sun constantly throws out flaming streamers of fire for many thousands of miles from its surface.

A layer of dust, composed of pumice, covers most of the moon surface. Present investigation supports the claim that this pumice layer is on the average a quarter of an inch deep; some scientists, however, insist that the covering may be several inches in thickness. Color will be conspicuously absent. Instead of the deep, rich shades familiar on earth, there will be a predominance of dull browns and grays, intermittently mixed with faded reds. The only relief will be the greenish earth, the black of space, and the glaring brilliance of the sun. Men walking across the surface will kick up clouds of fine pumice, which will settle almost as quickly as it rises.

There will be no sound on this airless, barren world, no covering of soil and plant life, no streams or lakes. The endless panorama will be one of crater walls, jagged mountain peaks, rills, and repeated crevasses. Thousands of meteorites, the majority microscopic in size, shower down incessantly upon the surface. The larger ones throw up spurts of pumice in a fine spray; an occasional shower sends a concentration of particles crashing silently across the plain.

The scientific expedition will utilize the space ship as its base of operations. Since its meteor bumper is as effective as that surrounding the satellite in space, the men are protected against all fast-moving particles of normal and expected size. The chances for collision with a meteor which could wreck the space ship are as remote on the moon as in the satellite orbit. . . .

Unless the space-suited explorers exercise constant vigilance, death can come easily and suddenly on the moon. A space suit torn by a jagged piece of rock will cause an agonizing explosive decompression. Unwary passage over thin-crusted, deep crevasses can mean death. A man who weighs 180 pounds on the earth, burdened with an equal 180 pounds of space suit, lead boots, oxygen tanks, radio, and other equipment, for a total 360 pounds, will weigh only 60 pounds on the moon. One might suppose, then, that a fall on the moon would not be dangerous, since its gravity is only one sixth that of earth. On our own planet, however, a man falling from a bed can sustain as much harm as he might suffer by falling off a ladder. The body still has inertia on the moon, and despite the lighter gravity a drop to the surface can be dangerous.

There will be no lack of spectacular sights on this unusual world, for lofty mountains towering even higher than the greatest peaks of earth stretch across the lunar surface. Two hundred miles in length and with peaks rising to a height of more than 20,000 feet, the Apennine mountain range forming the southwestern boundary of the Mare Imbrium is perhaps the most impressive on the moon. In the southern hemisphere the stupendous peaks of the Leibnitz Mountains tower more than 30,000 feet above the satellite's surface, reaching even higher than Asia's mighty Everest. The summit of Dorfel Mountain rises more than six miles from the flat lunar plain. Sharp, jagged, unscarred, and free from the eroding forces of wind and ice, these lunar peaks are comparatively more than four times as high as the tallest mountains on earth. To approximate (proportionately, that is) the incredible lunar mountain formation, Mount Everest would have to soar 116,564 feet above the earth.

RETURN TO EARTH

The return trip by shuttle rocket to the planet's surface [from the earth's space-ship satellite] will be a journey involving far greater tension than did the climb, during which the crew acted as passengers until the final power maneuver was made to settle into the orbit. To return to earth the space ship must eliminate the momentum of more than 18,000 miles per hour achieved during the ascent, when climbing energy in the form of velocity was imparted to the ship. While the space ship orbited about the earth in a vacuum, that energy as velocity was unimportant, but in the return to earth the energy is manifested as heat when the speeding space ship strikes the atmosphere. To prevent the ship from burning up like a meteor, the energy release must be gradual.

When leaving the satellite's position in space, the pilot operates the gimbal-system gyroscopes to turn the ship around so that the rocket tubes point in the direction of the orbital movement. After a short blast of power to reduce the speed of the space ship, it begins to fall back to earth. Climbing at a height of more than 20 miles, the V-2 rocket tumbles end over end if unbalanced; the atmosphere above that height is so tenuous that it cannot affect the movement of the rocket. The velocity of the V-2, however, is less than 4000 miles per hour; the returning space ship is moving at a speed of more than 18,000 miles per hour.

When the space ship passes through the extreme upper atmosphere and descends to a height of 50 miles, it is still moving at a velocity of more than 14,000 miles per hour. At an altitude of 50 miles, that velocity through the tenuous atmosphere is great enough to affect the ship's movement. By pushing the control stick all the way forward so that the elevators keep the speeding vessel moving downward, the pilot reduces altitude and lets air friction further slow the ship. A loss in velocity of 1000 miles per hour requires a forward movement of some 10,000 miles in the upper atmosphere. This is sufficiently slow to permit a further descent to even lower heights, where the atmosphere becomes "thick" enough to slow the ship to a forward velocity of 6000 miles per hour within a distance of 3000 miles.

Descending in this fashion through the atmosphere to lose the energy of its momentum through dissipation of heat, the space ship's outer skin is soon flowing a deep copper red. Skin temperatures, as calculated by Wernher von Braun, will run as high as 1300° Fahrenheit. Heat-resistant steels can withstand such temperatures without difficulty. Inside the sealed cabin the crew is protected by refrigeration equipment, glass-wool insulation, and other heat-resisting aids. The forward pilot's canopy and the navigator's bubble and portholes are double-layered sandwiched glass or other transparent material between which an invisible coolant is circulated to prevent their melting.

Fifteen miles above the earth, the space ship is flying like any supersonic, swept-wing airplane under power-off flight conditions. Before long it will slow down to the speed of sound. Unless the aerodynamic design permits an easy flow through Mach 1 speeds, the ship could be damaged or even broken up. . . .

Finally the ship approaches its landing base. Chase fighters, speedy jets which accompany the space ship in its approach and landing run to assist the pilot, are already in the air following and leading the great ship. At a speed comparable to present transport and bomber aircraft, the still-glowing space ship drops to the ground.

More than 1000 miles above, invisible to the naked eye except briefly at dawn and dusk, a giant station is whirling about the planet. Man has achieved the first of many steps in his struggle to conquer space.